For Mary, Rebecca, and Sara
(JO)

For Ben
(SB, EW)

About the Authors

James M. Olson

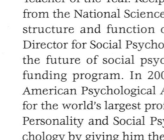

Steven J. Breckler

Elizabeth C. Wiggins

James Olson completed his undergraduate degree at Carleton University in Ottawa, Canada, and obtained his Ph.D. at the University of Waterloo. He was hired as an Assistant Professor at the University of Western Ontario in London, Canada, in 1978, where he has remained except for a year as a Visiting Professor at the University of California at Santa Barbara. Jim was promoted to Full Professor in 1990 and served as Chair of the Psychology Department from 1998 to 2003. He teaches social psychology and has twice been named Professor of the Year by the Undergraduate Psychology Club at Western Ontario. Jim has conducted research on many topics, including attitudes, social cognition, justice, and humor. He has published more than 100 articles and chapters and has edited 10 books. He is a co-organizer of the Ontario Symposium on Personality and Social Psychology, a well-known series of conferences on various topics in personality and social psychology. Jim has served as an Associate Editor of three scientific journals, including the *Journal of Personality and Social Psychology* (Attitudes and Social Cognition Section) from 1995 to 1998. He is a Fellow of the Canadian Psychological Association, the American Psychological Association, the Society for Personality and Social Psychology, and the Association for Psychological Science.

Steven Breckler was an undergraduate at UC San Diego, and completed his Ph.D. work at the Ohio State University. Following a post-doctoral year at Northwestern University, he joined the faculty of Johns Hopkins University, where he taught social psychology. In 1994, the students at Johns Hopkins selected Steve as Outstanding Teacher of the Year. Recipient of the prestigious Presidential Young Investigator Award from the National Science Foundation (NSF), Steve's research focuses primarily on the structure and function of social attitudes. In 1995, Steve was appointed Program Director for Social Psychology at NSF, where he then spent nine years helping to shape the future of social psychology through the management of a multimillion-dollar funding program. In 2004, Steve was made Executive Director for Science at the American Psychological Association, where he manages the science-related programs for the world's largest professional association of psychologists. In 2003, the Society for Personality and Social Psychology honoured Steve for his contributions to social psychology by giving him the Service Award on Behalf of the Discipline. In the same year, the American Psychological Association recognized Steve with a Meritorious Research Service Commendation, for his work on behalf of the entire discipline of psychology.

Elizabeth Wiggins was an undergraduate at the University of North Carolina at Chapel Hill, and received her Ph.D. from the Johns Hopkins University and her J.D. from the University of Maryland. Following a post-doctoral year at the Ohio State University, she joined the faculty at Barnard College of Columbia University, where she taught psychology and law and other courses. In 1989, Beth joined the research staff at the Federal Judicial Center and continues her career there today. The Center undertakes empirical research related to judicial processes and develops and administers educational programs for judges and other court personnel. Center projects often have policy significance and involve complex and innovative research methods, for which her social and quantitative psychology have proved invaluable. In 1998, the Judge John R. Brown Scholarship Foundation recognized her contributions to the judicial system with its Brown Award for Judicial Scholarship and Education. Beth is active in the American Psychology-Law Society, and has been a member of its Executive Committee. She recently served on a five-member international team under the auspices of the United Nations, U.S. Department of Justice, and the Council of Europe to make recommendations for restructuring the judicial and prosecutorial systems of Kosovo. Beth pursues filmmaking as a hobby, and recently co-wrote and produced the psychologically based documentary *The Building of a Sanctuary,* which was awarded a CINE Golden Eagle Award.

Brief Contents

Attitude Change

Conformity, Compliance, and Obedience

Stereotypes, Prejudice, and Discrimination

Chapter 9

323

Group Dynamics and Intergroup Relations

Chapter 10

371

Aggression and Violence

Chapter 11

417

Helpful Social Behaviour

Chapter 12

459

Liking, Loving, and Close Relationships

Chapter 13

505

Social Psychology in Your Life

Chapter 14

551

Preface

Social psychology today is a truly international discipline. Important and influential research is being done around the world, including North America, Europe, Asia, and Australia. As one of the places where social psychology flourishes, Canada boasts many productive social psychologists who have contributed to knowledge about almost every major topic in the field. A central purpose of this Canadian edition, therefore, is to describe research being done in Canada and to highlight the theoretical and empirical contributions of Canadian social psychologists. Canadian researchers are well known for work on many topics, some distinctly Canadian (e.g., acculturation, multiculturalism) and some traditional issues in the field (e.g., attitudes, close relationships). Students will learn that social psychology is thriving in Canadian universities. A second purpose of this Canadian edition is to illustrate important concepts with examples from the Canadian context. These examples include notable events (e.g., the school shooting in Taber, Alberta), famous Canadians (e.g., Pierre Elliott Trudeau), and distinctively Canadian issues (e.g., Quebec separatism). Students will see that social psychology is applicable to their personal experiences in Canada.

As indicated by its title, our most fundamental goal in this textbook and its supporting components is to bring social psychology *alive* for Canadian students. We want to communicate to students the enthusiasm that their professors have for the field. We want to get students excited about social psychology—to be fascinated by its experiments, to appreciate its relevance to everyday life, and to recognize that the field addresses questions we must answer to solve pressing social problems. From the inception of the *Social Psychology Alive* project, we developed the textbook, workbook, online labs, and videos in concert so that each component would work seamlessly with the other components to help students recognize social psychological phenomena in the world around them.

The textbook and supporting materials help instructors meet two key challenges of teaching social psychology. One challenge is that students resist seeing themselves as subject to the forces identified in social psychological research, perhaps especially to the power of the situation. They can understand the concepts and appreciate the cleverness of the research, but they do not really believe that they themselves would exhibit the predicted responses. A second challenge is that students often think that the findings of social psychology are obvious—the results simply confirm common sense and could have been predicted in advance. Students may recognize that the topics of research are important, but they view many results as unsurprising.

Social Psychology Alive, First Canadian Edition, and its supporting package correct these erroneous beliefs by having students experience social psychology for themselves. The book, workbook, videos, and online labs were designed to involve the students as researchers, as participants, and as critical observers of social psychology in Canadian life. For example, the workbook describes simple projects that students can do to illustrate social psychological processes (e.g., the correspondence bias, attitude change); these the coverage of cognitive dissonance theory begins with a description of Festinger and Carlsmith's (1959) famous $1/$20 experiment, and closes with a description of research conducted at the University of Waterloo on cultural differences in how dissonance is aroused (Hoshino-Browne et al., 2002).

- **Accessible Writing** Our descriptions of theories and studies are presented in a conversational writing style. Studies are described in enough detail that students get a clear idea of how participants in the research felt and how the procedures created the intended psychological conditions. Extensive use of graphs and figures makes findings easier to understand. By drawing connections between theories, experimental manipulations, and real-world variables, we help students relate social psychology to nonlaboratory settings.

- **Person in the Situation** A distinctive chapter titled "The Person in the Situation" reviews personal characteristics that are important for understanding social behaviour. The chapter begins with the *self,* describing research on self-concept, identity, and self-esteem. Gender is then discussed as a social psychological construct. Finally, a number of personality dispositions that have frequently been included in social psychological research are described, including self-monitoring, perfectionism, and dispositional optimism.

- **Know Yourself** Throughout the textbook, features labelled "Know Yourself" provide full or condensed versions of individual difference scales for students to complete. The items, response scales, and scoring instructions are provided. The dimensions presented include several measures developed by Canadian researchers, such as perfectionism and neosexism, as well as other scales such as self-esteem and empathy. Students learn about themselves while also getting a clearer idea of what each dimension represents.

- **Online Labs** Students have access to an online laboratory that allows them to participate in more than a dozen studies. These online experiments give students personal experience in social psychological research while expanding their knowledge of the topics addressed by the studies. Topics of the experiments include the universality of emotional expressions, evaluative conditioning as a source of attitudes, the effects of stereotypes on social perception, and cooperation/competition.

An Engaging, Multimedia Package of Ancillary Materials

Our supplementary materials are the best and broadest in the field. These components have been developed simultaneously to create a coherent and comprehensive package. They use various media to capture students' interest and to allow them to experience social psychology themselves. We list students' ancillaries first and then instructors' ancillaries.

Students' Ancillaries

- **Student Workbook** Written by Elizabeth C. Wiggins and Meghan Dunn, and adapted by Elizabeth Ridley, the Canadian edition of the workbook developed for this text is unique. In addition to being a study guide, it includes exercises that students can complete to learn more about social psychological principles and their application to everyday life and world events. The exercises include simple experiments and demonstrations (Try It Yourself), readings and analytical questions about social psychology as it relates to world events (Thinking Critically About Social Psychology), instructions to students for observing social psychology in their daily lives and the world around them (*Social Psychology Alive* Journal), and Internet-based activities (On the Web). Each workbook chapter includes an introduction to the Social Psychology Labs for the corresponding textbook chapter, and concludes with questions to guide the students' study of the text (Learning Objectives) and a test (Test Yourself) comprising multiple-choice, sentence-completion, and matching questions.

ISBN: 0-17-644149-2

- **Student Online Labs** Developed by Stephanie Goodwin, Greg Francis, and Ian Neath of Purdue University, this unique online laboratory component gives students firsthand experience in actual social psychological experiments. Students can participate in more than a dozen studies on a variety of topics, including priming effects, mere exposure, postdecisional dissonance, and interpersonal attraction. Students are randomly assigned to participate in one condition of a study, which usually takes 10–15 minutes. They can also run through other conditions if they wish to understand the nature of the manipulations. Students' responses are saved (from their first condition only), and they can view their own responses or a summary of all responses from their class or from all classes. Full explanations and expected findings are given for each study. Students will watch as research results are compiled at the online laboratory site, and they will see how data are summarized to test hypotheses. The online laboratory will give students a sense of personal involvement in social psychology. The labs are integrated into ThomsonNOW™ so it's easy for students to access them.

  Online Purchase ISBN: 0-495-12955-0

  Standalone ISBN: 0-495-12956-9

- **ThomsonNOW™** With pre- and posttests written by John Bickford and adapted by Joseph Snyder, this new diagnostic tool (http://hed.nelson.com) identifies each student's unique needs with a Pretest that generates a personalized Study Plan for each chapter, helping students focus on concepts they're having the most difficulty mastering. Students then take a Posttest to measure their understanding of the material. An instructor Gradebook is available to track and monitor student progress. A key component of the Study Plan is the inclusion of visually and pedagogically rich modules that begin with clearly stated learning objectives, followed by knowledge-building animations with audio to present key concepts. Modules also include discovery activities and self-check quizzes that confirm students' understanding of the module material.

  Online Purchase ISBN: 0-17-644181-6

  Standalone ISBN: 0-17-644189-1

- **Student CD-ROM** Developed by John Bickford of the University of Massachusetts—Amherst, a Student CD-ROM accompanies the textbook for those instructors who choose it. The CD includes videos from classic studies such as Milgram's obedience research and Bandura's bobo-doll studies. Other video segments show real-life settings that illustrate social psychological principles, such as military boot camp, job interviews, public service announcements, and video dating services. In addition, the videos present conversations with well-known researchers, including Craig Anderson, Mahzarin Banaji, Elizabeth Loftus, Claude Steele, Greg Herek, and Greg Mendoza-Denton. Each video segment on the student CD has associated multiple-choice questions and critical thinking questions for the student to answer, and the results can be e-mailed to the instructor, making it easy to assign.

  ISBN: 0-534-57836-5

- **Book Companion Web Site** Students will have access to a Web site (http://www .socialpsychologyalive.nelson.com) that provides several additional resources. Online quizzes and flash cards allow students to test their knowledge of textbook material (especially when combined with the guided study questions and sample test items presented in the workbook). Internet links to sites that are relevant to topics in the textbook are also provided.

- **InfoTrac® College Edition** *InfoTrac®* is a powerful online learning resource, consisting of thousands of full-text articles from hundreds of journals and periodicals. Students using *Social Psychology Alive* receive four months of free access to the *InfoTrac® College Edition* database (http://www.infotrac-nelson.com). By doing a simple keyword search, students quickly generate a list of relevant articles from thousands of possibilities. Then they select full-text articles to read, explore, and print for references or personal study. *InfoTrac®*'s continually updated collection of articles can be useful for doing reading and writing assignments that reach beyond the pages of this text.

Instructors' Ancillaries

- **Multimedia Manager Instructor's Resource CD-ROM** Written by Alan Swinkels and adapted by Joseph Mior, the *Instructor's Resource CD-ROM* provides a range of materials to assist instructors in the classroom. PowerPoint® summaries of principal ideas in each chapter are provided for use in lectures. PowerPoint reproductions of most figures in the textbook are also provided. The CD-ROM also includes a few sample video clips as well as a complete listing of available videos. The Multimedia Manager IRCD also contains the electronic Word files of the *Instructor's Resource Manual* and ExamView® *Test Bank*.

  ISBN: 0-17-644173-5

- **Instructor's Manual** Written by Gail Knapp and adapted by Saba Safdar, the *Instructor's Resource Manual* offers a variety of information to assist lecture preparation and classroom participation. It provides detailed teaching plans for every chapter, lists ideas for classroom activities, outlines possible assignments for students, and provides information about additional resources for lecture preparation.

  ISBN: 0-17-644165-4

- **Test Bank** Written by Eric Vanman and adapted by Saba Safdar, a comprehensive *Test Bank* provides 150 multiple-choice questions for every chapter, with textbook page references for each item. Some items are also provided to test information presented in the workbook, if instructors want to require workbook activities. In addition, 10 fill-in-the-blank, 20 true/false, and 10 essay questions are presented, again with textbook page references.

  Print Test Bank ISBN: 0-17-644157-3

- **Instructor Video** Consultant: John Bickford. This video contains all of the video that is featured on ThomsonNOW™ and the Student CD-ROM. It is available in VHS or DVD format for easy in-class viewing.

  VHS ISBN: 0-495-03110-0

  DVD ISBN: 0-495-03111-9

Distinctive Content

Our textbook provides comprehensive coverage of the basic content of social psychology, organized according to the major research areas in the field. The structure and order of the chapter topics are relatively traditional for an introductory social psychology textbook, although at least two chapters are unusual (The Person in the Situation, Social Psychology in Your Life). Every chapter, however, has some content that is distinctive from most textbooks in the field. We summarize some of the distinctive content in each chapter in the following paragraphs.

Chapter 1: Introducing Social Psychology

- We describe the hindsight bias in the context of discussing the fact that social psychological findings sometimes seem to be "obvious," and offer suggestions to students about how to avoid this bias when studying social psychology.
- We compare and contrast social psychology with other disciplines (e.g., sociology, anthropology) and other areas in psychology (e.g., personality psychology, cognitive psychology).
- We provide a brief history of social psychology, including its roots in philosophy and early, influential Canadian social psychologists.

Chapter 2: The Methods of Social Psychology

- In our coverage of experimental methods, we use the question "Does contact with members of a group cause more favourable attitudes toward that group?" as a recurring example when discussing many concepts, including independent variables, dependent variables, extraneous variables, random assignment, and factorial designs.

- We present a thorough discussion of ethical issues in social psychology, including deception, informed consent, debriefing, and the Tri-Council Policy Statement, which guides Research Ethics Boards in Canada.
- We discuss the implications of the Internet for social psychology, as well as how technology can be made to work for social psychology.

Chapter 3: Social Cognition

- We outline the workings of human memory as a background to social cognition, including the concepts of schemas, automatic and controlled processes, and accessibility.
- We include a section on counterfactual thinking, describing its causes and consequences.
- We include a section on reconstructive memory, which outlines social psychological research on this topic, much of it conducted in Canada; we then discuss related social issues including the validity of recovered memories of abuse and the accuracy of eyewitness testimony.

Chapter 4: Social Perception

- We describe Canadian research investigating cultural differences in social comparison processes.
- A recurrent question we ask is whether perceptual biases identified by social psychologists, including positive self-evaluations, optimism, and perceived control, reflect adaptive or maladaptive processes; in this context, we discuss both learned helplessness and the false hope syndrome.
- In the Know Yourself features, students learn about individual differences in (and their own standing on) unrealistic optimism and self-handicapping.

Chapter 5: The Person in the Situation

- This entire chapter is distinctive; we focus on personal characteristics that have been shown to influence social behaviour, including the self-concept, gender, and dispositions.
- We include a comprehensive section on identity and self-esteem, including the importance of social identity, cultural differences in self-concepts, and recent work in Canada and elsewhere on secure versus defensive high self-esteem.
- In the Know Yourself features, students learn about individual differences in (and their own standing on) self-esteem, self-monitoring, perfectionism, and dispositional optimism.

Chapter 6: Attitudes and Social Behaviour

- We discuss the measurement of attitudes, including the challenge of assessing implicit attitudes.
- We include a biological perspective on attitudes, including Canadian research on the effects of alcohol on attitudes and the role of genetic factors.
- We discuss the role of attitudes in sexual behaviour and how people can be induced to perform protective actions, such as using condoms consistently.

Chapter 7: Attitude Change

- We provide a detailed consideration of propaganda, including Canadian wartime propaganda, manipulative techniques used by cults, and examples of propaganda in everyday life.
- We discuss cultural factors in attitude change, including cultural differences in dissonance arousal and in responses to persuasive messages.
- In a Know Yourself feature, students learn about individual differences in (and their own standing on) preference for consistency.

Chapter 8: Conformity, Compliance, and Obedience

- We discuss the conformity pressure exerted on young Canadians to use tobacco, alcohol, and illegal drugs; we also describe prevention programs designed to teach social skills to resist this pressure.
- We discuss cultural factors in conformity and provide a Know Yourself feature that introduces students to individual differences in (and their own standing on) independent and interdependent self-construal.
- We discuss how obedience pressure could have led to some dark events in Canadian history, including the Solar Temple cult suicides and the murder of a Somalian prisoner by Canadian soldiers.

Chapter 9: Stereotypes, Prejudice, and Discrimination

- We present integrated threat theory as a comprehensive model of prejudice.
- We include a detailed discussion of gender stereotypes and sexism, including Know Yourself features that introduce students to individual differences in (and their own standing on) neosexism and ambivalent sexism.
- We contrast the Canadian model of multiculturalism and the American model of a melting pot as ways of reducing ethnic prejudice.

Chapter 10: Group Dynamics and Intergroup Conflict

- We cover the topic of leadership in detail, using Pierre Elliott Trudeau as an example of a charismatic leader.
- We discuss intergroup conflict, including conflict escalation and reduction and terrorism as a form of intergroup threat.
- We describe research, much of it Canadian, on the topic of acculturation, which refers to changes elicited by contact between cultural groups.

Chapter 11: Aggression and Violence

- We use the general aggression model (GAM) as a unifying framework for the chapter.
- We present a thorough discussion of the effects of the media on aggression, including recent data on the effects of television violence, the impact of violent video games, and the effects of pornography—drawing a distinction between erotica and violent pornography.
- We discuss gun control as a way of reducing violent aggression and contrast the Canadian and American policies on this issue.

Chapter 12: Helpful Social Behaviour

- We discuss whether there is an "altruistic personality" and provide a Know Yourself feature that introduces students to individual differences in (and their own standing on) interpersonal reactivity (empathy).
- We discuss cultural factors in helpful social behaviour.
- We present detailed coverage of social support, including recipients' reactions to being helped, the nature of social support networks, and the relation between social support and health.

Chapter 13: Liking, Loving, and Close Relationships

- We include an evolutionary perspective on interpersonal attraction and relationships.
- We review research, much of it Canadian, on adult attachment and provide a Know Yourself feature that introduces students to individual differences in (and their own standing on) the Adult Attachment Scale.
- We discuss same-sex attraction and relationships.

Chapter 14: Social Psychology in Your Life

- This entire chapter is distinctive. We discuss career opportunities in social psychology, as well as the applicability of social psychological knowledge to many occupations.
- We introduce some Canadian social psychologists who have taken unusual career paths, such as the insurance business.
- We describe some emerging new frontiers for social psychology.

We are excited about the Canadian edition of *Social Psychology Alive.* The diverse, multimedia elements of the package give students a unique introduction to social psychology by involving them directly in the learning process. The textbook emphasizes the relevance of the discipline, the workbook complements the text with custom-made, hands-on activities, Social Psychology Online Labs give students the experience of participating as subjects in experiments (as accessed through ThomsonNOW™), and the Instructor Video was built to give you the video that you want to show and discuss in class. (The same clips are featured on ThomsonNOW™ and the Student CD-ROM.) These various components combine to form an engrossing presentation of a vigorous field.

We invite feedback from students and instructors. We are eager to hear about users' experiences with all elements of the package. We have greatly enjoyed the challenge of preparing these materials and hope that you will be caught up in the fascinating science of social psychology.

Acknowledgments

The creation of a social psychology textbook with a full range of supplementary materials is a team effort. We are extremely fortunate to have had very talented people working with us on this project. Let us acknowledge the contributions of these individuals.

John Bickford of the University of Massachusetts–Amherst played a key role in the development of the Student CD-ROM; he also created the Social PsychologyNow™ quizzes which were adapted as ThomsonNOW™ for the Canadian market by Ken Cramer of the University of Windsor. Stephanie Goodwin, Greg Francis, and Ian Neath, all of Purdue University, set up the online experiments in Social Psychology Labs. Gail Knapp of Mott Community College authored the *Instructor's Resource Manual,* adapted by Saba Safdar of the University of Guelph who has also adapted the Test Bank to accompany the Canadian edition, originally authored by Eric Vanman of Georgia State University. Alan Swinkels of St. Edward's University developed the *Instructor's Resource CD-ROM.* Meghan Dunn of the Federal Judicial Center helped to create the *Student Workbook* which Elizabeth Ridley of the University of Toronto has adapted for Canadian students.

We also thank the illustrious researchers who agreed to be interviewed for the Student CD-ROM and Instructor Video: Craig Anderson, Iowa State University; Mahzarin Banaji, Harvard University; Sheldon Cohen, Carnegie-Mellon University; Vicki Helgeson, Carnegie-Mellon University; Greg Herek, University of California at Davis; Elizabeth Loftus, University of California at Irvine; Rodolfo Mendoza-Denton, University of California at Berkeley; Claude Steele, Stanford University; and Jeanne Tsai, Stanford University. We also want to express our appreciation to Alexandra Milgram, who graciously allowed footage of the famous studies by Stanley Milgram to be included in the video.

We are grateful to all of those who provided thoughtful reviews of the Canadian Edition and made numerous helpful suggestions:

Darryl Hill, Concordia University
Tara Burke, Ryerson University
Jennifer Campbell, University of British Columbia
Louis Schmidt, McMaster University
Doug McCann, York University
Saba Safdar, University of Guelph

Jayne Gackenbach, Grant MacEwan College

Delbert A. Brodie, St. Thomas University

Glenn Adams, University of Toronto

Rory Coughlan, Trent University

We also would like to acknowledge the invaluable contributions of several people at Thomson Nelson Canada who were involved in this project: Lenore Taylor-Atkins, Senior Marketing Manager; Alwynn Pinard, Senior Developmental Editor; and Carrie McGregor, Content Production Manager. Thanks also go to Valerie Adams for her copy-editing expertise, Liba Berry, proofreader, and Marianne Taflinger, Senior Editor at Thomson Wadsworth in California, without whom this book would not have happened.

Finally, our families know what it is for social psychology to come alive—they see it in us every day. As we worked on the book, they showed remarkable patience and understanding. As we go to press, they are also thrilled to see this book finally coming alive. It is to Mary, Rebecca, Sara, and Ben that we dedicate this First Canadian Edition of *Social Psychology Alive.*

Social Psychology Alive

NEL

Introducing Social Psychology

On September 11, 2001, international terrorism came to North America. A well-coordinated group of men managed to commandeer four commercial aircraft. They flew two of the planes directly into the twin towers of the World Trade Center in New York City—first the north tower, and then the south tower. Thousands of people were killed: the airline passengers, the people who occupied the buildings, the emergency rescue workers, and the terrorists themselves. A third plane was flown into the Pentagon building in Washington, DC, killing hundreds more. The fourth plane crashed outside of Pittsburgh, Pennsylvania, killing all aboard. Millions of people around the world witnessed these events as they were being broadcast on live television.

The victims included 24 Canadian citizens. Garnet (Ace) Bailey, a former star hockey player in the NHL, was employed as director of scouting for the Los Angeles Kings. The 53-year-old man was aboard United Airlines Flight 175 when it crashed into the south tower of the World Trade Center. Christine Eagan was a 55-year-old nurse from Winnipeg who was visiting her younger brother's office on the 105th floor of the south tower. Her brother Michael Eagan was 51 years old and worked at Aon Corporation. He was showing Christine the wonderful view of New York from his office when the first plane hit. Michel Pelletier was a 36-year-old broker for the trading firm Cantor Fitzgerald, located on the 105th floor of the north tower. He called his wife, Sophie, on the phone and calmly told her he was trapped in the building and he loved her. When he died, he had a three-month-old son and a two-year-old daughter.

In New York City and Washington, people responded swiftly. Emergency crews and ordinary citizens rushed to the scenes to help, often at great risk to their own lives. U.S. government officials ordered all aircraft to land at the nearest airport and closed American airspace to incoming international flights. These actions resulted in 224 flights being diverted to Canada, including 40 to Halifax, 38 to Gander, 33 to Vancouver, and 25 to St. John's. Canadian families opened their homes to stranded passengers, establishing relationships that often continued after the event.

As the days and weeks went by, people in both Canada and the United States tried to cope with the trauma of the events—the loss of loved ones, the fear and insecurity about whether more terrorist acts would occur, the anger aroused by an unknown enemy, and the need to understand why it happened. Many questions, few answers.

CP Photo/Jonathan Hayward

Kimmie Chedel leaves a plaque unveiling in Ottawa, September 15, 2002, with her children, Garette and Zoe Doyle. The plaque is in honour of the Canadians who died during the attacks on the World Trade Centre in New York on September 11, 2001. Chedel's husband, Frank Doyle, was one of the victims.

- *What could have motivated the terrorists to carry out their deadly plan? Whatever the motivation, it was strong enough that they were willing to die for it.*

- *How did these events change our perceptions of the risks associated with terrorism? Many people in North America and Europe suddenly felt vulnerable. Air traffic decreased dramatically as people stayed home rather than travel. Individuals of apparent Middle Eastern ancestry were regarded suspiciously.*

- *How did people cope with the stress and trauma brought on by these events? Thousands of families were shattered by the loss of loved ones. Almost everybody felt anxious and confused.*

- *What role did the media play in changing our attitudes and influencing our behaviours? Coverage of the immediate events was extensive, ranging from the bravery of the firefighters to the heartbreak of families. Both Canadian and American networks provided virtually continuous coverage of the tragedy for several days. Media stories subsequently turned to questions about who was responsible for the terrorism and what could be done to punish them.*

Knowing the answers to these questions would give us considerable insight into human motivation and behaviour. The answers might tell us how to prevent such attacks in the future, how to help victims cope more effectively if such a thing were to happen again, and how to shape social policy in democratic societies. The questions are difficult, and the answers are undoubtedly complex. But there are ways to gain insight. One way is called social psychology.

In this opening chapter, we introduce the field of social psychology. We begin by defining social psychology and describing a few studies that illustrate the field's breadth. Armed with these research examples, we next offer a couple of warnings about things you should keep in mind while studying the field. Notwithstanding these potential pitfalls, studying social psychology has many benefits, some of which we specify in the subsequent section. Then, to clarify the boundaries of social psychology, we explain how the field is different from other areas of psychology and from other disciplines. We next provide a brief history of social psychology. Finally, we outline the organization of the book and describe the supplementary materials that are available to enrich your understanding of the field.

What Is Social Psychology?

Our lives are *social:* they involve *other people.* We reside in societies that require us to interact many times every day with other people, including friends, teachers, partners, co-workers, and even enemies. We persuade (and are persuaded), we obey (and are obeyed), we love (and are loved)—all of these actions implicate other people. We cannot, nor would we want to, separate ourselves from the social groups to which we belong: families, neighbourhoods, schools, towns, provinces, nations. *We are social beings.* No matter what our pursuit in life, social settings and social problems will be important.

The Science of Social Behaviour

Social psychology can be considered the science of social behaviour (we give a formal definition in the next paragraph). It is a field dedicated to understanding the causes and consequences of social interactions between individuals or groups. The sorts of behaviours mentioned in the preceding paragraph—persuasion, obedience, love— are of great interest to social psychologists. In fact, entire chapters in this book are dedicated to attitude change and persuasion (Chapter 7), conformity and obedience (Chapter 8), and love and close relationships (Chapter 13). In these chapters, answers are provided to such questions as: What strategies do advertisers use to persuade viewers? When does social pressure produce conformity? How do people from different cultures think about love?

Probably the best way to get an appreciation of social psychology is via specific examples of research by social psychologists. Before we describe a few studies, however, we want to state and explain a formal definition of the field, adapted from one given by Gordon Allport (1985), which captures its pivotal elements:

> **Social psychology** *is the scientific study of how individuals' thoughts, feelings, and behaviours are influenced by other people.*

social psychology

the scientific study of how individuals' thoughts, feelings, and behaviours are influenced by other people

This definition has four key aspects, which we briefly explain in the following paragraphs, but in the reverse order of their appearance in the definition: (1) influenced by other people, (2) thoughts, feelings, and behaviours, (3) individuals' perspective, and (4) scientific study.

Influenced by Other People. Social psychology is the study of how other people affect us. It is *social* psychology. This "social" aspect is probably the single most important thing about social psychology and is true of all research in the field. Usually, the social component is obvious, as in research on aggression, altruism, intergroup relations, and interpersonal attraction. But sometimes the role of other people is less obvious. Have you ever had the experience of wondering what your mother, romantic partner, or close friend would think about your behaviour in a particular situation? Or have you ever prepared yourself mentally for a future interaction, such as an upcoming job interview or romantic date? These are common experiences, and they show that other people can influence us without having to be physically present. A specifically Canadian example is thinking about the separatist movement in Quebec: just the thought of a referendum on separation causes anxiety and distress in many Canadians. We do not have to be actually interacting with anyone to worry about the implications of Quebec leaving the confederation.

So long as someone is being affected in any way by other people, including their *imagined* presence or actions, the situation is relevant to social psychology. We will return to this "social" aspect of the field momentarily and give some examples of the broad influence of other people, including effects on how we interpret events, how we feel about ourselves, and how we behave.

Thoughts, Feelings, and Behaviours. Social psychologists are interested in how other people affect every aspect of individuals' lives, including thoughts (cognitions), feelings (affect), and behaviours. For example, social psychologists study how individuals process information about other people and how they store this information in memory (see Chapters 3 and 4). Social psychologists also examine people's feelings and emotions, such as their prejudice against outgroups and their affection for friends and lovers (see Chapters 9 and 13). Finally, social psychologists are, of course, interested in explaining social behaviour. The ultimate goal of the science is to understand why various kinds of actions toward other people occur or do not occur, such as conformity, aggression, helping, and discrimination. Every chapter in this book deals with social behaviour in some form.

Social psychology focuses on how individuals are influenced by other people.

Individuals' Perspective. Social psychologists take the perspective of individuals in a social setting, rather than focusing only on objective features of the situation. To understand behaviour, social psychologists believe that it is necessary to look at the world through the actor's eyes. Imagine that someone tries to give you a free gift (e.g., a small Canadian flag) while you are walking in a shopping mall. On the surface, this offer is generous, and you should accept the gift and respond with thanks. But if you suspect that the person is simply buttering you up before asking for a donation to some organization (e.g., an amateur hockey league), you might refuse the gift and respond with annoyance. Does it matter what the other person's *real* intentions are? Probably not, if the goal is simply to understand your response: whatever *you believe* to be the other person's motive will determine how you behave. Similarly, to understand many social events, it is more important to know individual actors' subjective *perceptions* of the situation than to know the setting's objective features. A term that is often used to refer to individuals' perceptions of a situation is **social construals**—how they construe (perceive, interpret) the situation. Social psychologists focus on actors' social construals to understand behaviour. Even when studying *group* processes, social psychologists adopt the perspective of individual members of the group. For instance, some groups have charismatic, powerful leaders who exert tremendous influence over members (e.g., the leaders of the Solar Temple cult in Quebec; see Chapter 7). To understand actions by these groups (e.g., mass suicides), social psychologists focus on individual members' thoughts and feelings about the leader, such as their beliefs about the leaders' goals, their feelings of loyalty to the leaders, and their perceptions of the leaders' relationships to God. Ultimately, group actions are made up of many actions by individuals.

social construals
how individuals personally interpret or perceive a social situation

Scientific Study. Finally, social psychology is a science. Social psychologists rely on direct tests of their ideas. Scientific evidence is necessary before a proposal will be taken seriously; it is not enough merely to speculate about an event and generate a plausible explanation. In Chapter 2, we discuss the scientific method and describe various methodologies used by social psychologists. For our present purposes, the important point is that, like any science, social psychology involves collecting data to test predictions. Throughout the book, you will read about experiments that have been conducted in the laboratory or in the field, wherein researchers have collected systematic information that bears on social behaviour. Social psychology has yielded many important insights and promises to advance our understanding of social behaviour further in the future.

The accompanying Concept Review table summarizes the key aspects of social psychology by asking the question "How would a social psychologist's perspective on understanding romantic dating be unique?"

How Other People Affect Us

We have noted that the key element of social psychology is that it investigates how individuals *are influenced by other people.* One reason the field is interesting and exciting is that most individuals don't recognize just how much they are affected by others. Many of us think of ourselves as strong individualists who make our own decisions based on our central values and do not worry much about what other people think. Is this how you think of yourself? Although individuals certainly do make personal decisions, most decisions are also influenced directly or indirectly by other people. Indeed, social psychologists have shown that other people influence virtually every aspect of life, including how we interpret events, how we feel about ourselves, and how we behave.

Other People Affect How We Interpret Events. Have you ever read about an accident or emergency where nobody stopped to help? Or have you wondered why one of the students in the crowded hallway didn't open the door for you when you were struggling toward it with a huge pile of textbooks you just purchased? Or have you yourself ever been uncertain about whether you should ask someone who looks distressed if he or she is okay? Social psychologists also wonder why people often do not offer help and have designed studies to explore this question.

CONCEPT REVIEW
How Would a Social Psychologist's Perspective on Understanding Romantic Dating Be Unique?

Key Element of Social Psychology	*Applied to Romantic Dating*
Influenced by other people	Romantic dating clearly fits into the domain of social psychology because the dating individuals are influenced by one another.
Thoughts, feelings, and behaviours	To understand dating, social psychologists would look at each person's thoughts about the other (e.g., first impressions), feelings toward the other (e.g., emotional passion toward the other), and behaviours toward the other (e.g., telephone calls, dates, gifts).
Individuals' perspective	Social psychologists would focus on each person's perceptions of the other, rather than on what the individuals are "really" like; the critical factor is what each person *believes* about the other.
Scientific study	Social psychologists would conduct experiments to learn about the processes underlying interpersonal attraction and love.

Researchers have conducted experiments in which they constructed fake emergencies and observed how people responded
who did not know that the situation was staged (e.g., Latané &
Darley, 1970). These studies on *bystander intervention* will be
discussed in detail in Chapter 12. By carefully controlling the
situation, including the behaviour of apparent observers who
were actually working for the experimenter, researchers determined that one important reason individuals fail to intervene is
that they rely on other people to interpret the event.

Other people can affect how bystanders interpret
a potential emergency.

   To understand this explanation, imagine that a few adults
(each walking alone) come upon a potential emergency at about
the same time, such as a man lying on the ground in downtown
Vancouver. They need to decide what is going on and what they
should do. Is the man sick? Is he drunk? Will he be angry if they
ask him questions? One source of information they might use is
how *other people* in the situation are responding: Do other people seem to think that
this is an emergency requiring intervention? If they are not doing anything about the
event, then perhaps it is not an emergency at all. Unfortunately for the victim, all of
the individuals may be looking at one another for cues about how to respond, with
the result that no one does anything! People may misinterpret the situation as a non-
emergency based on the inaction of other individuals. This analysis of emergency
situations is classic social psychology, providing a compelling example of how we use
other people to interpret our world.

Other People Affect How We Feel About Ourselves. We also rely on
other people to make judgments about ourselves. Consider: Are you generous? Do you
have a good sense of humour? Are you skilled at skating? Although these questions
refer to you as an individual, the answers rely partly on comparisons with other people.
Deciding whether you are generous, funny, or good at skating usually involves thinking
about whether you are better or worse than other people. Do you give more money to
charities than most people of your age? Do you tell more jokes than most of your
friends? Can you skate faster than most of your friends? Other people can have dramatic effects on how we feel about ourselves.

   This process of comparing ourselves to other people to make judgments about the
self is called *social comparison* (Festinger, 1954) and is discussed in detail in Chapter 4.
Social comparison occurs all the time and has many implications for daily life. For
example, have you ever wondered about the effects of extremely attractive men and
women in the media? We are constantly exposed to very attractive and very thin
models on television, in magazines, and at the movies. Do these attractive men and
women affect how we feel about ourselves?

   Some research in social psychology suggests that the answer to this question is *yes*.
For instance, Bill Thornton and Scott Moore (1993) had male and female undergraduates at the University of Southern Maine complete several questionnaires that assessed
a variety of self-perceptions, including ratings of their own physical attractiveness
and social skills. Some participants completed these questionnaires while seated
beside a large posterboard leaning against a wall, which allegedly was from a different
study that was being run in the same room at different times. This posterboard dis-
played 24 colour photographs of very physically attractive members of the same sex as
the participant. Participants who were exposed to these attractive photographs rated
themselves as less physically attractive and less socially competent than did participants in a control condition who were not exposed to the posterboard. Seeing very
attractive people made participants feel worse about themselves. Further, these effects
occurred for both men and women. This experiment is a good example of how an
issue from real life (media exposure to physically attractive models) can be studied in
the laboratory.

Other People Affect How We Behave.   Other people affect not only how we interpret events and how we feel about ourselves, but also our actions. This point was demonstrated indirectly in the bystander intervention studies, because bystanders' interpretations of the situation influenced their actions: they did not intervene. But other people can also affect how we behave more directly. That is, the presence of other people can elicit very different behaviour than would have occurred if individuals were alone. For example, have you ever been surprised by news reports of riots or other "mob" events? Perhaps football fans were celebrating their team's Grey Cup victory and started smashing windows and overturning cars, or perhaps workers on strike at a uranium mine were demonstrating peacefully but began to throw stones and attack police. Did you wonder how these escalations occurred, and whether you would have responded differently in the same situation? Social psychologists have been very interested in how individuals can be transformed in group settings, including the tendency for some large groups to exhibit aggressive behaviour.

One explanation for mob aggression focuses on feelings of anonymity. If people feel unidentifiable when they are immersed in a large group, they may be "released" from their normal inhibitions and do things they would not have done alone or in a smaller group. The term *deindividuation* has been used to refer to this feeling that people are unaccountable for their actions when in a large group; deindividuation will be discussed in detail in Chapter 10. The relation between group size and aggression is perhaps most clearly illustrated by an analysis of historical events conducted by Brian Mullen (1986). Mullen examined 60 newspaper reports of lynchings (mob executions) of Black men by White mobs in the southern United States between 1899 and 1946. The degree of viciousness or atrocity of each lynching was rated (e.g., based on whether the victim was burned or dismembered), as well as the size of the lynch mob relative to the number of victims. Results showed that as the lynchers became more numerous relative to the victims, the viciousness of the lynchings increased. That is, larger mobs were associated with more savage lynchings. Mullen hypothesized that people in the large mobs felt relatively anonymous, which led to a breakdown of normal inhibitory self-control. This study is a good example of how analyses of historical data can inform explanations of important social behaviours.

© AP/Wide World Photos/The Lantern, Zach Wittig

Sometimes large groups of people exhibit aggressive, destructive behaviour.

These examples of social psychological research illustrate the diverse ways individuals are affected by other people. Clearly, the field of social psychology can be applied to many settings in daily life. In a moment, we will discuss explicitly some benefits of studying social psychology, but first we need to identify some pitfalls to avoid.

Beware!

Social psychology deals with many topics that you will recognize as having been part of your life. Forming impressions of other people, reading persuasive messages, joining groups, helping those in need, falling in love—these (and other) settings and topics will be familiar to you. This everyday familiarity of social psychological content is, on the one hand, terrific, because it means that you will learn many things that are applicable to your life (more on this point soon). But there is a downside to the familiarity of the field's subject matter: you may think you know more than you do.

Social Psychology Is Not Just Common Sense. Over the course of our lives, we develop considerable expertise about our own behaviour: our preferences and desires, our strengths and shortcomings, and how we respond in different situations. Through our relationships with other people, we learn a lot about social interaction and what makes others tick. In a way, we are all social psychologists trying to understand and predict our world (see Chapter 4). Moreover, our beliefs and intuitions about social behaviour are often correct. Because of this overlap between social psychology and intuition, students sometimes claim that social psychology is little more than common sense.

It is true that some of social psychology is common sense and consistent with folk wisdom. There is a Chinese proverb that says a courtyard shared by all will be swept by none; this insight was offered long before social psychologists suggested that group settings tend to dilute feelings of personal responsibility (see Chapter 12). Similarly, a Spanish proverb suggests that flattery makes friends, whereas truth makes enemies; it may not be surprising that social psychologists found that people like others who say nice things about them (see Chapter 13).

Does this mean that social psychology is completely common sense, just bits of wisdom already well known? Don't be fooled. Consider the case of interpersonal attraction—how and why people like or dislike one another. Which of the following two sayings is correct? Is it that *birds of a feather flock together,* or is it that *opposites attract?* That is, do we most like others who are similar to us, who think like us and look like us? Or do we prefer those who complement rather than duplicate our own interests and needs? A common-sense case could be made for either view. As you will see in Chapter 13, however, social psychological research gives us a clear-cut answer: similarity wins the day.

As another example, common sense (and a good deal of psychological theory) tells us that rewards and reinforcement are the way to change behaviour. Give people money or prizes, and you can lead them to do almost anything. Social psychology, however, teaches a different lesson. It is sometimes the *absence* of an attractive reward that produces the greatest changes in attitudes and behaviour. You just need to get people started in the desired direction, and a sort of social momentum will take over from there. In fact, if rewards are used too much, they can actually reduce a person's interest in an activity. Not common sense at all, but it makes good social psychological sense, as you will learn in Chapters 4 and 7.

Thus, social psychology is more than common sense or folk wisdom. But even when research findings confirm our intuitions, there is considerable value in knowing

Sometimes pieces of "folk wisdom" offer conflicting advice.

for sure. One reason is that common sense often allows competing predictions, as in the similarity and liking example given earlier. Another reason is that because intuitions are *not* always right, we must conduct research to find out which ones are valid. A final reason is that folk wisdom is often vague and simplistic; real life is usually more complicated. So even when an adage has a kernel of truth, there may be exceptions or limitations that must be identified via scientific research. For example, although people generally like others who say nice things about them, if they suspect that the flattery was not genuine but was an attempt to manipulate them, it can lead to less rather than more liking (e.g., Jones & Wortman, 1973; see Chapter 4).

Hindsight Is Not Always Golden.   Predicting future, uncertain outcomes is often difficult. Who will win an election? What hockey team will win the Stanley Cup? How well will you do on an upcoming exam? In advance, these kinds of outcomes can seem highly unpredictable. Once we learn about an outcome, however, it often seems that it was obvious. We may experience the feeling that "we knew it all along." Beware—this is an illusion. Things that seem obvious in hindsight may not have been easily predicted in foresight. The tendency to think that a known outcome was obvious is called the *hindsight bias,* and how and why it happens is described in Chapter 3.

We mention the hindsight bias here because it can lead you astray when you are judging the importance and value of research findings. After reading about a study and its results, you may think that the findings were obvious—anyone could have predicted that! In actuality, though, the outcome might have been quite uncertain in advance. To counteract the bias, try this: as you read about an experiment, try predicting the result before you learn it. Don't peek! Very often you will be surprised at the difficulty of predicting a result before you know it, and it will confirm that perhaps a result is not something you knew all along. Or try this: after learning about an experiment, including its result, pretend that a different result had been obtained. See if you can invent a logical explanation for the different result. Many results can be explained in retrospect, once they are known. Predicting them ahead of time is far more challenging.

Now that you know some things to avoid while studying social psychology, let's discuss the benefits of exposure to this field. We think that learning about social psychology is important for several reasons.

Why Study Social Psychology?

The authors of this book are passionate about social psychology. We enjoy thinking about social psychological questions and conducting research on the topics covered in the book. We also delight in teaching social psychology to undergraduate and graduate students. To us, the question "Why study social psychology?" is a no-brainer—because it's interesting and useful at the same time! But we know that we may be biased (just a little), and the benefits of studying social psychology may not be so apparent to everyone. So let us articulate a few of the (many) benefits of learning about social psychology, not including our opinion that the field is truly fascinating.

Being an Informed Citizen. Think about the issues and problems that most concern you and your friends. Prominent among them are certain to be complex social issues and social problems. What should we, as citizens, do about national unity, the death penalty, or the widespread poverty of our First Nations and Inuit peoples? How should our country address terrorism internationally? What about anti-gay hate crimes: How can we minimize this problem? How can we stop the spread of AIDS, both within Canada and around the world?

This is where social psychology comes in. Most people have their own opinions about how to deal with some of these problems. Yet, as we noted earlier, intuition and common sense can sometimes lead us astray. If we really want to develop an informed and reasoned approach to dealing with social problems, we need to understand why people behave the way they do and the likely effectiveness of different solutions. Think about a parallel example: All of us have some intuition about how to build a bridge. We know what a bridge should look like, and we know what it is supposed to do. Does that mean that we could design and build a bridge that would work? Probably not. It takes a great deal of expertise from engineering and a deep understanding of physical forces before someone can build a bridge that will carry weight and last.

Developing effective social policies is a lot like building a bridge. For example, we may all share the goal of stopping the spread of AIDS, but we are unlikely to agree on how best to achieve that goal. Medical science and molecular biology have taught us a great deal about the virus that causes AIDS. The reality, however, is that this disease (like many others) spreads because of human social behaviour—such as unprotected sex and the sharing of intravenous needles. To many people, the solution may seem plain: tell people to stop doing these things. But to the knowledgeable student of social psychology, the problem is more complex and the solution less obvious. We need to understand how people judge their own susceptibility to the virus, and how those judgments influence behaviour. We need to recognize that situational factors can be very powerful, and emotions can override reason. We need to know how to change attitudes effectively. In Chapter 6, we describe research by social psychologists, including William Fisher at the University of Western Ontario, that has investigated the determinants of safer-sex behaviour. Just as the structural engineer relies on a myriad of

Social psychology can provide knowledge that might help us to deal with complex social issues.

Social psychology can provide insights about our close relationships.

details to design a bridge, so the social engineer needs a broad understanding of the determinants of behaviour to design a truly effective social policy. An informed citizen understands the principles of social psychology.

Applying Social Psychological Knowledge to Everyday Life. The principles of social psychology are relevant to understanding not only broad, complex social issues, but also more limited, everyday problems that many of us face. Elementary school teachers need to handle playground disputes and help underachieving students fulfill their true potential. Advertising and marketing executives need to design effective media campaigns. Doctors and health-care providers need to get patients to comply with drug regimens and therapies. Law enforcement officials need to control crowds and obtain accurate information from eyewitnesses. Employers must make hiring decisions on the basis of limited information and must organize the workplace to maximize productivity. And all of us experience problems occasionally in our close relationships with parents, friends, siblings, bosses, employees, or romantic partners. Despite the great diversity of these problems and their settings, each has been the focus of social psychological research designed to understand and solve them. You will learn about these literatures as you read this book.

The bottom line is that social psychology is relevant. Indeed, entire scientific journals are devoted to pursuing the applications of social psychology. See if your library subscribes to the *Journal of Applied Social Psychology* or the *Journal of Social Issues*. In these journals, you are sure to find applications that interest you and will be of value to you no matter what your field of study or career aspirations. But we need to be cautious. We do not want to promise more than social psychology can currently deliver. It may take dozens of studies to identify an effective strategy for solving a particular problem, and many interesting problems remain unexplored. As a science, social psychology is still in the earliest stages.

Understanding Yourself. Perhaps the best reason of all for studying social psychology is that you will learn some things about yourself. If you think of yourself as immune to advertising, you will learn that you may be more influenced than you believed. If you think that other people seem more poised, confident, or talented than you, you will find out that those others often harbour feelings of doubt, insecurity, and low self-esteem. If you wish you were better at handling conflict with others, you will learn some things to do and some things to avoid. If you wonder why you always seem to want what you can't have, you will discover that most people feel the same way—and you'll learn why. In sum, social psychology will help you to better understand yourself and your social world.

Thus, studying social psychology has many benefits. In part, these benefits derive from the fact that the field of social psychology is very broad. To help you understand the boundaries of social psychology, we next turn to how it connects to other fields.

Social Psychology's Connections to Other Areas of Psychology

We have defined social psychology as the scientific study of how individuals' thoughts, feelings, and behaviours are influenced by other people. This definition encompasses a large range of settings and topics. We need to specify the boundaries of the field. Let us begin with a discussion of how social psychology overlaps with some other areas of psychology that are related but distinct.

Personality Psychology. The area of psychology that is perhaps most closely related to social psychology is personality psychology. Personality psychologists study traits, or *dispositions,* that help to explain human behaviour. Dispositions are consistencies in thought or action that characterize an individual across time and settings and that make him or her different from other people (see Friedman & Schustack, 2003). The primary goal of personality psychologists is to identify the dispositions that are most useful for describing behaviour and for differentiating between individuals. In contrast, social psychologists want to understand the impact of external, situational factors on behaviour—in particular, how individuals are affected by other people. Nevertheless, social psychologists often include individual difference variables in their research, hoping they will improve the prediction of behaviour above and beyond the situational factors. For instance, a social psychologist might investigate aggression by manipulating a situational factor (e.g., whether or not participants are insulted by an accomplice of the experimenter), but also include a measure of a relevant individual difference variable (e.g., self-esteem) that might further improve prediction of participants' aggressive responses. In Chapter 5, "The Person in the Situation," we discuss numerous dispositional variables that have often been included in social psychological studies.

Developmental Psychology. Developmental psychologists study age-related changes in human abilities and behaviours, ranging from childhood to the end of the life span. Most developmental psychologists study children, often focusing on either social development (e.g., how friendships emerge, the importance of early attachments to other people) or cognitive development (e.g., how language emerges, intellectual skills). Although many social psychologists have used children as participants in research, the focus of these studies has typically been to understand a basic principle that was expected to apply to other age groups as well. Nevertheless, some research focusing specifically on developmental changes in social psychological processes will be described in various chapters of this book.

Cognitive Psychology. Cognitive psychologists study how the human mind works, including memory, information processing, consciousness, and decision making. This field has made important contributions to our understanding of how knowledge is organized in memory, as well as common errors in judgment and decision making. One area of social psychology overlaps substantially with cognitive psychology: *social cognition,* which is the study of how information about people is processed and stored (see Chapter 3). The "about people" (social) aspect of the definition of social cognition is critical; cognitive psychologists additionally study the processing of *non*social information. Both cognitive and social psychologists rely on experiments to test their ideas, and the two fields share some theories and models. A cognitive perspective is very common in social psychology, and the impact of information processing on social behaviour will be discussed many times in this book (particularly in Chapters 3 and 4).

Clinical and Counselling Psychology. Clinical and counselling psychologists study people who are having difficulty coping with life's demands. Sometimes also called *abnormal psychology,* these fields focus on individuals who are suffering from some kind of psychological or emotional problem. The problems can range from relatively minor ones like mild depression or anxiety to severe ones like schizophrenia or antisocial personality disorder. In contrast, social psychologists are primarily interested in "normal" individuals' behaviour in social settings. Nevertheless, there are points of contact between the fields. For example, social psychologists are

Area of Psychology	Primary Focus of the Field	Related Topics in Social Psychology
Personality psychology	Traits that help to explain human behaviour	Individual differences that affect social behaviour (e.g., self-esteem)
Developmental psychology	Age-related changes in human abilities and behaviour	Social development—how relationship skills emerge
Cognitive psychology	How the human mind works	Social cognition—how information about people is processed and stored
Clinical/counselling	Psychological or mental problems affecting people's well-being	Loneliness, shyness, and other relationship problems; depression and anxiety

interested in loneliness, shyness, relationship dissolution, and low self-esteem, all of which can lead to coping problems. Also, social psychologists have investigated whether certain styles of processing social information might predispose individuals to depression and anxiety.

The connections between social psychology and other areas of psychology are summarized in the accompanying Concept Review table.

Social Psychology's Connections to Other Disciplines

It is also helpful to know how social psychology is similar to and different from a few related disciplines. These are all subjects that are taught at colleges and universities. You may have taken courses on them or even be majoring in one of them.

Sociology. Sociology is the discipline most closely related to social psychology. Sociology is the study of how social and cultural forces influence behaviour. Sociologists focus on *groups* to understand phenomena, in contrast to social psychology's focus on the *individual*. For example, sociologists might compare the relative health standing of people from different socioeconomic levels (e.g., low vs. middle vs. upper classes) or the murder rate in countries with different laws (e.g., capital punishment vs. no capital punishment). Social psychologists, on the other hand, might examine whether specific beliefs and attitudes are associated with better health, or whether individuals are more aggressive under certain social conditions. Thus, sociologists are primarily interested in large social categories and groups, rather than individuals. Another important difference between sociology and social psychology is their preferred research methodologies. Sociologists typically study existing groups and measure the relevant characteristics. Social psychologists, on the other hand, often manipulate factors in experiments. Interestingly, there are textbooks on social psychology written by sociologists (e.g., Michener, DeLamater, & Myers, 2003), which differ quite dramatically from textbooks written by social psychologists.

Anthropology. Anthropology is the study of past and present cultures, particularly how cultural features influence behaviour. Archaeology is one branch of anthropology, which involves the investigation of past cultures through their physical remains. But many anthropologists study modern cultures, such as the First Nations in Canada, usually comparing the features of different groups (e.g., their customs or institutions) to understand a particular outcome (e.g., divorce rate, life expectancy). Although social

Discipline	Primary Focus of the Discipline	Differences from Social Psychology
Sociology	How social and cultural forces influence human behaviour	Focus on groups rather than individuals; measure relevant concepts rather than manipulate in experiments
Anthropology	The study of past and present cultures	Focus on cultures rather than individuals; rely on existing materials rather than conducting experiments
Political science	The study of methods of government	Exclusive focus on the political domain; study existing systems rather than conducting experiments

psychologists study some of the same outcomes as anthropologists, the two fields overlap very little in terms of theoretical perspective (cultures vs. individuals) or research approach (investigation of existing records and materials vs. experiments).

Political Science. Political science is the study of methods of government, including the principles and operations of political institutions. This field is more specialized than social psychology, which potentially addresses any behaviour that is influenced by other people. Although the political domain is certainly of interest to social psychologists (e.g., research on voting, leadership, and justice), political scientists engage primarily in theoretical analysis of governmental systems, rather than experiments on how factors influence individuals' perceptions. Interestingly, a hybrid subdiscipline known as *political psychology* has emerged in the past 20 years in which social psychologists and political scientists sometimes work together to understand human political behaviour (e.g., Ottati et al., 2002).

The differences between social psychology and other related disciplines are summarized in the accompanying Concept Review table.

Historical Background of Social Psychology

Social psychology emerged as a field distinct from other disciplines and from other areas of psychology sometime in the middle of the 20th century, perhaps most clearly during the 1950s. Important social psychological studies had been done prior to this time, but few specialized theories had appeared, and the field's reliance on the experimental method had not solidified. Thus, "modern" social psychology has existed only 50 or 60 years. In this section, we trace some of the historical roots of modern social psychology and outline briefly some of the major early developments in the field.

Social Psychology's Roots in Philosophy

Although we did not include philosophy in the disciplines whose connections to social psychology were described, the earliest sources of social psychology (and of psychology more generally) can be found in philosophy. In fact, several important social psychological concepts can be traced directly back to the work of philosophers.

For instance, modern social psychologists distinguish between thoughts, feelings, and behaviours—recall our definition of the field. The Greek philosopher Plato, generally considered the father of Western philosophy, suggested that people experience the world in three distinct ways: in thought, in emotion, and in action. Thus, the triumvirate of cognitive (thoughts), affective (feelings), and behavioural aspects of experience is very old; you will see that this conceptualization continues to appear in modern social psychological theories.

As another example, social psychology is based on the fundamental point that humans are social beings. Aristotle, one of Plato's students, argued forcefully that living a good life and achieving personal happiness are both dependent on providing benefits to other people in addition to the self. Aristotle's view was that connections with others form an essential part of who we are. This idea is consistent with social psychological work on the self-concept, which has shown that our social relationships are important components of how we define ourselves (e.g., see Baumeister & Twenge, 2003).

social contract

the idea that human societies have developed basic rules of social and moral conduct, which members of the societies implicitly agree to follow

Much attention in social psychology has been directed to *social norms,* which are perceived rules or guidelines about what behaviours are acceptable and unacceptable (see Chapter 8). The concept of social norms can be traced back to one of the great ideas of philosophy: the **social contract.** The social contract refers to the idea that, to survive and prosper, human groups had to develop some basic rules of social and moral conduct; an absence of rules would have led to societal breakdown. Thus, through the millennia, humans have evolved formalized codes and laws, which people in a society implicitly "agree" to follow (hence, the social *contract*). Modern social psychologists use the concept of norms to understand various social behaviours.

A final connection between social psychology and philosophy involves the concept of *identity.* Social psychologists have been very interested in issues related to how people see themselves (see Chapter 5). Similarly, perhaps the fundamental question in philosophy has been the essence of human existence: What is a person? What is the nature of consciousness? These questions clearly relate to self-perceptions. The issues are complex, and debate continues among philosophers. Nevertheless, social psychologists have made considerable progress in developing useful models of identity.

Social Psychology's Early History

The field of psychology (not just social psychology) separated from philosophy and became a distinct discipline in the middle of the 19th century, when a number of European researchers began to use scientific methods (e.g., experiments) to address questions about human perception and judgment, moving away from the introspective techniques (e.g., thought and speculation) used by philosophers. The earliest publication that is widely viewed as *social* psychological appeared in 1898 in the *American Journal of Psychology* (Triplett, 1898). This experiment addressed whether the presence of an audience improves individuals' performances and is described in the accompanying box, Social Psychology in Your Life: "The First Published Social Psychology Experiment."

In 1908, two textbooks with *social psychology* in their title appeared, one by a psychologist (McDougall, 1908) and one by a sociologist (Ross, 1908). These books were very different from one another. McDougall's text relied on the concept of *instincts* to explain much of human behaviour, whereas Ross's text emphasized imitation and learning. These authors were not hesitant about proclaiming the importance of social psychology; for example, McDougall wrote on his opening page that social psychology was "the essential common foundation on which all the social sciences . . . must be built up" (p. 1). Although these textbooks ushered in the

Social Psychology in Your Life
The First Published Social Psychology Experiment

Throughout the book, we have placed special boxes like this one to make connections between social psychology and your own life. Here, we tell you about a study that is generally regarded as the first social psychology experiment ever to be published. The issue addressed in this experiment remains relevant today: how performance is affected by the presence of other people. As you read about the study, see if you can relate the ideas to your own experiences.

Norman Triplett was a researcher at Indiana University in the late 1800s. Triplett was curious about a pattern he noticed in bicycle racing times: racing records showed faster times (about 20% faster) in multirider competitive races than in individual races against the clock. Triplett developed a variety of hypotheses that might explain this difference, including some that were based on the physics of bicycle racing. For example, in multirider races, the lead racer provides a shield against the wind for those following behind, whereas no such shelter is available when racers compete only against the clock.

Can you think of an explanation that is more social psychological in nature? Triplett could: he hypothesized that "the bodily presence of another rider is a stimulus to the racer in arousing the competitive instinct" (Triplett, 1898, p. 516). In other words, riders' competitive juices get flowing when they race against other riders. Triplett recognized that distinguishing among the competing hypotheses would require careful experimental work. Therefore, he designed a task in which children turned a crank on a fishing reel as quickly as possible. Sometimes the children did the task by themselves, and sometimes they competed against other children. The results showed clearly that the children were faster at turning the crank when they competed against other children than when they performed the task alone.

This early experiment eventually generated a fascinating line of research on how the presence of other people affects individuals' performances. This topic became known as *social facilitation* and will be discussed in detail in Chapter 10 on group dynamics. To foreshadow our later discussion a bit, can you think of any circumstances under which the presence of others is likely to make performance *worse* rather than better? It turns out that there are such conditions, which have to do primarily with the task being very complex or difficult.

Norman Triplett was intrigued in the 1890s by records showing that bicycle racers exhibited faster times in multirider competitions than in individual races against the clock.

© Hulton-Deutsch Collection/CORBIS

academic study of social psychology, the field was relatively undefined and did not yet have its own theoretical models.

An increasingly important view in psychology during the first few decades of the 20th century was **behaviourism,** which attempted to explain behaviour purely in terms of stimulus–response connections established through experience and reinforcement (e.g., if a certain behaviour occurs in a situation and produces a reward, the same behaviour is more likely to occur again in the future in the same or similar situations). Behaviourists dismissed the importance of unobservable mental

behaviourism

an approach in psychology that assumes that behaviour can be explained purely in terms of stimulus–response connections established through experience and reinforcement

Gestalt theory

an approach in psychology that assumes that people's overall, subjective interpretations of objects are more important than the objects' physical features, and that objects are perceived in their totality, as a unit, rather than in terms of their individual features

Kurt Lewin is often regarded as the father of modern social psychology.

During the Second World War, social psychologists directed their attention to practical questions like how to motivate people at home to conserve scarce resources.

concepts like thoughts and attitudes. This view influenced some early work in social psychology, particularly theories of human aggression (e.g., Dollard et al., 1939).

In the 1930s, Adolf Hitler and the Nazi party gained influence in Germany. The spreading racism of the Nazis and the threat of impending war led many European scientists to emigrate to North America, including several psychologists who made important contributions to social psychology. Perhaps the most notable example is Kurt Lewin, who is often regarded as the father of modern social psychology (for a collection of his influential articles, see Lewin, 1951). One significant characteristic of these European theorists, including Lewin, was that they were generally opposed to behaviourism, which had not achieved as much acceptance in Europe as in North America. Instead, these theorists were usually trained in **Gestalt theory,** which was based on the idea that people's overall, subjective interpretations of objects are more important than the objects' physical features. You will recognize the parallel between this approach in Gestalt theory and modern social psychology's focus on individuals' perspectives. Gestalt researchers also emphasized that objects are perceived in their totality, as a unit, rather than in terms of their individual features. For instance, we perceive an automobile as a complete, functioning unit, rather than as four tires, a hood, a steering wheel, and so on. Gestalt theorists were very interested in people's internal representations of objects—in contrast to behaviourism.

The rising influence of authoritarian dictators in such countries as Germany, the Soviet Union, and Italy in the 1930s and 1940s stimulated much interest among social psychologists in prejudice, discrimination, and totalitarianism. These topics became central issues investigated in early social psychology (e.g., Allport & Kramer, 1946; Adorno, Frenkel-Brunswik, Levinson, & Sanford, 1950).

The Second World War turned North American and European social psychologists' attention to practical questions relevant to the war effort, such as how to select good leaders from among army recruits, which leadership styles are most effective in small groups, how people could be encouraged to conserve essential war materials at home, and how messages could best be constructed to maintain morale. The immediate needs of the armed forces stimulated pragmatic, problem-focused research. It became apparent that social psychology offered techniques that could yield important insights about human behaviour.

Social Psychology's Emergence as a Distinct Area of Psychology

Social psychology came out of the Second World War as a field that used experimental techniques to study social behaviour. There were increasing numbers of social psychologists at Canadian and American universities, and specialized theories were beginning to appear. Social psychology was clearly emerging as a distinct area of psychology. The 1950s and 1960s were a time of excitement in social psychology, as researchers explored new topics and identified interesting phenomena.

Many researchers continued to investigate issues carrying over from the Second World War, such as conformity (e.g., Asch, 1956), obedience to authority (e.g., Milgram, 1963), attitude change (e.g., Hovland, Janis, & Kelley, 1953), and intergroup conflict (e.g., Sherif et al., 1961). In Canada, issues related to bilingualism and second-language learning were investigated by Wallace Lambert and his students at McGill University (e.g., Gardner & Lambert, 1959). John Arrowood and his students at the University of Toronto explored social comparison processes (e.g., Arrowood & Amoroso, 1965). The research programs of these and other scientists elevated social psychology to a new level of productivity as an experimental science.

The 1950s and 1960s also saw the appearance of many important theoretical models that gave social psychology a set of theories specifically related to social behaviour. The names of these theories (e.g., cognitive dissonance theory, Festinger, 1957; social learning theory, Bandura, Ross, & Ross, 1963) would probably mean little to you at this point, so we will not list them here. Suffice it to say that many models from this time period will be discussed.

Most of the theories and studies described in the remaining chapters of this book have been proposed or conducted since social psychology emerged as a vibrant, unique area of psychology in the 1950s. Our goal is to give you a comprehensive and up-to-date introduction to the field, though we must of course be selective to some extent. We focus on work done in the past 20 or 30 years (and especially in the last 10), but it is important to recognize that recent advances in understanding have been possible only because of the earlier contributions of researchers and research programs we have mentioned here.

Organization of the Book

We have 14 chapters in this book. These chapters cover all of the classical topics or problems of social psychology, such as social cognition, attitudes, aggression, and so on. Each chapter focuses on one topic or problem and reviews the social psychological research in that area. Cross-cutting the chapters are numerous contexts or settings to which social psychology can be applied. Many contexts will be discussed in the book, but three will be especially emphasized: culture, health, and the law.

Classical Problems of Social Psychology

Social psychology is a wonderfully—but sometimes bewilderingly—diverse field. Individuals' thoughts, feelings, and behaviours can be influenced by other people in many, many ways. Although social psychology potentially encompasses a nearly infinite number of topics, social psychologists have focused on a limited number of problems or issues in their research. We have organized this book to reflect these classical topics.

Setting the Stage. Chapters 1 and 2 set the stage for the remainder of the book. After the current chapter's introduction to the field, we turn in Chapter 2 to how social psychologists go about studying social behaviour. We discuss the scientific method and compare different approaches to research. We summarize the things you need to know to understand and appreciate the research findings described in subsequent chapters.

Perceiving the Social World. Chapters 3 and 4 introduce the processes involved in making sense of the social world. In Chapter 3, we survey social cognition, which refers to how information about people is processed and stored. We discuss memory, impressions, and some common errors that people make in everyday judgments. In Chapter 4, we address more complex decisions and judgments, such as attributions, which are judgments about why an event occurred or why someone behaved in a certain way. Chapter 4 also discusses how we perceive ourselves, including judgments of our abilities and future prospects.

The Person in the Situation. Chapters 5 and 6 discuss some important features of individuals that are stable across settings; these enduring characteristics differentiate one person from another and must be included in any attempt to understand social behaviour. In Chapter 5, we focus on the self-concept (identity), gender, and dispositions (personality traits). In Chapter 6, we focus on one of the most researched topics in social psychology: attitudes, which are good–bad evaluations of targets. We discuss where attitudes come from and how they affect behaviour.

Social Influence. Chapters 7 and 8 address social influence: how other people can change our opinions and actions. In Chapter 7, we discuss attitude change. We articulate some of the factors that affect the success of persuasive messages, including advertisements. We also discuss the topic of propaganda. In Chapter 8, we turn our attention to conformity and obedience. This chapter is where you will learn about some of the most famous experiments in social psychology.

Harmful Social Behaviour. Chapters 9, 10, and 11 cover some of the negative aspects of human behaviour. In Chapter 9, we discuss stereotypes, prejudice, and discrimination. We consider the sources of these constructs and how they might be reduced. We also discuss sexism, which is prejudice and discrimination directed against women. In Chapter 10, we review group processes, including how groups make decisions and what kinds of leaders are most effective. We also discuss intergroup conflict, which often can be traced back to stereotypes and prejudice. In Chapter 11, we review research and theories of human aggression. We discuss conditions that elicit violence and aggression, as well as strategies for controlling harmful behaviour.

Helpful Social Behaviour. Chapters 12 and 13 address some positive aspects of human behaviour. In Chapter 12, we discuss the conditions that promote helping in casual or in emergency situations. We also discuss the causes and benefits of social support. In Chapter 13, we take up the topics of liking, loving, and close relationships. From our earliest moments as infants, and continuing through to the end of our lives, the relationships and attachments we form with other people provide the foundation of social life.

Putting It All Together. The final chapter of most textbooks provides a summary and review of the entire book. And, in Chapter 14, we do provide a brief summary. But we do more than that. The aim of the last chapter is to show you how social psychology is relevant to your own life. By understanding social psychology, you are better informed about the determinants of behaviour and can use that knowledge to help yourself and others. Chapter 14 also tells you about career opportunities in social psychology. A background in social psychology will serve you well in many fields, including marketing, advertising, government, law, health, education, and business (not to mention psychology).

The Many Contexts of Social Psychology

One of the key features of social psychology is the diversity of contexts to which it applies. After all, social behaviour occurs in almost every conceivable setting. We will discuss many contexts throughout the book, but three will appear most frequently because they are especially interesting and important: culture, health, and the law.

The Culture Context. Much of social psychology has been built on studies of North American university students. These studies have identified many important principles of social behaviour, but there are reasons to question whether these principles always apply to other cultures. In the past two decades, social psychology has become much more international in scope, with research being conducted in many countries around the world. Some of these cross-cultural studies have identified limitations to social psychological findings from North America.

Cultures differ from one another in many ways, of course, so when a principle does not generalize to cultures outside North America, it is not always easy to know why. Also, understanding cultural differences is made more challenging by the fact that each of us is at least partly the product of our own culture, so it can be difficult to look at the world in other ways. Nevertheless, analyzing the role and influence of culture can provide significant insights into the dynamics of social behaviour. The importance of studying culture is brought home by the threat of terrorism. To understand and reduce this threat, we must look at the world through the eyes of terrorists—what motivates them, how they recruit new members, and so on. Why are these young people willing to die for their cause?

Social psychology has become more international and cross-cultural in scope over the past two decades.

Throughout this book, we will discuss cross-cultural limits that have been identified to social psychological findings and theories. For example, we will discuss cultural differences in the favourability of self-evaluations (Chapter 4), the nature of the self-concept (Chapter 5), the ways attitudes change (Chapter 7), rates of conformity (Chapter 8), and rates and forms of aggression (Chapter 11). We will also discuss numerous issues that are more specific to the Canadian cultural context, such as prejudice against Aboriginal Canadians and the French-speaking minority (Chapter 9), the feasibility of achieving a truly multicultural society (Chapter 9), and relations between the provinces and the federal government (Chapter 10).

These comments should not be taken to imply that every culture produces totally different patterns of social behaviour. Indeed, differences between cultures are often small compared to cross-cultural similarities. Thus, studying the cultural context of social behaviour also gives us a deeper appreciation for the qualities we *share* with all members of our species.

The Health Context. Some of the most important problems facing humans today centre on health and the prevention of disease. In many chapters of this book, we illustrate how social psychology offers insight and points the way to possible solutions. For example, depression and anxiety are related to whether people think they are measuring up to important standards (Chapter 4); optimism and other dispositions are related to well-being (Chapter 5); safer-sex campaigns that rely on principles of persuasion can be effective (Chapter 6); fear appeals can successfully motivate changes to unhealthy lifestyles (Chapter 7); and recovery from health-related problems is often improved by social support (Chapter 12).

The Law Context. As a society, we are governed and live by a system of rules and laws, both provincial and federal. You may not appreciate how your daily social behaviours are shaped and influenced by these rules and laws, but the influence is very powerful and based on principles of social psychology. From traffic regulations to criminal prosecutions, our legal institutions impose constraints and boundaries on social behaviour. And those institutions themselves—police, courts, juries, judges— provide rich and important contexts for studying social behaviour. For example, social psychologists have shown that eyewitness testimony is often unreliable (Chapter 3); rules and laws work, in part, because of conformity and obedience

(Chapter 8); principles of group dynamics explain how and why juries make their decisions (Chapter 10); and people sometimes violate rules and laws by harming one another (Chapter 11).

Social Psychology Alive

Social psychology is an exciting and vibrant discipline, and a rich theoretical tradition has evolved since the Second World War. The methods and experiments of social psychology create engaging social situations, and the problems addressed by social psychology are intrinsically interesting and relevant to people's lives. A textbook by itself can certainly provide the factual material, the theoretical models, graphs of results, and still photographs. But it takes more than that to truly appreciate and understand social psychology. You must experience experimental procedures and manipulations for yourself—you need to see social psychology in action. That's why we have developed a number of additional resources to accompany this book. Our aim is to make social psychology come *alive*.

Social Psychology in Action

The science of social psychology is built on a foundation of careful research. The pages of a textbook can give you an impression of these studies, but actually seeing a study in progress clarifies what they are really about. Meeting researchers and listening to them explain their studies can also be helpful. That is why we have produced *Social Psychology Alive: The Videos*. Several clips on this CD-ROM provide an inside look at actual or re-created experiments. For instance, you will see for yourself how participants behaved in Stanley Milgram's famous obedience experiments (Chapter 8) and how children responded when they observed an adult engaging in acts of aggression (Chapter 11). You will also listen to interviews with famous social psychologists talking about a variety of topics, including the unreliability of eyewitness testimony (Chapter 3), cultural influences on emotion (Chapter 4), and the devastating effects of racial stereotypes (Chapter 9). Finally, you will see real-life examples of social psychology in action, such as the challenges women face trying to juggle multiple social roles (Chapter 5), how military recruits feel after suffering through training (Chapter 7), and strategies used by video dating services to match partners (Chapter 13). These video clips will help you to visualize the materials in the textbook.

Try It Yourself

One thing we know from research in psychology and education is that active learning is often more effective than passive receipt of information. People are better able to learn and retain new knowledge when they can play with it and make connections to their own lives. We have done a variety of things to help you do that.

Learn About Yourself. Throughout the book, you will find commonly used scales in social psychology. These scales are presented in tables labelled "Know Yourself" and include all or some items from the original scale, as well as instructions for scoring your responses. For example, in Chapter 5, we discuss individual differences in *self-monitoring*. As described originally by Canadian social psychologist Mark Snyder (1974), the high self-monitor is a person who is especially sensitive to external, situational cues in interpersonal settings and who uses such cues as a guide to behaviour; the low self-monitor, on the other hand, is a person who uses internal cues and personal attributes (e.g., attitudes, feelings, values) as a guide to behaviour. Are you able to develop a clear sense of self-monitoring based on this conceptual description? Can you tell whether *you* are a high or low self-monitor? Perhaps. But the best way to find out is by completing items from the *Self-Monitoring Scale*, which you can do in Chapter 5 (see page 176).

Be a Research Participant. Another way to learn about social psychology is by experiencing the conditions and manipulations in actual experiments. Therefore, we have constructed a Web site, *Social Psychology Alive: Online Labs,* where you can be a participant in more than a dozen studies. These experiments relate to topics throughout the book; the titles of relevant studies are listed at the end of each chapter. For each experiment, you will be assigned to one condition and will complete the study like an actual participant. If you wish, you can subsequently run through the procedure for other conditions as well. Your data will be saved (only for the first condition you completed), and you can look at your responses when you are done. In addition, you can look at an anonymous summary of the responses of all students who have participated. A detailed explanation of the purpose and expected results of the study is available when you complete your participation. These online studies will give you the perspective of a research participant and make reading about social psychology experiments in the textbook more engaging.

Do Your Own Research. To make social psychology truly come alive, you also need to know what it is like to be a social psychologist. You need to conduct your own projects or experiments by developing the measures, collecting the data, and interpreting the results. To get you started, we have prepared a project-oriented workbook to accompany this textbook. *Social Psychology Alive: The Workbook* provides project ideas, sample stimulus materials, and help with interpreting data. A variety of possible projects are outlined, many of which can be done with the resources available to you. With the guidance and supervision of your instructor, you can personally do social psychology.

Dig Deeper. You will notice that, like most textbook writers, we provide many references and citations. We provide these references to give credit to the person or persons who proposed an idea or conducted a study, but also to allow you to dig a little deeper. These references generally follow the citation style of the American Psychological Association (2001), and the format we use is the same as the one you will find in scientific articles and books. All of these references are presented in alphabetical order in a list at the back of the book. If you are curious about the details of an experiment, want to get more information so you can conduct a similar study, or want to understand more fully the theoretical background to the research, the references are there to lead the way. With the citation in hand, you should be able to find the original article in your library, or have it ordered for you. Our goal is to make the social psychological literature accessible to you. For this reason, we only provide citations for articles or books that are readily found in Canadian university libraries.

There are two other ways you can dig deeper. First, at the end of each chapter, you will find sources listed under the heading *To Learn More.* These sources are ones that are particularly interesting or comprehensive for the topics in that chapter. They also should be available at most university libraries. Second, if your instructor ordered it with this book, you have access to *InfoTrac College Edition,* which is an online library of archived journal articles and periodicals dating back 22 years. You can access this information via your CD-ROM or by going directly to the Web site listed at the end of each chapter and using the passcode from the InfoTrac College Edition card that came with your book. To use the online library, enter a search term and see what comes up. This is an excellent way to find additional materials on specific topics in the chapters.

Social Psychology Is All Around You

As we noted earlier, social psychology is an exciting field to study because our lives are immersed in a social world. To maximize your appreciation of social psychology, you should pay special attention to your own life. The workbook provides many connections between the ideas in the textbook and daily life, such as newspaper articles, real-life examples of social psychological principles, and suggestions about things to watch for. Here are a few specific ways you can find social psychology in your own experiences.

Watch Television. Television is a rich source of social psychology in action. We posed a question at the beginning of the chapter about how the media affected people's responses to the terrorism of September 11, 2001. Constant replays of the attacks probably heightened feelings of threat and fear; stories of heroism probably heightened feelings of compassion and admiration. In many ways, reporters and commentators helped to define the events for the public.

So think about social psychology while you watch TV. Pay attention to commercials, sitcoms, the news, and (if you can) television programming in other countries and cultures. In commercials and advertisements, you will see in action the basic principles of persuasion (Chapter 7) and social influence (Chapter 8). So-called *infomercials* are especially interesting—see if you can connect this sales method to theories of persuasion. Television programs (especially dramas and situation comedies) often reflect or portray social stereotypes (Chapters 3 and 9) and close relationships (Chapter 13). The news often tells of intergroup conflict (Chapter 10) and violence (Chapter 11). More generally, do you think that the massive exposure of Canadians to American television networks and programs affects how we view the world?

Many principles of social psychology can be observed in television programs.

Read the Newspaper and Magazines. Newspapers and magazines are also brimming with rich examples of social psychology in action. Unlike television, newspaper editorials allow writers to present extended arguments. Think about the editorials you find most and least persuasive: What are the techniques used by effective writers (Chapter 7)? Study the cartoons. You will find that cartoonists often rely on basic social psychological concepts to create humour, such as the hindsight bias (Chapter 3), stereotypes (Chapters 3 and 9), social norms (Chapter 8), and close relationships (Chapter 13). You may want to develop a small portfolio of clippings from newspapers and magazines that illustrate basic social psychological principles.

Surf the Web. The Internet offers still another perspective on social psychology, in at least two distinct ways.

You can see social psychology in action by watching other people around you.

First, you will find numerous Web sites offering links and content relating to social psychology. For instance, a good place to get started is the Social Psychology Network: http://www.socialpsychology.org. Second, many Web sites are little more than persuasive communications; ask yourself how the sites use basic principles of persuasion (Chapter 7) and social influence (Chapter 8). The Internet is less restricted or filtered than other mass media, so it is also easier to find examples of social extremes—portrayals of violence, racism, and stereotypes abound on the Web (Chapters 9 and 11).

Observe Others. Part of the social psychologist's toolkit is the ability to observe the actions of others, especially in their natural environments. Watch your friends and family members as they go about their daily lives and interact with one another. Can you tell what people are thinking or feeling by simply observing their facial expressions or body language (Chapter 4)? Are people consistent in their actions and personal styles across time, places, and contexts (Chapter 5)? Can you see evidence of prejudice against ethnic minorities like Aboriginal peoples or Chinese Canadians (Chapter 9)? Do people behave differently when they are alone than when they are in groups (Chapter 10)? Why are some people attracted to one another and others not (Chapter 13)?

Observe Yourself. A little self-reflection and introspection will also make you a better social psychologist. Do you engage in much wishful thinking (Chapter 3)? Do you explain your own behaviour in the same way you explain others' actions (Chapter 4)? Do you tend to rationalize and justify your wasted effort (Chapter 7)? Do your moods influence how helpful you are to other people (Chapter 12)?

If you want to collect some data on yourself, consider keeping a personal diary. The method is described in Chapter 13 and in the workbook. At regular times each day, write down what you are doing, how you are feeling, and what you are thinking. After several weeks, you will be surprised to see how rich and complex your social world really is.

Chapter Summary

We end each chapter with a brief summary, which reviews the chapter's key terms and central ideas. In this chapter, we introduced **social psychology,** which is the scientific study of how individuals' thoughts, feelings, and behaviours are influenced by other people. Social psychologists take the perspective of individuals in a social setting, rather than focusing only on objective features of the situation. Put another way, social psychologists focus on **social construals,** which are individuals' personal perceptions or interpretations of the social situation. Other people can affect us in many ways, even without having to be physically present.

Some findings in social psychology are consistent with intuitive folk wisdom, but it is a mistake to think that social psychology is just common sense. Many findings are not common sense at all, often because folk wisdom is simplistic whereas real life is more complicated. Also, after reading about the results of a social psychology experiment, people may think that the findings were obvious, whereas the outcome was actually quite uncertain in advance. Studying social psychology has many benefits, including becoming an informed citizen, being able to apply social psychological knowledge to everyday life, and gaining a better understanding of yourself.

Social psychology's roots can be found in philosophy. For example, the concept of social norms can be traced back to the philosophical concept of the **social contract:** the idea that human societies have developed some basic rules of social and moral conduct, which members of the societies implicitly agree to follow. An influential approach in psychology during the first half of the 20th century was **behaviourism,** which attempts to explain behaviour purely in terms of stimulus–response connections established through experience and reinforcement. Several influential social psychologists who came to North America in the 1930s brought with them an alternative approach: **Gestalt theory.** Gestalt theory assumes that people's overall, subjective interpretations of objects are more important than the objects' external, physical features. The Second World War turned North American social psychologists' attention to practical questions regarding the war effort. By the time the war had ended, social psychology was emerging as a distinct area of psychology.

Each chapter in this book focuses on one of the classical topics or problems of social psychology and reviews the scientific literature in that area. Cross-cutting the chapters are many contexts to which social psychology can be applied, with special emphasis on culture, health, and the law. The approach of *Social Psychology Alive* is to encourage you to experience social psychology for yourself. We have prepared many supplementary materials to help, including *Social Psychology Alive: The Videos, Social Psychology Alive: The Workbook,* and *Social Psychology Alive: Online Labs.* We want you to pay attention to things in your own life, because social psychology is all around you.

Key Terms

behaviourism (19)

Gestalt theory (20)

social construals (7)

social contract (18)

social psychology (6)

Social Psychology Alive on the Web

SOCIAL PSYCHOLOGY ALIVE: QUIZZING AND PRACTICE TESTS

You can access our Web site directly by going to http://www.socialpsychologyalive.nelson.com for online quizzes, flash cards, and Internet links.

INFOTRAC® COLLEGE EDITION

For additional readings, explore InfoTrac® College Edition, your online library of archived journal articles and periodicals dating back 22 years. If your instructor ordered InfoTrac® College Edition with this book, you can access it from your CD-ROM, or go directly to http:// www.infotrac-college.com and use the passcode from the InfoTrac® College Edition card that came with your book. For this chapter, try these search terms: *social psychology, sociology, philosophy, social contract, behaviorism, Gestalt theory*.

Social Psychology Alive: The Workbook

Chapter 1 of *Social Psychology Alive: The Workbook* provides key terms, guided study, and sample test questions. It also provides suggestions for connecting social psychology to the real world and to your life:

- Social Psychology Alive Journal: Personal Experiences
- Social Psychology Alive Journal: Events in the Media

- Proverbs, Adages, and Platitudes: Which Do Social Psychology Support?
- How Does Social Psychology Compare to Other Areas of Psychology and Other Disciplines?

Social Psychology Alive: The Videos

To see video on the topics and experiments discussed in this chapter, you can go either to ThomsonNOW™ or to the CD-ROM, if your instructor assigned either one, to the following section:

- Social Psychology: It's All Around You

To Learn More

At the end of each chapter, we provide a few citations to books or articles that can help you learn more. These readings are good places to start if you want to gain a deeper understanding of the topics in that chapter. Here are three suggestions for Chapter 1:

- Allport, G. W. (1985). The historical background of social psychology. In G. Lindzey & E. Aronson (Eds.), *The handbook of social psychology* (3rd ed., Vol. 1, pp. 1–46). New York: Random House.

- Aron, A., & Aron, E. N. (1986). *The heart of social psychology*. Lexington, MA: Lexington Books.
- Taylor, S. E. (1998). The social being in social psychology. In D. T. Gilbert, S. T. Fiske, & G. Lindzey (Eds.), *The handbook of social psychology* (4th ed., Vol. 1, pp. 3–57). Boston: McGraw-Hill.

The Methods of Social Psychology

Veranna Johnson is a fourth-year student in accounting at the University of Waterloo. She receives a telephone call from a researcher in the Psychology Department, who offers her some money if she will participate in a study of the effects of "journalistic style on social perception." She agrees to participate.

A few days later in a psychology laboratory, Veranna is given an article to read from the campus newspaper, which describes a stellar fourth-year student at the university—who happens to be in the accounting program as well. This individual recently won an important award for outstanding academic achievement and was praised by the chair of the Accounting Department as "innovative and creative." In addition, the article describes in detail the individual's involvement in student government, volunteer activities, and various sports teams. Simply put, the student described in the article is extraordinary.

After reading the article, Veranna gives some ratings of the stellar student, which are, of course, very favourable. Then the experimenter asks Veranna to provide some ratings of herself on ten positive traits related to career success (e.g., bright, skillful) and ten negative traits (e.g., incompetent, unintelligent). Veranna isn't feeling very positive about herself and gives herself rather unfavourable ratings—low on the positive traits and high on the negative traits.

● ● ● The Scientific Method

The preceding story is true; only the name was changed to protect the innocent participant! The study was a social psychological investigation of the effects of information about "superstars"—one kind of *social comparison* information, which we mentioned briefly in Chapter 1. The experiment was conducted by Penelope Lockwood and Ziva Kunda at the University of Waterloo.

Lockwood and Kunda (1997) hypothesized that being exposed to information about an extremely successful person would make some participants feel negatively about themselves—like Veranna's reaction. This prediction is consistent with the study by Thornton and Moore (1993) that we described in Chapter 1, which showed that participants who sat beside a posterboard displaying photographs of very physically attractive persons rated themselves more negatively than did participants in a control condition (see page 9).

But Lockwood and Kunda also predicted that some other participants would actually feel *better* about themselves after exposure to a superstar. Who will feel better and who will feel worse? Lockwood and Kunda suggested that the critical factor is whether or not people think that they themselves have the potential to be very successful. For example, those who have many future opportunities to achieve success will be inspired by a superstar and rate themselves more positively, whereas those who have few opportunities for similar success will be distressed by a superstar and rate themselves more negatively.

Lockwood and Kunda predicted that students who were still in their *first* year of the accounting program at the university would be inspired by the stellar student because they still had lots of time to achieve similar success. Fourth-year students like Veranna, on the other hand, would feel worse about themselves because they had little or no chance of achieving similar success. The results confirmed these predictions. This study illustrates many of the principles and challenges of social psychological research, and we will refer back to it several times in the chapter.

We know from Chapter 1 that social psychology is a *science*—we defined the field as "the scientific study of how individuals' thoughts, feelings, and behaviours are influenced by other people." It is not simple, however, to study social behaviour scientifically. Unlike physical sciences such as biology and chemistry, in which researchers often have total control over the materials they are studying, social psychologists are interested in understanding spontaneous social behaviour, which is difficult to study in tightly controlled settings. Thus, social psychology is a tricky science. Social psychologists have to be very creative in using the scientific method to study how individuals are influenced by other people.

The scientific method is basically a tool (or, more correctly, a set of tools) that scientists use to find out about the world. Scientists are curious about why events occur, and the scientific method provides an objective, efficient way to answer questions. Just as early explorers used maps, telescopes, and compasses to discover things about the world, scientists use the scientific method to investigate issues in their own field. Scientists are like modern explorers trying to understand the causes of important events and phenomena. The scientific method gives them a way to collect impartial information about the world around them.

In this chapter, we discuss the research methods of social psychology. We begin by providing some general background about the scientific method. Specifically, we define *theories* and *hypotheses* and discuss issues involved in translating theories and hypotheses into testable questions. Armed with this background information, we turn to *correlational research*: studies that involve collecting two or more measures and seeing how they relate to one another. We describe three correlational methods— surveys, archival research, and observational studies—which differ primarily in terms of how researchers collect their data. Next, we discuss the most important method used by social psychologists: the *experiment*. In experiments, researchers *manipulate* independent variables, *measure* dependent variables, and *control* extraneous variables. We note that researchers want careful control in their experiment but also hope to be able to apply their findings to nonlaboratory settings—the sometimes-competing goals of *internal validity* and *external validity*. We then differentiate between *single-factor* and *factorial* experimental designs, discuss the issue of *realism* in experiments, and explain *field experiments*, which are experiments conducted in nonlaboratory settings. We then consider some implications of modern technologies for research in social psychology. Finally, we raise some ethical issues that are relevant to social psychological research and explain how investigators address these issues.

Theories and Hypotheses

Two key elements of the scientific method are *theories* and *hypotheses*. An excellent discussion of theories and hypotheses in social psychology can be found in a paper by Shelagh Towson (2005) of the University of Windsor. You can think about theories as *explanations,* and hypotheses as *predictions*. More specifically, a **theory** is a scientist's explanation of why an event or outcome occurs (see Pelham, 1999; Schmidt & Hunter, 2003); it identifies the underlying causes of something the scientist has observed. In psychology, theories typically focus on psychological processes to explain events. For instance, in attempting to explain how information about extremely successful people (superstars) can influence individuals, a social psychologist might propose that individuals who believe that they can be similarly successful themselves will be inspired by the superstar. This simple theory explains one possible response to superstars (inspiration) in terms of an underlying psychological mechanism (the belief that they can be successful too).

theory

an explanation of why an event or outcome occurs; it identifies the underlying causes of an event or phenomenon

hypothesis

a specific prediction about what should occur if a theory is valid; it provides the means by which a theory can be tested

Whereas theories provide a framework for understanding *why* something occurs, **hypotheses** are specific *predictions* about what should occur if a theory is valid. Hypotheses are derived from a theory and, therefore, provide a means for testing the theory. For example, if the belief that they can personally be successful causes individuals to be inspired by a superstar (theory), then increasing or decreasing individuals' belief that they can succeed should directly increase or decrease how much they are inspired by a superstar (hypothesis). If a test of this hypothesis confirmed it, then confidence in the validity of the theory would increase. A process of evaluating theories by confirming or disconfirming hypotheses forms the core of the scientific method— a point to which we will turn momentarily.

But, first, how do scientists develop theories? What are the sources of their ideas? (See Kruglanski & Higgins, 2004, for a series of articles discussing theory construction in social psychology.) Most theories build on prior scientific work, including previous theories that have been shown to be inaccurate or limited (Cacioppo, 2004). Theories often involve applying a concept or principle from one field to another related but distinct field (Zanna, 2004). Theories also frequently rely on scientists' intuitive analyses of problems, including their personal experiences (Fiske, 2004). Some theories are the result of collaborations between scientists who have different perspectives (Levine & Moreland, 2004). In developing a theory, scientists aim for simplicity, coherence, and testability (Fiske, 2004), because these features make it more likely that the theory will generate new ideas and new discoveries (Higgins, 2004).

To make the concepts of theories and hypotheses more concrete, let's briefly consider a fascinating theory from social psychology as an example. Melvin Lerner (1977, 1980), who spent most of his career at the University of Waterloo, proposed *just world theory,* in which he suggested that humans *need* to believe that the world is a fair and just place. Lerner proposed that we are all motivated to believe that people usually receive what they deserve: hard work and honesty bring rewards, whereas laziness and dishonesty do not pay. Lerner argued that if we did *not* believe that the world is largely fair, then we would fear that our *own* efforts and investments might not pay off. That is, if we believed that the world is unjust and that hard-working people do not necessarily succeed, then we would fear that our *own* hard work might be in vain! Lerner proposed that this possibility is threatening and anxiety-provoking, so we try to *protect* our belief in a just world.

What are some *hypotheses* that can be derived from just world theory? One rather straightforward hypothesis is that, when asked, most people will say that the world is generally fair. After all, if just world theory is valid, then people should report that the world is just. Lerner also derived a more indirect and interesting hypothesis from the theory's assumption that we want to *protect* our belief in a just world. Lerner made the provocative prediction that people would blame or derogate (evaluate negatively) victims who are suffering in negative circumstances (e.g., unemployed people, AIDS patients), especially when their suffering is expected to continue. This prediction was based on the logic that suffering victims threaten the belief that the world is fair, *unless the victims are either responsible for their suffering or are bad people who in some sense deserve their suffering.* Therefore, if we are truly motivated to defend our belief that the world is fair, we might try to convince ourselves that people who are suffering brought it on themselves or are bad people who deserve their fate. Can you think of victims who tend to be blamed or disparaged in our society? What about people living on welfare? Or what about sexual assault victims, who are sometimes

Just world theory predicts that people may blame and disparage victims.

© Tim Boyle/Getty Images

accused of having acted in ways that somehow "invited" the assault? Lerner's hypothesis seems consistent with some people's devaluation of these victims.

Just world theory is a good example of how theories can lead to interesting, possibly unexpected predictions. Just world theory offers a novel perspective on people's beliefs about fairness and justice. As a *theory*, it explains *why* people want to believe in a just world and proposes that this need is present, at least to some extent, in everyone. It identifies psychological mechanisms that are thought to account for important social behaviours. It also provides the basis for some intriguing *hypotheses*, including the prediction that people will blame or derogate victims whose suffering is expected to continue. We will return to this prediction later in the chapter when we discuss experimental research. First, though, we continue with background information about the scientific method and discuss another important component: operational definitions.

Translating Theoretical Ideas into Testable Questions: Operational Definitions

Theories and hypotheses in social psychology are typically expressed in *conceptual* terms: they refer to abstract ideas or concepts that cannot be observed directly. Therefore, to test theories or hypotheses, researchers must somehow translate the abstract ideas into concrete, objective measures. For instance, a researcher interested in *attitudes* cannot directly "see" participants' attitudes; this concept can only be measured indirectly. Or a researcher interested in the effects of information about outstanding performers must think of how to measure such effects in a consistent, objective way across participants.

An **operational definition** of a concept is a *specific, observable response* that will be used to measure the concept (see Dooley, 2001; Pelham, 1999). For instance, people's attitudes toward religion (which are unobservable but presumably exist in people's minds) could be operationally defined by asking respondents to indicate how unfavourable or favourable they are toward religion on a scale from 0 (very unfavourable) to 10 (very favourable). Table 2.1 illustrates what the scale could look like. The concept is *attitudes toward religion;* the operational definition (or measure) is *scores from 0 to 10* on a response scale.

As another example, one possible effect of information about superstars is to make people feel good about themselves (which might occur when they believe they, too, can succeed). But how can "feeling good about the self" be operationally defined? Lockwood and Kunda's (1997) strategy was to ask participants to rate themselves on a number of positive and negative traits: favourable ratings were assumed to reflect feeling good about the self. The concept was feeling good about the self; the operational definition (or measure) was favourability of self-ratings on positive and negative traits.

operational definition
a specific, observable response that is used to measure a concept

---

TABLE 2.1
Operational Definition of Attitudes Toward Religion

How unfavourable or favourable are you toward religion? Please circle the number that best represents your attitude.

My attitude toward religion is

0	1	2	3	4	5	6	7	8	9	10
Very Unfavourable		Unfavourable			Neutral		Favourable			Very Favourable

CONCEPT REVIEW
Theories, Hypotheses, and Operational Definitions

Concept	Description	Example
Theories	Explanations of why an outcome occurs	People who believe that they can be successful will be inspired by a superstar
Hypotheses	Predictions about what should happen if a theory is valid	Increasing individuals' belief that they can be successful will increase how much they are inspired by a superstar
Operational definitions	Specific, observable responses used to measure concepts	People who have many future opportunities to succeed will rate themselves more favourably on various traits after being exposed to information about a superstar

The accompanying Concept Review summarizes the meanings of theories, hypotheses, and operational definitions (measures).

Two types of measures are most common in social psychology: self-report measures and behavioural measures. We briefly address the advantages and disadvantages of each kind of measure in the following paragraphs. A detailed discussion of self-report and behavioural measures in the specific context of measuring attitudes is presented in Chapter 6 (see page 198). We also provide a more general description of how to develop measures of social psychological constructs in Appendix I of this book.

Self-Report Measures. To measure many social psychological concepts, the easiest strategy is to ask people directly. If you want to know whether individuals believe in God, ask them. If you want to know whether people are optimistic about their future, ask them. If you want to know how often people go to the dentist, ask them. So long as a concept is something that people are *able* and *willing* to report, measuring it via self-report questions makes sense. Belief in God, optimism about the future, and visits to the dentist probably satisfy these assumptions, because people are presumably aware of these concepts and seem unlikely to be dishonest in reporting them.

Of course, even when people are able and willing to report a concept, researchers must be careful to express self-report questions clearly. It is easy to understand questions such as "How old are you?" or "What is the date of your birth?" It is harder to understand questions such as "Are you favourable to legalized abortion?" People attempting to answer this question might wonder what is meant by "legalized abortion." Does it mean in the first trimester, or anytime during a pregnancy? Does it refer to across-the-board access to abortion so long as a woman wants it, or only in special circumstances that must be approved by a physician? It can be difficult to answer a question if the meaning is not well specified.

The same question can often be asked in different ways, and subtle changes in phrasing or wording can significantly affect responses. As an illustration of this, Elizabeth Loftus and John Palmer (1974) asked people to watch a short film depicting a car accident. Everybody saw the same film, but different questions were asked to different groups of viewers. One group of viewers was asked, "About how fast were the cars going when they hit each other?" On average, these viewers answered 13 kilometres per hour. Another group of viewers was asked a slightly different question: "About how fast were the cars going when they smashed each other?" The viewers in this group answered, on average, 18 kilometres per hour. Why did these different answers occur? It all had to do with the verb used to describe the accident: *hit* versus *smashed*. Even though all participants saw the same accident, the wording of the question influenced their answers. Similar concerns about wording are important in many occupations. For example, physicians interviewing patients must avoid leading questions if they want to diagnose problems accurately; they should ask patients to describe their symptoms, rather than inadvertently focusing patients' attention on particular sensations (e.g., "Does your stomach hurt?"). Social psychologists are very careful about how they word their questions. The answers they get may depend on it.

Sometimes the assumption that people are able and willing to report a concept is *not* valid. For instance, people may not be *aware* of some internal states, such as unconscious motives that can affect their actions (e.g., "Are you afraid of failure?") or memories that may no longer be available (e.g., "How did you feel about religion when you were a child?"). People may *believe* that they can answer these questions accurately, but their responses will probably be guesses.

Perhaps even more often than being unaware of a concept, participants in social psychological research may not *want* to report some things honestly. For instance, respondents may be motivated to create a positive impression of themselves. Responding in this manner is known as **socially desirable responding**—giving answers that portray the respondent in a favourable light. Questions like "How often do you put cans in recycling bins after finishing a drink?" and "How favourable are you toward Aboriginal Canadians?" are loaded—some answers are more socially valued than others. Everyone knows that the most desirable answer to the recycling question is "always" or "every time," and the most desirable answer to the Aboriginal Canadians question is "very favourable." Failing to recycle and being prejudiced are considered undesirable in our society. So people might not answer these kinds of questions honestly.

What can researchers do to control contamination of their measures by social desirability motives? One straightforward strategy is to avoid phrasing items in ways that make some responses more socially desirable than others. For example, if a researcher wants to measure participants' attitudes toward immigration, it is better to ask "Do you think that changing our immigration policies to be more restrictive

socially desirable responding
a form of responding that involves giving answers that portray the respondent in a positive light

Observers' judgments about a car accident were affected by the questions they were asked.

would strengthen Canada?" than a question like "Do you resent immigrants?" A second strategy is to obtain a measure of participants' general tendencies to respond in a desirable manner on all measures, which can then be used to control desirable responding on a specific measure. For example, Canadian social psychologist Delroy Paulhus (1984) at the University of British Columbia developed a scale called the *Balanced Inventory of Desirable Responding*, which provides scores for respondents' tendencies to present themselves in a favourable light. This scale is well known and has been used in many studies.

Behavioural Measures. Because people may be unable or unwilling to report some things accurately, researchers sometimes measure concepts by observing individuals' behaviours. For instance, continuing the examples of recycling and ethnic attitudes, researchers interested in people's recycling behaviour might give participants a canned drink while completing a questionnaire and then watch to see if they drop the can in a recycling bin on their way out of the room. For a behavioural measure of attitudes toward Aboriginal peoples, participants might be required to complete a task together with an Aboriginal partner, and the researcher would observe how often the participant smiles at the partner or assists the partner on the task.

unobtrusive measures

assessments that are taken without the realization of participants, thereby minimizing socially desirable responding

One advantage of behavioural measures is that they are often **unobtrusive measures,** which means that participants do not realize that the measure is being taken. If participants are unaware that a measure is being taken, then presumably they will not try to alter their actions to create a favourable impression. For instance, participants given a canned drink and then allowed to leave would not realize that the researcher was watching to see whether they would recycle the can. Similarly, participants interacting with a First Nations person would not realize that the researcher was watching to see how much they smiled or helped their partner.

A disadvantage of behavioural measures is that they can be difficult or time-consuming to obtain. For instance, the behavioural measure of favourability toward Aboriginal Canadians described above would require a complex cover story and the help of an experimental accomplice. A second disadvantage is that behavioural measures are very difficult or impossible for some concepts. For instance, how could a researcher measure participants' emotional responses to a past event using behaviour? Or how could a researcher measure participants' thoughts in response to a persuasive message using behaviour? These limitations of behavioural measures, together with the simplicity and directness of self-report measures, explain why self-report measures are much more common in social psychological research.

No matter how a concept is operationally defined (e.g., self-report or behavioural measures), the goal is to measure the concept *accurately*. This goal is not always simple in social psychology, nor indeed in psychology generally, because many of our concepts are complex, elusive, and buried deep beneath the surface. The problem of the accuracy of psychological measures is so challenging that an entire subdiscipline within psychology—**psychometrics**—is devoted to understanding and refining methods for psychological measurement. Psychometrics tells us to focus on two properties of measures that represent accuracy: reliability and validity. We turn to these properties next.

psychometrics

a subdiscipline within psychology that is devoted to understanding and refining methods for psychological measurement

Reliability. A good measure should be stable and steady. It should always give us the same answer (assuming, of course, that the concept does not change between measurements). Have you ever stood on the bathroom scale wondering if the number is really correct? You step off, let the pointer return to zero, and then step on again. Is it the same number? It will probably be very close. That's because the scale is reliable: it gives you the same answer over and over again. Perhaps you don't trust that scale, so you check out your weight on your friend's bathroom scale. Same answer again?

Reliability refers to the consistency or stability of scores on a measure. A reliable measure is one that produces consistent scores, free from "random" or unexplained fluctuations. We can think of consistency in at least two distinct ways. The first is consistency *over time*. In this sense, a reliable measure is one that produces stable scores for the same object on repeated use. Stepping off and then back on the same bathroom scale is an effort to assess consistency over time. Another form of consistency is *across judges*. In this sense, reliability occurs when an object receives similar scores from different judges. Tracking down that second scale is an effort to assess consistency across judges.

In measuring social behaviour, it is quite common to have several observers record or score a person's actions (e.g., rate the aggressiveness of a child in the playground). Why? Because ensuring that there is consistency across judges (observers) for the same person shows that the scoring system is reliable. If three or four independent judges assign the same scores to an individual, then we can have confidence in the reliability of the measure. Similarly, social psychologists often videotape the behaviour of research participants. This is done so that multiple observers can be used later to get repeated assessments of the same behaviour, all in an effort to establish the reliability of the measure.

Validity. A good measure (a good operational definition of a concept) does more than yield a reliable score. It also yields a score that truly reflects the concept it is intended to measure. This quality of measures is called **validity:** the extent to which scores on the measures really represent the underlying concept they are intended to represent. In other words, does a measure really assess what it is supposed to assess? When we step on a bathroom scale, we are pretty confident that the number it shows represents our weight and not, say, our body heat. Likewise, when we use a thermometer, we trust that the number corresponds to our body heat and not to our weight.

The validity of social psychological measures, however, is often more difficult to establish than the validity of instruments assessing physical characteristics like weight and temperature. For example, how do we know that answers to one or more self-report questions will really give us a good assessment of individuals' attitudes toward religion? Or how can we be confident that individuals' self-reports of how many hours a week they study really give us an accurate estimate of this behaviour? The most common way to demonstrate validity is by showing that scores on a measure correspond reasonably well to scores on other measures that *should* be related. These other measures presumably assess at least some aspects of the same concept, so showing that they overlap with the focal measure supports the validity of that measure.

For instance, to establish the validity of a measure of attitudes toward religion, a researcher might try to show that scores on the scale correspond quite closely to the following additional measures: ratings of participants' religiosity by their friends; records of charitable donations by participants to religious organizations; and participants' self-reports of how often they attend a religious service. None of these additional measures is itself a perfect reflection of attitudes toward religion, but they are all at least somewhat related; thus, if the attitude scores predict these other measures adequately, then it seems reasonable to conclude that the attitude scores are valid. To establish the

reliability
the extent to which a measure is free of "random" fluctuations, both over time and across judges

validity
the extent to which a measure really assesses what it is supposed to assess—whether scores on the measure actually reflect the assumed underlying concept

Scales generally provide *reliable* estimates of weight.

A valid measure of *attitudes toward religion* should predict how often a person attends a religious service.

validity of a self-reported estimate of time spent studying, a researcher might try to show that the self-reports of studying predict ratings of participants' studiousness by their friends, participants' academic grades, and participants' self-reports of how motivated they are to do well at school. Again, though none of these additional measures corresponds exactly with number of hours of study, they should all be at least moderately related to participants' actual studiousness and, therefore, provide appropriate checks on the validity of the self-report measure.

We have now discussed some of the key elements of the scientific method, including theories, hypotheses, operational definitions, reliability, and validity. If the scientific method produces support for a theory, then scientists begin to accept the theory as a valid basis for understanding the events to which it applies. A validated theory is very useful, because if we understand why something occurs, we may be able to encourage it (if it is beneficial) or discourage it (if it is detrimental). For instance, if we can develop valid theories of prejudice (valid explanations of why prejudice occurs), then we should be able to design programs to reduce prejudice. Given the practical value of theories, social psychologists are constantly proposing, testing, and revising theories about important social behaviours.

Armed with this background knowledge about the scientific method, we can now turn to specific methods that are used frequently by social psychologists. We will discuss two broad categories of research: correlational research and experimental research.

● ● ● Correlational Research

correlational research

studies in which investigators measure two or more concepts and see whether the concepts are associated with one another

In **correlational research,** investigators measure two or more concepts and see whether the concepts are associated with one another—that is, whether measures of the concepts go together, or co-relate (hence, *correlational* research). This focus on whether measures are associated with one another is true of all correlational research. The various kinds of correlational studies differ primarily in *how researchers obtain the data:* by asking questions, by using historical information, or by watching behaviour.

When two measures are correlated, it means that scores on the measures are systematically related: as scores on one measure change, scores on the other measure also change in a consistent fashion. If the two measures change in the *same* direction (i.e., as scores on one measure go up, scores on the other measure go up too), then the relation between the measures is called a *positive correlation*. For example, height and weight are positively correlated: taller people also tend to weigh more than shorter people. If two measures change in the *opposite* direction (i.e., as scores on one measure go up, scores on the other measure go down), then the relation between the measures is called a *negative correlation*. For example, altitude and temperature are negatively correlated: locations that are high in altitude, such as mountaintops, tend to have colder temperatures than lower locations.

Let's consider an example of a correlation from social psychological research. The University of Manitoba's Robert Altemeyer (1994) and other social psychologists have found that the amount of contact people have had with members of an ethnic group is negatively correlated with their prejudice toward that group: people who report *more contact* with members of an ethnic group also report *less prejudice* toward that group (we discuss this topic in Chapter 9; see page 361).

This correlation between contact and prejudice can be used to illustrate an important limitation of correlational research: *correlations do not show that measures are causally connected.* When two measures are correlated, the cause of this association cannot be known with certainty. Just because one measure correlates with another measure does not necessarily mean that the first measure causes the second, nor that the second measure necessarily causes the first. For instance, why does contact with an ethnic group correlate with prejudice? One possibility is that more frequent contact with a group causes a reduction in prejudice, perhaps because people learn that members of the ethnic group are nicer than they expected (contact reduces prejudice). But it is also possible that the *opposite* direction of cause explains the correlation: perhaps people who are prejudiced avoid contact with members of the minority group (prejudice reduces contact). It is even possible that some unidentified *third* factor causes the correlation between contact and prejudice.

The reason correlational research is ambiguous about cause is that the investigator does not (or cannot) control other factors in the environment that might partly

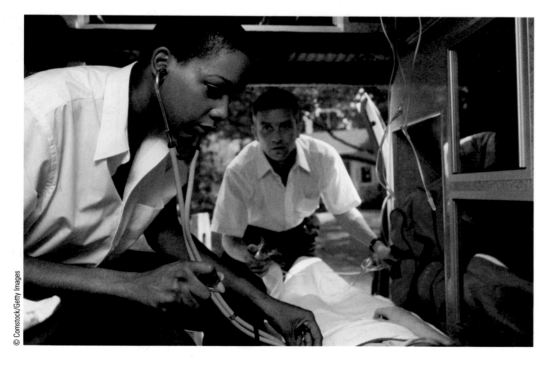

© Comstock/Getty Images

Why does contact with members of an ethnic group correlate with prejudice toward that group?

or completely explain an obtained correlation. Instead, the researcher simply measures two or more concepts and examines their associations. *Why* associations did or did not occur is unclear.

This problem with correlational data applies to all of the methods we describe in the following sections. As you are reading examples of research for each correlational method, see if you can explain the results in different ways. You may be able to generate more than one possible interpretation.

Notwithstanding this limitation of correlational research, these methods do have some real strengths. For example, they are quite flexible and can be designed to explore many different issues (as you will see from the examples we provide). Also, obtaining correlational data is often easier than trying to set up an experiment. Finally, correlational measures are sometimes obtained in naturalistic settings, as opposed to the potentially artificial settings of laboratory research.

Surveys

survey

a correlational study in which the researcher asks questions to respondents, either in a printed questionnaire, on a computer, over the telephone, or during an interview

The most common kind of correlational research in social psychology is the survey. A **survey** is a study in which the researcher asks questions to respondents. Survey researchers design questions to accurately assess concepts and then examine whether participants' answers to different questions are correlated.

Many surveys are conducted by distributing printed questionnaires to participants. For instance, questionnaires may be distributed in a laboratory, completed by participants, and handed back to the researcher; alternatively, questionnaires can be mailed to respondents, completed at their leisure, and mailed back to the researcher. Also common are computer-based surveys, which can be completed by participants either in the laboratory or at home (e.g., on the Internet). Another common type of survey is a telephone survey. In this case, the researcher telephones participants, asks them questions over the phone, and records their answers. Finally, face-to-face interviews are also a form of survey; researchers ask questions during an interview and record participants' answers.

All of these methods are common in social psychology. We will provide just one example. Carleton University's Christopher Davis and his colleagues (Davis et al., 1995) were interested in *counterfactual thinking,* which refers to thoughts about how past events could have turned out differently. We will discuss counterfactual thinking in detail in Chapter 3 (see page 93). Davis and his colleagues were interested in whether counterfactual thinking after a traumatic event correlated with emotional distress. Specifically, the researchers wondered whether people who frequently think about how a tragic event that occurred to them could have been avoided (one type of counterfactual thinking) would also report more emotional distress. To test this hypothesis, the researchers surveyed 93 people who had lost a loved one, either a spouse or a child, in a motor vehicle accident four to seven years previously. Names of possible participants were obtained from a list of all motor vehicle fatalities over a three-year period in a specific county. After agreeing to be interviewed, participants were visited in their homes by a researcher who asked them a number of questions. Some questions assessed how often participants found themselves thinking, "If only I had done something different, my child [spouse] would still be alive." Other questions concerned participants' current emotional states, such as their feelings of depression and anxiety.

Results showed that people who reported more frequent counterfactual thinking about the event also reported greater emotional distress. That is, people who frequently thought about how their loved one would still be alive if they had done something differently reported more symptoms of depression and anxiety. Based on these results, the researchers speculated that, to cope effectively with a traumatic event, people should not repeatedly chew over how the tragedy could have been avoided. This recommendation assumes that thinking about a past tragedy causes depression; can you think of an alternative interpretation of the findings? One alternative may be that depression causes people to think about unhappy events (see Chapter 3, page 103), including previous tragedies.

Before turning to the next type of correlational method, we need to discuss an issue that is specifically relevant to surveys but not to the other methods.

Representative Samples. Researchers who conduct surveys sometimes want to be able to generalize their results to a large population, such as all adult Canadians, or all adults living in a province. For instance, political pollsters may want to use their findings to predict the outcome of a federal or provincial election. If this ability to generalize is important, then the researcher must ensure that the sample of people who complete the survey is typical of the population. If researchers simply distribute questionnaires haphazardly to students at a university or to shoppers in a mall, they cannot assume that their findings will generalize to larger groups.

How can researchers make their findings generalizable to a large population? To achieve this goal, they must recruit a **representative sample** to complete the survey. A representative sample is a group of respondents that reflects the larger population accurately: it has ratios of various subgroups that are similar to those in the larger population. For instance, if researchers want to generalize to all adults in Canada, then equal numbers of men and women should complete the survey, as well as respondents from each province in approximately the same proportions as the provinces' populations. The typical way to obtain a representative sample is via **random sampling,** which refers to a recruitment process in which every person in the larger population has exactly the same probability of being in the study. For instance, random sampling of all Canadian adults would mean that every adult in Canada was equally likely to be recruited. As you can imagine, random sampling is a difficult and time-consuming procedure. Typically, social psychologists do not obtain random samples. Instead, they rely on replications of a study with different (nonrandom) samples to assess whether research findings generalize to other groups. For polling companies, however, it is usually so important to be able to generalize a survey's results to a larger population that they accept the necessary costs of time and money involved in obtaining a random sample.

representative sample

a group of respondents that accurately reflects a larger population from which it was drawn and to which the researcher wants to generalize the results

random sampling

a recruitment process in which every person in a particular population has exactly the same probability of being in the study; it produces a representative sample

Archival Research

Archival research refers to investigations that are based on pre-existing information obtained by the researcher. Archival research is common in social psychology and can utilize a wide variety of public data. For example, historical records, newspaper articles, police reports, and past speeches by politicians have all provided data for archival research by social psychologists. You may recall that, in Chapter 1, we mentioned an archival study by Brian Mullen (1986), which showed that lynchings of Black men by White mobs between 1899 and 1946 were more vicious when the mobs were larger in number, perhaps because larger mobs provided stronger feelings of anonymity.

Researchers have been very creative in testing interesting questions using archival information. David Phillips (1977) at the University of California at San Diego identified 20 highly publicized suicides that occurred between 1966 and 1973 (e.g., suicides by famous actors). Phillips also obtained information about motor vehicle fatalities in the days prior to and following the appearance of these suicide stories. Across the 20 suicides, Phillips found a consistent and significant rise in motor vehicle fatalities three days after the appearance of the story. Figure 2.1 presents the results of his

archival research

correlational investigations that are based on pre-existing information obtained by researchers, such as historical records, newspaper articles, or other forms of public data

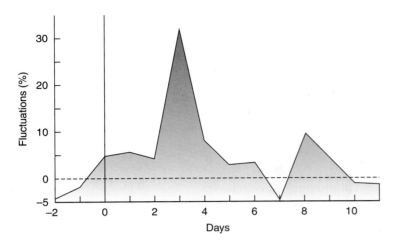

FIGURE 2.1 Motor vehicle fatalities following publicized suicides

From D. P. Phillips, "Motor vehicle fatalities increase just after publicized suicide stories," *Science*, 196, 1464–1465, 1977. Reprinted by permission of the American Association for the Advancement of Science.

archival research, showing the fluctuations from the normal rate of motor vehicle fatalities in the days surrounding the publicized suicides. Phillips speculated that the suicides by well-known individuals prompted copycat suicides using motor vehicles by depressed, vulnerable members of the public.

Another fascinating piece of archival research is described in the accompanying box, Social Psychology in Your Life: "The Effects of Name Similarity."

Observational Studies

Observational studies refer to research in which the investigator watches participants and codes measures from the observed behaviour. The scoring of behaviour can occur either "live," while the observer is actually watching participants, or later if participants are videotaped (in which case their behaviour can subsequently be evaluated and scored using the tapes). Participants in observational studies are sometimes aware that they are being observed and sometimes unaware. Also, observational studies can focus on behaviour in either a naturalistic setting or a laboratory setting. These features of observational studies are interconnected. For example, if behaviour

Social Psychology in Your Life   *The Effects of Name Similarity*

Brett Pelham, Matthew Mirenberg, and John Jones (2002) reported some fascinating archival data on people's names and the places they lived. Pelham and his colleagues noted that humans generally like themselves and think positively of themselves (a point we will make several times in Chapters 3 and 4) and suggested that this liking extends to their own names. The researchers further speculated that people might show enhanced liking for things that elicit connections to themselves (perhaps unconsciously), such as things that remind them of their own names. To test this idea, the researchers sifted through census data and telephone books to see whether people were more likely than would be expected by chance to live in cities that were similar to their own names. The researchers presented a

large array of relevant archival findings in their paper, but we will present only one example here.

In one set of data, the authors identified common surnames (family names) that shared the first three letters of one of eight large cities in Canada. For example, Edmiston and Edmunds share the first three letters of Edmonton, and Longhurst and Lonsdale share the first three letters of London. The researchers then searched telephone directories for these cities to see whether names that matched a city's first three letters were more common in that city than would be expected by chance. The results showed that, indeed, names sharing a city's first three letters were overrepresented in that city. For example, 836 listings of names beginning with *Tor* were found in

the Toronto directory, whereas only 611 such names would have been expected by chance. Similarly, 338 listings of names beginning with *Win* were found in the Winnipeg directory, whereas only 287 such names would have been expected by chance. Thus, the likelihood that families would live in cities that resembled their surname was greater than chance. The researchers argued that these findings occurred because people like things, including cities, that remind them of themselves.

Do you think that you like things that remind you of your name? For instance, do you like actors or musicians who have the same first or last name as you? The research by Pelham and his colleagues suggests that name similarity might even influence the places we decide to live.

is observed in a natural setting, then participants may be unaware that they are being watched, whereas laboratory settings usually require that participants know they are being observed. We will give examples of one observational study conducted in the laboratory and another conducted in a naturalistic setting.

Geraldine Downey and her colleagues at Columbia University (Downey, Freitas, Michaelis, & Khouri, 1998) were interested in the interaction styles of dating couples and whether certain styles were dysfunctional. Participants were 39 university-age couples who had been dating for an average of three months. Couples came to the laboratory and were asked to discuss for 20 minutes a topic that they often argued about; these discussions were videotaped. After the discussion, participants separately completed questionnaires in which they reported how angry they felt at that moment about the relationship. The videotaped discussions were later scored for the occurrence of specific interpersonal behaviours. Results revealed significant effects for the women's interaction styles but not the men's. Specifically, women who exhibited more frequent negative behaviours during the discussion (e.g., hostile voice tones, verbal put-downs, denials of responsibility for a problem, gestures that indicate disgust) tended to have male partners who reported greater anger after the discussion. Thus, a negative interpersonal style by the women during the discussion was associated with greater partner anger after the discussion. The authors speculated that the women's negative behaviours caused anger in their partners (negative behaviours caused anger). Can you think of an alternative interpretation? One possibility is that if partners started getting angry during the discussion, women responded with negative behaviours (anger caused negative behaviours).

An interesting observational study was conducted in a parking lot by Barry Ruback and Daniel Juieng (1997). These researchers suggested that most humans are naturally territorial and want to protect their own space from intruders. The researchers further speculated that these territorial inclinations are so strong that they may even carry over into the protection of *public* space that people have occupied only temporarily. To test this idea, Ruback and Juieng went to a parking lot in front of a shopping mall. They watched as 200 different drivers got into their

observational studies

correlational investigations in which researchers watch participants and code measures from the observed behaviour, either "live" or from videotapes

An observational study found that drivers took longer to leave their space when another car was waiting than when no car was waiting.

cars and drove away. The researchers noted two things: how long it took the driver to completely leave the parking space and whether another car was waiting for the space. To ensure that the driver of the departing car was aware that another car was waiting, the departing driver had to have turned his head in the direction of the waiting car before opening his or her driver's side door. Using these criteria, the results were clear: drivers took *longer* to depart their space when they knew another car was waiting (an average of 39 seconds) than when no car was waiting (an average of 32 seconds). Does this surprise you? The researchers suggested that the waiting car elicited territorial feelings, and drivers unconsciously wanted to protect their territory (parking space) longer. Before you reject this interpretation, think about your own behaviour in public spaces. For instance, consider escalators: when you are standing on an escalator going up or down, does it feel like you sort of "own" your step, and do you feel annoyed when other people intrude on your step?

Participant-Observation Research. One special kind of observational study deserves mention. Sometimes, if researchers want to observe behaviour in natural settings, they must participate actively in the settings themselves. For example, Robert Cialdini (2001), a well-known researcher in the area of social influence (whose work we discuss in Chapter 8), reported that he enrolled in several courses designed to train salespersons so that he could see whether specific persuasion strategies were being taught. This kind of investigation, when researchers actually join ongoing groups, is called **participant-observation research.**

participant-observation research

a special type of observational study in which a researcher actually joins an ongoing group to observe the members' behaviour

Perhaps the most famous example of participant-observation research in social psychology was conducted by Leon Festinger, Henry Riecken, and Stanley Schachter (1956), who saw a newspaper article and subsequently joined a doomsday cult that had predicted the end of the world; the researchers wanted to watch as members' beliefs were (hopefully) disconfirmed. Members of the group believed that they would be picked up by an alien spaceship at midnight of December 20, prior to the destruction of the world on December 21. (This information came from the group's leader, Marion Keech, who claimed to be able to communicate with aliens from the planet Clarion.) As the hours passed after midnight on December 20, Festinger and his colleagues watched as members slowly realized they were not to be rescued. Suddenly, at about 4:30 A.M., their leader received another "message" from the aliens, which said that because of the group's unwavering faith, the world had been spared—so now they did not need to be picked up after all.

Faced with this clear disconfirmation of their initial beliefs but also a face-saving excuse from their leader, what did group members do? Festinger and his colleagues reported that several members of the group actually became more active in their attempts to convince new people that they had saved the world. It seemed to the researchers that group members needed to justify the time and effort they had invested in the group, and one way to do this was to convince other people to join. This participant-observation study contributed to Festinger's development of *dissonance theory,* which we describe in Chapter 7 (see page 240).

Our discussion of correlational methods has illustrated the creative and interesting ways that social psychologists make use of surveys, archival records, and observational studies. Correlational studies are flexible and have been applied to many fascinating topics. They can provide important data on how various concepts are related. But correlational studies do not provide causal information—they do not show *why* concepts are related. To answer causal questions, researchers must use experimental research. Given that social psychologists want to understand the causes of social behaviour, experiments are frequently the method of choice. So, to experiments let us turn.

 # Experimental Research

We noted at the beginning of the chapter that theories are organized statements of the causal relations between two or more concepts. To test whether concepts are related in a causal manner (i.e., whether one concept causes another), it is necessary to use experiments. Thus, it is primarily through experimental research that social psychologists have been able to develop compelling theories about the causes of many important social behaviours. **Experimental research** refers to investigations in which the researcher manipulates one concept (or more than one) and assesses the impact of the manipulation(s) on one or more other concepts. This definition will become clearer as we explain its components.

In discussing the fundamental principles of experiments, we will use one continuing example that will hopefully illustrate both the advantages and challenges of experimentation. In the preceding section on correlational research, we stated that social psychologists have found that the amount of contact people have had with members of an ethnic group is correlated with their prejudice toward that group: people who report *more contact* with an ethnic group also report *less prejudice* toward that group (e.g., Altemeyer, 1994). We also pointed out that it is impossible to know why this correlation occurs. Perhaps contact with a group causes a reduction in prejudice; or perhaps strong prejudice causes people to avoid members of the group.

How could this issue be tested experimentally? If social psychologists want to go beyond correlations and use experiments to assess the relation between contact and prejudice, how could they do so? We will consider how an experiment could be designed to test the hypothesis that *more contact with Asian Canadians causes lower levels of prejudice toward Asian Canadians.*

Our first task is to define three kinds of *variables* (concepts or measures that can *vary*, or take on different values) that are important in experiments: independent variables, dependent variables, and extraneous variables (see Pelham, 1999; Solso & MacLin, 2002).

experimental research

investigations in which the researcher manipulates one concept (or more than one) and assesses the impact of the manipulation(s) on one or more other concepts

Independent, Dependent, and Extraneous Variables

The basic structure of experiments is quite simple: the researcher *manipulates* independent variables, *measures* dependent variables, and *controls* extraneous variables. This structure provides the potential for the study to yield causal information.

Independent Variables. Experiments are designed to test cause–effect relations; independent variables are the *causes* in these cause–effect sequences. An **independent variable** is a concept that the experimenter carefully manipulates so that participants in different conditions of the study are exposed to different levels of the independent variable.

For instance, if an experimenter wants to test whether contact with Asian Canadians reduces prejudice, then the independent variable is *contact with group members.* The experimenter must set up the study so that participants in different conditions are given different amounts of contact with Asian Canadians. One possibility would be for the experimenter to require some participants to interact with several Asian Canadians while discussing a neutral topic, whereas other participants would not meet any Asian Canadians during a similar discussion. In this case, there would be two levels of the independent variable: contact and no contact.

Why is the independent variable labelled the *independent* variable? Because it is independent of research participants' actions: participants have no control over what condition or group they are assigned to. It is the experimenter who manipulates the

independent variable

a concept or factor that is manipulated by the researcher in an experiment; its causal impact on one or more other variables is assessed in the experiment

Dependent variables are measures completed by participants after exposure to the *independent variable*.

dependent variable

a concept that is measured by the researcher after the manipulation(s) in an experiment; it is typically expected to be affected by the manipulation(s)

extraneous variables

potential sources of error in the experiment that should be controlled; they encompass everything in the experiment except the independent and dependent variables

independent variable, whereas participants have nothing to do with it (they are simply exposed to one version of the independent variable). We should note that experiments often involve two (or even more) independent variables, a point that we will elaborate in the section on *factorial designs*.

Dependent Variables. An experiment also always involves one or more dependent variables. A **dependent variable** is a concept that is *measured* by the experimenter because it might be affected by the manipulation. Dependent variables are the *effects* in cause–effect sequences. Therefore, dependent variables must be measured *after* the independent variable has been manipulated (that is, after participants have gone through one of the conditions in the experiment), because the researcher wants to see whether the independent variable causes the dependent variable.

For example, if a researcher wants to test whether contact with Asian Canadians reduces prejudice toward this group, then *prejudice toward Asian Canadians* is the dependent variable. You might think that prejudice is a difficult thing to measure, but social psychologists have actually developed many ways to assess negative attitudes toward ethnic groups (discussed in detail in Chapter 9, "Stereotypes, Prejudice, and Discrimination"). One option would be for the researcher to use a self-report measure by asking participants to rate how unfavourable or favourable their feelings are toward Asian Canadians on a scale from 1 (very unfavourable) to 10 (very favourable). The prediction would be that participants who were given contact with Asian Canadians would report less prejudice (more favourable attitudes) than participants who were not given any contact with members of the group.

Why is the dependent variable labelled the *dependent* variable? Because it is dependent on research participants' responses. That is, participants determine their "score" on the dependent variable by completing a questionnaire or behaving in some fashion. Another way to think about this label is that the dependent variable is often dependent on the independent variable (e.g., it is expected to be affected by the independent variable).

Extraneous Variables. **Extraneous variables** refer to everything in the experimental setting other than the independent and dependent variables. Extraneous variables are potential problems, or sources of error, in the experiment, so the experimenter must *control* them by holding them constant across conditions. The experimenter does *not* want the different conditions or groups in the experiment to differ on any extraneous variables; the experimenter wants the conditions to differ *only* on the independent variable.

For instance, if an experimenter wants to test whether contact with Asian Canadians reduces prejudice toward this group, then he or she must hold constant all aspects of the experiment except contact (all extraneous variables). Let's imagine a situation in which control did *not* occur. Imagine that participants in a condition involving contact with Asian Canadians were paid $25 for participating, whereas participants in a condition with no contact were not paid anything. (Exactly *how* this circumstance could arise is not entirely clear!) Can you see why this would be a serious problem? Perhaps this difference in payment could produce differences in reported prejudice without any effects of the contact manipulation. For instance, if participants in the contact condition felt really happy about making $25, then their good mood might induce them to report less prejudice against Asian Canadians than participants in the no-contact (and no-pay) condition. This differential payment across the two conditions would be an example of an extraneous variable that was *not* successfully controlled. Because it was not held constant across conditions, the researcher would not know whether differences in prejudice were due to the contact manipulation (the independent variable) or to the differing payments (an extraneous variable).

The key features of independent, dependent, and extraneous variables are summarized in the accompanying Concept Review.

In many fields of science, the control of extraneous variables is relatively easy. For instance, the physical sciences often allow tremendous control over the materials that are being studied (e.g., inanimate objects). But control in social psychological experiments is more challenging. Social psychologists study human social behaviour; it is difficult to construct settings in which everything is carefully controlled yet participants are free to behave naturally and spontaneously. Two strategies for controlling extraneous variables are most important in social psychology; indeed, these strategies are so critical and so common that they are true of virtually every experiment conducted in the field. The strategies are *standardized procedures* and *random assignment.*

Standardized Procedures. Researchers will always attempt to make all conditions in the study identical except for the manipulation of the independent variable. That is, as much as possible, the procedures in the study will be standardized across conditions. For example, all experimental sessions will usually be conducted by the same experimenter in the same laboratory. All participants will be recruited in the same way and offered the same payment. As much as possible, participants in all conditions will be given the same explanation of the study's purpose, and will expect similar kinds of feedback after the experiment is over. The researcher will be careful

CONCEPT REVIEW
Variables in Experiments

Concept	Description	Action by Experimenter	Example: Experiment Testing Whether Contact Reduces Prejudice
Independent variable	The *cause* in cause–effect hypotheses; the conditions in an experiment; participants are exposed to just one level	Manipulated by the experimenter	Contact with Asian Canadians
Dependent variable	The *effect* in cause–effect hypotheses; obtained after the independent variable; participants provide the dependent variable	Measured by the experimenter	Prejudice toward Asian Canadians
Extraneous variable	Potential source of error in experiment; must be held constant across conditions	Controlled by the experimenter	Amount of payment for participation

to avoid running one condition only in the morning and the other condition only in the afternoon. Even though the time of day probably doesn't matter, it is safest to control this extraneous variable by running all conditions both mornings and afternoons. Standardized procedures hold constant participants' external environment, so the experimental conditions will differ only in terms of the independent variable.

Random Assignment. Even if participants in all conditions are treated identically except for the independent variable, one category of extraneous variables might still be a problem. Specifically, even if the environment is carefully controlled by standardizing the procedures, the *participants* in the different conditions might still vary in their personal characteristics. Let's return to our example of testing the effects of contact on prejudice. Imagine that we have two conditions: some participants are given contact with Asian Canadians, whereas other participants do not meet anyone from the group (and payments are the same!). Imagine further that participants in both conditions report their attitudes toward Asian Canadians at the end of the session, and those in the contact condition report less prejudice than those in the no-contact condition. Although this result seems to indicate that contact caused reduced prejudice, perhaps participants in the contact condition *were less prejudiced even before the study began.* How can we rule out this possibility? That is, how can we be sure that the groups were equivalent in prejudice to begin with?

Fortunately, all extraneous variables related to characteristics of the participants can be controlled with a simple methodological procedure: **random assignment.** Random assignment means that each participant in an experiment is equally likely to take part in any of the experimental conditions. For instance, any prejudiced participant in our experiment on the effects of contact on prejudice is just as likely to be assigned to the contact condition as to the no-contact condition. This is a very simple and elegant procedure, which usually eliminates all extraneous variable problems coming from characteristics of the participants. If there are only two conditions, the experimenter might flip a coin, with heads meaning that the participant goes into one condition and tails meaning that the participant goes into the other condition. Alternatively, a computer program can be used to generate random numbers to assign participants to conditions.

How does random assignment address this extraneous variable problem? If we use enough participants, then we should end up with approximately the same number of prejudiced people in both conditions. Therefore, if the manipulation of contact still appears to reduce prejudice, we can be more confident this was not the result of a coincidence in which unprejudiced people were more likely to participate in the contact condition. In fact, random assignment will usually effectively control *all* of the individual characteristics that people might carry with them into an experiment and that might influence the dependent variable.

We should note, however, that the logic of random assignment is based on the laws of chance. For instance, in the long run, a fair coin will come up heads just as often as tails. In the long run, a random number generator will come up with different numbers equally often. *In the long run.* The point is that random assignment works better with a larger number of people to assign; for example, most social psychologists try to have at least 10 or 20 participants in each condition. Another check on the effectiveness of random assignment is provided when a finding is replicated in subsequent research.

Demand Characteristics. In social psychology experiments, the goal is to have participants respond naturally and spontaneously, rather than according to how they think the experimenter *wants* them to respond. Any cues in a study that suggest to participants how they are supposed to respond are called **demand characteristics** (labelled in this manner because the cues, or characteristics, "demand" a certain response). If demand characteristics guide participants' responses, then the experiment will not yield information about spontaneous

random assignment

a procedure by which each participant in an experiment is equally likely to take part in any of the experimental conditions; it controls extraneous variable problems arising from characteristics of the participants

demand characteristics

cues in a study that suggest to participants how they are supposed to respond

Welcome to the University of Toronto
214 College St.
Toronto, ON M5T 3A1

YPE: PURCHASE

CCT: CHEQUING $ 129.78

ard Type: Interac

ARD NUMBER: *************3058
ATE/TIME: 11/09/30 16:
EFERENCE #:   66198272 0010620010 C
UTHOR. #:   173464
NVOICE NUMBER: 001650073-14

ITERAC
000002771010

   00/001 APPROVED - THANK YOU

      -- IMPORTANT --
Retain This Copy For Your Rec

   *** CUSTOMER COPY ***

JTM Code: 173464

nge Due: $0.00

   You Saved: $30.90

Receipt required for all refunds
See reverse for full refund policy

o Returns on Print On Demand titles

Returns are allowed on Used books
Same Return Policy as New Textbooks

With new pin chip technology, the
credit/debit card used to purchase
must be present to process refund

All other returns must be
  in MINT CONDITION

K0001650073-14

e, researchers attempt to minimize any
earchers do not typically tell participants
study before beginning, because partici-
pected manner. Standardized procedures
istics by giving participants in all condi-
urpose of the research.

xperimental or correlational, investigators
that are truly informative about the con-
accurate, valid results was elegantly sum-
distinguished between two aspects of the
xternal validity. These kinds of validity are
that we discussed earlier in the section on

lo experiments is to establish whether the
e dependent variables. In essence, we want
ipulation caused differences on the meas-
cted properly, and all extraneous sources of
d, then we can be confident that any differ-
e to the experimental manipulation. This is
e extent to which the research yields clear
ernal validity is one in which differences on
differences on another measure (e.g., the

internal validity
the extent to which research yields clear causal information; it tends to be low in correlational research and high in experimental research

d by many things (see Aronson, Ellsworth,
ost common threat to internal validity in
is variables. When it is impossible to stan-
n participants, a study will have low internal
s, which do not control extraneous variables,
ty, whereas well-conducted experiments are

gy aspires to accomplish more than an accu-
xperiments (studies showing that one variable
etting). The promise and excitement of social
hed light on real-world problems: aggression,
rsuasion. Social psychologists are not solely
ms within the confines of carefully controlled
Ve want to know how these factors operate in
and real families. We ultimately want to under-
iean by **external validity:** the extent to which
yond the current sample, setting, and other

external validity
the extent to which research results can be generalized beyond the current sample, setting, and other characteristics of the study

idity: the people to whom the results can be
xperiment consist only of university students
ts be generalized? It may be safe to generalize
rsity. We may even feel confident in general-
But will the results of our experiment be valid
le who struggled just to complete high school?
iportant segment of the population, yet our
m.

It is unclear that research results based on a sample of university students will necessarily generalize to other segments of society.

It is not really fair to hold a single piece of research accountable for achieving high external validity. Indeed, it is probably impossible for a single study to generalize in all the ways we might desire. Nevertheless, researchers often try to increase the external validity of their study. One way is by using a more diverse sample of participants. Another way is by making the experimental setting as similar as possible to real-life situations (e.g., conducting the experiment in a field setting—an approach we will describe shortly). The main problem with this second strategy is that the increased external validity often comes at a price: decreased internal validity. The more you try to model the real world and include the "noise" and complexity of daily life, the more you lose control over extraneous variables and, therefore, the internal validity of the experiment.

How does social psychology try to resolve the trade-off between internal and external validity? Most often, external validity in social psychology is achieved not within single studies, but rather by the accumulation of research: experiments that vary in who the research participants are, who the experimenters are, where and when the studies are conducted, and the kinds of materials and topics that are used. When a theory has been supported by an array of studies using different procedures, samples, and settings, its external validity can more confidently be assumed.

Single-Factor Experiments

single-factor experiment

an experimental study that involves only one independent variable

Peer discussion groups [for cancer patients] are available in many communities throughout North America. The goal of such groups is to raise patients' quality of life. But do they?

When we first defined independent variables, we noted that researchers manipulate one *or more* independent variables. When an experiment involves only one independent variable, it is called a **single-factor experiment** ("factor" is another word for manipulation or independent variable).

Single-factor experiments are very common. Let's give a real example of a single-factor experiment in social psychology. For this experiment, we return to Melvin  Lerner's (1977, 1980) *just world theory*, which we described earlier in our discussion of theories and hypotheses. Lerner theorized that humans want to believe that the world is a fair and just place, because to believe otherwise would threaten the assumption that people's own efforts will be rewarded in life. Based on this theory, Lerner derived the hypothesis that people would evaluate suffering victims negatively, especially when their suffering is expected to continue. The rationale for this hypothesis is that by evaluating victims negatively, the victims' suffering no longer seems unfair—and, thus, no longer threatens observers' belief in a just world.

How could this hypothesis be tested experimentally? Lerner wanted to manipulate the extent to which a victim's suffering threatened participants' belief in a just world (independent variable) and see whether this manipulation influenced how much participants derogated the victim (dependent variable). Thus, the cause–effect sequence Lerner wanted to test was whether *threat to just world beliefs* causes *derogation of the victim*.

The experiment we will describe was conducted by Melvin Lerner and Carolyn Simmons (1966). These researchers set up a study in which female university undergraduates watched another young woman receive a series of painful electric shocks. The young woman appeared to be suffering quite severely. After participants had watched this suffering for ten minutes, there was a pause in the experiment, and participants could no longer see the victim. At this point, the manipulation of *threat to just world beliefs* was administered. Some of the participants (high-threat condition) were told that, in a few moments, they would watch the young woman go through another set of shock trials. This condition was expected to be very threatening to participants' beliefs in a just world, because the woman's suffering was expected to continue. Other participants (low-threat condition) were told that, in a few moments, the victim was going to participate in a *reward session* that would not involve shocks—in fact, she would earn between $2 and $8 based on her memory performance. This condition was expected to be much less threatening to participants' beliefs in a just world, because the woman's suffering was over and, indeed, she was going to be compensated by earning some money.

Participants were then asked, before watching the next set of trials, to rate the victim on a variety of scales, including judgments of her likeability, maturity, and admirability. Participants in the high-threat condition, who expected the victim's suffering to continue, rated her much more negatively than did participants in the low-threat condition, who expected the victim to earn money in the remaining learning trials. Thus, even though they watched the identical videotape, participants in the two conditions evaluated the victim very differently.

The researchers concluded that these results confirmed their hypothesis that people will evaluate victims negatively when the suffering is expected to continue. The researchers proposed that this effect occurs because derogating victims who are suffering makes the suffering seem less unfair. This single-factor experiment is an excellent illustration that complex concepts like "threat to beliefs in a just world" can be manipulated powerfully in a laboratory setting. If you want to learn more about just world theory, Carolyn Hafer of Brock University has written an excellent recent review of experiments on the theory (see Hafer & Bègue, 2005).

Factorial Design Experiments

Many experiments in social psychology involve more than one independent variable. In studies that include two or more manipulations, the experiment's structure is called a **factorial design.** This design of experiments allows the investigator to examine the *combined* influence of more than one independent variable (see Crano & Brewer, 2002; Kirk, 2003).

An important advantage of factorial design experiments is that they allow the investigator to test for possible **interactions** between independent variables. An interaction occurs when the effect of one experimental manipulation *depends on the level of another experimental manipulation.* For instance, the effect of contact with members of an ethnic group on prejudice may depend on the *type of contact* that is involved: perhaps *cooperative contact* (e.g., working together on a project) reduces prejudice, but *competitive contact* (e.g., playing a competitive game) does not. In fact, we discuss in Chapter 9 this exact hypothesis that different kinds of contact have different effects on prejudice (see page 362). This pattern represents an *interaction* between the amount of contact and the type of contact.

We need to address a potentially confusing issue here. We have been stressing throughout the section on experiments that everything in the study except the manipulation (i.e., all extraneous variables) must be controlled so the researcher can be confident that the independent variable caused the results. But now we are saying that researchers often include two or more independent variables in the same study. How can they know which manipulation is causing differences between conditions? It is true that when two manipulations are operating simultaneously, it is impossible to disentangle their effects completely; nevertheless, the

factorial design experiment
an experimental study that involves two or more independent variables

interaction
result showing that the effect of one experimental manipulation depends on the level of another experimental manipulation; it can only be observed in a factorial design experiment

main effect

the effect of one experimental manipulation on the dependent variable, averaged across all levels of other experimental manipulations

researcher can explore the effects of each independent variable separately *by averaging across all levels of the other independent variable*. This procedure is called looking at the **main effect** of a manipulation, which is the effect of one experimental manipulation on the dependent variable, averaged across all levels of other experimental manipulations. For example, imagine that an experimenter tested whether humour increases the effectiveness of an advertisement (interest in buying the product) by comparing serious and funny advertisements for two different kinds of products (e.g., shampoo versus beer). The experimenter could then examine whether the funny advertisement was more effective than the serious advertisement for both kinds of products (a main effect of humour) or whether humour interacted with product type. The important point is that in factorial design experiments, the separate effects of each independent variable, as well as their combined effects, can be examined.

To get a better handle on the notion of interactions, let's consider a real example of an experiment in social psychology that used a factorial design to uncover an interaction between two independent variables. Stephen Bochner and Chet Insko (1966) at the University of North Carolina were interested in the effects of *source credibility* on the effectiveness of a persuasive message. Previous researchers (e.g., Hovland & Weiss, 1951) had shown that the identical message produces more persuasion when it is believed to come from a highly credible source (e.g., an expert) than when it is believed to come from a source who is low in credibility. Bochner and Insko (1966) hypothesized that source credibility would be especially important when the position advocated in a message is relatively extreme. When an extreme view is advocated in a message, listeners are most likely to be skeptical about the information in the message. If the source is highly credible, then listeners may not reject extreme positions, whereas if the source is not credible, then an extreme message is likely to be rejected. For positions that are not extreme, however, source credibility might not matter so much. If a message advocates a position that is only slightly different from a listener's own views, the credibility of the source probably makes little difference because listeners will not be as skeptical about the information.

This reasoning suggests that source credibility might *interact* with the extremity of a message in affecting persuasion. When a message advocates a relatively extreme position, highly credible sources will be more persuasive than low-credibility sources; when a message advocates a moderate position, however, high- and low-credibility sources might not differ in persuasiveness. This hypothesis can be investigated only with a factorial design that includes two manipulations: the credibility of the source and the extremity of the message.

To test this analysis, Bochner and Insko (1966) gave participants a message that argued for a reduction in the number of hours young adults sleep. One independent variable was the credibility of the alleged author of the message. For some participants, the message was said to come from "Sir John Eccles, a Nobel Prize–winning physiologist" (high credibility), whereas other participants were told that the message came from "Mr. Harry Olsen, director of the Fort Worth YMCA" (low credibility). Actually, this "low credibility" source was probably at least *somewhat*

© Bill Varie/CORBIS

The persuasive message in the experiment by Bochner and Insko (1966) argued for a reduction in the number of hours young adults sleep.

credible—it seems reasonable that someone who works at a health facility might know something about health-related issues like getting enough sleep; indeed, Bochner and Insko labelled their conditions "high credibility" and "medium credibility." Nevertheless, the Nobel Prize–winning physiologist was certainly *more* credible than the YMCA director. The second independent variable was the extremity of the position argued in the message. For some participants, the message argued for a position that was only slightly discrepant from the common view that people need about eight hours of sleep: the message argued that people need seven hours of sleep (moderate position). For other participants, the message argued for a position that was extremely discrepant from the common view: the message argued that people need only one hour of sleep (extreme position).

After reading the message, all participants were asked how many hours of sleep they believed were necessary for the average young adult. Figure 2.2 presents participants' answers to this question. When the message took a moderate position, the credibility of the source made no difference whatsoever: participants in the high-credibility and the low-credibility conditions both estimated that people need 7.5 hours of sleep per night. When the message took an extreme position, however, the credibility of the source made a significant difference: participants in the high-credibility condition estimated that people need 5.9 hours of sleep, whereas participants in the low-credibility condition estimated that people need 6.7 hours of sleep. Thus, the effect of source credibility on attitude change *depended* on the extremity of the position in the message: credibility made a significant difference for the extreme message but not for the moderate message. This pattern of results reflects an *interaction* between source credibility and message extremity.

Most of the experiments we describe in this textbook are factorial designs that involve more than one independent variable. And the patterns of findings often reflect interactions between independent variables. Why is this complexity common in social psychology? Because *social behaviour* is complicated: people's actions often depend on a *combination* of factors.

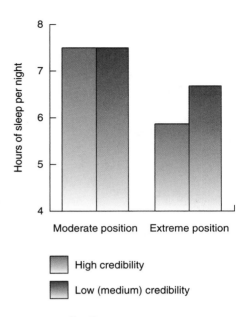

FIGURE 2.2 Participants' estimates of number of hours of sleep needed per night

From Bochner and Insko, "Communicator discrepancy, source credibility, and attitude change," *Journal of Personality and Social Psychology*, 4, 614–621, 1966. Copyright © 1966 by the American Psychological Association.

Making Experiments Real

The world of the experiment can be very artificial. In some fields of science, this artificiality is desired: much of physics, for example, is done in the context of a vacuum. The artificial world is created to control extraneous variables and to be sure that the only causal influences are those being manipulated by the physicist. As we noted in the opening to this chapter, however, it is not so easy to control the research environment when human social behaviour is the focus. Making the experiment too artificial can produce results that are not informative about behaviour in real life. This dilemma creates a special challenge for social psychology: How can we do carefully controlled experiments and still hope to generalize our results to conditions outside the research environment? Social psychologists have identified two aspects of *realism* that bear on this problem: *experimental realism* and *mundane realism* (see Aronson & Carlsmith, 1968).

Experimental Realism. A major goal within the world of a social psychology experiment is to engage the participants—to make the experiment real and involving for them. It is essential that participants believe that what is happening around them is real, so they will behave in natural, spontaneous ways rather than artificially. This quality is what we mean by **experimental realism:** the experimental situation feels realistic to the research participants and elicits spontaneous behaviour.

Many social psychology experiments create very high levels of experimental realism. A famous example is Stanley Milgram's (1963, 1974) research on obedience,

experimental realism

the extent to which the study's setting feels realistic and involving to participants and elicits spontaneous behaviour which we discuss in detail in Chapter 8. In Milgram's studies, participants were led to believe that the experimenter was investigating the effects of punishment on learning, and they were delivering real electric shocks to another person. Participants were highly engaged by the procedures and experienced strong emotions. Their responses were almost certainly spontaneous and honest.

Mundane Realism. Just because an experiment is high in experimental realism, however, does not mean that it looks or feels like the real world. The experimental setting in Milgram's studies did not actually resemble real-world settings: when do people ever deliver electric shocks to others? The success and importance of this experiment depended primarily on experimental realism. Yet a principal goal of research is to learn about life in the real world. We want to be able to generalize the results of experiments to settings beyond the confines of the university classroom or laboratory; this issue relates to the notion of *external validity,* which we discussed earlier.

One way to achieve the goal of generalizability is by creating experiments that look and feel like the outside world: a kind of realism that we call **mundane realism.** If you want to study how leaders emerge in groups, then set up groups that are given real tasks, and allow them to select someone to be in charge. If you want to study flirting behaviour, then have participants interact with people whom they believe to be romantically unattached. If you want to study alcohol consumption, then conduct the study in a campus pub. The important point is that the context of the experiment must be similar to relevant real-life settings.

Persuasion experiments often have relatively high levels of mundane realism: participants read messages that are similar to those they encounter in real life. So long as participants consider the message to be genuine and believe the cover story of the experiment, the experimental setting parallels real-life persuasion settings. For example, Bochner and Insko's (1966) experiment examining the effects of source credibility on persuasion had a reasonably high level of mundane realism. Participants almost certainly believed that the message came either from the Nobel Prize–winning physiologist or the director of the YMCA, and the message was typical of articles on social issues. These features increase our confidence that the findings will apply to real-life settings.

mundane realism

the extent to which the study's setting looks and feels like the outside world; it increases the external validity of research results

Experiments conducted in field settings have high *mundane realism.*

CONCEPT REVIEW
Internal/External Validity and Experimental/Mundane Realism

Concept	Description	Features That Enhance It
Internal validity	The extent to which the research yields clear causal information	Experiment (versus correlational research); random assignment; control of extraneous variables
External validity	The extent to which research results can be generalized beyond the current sample, setting, and other characteristics of the study	Realistic setting; diverse sample; replications across different studies
Experimental realism	The extent to which the experimental setting elicits spontaneous, natural behaviour	Involving procedure for participants; convincing cover story for participants; perception by participants that the study is addressing an important issue
Mundane realism	The extent to which the experimental setting is similar to nonlaboratory settings	Realistic setting; tasks and behaviours that occur in the real world; field experiment

The connections between internal/external validity and experimental/mundane realism are summarized in the accompanying Concept Review.

Field Experiments. One important way to increase mundane realism and external validity is to conduct experiments outside the laboratory in natural settings, which are called **field experiments.** We mentioned in Chapter 1 a very well-known set of field experiments: Latané and Darley's (1970) studies of bystander intervention. These investigators wanted to be sure that their findings would generalize to real-world emergency settings, so they conducted several field experiments in which apparent emergencies were staged in nonlaboratory settings, and participants' responses were observed. These experiments provided compelling demonstrations that individuals' interpretations of potential emergencies are influenced by the responses of other people.

A high level of mundane realism is an important advantage of field experiments compared to laboratory experiments. It is reassuring when investigators can confirm their hypotheses and theories in settings where behaviour is clearly natural. Field experiments also have some disadvantages, however. Most obviously, controlling extraneous variables in field settings is often difficult—for instance, unexpected interruptions are more likely than in the laboratory. Field settings also introduce complications regarding approval and access: investigators must inform and get approval from appropriate authorities before they can conduct research in natural settings. Finally, it is more costly in terms of time and money to conduct research in the field than in the laboratory. Notwithstanding these problems, field experiments are an important tool for social psychologists to document the practical relevance of their theories.

field experiment

an experimental study that is conducted in a setting outside the laboratory; it tends to produce high mundane realism and external validity

Social Psychology and the Internet

Ten years ago, it would have been very rare to mention the Internet in the context of research methods in social psychology. The Internet is a relatively recent phenomenon, and one that is worthy of study in its own right, but here we will briefly consider how the Internet might be used as a medium or vehicle for doing social psychological research (see Birnbaum, 2000, 2001).

The Internet has tremendous potential as a research tool for social psychologists, but it also has some serious limitations.

The Advantages. An exciting aspect of the Internet is the extent of its reach throughout the world. A tremendous infrastructure of computers, cables, satellites, and software allows us to reach into millions of homes, schools, and businesses. Social psychologists used to be satisfied to draw on first-year university students as their research participants. It took great effort to reach different populations and to draw samples from other places. The Internet now makes that relatively easy. Without leaving your computer, it is possible to set up a server that presents stimulus materials, collects answers to questions, and maintains the data. And anybody, almost anywhere in the world, can participate at very negligible cost. Software designed to create Web pages is very well suited for creating experiments, complete with colour graphics, animation, and user input.

The Disadvantages. The Internet may sound like a social psychologist's dream come true. But we also need to recognize the downside. Perhaps most important, Internet-based methods do not currently provide a good way to conduct true experiments. A Web server can certainly do random assignment of participants to conditions, but it is very difficult to control other important aspects of the research environment. How do we know who the person is on the other end? Is he sitting in a quiet room or a noisy Internet café? Is she responding alone or is she getting help from friends? Is this the first time the person has participated in your experiment, or is it the 50th?

Social psychologists are wrestling with these kinds of questions about Internet research. The potential of the Internet is almost unlimited, but the current reality is less glowing. It seems very likely, however, that the Internet will eventually become an important component of social psychological research.

Making Technology Work for Social Psychology

Technological advancements are providing new research instruments for social psychologists. We mention two here.

immersive virtual environments technology

computer programs that construct an imaginary setting in which participants behave; the computer controls the visual and auditory information and allows participants to respond as if the scene was real

Immersive Virtual Environments Technology. A relatively recent addition to the social psychologist's toolbox is the use of **immersive virtual environments technology** (e.g., Loomis, Blascovich, & Beall, 1999). This technology creates the experience of being surrounded by and immersed in a constructed environment. The computer controls the visual and auditory scene, and produces real-time feedback to give participants the sensation that they are actually there. It is only a matter of time before these synthetic environments are of such high quality that they virtually reproduce the real thing. Immersive environments offer tremendous potential for solving the problem of trade-offs between internal and external validity. Immersive environments would allow total experimental control (maximizing internal validity) while creating experiences that closely correspond to the real world (maximizing external validity).

To give you a sense of how social psychologists can utilize immersive virtual environments technology, consider a study by John Lydon and his colleagues at McGill University (reported in Lydon, Burton, & Menzies-Toman, 2005). These researchers found that participants who were currently in relationships (either dating or married) maintained greater distance in virtual reality from an attractive member of their preferred sex than did participants who were not currently in relationships. Presumably, commitment to their current partner motivated the

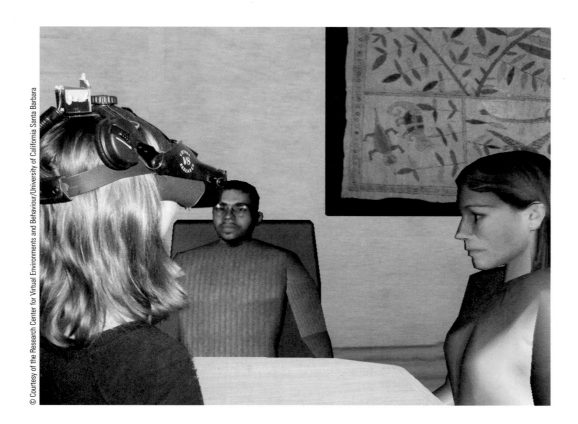

Immersive virtual environments technology offers the potential of highly controlled but realistic settings for studying social behaviour.

former participants to avoid close contact with potential alternative partners (see also Bailenson, Blascovich, Veall, & Loomis, 2003).

Keeping Track of Daily Events. Computer technology is also very useful when social psychology is taken into the real world. Later in the book, we will talk about *event sampling methods* (see Chapter 13). These methods allow researchers to

Computer technology provides sophisticated ways to record daily experiences.

record the momentary thoughts, emotions, and behaviours of people as they go about their daily lives. Our workbook suggests that you keep your own daily experiences diary. If you want to go high-tech, try using the software developed by Lisa Feldman Barrett, who obtained her doctoral degree at the University of Waterloo, and her husband, Daniel Barrett (2001). The Experience Sampling Program (ESP) lets you record simple ratings on a handheld computer such as a Palm Pilot. The software is available for free at http://www2.bc.edu/~barretli/esp/.

● ● ● Ethical Issues in Social Psychology

Social psychologists conduct research on human participants with the goal of understanding social behaviour. Researchers must take special care to protect the welfare of participants in their experiments. This goal is important, and it can be difficult. Researchers must carefully weigh the costs and benefits of their research, and take precautions to be sure that nobody gets hurt or otherwise experiences harm as a result of participating in a study. Think about Milgram's (1963) experiment on obedience to authority, in which participants were ordered to deliver what they thought were real electric shocks to another person. That experiment touched off a serious debate about ethics in research, and whether the participants in such experiments suffered serious psychological harm (e.g., Baumrind, 1964; Milgram, 1964).

Research Ethics Board (REB)

a committee that must approve all studies before they can be started; it ensures that the procedures will not cause unacceptable harm to participants

Three special procedures have been established to protect human participants in research. First, almost all research conducted in universities, research institutes, and companies must first be approved by a **Research Ethics Board (REB).** An REB is a committee given responsibility for reviewing the research protocol of an experiment or study, and making sure that the procedures will not cause unacceptable harm to the research participants (Wiggins, 2000). If you have participated in a psychology experiment at your school, it is almost certain that the experiment was approved by an REB. In most research settings, two review boards are maintained. One focuses on research being conducted with human participants, and the other on research with animal participants. In Canada, REBs are guided by the *Tri-Council Policy Statement: Ethical Conduct for Research Involving Humans,* which is a comprehensive policy document that specifies many rules and guidelines for how research should be conducted. Researchers and universities must follow these guidelines or their research funding will be withdrawn.

informed consent

a procedure by which participants are told beforehand what to expect in the study and are reminded that they can withdraw at any time

The second precaution is called **informed consent,** which means that people are told beforehand that they are participating in a study. They are told what to expect and, most importantly, that their participation is voluntary and they can withdraw at any time. This does not mean that every detail of the experimental design must be revealed at the outset. Indeed, this would severely undermine the logic of many social psychology experiments. Rather, it means that people are made aware of the general nature of what they will be asked to do and are assured that they will be treated reasonably.

debriefing

a postexperimental procedure in which participants are given a full and complete description of the study's design, purpose, and expected results; if there has been any deception during the study, it must be identified and explained in the debriefing

The third precaution is called **debriefing,** which means that a full and complete disclosure is made at the conclusion of the study. If the details of the entire experimental design and purpose of the study were not revealed beforehand, debriefing is the time to do so. The goals of a good debriefing procedure are to create a learning experience for the participants and to check for any signs of distress or harm.

In many social psychology experiments, the participants are deceived in some way. The simplest form of deception is hiding information about all of the various conditions of an experiment or not revealing the true purpose of the study. But sometimes deception is more substantial and has serious ethical considerations. Again, think about the deception involved in Milgram's obedience experiments: the entire scene was one big deception. As another example, we may wish to give people incorrect feedback about their performance on a test, and this feedback might sometimes be that the participant failed a test. Is such deception justified? Does it have any lasting consequences? Can we manage to do experiments without it? Read the *Workbook* for a more detailed discussion of these questions.

You will notice throughout this book that we refer to the people in studies as research participants or *participants* for short. Until recently, the terminology was a little different. In the "old days," we referred to participants as "subjects." Even though you will still find this term used occasionally, it has been properly recognized as a somewhat demeaning way to talk about people. They are not simply the objects of our research; they are individuals who deserve our respect and our appreciation for their participation.

Chapter Summary

In this chapter, we discussed the research methods used by social psychologists to study social behaviour. As in any science, social psychologists develop **theories,** which are explanations of why particular events or outcomes occur. Theories identify the underlying causes of events or phenomena. **Hypotheses** are specific predictions about what *should* occur if a theory is valid. Hypotheses are the means by which theories are tested.

It is often a challenge to translate theories and hypotheses, which are usually expressed in abstract, conceptual terms, into testable questions. **Operational definitions** are specific, observable responses that are used to measure a concept. In social psychology, researchers use both self-report measures and behavioural measures to operationally define important concepts. Self-report measures can be problematic if respondents are motivated to create a positive impression of themselves—a form of responding known as **socially desirable responding.** One strategy for reducing socially desirable responding is to use behavioural measures, which are often **unobtrusive measures**—meaning that participants do not realize that the measures are being taken.

Psychometrics is a subdiscipline within psychology that is devoted to understanding and refining measures for psychological measurement. This field has focused researchers' attention on the reliability and validity of measures. **Reliability** refers to the consistency or stability of scores on a measure, both over time and across judges. **Validity** refers to whether scores on a measure really represent the underlying concept they are supposed to represent.

Correlational research refers to studies in which investigators measure two or more concepts and see whether the concepts are associated with one another. The primary weakness of correlational research is that it cannot establish causal connections between concepts, but it is very flexible and has been used in creative ways to examine social behaviour. For example, **surveys** are correlational studies in which the researcher asks questions to respondents, either in a questionnaire, on a computer, over the telephone, or during an interview. If survey researchers want to generalize their findings to larger populations, then they must recruit a **representative sample,** which is a group of respondents that accurately reflects the larger population. A common way to obtain representative samples is via **random sampling,** which means that every person in a particular population has the same probability of being in the study.

Archival research refers to correlational investigations that are based on pre-existing information obtained by the researcher, such as historical records, newspaper articles, or other forms of public data. **Observational studies** refer to correlational investigations in which the researcher watches participants and codes measures from the observed behaviour, either "live" or from videotapes. **Participant-observation research** is a special kind of observational study, in which the researcher actually joins an ongoing group to observe the members' behaviour.

Experimental research refers to empirical investigations in which researchers manipulate one concept (or more than one) and assess the impact of the manipulation(s) on one or more other concepts. The manipulated factors in experiments are called the **independent variables.** The **dependent variables** are those concepts that are measured by the researcher and might be affected by the independent variables. **Extraneous variables** are potential sources of error in the experiment and should be controlled. One important strategy for controlling extraneous variables is *standardized procedures,* which means that participants in different conditions are treated exactly the same except for the manipulations. Another important strategy for controlling extraneous variables is **random assignment,** which means that each participant in the experiment is equally likely to take part in any of the experimental conditions. **Demand characteristics** are cues in a study that suggest to participants how they are supposed to respond; these cues must be minimized if the research is to provide information about spontaneous social behaviour.

Researchers strive for both internal validity and external validity in their research. **Internal validity** refers to the extent to which the research yields clear causal information. Correlational studies tend to have low internal validity, whereas experiments tend to have high internal validity. **External validity** refers to the extent to which research results can be generalized beyond the current sample, setting, and other characteristics of the study. In social psychology, external validity is typically established across numerous experiments.

When an experiment involves only one independent variable, it is called a **single-factor experiment.** When an experiment involves two or more independent variables, it is said to have a **factorial design.** Factorial designs allow the investigator to test for possible **interactions** between independent variables, which means that the effect of one manipulation depends on the level of another manipulation. In contrast to interactions, when an experimental manipulation has an overall effect on the dependent variable, averaged across all levels of other manipulations, the result is called a **main effect.** Factorial designs and interactions between variables are very common in social psychology.

Researchers also strive for realism in their experiments. **Experimental realism** refers to the extent to which the experimental setting feels realistic and involving to participants and elicits spontaneous behaviour. **Mundane realism** refers to the extent to which the experimental setting looks and feels like the outside world. Mundane realism is one quality that increases the external validity of research results. **Field experiments,** which are conducted in settings outside the laboratory, tend to increase both mundane realism and external validity.

A relatively recent methodological development has been **immersive virtual environments technology**, which creates the experience of being immersed in a constructed environment. This method allows total experimental control while creating experiences that closely correspond to the real world.

Social psychologists must take care to protect the welfare of participants in their research. One procedure that helps to achieve this goal is that all research must first be approved by a **Research Ethics Board (REB),** which is a committee that ensures the procedures will not cause unacceptable harm to participants. Another protective strategy is **informed consent,** whereby participants are told beforehand what to expect in the study and are reminded that they can withdraw at any time. A third protective strategy is **debriefing,** which means that a full and complete description of the study's design, purpose, and expected results are given to participants after the session is completed. If there has been any deception during the study, it must be identified and explained in the debriefing.

Key Terms

archival research (43)

correlational research (40)

debriefing (60)

demand characteristics (50)

dependent variable (48)

experimental realism (55)

experimental research (47)

external validity (51)

extraneous variables (48)

factorial design experiment (53)

field experiment (57)

hypothesis (34)

immersive virtual environments technology (58)

independent variable (47)

informed consent (60)

interaction (53)

internal validity (51)

main effect (54)

mundane realism (56)

observational studies (44)

operational definition (35)

participant-observation research (46)

psychometrics (38)

random assignment (50)

random sampling (43)

reliability (39)

representative sample (43)

Research Ethics Board (REB) (60)

Social Psychology Alive on the Web

SOCIAL PSYCHOLOGY ALIVE: QUIZZING AND PRACTICE TESTS

You can access our Web site directly by going to http://www.socialpsychologyalive.nelson.com for online quizzes, flash cards, and Internet links.

INFOTRAC® COLLEGE EDITION

For additional readings, explore InfoTrac® College Edition, your online library of archived journal articles and periodicals dating back 22 years. If your instructor ordered InfoTrac® College Edition with this book, you can access it from your CD-ROM, or go directly to http://www.infotrac-college.com and use the passcode from the InfoTrac® College Edition card that came with your book. For this chapter, try these search terms: *reliability, validity, just world theory, unobtrusive measures, psychometrics, archival research, participant-observation, internal validity, external validity, experimental realism, mundane realism, Internet research, informed consent.*

Social Psychology Alive: The Workbook

Chapter 2 of *Social Psychology Alive: The Workbook* provides key terms, guided study, and sample test questions. It also provides suggestions for connecting social psychology to the real world and to your life:

- The Rooster's Crow Raises the Sun (Or Does It?)
- What's in a Design? And Understanding the Results of Studies

- The Protection of Research Participants
- Selecting the Institutional Review Board
- Evaluating the Adequacy of Informed Consent

Social Psychology Alive: The Videos

To see video on the topics and experiments discussed in this chapter, you may go either to ThomsonNOW™ or to the CD-ROM, if your instructor assigned either one, to the section:

- Unmasking the Truth: Which Cancer Intervention Actually Works?

To Learn More

This list contains citations to books or articles that can help you learn more. These readings are good places to start if you want to gain a deeper understanding of the topics in this chapter.

- Crano, W. D., & Brewer, M. B. (2002). *Principles and methods of social research* (2nd ed.). Mahwah, NJ: Erlbaum.

- Pelham, B. W. (1999). *Conducting experiments in psychology: Measuring the weight of smoke*. Pacific Grove, CA: Brooks/Cole.
- Birnbaum, M. H. (2001). *Introduction to behavioral research on the Internet*. Upper Saddle River, NJ: Prentice Hall.

NEL

Social Cognition: Thinking About People

W alter Gretzky, the father of hockey great Wayne Gretzky, has always considered himself to be a lucky man. But on October 13, 1991, at the age of 58, his luck almost ran out. Walter was painting, when he suddenly felt dizzy and developed a splitting headache. He wanted to go to his bedroom and lie down for a while, but a friend of his daughter's was visiting and insisted on driving him to the hospital. She almost certainly saved his life. Walter immediately underwent five hours of emergency surgery for a burst blood vessel on the surface of his brain. The reduced blood supply to his brain caused a stroke. Strokes are the leading cause of disability in Canada and the fourth leading cause of death. Approximately 50 000 Canadians suffer a stroke each year, and about 16 000 of these individuals die.

Walter Gretzky had a long and difficult recovery period, during which he struggled to regain his physical and mental abilities. He suffered some permanent damage—for example, he lost many of his memories from the 1970s and 1980s. But he is alive and able to generate new memories with his children and grandchildren.

Walter's experience shows that it is sometimes a matter of life or death to identify quickly and correctly what is happening to you or to someone with you. Time is of the essence in the case of a stroke, because receiving treatment within the first three hours greatly increases the chances for a full recovery. Would you recognize the symptoms of a stroke? Common symptoms include numbness or weakness of one or both arms or legs, difficulty speaking, trouble seeing out of one or both eyes, severe headache, and nausea. The symptoms usually come on suddenly.

Why do we begin this chapter with a discussion of strokes? Labelling a set of symptoms as a stroke is one example of **categorization,** which is the process of recognizing and identifying something. Categorization is the most basic process we use to understand and structure our world. We are constantly identifying objects around us so we can know how to behave. The example of labelling symptoms as a stroke is a particularly dramatic one, because erroneous categorization can be fatal. The stroke example can also be an unusually difficult case of categorization, because we have so little relevant experience. Notwithstanding its drama and difficulty, identifying a stroke serves as a good example of how we categorize. We match features of an object (or symptoms being experienced) with our knowledge about the defining characteristics of various categories. Once we have categorized the object (or symptoms), we can make more informed decisions about what to do.

For the purposes of studying social psychology, you do not need to understand all the intricacies of the human mind, but you do need to have some basic knowledge about cognitive processes. In this chapter, we discuss **social cognition,** which is the study of how information about people is processed and stored. We begin by

categorization
the process of recognizing and identifying something

social cognition
the study of how information about people is processed and stored

Walter Gretzky, father of hockey legend Wayne Gretzky, suffered a stroke at the age of 58.

considering how the mind works—the basic elements of knowledge and the processes by which relevant knowledge is activated. We then discuss stereotypes, which are important in almost all perceptions of groups and individuals. Next, we describe some shortcuts that people use to make everyday judgments and a number of errors or biases that can occur when processing information about others. We also discuss how people think about events that could have happened but did not—called "what if" or counterfactual thinking. We close the chapter with a discussion of how motives and moods can influence social cognition. In Chapter 4, "Social Perception: Perceiving the Self and Others," we go beyond this chapter's description of social cognition to discuss how people draw inferences about causes and make complex judgments about themselves and others.

It might be helpful at the outset to note that there are generally thought to be two basic motives that underlie human information processing. One motive is to perceive the world accurately (Heider, 1958). We are more likely to survive if we categorize objects correctly (e.g., these are the symptoms of a stroke), draw valid inferences about other people, predict others' actions accurately, and so on. A second motive is to view the self positively (Sedikides & Strube, 1997). We want to see ourselves as good, worthy people who deserve to succeed. The various concepts and processes described in this chapter all flow from these two fundamental needs.

How Does the Mind Work?

The human mind is a marvellous thing—it perceives, imagines, expects, remembers, infers, controls, and does other complex processes. Moreover, it often does more than one of these things simultaneously. Let's consider some of the basic aspects of the mind.

Schemas: The Building Blocks of the Mind

All complex things are made up of simpler or more elementary things. Houses are made of bricks, bodies are made of cells, and so on. Although it is possible to break down the simpler things (bricks, cells) into even more basic elements, there are good reasons for using these particular levels of analysis for some purposes (e.g., for training bricklayers or for explaining the growth of the body to biology students). To understand the *mind* for the purposes of social psychology, we are less interested in its physical or biological elements than we are in its underlying *theoretical* elements. What are the elementary "building blocks" of the mind, beyond which we gain little by getting even simpler? For social psychologists, the building blocks of the mind are *schemas*.

Schemas are mental representations of objects or categories of objects (Fiske & Taylor, 1991; Hastie, 1981; Smith, 1998). You possess distinct schemas for televisions, fathers, your own father, justice, iPods, the moon, danger, your social psychology professor, and countless other things. Mark Baldwin (1992) of McGill University has noted that people also have schemas for specific interpersonal interactions, such as how doctors and patients are supposed to interact; Baldwin labelled these schemas *relational schemas* (see also Baldwin, 2005). Another term

schemas

mental representations of objects or categories, which contain the central features of the object or category as well as assumptions about how the object or category works

or Concepts

Your schema for iPod probably includes the points that they are small and can hold many songs.

that is sometimes used for schemas is *concepts* (see Kunda, 1999; Medin, 1989). Schemas or concepts contain the principal features of the object or category, as well as simple assumptions or "theories" about how the object or category functions. Your schema of iPods probably includes that they are small, they play MP3 audio files, they can hold many songs, and they come in various colours. When you encounter an object that might be classified as an iPod, you assess the similarity between the features of the object and the features in your schema of iPods; if most of the features match, then you categorize this particular instance as an iPod. This process is virtually instantaneous and effortless for distinctive objects like iPods.

Much of a child's early learning involves the formation of schemas. Parents teach their young children to identify types of animals, colours, foods, and flowers. Similarly, an important goal of the educational system is to expand students' knowledge of schemas, including some very specialized schemas. For instance, introductory social psychology teaches students precise meanings of schemas (concepts) like *attitudes, dissonance,* and, of course, *schemas.*

Categorization. Why do humans develop schemas? The basic function of schemas is to categorize objects in ways that impose meaning and predictability. When we encounter an object, we must identify what it is (categorize it) before we can behave effectively toward it. This process occurs automatically and effortlessly with the vast majority of things we encounter every day. In the morning in our kitchen, we know without conscious thought that our bowl is a bowl and our spoon is a spoon and our cereal is cereal, and we therefore smoothly put our cereal in our bowl and eat it with our spoon. We recognize our roommate and know that he is not a threat even though he looks cranky this morning. But sometimes categorization is less clear. What was that sound I just heard downstairs? Was it the floor creaking or is someone down there? What kind of insect just buzzed by? Was it a harmless ladybug or an angry hornet? These instances illustrate that the categorization of an object has important implications for behaviour.

Going Beyond the Information Given. How does categorization impose meaning on the world? The answer is that when we categorize something, we assume that it possesses the characteristics of the schema (or most of them) even if we cannot perceive those characteristics directly. Thus, we assume that this instance of fire is hot without touching it, that this apple tastes good before eating it, and that this hornet might sting us without swatting it. We are "going beyond the information given" in the sense that we are inferring other, nonvisible characteristics about the object on the basis of our categorization (Bruner, 1957). Categorization allows us to form impressions and make decisions quickly and efficiently, without having to think carefully about every object we encounter. Our world is so complex and everchanging that we absolutely have to make simplifying assumptions in order to cope. Categorization allows us to make assumptions about objects and to direct our attention to those aspects of the environment that are most important. Sometimes we make faulty assumptions about objects based on our schemas. For example, when we categorize a person into a group (lawyer, French Canadian, or movie star) and assume that he or she possesses particular characteristics, we can make errors. Nevertheless, categorization is a necessary and effective process, especially for inanimate objects.

Selective Information Processing. Schemas not only impose meaning on the world, they also influence how information is processed. For instance, many researchers have shown that the schema used to categorize an object can influence what is *noticed* about the object. A classic study was conducted by Claudia Cohen

(1981) at the University of California at San Diego. Participants watched a 15-minute videotape of a woman having a birthday dinner at home with her husband. The woman ate her dinner, talked with her husband, and opened some gifts. Half of the participants were told before watching the videotape that the woman was a server at a local coffee shop; the other half were told that the woman was a librarian at the city library. Thus, the schema of either server or librarian was activated. The videotape was specially constructed so that it included some elements that were consistent with the stereotype of servers and some elements that were consistent with the stereotype of librarians. For example, the woman drank beer and mentioned that she had not travelled to Europe (two elements consistent with the server label), and she wore glasses and listened to classical music (two elements consistent with the librarian label).

Participants' memory for information in the videotape was tested either immediately after viewing it, four days later, or seven days later. Nine items in the memory test related to elements that were consistent with the stereotype of servers, and nine items related to elements that were consistent with the stereotype of librarians. Figure 3.1 presents the percentage of correct responses at each testing time that participants made for elements that were consistent and inconsistent with the occupation label they were given. Participants were more accurate in their answers about things that fit their occupation label than about things that did not fit their label at every delay interval. For example, participants who believed that the woman was a server were more likely to recall correctly that

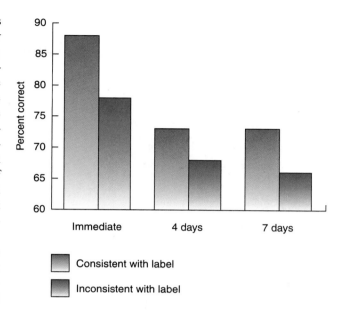

FIGURE 3.1 Percentage correct for items consistent and inconsistent with occupation label

From C. E. Cohen, "Person categories and social perception: Testing some boundaries of the processing effects of prior knowledge," *Journal of Personality and Social Psychology,* 40, 441–452, 1981. Copyright © 1981 by the American Psychological Association. Reprinted by permission.

she drank beer than were participants who believed she was a librarian; on the other hand, participants who believed that the woman was a librarian were more likely to recall correctly that she listened to classical music than were participants who believed she was a server. The schema that was activated for the woman (server or librarian) influenced what participants noticed and recalled from the videotape, whether recall was assessed immediately or up to a week later.

Schemas also influence the *interpretation* of information. Typically, their effect will be that ambiguous information is interpreted in accordance with the schema (Fiske & Taylor, 1991; Rothbart, Evans, & Fulero, 1979). A plant's foliage and blossom might seem prettier to us if we are told it is a wildflower than if we are told it is a weed. A more ominous example might be that if a man you encounter on the street in the evening evokes the schema of "mugger," then ambiguous actions by him are likely to be interpreted in threatening ways (e.g., he is following you). Schemas lead us to assume that the object possesses particular characteristics, and anything that vaguely implies those characteristics may be taken as evidence that our assumption is accurate.

The functions and consequences of schemas are summarized in the accompanying Concept Review.

Although *ambiguous* information will usually be interpreted as consistent with a schema, anything that obviously *contradicts* our expectancies will grab our attention (Olson, Roese, & Zanna, 1996; Stangor & McMillan, 1992). How do you think you would react if you were walking through a park and saw a raccoon running toward you? You would probably be startled, to say the least, whereas similar behaviour by your dog would hardly be noticed. Unexpected actions arouse our curiosity and lead to attempts to understand why the object is exhibiting characteristics that are inconsistent with its category. In the raccoon example, you might decide that the raccoon is approaching you without fear because it is rabid, so you had better run away. The

If a man is categorized as a *mugger,* his actions will probably be interpreted in ominous and threatening ways.

3.1
ONLINE
LAB

CONCEPT REVIEW
Functions and Consequences of Schemas

Definition of Schema:

Mental representations of objects or categories of objects, which contain the central features of the object or category as well as assumptions about how the object or category works

Function or Consequence	Description	Example
Function: Categorization	Identify the object	This man walking out of a hotel is probably a tourist.
Function: Information gain	Assume that the object probably possesses the typical characteristics of the schema	I bet he doesn't live in this city.
Function: Rapid, efficient decisions	Can decide quickly how to behave toward the object	I will ask him if he needs directions.
Consequence: Selective attention	More likely to notice information that is consistent with the schema (or that obviously contradicts it)	I see that he is carrying a camera and a map.
Consequence: Selective interpretation	Likely to interpret ambiguous information as consistent with the schema	He looks a bit confused, so he must be lost.

---

schema of *rabid animal* has been invoked to understand the raccoon, with the result that new characteristics have been attributed to it (e.g., sick, fearless, dangerous, and contagious).

Accessibility: What's on Your Mind?

When a schema is activated, it provides expectancies about the object's probable characteristics and influences the processing of information about the object. When you categorize an animal as a dog, you expect it to be sociable and loyal, and you may interpret its behaviour as reflecting these characteristics. Thus, the schema used to categorize an object is important; if two individuals categorize the same object differently (i.e., using different schemas), they may expect very different characteristics.

Given the significance of how an object is categorized, it is important to know the factors that influence whether a particular schema will be used. Sometimes a schema is directly activated by information, such as when participants are *told* that a woman is a server or a librarian. But what about "spontaneous" activation without information from others? One factor is very straightforward: a schema will be activated when the object's features match the features of the schema (e.g., when you see a friend holding something small against her ear and categorize it as a cell phone, or when you see a man behind the wheel of a truck and categorize him as a truck driver). Another, less obvious factor that influences whether a schema will be used is its **accessibility**—the ease with which the schema comes to awareness. People are more likely to use schemas that are highly accessible to them; these schemas are "on their mind." Let's consider factors that affect the accessibility of a schema (see Higgins, 1996).

accessibility

the ease with which a schema comes to awareness

Priming of Schemas. Have you ever noticed that one event can get you thinking about the same thing in other situations? If you read about a car accident in the morning newspaper, you might find yourself driving very cautiously all day. Or if someone compliments your haircut, you might find yourself looking at everyone's hair for the rest of the day. What is going on here? The initial event (e.g., the hair compliment) activates the schema of haircut or hair, and because this schema is "on your mind," it is more accessible and more likely to be activated again. Social and cognitive psychologists have shown that when a schema has been used recently, it is more accessible, an effect that is called **priming.** In the haircut example, the compliment primed the schema of hair or haircut. Many researchers have found that priming a schema in people's minds increases the likelihood that they will use that schema in a later task.

Charles Carver and his colleagues at the University of Miami (Carver, Ganellen, Froming, & Chambers, 1983) showed participants a videotape of a businessman asking his assistant about arrangements for a trip he was going to take. Participants were told that their memory for this videotape would be tested. Some participants saw a version of the tape in which the businessman was quite hostile and derogatory toward the assistant, whereas other participants saw a version of the tape in which the businessman was calm and relaxed toward the assistant. Carver and his colleagues assumed that the first version of the videotape would prime (activate) the schema of "hostile" or "aggressive," whereas the second version would not (it might instead prime "polite" or "friendly"). Participants then completed a second task that they believed was unrelated to the first one. They read a paragraph describing a young man who behaved in several ways that were ambiguous with respect to hostility—he engaged in actions that could be seen as hostile or could be interpreted in other ways. For example, the young man was said to be "refusing to pay his rent until the landlord had his plumbing repaired"; this action might reflect hostility or it might reflect standing up for one's rights. After reading this paragraph, participants were asked for their impressions of the young man, including the extent to which he was hostile and unfriendly. Participants who had been exposed to the hostile videotape in the first task rated the young man in the second task as more hostile than did participants who had been exposed to the nonhostile videotape in the first task. Priming the schema of hostile increased its use in a subsequent, unrelated task (see also Martin, Seta, & Crelia, 1990; Sedikides, 1990; Skowronski, Carlston, & Isham, 1993; Srull & Wyer, 1980; Strack, Schwarz, Bless, Kubler, & Wanke, 1993). Bertram Gawronski at the University of Western Ontario has conducted research exploring the basic mechanisms underlying priming and accessibility effects (e.g., Gawronski & Bodenhausen, 2005; Gawronski, Deutsch, & Seidel, 2005).

A powerful example of real-world priming, which many of you will experience one day or perhaps have experienced, occurs when you or your partner become(s) pregnant. Suddenly, pregnant women seem to be everywhere, and small infants in baby carriages have apparently multiplied. Indeed, the world seems to be populated primarily by pregnant women, mothers, and small children. One of the authors of this text (J.O.) suffered a very embarrassing consequence of this heightened accessibility of pregnancy while his wife was pregnant. He was proctoring an exam, daydreaming at the front of the room about what it was going to be like to have a child. Near the end of the allotted time, a female student in the class, who was perhaps 25 years old, came to the front to hand in her exam. Noticing a slight roundness in her belly that looked exactly like a pregnancy of four or five months, the daydreaming professor whispered excitedly to her, "Are you pregnant?" The words were barely out

3.2
ONLINE
LAB

priming
the process by which the activation of a schema increases the likelihood that the schema will be activated again in the future

© Photodisc Green/Getty Images

Being pregnant, or having one's partner pregnant, makes the schemas for pregnancy and children very accessible.

of his mouth when he knew that he had made a big mistake. Let his experience be a lesson for you: do not let accessible schemas take over your life!

Chronic Accessibility of Schemas. For each of us, some schemas are more accessible, in general, than are other schemas. The extent to which schemas are easy to activate for an individual across time and situations is termed **chronic accessibility.** People differ in the schemas that are most chronically accessible to them. A teacher at a high school who coaches the basketball team might have "height" as a chronically accessible schema when meeting new students—she might notice the height of students immediately, and she might categorize students as potential "post players," "guards," or "forwards" based on their height. The pregnancy example given a moment ago might seem to qualify as chronic accessibility, but it is actually initiated by a specific event (one's own involvement in a pregnancy) and fades over time, so it is probably better viewed as a case of strong priming.

chronic accessibility

the degree to which schemas are easily activated for an individual across time and situations

Tory Higgins, Gillian King, and Gregory Mavin (1982) asked students at the University of Western Ontario to describe themselves, two male friends, and two female friends using a maximum of ten traits in each description. The researchers looked for any traits (e.g., honest, intelligent, friendly) that participants used for themselves plus at least one friend or for at least three friends; these traits were considered to be chronically accessible for that participant. Two weeks later, participants were brought back for what they thought was a different experiment. They read a short essay that had been specially constructed for them (though they did not know this), which described several actions by another student; some of these actions exhibited traits that were chronically accessible for the participant, and other actions exhibited traits that were not chronically accessible for the participant. After a ten-minute delay, participants' memory for the essay was tested, and they were also asked to write a detailed description of the student. Figure 3.2 presents the percentage of the chronically accessible and nonaccessible traits that participants recalled and included in their descriptions. Results showed that participants were more likely to remember actions by the student that exhibited their own chronically accessible traits than actions that exhibited nonaccessible traits. For example, if a participant had used the trait *funny* to describe several friends at the first session, then he or she was likely to remember funny behaviours in the paragraph at the second session. Participants were also more likely to include chronically accessible traits than nonaccessible traits in their written descriptions of the student. Thus, participants' chronically accessible traits influenced both what they could remember about the student and how they described the student (see also Baldwin, Fehr, Keedian, Seidel, & Thomson, 1993; Bargh, Bond, Lombardi, & Tota, 1986).

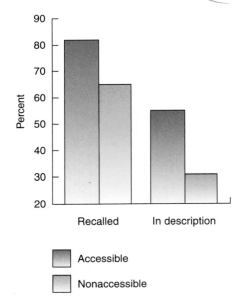

FIGURE 3.2 Percentage of accessible and nonaccessible traits recalled or included in description

From Higgins et al., "Individual construct accessibility and subjective impressions and recall," *Journal of Personality and Social Psychology,* 43, 35–47, p. 39, 1982. Copyright © 1981 by the American Psychological Association.

Cultural Differences in Accessible Schemas

Cultures differ in the schemas that are used most often to categorize both self and others. Western cultures (e.g., Canada, the United States, Great Britain, Australia) emphasize in their socialization individuality, freedom, and independence, whereas Eastern cultures (e.g., China, Japan, Korea, Indonesia) emphasize in their socialization harmony, obedience, and interdependence (e.g., Hofstede, 1980; Markus & Kitayama, 1991; Triandis, 1989). This independence–interdependence (also called individualism–collectivism) difference between Western and Eastern cultures will be mentioned numerous times in this book as we discuss specific topics in social psychology. For our present purposes, we mention this point because individuals from Western and Eastern cultures are likely to differ in the schemas that are most chronically accessible to them. Canadians, for example, may be more likely than Chinese persons to categorize people in terms of individual achievements ("he is a math wizard," "she is a natural comic"). In contrast, Chinese persons may be more likely than Canadians to categorize people in terms of group memberships ("his family is religious," "she comes from a small town"). These differences in accessible schemas imply that people from different cultures may perceive the same event or the same person quite differently.

In a study that yielded findings consistent with this reasoning, Joseph Forgas and Michael Bond (1985) asked university students from Australia and Hong Kong to sort a set of 27 different social events (e.g., studying with another student before an exam; arriving very late to a tutorial; comparing marks with other students after they have been posted on a notice board; taking a friend of the opposite sex to the movies) into sets of events that they considered to be similar to one another. To decide which events were similar, students could use whatever aspects of the 27 events they wished. The researchers assumed that students would use their most accessible schemas to define similarity between the events. Results showed that students from Australia (but not Hong Kong) tended to organize the different events in terms of how competitive the events were. This reliance on competitiveness to classify the events is consistent with the Western emphasis on individualism. In contrast, students from Hong Kong (but not Australia) tended to group the events in terms of the number of people involved in the events. This reliance on group size is consistent with the Eastern emphasis on collectivism. Thus, different schemas appeared to be chronically accessible in the two cultures (see also Gardner, Gabriel, & Yee, 1999).

Stereotypes: Schemas in the Social Domain

A **stereotype** is a set of characteristics that someone associates with members of a group; it is a cognitive structure containing the individual's beliefs that members of a group share particular attributes (Gardner, 1994; Hamilton & Sherman, 1994). Stereotypes are one kind of schema (defined earlier as mental representations of objects or categories of objects)—namely, schemas that represent human groups. All of us possess stereotypes of many groups, including occupations (lawyers, nurses, construction workers), racial or ethnic groups (French Canadians, Aboriginal peoples, immigrants), religious groups (Muslims, Roman Catholics, Jews), age groups (the elderly, infants, teenagers), and many other categories (women, gay men, Liberals). Sometimes the characteristics that we associate with a group are largely positive (e.g., doctors, firefighters), but they can also be negative (e.g., telemarketers, drug addicts). Social psychologists have been most interested in the latter, negative stereotypes, especially those directed at disadvantaged groups, because researchers want to understand and reduce the prevalence of phenomena such as prejudice and discrimination (discussed in detail in Chapter 9, "Stereotypes, Prejudice, and Discrimination"). Stereotypes have fundamental importance in social perception—they guide our perceptions and impressions of almost everyone we meet.

Going Beyond the Information Given. Just like other types of schemas, stereotypes reflect our attempt to categorize an object and draw inferences about it. When we learn that a woman is a lawyer, we use our lawyer categorization to infer that she is probably intelligent, persuasive, and wealthy (your stereotype of lawyers may be quite different from these features). These inferences provide us with a rapid guide for how to behave toward her. Unfortunately, the assumptions we make about members of human groups may often be oversimplified or even dead wrong.

An interesting aspect of stereotypes is that we ourselves are members of some groups about which we have stereotypes. A group to which a perceiver belongs is called his or her *ingroup.* Your ingroups probably include university students, people

stereotype

a set of characteristics that a perceiver associates with members of a group in your age group, your gender, and your ethnic identity (e.g., English Canadian, French Canadian). An *outgroup* is a group to which a perceiver does not belong. Outgroups for you probably include professors, elderly people, the opposite sex, and ethnic groups other than your own. Stereotypes of ingroups are generally favourable, whereas stereotypes of outgroups can sometimes be unfavourable. Bertram Gawronski at the University of Western Ontario has shown that perceivers habitually use perceptions of their ingroups as implicit standards of comparison when judging outgroups. Given that stereotypes about ingroups are generally favourable, this implicit comparison process can serve to make judgments about outgroups more negative.

Stereotypes usually include information about how much variability (difference on a characteristic) exists in the group (see Hamilton & Sherman, 1994). One individual might believe that almost all nurses are outgoing, but another individual might believe that some nurses are outgoing and other nurses are shy. There is a general tendency, however, for people to overestimate the similarity within groups. This tendency to overestimate the similarity within groups is much stronger for outgroups (especially disliked and little-known outgroups) than for one's own ingroups. That is, whereas people often view their ingroups as being quite diverse (see Brewer, 1993; Goethals, 1986b; Judd & Park, 1988), outgroups tend to be seen as more uniform ("They're all alike!"). For example, think about how most Canadians view people who live in Iran or in North Korea; people within these relatively unfamiliar countries are often seen as quite similar to one another. The exaggeration of similarity within groups to which we do not belong is called the **outgroup homogeneity effect** ("homogeneity" means similarity or uniformity). They're all alike.

outgroup homogeneity effect
the tendency for people to overestimate the similarity within groups to which they do not belong

Selective Information Processing. If you see a young man with a shaved head, leather clothes, several tattoos, and multiple body piercings, you may classify him as a skinhead. Once this stereotype has been activated, do you think that it will influence what else you *notice* about the man? Will you, for example, be particularly attentive for signs of aggression or hostility?

Social psychologists have argued that stereotypes can guide our attention in this manner (e.g., Plaks, Stroessner, Dweck, & Sherman, 2001). Recall the study by Cohen (1981), in which participants were more likely to recall things in a videotape that were consistent with a woman's alleged occupation (server or librarian). Presumably, participants were more likely to notice the occupation-consistent information while watching the video.

What about your *interpretation* of ambiguous behaviour—will this be affected by stereotypic expectancies? Returning to the skinhead, will you interpret ambiguous behaviour by him as aggressive and hostile? Imagine that he asks a passer-by for money. Are you likely to interpret his action as threatening and intimidating, compared to how you would interpret exactly the same behaviour exhibited by someone who was not a skinhead?

Again, social psychologists would answer this question affirmatively (see Kunda & Thagard, 1996); our stereotypes can change how we interpret ambiguous behaviour. An interesting experimental demonstration of this effect was provided by Princeton University social psychologists John Darley and Paget Gross (1983), who investigated social class stereotypes. The researchers showed participants a short videotape of a nine-year-old Caucasian girl named Hannah. The videotape showed Hannah playing in her schoolyard and outside her home. Half of the participants saw a version of the tape that depicted Hannah in an inner-city, run-down area (the negative expectancy condition), whereas the other half of the participants saw a version of the tape that depicted Hannah in a wealthy, suburban area (the positive expectancy condition).

Some participants were then immediately asked to rate Hannah's academic ability (the baseline condition). Other participants watched a second videotape of Hannah before rating her academic ability. On this second videotape, Hannah responded to 25 general knowledge questions (the performance condition). Her performance on these questions was inconsistent and ambiguous; she answered some items correctly, including some difficult items, but she also made some mistakes on both simple and difficult items.

How did the negative and positive expectancies influence participants' ratings of Hannah's academic abilities? Figure 3.3 presents the ratings of Hannah's academic ability. Participants who believed Hannah to be from a wealthy background (positive expectancy) consistently rated her as more skilled than did participants who believed Hannah to be from a poor background (negative expectancy). But the effect of expectancies was much stronger when participants watched Hannah answer some test items (the performance condition) than when they rated her abilities based only on the background information (the baseline condition). Among those participants who watched Hannah answer questions, those in the positive expectancy condition rated her much more positively than did those in the negative expectancy condition. Why did watching Hannah's performance increase the impact of the expectancies manipulation? The researchers suggested that participants' interpretations of Hannah's inconsistent performance differed based on their expectancies. If participants had positive expectancies, they probably focused on her correct answers to difficult questions when assessing her ability, whereas if participants had negative expectancies, they probably focused on her incorrect answers to easy questions when assessing her ability. Exactly the same performance was interpreted differently based on expectancies derived from social class stereotypes.

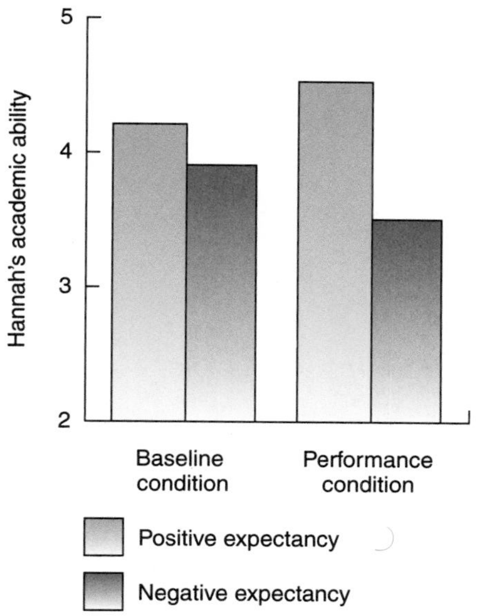

Barry Corenblum of Brandon University has conducted studies with White and Aboriginal Canadian elementary school children (who attended integrated inner-city schools) in which participants either watched a video or read information about another child (Corenblum, 2003; Corenblum, Annis, & Young, 1996). Both White and Aboriginal participants tended to recall positive information about White models but negative information about Aboriginal models. Interestingly, the bias against their own group shown by Aboriginal children disappeared among those who were attending a heritage school on their own reserve, which presumably affirmed and promoted First Nations cultures.

FIGURE 3.3 Ratings of Hannah's academic ability

From Darley and Gross, "A hypothesis-confirming bias in labeling effects," *Journal of Personality and Social Psychology*, 24, 20–33, Fig. 1, p. 24, 1983. Copyright © 1983 by the American Psychological Association. Reprinted by permission.

Automatic Versus Controlled Processes

Most of us believe that we have full control over our mental processes. We can focus our attention *wherever* we wish; we can think about *whatever* we wish; and we can make judgments *whenever* we wish. We are completely in control. Right? Not always. Cognitive and social psychologists have come to realize that people do *not* have full control over all of their mental processes. Many thoughts and judgments occur whether we want them to or not. In fact, we are not even aware of some of our cognitive processes (see Nisbett & Wilson, 1977).

Theorists have proposed an important distinction based on the controllability or reflectiveness of a mental process (see Smith & DeCoster, 2000; Strack & Deutsch, 2004). An **automatic process** is a judgment or thought that we cannot control: it occurs without intention, very efficiently (demanding few cognitive resources), and sometimes beneath our awareness (Bargh, 1994; Gilbert, 1989). Thus, we cannot "turn on" and "turn off" an automatic process. It is spontaneous and not subject to intentional control; we may sometimes not even realize that it has occurred. An automatic process is also very efficient: it can occur at the same time as other processes. A **controlled process** is a judgment or thought that we command: it is intentional, requires significant cognitive resources, and occurs within our awareness. We can

automatic process

a judgment or thought that we cannot control, which occurs without intention, very efficiently, and sometimes beneath our awareness

controlled process

a judgment or thought that we command, which is intentional, requires significant cognitive resources, and occurs within our awareness turn it on or off at will. Because a controlled process requires mental resources, it may not occur if we are engaged in other processes. We are consciously aware of engaging in a controlled process.

What processes occur automatically? Perhaps the clearest example of automatic processing is categorization—recognizing and identifying an object. We do not have to stop and think, "What is that rectangular piece of wood over there with four other pieces of wood going down from its corners?"; we automatically categorize the object as a table. This labelling is involuntary, immediate, and effortless. Categorization must be rapid and effortless so we can assign our limited attentional resources to more demanding tasks.

Categorization of people also occurs automatically. We perceive instantly and effortlessly various characteristics of others, including their age, sex, racial group, and physical appearance. The relevant schemas, or stereotypes, are activated automatically, whether we "want" them to be activated or not. Like other schemas, stereotypes allow us to draw inferences about individuals based on the assumption that they possess the central features of the category. In Chapter 9, we will discuss research suggesting that when people meet another individual, they cannot stop or inhibit relevant stereotypes from being activated in their minds (e.g., woman, elderly, Black), even if they reject the validity of those stereotypes. Researchers have also argued that the simple observation of an action (e.g., someone swearing at another person) leads us to label that action automatically, or spontaneously, in terms of relevant traits (e.g., as a hostile act). These "spontaneous trait inferences" can occur instantly and effortlessly (Carlston & Skowronski, 1994; Newman, 1991; Uleman, Newman, & Moskowitz, 1996; but see Bassili & Smith, 1986).

Of course, some cognitive processes are controlled—we can initiate them deliberately and focus them on whatever problem we need to solve. For example, thinking carefully about why someone behaved in a certain fashion is a controlled process. Similarly, deciding how to behave toward another person is often an effortful, deliberate process. One function of controlled thinking is to correct errors from automatic processes if we suspect that errors may have occurred. For instance, we may decide that someone who acted in a hostile fashion (e.g., swore at another person) is not really hostile because he or she was responding to a prior threat. We will talk in Chapter 9 about research showing that people can consciously override the effects of stereotypes that have been elicited automatically.

Reconstructive Memory

Retrieval of information from memory can be a challenging task. We have tens of thousands of schemas stored in memory, as well as tens of thousands of recollections of our own experiences. How do we get information out of this massive storage system? Let's think of a simple example. Try to recall the last movie you saw. How did you retrieve this memory? Most social cognition theorists assume that retrieval occurs by using schemas to search memory. For instance, we begin by thinking about a schema related to our memory goal (e.g., movies), which then activates other related schemas (comedies, dramas), which ultimately activate the information you need (the name of your most recent movie).

This example illustrates the retrieval of concrete, objective information. Sometimes, however, memory retrieval must be a "reconstructive" process. By reconstructive, we mean that cues or strategies must be used to search memory and to estimate the correct answer. **Reconstructive memory** is trying to cognitively rebuild the past based on cues and estimates. Although retrieval of things like the last movie you saw may not be susceptible to much distortion, many things in memory are less

reconstructive memory
the process of trying to rebuild the past based on cues and estimates

concrete and verifiable. How many soft drinks did you consume last month? How good were your study habits in high school? These sorts of questions cannot be answered solely by direct access to objective, concrete memories. They require estimations or interpretations that can be quite subjective. Therefore, the schemas, goals, and expectations that are active while you try to retrieve the information and estimate the answer can influence the outcome. John Kihlstrom (1994) captured this reconstructive aspect of memory very nicely: "memory is not so much like reading a book as it is like writing one from fragmentary notes" (p. 341).

Autobiographical Memory

Autobiographical memory is stored information about the self—our goals, personality traits, past experiences, and other qualities. Autobiographical memory comprises our knowledge about the self, including our personal history. Because our own experiences make up so many of our memories, and because information about the self has major implications for identity and self-esteem, autobiographical memory is an important component of our memory system.

Michael Ross (1989), who is at the University of Waterloo, has proposed a model of autobiographical memory that is based on the notion of reconstruction. Together with Canadian colleagues Michael Conway of Concordia University, Cathy McFarland of Simon Fraser University, and Anne Wilson of Wilfrid Laurier University (Conway & Ross, 1984; McFarland & Ross, 1987; Wilson & Ross, 2001), Ross has demonstrated that autobiographical memory often involves *estimating* what we were like in the past, because we may not be able to retrieve actual, concrete information. Thus, autobiographical memory is rather slippery—it involves guesswork, which can be influenced by our motives and beliefs.

Before continuing to read, look at Know Yourself 3.1: "Current and Past Self." This questionnaire asks you to rate yourself on a number of characteristics at two points in time: now and when you were 16 years old. Take a look at the dimensions and rate yourself honestly in terms of how much you possess these qualities now and how much you possessed them when you were 16. After you have completed the ratings, come back to this point and continue reading.

In a series of studies, Anne Wilson and Michael Ross (2001) asked college students to rate themselves on a variety of traits like those in the Know Yourself 3.1 feature. Participants rated both their current self and the way they were at a certain point in the past (e.g., when they were 16 years old). Some participants rated the current self before the past self, whereas others rated the past self before the current self. Irrespective of the order of the two ratings, the results were clear and consistent: participants rated the current self more positively than the past self. Was this also true for you? Did you rate your current self more favourably than your 16-year-old self?

It is possible that the students in Wilson and Ross's research (and perhaps you) really did improve on these characteristics over the years, and their (or your) ratings were based on accurate, concrete memories. Wilson and Ross, however, proposed a second interpretation: many of their participants did not really access valid memories about themselves in the past, but instead estimated the past self based on a desire to see the current self positively. All of us want to think that we are good, worthwhile individuals. One way to feel good about ourselves is to believe that we are steadily improving over time: we are getting better and better on most qualities.

autobiographical memory
stored information about the self, such as goals, personality traits, past experiences, and other qualities

Autobiographical memory includes our memories of childhood experiences.

Know Yourself 3.1
Current and Past Self

Please rate yourself on each of the following dimensions by circling the appropriate number on the answer scale. First rate yourself as you are *now* (that is, your *current self*). Then rate yourself on the same dimensions as you were *when you were 16* (that is, a *past self*).

How much do these characteristics describe you **now**?

1. Broad-minded:

1	2	3	(4)	5
Not at all	Slightly	Somewhat	Moderately	Extremely

2. Socially skilled:

1	2	3	(4)	5
Not at all	Slightly	Somewhat	Moderately	Extremely

3. Self-confident:

1	2	3	(4)	5
Not at all	Slightly	Somewhat	Moderately	Extremely

4. Thoughtful:

1	2	3	(4)	5
Not at all	Slightly	Somewhat	Moderately	Extremely

5. Resourceful:

1	2	(3)	4	5
Not at all	Slightly	Somewhat	Moderately	Extremely

How much did these characteristics describe you **when you were 16 years old**?

1. Broad-minded:

1	(2)	3	4	5
Not at all	Slightly	Somewhat	Moderately	Extremely

2. Socially skilled:

1	2	(3)	4	5
Not at all	Slightly	Somewhat	Moderately	Extremely

3. Self-confident:

1	(2)	3	4	5
Not at all	Slightly	Somewhat	Moderately	Extremely

4. Thoughtful:

1	2	(3)	4	5
Not at all	Slightly	Somewhat	Moderately	Extremely

5. Resourceful:

1	(2)	3	4	5
Not at all	Slightly	Somewhat	Moderately	Extremely

SCORING: Look at your ratings on each dimension for the two time periods. Was one set of ratings consistently higher than another? Return to the text for relevant discussion.

A third possible interpretation of Wilson and Ross's findings is that participants' past and present ratings were guided by their beliefs about the effects of time. For example, most of us believe that people generally improve over time on most characteristics. Thus, perhaps participants rated the past self lower than the present self because they assumed that improvement had occurred, which means that the past self must have been somewhat worse than the current self.

Which of these alternative interpretations is most plausible? In one of Wilson and Ross's (2001) studies, participants at the University of Waterloo rated themselves at the beginning of the school term and then returned to the laboratory two months later. At this second session, participants rated the current self and then were asked to think back to how they were at the beginning of the term and to rate themselves again *as they were at that time*. Results showed that participants at the second session rated the past self (at the beginning of the term) less positively than the current self, whereas participants' *actual* self-ratings obtained at the beginning of the term were just as positive as the "current self" ratings at the second session. Thus, participants estimated at the second session that they had improved over the two-month period, but their original ratings indicated that they did not actually improve. This finding suggests that differences between the ratings of current and past selves do *not* necessarily reflect actual changes (improvements).

But this study did not distinguish between the second and third possibilities: perhaps participants simply wanted to see themselves favourably, or perhaps, when rating the past self, participants simply assumed that people improve over time. Therefore, in another study, Wilson and Ross (2001) asked participants to rate either themselves or an *acquaintance* (who was in the same year) on several traits; participants rated the target (self or acquaintance) both currently and when the target was 16 years old. Presumably, if people believe that everyone improves over time, then ratings of an acquaintance should show the same pattern as ratings of the self. The average ratings provided by participants are presented in Figure 3.4. These ratings revealed perceived improvement over time for the self, but *not* for the acquaintance, which suggests that the ratings of the self were caused by a desire to see the current self positively (see also Ross & Wilson, 2002). We will elaborate on this motive to see the current self positively later in this chapter.

Given that autobiographical memory is often reconstructive, an important question is whether *false* memories can be implanted in people's minds. Is it possible to make people believe that something happened to them that did not? Can people be influenced in such a way as to guide their reconstruction of the past in false directions? Think about some of your earliest memories. Are you certain that these memories are real and concrete, or could they possibly be your reconstructions based on things you have heard from your parents?

Some evidence suggests that yes, in fact, it may be possible to tamper with autobiographical memory (see Kunda, 1999; Loftus, 2004; Schacter, 1996). For example, Stephen Lindsay and his colleagues at the University of Victoria (Lindsay, Hagen, Read, Wade, & Garry, 2004) contacted the parents of university students and obtained descriptions of a few events that had occurred in their child's life. The researchers then interviewed the students and asked them questions about these factual events and about one fictitious event that did not actually occur (fabricated by the researchers—putting Slime, a brightly coloured, sticky substance made by Mattel as a toy, in the teacher's desk in Grade 1 or 2). Some participants were also given a copy of their class photo from the appropriate grade. At this initial interview, very few participants claimed to remember the fictitious event. The students were interviewed a second time, however, during the following week. At this second interview, 47% of the students reported some memories of the fabricated event, including 65% of the students who had been given a class photo! Presumably, the first

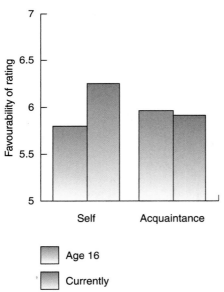

FIGURE 3.4 Ratings of self and acquaintance currently and at age 16

From Wilson and Ross, "From chump to champ: People's appraisals of their earlier and present selves," *Journal of Personality and Social Psychology*, 80, 572–584, Table 2, p. 578, 2001. Copyright © 2001 by the American Psychological Association. Reprinted by permission.

interview, especially when a class photo was also provided, put images into participants' minds that were now confused with real memories (see also Hyman, Husband, & Billings, 1995).

We should not overstate the problem: human memory provides an amazing storage system for recollections of our past experiences. But human memory is *not* infallible. We often reconstruct personal memories based on information that is currently accessible to us. It is also possible for us to have seemingly real memories of events that we simply heard about or imagined occurring. Kenneth Bowers and Peter Farvolden (1996) of the University of Waterloo have pointed out that dreams can also provide fodder for erroneous memories. Have you ever found yourself thinking about an event but then realized that you only dreamed about it? These points underscore that memory can be misleading—we may believe that something happened when, in fact, it did not.

A highly controversial question regarding the accuracy of autobiographical memory is whether "recovered" memories of childhood sexual abuse can be false. This emotionally charged issue has generated both vigorous debate and significant anger—but few empirical data. The conflicting perspectives on this question are outlined briefly in the accompanying box, "Social Psychology in Your Life: Are Recovered Memories of Abuse Fact or Fiction?"

The Accuracy of Eyewitness Testimony

If human memory is unreliable, it may be risky to rely solely on one person's memory of a complex event to make an important decision. A domain in which exactly this circumstance can happen is legal settings. Many criminal cases are built around the testimony of an eyewitness to convict an accused person. In many trials, the eyewitness is the victim of the crime, and his or her principal role is to identify the accused person as the perpetrator of the crime. Jurors usually weigh eyewitness testimony very heavily; after all, if someone *saw* this person committing the crime (especially the victim), then he or she *must* be guilty. But how much confidence should we have in eyewitness identifications? Do errors occur?

Looking at documented cases of wrongful conviction makes the significance of erroneous eyewitness testimony very clear. There have been hundreds of examples of people who were convicted of a crime but later proven to be innocent. Legal experts have concluded that the single largest cause of these demonstrably false convictions has been eyewitness error (e.g., Brandon & Davies, 1973; Huff, Rattner, & Sagarin, 1986). Not only is eyewitness testimony compelling to judges and jurors, but when an eyewitness positively identifies a suspect, the police often stop investigating all other leads (Wrightsman, 1991). The consequence is that an eyewitness identification can dramatically affect the course of the investigation and the trial. Unfortunately, eyewitnesses can sometimes be mistaken. Human memory is fallible, perhaps especially when the eyewitness was emotionally fearful or upset (e.g., was the victim of an assault).

One factor that has dramatically increased the number of overturned convictions has been the advent of DNA testing. By matching inmates' DNA to samples obtained from the crime scene (e.g., using hairs from the scene), this form of testing can positively show that an individual is innocent. It can also sometimes positively identify someone else as the person who committed the crime.

The case of Thomas Sophonow is typical of a wrongful conviction. This Winnipeg man served almost four years in prison for a murder he did not commit. On what basis was Sophonow found guilty? Several eyewitnesses identified him as the person they saw coming out of a donut shop where the murder occurred. Despite other evidence that placed Sophonow at a different location, the jury was swayed by the

Social Psychology in Your Life   *Are Recovered Memories of Abuse Fact or Fiction?*

Sexual abuse is a major social problem and is especially tragic when it involves children. Every year in Canada, thousands of children are abused by a parent, other relative, or acquaintance, and the consequences of this abuse can be terrible. In addition to the immediate fear, pain, and humiliation, victims often experience long-term problems including depression, post-traumatic stress disorder, and difficulty establishing relationships with others (see Cardeña, Butler, & Spiegel, 2003; Wolfe, 1999).

In the past 20 years, increasing numbers of adults, usually women, have reported suddenly remembering childhood abuse after years of no such memory. Often, these recovered memories have appeared during psychotherapy, when therapists probed for possible abuse in the patient's past to explain her or his current difficulties. Sometimes, the memories have included bizarre elements like satanic cults and ritualistic torture. Typically, the people accused of committing these crimes have vehemently denied their guilt, claiming instead that the alleged events were somehow planted in the minds of the patients.

What should we conclude about these recovered memories? Is it possible that people can be induced to believe firmly that such violent acts occurred when they did not? Can therapists unknowingly elicit false memories of awful traumas?

Unfortunately, this question is extremely difficult to answer. For one thing, there are no objective, agreed-upon criteria for distinguishing true

memories from false memories, even within more mundane domains than abuse. So unless physical evidence is available (which is unlikely for events that allegedly occurred many years ago), absolute certainty is impossible. Also, no empirical research has directly tested whether memories of sexual abuse can be implanted—nor will such research *ever* be conducted, because of the obvious ethical problems (Kunda, 1999). It is debatable whether research on less emotional issues should be generalized to the domain of recovered memories of sexual abuse (Pope, 1996). Harvard cognitive psychologist Daniel Schacter (1996) commented on the absence of relevant data: "Few times in the history of psychology or psychiatry has the ratio of data to impassioned argument been so low" (p. 277). Canadian psychologists Clare MacMartin and A. Daniel Yarmey (1999) of the University of Guelph have pointed out that people on both sides of the issue sometimes use the same evidence to argue for opposite conclusions.

The stakes are very high on this issue. People accused of sexual abuse on the basis of recovered memories can go to jail—and some have. On the other side of the issue, victims of abuse worry that if recovered memories are discredited, a cloud of uncertainty will descend on *all* who claim to have been sexually abused. It is important to recognize, however, that most critics of recovered memories have limited their criticisms to allegedly forgotten memories that

were drawn out in psychotherapy. They have *not* questioned the veracity of victims' claims who have always remembered their abuse.

So what is the truth? Although not everyone agrees, many psychologists who study memory have concluded that psychotherapy can potentially generate false memories in some cases (Bowers & Farvolden, 1996; Kunda, 1999; Schacter, 1996). For example, patients may be asked to imagine specific events and report how they would feel. This procedure may result in their subsequently perceiving their imagined experiences as real. Also, hypnosis may be employed, such as asking patients to write down whatever comes to mind while in a hypnotic trance. This procedure may result in some highly suggestible patients believing that something happened when it actually did not.

There have been a few cases in which people who were convicted of sexual assault on the basis of recovered memories have subsequently been proven innocent, or victims have recanted their testimony and sometimes even sued their therapists. Because of these cases, it is unlikely today that someone would be convicted and sentenced to prison based *solely* on the alleged victim's recovered memories, without any other corroborating evidence. Nevertheless, the issue remains highly charged and seems likely to continue to elicit spirited exchanges (e.g., Brown, 1997; de Rivera, 1997; Loftus & Ketcham, 1994; Pope, 1996).

eyewitnesses and reached a guilty verdict. This verdict was eventually overturned on appeal. Since his release, DNA evidence has positively cleared Sophonow of involvement in the murder.

The issue of eyewitness identification has been studied systematically by social psychologists for more than 25 years, and we have learned a great deal about how false

Thomas Sophonow served four years for a murder that he did not commit. Mistaken eyewitness identification sent him to jail.

identifications can occur. David Day (2005), who is at Ryerson University in Toronto, has written an excellent chapter summarizing the application of social psychology to the criminal justice system, including eyewitness testimony. The most common experimental procedure for studying eyewitness identification has been to create a simulated event that is meticulously controlled by the researcher. In some studies, participants watch a film, slide show, or video, not knowing that they will later be asked to identify someone in the film. In other studies, participants are actually exposed to an unexpected, real-life event (e.g., a purse snatching) while they are waiting for the study to begin. Because participants do not know that they will later be asked to identify someone, their reactions during the event are very similar to those of real eyewitnesses of actual crimes. Two influential researchers in the area of eyewitness recall are Canadians Rod Lindsay of Queen's University and A. Daniel Yarmey of the University of Guelph, who have manipulated various factors in their studies, including the amount of time people are exposed to a target, the clothing worn by the target, and whether people looked at mug shots before seeing the police lineup (e.g., Lindsay, Nosworthy, Martin, & Martynuck, 1994; Lindsay, Pozzulo, Craig, Lee, & Corber, 1997; Yarmey, 2004; Yarmey, Jacob, & Porter, 2002).

What has this research found? Numerous studies have shown that people exposed to an event and later asked to identify the perpetrator often select the wrong individual (e.g., Buckhout, 1974; Cutler & Penrod, 1995; Lindsay et al., 1997; Yarmey et al., 2002). The rate of erroneous identification has ranged from less than 10% to more than 90% (Wells, 1993), depending on such factors as the duration of the event and the setting in which it occurred. Of course, even the lower end of this distribution (10% or 20%) is high enough to produce many false convictions. There appears to be an ingroup advantage (or outgroup disadvantage) in eyewitness identification: members of a particular racial group tend to be better at identifying people from their own racial group than people from other racial groups (MacLin, MacLin, & Malpass, 2001; Meissner & Brigham, 2001; Sporer, 2001; Wells & Olson, 2001), though errors can certainly occur even with ingroup targets.

Given that erroneous eyewitness identifications appear to occur frequently, an important question then becomes whether erroneous identifications differ from accurate identifications in some way that might allow us to weed out the former in real-life trials. Perhaps the most obvious candidate is the *confidence* an eyewitness expresses in his or her identification: if eyewitnesses are very confident that the accused person committed the crime, then it seems reasonable to conclude that they are probably correct. Unfortunately, research has shown that the confidence with which eyewitnesses identify the perpetrator is *not* a strong indication of their accuracy. Although there is a small correlation between confidence and accuracy, people who misidentify the perpetrator are often just as confident as people who identify the correct individual (see Brigham, 1990; Smith, Lindsay, Pryke, & Dysart, 2001; Sporer, Penrod, Read, & Cutler, 1995; Wells, Olson, & Charman, 2002). Therefore, it is *not* the case that highly confident eyewitnesses can necessarily be trusted. Ironically, highly confident eyewitnesses *do* have more impact on jurors' decisions than do less confident eyewitnesses.

One quality that might be better than confidence is the *speed* with which eyewitnesses make their identification. Steven Smith of St. Mary's University in Halifax, together with Rod Lindsay and Sean Pryke of Queen's University, had university students watch a video of a staged crime, in which a man stole money from a woman's purse (Smith, Lindsay, & Pryke, 2000). Participants later tried to identify the criminal from a six-person lineup photo. These researchers found that eyewitnesses who identified someone as the target person in 15 seconds or less were correct 69% of the time, whereas eyewitnesses who took between 16 and 30 seconds were correct only 43% of the time, and eyewitnesses who took more than 30 seconds were correct only 18% of the time (see also Dunning & Perretta, 2002; Sporer, 1993).

We have focused on the implications of unreliable memory for eyewitness identification of a perpetrator. Other aspects of eyewitness memory might also be open to distortion. For example, work by Elizabeth Loftus (1979; Loftus, Miller, & Burns, 1978), who is at the University of California at Irvine, has shown that leading or suggestive questions can introduce errors into eyewitnesses' accounts of events. Participants in one study watched a slide show presentation of an accident that involved an automobile striking a pedestrian. If a false element was inserted into a question about the event, participants often later included the false element in their memories. For example, if participants were asked a question about whether something happened while the car in the slide show "was stopped at the yield sign," even though the original slides actually showed the car stopping at a stop sign, the majority of participants later believed that a yield sign had been part of the slide presentation. These findings reflect that when people cognitively reconstruct past events, they rely on cues as a starting point for retrieving memories.

You don't just record the event and play it back the way a videotape would work—the process is much more complex.

Reducing Eyewitness Errors. Despite the limitations of eyewitness testimony, eyewitnesses continue to play a key role in many trials. Psychological researchers have argued that the traditional safeguards against eyewitness errors are relatively ineffective. For instance, defence lawyers can cross-examine the witness to try to raise doubts about the identification. Also, judges usually give instructions to the jury to come to a guilty verdict only when they are convinced beyond a "reasonable doubt." Psychologists have argued that these procedures are unlikely to make jurors appropriately cautious about eyewitness identifications.

What can the legal system do to reduce both the rate of eyewitness errors and jurors' reliance on eyewitness testimony? Rod Lindsay of Queen's University and his colleagues (Lindsay, Brigham, Brimacombe, & Wells, 2002) wrote a chapter that summarized the practical implications of the eyewitness literature. A. Daniel Yarmey of the University of Guelph has also made recommendations about how to improve eyewitness procedures (e.g., Yarmey, 2001, 2003). With regard to reducing false identifications, these researchers have suggested that police "lineup" procedures, in which witnesses are asked to identify the suspect from a line of individuals, need to be altered. For instance, exposing witnesses to a **blank lineup** is a good way to assess their credibility. A blank lineup is a group of individuals (lineup) that does *not* include the suspect; everyone in the lineup is known to be innocent. If the eyewitness identifies someone in this blank lineup as the perpetrator, he or she should be dismissed. If the eyewitness states that no one in the blank lineup is the perpetrator and then identifies the true suspect in another lineup, he or she is more likely to have made an accurate identification. Another recommendation is that a **sequential lineup** is better than the traditional, simultaneous lineup. A sequential lineup is a procedure in which the eyewitness is presented with each person in the group (lineup) individually, rather than with the entire lineup together (simultaneously). Evidence suggests that when eyewitnesses see a traditional simultaneous lineup, they try to find the person who looks *most like* the perpetrator, which can lead to erroneous identifications; eyewitnesses may assume that the police have arrested the guilty person, who must, therefore, be in the lineup. In contrast, eyewitnesses exposed to a sequential lineup judge each person separately,

blank lineup

a group of individuals that does not include the suspect; everyone in the lineup is known to be innocent

sequential lineup

the procedure of showing an eyewitness each individual in the group separately rather than together in a simultaneous lineup

Courtesy of the Manitowoc County Sheriff's Department

Psychologists have suggested that traditional police lineup procedures need to be changed. This photo shows a typical lineup used by police.

which reduces errors. They tend to wait until they see someone whose face "pops out" at them—someone whose face automatically elicits recognition.

In addition to these changes to how lineups are presented, researchers have suggested that it might be possible to reduce jurors' confidence in eyewitness testimony by introducing expert psychological evidence at the trial. This expert should try to educate the jury about how reconstructive memory works, the potential inaccuracy of eyewitness identifications, and how to evaluate eyewitness testimony more effectively (see Cutler & Penrod, 1995). The domain of eyewitness testimony illustrates how social psychology can contribute to more effective functioning of the legal system. For a Canadian perspective on the interface of social psychology and the law, we recommend an excellent 2001 volume edited by Regina Schuller of York University and James Ogloff of Simon Fraser University (now at Monash University in Australia).

Heuristics and Biases in Everyday Judgments

All of us make many ordinary, everyday judgments quickly and without much effort. These judgments may come in response to a question from others, or simply from our own reflections: Does your roommate have a bad temper? What was the breed of the dog you saw in the park last night?

How do we make routine judgments of these kinds? It turns out that we typically use informal rules or shortcuts to come up with quick, "intuitive" answers. These informal rules or shortcuts in everyday judgments are called **heuristics.** Heuristics are "rules of thumb" or simplifying strategies for making judgments quickly. Because we cannot afford to expend large amounts of time or energy making every judgment

heuristic

an informal rule or shortcut that is used to make everyday judgments required during the day, we rely on simple shortcuts to make reasonable guesses. Sometimes, if the decision is particularly important or if we believe we are on the wrong track, we may subsequently think more carefully and deliberatively about our initial judgment. But most of the time, we will stick with our first, intuitive judgment—and most of the time, this judgment will be reasonably accurate (see Goldstein & Gigerenzer, 2002; Kahneman, 2003). Thus, heuristics usually work well and yield fairly accurate judgments, but sometimes they can lead us astray and result in errors. The distinction we described earlier between *automatic* and *controlled* processes is similar in many respects to this distinction between heuristics and deliberative judgments.

The hypothesis that perceivers usually rely on simple rules to make judgments and engage in careful, thoughtful processing only when necessary has been called the **cognitive miser model** of information processing (see Fiske & Taylor, 1991). This perspective assumes that detailed, deliberative processing is costly or expensive in terms of psychological resources, and our resource capacity is limited. Therefore, we try to "spend" as little as possible in most cases—we are *misers* who try to protect our resources for important judgments. Heuristics are one way that we save resources.

The term *heuristics* was made famous by two cognitive psychologists, Amos Tversky and Daniel Kahneman, whose work on intuitive reasoning also captured the interest of many social psychologists. Indeed, the field of social cognition owes a great deal to Tversky and Kahneman for showing that everyday judgments are both fascinating and important to study. All psychologists were proud when Daniel Kahneman was awarded the 2002 Nobel Prize for Economics, based on the work he did with Tversky (who died in 1996; the Nobel Prize cannot be awarded posthumously).

Returning to the examples given above, your judgment of whether your roommate has a temper will probably be based on how easily you can bring to mind times when he or she has exhibited angry behaviour. If you can easily think of examples of your roommate yelling or swearing, you will answer affirmatively that, yes, he or she does have a bad temper, whereas if you cannot think of such incidents, you will state that he or she is even-tempered. A different rule will guide your judgment of the breed of the dog you saw last night. This answer will probably be based on the dog's similarity to your images (schemas) of various breeds—poodles, German shepherds, and so on. If the dog resembled a particular breed or mix of breeds, then that will be your guess.

These examples illustrate the application of two heuristics that are described in the following paragraphs: the availability heuristic and the representativeness heuristic. Although we limit our consideration to these two heuristics (which are the best known and most researched heuristics), there are others that also influence everyday judgments (for additional examples, see Gilovich, Griffin, & Kahneman, 2002; Lassiter, Geers, Munhall, Ploutz-Snyder, & Breitenbecher, 2002). After describing the availability and representativeness heuristics, we discuss several other processes in social cognition that can produce errors or biases.

Psychologist Daniel Kahneman was awarded the 2002 Nobel Prize for Economics based on the work he did with Amos Tversky on heuristics.

cognitive miser model

a view of information processing that assumes people usually rely on heuristics to make judgments and only engage in careful, thoughtful processing when necessary

The Availability Heuristic

Tversky and Kahneman (1973) defined the **availability heuristic** as the tendency to base a judgment on how easily relevant examples can be generated. For instance, basing a judgment about your roommate's temper on how easy it is for you to recall temper tantrums would illustrate the availability heuristic. This heuristic makes a lot of sense. After all, it usually *is* easier to think of tantrums by an ill-tempered person than by an even-tempered person, because ill-tempered people *do* throw more tantrums (by definition)! As another example, if you were asked what percentage of municipal politicians in your city are women, it would make sense to bring to mind as many local politicians as possible and use this mental sample to make your judgment.

availability heuristic

the tendency to base a judgment on how easily relevant examples can be generated

After all, the greater the proportion of politicians in your city who are women, the easier it *should* be to think of examples.

Australian social psychologists Colin MacLeod and Lynlee Campbell (1992) provided direct evidence that people base judgments about the likelihood of future events on the ease with which they can think of examples of these events in the past. Participants read three-word descriptions of common pleasant and unpleasant events, such as "an unexpected gift," "a welcome visitor," "a painful injury," and "a disappointing vacation." As each event was presented, participants were asked to think of a specific example of that event in their own life and to immediately press a button, which allowed the computer to record how long it took them to think of the example. Participants were then asked to rate how likely it was that they would experience this event sometime in the next six months. Results showed a strong correlation between how quickly participants could think of a relevant example in their own life and their estimated likelihood that they would experience the event in the next six months: the *faster* they thought of an example, the *more likely* they judged another experience to be. The availability heuristic in action.

The availability heuristic is a sensible, useful shortcut for making many judgments. The actual frequency of an event or object *will* be related in most circumstances to the ease with which such events or objects can be brought to mind. The availability heuristic can lead to problems, however, when the examples that come to mind most easily are slanted or atypical. For instance, a recent event might have substantially increased the accessibility of a particular concept in memory. The pregnancy situation described in the earlier accessibility section illustrates this point. Being pregnant or being the partner of someone who is pregnant greatly increases the salience of pregnant women in one's environment. If someone in this condition were asked to estimate the percentage of women in the local community who are pregnant at the current time, he or she could probably think of many examples and might therefore overestimate the actual percentage.

In one of the original studies on availability, Tversky and Kahneman (1973) asked participants to read a list of 39 names: either 19 men and 20 women or 20 men and 19 women. These lists included the names of some famous people and some nonfamous people. For some participants, all of the men in the list were famous whereas the women were not; for the remaining participants, all of the women in the list were famous whereas the men were not. After reading the list, participants were asked to estimate how many men and how many women had been in the list (participants were *not* forewarned that they would be asked this question). The researchers assumed that participants would more easily recall famous names than nonfamous names. Thus, if the famous names had been men, participants were expected to be able to recall more men than women from the list, which would lead them to guess that the list contained mostly men. If the famous names had been women, however, participants were expected to be able to recall more women than men from the list, which would lead them to guess that the list contained mostly women. The results conformed exactly to these predictions. Note that the researchers deliberately constructed these lists to slant participants' recall of one of the sexes; thus, the researchers set up the situation in such a way as to make the availability heuristic misleading.

In most cases, the availability heuristic will rely on the total number of examples that can be recalled (e.g., how many men vs. women from the list are recalled). Recent research has shown, however, that people are sometimes influenced directly by the *ease* with which they can recall something, independently of the number or content of what they recall (see Haddock, Rothman, Reber, & Schwarz, 1999; Schwarz & Vaughn, 2002). For instance, University of Michigan social psychologist Norbert Schwarz and his colleagues (Schwarz, Bless, Strack, Klumpp, Rittenauer-Schatka, & Simons, 1991) investigated the availability heuristic in the context of judgments of assertiveness. The researchers asked participants to recall and describe either 6 times they had acted assertively, 12 times they had acted assertively, 6 times they had acted unassertively, or 12 times they had acted unassertively. Pilot testing had shown that most people can think of 6 examples of their own assertive or unassertive behaviour relatively easily, but it is very difficult to come up with 12 examples of either kind of behaviour. The researchers therefore predicted that when participants were asked to describe 6 examples of assertive (or unassertive) behaviours, they would be able to do so relatively easily and would conclude, based on the availability heuristic, that their personality was assertive (or unassertive). In contrast, the researchers predicted that when participants were asked to describe 12 examples of assertive (or unassertive) behaviour, they would find the task very difficult and show a boomerang effect, such that they would conclude that they do *not* possess that characteristic. For instance, participants asked to describe 12 examples of assertive behaviour were expected to say to themselves, "I can't come up with as many examples of assertive behaviour as the experimenter wants, so I guess I'm not very assertive." These inferences would be based directly on how difficult it was to recall the requested behaviours.

Figure 3.5 presents the results of the study on ratings of assertiveness of the self. As predicted, participants rated themselves as more assertive when they were asked to recall 6 examples of assertive actions than when they were asked to recall 12 examples of assertive actions, even though the latter individuals generated more total examples of assertiveness. Conversely, participants rated themselves as less assertive (more unassertive) when they were asked to recall 6 unassertive actions than when they were asked to recall 12 examples of unassertive actions. The ease of completing the task was used by participants to infer their own assertiveness.

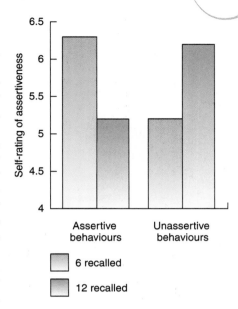

FIGURE 3.5 Self-ratings of assertiveness after behaviour recall

From Schwarz et al., "Ease of retrieval of information: Another look at the availability heuristic," *Journal of Personality and Social Psychology*, 61, 195–202, Table 1, p. 197, 1991. Copyright © 1991 by the American Psychological Association. Reprinted by permission.

The Representativeness Heuristic

Another shortcut that people use to make everyday judgments is the **representativeness heuristic** (see Kahneman & Frederick, 2002). Kahneman and Tversky (1973) defined this heuristic as the tendency to judge the likelihood that an object belongs to a certain category based on how similar the object is to the typical features of the category (how *representative* it is of the category). For instance, deciding that the dog you saw last night in the park was probably a poodle because it had curly hair that was cut in a poodle style illustrates the representativeness heuristic. This process is akin to categorization—the most basic of our cognitive processes. Thus, like the availability heuristic, this heuristic makes a lot of sense. Categorizing an object by assessing the overlap between its features and the defining features of a category is perfectly reasonable—this is precisely how we use schemas to categorize an object so we can predict its behaviour (Fiske & Taylor, 1991). A small animal that looks like a cat and meows like a cat probably *is* a cat. The representativeness heuristic usually serves us well.

Problems can arise, however, when perceivers ignore everything *except* representativeness. That is, people sometimes base their judgments *only* on the overlap between an object's characteristics and the defining features of a category, even when other kinds of information could (and should) also be employed. For instance, people should pay attention to the initial, baseline probability of different categories. Imagine that you are on a bus or train and overhear a young man sitting in front of you speaking with an accent that you can identify as European—perhaps German, Swiss, Austrian, or French. He talks to his acquaintance about his love of downhill skiing and how he has skied since he was very young. What country would you guess he is from? You might think of countries known especially for downhill skiing, such as Switzerland or Austria, and guess that he is from one of these countries. But these are actually poor choices, based simply on the total populations of the four countries. Switzerland has a population of

representativeness heuristic
the tendency to judge the likelihood that a target belongs to a category based on how similar the target is to the typical features of the category

Based on the *representativeness heuristic,* you might guess that this man is from Switzerland or Austria.

7 million, and Austria has a population of 8 million. In contrast, Germany has a population of 82 million, and France has a population of 60 million. Although a love of skiing may be associated in our minds more closely with Switzerland and Austria than with Germany and France, the latter countries have almost 10 times as many people as the former—and, of course, there are plenty of people in Germany and France who also love skiing.

In a classic demonstration of the representativeness heuristic, Kahneman and Tversky (1973) gave participants brief descriptions of individuals who were (allegedly) either engineers or lawyers and asked them to predict each stimulus person's occupation. Participants were told that each description was randomly selected from a group of 100 individuals. Some participants were told that the group was composed of 70 engineers and 30 lawyers, whereas other participants were told that the group was composed of 30 engineers and 70 lawyers. Thus, the baseline probability that a randomly selected individual would be an engineer was either 70% or 30% in the two conditions.

The brief descriptions given to participants were constructed by the researchers to be more or less representative of the stereotypes of engineers or lawyers. For instance, a stimulus person might be described as having a strong need for order and clarity, being a loner, and having hobbies that included computers and math puzzles—features chosen to resemble the stereotype of engineers. Kahneman and Tversky found that participants almost always based their predictions entirely on representativeness and not at all on the overall ratio of engineers to lawyers. That is, someone described as having a strong need for order and clarity, being a loner, and enjoying computers and math puzzles was usually classified as an engineer no matter what the baseline probabilities—it did not matter whether participants believed that engineers constituted 70% or 30% of the sample. Of course, it was reasonable for participants to base their predictions at least partly on the descriptions, but they should *also* have given some weight to the baseline probabilities of each occupation. The representativeness heuristic can lead us astray when we rely on it exclusively.

Illusory Correlations

illusory correlation

the belief that two variables are related to one another when, in fact, they are not

A correlation exists when two variables are associated with one another, such as height and weight or class attendance and exam performance. As we noted in Chapter 2, correlations do not necessarily reflect cause, although causal relations between the variables may sometimes account for some or all of the correlation (e.g., class attendance definitely improves exam performance).

An **illusory correlation** occurs when an individual believes that two variables are related to one another when, in fact, they are not (Hamilton & Gifford, 1976). For example, athletes often believe that they perform better when they follow some ritual. Basketball legend Michael Jordan wore his college shorts under his professional uniform. Would an objective test of his superstitious behaviour have shown that he would have performed just as well without the college shorts? We suspect so.

Seeing What We Expect to See. Why or when do illusory correlations occur? Loren Chapman and Jean Chapman (1967, 1969) at the University of Wisconsin suggested that people are especially likely to notice events that confirm their expectancies, which leads them to overestimate the frequency of such confirmations (see also Stroessner & Plaks, 2001). People tend to see what they expect to see.

For example, some people believe in astrology. Such individuals might read their daily horoscope every morning. Chapman and Chapman would suggest that if something happens that is congruent with the individual's horoscope for that day, he or she is more likely to notice than if nothing happens to confirm the horoscope. Therefore, those days when something confirmatory happened will be recalled better than those days when nothing happened, and the person will overestimate the accuracy of the horoscopes.

In a test of the role of expectancies in illusory correlations, Loren Chapman (1967) asked participants to read a series of word pairs (*bacon-notebook, blossoms-tiger,* etc.), which were presented several times. Some of the word pairs consisted of commonly associated words, such as *bacon-eggs* and *lion-tiger,* whereas other pairs combined unrelated words, such as *bacon-tiger* and *lion-eggs.* The commonly associated word pairs (the expected pairings) were not presented any more often than the unrelated word pairs. When participants were asked to estimate the frequency of various word pairings, however, they overestimated the frequency of the expected pairings. For example, they tended to overestimate the frequency with which bacon and eggs or lion and tiger had been paired in the trials. Chapman suggested that these illusory correlations occurred because the expected pairings were more likely to be noticed and thus were easier to retrieve from memory.

The "Hot Hand" in Sports.

Do you think that sports athletes can get "hot" or go "cold" in their performance? Do basketball players sometimes have a "hot hand" such that they just can't miss in a particular game? Do hockey players go on scoring streaks where they shoot the puck well for an extended period of time? The hypothesis of the hot hand is widely accepted in sports, perhaps especially in basketball. Most basketball players and fans believe that players shoot in streaks, such that they are more likely to make a shot if they have previously made a shot than if they have previously missed a shot. Coaches also subscribe to this hypothesis, instructing teammates to get the ball to a player who has made a high percentage of shots in the game.

Ray Stubblebine/Reuters/Landov

Most basketball players and fans believe that players can have a "hot hand," but the data suggest otherwise.

Cornell University social psychologist Thomas Gilovich and his colleagues (Gilovich, Vallone, & Tversky, 1985; see also Gilovich, 1991) examined the validity of this hypothesis by obtaining empirical data from the National Basketball Association. Interestingly, the researchers found no evidence for a hot hand. The probability of making a shot was unrelated to whether a previous shot had been made. Figure 3.6 depicts the percentage of shots that players made, either from the floor or from the foul line, based on the outcome of their previous shot. Players made 51% of their shots from the floor after making their previous shot, compared to 54% after missing their previous shot—a tendency in the *opposite direction* of a hot hand. The most compelling test of the hot hand hypothesis is probably provided by foul shooting, because players were always shooting from the same place. But again the evidence was clearly inconsistent with the notion of a hot hand: players made 75% of their foul shots after making the previous foul shot, and 75% of their foul shots after missing the previous foul shot. No difference whatsoever.

Why do players and fans believe in the hot hand? Gilovich (1991) provided several possible reasons. Perhaps the most plausible explanation is that people notice when

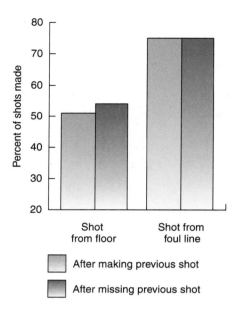

FIGURE 3.6 Percentage of shots made after hits and misses

From Gilovich et al., "The hot hand in basketball: On the misperception of random sequences," *Cognitive Psychology*, 17, 295–314. Copyright © 1985. Reprinted by permission of Elsevier.

hindsight bias

the tendency for people to overestimate the predictability of known outcomes

a player hits several shots in a row or misses several shots in a row, whereas they do not notice when hits and misses are intermixed. Thus, people's belief in the hot hand may constitute an example of seeing what we expect to see—an illusory correlation. Another possibility is that people fail to realize that occasional "runs" of consecutive hits or consecutive misses will occur even when events are truly independent—that is, people have a misperception of what "random" sequences look like. As a result, runs that are actually random may appear to many people to be more representative of nonrandom sequences, such as a series of hot and cold streaks. Thus, people's belief in the hot hand may also reflect the operation of the representativeness heuristic.

The Hindsight Bias: I Knew It All Along

Think about a recent test that you took in a challenging course (and for which you have received your grade). How predictable in advance was your performance? If you had been asked before the test to predict your grade, what would you have said?

According to research in social and cognitive psychology, you are likely to think now that your performance was more predictable than it actually was. That is, you probably now think that if you had been asked before the test to predict the grade, you would have predicted a grade relatively close to the one you actually received. But if you had *really* been asked before the test, you would have expressed more uncertainty about how you would do.

What is different between now and before the test? *You know how you did.* This "outcome information" is very difficult to ignore and colours your judgment of what you believed before the event. This tendency for people to overestimate the predictability of known outcomes, called the **hindsight bias** (Fischhoff, 1975), has been shown to occur in both children and adults (e.g., Bernstein, Atance, Loftus, & Meltzoff, 2004). It is captured in common phrases like "I knew it all along" and "Hindsight is 20/20."

Outcomes of events such as elections tend to look more predictable in retrospect, a phenomenon known as the *hindsight bias.*

Armchair Quarterbacks. A vintage example of the hindsight bias comes from sports fans, who regularly blame coaches and players for bad decisions. "That idiot coach should have changed goalies," "What a stupid call to make on first down," "It was obvious that a zone defence would be murdered by the other team." Armchair quarterbacks benefit from hindsight and fail to recognize that things were not really so predictable before the event.

In a classic experimental demonstration of the hindsight bias, Baruch Fischhoff (1975) gave students at Carnegie-Mellon University information about little-known historical events, such as a war between British soldiers and fighters from Nepal in the 19th century. Some participants (the "foresight" condition) received the background information and were asked to predict the likelihood of each of a set of possible outcomes (a British victory, a Nepalese victory, a stalemate, a peace settlement). Other participants (the "hindsight" conditions) received the background information along with a sentence allegedly presenting the actual outcome (some were told that the British won, some were told the Nepalese won, etc.). When these hindsight participants were asked to rate the pre-outcome likelihood of each of the possible outcomes, they gave higher probability ratings to the outcome that they believed had occurred than did participants in the foresight condition. For example, participants who believed the British won rated a British victory as a more likely outcome than did participants who received no outcome information. This effect occurred even though participants in the hindsight conditions were explicitly told to answer as if they did not know the actual outcome.

Hal Arkes and his colleagues at Ohio State University (Arkes, Wortmann, Saville, & Harkness, 1981) asked physicians to read a case history and to indicate what their diagnosis would have been. Some physicians were given only the case history with no diagnosis, whereas other physicians were told what diagnosis allegedly had been made. When asked how likely it was that they would have made a particular diagnosis based only on the case history, physicians who thought they knew the diagnosis reported a higher probability of that diagnosis than did physicians who received no diagnosis information.

Why does the hindsight bias occur? Several processes might contribute, but we will mention just two (see also Hawkins & Hastie, 1990; Werth, Strack, & Forster, 2002). One important cause is that people reinterpret pre-outcome information based on knowing the outcome. If you learn that a friend has dropped out of school, you might reinterpret his or her past behaviours as reflecting unhappiness or disillusionment. These reinterpretations make it seem more obvious that the decision to drop out would happen. Second, people generate explanations that would not have occurred to them if they had not known the outcome. You might think about your friend's academic history and realize that his performance has been declining since starting university. This realization might lead you to conclude that poor grades caused your friend to drop out and his decision was foreseeable. The flowchart in Figure 3.7 illustrates how the hindsight bias occurs.

Another domain in which the hindsight bias may occur is accusations of medical malpractice. If a patient has been seen by a physician but then suddenly deteriorates, his or her family may later look back and conclude that the correct diagnosis was obvious, whereas it may actually have been unclear. Moreover, other physicians may examine the case and also conclude that the diagnosis was more obvious than it actually was (as in Arkes et al., 1981).

The Planning Fallacy

The final bias that we will discuss is one that you will probably recognize in yourself. People consistently *underestimate* how long it will take to complete a task. This **planning fallacy** occurs for relatively straightforward and familiar tasks like reading a

planning fallacy
the tendency for people to underestimate how long it will take to complete a task

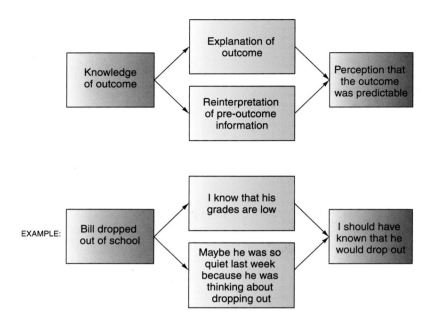

FIGURE 3.7 Hindsight bias

chapter of a textbook or shopping for holiday gifts, as well as for more complex tasks like writing an essay or renovating a kitchen. Who hasn't found himself or herself wondering on Sunday evening how the weekend could have passed by with so little accomplished? It seems that when we plan a task, we are almost always overly optimistic about the speed with which it will be accomplished.

One especially interesting aspect of the planning fallacy is that we make it over and over again—we don't seem to learn from experience. For instance, even when previous chapters of a textbook have taken authors longer to write than expected, those authors will probably remain irrationally confident that the *next* chapter will be completed much more quickly! (This example is purely hypothetical.) Or even when students have experienced many summer vacations during which they did not read as many novels as planned, the students will be optimistic that *this* summer will be different, and they will find more time for pleasure reading.

Arguably the pre-eminent investigator of the planning fallacy is Roger Buehler of Wilfrid Laurier University in Waterloo. Buehler and his colleagues (e.g., Buehler & Griffin, 2003; Buehler, Griffin, & MacDonald, 1997; Buehler, Griffin, & Ross, 1994, 2002) have documented the planning fallacy in many studies and across a wide variety of tasks. For instance, these researchers have asked participants to predict when a specific task will be finished (e.g., students' fourth-year honours thesis projects; income tax returns; holiday shopping) and then followed up to learn when the task was actually done. Typically, only about 30% of respondents will have completed the task by the predicted deadline, and most will take substantially longer than they estimated.

What causes the planning fallacy? Buehler and his colleagues have suggested that when people estimate how long a task will take, they focus on specific ways the task can be accomplished without considering potential problems that might occur. For example, Buehler and his colleagues (1994) asked participants to "think aloud" while predicting when a task would be completed. Analysis of the content of these thoughts showed that participants directed most of their thoughts (about 75%) to the future, especially plans for how to accomplish the task. Very few thoughts considered problems that might occur (about 3%) or participants' own past experiences with similar tasks (about 7%). The biased production of thoughts directed toward successful completion of the task presumably led participants to be overly optimistic about when it would be done (see

CONCEPT REVIEW
Heuristics and Biases

Heuristic or Bias	Description	Example
Availability heuristic	The tendency to base a judgment on how easily relevant examples can be generated	Someone decides that the level of violence on television is very high because she can think of many examples of violence she has seen on television programs.
Representativeness heuristic	The tendency to judge the likelihood that a target belongs to a category based on how similar the target is to typical features of the category	Someone decides that a woman is probably Irish because she is wearing a green dress on St. Patrick's Day.
Illusory correlation	The belief that two variables are related to one another when, in fact, they are not	A man believes that women are worse drivers than men because he notices whenever female drivers, but not male drivers, annoy him.
Hindsight bias	The tendency for people to over-estimate the predictability of known outcomes	Looking back, a woman thinks that she should have been able to predict her husband's descent into alcoholism.
Planning fallacy	The tendency for people to underestimate how long it will take to complete a task	A student expects to complete an essay in one week, even though past essays have taken longer than that to complete.

also Roy, Christenfeld, & McKenzie, 2005). Ian Newby-Clark, who is at the University of Guelph, has similarly found that people focus on optimistic, best-case scenarios when considering the future (Newby-Clark, Ross, Buehler, Koehler, & Griffin, 2000).

So how can you avoid making unrealistically rosy predictions about your own completion of tasks? It isn't easy. Buehler and his colleagues (2002) suggested that you should think carefully about why or how, based on your own past experiences, you might complete the task *in your typical fashion* (that is, taking longer than you originally planned). For instance, based on your past experiences, what kinds of problems might occur that could delay completion of the task? By connecting your past experiences with this specific task, you will be more likely to consider obstacles that might slow you down. The result may be a more accurate prediction.

The accompanying Concept Review summarizes the heuristics and biases we have described.

What Might Have Been: Counterfactual Thinking

Do you ever think about how your life might have been different? Perhaps you've thought about what your life would be like if you'd gone to a different university or if you'd continued a relationship with someone who is not part of your current life. Do you ever wish that you had taken different courses in high school or university? (We hope that such a thought is not too applicable at the present moment.) Your thoughts will not always be regretful in tone—you may sometimes think about how things could have been worse. If you hadn't studied so hard, perhaps you would have failed an exam, or if you hadn't gone to your friend's party, perhaps you wouldn't have met your romantic partner.

counterfactual thoughts

reflections on how past events might have turned out differently

All of these thoughts about "what might have been" qualify as **counterfactual thoughts.** Counterfactual thoughts are reflections on how past events might have turned out differently. They are called "counterfactual" because they are counter to the facts (they imagine things that did not really happen). Counterfactual thinking is a relatively recent topic in social cognition, having received significant attention only during the past 15 to 20 years (see Roese & Olson, 1995), although it has interested philosophers for much longer.

Wishful Thinking in Everyday Life

Counterfactual thoughts are very common and may be uniquely human—the capacity to think about alternative realities is probably something that distinguishes humans from other species. Some counterfactual thoughts are playful and fanciful, such as children imagining themselves having grown up on a pirate ship; other counterfactual thoughts are excruciatingly painful, such as parents thinking again and again how their child might still be alive if they had only taken her sooner to the hospital emergency room. The vast majority of counterfactual thoughts, however, are quite ordinary and involve thinking about how commonplace events might have been different. Counterfactual thoughts are more likely to occur when it is *easy* for the person to imagine how things could have been different—when it is easy to "undo" the event mentally (Kahneman & Miller, 1986). If a woman decides at the last minute to go to a public lecture that turns out to be dreadfully boring, she will probably think about how she could be at home relaxing, because she almost did stay home—thus, being at the lecture is easy for her to undo mentally.

Many counterfactual thoughts change something that occurred prior to an event and then imagine how the event could have turned out differently. A student might think, "If I had stayed home last night to study, I bet I would've done better on the test today." Or a woman at her place of work might think, "I wish that I'd listened to the weather this morning, because then I would've brought an umbrella and not gotten soaked by the rain at lunchtime."

Why are counterfactual thoughts important? Canadian social psychologists Dale Miller, William Turnbull, and Cathy McFarland (1990) at Simon Fraser University argued that counterfactual thoughts have important consequences for emotions, beliefs, and behaviour. These consequences depend in important ways on the *type* of counterfactual thoughts that occur.

Upward Counterfactual Thoughts: Wanting to Improve

upward counterfactual thoughts

reflections on how past events might have turned out better

The most common type of counterfactual thought has been labelled **upward counterfactual thoughts.** Upward counterfactual thoughts involve reflecting on how things could have turned out *better*. Most of the examples we have given to this point have been upward counterfactual thoughts—such as the student wishing he had stayed home to study last night, and the woman wishing she had brought an umbrella to work. These alternative realities would have been preferable to what actually occurred.

Upward counterfactual thoughts are particularly likely to occur after a negative outcome (Roese & Olson, 1997; Sanna & Turley, 1996). When something bad happens, it seems almost inevitable that people will think about how the event could have been avoided, especially when it was unexpected (Shepperd & McNulty, 2002). Notice that this process can be very adaptive—people may be able to think of ways to prevent a recurrence of the negative outcome (i.e., ways to avoid a similar event in the future). When a student thinks, "I wish I had studied the textbook more instead of the lectures—I would have done better on the test," she has identified a way to improve her grade on the next exam (namely, by studying the textbook more).

Given these possible benefits of upward counterfactual thoughts, Neal Roese at the University of Western Ontario (who is now at the University of Illinois) argued that the motive or desire to improve explains why upward counterfactual thoughts occur (Roese, 1994, 1997, 2005). That is, the reason we engage in upward counterfactual thinking after a negative outcome is because it helps us to avoid similar negative outcomes in the future (we want to improve; see also Markman, Gavanski, Sherman, & McMullen, 1993).

When something bad happens, people tend to generate *upward counterfactual thoughts.*

In a study examining this possible functional benefit of upward counterfactual thinking, Suzanne Nasco and Kerry Marsh (1999) asked introductory psychology students at the University of Notre Dame to complete a questionnaire immediately after receiving their grade on a class test. Among other things, the questionnaire measured counterfactual thinking by asking the students to "list any things that might have occurred differently that would have resulted in a different grade on the test." The students' lists were later scored for the total number of upward counterfactual thoughts that were given (thoughts about how their grade could have been better).

Approximately one month later, the day before their next test, students completed another questionnaire in which they reported how much their circumstances had changed since the first test (e.g., whether they were able to study more than last time). The next day, participants reported how much control they felt they had over their performance on the second test and then took the test.

Results showed that the number of upward counterfactual thoughts students generated after the first test predicted the extent of reported changes in circumstances prior to the second test. Students who, after the first test, generated many ways that their grade could have been better (i.e., who generated many upward counterfactual thoughts) reported, prior to the second test, that their circumstances had changed a lot. Why? Presumably, things had changed because participants had implemented some of the ideas they generated after the first test. Upward counterfactual thinking generated ideas for improved performance, which were later implemented.

Importantly, the extent of reported changes in circumstances predicted how much control students felt they had over the second test, and perceived control predicted how well the students actually did on the second test. Thus, upward counterfactual thoughts after the first test were ultimately associated with better performance on the second test, with the improved performance apparently due to changes implemented after the first test (see also Roese, 1994).

Sometimes, upward counterfactual thoughts will not provide useful ideas for how to improve outcomes. A young man who has been paralyzed in a car accident may think repeatedly about how he could have avoided the accident, but nothing can bring back his mobility. The example given in Chapter 2 (see page 42) of parents who lost a child is another case in which upward counterfactual thoughts (thinking about how the death could have been avoided) are unlikely to be useful. In these circumstances, ruminating about how the traumatic event could have been avoided may only rub salt in the wound (see Davis, Lehman, Wortman, Silver, & Thompson, 1995).

Downward Counterfactual Thoughts: Wanting to Feel Better

downward counterfactual thoughts

reflections on how past events might have turned out worse

Some counterfactual thoughts involve imagining how things could have been *worse*. These reflections are called **downward counterfactual thoughts.** These kinds of thoughts usually make people feel fortunate, because their present condition is better than what it could have been. Sometimes these thoughts occur spontaneously, such as when something bad *almost* happens. Coming upon a grisly car accident scene just moments after it occurred can engender the thought "it could have been me," which is a downward counterfactual thought that causes feelings of relief. Downward counterfactual thoughts can also be generated deliberately or strategically, when people want to make themselves feel better. Someone who is not selected for a promotion might think, "Well, things could be worse—I could be unemployed," which is a downward counterfactual thought that causes feelings of satisfaction that raise the individual's injured self-image. Thus, one possible benefit of downward counterfactual thoughts is that they can make people feel better.

Whereas downward counterfactual thoughts can make people feel better (cause positive emotions), upward counterfactual thoughts can make people feel worse (cause negative emotions). We touched on this point earlier when discussing rumination about traumatic events. By thinking about how things could have been better (upward counterfactual thoughts), people make their actual situation seem worse by comparison, which can arouse dissatisfaction or unhappiness. But recall that upward counterfactual thoughts often have important benefits—they generate useful ideas for how to avoid negative outcomes. Nevertheless, upward counterfactual thoughts can make people feel bad, so the benefits come with an emotional price.

Newspaper stories after tragic events often articulate counterfactual possibilities that elicit strong emotions. For example, after the terrorism of September 11, 2001, many stories appeared in the media describing victims who did not need to be in the World Trade Center at all, such as the Canadian woman we mentioned in the opening of Chapter 1—Christine Eagan—who was visiting her brother's office on the 105th floor. On a happier note, one young father who worked near the top of one of the towers drove his children to preschool in the morning because his wife was sick; he was late getting to work and missed the attack. These stories, tragic or happy, derive their emotional impact partly from the fact that it is so easy to imagine how things could have been different.

The two categories of counterfactual thoughts are summarized in the accompanying Concept Review.

Students' performances on multiple-choice tests may be influenced by counterfactual thinking. When you take a multiple-choice test, do you think that you should

CONCEPT REVIEW
Counterfactual Thinking

Type of Thought	Description	Emotional Consequences	Possible Benefits	Example
Upward counterfactual thoughts	Thoughts about how things could have been better	Often arouse negative emotions	Provide ideas about how to avoid negative outcomes in the future	"If only I had been driving more slowly, I would have avoided the car accident."
Downward counterfactual thoughts	Thoughts about how things could have been worse	Often arouse positive emotions	Can be used strategically to repair self-image or improve mood	"If I lived in many other countries, I would have less freedom."

avoid changing your answers, because you are more likely to change an answer from right to wrong than from wrong to right? Most students believe that they should "go with their first instinct" and avoid changing answers. In fact, however, evidence clearly shows that students *should* change their answers if they decide that another answer is better (e.g., see Benjamin, Cavell, & Shallenberger, 1984; Vispoel, 1998). That is, when students do change an answer on a multiple-choice question, they are more likely to raise their mark than to lower their mark. So why, then, do most students believe otherwise? Justin Kruger at the University of Illinois and his colleagues (Kruger, Wirtz, & Miller, 2005) argued that counterfactual thinking explains students' erroneous beliefs. These authors suggested that changing an answer from right to wrong is very upsetting because it is easy to imagine how one might *not* have changed the answer. Thus, students tend to remember such experiences very well (better than they recall sticking with wrong answers), which causes them to be leery of changing any answers. But do not let counterfactual thinking affect your performance. The data are clear: if you believe that an answer to a multiple-choice question should be changed, go ahead and just do it.

In sum, counterfactual thoughts can influence people's emotional reactions to events in their lives. An interesting demonstration of the real-life consequences of counterfactual thinking is described in the accompanying box, "Social Psychology in Your Life: Agony and Ecstasy at the Olympics."

Hot Cognition: Adding Motives and Mood to the Cognitive Mix

To this point in the chapter, we have emphasized cognitive processes, such as categorization, retrieval cues, and counterfactual thinking, and have not paid much attention to feelings or affect. But emotions, motives, and moods are key parts of our lives. How do these "hot," emotional processes influence the "cold," cognitive processing of information about people? In this section, we take a detour from the strictly cognitive terrain to describe briefly how motives and moods can influence social cognition (see also Kruglanski, 1996; Kunda, 1990; Sorrentino & Higgins, 1986).

Self-Serving Judgments

We noted at the beginning of the chapter that two basic goals are generally presumed to underlie social cognition: the need to perceive the world accurately and the desire to perceive the self positively. We mentioned the second goal briefly when we discussed work showing that people want to regard the "present self" as better than the "past self" (e.g., Wilson & Ross, 2001). Let us now consider two examples of how this motive to see the self positively can cause **self-serving judgments,** which are perceptions or comparisons that enhance the perceived worth of the self (Gilovich, 1991; Greenwald, Banaji, Rudman, Farnham, Nosek, & Mellott, 2002; Tesser, 2000).

self-serving judgments
perceptions or comparisons that enhance the perceived worth of the self

Self-Serving Perceptions of Others. If you knew that you would have to work with another person, you would probably hope that the person would be pleasant and competent. If a friend set up a blind date for you, you would probably hope that the date would be friendly and attractive. These hopes are understandable—we don't want to work with or date someone who is unpleasant. But do you think that these hopes might lead you to perceive the individuals more positively than they really are?

Social Psychology in Your Life   *Agony and Ecstasy at the Olympics*

One of the most intriguing demonstrations of how upward counterfactual thoughts can produce unhappiness and downward counterfactual thoughts can produce happiness was provided by Cornell University social psychologists Victoria Medvec, Scott Madey, and Thomas Gilovich (1995). These researchers obtained videotapes of all NBC television coverage of the 1992 summer Olympic games in Barcelona, Spain. The researchers selected from these tapes all coverage of silver medal winners or bronze medal winners showing the athletes either completing their event (and finishing second or third) or receiving their medals on the medal stand.

The researchers showed these selections to judges and asked the judges to rate each athlete's emotional reaction on a scale from 1 to 10, with the endpoints labelled *agony* and *ecstasy*.

A study of medal winners at the 1992 summer Olympics showed that bronze medallists appeared happier than did silver medallists.

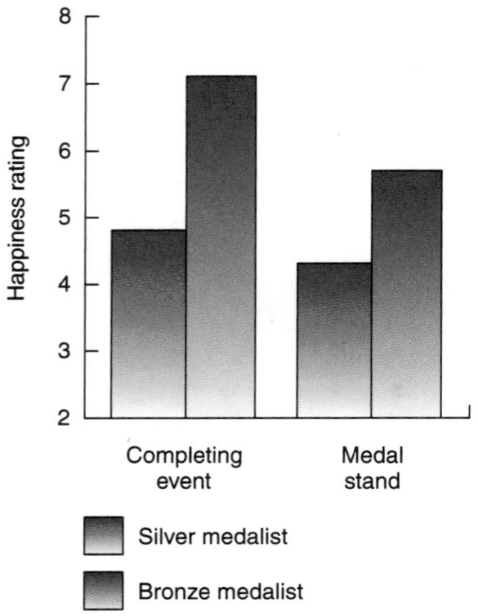

The judges were chosen because they stated they were uninterested in and uninformed about sports—the researchers did not want judges whose ratings might be influenced by prior knowledge about the athletes or the Olympics. Thus, all silver and bronze medallists were rated for how happy they appeared to be.

The results, depicted in Figure 3.8, revealed a fascinating difference: bronze medallists were judged to be happier than silver medallists, even though the bronze medallists had actually done worse than the silver medallists! This difference occurred both when the athletes completed their event and when they received their medal.

What was going on here? The researchers hypothesized that bronze and silver medallists generated different kinds of counterfactual thoughts. For bronze medallists, the most compelling or vivid alternative outcome was probably finishing fourth, out of the medals—a *downward* counterfactual thought. Compared to the possibility of finishing fourth, winning a bronze medal seemed great, and the athletes were ecstatic. But for silver medallists, the most obvious alternative outcome was probably finishing first and winning the gold medal—an *upward* counterfactual thought. Compared to the possibility of finishing first, winning a silver medal didn't seem so great, and the athletes were disappointed.

Thus, how well the athletes did and how happy they felt were not equivalent. These data make the point that people's emotional reactions to an event depend, at least in part, on alternative possible outcomes that are conspicuous to them (for another fascinating example of how counterfactual thoughts can influence emotional responses to wins and losses, see Larsen, McGraw, Mellers, & Cacioppo, 2004).

FIGURE 3.8 Happiness ratings of silver and bronze medallists

From Medvec et al., "When less is more: Counterfactual thinking and satisfaction among Olympic medallists," *Journal of Personality and Social Psychology, 69*, 603–610, Fig. 1, p. 605, 1995. Copyright © 1995 by the American Psychological Association. Reprinted by permission.

Social psychologists have shown that when people believe that they will interact with or be dependent on another individual, they tend to view that individual more positively than do people who are not expecting to interact with or be dependent on the individual. In a classic experiment, Ellen Berscheid, William Graziano, Thomas Monson, and Marshall Dermer (1976) recruited participants for a dating study at the University of Minnesota and showed them a videotape of three people having a discussion. One of the three persons on the tape was allegedly going to be the participant's dating partner for at least one date (and sometimes up to five dates). After watching the videotape, participants rated the three individuals. Compared to ratings by participants who were not expecting to date that individual, participants who were expecting one or more dates rated their expected partner significantly more positively. The researchers argued that participants *wanted* to see their future partner as likeable and pleasant (see also Wilson, Wheatly, Kurtz, Dunn, & Gilbert, 2004).

Self-Serving Activation of Stereotypes. Imagine that you submit some poetry to a local poetry competition. Imagine further that the written feedback you receive from the judge of the competition is negative—the feedback states that your poems are confusing and difficult to understand. Imagine finally that you learn that the judge who was supposed to evaluate the poems, a high school English teacher, fell ill and was replaced at the last minute by one of his high school students. Do you think that you would discredit the feedback because it came from a high school student? Would you conclude that the judge was too immature to understand your poetry?

But imagine for a moment that the same events occur except you receive *positive* feedback from the judge, who states that your poems are clear and interesting. Do you think that you would discredit this feedback because it came from a high school student? Would you even consider the questionable status of the judge?

Most of us would focus on the judge's high school status more in the first case than in the second case. We would be motivated to use our stereotype of high school students (that they are younger and more immature than adults) to discredit the negative feedback but not the positive feedback. We would use the stereotype selectively to enhance our self-worth.

Lisa Sinclair and Ziva Kunda (1999, 2000) argued precisely this point—that people can activate a stereotype strategically, based on its implications for feedback they have received. In one experiment at the University of Waterloo (Sinclair & Kunda, 2000), male participants provided answers to several interpersonal skills questions (e.g., "How would you motivate your employees to complete an important project on time?"). These responses were then assessed by another participant, who was allegedly training to be a manager. This manager-in-training provided either positive or negative feedback via videotape to the participant. For half of the participants, the videotaped evaluator was a man, whereas for the remaining participants, the evaluator was a woman. All participants then rated the manager's skill at evaluating them.

The researchers predicted that participants who received negative feedback from a female evaluator would be motivated to activate a negative stereotype of women that is held by some people, which includes the invalid notion that women may not be as competent as men at assessing managerial skill (e.g., Heilman, Block, & Martell, 1995). Derogating the woman's competence at this task would negate the validity of her feedback. These participants could then attribute the negative feedback to the incompetence of the female evaluator rather than to their own poor performance. Although participants who received negative feedback from a male evaluator would also want to discredit his feedback, their stereotype of men would not allow them to do so as easily, because they see men as more competent at assessing managerial skill. In contrast, the researchers predicted that participants

Sinclair and Kunda (2000) found that some men selectively activated a negative stereotype of women to disparage a female manager's unfavourable evaluation of them.

© Royalty-Free/CORBIS

who received positive feedback from a female evaluator would be motivated to see her as highly competent. Figure 3.9 presents participants' mean ratings of the manager's skill at evaluating them. As predicted, participants rated the female evaluator who provided negative feedback as significantly less skilled than the male evaluator who provided negative feedback; ratings of the male and female evaluators did not differ when they provided positive feedback. Thus, it seemed that at least some participants conveniently activated their stereotype of women only when necessary to protect their self-esteem. There was self-serving activation of stereotypes.

Mood and Social Cognition

Another way that social cognition can be "hot" is through mood effects. Whether we are in a happy, neutral, or negative mood can influence a variety of perceptions and judgments (see Bless, 2001; Clore, Schwarz, & Conway, 1994; Fiske & Taylor, 1991; Forgas, 1992; Schwarz, 1990; Schwarz & Clore, 1996). We give a few examples in this section.

Mood and Stereotypes. Do you think that your mood influences your perceptions of members of minority groups? Are you less positive toward out-groups when you are angry or depressed than when you are in a good mood?

In research conducted at the University of Western Ontario and the University of Waterloo, Victoria Esses, Geoffrey Haddock, and Mark Zanna (1994) investigated whether mood influenced the stereotypes that White Canadians expressed about minority groups (see also Esses & Zanna, 1995). The researchers hypothesized that negative mood would evoke more negative stereotypes of minority groups. In one experiment, participants listened to mood-inducing music for ten minutes, either uplifting and joyous music (positive mood condition), sad and depressing music (negative mood condition), or neutral and innocuous music (neutral mood condition). Participants then

FIGURE 3.9 Ratings of manager's skill

From Sinclair and Kunda, "Motivated stereotyping of women: She's fine if she praised me but incompetent if she criticized me," *Personality and Social Psychology Bulletin*, 26, 1329–1342, Fig. 1, p. 1336, 2000. Reprinted by permission of Sage Publications.

(Bar graph: Y-axis labelled "Rating of manager's skill" ranging from 6 to 10. X-axis groups "Positive feedback" and "Negative feedback". Legend: light bar = Male manager, dark bar = Female manager. Positive feedback: Male ≈ 8.9, Female ≈ 9.3. Negative feedback: Male ≈ 8.0, Female ≈ 6.9.)

provided their stereotypes of several ethnic groups by listing, for each group, characteristics that they would use to describe typical members of that group. After listing characteristics for all of the groups, participants went back over their characteristics and rated each one for how positive or negative it was and for how common it was in the group. The researchers were able to use these ratings to calculate an overall score to reflect the extent to which positive or negative characteristics were ascribed to typical members of that group.

Figure 3.10 presents the average ratings by majority group members of four ethnic minority groups. In the neutral mood condition (the "baseline" condition), two of the groups—Jewish and Chinese persons—elicited relatively positive stereotypes, whereas two other groups—Pakistanis and Aboriginal Canadians—elicited more neutral ratings. Ratings in the positive mood condition were virtually identical to ratings in the neutral mood condition for all four ethnic groups, so people did not become more positive toward minority groups when they were in a happy mood. Unfortunately, negative mood did have an effect, and it was a negative one. Participants in the negative mood condition generated significantly more negative stereotypes of the two lower-rated groups, Pakistanis and Aboriginal Canadians, than did participants in the neutral or positive mood conditions. Negative mood did not affect the ratings of the higher-rated groups, Jewish and Chinese persons. Thus, when people were made to feel sad or depressed, their views of some minority groups became more negative. The researchers speculated that the negative mood made negative stereotype content more accessible in memory.

These findings are rather disturbing, because negative moods can occur for many different reasons. It is conceivable that anxiety about the future, sadness about the death of a loved one, or frustration from work-related problems could all potentially elicit negative stereotypes of minority groups. At a societal level, perhaps economic downturns, which produce increased unemployment and stress, will elicit more negative stereotypes and provoke racial and ethnic hostility (see Berkowitz, 1989; Hovland & Sears, 1940; Zawadzki, 1948).

Mood-Congruent Recall. The findings by Esses and her colleagues (1994) suggested that negative moods can make negative stereotypes more accessible in memory. What about other kinds of information in memory? Does mood heighten the accessibility of all material that is compatible with it, such that positive mood

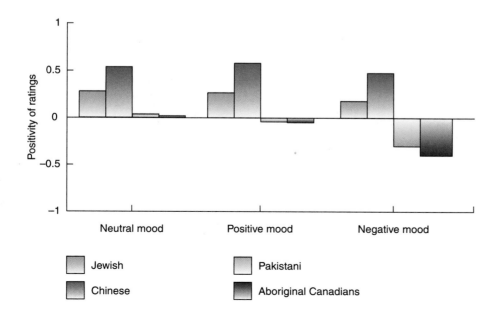

FIGURE 3.10 Ratings of ethnic minority groups while in neutral, positive, and negative mood

From Esses et al., "The role of mood in the expression of intergroup stereotypes." In M. P. Zanna and J. M. Olson, eds., *The Psychology of Prejudice: The Ontario Symposium,* p. 86, 1994. Reprinted by permission of Lawrence Erlbaum Associates.

makes positive information more accessible and negative mood makes negative information more accessible? This idea that positive feelings will activate positive memories and negative feelings will activate negative memories is called **mood-congruent recall** (Bower, 1981).

If you were asked to rate the performance of your car or your television set, would your mood play a role? If you just found out that you did well on a test, would you rate your car and your television set more positively than if you had not received feedback on the test? Although this may seem unlikely, evidence suggests that, in fact, you would. People do seem to give more positive evaluations of stimuli when they are in a positive mood than when they are in a neutral mood—and the positive mood does not have to be very strong! In an early, classic study of the effects of a small gift on memory, Cornell University's Alice Isen and her colleagues (Isen, Shalker, Clark, & Karp, 1978) approached shoppers at a mall. Some shoppers were approached by a confederate of the researchers and given a "free sample" of either a notepad or a nail clipper. The confederate told recipients that the free sample was meant to introduce potential customers to the company's product. Each sample was said to be worth 29 cents (about $1 today). Approximately 50 metres beyond the first confederate, another (seemingly unassociated) experimenter approached the shoppers and asked whether they would be willing to complete a "consumer survey." If shoppers agreed to participate, they answered several questions about their automobile and television set, including evaluations of the performance of these products. Compared to shoppers who were *not* given a free sample, participants who received a free sample rated the performance of their automobile and television set more favourably. The small, free gift presumably induced a mildly positive mood, which made positive memories of the products more accessible in memory.

People report being happier with their life on a sunny day than on a rainy day, presumably because they use their mood as a source of information to infer their happiness with life.

In a study that yielded a similar effect but used a different cause of moods, Joseph Forgas, George Levinger, and Stephanie Moylan (1994) asked people coming out of either a happy or a sad movie in Australia to evaluate their current (or a recent) relationship. Participants provided more favourable evaluations of their relationship after a happy movie than after a sad one. Positive feelings presumably made positive thoughts about the relationship more accessible than did negative feelings (see also Fiedler, Nickel, Muehlfriedel, & Unkelbach, 2001). There are some conditions under which mood-congruent recall may not occur (see McFarland & Buehler, 1998), but the typical effect of mood on memory is to improve recall of congruent thoughts.

Mood and Information Processing. Have you noticed that when you are in a good mood, you take other people's word for things and are just generally more agreeable than usual? Positive moods seem to reduce our need for compelling evidence or arguments before we will agree to something. After learning that we did well on a test, we'll respond to a friend's request with "Yeah, sure, I'll go to that movie with you—or to another one if you'd prefer."

Several studies have supported the idea that positive moods reduce the tendency to use detailed information to make decisions (e.g., Bodenhausen, Kramer, & Susser, 1994; Sinclair, 1988), although there may be circumstances under which good moods do not lead to superficial processing (e.g., Isbell, 2004). For example, in a simulated work appraisal setting, Robert Sinclair (1988), who is at Laurentian University in Sudbury, gave participants information about the quality of several individuals' performances and then asked participants to evaluate those performances. He found that participants in a good mood relied *less* on the information about the others' behaviour to make their performance appraisals than did participants in neutral or negative moods. Participants in a good mood also made less accurate appraisals overall than did participants in neutral or negative moods, presumably because the former individuals ignored (or underutilized) useful information.

If people in a good mood do not focus on detailed information to make judgments, what *do* they base their judgments on? The answer is heuristics, at least in some situations. Alice Isen and her colleagues (Isen, Means, Patrick, & Nowicky, 1982) found that participants who were in a good mood relied on the availability heuristic more than did participants who were in a neutral mood. Specifically, a good mood increased participants' tendency to base judgments of how often something occurs on the ease with which examples could be brought to mind. Good moods increased reliance on this judgmental shortcut.

What about negative moods? There has been considerable interest in how people who are depressed process information (e.g., see the book edited by York University social psychologists C. Douglas McCann and Norman Endler, 1990). In general, researchers have found that depressed individuals are more sensitive to negative information about themselves and others than are nondepressed individuals. For instance, Simon Fraser University's Marlene Moretti and her colleagues found that people who are depressed consider negative information about the self to be more useful or accurate than do people who are not depressed (Moretti, Segal, McCann, Shaw, Miller, & Vella, 1996). These findings are worrisome because they imply that depressed persons may process information in ways that maintain or even worsen their depression. Thus, one goal of therapy for depression should be to reduce depressed patients' uncritical acceptance of negative information about themselves.

Chapter Summary

In this chapter, we discussed **social cognition,** which is the study of how information about people is processed and stored. The fundamental building blocks of human cognition are **schemas**—mental representations of objects or categories. Schemas contain the principal features of the object or category, as well as simple assumptions about how the object or category works. The primary function of schemas is to categorize objects in ways that impose meaning and predictability. **Categorization** is the process of recognizing and identifying something. When we categorize a target, we assume that it possesses the characteristics of the schema (or most of them) even if we cannot perceive those characteristics directly.

The **accessibility** of a schema is the ease with which the schema comes to awareness; more accessible schemas are more likely to be activated than are less accessible

schemas. **Priming** is one process that increases the accessibility of a schema; it refers to the fact that the activation of a schema increases the likelihood of that schema's being activated again in the future. Schemas also differ in the extent to which they are easily activated for an individual across time and situations, which is termed their **chronic accessibility.**

A **stereotype** is a set of characteristics that a perceiver associates with members of a group. Stereotypes are one kind of schema—namely, schemas that represent human groups. Stereotypes usually include information about how much variability exists in the group; there is a general tendency for people to overestimate the similarity within groups to which they do not belong, which is called the **outgroup homogeneity effect.** Just like other schemas, stereotypes reflect our attempt to categorize an object (a person) and draw inferences about him or her.

Researchers have recognized that people do not have full control over all of their mental processes. An **automatic process** is a judgment or thought that we cannot control—it occurs without intention, very efficiently, and sometimes beneath our awareness. A **controlled process** is a judgment or thought that we command—it is intentional, requires significant cognitive resources, and occurs within our awareness.

Sometimes, memories cannot be retrieved directly, so retrieval must involve a "reconstructive" process. **Reconstructive memory** is trying to cognitively rebuild the past based on cues and estimates. **Autobiographical memory** refers to information in the brain that is related to the self. Autobiographical memory often involves estimating what we were like in the past.

Because human memory is fallible, eyewitnesses in trial settings sometimes make errors in identifying suspects. Experts have suggested that police lineup procedures should be changed to reduce the rate of eyewitness errors. For instance, a **blank lineup** is a good way to test the credibility of an eyewitness. A blank lineup is a group of individuals (lineup) that does not include the suspect—everyone in the lineup is known to be innocent. If the eyewitness identifies someone in the blank lineup, he or she should be dismissed. Also, it has been found that eyewitness identification errors are reduced if the eyewitness sees each person in the group (lineup) separately, a procedure that is called a **sequential lineup.**

Heuristics are informal rules or shortcuts that are used to make everyday judgments. Researchers have hypothesized that people usually rely on heuristics to make judgments and will engage in careful, thoughtful processing only when necessary—a view that has been termed the **cognitive miser model** of information processing. The **availability heuristic** is the tendency to base a judgment on how easily relevant examples can be generated. The **representativeness heuristic** is the tendency to judge the likelihood that a target belongs to a certain category based on how similar the target is to the typical features of the category.

An **illusory correlation** occurs when individuals believe that two variables are related to one another when, in fact, they are not. One cause of illusory correlations is that people are more likely to notice events that confirm their expectancies than nonconfirming events.

The **hindsight bias** refers to the tendency for people to overestimate the predictability of known outcomes. The **planning fallacy** is the tendency for people to underestimate how long it will take to complete a task.

Counterfactual thoughts are reflections on how past events might have turned out differently. **Upward counterfactual thoughts** involve reflecting on how things could have turned out better, whereas **downward counterfactual thoughts** involve reflecting on how things could have been worse.

Self-serving judgments are perceptions or comparisons that enhance the perceived worth of the self. Researchers have identified numerous self-serving judgments, including tendencies to define trait terms in ways that flatter the self and to activate stereotypes strategically to protect the self.

Moods can influence social cognition. For example, negative moods can elicit more unfavourable stereotypes of minority groups, and positive moods can make positive information more accessible in memory. The tendency for positive or negative feelings to make similarly valenced information more accessible in memory is called **mood-congruent recall.**

Key Terms

accessibility (70)

autobiographical memory (77)

automatic process (75)

availability heuristic (85)

blank lineup (83)

categorization (66)

chronic accessibility (72)

cognitive miser model (85)

controlled process (75)

counterfactual thoughts (94)

downward counterfactual thoughts (96)

heuristic (84)

hindsight bias (90)

illusory correlation (88)

mood-congruent recall (102)

outgroup homogeneity effect (74)

planning fallacy (91)

priming (71)

reconstructive memory (76)

representativeness heuristic (87)

schemas (67)

self-serving judgments (97)

sequential lineup (83)

social cognition (66)

stereotype (73)

upward counterfactual thoughts (94)

Social Psychology Alive on the Web

SOCIAL PSYCHOLOGY ALIVE: ONLINE LABS

To perform the following experiments and see how you compare to other students, go to Social Psychology Lab, which can be accessed through ThomsonNOW™:

- 3.1 Lexical Decisions
- 3.2 Impression Formation

SOCIAL PSYCHOLOGY ALIVE: QUIZZING AND PRACTICE TESTS

You can access our Web site directly by going to http://www.socialpsychologyalive.nelson.com for online quizzes, flash cards, and Internet links.

INFOTRAC® COLLEGE EDITION

For additional readings, explore InfoTrac® College Edition, your online library of archived journal articles and periodicals dating back 22 years. If your instructor ordered InfoTrac® College Edition with this book, you can access it from your CD-ROM, or go directly to http://www.infotrac-college.com and use the passcode from the InfoTrac® College Edition card that came with your book. For this chapter, try these search terms: *social cognition, schema, accessibility, priming, stereotype, reconstructive memory, availability heuristic, representativeness heuristic, illusory correlation, hindsight bias, counterfactual thinking, mood-congruent recall.*

Social Psychology Alive: The Workbook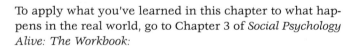

To apply what you've learned in this chapter to what happens in the real world, go to Chapter 3 of *Social Psychology Alive: The Workbook*:

- The *Sports Illustrated* Jinx: Does Appearance on the Cover Doom the Featured Athlete to a Terrible Fate?
- Spreading Activation of Schemas in Memory

- Priming Effects in Impression Formation
- Try These Experiments!
- Eyewitness Testimony and Reconstructive Memory
- Is It a Hot Hand or an Illusory Correlation?
- Have You and Your Friends Experienced These Social Cognition Phenomena?

Social Psychology Alive: The Videos

To see video on the topics and experiments discussed in this chapter, you can go either to ThomsonNOW™ or to the CD-ROM, if your instructor assigned either one, to the following section:

- Reconstructive Memory: Recalling What Never Happened

To Learn More

This list contains citations to books or articles that can help you learn more. These readings are good places to start if you want to gain a deeper understanding of the topics in this chapter.

- Gilovich, T. (1991). *How we know what isn't so: The fallibility of human reason in everyday life.* New York: Free Press.

- Moskowitz, G. B. (2005). *Social cognition: Understanding self and others.* New York: Guilford.
- Roese, N. J. (2005). *If only: How to turn regret into opportunity.* New York: Broadway Books.

Social Perception: Perceiving the Self and Others

In Catherine Ryan Hyde's novel *Pay It Forward* (1999), an investigative reporter by the name of Chris Chandler stumbles onto a plan that was initiated by a 12-year-old boy, Trevor McKinney, for his social studies class. The plan was designed to make the world a better place, and it involved doing favours for other people. Trevor (played by Haley Joel Osment in a movie version of the book) decided to do an unrequested and substantial favour for three different people and to ask in return only that they do a similar unrequested favour for three other people (that they pay it forward). If everyone followed through on these commitments, there would soon be large numbers of people doing favours for others.

The event that initially alerted Chris to the plan occurred while he was standing in an intersection looking under his car's hood at the engine of his old, stalled vehicle. A complete stranger came up to him, helped him push his car out of the intersection, and said that they should trade cars. Chris eventually drove away in a nice two-year-old silver Acura, but not before feeling very confused about what was going on.

Imagine yourself in Chris's position. How would you respond if a stranger tried to give you his car when yours stalled? Wouldn't you wonder why he was doing this? You might even suspect that it was a trick—perhaps "his" car was stolen, or perhaps he was trying to make you feel indebted to him for some reason. Ultimately, your actions would depend on your conclusion about the cause of his apparent generosity. If you decided that the gift was sincere, you might eventually drive off in the car, but if you remained suspicious that all was not well, you would probably decline the offer and pursue more traditional ways of dealing with a stalled car (such as phoning for a tow truck).

© Lucinda Dowell Photographs

How would you respond if a stranger offered to trade cars when yours stalled?

In this chapter, we discuss these sorts of judgments about the causes of behaviour, as well as other inferences that are made in daily life. The topics covered in this chapter extend the basic processes described in the previous chapter on social cognition to more complex judgments. We discuss perceptions of other people (e.g., judgments about what caused them to act in a certain way), perceptions of ourselves (e.g., judgments of our own abilities), and other people's perceptions of us (e.g., others' judgments of our likeability and competence). Taken together, these topics provide a broad overview of social psychological research on social perception and self-perception.

What We See in Others: Social Perception

The most important things in our lives are other people. Our family, friends, children, and colleagues give our lives meaning, security, and happiness—and bring us our most intense pain as well. For us to cope effectively in a social world, it is essential that we predict other people's actions reasonably well. Such knowledge will help us control our environment. Perhaps a few hermits and religious isolates do not need to deal with other people, but for the rest of us, predicting the actions of those we meet is an important goal. How can we predict what people will do? First, we need to understand *why* they acted as they did in the present and the past—we need to figure out what their present or previous actions tell us about their personality, attitudes, and other personal characteristics. It is also important to have a good understanding of how various external or situational forces influence people's behaviour (e.g., money, situational norms, laws). These judgments about personal qualities and external forces fall into the domain of *attribution theories*.

Attribution Theories: Explaining Social Behaviour

Judgments about why an event occurred or why someone behaved in a certain way are called **attributions.** Thus, attributions are causal judgments. As illustrated in the *Pay It Forward* example given above, the causal judgment we make about another person's behaviour influences how we behave toward him or her (e.g., whether we accept a gift automobile from him). More mundane examples of actions that require causal analysis are abundant. If your housemate gets angry with you one afternoon for not keeping the kitchen clean, you must decide whether he or she is in a bad mood (and will get over it) or whether the state of the kitchen really does upset him or her (in which case you will have to be cleaner). If someone you are attracted to is very friendly to you late in the evening at the university pub, you must decide whether he or she likes you (in which case you will definitely ask for a date) or is being so friendly because he or she has consumed several alcoholic drinks (in which case you will be more cautious in your approach). Judgments about the causes of people's actions and outcomes are made constantly and have important implications for our own behaviour.

attributions
causal judgments about why an event or behaviour occurred

Many social psychologists have studied how people make attributions for others' behaviour. Indeed, interest in the attribution process in the 1970s was one of the first steps toward a "cognitive" perspective in social psychology, which is now probably the dominant approach in the field. Attribution theories are models that attempt to delineate the processes underlying judgments of cause.

intuitive scientists
untrained scientists who try to make causal judgments in a rational, scientific manner

⊛ **The Intuitive Scientist.** One of the best-known attribution theories was proposed by Harold Kelley (1967, 1973), who suggested that people often make causal judgments in a relatively scientific manner—as if they were **intuitive scientists** (i.e., untrained or lay scientists). How do scientists test their ideas? They make repeated observations (e.g., across many trials or across many participants) and determine whether certain events or responses reliably occur under certain conditions. For example, a medical scientist might recruit a large number of patients with a particular medical problem and test whether giving them Medicine A improves their condition, whereas Medicine B does not.

Building on earlier work by Fritz Heider (1958), Kelley suggested that people behave as intuitive scientists in testing everyday causal questions. For example, imagine that you went to a friend's place and found him or her crying in front of the television as a DVD of the movie *Million Dollar Baby* (a drama about a female boxer, released in 2004, starring Hilary Swank and Clint Eastwood) came to an end. Imagine also that you had never seen *Million Dollar Baby*, so you did not have a personal opinion about whether it was a sad movie. What attribution would you make for your friend's behaviour? Two obvious possibilities would be that the movie is sad (an *external* attribution) or that your friend is a sentimental person who cries easily at movies (an *internal* attribution). How would you decide which of these possibilities was more plausible? Kelley suggested that you would think back over how your friend has behaved during other movies in the past and how other people you know have responded to *Million Dollar Baby*. Thus, for example, if you could think of several occasions when your friend cried at movies, you would be more likely to conclude that your friend cried this time because he or she is sentimental. If you knew several other people who had seen *Million Dollar Baby* and also happened to know that none of them cried (we will finesse the issue of how you could know this if you hadn't been there watching the movie!), you would again be inclined to conclude that your friend cried because he or she is sentimental. On the other hand, if you had never seen your friend cry at any movie before, and if several people had told you they cried at the end of *Million Dollar Baby*, you would probably conclude that your friend cried because the

Hilary Swank and Clint Eastwood played the lead roles in the 2004 movie *Million Dollar Baby*.

movie is sad. Notice how rational this process is: you are systematically testing whether crying was associated with your friend or with *Million Dollar Baby*.

Kelley suggested that we use this kind of reasoning when we have multiple observations of several individuals across several settings. He proposed that we think back over all our relevant observations and try to figure out whether the behaviour was associated with a particular person, with a particular situation (or object), or with some combination of persons and situations. Kelley labelled this theory the **covariation model of attribution,** because it assumes that people try to determine whether a behaviour *covaried* (correlated, was associated) with a person, a situation, or some combination of persons and situations. Many researchers have obtained evidence that is consistent with Kelley's covariation model (e.g., Hazlewood & Olson, 1986; Hewstone & Jaspars, 1983; McArthur, 1972). Thus, ordinary people sometimes test causal questions in a relatively scientific manner (but for limitations, see Cheng & Novick, 1992; Forsterling, 2001; Hilton & Slugoski, 1986; Johnson, Boyd, & Magnani, 1994; Smith, 1994).

The False Consensus Effect. What would happen if you had seen *Million Dollar Baby* before you found your friend crying at the end of the movie? Would your own reaction to the movie influence how you interpreted your friend's reaction? Research on the attribution process suggests that the answer to this question is yes. When individuals have personal experience with a situation, they usually assume that most other people would respond similarly to themselves, and they draw conclusions about the cause of behaviour based on this assumption. For example, if you did *not* cry while watching the movie, you would probably decide that your friend cried because he or she is sentimental. If you *did* cry at the end of the movie, however, you would probably decide that your friend cried because the movie is sad (unless you view yourself as a sentimental softie!). These inferences reflect an assumption that most people would respond to the movie the same way that you did.

There is, in fact, a general tendency for individuals to assume that other people share their attitudes and behaviours to a greater extent than is actually the case; this tendency is called the **false consensus effect.** Perceivers overestimate the "consensus" (agreement) that exists for their attitudes and actions (for reviews, see Kreuger, 1988; Marks & Miller, 1987).

Imagine yourself in the following situation: You arrive at an experiment and learn that the purpose of the study is to investigate how people respond to different types of messages. If you are willing, your task will be to wear a "sandwich board" sign and walk around the campus for 30 minutes keeping track of how people respond to you. The message board that you will be wearing says "Repent" on the front and on the back. The experimenter states that if you do not want to do this task, you can decline and still receive your experimental credit. What would you do? Would you agree to wear the sign or decline to wear it?

Now answer another question: What percentage of students at your university do you think would make the *same* decision as you? Lee Ross, a Canadian who obtained his undergraduate degree at the University of Toronto, conducted a study with colleagues David Greene and Pamela House (1977) that did exactly what you have just imagined. They asked students at Stanford University to walk around the campus wearing unusual messages on sandwich boards (either "Repent" or "Eat at Joe's"). After making their decision, participants were asked to predict what percentage of other participants would agree to wear the sign.

covariation model of attribution

an attribution theory proposing that we make causal judgments by determining whether a particular behaviour correlated with a person, a situation, or some combination of persons and situations

false consensus effect

the tendency to assume that other people share our own attitudes and behaviours to a greater extent than is actually the case

Would you agree to wear a sign like this for an experimenter?

Table 4.1 presents the results of Ross and his colleagues' (1977) experiment. Exactly 50% of the participants agreed to wear the "Repent" sign (and 50% refused), whereas 70% of the participants agreed to wear the "Eat at Joe's" sign (and 30% refused). With the one exception of participants who agreed to wear the "Eat at Joe's" sign, all groups overestimated the number of participants who would do whatever they had done themselves. For example, participants who agreed to wear the "Repent" sign predicted, on average, that 63% of other people would also agree, whereas participants who refused to wear the "Repent" sign predicted that 77% of other people would similarly refuse. These overestimates are examples of the false consensus effect.

Why does the false consensus effect occur? There are probably several reasons (see Dawes, 1989; Gilovich, 1991; Kunda, 1999; Nickerson, 2001). One reason for the bias is that we tend to interact mainly with other people who agree with us. Think about your friends. Most of them are probably quite similar to you in terms of interests, attitudes, and values. Indeed, as we will see in Chapter 13, "Liking, Loving, and Close Relationships," attitude similarity is a strong predictor of liking and friendship. The people you interact with the most, therefore, are not representative of the general population—they are more similar to you than is the average person. But we do not always recognize this fact, so we tend to overestimate the degree of agreement that exists in the general population for our attitudes and behaviours. A second reason is a motivational one—we *want* to believe that others agree with us. We are motivated to believe that our opinions are accurate and our actions are appropriate (e.g., Festinger, 1957). If lots of other people agree with us, it seems likely that our attitudes and actions are good ones. Therefore, people may overestimate consensus because it makes them feel good about their attitudes and behaviours (Sherman, Presson, & Chassin, 1984). Consistent with this second, motivational explanation of the false consensus effect is evidence that people sometimes *under*estimate consensus when it makes them look good. For example, people who report that they would perform altruistic acts such as stopping to help a stranded motorist tend to

TABLE 4.1
Predictions for Other Participants' Decisions About Wearing a Sign

Participant's Own Decision	Predictions for What Other Participants Will Decide	
	Will Agree to Wear Sign	**Will Refuse to Wear Sign**
"Repent"		
Agreed to Wear Sign (50%)	63%	37%
Refused to Wear Sign (50%)	23%	77%
"Eat at Joe's"		
Agreed to Wear Sign (70%)	61%	39%
Refused to Wear Sign (30%)	43%	57%

Adapted from Ross et al., 1977 (Study 4, p. 292)

underestimate how many other people would behave in the same way, perhaps because this perception of uniqueness makes them feel good about themselves (see Goethals, 1986a; Kernis, 1984; Tesser, 1988).

Discounting and Augmentation.

The covariation model of attribution assumes that people have multiple observations of the target person (e.g., how your friend has reacted to other movies). But, of course, we often encounter complete strangers in our daily lives, and we certainly do make attributions about their behaviour. How do we make judgments about why a stranger acted in a particular way? Kelley (1973) suggested that when we make attributions about a person based on just one observation, we rely on our knowledge of "plausible causes" in the situation. That is, we use our general knowledge to infer one or more causes that might explain the behaviour and then simply look to see whether those plausible causes were, in fact, present.

Imagine that you are walking home one fine Canadian winter day and come upon a car in the ditch at the side of the road. Your general knowledge of why cars leave the road in the winter will probably identify at least two plausible causes: bad driving (e.g., the driver was inattentive) and bad conditions (e.g., the road was snow-covered and icy). You cannot "see" the driver's skill or attentiveness, so you instead look at the road to see if it is covered with ice. If you see a patch of ice, you will probably conclude that the car left the road because of bad conditions, whereas if there is no ice, you will probably conclude that the car left the road because of bad driving.

Many everyday attribution situations conform to the car example just given: there is a plausible *internal* or dispositional cause, which is often nonobservable (e.g., poor driving skills), and one or more plausible *external* or situational causes, which are normally observable (e.g., bad road conditions). Therefore, the attribution process based on a single observation frequently involves looking to see whether a plausible external cause is present. If an external cause *is* present, then the behaviour is attributed, at least partly, to that cause, but if there is *no* external cause present, then the behaviour is attributed to an internal cause.

The sequence of looking for an external cause and, if one is present, reducing the perceived importance of internal causes, is an example of the **discounting principle.** The discounting principle states that the perceived role of one cause will be diminished if other plausible causes are also present. Usually, discounting involves reducing the perceived role of an *internal* cause because an *external* cause is known to be present (e.g., inferring that a traffic accident was *not* caused by poor driving skills, because you can see that the road is icy). There are many, many examples of discounting in everyday life. When an attractive young woman or man marries a wealthy older man or woman, observers discount the importance of love (an internal factor causing marriage) and attribute the younger person's behaviour to the external force of money. When a student does well on a test that yielded a class average of 85%, observers reduce the perceived role of intelligence (an internal factor causing good test performance) and attribute his or her high score, at least partly, to the external factor of an easy test. Numerous researchers have obtained empirical evidence of discounting effects (see Hansen & Hall, 1985; Hull & West, 1982; Morris & Larrick, 1995).

The discounting principle implies that internal factors will be downplayed when plausible external causes are present. The flip side of the discounting principle is the **augmentation principle.** The augmentation principle applies to situations in which there are factors present that should have worked *against* the behaviour

discounting principle
a rule of attribution that states that the perceived role of a cause will be discounted (reduced) if other plausible causes are also present

augmentation principle
a rule of attribution that states that the perceived role of a cause will be augmented (increased) if other factors are present that would work against the behaviour

© Jimmy Chin/Outdoor Collection/Aurora Photos

Reaching the top of Mount Everest is extremely difficult, so anyone who does so will be seen as an extremely talented climber—an inference that reflects the *augmentation principle.*

(rather than factors that might have *caused* the behaviour). The augmentation principle states that the perceived role of a cause will be *increased* when other causes are present that would work against the behaviour. For example, behaviour sometimes occurs despite the presence of difficult, inhibitory external circumstances. In such cases, observers attribute the behaviour to especially strong internal causes (see Mills & Jellison, 1967; Trope, Cohen, & Maoz, 1988). If a student does very well on a test that yielded a class average of 45%, observers "augment" the role of intelligence and conclude that he or she is *extremely* smart. If a climber successfully reaches the top of Mount Everest, observers conclude that he or she is an *extremely* talented or determined climber. The flowchart in Figure 4.1 illustrates the processes underlying the discounting and augmentation principles.

The Correspondence Bias: A Fundamental Attribution Error

The intuitive scientist perspective on attribution emphasizes the relatively rational processes involved in deciding why someone behaved in a particular way. In the present section, we discuss an important error that is very common in our perceptions of others—so common that it has been called the *fundamental attribution error* (Ross, 1977). We will refer to it as the **correspondence bias,** which is the label preferred by the researcher who initially identified it, Edward (Ned) Jones (e.g., Jones, 1979, 1990; Jones & Harris, 1967; Snyder & Jones, 1974).

If we asked you to describe one of your close friends, how would you do so? A major part of your description would probably involve personality traits—things like funny, honest, and reliable (Park, 1986). You could likely generate a large number of relevant traits for almost everyone you know well (Ross & Nisbett, 1991) and even for celebrities and public figures you have never met personally but have seen in the media. All of us believe that other people possess many stable personality traits (Kunda & Nisbett, 1986). Of course, people *do* possess some personality traits, as we

correspondence bias

the tendency to assume that people's actions and words reflect their personality, their attitudes, or some other internal factor, rather than external or situational factors

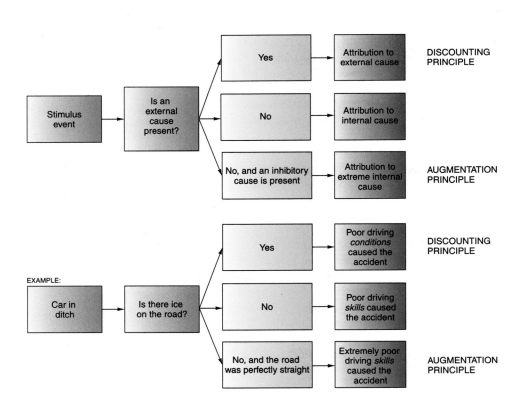

FIGURE 4.1 Processes underlying the discounting and augmentation principles

will discuss in Chapter 5, "The Person in the Situation." But we tend to rely *too much* on personality to explain other people's actions. When someone is late, we tend to assume that he or she is a tardy person, rather than late on this one occasion. When someone does well on a test, we tend to assume that he or she is intelligent, rather than wondering whether the test was easy. When someone is friendly to us, we tend to assume that he or she is a friendly person and not just conforming to a norm of politeness.

The overreliance on personality traits to understand behaviour is an example of the correspondence bias. The correspondence bias is "the tendency to see behaviour as caused by a stable personal disposition of the actor when it can just as easily be explained as a natural response to situational pressures" (Jones, 1990, p. 138). In other words, the correspondence bias is the tendency to assume that people's actions and words reflect their personality, their attitudes, or some other internal factor, even when there are plausible external or situational factors. You may have noted that the correspondence bias represents a failure to use the *discounting principle* (a failure to discount internal factors when plausible external factors are present). The correspondence bias can involve both overestimating the role of personality factors and underestimating the role of situational factors.

A Laboratory Demonstration of the Correspondence Bias.

Imagine that you participated in an experiment where you and another student played a simulated quiz-show game. The experimenter flipped a coin, and the other student was assigned to be the "questioner" and you were assigned to be the "contestant." The experimenter then told the questioner to think of ten questions to ask you, which should be "challenging but not impossible." How do you think you would do in answering these questions? How many of your answers would you expect to be correct? Imagine that you were able to answer just four of the ten questions correctly. Would you feel smart or stupid? Would you think that you were less intelligent than the questioner?

But now think about the reverse role assignment. If you were the one who thought of ten questions for the other participant, how many do you think he or she would get correct? Would you feel smarter than the other participant if he or she got just four of the ten questions correct?

Lee Ross (the researcher who designed the "sandwich board" study described earlier) conducted another study at Stanford University, this time with Teresa Amabile and Julia Steinmetz (1977), which used this quiz-show procedure. Pairs of student participants came to the lab and were randomly assigned to be either the "questioner" or the "contestant" in a simulated quiz-show game. Because the participants were *randomly assigned* to the two roles, the groups of questioners and contestants were presumably comparable in intelligence. There was also a group of uninvolved observers who watched the questioners and contestants on videotape. Questioners thought of ten questions that would be "challenging but not impossible." The contestants were able to answer an average of only four of the ten questions correctly. When later asked to estimate the intelligence of the questioner and the contestant, contestants and uninvolved observers both estimated that the questioner was more intelligent than the contestant (see Figure 4.2). Interestingly, questioners did not show this bias, perhaps recognizing that everyone has some relatively obscure knowledge and they appeared intelligent only because they were given the questioner role.

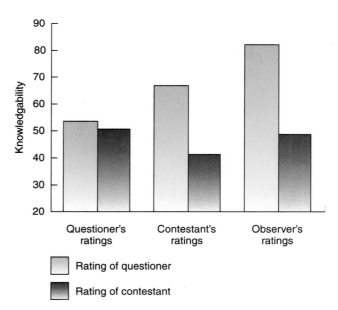

FIGURE 4.2 Ratings of questioner's and contestant's general knowledge

From Ross et al., "Social roles, social control, and biases in social-perception processes," *Journal of Personality and Social Psychology,* 35, 485–494, Table 1, p. 489, 1977. Copyright © 1977 by the American Psychological Association.

The contestants and observers did not seem to recognize that the apparent knowledge difference between the questioner and the contestant occurred only because of the role assignments: if the contestant had been assigned to the role of questioner, he or she would have appeared more intelligent than the other participant. Why is this an example of the correspondence bias? Because people saw the poor performance of the contestant as being caused by the internal characteristic of low intelligence (compared to the questioner) when it could just as easily be explained by the external factor of being assigned to the role of contestant.

Causes of the Correspondence Bias. Why is the correspondence bias common in our perceptions of other people? There are probably several processes or mechanisms that contribute to our tendency to see others' behaviour as caused by stable internal characteristics even when there are plausible external explanations (see Fiske & Taylor, 1991; Gilbert & Malone, 1995; Jones, 1990; Ross & Nisbett, 1991). First, we may simply *overlook* or be unaware of situational factors that influence other people's behaviour. Situational factors guiding behaviour are often subtle or nonobvious. For example, many behaviours are guided by norms that specify how to behave in a particular situation: people listen quietly in class because students are supposed to be attentive, people line up in an orderly way at the cash register because that is how they are supposed to act in a store, and so on. We are not generally aware of these external norms even though they guide everyone's behaviour, so we may not consider them when trying to determine why someone behaved in a particular fashion.

A second cause of the correspondence bias is that we simply underestimate the *power* of situational factors. Even when we notice external factors (which, as just noted, will *not* always be the case), we might still underestimate their strength and therefore fail to discount internal factors enough (Trope, 1986). For example, contestants and observers in the quiz-show experiment by Ross and his colleagues (1977) clearly underestimated the ability of people to come up with challenging questions if assigned to the role of questioner.

A third factor contributing to the correspondence bias is that the process of taking situational factors into account requires cognitive resources, which may not always be available. Harvard University social psychologist Daniel Gilbert and his colleagues (Gilbert & Malone, 1995; Gilbert, Pelham, & Krull, 1988) hypothesized that when perceivers observe another individual's actions, they first assume that the behaviour reflected the individual's dispositions, but then adjust this initial assumption, if necessary, based on situational information about possible external causes of the behaviour. For example, seeing a man yell at his neighbour will initially create the impression of hostility or aggressiveness, but perceivers might subsequently adjust this impression based on situational information; if they know, for instance, that the neighbour stole tomatoes from the man's garden, they will probably adjust their initial inference of a hostile disposition and instead attribute the man's behaviour to his neighbour's provocation. How can this two-stage model of the attribution process explain the correspondence bias? It turns out that the initial step of assuming that a behaviour reflected an internal disposition is relatively *automatic* and spontaneous (e.g., see Winter & Uleman, 1984). The second step of using situational information to adjust the initial impression, however, is not automatic and in fact requires significant cognitive resources (e.g., thinking about the possible role of situational factors). Because the second step requires deliberative thought, it is much more susceptible to disruption than is the first step (see Gilbert et al., 1988). For example, distraction or multitasking can interfere with the second step, which will leave perceivers with their initial impression that the target's behaviour reflected an internal disposition (i.e., the correspondence bias). From this perspective, the correspondence bias is not inevitable in social perception, but instead will occur mainly when perceivers lack either the motivation or the cognitive resources necessary to use situational information to adjust initial, automatic, dispositional inferences.

Culture and the Correspondence Bias. A fourth possible cause of the correspondence bias is cultural influences. Specifically, the emphasis in Western cultures on individualism and personal accomplishments may account, in part, for the frequent appearance of the correspondence bias in research conducted in Canada and the United States. Western cultures preach that anyone can be successful if they try hard enough, and values like personal freedom and liberty are held very high in Western cultures. It is possible that this emphasis on individualism causes people from Western cultures to focus on internal, personal variables like personality traits, attitudes, and values when explaining behaviour.

But what about cultures in which there is less emphasis on individuality and more emphasis on such things as group harmony, social obligations, and conformity to tradition (collectivism)? Perhaps members of these cultures will be *less* likely to explain behaviour in terms of personal, internal characteristics (i.e., they will be less likely to exhibit the correspondence bias). We will discuss the individualism versus collectivism dimension in more detail later in this chapter. For our present purposes, it is necessary only to note that several researchers have compared individualist North American and collectivist Asian participants in experiments investigating the correspondence bias (e.g., Choi & Nisbett, 1998; Krull, Loy, Lin, Wang, Chen, & Zhao, 1999; Masuda & Kitayama, 2004; Miller, 1984; Miyamoto & Kitayama, 2002; Morris & Peng, 1994; Norenzayan, Choi, & Nisbett, 2002). Although the findings have not been perfectly consistent, most researchers have found that Asian participants exhibited a significantly weaker correspondence bias than did North American participants. The bias did not usually disappear altogether in Asian participants, but these individuals were consistently less likely to make internal attributions than were North Americans. These findings suggest that cultural factors do contribute to the correspondence bias, but do not explain it entirely (see also Peng & Knowles, 2003).

The various causes of the correspondence bias are summarized in the accompanying Concept Review.

A fascinating real-life illustration of cultural differences in the correspondence bias has been documented in newspaper reports of murders. For a description of this phenomenon, see "Social Psychology in Your Life: Cultural Differences in the Correspondence Bias."

CONCEPT REVIEW
Causes of the Correspondence Bias

Cause	Example
We are unaware of subtle external factors that influence behaviour.	We conclude that a student who failed a test lacks ability because we are unaware that she felt sick during the exam.
We underestimate the power of external factors on behaviour.	We conclude that a man who put money into a Salvation Army kettle is generous because we do not believe that seeing a previous person donate could have influenced him.
We do not have the cognitive resources necessary to take situational factors into account when explaining behaviour.	We conclude that a student who slipped and fell at the other end of the cafeteria is uncoordinated because we are distracted by a conversation with a friend and do not bother to look for possible external causes like a wet floor.
Western culture emphasizes the importance of personal, internal causes of behaviour.	We conclude that a successful businessman is hardworking because we believe that individuals in our society can accomplish anything if they work hard enough.

Social Psychology in Your Life   *Cultural Differences in the Correspondence Bias*

Comparisons of actual newspaper articles have revealed fascinating cultural differences in the causal explanations for behaviour offered by reporters: North American reporters exhibit the correspondence bias (the tendency to attribute others' actions to internal causes) more than do Asian reporters. For example, Michael Morris and Kaiping Peng (1994) examined newspaper articles about two U.S. murders, one committed by a Chinese man in Iowa and one committed by an American man in Michigan. The newspaper articles appeared either in the *New York Times,* an English-language paper, or in *World Journal,* a Chinese-language paper based in New York. A total of 22 articles in the two newspapers dealing with the murders were examined. Analysis of the articles showed that the English-language reporters focused on internal characteristics of the murderers (e.g., "very bad temper," "martial arts enthusiast," and "darkly disturbed man who drove himself to success and destruction"), whereas the Chinese-language reporters stressed external factors that precipitated the murders (e.g., "did not get along with his advisor," "isolation from Chinese community," and "gunman had recently been fired").

In another survey of newspaper articles on a very different topic, Fiona Lee, Mark Hallahan, and Thaddeus Herzog (1996) examined sports coverage of soccer games. The newspaper reports appeared in one of three U.S. newspapers (e.g., *Los Angeles Times*) or in an English-language Hong Kong newspaper (*South China Morning Post*). A total of 39 articles about soccer, all written by local reporters, were compared. Analysis of the articles showed that the American reporters tended to focus on internal explanations of events in the soccer games (e.g., "The more talented team was victorious"; "He was ejected from the game because he didn't control his hot temper"). In contrast, Hong Kong reporters tended to focus on external explanations of events in the games (e.g., "The winning team defeated an exhausted opponent at the end of a long road trip"; "He was ejected from the game because he retaliated when an opposing player insulted him").

The Appeal of Social Psychology? It is probably accurate to say that the correspondence bias contributes to the appeal of social psychology. By this we mean that the correspondence bias helps to explain why so many findings in social psychology are surprising (see Gilbert & Malone, 1995; Jones, 1990; Ross, 1977). People often overlook the situational forces that influence behaviour and instead interpret others' behaviour in terms of internal, dispositional factors. For example, one of the most famous research programs in social psychology is Stanley Milgram's (1963, 1974) research on obedience, which showed that ordinary people will follow the orders of an experimenter to deliver intense electric shocks to another person (this research is discussed in Chapter 8, "Conformity, Compliance, and Obedience"). Why did this research have such an impact? Because people were surprised that the situational pressure provided by the authority of an experimenter was sufficient to produce such obedience. In other words, people were surprised by the influence of an external factor (authority) on behaviour. Another research program that generated a lot of attention was conducted by Bibb Latané and John Darley (1970) on bystander intervention; these studies showed that people who witness an emergency situation often fail to help because of situational factors such as the presence of other bystanders (this research is discussed in Chapter 12, "Helpful Social Behaviour"). This research was interesting to nonpsychologists because they were surprised by the failure of bystanders to intervene; the situational forces inhibiting assistance seemed relatively weak on the surface, yet exerted strong effects on behaviour.

Beyond Words: Understanding Nonverbal Behaviour

One important determinant of how we interpret other people's words and actions (and, therefore, one determinant of the impressions we form) is their **nonverbal behaviour:** actions and cues that communicate meaning in ways other than direct verbal statements. Do you pay attention to the little signs people exhibit in their eyes, voice, or hands that suggest their mood? Do you watch for clues that your romantic partner is happy, unhappy, or bored with you? Nonverbal behaviour comprises everything other than the words themselves. Thus, nonverbal behaviour includes a multitude of cues such as facial expressions, vocal qualities like pitch and intensity, interpersonal space, eye gaze, and gestures (see DePaulo & Friedman, 1998). We comment below on a few interesting questions about nonverbal behaviour that have been investigated by social psychologists.

nonverbal behaviour
actions and cues that communicate meaning in ways other than by words

We often infer how people are feeling based on their nonverbal actions.

It's Not Only What You Say, It's Also How You Say It. Words are important. When we say "I love you" to our partner, parents, or children, it communicates something meaningful and important. But there is another aspect of interpersonal communication that often matters just as much, and sometimes more, than the words themselves: *how* the words are expressed.

Consider the following situation: You overhear someone saying "What a *nice* haircut!" to another person in a mocking tone with a quick laugh at the end. How would you interpret the speaker's meaning? Would you rely on the words themselves, which are positive, or the tone of the words, which is negative? Research evidence suggests that when verbal and nonverbal cues directly conflict like this, observers rely more on the nonverbal cues in interpreting the message's meaning (e.g., Argyle, Alkema, & Gilmour, 1971; Mehrabian, 1972). Thus, the haircut comment would be interpreted as a statement that was meant to be sarcastic and negative.

Typically, nonverbal cues do not directly conflict with verbal content, but instead provide additional information. Researchers have found that nonverbal information does enhance our understanding of interactions. For example, Dane Archer and Robin Akert (1977) showed students at the University of California at Santa Cruz brief videotapes of two or three people talking or interacting and then asked participants questions that were not specifically answered in the videotapes (thus, participants had to infer the answers from things in the videotapes). The videotapes were genuine, spontaneous interactions among two or three individuals, which lasted between 30 and 60 seconds. For example, one scene depicted two women playing with a seven-month-old baby, and participants were later asked to predict which of the women was the baby's mother. Another scene involved two men discussing a game of basketball they had played, and participants were later asked to predict which of the men had won the game. Participants who simply read a written transcript of the verbal communications did not differ from chance in answering the questions correctly, whereas participants who watched the videotapes performed much better (about 50% better). Thus, nonverbal information was helpful to participants and improved their comprehension of the social interactions.

Nonverbal cues are particularly useful in judging the emotion of speakers—how other people are feeling. The most obvious nonverbal cues for inferring emotions are facial expressions, such as smiling and frowning. But other cues like a quivering voice, shaking hands, and frequent shifting of body posture reflect such emotions as nervousness and embarrassment. One of the reasons nonverbal cues are seen as informative about true feelings is that they are not completely under voluntary control. Even when people try to mask their feelings, nonverbal cues can "leak" their emotions (e.g., Ekman & Friesen, 1969a). If someone is very upset but denying it ("I'm not upset"), their voice may quiver or their hands may shake no matter what they do to try to hide their feelings. Nonverbal cues are usually taken as a more accurate sign of underlying emotions than are words themselves.

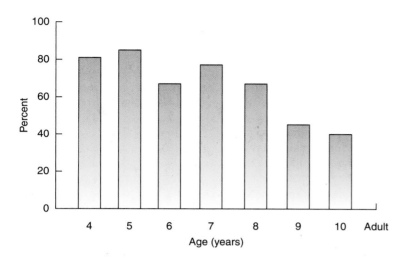

FIGURE 4.3 Percent of respondents at each age who relied on verbal content (words) to judge emotion

From Morton and Trehub, "Children's understanding of emotion in speech," *Child Development*, 72, 834–843, Table 2, p. 837, 2001. Reprinted by permission of Blackwell Publishing.

Developmental Changes in the Weighting of Verbal and Nonverbal Cues. We have noted that when verbal and nonverbal cues directly conflict, such as in a sarcastic compliment ("What a *nice* haircut!") or an unsuccessful attempt to mask one's feelings ("I'm not upset"), perceivers rely on the nonverbal cues to interpret the speaker's meaning or emotional state. This use of nonverbal cues to qualify verbal meaning requires a relatively sophisticated understanding of how emotions are expressed nonverbally. Research with children indicates that very young children do not possess such understanding.

Bruce Morton of the University of Western Ontario and Sandra Trehub of the University of Toronto (2001) asked children between the ages of four and ten, as well as university students, to judge whether a speaker was feeling happy or sad. Participants listened to 40 utterances in which the speaker stated something happy (e.g., "My soccer team just won the championship") or sad (e.g., "I lost my sticker collection") in a tone of voice that was either happy or sad. Twenty of the utterances presented consistent verbal and nonverbal cues, and 20 presented inconsistent cues (e.g., happy content expressed in a sad voice). Figure 4.3 summarizes the results. On the utterances that involved conflicting cues, more than 80% of the youngest children (ages four and five) relied on the verbal content to judge the speaker's emotion (e.g., judging someone who expressed happy content in a sad voice to be feeling happy). This tendency fell to approximately 40% by the time children were nine or ten years old. In contrast, 100% of the adults relied exclusively on the nonverbal cues in making their judgments. Presumably, children must learn such things as the difficulty of hiding emotions before they can judge the appropriate weight to give to verbal content and nonverbal cues in spoken communication. Interpretation of nonverbal cues is a skill that slowly develops over children's early years.

Facial Expressions. Charles Darwin proposed in 1872 that facial expressions in humans are biologically based and universal. Darwin believed that facial expressions evolved from more primitive behaviours (e.g., the expression for disgust is a simplified derivative of vomiting or spitting) and all humans expressed their emotions similarly (although, of course, people might attempt to hide their emotions). Darwin believed that the ability to recognize emotions in others' faces was adaptive; for example, if someone shows a fear or anger expression, other people can infer that a threat is present and either address the threat or escape (see Hansen & Hansen, 1988).

If facial expressions are biologically based and have evolved from primitive behaviours, then people from different cultures should be able to recognize facial expressions from other cultures relatively accurately. This hypothesis has, in fact, been tested many times. For example, Paul Ekman of the University of California at San Francisco and a large number of collaborators (Ekman et al., 1987) conducted a cross-cultural study involving ten countries, in which university-age participants were shown 18 facial photographs of Caucasian men and women expressing one of six emotions. For each photograph, participants were asked to select which emotion was being expressed. Although there were some variations across cultures, all of the emotions were correctly identified by the majority of participants from

4.1
ONLINE
LAB

every culture. Considering the limitations of these two-dimensional photographs (e.g., real-life emotional expressions change dynamically over time and are three-dimensional), the level of accuracy was quite remarkable.

Some researchers have criticized this study, however. James Russell of the University of British Columbia has conducted several studies on the recognition of facial expressions that raise questions about the universality issue (e.g., Russell, 1994; Russell, Suzuki, & Ishida, 1993). For example, Russell and his colleagues (1993) asked adult participants in Canada, Japan, and Greece to *generate their own term or label* for photographs of the same emotions studied by Ekman and his colleagues (1987). When participants had to generate their own labels for emotions, agreement dropped substantially, especially for negative emotions. In another set of studies, Russell and his colleague Beverly Fehr of the University of Winnipeg found that participants' judgments of the emotion being expressed in a photograph were influenced by the other photographs in the set (Russell & Fehr, 1987). For instance, the same neutral facial expression was judged as sad if participants had previously seen a happy face but as happy if participants had previously seen a sad face.

These studies show that the recognition of facial expressions is far from perfect, but evidence for at least some universality of emotion recognition is accumulating. After a comprehensive review of 87 articles, Harvard University's Hillary Elfenbein and Nalini Ambady (2002) concluded that cross-cultural recognition accuracy was substantially above chance on every one of seven basic emotions: anger, contempt, disgust, fear, happiness, sadness, and surprise. Some emotions have been recognized in research better than others (e.g., across studies, happiness and anger have been the best-recognized emotions), but all have shown substantial cross-cultural generalizability. This pattern of findings supports Darwin's argument that facial expressions of certain fundamental emotions are biologically based and mostly similar in all cultures (see also Elfenbein & Ambady, 2003; Rozin, Lowery, Imada, & Haidt, 1999).

Gender and Cultural Differences in Nonverbal Behaviour

Although facial expressions and other nonverbal behaviours have been shown to be similar across many groups, there are also differences in the ways that people express emotions and communicate nonverbally. We will discuss two sources of differences: gender and culture.

Gender Differences in Nonverbal Behaviour. Do you think that men and women differ in their nonverbal behaviour? A common stereotype is that women are more emotional and are allowed to express more emotion (men should be "stoic" and unemotional); do you think that this stereotype occurs in real life?

Researchers have identified a number of interesting gender differences in nonverbal behaviour. First, women are better judges than men of *other people's* emotions (e.g., Hall, 1984). This tendency for women to identify emotions in others more accurately than men may reflect that women are more oriented toward interpersonal harmony than men; alternatively, it may be that women must be more vigilant about others' emotions because they are less physically powerful and therefore more vulnerable than men (Deaux & LaFrance, 1998). Second, whereas women are better judges of emotions than are men, women's own facial expressions of emotion are generally easier to judge than are men's expressions (Hall, 1984; DePaulo & Friedman, 1998). This difference may reflect the stereotype that it is more socially acceptable for women to express their emotions than it is for men (Mayo & Henley, 1981).

Women gaze at other people more than men, smile more often than men, and are gazed at by other people more than men (Hall, 1984; LaFrance, Hecht, & Paluck, 2003).

display rules

norms in a culture for how and when emotions should be expressed

In Japan, it is considered inappropriate to show strong negative emotions—one of the *display rules* in that culture.

Culture seems to shape how we express our emotions on our faces as well as how we talk about our emotions when we're in the throes of an emotional event.

Women also approach other people more closely than do men and are approached by other people more closely than men (Hall, 1984). These various tendencies reflect women's greater expressions of behaviours that reflect intimacy and liking (Mehrabian, 1972; Mayo & Henley, 1981). Women may express greater nonverbal intimacy than men because women are more concerned about interpersonal relationships, or because men are not supposed to show their feelings.

Cultural Differences in Nonverbal Behaviour. There are also many cultural differences in nonverbal behaviour. In particular, cultures differ in their **display rules**—norms for how and when emotions should be expressed (Ekman & Friesen, 1969b). For example, it is considered inappropriate in Japan to show strong emotions, especially strong negative emotions (Leathers, 1997), whereas Canadian culture allows freer expression of emotional states.

Cultures also differ in nonverbal gestures and greetings (see Archer, 1997; Axtell, 1991; Leathers, 1997). For example, in Canada and the United States, it is traditional to shake hands when greeting others, whereas people in Japan bow to one another, and people in Eastern Europe often exchange kisses on the cheek. Hand signals are almost always culture-specific, such as the North American "thumbs up" sign, which is obscene in some Middle Eastern countries. It is acceptable in Canada to point and wave at other people from a distance, whereas these actions are considered impolite in many Asian countries.

 Finally, there are substantial differences in how close or far apart individuals stand in different cultures. Have you ever felt "crowded" by someone who talked to you while standing nose to nose? In Canada, people have a relatively large "personal space" zone (Hall, 1984), which is not supposed to be entered except by individuals who have an intimate relationship (e.g., family members) or who don't know any better (e.g., children). In some Middle Eastern cultures, in contrast, people stand very closely to one another even during casual conversation. There is also more touching by Middle Eastern acquaintances than by acquaintances in Canada. These differences can create considerable discomfort when two people from cultures with different norms for personal space and touching interact.

What We See in Ourselves: Self-Perception

Do you have a clear conception of who you are? Can you describe your strengths and weaknesses, your important attitudes and values, your goals and dreams? These are questions about self-perception. We will discuss issues related specifically to *identity* in Chapter 5, but first we want to consider more generally how people make judgments about their abilities, ambitions, and attitudes. What kind of information do we seek to assess our strengths and weaknesses? In this section, we discuss the important role of comparisons to other people in judgments about the self. We also propose that people sometimes make judgments about themselves in a detached, logical manner that closely parallels how they make judgments about other people.

The Looking Glass Self

We rely on other people for much of our self-concept. It may seem ironic that judgments about the self rely heavily on other people, but it is true nonetheless. We rely on others in at least two ways. First, other people sometimes *tell us* about ourselves. Our mother will say, "You are such a thoughtful child"; our teacher will say, "You are a good speller"; a friend will say, "You're so funny!" These judgments by other people may be internalized into the self-concept, especially if they come from more than one person. This idea that other people's judgments about us will be integrated into our self-concept was labelled the **looking glass self** (we see ourselves as others see us) in an early, influential book by Charles Cooley (1902). A classic example of the looking glass self is children's internalization of their parents' labels.

In a well-known study of the looking glass self, Richard Miller, Philip Brickman, and Diana Bolen (1975) tried to teach children in the fifth grade not to litter and to clean up after others. Some children were repeatedly told that they were neat and tidy people (the labelling condition), whereas others were told that they *should* be neat and tidy (the persuasion condition). Results showed that children in the labelling condition changed their behaviour more than children in the persuasion condition. The authors hypothesized that children in the labelling condition internalized the labels, at least to some extent (see also Jussim, Soffin, Brown, Ley, & Kohlhepp, 1992; Tschanz & Rhodewalt, 2001).

looking glass self
the tendency to internalize other people's judgments about us into our self-concept

Social Comparison

A second way that other people are involved in judgments about the self is that we often compare ourselves to other people. Let's consider an example of self-assessment borrowed from the book *Pay It Forward*. Think about your own helpfulness toward others. Do you consider yourself to be a helpful person? What is the extent or degree of your helpfulness? Now an important question: *How* did you come to the conclusion that you are helpful or not?

If you're like most people judging themselves, you probably tried to think of examples of helpful behaviours that you have performed, such as volunteering, helping your friends move, lending your study notes in class, and so on. Then you probably compared your own helpful behaviours to the amount of helpful behaviours that you have seen your friends and acquaintances exhibit (or perhaps the amount of helpful behaviours that you believe the average person your age exhibits). If you estimated that you have exhibited more helpful behaviours than most of your acquaintances, then you judged yourself to be high in helpfulness, whereas if you estimated that your acquaintances' helpful behaviours have exceeded your own, then you judged yourself to be lower in helpfulness. The important point is that it was informative to compare yourself to other people in order to make a judgment about the self.

This process of explicitly comparing ourselves to other people in order to judge the self is called **social comparison.** The term was coined by Leon Festinger (1954), who proposed that we often rely on comparisons with other people to assess our abilities and our attitudes. Festinger hypothesized that, if possible, we test our abilities or beliefs in an objective, physical way. We can test whether our prediction for a federal election is accurate by waiting to see if it comes true, or we can test our ability to sing on tune by trying to sing "O Canada" to a friend. But often we cannot test our abilities or beliefs in a direct, physical manner. In these cases, we compare our performance or belief to the performances or beliefs of others. To assess our helpfulness, we must compare the frequency of our helpful behaviours to the frequency of helpful behaviours by others, as in the example above; to assess the validity of our

social comparison
the process of comparing ourselves to others in order to judge the self

We would not compare ourselves to Andy Roddick to judge our ability at tennis.

belief in an afterlife, we must compare our belief to the beliefs of others to see whether others agree with us (see Suls, Martin, & Wheeler, 2002). Because social comparisons often provide the only way for us to make important judgments about the self, we engage in the process of social comparison frequently and automatically (i.e., often without consciously intending to do so, see Mussweiler, Rüter, & Epstude, 2004; Wilson & Ross, 2000).

Social Comparison with Similar Others: Wanting to Assess Oneself Accurately. Festinger's theory of social comparison was based on the assumption that people are motivated to make *accurate* judgments about their abilities and opinions. He assumed that we want to know our true strengths and weaknesses and the actual validity of our attitudes and opinions. This desire to make accurate judgments about the self is highly adaptive, because a mistaken view of the self might lead to serious problems (Buunk, 1995; Sedikides & Strube, 1997; Wheeler, Martin, & Suls, 1997). If we assess our abilities too optimistically, we might get ourselves into situations that are above our heads (e.g., taking a course in mathematics that is too difficult for us). If we assess our abilities too harshly, we might avoid challenging ourselves in productive ways (e.g., deciding not to attend college or university).

The goal of assessing our abilities accurately is usually best achieved by comparing ourselves with other people who are *similar* to us on dimensions that are relevant to performance (Goethals & Darley, 1977; Goethals & Klein, 2000; Smith & Arnkelsson, 2000). If you wanted to assess your level of ability in skating, to whom would you compare yourself? Comparing yourself to a five-year-old child would not be informative because you are older, stronger, and more experienced at skating. Comparing yourself to hockey player Jarome Iginla or speed skater Cindy Klassen would also not be informative because they have tremendous natural ability and have skated much more than you. You would probably choose one or more persons who are about the same age as you and have skated about the same length of time as you. These characteristics of age and experience affect skating performance and need to be taken into account when assessing natural ability. If you are better than these similar persons, then you probably have a natural talent for skating, whereas if you are worse than these similar persons, then you probably lack natural ability at skating.

The flowchart in Figure 4.4 depicts how social comparisons are used to make judgments about the self.

Upward Social Comparison: Wanting to Improve. Having an accurate view of our strengths and weaknesses is probably beneficial in most cases. But performance is not static: we can become better at many things, even when our ability is low. If we want to improve ourselves, one excellent source of information about how to do so is other people (Collins, 1996; Taylor, Wayment, & Carrillo, 1996; Wood, 1989).

What kind of social comparisons will be stimulated by the desire to improve? Let's imagine that you wanted to improve your study habits; whom would you choose for social comparison in this case? The most likely choice would be someone who has *better* study habits than you: someone who studies more effectively and gets better grades. You would be able to copy this person's behaviour and discuss strategies for improving your habits, whereas someone who has worse study habits would not provide useful ideas. "Gilles is much more focused than I am when he studies; I need to change my habits so I'm more like Gilles." This kind of social comparison is labelled **upward social comparison.** Upward social comparison involves comparing yourself to someone who is better off than you are (better performance, better outcomes) and can provide useful ideas for how to improve. The link between upward social comparison and the desire to improve parallels our discussion of upward counterfactual thoughts in Chapter 3 (see Olson, Buhrmann, & Roese, 2000).

upward social comparison

social comparison with people who are better off or more skilled than we are

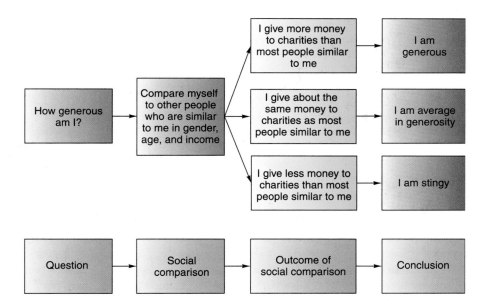

FIGURE 4.4 Social comparison processes

Downward Social Comparison: Wanting to Feel Better. The desire to assess one's abilities accurately and the desire to improve are two important motives that occur in many settings in everyday life. There is at least one additional motivation, however, that also occurs frequently: the desire to feel good (or to feel better). We like to feel good about ourselves, and this motive can be particularly strong if something bad has happened, such as if we have performed poorly or experienced an unfavourable outcome (Helgeson & Mickelson, 1995; Taylor & Brown, 1988; Taylor & Lobel, 1989; Wills, 1981).

What kind of social comparisons will be stimulated by the desire to feel good about oneself? Let's imagine that you wanted to feel good about your performance on an exam. Whom would you seek out? The most likely choice would be someone you think probably did *worse* than you on the test. Exposure to people whose performances or outcomes are less positive than our own makes our situation seem better in contrast. "I didn't do great, but at least I did better than my friends in the class." This kind of social comparison is labelled **downward social comparison.** Again, this link between downward social comparison and feeling good parallels our discussion of downward counterfactual thoughts in Chapter 3.

Joanne Wood, John Michela, and Caterina Giordano (2000) conducted a study at the University of Waterloo in which participants were asked to use a diary to keep track of all their social comparisons for a period of three weeks. Each time they compared themselves to another person, they recorded why they made the comparison (to evaluate themselves on a dimension, to learn something from this person, to feel better about themselves, or no specific goal); they also recorded whether they compared themselves to someone who was better off, similar to, or worse off than themselves. Results showed that when participants engaged in social comparison to feel better about themselves, they usually compared themselves to someone who was worse off than themselves (a downward comparison). Thus, downward social comparison seemed to serve as a strategy to feel better (see also Buunk, Oldersma, & de Dreu, 2001).

In research conducted at Simon Fraser University, Cathy McFarland and Dale Miller (1994) found that some people are more likely than others to engage in downward social comparison (and therefore to feel good about themselves). Specifically, these researchers found that people who were optimists tended to focus on others

downward social comparison
social comparison with people who are worse off or less skilled than we are

who did worse than themselves on a test and consequently felt good about their own ability, whereas people who were pessimists tended to focus on others who did better than themselves on a test and consequently felt bad about their own ability. (For further information about optimists and pessimists, see pages 181–183 in Chapter 5.)

Diverse Consequences of Upward Social Comparisons. As just noted, when we compare ourselves to people who are better off or who perform better than we do, we may feel bad (see Thornton & Moore, 1993). Although upward comparisons often provide useful information, we can also experience negative affect because our circumstances or our performances seem worse in contrast to those of someone more accomplished. These upward comparisons can make us feel depressed or inadequate because others are more successful than we are.

On the other hand, upward comparisons can sometimes make us angry and resentful, if we think that we *should* be doing as well as other people who are better off. When we feel that we *deserve* better outcomes than we are receiving, we experience **relative deprivation,** which is a feeling of anger or resentment about one's outcomes based on comparisons with others. For example, if workers in another company are making more money for doing the same job we do, we may feel unfairly treated. The emotion of relative deprivation can lead to actions intended to improve our status, such as complaining to our boss or looking for another job (see Crosby, 1976; Walker & Smith, 2002).

Serge Guimond and Lise Dubé-Simard (1983), social psychologists at the University of Montreal, found that supporters of Quebec separatism tended to believe that Francophones (French-speaking Canadians) have historically been disadvantaged in Quebec compared to Anglophones (English-speaking Canadians). This belief that Francophones have not had equal opportunities was associated with feelings of relative deprivation (resentment) about the status of Francophones. This relative deprivation presumably motivated support for the separatist movement.

There are also some conditions, however, under which upward social comparisons may not elicit negative affect at all, but instead might produce hope or optimism about the future (see Collins, 2000; Gardner, Gabriel, & Hochschild, 2002; Lockwood & Kunda, 1997; Mussweiler, 2003; Mussweiler & Strack, 2000; Smith, 2000). Cancer patients, for example, have been shown to prefer comparisons with other patients who are doing well (e.g., Taylor & Lobel, 1989; Wood & Van der Zee, 1997), presumably because such persons give them hope for improvement.

Another interesting circumstance is when someone who is close to us does extremely well. How do you think you would feel if a close friend of yours achieved success and fame? Would you be jealous, or would you feel proud that you were friends with a famous person? Abraham Tesser and his colleagues at the University of Georgia (Beach & Tesser, 2000; Tesser, 1988; Tesser, Millar, & Moore, 1988), in their *self-evaluation maintenance* model, have argued that it might depend on whether your friend was successful in a domain that you also were pursuing or in a domain very different from your own pursuits. Imagine that your occupational goal is to establish your own software company in the computer field. If your friend achieves success and fame in the software field, it might make you feel like a failure in comparison, and you might be jealous. But if your friend achieves success and fame in another field, such as music, you might be happy about his or her success and feel proud of your friendship. Robert Cialdini and his colleagues (Cialdini, Borden, Thorne, Walker, Freeman, & Sloan, 1976) labelled this latter process "basking in the reflected glory" of the other person.

How we react to the success of someone close to us also depends on *how* close we are to them. Cathy McFarland, Roger Buehler, and Laura McKay (2001) found that students at Simon Fraser University reported strong feelings of happiness when a person with whom they had a very close emotional bond succeeded (e.g., a romantic

relative deprivation
a feeling of anger or resentment about our outcomes based on comparisons with better-off others

partner or a parent), but participants' responses were less consistently positive when a person with whom they had a less intimate relationship succeeded (e.g., a friend or co-worker). Presumably, when we identify closely with another person, we vicariously enjoy his or her success as if it were our own.

Cultural Differences in Social Comparison

Recent research by several Canadian social psychologists has uncovered cultural differences in social comparison. Cultural differences exist both in the frequency of social comparison and in how individuals respond to different kinds of social comparison information.

Individualist Versus Collectivist Cultures. Most social psychologists interested in cultural differences have compared two types of societies: individualist and collectivist (see Fiske, Kitayama, Markus, & Nisbett, 1998; Hui, 1988; Oyserman, Coon, & Kemmelmeier, 2002; Sorrentino, Cohen, Olson, & Zanna, 2005; Triandis, 1995). Individualist cultures include most Western European (e.g., United Kingdom, Germany) and North American countries (e.g., Canada, United States), whereas collectivist cultures include most East Asian (e.g., China, Japan), South American (e.g., Guatemala, Ecuador), and African (e.g., Nigeria, Egypt) countries. We should note, however, that subgroups within countries sometimes differ from the predominant approaches. For example, many First Nations groups in Canada have traditionally had collectivist rather than individualist social structures.

Individualist and collectivist societies have different views of the "self," as well as different views of what is good and what is healthy for people in society. In Chapter 5, "The Person in the Situation," we will discuss cultural differences in identity and the self-concept. In the current section, we consider the implications of this dimension for self-serving judgments.

But first, we need to describe the individualism–collectivism dimension in a little more detail (see Fiske et al., 1998; Markus & Kitayama, 1991). Let's begin with individualism: What are some of the key beliefs and attitudes in these societies? In **individualist cultures,** people are seen as free, independent beings who possess stable abilities, traits, and attitudes. "Healthy individuals" are considered to be those who have a strong sense of identity, who feel good about themselves, and who have achieved individual success (e.g., personal wealth, fame). Personal identity is defined largely in terms of how people are unique and different from others.

In **collectivist cultures,** however, people are seen as part of a social fabric that joins individuals together. Group needs are emphasized above individual needs. People are seen as *interdependent* rather than independent. "Healthy individuals" are considered to be those who understand their connections to others, who feel good about their social roles, and who contribute effectively to harmonious group functioning. Group achievements are valued above individual achievements. Personal identity is defined largely in terms of people's social roles and relationships.

Cultural Differences in the Frequency of Social Comparison.
Katherine White and Darrin Lehman (2005) of the University of British Columbia compared European Canadians (e.g., British, French, German descent), who tend to have an individualist perspective, with Asian Canadians (e.g., Chinese, Korean, Japanese descent), who tend to have a collectivist perspective. These researchers found that Asian Canadians engaged in more social comparison than did European Canadians. For example, in one study, participants completed a spatial reasoning test and were told that they had performed "about average." Participants were then given the opportunity to view other students' scores. Asian Canadians chose to view more

individualist cultures

cultures in which people are seen as independent beings who possess stable abilities, traits, and attitudes

collectivist cultures

cultures in which people are seen as interdependent beings who should contribute to harmonious group functioning students' scores (an average of approximately four scores) than did European Canadians (an average of approximately one score). Subsequent studies showed that this cultural difference in the frequency of social comparison was heightened after poor performance: Asian Canadians differed from European Canadians most dramatically when participants were told that they had performed poorly. The researchers suggested that people from collectivist cultures (such as Asian Canadians) are more motivated to improve themselves than are people from individualist cultures (such as European Canadians); this heightened desire for self-improvement leads people from collectivist cultures to engage in more social comparison, especially after poor performance.

Cultural Differences in Responses to Social Comparison. Penelope Lockwood and her colleagues at the University of Toronto (Lockwood, Marshall, & Sadler, 2005) identified a cultural difference in responses to social comparison that is compatible with White and Lehman's (2005) findings. Lockwood and her colleagues compared European Canadians with Asian Canadians in terms of how they responded to information about another person's positive or negative performance. Participants were undergraduate students at the beginning of the fall term who read a self-description allegedly written the previous academic year by another student of the same gender, academic major, and cultural background as themselves. This self-description was either positive or negative. The positive self-description included comments that the second term went better than the first term, and, overall, the year was fantastic. The negative self-description included comments that the second term went worse than the first term, and, overall, the year was a disaster. Participants then completed a series of questions about their own motivation, such as "I plan to study harder" and "I plan to keep up with my reading assignments." Results showed that European Canadians were more motivated by a positive than a negative role model, whereas Asian Canadians were more motivated by a negative than a positive role model. That is, information about another student who succeeded led European Canadians to intend to work harder, whereas information about another student who failed led Asian Canadians to intend to work harder. The researchers suggested that people from individualist cultures are primarily motivated to pursue success, whereas people from collectivist cultures are primarily motivated to avoid failure. This difference in motivation may help to explain the previous findings by White and Lehman (2005) that Asian Canadians engage in more social comparison following poor performance than do European Canadians.

Self-Perception Theory

We asked you earlier in this chapter to think about how helpful you are. We speculated that you would make this judgment by thinking about your helpful behaviours in the past and comparing your actions to the rate of helpful behaviours you have seen exhibited by other people. Our point was to illustrate the importance of social comparison in judgments about the self. But this process of using our own behaviour to infer helpfulness also illustrates another important theory in social psychology: **self-perception theory.**

Darryl Bem (1967, 1972) developed self-perception theory to describe how we make judgments about our internal states, such as our attitudes, emotions, and personality traits. He proposed that we often judge our own internal states in a manner exactly parallel to how we judge other people's internal states: we review our behaviour and the situation in which it occurred and infer an internal state consistent with the behaviour unless there were clear external causes of our behaviour. This idea seems relatively straightforward for some internal states, such as general personality traits like helpfulness.

self-perception theory

a theory proposing that we often judge our own internal states by reviewing our past behaviour and inferring internal states consistent with our behaviour unless there were clear external causes of our behaviour

But Bem (1972) proposed a more controversial hypothesis, which was that we use this same process for almost all internal states, including some that are normally thought to include an affective component that people can access directly. For instance, Bem proposed that we use self-perception logic to infer many of our likes and dislikes. The notion that we need to infer from our behaviour how much we like or dislike something strikes most people as implausible. Most of us believe that we can make judgments about these internal states by accessing them directly. We judge our liking for apple pie by thinking about apple pie and appraising how this image makes us feel (good or bad).

Can you "feel" your liking for these puppies?

Think about some of your own likes and dislikes: Can you directly "sense" them? Do you like or dislike puppies? Worms? Chocolate? Speaking in front of an audience? We suspect that you believe you can access these feelings directly. These targets elicit clear and strong affective reactions from most people. But let's think of some other examples. Do you like or dislike brown bread? Biographical books? Genetically engineered foods? We suspect that your likes and dislikes for these targets may be more difficult to sense directly.

What was different about the second set of examples? These examples probably involved targets toward which you have weaker or more ambiguous feelings. You may not yet have developed clear feelings toward genetically engineered foods. Your feelings may be neutral toward brown bread, which is a target that does not evoke strong feelings either way in many people. And your feelings about biographies may include both positive and negative elements, because you have enjoyed some biographies but found others boring. Consequently, liking for these targets cannot simply be accessed; we must estimate our liking for them in some other manner. Perhaps self-perception theory describes how.

Inferring Our Own Attitudes from Our Behaviour. Bem (1967) originally proposed that we infer almost *all* of our internal states from our behaviour. This provocative proposal was subsequently revised, however, to the hypothesis that self-perception occurs for internal states that are *weak or ambiguous*. When we do not have a clearly defined evaluation of a target, we infer our attitude (or like/dislike) from our past actions toward the target. Eventually, our attitude becomes strong and clear enough for us to be able to access it directly without self-perception.

A clever study by Shelly Chaiken and Mark Baldwin (1981) at the University of Toronto provided empirical evidence that self-perception occurs for ambiguous attitudes but not for well-defined attitudes. Participants had previously completed a questionnaire that assessed their feelings and beliefs about the environment (feelings and beliefs about acting in a pro-ecology way, such as recycling and minimizing energy use). Some participants were identified as having "well-defined" views because they had feelings and beliefs that either consistently supported or consistently opposed behaving in a pro-ecology manner. Other participants were identified as having "poorly defined" views because their feelings and beliefs were inconsistent; for instance, some of these individuals had positive beliefs about the benefits of behaving in a pro-ecology way but reported that they disliked doing things like recycling and turning down the thermostat at night.

Chaiken and Baldwin gave participants a questionnaire to complete that required them to review their past behaviours in the environmental domain (e.g., recycling, conserving energy). The questionnaire was intentionally constructed, however, to produce a *biased* review of past behaviour: one version of the questionnaire forced participants to focus on their pro-environmental actions, whereas the second version focused participants' attention on anti-environmental actions. The authors hypothesized that if participants used a self-perception process to infer their environmental attitude, then the questionnaire that highlighted pro-environmental actions would lead them to report that their attitude was pro-environment, whereas the questionnaire that highlighted anti-environmental actions would lead them to report that

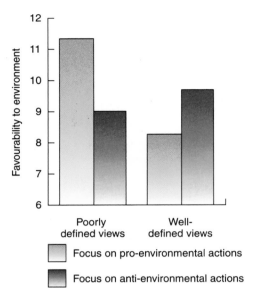

FIGURE 4.5 Favourability of reported attitudes toward the environment

From Chaiken and Baldwin, "Affective-cognitive consistency and the effect of salient behavioral information on the self-perception of attitudes," *Journal of Personality and Social Psychology*, 41, 1–12, Table 1, p. 6, 1981. Copyright © 1981 by the American Psychological Association. Reprinted by permission.

overjustification effect

an inference that we performed a potentially enjoyable activity for external reasons (e.g., for a reward) rather than because we enjoyed it

their attitude was anti-environment (or, at least, less pro-environment). After completing one of the two questionnaires, participants reported their attitude toward environmental issues.

Figure 4.5 presents the mean ratings of environmental attitudes by participants with poorly defined and well-defined views after completing one of the questionnaires. The figure shows that the questionnaire that focused attention on pro-environmental actions led to more pro-environmental attitudes than the questionnaire that focused attention on anti-environmental actions, but *only* for participants who had *poorly* defined attitudes. Participants who had well-defined views were not significantly influenced by the biased review of past behaviours. Chaiken and Baldwin hypothesized that participants with well-defined views were able to access their attitude directly and did not need to use their past behaviours to make the judgment, whereas participants with poorly defined views had to rely on their past behaviours to infer their attitude (and the questionnaire led them to review their past behaviours in a biased way).

The Overjustification Effect. One of the most interesting applications of self-perception theory has been to understanding the effects of rewards on liking for an activity or task. Sometimes people perform activities because they must do so (e.g., schoolwork, job responsibilities). At other times, however, they engage in activities for *intrinsic* reasons— because they enjoy the activities or find them fulfilling in some way. Let's begin our discussion of this topic with a thought experiment. If you saw a boy who lives next door to you playing the piano as you walked by his house in the evening, would you think that he enjoys playing the piano? Why? What if you learned that his parents had told him that he could watch his favourite television show later in the evening if he played the piano for an hour? Would you then conclude that he enjoys the piano?

Now think about yourself. If you pick up a friend's book that he or she recommended and spend a couple of hours reading it, what is the best explanation for your behaviour? If someone asked you, "Did you read the book because you wanted to read it?" what would you say? But what if the book was not your friend's but one that you were assigned to read for an English course? Now how would you answer the question about whether you wanted to read it?

Both of these examples illustrate that when there is a good external reason for a behaviour (e.g., to be able to watch a favourite television show, or to prepare for an English test), we tend to downplay internal causes (e.g., enjoyment). The **overjustification effect** occurs when people decide that they performed a potentially enjoyable task for external reasons rather than because they enjoyed it. A reward (or threat) provides sufficient justification for performing the task, so the individual infers that he or she did not really enjoy the task. The overjustification effect is an example of the *discounting principle* that we discussed earlier.

Mark Lepper, David Greene, and Richard Nisbett (1973) conducted a well-known experiment with children in a nursery school in the San Francisco area. All of the children (ages three to five) were given an opportunity to draw some pictures using a really attractive set of marker pens. Before using the pens, children in one condition were told that they would be given a Good Player Award if they drew some pictures for the experimenter with the pens. These children were shown the award in advance so it would be salient in their minds (it was a small certificate with a gold star, spaces to write the child's name and school, and a red ribbon). Children in a second group were not told about the Good Player Award in advance, but were unexpectedly given the award after using the marker pens. Children in a third condition were not told about the award and did not receive one unexpectedly after using the pens.

Between one and two weeks after the children drew pictures for the experimenter, the marker pens were placed on a table in the nursery school for one hour on three different days and left for the children to use or not. Observers recorded how long each child played with the pens during the free-play periods. Figure 4.6 presents the percentage of their free-play time that children spent drawing with the pens. Children who were promised a Good Player Award in advance if they used the pens subsequently spent less of their free time using the pens than did children who received an unexpected award or who did not hear anything about an award.

What was going on in the minds of the children? Lepper and his colleagues suggested that the children who were promised the award concluded that they were using the pens *in order to get the reward,* so the pens were not "toys" that were fun to use. The extrinsic reward of the Good Player Award was enough to produce an overjustification effect: the children believed that the pens were simply a way of getting the award, which reduced their perception of being intrinsically motivated to use the pens.

These findings are disturbing for parents and teachers who use rewards or other external incentives to encourage their children and students to engage in important activities such as reading or playing a musical instrument. The goal of parents and educators should be to produce intrinsic motivation in their children and students, because liking for a task enhances persistence and improves performance (e.g., see Deci & Flaste, 1995; Harackiewicz & Elliot, 1998; Henderlong & Lepper, 2002; Losier & Koestner, 1999). If offering rewards to encourage the activity, or forcing the activity via some other external pressure, leads people to conclude that the activity is not enjoyable, then the rewards or pressure may be counterproductive in the long run (see Lepper & Greene, 1978).

Are rewards or other incentives always a bad idea when the activity is one for which we want intrinsic motivation to develop? No, not necessarily. It turns out that if the reward is given only when performance is good, then the reward may not have a negative effect. Rewards given for good performance show recipients that they are skilled at an activity, which can actually increase personal motivation (Tang & Hall, 1995). Think about times that you have been given a reward or recognition because you did something extremely well—it made you feel good about yourself and the activity, didn't it? On the other hand, if rewards are given simply because the activity was undertaken, the rewards will not show recipients that they performed well, but instead will be seen as "controlling," which will serve to reduce perceived enjoyment (Deci & Flaste, 1995; Deci & Ryan, 1985). Parents should *not* say "Play the piano for one hour, and you can watch television" and then let the child plunk away randomly on the keys for an hour. Instead, parents should say "If you can play all of your songs at least once without any major mistakes, you can watch television" and then comment on the child's good performance when the reward criterion is reached. Thus, rewards are not necessarily bad, even when the activity for which they are given is enjoyable. Nevertheless, rewards should be used cautiously and given only for good performance. If there is no need of reward to encourage the activity in the first place (e.g., if a child is certain to read a colourful book without any pressure), then it is probably best to avoid rewards altogether.

University of Western Ontario social psychologist Clive Seligman and his colleagues (Seligman, Fazio, &

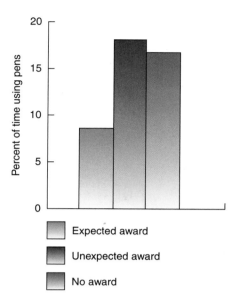

FIGURE 4.6 Percent of free-play time spent drawing with pens

From Lepper et al., "Undermining children's interest with extrinsic rewards: A test of the 'overjustification effect,'" *Journal of Personality and Social Psychology,* 28, 129–137, Table 1, p. 134, 1973. Copyright © 1973 by the American Psychological Association. Reprinted by permission.

Lepper, Greene, and Nisbett (1973) found that giving children a reward for drawing with pens reduced the children's interest in using the pens during a subsequent free-play period.

Zanna, 1980) extended the overjustification effect to interpersonal relationships. These researchers showed that when people in a romantic relationship were induced to think about extrinsic reasons for their relationship (e.g., to list extrinsic benefits they obtained from the relationship), they reported less love, which is an intrinsic reason for a romantic relationship. Presumably, thinking about extrinsic benefits led participants to infer that their relationship was not necessarily based exclusively on love.

Robert Vallerand (1997), who is at the University of Quebec at Montreal, developed a comprehensive model of intrinsic and extrinsic motivation that integrates many of the points we have made. Vallerand argued that intrinsic motivation can occur at the level of personality traits (e.g., some people are intrinsically motivated in almost everything they do), at the level of life domains (e.g., some people are intrinsically motivated in all of their academic activities), and at the level of specific tasks (e.g., some people are intrinsically motivated to play the piano). Vallerand suggested that, at each level, intrinsic motivation will occur when people have feelings of autonomy (freedom to choose), competence (effectiveness), and relatedness (being connected to others). This analysis suggests that parents and educators need to avoid actions that make children feel controlled (e.g., concrete rewards) or disconnected from others (e.g., threats of punishment) to motivate activities that are potentially intrinsically enjoyable.

An interesting application of the concept of intrinsic motivation has been to the domain of second language learning. Several Canadian social psychologists have shown that people's motivation for learning a second language predicts their success. In particular, individuals who study a second language for intrinsic, autonomous reasons (e.g., to achieve a sense of mastery, to be able to travel, to establish friendships with people who speak the language) tend to perform better than individuals who have more extrinsic, controlling reasons for studying the language (e.g., to get a job, to be a good citizen, to please one's parents). Individuals with autonomous motivation tend to be more confident about their language skills and more willing to use the second language. The researchers involved in this research have included Robert Gardner at the University of Western Ontario, Richard Clément and Luc Pelletier at the University of Ottawa, Kimberly Noels at the University of Alberta, and Peter MacIntyre at the University College of Cape Breton (e.g., Clément, Baker, & MacIntyre, 2003; Clément, Noels, & Deneault, 2001; Gardner, 1985; Gardner & Clément, 1990; MacIntyre, Clément, Baker, & Conrod, 2001; MacIntyre, Clément, Dörnyei, & Noels, 1998; Noels, 2003; Noels, Pelletier, Clément, & Vallerand, 2000; Pelletier, Séguin-Lévesque, & Legault, 2002). Canada's bilingual character makes second language learning a natural topic for Canadian researchers.

Self-Serving Judgments

In Chapter 3, we defined *self-serving judgments* as perceptions or comparisons that enhance the perceived worth of the self. We all want to believe that we are good people, and this desire colours many of our judgments (Gilovich, 1991; Tesser, 2000). Earlier in this chapter, we described downward social comparison, which is often motivated by self-enhancement and makes people feel good about themselves. In the present section, we provide additional examples of self-serving judgments about the self.

I'm Better than Average: Unrealistic Self-Evaluation. How do you think you compare to the average person on such dimensions as honesty, friendliness, and compassion? Would you say that you are above average? But perhaps we should restrict our comparisons to similar others, because you are, after all, a university or college student, which suggests that you may well be more talented than the average person in our society. Okay, let's think only about other similar students. How would you compare yourself to other students in terms of honesty, friendliness, and compassion? Would you say that you are above average?

If you are like most other people, you would rate yourself as above average on all of these dimensions. Almost all of us think that we are above average in our group, which, of course, is statistically impossible. Somebody must be below average! The range of traits on which self-serving evaluations have been obtained is very wide. Researchers have found that most of us rate ourselves as more honest, more fair, more loyal, more considerate, less lazy, less deceitful, more polite, and more capable than the average person (e.g., Alicke, 1985; Allison, Messick, & Goethals, 1989; Brown, 1986; Dunning, 1993; Dunning, Meyerowitz, & Holzberg, 1989; Goethals, Messick, & Allison, 1991; Kreuger, 1998; Van Lange & Sedikides, 1998). We also perceive ourselves as less persuasible than average by negative media communications such as advertising and political appeals, though we consider ourselves just as responsive as other people to positive communications such as health information (e.g., Brosius & Engel, 1996; Duck, Hogg, & Terry, 1998; Hoorens & Ruiter, 1996). Tom Gilovich (1991, p. 77) described a particularly interesting survey of 1 million high school seniors, which found that 70% of the respondents thought they were above average in leadership ability, and only 2% thought they were below average. On the dimension of ability to get along with others, 100% of the high school respondents thought they were above average, 60% thought they were in the top 10%, and 25% thought they were in the top 1%!

Let's take a final example. How do you honestly think you compare to other students in how much you engage in self-enhancing evaluations? Do you think that you engage in this bias less than the average student at your school? Most of us would probably answer this question affirmatively, providing an ironic illustration of the strength of the bias. In fact, Emily Pronin, Daniel Lin, and Lee Ross (2002) coined the term the **bias blind spot** to refer to the tendency for people to think that biases and errors in judgments are more common in others than in themselves (we have a "blind spot" when it comes to our own biases). In one study, Pronin and her colleagues described eight different cognitive and motivational biases to participants, including the correspondence bias and self-enhancing evaluations, and found that respondents reported greater tendencies toward bias by others than by the self on all eight biases.

bias blind spot
the tendency to think that biases and errors in judgments are more common in others than in ourselves

If we exaggerate the extent to which we are better than others, is it because we have inflated views of our own characteristics, or are we too critical of other people? Nicholas Epley and David Dunning (2000) at Cornell University explored this question by comparing people's responses with actual data. For example, participants in one study were given $5 for taking part in the experiment and were then asked how much of this $5 they would have been willing to donate to one of three charities (e.g., the American Red Cross) if they had been given this opportunity. Participants also predicted how much the average student at their university would give in such a situation. Participants' mean estimates were $2.44 for themselves and $1.83 for the average student. To assess the accuracy of these predictions, Epley and Dunning also ran a group of participants who were actually given the opportunity to donate money to the charities. The average actual donation was $1.53. These data suggest that the original participants had inflated views of their own generosity and more accurate views of other people (though still somewhat inflated).

My Future Is Better than Average: Unrealistic Optimism. Before continuing to read, try answering the questions in Know Yourself 4.1: "The Likelihood of Events for Yourself and Other Students." For each event listed, choose a percent between 0 and 100 to represent the likelihood that the event will happen to you and another percent to represent the likelihood that the event will happen to other students at your university or college. After you have completed the ratings, come back to this point and continue reading.

Know Yourself 4.1
The Likelihood of Events for Yourself and Other Students

What do you think is the likelihood that each of the following events will happen to you, and what is the likelihood that they will happen to other students at your university or college? Choose a percent between 0 and 100 to show the probability that the events will happen to you or to other students, where 0% would mean no chance at all, 50% would mean an equal chance that it will happen or it won't happen, and 100% would mean a sure thing.

	YOURSELF	OTHER STUDENTS
1. Having a heart attack	_____	_____
2. Being happy with your romantic or marital partner in later life	_____	_____
3. Being physically healthy in middle age	_____	_____
4. Being refused a bank loan	_____	_____
5. Having a mentally gifted child	_____	_____
6. Being killed in a car accident	_____	_____
7. Becoming alcoholic	_____	_____
8. Developing arthritis	_____	_____
9. Having your work recognized with an award	_____	_____
10. Becoming actively involved in a charitable organization	_____	_____

SCORING: Compare the likelihood ratings you gave to yourself and other students for positive events (2, 3, 5, 9, and 10). Did you tend to give yourself higher probabilities? Now compare the likelihood ratings you gave to yourself and other students for negative events (1, 4, 6, 7, and 8). Did you tend to give yourself lower probabilities? Return to the text for relevant discussion.

Most of us believe that we are more likely than average to experience positive events in our lives, an optimism that may often be unrealistic.

When people are asked to answer these sorts of questions, most show an optimistic bias: they estimate that they are *more* likely than average to experience *positive* events and *less* likely than average to experience *negative* events (e.g., Brinthaupt, Moreland, & Levine, 1991; Harris, 1996; Price, Pentecost, & Voth, 2002; Regan, Snyder, & Kassin, 1995; Weinstein, 1980, 1984; Weinstein & Klein, 1996). Did your responses correspond to this pattern? The optimistic bias appears to occur mainly in overestimating our chances of *common* positive events and underestimating our chances of *rare* negative events (see Kruger & Burrus, 2004).

Tara MacDonald of Queen's University and Michael Ross of the University of Waterloo (1999) asked Canadian students involved in a dating relationship to predict whether their relationship would be together at several points in the future, including six months and one year later (see Figure 4.7). Participants estimated a likelihood of 83% that they would be together in six months and 68% that they would be together in one year. The researchers also interviewed participants' roommates and parents, who provided lower estimates of the likelihood that participants' relationships would survive (approximately 10–20% lower). The researchers subsequently contacted the participants six months and one year later, and found that the *actual* survival rates for the relationships were 61% at six months and 48% at one year. Thus, the students were more unrealistically optimistic about the stability of their relationship than were their roommates or their parents.

Why are we unrealistically optimistic about our future? One possible factor is a motivational one: we *want* our futures to be rosy and are threatened by the possibility of negative life events (Sherman & Cohen, 2002; Sherman, Nelson, & Steele, 2000). Therefore, we convince ourselves that good things are in store for us. A second possibility is we think that we *deserve* positive outcomes because we are, after all, good people (this possibility draws a connection between unrealistic self-evaluation and unrealistic optimism). Most of us believe that the world is, in general, a fair and just place, where good things happen to good people and bad things happen to bad people (see Lerner, 1980; Montada & Lerner, 1998). Because we are good people, good things will happen to us. A third possibility is that we are aware of factors that might reduce our own risk for certain problems (e.g., we do not smoke, we exercise at least occasionally), but we do not realize that many other people also possess these risk-reducing features (Weinstein, 1980). Predictions for our own outcomes relative to others' outcomes, therefore, tend to be too optimistic.

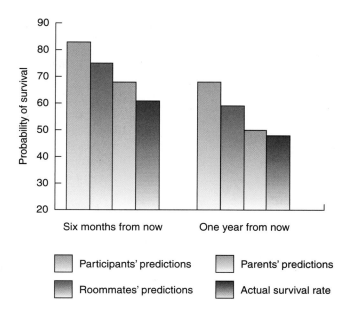

FIGURE 4.7 Predicted likelihood of survival of relationship in six months and one year

From MacDonald and Ross, "Assessing the accuracy of predictions about dating relationships: How and why do lovers' predictions differ from those made by observers?" *Personality and Social Psychology Bulletin*, 25, 1417–1429, Table 2, p. 1422, 1999. Reprinted by permission of Sage Publications.

Are Unrealistic Self-Evaluation and Unrealistic Optimism Adaptive or Maladaptive? Accurate perceptions of the self would seem to be adaptive. Accurate perceptions should facilitate successful prediction of our own outcomes and of others' behaviour toward us. The more accurately we see ourselves, the more effectively we should be able to deal with the world. Also, if we are too optimistic about the future, we may fail to perform preventive health behaviours. From this perspective, unrealistically positive self-evaluations and unrealistically optimistic predictions for the future would be expected to be maladaptive (see Radcliffe & Klein, 2002).

What do you think? Do you think that it is a bad thing for people to have an overly positive view of themselves? Can you see any potential benefits of self-enhancement?

Some theorists have proposed that self-enhancement can be adaptive. Shelley Taylor and Jonathon Brown (1988, 1994) argued that self-enhancement is associated with mental well-being. These researchers proposed that "positive illusions" about the self are associated with contentment, high self-esteem, creativity, high effort, persistence at tasks, and coping effectively with stressful events (see also Oettingen & Mayer, 2002). Many findings are consistent with this view. Canadians Sandra Murray and John Holmes (1997) at the University of Waterloo found that people in a dating relationship who were very optimistic about the stability of the relationship and who idealized their partner (i.e., who rated their partner more positively than they rated the typical partner) were more likely to remain in that relationship than less optimistic individuals. Perhaps the positive impressions of their partner protected against conflicts and doubts that damaged other relationships. Studies have also linked self-enhancement to better coping with serious illness (e.g., Helgeson & Taylor, 1993), better coping with stressful life events such as the death of a spouse (e.g., Bonanno, Field, Kovacevic, & Kaltman, 2002), and success in achievement settings (see Sternberg & Kolligan, 1990).

Other researchers have argued that self-enhancement is not always, or even not usually, adaptive. Instead, these theorists have argued that excessive self-enhancers will be seen as arrogant and selfish (Colvin & Block, 1994; Colvin, Block, & Funder, 1995; Paulhus, 1998). Why would self-enhancement lead to negative impressions of the individual? One possibility is that the negative impressions are caused by unrelenting self-promotion (e.g., bragging), which becomes tiresome over time. It has also been suggested that narcissism (excessive self-admiration) interferes with the establishment of meaningful social relationships with others; people who are overly fond of themselves may fail to make others feel valued and respected.

Nevertheless, greater self-enhancement has been shown to be associated with numerous positive states, including higher self-esteem, lower depression, and greater perceived purpose in life (e.g., Taylor, Kemeny, Reed, Bower, & Gruenewald, 2000; Taylor, Lerner, Sherman, Sage, & McDowell, 2003a). There is even evidence that self-serving tendencies are positively correlated with some biological signs of well-being, including lower cardiovascular responses to stress, more rapid cardiovascular recovery from stress, and lower baseline levels of cortisol—a steroid hormone associated with high chronic levels of stress (Taylor, Lerner, Sherman, Sage, & McDowell, 2003b). It seems likely that at least moderate self-enhancement is beneficial without having negative consequences such as being seen as arrogant and self-absorbed.

Cultural Differences in Self-Serving Judgments

All of the research on self-serving judgments that we have described to this point was based on North American samples. There are reasons to believe, however, that the tendency toward self-enhancement may differ across cultures.

Cultural Differences in Unrealistic Self-Evaluation.
University of British Columbia social psychologists Steve Heine and Darrin Lehman (1997b) proposed that data showing excessively positive self-evaluation by North American students reflected the fact that Western society "encourages people to think positively about themselves as a means to approach the culturally defined ideals of independence and autonomy" (p. 1269). They argued that, in contrast, people from collectivist cultures are encouraged to gain a sense of belongingness, which is not achieved by perceiving the self as better than other people.

Interviewer: "I see that you designed a computer program for academic advising. Can you tell me what you did to develop that program?"

Job candidate: "Not really so much. I could see that much of advising is based on rules, so I only needed to write a program simple enough for advisors to use. It was not that hard."

To test the prediction that unrealistic self-evaluation is absent or weaker in collectivist cultures, Heine and Lehman (1997b) collected data from university students in Canada and Japan. On one task, participants were asked to estimate the percentage of the population of the same age and gender as themselves who were better than they on ten desirable traits, five of which were selected to be "independent" or "individualistic" in nature (attractive, interesting, independent, confident, and intelligent) and five of which were selected to be "interdependent" or "collectivistic" in nature (cooperative, loyal, considerate, hardworking, and dependable). Participants were also asked to identify the member of their own family to whom they "felt closest." They then estimated the percentage of the population of the same age and gender as their family member who were better than this family member on each of the ten traits. These judgments about a family member were included as another test of self-enhancement, because believing that one's family members are better than average should make people feel good about themselves as well.

The researchers calculated the percentages of the matched population that participants believed were better than they (or their family member) on the five independent traits and on the five interdependent traits. Estimates would be expected to hover around 50% if people were making unbiased judgments. Estimates substantially smaller than 50% would suggest unrealistically positive self-evaluations—relatively few people are better than you (or your family member).

Figure 4.8 presents the average estimates for Canadian and Japanese participants on the four principal measures. Notice that the Canadian respondents showed biased self-evaluations on *all* of the judgments: both self and family member on both independent and interdependent traits, with an average of approximately 25% of the population estimated to be better than the self or family member. In contrast, Japanese respondents gave higher (more modest) estimates on all of the items, with an average of approximately 40% of the population estimated to be better than the self or family member. For judgments about the self, Japanese participants showed almost no unrealistic self-evaluation at all, with their estimates coming quite close to 50%. For judgments about their family member, Japanese participants did show some positive enhancement, but less than was exhibited by Canadian respondents. It is interesting that even on *interdependent* traits, Japanese respondents showed less self-evaluative bias than Canadian respondents. Given that interdependent traits are highly valued in collectivist cultures, a positive bias by Japanese respondents might be expected, but this did not occur.

A different pattern of findings was obtained, however, by Constantine Sedikides, Lowell Gaertner, and Yoshiyasu Toguchi (2003). These researchers asked American and Japanese university students to rate themselves on a number of desirable personality traits, compared to the typical member of their group. Some traits were individualistic (e.g., independent, original) and others were collectivistic (e.g., respectful, good listener). Figure 4.9 depicts the findings. Both cultural groups self-enhanced (rated themselves as significantly higher than the average member of their group) on both kinds of traits. American students self-enhanced more than Japanese students on the individualistic traits, whereas Japanese students self-enhanced more than American students on the collectivistic traits. Thus, both American and Japanese respondents showed self-enhancement, especially on the traits that were most valued in their culture.

What are we to conclude from these conflicting results? Clearly, the issue is not settled. On balance, however, it seems likely that members of collectivist cultures engage in *less* unrealistic self-evaluation than do members of individualist cultures, but they still self-enhance to some degree (see also Kitayama & Uchida, 2003). Also, there may be some collectivist cultures whose self-evaluations are very similar to those in individualist cultures (e.g., see Kurman, 2001).

Cultural Differences in Unrealistic Optimism. Steve Heine and Darrin Lehman (1995) also suggested that members of collectivist cultures might not show unrealistic optimism about their future because they do not

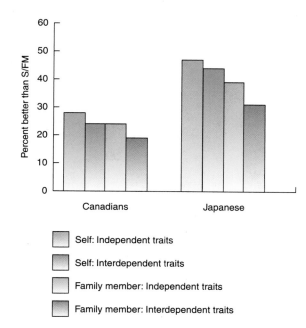

FIGURE 4.8 Estimated percent of matched population who are better than self or family member

From Heine and Lehman, "The cultural construction of self-enhancement: An examination of group-serving biases," *Journal of Personality and Social Psychology*, 72, 1268–1283, Table 1, p. 1272, 1997. Copyright © 1997 by the American Psychological Association. Reprinted by permission.

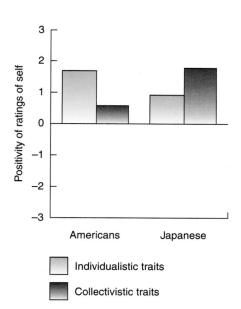

FIGURE 4.9 Ratings of self versus typical group member on desirable personality traits

From Sedikides et al., "Pancultural self-enhancement," *Journal of Personality and Social Psychology*, 84, 60–79, Table 3, p. 66, 2003. Copyright © 2003 by the American Psychological Association. Reprinted by permission.

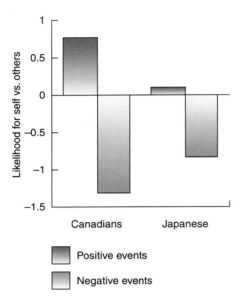

FIGURE 4.10 Predicted likelihood of positive and negative events for self versus others

From Heine and Lehman, "Cultural variation in unrealistic optimism: Does the West feel more invulnerable than the East?" *Journal of Personality and Social Psychology*, 68, 595–607, Table 1, p. 599, 1995. Copyright © 1995 by the American Psychological Association. Reprinted by permission.

want to isolate themselves from others in their culture by perceiving themselves and their futures much more favourably than average.

To test this reasoning, Heine and Lehman (1995) recruited Canadian and Japanese university students and asked them to estimate the likelihood that they would experience a variety of positive and negative life events. They were specifically asked, "Compared to other university students of the same sex as you, what do you think are the chances that the following events will happen to you?" Possible answers ranged from –3 (much below average) to 0 (average for other university students of your sex) to +3 (much above average). The events that people estimated included five positive events, such as "You will live past the age of 80" and "Sometime in the future you will own your own home," and ten negative events, such as "Sometime in the future you will become an alcoholic" and "You will have a heart attack before the age of 50."

For the positive events, positive scores reflected optimism (more likely to happen to self), whereas for the negative events, negative scores reflected optimism (less likely to happen to self). Answers close to 0 constituted unbiased estimates. Figure 4.10 presents the mean likelihood ratings for Canadian and Japanese respondents. The results showed that Canadian participants were unrealistically optimistic about both positive and negative events. Japanese participants, on the other hand, showed no optimistic bias for positive events, and a weaker optimistic bias for negative events than did Canadian respondents. Thus, participants from a collectivist culture showed less unrealistic optimism than did participants from an individualist culture, as the researchers had predicted.

These and other data (see also Chang & Asakawa, 2003; Chang, Asakawa, & Sanna, 2001) have indicated that members of collectivist cultures exhibit weaker optimistic biases than do members of individualist cultures. These differences are consistent with the reduced tendency for unrealistic self-evaluation outlined in the previous section. Presumably, the interdependent self that is fostered in collectivist cultures minimizes perceived differences between the self and others, even in predictions for the future (see also Cohen & Hoshino-Browne, 2005).

Members of *collectivist cultures*, such as these Chinese students, tend to show less positive self-evaluations and less optimism about their future than do members of *individualist cultures*, such as North American students.

I Think I Can: Self-Efficacy in Everyday Life

Have you ever had the sinking feeling that you would probably *not* be able to do something that you were supposed to do (or something that you wanted to do)? Perhaps you avoided your textbook readings for a course until the day before the exam and then realized that there was no way you'd be able to read all of the chapters carefully. Or perhaps, in a moment of enthusiasm on New Year's Eve, you publicly resolved that you would start exercising regularly, but the next morning you were not at all confident that your exercise commitment would last very long. Each of these situations involves the belief that you are not capable of performing particular behaviours (reading all chapters carefully, exercising regularly). Now an important question: How would your belief affect your actual behaviour? Would you try even harder to succeed? Or, instead, would you give up quickly and stop trying?

Albert Bandura (1977, 1991), a Canadian who is a social psychology professor at Stanford University, proposed that feelings of **self-efficacy** are very important determinants of whether people achieve goals that they have set for themselves. Self-efficacy refers to the belief that you are capable of performing a particular behaviour that is required for a particular goal. Bandura argued that when people doubt that they can perform a behaviour, they are less likely to attempt it and are less likely to persist in the face of obstacles or failure. Bandura, therefore, would predict that you would quickly give up in the situations described above. You would try to read some of the textbook chapters carefully but quit when you began to feel confused; you would exercise once or twice but then stop as soon as you found it slightly inconvenient to continue. Note that these decisions to stop would occur in response to events that virtually everyone would experience in the situations. *Everyone* feels confused when initially trying to read a large number of chapters; exercise will *inevitably* be inconvenient sometimes. Thus, the lack of self-efficacy almost guarantees that the goal will not be achieved.

self-efficacy
the belief that we are capable of performing a particular behaviour that is required for a certain goal

High self-efficacy, relative to low, has been shown in many studies to predict both undertaking a behaviour and continuing a behaviour despite negative feedback (see Bandura, 1986; Mischel, Cantor, & Feldman, 1996). If you are confident that you will be able to perform the necessary things to do well in a math course, such as reading and understanding the textbook, completing assignments successfully, and solving questions on exams, then you are more likely to enroll in the course and more likely to stay in the course even if an early test goes poorly than if you lack such confidence. When we have high self-efficacy, we interpret problems and failures as temporary and correctable—after all, we believe that we are capable of performing the necessary behaviours. This perception that failure can be overcome is associated with increased effort and persistence (e.g., Dweck, 1986; Dweck & Leggett, 1988; Oettingen & Mayer, 2002).

The concept of self-efficacy has also been applied to understanding why some people cope with adversity better than do others. When people feel confident that they can perform actions that are necessary for coping, they show better adjustment to such stressors as the pain of rheumatoid arthritis, coping with abortion, and adjusting to new parenthood (e.g., Cozzarelli, 1993; Cutrona & Troutman, 1986; Major, Cozzarelli, Sciacchitano, Cooper, Testa, & Mueller, 1990; Schiaffino & Revenson, 1992).

Illusions of Control? Self-efficacy is a form of control: people believe that they can perform an action successfully. In general, people are motivated to believe that they have control over their environment. What about you? Do you feel that you have control over your outcomes in most situations? An absence of control would clearly be undesirable, because then you might not be able to obtain necessary resources and avoid negative events.

Given that we want to see ourselves as having control, it may not be surprising to learn that we often think we have *more* control than we really do. There is a general tendency for people to overestimate their control of situations and events. This **illusion of control** has been documented by several researchers (see Crocker, 1981; Langer, 1975; Taylor & Brown, 1988). A good example of the illusion of control is superstitious beliefs. Many people believe that certain rituals are associated with better outcomes (e.g., wearing your "lucky socks" when you play baseball). In reality, these superstitious beliefs are erroneous (except, perhaps, your lucky socks) and reflect, at least in part, our desire to perceive ourselves as in control. Another example of the illusion of control occurs in gambling behaviour. Gamblers often believe that they can control chance events, such as predicting the next card in a sequence, pulling a winning outcome on a slot machine, or selecting a series of numbers on a lottery ticket (see Langer, 1977). As the availability of gambling has increased over the past 15 years in Canada, it has become an increasingly serious social problem. The fallacy that gamblers have control over chance events explains, in part, the lure of gambling.

illusion of control
the tendency to overestimate our control of situations and events

We noted earlier that theorists have argued about whether self-enhancement is associated with better or worse functioning (e.g., Colvin & Block, 1994; Taylor & Brown, 1988). Illusions of control are another form of self-enhancing response that could potentially have either adaptive or maladaptive consequences. Perceived control might be adaptive because believing that one has control will encourage persistence at an activity: we may try again if we did not initially succeed. Indeed, when people believe that they have no control over events in their life, they often show symptoms of **learned helplessness**: a state of apathy, in which people simply give up trying to achieve their goals because they believe they lack control (Seligman, 1975). Learned helplessness is one possible cause of depression (Abramson, Metalsky, & Alloy, 1989).

On the other hand, it is probably maladaptive to keep attempting behaviours that are completely beyond our control. Believing that we have control when we do not may lead to repeated failure. University of Toronto social psychologists Janet Polivy and Peter Herman (2002) coined the term **false hope syndrome** to refer to cases in which individuals repeatedly try and fail to achieve a goal (e.g., losing weight, stopping smoking) because they have unrealistic expectations about their likelihood of success. This syndrome is described in the accompanying box, "Social Psychology in Your Life: The False Hope Syndrome."

learned helplessness

a state of apathy in which we simply give up trying to achieve our goals

false hope syndrome

the tendency to try repeatedly but unsuccessfully to achieve a goal because of unrealistic expectations about the likelihood of success

Self-Perception in the Health Domain: Self-Discrepancy Theory

Do you ever think about characteristics that you *wish* you had? Perhaps you wish that you were more extraverted, or that you were better in math, or that you could sing. We already know from Chapter 3 that these thoughts qualify as *counterfactual thoughts* because they refer to how things could have been different. In the present context, these thoughts are important because they refer to an alternative conception of yourself: the way that you would ideally like to be. How does it make you feel when you think about the features that you would like to possess but do not?

Let's take another perspective on the self. Are there qualities that you think you *ought* to possess but do not? These characteristics are things that you *should* do or be. Perhaps you think that you should be less selfish, or that you should work harder, or that you should exercise more often. These features represent yet another alternative conception of yourself: the way you think you ought to be. How does it make you feel when you think about the features that you ought to possess but do not? Are these feelings different from the ones you imagined in the preceding paragraph?

Actual, Ideal, and Ought Selves. Psychologists have recognized for a long time that people have multiple conceptions of themselves (e.g., Cooley, 1902; James, 1890). The most frequently discussed self-conceptions have been the **actual self,** how people believe they really are, and the **ideal self,** how people would ideally like themselves to be (e.g., Colby, 1968; Rogers, 1961). Theorists have predicted that when the actual and ideal selves differ substantially, people will have low self-esteem.

Canadian social psychologist Tory Higgins (1987, 1989) was a professor at the University of Western Ontario and is now at Columbia University. Higgins was awarded the career achievement award in 2005 by the Society for Experimental Social Psychology, which is the most prestigious scientific organization in social psychology. Higgins agreed with previous theorists that the actual and ideal selves are important but added another self-conception to the mix: the **ought self,** how people think they should or ought to be (see also Ausubel, 1955; Schafer, 1967). The ought

ideal self

a conception of the self describing our perception of how we would ideally like to be

actual self

a conception of the self describing our perception of how we really are

ought self

a conception of the self describing our perception of how we think we should or ought to be

Social Psychology in Your Life   *The False Hope Syndrome*

Do you make New Year's resolutions? Most adults do. How successful have you been in keeping your resolutions? If you're like most people, you haven't done very well. In fact, you may have failed numerous times with the same resolution. James Prochaska, Carlo DiClemente, and John Norcross (1992) reported that, on average, people make the same pledge for five or more years before they manage to keep their resolution for six months. Also, approximately 60% of those who break their resolution will make the same one again the next year.

Why do we so often fail to keep our resolutions? Janet Polivy and Peter Herman (2002) suggested that most of us have unrealistic expectations about our ability to change our behaviour (in general, not only at New Year's), which produce what they termed the *false hope syndrome.* This syndrome involves exaggerated feelings of control and overconfidence about our ability to change our behaviour successfully. We often begin with an unrealistic goal (e.g., "I will exercise for two hours every day!"). We also underestimate how difficult it will be to change our behaviour (e.g., "I'll have no trouble stopping smoking!"). Finally, we tend to expect dramatic, rapid results (e.g., "I'll probably lose about five kilograms a week!"). Given these erroneous expectations, it is not surprising that we usually fail. When the new behaviour proves to be more difficult than we

anticipated, and when visible results turn out to be slow, we often abandon our attempt to change.

But why doesn't the false hope syndrome disappear? Why do we *keep* trying again and again to achieve the same goals? Why don't we learn from our failures and direct our energies elsewhere? (This may remind you of the *planning fallacy,* discussed in Chapter 3, where people's tendency to underestimate the time it will take to complete a task does not seem to weaken with experience.) Polivy and Herman argued that we often explain our failures in ways that maintain false hope for the future. For instance, we often blame ourselves for not trying hard enough (e.g., "If only I try a bit harder next time, I'm sure I'll succeed"). We may also blame external circumstances for our failure and decide that these circumstance are unlikely to occur again (e.g., "I won't be as busy next year as I have been this year, so I'll have more time to exercise"). Thus, we remain hopeful—often unrealistically hopeful—that we'll succeed in our next attempt. We convince ourselves that *this* diet will be easier to follow than the Atkins diet, or *this* method for quitting smoking will be more effective than going cold turkey, or *this* kind of exercise will be less boring than using a stationary bicycle. Unfortunately, the new strategy

People often make the same resolution year after year to change their behaviour despite previous failures, which might reflect the false hope syndrome.

is often no easier, no more effective, or no less boring than the last one, and we fail again.

Polivy and Herman (2002) did not argue that we should give up attempting self-improvement. Rather, they suggested that we adopt realistic goals (thereby avoiding overly ambitious plans) and recognize that success will be difficult. If we understand that changing our behaviour will be challenging and results may be slow, we are less likely to become discouraged quickly and more likely to structure our environment to encourage our new lifestyle (e.g., by convincing another person to join us or help us). The key is to recognize false hopes and work to replace them with realistic determination.

self is similar to the notion of a conscience. Higgins integrated these ideas in his **self-discrepancy theory,** which hypothesized that perceived discrepancies between the actual self and either the ideal self or the ought self have important (and different) consequences.

Before we discuss the consequences of self-discrepancies, let's describe how the different selves can be measured. In one procedure, participants are asked to list up to ten attributes that they think they *actually* possess, up to ten attributes that they

self-discrepancy theory
a theory proposing that perceived differences between the actual self, the ideal self, and the ought self produce emotional consequences

would like *ideally* to possess, and up to ten attributes that they believe they *should* or *ought* to possess. Participants are told that they can use the same or different attributes in more than one category. The researcher then compares participants' responses to the different selves. If attributes listed for the actual self and the ideal or ought self are similar, then discrepancy scores are low. If attributes listed for the actual self are opposite from attributes listed for the ideal or ought self, then discrepancy scores are high. The scores can be conceptualized as representing the extent to which people believe that they have failed to measure up to what they would ideally like to be or to how they think they ought to be.

Implications for Depression and Anxiety. We asked you to reflect on how you feel when you think about characteristics that you would like to possess but do not and when you think about characteristics that you ought to possess but do not. Did you imagine that the feelings were different? In self-discrepancy theory, Higgins predicted that the two kinds of discrepancies have very different emotional consequences, and empirical tests have supported his predictions (e.g., Higgins, Bond, Klein, & Strauman, 1986; Higgins, Klein, & Strauman, 1985).

Higgins proposed that when we fail to achieve our ideals (the things we want to be), we experience negative emotion along a *dejection* dimension. He suggested that this situation is psychologically experienced as the absence of positive things: we do not possess things that we want to possess. We therefore feel unhappy, disappointed, sad, and depressed (negative dejection emotions). In contrast, Higgins proposed that when we fail to live up to our ought self (the things we should be, our conscience), we experience negative emotion along an *agitation* dimension. He suggested that this situation is psychologically experienced as the presence of negative things: we believe that we have behaved inappropriately and are worried that we may be punished or criticized. We therefore feel anxious, guilty, nervous, and ashamed (negative agitation emotions). Thus, discrepancy between the actual and ideal selves is expected to produce depression, whereas discrepancy between the actual and ought selves is expected to produce anxiety. The key elements of self-discrepancy theory are summarized in the accompanying Concept Review.

The most frequent psychological complaints reported to clinical psychologists and psychiatrists are depression and anxiety. Depression and anxiety are extremely common problems, which are experienced by most of us sometime during our lifetime. Higgins's work on self-discrepancy theory links a particular pattern of self-perceptions to each of these two states. He proposed that failure to reach our ideals can lead to

CONCEPT REVIEW
Self-Discrepancy Theory

Concept	Description	Example	Consequences of Discrepancies
Actual self	How we believe we actually are	I am intelligent.	
Ideal self	How we would ideally like to be	I would like to be a good singer.	
Ought self	How we think we should or ought to be	I should attend a religious service at least once a week.	
Discrepancy between actual and ideal selves	Failing to achieve our ideals	I will never be a good singer.	Depression and sadness
Discrepancy between actual and ought selves	Failing to fulfill our obligations	I almost never attend a religious service.	Anxiety and guilt

depression, whereas failure to live up to our obligations can lead to anxiety. This reasoning provides possible clues to clinical psychologists about where they might focus their treatment of these common problems.

 ## What Others See in Us

Do you often think about the fact that other people make judgments about *you*? Do you wonder what sort of impression you make on people you meet for the first time? Do you sometimes try to *create* a certain impression?

In this section, we consider some of these issues. We describe how people present themselves publicly, especially to achieve the goals of appearing likable and competent. We also discuss a potentially maladaptive strategy that people sometimes use to give themselves an excuse for failure.

All the World's a Stage: Managing Others' Impressions

Professional actors deliberately portray roles they are given. They make themselves appear angry, happy, or depressed, depending on the character and the setting they are depicting. There is skill and artistry in the acting trade.

Does your life sometimes feel like it is on a stage? Are you an actor portraying your life in a certain manner? Or, instead, is your public life always fully spontaneous and "honest"? Sociologists and social psychologists have suggested that most of us fall in between these extremes: we do not always monitor our behaviour and try to make a particular impression, but neither do we always behave in an open, unrestrained fashion. We are selective actors; when it is important, we adopt deliberate guises to achieve particular goals.

Erving Goffman, a Canadian citizen who obtained his undergraduate degree at the University of Toronto, was an eminent sociologist. Goffman (1959, 1967) coined the term **impression management** to refer to the deliberate control of one's public behaviour to create a certain impression in others' minds. Another term for impression management is **self-presentation:** people "present" the self to others (Baumeister, 1982, 1998; Leary, 1995; Schlenker, 1980). All of us engage in self-presentation in many different settings with many different people.

How can a researcher show that someone is engaging in self-presentation? People are unlikely to admit that they are trying to manage someone's impression of them, so evidence must be obtained in an indirect way. The most common strategy for testing self-presentation predictions has been to compare situations in which people's behaviour is public with situations in which their behaviour is private. If public behaviour differs from private behaviour, then individuals are modifying their actions because someone can observe them, which constitutes self-presentation (Baumeister, 1982; Leary, 1995). For example, Kay Satow (1975) showed that public donations to charities were larger than private donations, presumably because people were trying to appear generous in the public condition (see also Olson, Hafer, Couzens, & Kramins, 2000).

Think about your own public behaviour. Do you ever act differently when other people can see you? Do you express somewhat different attitudes to different people? If so (and almost all of us do), then your public behaviour sometimes reflects impression management.

Self-Presentation Goals. Think about the times that you have tried to make a certain impression on someone. What were your goals? Can you think of an occasion when you wanted to appear dangerous or strong so others would be afraid of you

impression management
the deliberate control of one's public behaviour to create a certain impression

self-presentation
impression management

(e.g., to intimidate members of an opposing sports team)? Can you think of another time when you wanted someone to think you were moral and virtuous (e.g., to impress your imam, priest, or rabbi)?

Although appearing dangerous or virtuous can serve as self-presentation goals in some circumstances, Ned Jones at Princeton University (the same person who identified the correspondence bias) and Thane Pittman at Gettysburg College (1982) proposed that two other goals are more common. Indeed, Jones and Pittman argued that these two goals are operative almost *all* of the time—they are so basic that they are virtually "automatic" parts of our public personae. The two self-presentation goals are to appear *likable* and to appear *competent*.

ingratiation

behaviour designed to make someone like us

Ingratiation is behaviour that is designed to make someone like us. What actions are common examples of ingratiation? Flattery is one; friendliness is another; giving gifts and doing favours are still others. Jones and Pittman suggested that we almost always want to appear likable, so our public behaviour follows certain rules without our even thinking about it. For example, we are polite to everyone, unless there is pre-existing dislike or a conflict of interest between us and another person. Our public face is almost always happy, friendly, and relaxed; we want to appear well adjusted and comfortable with ourselves and others (even when we may not *feel* comfortable).

Ingratiation has some risks, because other people may know that we want them to like us. Excessive flattery and syrupy friendliness can elicit suspicion, which can actually lead to less rather than more liking (Jones & Wortman, 1973). When you walk into a store and a salesperson walks up and greets you warmly, do you believe that he or she really likes you a lot? Probably not. This risk of appearing false is particularly great when we are highly dependent on someone, because the person will be more aware that we might be trying to evoke liking. Imagine that you have a part-time job at a grocery store. It is more important for you to get your boss to like you than it is to get a co-worker to like you. Unfortunately, flattering your boss is more likely to be suspected than flattering your co-worker. Ironically, then, when ingratiation is most important (because we are highly dependent on someone), it is most likely to arouse suspicion. Fortunately, most people like being flattered or receiving gifts, so they are often quite willing to overlook the possibility that our friendly behaviour is based on ulterior motives (see Vonk, 2002).

self-promotion

behaviour designed to make someone respect us

Self-promotion is behaviour that is designed to make someone respect you. What actions exemplify self-promotion? Bragging is an obvious example, but it can elicit negative reactions. What can you do besides boasting if you want to look competent? *Performing well* is a good start! Showing effort also engenders respect, and self-confidence is helpful as well. Jones and Pittman proposed that, similar to likability, we virtually always want to be seen as competent. As a result, we automatically try to appear intelligent, motivated, and competent.

Job interviews are a wonderful place to investigate self-promotion because candidates are trying very hard to look competent. Researchers who have studied job interviews have found that self-promotion strategies generally do increase the perceived competence of the candidate (e.g., Kacmar, Delery, & Ferris, 1992; Stevens & Kristof, 1995). Self-promotion can also have the unintended effect, however, of reducing liking, especially for female candidates (Rudman, 1998). Why would women be particularly vulnerable to this unintended effect of reduced liking? Perhaps because frankly stating one's accomplishments is inconsistent with the stereotypical expectation that women will be modest (Miller, Cooke, Tsang, & Morgan, 1992).

Candidates in job interviews try to appear competent, which is a form of *self-presentation* known as *self-promotion*.

Self-Handicapping: Setting Yourself Up for Failure

Imagine that you report for an experiment and are given a test of analogical reasoning, which requires you to select the correct answer for questions like "Puppy is to dog as _____ is to cow," with the possible answers being *meat, milk, calf,* and *bull* (the correct answer is *calf*). For almost all of the items, however, you cannot identify any response that makes sense, so you end up just guessing. You give your response sheet to the experimenter and wait for the bad news while he scores it in another room. To your considerable surprise, when the experimenter returns, he congratulates you on your outstanding performance and says that your score is one of the best he has seen. You can only conclude that you were lucky enough to guess right on a lot of the items.

Now comes the interesting part. The experimenter says that you will be taking another test of analogical reasoning because he is studying the effects of drugs on performance. You will therefore ingest a drug and take another test. The experimenter says he does not care which specific drug you take, so you can select between two drugs: *pandocrin* and *actavil*. One of the drugs is expected to improve performance on analogical reasoning, and the other is expected to impair or worsen performance. You can choose whichever one you like.

Which drug would you choose? The one that is expected to improve your performance or the one that is expected to worsen your performance? Why?

When Steven Berglas and Ned Jones (yes, the same person who studied the correspondence bias and self-presentation motives) conducted a study that used a similar procedure at Duke University (Berglas & Jones, 1978), most participants chose the drug that was expected to *hurt* their performance—the drug that would actually increase their chances of performing *poorly*. Why did this pattern occur? The authors suggested that participants were worried that they would not perform well on the next test (because they were just lucky on the first test) and wanted to give themselves an *excuse* for doing badly. By taking the performance-impairing drug, participants could blame their poor performance on the drug rather than on their lack of analogical reasoning skill.

This tendency to seek or create inhibitory factors that interfere with performance and thus provide an explanation for potential failure has been termed **self-handicapping** (Higgins, Snyder, & Berglas, 1990; Jones & Berglas, 1978). This strategy involves deliberately doing something that can hurt performance so that failure will not imply low ability. Self-handicapping is often employed in the service of protecting the public appearance of competence and represents a clear example of self-presentation (Arkin & Baumgardner, 1985; Rhodewalt, 1990).

self-handicapping
the tendency to seek, create, or claim inhibitory factors that interfere with performance and thus provide an explanation for potential failure

It is assumed that people self-handicap because they lack confidence that they can perform well on a task or test and want to have an excuse for the feared failure. Jeff Schimel at the University of Alberta and his colleagues have shown that increasing people's feelings of intrinsic self-worth makes them less defensive, including reduced self-handicapping (Arndt, Schimel, Greenberg, & Pyszczynski, 2002; Schimel, Arndt, Pyszczynski, & Greenberg, 2001).

Can you think of methods of self-handicapping that you have used or that you have seen others use? One technique is simply not preparing—not studying for a test or not practising a task. If people know that Rachel was out late at a movie and did not study before a math test, they will not necessarily infer from poor performance that she is poor at math (although they might draw *other* negative inferences about her, such as being unmotivated—see Luginbuhl & Palmer, 1991; Rhodewalt, Sanbonmatsu, Tschanz, Feick, & Waller, 1995). Another possibility is taking on an obstacle that must be overcome. If a boy is worried that he might lose a one-on-one game of basketball to a girl, he might say "I'll play you with one hand held behind my back!" If he loses this game, it does not mean that the girl is better at basketball—after all, he had one hand behind his back. And if he happens to win, he will look *really* good. A third possible self-handicapping strategy is to simply *claim* that you did not prepare, or that you are sick, or that you have been under

Drinking heavily the night before an exam might reflect *self-handicapping*.

a lot of stress. These claimed impediments provide you with an excuse that, depending on the situation, can be effective in protecting your public image of competence (e.g., Leary & Shepperd, 1986; Smith, Snyder, & Perkins, 1983). The first two methods of self-handicapping (not preparing and taking on an obstacle) have been termed *behavioural* self-handicapping because they involve actually creating impediments to performance, whereas the third method has been called *self-reported* self-handicapping because it involves simply claiming that an impediment was present (Arkin & Baumgardner, 1985; Leary & Shepperd, 1986).

It may seem as though self-handicapping has no downside. If people fail, it doesn't reflect badly on them, and if they succeed, they look great. But behavioural self-handicapping does have a downside, a *big* downside: it increases the actual likelihood of poor performance (e.g., Rhodewalt & Fairfield, 1991; Tice & Baumeister, 1990). By failing to study for a test, for example, individuals might directly cause their own failure, which might *not* have occurred if they had studied; thus, the individuals generated an excuse for failure, but no excuse would have been necessary if the excuse hadn't been generated! (Whew. Did you follow that?) To put it another way, if people think that they might need an excuse for failure and take steps to create such an excuse, they might *cause* the very failure that they fear.

Researchers, including Leslie Janes at Brescia University College in London, Ontario, have uncovered a gender difference in self-handicapping: men are more likely to *behaviourally* self-handicap (i.e., take on actual impediments) than are women (see Hirt, Deppe, & Gordon, 1991; Hirt, McCrea, & Kimble, 2000; Janes, 2003). The two sexes engage in *self-reported* self-handicapping about equally. Why do men engage in behavioural self-handicapping more than women? One possibility is that men are more threatened by potential failure than are women, which makes them more willing to risk damaging their own performance. A second possibility is that women know that self-handicapping is ineffective for them because observers tend to attribute women's failures to lack of ability even when external impediments are present (e.g., Dweck, Goetz, & Strauss, 1980; Hirt et al., 1991). If self-handicapping is unlikely to work for women in the first place, then there is little reason to absorb the real costs of taking on an impediment.

Individual Differences in the Tendency to Engage in Self-Handicapping.
In addition to a gender difference in self-handicapping, there are differences between individuals in their general tendency to engage in this behaviour. That is, some people self-handicap more often than do other people. Ned Jones and Frederick Rhodewalt (1982) at Princeton University developed the **self-handicapping scale** to measure this tendency. Sample items from the scale are presented in Know Yourself 4.2: "The Self-Handicapping Scale." Answer the items to see whether you tend to score high or low on this dimension.

Researchers have found that scores on this scale predict whether people will actually engage in self-handicapping behaviour in experimental settings (for a review, see Rhodewalt, 1990). High scorers are more likely than low scorers to take on handicaps that provide excuses for poor performance.

Most research on self-handicapping has focused on university students or older adults. In a paper published in 2000, however, Sonia Greaven and Darcy Santor of Dalhousie University in Halifax, together with Richard Thompson and David Zuroff of McGill University in Montreal, examined self-handicapping among adolescents. Boys and girls aged 12 to 15 were asked to complete a modified version of the Self-Handicapping Scale (a few items were altered to make them more age appropriate),

self-handicapping scale

a scale that measures how often people engage in self-handicapping behaviour

Know Yourself 4.2
The Self-Handicapping Scale

Please indicate the extent to which you agree or disagree with each of the following statements by circling the appropriate number on the answer scale.

1. When I do something wrong, my first impulse is to blame the circumstances.

0	1	2	3	4	5
Disagree very much	Disagree pretty much	Disagree a little	Agree a little	Agree pretty much	Agree very much

2. I tend to put things off to the last moment.

0	1	2	3	4	5
Disagree very much	Disagree pretty much	Disagree a little	Agree a little	Agree pretty much	Agree very much

3. I always try to do my best, no matter what.

0	1	2	3	4	5
Disagree very much	Disagree pretty much	Disagree a little	Agree a little	Agree pretty much	Agree very much

4. I tend to get very anxious before an exam or "performance."

0	1	2	3	4	5
Disagree very much	Disagree pretty much	Disagree a little	Agree a little	Agree pretty much	Agree very much

5. I would rather be respected for doing my best than admired for my potential.

0	1	2	3	4	5
Disagree very much	Disagree pretty much	Disagree a little	Agree a little	Agree pretty much	Agree very much

6. I sometimes enjoy being mildly ill for a day or two because it takes off the pressure.

0	1	2	3	4	5
Disagree very much	Disagree pretty much	Disagree a little	Agree a little	Agree pretty much	Agree very much

7. I would rather not take any drug that interfered with my ability to think clearly and do the right thing.

0	1	2	3	4	5
Disagree very much	Disagree pretty much	Disagree a little	Agree a little	Agree pretty much	Agree very much

8. I admit that I am tempted to rationalize when I don't live up to others' expectations.

0	1	2	3	4	5
Disagree very much	Disagree pretty much	Disagree a little	Agree a little	Agree pretty much	Agree very much

9. When something important is coming up, like an exam or a job interview, I try to get as much sleep as possible the night before.

0	1	2	3	4	5
Disagree very much	Disagree pretty much	Disagree a little	Agree a little	Agree pretty much	Agree very much

10. I often think that I have more than my share of bad luck in sports, card games, and other measures of talent.

0	1	2	3	4	5
Disagree very much	Disagree pretty much	Disagree a little	Agree a little	Agree pretty much	Agree very much

SCORING: Items 1, 2, 4, 6, 8, and 10 are scored using the answer scales as provided (0-1-2-3-4-5); Items 3, 5, 7, and 9 are reverse-scored (that is, 5-4-3-2-1-0). Add up all of the items for your self-handicapping score. Possible scores range from 0 to 50, and higher scores represent stronger tendencies to engage in self-handicapping.

Sample items from Jones and Rhodewalt, "Self-handicapping scale," 1982 (unpublished). Department of Psychology, Princeton University, and Department of Psychology, University of Utah. Reprinted by permission of the authors.

as well as a measure of depression symptoms (e.g., feeling sad, sleeping problems). Results showed that children who reported more depression symptoms also reported more self-handicapping. The authors speculated that children who are feeling depressed may use escape-type mechanisms for dealing with stress, including self-handicapping—such as drinking alcohol or avoiding studying before academic tests (see also Adams & Adams, 1991; Midgley & Urdan, 1995).

Return to the Correspondence Bias

No discussion of "what others see in us" would be complete without consideration of the correspondence bias. Recall from earlier in the chapter that the correspondence bias refers to the tendency to explain other people's actions using internal concepts, such as personality traits and attitudes, more than we should. We tend to see other people's behaviour as reflecting stable, internal characteristics.

Guess what? Other people are committing the correspondence bias with *you* as the target. Your friends and acquaintances are forming (or have formed) clear and confident impressions of your personality. Some of these impressions are undoubtedly accurate: we do differ in shyness, self-esteem, and other characteristics (see Chapter 5). But you would probably be surprised by some people's impressions of you. In fact, it is quite likely that different people have opposing impressions of you, which means that someone *must* be wrong. You are probably seen as friendly by some people but aloof by others, helpful by some people but selfish by others, and mature by some people but self-centred by others. Where do these competing impressions come from? Perceivers are willing to draw inferences about personality traits based on very little evidence, so small snippets of behaviour will suffice to form an impression. If different people are exposed to different snippets, they may come to differing conclusions about your personality. Also, people tend to see you in one particular situation: your siblings see you mainly at home, your teachers see you mainly at school, and your friends see you mainly in social settings. Do your siblings, teachers, and friends have the same impressions of you? Unlikely.

What can you do about people forming quick or erroneous impressions of your personality? Probably very little. For people who are important to you, you might monitor whether they have drawn a trait inference that you think is wrong. In such cases, calm discussion of their impression might be warranted. You might also want to keep in mind, however, the evidence presented earlier on self-serving tendencies in self-perception: your own view of your qualities might be enhanced to some extent by rose-coloured glasses.

The Actor–Observer Difference. Other people tend to attribute your behaviour to your internal dispositions and traits, and, in return, you tend to attribute their behaviour to their internal dispositions and traits; these patterns constitute the correspondence bias. But how do people view the causes of their *own* behaviour? Does the correspondence bias occur for self-attributions? No. To explain their own behaviour, people tend to focus on *external* factors. This pattern of differences in attributions has been called the **actor–observer difference:** actors tend to make external attributions for their own behaviour, whereas observers tend to make internal attributions for the same actions (Jones & Nisbett, 1972).

Why does the actor–observer difference occur? The "observer" part of the phenomenon reflects the correspondence bias, which we have already said occurs for several reasons (e.g., the situational factors guiding other people's behaviour are often subtle or nonobvious). Where does the "actor" part come from? Why do we attribute our own behaviour more externally than do observers? Think about yourself: Why might you give greater weight than observers to environmental causes for your own behaviour? Social psychologists have suggested one important reason is

actor–observer difference

a pattern of differences in attributions in which actors tend to make external attributions for their own behaviour, whereas observers tend to make internal attributions for the same actions that we have a lot of knowledge about our own behaviour in the past. We know that we have been outgoing in one social situation but reserved in another, that we have been kind and generous toward one person but more selfish toward another, and that we have been happy and contented sometimes but unhappy and depressed at other times. Knowing these variations across time and settings makes clear to us that we are *not* as consistent or stable as implied by a trait attribution. Canadian social psychologist Gerald Sande of the University of Manitoba and his colleagues (Sande, Goethals, & Radloff, 1988) offered a second reason for viewing our own behaviour as externally caused: we *want* to view ourselves as flexible—we want to believe that we can respond appropriately to different situational contexts. If we possess strong, stable personality traits, we may not have the capacity to respond flexibly to environmental demands. A third reason for the actor–observer difference is that our visual focus while we behave is on the environment, whereas the visual focus of observers is on us (on our behaviour); consequently, the environment is more salient to us, whereas we (as persons) are more salient to observers. Thus, there are informational, motivational, and perceptual reasons for actors' tendency to focus on external causes of their own behaviour compared to observers.

Chapter Summary

This chapter describes social and self-perception—how we make judgments about others and ourselves. Causal judgments about why an event occurred or why someone behaved in a particular way are called **attributions.** Attribution theories are models that attempt to delineate the processes underlying causal judgments. One of the best-known attribution theories portrays people as **intuitive scientists**—untrained scientists who try to make causal judgments in a rational, scientific manner. This theory is labelled the **covariation model of attribution** because it assumes that people try to determine whether a particular kind of behaviour covaried (correlated) with a person, a situation, or some combination of persons and situations.

People tend to assume that other people share their attitudes and behaviours to a greater extent than is actually the case. This tendency is called the **false consensus effect.**

When individuals make causal judgments about a person based on just one observation, they rely on their knowledge of plausible causes in the situation. Perceivers look to see whether plausible external causes are present and make their causal judgments based on this information. The **discounting principle** states that the perceived role of a cause will be discounted (reduced) if other plausible causes are also present. The **augmentation principle** states that the perceived role of a cause will be augmented (increased) if other factors are present that would work against the behaviour.

The **correspondence bias** is the tendency to see other people's behaviour as caused by internal factors, such as their personality traits and attitudes, even when plausible external causes are present. The correspondence bias is so common that it has been called the *fundamental attribution error.*

Nonverbal behaviour refers to actions and cues that communicate meaning in ways other than direct verbal statements, such as facial expressions, voice cues, interpersonal space, eye gaze, and hand gestures. Nonverbal cues are particularly useful in judging the emotions of speakers.

Researchers have identified numerous gender differences and cultural differences in nonverbal behaviour. For example, women are better judges than men of other people's emotions. One important difference between cultures is in their **display rules,** which are their norms for how and when emotions should be expressed.

We rely on other people for many judgments about ourselves. For example, we may internalize other people's judgments about us into our self-concept, a process that has been called the **looking glass self.** We also explicitly compare ourselves to other people in order to make judgments about ourselves, a process labelled **social comparison.** One reason we engage in social comparison is to improve ourselves. This motive is usually best served by **upward social comparison**—comparisons with people who are better off or more skilled than we are. Yet another motive for social comparison is to feel good about ourselves. This motive is usually best served by **downward social comparison**—comparisons with people who are worse off than we are. Upward social comparison can have diverse emotional consequences: sometimes it produces hope for the future, but sometimes it causes **relative deprivation,** which is a feeling of anger or resentment about one's outcomes based on comparisons with better-off others.

A distinction between individualist and collectivist cultures may have implications for social comparison. In **individualist cultures,** people are seen as free, independent beings who possess stable abilities, traits, and attitudes. In **collectivist cultures,** people are seen as part of a social fabric—as *inter*dependent rather than independent. Some evidence suggests that people in collectivist cultures engage in social comparison more often than do people in individualist cultures.

Self-perception theory proposes that we often judge our own internal states by reviewing our past behaviour and the situation in which it occurred and inferring internal states consistent with the behaviour unless there were clear external causes of our behaviour. The **overjustification effect** occurs when people decide that they performed a potentially enjoyable activity for external reasons rather than because they enjoyed it, which can occur when people are offered a reward for engaging in the activity.

Most people think that they are above average on many dimensions, including honesty, fairness, and ability to get along with others. An example of this unrealistically positive self-evaluation is the **bias blind spot,** which refers to the tendency for people to think that biases and errors in judgments are more common in others than in themselves. Most people are also overly optimistic about their own futures—good things are more likely to occur to them than to other people, whereas bad things are less likely to occur to them than to other people.

Self-efficacy refers to the belief that you are capable of performing a particular behaviour that is required for a certain goal. High self-efficacy has been shown to increase the likelihood that people will undertake a behaviour and continue it despite negative feedback. People tend to have **illusions of control:** they overestimate their control of situations and events. This bias may often be adaptive, because when people believe that they have no control over events in their life, they may show symptoms of **learned helplessness,** which is a state of apathy wherein people simply give up trying to achieve their goals. On the other hand, excessive perceptions of control can also cause problems; for example, overconfidence can lead to the **false hope syndrome,** in which individuals repeatedly try (unsuccessfully) to achieve a goal despite previous failures.

The **actual self** is how people believe they really are. The **ideal self** is how people would ideally like themselves to be. The **ought self** is how people think they should or ought to be. **Self-discrepancy theory** hypothesizes that perceived differences between the actual and ideal selves produce depression, and perceived differences between the actual and ought selves produce anxiety.

Impression management refers to the deliberate control of our public behaviour to create a certain impression. This kind of behaviour is also called **self-presentation.** Two very common self-presentation goals are to appear likable and to appear competent. Behaviour that is designed to make someone like you is called **ingratiation;** behaviour that is designed to make someone think you are competent is called **self-promotion. Self-handicapping** occurs when people create or claim an impediment to their own performance, which gives them an excuse for failure (e.g., not studying for a test). The **self-handicapping scale** measures individuals' tendencies to engage frequently in self-handicapping.

The **actor–observer difference** refers to the differing patterns of attribution for one's own versus others' behaviour. Actors tend to make external attributions for their own behaviour, whereas observers tend to make internal attributions for actors' behaviour (this latter tendency constitutes the correspondence bias).

Key Terms

actor–observer difference (148)

actual self (140)

attributions (109)

augmentation principle (113)

bias blind spot (133)

collectivist cultures (127)

correspondence bias (114)

covariation model of attribution (111)

discounting principle (113)

display rules (122)

downward social comparison (125)

false consensus effect (111)

false hope syndrome (140)

ideal self (140)

illusion of control (139)

impression management (143)

individualist cultures (127)

ingratiation (144)

intuitive scientists (110)

learned helplessness (140)

looking glass self (123)

nonverbal behaviour (119)

ought self (140)

overjustification effect (130)

relative deprivation (126)

self-discrepancy theory (141)

self-efficacy (139)

self-handicapping (145)

Social Psychology Alive on the Web

SOCIAL PSYCHOLOGY ALIVE: ONLINE LABS

To perform the following experiment and see how you compare to other students, go to Social Psychology Lab, which can be accessed through ThomsonNOW™.

- 4.1 Facial Expressions

SOCIAL PSYCHOLOGY ALIVE: QUIZZING AND PRACTICE TESTS

You can access our Web site directly by going to http://www.socialpsychologyalive.nelson.com for online quizzes, flash cards, and Internet links.

•INFOTRAC® COLLEGE EDITION

For additional readings, explore InfoTrac® College Edition, your online library of archived journal articles and periodicals dating back 22 years. If your instructor ordered InfoTrac® College Edition with this book, you can access it from your CD-ROM, or go directly to http://www.infotrac-college.com and use the passcode from the InfoTrac® College Edition card that came with your book. For this chapter, try these search terms: *attribution, discounting, correspondence bias, nonverbal behaviour, social comparison, self-perception, unrealistic optimism, individualism–collectivism, self-efficacy, self-discrepancy theory, self-presentation, self-handicapping.*

Social Psychology Alive: The Workbook

To apply what you've learned in this chapter to what happens in the real world, go to Chapter 4 of *Social Psychology Alive: The Workbook*:

- The Intuitive Scientist
- "We Just Didn't Bring Our 'A' Game Today"
- Are Facial Expressions Universal?

- The Alex Trebek Effect: Replicating the Quiz Show Study
- Encouraging Children to Read: Can You Design a Better Program?
- Unrealistic Optimism
- School Spirit
- Measuring Our Different Selves

Social Psychology Alive: The Videos

To see video on the topics and experiments discussed in this chapter, you can go either to ThomsonNOW™ or to the CD-ROM, if your instructor assigned either one, to the following sections:

- We Don't Feel the Same Way: Cultural Influences on Emotion
- Getting the Job: Self-Presentation in the Job Interview

To Learn More

This list contains citations to books or articles that can help you learn more. These readings are good places to start if you want to gain a deeper understanding of the topics in this chapter.

- Leary, M. R. (1995). *Self-presentation: Impression management and interpersonal behaviour.* Madison, WI: Brown & Benchmark.

- Ross, L., & Nisbett, R. E. (1991). *The person and the situation: Perspectives of social psychology.* New York: McGraw-Hill.
- Suls, J. M., & Wheeler, L. (Eds.). (2000). *Handbook of social comparison: Theory and research.* New York: Kluwer Academic/Plenum Press.

The Person in the Situation: Self-Concept, Gender, and Dispositions

Monique and Courtney are two second-year university students taking the same course in Canadian history, who do not know one another. They both earned a "B" average in their first year. The course is an elective for both women, and, after the first four weeks, they are enjoying the course. The professor is a good lecturer, and the textbook is interesting to read. Everything is going smoothly—until the first exam.

The first test in the course consists of multiple-choice and short-answer questions, many of which seem very difficult to Monique and Courtney. Both women leave the exam uncertain about their performance. At class the following week, the professor returns the exams, and the news isn't good: both women learn that their mark was 55%.

Monique responds to this outcome with disappointment mixed with determination. She feels that the exam was difficult and did not allow her to show her knowledge, but is confident she can prepare better now that she knows the professor's exam style. She is resolved to do better on the next test and prove to herself—and the professor—that she is a strong student in this subject. She does not doubt for a moment that she is capable of a much better performance.

Courtney, on the other hand, feels very discouraged by her mark. She blames herself for her poor performance and wonders whether she lacks natural ability in this subject. She hopes that she will do better on the next test but does not feel confident that such will be the case. She wonders whether she should have taken a different course.

Monique and Courtney responded very differently to the same circumstance of a poor exam mark. Monique was disappointed by her grade, attributed it to a difficult exam, and was determined to improve. Courtney was discouraged by her mark, blamed herself for it, and was not confident that she could do much better. How can we understand the differing responses of these two women?

Social psychologists typically focus on external, situational factors to understand social behaviour (see Ross & Nisbett, 1991). Indeed, we noted in the preceding chapter that social psychological findings are often surprising to nonpsychologists precisely because the findings demonstrate the powerful effects of the situation on human behaviour (e.g., Milgram's work on obedience). But social psychologists also recognize that behaviour reflects the person in the situation. That is, individuals' personal characteristics affect how social events unfold.

Clearly, the critical difference between Monique and Courtney was an internal, personal characteristic that influenced how they interpreted and responded to the same situational event. Psychologists define **dispositions** (also called individual difference variables or personality traits) as consistencies across time and settings in a specific type of feeling, thought, and/or action, which make individuals different from other people (Friedman & Schustack, 2003; Snyder & Cantor, 1998). Dispositions reflect stable differences in a particular domain between persons (e.g., friendliness, generosity, athleticism).

What disposition might help us to understand the differing responses of Monique and Courtney? Perhaps the most studied

dispositions

individuals' consistencies across time and settings in a specific type of feeling, thought, and/or action, which make individuals different from other people

Individual students may respond very differently to the same exam result.

*disposition in social psychology is **self-esteem,** which refers to people's judgments of their own worthiness. People with high self-esteem think positively about themselves and consider themselves to be worthwhile individuals, whereas people with low self-esteem evaluate themselves negatively and are less confident about their self-worth. Later in this chapter, we will describe some of the many implications of self-esteem.*

Monique has high self-esteem, whereas Courtney has low self-esteem. This difference was associated with divergent patterns of emotional reactions, causal attributions, and expectations for the future. Monique was disappointed, deflected blame from herself, and remained confident of her own abilities, whereas Courtney was discouraged, blamed herself, and was uncertain about her ability to improve her grade. Looking at the disposition of self-esteem renders the two different responses to the same situational event understandable.

In their research, social psychologists frequently measure individual difference variables that, together with situational factors, might influence behaviour. These personal characteristics are diverse, ranging from demographic variables like gender to psychological dispositions like self-esteem. The purpose of this chapter is to describe some of the personal characteristics that have been studied most often by social psychologists (see Judge, Erez, Bono, & Thorsen, 2002). We begin with variables related to the self-concept, including identity and self-esteem. We then turn to the issue of gender, discussing some of the characteristics on which women and men are either similar or different. The third section describes several interactions between "person" factors and "situation" factors, representing the most common perspective on individual difference variables in social psychology. Finally, we discuss the interesting issue of how personal dispositions are related to health. The goal of the chapter is to introduce you to how social psychologists investigate the person in the situation.

self-esteem

a disposition that represents people's judgments of their own worthiness

Self-Concept and Identity

Humans are probably unique among species in their ability to be self-reflective—to view themselves as objects of categorization and evaluation. Much of what is thought of as *being human* has to do with self-reflection: thinking about one's past and future, wondering how one is viewed by other people, and assessing one's own strengths and weaknesses (see Owens, 2003). These points underscore the importance of the self as a psychological construct.

The product of self-reflection is our *self-concept*, which encompasses the most fundamental aspects of our psychological makeup, including how we identify ourselves, the values we endorse most strongly, and how we feel about ourselves. In this section, we describe how social psychologists have studied the self-concept.

Who Am I? The Self in Me

The **self-concept** refers to all information about the self in memory (Baumeister, 1998). The self-concept contains memories of one's past behaviour, beliefs about one's current qualities, expectations for one's future, and many other self-oriented bits of knowledge. A closely related but narrower construct is **identity,** which

self-concept

all information about the self in memory

identity

the characteristics that individuals think define them and make up their most important qualities refers to those characteristics that individuals think define them and make up their most important qualities. If someone asked you to describe who you are, your answer would constitute your identity. You might identify yourself as a university student, an honest person, a cousin of someone famous, a lacrosse player, or a redhead; your identity consists of whatever characteristics you see as highly self-descriptive.

Attitudes, Gender, and Dispositions. What are some of the specific contents of your identity? Your attitudes and values are certainly important. You might identify yourself as conservative or liberal, as supporting or opposing the hunting of baby seals in Newfoundland, and as religious or nonreligious. In Chapter 6, we will describe social psychological research on attitudes. Another key element of your identity is probably your gender; people frequently identify themselves as a woman or a man (Deaux & LaFrance, 1998). We discuss some research on gender later in this chapter. Finally, your dispositions, or traits, are also probably central to your identity. You may describe yourself as shy or outgoing, as optimistic or pessimistic, and as competitive or cooperative. We discuss several dispositions that have been studied by social psychologists later in this chapter.

But where do these elements of identity come from? How do we come to see ourselves in a particular way? We discussed some important processes in Chapter 4, "Social Perception: Perceiving the Self and Others." For example, *social comparison* is one way that we evaluate and define ourselves: we compare ourselves to other people and assess whether we are strong or weak in a certain ability, and whether our attitudes are shared or unusual. We observe that we do better than most other kids at school and decide that we are intelligent. We notice that we are shorter than most of our friends and label ourselves as short.

A second process is *self-perception:* we infer our attitudes and feelings directly from our own experiences and behaviour. For instance, we know that we love chocolate because we have tasted it. We label ourselves as athletic because we participate successfully in many sports. We decide that we are helpful because we volunteer at a hospital. Once we have applied a label to ourselves via self-perception, we can access the label directly and do not have to repeat the inference process.

5.1
ONLINE LAB

5.2
ONLINE LAB

Individuals' *identity* refers to the characteristics that they think describe their most important qualities, such as their religious and ethnic affiliations.

© Richard T. Nowitz/CORBIS

Priming and Situational Distinctiveness. Although it is true that everyone has certain traits and characteristics that are central to his or her identity, there is also some variability over time and across situations in how people see themselves. For instance, a young woman might think of herself as a student while on her way to school, but as a figure skater while on her way to figure skating classes. People juggle numerous identities, which can sometimes even conflict with one another (e.g., the challenge of integrating professional careers and parenthood). Changes over time and settings reflect, in part, that only limited portions of the self-concept can be accessible at any specific moment.

The aspects of identity that are in conscious awareness at a given point in time make up what is called the **spontaneous self-concept** (McGuire & Padawer-Singer, 1976). The spontaneous self-concept changes in response to personal and situational factors. For example, the accessibility of a particular feature of the self will depend on how recently it has been activated. If someone spends a weekend at a dog show, the feature *pet owner* will be more accessible to him or her during the following week than if the dog show had been held several months ago. This example shows how recent activation can increase the likelihood of subsequent activation, which is called *priming,* as we discussed in Chapter 3 (see p. 71).

Another variable that influences the spontaneous self-concept is the distinctiveness of a feature in a particular setting. Which of the following situations would make you more conscious of your gender? In one situation, you are discussing a topic in class with a group of three other individuals of your own sex. In the second situation, you are discussing a topic in class with a group of three individuals of the opposite sex.

William McGuire and his colleagues at Yale University (e.g., McGuire, McGuire, & Winton, 1979; McGuire & Padawer-Singer, 1976) hypothesized that people are more aware of a specific characteristic when it makes them distinctive from other people in the situation. Any feature that distinguishes individuals from others in the setting is expected to become more accessible. Thus, in the question just posed, McGuire would predict that you will be more aware of your gender when you are the only member of your sex than when you are in a group of same-sex individuals. Is this consistent with your own intuition?

McGuire conducted several interesting studies to test his hypothesis. McGuire and his colleagues (1979) interviewed 560 schoolchildren (grades 1, 3, 7, or 11) and asked them to "Tell us about yourself" for five minutes. The boys and girls talked spontaneously into a tape recorder, and their self-descriptions were later scored for whether or not the child mentioned his or her sex. Information was also obtained about the sex composition of the child's home—how many males and females lived with the child (parents, siblings, or others). Figure 5.1 provides the percentages of children who mentioned their own gender, broken down by sex composition at home. The figure shows that *boys* were much more likely to mention their sex when *females* were in the majority at home than when males were equal or in the majority at home. *Girls* were much more likely to mention their sex when *males* were in the majority at home than when females were equal or in the majority at home.

In another study, William McGuire and Alice Padawer-Singer (1976) interviewed 252 boys and girls in grade 6 and used the same "Tell us about yourself" method to elicit their spontaneous self-concepts, except this time participants were given seven minutes to provide their answers in writing. Participants were then given another sheet of paper and were asked to "Describe what you look like." The researchers then looked to see whether students were more likely on these two tasks to mention

spontaneous self-concept
the aspects of identity that are in conscious awareness at a given point in time

© MediaImages/Getty Images

A woman's spontaneous self-concept is more likely to include her sex when she is the only woman in a group.

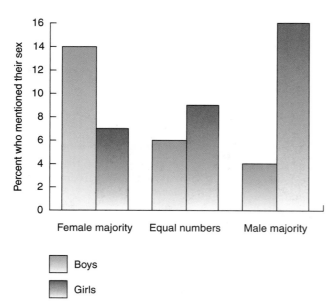

FIGURE 5.1 Percent of schoolchildren who mentioned their sex in spontaneous self-description

From McGuire et al., "Effects of household sex composition on the salience of one's gender in the spontaneous self-concept," *Journal of Experimental Social Psychology*, 15, 77–90, Table 2, p. 86, 1979. Reprinted by permission of Elsevier.

characteristics on which they were relatively unusual. This hypothesis was confirmed for several features. For example, most of the children (70%) were born in the city where their school was located. Only 6% of these children (born in the same city) spontaneously mentioned their place of birth in their self-description, whereas 22% of the children who were born elsewhere mentioned their birthplace (e.g., "I was born in Halifax"). Mention of physical characteristics was also influenced by the distinctiveness of the feature. Most children in the sample had brown or black hair (88%) and most had brown eyes (70%). When asked to describe their appearance, only 54% of the children with brown or black hair mentioned their hair colour, whereas 79% of the children with red or blond hair mentioned their hair colour. Only 56% of the children with brown eyes mentioned their eye colour, whereas 77% of the children with blue or green eyes mentioned their eye colour.

These studies suggest that situational factors can make features more prominent, which increases the likelihood that those features will be activated and become part of the spontaneous self-concept. In different situations or at different times, we may see ourselves quite differently. Sometimes our height or weight may seem most important, and other times we will be conscious of our sex or age. Even personality characteristics like helpfulness or assertiveness can become more accessible when the features differentiate us from others. If we are the only person in our class who volunteers to stay late to help the teacher clean up the classroom, we may feel quite helpful or unselfish. If we are the only person in our class to tell the teacher that a test was unfair when we know our friends agree with us, we will feel quite assertive. The spontaneous self-concept is fluid.

Is It Me or We?

Our identity consists of the characteristics that we believe define us and describe our most important qualities. These qualities can include our personal traits, attitudes, abilities, and physical characteristics. But our identity can also include *group memberships*—we see ourselves as a student, a hockey fan, a French Canadian, a young person, a woman. These groups define some of our most valued characteristics (see Ashmore, Deaux, & McLaughlin-Volpe, 2004). In a very real sense, *me* is often *we*.

". . . I get stressed and it's sometimes really hard to balance everything. When I'm an employee, I'm an employee, and I concentrate on that. When I'm a mom, I'm a mom, and when I'm a wife, I'm a wife."

In the following paragraphs, we describe a theory that assumes group memberships are central to our identities, called *social identity theory*. We then turn to a theory that hypothesizes that individuals need to feel both similar to other people and different from other people, called *optimal distinctiveness theory*. Both theories address the role of group memberships in the self-concept.

social identity theory

a model hypothesizing that people want to have positive appraisals of groups to which they belong

Social Identity Theory.   Social identity theory was proposed by Henri Tajfel (1970, 1978; Tajfel & Turner, 1986), who spent most of his career at the University of Bristol in the United Kingdom. Tajfel hypothesized that an important component of individuals' identity comes from their group memberships. Tajfel assumed that we want to maintain a positive identity, including a positive group (social) identity. How can a positive social identity be achieved? Tajfel suggested that we achieve this goal by judging our groups to be superior to other groups. Just as social comparison makes us feel good when we outperform another individual, so, too, comparisons between our group and other groups make us feel good when our group outperforms the other groups.

The most provocative finding from research on social identity theory has been that when people are given an opportunity to distribute resources between members of their ingroup and members of an outgroup, they systematically favour their ingroup (see Bourhis, 1994; Taylor & Moghaddam, 1994). Tajfel interpreted these data as reflecting people's desire to make their group superior to the outgroup—to *create* a positive social identity.

For example, one of the earliest studies of social identity theory (Tajfel, 1970) involved British teenage boys, who began the study by completing a dot estimation task in which they guessed how many dots were flashed briefly on a screen. Participants were told that some people consistently overestimate the number of dots and some people consistently underestimate the number of dots. Half of the participants (randomly selected) were told at the completion of the dot estimation task that they were a consistent overestimator, and half were told that they were a consistent underestimator. The boys then learned that they would perform a completely different kind of judgment task, which would require them to divide rewards between other partici-

An important part of our identity comes from the groups to which we belong.

pants. The boys were told that their decisions would have no effect on their own reward, and they would not know the individual identities of the other participants but would know only whether the others were overestimators or underestimators. Participants then made a series of decisions about allocating rewards to other boys. Results showed that when participants made an allocation decision that involved an ingroup member and an outgroup member, they consistently favoured the ingroup member. For example, when a participant who believed himself to be an overestimator was asked to divide resources between another overestimator and an underestimator, the participant tended to give more reward to the overestimator.

These kinds of studies use a method called the **minimal group paradigm,** because the "groups" that are created are trivial and meaningless (they are "minimal" groups). In the overestimator–underestimator study, for example, participants did not even know who the other ingroup members were. Also, the basis for the discrimination, overestimating versus underestimating, was pretty ridiculous—why did the boys care whether another person was similar or different on this dimension anyway? Research since this early study has shown that ingroup bias occurs even when groups are formed randomly—by the flip of a coin! Tajfel argued that if ingroup bias occurs in these trivial situations, then very strong bias probably occurs when groups are formed on the basis of characteristics that people truly value (e.g., religion, nationality).

minimal group paradigm

a procedure in which participants are divided into groups based on trivial features or information

Optimal Distinctiveness Theory.

In social identity theory, Tajfel (1970, 1978) hypothesized that people want to create a *distinctive* group identity, and one that is also *positive.* That is, people want their ingroup to be both different from and better than other groups. The distinctiveness element, however, was not pursued in depth in social identity theory.

optimal distinctiveness theory

a model hypothesizing that people want to maintain a balance between similarity to other people and individuality from other people

Other theorists have argued that although distinctiveness is an important goal in social identity, it coexists with a need to belong to groups (e.g., Brewer, 1991; Pickett, Gardner, & Knowles, 2004; Snyder & Fromkin, 1980; Vignoles, Chryssochoou, & Breakwell, 2000). These theorists have suggested that people want a *balance* between similarity and distinctiveness—that is, people want to feel similar to other members of their group, but not *too* similar, because they also want to feel like an individual with a distinct identity. This struggle for a balance or equilibrium between similarity and distinctiveness is the focus of **optimal distinctiveness theory** (Brewer, 1991). Marilyn Brewer at Ohio State University hypothesized that people are constantly adjusting their perceived similarity or perceived distinctiveness in order to maintain the optimal level. If people are exposed to a situation that makes them feel indistinguishable from other people, they will want to re-establish their unique identity. If people are exposed to a situation that makes them feel very different from other people, they will want to re-establish their group belongingness.

An interesting example of the push-and-pull between the competing motives for similarity and distinctiveness was documented in a study by Hazel Markus and Ziva Kunda (1986). Female students at the University of Michigan were shown 18 different sets of three items each and were asked to identify from each set the one they liked the best. For example, they were shown three cartoons and asked to select their favourite; they were shown three greeting cards and asked to select their favourite; and they were shown three colours and asked to select their favourite. Participants completed this task together with three other alleged participants, who were actually confederates of the experimenter. The real participant always answered first, followed by the three confederates. In the *unique condition,* the confederates all disagreed with the participant on 15 of the 18 trials and agreed with each other. For example, if the participant selected option A, the three confederates might all select option C. On the remaining three trials (included to increase the plausibility of the confederates' responses), one of the confederates agreed with the participant but the other two confederates disagreed. In the *similar condition,* all three confederates agreed with the real participant on 15 of the 18 trials. On the remaining three trials (again included for plausibility reasons), none of the confederates agreed with the participant.

If people feel too similar to other members of their group, they will be motivated to establish their unique or distinctive characteristics.

Ron Hilton /Shutterstock

Immediately after completing this task, participants rated their own similarity to several groups; we will focus here on participants' ratings of *ingroups*—that is, groups to which they belonged (e.g., women, Michigan students). The authors predicted that participants in the unique condition would be feeling very dissimilar from other people and would want to emphasize their similarity to their ingroups, whereas participants in the similar condition would be feeling nearly identical to other people and would want to downplay their similarity to their ingroups. As predicted, the unique condition produced higher ratings of similarity to ingroups than did the similar condition. These data indicate that people try to balance the needs to be similar to others and to have a unique identity (see also Hornsey & Jetten, 2004). The flowchart in Figure 5.2 diagrams the hypothesized processes in each condition.

Cultural Differences in Identity

Almost all of the research on identity we have described to this point was based on North American or Western European samples. This fact raises questions about whether the principles we have delineated, such as optimal distinctiveness, may reflect specific aspects of Western cultures—and, perhaps, be limited to those cultures. In this section, we consider how other cultures might differ from the North American and European findings for identity (see also Kashima, Kokubo, Kashima, Boxall, Yamaguchi, & Macrae, 2004, for data on cultural differences in identity between people who live in large urban areas and people who live in smaller, regional cities).

Independent Versus Interdependent Selves. In Chapter 4, we described the dimension that has been used most often to distinguish between cultures: the individualist–collectivist dimension (Fiske, Kitayama, Markus, & Nisbett, 1998; Triandis, 1995). Individualist cultures, such as Canada, the United States, and Western Europe, conceptualize people as possessing stable abilities, traits, and attitudes. Collectivist cultures, such as most East Asian countries, conceptualize people as fitting into social roles and following important communal norms.

It seems obvious that these different perspectives should affect members' personal identities. Perhaps most fundamental is the relative emphasis on an independent self versus an interdependent self. In individualist cultures, the self is seen as independent from other people, whereas in collectivist cultures, the self is seen as interdependent with other people.

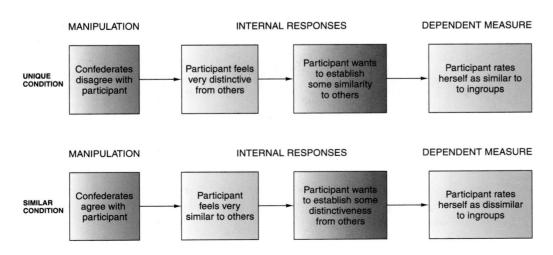

FIGURE 5.2
Conditions in experiment by Markus and Kunda (1986)

Is It Me or We? In our previous discussion of *me* versus *we*, we described optimal distinctiveness theory, which hypothesizes that people want to achieve a moderate degree of differentiation from others. Too much similarity to other people threatens our sense of uniqueness, whereas too much difference from other people threatens our sense of belonging. Researchers have shown that individuals prefer to maintain a moderate or intermediate level of distinctiveness from other people—enough uniqueness to have their own identity but not so much that they feel disconnected.

Is it possible that the greater emphasis on interdependence and social relationships in collectivist cultures reduces the importance of personal distinctiveness? Do people in collectivist cultures have a lower level of optimal distinctiveness, compared to the level desired in individualist cultures?

Harry Triandis at the University of Illinois was one of the first social psychologists to study cross-cultural differences and made important contributions to the literature on individualism versus collectivism (e.g., Triandis, 1995). In a 1990 paper, Triandis and his colleagues investigated whether the identities of members of collectivist cultures are more interpersonal (*we* rather than *me*) than the identities of members of individualist cultures (Triandis, McCusker, & Hui, 1990). On one task, the researchers asked participants from several different cultures to give 20 completions to the statement, "I am . . ." (Kuhn & McPartland, 1954). The percentage of these statements that referred to social groups was calculated for each respondent. For example, social group completions might include "I am a daughter," "I am a Roman Catholic," or "I am the captain of my hockey team," whereas nonsocial completions might include "I am honest," "I am interested in astronomy," or "I am a fast runner." Respondents from Illinois gave an average of only 19% social group completions; similarly, respondents from Greece, another individualist culture, gave an average of only 15% social group completions. In contrast, participants from collectivist cultures listed more social groups in their answers. For example, respondents from Hawaii who were of Japanese origin gave an average of 28% social group completions, and respondents from the People's Republic of China gave an average of 52% social group completions. These data indicate that people from collectivist cultures define themselves in terms of their relationships to others more than do people from individualist cultures.

People from China define themselves in terms of social groups more than do people from North America.

In a study conducted at the University of Waterloo, Michael Ross, Elaine Xun, and Anne Wilson (2002) recruited bilingual Chinese Canadians and asked them to write a description of themselves ("Describe what you are like as a person"). Half of the participants responded in Chinese and half responded in English. Results showed that participants who responded in Chinese included more references to groups (e.g., "I am a student at the University of Waterloo"), more references to other people (e.g., "My parents are still in Hong Kong"), and fewer statements about their private characteristics (e.g., "I am intelligent") than did participants who responded in English. Thus, when participants responded in the language associated with a collectivist perspective, they defined themselves in social terms more than when they responded in the language associated with an individualist perspective. These data suggest that participants had separate identities stored in memory, one reflecting their family's Chinese culture and one reflecting the dominant English culture, which were activated by the associated language (see also Vignoles et al., 2000).

Self-Esteem: Liking for the Self

Do you know someone who is always hard on himself or herself? These individuals don't give themselves a break and criticize themselves frequently. They often take negative feedback to heart and are devastated by it, even when the feedback is presented constructively. Individuals who are hard on themselves in this manner have very low *self-esteem*—the disposition we used to understand the differences between Monique and Courtney in the example given at the beginning of the chapter. Self-esteem refers to an individual's evaluation (good–bad judgment) of himself or herself. Self-esteem can be conceptualized as an *attitude* toward the self—a judgment that the self is worthy or unworthy.

Most people have reasonably high self-esteem—most have positive views of themselves, a point we have made several times in previous chapters. Humans appear to be motivated to strive for high self-esteem (e.g., Crocker & Park, 2004; Sheldon, Elliot, Kim, & Kasser, 2001), and most people rate themselves as above average on most positive traits. Nevertheless, there are some people who have negative self-views.

Self-esteem is usually assessed with a self-report scale. In Know Yourself 5.1: "Self-Esteem Scale," you can measure your own self-esteem using a well-known scale developed by Morris Rosenberg (1979). A recent series of studies (Robins, Hendin, & Trzesniewski, 2001) tested the validity of the Rosenberg Self-Esteem Scale and found that it successfully predicted numerous relevant variables, including friends' ratings of the target's behaviour. Moreover, the scale predicted well for both men and women, for different ethnic groups, and for different age samples.

Sources of Self-Esteem. Where do people's positive or negative evaluations of themselves come from? Why do some people consider themselves worthy and some consider themselves unworthy?

Personal experiences are one obvious source of attitudes toward the self. To the extent that people experience many positive outcomes (e.g., success, praise) across varied situations, they are likely to develop favourable beliefs about themselves and positive feelings about their personal worthiness, whereas to the extent that they experience many negative outcomes (e.g., failure, criticism), they are likely to develop unfavourable beliefs about themselves and negative feelings about their personal worthiness. In children's early years, parents are an important source of these positive or negative experiences. Many parenting books emphasize the importance of unconditional love for the child, so that he or she develops a stable sense of being cared for and respected. Recall also the concept of the *looking glass self* in Chapter 4 (see p. 123), which refers to the idea that people may internalize others' views of them—such as children internalizing their parents' labels.

Know Yourself 5.1
Self-Esteem Scale

Please indicate the extent to which you agree or disagree with each of the following statements by circling the appropriate number on the answer scale.

1. On the whole, I am satisfied with myself.

1	2	3	4
Strongly agree	Agree	Disagree	Strongly disagree

2. At times, I think I am no good at all.

1	2	3	4
Strongly agree	Agree	Disagree	Strongly disagree

3. I feel that I have a number of good qualities.

1	2	3	4
Strongly agree	Agree	Disagree	Strongly disagree

4. I am able to do things as well as most other people.

1	2	3	4
Strongly agree	Agree	Disagree	Strongly disagree

5. I feel that I do not have much to be proud of.

1	2	3	4
Strongly agree	Agree	Disagree	Strongly disagree

6. I certainly feel useless at times.

1	2	3	4
Strongly agree	Agree	Disagree	Strongly disagree

7. I feel that I'm a person of worth, at least on an equal plane with others.

1	2	3	4
Strongly agree	Agree	Disagree	Strongly disagree

8. I wish I could have more respect for myself.

1	2	3	4
Strongly agree	Agree	Disagree	Strongly disagree

9. All in all, I am inclined to think I am a failure.

1	2	3	4
Strongly agree	Agree	Disagree	Strongly disagree

10. I take a positive attitude toward myself.

1	2	3	4
Strongly agree	Agree	Disagree	Strongly disagree

SCORING: Items 2, 5, 6, 8, and 9 are scored using the answer scales as presented (1-2-3-4); Items 1, 3, 4, 6, and 10 are reverse-scored (that is, 4-3-2-1). Add up all of the items for your overall self-esteem score. Possible scores range from 10 to 40, and higher scores represent higher self-esteem.

Sample items from Morris Rosenberg, *Society and the Adolescent Self-Image*, Revised Edition (Middletown, CT: Wesleyan University Press, 1989).

Personal experiences of successful or unsuccessful social relationships are very important for self-esteem: friendships and social acceptance produce self-confidence and high self-esteem, whereas loneliness and social rejection produce self-doubts and low self-esteem (see Leary & Baumeister, 2000). Academic achievement at school also affects people's sense of self-worth: consistent success or consistent failure at school can strongly affect individuals' self-esteem (see Crocker, Sommers, & Luhtanen, 2002).

Mark Baldwin at McGill University and Lisa Sinclair at the University of Winnipeg have shown that individuals with low self-esteem are more likely than those with high self-esteem to believe that other people's liking for them depends on their performance: others will accept them if they succeed but reject them if they fail (Baldwin & Sinclair, 1996). This belief in the contingency of others' approval makes low-self esteem individuals very self-critical and anxious in performance settings. Everybody fails occasionally, but those with low self-esteem are more likely than those with high self-esteem to conclude from such failure that others dislike and disrespect them.

Social comparison is also involved in the development of self-esteem. People compare themselves to others on performance, traits, and attitudes, and the results of these comparisons influence judgments of self-worth (e.g., Alicke, 2000; Smith, 2000). When social comparisons indicate that the self has outperformed others, self-esteem is raised. When social comparisons show that the self has fallen below others, self-esteem suffers. Of course, most of us tend to focus on our positive accomplishments and downplay our failures (see Mezulis, Abramson, Hyde, & Hankin, 2004), so most of us maintain a reasonably high level of self-esteem.

Experiences of success at school can contribute to high self-esteem.

Correlates of Self-Esteem. What are the correlates of high or low self-esteem? How does this dimension relate to other aspects of people's lives? It turns out to have wide-ranging associations.

First, people with high self-esteem have clearer and more certain views of themselves than do people with low self-esteem (Baumgardner, 1990; Campbell, 1990). Self-esteem is also correlated with expectancies for success: although low–self-esteem individuals *want* to succeed just as much as people with high self-esteem, those with low self-esteem do not really *expect* to succeed, whereas people with high self-esteem anticipate success. Because of these differences in expectancies, people with high self-esteem approach situations hoping to demonstrate their skill and garner praise, whereas people with low self-esteem approach situations simply hoping to avoid failure and escape without looking bad (see Baumeister, 1998).

Perhaps the most consistent findings in the self-esteem literature have concerned the issue of self-serving judgments. People with high self-esteem exhibit more self-enhancement in a variety of ways (see Blaine & Crocker, 1993, for a review). Compared to people with low self-esteem, people with high self-esteem are more likely (1) to attribute success to internal factors, (2) to attribute failure to external factors, (3) to recall information about personal successes better than information about personal failures, and (4) to exaggerate their control over situations. Thus, people with high self-esteem process information in ways that magnify their virtues. Note, however, that the direction of causality in these findings is unclear. Does high self-esteem lead to more self-enhancement, or does self-enhancement lead to higher self-esteem? Perhaps both directions occur.

Romin Tafarodi (1998), a social psychologist at the University of Toronto, noted that some people with low self-esteem consider themselves competent and capable but do not *like* themselves. He showed that, rather than exhibiting self-enhancement, these individuals instead processed information in a *negatively* biased fashion. For instance, they were especially likely to recall *negative* information they had been given about themselves. Thus, an absence of self-enhancement was associated with lower liking for the self.

People with high self-esteem tend to be happier than people with low self-esteem. Self-esteem correlates negatively with depression and anxiety, and positively with life satisfaction (Baumeister, 1998; Leary & Kowalski, 1995; Sedikides, Rudich, Gregg, Kumashiro, & Rusbult, 2004; Tennen & Affleck, 1993).

What about personal relationships? Here, again, high self-esteem is associated with greater satisfaction. People with high self-esteem have more stable dating relationships and report happier marriages than do people with low self-esteem (Fincham & Bradbury, 1993; Hendrick, Hendrick, & Adler, 1988). The former individuals also rate their romantic partners more positively, focusing on their partner's virtues rather than deficiencies (Murray, Holmes, & Griffin, 1996a, 1996b). People with high self-esteem also seem to use their romantic relationships as a way to cope with threats to their sense of self-worth. Sandra Murray, John Holmes, and their colleagues at the University of Waterloo (Murray, Holmes, MacDonald, & Ellsworth, 1998) gave people negative feedback about either their considerateness in their romantic relationship or their intellectual abilities. In subsequent ratings of their partner, high–self-esteem individuals responded to these threats by becoming more confident about their partner's commitment to the relationship and by rating their partner more positively, whereas low–self-esteem individuals responded to the threats with greater doubts about their partner's commitment to the relationship and by rating their partner more negatively. We will return to these findings for self-esteem in Chapter 13 when we discuss close relationships.

The various correlates of high self-esteem we have described are summarized in the accompanying Concept Review.

CONCEPT REVIEW
Correlates of High Self-Esteem (Relative to Low Self-Esteem)

Clear and certain views of the self	Stable dating relationships
Expect to succeed	Happy marriages
Approach situations hoping to demonstrate skill	Rate romantic partners positively
High self-enhancement and self-serving judgments:	Use relationships as a way to cope with threats
• Attribute success internally	
• Attribute failure externally	
• Recall information about personal successes	
• Exaggerate personal control over situations	
High happiness:	
• Low depression	
• Low anxiety	
• High satisfaction with life	

All of this sounds pretty good for high self-esteem, doesn't it? High self-esteem appears to be a terrific quality to possess. The world would be a better place if we could raise every child to have high self-esteem. But wait a minute—do these conclusions fit comfortably with your own experiences? Do you think that the world would be better off if everyone had high self-esteem? Have you always found people with high self-esteem to be the most admirable and thoughtful individuals? What about that conceited jerk back in high school who treated everyone like dirt? Or what about that arrogant teacher who was so obnoxious about his knowledge and training?

These hypothetical examples of conceited individuals illustrate the point that high self-esteem may be a mixed bag (see Crocker & Park, 2004; Kernis & Paradise, 2002; Kernis & Waschull, 1995). Yes, some people with high self-esteem are self-confident, well-adjusted, and optimistic without being nasty or arrogant. But other people with high self-esteem are not so pleasant: they brag, make other people feel inferior, and are hostile if they don't get their own way. How can we distinguish between these two conflicting types of high self-esteem?

One dimension that might help is **narcissism,** which refers to an *excessive* love for the self. People who are high in narcissism have inflated views of their self-worth, which are not connected to reality. Narcissism can be measured by a self-report scale developed by Robert Raskin (Raskin & Hall, 1979; Raskin & Terry, 1988), which contains 40 items that are answered either *true* or *false*. People who score high on this scale answer *true* to items like "I am going to be a great person" and "If I ruled the world, it would be a much better place." It turns out that narcissism correlates with self-esteem, but only moderately, which means that people with high self-esteem are *not* always high in narcissism (Sedikides et al., 2004). Perhaps well-adjusted individuals are high in self-esteem and low in narcissism, whereas obnoxious, conceited people are high in both self-esteem and narcissism.

Some data consistent with the view that narcissists can be hostile was obtained by Brad Bushman, who is at the University of Michigan, and Roy Baumeister, who is at Florida State University (1998). Participants in this study received from another person a negative, critical evaluation of an essay they had written. Later, participants had the opportunity to make the critic listen to loud, unpleasant noise while trying to perform a competitive task. Participants who were high in narcissism made the critic listen to louder and longer bursts of noise than did participants who were low in narcissism. In contrast, self-esteem was unrelated to aggression. The authors suggested that narcissists are defensive about criticism that threatens their ego and respond with aggression. This process of self-threat leading to aggression by narcissists was termed **threatened egotism** (Baumeister, Smart, & Boden, 1996; see also Morf & Rhodewalt, 1993; Twenge & Campbell, 2003). Although it might be desirable to have more people who have high self-esteem without being arrogant, more narcissists would not make the world a better place.

In a study at the University of British Columbia, Delroy Paulhus (1998) brought small groups of four to six students together for 20 minutes on seven different occasions. All participants had previously completed a number of personality measures, including a narcissism scale. At each meeting, the group members discussed an assigned topic (e.g., worries and concerns; the characteristics of well-adjusted persons). At the end of the first and seventh sessions, participants rated one another on a variety of adjustment and likeability dimensions. Results showed that narcissistic individuals made a positive impression at the first session: narcissists tended to be rated as more agreeable and well adjusted than non-narcissists. However, liking for narcissists declined over the seven sessions, as participants got to know one another better. In fact, after the seventh session, narcissists tended to be rated as less agreeable and less well adjusted than non-narcissists. Thus, excessive self-love became tiresome and unattractive to others over time.

narcissism

a disposition that represents the extent to which people have excessive love for themselves

threatened egotism

a hostile, aggressive response to criticism from others, which has been linked to narcissism

Narcissists have excessively positive views of themselves and may respond in a hostile way to criticism.

secure high self-esteem

a positive self-view that is confidently held

defensive high self-esteem

a positive self-view that is fragile and vulnerable to threat

Secure and Defensive High Self-Esteem. Another perspective on this issue of the good and bad sides of high self-esteem was provided by Christian Jordan, who is now at Wilfrid Laurier University, and his colleagues Steve Spencer and Mark Zanna of the University of Waterloo (Jordan, Spencer, & Zanna, 2003; Jordan, Spencer, Zanna, Hoshino-Browne, & Correll, 2003). These researchers distinguished between people who have **secure high self-esteem** and those who have **defensive high self-esteem** (see also Kernis & Paradise, 2002). Both groups report positive self-evaluations on self-report measures of self-esteem such as Rosenberg's (1979) scale. However, people with *secure* high self-esteem possess positive self-views that are *confidently* held; these individuals feel good about themselves and do not need constant reassurance from others to maintain their high self-esteem. In contrast, people with *defensive* high self-esteem possess positive self-views that are *fragile* and vulnerable to threat; these individuals harbour subconscious self-doubts and insecurities, which can lead them to react very negatively to criticism. People with defensive high self-esteem need repeated positive feedback from others to maintain their uncertain feelings of self-worth. This unending need for praise can be associated with boastful, arrogant behaviour, as well as hostility and aggression toward anyone who questions the perceiver's self-worth (threatened egotism).

How can secure and defensive high self-esteem be distinguished empirically? Jordan and his colleagues proposed that a measure of an individual's automatic, spontaneous self-evaluation was necessary. Recall our discussion of *automatic processes* in Chapter 3 (see p. 75); these processes cannot be controlled deliberately. In the domain of self-esteem, automatic (also called *implicit*) self-evaluations refer to people's uncontrolled, spontaneous feelings about the self (positive or negative). People may not be aware of their automatic, implicit self-evaluations. Therefore, whereas explicit self-evaluations are conscious and can be measured with self-report scales, implicit self-evaluations are often unconscious and can only be measured by indirect means. The technique used by Jordan and his colleagues to assess implicit self-evaluations was a reaction-time task that we will describe in detail in the next chapter (the *Implicit Association Test*); for our present purposes, we need only know that this task assesses the extent to which people automatically associate positive or negative feelings with a target—in this case, the target was the self (see also Pelham, Koole, Hardin, Hetts, Seah, & Dettart, 2005).

In a series of studies at the University of Waterloo, Jordan and his colleagues showed that people who scored high on a self-report scale of self-esteem but who exhibited negative self-evaluation on an implicit measure of self-esteem (i.e., those with *defensive high self-esteem*) behaved more self-protectively in several contexts than did people who scored high on a self-report scale of self-esteem and who exhibited positive self-evaluation on an implicit measure of self-esteem (i.e., those with *secure high self-esteem*). The researchers also found that people with defensive high self-esteem scored higher on a *narcissism* scale than did people with secure high self-esteem; thus, narcissists may be insecure about themselves on a subconscious level.

These findings suggest that secure high self-esteem is generally a good thing, whereas defensive high self-esteem has some undesirable correlates. Thus, encouraging positive *automatic* or *implicit* self-regard might be beneficial, if it would increase the number of individuals with secure high self-esteem. How this goal can best be reached, however, has received little attention. McGill University social psychologists Jodene Baccus, Mark Baldwin, and Dominic Packer (2004) conducted one of the few studies on this issue. These Canadian researchers found that participants' implicit self-esteem could be increased using a computer game that repeatedly paired self-relevant information (e.g., a participant's name) with photos of smiling faces. Whether this procedure could be used to improve the implicit self-esteem of people with defensive high self-esteem is a question that awaits further research.

Gender and Social Behaviour

Another "person" factor that social psychologists often study is gender. How important is this characteristic for understanding social behaviour? For example, does gender influence people's social lives, such as dictating the settings they enter or the roles they adopt? Do women and men differ reliably across time and settings in their feelings, thoughts, and actions? Are women and men mostly similar or mostly different on important dispositions and abilities?

We should distinguish at the outset between the terms *sex* and *gender*. Sex is a biological characteristic and a naturally occurring category, which refers to an individual's reproductive status as female or male. Gender, on the other hand, is a psychological characteristic and a socially constructed category, which refers to all of the things it means to be a woman or a man in our society. Thus, the concept of gender includes such variables as masculinity and femininity, differential expectations for boys and girls, and so on.

Let's begin our discussion with some self-analysis. How central is your gender identity in your self-concept? For example, if you were asked to define yourself, how early would your gender as a man or a woman be mentioned? Now think about your personality traits. Do you suppose that your dispositions and abilities reflect your biological sex and/or your gender socialization? More broadly, do you think that any particular traits occur much more often in one gender than the other?

In the following sections, we discuss some of the most interesting findings by social psychologists regarding sex differences and similarities. We consider both the nature and the possible causes of differences between men and women.

Gender Differences and Similarities

The issue of differences and similarities between women and men is both fascinating and complex. Gender roles and expectations have a large impact on our lives, affecting our identity, our relationships with others, and our views of the world. Any differences between women and men could reflect both biological factors (e.g., differences in hormones, or different evolutionary pressures on women and men) and socialization factors (e.g., different gender roles or institutional forces).

The Importance of Gender in Everyday Life. There is no doubt that, right from birth, our lives are affected by our sex and our gender socialization. Boys and girls are almost always treated differently, encouraged to pursue divergent interests, and socialized differently by parents, peers, and societal institutions. Think about your own daily experiences and how they are affected by your gender. It is typical for women and men to wear different clothes, to have mostly same-sex friends, to use separate bathrooms, to watch different television shows, to play sports separately, and so on—gender is an enormously influential "gate" to specific environments and activities.

The significance of gender in our society is humorously illustrated in parents' reactions to misperceptions of their baby's sex. An infant girl whose hair has not started to grow may elicit "What a cute little boy!" from observers, with an immediate correction from the parents, "Oh no, she is a girl." Why should this sort of mistake bother parents? Why do they care whether their child's sex is perceived accurately by strangers? The fact is that gender is a fundamental element of our conceptions of people. Indeed, there is evidence that gender is the characteristic that is used *more often than any other characteristic* to spontaneously categorize people we encounter (Fiske, Haslam, & Fiske, 1991; Stangor, Lynch, Duan, & Glass, 1992). Gender seems

Our lives are affected by our gender right from the beginning.

more basic even than age, occupation, or ethnic category. Thus, more than anything else, we categorize people as men and women, boys and girls.

It is also the case that most people *believe* that there are at least some sex differences in personality. These expectations constitute *gender stereotypes:* beliefs about the characteristics that are associated with men and women. For example, men are often believed to be more aggressive than women, whereas women are often believed to be more emotional than men (e.g., Bergen & Williams, 1991). As we note below, there may be some truth in these beliefs, but gender stereotypes substantially exaggerate any actual differences (see Martin, 1987). Also, even if men and women currently differ on particular characteristics, this does not mean that such differences are inevitable or "natural"; they might disappear if gender socialization were changed. We will talk about gender stereotypes in detail in Chapter 9 when we discuss sexism.

There is also considerable evidence that people's *identity* as a man or a woman is important to them. Children learn that they are male or female at an early age and incorporate this feature as a central aspect of their identity (Deaux & LaFrance, 1998; Martin, Ruble, & Szkrybalo, 2002). People also come to view many of their other characteristics as related to their gender (Spence, 1993). The extent to which individuals view themselves in ways that are consistent with sex-role stereotypes can be measured using Sandra Bem's Sex Role Inventory (see Bem, 1981, 1984). It turns out that most women and men do *not* fall neatly into "feminine" and "masculine" categories. In fact, only a minority of women score both high in femininity and low in masculinity, and only a minority of men score both high in masculinity and low in femininity (e.g., Choi & Fuqua, 2003; Todman & Day, 2006). It is more common for people to show patterns of scores that do *not* reflect traditional Western sex-role stereotypes (e.g., high or low in both femininity and masculinity).

Gender Similarities in Dispositions.   Given the importance of gender as a gate to environments and activities in everyday life, it may be surprising that empirical data have shown that men and women do *not* differ significantly on most dispositions that have been investigated by social psychologists. For example, approximately equal proportions of men and women have high (or low) self-esteem; similar proportions of men and women are extraverted (or introverted); and men and women are equally intelligent (though men tend to score higher than women on visual-spatial tasks, and women tend to score higher than men on verbal tasks; see Halpern, 1992, 2004; Silverman, Choi, Mackewn, Fisher, Moro, & Olshansky, 2000; Weiss, Kemmier, Deisenhammer, Fleischhacker, & Delazer, 2003). Thus, although men and women experience different patterns of daily experiences (e.g., interacting with mostly same-sex friends), these gender-based experiences do not produce reliable sex differences on most personality traits. Presumably, the general absence of sex differences reflects that the settings encountered by women and men produce approximately equal rates of success and failure, provide similar numbers of interpersonal interactions, and involve comparable opportunities for intellectual growth (see Friedman & Schustack, 2003).

Gender Differences in Dispositions.   As mentioned, many people believe that women and men differ in some traits (gender stereotypes). For instance, men are often thought to be more dominant than women, who, in contrast, are thought to be more nurturing than men. Empirical investigations of these expected gender differences, using participants' self-ratings, have often supported parts of the stereotypes,

H H H Ex
L H L In

Consensus
Consistency.
Distinctiveness

but the differences tend to be small (e.g., Martin, 1987; White, 2003). In an illustrative study, Yoshihisa Kashima at La Trobe University in Australia and his colleagues (Kashima, Yamaguchi, Kim, Choi, Gelfand, & Yuki, 1995) used a 12-item questionnaire in several countries to assess the extent to which respondents felt compassion toward other people and reported experiencing their feelings. Items included "I feel like doing something for people in trouble because I can almost feel their pain," "I often do what I feel like doing without paying attention to others' feelings" (reverse scored), and "I am not too concerned about other people's worries" (reverse scored). Kashima and his colleagues found that women scored significantly higher on these items than did men in Australia, the United States, and Japan. Thus, women reported feeling closer to other people than did men—a difference that is consistent with the gender stereotype of women as more nurturing than men.

Gender Differences in Homicidal Aggression.   Perhaps the clearest difference between men and women is in violent physical aggression. Men commit between 70% and 90% of murders around the world (see Archer, 1994; Daly & Wilson, 1988; Knight, Fabes, & Higgins, 1996). This is not to say that women are never aggressive—in fact, women engage in some kinds of aggressive behaviours almost as often as men, including verbal insults and slapping (see Bjorkvist, Osterman, & Lagerspetz, 1994; Ramirez, 1993). But in terms of homicidal aggression, men—particularly, young men between the ages of 18 and 30—are much more likely than women to be perpetrators. The greater physical strength of men may explain part of this pattern; a man is more likely to cause serious injury or death when he strikes another person with a fist or weapon than is a woman. But more than just strength is at play. Men consider violence to be a more acceptable response to many kinds of provocations than do women, including insults to their reputation, masculinity, or "honour" (especially when they come from certain cultural backgrounds; see Cohen & Nisbett, 1997). Men also have higher levels of certain hormones that have been implicated in physical aggression, especially testosterone. We will return to some of these determinants of aggression in Chapter 11.

Gender Differences in Romantic Attraction.   Another area that has revealed gender differences is romantic attraction. Let's begin, however, with some noteworthy *similarities* in this realm: when asked to describe the ideal mate, women and men across many cultures agree that three extremely important characteristics are honesty, kindness, and intelligence (see Berscheid & Reis, 1998; Buss, 1989). Thus, everybody wants a truthful, generous, and smart mate.

But women and men disagree about the importance of some other qualities. In particular, women place more weight than men on the status and material wealth of possible mates, whereas men place more weight than women on the physical attractiveness of possible mates (e.g., Buss, 1999; Feingold, 1992a; Kenrick, Ackerman, & Ledlow, 2003; Townsend & Wasserman, 1998). For example, women rate male targets who are ambitious and well educated more highly as mates than targets who do not possess these qualities, whereas men are less influenced by information about the ambitiousness or education of possible female mates. In contrast, men rate female targets who are youthful and physically attractive more positively as mates than older and less attractive targets, whereas women are less influenced by the age and physical attractiveness of potential male mates. These differences have been found in many different cultures; we offer possible explanations shortly.

Another gender difference in the romantic/sexual domain that is worth mentioning concerns the intentions that are inferred from friendly behaviour in a heterosexual interaction.

Men commit the vast majority of homicides.

Antonia Abbey (1987) at Wayne State University found that men were more likely than women to interpret a woman's friendly behaviour toward a man as indicating some sexual interest (i.e., as indicating potential willingness to engage in sexual behaviours). The erroneous assumption of a woman's sexual interest by men might cause them to initiate sexual behaviour that is more intimate than what a woman actually wants to do. This gender difference might explain why there are many more women who say that they have been forced into unwanted sexual behaviour than there are men who say that they have forced sexual behaviour on women.

We discuss a final interesting difference between the sexes in "Social Psychology in Your Life: Gender Differences in Responses to Threats." The box describes a recent hypothesis that women and men have fundamentally different automatic responses to threats and stress.

Social Psychology in Your Life   *Gender Differences in Responses to Threats*

It has long been assumed that all humans have a natural reaction to threat that can be characterized as a *fight-or-flight* response (Cannon, 1932). This response begins when the perception of a threat stimulates the release of adrenalin into the blood, which provides a surge of energy and strength. The surge of energy can be used either to confront the threat directly (fight) or to flee the threat (flight). The fight response will occur when the individual either has no escape or thinks that the threat (e.g., a predator) can be overcome physically; the flight response will occur when escape is possible and direct confrontation is judged likely to be either unsuccessful or extremely costly. For example, seeing a bear while strolling through the woods will cause a rush of fear and adrenalin that will facilitate a hasty retreat from the situation. Presumably, the fight-or-flight response evolved because it increased humans' survival rates by helping them to overcome or escape from dangerous situations.

Shelley Taylor and her colleagues at the University of California at Los Angeles (Taylor, Klein, Lewis, Gruenewald, Gurung, & Updegraff, 2000) made the interesting proposal that the fight-or-flight response is how men react to

threat, but not how women react. These researchers noted that most prior research testing the fight-or-flight response focused on men, and the relatively few studies that included women yielded inconsistent findings. They suggested that the inconsistent results occurred because women's reactions to threat are fundamentally different from men's. Throughout human history, women have been primarily responsible for the care of infants and children. Being pregnant or being burdened with infants and children would greatly interfere with women's capacity to fight, as well as reducing their chances of successful escape from the situation. Therefore, a fight-or-flight response to threat might not have been adaptive for ancestral women.

Instead, Taylor and her colleagues proposed that women show a *tend-and-befriend* response to threat. The *tend* component refers to looking after offspring. For many kinds of threats, it was probably adaptive for women to focus on their children—for example, to hide from the threat by quieting their children and blending into the environment. The *befriend* component refers to affiliating with others when threatened. It was also probably adaptive in response

Women may show a tend-and-befriend response to threats.

to many threats for women to seek other humans who could provide resources and protection for them and their offspring. As a result, gathering into groups may have become a natural response of women to threats.

Taylor and her colleagues proposed that both men and women experience arousal when threatened, but the consequences of this arousal and the hormones that are released differ between the sexes. They suggested that men's fight-or-flight responses to threat are guided by male androgen hormones, especially testosterone, which are present only in low levels in women. In contrast, they suggested that women's tend-and-befriend responses to threat are guided by the female hormones of estrogen and oxytocin, which are largely absent in men.

Causes of Gender Differences

Although women and men are similar on most qualities, we have identified a few areas where, on average, they currently differ, including nurturance, homicidal aggression, and romantic attraction. An important question—and a politically charged one (e.g., see Brescoll & LaFrance, 2004)—is *why* these sex differences occur. This issue is very complex, because gender differences reflect many factors, including social, biological, political, and institutional processes. Although it is an oversimplification, we will focus on two broad categories of variables that may contribute to gender differences: biological processes and social processes.

Some researchers have identified possible *biological* sources of gender differences, arguing that genetic and physiological differences between the sexes play a role. For example, Sarah Duff and Elizabeth Hampson (Duff & Hampson, 2000, 2001; Hampson, 2002) at the University of Western Ontario obtained evidence that hormonal differences between women and men (e.g., levels of estrogen and androgen) may contribute to the sexes' differential performance on specific kinds of ability tests, such as women's superiority on verbal measures and men's superiority on spatial measures.

Another biological perspective on gender differences comes from evolutionary theory (see Buss, 1996; Buss & Kenrick, 1998; Gangestad & Simpson, 2000; Geary, 1999; Kenrick et al., 2003). This perspective assumes that, in our distant ancestral past, men and women faced different reproductive pressures, which led to the evolution of certain gender differences. For example, the **parental investment hypothesis** (Trivers, 1972) contends that having children is more costly for women than for men (women must *invest* more to be a *parent*, hence *parental investment* hypothesis). Women carry the fetus during pregnancy and typically nurse the baby for some time after birth; women also provide most of the postnatal care and socialization of infants and young children. These high costs of parenting make women more selective than men about potential sexual mates; the costs also induce women to focus especially on characteristics that suggest a man will be able and willing to provide support and protection for the mother and child. These pressures may explain the findings described earlier that women put more emphasis on status and wealth cues in rating the attractiveness of potential mates than do men: mates who are high in status and wealth should be able to provide excellent support for mother and child. In contrast, because men invest less in becoming a parent, they are less selective about potential sexual mates and emphasize characteristics that imply reproductive fertility, such as youth and physical attractiveness.

Other researchers have identified *social,* or *cultural,* sources of gender differences, noting that men and women are socialized to behave differently, to want different things, and to expect different actions from other men and women (e.g., Deaux & LaFrance, 1998; Eagly, 1987). We observed earlier that gender has profound effects on the daily experiences of men and women. The cultural perspective argues that these different experiences, which are assumed to result mainly from society's gender stereotypes, produce some differences between men and women (see Abele, 2003). For example, women may be more nurturing than men because, from infancy, girls are socialized more than boys to be compassionate and supportive; these gender-based socialization practices lead to differences in adult personalities.

Socialization explanations for gender differences in romantic attraction have also been proposed (e.g., Caporael & Brewer, 1995; Eagly, 1995). For example, theorists have noted that everyone, at least in Western cultures, is bombarded with messages in the media that emphasize the importance of women's physical beauty; these messages may convince both women and men that beauty is important in determining the worth of women. Also, women's socialization toward domestic roles may lead

parental investment hypothesis
the idea that having children is more costly for women than for men, which has led to the evolution of some differences between the sexes in the characteristics they seek in mates

Men and women differ in the roles they are assigned in our culture.

them to assume that they should rely on men for financial support; this belief might explain the greater weight put on resources by women than by men in evaluating possible mates.

It seems likely that biological, social, and other processes all play some role in gender differences. Wendy Wood at Duke University and Alice Eagly at Northwestern University (2002; Eagly & Wood, 1999) argued that women and men have been assigned different social roles throughout history based, in part, on biological demands: women must bear children and care for infants, and men can use their superior speed and strength for certain kinds of hunting and fighting. These biological facts have encouraged the evolution of a few differences between the two sexes across all cultures. But most roles assigned to women and men within specific cultures do not follow directly from biological characteristics. Indeed, Wood and Eagly (2002) noted that there are substantial differences between cultures in some of the specific roles and duties assigned to women and men. They concluded from these cultural differences that women and men both "appear to possess sufficient psychological flexibility to accommodate to a wide range of socioeconomic roles" (p. 718). In sum, although biology places a few inevitable constraints on gender roles, most current differences between men and women probably reflect gender-specific socialization.

Interactions Between Persons and Situations

Social psychologists focus on situational factors that influence behaviour. When social psychologists include "person" variables in their studies, they typically conceptualize the dispositions' effects in terms of *interactions between persons and situations*.

This interactionist approach to understanding social behaviour assumes that situational factors can have different effects on people with dissimilar personal characteristics—that is, dissimilar people can act differently in the same situation.

In the current section, we present three examples of this interactionist perspective on social behaviour. Although there are dozens of individual difference variables that have been studied by social psychologists, we will focus on these three variables in depth.

So, if she's friendly with her peers but not with her professors, we know a little bit about her psychology . . .

Self-Monitoring

Mark Snyder, a Canadian who obtained his undergraduate degree at McGill University and is currently a professor at the University of Minnesota, developed a scale to measure the dimension of **self-monitoring** (Snyder, 1974, 1987; Snyder & Gangestad, 1986). Self-monitoring refers to the extent to which people rely on external or internal cues to guide their behaviour. People who are high self-monitors pay attention to external cues, such as group norms or what other people want, in deciding how to behave. High self-monitors shape their behaviour to fit the external guidelines: they conform to group norms and rules, or they tailor their words to avoid offending someone who disagrees with them. In contrast, low self-monitors are largely insensitive to external cues, instead deciding how to behave based on internal states like attitudes and values (Kardes, Sanbonmatsu, Voss, & Fazio, 1986; Snyder & Swann, 1976). Low self-monitors are less likely to follow group norms or to tailor their public behaviour: they "say what they believe" without much regard for the consequences. As is the case with most dispositional variables, there is no "good" or "bad" level of self-monitoring.

self-monitoring

a disposition that represents the extent to which people rely on external or internal cues to guide their behaviour

Self-monitoring can be measured with an 18-item, self-report questionnaire in which respondents answer either *true* or *false* to each item. Sample items are presented in Know Yourself 5.2: "Self-Monitoring Scale." How would you answer these items?

Scores on the self-monitoring scale have been shown to interact with situational factors to influence behaviour. For example, one application has been to the area of interpersonal attraction. Imagine yourself in the following situation: You have an opportunity to go on a date with one of two individuals. One possible dating partner is someone who is very attractive physically but has a number of undesirable personal characteristics: he or she is reserved toward strangers, is more concerned about himself or herself than other people, and has a tendency toward moodiness. The second possible dating partner is someone who is physically unattractive but has highly positive personal characteristics: he or she is outgoing, listens well to other people, and values a sense of humour. Which of these two persons would you choose for a date?

Mark Snyder, Ellen Berscheid, and Peter Glick (1985) conducted a study at the University of Minnesota in which male participants were given exactly this choice: they could date either a physically attractive woman who had the undesirable characteristics noted above or a physically unattractive woman who had the desirable characteristics noted above. Participants also completed the self-monitoring scale. The findings were dramatic: low self-monitors chose the partner with the desirable personal characteristics 81% of the time, whereas high self-monitors chose the

High self-monitors are more concerned about the physical attractiveness of their date than are low self-monitors.

Know Yourself 5.2
Self-Monitoring Scale

Please indicate whether each of the following sentences is more true or more false about you.

1. I find it hard to imitate the behaviour of other people.

   True   False

2. I can only argue for ideas that I already believe.

   True   False

3. I would probably make a good actor.

   True   False

4. In different situations and with different people, I often act like very different persons.

   True   False

5. I am not particularly good at making people like me.

   True   False

6. I'm not always the person I appear to be.

   True   False

7. I would not change my opinions (or the way I do things) in order to please someone or win their favour.

   True   False

8. At a party, I let others keep the jokes and stories going.

   True   False

9. I can look anyone in the eye and tell a lie with a straight face (if for a good cause).

   True   False

10. I may deceive people by being friendly when I really dislike them.

    True   False

SCORING: One point is assigned for answering *True* to Items 3, 4, 6, 9, or 10; one point is assigned for answering *False* to Items 1, 2, 5, 7, or 8. Possible scores range from 0 to 10, and higher scores indicate that the respondent is a high self-monitor.

Sample items from Snyder and Gangestad, "On the nature of self-monitoring: Matters of assessment, matters of validity," *Journal of Personality and Social Psychology,* 51, 125–139, 1986. Copyright © 1986 by the American Psychological Association. Reprinted by permission.

partner who was physically attractive 69% of the time. Why did this division along self-monitoring lines occur? The authors speculated that because low self-monitors behave on the basis of internal cues like attitudes and beliefs, they focus on the internal characteristics of other people as well (see also Jamieson, Lydon, & Zanna, 1987). High self-monitors, on the other hand, are more concerned about external cues, such as physical attractiveness. High self-monitors also care more about making a good impression on other people than do low self-monitors, and an attractive partner enhances one's public image (see also Glick, DeMorest, & Hotze, 1988; Sharp & Getz, 1996).

This example of research on self-monitoring illustrates nicely how dispositions can interact with other factors to predict behaviour. The physical attractiveness of a potential date influenced choices by high but not low self-monitors, whereas the personality characteristics of a potential date influenced choices by low but not high self-monitors.

Uncertainty Orientation

Richard Sorrentino and his colleagues at the University of Western Ontario (Sorrentino & Roney, 2000; Sorrentino, Short, & Raynor, 1984) have identified the trait of **uncertainty orientation,** an individual difference variable that reflects people's interest in learning new things about themselves and their environment. Research on uncertainty orientation has focused on two groups of people: those who are oriented either toward uncertainty or toward certainty. People who are *uncertainty-oriented* want to learn new things about themselves and are attracted by novelty and unpredictability. People who are *certainty-oriented* want to maintain their current conceptualizations of themselves and the environment and are attracted by familiarity and predictability.

Uncertainty orientation is measured by asking participants to write brief stories based on an opening sentence, such as "Several people are sitting in a lounge talking" or "A person is sitting wondering about what may happen." Participants are asked to describe what led up to the current situation, what the characters are doing and thinking, and what will happen in the future. Because the lead-in sentences are ambiguous, they allow participants to take the stories in many different directions; therefore, the stories are expected to reflect the storytellers' underlying motivations (see Smith, 1992). To score uncertainty orientation, the stories are examined by trained judges who look for the presence of uncertainty "themes." For example, a story in which a character imagines something that might happen in the future and looks forward to a new environment would generate a high uncertainty score. In contrast, a story in which the character focuses on the past and thinks only about events that have already taken place would generate a low uncertainty score. Participants are normally asked to write several stories, and their uncertainty scores are averaged or summed across all stories.

Sorrentino and his colleagues have conducted a diverse research program over the past 20 years investigating the implications of uncertainty orientation (for a review, see Sorrentino & Roney, 2000). These researchers have identified numerous situational factors that interact with uncertainty orientation to predict behaviour. We will describe one example here.

Richard Sorrentino and Erin Hewitt (1984) showed that uncertainty-oriented and certainty-oriented individuals responded very differently to an opportunity to learn about themselves. These researchers had participants complete a task that allegedly measured a new aspect of their mental abilities. They were given feedback that was somewhat unclear and uncertain. Some participants were told that their performance showed that they were *not low* in this ability, but it was unclear whether they were *average* or *high* in the ability. Other participants were informed that their performance showed that they were *not high* in this ability, but it was unclear whether they were *low* or *average.*

All participants then learned that they would be performing another test of this same mental ability, but this time they would have some input into the makeup of the test. They were informed that there were two different sets of test items from which they could choose. One set of test items was very good at distinguishing between *low* and *average* ability, whereas the other set of test items was very good at distinguishing between *average* and *high* ability. Participants were instructed that they could select items from either set for their next test.

Participants who were uncertainty-oriented (UOs) tended to choose items that would clarify their uncertainty. UOs who had been told that they did not have low ability (but did not know whether they were average or high in ability) selected most of their items from the set that was good at distinguishing between average and high ability; UOs who had been told that they did not have high ability (but did not know whether they were low or average in ability) selected most items from the set that was good at distinguishing between low and average ability. Obviously, these uncertainty-oriented

uncertainty orientation

a disposition that represents the extent to which people want to learn new things about themselves and their environment participants wanted to zero in on their actual level of ability, so they could find out exactly where they stood.

On the other hand, certainty-oriented participants (COs) tended to *avoid* the most diagnostic items. If they knew they were not low in ability (but did not know whether they were average or high), COs chose most of their items from the set that was good at distinguishing between low and average ability, which would not clarify their own ability. If they knew they were not high in ability (but did not know whether they were low or average), COs chose most of their items from the set that was good at distinguishing between average and high ability—again, selecting items that would not clarify their own ability. Obviously, these certainty-oriented participants simply did not want to learn anything new about this aspect of their mental abilities. The personal disposition of uncertainty orientation predicted how individuals behaved in the same situation. The flowchart in Figure 5.3 depicts the hypothesized responses of uncertainty-oriented and certainty-oriented participants.

Perfectionism

Some people strive for perfection in everything they do. They are personally satisfied only when their work is flawless and believe that others will judge them negatively unless everything they do is a masterpiece. The trait of **perfectionism** captures this striving for excellence. The best-known scale to measure perfectionism was developed by Paul Hewitt of the University of British Columbia and Gordon Flett of York University (Hewitt & Flett, 1991). Their scale distinguished between three kinds of perfectionism, but we will discuss only two. **Self-oriented perfectionism** refers to the tendency to set extremely high standards for yourself and to be satisfied only when your performance is flawless. **Socially prescribed perfectionism** refers to believing that other people expect your performance to be outstanding and will judge you negatively unless such high standards are achieved.

These two types of perfectionism can be measured with a 30-item scale (15 items for each type). Respondents indicate the extent to which they agree or disagree with each item on a 7-point scale from *Disagree strongly* (1) to *Agree strongly* (7). Sample items are presented in Know Yourself 5.3: "Perfectionism Scale." See how you score on these characteristics.

perfectionism

a disposition that represents the extent to which individuals strive for error-free performance

self-oriented perfectionism

a disposition that represents the extent to which individuals set extremely high standards for themselves and are satisfied only when their performance is flawless

socially prescribed perfectionism

a disposition that represents the extent to which individuals believe that other people expect exceptional performance from them and will judge them negatively if such standards are not achieved

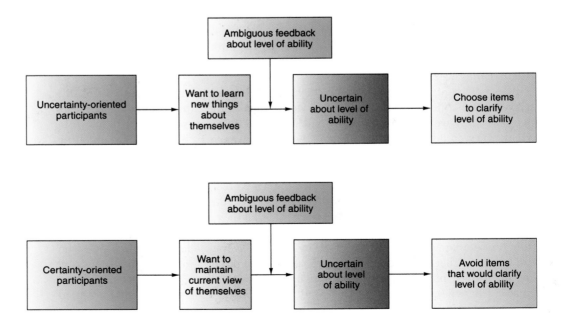

FIGURE 5.3

Hypothesized responses of uncertainty-oriented and certainty-oriented participants in experiment by Sorrentino and Hewitt (1984)

Know Yourself 5.3
Perfectionism Scale

Please indicate the extent to which you agree or disagree with each statement by circling the appropriate number on the answer scale.

1. It makes me uneasy to see an error in my work.

1	2	3	4	5	6	7
Disagree strongly						Agree strongly

2. The better I do, the better I am expected to do.

1	2	3	4	5	6	7
Disagree strongly						Agree strongly

3. One of my goals is to be perfect in everything I do.

1	2	3	4	5	6	7
Disagree strongly						Agree strongly

4. My family expects me to be perfect.

1	2	3	4	5	6	7
Disagree strongly						Agree strongly

5. I never aim for perfection in my work.

1	2	3	4	5	6	7
Disagree strongly						Agree strongly

6. Those around me readily accept that I can make mistakes too.

1	2	3	4	5	6	7
Disagree strongly						Agree strongly

7. I must work to my full potential at all times.

1	2	3	4	5	6	7
Disagree strongly						Agree strongly

8. The people around me expect me to succeed at everything I do.

1	2	3	4	5	6	7
Disagree strongly						Agree strongly

9. I must always be successful at school or work.

1	2	3	4	5	6	7
Disagree strongly						Agree strongly

10. Anything that I do that is less than excellent will be seen as poor work by those around me.

1	2	3	4	5	6	7
Disagree strongly						Agree strongly

SCORING:

1. *Self-oriented perfectionism:* Items 1, 3, 7, and 9 are scored using the answer scales as presented (1-2-3-4-5-6-7); Item 5 is reverse-scored (that is, 7-6-5-4-3-2-1). Add up all of these items for your overall self-oriented perfectionism score. Possible scores range from 5 to 35, and higher scores represent more self-oriented perfectionism.

2. *Socially prescribed perfectionism:* Items 2, 4, 8, and 10 are scored using the answer scales as presented; Item 6 is reverse-scored. Add up all of these items for your overall socially prescribed perfectionism score. Possible scores range from 5 to 35, and higher scores represent more socially prescribed perfectionism.

Researchers have investigated whether the two types of perfectionism—self-oriented and socially prescribed—are associated with other desirable or undesirable characteristics. Socially prescribed perfectionism has typically been found to be correlated with negative emotional states like depression and anxiety, presumably because socially prescribed perfectionists are fearful of negative evaluations by other people if they fail to perform flawlessly (e.g., Chang & Sanna, 2001; Hewitt & Flett, 1991; Powers, Zuroff, & Topciu, 2004). In contrast, self-oriented perfectionism has been found to be correlated with some positive outcomes (e.g., Dunkley, Blankstein, Halsall, Williams, & Winkworth, 2000; Mills & Blankstein, 2000). For instance, in a study conducted at the University of Quebec at Montreal, Paule Miquelon, Robert Vallerand, and their colleagues (Miquelon, Vallerand, Grouzet, & Cardinal, 2005) found that higher levels of self-oriented perfectionism were associated with higher levels of intrinsic motivation for school activities and academic achievement. That is, self-oriented perfectionists were more likely to complete schoolwork because they *wanted* to complete it, compared to participants who were low on this dimension. Presumably, self-oriented perfectionism has more positive correlates than socially prescribed perfectionism because, in the former case, the high standards are personally chosen rather than imposed by others' expectations.

In a recent study, perfectionism was shown to interact with another factor in the domain of goal attainment. Richard Koestner, a social psychologist at McGill University, previously conducted research showing that people are more likely to successfully achieve a goal if they make specific plans about *how* to do so; such action plans are called *implementation intentions* (e.g., Koestner, Lekes, Powers, & Chicoine, 2002). Presumably, planning helps people to focus on the goal and facilitates efficient task completion (see Gollwitzer, 1999).

Recently, however, Koestner and his colleagues (Powers, Koestner, & Topciu, 2005) found that one type of perfectionism *interferes* with the positive effect of planning. Students at McGill University who had made at least one New Year's resolution (e.g., to become more physically active, to spend more time studying) were recruited in early January to participate in this study. Half of the participants were asked to develop specific implementation intentions for their most important resolution—to think about concrete ways they could achieve their goal. The remaining participants completed a control task that did not involve making any plans for achieving their resolution. Four weeks later, participants were contacted and asked how much progress they had made toward achieving their resolution. Results showed that, in the implementation condition, people who were high in socially prescribed perfectionism reported *less* progress toward their goal than did people who were low in socially prescribed perfectionism. In other words, advance planning appeared to backfire for socially prescribed perfectionists. The researchers speculated that these individuals were so concerned about how others would evaluate them that each specific plan triggered worry and self-criticism, thus interfering with effective goal accomplishment. People who were high in self-oriented perfectionism reported more progress toward their resolution than people who were low in self-oriented perfectionism, and planning had a generally positive effect on these self-oriented perfectionists. Thus, the effect of planning on goal achievement depended on individuals' levels of perfectionism.

Dispositions and Health

Some of the most interesting research in the area of individual differences has addressed the issue of health, specifically the connections between dispositions and well-being. Are people with particular traits more likely to be in good health? "Good health" can be defined in terms of objective health outcomes (e.g., physical symptoms, behavioural recovery, admission to hospital) or in terms of subjective judgments (e.g., distress, happiness, satisfaction with life). This distinction between objective and subjective well-being may be important. For example, Dave Korotkov and T. Edward Hannah (2004) at Memorial University in St. John's, Newfoundland, found that measures of several personality traits predicted respondents' subjective well-being over a six-month period better than they predicted objective health outcomes. It seems plausible that feelings of distress or happiness may be more susceptible to influence by individuals' personal qualities (e.g., their outlook on life) than objective outcomes like recovery from illness.

You may have heard of Norman Cousins, who wrote a book titled *Anatomy of an Illness,* which was published in 1979 and received wide popular acclaim. Cousins wrote about his personal battle with an inflammatory illness of the spine and joints. In particular, the book focused on Cousins's use of humour and laughter to fight the disease. He deliberately sought out humour and comedy to maintain his spirits; he also believed that laughter directly reduced his pain. Cousins's book stimulated considerable interest in the role of humour and optimism in health. An excellent review of the literature on the relation between humour and well-being was written by Rod Martin (2001) of the University of Western Ontario.

How accurate is this view of fighting disease? Can an individual's emotional state or outlook play a role in his or her health outcomes? We need to be careful not to "blame the victim" by concluding that people who do not recover from illnesses are somehow responsible for their negative outcome because they were not optimistic enough in their outlook. On the other hand, emotional states can affect physical processes, and there may also be personal qualities that facilitate healthier lifestyles, such as a conscientious person who carefully follows doctors' orders.

In the following sections, we discuss three individual differences that have been shown by researchers to be related to well-being: optimism, intelligence, and the Type A coronary-prone behaviour pattern (see also Kling, Ryff, Love, & Essex, 2003). Keep in mind that data involving personal dispositions are correlational, so we must be careful about drawing causal conclusions.

Dispositional Optimism

In 1985, Michael Scheier at Carnegie-Mellon University and Charles Carver at the University of Miami published a paper that introduced an eight-item scale to measure **dispositional optimism,** which they defined as the tendency to have positive, confident expectations about one's own future outcomes. Scheier and Carver labelled their scale the **Life Orientation Test (LOT).** People who are optimistic generally expect things to go well, whereas people who are pessimistic generally expect things to go poorly. Note that optimists do not necessarily believe that they have *personal control* over their outcomes (i.e., they do not necessarily have high self-efficacy; see Chapter 4)—they are simply optimistic that things will go well, for whatever reason (e.g., they might believe they are "lucky people").

Are you generally an optimist or a pessimist? In Know Yourself 5.4: "Life Orientation Test," you can measure your own dispositional optimism.

In their initial research, Scheier and Carver (1985) surveyed university students twice, the second time four weeks after the first. A measure of optimism was obtained at the first session, and at both sessions participants reported their level of several common symptoms, such as dizziness, muscle soreness, fatigue, and blurred vision. The researchers found that optimistic respondents were less likely

dispositional optimism
a disposition that represents the extent to which people have positive, confident expectations about their own future outcomes

Life Orientation Test (LOT)
a measure of dispositional optimism

Know Yourself 5.4
Life Orientation Test (LOT)

Please indicate the extent to which you agree or disagree with each of the following statements by circling the appropriate number on the answer scale.

1. In uncertain times, I usually expect the best.

0	1	2	3	4
Strongly disagree	Disagree	Neutral	Agree	Strongly agree

2. If something can go wrong for me, it will.

0	1	2	3	4
Strongly disagree	Disagree	Neutral	Agree	Strongly agree

3. I always look on the bright side of things.

0	1	2	3	4
Strongly disagree	Disagree	Neutral	Agree	Strongly agree

4. I'm always optimistic about my future.

0	1	2	3	4
Strongly disagree	Disagree	Neutral	Agree	Strongly agree

5. I hardly ever expect things to go my way.

0	1	2	3	4
Strongly disagree	Disagree	Neutral	Agree	Strongly agree

6. Things never work out the way I want them to.

0	1	2	3	4
Strongly disagree	Disagree	Neutral	Agree	Strongly agree

7. I'm a believer in the idea that "every cloud has a silver lining."

0	1	2	3	4
Strongly disagree	Disagree	Neutral	Agree	Strongly agree

8. I rarely count on good things happening to me.

0	1	2	3	4
Strongly disagree	Disagree	Neutral	Agree	Strongly agree

SCORING: Items 1, 3, 4, and 7 are scored using the answer scales as presented (0-1-2-3-4); Items 2, 5, 6, and 8 are reverse-scored (that is, 4-3-2-1-0). Add up all of the items for your overall dispositional optimism score. Possible scores range from 0 to 32, and higher total scores represent stronger optimism.

Sample items from Scheier and Carver, "Optimism, coping and health: Assessment and implications of generalized outcome expectancies," *Health Psychology*, 4, 219–247. Copyright © 1985 by the American Psychological Association. Reprinted by permission.

to show an increase in reported symptoms between sessions than were pessimistic respondents. Thus, optimism was associated with fewer newly reported physical complaints.

In another study, Scheier and his colleagues administered the LOT to 51 men on the day before they underwent coronary artery bypass surgery (Scheier et al., 1989). The men were interviewed two more times: one week and six months after surgery. Findings showed that men who scored high on optimism before surgery recovered faster, as indicated by such behaviours as walking, returning to work, and resuming vigorous exercise, than did men who scored low on optimism. Also, men who scored high on optimism before surgery reported greater satisfaction with their recovery and less distress about their condition six months after surgery, compared to men who scored low on optimism.

Other researchers have also found that optimism is associated with lower distress after surgery or stressful life events (e.g., Carver et al., 1993; Kaiser, Major, & McCoy, 2004; Litt, Tennen, Affleck, & Klock, 1992), although it is important to note that the correlations between optimism and healthy outcomes are sometimes small and occasionally absent altogether (see Salovey, Rothman, & Rodin, 1998). Notwithstanding the occasional null result, the findings for optimism are impressive.

Why might a confident outlook predict heightened well-being? One possibility is that optimists may be more likely to engage in healthy behaviours than pessimists (e.g., Shepperd, Maroto, & Pbert, 1996), such as lowering their intake of saturated fats, perhaps because they expect those behaviours to be effective (after all, they *are* optimistic). Second, optimists avoid dwelling on negative affect (e.g., Scheier et al., 1989), which can reduce the sense of well-being directly. In this context, Ulrich Schimmack of the University of Toronto and his colleagues (Schimmack, Oishi, Furr, & Funder, 2004) found that a cheerful disposition was a strong predictor of life satisfaction.

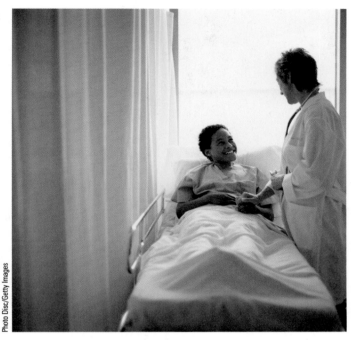

People who are optimistic about the future may recover from surgery more quickly than people who are pessimistic.

But what about the research on *unrealistic optimism* we described in Chapter 4 (see page 135)? Recall that most people predict that they are less likely than average to experience negative life events and more likely than average to experience positive life events (e.g., Weinstein & Klein, 1996). There is some evidence that unrealistic optimism is associated with fewer health-protective behaviours, perhaps because unrealistically optimistic individuals do not feel vulnerable to health threats (e.g., Perloff, 1983; Tennen & Affleck, 1987).

Are people who score high on dispositional optimism also more unrealistically optimistic about specific negative and positive events? At least concerning heart disease, the answer appears to be no! Nathan Radcliffe and William Klein (2002) studied 146 middle-aged adults in Waterville, Maine, who completed the LOT as a measure of dispositional optimism. Respondents also provided detailed personal information (e.g., family history, blood pressure, cholesterol level) that allowed the researchers to calculate their actual risk of suffering a fatal heart attack, based on data from large-scale studies of heart disease. Respondents were also asked to estimate the likelihood that they would have a fatal heart attack. It was then possible to calculate objectively the degree to which respondents were unrealistically optimistic—the extent to which their estimates were lower than their actual risk. Results showed that participants who were high in dispositional optimism were *not* more unrealistic about their vulnerability to heart disease than were pessimistic participants. In fact, optimistic respondents had more knowledge about heart disease than did pessimistic respondents. Thus, being optimistic and being unrealistic were not the same.

These findings are interesting because they suggest that optimism as measured by the LOT does not involve "sticking one's head in the sand" like an ostrich and simply denying real risks or refusing to obtain information about risks. Instead, dispositional optimism seems to be an outlook or approach to life that tries to focus on the positive aspects of events, including positive ways of dealing with real risks.

Intelligence

On June 1, 1932, almost every child attending school in Scotland who was born in 1921 (then either 10 or 11 years old) took an intelligence test. This process was repeated in 1947, testing all children attending school in Scotland who were born in 1936. These two huge samples of boys and girls have been followed into adulthood, completing several surveys since the initial interviews. The resulting data have allowed researchers to examine the long-term health implications of intelligence scores. Follow-up studies have examined rates of illness and death from various causes, including cancer and cardiovascular disease.

These studies have consistently shown that intelligence (measured in childhood) is positively correlated with subsequent health (freedom from illness) and longevity (life span). For example, Lawrence Whalley and Ian Deary (2001) traced the records of 2185 men and women in 1997 who had taken the intelligence test as children living in 1932 in the city of Aberdeen, Scotland. Of this total, 1101 were alive and 1084 were dead at age 76. Intelligence scores as children predicted survival: every 15-point increase in IQ scores was associated with a 20% increase in survival rate.

Specific illnesses that have been shown to be predictable from childhood intelligence scores include lung cancer, stomach cancer, and heart disease (e.g., Deary, Whiteman, Starr, Whalley, & Fox, 2004). One possible explanation of these findings is that higher intelligence is associated with higher socioeconomic status (SES). That is, individuals who are highly intelligent also tend to be wealthier, which might improve their health through better nutrition, better access to health services, and so on. However, SES cannot entirely explain the findings because the correlation between intelligence scores and longevity remains significant even when individuals who are equal in SES are examined.

What other factors might explain the correlations between childhood intelligence scores and length of life? Linda Gottfredson and Ian Deary (2004) suggested that intelligence may increase people's skill at maintaining their own health. For example, intelligent people may recognize possible risks quickly and thereby avoid accidental injuries. Intelligent people may also understand the significant health implications of lifestyle choices such as smoking or eating fatty foods. Finally, intelligent people may be good at implementing and maintaining complex treatment programs, such as remembering to take medications at specific times and monitoring their physical status (e.g., blood sugar levels for diabetics).

"Type A" Coronary-Prone Behaviour Pattern

"Type A" coronary-prone behaviour pattern

a constellation of characteristics, including impatience, anger, and hostility, that has been linked to heart disease

The **"Type A" coronary-prone behaviour pattern** refers to a constellation of characteristics that has been linked with heart disease (e.g., Chesney & Rosenman, 1985; Friedman & Rosenman, 1974; Glass, 1977). It represents a hard-driving, competitive style, as reflected in impatience, time urgency, competitiveness, ambitiousness, anger, and hostility.

The Type A pattern is usually assessed by interviewing individuals and posing a set of standard questions. The questions mostly concern competitive situations, such as whether the person always plays games to win. The individual's verbal and nonverbal responses are used to decide whether he or she meets the criteria for classification as Type A. For example, if someone answers the question about playing to win affirmatively, and if his or her response is immediate and forceful (e.g., "You bet I do!"), then classification as a Type A person is more likely. In general, nonverbal cues indicating tension, aggressiveness, time urgency, and anger increase the likelihood of a Type A label. Self-report measures have also been developed to assess the Type A pattern (e.g., Krantz, Glass, & Snyder, 1974), but the interview procedure is generally regarded as the most valid diagnostic method (see Matthews, 1982, 1988).

The assumption underlying research on the Type A pattern has been that the emotional volatility of these individuals (due to impatience, competitiveness, hostility, etc.) produces frequent states of arousal and stress, which increase blood pressure, stimulate the release of stress hormones, and generally hasten the onset of cardiopulmonary problems. Type A individuals respond to many situations more intensely than the average person. All of us can think of times when we have felt stressed and under pressure; we know that the pounding heart, aching gut, and suppressed emotions cannot be healthy. This stress is experienced quite frequently by individuals who are Type A.

To make matters even worse, Type A individuals also tend to have unhealthy lifestyles (e.g., to smoke and drink more than average) and to ignore physical warning signals they may experience (e.g., Carver, Coleman, & Glass, 1976; Matthews, 1982). Obviously, these lifestyle issues can amplify the physical vulnerability of those with a Type A disposition.

The Type A pattern is a very broad one, incorporating emotions, behaviours, and personality. Some researchers have argued that only certain portions of the behaviour pattern are unhealthy, whereas other portions may be innocuous (Booth-Kewley & Friedman, 1987; Salovey et al., 1998). There is some evidence that the major risk factor in the Type A pattern is the tendency toward anger and hostility. The emotional reactivity of angry and hostile people may increase their susceptibility to heart disease, whereas there may not be serious negative health implications of ambitiousness or competitiveness per se (Barefoot, 1992; Friedman, 1992; Smith, 1992). Future research will explore further whether anger and hostility are the key negative aspects of the broader concept of the Type A behaviour pattern.

People who fit the "Type A" coronary-prone behaviour pattern experience anger more often than most people.

Chapter Summary

Dispositions refer to individuals' consistencies across time and settings in a specific type of feeling, thought, and/or action, which make individuals different from other people. For example, **self-esteem** represents people's judgments of their own worthiness; people with high self-esteem think positively about themselves, but people with low self-esteem evaluate themselves negatively.

The **self-concept** refers to all information about the self in memory. **Identity** is a narrower construct, which refers to the characteristics that individuals think define them and make up their most important qualities. The **spontaneous self-concept** refers to those aspects of the identity that are in conscious awareness at a given point in time. Aspects of the self that have been recently activated and

aspects that make the self distinctive from others in the situation are especially likely to be part of the spontaneous self-concept.

Identity consists of both personal qualities and group memberships. **Social identity theory** proposes that people want to maintain a positive social (group) identity, which can be achieved via the perception that groups to which they belong are superior to other groups. Several **minimal group studies,** which assign participants to arbitrary and meaningless groups, have shown that participants generally treat ingroup members more favourably than outgroup members.

Optimal distinctiveness theory proposes that individuals want a balance between similarity to other people and separateness from other people; they want enough individuality to have their own identity but not so much that they feel disconnected from others. People from collectivist cultures are more likely to define themselves in terms of their social relationships than are people from individualist cultures.

Individuals' levels of self-esteem predict a variety of psychological processes. For example, higher self-esteem is associated with greater optimism about the future, more self-serving judgments, greater reported happiness, and more confidence in one's relationships. But high self-esteem can have negative associations: some people with high self-esteem are also high in **narcissism,** which refers to an excessive love for the self. People who are high in narcissism have been shown to respond with greater aggression to personal threat than people who are low in narcissism—a response that has been labelled **threatened egotism.** A distinction can also be made between **secure high self-esteem,** which refers to a positive self-view that is confidently held, and **defensive high self-esteem,** which refers to a positive self-view that is fragile and vulnerable to threat. People with defensive high self-esteem need repeated praise from others, which can be associated with boastful, arrogant behaviour and hostility toward anyone who questions their self-worth.

Gender is another "person" factor that affects many aspects of our daily lives. Although women and men do not differ on most dispositions, there are sex differences in some traits, as well as in homicidal aggression, romantic attraction, and behavioural responses to threat. The differences between women and men probably reflect a combination of biological and social processes. An example of a biological process is the **parental investment hypothesis,** which contends that having children is more costly for women than for men; these differential costs are hypothesized to have led to the evolution of some differences between the sexes in the characteristics they seek in mates.

Social psychologists often conceptualize social behaviour in terms of *interactions between persons and situations;* this perspective assumes that situational factors can have different effects on people with dissimilar personal characteristics. Illustrative dimensions discussed in the chapter include **self-monitoring,** which refers to the extent to which people rely on external or internal cues to guide their behaviour; **uncertainty orientation,** which distinguishes between people who want to learn new things about themselves and the environment (labelled *uncertainty-oriented* individuals) and people who want to maintain their current conceptualizations of themselves and are attracted by familiarity and predictability (labelled *certainty-oriented* individuals); and **perfectionism,** which refers to how much people strive for flawless performance. Different types of perfectionism can be distinguished, including **self-oriented perfectionism** (people expect perfection from themselves) and **socially prescribed perfectionism** (people believe that others expect them to be perfect).

Several dispositions have been shown to be related to health and well-being. For instance, **dispositional optimism,** which is the tendency to have positive, confident expectations about one's own future outcomes, has been found to predict both physical and psychological well-being. Dispositional optimism is usually measured using the **Life Orientation Test** (or **LOT**). The **"Type A" coronary-prone behaviour pattern** refers to a constellation of characteristics, including impatience, anger, and hostility, that has been linked to heart disease.

Key Terms

defensive high self-esteem (168)

dispositional optimism (181)

dispositions (154)

identity (155)

Life Orientation Test (LOT) (181)

minimal group paradigm (159)

narcissism (167)

optimal distinctiveness theory (160)

parental investment hypothesis (173)

perfectionism (178)

secure high self-esteem (168)

self-concept (155)

self-esteem (155)

self-monitoring (175)

self-oriented perfectionism (178)

social identity theory (158)

socially prescribed perfectionism (178)

spontaneous self-concept (157)

threatened egotism (167)

"Type A" coronary-prone behaviour pattern (184)

uncertainty orientation (177)

Social Psychology Alive on the Web

SOCIAL PSYCHOLOGY ALIVE: ONLINE LABS

To perform the following experiments and see how you compare to other students, go to Social Psychology Lab, which can be accessed through ThomsonNOW™

- 5.1 Personality Test
- 5.2 Self-Description

SOCIAL PSYCHOLOGY ALIVE: QUIZZING AND PRACTICE TESTS

You can access our Web site directly by going to http://www.socialpsychologyalive.nelson.com for online quizzes, flash cards, and Internet links.

INFOTRAC® COLLEGE EDITION

For additional readings, explore InfoTrac® College Edition, your online library of archived journal articles and periodicals dating back 22 years. If your instructor ordered InfoTrac® College Edition with this book, you can access it from your CD-ROM, or go directly to http://www .infotrac-college.com and use the passcode from the InfoTrac® College Edition card that came with your book. For this chapter, try these search terms: *self-concept, identity, social identity theory, self-esteem, narcissism, self-monitoring, optimism, Type A.*

Social Psychology Alive: The Workbook

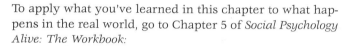

To apply what you've learned in this chapter to what happens in the real world, go to Chapter 5 of *Social Psychology Alive: The Workbook:*

- Did Martha Get Shafted?
- Who Am I?
- Self-Monitoring and Finding Mr. or Ms. Right
- Assessing Your Personality: Are You a Thrill-Seeker?

- Does Your Life Orientation Affect Your Health?
- Assessing Your Personality: Are You a Type A Personality?
- The Barnum Effect
- Processing Information About Oneself

Social Psychology Alive: The Videos

To see video on the topics and experiments discussed in this chapter, you may go either to ThomsonNOW™ or to the CD-ROM, if your instructor assigned either one, to the following section:

- Which Is the Real Me? Being One Woman with Many Hats
- It's Not All About You: Knowing When to Blame Your Circumstances

To Learn More

This list contains citations to books or articles that can help you learn more. These readings are good places to start if you want to gain a deeper understanding of the topics in this chapter.

- Baumeister, R. F. (Ed.). (1993). *Self-esteem: The puzzle of low self-regard.* New York: Plenum.

- Hunter, A. E., & Forden, C. (Eds.). (2002). *Readings in the psychology of gender: Exploring our differences and our commonalities.* Needham Heights, MA: Allyn & Bacon.
- Salovey, P., & Rothman, A. J. (Eds.). (2003). *Social psychology of health.* New York: Psychology Press.

RATHER GO NAKED THAN WEAR FUR

WE'D RATHER GO NAKED THAN WEAR FUR

SEARS SUPPORT THE TORTURE OF INNOCENT ANIMA

WEAR YOUR OWN

NEL

Attitudes and Social Behaviour

P*hillip occasionally drives his car after drinking alcohol. He doesn't drink very much, but when he does, he never really thinks about the possibility that he shouldn't drive—the idea of taking a taxi just doesn't occur to him.*

Phillip also smokes cigarettes. He smokes about a pack a day and feels free to smoke wherever he wants. He often smokes in the presence of nonsmokers, although he'll extinguish his cigarette if someone asks him to. He smoked throughout his wife's pregnancies.

Phillip never wears a seatbelt while driving. It doesn't feel comfortable, so he doesn't use it. He also never makes his children buckle up in the car.

What is your impression of Phillip? Is he someone to be admired or to be condemned? Do you think that he is a responsible person? What other characteristics do you think he might possess?

Our description of Phillip is based on a real person. If you thought that Phillip sounded a bit old-fashioned, you were right—he lived from 1910 to 1985. He was caring, funny, and kind. He was a good father and a good husband. But he also sometimes drove after drinking, smoked wherever he wished, and never used seatbelts even after they became standard equipment in the early 1960s.

Do you want to know something else? Your grandfathers were probably a lot like Phillip. Phillip reflected the attitudes of his times, and it is a testament to how much attitudes have changed that Phillip now sounds rather irresponsible. In the 1950s and 1960s people routinely drove their cars after drinking, smokers thought it was their right to smoke anywhere, and almost no one used seatbelts. But today? Driving after drinking is evaluated negatively by most people, and the concept of designated drivers has caught on. Nonsmokers insist on their right to healthy air, and most smokers agree that they should not smoke around nonsmokers. Most people use seatbelts consistently and feel vulnerable if they are not buckled up. The different prevailing attitudes of the two time periods help us to understand the different patterns of behaviour.

Attitudes may be the most studied topic in social psychology. Back in 1935, Gordon Allport stated that attitudes were the most indispensable concept in social psychology. Many social psychologists would argue that this statement is still true today (e.g., Albarracin, Johnson, & Zanna, 2005; Perloff, 2003). Literally thousands of experiments have been conducted exploring various aspects of attitudes.

This chapter describes some of the social psychological research and theory on attitudes, particularly attitude formation and the relation between attitudes and behaviour. (In Chapter 7, we discuss attitude change.) We begin the current chapter by defining attitudes and considering why humans have evolved to possess attitudes. We then describe how attitudes are measured by social psychologists. Next, we address how attitudes form, and we identify some developmental trends in attitudes across the life span. We then turn to the effects of attitudes on behaviour, addressing both how attitudes affect behaviour and when they do so. We close the chapter with a discussion of culture and attitudes.

Simone van den Berg/Shutterstock

Today, attitudes toward smoking require that smokers indulge their habit outside of buildings.

What Are Attitudes?

Jeff Keller is president of the company Attitude Is Everything, Inc. He says that success "is a matter of having a positive attitude." He sells lots of materials that encourage people to "build a positive attitude" (e.g., motivational music, with titles like "Born for Greatness" and "Bitter or Better?").

What does Jeff Keller mean by the term *attitude*? He means a general perspective on life, an outlook that can be positive (leading to success) or negative (leading to failure). The "attitude" he prescribes corresponds reasonably closely to the dimension of *dispositional optimism* that we discussed in Chapter 5 (see page 181).

Social psychologists do *not* use the term *attitude* to refer to a general perspective, outlook, or approach to life. Social psychologists have a much more specific meaning for the term.

Attitudes: Evaluations of Targets

An **attitude** is *an individual's evaluation of a target* (Eagly & Chaiken, 1993; Oskamp & Schultz, 2005; Wood, 2000; Zanna & Rempel, 1988). The target can be an object, an issue, a person, a group, a behaviour, or any other identifiable aspect of the environment (e.g., a colour, an emotion). By calling it an *evaluation,* theorists mean that an attitude is a *good–bad* judgment: it represents the individual's overall assessment of whether a particular target is positive or negative. As we mentioned in Chapter 2 (see page 35), attitudes cannot be seen directly, so researchers must infer attitudes from individuals' observable responses. A thorough discussion of the structure of attitudes is provided by Leandre Fabrigar, Tara MacDonald (both of whom are at Queen's University in Kingston, Ontario), and Duane Wegener (2005).

Attitudes *always* have a target—they are directed *at* something. People have attitudes toward many, many targets, ranging from broad *ideologies or values* (e.g., democracy, multiculturalism) to *controversial issues* (e.g., stem cell research, the separatist movement in Quebec) to *individual people* (e.g., your mother, Shania Twain) to *groups* (e.g., computer programmers, hockey players) to *objects* (e.g., cars, the Canadian flag) to *behaviours* (e.g., exercising, drinking Tim Hortons coffee). Obviously, the concept of attitude is very broad; there are an almost infinite number of targets toward which someone might have an attitude (e.g., green bicycles, china teapots, paper clips). Although it is true that people can have an attitude toward almost anything, social psychologists have been interested mainly in attitudes that are directed at important targets, such as controversial issues, ethnic groups, and consequential behaviours.

Think about some of your own attitudes. Which ones do you think are most important in your daily life? Your attitudes toward individual people? Your attitudes toward foods? Your attitudes toward broad goals like getting an education and staying healthy? Your attitudes toward specific activities like watching television and studying? Your attitudes toward social and ethnic groups? You can probably think of examples of attitudes from each of these categories that influence your behaviour in everyday settings. By understanding where these attitudes come from and how they affect us, you can gain insight into the causes of your daily actions.

attitude

an individual's evaluation of a target along a good–bad dimension

Three Parts of Attitudes

Cockroaches . . . big cockroaches crawling on your floor. How would you feel about this situation? Probably not too good. Let's analyze your reaction in terms of attitudes. What is your attitude toward cockroaches? How do you evaluate this species

Most people have a negative attitude toward cockroaches.

of insects? Almost certainly, you will say that your attitude is negative. But *why* is it negative? What things about cockroaches make your evaluation negative? It turns out that attitudes can come from sources: emotional reactions, cognitive information, and past behaviour.

One aspect of your negative reaction to cockroaches is probably based on the fact that cockroaches (or even *thoughts* of cockroaches) make you feel rather sick. Cockroaches are disgusting. These are your affective or emotional reactions to cockroaches.

Another aspect of your evaluation is probably based on information you have about cockroaches. You know that they are likely to infest dirty or old buildings, and you believe that they can spread disease. You know that cockroaches crawl around at night, which makes them seem secretive and frightening. You also know that they are hard to get rid of—they can be a very persistent pest. These are some of the cognitive elements contributing to your negative attitude.

A third part of your reaction to cockroaches may be based on your past behaviour toward them. You may be able to remember recoiling from a cockroach (or a similar large beetle) and expressing disgust or even screaming involuntarily. You might also have killed a cockroach in the past by stepping on it or by spraying pesticide in the cracks where the insects can live. If you are asked whether you like or dislike cockroaches and think about having killed them in the past, you are likely to decide that you dislike them.

In trying to dissect attitudes into their components, social psychologists have identified the three elements just described: affect, cognition, and past behaviour (e.g., Breckler, 1984; Crites, Fabrigar, & Petty, 1994; Rosenberg & Hovland, 1960). For example, University of Waterloo social psychologists Mark Zanna and John Rempel have proposed that whether an individual evaluates a target positively or negatively will depend on three things: (1) how the object makes the person feel, (2) the person's beliefs about the object, and (3) the person's previous actions toward the object (Zanna & Rempel, 1988). Targets that arouse negative feelings and emotions (e.g., snakes, hypodermic needles) are more likely to generate unfavourable attitudes than are targets that arouse positive feelings and emotions (e.g., puppies, chocolate). Targets that are known or believed to possess negative characteristics (e.g., criminals, cholesterol) are more likely to generate unfavourable attitudes than are targets that are known or believed to possess positive characteristics (e.g., medical doctors, healthy foods). Targets toward which someone has behaved negatively in the past (e.g., enemies, weeds) are more likely to be seen as disliked than are targets toward which someone has behaved positively in the past (e.g., friends, kittens). When we discuss attitude formation later in this chapter, we organize the material in terms of affective, cognitive, and behavioural sources of attitudes.

It might be helpful at this point to acknowledge a potentially confusing issue in the attitudes literature: the *two-way* relation between attitudes and behaviour. We have just noted that *previous behaviour* toward a target may contribute to an individual's *current attitude* toward the target. Thinking about the fact that she or he has killed cockroaches in the past might actually strengthen a person's negative attitude toward them ("I must really hate cockroaches because I have killed them in the past"). But don't *current attitudes* also cause *future behaviour*? Our opening example of Phillip's behaviour was explained by stating that attitudes in his time were different from prevailing attitudes today, an explanation that implies that attitudes cause behaviour. Doesn't the fact that someone is negative toward cockroaches increase the likelihood that she or he will kill them in the future?

The answer is that *both* directions of influence can occur, which can be confusing for students learning about attitudes. Past behaviours influence current attitudes, and current attitudes influence future behaviour. If people have behaved positively toward something in the past, they are more likely to judge that they like it, whereas if they have behaved negatively toward something, they are more likely to judge that they dislike it. But people also will behave in the future in ways that reflect their current attitudes: they will approach things they like and avoid things they don't like. We will talk about each of these directions of influence in this chapter.

Let's now return to the idea that attitudes can have three components or sources: feelings, beliefs, and past behaviour. Canadian social psychologists Victoria Esses and Greg Maio (2002) argued that attitudes toward certain targets depend mostly on people's feelings toward those targets, whereas attitudes toward other targets depend mostly on people's knowledge and beliefs (see also Breckler & Wiggins, 1989; Haddock & Zanna, 1998; Trafimow & Sheeran, 1998). For instance, attitudes toward blood donation tend to rely heavily on people's feelings (e.g., their level of fear at the thought of giving blood), whereas attitudes toward controversial social issues are heavily reliant on people's beliefs (e.g., their agreement with arguments supporting each side of the issue). Which of these sources is most important for attitudes toward cockroaches, do you think? It seems likely that emotions and feelings usually dominate.

Often, people's feelings, beliefs, and past actions toward a target are reasonably consistent with one another—either mostly positive or mostly negative. Think about your attitude toward a close friend: you probably feel affection for this person, believe that he or she possesses many desirable characteristics, and have behaved in friendly, positive ways toward him or her in the past. Your attitude toward garbage is also probably based on relatively uniform components, but this time negative ones: you have negative feelings about the unpleasant smell of garbage, you believe that garbage can grow unhealthy bacteria, and your principal action toward garbage in the past has been to dispose of it.

But now think about your attitude toward chocolate cake. Is it also based on uniformly positive or uniformly negative elements? If you are like most people, you may *feel* positively toward chocolate cake (e.g., you love the taste) but *believe* that chocolate cake has some negative characteristics (e.g., it is high in calories and generally not a healthy thing to eat). Your attitude toward many individuals and social groups may similarly include a mix of positive and negative feelings and beliefs: you believe that many rock musicians are talented but egotistical; Susan's jokes make you laugh but she can also be immature; you respect Etienne but know that he can be selfish. When, as in these examples, attitudes contain conflicting elements (both positive and negative), they are called **ambivalent attitudes** (Kaplan, 1972; Katz & Hass, 1988). Canadian social psychologists Ian Newby-Clark of the University of Guelph, Ian McGregor of York University, and Mark Zanna of the University of Waterloo (2002) noted that many people do not *like* attitudinal ambivalence—the conflict among the attitudinal elements is experienced as unpleasant.

We will talk a bit more about ambivalence in the next section on how to measure attitudes. For now, let's just consider briefly why ambivalence is an important concept. Mark Zanna and his colleagues (Lavine, Thomsen, Zanna, & Borgida, 1998; Thompson, Zanna, & Griffin, 1995) have argued that a key implication of ambivalence is for the consistency of behaviour. What kind of behaviour do you think an ambivalent attitude will produce? If an individual has both positive and negative feelings/thoughts about another person, will the individual's behaviour be constant (the same) or variable (changing) toward the other? If you said variable, you predicted what has been found by social psychologists (e.g., Armitage & Conner, 2000; Lavine et al., 1998). Ambivalent attitudes can lead to different behaviour over time because either the positive or the negative elements about the target may come to mind at a particular point, and whichever type of element is dominant will drive behaviour. In contrast, attitudes that are low in ambivalence (all positive or all negative elements) will not produce such variable responses. A good example of this latter case is your attitude toward cockroaches: it is probably low in ambivalence (all of the elements are negative), and your behaviour toward cockroaches will probably be negative every time you encounter them!

ambivalent attitudes
evaluations of targets that include both positive and negative elements

Many people have an *ambivalent attitude* toward chocolate cake, which means that it contains both positive and negative elements.

Explicit Versus Implicit Attitudes

explicit attitudes

evaluations that people can report consciously

Explicit attitudes are those that people can report consciously. Most of the examples we have given so far represent explicit attitudes. You are aware that you dislike cockroaches and that you like puppies, and you can report these attitudes confidently on a self-report scale. Explicit attitudes have been the focus of the vast majority of social psychological research on attitudes, so the remainder of this chapter will deal mainly with explicit attitudes.

Recently, however, researchers have identified another, more subtle effect of attitudes on cognition and behaviour, which has led to the term *implicit* attitudes. An **implicit attitude** is an individual's automatic evaluative response to a target, which can occur without awareness (Blair, 2001; Dasgupta & Greenwald, 2001; Greenwald & Banaji, 1995; Wilson, Lindsey, & Schooler, 2000). An implicit attitude is a spontaneous, immediate, good–bad response to the target that cannot be consciously controlled. It reflects how the individual evaluates the target at a subconscious level. Recall our discussion of *automatic processes* in Chapter 3 (page 75), which cannot be controlled. Implicit attitudes are automatic. Bertram Gawronski at the University of Western Ontario has argued that implicit attitudes reflect "low-level" (minimal processing) associations between objects and evaluations, whereas explicit attitudes reflect "higher-level" (more extensive processing) evaluations that are based on rational beliefs about the object and its features (Gawronski, Strack, & Bodenhausen, in press).

implicit attitudes

automatic evaluative responses to a target, which may occur without awareness

Typically, implicit attitudes conform to explicit attitudes; that is, our spontaneous, automatic response to a target typically parallels our conscious evaluation of the target. Cockroaches elicit an *implicit* negative response that is consistent with our *explicit* negative attitude. Thus, the distinction between explicit and implicit attitudes will not always be important.

Inconsistency between explicit and implicit attitudes can occur, however. An individual might consciously support an issue or policy (e.g., a bilingualism policy that requires service in French to be available to all citizens in the province) but feel anxious about it at a subconscious level (e.g., be worried about its implications for his or her taxes). Or someone might express liking for an individual whom he or she subconsciously envies. Because implicit attitudes are automatic and subconscious, people may not realize that their implicit and explicit attitudes toward a target differ. Later in this chapter, we will discuss at least one way that implicit attitudes might affect behaviour without an individual's awareness. University of Toronto social psychologist John Bassili and his colleague Rick Brown (2005) have provided a comprehensive review of work on implicit attitudes.

Perceptions of Others' Attitudes

Social psychologists interested in attitudes have focused primarily on understanding individuals' own attitudes—how people's attitudes form, the relation between attitudes and behaviour, and so on. A few researchers, however, have investigated individuals' *perceptions* of the attitudes of *other people*. In particular, an interesting program of research at Memorial University in St. John's, Newfoundland, has examined the dimensions that underlie perceptions of others' attitudes. Cathryn Button, Malcolm Grant, T. Edward Hannah, and Abraham Ross (1993) have found that there is a common structure to people's perceptions of others' attitudes. Two dimensions are most important: liberal versus conservative and traditional versus novel (or radical). Thus, perceptions of other people's attitudes tend to be guided by consideration of the extent to which the others are liberal or conservative and traditional or innovative. In a series of studies, these researchers have shown that the two dimensions are fundamental in perceptions of others' attitudes in many different domains (e.g., Button et al., 1993; Grant, Button, Hannah, & Ross, 2003; Grant, Hannah, Ross, & Button, 1995).

In the remaining sections of this chapter, we return to the more typical focus in attitudes research, namely understanding people's own attitudes.

Why Do We Evaluate?

Why have humans evolved to form attitudes? What useful functions are served by storing thousands of evaluations of different targets in our brains? Although social psychologists have proposed numerous functions of attitudes, two in particular have been emphasized in research and theory. Let's begin our consideration of this "why" question by putting ourselves in the role of a master designer.

Imagine that you are a brilliant scientist who is developing a robot that must be able to survive on its own in the world. The robot must be able to learn and perform some simple tasks and respond adaptively to the demands of the environment. The robot must be able to seek help when necessary and recognize dangerous situations that should be avoided.

Besides the ability to move and manipulate objects, what senses and abilities would you need to give your robot? What kinds of skills would be essential for it to cope effectively in a changing environment?

Sight and hearing are probably two critical senses; if the robot were unable to visually scan the environment or to hear auditory stimuli, it would be severely limited. Another necessity would be some sort of memory system, whereby the robot could recognize objects that it had encountered before. But would a simple memory system be enough? Recognition, per se, is not very informative unless the memory system also triggers some sort of *evaluation* of the object. The robot would need to be able to recall how the object had behaved in the past and to predict whether it is likely to be helpful or harmful in the present situation. A rapid appraisal of the object's implications for the robot (i.e., a rapid good–bad judgment) would be extremely useful. This evaluative judgment would then allow the robot to approach, or to flee from, the object.

Assessing Objects

Just like our hypothetical robot, humans benefit from quick assessments of the positive or negative implications of objects that they encounter in the environment. In humans, *attitudes* provide these rapid evaluations of objects, people, and issues; this has been termed the **object-appraisal function** of attitudes (Fazio, 2000; Smith, Bruner, & White, 1956). These attitudes give the individual a quick assessment (*appraisal*) of whether targets are likely to be helpful or hurtful. Almost all attitudes serve this function at least to some extent, because attitudes always provide a summary good–bad judgment of a target. Object appraisal is the most basic function of attitudes and probably the principal reason why humans have evolved to form attitudes. In our distant evolutionary past, ancestors who formed and stored evaluations of objects in their brains were more likely to survive than would-be ancestors who did not form attitudes; for instance, the former individuals avoided objects that elicited negative evaluations (e.g., sabre-toothed tigers) while their less evaluative peers occasionally suffered nasty outcomes.

You might be thinking that this object-appraisal function should generalize beyond humans. Wouldn't other animals also benefit from forming positive or

object-appraisal function
a function of attitudes in which attitudes provide rapid evaluative judgments of targets, facilitating approach or avoidance

negative evaluations of objects and basing their actions on those evaluations? Yes, absolutely. Think about dogs: Do you believe that they have attitudes? When a dog wags its tail and runs toward its owner, or when it bares its teeth and snarls at a threatening stranger, or when it jumps up and down with excitement while its food dish is being prepared—these seem to be clear behavioural manifestations of attitudes. So dogs probably do possess attitudes. If so, dogs undoubtedly experience attitudes differently from humans, because we have a complex cognitive component of attitudes that is presumably missing in dogs. But the fundamental goal of object appraisal can be served by simple, affective responses that do not rely on complex cognition. If they exist, dogs' attitudes must be based more on affect than on cognition, but they are attitudes nonetheless, and they serve an object-appraisal function.

Expressing Values

values

broad, abstract standards or goals that people consider to be important guiding principles in their life

People sometimes adopt attitudes to express their underlying values. **Values** can be defined as broad, abstract standards or goals that people consider to be important guiding principles in their life (Maio & Olson, 1998; Rokeach, 1973; Schwartz, 1992). Examples of values include freedom, equality, and happiness. Clive Seligman and Albert Katz of the University of Western Ontario have argued that people's values are related to their attitudes toward specific issues (Seligman & Katz, 1996). For example, religious individuals might adopt specific positions on issues such as birth control or gay marriage to display their support for their faith. Parents might express contempt for cheaters to communicate the importance of honesty to their children. Teenagers might wear certain clothing or pierce certain body parts to show their commitment to a desired group.

value-expressive function

a function of attitudes in which attitudes communicate individuals' identity and values

In each of these cases, the attitudes serve, at least in part, *symbolic* functions for the holders—symbolizing support for and commitment to particular religions, values, or groups. These symbolic attitudes have a **value-expressive function** (Herek, 1986; Katz, 1960; Maio & Olson, 2000b), which means that they allow people to convey an identity that connects them to some groups and makes them distinct from other groups (Brewer, 1991). For example, teenagers may embrace a particular musical style (e.g., heavy metal) because they want to associate themselves with a peer group and dissociate themselves from their parents.

Teenagers' attitudes toward clothing sometimes serve a *value-expressive function.*

Testing the Functions of Attitudes

Although social psychologists have talked about the functions of attitudes for a long time (e.g., Katz, 1960; Smith et al., 1956), there was for many years little research on this topic. The main reason for the lack of research was the perceived difficulty of measuring attitude functions: How can an investigator determine whether a particular attitude fulfills an object-appraisal or a value-expressive function?

Over the past 15 years, however, there has been an increase in research on the functions of attitudes (e.g., see the book edited by Maio & Olson, 2000a, in which numerous researchers describe their work in this area). Researchers have developed several novel and creative ways of investigating the functions fulfilled by attitudes (e.g., DeBono & Packer, 1991; Herek & Capitanio, 1998;

Murray, Haddock, & Zanna, 1996). For example, Gregory Maio, a Canadian who obtained his Ph.D. at the University of Western Ontario and is now a professor at the University of Wales at Cardiff, conducted several studies in which participants were induced to form attitudes that served either object-appraisal or value-expressive functions (see Maio & Olson, 2000b). These studies confirmed the assumption that the motivations underlying object-appraisal attitudes differ from those underlying value-expressive attitudes.

In another research program on the functions of attitudes, Sharon Shavitt (1990), who is at the University of Illinois, had the clever idea that attitudes toward a particular object may fulfill the *same* function for almost everyone. Let's think about two examples of the attitudes she studied: attitudes toward *coffee* and attitudes toward *perfume.* Shavitt proposed that one of these attitudes typically fulfills an object-appraisal function, and the other typically fulfills a value-expressive function. Can you guess which is which? Object-appraisal attitudes give the individual a quick evaluation of the target, whereas value-expressive attitudes tell other people about the individual's identity or values. Shavitt hypothesized that attitudes toward coffee typically fulfill an object-appraisal function: people either like or dislike the taste of coffee (as well as its dose of caffeine). Shavitt hypothesized that attitudes toward perfume, on the other hand, often fulfill a value-expressive function: many people purchase a particular brand of perfume because it projects a desired image or because it is promoted by a beautiful model or movie star with whom they identify.

In one study, Shavitt (1990) asked participants to write down thoughts about their attitudes toward a particular target (e.g., coffee, perfume) and to explain why they felt that way. These thoughts were later examined by judges who recorded how often the participants mentioned specific themes. The results were consistent with Shavitt's predictions. When participants described an object-appraisal attitude (e.g., their attitude toward coffee), they were likely to mention positive or negative features of the object. In contrast, when participants described a value-expressive attitude (e.g., their attitude toward perfume), they were likely to mention their values, their identity, and what the object communicated to others.

In a second study, Shavitt (1990) tested the implications of attitude functions for the effectiveness of persuasive messages—in this case, advertisements. If attitudes toward coffee give people a quick evaluation of this target, how do you think an advertisement should be constructed to promote a new brand of coffee effectively? Shavitt proposed that the most effective strategy would be to focus on the positive features of the coffee and the rewards it will bring. But if attitudes toward perfume reflect individuals' identities and desired images, how should an advertisement for a new brand of perfume be constructed? Shavitt proposed that the most effective strategy would be to focus on the desirable impression the perfume will make on others.

To test these predictions, Shavitt created two different versions of advertisements for a fictitious brand of coffee and a fictitious brand of perfume. One version of the advertisements stressed the rewards provided by the product, such as "The delicious, hearty flavour and aroma of Sterling Blend coffee come from a blend of the freshest coffee beans," or "The fresh, floral scent of Cadeau perfume comes from a balanced blend of oils and essences." The second version of the advertisements emphasized how the product created a particular image in others' minds, such as "The coffee you drink can reveal your rare, discriminating taste," or "Cadeau perfume is the sophisticated scent that tells people that you are *not* one of the crowd." Participants read one of these advertisements and were asked how much they wanted to try the product (coffee or perfume). The coffee ad focusing on *rewards* generated more interest than did the coffee ad focusing on *image.* In contrast, the perfume ad focusing on *image* generated more interest than did the perfume ad focusing on *rewards.* Thus, the advertisements were more effective when they were consistent with the function fulfilled by the attitude: object-appraisal attitudes responded to information about rewards, whereas value-expressive attitudes responded to information about image. These findings show that the function an attitude fulfills has important implications for other psychological processes.

   ## Measuring Attitudes

Social psychologists who want to study attitudes must measure them accurately. In Chapter 2, we introduced the concepts of *validity* and *reliability* (see pages 39–40), both of which are necessary for accurate measurement. Validity refers to whether a measure actually assesses what it is supposed to assess, and reliability refers to whether participants' scores on the measure are stable and free from "random" fluctuations. In striving for these goals of validity and reliability, attitude researchers have developed numerous measurement techniques. We briefly describe some of the most common methods in this section.

Self-Report Measures of Attitudes

An attitude is an individual's evaluation of a target: his or her judgment of an object, issue, or person on a "good–bad" dimension. Because people are usually aware of their attitudes (or, at least, their *explicit* attitudes), it seems sensible to ask them directly to report their evaluations. And, indeed, most attitude measurement techniques are *self-report* in nature. Items are administered either in a paper-and-pencil questionnaire or on a computer. Respondents indicate their attitudes by circling a number or word on a response scale (or typing a number or word on the computer) or by placing an *X* along a response dimension. In the following paragraphs, we describe three common self-report techniques and then discuss some limitations to self-report measures. You can find a more general description of how to develop self-report measures of social psychological constructs in Appendix I of this book.

Likert-type scale

an attitude measurement technique that requires respondents to indicate the extent of their agreement or disagreement with several statements on an issue

Likert-Type Scales. Over the past 70 years, researchers have probably used **Likert-type scales** more than any other technique to measure attitudes. This method evolved from early work by Rensis Likert (1932), who made many contributions to survey methodology. In a Likert-type attitude scale, respondents read a number of statements, each of which expresses a clear position (pro or con) on an issue, or a clear attitude (favourable or unfavourable) toward a target. Respondents are asked to indicate their agreement or disagreement with each item. For example, if a researcher wanted to measure participants' attitudes toward the Canadian health-care system, he or she might ask them to indicate their agreement or disagreement with such statements as "The Canadian health-care system is excellent," "Universal access to health care is important," "Patients often have to wait too long for needed surgery in Canada," and "The Canadian health-care system is too expensive." The first two statements express clearly favourable aspects of the Canadian health-care system, whereas the last two statements express clearly unfavourable aspects. Respondents would indicate their agreement with each statement by circling one of five possible responses: *Disagree Strongly, Disagree, Undecided, Agree,* or *Agree Strongly.* Participants' attitudes would be calculated by scoring responses to each question from 1 to 5, with higher numbers always reflecting the same direction of attitude (e.g., with higher numbers always reflecting a favourable attitude) and then summing all of the items. For example, the statement "The Canadian health-care system is excellent" could be scored such that *Agree Strongly* would get a score of 5 and *Disagree Strongly* would get a score of 1; the statement "Patients often have to wait too long for needed surgery in Canada" would then be scored such that *Disagree Strongly* would get a score of 5 and *Agree Strongly* would get a score of 1. (For both items, the response *Undecided* would get a score of 3.) Participants' total scores across all items would represent their attitude score.

Typically, researchers constructing a Likert-type scale conduct analyses to ensure that all of the items are valid reflections of the target attitude. For example, the correlations between participants' responses to each individual item and their total scores (based on all items) may be calculated, and any items that do not correlate significantly with total scores are dropped from the scale. Some advantages of Likert-type scales for measuring attitudes are that they are relatively easy for researchers to construct, are clear and simple for respondents to complete, and have been shown to produce reliable scores.

Semantic Differential Scales.   A simple but effective method for measuring attitudes is a **semantic differential scale** (Osgood, Suci, & Tannenbaum, 1957). This procedure asks respondents to rate an attitude object on several evaluative dimensions. The target of the attitude is written at the top of the page, and several rating scales are presented below the target. For example, "The Canadian Health-Care System" is written at the top, with such dimensions as "good–bad," "favourable–unfavourable," "effective-ineffective," and "fair–unfair" written below it. The opposing adjectives appear at each end of a 5-point response scale, and the respondent is instructed to put an *X* or a check mark somewhere on the scale to indicate his or her evaluation. Participants' attitudes are calculated by summing their ratings across all of the evaluative dimensions, with responses for each dimension scored so that high scores always reflect the same direction of attitude. For example, the items might be scored so that high scores reflect favourable attitudes toward the health-care system: if respondents put an *X* immediately beside the adjective "good" or "fair," they are given a score of 5, but if they put an *X* immediately beside the adjectives "bad" or "unfair," they receive a score of 1 (an *X* in the middle of either scale gets a score of 3). The total scores across all items represent participants' attitude scores.

Some advantages of semantic differential scales are that they are easy for researchers to construct and straightforward for respondents to complete. Also, a semantic differential scale assesses evaluations very directly, because participants rate the attitude object on dimensions that are explicitly evaluative (including the fundamental dimension underlying attitudes, the *good–bad* dimension).

In Know Yourself 6.1: "Attitudes Toward Watching Television," you can measure your favourability toward watching television using the two most common kinds of scales in social psychology. The first set of items constitutes a Likert-type scale, and the second set of items constitutes a semantic differential scale.

Opinion Surveys.   A final type of self-report measure is one that you are probably familiar with: the opinion survey. Opinion surveys are designed to assess public opinion about an issue, event, or group. Sometimes, the survey researcher wants to be able to generalize the findings to a larger population (e.g., all adults in Canada), in which case the sample must be representative of that population. But on other occasions, survey researchers simply want a "snippet" of public opinion and will not present their findings as necessarily applicable to larger populations. Most opinion surveys contain just one or two items on a particular issue, and responses are often limited to "yes" or "no." For example, an opinion survey on the Canadian health-care system might ask respondents, "Do you consider the Canadian health-care system to be working effectively?" or "Do you think that wait times for medical treatment are too long in Canada?" with possible responses being *yes* or *no* (and perhaps also *undecided*).

semantic differential scale
an attitude measurement technique that requires respondents to rate a target on several evaluative dimensions (such as good–bad and favourable–unfavourable)

Know Yourself 6.1
Attitudes Toward Watching Television

LIKERT-TYPE SCALE:

Please indicate the extent to which you agree or disagree with each of the following statements by circling the appropriate number on the answer scale.

1. Many programs that I watch on television are educational and informative.

1	2	3	4	5
Disagree strongly	Disagree	Undecided	Agree	Agree strongly

2. Watching television is a big waste of time.

1	2	3	4	5
Disagree strongly	Disagree	Undecided	Agree	Agree strongly

3. I enjoy watching television.

1	2	3	4	5
Disagree strongly	Disagree	Undecided	Agree	Agree strongly

4. Society would be better off if people watched less television.

1	2	3	4	5
Disagree strongly	Disagree	Undecided	Agree	Agree strongly

5. Television portrays too much violence and aggression.

1	2	3	4	5
Disagree strongly	Disagree	Undecided	Agree	Agree strongly

6. Watching television is a good way to relax.

1	2	3	4	5
Disagree strongly	Disagree	Undecided	Agree	Agree strongly

SCORING: Items 1, 3, and 6 are scored using the answer scales as presented (1-2-3-4-5); Items 2, 4, and 5 are reverse-scored (that is, 5-4-3-2-1). Add up all of the items for your overall attitude score. Possible scores range from 6 to 30, and higher scores represent more favourable attitudes toward television.

SEMANTIC DIFFERENTIAL SCALE:

Please put an *X* or a check mark on each of the following scales to indicate how you evaluate *watching television*.

Watching Television:

Bad	____ : ____ : ____ : ____ : ____	Good
Worthless	____ : ____ : ____ : ____ : ____	Valuable
Unpleasant	____ : ____ : ____ : ____ : ____	Pleasant
Boring	____ : ____ : ____ : ____ : ____	Interesting
Unfavourable	____ : ____ : ____ : ____ : ____	Favourable
Harmful	____ : ____ : ____ : ____ : ____	Beneficial

SCORING: Score all items 1-2-3-4-5 from left to right. Add up all of the items for your overall attitude score. Possible scores range from 6 to 30, and higher scores represent more favourable attitudes toward television.

Opinion surveys are very useful for gathering information about public opinion, but social psychologists rarely use them. Empirical research on attitudes generally requires the more elaborate techniques described earlier.

The accompanying Concept Review summarizes the key features of the three self-report measures of attitudes.

CONCEPT REVIEW
Self-Report Measures of Attitudes

Measurement Technique	Key Features	Advantages and Disadvantages
Likert-type scale	Respondent rates agreement or disagreement with attitude statements All statements are clearly favourable or clearly unfavourable Researcher must identify nonvalid items and eliminate them	Relatively easy to construct Clear and simple to answer Reliable scores
Semantic differential scale	Respondent rates attitude object on evaluative dimensions All dimensions reflect the good–bad dimension Score is sum of the respondent's ratings	Very simple to construct Clear and simple to answer Very direct measure of evaluations
Opinion survey	Respondent answers just one or two items on each issue Responses are usually yes, undecided, or no Researchers sometimes obtain a representative sample	Very simple to construct Useful for gathering information about public opinion Usually not detailed enough for use in psychological research

Problems with Self-Report Measures. All of the self-report techniques we have described rest on at least two assumptions: (1) people know what their attitudes are, and (2) they will report those attitudes honestly. Sometimes these assumptions are doubtful. If researchers are interested in *implicit attitudes,* for example, then they cannot use self-report measures. Recall that an implicit attitude is an individual's automatic evaluative response to a target, which can occur without his or her awareness. By definition, people do not have direct access to their implicit attitudes. To deal with this problem, researchers have developed specific techniques to measure implicit attitudes, which we describe in the next section.

The second assumption underlying self-report measures—that people will report their attitudes honestly—is also questionable in some cases. For instance, often one position on an issue is more socially desirable than other positions (recall our discussion of *socially desirable responding* in Chapter 2; see page 37). In the domain of ethnic attitudes, for example, the socially desirable position is to express positive attitudes toward all ethnic groups. Other topics that can be influenced by social desirability include attitudes toward illegal activities (e.g., illicit drug use, cheating on taxes), attitudes toward harmful behaviours (e.g., aggression, gossiping), and attitudes toward helpful but costly or time-consuming actions (e.g., donating money to charities, volunteering). Given that people want to appear likeable, moral, and competent, they may be tempted to shift their answers on attitude scales in the direction of the socially desirable position. Simply put, people may lie a little bit to make themselves look better, which will reduce the accuracy of the measure of attitudes. Partly to inhibit socially desirable responding, some researchers have developed alternative measures of attitudes (e.g., Vargas, von Hippel, & Petty, 2004). In the next section, we describe several alternative strategies that employ nonverbal responses.

Another problem with self-report techniques is that they typically do not yield a clear and easy way to measure the *ambivalence* of an individual's attitude.

Recall that an ambivalent attitude includes both positive and negative elements, such as positive feelings but negative beliefs (e.g., someone who loves the taste of banana cream pie but knows it is high in fat and calories). The techniques we have described yield a single, overall score to represent the attitude. Semantic differential scales explicitly require respondents to indicate their evaluations along scales like *good–bad* and *favourable–unfavourable.* Someone whose attitude has both good *and* bad elements cannot express such ambivalence on these sorts of scales.

To measure ambivalence, some researchers have asked respondents to rate the target on *both* positive scales *and* negative scales separately (e.g., Maio, Esses, & Bell, 2000; Priester & Petty, 1996; Thompson et al., 1995). For instance, participants might rate the target on a scale from *not at all good* to *extremely good* and on another scale from *not at all bad* to *extremely bad.* In this way, participants can indicate that they have mixed reactions to the target.

Nonverbal Measures of Attitudes

In response to the first two problems with self-report measures mentioned above, social psychologists have developed several nonverbal measures of attitudes. These methods do not rely on participants' ability or willingness to report their attitudes. Also, nonverbal measures may provide better assessments of people's unconscious, affective responses to objects than self-report measures (which reflect people's conscious, often primarily cognitive, evaluations). On the negative side, these measures are often difficult to obtain and may not be as sensitive for assessing explicit attitudes as self-report measures. Nonverbal measures include behavioural measures, physiological measures, and implicit measures.

Behavioural Measures. Some researchers have used participants' overt behaviour to infer their attitude toward an object. For instance, Steven Breckler (1984) used people's willingness to approach a live snake as a behavioural measure of their attitudes. He assumed that people who were unwilling to come close to a snake possessed more negative attitudes than did people who would come right up to a snake (an assumption that was supported by self-report measures that were also obtained).

Douglas Hazlewood and James Olson (1986) required participants at the University of Western Ontario to go into a room where another person (the target) was waiting and conduct a brief interview with that individual. Participants had been given information about the target person that was expected to produce positive or negative attitudes. Results showed that participants in the negative attitude condition sat further away from the individual and smiled less often than did participants in the positive attitude condition.

One advantage of behavioural measures of attitudes is that they are usually *unobtrusive measures:* participants usually do not realize that their attitudes are being assessed. By being unobtrusive, behavioural measures reduce problems of self-presentation and social desirability (see Word, Zanna, & Cooper, 1974). Unfortunately, it is often difficult to design a behavioural measure of an attitude. For example, how could attitudes toward nuclear power plants be inferred from behaviour? Also, using behaviour to measure attitudes assumes that there is a strong, inevitable link between attitudes and actions. As we will see in the section entitled "When Do Attitudes Predict Behaviour?" there are conditions under which attitudes do not predict behaviour very well.

Physiological Measures. Is it possible that there are objective, physiological reactions that reveal positive or negative evaluations? One category of physiological reactions that has received attention is symptoms of arousal, such as heart rate and blood pressure. Some researchers have found that exposure to negative or disliked objects increases arousal as measured by these symptoms (e.g., Clore & Gormly, 1974; Rankin & Campbell, 1955). These findings make sense if exposure to a negative object is conceptualized as a threat: arousal would prepare the individual for possible "fight or flight." Other researchers, however, have obtained nonsignificant results for arousal symptoms as measures of attitudes (see Zanna, Detweiler, & Olson, 1984). It appears that although heart rate and blood pressure may sometimes indicate the *intensity* of people's feelings about a target, arousal symptoms are poor at distinguishing between positive and negative evaluations (Guglielmi, 1999). That is, strong feelings of liking and strong feelings of disliking may produce similar levels of physiological arousal—a very serious limitation to the usefulness of these measures as indicators of attitudes!

Another category of physiological responses that has been explored as a measure of attitudes is muscle movements in the face, especially in the eye and cheek regions. These movements can be monitored by putting electrodes at certain places on the face—a procedure known as **facial electromyography** (or **facial EMG**). Facial EMG can record very small muscle contractions. Work by John Cacioppo and his colleagues has shown that specific patterns of facial muscle contractions are associated with positive versus negative emotional responses to a stimulus (e.g., Cacioppo, Bush, & Tassinary, 1992; Cacioppo, Martzke, Petty, & Tassinary, 1988; Cacioppo, Petty, Losch, & Kim, 1986). There is also some evidence that the magnitude of people's eye-blink response to a puff of air directed at their eye while they are looking at a target object (e.g., a White face or a Black face) reveals their affective response (e.g., Amodio, Harmon-Jones, & Devine, 2003). Although these findings are interesting and provocative, there are several challenges to using physiological measures of attitudes. First, obtaining physiological measures is a complex and time-consuming procedure. Second, facial EMG appears to be quite sensitive to emotional reactions, but less sensitive to evaluations that lack a strong affective component (e.g., attitudes that are based primarily on cognitive beliefs, such as attitudes toward many consumer products). Third, it is possible for people to deliberately alter or inhibit some of their facial responses, thereby making facial EMG less accurate.

facial electromyography (facial EMG)

a procedure for measuring muscle contractions in the face that may be sensitive to positive versus negative responses to a stimulus

Implicit Association Test (IAT)

a reaction time procedure that provides a measure of implicit attitudes; participants sort targets into a "good" category or a "bad" category, and the speed at which the sorting is completed is taken as a measurement of implicit attitude toward the object

Implicit Measures. Implicit attitudes are people's automatic evaluative responses to a target. Implicit attitudes cannot be measured by simply asking people about them, because the responses can occur without awareness (e.g., people's spontaneous, uncontrollable responses to spiders). To measure implicit attitudes, therefore, researchers have designed procedures that assess the extent to which people have an automatic positive or negative response to an object.

How can automatic responses be measured? Researchers have proposed that *reaction times* provide a way (e.g., Cunningham, Preacher, & Banaji, 2001; Fazio, Jackson, Dunton, & Williams, 1995; Kawakami & Dovidio, 2001). The most common reaction time procedure for measuring implicit attitudes is the **Implicit Association Test,** or **IAT** (Greenwald, McGhee, & Schwartz, 1998). In essence, this procedure requires participants to complete two sorting tasks as quickly as possible. On one sorting task, the target of the attitude

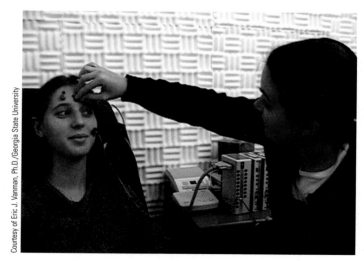

Courtesy of Eric J. Vanman, Ph.D./Georgia State University

Facial EMG records muscle contractions in the face that are associated with positive or negative reactions to a stimulus.

(e.g., elderly persons, automobiles) must be sorted into the same category as some "good" objects (e.g., words with positive meanings, such as *good, beautiful,* and *honest*). On the second sorting task, the target must be sorted into the same category as some "bad" objects (e.g., words with negative meanings, such as *bad, ugly,* and *dishonest*). We need not go into the details of the methodology here. The basic idea is that if participants complete the task in which the target is associated with "good" things *more quickly* than the task in which the target is associated with "bad" things, they are assumed to have a *positive* implicit attitude toward the target.

"I might report having a feeling of a certain kind. I might say, 'I really like X.' But the implicit attitude need not always fit with that. In other words, it's something that resides a little bit below the surface of conscious awareness."

If, on the other hand, they complete the task in which the target of the attitude is associated with "bad" things *more quickly* than the task where the target of the attitude is associated with "good" things, they are assumed to have a *negative* implicit attitude toward the target.

The IAT has been the target of some criticism (e.g., Brendl, Markman, & Messner, 2001; Govan & Williams, 2004; Olson & Fazio, 2004). For example, Bertram Gawronski of the University of Western Ontario has shown that responses on the IAT and other implicit measures are influenced by idiosyncratic factors, such as recently generated thoughts by the respondents (Gawronski & Bodenhausen, 2005; Gawronski, Deutsch, & Seidel, 2005). Notwithstanding these criticisms, the IAT and other implicit measures of attitudes have been shown to predict individuals' responses, especially spontaneous, nonverbal reactions to targets, such as eye contact, speech hesitations, and smiling (e.g., Dovidio, Kawakami, Johnson, Johnson, & Howard, 1997; Fazio et al., 1995; McConnell & Leibold, 2001; Neumann, Hülsenbeck, & Seibt, 2004). Because these measures are presumed to reflect people's automatic evaluations, they would not be used to measure explicit attitudes.

The key features of different nonverbal measures of attitudes are summarized in the accompanying Concept Review.

CONCEPT REVIEW
Nonverbal Measures of Attitudes

Measurement Technique	Key Features	Advantages and Disadvantages
Behavioural measures	Observe respondent's actions toward attitude object	Unobtrusive (respondent unaware)
	Favourable actions (e.g., approach object, smile at object) are assumed to reflect favourable attitudes	Not possible for all attitude objects
		Assumes inevitable link between attitudes and behaviour
		Time-consuming to obtain
Physiological measures	Assess respondent's physiological reactions to object	May reflect intensity but not direction of attitude
	Examples include arousal symptoms and facial EMG	May not be very sensitive
Implicit measures	Respondent's reaction times are used to infer automatic responses	Respondent cannot easily distort answers
	Example is the Implicit Association Test (IAT)	Shown to predict spontaneous, nonverbal reactions to attitude object
	Implicit attitudes are assumed to influence the speed with which the attitude object can be paired with good or bad things	Time-consuming to obtain

How Do Attitudes Form?

When we discussed the structure of your attitude toward cockroaches, we suggested that it contained three components: an affective component (e.g., feelings of disgust, fear), a cognitive component (e.g., beliefs about cockroaches, such as their potential to spread disease), and a behavioural component (e.g., a history of killing them). These three sources (affect, cognition, behaviour) can each contribute to the development of an evaluative response (Zanna & Rempel, 1988). Thus, if we want to understand how attitudes form, we need to discuss each source separately.

We develop negative attitudes toward colds because they make us feel sick.

Affective Sources of Attitudes

Humans are emotional animals. We like to feel good and do not like to feel bad. It is not surprising, therefore, that *affect*—feelings and emotions—influences our attitudes. Think about a food that you dislike because of its taste or smell: it is difficult to evaluate such foods positively even if we know that they are good for us. Now think about a location that is always associated with positive feelings, such as a ski lodge: it is difficult to evaluate such places negatively even if we know that they are expensive.

When an object, event, or action consistently produces positive feelings or pleasurable biological responses, we will form a favourable attitude toward it. Maple syrup tastes sweet, massages feel good, and cold water quenches our thirst, so we develop positive attitudes toward maple syrup, massages, and drinking water. When an object, event, or action consistently produces unpleasant feelings or aversive biological responses, we will form an unfavourable attitude toward it. Shovelling snow makes our arms ache, spoiled milk smells bad, and getting a cold makes us feel lousy, so we develop negative attitudes toward shovelling snow, spoiled milk, and colds.

Evaluative Conditioning. The examples we just gave represent straightforward effects of feelings and emotions on attitudes: when an object or event directly causes positive or negative affect, our attitudes are influenced in the corresponding positive or negative direction. But there is another way that feelings can be linked to targets and thus influence attitudes, in which the target is not the direct cause of the feelings.

Have you ever noticed that things that coincide with a pleasant event can evoke happy feelings? Perhaps you have special feelings for the song that was playing when you first met your romantic partner. Perhaps you think fondly of the coffee shop where a good friend gave you a surprise gift. In contrast, have you noticed that things that coincide with an unpleasant event sometimes evoke negative feelings? Perhaps you harbour negative feelings for the city you were visiting when you lost your wallet. Perhaps you dislike a television show that you were watching when you received a phone call delivering bad news.

In these examples, an object that had no causal role in the outcome nevertheless comes to evoke positive or negative feelings simply by its association with the affect-arousing event. This process is called **evaluative conditioning** and is a common source of feelings toward objects, settings, and people (for a review, see De Houwer, Thomas, & Baeyens, 2001). A famous example of research on conditioning is Ivan Pavlov's (1927) work with dogs, in which he showed that if a bell was rung together with the presentation of meat powder several times, then simply ringing the bell would cause the dogs to salivate in anticipation (a conditioned response to the bell).

evaluative conditioning
a process by which objects come to evoke positive or negative affect simply by their association with affect-inducing events

6.1
ONLINE
LAB

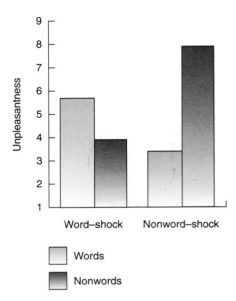

FIGURE 6.1 Unpleasantness ratings of words and nonwords

From Cacioppo et al., "Microexpressive facial actions as a function of affective stimuli: Replication and extension," *Personality and Social Psychology Bulletin, 28*, 207–233, Fig. 1, p. 218, 1992. Reprinted by permission of Sage Publications.

mere exposure effect

the tendency for repeated contact with an object, even without reinforcement, to increase liking for the object

Humans are very easily conditioned (e.g., see Blair & Shimp, 1992; Van Reekum, Van den Berg, & Frijda, 1999; Walther, 2002; Zanna, Kiesler, & Pilkonis, 1970). Many of your attitudes probably reflect, in part, conditioned positive or negative feelings. One interesting experiment that documented evaluative conditioning in humans was conducted by John Cacioppo, Beverly Marshall-Goodell, Louis Tassinary, and Richard Petty (1992) at Ohio State University. These researchers asked participants to read a series of six-letter words (e.g., *reason, finger, winter*) and six-letter nonwords (e.g., *petory, triwen, begrid*), which were projected onto a screen in front of participants for seven seconds. Now for the interesting part: mild electric shocks were delivered to the leg of participants in association with either the words or the nonwords. (Participants selected the level of shock in pretesting so that it was "annoying but not painful.") For some participants, a shock was delivered with every real word but with none of the nonwords. For other participants, a shock was delivered with every nonword but with none of the real words. After the exposure trials were completed, participants were asked to rate each of the words and nonwords for how unpleasant it was on a scale from 1 ("very pleasant") to 9 ("very unpleasant"). Figure 6.1 presents the results. As you can see from the figure, nonwords were rated as much more unpleasant when they were associated with shock than when they were not. The same effect occurred for real words: they were rated as more unpleasant when they were associated with shock than when they were not. Thus, participants' ratings of both nonwords and words were influenced by the electric shocks, consistent with an evaluative conditioning perspective. You might also have noticed in the figure that the effect of shock on participants' ratings was stronger for nonwords than for words. The authors speculated that conditioning was stronger for nonwords because participants had never seen them before, whereas they had a long history of exposure to the real words, which interfered to some extent with the conditioning.

Mere Exposure Effect. "Familiarity breeds contempt." Do you agree with this well-known saying? Do you think that becoming more familiar with an object or a person leads to unfavourable (or, at least, less favourable) attitudes? Perhaps boredom sets in, or perhaps we learn things about people that reflect negatively on them. For instance, we get tired of songs that have been played too much on the radio, and friendships can wane over time as an acquaintance's habits become increasingly annoying (we will skirt the issue of whether *we* become increasingly annoying to others).

But what about the feelings of comfort and ease that develop when we know someone well? And can't you think of examples of highly familiar things that are very dear to you, such as a childhood toy or a long-time pet? Also, strange or new situations are often intimidating until we become familiar with them. These examples seem inconsistent with the "familiarity breeds contempt" saying.

Robert Zajonc (1968) argued that exposure to an object generally leads to a *more favourable* attitude toward it, especially for relatively novel objects. He proposed that the more often we are exposed to something, even without reinforcement, the more we will tend to like it. Zajonc labelled this effect the **mere exposure effect** and suggested that the well-known phrase about familiarity should be changed to "familiarity breeds *content*."

Why does the mere exposure effect occur? One possibility is that we are uncertain about how to respond to novel objects, and this uncertainty is unpleasant. When we come to know the object better, there is less uncertainty about how to respond to it. Another possibility is that when we are familiar with an object, we can perceive and categorize it more quickly and easily than unfamiliar objects. This ease of recognition is pleasing, so we come to feel good about familiar things. Through mere exposure, positive affect can be linked with an object, which will increase the favourability of the person's attitude toward the object.

Zajonc tested his hypothesis in several experiments at the University of Michigan and obtained supportive results. In one study, he showed participants photographs of human faces and asked them how much they thought they would like each person. Some of the faces were shown numerous times before being rated, whereas others were seen only once or twice before rating. The results showed that participants gave more favourable ratings to faces that they had seen more often (see also Bornstein, 1989; Bornstein & D'Agostino, 1992; Murphy, Monahan, & Zajonc, 1995).

An interesting phenomenon that might reflect the mere exposure effect is the finding that people tend to like the letters that appear in their own name more than do people whose names do not include those letters (Hodson & Olson, 2005; Hoorens & Nuttin, 1993; Nuttin, 1987). For example, people named Paul will tend to rate the letters *a, l, p,* and *u* more favourably than people whose names do not include these letters. The effect is especially strong for people's first and last initials. One explanation for this finding is

6.2
ONLINE
LAB

Social Psychology in Your Life *Familiarity Effects in the Classroom*

Do you think that you would like a person better if you'd seen him or her several times before? In a test of this idea in a natural social setting, Richard Moreland and Scott Beach (1992) hired four young women to serve as confederates in a study conducted at the University of Pittsburgh. The women were rated as equally attractive by undergraduate students in a pretest. The women posed as students and attended an undergraduate course on personality psychology—a large class consisting of 191 students. The lectures took place in a 200-seat classroom that was fan-shaped, narrower at the front than the back, and sloping upward from the front to the back. Anyone seated in the front rows was visible to the rest of the class.

On the days that they attended, the women entered the hall a few minutes before the class was to begin, walked slowly down the stairs to a front row, and sat where they could be seen by everyone. During the class, they listened and took notes quietly. At the end of the class, they rose, walked slowly up the stairs to the back of the hall, and left without speaking to any other students. A total of 40 class sessions were held during the term, with a

typical attendance rate by the real students of about 75%. One of the target women attended 15 lectures in the course, another attended 10 lectures, another attended 5 lectures, and another did not attend any lectures at all. Only one target woman attended any particular lecture.

After the term ended, students in the course were shown photos of each of the four women's faces and were asked to rate her on ten scales that reflected liking and attraction (e.g., ranging from cold to warm, unattractive to attractive, and dishonest to honest). The results are presented in Figure 6.2. The results were simple and clear: the more often the woman had attended the class, the more positively she was rated. Even though no one in the class had even spoken to any of the women, visual exposure led to more liking.

After making the liking ratings, students in the class were also asked whether they had ever seen each target woman.

Only about 10% of the students reported recognizing any of the women, and this rate was similar for all four targets. Thus, the effects of exposure on liking occurred even though most participants could not actually recall seeing the women who attended most often.

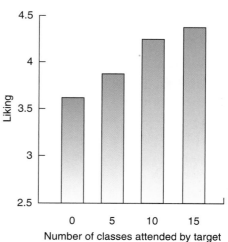

FIGURE 6.2 Liking for target women based on their class attendance

From Moreland and Beach, "Exposure effects in the classroom: The development of affinity among students," *Journal of Experimental Social Psychology*, 28, 255–276, Table 2, p. 262, 1992. Reprinted by permission of Elsevier.

that people are more familiar with the letters in their own name. (Another possibility is that the letters of one's own name are linked to one's identity, and people like the letters because they view themselves positively—recall the discussions of *self-serving judgments* in Chapters 3 and 4, pages 97 and 132; see Jones, Pelham, & Mirenberg, 2002.)

What about the possible negative effects of repeated exposure mentioned at the beginning of this section? It is true that repeated exposure to a stimulus can sometimes lead to boredom or satiation, such as hearing a song on the radio too many times. Consumer and marketing psychologists have commented on the problem of "wear-out," which occurs when advertising exposure of a product goes beyond the limit and begins to cause a reduction in attitude favourability. But these effects are the exception rather than the rule and occur only after many, many exposures. For most targets, our attitude becomes more positive as we are exposed to it more frequently.

Mere exposure is a phenomenon that is easy to find in everyday life outside the laboratory. One interesting study that tested the effect in a classroom setting is described in Social Psychology in Your Life: "Familiarity Effects in the Classroom."

Can you think of other examples of the mere exposure effect in real life? Have you ever noticed that something that seemed strange at first eventually became familiar and likeable? In Table 6.1, we provide a few examples of everyday experiences that show the mere exposure effect. Perhaps you will recognize your own experiences in some of these examples. Politicians certainly seem to believe in the mere exposure effect: they do everything they can to put their names and photos everywhere, especially during election campaigns.

Cognitive Sources of Attitudes

What is your attitude toward taking vitamin supplements? Are you favourable or unfavourable? Now consider: *Why* are you favourable or unfavourable toward taking vitamin supplements?

Most people would answer this question by referring to their beliefs about the health consequences of taking vitamin supplements. If they believe that vitamin supplements

TABLE 6.1
Some Everyday Examples of the Mere Exposure Effect

You do not really like a new song that you hear for the first time, but after a number of exposures, you come to love the song.

Wine usually tastes awful to people when they first try it as children or teenagers, but many people develop a liking for wine over time.

New fashions can look ridiculous when you see them for the first time, but soon they evoke more positive reactions.

You don't like your new hairstyle at all, but as you get used to it, you begin to like it.

You are introduced to someone at work with the first name of Lydellium; you think the name is really strange, but as you hear the name used occasionally over the next few weeks, you come to think of it as quite natural.

New foods often taste strange at first, but people can come to love unusual foods eventually.

Brand names that are very familiar (e.g., Kleenex, Xerox, Canada Dry) are usually perceived as trustworthy and high in quality.

Your new neighbour looks rather weird to you the first time you see him, but after you've seen him working in his yard several times, he looks more normal to you.

Abstract art often seems jarring or unattractive when viewed for the first time, but is appreciated more after several viewings.

A foreign language can sound bizarre and undecipherable when you first visit a country, but as your visit continues, the language comes to sound more structured and attractive.

strengthen the body and increase resistance to disease, they will be favourable to vitamin supplements. If, on the other hand, they believe that vitamin supplements do not improve health and might even produce toxic levels of some vitamins, they will be unfavourable to vitamin supplements.

As these comments indicate, your attitude toward vitamin supplements probably depends to a significant degree on your analysis of the rational arguments for and against taking supplements. If you think that vitamin supplements have more positive consequences than negative consequences, you are likely to be favourable toward them, whereas if you think that vitamin supplements have more negative consequences than positive ones, you are likely to be unfavourable toward them.

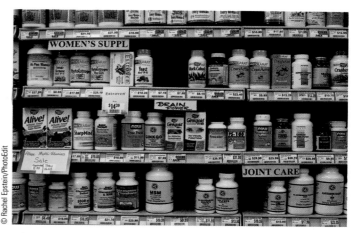

What is your attitude toward taking vitamin supplements?

This influence of cognitive information occurs in many attitudes. Your attitudes toward people you know are influenced by your beliefs about their positive and negative characteristics. If you think that Danielle is friendly and honest, your attitude toward her will be favourable; if you think that she is conceited and a troublemaker, your attitude toward her will be negative. Your attitudes toward consumer products are influenced by your perceptions of their quality and performance. If you believe that your refrigerator has been reliable and economical, your attitude toward it will be positive; if you know that it has been unreliable and required expensive repairs, your attitude toward it will be negative.

This idea that our beliefs about an object, person, or issue influence our attitude toward it may seem a bit obvious, but the idea is important nonetheless. We tend to evaluate objects, people, and policies positively when we believe that they possess mostly positive characteristics, and we tend to evaluate them negatively when we believe that they possess mostly negative characteristics.

This link between beliefs and attitudes has been documented in many studies (see Ajzen & Fishbein, 1980; Doll & Orth, 1993; Eagly & Chaiken, 1993; Sheppard, Hartwick, & Warshaw, 1988). For example, William Fisher, Jeffrey Fisher, and Barbara Rye (1995) conducted a study at the University of Western Ontario in which they measured participants' attitudes toward several "safer sex behaviours," such as *using condoms during intercourse* and *discussing contraception with partners*. Participants were asked to rate these behaviours on good–bad evaluative scales. The researchers also measured participants' beliefs about the consequences of the various behaviours. For example, they measured whether participants believed that using condoms would effectively protect against AIDS and other sexually transmitted diseases. Results showed that participants' attitudes toward these safer sex behaviours were strongly correlated with their beliefs about the positive and negative consequences of the behaviours. For example, participants who knew that condoms provide effective protection against sexually transmitted diseases expressed more favourable evaluations of using condoms than participants who were uncertain of the effectiveness of condoms for avoiding STDs. Thus, participants' attitudes were directly and logically related to their beliefs.

In an interesting set of experiments, York University social psychologist Kerry Kawakami and her colleagues (Kawakami, Dovidio, & Dijksterhuis, 2003) documented another cognitive influence on attitudes. These researchers showed that priming a schema (see Chapter 3) caused attitude ratings to move in the direction of the schema. For example, priming the schema of *elderly persons* led university students to express more conservative attitudes than participants in a control, no-priming condition. Presumably, priming the schema increased the accessibility of cognitive information that was consistent with the schema, which then influenced attitudes.

Behavioural Sources of Attitudes

In Chapter 4, we discussed several processes involved in making judgments about ourselves. One of the theories described was *self-perception theory* by Daryl Bem (1967, 1972). Self-perception theory is based on the intriguing hypothesis that if we cannot directly access our internal states, we may *infer* them from our actions. For example, if we are asked about our attitude toward seatbelts, and our attitude is weak or ambiguous, we may think about how we have behaved with regard to seatbelts in the past. If our behaviour has been predominantly positive (e.g., we have typically used seatbelts in cars and taxis), we will infer that we are favourable toward using seatbelts; if our behaviour has been more negative (e.g., we have often failed to use seatbelts in cars and taxis), we will infer that our attitude toward using seatbelts is unfavourable.

Thus, attitudes can be based on behavioural information—specifically, information about our own past behaviour toward the target (see Albarracín & Wyer, 2000; Olson, 1992). This process is unlikely to occur when we have strong and well-developed attitudes (Chaiken & Baldwin, 1981; Holland, Verplanken, & van Knippenberg, 2002). For example, we do not need to review how we have acted toward ice cream before we can report our evaluation: we *know* we love it! We also do not need to review our past actions toward mosquitoes before we can report our evaluation: we *know* we hate them!

Can you think of an attitude domain in which you might use your own behaviour to infer your evaluation? What about an activity that you perform only occasionally? For example, if asked the question "Do you like hiking?" you might reply by referring to your behaviour: "Yeah, I guess so—I go hiking several times a year" or "No, not really—I haven't gone hiking for a couple of years." Some people, of course, know that they love or hate hiking, but others may gauge their attitudes toward the activity by reflecting on their actions.

Physiological Processes and Attitudes

We have addressed three sources of attitudes that have been studied by attitude theorists: affective, cognitive, and behavioural sources. There is another domain, however, that also has implications for attitudes: physiological or biological processes. The topic of the biology of attitudes has historically received little attention from social psychologists, but it has been the focus of more research recently.

It may seem implausible to you that biological processes are important for understanding people's attitudes. After all, don't attitudes have to be learned? We are not born liking or disliking objects and issues. If attitudes are learned, doesn't this mean that they must be environmentally caused?

But let's think about this for a moment. Have you ever been intoxicated with alcohol? If so, did this drug affect your behaviour—for example, did you do anything that you wouldn't normally have done? Humorous examples of this phenomenon might include dancing more energetically than usual at the bar or singing on the way home on the bus with your friends. More ominous examples might include getting involved in a violent confrontation in the bar or having unprotected sex—actions that can kill.

Statistics suggest that most Canadian university students drink alcohol. Andrée Demars at the University of Montreal and his colleagues (Demers, Kairouz, Adlaf, Gliksman, Newton-Taylor, & Marchand, 2002) reported data from a 1998 survey of students at 18 Canadian universities. Among the 8864 undergraduates who completed the survey, 83% reported drinking alcohol since the beginning of the term. Also, the more students thought that drinking was the norm in university life, the more they reported drinking, especially for males.

How does alcohol affect behaviour? For one thing, alcohol changes how people feel about various actions (i.e., it changes their attitudes toward the actions, at least temporarily); it also impairs their ability to think rationally about the consequences of different actions. The fact that alcohol has these effects underscores that humans are biological beings, whose cognitive and emotional systems are influenced by chemicals in the blood and brain. These effects of alcohol and other drugs show that physiological processes have important implications for attitudes.

Alcohol Myopia. The effect of alcohol on information processing has been termed **alcohol myopia** (Steele & Josephs, 1990). Alcohol myopia refers to the fact that intoxication reduces cognitive capacity, which results in a narrowing of attention (hence, *myopia*). When individuals are intoxicated, their ability to pay attention to multiple cues is impaired. As a result, only the most obvious and strongest cues, external or internal, will be perceived, which will increase the impact of these cues compared to times when the individual is sober. For instance, if the obvious external cues are consistent with aggressive behaviour (e.g., someone insults and shoves another person), then aggression is more likely when an individual is intoxicated than when he or she is sober. Or if the strongest external and internal cues are consistent with having sex (e.g., the individual is alone with the potential partner and is sexually aroused), then unprotected sexual behaviour is more likely when an individual is intoxicated than when he or she is sober.

> **alcohol myopia**
>
> *the tendency for intoxication to reduce cognitive capacity, which results in a narrowing of attention*

Several interesting studies by Tara MacDonald, who is at Queen's University, and her colleagues Mark Zanna and Geoff Fong (1996), who are at the University of Waterloo, tested whether alcohol intoxication influenced university students' willingness to have unprotected sexual intercourse. In one experiment, male students were randomly assigned to either a *sober* or *intoxicated* condition (women were not included because of concerns about possible negative health effects of consuming alcohol while pregnant). In the sober condition, participants viewed a videotape and answered some questions without having consumed any alcohol. In the intoxicated condition, participants consumed three alcoholic drinks, spaced 20 minutes apart, and then viewed the same videotape and answered the same questions. The ten-minute videotape portrayed two undergraduates, Mike and Rebecca, in a situation in which sexual intercourse without using a condom was possible. The videotape showed the two individuals talking in a hallway after writing an exam, where Mike asked Rebecca out on a date. The next scene showed the couple at the campus bar, where they were drinking and dancing, including a slow dance during which they kissed. In the next scene, the couple was kissing passionately on a couch at Rebecca's apartment, and Rebecca suggested they move to her bedroom. Mike awkwardly stated that he didn't have any condoms, but Rebecca said that she was on the pill. The two then discussed that they were "clean" and did not "sleep around." Mike then asked Rebecca what she wanted to do. She kissed him and replied, "I don't know. What do *you* want to do?" The video then ended with a freeze frame.

Participants had been instructed to imagine themselves in the role of Mike as they watched the video. Do you think that this procedure was involving and engaging for participants? That is, did it create *experimental realism* (see Chapter 2, page 55)? Because the video was very well done, an acceptable level of experimental realism was probably achieved.

When the video ended, participants completed a questionnaire that assessed their willingness to have unprotected sexual intercourse if they were in Mike's position. Results showed that intoxicated participants expressed greater willingness to have unprotected sex with Rebecca than did sober participants. Intoxicated participants also expressed stronger agreement with a

Alcohol myopia results in a narrowing of attention.

number of questionable "justifications" for having unprotected sex, such as "Rebecca looks totally healthy, so it's unlikely that she has AIDS or other sexually transmitted diseases." Thus, intoxication increased the likelihood that participants would act in a risky fashion when the most obvious cues supported such behaviour.

A study by Kathy Denton, who is at Douglas College in New Westminster, British Columbia, and Dennis Krebs, who is at Simon Fraser University in Burnaby, British Columbia, found that virtually all university students who were sober reported in a laboratory setting that they would *not* drive while impaired, whereas most university students at bars who were actually intoxicated did, in fact, drive themselves home if they had come by car (Denton & Krebs, 1990). A similar pattern of results was obtained at the University of Waterloo by Tara MacDonald, Mark Zanna, and Geoff Fong (1995), who found that intoxicated participants expressed greater willingness to drive after drinking than did sober participants.

These studies have an important message: we must realize that we are, quite literally, *different people* when we are intoxicated—with different attitudes and different behavioural inclinations. We must either avoid becoming heavily intoxicated or arrange to have someone else help us when we are impaired (e.g., by serving as a designated driver).

Attitude Heritability. Many characteristics are inherited from our parents (who may have inherited them from their parents). Obvious examples include hair colour, eye colour, and height. The physical characteristics shared by almost all humans, such as having two eyes, two ears, and two legs, are also inherited. Interest in the genetic determination of things other than physical characteristics has greatly increased in the past 20 or 30 years, with important discoveries identifying genetic "markers" for a number of illnesses or conditions (e.g., breast cancer, muscular dystrophy).

What about attitudes? Is it possible that we inherit some of our attitudes from our parents? For instance, if someone has a positive attitude toward sports, could the person have inherited this attitude from his or her parents? The answer is almost certainly no if, by inherited, we mean that a particular gene caused the attitude (e.g., a gene caused the person to be favourable toward sports). But the answer is very possibly yes if we mean that biological characteristics (e.g., strength, coordination) partly inherited from the parents made it more *likely* that he or she would develop a favourable attitude toward sports.

Think about yourself. What are some important features or abilities that you think you probably inherited from your parents? Such features or abilities might include your height, facial features, intelligence, shyness, or musical ability. (We should note that not all scientists would agree that such things as intelligence, shyness, or musical ability are highly heritable.) Now think about whether the features or abilities that you inherited might have influenced your attitudes. Is it possible that some of your attitudes were shaped by your inherited features or abilities?

Let's consider some feasible hypothetical examples. John inherited unusual physical strength and coordination from his parents. These abilities made him successful in various sports. Because of this success, he developed positive attitudes toward athletic activities.

Mohini inherited high intellectual abilities from her parents. Because she was so intelligent, she did extremely well at school and also became an excellent chess player. These achievements fostered positive attitudes toward education and intellectual pursuits.

Pierre inherited from his parents an inner-ear structure that was very sensitive to changes in balance.

Do you think that characteristics you inherited from your parents affected any of your attitudes?

As a result, he felt nauseated quite easily. This tendency toward nausea made him dislike roller coasters, boats, and airplane rides.

Sara inherited an outgoing, extraverted disposition from her parents. This sociability meant that she felt very comfortable in social surroundings and interpersonal interactions. Her extraversion fostered positive attitudes toward parties, group activities, and other social settings.

Do these examples clarify how people's inherited abilities and characteristics might predispose them to having certain kinds of experiences, such as success at sports or success at school, which then foster certain attitudes? Although the experiences (e.g., success at sports) are the specific events that cause the attitudes (e.g., positive attitudes toward sports), the experiences occur partly *because of the inherited characteristics* (e.g., natural athletic ability). Thus, the final attitudes reflect a combination of biology and experience. The flowchart in Figure 6.3 depicts the hypothesized process.

James Olson, Anthony Vernon, Julie Harris, and Kerry Jang (2001) at the University of Western Ontario distributed an attitude survey that measured attitudes toward 30 different targets to a total of 336 pairs of twins: 195 pairs of identical twins (who share all of their genes) and 141 pairs of same-sex fraternal twins (who share some but not all genes). Research using samples of twins is based on the idea that by comparing the responses of identical and same-sex fraternal twins, it is possible to estimate the extent to which differences between the respondents can be attributed to genetic factors. Specifically, if identical twins report more similar attitudes to one another than do fraternal twins, then a genetic component in attitudes is indicated. The researchers found that almost all of the attitudes (26 of 30) showed at least some genetic component, supporting the hypothesis that many attitude differences between individuals are partly due to genetic differences (see also Abrahamson, Baker, & Caspi, 2002; Eaves, Eysenck, & Martin, 1989; Waller, Kojetin, Bouchard, Lykken, & Tellegen, 1990; Zuckerman, 1995). The five attitudes that yielded the highest genetic influence were attitudes toward reading books, abortion on demand, playing organized sports, roller-coaster rides, and the death penalty for murder.

Researchers do not yet understand why particular attitudes have a large genetic component (e.g., attitudes toward the death penalty) and why other particular attitudes have little or no genetic component (e.g., attitudes toward capitalism). Research to date has focused on identifying *which* attitudes are heritable, rather than *why* they are heritable. One goal of future research will be to understand the mechanisms that make some attitudes more heritable than others.

University of Georgia social psychologist Abraham Tesser (1993; Crelia & Tesser, 1996) proposed that attitudes with a substantial biological component might be more

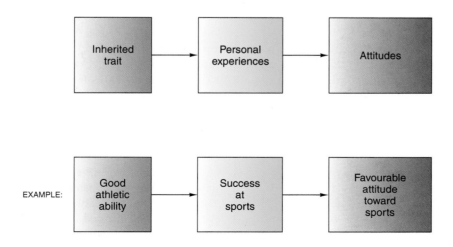

FIGURE 6.3 How attitudes could be partly inherited

important to people than attitudes with very little biological component. To test this hypothesis, he measured the speed with which people could state their attitudes; he assumed that important attitudes can be stated more quickly than unimportant attitudes. Therefore, Tesser asked participants to report several attitudes that had been shown in previous studies to be highly heritable (e.g., attitudes toward the death penalty and attitudes toward the use of birth control) and to report several attitudes that had been shown in previous studies to be very low in heritability (e.g., attitudes toward capitalism and attitudes toward social support for immigrants). As predicted, people could report the highly heritable attitudes more quickly than the attitudes with little heritable component. In another study, Tesser showed that people were more attracted to someone else who was similar to them on highly heritable attitudes than to someone who was similar to them on low-heritability attitudes. Again, this finding supports the idea that people care more about highly heritable attitudes than attitudes low in heritability.

Parents, Peers, and Attitudes

Other people have major effects on individuals' attitudes, beliefs, and values. In the earliest years of childhood, parents and family are extremely important. As children approach adolescence, their peer groups become increasingly significant. In this section, we briefly discuss these two sources of influence.

Parental Socialization

socialization

the process by which infants are moulded into acceptable members of their society

Socialization is "the process by which an infant becomes an acceptable member of his or her society—one who behaves appropriately, knows the language, possesses the requisite skills, and holds the prevailing beliefs and attitudes" (Harris, 1995, pp. 461–462). For the first few years of life, the family is the most important source of socialization, especially parents.

Researchers have shown that parents exert influence over their children in a variety of ways. Parents express opinions and values that children may internalize. Can you think of times when your parents expressed a value such as honesty and tried to explain why it was important? Parents also model behaviour, which children may imitate. Can you think of times when you imitated your parents' actions, such as treating toys as if they were your children? Parents also provide much of the information that young children obtain about the world. Can you think of topics that you first learned about primarily from your parents, such as religious issues and educational values? Given these various modes of influence, it is not terribly surprising that children express attitudes that are similar to those of their parents on a variety of issues, including gender roles, cigarette smoking, political views, and values (e.g., Chassin, Presson, & Sherman, 1984; Cunningham, 2001; Jessop, 1982; Rohan & Zanna, 1996; Ruble & Goodnow, 1998).

There is also evidence that parenting styles influence children's values in adulthood. Tim Kasser, who is at Knox College, together with Richard Koestner and Natasha Lekes (2002), who are at McGill University, reported data from a sample of individuals whose values were measured at age 31 and whose parents had been interviewed 26 years earlier (when the participants were five years old). Based on the early interviews, parents were classified in terms of restrictiveness (e.g., their use of physical punishment, their demands for sexual modesty) and in terms of coldness (e.g., their avoidance of physical affection, their limited use of praise). Results showed that *nonrestrictive* parenting was associated with greater emphasis at age 31 on imaginativeness and independence, whereas *restrictive* parenting was associated with greater emphasis at age 31 on obedience and politeness. Results also showed that a *warm* parenting style was associated with greater emphasis at age 31 on freedom and personal responsibility, whereas a *cold* parenting style was associated with greater emphasis at age 31 on safety issues such as family and national security. These findings suggest that nonrestrictive and warm parenting styles, which give children autonomy and acceptance, are more likely to instill adult values that encourage independence and caring relationships with others (see also Kasser, Ryan, Zax, & Sameroff, 1995; Williams, Cox, Hedberg, & Deci, 2000).

One rather surprising domain in which researchers have *not* always found strong correlations between children's and parents' attitudes is racial attitudes. Canadian social/developmental psychologists Frances Aboud and Anna-Beth Doyle (1996), for example, found no relation between the racial attitudes of third-grade children and their mothers in Montreal. At the University of Indiana, Tamara Towles-Schwen and Russell Fazio (2001) found no relation between White students' implicit attitudes toward Blacks and their reports of their parents' racial attitudes. Instead, these latter researchers found that implicit attitudes toward Blacks were correlated with positive interactions with Blacks in high school, suggesting the importance of personal experiences.

Reference Groups

Parents do not always rule our world. Developmental psychologists have found that as children's exposure to people outside the family increases, parental influence is gradually overtaken by peer influence, most notably in the form of reference groups. In fact, some theorists have argued that, in the long run, peer groups are more important agents of socialization than are parents. For example, Judith Harris (1995, 1998) has argued that parents do not socialize children—*children* socialize children. She believes that children's experiences outside the home, in the company of their peers, are very influential in determining attitudes, beliefs, and personality traits.

A **reference group** is a group that serves as a standard of comparison for an individual, whether in terms of attitudes, values, or behaviour. Individuals try to conform to the norms and values of their main reference groups. A reference group can be any collective that an individual recognizes: a group of friends, people who prefer a certain musical style, a club, a gang, a team, a political party, or any other identifiable group. The most obvious ways that people conform to reference groups is by joining them, if possible (e.g., a friendship group or a club), or by copying their appearance and behaviour. Thus, adolescents may adopt the dress and language of goths, rappers, preppies, or skaters—sometimes to the horror of their parents. Susan Boon and Christine Lomore (2001) of the University of Calgary found that celebrities (e.g., movie stars, musicians) also serve as important referents for many young people; indeed, more than 90% of their respondents said that one or more celebrities had influenced their attitudes and sense of identity.

Theodore Newcomb (1943) conducted a famous early study of reference groups by following an entire class of students at Bennington College in Vermont (an all-women school at that time) through their four years at the university. The prevailing values at the college were very liberal, whereas most of the students came from wealthy, conservative backgrounds. Newcomb found that most students became increasingly liberal over their four-year period at the college. He also found that students who expressed liberal views tended to be more popular on campus than those who expressed conservative views, and the latter students (those who expressed conservative views) tended to identify strongly with their family. These data show the power of reference groups.

reference group

a collection of people that serves as a standard of comparison for an individual, whether in terms of attitudes, values, or behaviour

Newcomb and his colleagues followed up his original survey approximately 25 and 50 years later and compared the Bennington College graduates with a comparable group of women from similar socioeconomic backgrounds who did not attend the college (Alwin, Cohen, & Newcomb, 1991; Newcomb, 1963; Newcomb, Koeing, Flacks, & Warwick, 1967). At both follow-ups, these researchers found that the Bennington graduates expressed more liberal attitudes than the comparison group. Bennington graduates also tended to marry men who had liberal attitudes. It appears that their experiences at Bennington College had a long-lasting impact on the women's attitudes and lives.

Jeer Pressure. Think back to when you were in high school (which may not be very long ago!). What do you remember as your *greatest fear* at that time in your life? What possible event caused you to lose the most sleep? Being a victim of crime? Global nuclear war? Having a car accident? Failing at school? Coming down with a serious illness?

Based on a survey of high school students conducted by Jeremy Shapiro, Roy Baumeister, and Jane Kessler (1991) in Cleveland, there is a good chance that you chose "none of the above" for your greatest fear. Instead, the most common answer given by high school students asked to identify their greatest fear was *being ridiculed.* Does this surprise you? This finding shows how important it is to teenagers to be accepted by their peer group.

Ridicule is derogatory humour directed at an individual concerning some aspect of his or her behaviour or appearance. It occurs in many forms: laughing at someone's looks or clothes, mocking someone's values, insulting someone's family, or otherwise humiliating someone, usually in public. Ridicule is very common in our society, but its frequency and emotional impact are greatest during adolescence and the teenage years, when the desire to belong and to be popular is at its peak. Being the target of ridicule is extremely painful, as most of us know from personal experience. Being a constant target of ridicule can lead to withdrawal, depression, and even suicide. It can also lead to violence, in which the target of ridicule exacts revenge on his or her tormentors by fighting or, in extreme cases, shooting them in the school or schoolyard.

Why do people ridicule others? One reason is that, by mocking another person, the individual doing the ridiculing feels superior and may be seen as clever by people in his or her clique who witness it. But the more common reason is, quite simply, to gain or establish control. Peer pressure involving ridicule can be a powerful way to enforce conformity to group norms. Ridicule can be an effective tool for influencing others—both the target of the ridicule and observers. Research on the intentional use of embarrassment (which is often milder than true ridicule) has shown that more than 90% of people who use embarrassment to establish control say that they successfully achieved their goals (Sharkey, 1992). Darcy Santor and his colleagues at Dalhousie University in Halifax found that reports of stronger peer pressure among high school students were associated with more risky behaviours such as alcohol and drug use (Santor, Messervey, & Kusumakar, 2000).

jeer pressure

the conformity pressure that is produced by seeing someone ridiculed by another person

Leslie Janes, who is at Brescia University College in London, Ontario (affiliated with the University of Western Ontario), coined the term **jeer pressure** to refer to the conformity pressure that is produced by seeing someone ridiculed by another person (Janes & Olson, 2000). People do not have to be the direct target of ridicule to feel jeer pressure; even observers of the ridicule will conform to norms so that they will not be ridiculed too. Think of a group of teenagers sitting outside a high school. If one of the individuals ridicules a student walking by who isn't wearing the newest fashions, other members of the group are unlikely to say anything that will draw notice to themselves—instead, they will quietly conform to the clique's norms. Similarly, other bystanders are unlikely to intervene, opting instead to try to sneak away without being ridiculed as well.

Janes and Olson (2000) showed that jeer pressure can make people express public attitudes and opinions that conform to other people's views. (We discuss conformity in greater detail in Chapter 8.) In one study, university students watched a videotape showing two men changing a tire on a bicycle. In the process of changing the tire, one of the men made a number of mistakes, such as pinching his finger in a pump. In one version of the videotape, the second man ridiculed the mistakes (e.g., "I guess that's why they call it a *foot* pump!") and made other, generally derogatory but potentially humorous comments (e.g., "If a loser like him can fix a tire, so can you"). In another version of the videotape, the man who made the mistakes expressed the same derogatory comments, but this time *directed at himself* (e.g., "If a loser like me can fix a tire, so can you"). This self-ridicule condition was not expected to create jeer pressure, because making fun of oneself is not threatening to others. Finally, in a third version of the videotape, no ridicule or derogatory comments occurred. After watching the videotape, participants were asked to evaluate it on a number of dimensions, such as clarity, enjoyability, and overall educational value. They recorded their ratings on sheets that already included the alleged answers of two previous participants. These "previous ratings" were actually made by the experimenter and were designed to be inaccurate (e.g., these answers rated the tape as low in clarity and high in enjoyability, whereas actual pilot testing had shown that students rated all three versions of the tape as high in clarity and low in enjoyability). Participants who had observed one person ridiculing someone else on the videotape conformed more closely to the ratings of the alleged previous subjects than did participants who had observed self-ridicule or

© Michael Newman/PhotoEdit

Jeer pressure is pressure to conform that is produced by seeing someone ridiculed.

no ridicule at all. Thus, observing an individual being ridiculed by another individual led to conforming responses on the questionnaire—jeer pressure altered the public expressions of attitudes.

How Do Attitudes Affect Behaviour?

One reason that social psychologists are interested in attitudes is that attitudes are presumed to influence behaviour. We opened the chapter with a description of Phillip, whose actions seem surprising or inappropriate when viewed in the context of today's attitudes and beliefs. We suggested, however, that Phillip's behaviour was quite understandable given the prevalent attitudes of his time. Our comments assumed that attitudes are an important cause of people's behaviour—an assumption that has motivated much of the research in this chapter.

Let us mention once again the potentially confusing two-way relationship between attitudes and behaviour. We discussed earlier how someone might use his or her past behaviour to infer an attitude (e.g., "I guess I don't like peanut butter, because I almost never eat it"). This reasoning reveals that past behaviour can influence judgments about current attitudes. But current attitudes can also affect future behaviour—the focus of the present section. For instance, someone's current attitude toward peanut butter can influence how often he or she eats it in the future.

But *how* do current attitudes affect future behaviour? What are the psychological mechanisms that might explain the effects of attitudes on actions? We describe in this section two principal mechanisms: *rational choice* and *selective perception*. Rational choice refers to making deliberate, reasoned decisions based on our attitudes. Selective perception refers to a more subtle process: the biasing effect of our attitudes on how we interpret and understand the world.

Rational Choice

One source of attitudes (the *cognitive component*) is information—beliefs about the target. You believe that skating is fun and good for your health. You believe that cars made by Mercedes-Benz are high in quality but very expensive. You believe that cockroaches are dirty and hide in dark corners. These pieces of information about the targets can guide your behaviour in a rational manner. You will skate regularly. You will pass on buying a Mercedes-Benz until you've made your first million (just a matter of time, right?). If you find cockroaches in your apartment, you will try to kill them and to spray pesticide into dark corners. These examples represent actions that are rationally based on our beliefs.

The Theory of Reasoned Action. This idea that behaviour is often rational forms the core of Martin Fishbein and Icek Ajzen's (1975) **theory of reasoned action.** This model views humans as rational decision makers who behave on the basis of logical beliefs (hence its name, *reasoned action*). The theory is one of the most influential models in the history of research on attitudes.

theory of reasoned action

a model of behaviour that views humans as rational decision makers who behave on the basis of logical beliefs

behavioural intention

an individual's plan to perform or not perform an action

Figure 6.4 presents the key concepts in the theory of reasoned action. Let's work backwards from behaviour in the model. Fishbein and Ajzen proposed that the most immediate cause of a behaviour is a **behavioural intention,** which refers to the individual's plan to perform or not perform the action. When you took a can of ginger ale from the refrigerator last night and drank it, you *intended* to do so—your behaviour of drinking ginger ale was preceded by the behavioural intention to drink ginger ale ("I think I'll have a ginger ale now"). Most of our actions are based on intentions in this manner because most of our actions are voluntary (we can either do them or not do them).

The idea that behaviour normally follows from intentions is not really very useful for understanding *why* people do things; stating that people do things "because they intend to do them" seems rather circular. To understand behaviour

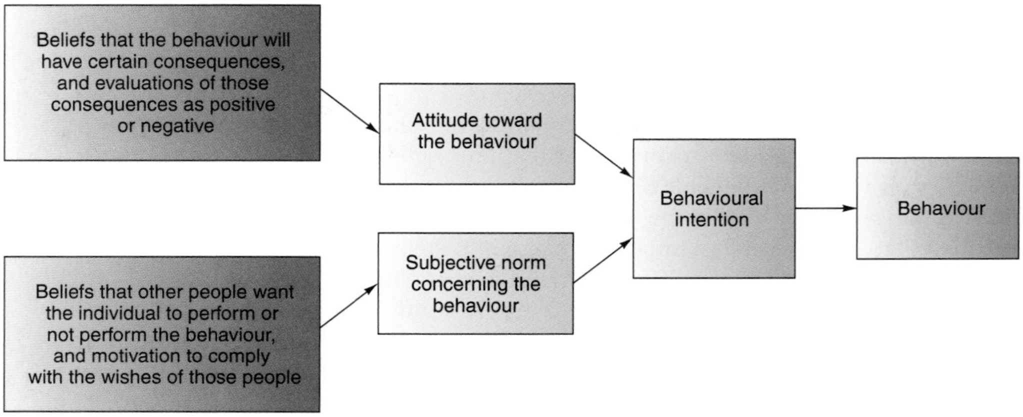

FIGURE 6.4 The theory of reasoned action

Adapted from Ajzen & Fishbein, 1980, p. 8.

better, it is necessary to look at the factors that cause intentions. Fishbein and Ajzen proposed that behavioural intentions are caused by two variables: the individual's attitude toward the behaviour and the individual's subjective norm concerning the behaviour.

In their model, an attitude is an individual's overall evaluation (good–bad judgment) of a particular behaviour, which is based on the individual's beliefs about the *consequences* of the behaviour. Their model parallels the perspective we presented earlier when discussing cognitive sources of attitudes: attitudes represent the overall favourability of someone's beliefs. Table 6.2 provides a set of illustrative beliefs that might underlie someone's attitude toward *doing volunteer work*. This hypothetical individual has seven beliefs about the consequences of doing volunteer work, which include "helps others," "makes me feel good about myself," and "takes time away from other activities." Most of these consequences are evaluated positively by the individual. As a result, his or her overall attitude toward doing volunteer work is also positive.

What are **subjective norms?** Let's begin with the more general concept of *norms*, which are cultural standards that define proper behaviour (e.g., we should wait our turn when there is a lineup at the grocery store; we should tell the truth); people feel social pressure to follow norms (see Chapter 8). In the theory of reasoned action, *subjective norms* are individuals' feelings of social pressure to perform or not perform an action. They are based on individuals' beliefs that other people want them to perform the action or do not want them to perform the action, as well as their motivation to do what these other people want. A husband might feel social pressure from his wife and children to stop smoking; he knows that they want him to stop, and he generally tries to comply with his family's wishes. A woman might feel pressure from her doctor to perform regular breast self-examinations; she knows that her doctor wants her to do these examinations regularly, and she doesn't want to disappoint him or her. In both of these cases, the individuals will feel some social pressure to act in a particular way, either to stop a behaviour or to perform a behaviour.

In the theory of reasoned action, behavioural intentions depend on attitudes and subjective norms. Favourable attitudes and favourable subjective norms foster intentions to perform a behaviour, whereas unfavourable attitudes and unfavourable subjective norms foster intentions to avoid performing it. If attitudes and subjective norms are consistent with one another, then behavioural intentions will be strong and

subjective norm
an individual's feelings of social pressure to perform or not perform an action

TABLE 6.2
Attitudes Toward Doing Volunteer Work in the Theory of Reasoned Action: Attitudes Are Based on the Individual's Beliefs About the Consequences of the Behaviour

Belief About a Consequence of Doing Volunteer Work	Evaluation of the Consequence
Helps others	Very good
Makes me feel good about myself	Good
Introduces me to new people	Very good
Takes time away from other activities	Bad
Gives me useful skills and experiences	Good
Sometimes makes me tired	Bad
Provides a good example to others	Good
Overall Attitude Toward Doing Volunteer Work = Positive	

actions will be consistent. If, on the other hand, attitudes and subjective norms conflict, then behavioural intentions may be uncertain and actions may be inconsistent. A man who wants to smoke but knows that his family wants him to stop will feel very conflicted about smoking. His intentions (and behaviour) may vacillate depending on whether he thinks about his personal preferences or his family's wishes. (This example might remind you of the concept of *ambivalent attitudes,* which contain both positive and negative elements about a target and can lead to inconsistent behaviour.)

The theory of reasoned action has been tested and supported in many different domains, including voting behaviour, donating blood, consumer purchases, eating at fast-food restaurants, and participating in political protest marches (see Ajzen & Fishbein, 1980; Brindberg & Durand, 1983; Eagly & Chaiken, 1993; Kelly & Breinlinger, 1995; McCaul, O'Neill, & Glasgow, 1988). These tests of the theory have shown that attitudes and subjective norms predict behavioural intentions, and behavioural intentions predict behaviour. People make rational choices in deciding how to behave, and their choices are based on both personal attitudes and social pressure.

There is some evidence that subjective norms—perceived pressure from other people—are more influential in collectivist cultures, where social roles and relationships are emphasized, than in individualist cultures, where personal goals and achievements are emphasized. For example, Dominic Abrams, Kaori Ando, and Steve Hinkle (1998) surveyed workers in Great Britain and Japan about their turnover intentions (intentions to leave or remain at their current job). Respondents reported their attitudes toward leaving and their perceived pressure from others to leave or stay (subjective norms). Subjective norms predicted participants' behavioural intentions more strongly within the Japanese sample than within the British sample (see also Chan, Cheung, Gray, Ip, & Lee, 2004; Giles, Liddell, & Bydawell, 2005).

IMB model of AIDS-preventive behaviour

a theory postulating that information, motivation, and behavioural skills guide individuals' protective actions in the sexual domain

Attitudes and Behaviour in the Health Domain: The IMB Model.

A second model that analyzes behaviour in terms of rational choices is the **IMB model of AIDS-preventive behaviour** (Fisher & Fisher, 1992). Jeffrey Fisher and William Fisher, who are at the University of Connecticut and the University of Western Ontario, respectively, proposed the IMB model (the letters stand for Information, Motivation,

Research has shown that people are more likely to donate blood when they have a positive attitude toward this behaviour and when their subjective norms support this behaviour.

PhotoCreate/Shutterstock

and Behavioural skills), which is based partly on the theory of reasoned action. These researchers wanted to identify the most important determinants of "safer sex behaviours," such as using a condom during intercourse and refusing to have unsafe sex.

Figure 6.5 presents the key concepts in the IMB model. The authors proposed that three major elements contribute to safer sex behaviours. *Information* refers to basic knowledge about sexually transmitted diseases, contraception, and protective methods. For example, unless people have a general understanding of AIDS, how it is transmitted, and how it can be prevented, they cannot engage in protective behaviours. *Motivation* encompasses the concepts of attitudes and subjective norms from the theory of reasoned action. Fisher and Fisher proposed that both favourable attitudes toward safer sex behaviours and perceived pressure from others to perform these behaviours would increase individuals' motivation to engage in the preventive behaviours. Finally, *behavioural skills* refer to the ability to perform safer sex behaviours effectively. For example, people must be able to use condoms correctly and be able to discuss and negotiate safer sex with their partner (e.g., to raise the issue and to discuss it openly) in order for unsafe sex to be avoided.

Like the theory of reasoned action, the IMB model conceptualizes behaviour as involving deliberate choices among options. Ultimately, individuals must decide themselves whether to engage in risky sexual behaviours or instead to behave safely. Their choices will depend on the information they possess, their motivation to perform risky or safer behaviours, and their skill at performing preventive behaviours correctly.

A fascinating test of the IMB model was conducted by the Fishers and their colleagues (Fisher, Fisher, Misovich, Kimble, & Malloy, 1996). These researchers developed an educational program that was designed to improve every component of the theoretical model. A slide show provided basic information about AIDS and about contraceptive methods. A small group discussion was designed to make participants' attitudes toward safer sex behaviours more favourable. Videos of using condoms and live portrayals of negotiating safer sex with a partner were designed to improve participants' behavioural skills. The educational program consisted of three two-hour sessions that were held one week apart. The program was offered on some floors, but not all, of several dormitories at the University of Connecticut. More than 500 students completed the program.

Two months later, these students were contacted and compared to other students who lived on floors of the dormitories where the program was not available. Results showed that students who completed the program were more likely to have protected themselves by using condoms during sexual intercourse than were students who did not participate in the program. Thus, a critical risk-reducing behaviour was more common after the educational program (see also Jemmott, Jemmott, & Fong, 1992).

Think for a moment about your own actions in the domain of sexual behaviour. Have you ever behaved in a risky manner, such as not using a condom during intercourse? If the answer is yes, does the IMB model help you to understand your actions? Do you think you fell short in terms of information, motivation, or behavioural skills?

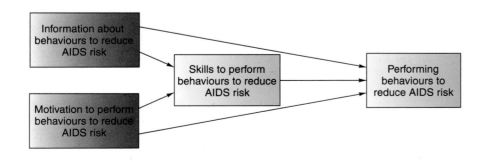

FIGURE 6.5 The IMB model of AIDS-preventive behaviours

Adapted from Fisher, Fisher, Misovich, Kimble, & Malloy, 1996.

Selective Perception

Attitudes can guide behaviour in a second, more subtle way than rational choice. Attitudes are a lens through which we view the world. Attitudes can influence what we notice, how we interpret information, and what we remember (e.g., Eagly & Chaiken, 1998; Eagly, Chen, Chaiken, & Shaw-Barnes, 1999; Fazio, 1990; Fazio & Williams, 1986; Frey, 1986; Kennamer, 1990; Schuette & Fazio, 1995). Attitudes can also affect the counterfactual thoughts we generate about past events (e.g., Crawford & McCrea, 2004). By changing our perceptions of the world around us, attitudes can influence our actions.

Have you ever listened to political commentators after a candidates' debate? If so, you may have noticed that commentators from different political leanings gave very different evaluations of the debate. After a federal leaders' debate, for example, representatives of a given party (Bloc Québécois, Conservatives, Liberals, or New Democrats) may compliment their own candidate's performance and criticize the other candidates. The wildly different evaluations can leave viewers wondering, "Did these people watch the same debate?"

Of course, we tend to be suspicious of representatives of political parties because their allegiances might cause them to be untruthful about how they actually think the candidates performed. But sometimes the differences of opinion are real—commentators from the different parties truly believe that their own candidate was more effective. How do these contrasting perceptions of the same event occur?

Biasing Effect of Attitudes. The bottom line is that people often see what they *expect* to see and what they *want* to see, based on their attitudes. You may recall from Chapter 3 (see page 67) that *schemas,* or *concepts,* can produce selective information processing, such that information that is consistent with an activated schema is more likely to be noticed and recalled. Claudia Cohen's (1981) experiment, in which participants watched a videotape of a woman and tended to recall information consistent with her alleged occupation (server or librarian), illustrated this phenomenon. We also discussed in Chapter 3 how *stereotypes* (which are a type of schema—namely, schemas representing human groups) can guide interpretation (see page 73). If a young man is categorized as a skinhead, the negative stereotype of skinheads will lead people to interpret ambiguous actions as hostile. These processes reflect that people often see what they expect to see (recall also *illusory correlations* from Chapter 3, see page 88, which occur when someone believes that two things are correlated when, in fact, they are independent).

In the same fashion, *attitudes* can influence what we notice and how we interpret events. If we have a positive attitude toward a co-worker, we will be predisposed to notice positive things about him or her and to interpret ambiguous information positively; exactly the opposite will occur if we have a negative attitude toward the co-worker. These biases reflect the tendency to see what we *expect* to see. Thus, attitudes can influence how we see the world. Our perceptions of the co-worker would have been different if we did not have our existing attitude toward him or her. Given that our impressions affect how we behave, attitudes can influence behaviour by changing our perceptions.

Note that this biasing effect of attitudes can occur for both *explicit* and *implicit* attitudes (see Strack & Deutsch, 2004). Even when individuals are unaware that they have an automatic positive or negative evaluative response to an object, the implicit attitude may affect their perceptions of the object. Bertram Gawronski, who is at the University of Western Ontario, and his colleagues (Gawronski, Walther, & Blank, 2005) showed that perceivers' implicit attitudes toward another person can affect how social information is encoded. For instance, if someone has an implicit negative response to members of a minority group, this automatic evaluative response may lead him or her to interpret actions by members of the group as negative. In turn, these unfavourable interpretations of behaviour may cause the perceiver to behave negatively toward members of the group. Thus, selective perception represents one way that implicit attitudes can subtly affect behaviour without the individual's awareness.

We also tend to see what we *want* to see, based on our attitudes. For instance, we are generally motivated to interpret information as *supporting* our attitudes. After all, we want to believe that our attitudes are correct, and information that supports our views implies that we are correct. Also, some attitudes express important aspects of our identity (recall the *value-expressive function* of attitudes), so information that supports our attitudes can serve to validate our identity.

Charles Lord, Lee Ross, and Mark Lepper (1979) conducted a well-known study at Stanford University that showed selective perception of information based on participants' attitudes toward the death penalty. Participants were selected because they had previously expressed either clearly favourable or clearly unfavourable attitudes toward capital punishment. When they came to the experimental session, they were given two articles to read and evaluate, each of which described a study that had investigated whether the death penalty deters people from committing murder. These two articles had actually been constructed by the experimenter to present opposing views of capital punishment. One study (article) concluded that capital punishment does reduce the murder rate (it is an effective deterrent), whereas the other study concluded that the murder rate was unaffected by capital punishment (it does not have any deterrent effect). Participants were asked to evaluate and comment on each article and then to report their current attitude on this issue.

What should have happened in this study if people processed the articles objectively? All participants were given mixed information, some supporting and some opposing capital punishment. The most sensible outcome, therefore, would seem to be to become *less extreme* on the issue—less certain about which side is correct. After all, the contradictory research findings showed that it is unclear whether or not the death penalty is effective as a deterrent. If people processed the material in an unbiased manner, pro–capital punishment participants should have become less pro, and anti–capital punishment participants should have become less anti.

But what actually happened? Pro–capital punishment participants became *more pro,* and anti–capital punishment participants became *more anti.* People became *more extreme* after reading the mixed information on the issue! Why? It turns out that participants evaluated the study that supported their own view more positively than the study that opposed their view (see also Edwards & Smith, 1996). They thought that the study supporting their view was methodologically strong, whereas they saw problems in the study opposing their view. Table 6.3 presents a few examples of actual comments that participants wrote about each study.

Although the information given to participants was mixed, it did not *seem* mixed to participants themselves. In their eyes, the evidence consisted of one strong study supporting their view and one weak study opposing their view. Obviously, then, their own view was correct! These findings illustrate rather dramatically how people's attitudes can influence the interpretation of attitude-relevant information. If the researchers had followed the participants and watched their behaviour with regard to the death penalty (e.g., how strongly the participants argued for their own position with other people), those who originally favoured the death penalty would presumably have argued for it even more strongly, whereas those who originally opposed the death penalty would have argued against it even more strongly. By changing perceptions of information, attitudes can ultimately change our behaviour (see also Cohen, Aronson, & Steele, 2000; Sherman & Cohen, 2002; Sherman, Nelson, & Steele, 2000).

Perceiving Media Coverage. One of the most longstanding, bitter, and complex political issues of our generation has been the situation in the Middle East. Many people have very strong views and high emotional involvement in this issue. Based on the notion of selective perception, it might be expected that individuals on

---

TABLE 6.3

Selected Comments by Pro— and Anti—Capital Punishment Participants on Pro— and Anti—Capital Punishment Studies

	Comments On	
Participant's Attitude	**Pro—Capital Punishment Study**	**Anti—Capital Punishment Study**
Pro–capital punishment	"The experiment was well thought out, the data collected was valid, and they were able to come up with responses to all criticisms."	"There were too many flaws in the picking of the states and too many variables involved in the experiment as a whole to change my opinion."
Pro–capital punishment	"It seems that the researchers studied a carefully selected group of states and that they were careful in interpreting their results."	"The research didn't cover a long enough period to prove that capital punishment is not a deterrent to murder."
Anti–capital punishment	"The study was taken only 1 year before and 1 year after capital punishment was reinstated. To be a more effective study, they should have taken data from at least 10 years before and as many years as possible after."	"The states were chosen at random, so results show the average effect capital punishment has across the nation. The fact that 8 out of 10 states show a rise in murders stands as good evidence."
Anti–capital punishment	"I don't feel such a straightforward conclusion can be made from the data collected."	"There aren't as many uncontrolled variables in this experiment as in the other one, so I'm still willing to believe the conclusion made."

Adapted from Lord, Ross, & Lepper, 1979, Table 2, page 2103.

---

different sides of the Israeli–Palestinian conflict would interpret similar information differently. In fact, this pattern has been documented in several studies of people's perceptions of the media (Giner-Sorolla & Chaiken, 1994; Perloff, 1989; Vallone, Ross, & Lepper, 1985).

For instance, Roger Giner-Sorolla and Shelly Chaiken (1994) asked participants at New York University to watch a videotape compiled from American national news broadcasts (CBS and NBC evening reports) on two consecutive evenings, which included 11 minutes of coverage of the Middle East. The coverage reported the killings of an Israeli settler and two Palestinian men in a confrontation in the West Bank, along with the reactions of Israeli settlers and Palestinian militants. Coverage also included scenes from the funeral of the settler and scenes of the Israeli Army destroying Arab homes in retaliation.

Participants' attitudes on the Middle East conflict were measured in a pretest, and approximately equal numbers of pro-Israeli, pro-Palestinian, and neutral individuals were brought to the laboratory. After watching the videotape, participants answered several questions about the news coverage, including a key question about whether the coverage was biased toward one side or the other. The results showed that participants' perceptions of the coverage were strongly correlated with their personal views on the issue. Pro-Israeli respondents judged the news coverage to be biased against the Israeli side and in favour of the Palestinian side. Pro-Palestinian respondents, on the other hand, judged the news coverage to be biased against the Palestinian side and in favour of the Israeli side. Neutral respondents fell in between the two groups of partisans. Thus, participants who had strong initial attitudes regarded the media coverage as unfair to their own side. This phenomenon of both sides viewing the media as biased against them was labelled the **hostile media phenomenon** (Vallone et al., 1985; see also Matheson & Durson, 2001).

hostile media phenomenon

the tendency for people who feel strongly about an issue to believe that the media coverage of the issue is biased against their side

In a similar study conducted at Carleton University in Ottawa by Kimberly Matheson and Sanela Dursun (2001), newspaper stories related to the conflict in the former Yugoslavia between Bosnian Serbs and Bosnian Muslims were shown to supporters of each side, as well as a neutral control group. Results showed that both groups of partisans (Serbs and Muslims) saw the media coverage as biased against their own side, whereas the neutral participants saw the coverage as unbiased. Also, those supporters who identified most strongly with their ingroup rated the media coverage as most biased.

Why did these perceptions of "hostile media" occur? One possibility is that individuals with strong attitudes believed that most of the evidence presented in the news reports should have favoured their own side, because, after all, their side was right and occupied the higher moral ground. Thus, to be "fair" in these partisans' eyes, the news coverage should have presented more evidence for their own side

People on both sides of the Middle East conflict believe that the mass media are hostile toward their own side.

than for the other side. But the impartial news reporters presented an equal, balanced account of both sides—which did not satisfy *either* group of partisans. Each group saw the coverage as biased because the weight of the information did not favour their own side of the conflict.

Together with the capital punishment results described earlier, these differences in perceptions of the media illustrate how individuals' attitudes can affect their perception of information. Exactly the same material can be seen very differently by participants with opposing attitudes. For example, people who support the separatist movement in Quebec might interpret information about the federal government's contributions to the province differently from those who oppose separation. Supporters of separatism might perceive federal funding for a specific program in Quebec as an attempt to bribe Quebec to stay in confederation, whereas those who oppose separation might perceive such funding as evidence that the country is truly committed to meeting Quebec's needs within Canada.

When Do Attitudes Predict Behaviour?

In our discussion of *how* attitudes influence behaviour, we identified rational choice and selective perception as the two principal mechanisms. The first of these processes is relatively direct and presumably occurs at a conscious level (e.g., skating frequently because we think it is good for us), whereas the second is more subtle and spontaneous—in fact, we may not even be aware of it (e.g., changing how we interpret media coverage).

In this section, we examine the related question of *when* attitudes predict behaviour. Our goal here is to specify some of the conditions under which attitudes predict behaviour strongly. Let's begin our discussion by generating some nonlaboratory examples of attitude-based actions. If we asked you to think of some instances of behaviour by other people that obviously reflected their attitudes (rather than external factors, such as following a rule or earning money), what actions would come to your mind?

Here are two examples. One is the behaviour of social activists, such as environmental activists who use their bodies to block lumber trucks from entering a tree-cutting area, or anti-abortion advocates who picket abortion clinics. These behaviours seem attitude-driven because they are both unusual and costly (e.g., potentially injurious, time-consuming); observers assume, therefore, that the individuals must feel very strongly about the issue. A second domain of behaviour that is commonly presumed to reflect attitudes is leisure activities, such as cross-country skiing, reading, or fishing. We believe that most people are basically free to do whatever they want during their time off, so they probably have positive attitudes toward their hobbies and leisure activities. If someone goes fishing regularly, we assume that he or she must like fishing.

These examples of attitude-driven behaviour domains (activism, leisure) can be used to illustrate some important principles about *when* attitudes will predict behaviour. In particular, they highlight the fact that certain kinds of attitudes and certain kinds of behaviour are especially likely to yield high attitude–behaviour correlations. We elaborate on these points below.

When the Attitude Is Strong

Strong attitudes predict behaviour better than weak attitudes. The activism example illustrates this idea nicely. Activists care a lot about the issue and usually possess relatively extreme attitudes (they are *extremely* pro or *extremely* anti). When people are willing to risk physical injury by blocking trucks or engaging in some other form of protest, it is abundantly clear that their attitudes are strong.

What do social psychologists mean, exactly, by a *strong* attitude? The concept of attitude strength actually incorporates several qualities, as has been shown by University of Toronto researcher John Bassili (1996) and others (e.g., Bizer & Krosnick, 2001; Petty & Krosnick, 1995; Visser & Mirabile, 2004). We just mentioned the feature of *extremity:* people with strong attitudes often endorse extreme positions near the end of the scale. A second feature that reflects the strength of the attitude is *importance:* the individual says that the attitude is very important to him or her. A third quality of strong attitudes is *accessibility,* which is a characteristic that we discussed in Chapter 3 (see page 70). Accessibility refers to how easy it is to activate a schema or attitude (Bassili, 1996; Higgins, 1996). Highly accessible attitudes come to mind quickly and spontaneously when we encounter or think about the target. Finally, a fourth feature of strong attitudes is that they are often based on *direct experience* with the attitude object, rather than on indirect information obtained from other people. For example, if a perceiver's attitude toward a young man is based on actual interactions with him, it is likely to be stronger and more confidently held than if it is based on information about him provided by an acquaintance of the perceiver. These aspects of attitude strength are summarized in the accompanying Concept Review.

Findings in numerous studies have supported the idea that extreme, important, accessible, and direct-experience attitudes predict behaviour better than do moderate, unimportant, less accessible, and indirect-experience attitudes (Bassili, 1996; Doll & Ajzen, 1992; Fazio, 1990; Fazio & Williams, 1986; Fazio & Zanna, 1981; Houston & Fazio, 1989; Kraus, 1995). Each of these findings can be interpreted as showing that when an attitude is strong, it predicts behaviour better than when it is weak.

When the Behaviour Is Controllable

If someone held a gun to your head and said that you had to write a letter to the local newspaper stating that automobiles should be banned, would you comply? Of course you would. Would your letter reflect your actual attitude toward automobiles? No, it would not. Does the fact that you behaved inconsistently with your attitude pose problems for social psychologists who argue that attitudes predict behaviour? Again, no. You had *no choice* but to comply with the demand to write the letter.

Attitudes are assumed to guide behaviour when the individual has the freedom to behave in whatever way he or she chooses. The example of leisure activities given

CONCEPT REVIEW
Aspects of Attitude Strength

Feature	Explanation	Feature of Strong Attitudes
Extremity	Extreme attitudes are very unfavourable or very favourable.	Strong attitudes tend to be extreme.
Importance	Important attitudes are ones that the individual cares about.	Strong attitudes tend to be very important.
Accessibility	Accessible attitudes are ones that can be activated quickly and easily.	Strong attitudes tend to be highly accessible.
Direct experience	Attitudes based on direct experience come from personal contact with the attitude object.	Strong attitudes tend to be based on direct experience.

earlier illustrates this point. Behaviour must be voluntary, or controllable, in order for the individual's personal preferences to play a role. If the person is not allowed to choose how to behave, then his or her attitudes are irrelevant (he or she doesn't have any choice!). In contrast, if the person is free to decide how to behave, then his or her attitudes will presumably guide behaviour, at least in part. For instance, people are generally free to engage in whatever leisure activities they most enjoy.

It turns out that many domains of behaviour are *not* completely controllable. People quite often lack—or *believe* that they lack—behavioural control, thus perceiving that they are not free to behave as they choose. Under these conditions, attitudes may not predict behaviour because individuals do not feel completely free to choose their actions. In fact, Icek Ajzen, who developed the theory of reasoned action together with Martin Fishbein (Fishbein & Ajzen, 1975), thought that perceptions of control are so important that he proposed a revised model labelled the *theory of planned behaviour* (Ajzen, 1985, 1991). The theory of planned behaviour retained the constructs of attitudes and subjective norms as predictors of behavioural intentions, but added the construct of *perceived behavioural control* as a third predictor of intentions. Ajzen hypothesized that people will intend to perform a particular behaviour when they have a favourable attitude toward the behaviour, when they feel social pressure to perform the behaviour, and when they perceive that they have control over the behaviour (e.g., are capable of performing it). If perceived behavioural control is low, then favourable attitudes and subjective norms may not be enough to produce intentions to perform the behaviour.

What are some everyday examples of situations in which people lack or believe that they lack control, which can lead to attitude-inconsistent behaviour?

1. *External threat.* Sometimes there are strong external threats or pressures that force us to behave in a certain way whether we want to or not. As a teenager, did you avoid doing some things that you were tempted to do (e.g., drinking alcohol at a party) because you were afraid of the punishment you'd receive if your parents found out? If so, these cases represented acting in ways that were inconsistent with your attitudes because threat of punishment took away your freedom to do what you wanted.

2. *Lack of alternatives.* Sometimes a lack of alternative choices can take away our behavioural freedom. Have you ever hung around with someone you didn't really like because he or she was the only person available? Or, if you live in

a small city or town, you may have only one local newspaper. Everyone in the town must read that newspaper or none at all (at least for local news). Someone might have a negative attitude toward the local paper but read it anyway because there is no other way to keep up to date on local events.

3. *Biological needs or addictions.* Sometimes biological needs force us to do things we do not really want to do. Can you remember when you were a child and your parents tried to get you to eat healthy foods that you did not like? Did your parents try the old trick of not giving you any options for eating? You had to eat the fish or nothing at all. For most kids, hunger eventually motivates the attitude-inconsistent behaviour of eating the disliked food. Another example of biological pressure is addiction—smokers might desperately want to quit smoking but not even try because they believe they are so addicted that stopping is impossible. A perceived lack of control "forces" them to smoke despite a desire to stop.

4. *Lack of time.* Let's close with a factor that is common for university students. Most university students report favourable attitudes toward exercising regularly. Yet most university students do not engage in regular exercise. Why? One common reason given by students is that they simply "do not have the time" to exercise. University students are busy at school and sometimes at a part-time job as well. Although they wish they could exercise, they often feel that it is simply impossible given their busy schedule. This belief may well be true for some students, but other students might be able to incorporate exercise into their schedule if they really tried. Unfortunately, if individuals *believe* that they do not have the time to exercise, they may not even try to do so, irrespective of their favourable attitudes. The lack of perceived behavioural control will mean that their favourable attitudes are irrelevant and do not predict behaviour.

When the Measures Match

Some famous early studies on attitudes appeared to show that attitudes do not predict behaviour very well (for a review, see Wicker, 1969). For instance, Richard LaPiere (1934) took a well-dressed Chinese couple on a tour of the United States, visiting more than 250 restaurants and hotels. Sometimes the Chinese couple went into the establishment alone, and sometimes LaPiere accompanied them. At the time the study was conducted, anti-Chinese sentiment was quite common in the United States. Nevertheless, only one of the 250+ establishments refused to serve the Chinese couple. After the tour was completed, LaPiere sent a letter to each establishment asking whether they served members of the Chinese race. Approximately 50% of the establishments replied. Surprisingly, more than 90% of those who replied said they would *not* serve Chinese guests. Thus, most of the responders expressed negative attitudes toward Chinese guests even though LaPiere had already found that their establishment would serve his Chinese couple. These results certainly seem to imply that attitudes do not predict behaviour strongly.

There was a consistent problem in many of these early studies, however, including LaPiere's work. Most of the studies involved correlating a measure of a broad attitude (e.g., attitudes toward members of the Chinese race) with a measure of a single, specific behaviour (e.g., serving a specific, well-dressed Chinese couple). It is inappropriate to use a general attitude to predict a specific behaviour. The two measures do not *match*—one is general (broad) and one is specific (narrow). When the measures do match, attitudes will predict behaviour strongly.

An example will illustrate this point. Imagine that you are doing a research project on the relation between attitudes and behaviour. You interview two individuals, Marie and Robert, and ask them to report their attitudes toward "living a healthy lifestyle" on a scale from 1 to 10. They report somewhat different attitudes: Marie states that she is very favourable toward living a healthy lifestyle (9 on the 10-point scale), and Robert states that he is moderately favourable (7 on the 10-point scale). To measure a behaviour that should be related to this attitude, you ask Marie and Robert whether they exercise regularly, with possible answers being "always," "usually," "sometimes," and "never." Surprisingly, Marie reports that she "usually" exercises regularly, whereas Robert reports that he "always" exercises regularly.

But notice that a relatively general attitude (toward "living a healthy lifestyle") is being used to predict a narrower, more specific behavioural measure (the regularity of exercise). Table 6.4 lists a number of behaviours that all represent "living a healthy lifestyle." Healthy behaviours can include exercising regularly, eating healthy foods, not smoking, avoiding too much alcohol,

Exercising regularly is only one aspect of living a healthy lifestyle.

getting enough sleep, and so on. The table shows that although Marie reports exercising less regularly than Robert, she performs most of the other healthy behaviours *more* regularly than Robert. For example, she "always" eats healthy foods and avoids excess alcohol, whereas Robert only "usually" eats healthy foods and avoids excess alcohol. A measure of healthy living that included *all* of these domains would show that Marie lives a healthier lifestyle, overall, than does Robert, consistent with Marie's more favourable attitude. Thus, to test whether a broad, general attitude (e.g., toward living a healthy lifestyle) predicts behaviour, the behaviour measure must also be broad and general, sampling from most or all of the relevant specific behaviours (e.g., exercising, eating healthy foods, not smoking, etc.).

A classic and compelling empirical demonstration of the idea that broad attitudes predict broad measures of behaviour was conducted by Russell Weigel and Lee Newman (1976). These researchers studied a group of residents of a small town in New England, assessing their attitudes and behaviours relating to environmental issues. First, participants completed a measure of attitudes toward a variety of topics, including their attitudes toward protecting the environment. Over the next six months, several measures of pro-environmental behaviours were obtained in unobtrusive ways (i.e., without the participants knowing that the measures were part of a study). The first behavioural measures were taken three months after participants' attitudes were assessed. An alleged member of an environmental protection organization (actually an experimental

TABLE 6.4
Living a Healthy Lifestyle: Marie Versus Robert

	Always, Usually, Sometimes, or Never?	
Healthy Behaviours	**Marie**	**Robert**
Exercising regularly	Usually	Always
Eating healthy foods	Always	Usually
Not smoking	Always	Always
Avoiding too much alcohol	Always	Usually
Getting enough sleep	Usually	Sometimes
Using sunscreen	Always	Always
Seeing a doctor annually	Usually	Never
Wearing a seatbelt	Always	Always

assistant) came to the door of each resident and asked him or her to sign three petitions on environmental issues. One petition opposed offshore drilling along the New England coast, one opposed construction of nuclear power plants, and one proposed tougher laws for cars' exhaust systems. Participants could sign each petition and were also asked whether they would be willing to circulate the petitions to family or friends. Six weeks later, another set of behavioural measures was obtained. Participants were contacted by a different individual and asked to participate in a roadside litter pickup program in the town. Three possible times were specified, and participants were encouraged to bring a friend or family member to the pickup as well. The behavioural measures were whether individuals attended at least one of the sessions and whether they brought another person to one of the sessions. Finally, two months after the litter pickup request, participants were contacted by yet another person, who asked them to participate in a test program for recycling newspapers and glass (the study was conducted before such programs were common). Residents were asked to put out recyclable materials on the same day each week. A behavioural measure was then obtained for each of eight weeks, reflecting whether or not participants put out any materials that week.

Weigel and Newman computed the correlations between participants' attitudes toward protecting the environment and various measures of behaviour. Table 6.5 presents the correlations from the study. The first column of 14 correlations shows how well the measure of attitudes toward protecting the environment (a broad, general attitude) predicted each of the specific, *single* behaviour items. As expected when a general attitude is used to predict a specific behaviour, these correlations were

TABLE 6.5
Correlations Between Attitudes Toward Protecting the Environment and Various Behavioural Measures

Single Behaviours	r^a	Categories of Behaviour	r^b	Behavioural Index	r^b
Offshore oil	.41**				
Nuclear power	.36*	Petitioning behaviour	.50**		
Auto exhaust	.39**	scale (0–4)			
Circulate petitions	.27				
Individual participation	.34*	Litter pickup	.36*		
Recruit friend	.22	scale (0–2)			
Week 1	.34*			Comprehensive behavioural index	.62***
Week 2	.57***				
Week 3	.34*				
Week 4	.33*	Recycling behaviour	.39**		
Week 5	.12	scale (0–8)			
Week 6	.20				
Week 7	.20				
Week 8	.34*				

Note: $N = 44$
a. Point-biserial correlations are reported in this column.
b. Pearson product-moment correlations are reported in this column.
*$p < .05$
**$p < .01$
***$p < .001$

From Weigel and Newman, "Increasing attitude-behavior consistency by broadening the scope of the behavioral measure," *Journal of Personality and Social Psychology*, 33, 793–802, Table 1, p. 799, 1976. Copyright © 1976 by the American Psychological Association. Reprinted by permission.

not very large, with an average r = .32 (correlations of .3 indicate relatively weak relationships). The second column of three correlations shows how well the measure of attitudes toward protecting the environment predicted each of the three *categories* of behaviour (petitions, litter pickup, and recycling); these categories represented somewhat broader and more general measures of behaviour. As expected, these correlations were larger than those in the first column, with an average r = .42. Finally, the third column of just one correlation shows how well the measure of attitudes toward protecting the environment predicted a measure of behaviour that combined *all* of the single behaviours together. This last correlation was between a general measure of attitudes and a general measure of behaviour, and it was very strong, r = .62. Thus, as the measures of behaviour became broader and more inclusive, they correlated more strongly with the measure of broad attitudes toward protecting the environment.

We have explained that a measure of a broad, general attitude will predict a broad, general measure of behaviour that samples across most or all of the relevant domains. The reverse is also true: a measure of a narrow, specific attitude will predict a narrow measure of behaviour that is limited to one domain. For instance, if a researcher measured individuals' attitudes toward *using sunscreen,* these attitudes should predict the extent to which the individuals actually use sunscreen over a certain period of time. Returning to our earlier example, if a researcher wanted to predict whether Marie and Robert exercise regularly, then he or she should measure their attitudes toward *exercising regularly* (rather than their attitudes toward living a healthy lifestyle).

This matching effect of measures of attitudes and behaviour is called the **compatibility principle.** The compatibility principle refers to the fact that measures of attitudes and measures of behaviour must be matched in terms of generality (they must be compatible: both measures should be general or both should be specific). Reviews of the literature have shown that, across many studies, when attitudes and behaviour are measured at similar levels of generality, they correlate strongly, whereas mismatched or incompatible measures of attitudes and behaviour yield much lower correlations (e.g., Ajzen & Fishbein, 1977; Eagly & Chaiken, 1993, 1998; Kim & Hunter, 1993; Kraus, 1995).

compatibility principle

a theory stating that a measure of attitudes will correlate highly with a measure of behaviour only when the two measures are matched in terms of being general/broad or specific/narrow

Culture and Attitudes

David Matsumoto (1996) of San Francisco State University defined **culture** as "the set of attitudes, values, beliefs, and behaviors shared by a group of people . . . [and] communicated from one generation to the next" (p. 32). Recall that we defined socialization earlier in this chapter as the process by which individuals are made into acceptable members of their society, which includes holding the prevailing beliefs and attitudes (Harris, 1995). These two definitions underscore how central attitudes are to the concept of culture. Social psychologists assume that when people from different cultures respond differently to the same event, it is *because* their perceptions and reactions are guided by different attitudes, values, and norms.

Culture-specific attitudes and values occur because cultures communicate several "core ideas" to their members, such as what is good and what is moral (Fiske, Kitayama, Markus, & Nisbett, 1998; Kitayama & Markus, 1994). These core ideas and beliefs help to shape the customs, norms, and institutions of the culture (e.g., family structures, the educational system), which then socialize individuals to adopt the prescribed attitudes and values.

The best-known analysis and comparison of cultures was conducted by Geert Hofstede (1980, 2001), who assessed the work-related values of IBM marketing managers in 40 countries around the world, including Canada. He proposed that the different countries could be characterized in terms of several underlying dimensions

culture

the set of values, beliefs, and behaviours shared by a group of people and communicated from one generation to the next of culture. The dimension that has received the most attention (and which we have discussed several times) is *individualism* versus *collectivism*. Individualist cultures emphasize individual identity and achievement, whereas collectivist cultures emphasize group harmony and tradition. North American and European countries tend to be individualistic, whereas East Asian, South American, and African countries tend to be collectivistic.

power distance

the extent to which a culture accepts an unequal distribution of influence within the society

Another interesting dimension identified by Hofstede was **power distance,** which refers to the extent to which a culture accepts unequal power distribution among individuals and institutions. Cultures that are high in power distance accept and support unequal power distribution, where some individuals have much more influence than others. In contrast, cultures that are low in power distance prefer equal distributions of influence, where everyone has the same opportunity to affect decisions. East Asian and East European countries tend to be high in power distance, whereas Canada, the United States, and West European countries tend to be low in power distance. Does it surprise you that Canada is characterized as preferring equal rather than unequal power, given the wide disparity in wealth that exists in our society? The dimension of power distance refers to the distribution of *influence,* such as the ability to "have one's say," rather than to the distribution of income. Canadians value democracy and individual freedom very highly—principles that are based on the idea that everyone should be treated equally under the law. Canadians also pride themselves on living in a "land of opportunity," where people can achieve whatever they like if only they work hard enough. Whether these perceptions are true or not may be arguable, but Canadians do fall more toward the low than the high end of the power distance dimension.

Many researchers have investigated cultural differences in specific attitudes and values (e.g., see Hofstede, 1991, 2001; Schwartz & Bardi, 1997; Schwartz & Sagiv, 1995; Smith & Bond, 1994; Triandis, 1994, 1995). In one interesting study, Jennifer Aaker, Verónica Benet-Martínez, and Jordi Garolera (2001) surveyed adults in the United States, Japan, and Spain, who were asked to report their perceptions of several *commercial brand names* that were well known in their country (e.g., Americans rated Marlboro cigarettes, Coca-Cola, Levi's jeans, etc.). The researchers found that Americans responded positively to brand names that evoked perceptions of "ruggedness" (e.g., masculine, outdoorsy, tough); Japanese participants responded positively

Cultures communicate core beliefs about what is good and moral.

© Mark Edwards/Peter Arnold, Inc.

to brand names that evoked perceptions of "peacefulness" (e.g., mild-mannered, shy, naïve); and Spanish participants responded positively to brand names that evoked perceptions of "passion" (e.g., intense, passionate, spiritual). The authors proposed that these differences in preferences for brand names reflected cultural differences in attitudes and values: Americans appreciate rugged independence, Japanese individuals cherish peaceful harmony, and Spaniards value passionate emotions.

Cross-Cultural Commonalities in Attitudes: We Are More Alike than Different

We have focused on differences between cultures in attitudes and values, but it is important to recognize that there are many cross-cultural similarities as well. Although cultures differ in the average ratings or rankings of some goals, all cultures place positive worth on most of the same goals. For example, although Koreans tend to place greater value on interpersonal harmony than do Canadians, both cultures consider harmony to be a desirable goal. Although Canadians tend to value freedom more than do Koreans, both cultures consider freedom to be desirable. For the most part, cultures differ in the *degree* to which they endorse particular goals or in how their values are *expressed*, not in whether the goals are worthwhile (see Schwartz, 1992, 1996). This point about cross-cultural similarity is particularly true when relatively specific attitudes and values are considered, such as honesty, reliability, compassion, and peace. Thus, we should keep in mind that humans around the world are much more alike than they are different.

Also, even when cultures yield average differences in an attitude or in the importance rating of a value, there is almost always substantial overlap in the ratings across cultures (Fiske et al., 1998; Triandis, 1994). For instance, although the average rating of the importance of freedom by Canadian respondents is higher than the average rating of the importance of freedom by Korean respondents, there are many individual Koreans who consider freedom to be more important than do many individual Canadians. Overlapping distributions mean that cultures differ on average, but individuals from the two cultures do not necessarily differ.

In conclusion, cultures vary in several important ways, such as their perception of the individual as independent or interdependent and their acceptance of power differences between people. These differences affect the attitudes and norms that develop in the culture, as well as the psychological makeup of its members. Nevertheless, people from all cultures share many fundamental beliefs, including the desirability of such values as honesty and compassion.

Chapter Summary

An **attitude** is an individual's evaluation of a target along a good–bad dimension. Attitudes are always directed *at* something—they have a target. Sometimes attitudes contain both positive and negative elements, in which case they are labelled **ambivalent attitudes. Explicit attitudes** are those that people can report consciously.

Implicit attitudes are individuals' automatic evaluative responses to a target, which can occur without awareness.

Attitudes serve at least two important functions for the individual. First, an attitude provides a rapid evaluation of an object, person, or issue, which allows the individual to decide whether to approach or avoid it. This function is called the **object appraisal function** of attitudes. Second, some attitudes communicate the individual's identity and **values,** which is called the **value-expressive function.**

The most common techniques for measuring attitudes use self-report approaches. **Likert-type scales** require respondents to indicate the extent of their agreement or disagreement with several statements on an issue. **Semantic differential scales** require respondents to rate an attitude object on evaluative dimensions, such as good–bad and favourable–unfavourable. Nonverbal measures of attitudes have also been developed. For instance, **facial electromyography (facial EMG)** records muscle contractions in the face that may be sensitive to positive versus negative responses to a stimulus. Reaction time procedures have been used to measure implicit attitudes, including the **Implicit Association Test (IAT).**

One possible source of attitudes is affect. Affect can become linked to objects through a process of **evaluative conditioning,** whereby objects that had no causal role in producing positive or negative affect nevertheless come to evoke affect simply by being associated with the affect-arousing events. Another source of affect is the familiarity of an object. The **mere exposure effect** is that repeated exposure to an object, even without reinforcement, will increase liking for the object. Attitudes can also be influenced by physiological and biological processes. For example, alcohol intoxication reduces cognitive capacity, which results in a narrowing of attention—an effect that has been labelled **alcohol myopia.**

Socialization is the process by which infants are moulded into acceptable members of their society. A **reference group** is a group that serves as a standard of comparison for an individual. Ridicule is derogatory humour directed at an individual concerning some aspect of his or her behaviour or appearance. Ridicule produces **jeer pressure,** which is conformity pressure that is caused by seeing someone ridiculed by another person.

Attitudes influence behaviour in two primary ways: rational choice and selective perception. The **theory of reasoned action** epitomizes the rational choice perspective; it views humans as rational decision makers who behave on the basis of logical beliefs. According to this theory, the most immediate cause of a behaviour is a **behavioural intention,** which refers to the individual's plan to perform or not perform the action. Two concepts are assumed to cause behavioural intentions: attitudes toward the behaviour and subjective norms concerning the behaviour. **Subjective norms** are individuals' feelings of social pressure to perform or not perform an action, which are based on their beliefs about how significant others want them to behave. Another model that focuses on rational choice is the **IMB model of AIDS-preventive behaviour.** This model proposes that three major elements contribute to safer sex behaviours: information, motivation, and behavioural skills.

Selective perception refers to the biasing effect of our attitudes on how we interpret and understand the world. One example of selective perception is the **hostile media phenomenon,** which refers to the tendency for people who feel strongly about an issue to believe that the media coverage of the issue is biased against their own side.

Attitudes predict behaviour best under certain conditions. One condition of attitude–behaviour consistency is the **compatibility principle,** which refers to the fact that measures of attitudes and measures of behaviour must be matched in terms of generality: both must be broad and general or both must be narrow and specific.

Culture can be defined as the set of values, beliefs, and behaviours shared by a group of people and communicated from one generation to the next. One dimension along which cultures differ is **power distance,** which refers to the extent to which a culture accepts unequal distribution of influence among individuals and institutions.

Key Terms

alcohol myopia (211)

ambivalent attitudes (193)

attitude (191)

behavioural intention (218)

compatibility principle (231)

culture (231)

evaluative conditioning (205)

explicit attitudes (194)

facial electromyography (facial EMG) (203)

hostile media phenomenon (224)

IMB model of AIDS-preventive behaviour (220)

Implicit Association Test (IAT) (203)

implicit attitudes (194)

jeer pressure (216)

Likert-type scale (198)

mere exposure effect (206)

object-appraisal function (195)

power distance (232)

reference group (215)

semantic differential scale (199)

socialization (214)

subjective norm (219)

theory of reasoned action (218)

value-expressive function (196)

values (196)

Social Psychology Alive on the Web

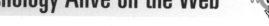

SOCIAL PSYCHOLOGY ALIVE: ONLINE LABS

To perform the following experiments and see how you compare to other students, go to Social Psychology Lab, which can be accessed through ThomsonNOW™.

- 6.1 Word Evaluation
- 6.2 Shape Judgment

SOCIAL PSYCHOLOGY ALIVE: QUIZZING AND PRACTICE TESTS

You can access our Web site directly by going to http://www.socialpsychologyalive.nelson.com for online quizzes, flash cards, and Internet links.

°INFOTRAC® COLLEGE EDITION

For additional readings, explore InfoTrac® College Edition, your online library of archived journal articles and periodicals dating back 22 years. If your instructor ordered InfoTrac® College Edition with this book, you can access it from your CD-ROM, or go directly to http://www.infotrac-college.com and use the passcode from the InfoTrac® College Edition card that came with your book. For this chapter, try these search terms: *attitudes, ambivalent attitudes, implicit attitudes, attitude functions, Likert scale, semantic differential, Implicit Association Test, mere exposure, reference groups, theory of reasoned action, hostile media phenomenon, compatibility principle.*

Social Psychology Alive: The Workbook

To apply what you've learned in this chapter to what happens in the real world, go to Chapter 6 of *Social Psychology Alive: The Workbook:*

- *Lockhart v. McCree:* Social Science Evidence and the Supreme Court
- Caffeine and Patriotism: Demonstrating the Function of Attitudes
- Measuring Attitudes Using a Single-Item Scale and a Likert Scale
- Measuring Attitudes: Do Semantic Differentials Measure Affect or Cognition?

- Implicit Intergroup Bias and the Implicit Association Test
- Evaluative Conditioning
- What's in a Name? Demonstrate the Mere Exposure Effect
- Do Attitudes Predict Behaviour? The Theory of Reasoned Action
- Do Attitudes Predict Behaviour? The Compatibility Principle

Social Psychology Alive: The Videos

To see video on the topics and experiments discussed in this chapter, you can go either to ThomsonNOW™ or to the CD-ROM, if your instructor assigned either one, to the following section:

- Reading the Unconscious Mind: The Implicit Association Test

To Learn More

This list contains citations to books or articles that can help you learn more. These readings are good places to start if you want to gain a deeper understanding of the topics in this chapter.

- Oskamp, S., & Schultz, P. W. (2005). *Attitudes and opinions* (3rd ed.). Mahwah, NJ: Erlbaum.

- Perloff, R. M. (2003). *The dynamics of persuasion: Communication and attitudes in the 21st Century* (2nd ed.). Mahwah, NJ: Erlbaum.
- Albarracin, D., Johnson, B. T., & Zanna, M. P. (Eds.). (2005). *Handbook of attitudes and attitude change.* Mahwah, NJ: Erlbaum.

I was a victim of CARELESS TALK

Attitude Change

Imagine how different your life would be if there were no advertisements. Newspapers would certainly be shorter without their ads for grocery stores, movie theatres, department stores, and other products. You would check your e-mail and not be inundated with spam messages selling everything from mortgages to get-rich-quick schemes to alleged wonder drugs. When you watched television, you would not be forced to view approximately 20 commercials per hour. When you rented a movie on videotape, you would not have to fast-forward through a series of "coming soon" theatrical trailers. You would not see billboards signs on buildings. You would not get phone calls in the evening from marketing companies offering you a deal on rug cleaning or some other service.

Sounds rather appealing, doesn't it? Unfortunately, the truth is that we cannot escape from advertisements in our society—they are everywhere. It has been estimated that the average North American is exposed to more than 200 advertisements per day (Pratkanis & Aronson, 2001), which would come to a total of more than 73 000 per year! Although many of us complain about the glut of ads, we're generally pretty apathetic about our level of exposure. Young people, in particular, even seem comfortable with the surplus of advertising. One of the authors of this book (JO) has a 17-year-old daughter who says she loves to read ads, especially in magazines for young women. He recently looked at one of her magazines—an issue of Elle Canada—and counted the number of pages that were dedicated to advertisements. The count showed that 322 of the 398 pages in the magazine were taken up either by explicit advertisements (211 pages) or by "articles" that consisted only of photographs of models wearing clothes, with the prices and store locations listed at the bottom of the page (111 pages). The first real article in the magazine (with any written content) began on page 115!

Advertisements are designed to create positive attitudes toward a product, with the ultimate goal being to induce people to buy that product. They are the most common and visible form of persuasive communication that we encounter in our daily lives. But ads are certainly not the only example of attempts to change attitudes and behaviour. Interpersonal influence is another important category: your friends may try to convince you to come with them to a movie; your doctor may suggest that you exercise more often; your romantic partner may argue with you about the pros and cons of the Canadian health-care system. Of course, you also initiate attempts to persuade others, including your friends, family, and romantic partner. Institutions in society are another source of persuasion attempts, including schools (e.g., sex education classes), religious institutions (e.g., sermons), and the military (e.g., basic training).

Imagine how different life would be if there were no advertisements.

The goal of the present chapter is to describe research in social psychology that has investigated attitude change. We already know from Chapter 6 that attitudes are an important determinant of behaviour. We discussed attitude formation in Chapter 6 but did not consider how attitudes, once formed, can change. In this chapter, we tackle this topic. As the chapter outline suggests, there are numerous ways that attitudes can change, including rationalization, persuasion, and propaganda. Rationalization constitutes a form of self-persuasion, whereby people convince themselves that their decisions or actions are justified. Persuasion refers to attitude change that results from a communication initiated by someone else. Sometimes persuasion occurs because information in the message convinces the individual that the recommendation is a good one. But sometimes persuasion occurs simply because the individual assumes that the recommendation is probably valid, without considering arguments for or against it. Propaganda is a persuasion attempt that is ideologically motivated and often intentionally misleading. Sometimes propaganda can convince people to make huge changes to their attitudes and behaviour, as when individuals join a cult.

We begin this chapter with perhaps the most famous theory in social psychology, cognitive dissonance theory, which addresses how attitude change can occur through a process of rationalization. We then turn to attitude change resulting from persuasive communications and describe several different perspectives on this phenomenon. We also discuss cultural differences in attitude change, as well as the effectiveness of fear appeals in changing health-related attitudes. We close the chapter with a discussion of the psychology of propaganda.

Rationalizing Our Own Behaviour: Cognitive Dissonance Theory

Would you be willing to eat a grasshopper? That's right, eat a grasshopper—fried. These insects can, in fact, be eaten safely, although they do not appear on most people's food lists.

Imagine that you were asked to eat a grasshopper for a researcher who said he was investigating whether grasshoppers could serve as a suitable survival food for soldiers in extreme circumstances. If given a choice, do you think that you would agree to eat one? Now imagine that you *did* eat one; would you feel a need to *rationalize* your behaviour—to justify the behaviour to yourself?

Phillip Zimbardo and his colleagues (Zimbardo, Weisenberg, & Firestone, 1965) conducted a classic study in New York City in which young men were asked to eat a fried grasshopper. For half of the participants, the experimenter was extremely polite and pleasant prior to asking them to eat a grasshopper, whereas for the remaining participants, the experimenter acted like an arrogant, cold, and thoroughly unpleasant person before he asked them to eat a grasshopper. It turned out that about 50% of the participants in each of these two conditions actually ate a grasshopper, so the likeable and unlikeable experimenters were equally successful in getting participants to comply with their request. Now for the interesting part: after they ate the grasshopper, participants were asked to evaluate the insect as a food source. Who do you think gave more favourable ratings of grasshoppers: participants who ate the grasshopper for the pleasant or the unpleasant experimenter?

Would you be willing to eat a grasshopper?

Results showed that the *unpleasant* experimenter produced more favourable ratings than the pleasant experimenter. Those participants who ate a grasshopper for the rude and unlikeable experimenter said grasshoppers were a more feasible food source than did participants who ate a grasshopper for the polite and likeable experimenter. Does this result surprise you? We will return to the study shortly and give the authors' explanation.

The grasshopper experiment is one of the many colourful studies that have tested one of the most colourful and famous theories in social psychology: cognitive dissonance theory. Dissonance theory has achieved fame not only among social psychologists but also in the general public, where terms like *dissonance* appear in normal conversation. Dissonance theory has achieved a level of public recognition that rivals such famous psychological models as reinforcement theory and Freudian psychoanalysis. Within social psychology, dissonance theory has had a fascinating history, which has included periods of intense interest, periods of virtual neglect, heated disagreements between researchers, and numerous proposed alternative explanations for findings.

Feeling Bad About Irrational Behaviour: The Arousal of Dissonance

cognitive dissonance theory

a model proposed by Leon Festinger, which states that awareness of consonant cognitions makes us feel good, whereas awareness of dissonant cognitions makes us feel bad. Further, the unpleasant feelings produced by dissonant cognitions motivate us to do something to change our state.

consonant cognitions

beliefs that are consistent or compatible with one another

dissonant cognitions

beliefs that are inconsistent or logically discrepant with one another

Leon Festinger proposed **cognitive dissonance theory** in 1957. Festinger worked at several universities during his career, including the University of Michigan, the University of Minnesota, Stanford University, and the New School for Social Research in New York City. Festinger was interested in the consequences of the "fit" or consistency between different *cognitions* in people's minds. He defined a cognition as a belief or piece of knowledge, such as "My name is Kierstin," "Peter Mansbridge reads the CBC news," "It snowed last night," and "I brush my teeth twice a day." People have thousands of cognitions stored in their memories, but will be aware of only a small number at any one time. Most cognitions are irrelevant to one another. The cognitions "Peter Mansbridge reads the CBC news" and "It snowed last night" have no implications for each other. But some cognitions are logically connected, either positively or negatively. **Consonant cognitions** are *consistent* with one another; they imply that the other is valid or good. The two cognitions "I brush my teeth twice a day" and "Toothbrushing prevents cavities" support one another. **Dissonant cognitions,** on the other hand, are *inconsistent* with one another; they imply that the other is wrong or bad. The two cognitions "I smoke" and "Smoking causes cancer" are logically discrepant.

Festinger hypothesized that awareness of consonant cognitions makes us feel good, whereas awareness of dissonant cognitions makes us feel bad. The fact that he named his theory *dissonance theory* shows that he was particularly interested in the latter case, involving inconsistent cognitions. Festinger proposed that the unpleasant feelings produced by dissonant cognitions motivate people to do something to change their state. His research was designed to investigate these attempts to deal with dissonance.

Our example of dissonant cognitions about smoking illustrates an important feature of research on dissonance theory. Although it is theoretically possible to experience dissonance between many different kinds of cognitions, Festinger focused on inconsistencies that involved cognitions about one's own *behaviour*. Specifically, he focused on dissonance between knowing that you behave or have behaved in a certain way (e.g., "I smoke"; "I hurt Sara's feelings") and another piece of knowledge implying that your behaviour was wrong or illogical or otherwise inappropriate (e.g., "Smoking causes cancer"; "I like Sara"). Researchers since Festinger have maintained this focus on cognitions about behaviour. Thus, for the purposes of research by social psychologists, dissonance can be defined as the state of feeling bad or conflicted about one's own irrational behaviour.

Let's generate a few examples of dissonance in everyday life. Someone who pays a substantial registration fee for a workshop on using computers and then finds the workshop useless will feel dissonance between the cognitions "I paid $100 to take this course" and "This course didn't teach me anything." A student who performs poorly on an important test may feel dissonance between the cognitions "I did badly on this test" and "I expected to do well on the test." Someone who buys a stylish winter parka and then realizes that the fur around the hood is from baby seals might feel dissonance between the cognitions "I bought this parka" and "I oppose the baby seal hunt in Newfoundland." Can you generate some examples of times when you have experienced dissonance? We all occasionally behave in ways that might be considered irrational or unproductive, so we all know how dissonance feels.

Festinger also proposed that the *importance* of the cognitions influences the amount of dissonance. Dissonance between very important cognitions causes more intense negative feelings than does dissonance between less important cognitions. Spending $1000 on a useless workshop will arouse more dissonance than spending $100 on the workshop. Thinking that you chose the wrong university will arouse more dissonance than thinking that you chose the wrong shirt to wear today. Hurting the feelings of your best friend will arouse more dissonance than hurting the feelings of a stranger.

Making Irrational Behaviour Rational: The Reduction of Dissonance

We don't like the feeling of dissonance. Festinger described dissonance as a state of "aversive arousal" and said that we are motivated to reduce it. How can this goal be accomplished? How can we reduce cognitive dissonance?

If dissonance represents feeling bad about one's own irrational behaviour, then reducing dissonance must somehow involve making the irrational behaviour seem rational (or, at least, making it seem *less* irrational). In other words, dissonance reduction must involve *rationalization:* convincing ourselves that our current or past behaviour made sense after all. Dissonance theory, then, is a motivational model focusing on self-persuasion in the form of rationalization.

The specific ways that dissonance can be reduced are best understood in the context of an example, such as dissonance between the two cognitions "I smoke" and "Smoking causes cancer." Festinger hypothesized that one way to reduce dissonance is to change one of the dissonant cognitions directly. The individual might stop smoking, in which case the cognition "I smoke" becomes "I do not smoke," which is consonant with the cognition "Smoking causes cancer." Or the individual might decide that the research on smoking is not definitive or that smoking is unlikely to affect him or her personally, in which case the cognition "Smoking causes cancer" becomes "Smoking will not cause cancer in me," which is more consonant with the cognition "I smoke." As you will see when we review the empirical research on dissonance, the dissonance-reduction strategy of changing one of the dissonant cognitions is the strategy that has been studied most often.

Directly reducing dissonance may not always be possible, however. Changing one's behaviour can be challenging, and many cognitions are based on strong evidence that we cannot easily distort or deny (e.g., the link between smoking and cancer). If changing one of the dissonant cognitions is difficult, then another way that people can reduce dissonance is by adding consonant cognitions. These cognitions support the person's behaviour and make it seem more reasonable. For example, a smoker might think "Smoking is enjoyable" or "Smoking keeps my weight down," which are consonant with the cognition "I smoke." In this way, the behaviour of smoking appears more rational or justified. Adding consonant cognitions is a common way to deal with dissonance in everyday life—people often rationalize undesirable behaviour by arguing that it has some positive benefits. For instance, politicians from tobacco-producing areas in Ontario or Quebec may oppose legislation that would restrict smoking by saying that the tobacco industry has economic benefits for their constituents. The flowchart in Figure 7.1 illustrates the application of dissonance theory to smoking behaviour.

Festinger proposed that there is one other way to reduce dissonance besides changing one of the dissonant cognitions or adding consonant cognitions. Recall that dissonance between important cognitions is more intense than dissonance between unimportant cognitions. Dissonance can be reduced, therefore, by reducing the importance of one of the dissonant cognitions and/or increasing the importance of one of the consonant cognitions. A smoker might accept the link between smoking and cancer but decide that he or she doesn't really want to live forever anyway—he or she wants to "live fast and die young!" (This philosophy tends to lose its appeal as one grows older.) Or a smoker might accept the smoking–cancer link but decide that the pleasure of smoking more than compensates for its risks. These rationalizations involve reducing the importance of the cognition "Smoking causes cancer" or increasing the importance of the cognition "Smoking is enjoyable."

Early Research on Dissonance Theory

We mentioned earlier that dissonance theory has had a colourful history. We can summarize here only a small part of the literature—published experiments on dissonance theory number in the hundreds, probably even the thousands. We begin our review of dissonance research by describing three major domains of the theory. These domains have been studied using different *experimental paradigms,* or research methodologies. Each of the three paradigms—induced compliance, effort justification, and free choice—explored one important application of dissonance theory. Table 7.1 summarizes the key features of these three paradigms, which are described in more detail in the following paragraphs.

Induced Compliance: Dissonance from Counterattitudinal Behaviour. To capture dissonance in an experiment, a researcher must elicit behaviour from participants that they will perceive as irrational or otherwise inappropriate. This is not easy to do. One category of behaviour that usually fits this requirement is *counterattitudinal behaviour*—behaviour that is counter to, or inconsistent with, an individual's attitudes, values, or beliefs. Most of us feel bad when we do

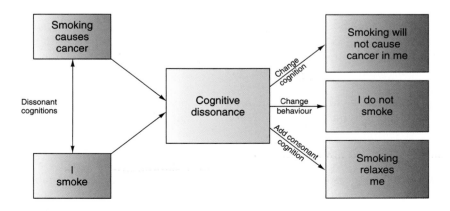

FIGURE 7.1 Arousal and reduction of dissonance related to smoking

TABLE 7.1
Three Research Paradigms Used to Test Dissonance Theory

Research Paradigm	Nature of Behaviour That Arouses Dissonance	Examples
Induced compliance paradigm	Counterattitudinal behaviour	Knowingly lie to another person Write an essay supporting a position that is discrepant with one's attitude Eat a disgusting food
Effort justification paradigm	Wasted effort or money	Endure a severe initiation to join a group that turns out to be boring Pay for admission to a movie that turns out to be unenjoyable
Free choice paradigm	Making a decision	Choose between two or more alternatives (chosen option will usually have some negative features, and rejected options will usually have some positive features)

induced compliance paradigm

a research methodology used to test dissonance theory that arouses dissonance by getting people to engage in counterattitudinal behaviour. In this paradigm, participants are induced to comply with an experimenter's request that they behave in a way that is inconsistent with their attitudes.

something that conflicts with our attitudes, such as accidentally hurting the feelings of someone we like or pretending to agree with someone on an issue simply because we don't want to argue.

Dissonance researchers have taken advantage of this type of behaviour in the **induced compliance paradigm.** This paradigm investigates dissonance that results from counterattitudinal behaviour. Participants are *induced* to *comply* with the experimenter's request that they behave in a way that is known to be inconsistent with their attitudes. Most often, the paradigm involves either getting people to say something they know is untrue or asking them to generate arguments against a position they personally support. The dissonance is created between the two cognitions "I believe X" and "I knowingly stated that I do not believe X" (or "I argued against X").

In one of the earliest dissonance experiments, Leon Festinger and J. Merrill Carlsmith (1959) made participants work for an hour on two very boring tasks: turning pegs on a board and placing spools on and off another board. After completing these tasks, participants were told that the purpose of the study was to investigate the effects of expectancies on task performance, and they had been in a control condition where no pre-task expectancies were created. But there was another condition, participants were told, in which people were being given positive expectancies about the enjoyability of the tasks. These positive expectancies were being created by having an experimental confederate sit beside subjects in the waiting room, pretend that he or she has just completed the study, and tell them that the tasks would be fun and exciting. The experimenter then made an unexpected request of the current participant: the usual confederate was unavailable, and there was someone in the waiting room who was supposed to be in the positive expectancies condition. Would they be willing to go into the waiting room and tell the person that the tasks were fun and exciting? (Participants were also told that if they agreed to do this task, the experimenter would keep their name on file as a possible replacement for the confederate in the future.) Almost all participants agreed to tell this lie and then went into the next room and told the waiting subject (who was actually a confederate of the experimenter) that the study was fun and exciting.

Participants were thereby induced to behave in a counterattitudinal fashion. The cognitions "The tasks were boring" and "I told someone that the tasks were fun"

© Karen Zebulon

Leon Festinger (in photo) conducted a famous experiment with J. Merrill Carlsmith (1959), in which participants completed two boring tasks and were then induced to tell someone else that the tasks were fun.

were expected to produce dissonance. How could this dissonance be reduced? It would be difficult for participants to convince themselves that they didn't tell another person that the tasks were fun—this behaviour had just occurred. But dissonance could be reduced by changing the cognition "The tasks were boring" by deciding that maybe the tasks weren't so bad after all. If the tasks were somewhat enjoyable, then telling someone that they were fun is less discrepant.

Another manipulation in the experiment was expected to influence the *amount* of dissonance people would feel. Participants were told that they would be *paid* for serving as the confederate, but the amounts they would be paid differed. Some participants were told that they would be paid $20 for telling the lie—a huge amount in the 1950s when the study was conducted. Other participants were told that they would be paid only $1 for serving as the confederate. Participants who were paid $20 were expected to feel less dissonance than those who were paid $1. Why? Because those paid $20 would have a strong, consonant cognition to support their behaviour: "I was paid a lot of money to say the tasks were fun." Thus, individuals paid $20 were not expected to have to convince themselves that the tasks were fun, whereas those paid $1 were expected to reduce dissonance by evaluating the tasks more positively.

After telling the lie, participants were told that the experiment was over and were asked to visit a secretary in the psychology department, who would give them a questionnaire that was being completed by all participants in all experiments. This questionnaire asked participants to rate how interesting and enjoyable the tasks in their experiment had been. Figure 7.2 presents the results for the $1 and $20 conditions, as well as for a control condition in which participants completed the tasks but did not tell anyone that the tasks were fun (this condition presumably showed how interesting or enjoyable the tasks really were). As predicted, participants in the $1 condition rated the tasks as more enjoyable than did control participants; telling the lie appeared to arouse dissonance, which was reduced by deciding that the tasks were somewhat enjoyable. Also as predicted, participants in the $20 condition did not differ from control participants; the large payment appeared to serve as a strong consonant cognition for telling the lie, which meant that participants did not have to re-evaluate the tasks.

The Festinger and Carlsmith (1959) experiment was the first of many to document dissonance using an induced compliance paradigm. Another common procedure was to ask participants to write a counterattitudinal essay arguing against their own view (e.g., asking university undergraduates to write an essay supporting tuition increases for university students). If participants were given a choice and willingly agreed to write such an essay (rather than simply being instructed to write it or being highly paid to write it), they tended to move their own attitude in the direction of their essay (e.g., Cohen, 1962; Stone, 1999; Zanna & Cooper, 1974). Presumably, participants in these studies reduced dissonance between "I believe X" and "I willingly wrote an essay arguing against X" by altering their initial cognition to be something closer to "I am against X."

Now let's return to the grasshopper experiment with which we opened our discussion of dissonance theory. Recall that Zimbardo and his colleagues (1965) found that people who ate a grasshopper for a rude and unlikeable experimenter rated grasshoppers more favourably as a food source than did people who ate a grasshopper for a polite and likeable experimenter. How do these data support dissonance theory?

First, eating the grasshopper was counterattitudinal behaviour: it seems safe to say that none of the participants came to the study with a favourable attitude toward eating insects of any kind. Thus, the study utilized an induced compliance paradigm to create dissonance between the cognitions "Eating grasshoppers is gross" and "I ate a grasshopper." But those participants who ate a grasshopper for a likeable experimenter at least had the cognition "I helped a nice person," which was consonant with their behaviour. The experimenter's pleasant personality served as a justification or reason for the participant's decision to eat a grasshopper. Those participants who ate a grasshopper for an unlikeable experimenter, however, had no such cognition;

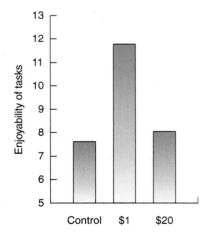

FIGURE 7.2 Ratings of enjoyability of tasks

Adapted from Festinger and Carlsmith, "Cognitive consequences of forced compliance," *Journal of Abnormal and Social Psychology,* 58, 203–210, 1959. Copyright © 1959 by the American Psychological Association.

indeed, they may have been thinking "Why am I helping this obnoxious person?" To reduce their dissonance, they were forced to change their evaluation of eating grasshoppers to "Eating grasshoppers isn't so bad." (Steak sauce, anyone?)

Effort Justification: Dissonance from Wasted Effort. How do you feel when you have worked hard on something but then received little in return? Have you studied hard for a test but nevertheless done poorly? Have you spent a lot of money on something that you subsequently used very little? Have you put a lot into a dating relationship but eventually realized that the other person wasn't reciprocating? Suspecting that we have wasted time, effort, or money on something is upsetting. "I worked hard" and "I gained nothing" are highly dissonant cognitions. Dissonance theory predicts that people who suspect they have wasted effort will be motivated to change one of the dissonant cognitions or to add consonant cognitions. For example, individuals might change the cognition about effort, deciding that they didn't really exert too much effort after all. Alternatively, individuals might change the cognition about having gained nothing, deciding instead that their payoff was worthwhile. Finally, individuals might add consonant cognitions, deciding that they learned an important lesson or benefited in some other way from the experience.

Recognizing that wasted effort was a form of dissonance that could be experimentally manipulated, dissonance researchers designed the **effort justification paradigm.** The effort justification paradigm involved leading participants to suspect that effort they had invested may have been worthless. The prediction was that participants would reduce dissonance by convincing themselves that the goal was actually worthwhile.

Elliot Aronson and Judson Mills (1959) published the first study using the effort justification paradigm. Female students at Stanford University were asked whether they wanted to join a "sexual discussion group"—an opportunity that interested many of them. Those who applied for the group were told that they had to undergo a "screening test" to ensure that they would be able to participate fully in the group. Some participants were then put through a "severe" test that required them to read out loud a list of obscene words and detailed descriptions of sexual activity. Other participants were put through only a "mild" test that required them to read out loud more ordinary words like *petting* and *prostitute*. After completing either the severe or the mild screening test, participants were told that they would join the group next week, but they would listen to the first week's discussion over headphones. Participants then listened to a tape recording of a discussion that had been created to be hideously boring. Aronson and Mills described the discussion by saying that it concerned "secondary sex behavior in the lower animals. [The people on the tape] inadvertently contradicted themselves and one another, mumbled several non sequiturs, started sentences that they never finished, hemmed, hawed, and in general conducted one of the most worthless and uninteresting discussions imaginable" (p. 179).

After listening to the tape, participants were asked to rate how interesting they found the discussion and the group members. Aronson and Mills predicted that participants who went through the severe screening test would experience dissonance between the cognitions "I went through an embarrassing test to join this group" and "This group is boring." To reduce their dissonance, these participants were expected to change the cognition "This group is boring" to "This group is somewhat interesting." Figure 7.3 presents the mean ratings of the discussion and of the group members by participants in the mild and severe screening test conditions, as well as ratings by participants in a control condition who simply listened to the taped discussion without going through any screening test (this condition presumably

effort justification paradigm
a research methodology used to test dissonance theory that arouses dissonance by getting people to invest time or energy to achieve a goal that may not be worthwhile

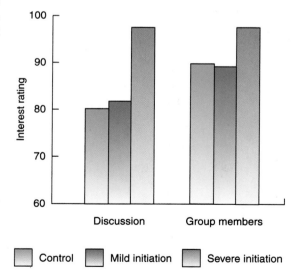

FIGURE 7.3 Interest ratings of discussion and group members

From Aronson and Mills, "The effect of severity of initiation on liking for a group," *Journal of Abnormal and Social Psychology*, 59, 177–181, 1959. Copyright © 1959 by the American Psychological Association. Reprinted by permission.

showed how boring the discussion really was). As predicted, participants in the severe test condition rated both the discussion and the group members as more interesting than did participants in the control condition. Thus, it appears that the severe test aroused dissonance, which was reduced by perceiving the discussion as more interesting than it really was. Participants in the mild test condition did not differ from control participants in their ratings of the discussion or group members. It appears that the mild test was not effortful or embarrassing enough to arouse dissonance when the discussion group turned out to be boring.

Has it occurred to you that these findings suggest that a severe "initiation" to join a group might, paradoxically, increase recruits' evaluations of the group? If individuals willingly go through a painful or embarrassing initiation to join a hockey team, a fraternity, or some other group, they will be motivated to justify their suffering by perceiving the group as attractive and worthwhile. So a painful initiation might actually increase the commitment of new members to the group, which may explain why some groups have such procedures. Similarly, if someone spends a lot of money to join a golf club or to undergo prolonged psychotherapy, he or she will be motivated to see the golf club as prestigious or the psychotherapy as helpful. We are motivated to come to like or value things we have invested time and effort to attain (see also Axsom & Cooper, 1985; Cooper, 1980).

It may interest you to know that feelings of dissonance from potentially wasted effort are quite common among research scientists (even dissonance researchers!). Many scientific activities are time-consuming and expensive but can sometimes bear little fruit. A series of experiments can yield null results; a long and detailed grant

How can some people such as these coal miners persist with an occupation that entails strenuous work, hazardous conditions, and often low pay?

proposal seeking financial support for research can be turned down; a paper submitted for publication can be rejected from one journal after another. Each of these experiences is very frustrating. How do scientists deal with their dissonance? It is difficult for them to change the dissonant cognitions directly—the effort that has been invested and the lack of output are both quite obvious and undeniable. Instead, scientists often add consonant cognitions: they rationalize that the effort was worthwhile because it "clarified their thinking" or "forced them to move in new research directions" or "motivated them to establish connections with other researchers." All of these observations may be true, of course, but they also constitute consonant cognitions that help to alleviate feelings of dissonance. No one is immune to dissonance, not even social psychologists who know what it is.

Free Choice: Dissonance from Making a Decision. Decisions always involve choosing one option from various alternatives: deciding which automobile to buy, deciding whom to ask out on a date, or deciding how to solve a problem. Thus, decisions always involve a *chosen option* and at least one *rejected option*. Festinger (1957) hypothesized that after making a decision, people almost always experience some dissonance; this kind of dissonance has (logically) been labelled *postdecisional dissonance*.

Why do people experience dissonance after most decisions? Because the chosen option will usually have some negative features, and the rejected option will usually have some positive features. Imagine that you are choosing between two cars: car A performs better and is more attractive than car B, but car A is also more expensive and less fuel efficient than car B. If you choose car A, its costliness will

Enduring a difficult or embarrassing initiation can motivate people to believe that the group is worthwhile.

arouse dissonance, and the fuel efficiency of car B will also arouse dissonance. If you choose car B, its low attractiveness will arouse dissonance, and the better performance of car A will also arouse dissonance. So no matter which car you choose, there will be some dissonant cognitions. (Of course, there will also be some consonant cognitions, such as the performance and attractiveness of car A if you choose it, so you will probably focus on these qualities after making your decision.)

The **free choice paradigm** is used to study postdecisional dissonance in the lab. It involves asking participants to make a choice between two or more alternatives. Participants' evaluations of the alternatives are assessed before making the decision and then again after the decision. Dissonance theory predicts that thinking about the negative features of the chosen alternative or the positive features of the rejected alternative will arouse dissonance after the decision is made. People will reduce this dissonance by focusing on the positive features of the chosen alternative and the negative features of the rejected alternative. As a result, after making a decision, people will tend to evaluate the chosen alternative even more positively and the rejected alternative even more negatively than before making the decision.

Deciding which appliance to buy can arouse *postdecisional dissonance.*

free choice paradigm

a research methodology used to test dissonance theory that arouses dissonance by getting people to choose between two or more alternatives

Jack Brehm (1956) published the first study employing the free choice paradigm to study postdecisional dissonance. Women at the University of Minnesota were asked to rate a number of consumer items, including a toaster, an electric coffeepot, and a silk-screen print, on evaluation scales. They were then given the opportunity to choose one of two items as a gift for taking part in the study. Some participants were given a difficult choice: they had to select between two items that they had rated very closely on the evaluation scales. Other participants were given an easy choice: they had rated one of the items much more favourably than the other. Difficult choices (between alternatives that were equally attractive) were expected to cause more postdecisional dissonance than easy choices.

After making their choice, all participants were asked to rate the items again on the same evaluation scales. Brehm could then examine whether participants had changed their ratings from before the decision to after the decision. Figure 7.4 presents the mean changes in ratings in the difficult (high-dissonance) and easy (low-dissonance) conditions. As predicted, participants in the high-dissonance condition increased their rating of the chosen item and decreased their rating of the rejected item, whereas participants in the low-dissonance condition did not show much change in ratings of either the chosen or the rejected item. The difficult condition aroused more postdecisional dissonance, which was reduced by exaggerating the difference between the chosen and rejected items. This tendency to rate the chosen item more favourably and the rejected item less favourably after a decision has been termed *spreading of the alternatives*—that is, the evaluations of the chosen and rejected items are spread further apart (see also Johnson & Rusbult, 1989; Shultz, Leveille, & Lepper, 1999; Zanna & Sande, 1987).

7.1
ONLINE LAB

Alternative Interpretations of Dissonance Findings

Despite the supportive experiments we have described, alternative interpretations of dissonance findings began to appear about a decade after Festinger's (1957) book was published. We describe three alternative interpretations here. The

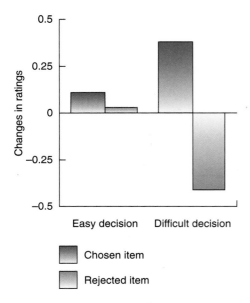

FIGURE 7.4 Changes in ratings of chosen and rejected items after decision

From Brehm, "Post-decision changes in desirability of alternatives," *Journal of Abnormal and Social Psychology,* 52, 384–389, Table 1, 1956.

key points of these alternatives, and of dissonance theory itself, are summarized in Table 7.2.

Self-Perception Theory. The first serious attack on dissonance theory came from Daryl Bem (1967, 1972) when he proposed *self-perception theory.* We discussed this theory in Chapter 4 (see pages 128–132) and again briefly in Chapter 6 (see page 210). Bem hypothesized that people sometimes infer their internal states, such as attitudes and emotions, from their behaviour and the situation in which the behaviour occurred. For instance, individuals might infer that their attitude toward golfing is unfavourable because they have rarely golfed despite having had opportunities to do so. Using behaviour to infer internal states is presumed to occur mainly when the internal states are weak or ambiguous.

How does self-perception theory offer an alternative interpretation of dissonance findings? Let's focus on just one of the dissonance paradigms: induced compliance. Recall that Festinger and Carlsmith (1959) induced participants to tell another person that some boring tasks were interesting. So long as they were not paid much for telling this lie (the $1 condition), participants subsequently reported that the tasks were somewhat interesting. According to the original researchers, this relatively favourable evaluation of the tasks reflected that participants felt dissonance between the cognitions "the tasks were boring" and "I told someone that the tasks were interesting"; participants reduced dissonance by changing one of the dissonant cognitions (from "the tasks were boring" to "the tasks were somewhat interesting") so that it would be more consonant with the other cognition ("I told someone that the tasks were interesting").

Bem (1967) suggested, however, that participants in the $1 condition (high dissonance) in Festinger and Carlsmith's (1959) study rated the tasks as somewhat interesting *because they inferred this attitude from the fact that they told someone the tasks were interesting without much justification for doing so.* From this perspective, participants were not upset by their lie or motivated to distort their evaluation of the tasks; rather, they simply inferred in a logical manner that the tasks must have been interesting because they willingly told someone the tasks were interesting. Participants in the $20 condition did not infer that they liked the tasks because the large payment provided a very plausible explanation of their behaviour.

TABLE 7.2
Key Points of Dissonance Theory and Alternative Interpretations

Theory	Key Points/Assumptions
Dissonance theory	Recognition that their actions have been irrational or erroneous makes people feel unpleasant arousal, which motivates them to change a dissonant cognition or to add consonant cognitions.
Self-perception theory	People logically infer their attitudes from their behaviour and the circumstances in which the behaviour occurred, without the occurrence of any arousal.
Impression management theory	People in dissonance experiments want to appear consistent to the researcher and therefore lie about their attitudes: they falsely report attitudes that are relatively consistent with their behaviour in the study.
Self-affirmation theory	Recognition that their actions have been irrational or erroneous threatens people's positive self-views, which causes unpleasant arousal; people can reduce this arousal by doing anything that reaffirms their value and worth as individuals.

Does this interpretation make sense to you? Do you think that participants were unaware of how interesting or boring the tasks were? Imagine yourself turning pegs for an hour. Would you know that you were bored? Dissonance researchers thought so. They responded to Bem's critique by arguing that participants knew perfectly well that the tasks were boring and felt bad after telling the lie; this aversive arousal motivated the favourable evaluation of the tasks in order to reduce the arousal.

This last comment highlights an important difference between dissonance and self-perception theories: the role of unpleasant arousal. Dissonance theorists hypothesized that aversive arousal motivated the attitude change, whereas self-perception theorists hypothesized that there was no arousal at all. Numerous experiments were conducted over the next few years to investigate the role of aversive arousal, including several by Mark Zanna at the University of Waterloo and his colleague Joel Cooper at Princeton University. These experiments consistently supported dissonance theory and thereby cast doubt on a self-perception interpretation of dissonance findings. For example, researchers found that if participants in high-dissonance conditions were given alcohol or a tranquillizer, either of which reduces arousal, they did not exhibit the usual attitude change (e.g., Cooper, Zanna, & Taves, 1978; Steele, Southwick, & Critchlow, 1981). Other studies used different methodologies to reach the same conclusion that aversive arousal is necessary for attitude change to occur (e.g., see Croyle & Cooper, 1982; Fazio, Zanna, & Cooper, 1977; Zanna & Cooper, 1974).

Although it has not fared well as an alternative to dissonance theory, self-perception theory made important contributions to the study of other phenomena in social psychology. For example, we discussed in Chapter 4 the usefulness of self-perception theory for understanding the effects of rewards, especially the *overjustification effect* (the finding that giving people a reward for an enjoyable activity can reduce their intrinsic interest in the activity; see page 130).

Impression Management Theory. A second alternative interpretation of dissonance findings made the provocative proposal that participants in dissonance experiments were often simply *faking* attitude change. **Impression management theory** (Tedeschi, Schlenker, & Bonoma, 1971) proposed that participants in dissonance studies did not want to appear inconsistent to the experimenter and therefore *falsely* reported attitudes that were relatively consistent with the counterattitudinal behaviour that they had exhibited. These researchers argued that participants were just trying to manage the experimenter's impression of them, and the reported attitudes were not genuine.

Imagine yourself in an induced compliance experiment in which you voluntarily agreed to write an essay arguing in favour of tuition increases for university students. After writing this essay, the experimenter asked you to report your own attitude toward tuition increases. Would you feel that you'd look stupid or weak to the experimenter if you admitted that you were actually against tuition increases? If so, perhaps you would decide to lie about your attitude—to state that you think that tuition increases are a good idea.

There is no doubt that research participants want experimenters to view them positively. Recall from Chapter 4 our discussion of *self-presentation goals* (see page 143). Common self-presentation goals include being seen as likeable and competent: we want others to think of us as nice and talented people. It is also true that some dissonance experiments have elicited counterattitudinal behaviour under very public conditions that probably aroused the motive to report an attitude consistent with the behaviour even if that attitude was not truthful.

But it is unlikely that impression management theory can explain all dissonance findings. For one thing, participants in some studies reported attitudes that were consistent with their counterattitudinal behaviour even though the person who took the attitude measure was not the same person who observed the counterattitudinal

impression management theory
an alternative to dissonance theory that argues that participants in dissonance experiments want to appear consistent to the experimenter and therefore lie about their attitudes

behaviour (e.g., Linder, Cooper, & Jones, 1967); there should have been no need to lie about one's attitude to someone who didn't even observe the counterattitudinal behaviour. Also, attitudes consistent with counterattitudinal behaviour have been obtained even when the counterattitudinal behaviour occurred in very private settings that virtually eliminated any impression management motives (e.g., Harmon-Jones, Brehm, Greenberg, Simon, & Nelson, 1996). These findings indicate that, although impression management motives do influence public behaviour, the attitude change that occurs in dissonance-arousing situations is almost certainly real.

Self-Affirmation Theory. Perhaps the most compelling alternative to dissonance theory was proposed by Stanford University social psychologist Claude Steele (1988; Steele & Liu, 1981), building on earlier work by Elliot Aronson (1968). **Self-affirmation theory** argues that people want to view themselves as moral, capable individuals. Extrapolating from this idea that people want to see themselves positively, Steele and his colleagues argued that counterattitudinal or irrational behaviour threatens participants' views of themselves as honest and intelligent. That is, counterattitudinal behaviour is upsetting because it *threatens self-worth*—it implies that participants are dishonest or foolish. For instance, self-affirmation researchers proposed that people in the Festinger and Carlsmith (1959) study were not upset about the inconsistency between "The tasks were boring" and "I told someone that the tasks were fun," but instead were disturbed by the inconsistency between "I am an honest person" and "I lied to someone." The flowchart in Figure 7.5 depicts the self-affirmation reinterpretation of Festinger and Carlsmith's experiment.

Self-affirmation theorists predicted that people can deal with threats to their self-worth in ways other than changing their attitudes. After all, if people are upset by counterattitudinal behaviour because it implies they are dishonest, then they should be able to make themselves feel better by doing something honest or good even without changing their attitudes. Prior to Steele's research, however, dissonance researchers did not provide such alternatives in their experiments.

In several studies, Steele and his colleagues showed that giving people an opportunity to demonstrate their self-worth after counterattitudinal behaviour reduces or eliminates attitude change (Steele, 1988; Steele & Liu, 1981, 1983; Steele, Spencer, & Lynch, 1993). For example, in one study (Steele & Liu, 1981), university students were asked to write an essay arguing against government funding of facilities for the disabled—a position that was counterattitudinal for the participants. Prior to writing the essay, some participants were told that they would later be asked to help a blind student, whereas other participants were not told about such an opportunity. After writing the essay, participants' attitudes toward the issue of government funding for the handicapped were measured. Those participants who did *not* expect to help a blind student reported more negative attitudes toward government assistance for the disabled (consistent with their essay) than did participants who expected to help

self-affirmation theory

an alternative to dissonance theory that argues that people are threatened by behaviour that challenges their self-worth and can deal with this threat by reaffirming an important value

FIGURE 7.5 Self-affirmation theory reinterpretation of Festinger and Carlsmith (1959) experiment

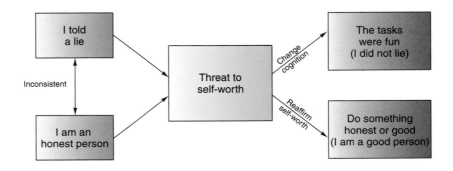

a blind student. The researchers proposed that the latter participants knew that they would soon be able to demonstrate their positive worth by helping the blind student and, therefore, were not disturbed by their counterattitudinal essay.

Summary. What should we conclude about the various alternative interpretations that have been proposed for dissonance theory? Perhaps the most sensible conclusion at the present time is that each alternative has a "kernel of truth," but none provides a complete account of all dissonance findings. Self-perception theory, impression management theory, and self-affirmation theory all describe psychological processes that occur under certain conditions. Each perspective can account for some dissonance findings and has implications for some nondissonance settings as well. But the full range of experimental paradigms used by dissonance researchers is still explained

Self-affirmation theory predicts that helping a blind person can reduce dissonance caused by a prior, unrelated behaviour.

most simply by dissonance theory itself. It is a testament to the creativity of Leon Festinger both that his model has generated so much attention and that it remains a viable theory today.

Recent Research on Dissonance Theory

Dissonance theory continues to interest social psychologists today (for recent reviews, see Harmon-Jones & Mills, 1999; Olson & Stone, 2005). Innovative developments have included investigations of how people learn to experience dissonance (Cooper, 1998) and attempts to integrate dissonance and self-affirmation theories (e.g., Blanton, Cooper, Skurnik, & Aronson, 1997; Stone, Wiegand, Cooper, & Aronson, 1997). Researchers have also proposed sophisticated, formal models that aim to specify the psychological mechanisms that underlie dissonance effects (e.g., Harmon-Jones & Harmon-Jones, 2002; Shultz & Lepper, 1996; Stone, 2001, 2003; Stone & Cooper, 2001, 2003; Van Overwalle & Jordens, 2002).

One issue that has received attention is whether the arousal of dissonance requires that bad consequences result from the individual's actions. Some theorists have proposed that people will not feel upset about behaving in a counterattitudinal way unless something negative happens, such as the behaviour hurts another person (Cooper & Fazio, 1984). Recent research has indicated, however, that negative consequences are *not* necessary for dissonance to occur (e.g., Harmon-Jones et al., 1996). In fact, researchers have identified a new paradigm for studying dissonance in which the individual's behaviour has no aversive consequences whatsoever.

The Hypocrisy Paradigm. Earlier, we described three paradigms—induced compliance, effort justification, and free choice—that have been used to study dissonance experimentally. More recent research by Elliot Aronson and his students at the University of California at Santa Cruz (e.g., Aronson, Fried, & Stone, 1991; Dickerson, Thibodeau, Aronson, & Miller, 1992) has added a fourth paradigm, which they labelled the **hypocrisy paradigm.** Imagine that you arrive for an experiment and are asked to prepare and deliver a speech about the importance of supporting Canadian businesses by purchasing Canadian-made goods. You are told that this speech might be included in a videotape being developed for viewing by high school students (to increase their awareness of the problem). The experimenter gives you a sheet with some relevant information on it about the positive impact on Canadian

hypocrisy paradigm

a research methodology used to test dissonance theory that arouses dissonance by having people publicly promote a socially desirable behaviour and then be made aware that they have not always exhibited the behaviour themselves in the past businesses that can come from purchases by Canadian consumers, and you spend a few minutes organizing your thoughts. The experimenter then videotapes you while you explain why it is important to buy Canadian goods. Now the interesting part. After giving this little speech, you are asked to complete a questionnaire about your own behaviour related to buying Canadian-made products. In answering these questions, you realize that you often purchase goods made in the United States, China, and other countries, even when Canadian alternatives are available. How do you think these realizations would make you feel?

Aronson and his students hypothesized that this kind of situation arouses dissonance. The situation makes people aware that they have sometimes failed to perform the behaviours they just recommended on the videotape. For example, your realization that you purchase many non-Canadian goods would arouse dissonance between the cognitions "I publicly recommended buying Canadian-made goods" and "I sometimes fail to buy Canadian products when I could do so."

This is an interesting form of dissonance because the public behaviour that provokes it is completely *pro*attitudinal—the individual recommends a behaviour that he or she already supports such as purchasing Canadian products. Yet privately knowing that he or she has not always performed the behaviour makes the individual feel hypocritical (because people should "practise what they preach"). Aronson and his colleagues predicted that dissonance aroused by hypocrisy would motivate individuals to change their behaviour to be more consistent with what they publicly promoted.

In one experiment using the hypocrisy paradigm, Jeff Stone, Elliot Aronson, and their colleagues (Stone, Aronson, Crain, Winslow, & Fried, 1994) recruited university students who had been sexually active in the previous three months and asked them to prepare a speech about the importance of safer sexual behaviours, such as always using a condom during sex. Participants were told that these speeches would be shown to high school students to promote the safer behaviours. Participants were given some information to help them prepare the speech, which they wrote and then delivered in front of a camera. After the speech was videotaped, participants completed a questionnaire that was designed to make them aware of their own failures to practise safer sex behaviours. For example, the questionnaire listed ten common reasons why people do not use condoms, and participants were asked whether any of these reasons applied to their own past failures to use condoms; they were also encouraged to generate additional reasons why they had failed to use condoms in the past.

Participants were then told that the experiment was finished and were given four $1 bills as payment for their participation. The experimenter then explained that when the campus health centre heard that this study was focused on safer sex behaviours, it made available a supply of condoms at a price of 10 cents each. The experimenter pointed to a table in the room where a clear plastic container was filled with 140 condoms in individual packages. A bowl of loose change was beside the container, as well as an envelope with numerous $1 bills. The experimenter said that if the participant wanted to buy any condoms, he or she could put a bill in the envelope and take the necessary change from the bowl. The experimenter then left the room, and the participant was able to purchase condoms privately and anonymously if he or she wished before leaving the room.

After delivering a speech advocating safer sex behaviours and then being reminded of past personal failures to use condoms, 83% of participants purchased at least one condom. Thus, most individuals in this condition apparently wanted to make their future sexual behaviour safer. In three control conditions in which participants (1) delivered a similar speech but were not reminded of past failures, (2) were reminded of past failures but did not deliver a speech, or (3) were simply given the opportunity to purchase condoms (without delivering a speech or being reminded of past failures), less than 50% of participants purchased at least one condom. These findings are presented in Figure 7.6. The results showed that the feeling of hypocrisy created by the *combination* of delivering the speech *and* being reminded of past failures was necessary to arouse dissonance; the dissonance then motivated people to make their sexual behaviour safer in the future.

Leanne Son Hing, who is at the University of Guelph, and Winnie Li and Mark Zanna, who are at the University of Waterloo, conducted a study in which the hypocrisy paradigm was applied to racial attitudes and discrimination (Son Hing, Li, & Zanna, 2002). We will focus on one subgroup of participants, who were chosen because they showed mild, but not extreme, prejudice against Asian Canadians. These participants were asked to write a persuasive essay on why they believed it is important to treat minority students on campus fairly. Participants were then asked to write briefly about two situations in which they had reacted negatively to an Asian person or treated an Asian person in a prejudiced manner (which was expected to make participants feel hypocritical regarding the persuasive essay they had just written). Finally, participants were told that the school's student federation was trying to decide how to distribute budget cuts across various clubs on campus. Participants were asked to give their own recommendations for the budget cuts that should be made to various clubs, including the Asian Students' Association (ASA). Participants who completed the hypocrisy procedure recommended significantly smaller budget cuts to the ASA than did control participants. Thus, the hypocrisy paradigm was shown to be capable of reducing racial discrimination.

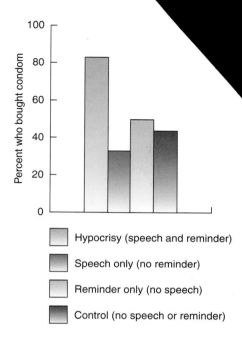

FIGURE 7.6 Percentage of participants who bought condom

From Stone et al., "Inducing hypocrisy as a means of encouraging young adults to use condoms," *Personality and Social Psychology Bulletin*, 20, 116–128, Fig. 1, p. 121, 1994. Reprinted by permission of Sage Publications.

Individual Differences in Preferences for Consistency. Are some people more sensitive to dissonance than others? Arizona State University social psychologists Robert Cialdini, Melanie Trost, and Jason Newsom (1995) thought so and developed a scale to measure such differences. They labelled the dimension **preference for consistency (PFC)** and hypothesized that scores on the scale revealed the extent to which people desired predictability and consistency within their own responses and within others' responses. For instance, people who score high in PFC are presumed to want their actions and attitudes to be consistent with one another (as assumed by dissonance theory), whereas people who score low in PFC are presumed to be less concerned about such consistency (in contrast to the assumptions of dissonance theory).

Ian Newby-Clark of the University of Guelph, Ian McGregor of York University, and Mark Zanna of the University of Waterloo (2002) showed that people who score high in PFC are more bothered than people who score low in PFC by *ambivalent attitudes*, which we defined in Chapter 6 as attitudes that include both positive and negative components (see page 193). This finding seems compatible with the prediction that people who score high in PFC will be more sensitive to dissonance, which involves contradictory cognitions, than will people who score low in PFC.

Know Yourself 7.1: "Preference for Consistency" presents the nine items from the brief form of the PFC scale (Cialdini et al., 1995). Answer the items and see whether you score high or low on this dimension.

Cialdini and his colleagues hypothesized that typical findings in dissonance experiments would be stronger for people who are high in the preference for consistency than for those who are low in this disposition. In a test of this hypothesis, students were asked to write an essay in favour of a tuition increase—a position that was assumed to be counterattitudinal for all participants. Those in the choice (high-dissonance) condition were asked whether they would be willing to write this essay, whereas those in the no-choice (low-dissonance) condition were simply told to write the essay. After preparing the essay, participants reported their own attitudes toward a tuition increase. As predicted by Cialdini and his colleagues, participants who were high in the preference for consistency reported more favourable attitudes toward

preference for consistency (PFC)

a disposition that represents the extent to which people desire predictability and consistency within their own responses and within others' responses

w Yourself 7.1
Preference for Consistency

Please indicate the extent to which you agree or disagree with each of the following statements by circling the appropriate number on the answer scale.

1. It is important to me that those who know me can predict what I will do.

1	2	3	4	5	6	7	8	9
Strongly disagree	Disagree	Somewhat disagree	Slightly disagree	Neither agree nor disagree	Slightly agree	Somewhat agree	Agree	Strongly agree

2. I want to be described by others as a stable, predictable person.

1	2	3	4	5	6	7	8	9
Strongly disagree	Disagree	Somewhat disagree	Slightly disagree	Neither agree nor disagree	Slightly agree	Somewhat agree	Agree	Strongly agree

3. The appearance of consistency is an important part of the image I present to the world.

1	2	3	4	5	6	7	8	9
Strongly disagree	Disagree	Somewhat disagree	Slightly disagree	Neither agree nor disagree	Slightly agree	Somewhat agree	Agree	Strongly agree

4. An important requirement for any friend of mine is personal consistency.

1	2	3	4	5	6	7	8	9
Strongly disagree	Disagree	Somewhat disagree	Slightly disagree	Neither agree nor disagree	Slightly agree	Somewhat agree	Agree	Strongly agree

5. I typically prefer to do things the same way.

1	2	3	4	5	6	7	8	9
Strongly disagree	Disagree	Somewhat disagree	Slightly disagree	Neither agree nor disagree	Slightly agree	Somewhat agree	Agree	Strongly agree

6. I want my close friends to be predictable.

1	2	3	4	5	6	7	8	9
Strongly disagree	Disagree	Somewhat disagree	Slightly disagree	Neither agree nor disagree	Slightly agree	Somewhat agree	Agree	Strongly agree

7. It is important to me that others view me as a stable person.

1	2	3	4	5	6	7	8	9
Strongly disagree	Disagree	Somewhat disagree	Slightly disagree	Neither agree nor disagree	Slightly agree	Somewhat agree	Agree	Strongly agree

8. I make an effort to appear consistent to others.

1	2	3	4	5	6	7	8	9
Strongly disagree	Disagree	Somewhat disagree	Slightly disagree	Neither agree nor disagree	Slightly agree	Somewhat agree	Agree	Strongly agree

9. It doesn't bother me much if my actions are inconsistent.

1	2	3	4	5	6	7	8	9
Strongly disagree	Disagree	Somewhat disagree	Slightly disagree	Neither agree nor disagree	Slightly agree	Somewhat agree	Agree	Strongly agree

SCORING: Items 1–8 are scored using the answer scales as presented (1-2-3-4-5-6-7-8-9), but Item 9 is scored in the reverse direction (that is, 9-8-7-6-5-4-3-2-1). Add up all of the items for your overall preference for consistency score. Possible scores range from 9 to 81, and higher scores represent stronger preferences for consistency.

Sample items from Cialdini et al., "Preference for consistency: The development of a valid measure and the discovery of surprising behavioral implications," *Journal of Personality and Social Psychology, 69,* 318–328, 1995. Copyright © 1995 by the American Psychological Association. Reprinted by permission.

a tuition increase in the choice condition than in the no-choice condition, whereas participants who were low in the preference for consistency reported equivalent attitudes in the two conditions. Thus, using an induced compliance paradigm, dissonance theory was supported only for high-PFC individuals.

This individual differences perspective on dissonance theory opens up many possibilities for future research. It will be interesting to see whether other dissonance paradigms also work better for people who are high rather than low in preference for consistency.

Dissonance and Explicit Versus Implicit Attitudes. In Chapter 6, we distinguished between *explicit attitudes* and *implicit attitudes* (see page 194). Explicit attitudes refer to people's *conscious* evaluations of a target, whereas implicit attitudes refer to people's *automatic* evaluative responses to a target, which can occur without awareness. All of the research on dissonance theory that we have described thus far used explicit measures of attitudes.

Bertram Gawronski, who is at the University of Western Ontario, and his colleague Fritz Strack at the University of Würzburg in Germany (2004) hypothesized that dissonance might *not* affect implicit attitudes. Why? Dissonance arousal and reduction rely on conscious mental inferences. For instance, counterattitudinal behaviour is assumed to motivate attitude change when people consciously recognize that their behaviour has been inconsistent with their attitude. Awareness of this inconsistency causes people to alter their conscious attitudes. But perhaps implicit attitudes, which are spontaneous and automatic, are not directly affected by conscious inferences.

Gawronski and Strack (2004) tested this reasoning by asking German university students to write an essay in favour of banning alcoholic beverages in their country (a counterattitudinal position). Some participants (high-dissonance condition) were asked whether they would be willing to write the essay, whereas others (low-dissonance condition) were simply told to write the essay. After generating the message, participants' explicit attitudes were assessed using self-report items, and their implicit attitudes were assessed using the Implicit Association Test (see page 203). Results showed that, consistent with dissonance theory, participants in the high-dissonance condition reported more favourable explicit attitudes toward banning alcoholic beverages than did participants in the low-dissonance condition. The two groups did not differ, however, in their implicit attitudes toward alcoholic beverages. Thus, dissonance changed explicit, but not implicit, attitudes. An interesting question for future research will be whether people's implicit attitudes might, over time, become consistent with their new explicit attitudes.

In closing, dissonance theory has stimulated a great deal of research and has provided a useful analysis of how everyday actions can change attitudes. The theory continues to inspire innovative experiments and seems likely to remain a vibrant theory in social psychology for many years to come.

Information-Based Persuasion: Cognitive Response Theory

As noted at the beginning of this chapter, attitude change can occur in many ways. Dissonance theory deals with one way—namely, self-persuasion: we sometimes change our attitudes to rationalize our own behaviour so that we feel better about it. Another way that attitudes change—perhaps the most common way—is as a result of *persuasive communications,* which are attempts (oral, written, face-to-face, media-based) by an individual or group to convince another person or persons to adopt a particular position. Many theories of attitude change in social psychology are designed to understand the factors that influence the success or failure of persuasive communications. Persuasive communications can be aimed at any kind of attitude: political views, evaluations of people, food preferences, or other targets (see Perloff, 2003; Seiter & Gass, 2004).

What are some common examples of persuasive communications? Let's begin by thinking about persuasive communications that you are exposed to regularly. Advertising is one category of such messages, with ads intended to make you more favourable toward a product. Education is another domain in which persuasive communications are frequent; for instance, your professors (and textbook authors) try to persuade you that their science is important. Family and friends also direct persuasive communications at you: your family tries to convince you to work hard at school, and your friends try to convince you to play hard after school.

What about persuasive communications that *you* initiate? What are some examples of your attempts to influence other people's opinions? You almost certainly generate many persuasive communications, even if you don't recognize them as such: you try to convince your housemate that she should take a course in psychology; you try to convince a friend to go to a movie with you; you try to convince an acquaintance that someone he currently dislikes is actually very nice. Often these communications are designed to change people's behaviour toward you, such as going to a movie with you or helping you in some way.

Many (but *not* all) persuasive communications rely on *information* to convince the recipient to adopt the advocated position. Information-based messages consist of arguments about an issue and/or evidence supporting a position; they try to use reason or logic to make their case.

cognitive response theory

a model of persuasion that assumes that the impact of a message on attitudes depends on the thoughts evoked by the message

The social psychology theory that focuses most directly on information-based persuasion is **cognitive response theory** (Eagly & Chaiken, 1984; Greenwald, 1968; Petty & Cacioppo, 1981). Cognitive response theory assumes that the effectiveness of a message in causing attitude change is determined by the thoughts evoked by the message. The thoughts can be about the communicator, the issue, or the message. If the message elicits mostly positive thoughts (called *proarguments* in the theory), then the individual will be inclined to adopt the position advocated in the message. If the message elicits mostly negative thoughts (called *counterarguments* in the theory), then the individual will be inclined to reject the position advocated in the message. In both cases, the cognitive responses (or thoughts) are assumed to cause the acceptance or rejection of the advocated position. For instance, if a message evokes thoughts about how intelligent the communicator is and how convincing the arguments are, then the recipient is likely to adopt the recommended position. If, on the other hand, a message evokes thoughts about how biased the communicator is and how weak the arguments are, then the recipient is likely to reject the recommended position.

Think about your own reactions to persuasive communications, such as advertisements, in-class discussions about politics, or arguments about the best movie of the year. Sometimes you probably find yourself thinking, "This product has some great features," or "What an interesting argument—I never thought of that before," or "This person is really smart." These kinds of thoughts are normally associated with being persuaded by the ad, discussion, or argument. But other times you probably find yourself thinking, "This is a useless product," or "What a stupid argument," or "What a loser this guy is." These kinds of thoughts are normally associated with rejecting the recommendations of the ad, discussion, or argument. We should all keep in mind that when we try to persuade others, they are silently generating thoughts about us and our message—and those thoughts may not always be flattering!

Strong Arguments, Strong Attitudes

What factors determine whether a message will elicit positive or negative thoughts? Once again, think about your own reactions to persuasive communications. What features characterize successful communications? Humorous? Eye-grabbing? Interesting?

All of these factors probably have some impact, as do characteristics of the recipient such as mood and amount of knowledge about the issue. But perhaps the most important factor is a simple and straightforward one: the *strength of the arguments* in the message. When a message contains strong arguments, it usually elicits positive thoughts about the communicator, the issue, and the message. By definition, strong arguments provide compelling reasons for adopting the advocated position. Thus, strong arguments tend to produce correspondingly strong attitudes that are consistent with the recommended position. In contrast, weak arguments provide poor support for the advocated position and usually elicit negative thoughts. Weak arguments do not typically move the recipient's attitude in the direction of the message. The flowchart in Figure 7.7 depicts these effects of strong and weak arguments.

John Cacioppo and Richard Petty (1985) conducted a study that illustrated nicely the importance of the strength of the arguments in a message. University students listened to a message arguing that seniors at their university should have a new requirement that they must pass a comprehensive examination in their major area before they can graduate. Needless to say, almost all students opposed this idea. Two messages were used, one containing strong arguments and the other containing weak arguments. An example of a strong argument was "Graduates from universities with comprehensive exams are recruited more heavily by employers." An example of a weak argument was "Comprehensive exams maintain a tradition dating back to the ancient Greeks." A second independent variable was also manipulated in the experiment: participants heard the message either once or three times. The researchers hypothesized that repeating the message three times should heighten the impact of argument strength because participants would have three chances to think about how convincing or how stupid the arguments were.

After hearing the strong or weak message once or three times, participants were asked to report their own attitude toward instituting comprehensive exams for

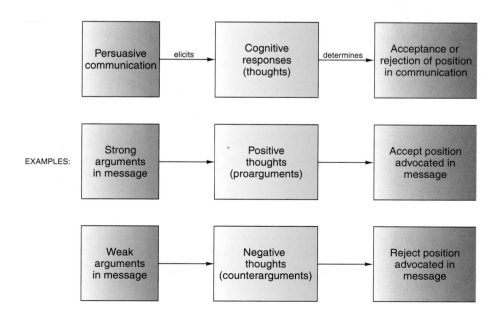

FIGURE 7.7 Cognitive response theory and persuasive communications

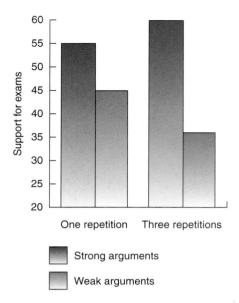

FIGURE 7.8 Favourability of attitudes toward comprehensive exams: Repetition

From Petty and Cacioppo, "The elaboration likelihood model of persuasion," in L. Berkowitz, ed., *Advances in Experimental Social Psychology* (Vol. 19, pp. 123–205), p. 142, 1986. Reprinted by permission of Elsevier.

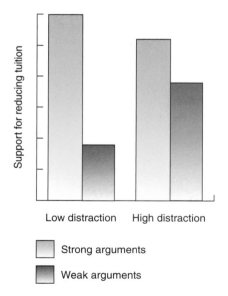

FIGURE 7.9 Favourability of attitudes toward reducing tuition

From Petty et al., "Distraction can enhance or reduce yielding to propaganda: Thought disruption versus effort justification," *Journal of Personality and Social Psychology*, 34, 874–888, 1976. Copyright © 1976 by the American Psychological Association.

seniors. In addition, their memory for the message was tested. Figure 7.8 presents the attitude findings from the experiment. When participants heard the message just once, the strong arguments produced more positive attitudes toward comprehensive exams than did the weak message, as would be expected. When participants heard the message three times, this difference was exaggerated: the strong message produced even more positive attitudes, and the weak message produced even more negative attitudes. Thus, the impact of the message in this study depended on its quality, as well as participants' opportunities to consider it carefully.

The researchers also analyzed participants' memory for the message. The memory data showed that repeated exposure improved recall of the arguments, whether strong or weak. Participants who heard the strong message three times recalled more strong arguments than did those who heard the strong message just once; participants who heard the weak message three times recalled more weak arguments than did those who heard the weak message just once. Thus, participants were paying attention to the message, and repeated exposure allowed them to analyze the message more thoroughly. Have you ever noticed that many commercials are shown more than once during the same TV show? These repetitions reflect the assumption by many advertisers that repeated exposure will enhance the impact of positive information about their products.

Are You Listening?

The experiment we just described manipulated how many times participants heard the message. This manipulation influenced how carefully the participants were able to process the message. The more opportunities they had to hear the message, the greater was the impact of argument strength. What about a manipulation that went in the opposite direction, in which participants were *inhibited* from processing the message? How would this manipulation affect the impact of argument strength? Richard Petty, Gary Wells, and Timothy Brock (1976) predicted that if participants were inhibited from paying close attention to a message, then the strength of the arguments would be less important. After all, unless recipients have the opportunity to process a message carefully, its content will make little difference.

To test this reasoning, Petty and his colleagues (1976) asked students at Ohio State University to listen to a message arguing for a reduction in tuition—a position that most participants supported. The message contained either strong arguments for a tuition reduction, such as reducing students' debt load, or weak arguments, such as giving students more money for leisure activities. The researchers also asked participants to complete a second task while listening to the message. This second task required participants to record on a sheet the quadrant in which Xs appeared on a screen in front of them (e.g., upper left quadrant, lower right quadrant, etc.). For some participants (the *low-distraction* condition), the Xs appeared at 15-second intervals—a frequency that was not disruptive to listening to the message. But for other participants (the *high-distraction* condition), the Xs appeared at 5-second intervals—a frequency that was very disruptive to processing the message. After hearing the message once while performing this low- or high-distraction task, participants reported their own attitude toward a tuition reduction. They were also asked to write down any thoughts that had occurred to them during the message.

Figure 7.9 presents the results on the attitude measure. In the low-distraction condition, participants who heard a strong message were more favourable toward reducing tuition than were participants who heard a weak message, as expected.

But in the high-distraction condition, the impact of argument strength was greatly reduced: the strong message was only slightly more persuasive than the weak message. If you compare the two strong argument bars, you will see that the strong message was somewhat less persuasive when participants were more distracted, which makes sense because distracted participants were not able to think about the arguments.

But the most interesting result was for weak arguments: notice that the weak message was actually somewhat *more persuasive* in the high-distraction condition than in the low-distraction condition. When participants were distracted from a weak message, its impact actually increased. Why did this effect occur? Examination of the thoughts that participants generated gives us a clue. Recall that participants were asked to write down any thoughts that had occurred to them while they listened to the message. The researchers coded each thought as favourable (a *proargument*) or unfavourable (a *counterargument*). For the weak message, the high-distraction condition yielded fewer counterarguments than did the low-distraction condition. Thus, the weak message was more persuasive in the high-distraction condition than in the low-distraction condition because participants had fewer chances to generate criticisms of the arguments. In a sense, participants were less able to determine just how bad the arguments were.

This finding has an interesting implication. If you want to convince people of something but do not have any strong arguments, then it might be a good idea to talk to them while the television is blaring or some other distraction is interfering with their ability to counterargue your reasoning!

Advertisers use a number of strategies to promote products. One general approach to advertising, which is consistent with the predictions of cognitive response theory, is known as the **hard sell.** It is described in Social Psychology in Your Life: "Advertising the Old-Fashioned Way: The Hard Sell."

If you want to convince someone of a position for which you have only weak arguments, it might be a good idea to present the arguments while the person is being distracted by something else, such as a newspaper.

hard sell

an advertising strategy that relies on presenting information about the positive features of a product

If You Say So: Heuristic Persuasion

Most people would use the term *persuasion* in a manner consistent with the preceding section: it is the result of reasoned thinking and occurs when people are convinced by strong arguments in a message. But there is another way that persuasion can occur, which is very different from the information-based process. This second mode of persuasion has been labelled **heuristic persuasion** by Shelly Chaiken (1980, 1987).

Heuristic persuasion is so named because it focuses on attitude change that results from the use of *heuristics,* which are simple rules, shortcuts, or assumptions that individuals have been taught or have learned from experience. In Chapter 3, we discussed the *availability heuristic* (see page 85) and the *representativeness heuristic* (see page 87). People often use heuristics to help them make decisions and judgments. With respect to attitude change, this perspective recognizes that people do not always exert a lot of effort to judge the validity of a persuasive message, but may instead base their agreement or disagreement on rather superficial cues, or informal rules, that are assumed to be instructive about the message's validity. These cues or heuristics can include things like "Experts are reliable sources of information," "People I like usually have correct opinions," and "Mom always knows best." People

heuristic persuasion

attitude change resulting from cues that indicate that the position advocated in a message is valid

Social Psychology in Your Life   *Advertising the Old-Fashioned Way: The Hard Sell*

When advertisers talk about the hard sell as one possible technique for promoting a product, they are referring to the use of information about the quality of a product to market it. The positive characteristics of the product are front and centre: the message attempts to convince the recipients that the product is a good one. The appeal is rational and logical, rather than emotional or symbolic. The hard sell relies on information about the product, and it adopts a model of persuasion very much like cognitive response theory. The hard sell assumes that people process advertisements carefully and can be convinced by information to purchase or use the product.

Some types of products are more easily promoted with a hard sell than others. First, products whose performance can be objectively specified—such as stereo equipment, computers, appliances, and automobiles—lend themselves well to the hard sell. These products can be promoted by comparing their performance to that of other brands and highlighting their advantages. A written mode of communication, such as newspaper ads, is often an effective way to present this information. Second, products that are strictly functional and do not have any status or symbolic value—such as garden tools, insect repellents, air conditioners, and surge protectors—also lend themselves well to the hard sell. Let's face it—we don't buy a spade or an insect repellent to make an impression on other people. With these kinds of products, people are simply looking for ones that work effectively, so the only relevant consideration is informa-

tion about their features (Shavitt, 1990). An example of a magazine advertisement that uses the hard sell is presented in Figure 7.10. Allergy medications are purchased for a specific purpose—to relieve congestion. The way to convince people to buy the product is to tell them why and how it works. This ad presents information about the speed and duration of relief as well as a toll-free number and a Web site where additional information can be found.

Public information campaigns, such as mass media campaigns to promote a healthy lifestyle, also frequently use the hard sell (Mendelsohn, 1973). These campaigns present information explaining the benefits of adopting a certain lifestyle: "You'll feel better if you exercise regularly";

FIGURE 7.10 Magazine advertisement that uses the hard sell

"You'll save money if you stop smoking." The assumption is that people will change their lifestyle if they can be convinced that there will be significant benefits. Another important component is often to provide specific advice about how to undertake new behaviours, such as how to exercise without injury or whom to contact for help in stopping smoking (Backer, Rogers, & Sopory, 1992; Leventhal & Cameron, 1994; Olson & Zanna, 1987).

Political advertisements also frequently adopt the hard sell. Think about the political campaign ads you have seen. The most common strategy in political ads seems to be to describe the candidate's positions on important issues and to extol his or her integrity and honesty. Negative ads about opponents are also quite common, which usually ascribe negative qualities to those individuals (they are "weak on crime," "intolerant of diversity," or "puppets of the big corporations"). Both types of political ads are based on the assumption that *information* about the candidates will alter voters' attitudes.

Information-based campaigns can be very successful, as some researchers have documented. Mass media campaigns designed to increase public knowledge about heart disease, to enhance public awareness of crime prevention, or to sell political candidates have all been shown to have statistically significant effects on public opinion and relevant behaviour (e.g., Kinder, 1998; Meyer, Nash, McAlister, Maccoby, & Farquhar, 1980; O'Keefe, 1985).

can use these rules to decide whether a particular message or recommendation is likely to be valid. For instance, the heuristic "Mom always knows best" implies that any communication from Mom should be accepted as accurate.

Do you think that *you* sometimes use heuristics to decide whether a persuasive communication is valid, rather than analyzing the arguments carefully? You may doubt that you accept or reject recommendations based on simple cues or clues. But let's think of some possible examples. You visit your family doctor because you have a persistent cough, and she or he tells you to take a certain medicine and reduce your physical activity for a week or two. Would you try to analyze the validity of these instructions? Most of us accept our doctor's recommendations without debate, because we assume that she or he is the expert. We may even think it would be inappropriate to question her or his instructions. The relevant heuristic here is "Experts are reliable sources of information."

Or imagine that you are watching television, and a story comes on about legal fees. One of the people interviewed is a lawyer, who presents some arguments in favour of increasing legal fees. How would you respond to this interview? Most of us are automatically suspicious of arguments that are delivered by someone who stands to gain or lose from an issue, because we believe that people often argue in self-serving ways even if evidence for their position is lacking. The relevant heuristic here is "People who argue for something that will benefit them personally are not reliable sources of information." Thus, you may simply ignore the interview with the lawyer or reject his or her arguments without careful thought.

As a third example, imagine that you open the local newspaper and see an unusually long and detailed editorial with the title "Using Cell Phones While Driving Should Be Banned." You don't really feel like reading the editorial carefully, so you just skim it and turn to the next page. Would seeing this article influence your attitude toward this issue? Most of us assume that long and detailed messages are probably based on lots of good evidence. After all, don't long messages require more arguments and more substance than short messages? The relevant heuristic here is "Long messages are valid." Thus, you might not read the editorial carefully, but nevertheless assume that it is probably accurate. Simply seeing the long editorial might make you more favourable toward banning the use of cell phones while driving.

Says Who?

Does it matter *who* says something? Are messages from some sources more likely to elicit agreement than identical messages from other sources? The answer to this question is *yes*. Source characteristics can serve as heuristic cues that lead people to agree with a message. As an example of heuristic persuasion, we gave the case of obeying without question our doctor's orders. This example illustrates one of the most researched heuristic cues: the credibility or expertise of the source of the message (see Benoit & Strathman, 2004). The prediction is that people may agree with a message based simply on the credibility of the source rather than on the strength of the arguments. Using this rule probably makes sense in many cases, but it can also lead people to ignore the quality of the message, which may have negative consequences.

In an experiment by Richard Petty, John Cacioppo, and Rachel Goldman (1981), students at the University of Missouri listened to a message arguing that graduating

Expert, authoritative sources can produce agreement through *heuristic persuasion*, based on the idea that experts are reliable sources of information.

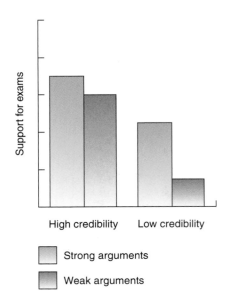

FIGURE 7.11 Favourability of attitudes toward comprehensive exams: Source credibility

From Petty et al., "Personal involvement as a determinant of argument-based persuasion," *Journal of Personality and Social Psychology,* 41, 847–855, 1981. Copyright © 1981 by the American Psychological Association.

soft sell

an advertising strategy that relies on the use of images, emotions, symbols, or values to promote a product

systematic-heuristic model

a theory of attitude change that distinguishes between two types of processing that can occur in response to a persuasive message: systematic processing and heuristic processing

elaboration likelihood model

a theory of attitude change that specifies the conditions under which people will think carefully about the content of a persuasive message. It distinguishes between two types of processing: the central route to persuasion and the peripheral route to persuasion.

seniors should be required to pass a comprehensive examination—a position that was counterattitudinal for almost all students (this topic was also used in a previously described study). The message contained either eight strong arguments or eight weak arguments. Also, the message was said to have been prepared either by "The Carnegie Commission on Higher Education, chaired by a Princeton University professor" (high-credibility condition) or by "a local high school class" (low-credibility condition). We want to focus here on a subset of the conditions in the experiment, in which participants were told that *comprehensive exams would not be instituted for at least a decade*—which meant that the participants would not be affected themselves. These conditions were expected to reduce the threat of the message, because the issue of comprehensive exams would not be personally relevant to the participants. The researchers predicted that these "low-relevance" participants would not really care about the issue and, therefore, would use the heuristic cue of source credibility to judge the message, rather than the strength of the arguments. After listening to the message, participants reported their attitude toward the idea of comprehensive exams for seniors.

Figure 7.11 presents the relevant attitude data. As predicted, participants in these low relevance conditions were more favourable toward comprehensive exams when the message came from the Carnegie Commission on Higher Education (the two left-hand bars) than when it came from a local high school class (the two right-hand bars). In contrast, the manipulation of argument strength had less effect on attitudes: strong arguments produced only slightly more favourable attitudes than did weak arguments. Thus, it didn't matter very much whether the message was strong or weak—what mattered was whether the source was credible or not (see also Chaiken & Maheswaran, 1994; Kumkale & Albarracín, 2004; Wood & Kallgren, 1988).

Credibility is not the only characteristic of the source that influences agreement. We are also more likely to agree with likeable people, with attractive people, and with famous people, compared to unlikeable, unattractive, and unknown people (e.g., Chaiken, 1980; Petty, Cacioppo, & Schumann, 1983; Shavitt, Swan, Lowery, & Wanke, 1994; Wegener & Petty, 1997). Why? The heuristic model of persuasion explains these effects in terms of our assumptions (heuristics) that likeable, attractive, and famous people are usually reliable sources of information.

Earlier, we described the *hard sell* approach to advertising, which is consistent with the predictions of cognitive response theory. A second general approach to advertising, which is consistent with the concept of heuristic persuasion, is known as the **soft sell.** It is described in Social Psychology in Your Life: "Advertising by Association: The Soft Sell."

Two Models of Persuasive Messages

We have described two ways that persuasive communications can produce agreement. One way is via strong arguments that elicit positive thoughts from the recipient. The other way is via superficial cues or heuristics that the recipient assumes indicate that the message is valid, such as an expert source. The first way is described by cognitive response theory, and the second way has been called heuristic persuasion.

Can these different perspectives on persuasive communications be integrated in a single theoretical model? In fact, attitudes researchers have proposed two theories that encompass both ways that messages can elicit agreement: the **systematic-heuristic model** (Chaiken, 1980, 1987) and the **elaboration likelihood model**

Social Psychology in Your Life

Advertising by Association: The Soft Sell

We previously described the hard sell, which involves promoting a product by stressing its positive characteristics and performance. Advertisers do not always try to sell products in this manner, however. In fact, they probably use the soft sell just as often as the hard sell. What is the soft sell? It refers to the use of images, emotions, symbols, or values to sell a product. The advertiser tries to associate the product with positive feelings or images, in the hope that consumers will come to like the product. The soft sell relies, in many cases, on heuristic cues implying that the product is a good one without necessarily providing relevant information.

Examples of the soft sell are easy to find. Many advertisements try to arouse positive emotions or moods, which will then be associated with the product in consumers' minds: humorous ads use jokes or slapstick to evoke positive affect; sentimental ads use babies or puppies to arouse warm feelings and happy memories; and many ads use cheerful or lively music to elicit good moods. These ads often have little information about the product—the goal of the ad is simply to make viewers feel good.

Other advertisements try to link a product with success, attractiveness, or high status without providing specific facts. For instance, beer ads show attractive young people having lots of fun at a party; car ads portray the handsome drivers as popular and successful; and clothing ads show beautiful models in prestigious settings. These images are intended to evoke impressions of happiness, attractiveness, prosperity, and status, which consumers will subconsciously associate with the product. An example of a magazine advertisement that uses the soft sell is presented in Figure 7.12. This advertisement for sunglasses simply shows a beautiful young woman wearing the glasses—no information whatsoever is presented about the features or effectiveness of the sunglasses. The image *is* the message.

FIGURE 7.12 Magazine advertisement that uses the soft sell

Courtesy of The Advertising Archives

Soft sell advertisements sometimes use heuristics about the source to influence consumers. Recall that likeable, credible, and famous people often elicit stronger agreement than unqualified or unknown people, even when the message is identical. Advertisers recognize this fact and hire likeable celebrities, known experts, and famous athletes to promote their products. They hope that the positive evaluation of the celebrity endorser will serve as a heuristic cue to accept his or her recommendation.

What do you think of the soft sell? Do these factors affect you? Are you more likely to buy a product if you find its ads funny? Do cute babies give you a warm glow that generalizes to the product? Do your emotional responses influence your response to messages (see DeSteno, Petty, Rucker, Wegener, & Braverman, 2004)? Are you more likely to try something if it is endorsed by Wayne Gretzky or Shania Twain than if it is endorsed by someone you don't know? Most of us probably think we are relatively immune to these effects, but research suggests that the techniques can be effective. For example, celebrity endorsements, humorous content, and physically attractive sources have all been shown empirically to elicit more favourable attitudes toward advertised products, at least in some circumstances (e.g., Atkin & Block, 1983; Duncan & Nelson, 1985; Petty & Cacioppo, 1983; Wilcox, Murphy, & Sheldon, 1985).

(Petty & Cacioppo, 1981, 1986; Petty, Rucker, Bizer, & Cacioppo, 2004). These theories are similar, though not identical (see Eagly & Chaiken, 1993). They were developed independently by the researchers and appeared at nearly the same time in the published literature. This is an interesting case of different researchers coming to the same conclusions about how to make sense of a diverse set of findings.

Two Types of Processing or Two Routes to Persuasion

systematic processing

careful, deliberative analysis of the arguments in a message

heuristic processing

superficial analysis of a message that focuses on cues indicating the validity or invalidity of the advocated position

central route to persuasion

persuasion that occurs when attitude change results from a careful analysis of the information in a persuasive communication

peripheral route to persuasion

persuasion that occurs when attitude change results from noncognitive factors; it encompasses evaluative conditioning and mere exposure

peripheral cues

simple features or heuristics that are assumed to indicate that a message is valid

The systematic-heuristic model of persuasion is designed to explain the effectiveness of persuasive messages. The model distinguishes between two types of processing that can occur when people encounter a persuasive communication. **Systematic processing** occurs when people think earnestly about the message; it involves a thoughtful analysis of the relevant information. **Heuristic processing** occurs when people rely on cues (heuristics) to make judgments about the message, without thinking carefully about the arguments that are presented.

Similarly, the elaboration likelihood model of persuasion is designed to explain the effectiveness of persuasive messages and distinguishes between two "routes to persuasion," which correspond closely to the types of processing identified in the systematic-heuristic model. The **central route to persuasion** occurs when attitude change results from a careful analysis of the information in a persuasive communication; it parallels systematic processing. The **peripheral route to persuasion** occurs when attitude change results from noncognitive factors; it parallels heuristic processing, although it also encompasses other affective processes like evaluative conditioning and mere exposure (see Chapter 6). This model was called the *elaboration likelihood model* because it specifies the conditions under which people are *likely* to *elaborate* on a message (i.e., to think about the message's arguments).

Each theory hypothesizes that the effectiveness of messages depends on different factors in the two types of processing or routes to persuasion. When recipients of a message are processing systematically (which activates the central route to persuasion), the main determinant of attitude change is the strength of the arguments. Strong arguments elicit agreement, whereas weak arguments elicit disagreement. On the other hand, when recipients of a message are processing heuristically (which activates the peripheral route to persuasion), the main determinant of attitude change is the presence of simple features or heuristics (labelled **peripheral cues** in the elaboration likelihood model) that the recipient assumes indicate that the message is valid, such as a famous source or a long message. If such cues are present, the recipient agrees with the message, but if such cues are absent, the recipient rejects the message.

The accompanying Concept Review summarizes the key features of the systematic-heuristic and elaboration likelihood models.

Do you think that persuasion that results from one type of processing will be more enduring than persuasion that results from the other type of processing? Will someone's endorsement of a position be more stable if it resulted from thinking about the arguments (systematic processing; the central route) or if it resulted from adopting a position because of the source or the length of the message (heuristic processing; the peripheral route)? If you said that systematic processing will produce more enduring attitude change than heuristic processing, your prediction matches

CONCEPT REVIEW
Two Models of Persuasive Messages

Theory	Key Processes	Nature of Processing	Determinants of Persuasion
Systematic-heuristic model	Systematic processing	Rational, information-based	Argument strength
	Heuristic processing	Superficial, simple cues	Heuristic cues
Elaboration likelihood model	Central route to persuasion	Rational, information-based	Argument strength
	Peripheral route to persuasion	Superficial, noncognitive	Peripheral cues

that of the original theorists (see Chaiken, 1987; Petty & Cacioppo, 1986). Why would this difference in stability occur? When we think carefully about the arguments on an issue and decide that they are compelling, we can use those arguments to resist subsequent attacks on our new position. But if we simply adopt a position because the source is famous or the message is long, we do not have any arguments that we can use to resist new persuasive attacks; thus, our new attitude is less likely to survive over time.

Motivation and Ability

The key contribution of the systematic-heuristic and elaboration likelihood models was that they specified *when* each kind of persuasion is likely to occur. Both models predict that the recipient's *motivation* and *ability* jointly determine which route is activated.

These predictions are based on the idea that the process of thinking carefully about a message and analyzing the strength of the arguments is effortful and potentially difficult. Therefore, people will engage in this kind of demanding thought only when it is necessary (recall the *cognitive miser model* of information processing in Chapter 3; see page 85). Why tire yourself out thinking about issues that won't affect you? Why bother analyzing a message carefully that addresses a problem you will never have? In these sorts of situations, people will opt for the easier route of looking for heuristics that give them clues about the message's validity.

Each model predicts that systematic processing (the central route) will occur *only* when the individual (1) is *motivated* to exert the necessary effort *and* (2) has the *ability* to process the message carefully (e.g., can pay attention and understand the arguments). If either motivation *or* ability is missing, then the only way that persuasion can occur is via the peripheral route (heuristic processing).

Thus, both motivation and ability are necessary for systematic processing to occur. When are these conditions likely to be present? Researchers have identified several variables that affect either recipients' motivation or their ability to process a message carefully. We will discuss two of these factors: personal relevance and message complexity.

Personal Relevance. The most studied factor affecting people's motivation to process a message carefully has been personal relevance: whether or not the topic or issue will affect someone directly. If the topic of a persuasive communication has implications for someone's personal outcomes, then it is high in personal relevance, and the individual is likely to be motivated to process the message carefully. If a persuasive communication addresses something that will not affect the recipient, then it is low in personal relevance, and the individual will probably not be motivated to think about the arguments carefully.

Imagine that you are looking to buy snow tires for your car and have definitely narrowed your choice to Bridgestone Blizzaks or Michelin Alpins. If you are sitting in your doctor's waiting room and see a magazine story on Bridgestone Blizzaks, you will be very motivated to read it carefully because it might give you information that is important for your decision. But if you see a magazine story on Goodyear Ultra Grips, you will be less likely to read it carefully because it does not have personal implications for you. In the former case, when the message is high in personal relevance, your response to the article (e.g., your evaluation of Blizzaks) will be based on the strength of the arguments. In the latter case, when the message is low in personal relevance, your response to the article (e.g., your evaluation of Ultra Grips) may be based on heuristic cues like the expertise of the author or the attractiveness of the models in the photographs.

Researchers testing the heuristic-systematic or elaboration likelihood models have conducted experiments in which they manipulated the personal relevance of a persuasive message for participants. The prediction of the researchers was that when a message was high in personal relevance, persuasion would depend on the strength of the arguments, whereas when a message was low in personal relevance, persuasion would depend on the presence of heuristic cues like source expertise.

In fact, the experiment by Richard Petty and his colleagues (1981) that we described earlier for the heuristic model of persuasion actually tested the larger, integrative theories. Recall that participants heard a message arguing that graduating seniors should be required to pass a comprehensive examination. The message contained either strong arguments or weak arguments, and was allegedly prepared either by a Princeton University professor (a high-credibility source) or by a local high school class (a low-credibility source). When participants were told that the comprehensive examinations would not be instituted for at least ten years (the low–personal-relevance conditions; Figure 7.11), participants were somewhat more persuaded by strong arguments than by weak arguments, but the credibility of the source made even more difference: the message from the high-credibility source produced much more favourable attitudes toward comprehensive exams than did the message from the low-credibility source. We have reproduced these low-relevance data again in Figure 7.13 (the four bars on the left half of the figure). But we also have included in Figure 7.13 the attitude findings for another set of conditions, in which participants were told that comprehensive exams were being considered for possible adoption *at their own university in the coming year.* This information meant that the exams could affect the participants directly, which made the topic high in personal relevance. Figure 7.13 shows that in these high–personal-relevance conditions (the four bars on the right half of the figure), the expertise of the source made almost no difference whatsoever; all that mattered was the strength of the arguments. When participants were motivated to process the message carefully, they were persuaded by strong arguments and rejected weak arguments, irrespective of the source of the arguments. These findings suggest that the high–personal-relevance conditions elicited systematic processing (or activated the central route to persuasion). In contrast, the low–personal-relevance conditions elicited heuristic processing (or activated the peripheral route to persuasion).

Leandre Fabrigar, who is at Queen's University in Kingston, Ontario, and his colleagues investigated the effects on persuasion of a factor that is related to personal relevance: attitude accessibility (Fabrigar, Priester, Petty, & Wegener, 1998). When an issue is personally relevant to someone, his or her attitude on that issue tends to be highly accessible (we defined attitude accessibility in Chapter 6 as the ease or speed with which an attitude comes to mind; see page 226). Thus, individuals with very accessible attitudes on an issue might be expected to process messages related to the issue more carefully or systematically than individuals with less accessible attitudes. Consistent with this reasoning, Fabrigar and his colleagues showed that the strength of the arguments in a message about nuclear power was more important for people with highly accessible

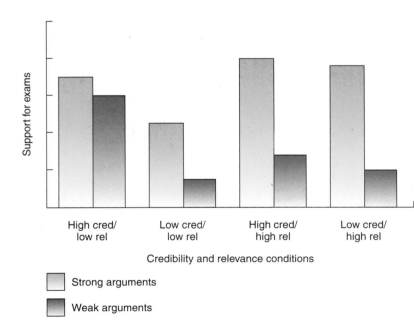

FIGURE 7.13 Favourability of attitudes toward comprehensive exams: Low- and high-relevance conditions

From Petty et al., "Personal involvement as a determinant of argument-based persuasion," *Journal of Personality and Social Psychology,* 41, 847–855, 1981. Copyright © 1981 by the American Psychological Association.

attitudes than for people with less accessible attitudes. That is, people with highly accessible attitudes were persuaded by messages with strong arguments but not by messages with weak arguments, whereas people with low-accessibility attitudes were about equally persuaded by messages with either strong or weak arguments.

Message Complexity. The personal relevance of a topic influences whether people will be *motivated* to process a persuasive communication carefully. Other factors influence whether people will be *able* to process a message carefully. For example, people who are being distracted from a message cannot pay close attention to its content. But perhaps the clearest example of a factor that influences the ability to process carefully is the complexity or comprehensibility of the message (Cooper, Bennett, & Sukel, 1996; Hafer, Reynolds, & Obertynski, 1996).

Carolyn Hafer and her students (1996) conducted an interesting experiment at Brock University in St. Catharines, Ontario, that tested students' responses to a persuasive message on *plea bargaining*. Plea bargaining occurs when a person accused of a crime agrees to plead guilty in return for getting a reduced charge or a shorter sentence. At the time the study was conducted, the highly publicized case of Karla Homolka's plea bargain was still fresh in people's memories in St. Catharines. Karla Homolka was the wife of Paul Bernardo. This couple kidnapped, sexually assaulted, and murdered two teenaged girls in St. Catharines. Homolka claimed that she was coerced by her husband to participate in the murders. In a plea bargain, she agreed to plead guilty and testify against her husband in return for a relatively short sentence. Shortly after the plea bargain was reached, however, videotapes of the murders were found, which showed that Homolka was more involved in the events than she had stated and which also made her testimony against her husband much less important in the case against him. Almost everyone in St. Catharines thought that Homolka's plea bargain was too lenient; thus, almost everyone had a negative attitude toward plea bargaining. (Homolka served 12 years in prison for the murders. She was released in July 2005.)

Participants listened to a taped message that argued in favour of plea bargaining. The credibility of the source was manipulated: some participants were told that the speaker was His Honour Judge William Grovestead, a summa cum laude graduate of Harvard Law School, who had been sitting on the bench for 15 years and was an expert on plea bargaining, whereas other participants were told that the speaker was William Grovestead, a second-year law student at Rockway University, who had recently become interested in plea bargaining. The strength of the arguments was also manipulated: the message contained either five strong arguments or five weak arguments supporting plea bargaining. Finally, and most importantly for our current focus, the complexity or comprehensibility of the message was manipulated: the arguments were stated either in clear and straightforward language (e.g., "Plea bargaining may make a charge more appropriate to the circumstances of a crime") or in complex and difficult-to-understand language (e.g., "Plea bargaining can acquire a conviction by obtaining a guilty plea in a weak case that may otherwise yield an acquittal, should the case be held over for trial").

The researchers predicted that even though the message would be high in relevance to everyone because of the well-publicized local trial, participants who listened to the complex message would not be *able* to understand what the speaker was saying; thus, the strength of the arguments would not matter, and the only factor that would influence persuasion would be the expertise of the source (a heuristic cue). In contrast, participants who listened to the simpler and clearer version of the message *would* be able to understand the arguments, so strong arguments would produce more persuasion than weak arguments, and the expertise of the source would be relatively unimportant. These patterns were exactly what the results showed (see Figure 7.14). When participants were unable to process the message carefully because it was so complex (the four bars on the right side of the figure), they were

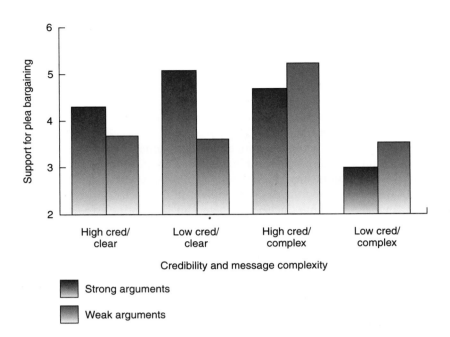

FIGURE 7.14

Favourability of attitudes toward plea bargaining

From Hafer et al., "Message comprehensibility and persuasion: Effects of complex language in counterattitudinal appeals to laypeople," *Social Cognition*, 14, 317–337, 1996. Reprinted by permission of Guilford Publications.

more favourable toward plea bargaining when the source was Judge Grovestead than when the source was student Grovestead, but the strength of the arguments did not affect persuasion. When participants listened to the easy-to-understand message (the four left-most bars), they were more favourable toward plea bargaining when the arguments were strong than when the arguments were weak, and the credibility of the source did not affect persuasion.

Cultural Differences in Attitude Change

Most empirical studies of persuasion have been conducted in North America, which raises questions about the generalizability of the findings to other cultures. In this section, we consider some possible differences in attitude change processes based on cultural factors.

In Chapters 4 and 5, we noted that the *self* is viewed as independent and autonomous in *individualist cultures* (e.g., Western Europe and North America) but as interdependent and role-based in *collectivist cultures* (e.g., East Asian and South American countries). Are these cultural differences relevant to any processes involved in attitude change? In this section, we discuss two possible cultural differences: in dissonance arousal and in responses to persuasive messages.

Cultural Differences in Dissonance Arousal

Dissonance theory suggests that people feel bad when they behave in ways that are inconsistent with their attitudes and, as a result, may change their attitudes to be more consistent with their actions. For example, asking people to tell someone else that a boring task is interesting causes them to rate the task as more enjoyable (e.g., Festinger & Carlsmith, 1959), or inducing people to write a counterattitudinal essay sways them to become more favourable to the position they argued in the essay (e.g., Cohen, 1962). These effects are presumed to reflect that people believe that they *should* behave in ways that are consistent with their attitudes and values.

But do the assumptions underlying dissonance theory generalize to collectivist cultures? Do people who have an interdependent self feel the same need to behave in ways that are consistent with their attitudes? Some evidence suggests that they might not.

Steve Heine and Darrin Lehman at the University of British Columbia (1997a) hypothesized that people from collectivist cultures would experience less dissonance arousal following a standard dissonance manipulation than people from individualist cultures. Heine and Lehman tested this prediction in a study of postdecisional dissonance using the free choice paradigm. Canadian and Japanese participants were given a choice between one of two music CDs as payment for their participation. The two CDs (along with eight others) had been evaluated previously by the participant and were always approximately equal in attractiveness. Shortly after their selection of one CD, participants re-evaluated all ten CDs that they had rated earlier (including the chosen and rejected CDs). Dissonance theory predicts that after making a decision, people are motivated to evaluate the chosen alternative more positively and the rejected alternative more negatively (e.g., Brehm, 1956; Zanna & Sande, 1987). Heine and Lehman found that Canadian participants exhibited this "spreading of alternatives," with the chosen CD going up in attractiveness and the rejected CD going down in attractiveness. Japanese participants, however, did not show significant changes in their evaluations of either CD. The authors concluded that dissonance theory might not generalize to collectivist cultures.

University of Waterloo researchers Etsuko Hoshino-Browne, Adam Zanna, Steve Spencer, and Mark Zanna (2004), however, challenged the conclusion that people from collectivist cultures do not experience dissonance. These researchers suggested instead that *different kinds of events cause dissonance* in collectivist cultures. They proposed that people in all cultures experience dissonance when their culturally valued self-views are threatened by their own behaviour. In Canada, the culturally valued self-view is an *independent* self, which is threatened when behaviour is inconsistent with personal attitudes or goals. But in collectivist cultures, the culturally valued self-view is an *interdependent* self. When will an interdependent self be threatened? Hoshino-Browne and her colleagues had the clever idea that asking collectivist participants to make a decision that has implications *for someone else* might arouse postdecisional dissonance. After all, people from collectivist cultures define the self in terms of relations with other people, so they might feel threatened when someone else is disappointed with a decision they made.

Hoshino-Browne and her colleagues (2004) included as participants both Asian Canadians born in Asia who identified strongly with their Asian culture and European Canadians born in Canada. Participants were told that they were helping a Chinese restaurant develop a special lunch menu. Some participants rated how much they would like each of ten Chinese dishes. They were then told that they would receive a gift certificate for one of two dishes and made a choice between two of the dishes that were approximately equally attractive. Other participants were asked to rate how much *a close friend* would like each of the ten dishes. They were then told that their friend would receive a gift certificate for one of two dishes and made a choice between two equally attractive dishes *for their friend*. All participants subsequently re-rated the ten dishes for how much they or their friend would like them, including the chosen and rejected dishes.

Figure 7.15 shows how much participants exhibited attitude change (a "spreading of alternatives," presumably to reduce dissonance) after their decision—that is, the extent to which they rated the chosen dish more positively and/or the rejected dish less positively after the decision. European Canadians showed more attitude change (spreading of alternatives) after making a choice for themselves than after making a choice for a close friend. Asian Canadians, however, showed more attitude change

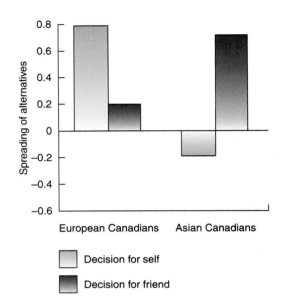

FIGURE 7.15 Attitude change after decision by European Canadians and Asian Canadians

From Hoshino-Browne, et al., "Investigating attitudes cross-culturally: A case of cognitive dissonance among East Asians and North Americans," in Haddock and Maio, eds., *Contemporary Perspectives on the Psychology of Attitudes* (pp. 375–398), Fig. 4, 2002. Reprinted by permission of the Taylor & Francis Group.

after making a choice for a close friend than after making a choice for themselves. In fact, the Asian Canadians did not show any dissonance reduction at all when choosing for themselves—a finding that replicated the results for Japanese participants by Heine and Lehman (1997a). Asian Canadians apparently experienced postdecisional dissonance only when their decision had implications for another person.

These data suggest that dissonance arousal does occur in people from collectivist cultures, but the types of behaviour that produce it are different than in individualist cultures (see also Hoshino-Browne, Zanna, Spencer, Zanna, Kitayama, & Lackenbauer, 2005; Kitayama, Snibbe, Markus, & Suzuki, 2004). In collectivist cultures, actions may have to relate to other people in order to threaten the individual's "interdependent" self.

Cultural Differences in Responses to Persuasive Messages

As we noted in the earlier section on cognitive response theory, persuasive messages often rely on information. Information-based communications are effective when they present strong evidence or compelling arguments that there will be positive consequences associated with accepting the recommendations in the message (e.g., positive consequences will be associated with abolishing the death penalty, or with buying this product). But is it possible that people in different cultures will find different evidence or arguments compelling? Will people in individualist versus collectivist cultures respond favourably to different kinds of information?

Sang-pil Han and Sharon Shavitt at the University of Illinois (1994) predicted that people from individualist cultures would respond most favourably to messages describing positive *personal* consequences of the recommendations because such appeals are consistent with the "independent self" that is encouraged in these cultures. In contrast, Han and Shavitt predicted that people from collectivist cultures would respond most favourably to messages describing positive *interpersonal* consequences of the recommendations because such appeals are consistent with the "interdependent self" that is encouraged in these cultures.

To test this reasoning, the researchers looked at magazine advertisements in the United States (an individualist culture) and Korea (a collectivist culture). They sampled a total of 100 ads from each of two American and two Korean magazines (*Newsweek, Redbook, Wolgan Chosun,* and *Yosong Donga*). They then showed these ads to bilingual judges, who scored each ad for individualism and collectivism. An ad received a high score for individualism when it appealed to independence (e.g., "She's got a style all her own"), personal benefits (e.g., "A quick return for your investment"), or personal goals (e.g., "Make your way through the crowd"). An ad received a high score for collectivism when it appealed to family or group cohesiveness (e.g., "We have a way of bringing people closer together"), interdependent relationships (e.g., "Successful partnerships"), or group goals (e.g., "The dream of prosperity for all of us").

Results showed that, overall, the ads were rated as more individualistic than collectivistic, which probably reflected that everyone buys products for personal benefits, at least in part. However, American ads were rated as significantly more individualistic than were Korean ads, whereas Korean ads were rated as significantly more collectivistic than were American ads. Thus, the nature of the advertisements in each country reflected, to some extent, the individualism–collectivism of the culture.

Han and Shavitt (1994) followed up their survey of American and Korean magazines with a controlled experiment that tested the same reasoning. The researchers created two versions of advertisements for four products (chewing gum, running shoes, detergents, and clothes irons). All of the ads contained a headline and illustrations. One version presented an "individualistic" headline (e.g., "Treat yourself to a breath freshening experience") and a picture of an individual using the product, whereas the second version presented a "collectivistic" headline (e.g., "Share the Freedent breath freshening experience") and a picture of a group of people. Participants from the United States and Korea rated each ad for how persuasive it was and how much they would like to try the product. Americans responded to the individualistic versions of the ads more favourably than the collectivistic versions, whereas Koreans showed the opposite pattern—more favourable responses to the collectivistic versions of the ads. These data show that cultural differences can occur in responses to persuasive messages.

Persuasion in the Health Domain: Fear Appeals

Have you ever looked at the warnings that are printed on Canadian cigarette packages? If you are a smoker, you will certainly have seen them, but if you are a nonsmoker, you might not know much about them. Beginning in 2000, tobacco companies were required to put explicit, full-colour, and sometimes graphic photos on their cigarette packages—things like a cancerous lung or a damaged heart—along with appropriate text (e.g., "Warning: CIGARETTES CAUSE LUNG CANCER. Every cigarette you smoke increases your chances of getting lung cancer"). Another photo shows a curled, limp cigarette, along with a warning that smoking can cause impotence. The photos and statements completely fill the top half of both the front and the back of the package. Inside the cigarette package, another written message is presented, which often contains tips about how to quit.

Do you think that these warnings will motivate smokers to quit smoking? In 2001, the Canadian Cancer Society conducted a national survey of smokers to assess the impact of the new, vivid warnings. The survey showed that 90% of Canadian smokers had noticed the new warnings (what on earth were the other 10% doing?), 44% said that the warnings increased their motivation to quit smoking, 43% said that they were more concerned about the health effects of smoking because of the warnings, and among those people who had attempted to quit smoking, 38% said that the warnings were a motivating factor. These data indicate that the warnings were having considerable impact on smokers.

Questions about effective persuasion concerning health issues are very important. How can the government motivate healthy lifestyles, both to improve the quality of

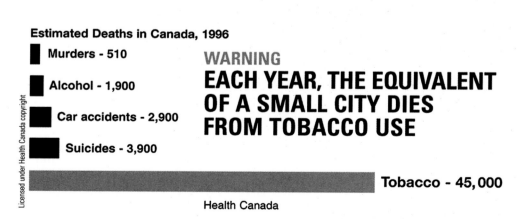

Estimated Deaths in Canada, 1996

Murders - 510

Alcohol - 1,900

Car accidents - 2,900

Suicides - 3,900

Tobacco - 45,000

Health Canada

Do fear-provoking images on cigarette packages convince smokers to quit?

WARNING
EACH YEAR, THE EQUIVALENT OF A SMALL CITY DIES FROM TOBACCO USE

people's lives and to save money on health care? How can spouses or parents convince a family member to stop smoking or avoid drug use? How can doctors motivate their patients to stay on a medication or perform simple self-examinations? Answers to these questions are, quite literally, life-and-death.

In most cases, health campaigns seem designed to threaten people with the dire consequences of performing, or of failing to perform, certain actions (Salovey & Wegener, 2002). Anti-drug campaigns illustrate "your brain on drugs" as an egg sizzling loudly in a frying pan. Pro-exercise campaigns identify obesity and heart disease as consequences of inactivity. Anti–drunk-driving campaigns show home videos of young children or young families who were subsequently killed by a drunk driver. Clearly, one goal of these messages is to arouse the emotion of fear in the audience.

Effectiveness of Fear Appeals

Is arousing fear an effective way to change your attitudes and behaviour? Are you more likely to follow the recommendations of a message when it has frightened you about what might happen if you don't?

Social psychologists have been interested in the effectiveness of fear appeals for many decades. The results of early studies were inconsistent (see Janis & Feshbach, 1953; McGuire, 1969), but there is now little doubt that the arousal of fear generally *increases* the impact of messages on attitudes and behavioural intentions (see Cho & Witte, 2004; Das, de Wit, & Stroebe, 2003; Eagly & Chaiken, 1993; Perloff, 2003). The usual explanation of this finding is that fear is an aversive state, which people want to reduce; people accept the recommendations of the message because doing so diminishes their fear (this is called a "drive reduction" hypothesis).

Does this conclusion surprise you? Some social commentators argue that fear is a poor way to motivate people because it is a "negative" and "extrinsic" motivator that will not have lasting effects. These observers suggest that because fear is unpleasant, people either will try to escape or will be so distracted that they won't listen to the message. But the empirical data indicate that fear does *not* typically reduce attention or comprehension of information related to the fear; if anything, fear tends to increase attention (e.g., Baron, Logan, Lilly, Inman, & Brennan, 1994; Gleicher & Petty, 1992; Salovey, Rothman, & Rodin, 1998).

Protection Motivation Theory

What kinds of health problems (or other threats) arouse the most fear? Think about your own reactions to information about illnesses such as cancer, heart disease, mental illness, and Alzheimer's disease: What specific aspects of these problems are fear-arousing? For instance, why are people more afraid of cancer than colds? Why are Canadians more afraid of heart disease than leprosy?

Ronald Rogers (1983) at the University of Alabama suggested that two specific beliefs arouse threat: (1) the problem is *severe,* and (2) you are *susceptible* to the problem. For instance, cancer is more fear-provoking than colds because cancer is more severe: cancer can kill you, but colds only make you uncomfortable. Heart disease is more fear-arousing in our culture than leprosy not because it is necessarily more severe, but rather because we feel susceptible to heart disease but not to leprosy: we can easily imagine how we might develop heart disease, but cannot easily imagine how we would get leprosy.

Rogers proposed that these perceptions of severity and susceptibility are threatening and arouse fear (see Das et al., 2003). But two additional factors are necessary before the fear will translate into attitude and behaviour change. In order for a message about a health problem to actually change listeners' behaviour, they must also believe (3) the *recommendations will be effective* in avoiding the problem, and (4) they are *personally capable* of performing the recommended behaviours. If the recommendations will not necessarily reduce listeners' risk, or if they feel incapable of doing the recommended behaviours, then they will not change their lifestyle. For instance, people who feel threatened by heart disease won't start exercising as a solution unless they believe that exercise will definitely reduce their risk. If it might not work, why bother? Also, people who feel threatened by lung cancer won't try to quit smoking as a solution unless they believe that they are personally capable of quitting successfully. If they're just going to fail, what's the point?

Rogers (1983; Maddux & Rogers, 1983) combined these four principles into **protection motivation theory,** which is a model that articulates how threatening messages can influence attitudes and behaviour. Rogers proposed that people will change attitudes and behaviour only when they are *motivated* to *protect* themselves (hence, *protection motivation* theory). Such motivation will be greatest when all four beliefs are present.

Table 7.3 provides an analysis of how, based on protection motivation theory, a message could be designed to convince university students *to reduce their unprotected exposure to the sun and their visits to tanning salons* (see also Witte, Meyer, & Martell, 2001). First, they must believe that the problem is severe. Skin cancer is definitely severe. Even leathery, wrinkled skin at an early age is pretty severe to young people concerned about their appearance. Second, they must believe that they

protection motivation theory
a model that articulates how threatening messages can influence attitudes and behaviour

---

TABLE 7.3
Using Protection Motivation Theory to Create a Message About Sun Exposure

Belief That Must Be Created	*Possible Arguments*
1. The problem is severe.	Exposure to the sun can cause skin cancer, which can disfigure and even kill. Exposure to the sun causes the skin to become leathery and wrinkled at an early age.
2. They are susceptible to the problem.	Suffering just a few serious sunburns greatly increases the probability of skin cancer. People with all hair colours and skin shades can develop skin cancer from too much sun.
3. The recommended behaviours will be effective in avoiding the problem.	Statistics show that smaller numbers of sunburns over one's lifetime are associated with lower rates of skin cancer. Applying sunscreen virtually eliminates harmful rays from the sun.
4. They are capable of performing the recommended behaviours.	If someone wants a tanned appearance, it can be safely achieved with skin-darkening creams. Applying sunscreen is simple and can even be fun when members of a couple apply it to one another.

are personally susceptible to the problem. This goal might be accomplished by explaining that even a small number of serious sunburns dramatically increases the probability of eventually developing skin cancer. Perceived susceptibility might also be increased by stating that people with all hair colours and skin shades, even those with dark hair and skin, can develop skin cancer from too much sun exposure. Third, they must be convinced that staying out of the sun and using sunscreen when exposure is unavoidable will significantly reduce their chances of developing a problem. Statistics about relative risk, focusing on how the probability of skin cancer decreases with decreased exposure, might achieve this goal. Also, explaining that applying sunscreen virtually eliminates harmful rays will increase perceived effectiveness. Finally, they must believe that they are capable of performing the recommended actions. Some people will argue, for example, that they simply must look good and, therefore, cannot give up the sun. Perhaps these individuals could be told that they can use products to darken their skin without sun exposure and still achieve the "golden" look they desire. They can also be told that applying sunscreen is simple—and can even be *fun* when members of a couple apply it to one another!

Tests of protection motivation theory have been largely supportive (see Aspinwall, Kemeny, Taylor, Schneider, & Dudley, 1991; Das et al., 2003; Rogers & Mewborn, 1976; Sturges & Rogers, 1996; van der Velde & van der Pligt, 1991; Witte & Allen, 2000). Fear appeals seem to be most effective when they successfully create the four beliefs identified by the theory.

   ## Propaganda

We have discussed a variety of ways that attitudes can change. For the most part, our examples have focused on "legitimate" persuasion: attitude change that occurs in normal, familiar sorts of situations, such as postdecisional dissonance, interpersonal influence, and persuasive messages in the media (although some of our examples have admittedly been unusual, such as the grasshopper-eating study). Our goal has been to understand rationalization and persuasion in everyday life.

But some kinds of influence go beyond the usual limits. The person or group doing the persuading may have selfish motives that are kept secret, or may intentionally distort the facts to achieve persuasion. These examples move into the domain of propaganda.

What Is Propaganda?

propaganda

a persuasive attempt that is motivated by an ideology, or set of values, and that is deliberately biased in its presentation of information

Propaganda is a persuasive attempt (or a campaign of many persuasive attempts) that is motivated by a specific ideology, or set of values, and that is deliberately biased in its presentation of the issues. The source of the propaganda has a value-based agenda (e.g., a religious view, a political position, or some other value system) and is willing to distort the facts to convince others to adopt the same view. Anthony Pratkanis and Elliot Aronson (2001) of the University of California at Santa Cruz described propaganda as attempted influence through "the use of images, slogans, and symbols that play on our prejudices and emotions . . . with the ultimate goal of having the recipient of the appeal come to 'voluntarily' accept this position as if it were his or her own" (p. 11). A key element of propaganda, then, is that the source does not present a balanced treatment of the issues and allow listeners to weigh the arguments for each side in a rational manner; instead, the propagandist presents only his or her desired side and usually appeals to emotions rather than to reason.

Of course, judgments about whether a person or group has "a value-based agenda" and is "willing to distort the facts" are subjective. Are political campaigns value-based, and do political candidates knowingly distort the facts? What about advertising: Is the goal of profit an ideology? And do advertisers care if consumers are fooled into buying something they don't want or don't need? What about established, organized religions: are they deliberately selective in presenting religious information to members?

Rather than classifying persuasive attempts as either propaganda or nonpropaganda, it makes sense to think about them as being *more* or *less* "propagandistic"—a dimension from *not at all* to *extremely* propagandistic. An example of a persuasive attempt that is not at all propagandistic would be a two-sided, argument-based message that is presented without extrinsic pressure (e.g., an article in *Consumer Reports* outlining the strengths and weaknesses of a product, or a lecture in a class presenting supportive and nonsupportive evidence for a scientific theory). An example of a persuasive attempt that is somewhat propagandistic would be an emotional appeal that is unabashedly one-sided (e.g., an advertisement for a charity that is designed to arouse guilt, or a "soft sell" advertisement that uses images to sell a product). An example of a persuasive attempt that is extremely propagandistic would be a deliberately deceptive presentation that promotes an ideology (e.g., a regimented program of indoctrination in a cult, or an advertisement in a political campaign that knowingly distorts the facts to arouse fear about an opponent).

Propaganda, then, is a matter of degree. In the following sections, we describe examples of propaganda, beginning with some extreme or obvious cases and then moving to some everyday and more subtle cases.

War and Propaganda

One event that is a reliable cause of unambiguous propaganda is war. The saying "All is fair in love and war" seems to be embraced by all governments during wartime. There is usually deliberate manipulation of the media at home, as well as distribution of propagandistic materials in enemy territories. For example, during the Second World War, allied military sources strictly controlled all information about the war that was given to the media; the information was manipulated to maintain morale and support for the war effort. The allies also sent radio broadcasts and dropped leaflets into enemy areas, which were designed to lower morale and to encourage resistance.

More recently, in the war in Iraq, American media correspondents were "embedded" into military units and actually accompanied soldiers into battle areas. The reporters were strictly controlled, however, in terms of the information they could convey to viewers. For example, one correspondent, Geraldo Rivera, was thrown out of Iraq after he used a stick to draw a rough map in the sand to show on camera the movements of his unit.

Prisoners of war (POWs) have sometimes been exposed to "indoctrination" procedures, designed either to create total obedience or to generate sympathy toward the captors' cause. For instance, Nazi treatment of Jewish prisoners and, to a lesser extent, allied military prisoners was brutal, with physical punishment and executions used frequently and openly to produce terror and obedience. There was little attempt by the Nazis to change their POWs' attitudes—many of them regarded their prisoners as subhuman (Welch, 1983). In the Korean War, however, Chinese captors exposed American POWs to more humane, but nevertheless manipulative, propaganda techniques (see Lifton, 1961). The Chinese did not try to convince American soldiers that Communism was the best thing for the United States, but they did try to convince them that Communism was right for China. The Chinese captors (1) made prisoners listen to repeated information sessions, (2) spread rumours about

During wartime, governments and military authorities exert tight control over information provided to the media.

AP Photo/Dusan Vranic

American actions in the war, and (3) carefully rewarded any positive comments about the Communist system. The result of these techniques was that when the soldiers returned to the United States after the war, some expressed sympathy for Communism in China. The American military became very concerned about the "brainwashing" that had been performed, although further investigation showed that very few soldiers were strongly affected.

Cults and Propaganda

destructive cult

a rigidly structured group, led by a charismatic leader, that recruits and retains members using manipulative, deceptive techniques

Another source of unambiguous propaganda is cults. Although the term *cult* is familiar to most people, we need to provide a specific definition. We adopt the perspective of Frank MacHovec (1989), who defined a **destructive cult** as "a rigidly structured group . . . under a charismatic leader, which isolates itself from established societal traditions, values, and norms, recruits members deceptively without informed consent, and retains them by . . . manipulative techniques which deny freedom of choice" (p. 10). Thus, cults normally revolve around a persuasive, magnetic figure who preaches that contact with the rest of society must be minimized, often describing people outside the cult as evil and dangerous. Perhaps most important, cults use techniques for recruitment and retention that are knowingly designed to induce people to join and stay even if they don't really want to.

What are some well-known cults that operate in Canada? One is the Unification Church, whose members are also known as "Moonies" (see Clay, 1987; Hassan, 1988; Swenson, 1987). The Unification Church is led by Sun Myung Moon, who was born in Korea in 1920. Moon established the church in 1954, claiming that Jesus came to him in a vision when he was 16 years old and told him that he was the second Messiah, who would form the nucleus of God's family on earth. In 1957, Moon published *The Divine Principle,* which became the bible of his movement. In 1972, with the church well established in South Korea, Moon moved to the United States, where he purchased a US$625 000 estate in northern New York. In the 1970s, the Unification Church expanded into Canada and invested in many businesses, including hotels, newspapers, and fish-processing plants. It also expanded to other countries, including

Nigeria, Japan, and Uruguay. In 1982, Moon was convicted of conspiracy, obstruction of justice, and perjury relating to his failure to pay taxes on interest income from a US$1.6 million bank account. He spent 13 months in prison—a sentence that his followers declared was the result of religious prejudice.

The church's income is currently in the hundreds of millions of dollars annually. Estimated membership is approximately 2 million worldwide. Members receive only food and shelter—all earned income goes to the church. Much of the money earned by the church is tax-free because of the organization's religious status. Members live in communal groups, segregated by sex. Marriage is allowed only by the personal decision of Moon, who matches partners. In one particularly extraordinary marriage ceremony in 1997, Moon officiated at the simultaneous weddings of 28 000 couples at the Robert F. Kennedy Stadium in Washington, DC.

How do cults obtain such obedience and sacrifice? How do they convince people to change their lifestyle completely and to give control over their life to the cult's leader? We describe in the following paragraphs some of the techniques used by cults (see Baron, 2000; Clay, 1987; Galanter, 1989; Hassan, 1988; Pratkanis & Aronson, 2001; Swenson, 1987). These techniques are neither unusual nor extremely powerful individually; indeed, the techniques are used routinely by salespersons, advertisers, and religious and nonreligious groups that we would not consider cults. But cults use the techniques simultaneously, deliberately, and forcefully, which can be very powerful.

Selective Targeting of Potential Recruits. In seeking potential recruits, cults target young people between the ages of 18 and 30, especially those with a strong social conscience who are looking for a "cause" to follow. Cults will focus on people who have experienced a recent trauma or loss, such as the death of a loved one, the dissolution of a relationship, or a significant failure at school or work. People who have suffered a recent loss are emotionally vulnerable and may be easier to manipulate than people who feel satisfied with their current lifestyle.

Young people are often uncertain about their identity and values. Ian McGregor, a social psychologist at York University in Toronto, has conducted a fascinating program of research demonstrating that feelings of personal uncertainty can cause individuals to embrace extremist, rigid views (e.g., McGregor, 2003; McGregor & Marigold, 2003; McGregor, Zanna, Holmes, & Spencer, 2001). McGregor has argued and shown that personal uncertainty causes discomfort, which can be relieved by endorsing a set of beliefs with conviction. Thus, young people may endorse extremist ideologies (e.g., a cult's doctrine) with conviction because such zeal compensates for personal uncertainty.

Isolation of Recruits Away from Noncult Influences. Cults try to bring recruits to locations that are removed from their familiar surroundings. For instance, young people will be invited to attend a "weekend retreat," where they can learn more about the group. These retreats give the cult complete control over the recruits' environment, allowing extensive socialization procedures and significant interpersonal pressure to be applied. If someone does join a cult, he or she is almost always forced to move into a cult-controlled environment (e.g., a commune) and to sever all contact with noncult friends and family.

Sleep Deprivation. At weekend retreats, cults often deprive potential recruits of sleep for 36 or 48 hours. The resulting fatigue induces both mental confusion and emotional vulnerability. Cults do not want recruits thinking carefully and logically about whether or not to join; they want recruits to accept the cult's messages uncritically. Fatigue and stress can reduce the attentional capacity of recruits, causing them to overlook the negative consequences of joining the cult and to be swept away by the emotion of the moment (see Baron, 2000).

Cults use a variety of persuasion techniques to recruit and retain members.

Love Bombing. A powerful technique that cults use is to shower potential recruits with "love": physical affection (e.g., hugs, hand-holding), flattery (e.g., "You're so talented"), and unconditional caring and security (e.g., "You will always be loved and protected in our group"). These sorts of words and actions can affect young people very strongly, especially those who have experienced a recent breakup or who have suffered from long-term loneliness. Many cults also adopt a "buddy system" at recruitment meetings, whereby one member of the cult is assigned to each recruit. This buddy tries to establish an emotional bond with the recruit, in the hopes of creating greater commitment to the cult.

Repetition. Recruits are exposed to long, repetitive lectures that regurgitate the doctrine of the cult (undiluted propaganda). These lectures often contain little substance, but lots of catchwords and clichés. When information is heard many times, it begins to sound plausible and to develop an aura of legitimacy. Increasing familiarity with the material can produce a more positive attitude toward it (recall the *mere exposure effect* from Chapter 6).

Foot-in-the-Door Technique. The foot-in-the-door technique refers to the fact that if you can get someone to agree to a small request, he or she is more likely to also agree to a much larger, related request (we will describe research documenting this technique in Chapter 8). Cults take advantage of this technique by initially requesting only small things from potential recruits: come to the meeting, introduce yourself to others, listen to the lecture. Gradually, the requests get larger: talk about your past experiences, make a donation to the group. Eventually, the requests become extreme: quit your job and join the group! Recruits would never have agreed to the extreme requests at the beginning of the process, but each of their small actions increases the likelihood of subsequent compliance with larger requests.

Denial of Privacy. During weekend retreats, potential recruits are never left alone. They are kept involved in group activities or discussions with at least one member of the cult (often the "buddy" we mentioned earlier). The cult does not want people to be able to sit and think quietly about the situation. Instead, the cult wants constant social pressure on the recruit to join.

Reciprocity. There is a norm in our society that when someone does a favour for you, you should repay that favour in kind. This *norm of reciprocity* will be discussed in Chapter 8. Cults take advantage of this norm to pressure potential recruits to join. Recruits are subtly reminded that they are guests of the cult, are receiving free food and accommodation, and have been treated well by everyone. The idealistic, vulnerable young people who are brought to retreats have a strong conscience and do not want to appear to be ungrateful guests. How can they repay all the favours done for them? Easy: join the group.

Fear Mongering. In their lectures and discussions, cults often appeal to fears about the future, such as nuclear war, financial collapse, or the disintegration of society into anarchy. The government is said to be corrupt and evil; powerful members of society are labelled selfish and dangerous; and the future is portrayed as bleak and ominous. In the context of this apocalyptic outlook, the cult provides stability, security, and even a possible solution to society's problems. Joining the cult therefore becomes a way for the recruit to reduce the fear that has been aroused.

Summary. We have described nine techniques that are used by many cults to recruit and retain members. The simultaneous application of these strategies can be very effective, especially when the potential recruits' environment is completely controlled by the cult, as at weekend retreats. There is nothing magical in these techniques—their effects can all be understood from a social psychological perspective. The use of the techniques by cults is unethical, however, because cults apply the techniques deliberately to overwhelm freedom of choice—to confuse and pressure vulnerable young people into joining the cult whether they really want to or not. Members who are "true believers" rationalize these strategies by saying that the end justifies the means: by joining the movement, people will be better off even if they might not have joined without the pressure. For the leader and others who benefit personally from the members, the motivation may be darker: greed.

Everyday Propaganda

Wartime propaganda and cult propaganda are pretty extreme. But other, more mundane examples of influence attempts that are moderately propagandistic are all around us. Let's consider some of these "everyday" examples of propaganda (see also Levine, 2003; Pratkanis & Aronson, 2001).

Advertising. Advertisements are openly one-sided. They rarely present the weaknesses of a product alongside its strengths. They often appeal to emotions and symbols, rather than to reason (e.g., advertisements that use the soft sell). Advertisements also reflect an ideology—namely, materialism. Although companies do not usually design their ads to promote materialism per se, there are implicit messages that spending is good and the way to be happy is to get or consume more things.

Interest groups are like any other entity with an agenda that includes changing your attitude, in that they all have a varied bag of tricks to use in their efforts to persuade you.

Advertisements also communicate other, unintended messages. Clothing designers have used skinny models so exclusively that women have developed unrealistic beliefs about their ideal weight. The nearly complete absence of anyone over 50 in advertisements contributes to our culture's negative stereotypes of aging and the elderly. Racial minorities are also underrepresented in advertisements, which implicitly endorses the existing hierarchical status structure in society.

Television and Movies. Directors and producers of television shows and movies sometimes create products that are propagandistic. War movies may portray historical events in a one-sided and emotional way. Televised sporting events like the Grey Cup may open with patriotic music and images (e.g., featuring the Canadian flag). News stories about an international event sometimes take a narrow view of the history of a conflict or issue.

Like advertisements, television shows and movies can communicate unintended messages. The professional and domestic roles of men and women in television programming generally conform to stereotypic divisions of labour, thereby reinforcing the stereotypes. Music videos often portray women as sexual objects, who use their physical beauty to attract and control men. The focus on negative events in news programs can lead viewers to overestimate the dangers they face in daily life, causing both unnecessary fear and withdrawal from the community.

Is education a form of propaganda?

Education. You may be wondering how education can be propagandistic. After all, isn't "education" by definition open-minded and information-based? Maybe not. (For an interesting discussion of this issue, see "Education or Propaganda?" in Pratkanis & Aronson, 2001, pp. 261–268.) Judgments of whether a topic belongs in the classroom often depend on whom you ask. For instance, fundamentalist Christians and left-wing liberals will probably differ in their judgments about whether the theory of evolution or the Ten Commandments are (1) "facts" that must be presented or (2) "ideologically based ideas" that should be excluded from the curriculum.

It is undeniable that the education system shapes and strengthens students' values. In Canada, for example, the school system deliberately advocates values such as democracy, religious tolerance, and individualism. Social institutions such as marriage, the family, and the legal system are also actively promoted. And the field of science is generally presented as objective and trustworthy—judgments with which your text's authors largely concur, but we also know that personal biases can and do affect scientists' work and conclusions.

Unintentional effects on beliefs and values also come from the school system. For instance, educators do not intend to contribute to a fear of other cultures or religions because of limited knowledge. Nor do they intend to confirm sex role stereotypes by failing to teach about the role of women in history. Yet decisions about the curriculum can have these sorts of indirect effects.

Religious Institutions. Most of us accept the principle of religious freedom. People should be able to practise religion (or not) in their own way. But do our organized religions really encourage choice and freedom? Most practising people are raised in their parents' places of worship and are never exposed to other religious views. Within religious organizations themselves, classes and sermons are exclusively based on the ideology and values of that particular church, temple, or mosque. Should this be considered propaganda? On the one hand, information presented by religions is one-sided. On the other hand, everyone *knows* that religions teach within the framework of their beliefs, and no one expects religious institutions to talk about alternative views. Clearly, this issue is difficult to settle.

Religious training does not only affect religious beliefs, of course. Different religions also influence attitudes and values regarding the roles of women and men, the morality of birth control, whether homosexuality is accepted or denounced, and the value of diversity. These broader effects are less obvious but no less important.

Summary. The "everyday" sources of propaganda that we have discussed may not present biased views *intentionally*. For instance, news coverage may reflect a reporter's values without his or her awareness. Advertisers may not realize that they are causing eating disorders in young women. Educators may not recognize that they are teaching more than the designated curriculum in their classes. Therefore, these examples do *not* represent the more extreme forms of propaganda, in which a communicator deliberately omits relevant information or intentionally misrepresents the facts. Nevertheless, these forms of influence rest on ideological foundations and do not always involve an objective presentation of the facts. It is useful for us to recognize how our social institutions shape our perceptions of the world.

A Final Comment: Resisting Illegitimate Authority-Based Appeals

In an interesting set of studies conducted at Arizona State University, Brad Sagarin, Robert Cialdini, William Rice, and Sherman Serna (2002) developed and tested a "treatment" that was designed to make students better able to identify and resist deceptive advertisements. In particular, the treatment focused on appeals that used illegitimate authority figures. *Illegitimate* was defined as using sources who had no real expertise related to the product. For instance, illegitimate advertisements used in the study included ones in which celebrities promoted something about which they had no expertise (e.g., Ivana Trump promoting the National Fluid Milk Processor Promotion Board) and ones in which actors portrayed the role of an expert (e.g., a model dressed as a stockbroker promoting the *Wall Street Journal*). Some participants in this research read a six-page discussion of legitimate and illegitimate uses of authorities in advertisements, which included several sample magazine ads. Compared to control participants who did not read these materials, participants who completed the treatment subsequently rated illegitimate magazine ads as less persuasive and legitimate magazine ads as more persuasive. Thus, it proved possible to sensitize people to illegitimate uses of authority. These findings are encouraging for attempts to educate consumers about deceptive advertising. It may be possible to teach people to be skeptical about advertisers who use manipulative techniques in their appeals.

Chapter Summary

This chapter described research and theory on the many ways that attitudes can change. One way that attitudes can change is through rationalization—convincing ourselves that our decisions or actions are justified. This process of rationalization is described by **cognitive dissonance theory.** Dissonance theory deals with the consequences of being aware of **dissonant cognitions,** which are beliefs that are inconsistent with one another, such as "I smoke" and "Smoking causes cancer." In contrast, **consonant cognitions** support one another, such as "I eat apples" and "Apples are good for me." Dissonance theory proposes that the awareness of dissonant cognitions produces an unpleasant state of arousal, which people are motivated to reduce. Dissonance can be reduced by changing one of the dissonant cognitions, adding consonant cognitions, or changing the importance of one or more of the relevant cognitions.

Dissonance theory has been tested in several different experimental *paradigms,* or research methodologies. The **induced compliance paradigm** investigates dissonance that results from counterattitudinal behaviour. It involves inducing participants to behave in a way that is inconsistent with their attitudes. To reduce dissonance, participants often change their attitude in the direction of their behaviour. The **effort justification paradigm** investigates dissonance that results from wasted effort. It involves leading participants to incur some costs for a goal that might not be worthwhile. To reduce dissonance, participants often increase the perceived value of the goal. The **free choice paradigm** investigates dissonance that results from making a decision or choice, which is termed *postdecisional dissonance.* It involves asking participants to choose between two or more alternatives. To reduce dissonance, participants often increase the perceived attractiveness of the chosen alternative and decrease the perceived attractiveness of the rejected alternative—a pattern of re-evaluation that is termed *spreading of the alternatives.*

Several alternative interpretations of dissonance findings have been proposed. *Self-perception theory* proposes that people change their attitudes after counterattitudinal behaviour because they logically infer their attitudes from their behaviour. **Impression management theory** proposes that people in dissonance experiments may not change their attitudes at all, but simply *report* new attitudes so they will not appear inconsistent to the experimenter. **Self-affirmation theory** proposes that counterattitudinal behaviour induces attitude change because it threatens people's sense of self-worth, and they can reduce the threat by reaffirming an important value.

Recent research on dissonance has produced the **hypocrisy paradigm,** in which participants deliver a speech arguing for a prosocial behaviour and are then made aware that they have not always exhibited the behaviour themselves in the past. People differ in their **preference for consistency (PFC),** which refers to their desire for predictability and consistency within their own responses and within others' responses. People who are high in PFC exhibit dissonance effects more strongly than people who are low in PFC.

Another way that attitudes can change is via *persuasive communications,* which are attempts by individuals or groups to convince another person or persons to adopt a particular position. **Cognitive response theory** suggests that an information-based message is effective at changing attitudes when it elicits mostly positive thoughts (termed *proarguments* in the theory), but does not change attitudes when it elicits mostly negative thoughts (termed *counterarguments* in the theory). In the domain of advertising, some advertisers use information about the quality and features of their product to generate strong rational arguments in favour of buying it; this strategy is called the **hard sell.**

A persuasive communication can also produce attitude change by **heuristic persuasion,** which results from the use of *heuristics:* simple rules or assumptions such as "Experts are reliable sources of information." In the domain of advertising, some advertisers use emotions, symbols, or images to sell a product; this strategy is called the **soft sell.**

Two theories of persuasive communications can encompass attitude change resulting from both strong arguments and the use of heuristics. One is the **systematic-heuristic model.** This model distinguishes between **systematic processing,** which occurs when people think carefully about the arguments in a message, and **heuristic processing,** which occurs when people rely on heuristics to make judgments about the message. The second theory, the **elaboration likelihood model,** distinguishes between the **central route to persuasion** and the **peripheral route to persuasion.** The central route occurs when attitude change results from a careful analysis of the information in the message; the peripheral route occurs when attitude change results from the use of heuristics or other noncognitive factors (which are termed **peripheral cues** in the model).

In the health domain, persuasive messages often try to arouse fear. **Protection motivation theory** provides an analysis of how threatening messages produce attitude change. It predicts that changes in attitudes and behaviours are more likely when recipients of a message are convinced that (1) the problem is serious, (2) they are personally susceptible to the problem, (3) the recommended behaviours will be effective in avoiding the problem, and (4) they are personally capable of performing the recommended behaviours.

Propaganda is a persuasive attempt that is motivated by an ideology, or set of values, and is deliberately biased in its presentation of information. Propaganda is employed by **destructive cults,** which can be defined as groups led by a charismatic leader that isolate themselves from the rest of society and use deceptive techniques to recruit and retain members. It is also possible to consider messages from many "legitimate" sources to be somewhat propagandistic.

Key Terms

central route to persuasion (264)

cognitive dissonance theory (240)

cognitive response theory (256)

consonant cognitions (240)

destructive cult (276)

dissonant cognitions (240)

effort justification paradigm (245)

elaboration likelihood model (262)

free choice paradigm (247)

hard sell (259)

heuristic persuasion (259)

heuristic processing (264)

hypocrisy paradigm (251)

impression management theory (249)

induced compliance paradigm (243)

peripheral cues (264)

peripheral route to persuasion (264)

preference for consistency (PFC) (253)

propaganda (274)

protection motivation theory (273)

self-affirmation theory (250)

soft sell (262)

systematic processing (264)

systematic-heuristic model (262)

Social Psychology Alive on the Web

SOCIAL PSYCHOLOGY ALIVE: ONLINE LABS

To perform the following experiment and see how you compare to other students, go to Social Psychology Lab, which can be accessed through ThomsonNOW™.

- 7.1 Travel Planner

SOCIAL PSYCHOLOGY ALIVE: QUIZZING AND PRACTICE TESTS

You can access our Web site directly by going to http://www.socialpsychologyalive.nelson.com for online quizzes, flash cards, and Internet links.

INFOTRAC® COLLEGE EDITION

For additional readings, explore InfoTrac® College Edition, your online library of archived journal articles and periodicals dating back 22 years. If your instructor ordered InfoTrac® College Edition with this book, you can access it from your CD-ROM, or go directly to http://www.infotrac-college.com and use the passcode from the InfoTrac® College Edition card that came with your book. For this chapter, try these search terms: *dissonance, rationalization, induced compliance, effort justification, impression management, self-affirmation, hypocrisy, systematic processing, heuristic processing, elaboration likelihood model, fear appeals, protection motivation, propaganda.*

Social Psychology Alive: The Workbook

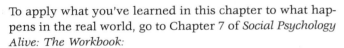

To apply what you've learned in this chapter to what happens in the real world, go to Chapter 7 of *Social Psychology Alive: The Workbook*:

- Does Hazing Enhance the Attractiveness and Worth of Fraternities and Sororities to Their Members?
- Postdecisional Dissonance: How to Make a Candy Bar Taste Better

- Making Choices
- Advertising in Daily Life
- Need for Cognition and Persuasive Communications
- How to Persuade People Not to Smoke
- What Is a Cult?

Social Psychology Alive: The Videos

To see video on the topics and experiments discussed in this chapter, you can go either to ThomsonNOW™ or to the CD-ROM, if your instructor assigned either one, to the following sections:

- When Trauma Makes the Heart Grow Fonder: Cognitive Dissonance and the Justification of Effort
- Moving the Masses: Public Service Announcements

To Learn More

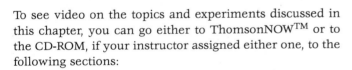

This list contains citations to books or articles that can help you learn more. These readings are good places to start if you want to gain a deeper understanding of the topics in this chapter.

- Seiter, J. S., & Gass, R. H. (Eds.). (2004). *Perspectives on persuasion, social influence, and compliance gaining.* Boston: Pearson Education.

- Levine, R. (2003). *The power of persuasion: How we are bought and sold.* Hoboken, NJ: Wiley.
- Pratkanis, A., & Aronson, E. (2001). *Age of propaganda: The everyday use and abuse of persuasion* (rev. ed.). New York: Freeman.

1945 - 2005

Conformity, Compliance, and Obedience

The Order of the Solar Temple was founded by Joseph Di Mambro and Dr. Luc Jouret in Switzerland in 1984. It spread to Canada in 1986, with Jouret establishing a chapter in Morin Heights, a ski resort north of Montreal.

The charismatic Jouret claimed to be the third reincarnation of Jesus Christ. The group had a number of strange beliefs, including that the world would end in a terrible fire. Members believed that being consumed by fire would initiate a "death voyage" leading to rebirth on a planet orbiting the star Sirius. They also believed that Di Mambro's daughter Emmanuelle was a "cosmic child" who would lead them on this death voyage.

On the night of October 4, 1994, two groups of followers committed mass suicide in Cheiry and Granges-sur-Salvan, two small towns in Switzerland. At one location, police discovered 22 bodies arranged in a circle with their feet pointing inward. At the other location, 25 bodies were found, including those of Jouret, Di Mambro, and Emmanuelle. At both locations, drugs were found in most bodies, and plastic bags had been pulled over most victims' heads. Also at both locations, fires had been set to consume the bodies (presumably so the death voyage would be initiated), but the incendiary devices failed to engulf the buildings fully.

Although the founders were dead, the Order of the Solar Temple continued to have followers in Canada and France. On March 22, 1997, a final mass suicide claimed five Canadians, whose bodies were found arranged in the shape of a cross inside a burning house in St. Casimir, a village west of Quebec City. Again, the victims had intended to be consumed by fire, but firefighters were able to bring the blaze under control before the bodies were burned.

What could possibly account for this behaviour? Why would so many people willingly give up their lives? Were they all suffering from some deep psychological problems? No. They were ordinary people who became victims of powerful pressures for conformity and obedience (see Osherow, 1999). Before you write off the Solar Temple suicides as an oddity, consider that you, too, are subject to some of the very same forces. These social pressures are with you every day, and they influence much of what you do.

Five Canadian members of the Solar Temple cult committed simultaneous suicide in March 1997.

Luc Jouret was the charismatic leader of the Solar Temple cult.

Defining Conformity, Compliance, and Obedience

In this chapter, we review social psychological research on three specific kinds of *social influence* (i.e., influence from other people): conformity, compliance, and obedience. These terms all refer to *changes in behaviour caused by other people,* but they differ in their breadth. Let us first define each term and then explain the differences between them. **Conformity** is the most general concept and refers to any change in behaviour caused by another person or group; the individual acted in some way because of influence from others. For example, a spectator at an Edmonton Oilers hockey game might boo the referee because other fans are booing. Note that conformity is limited to changes in *behaviour* caused by other people; it does not refer to effects of other people on internal concepts like attitudes and beliefs. **Compliance** refers to a change in behaviour that is *requested* by another person or group; the individual acted in some way because others asked him or her to do so (but it was possible to refuse or decline). For example, during an election campaign, a supporter of the New Democratic Party might agree to put a sign on her lawn supporting the NDP candidate in her riding because she was asked to do so by a party official. **Obedience** refers to a change in behaviour that is *ordered* by another person or group; the individual acted in some way because others commanded him or her to do so (failing to obey was not presented as an option, though it may have been considered by the individual). For example, a child might clean up his bedroom because he was ordered to do so by his parents.

Conformity encompasses compliance and obedience because it refers to *any* behaviour that occurs as a result of others' influence—no matter what the nature of that influence. For example, there may not have been any request or order given to the individual; the behaviour might have occurred because the person copied, learned from, wanted to impress, or was in some other way influenced by another person. Compliance and obedience refer to behaviour that resulted specifically from requests or orders. Even though the concept of conformity technically encompasses these other concepts, we will limit discussion in the section on conformity to studies focused on behaviour that was *not* specifically requested or ordered by others (because, after all, requests or orders would move the behaviour into the more specific literatures on compliance or obedience). We will particularly emphasize in the conformity section studies that involve people behaving in ways that are similar to how others are behaving (*doing as others do*) without any preceding request or order. For example, an adolescent girl might wear a piece of clothing because she saw Avril Lavigne wearing it in a music video. Or a new Member of Parliament will probably follow the example of his or her more experienced colleagues in terms of when to stand, sit, pound the desk, and cheer during parliamentary sessions.

Why would this kind of *conformity*—doing as others do without any request—occur? For one thing, when you find yourself in a new or unusual situation, it is natural—even sensible—to look to others in deciding what to do. Other people may have more experience, more information, or better skills than you do. Going along with others may be the best way to do the right thing or to avoid appearing foolish, especially when the situation is ambiguous and you are uncertain about your own judgment and experience. Our example of a new Member of Parliament illustrates this kind of circumstance. But suppose the other people around you are doing things that just don't make sense. Would you go along then? Would you try to "fit in" with the crowd? Research on conformity provides some surprising answers: people often go along with the incorrect responses of others, even when reality is as plain as it can be.

What about *compliance,* which refers to actions caused by a request? Even in everyday and familiar situations, we are susceptible to the requests of others. Indeed,

conformity
any change in behaviour caused by another person or group

compliance
a change in behaviour that is requested by another person or group

obedience
a change in behaviour that is ordered by another person or group

Panhandlers try to get you to comply with their request for money.

some people we encounter are compliance professionals—getting us to do things, to buy things, and to say things that we would not otherwise have done or bought or said. Has a salesperson ever convinced you to spend more money on something than you intended? Have you ever given in to a panhandler's request? Have you ever agreed to accompany a friend to an event that you would really rather have avoided? All of these situations represent cases of compliance. Research on compliance has identified some fascinating strategies that are effective in eliciting compliance with requests.

Obedience refers to a more extreme form of social influence, when another person simply tells someone to do something. Obedience commands start early in childhood, when we are socialized to follow the orders of parents and teachers. By the time we are adults, most of us have learned to be relatively obedient—to follow the orders of police, government officials, higher-ranking military officers, the boss, and, indeed, most people who wear a uniform or hold a position of authority. We don't question the police officer who directs traffic around an accident; we don't resist when a security guard tells us to leave an area; and we don't make a fuss when our boss orders us to take on a task that we were hoping to avoid. But how far does this go? We know that members of the Solar Temple followed orders to take their own lives. Would you obey the orders of an authority even if that meant causing harm to yourself or to another person? Again, the answer may surprise you: research on obedience to authority has shown that people are remarkably susceptible to this form of social influence.

The three varieties of social influence we describe in this chapter are not the only ways we are influenced by others (e.g., see Nail, MacDonald, & Levy, 2000). Indeed, virtually all of social psychology deals with social influence in some fashion (how individuals' thoughts, feelings, and behaviours are influenced by other people). For instance, in Chapter 7, we looked at how other people can affect attitudes and beliefs through such mechanisms as advertising, persuasive appeals, and propaganda. In Chapter 10, we will see how the dynamics of social groups shape our identity and influence our judgments. But in the present chapter, you will learn about some of the best-known—and most disturbing—results of social psychological research.

informational influence

influence from other people that is motivated by a desire to be correct and to obtain accurate information

We normally obey the commands of police officers.

Why Do We Conform?

Conforming behaviours occur for two principal reasons, which are captured by the terms *informational influence* and *normative influence* (coined by Deutsch & Gerard, 1955). **Informational influence** occurs when people are influenced by others because of a desire to be correct and to obtain valid information. This kind of influence reflects that people often rely on others as a source of information—they trust others' judgments to be useful in a particular context. Perhaps the other people are more knowledgeable, such as when young drivers alter their behaviour to conform to the suggestions of their driving instructor. Or perhaps the judgment is ambiguous and the person is unsure about the correct answer, such as when contestants on *The Price Is Right* use audience reactions to guide their estimate of the price of an item.

Normative influence, on the other hand, occurs when people are influenced by others to gain rewards or to avoid punishment. They might not necessarily think that others' judgments or behaviours are correct; they might simply want to be liked or to avoid conflict. For example, people sometimes obey laws simply to avoid being punished, such as driving on a highway at or near the 100 km/hr speed limit when they would actually like to go faster. We see another example when teenagers conform in words, deeds, or appearance to popular peers whom they hope to befriend.

Informational and normative influence can occur simultaneously. For instance, a novice automobile mechanic at a Canadian Tire store might ask for advice from the supervisor partly because the supervisor is an expert and partly because the mechanic hopes to be rewarded for showing such respect. Indeed, we often want to please other people (normative influence) whose judgments we seek (informational influence).

We will mention the distinction between informational and normative influence several times in the chapter as we discuss conformity, compliance, and obedience. We will also return to the distinction for a more thorough analysis in the final section, where we discuss general mechanisms underlying the three topics described in the chapter.

normative influence
influence from other people that is motivated by a desire to gain rewards or avoid punishment

Conformity: Doing as Others Do

We often find ourselves going along with the behaviour of others—doing as others do. This behavioural conformity can occur without our even realizing that we are doing it. Sometimes we go along with others because we do not understand what is happening or we are unsure what to do. But sometimes we go along when we know we shouldn't. Two famous early series of experiments in social psychology looked at these different kinds of conformity: Muzafer Sherif's (1935, 1936, 1937) work on the *autokinetic effect* and Solomon Asch's (1951, 1952, 1956) work on judgments of line lengths. These studies provide a nice package, because Sherif investigated conformity in situations where the correct judgment was ambiguous, whereas Asch investigated conformity in situations where the correct judgment was obvious.

Sherif's Autokinetic Effect Studies

Muzafer Sherif (1935, 1936, 1937), who spent most of his career at the University of Oklahoma and then Pennsylvania State University, conceptualized his research on conformity as addressing the development of *social norms*. A **social norm** is a rule or guideline about what behaviours are proper and improper. Norms can be formal, such as laws and contracts, or informal, such as customs and traditions within small groups (families, peer groups, etc.). Typically, the reward for following a norm is social acceptance or approval, whereas the punishment for breaking a norm is social rejection or disapproval. Social norms govern the way we dress, the way we speak, and the way we behave. An example of a formal norm is the law in Canada to drive on the right-hand side of the road. Violating this norm is usually met with swift punishment, not to mention dirty looks and gestures from other drivers. But in other parts of the world, the norm is exactly the opposite—driving on the left-hand rather than right-hand side of the road keeps you out of trouble. Examples of more informal norms are everywhere. In some business communities, the expected business attire for men includes a suit and tie (think of Bay Street in Toronto), whereas in other places, every day is "casual Friday" (think of the fashion industry in Montreal). Similarly, in some families, children are allowed significant input into decisions,

social norm
a rule or guideline in a group or culture about what behaviours are proper and improper

The norm in the United Kingdom is for people to drive on the left-hand side of the road.

autokinetic effect

in a darkened room, a stationary point of light will appear to move periodically

Alone, Then Together

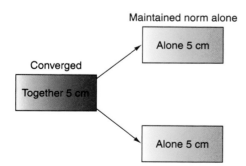

FIGURE 8.1 Conditions in Sherif's (1936) second study of social norms

whereas in other families, parents are the sole decision makers. The social norms on some Canadian university campuses promote serious studying and on others promote intense socializing (we leave the identification of specific instances of these campuses to the reader).

Social norms are one source of conformity (they represent influence from other people and guide behaviour). Sherif wanted to study the development and influence of social norms. He did so by setting up a novel situation in which most of the research participants had little or no prior experience. Under these conditions, he expected norms to emerge.

The Autokinetic Effect. Imagine that you are sitting in a completely darkened room. The only visible thing is a tiny point of light projected on the wall 5 metres in front of you. If you watch that point of light, it will appear to move, and it may even seem to be periodically jumping about in different directions. The light is not really moving; it is an illusion. This is known as the **autokinetic effect,** and it occurs partly because no other visual frame of reference is available to locate the light and partly because of occasional rapid movements of your eye.

In his first study, Sherif (1935) asked 19 men, participating individually, to report how far the light appeared to move. Other than the experimenter, no one except the person making the judgment was in the room. Over the course of 100 judgments, each man settled on a relatively stable distance, but these average estimates of movement ranged widely, from a low of 1 cm for one man to a high of 25 cm for another. Thus, a relatively wide range of perceived movement occurred from person to person—just the results Sherif needed to study the formation and influence of a group norm.

In a second study, Sherif (1936) assembled people in groups of two or three (see Figure 8.1). The task was the same as before: to announce out loud the distance of perceived motion of what was really a stationary point of light. Judgments were recorded in four sessions on four different days. For half of the participants, the first session involved making judgments alone, and then being joined by the other participants in the following three sessions. When they started alone, a wide range of perceived movement was observed, as expected from the first study (averages from less than 2.5 cm to more than 23 cm). But when the participants began making their judgments in groups of two or three, judgments of perceived movement began to converge. By the end of three sessions together, judgments of the two or three people in a group were very similar (typically differing by less than 2.5 cm), although the different groups tended to converge on different norms. For instance, one two-person group converged on a norm of about 2.5 cm, whereas another converged on a norm of about 13 cm.

The other half of the participants made their judgments in the group situation from the very beginning. These groups converged very rapidly on their own group norms. It was in these groups that a very interesting result was obtained. During the last (fourth) session, the participants in these groups were broken up and made their judgments alone. Yet the group norm carried on: the judgments now being made individually were nearly identical to the standard that had been established for the group. The flowchart in Figure 8.1 depicts the two conditions in this experiment.

Having observed the development and subsequent impact of a group norm, Sherif (1937) wanted to know if such "standards" could be arbitrarily established by experimental assistants (confederates). In one of the best-known autokinetic experiments, participants were assembled in groups of two. But only one member of each pair was naïve about the procedure; the other member was planted by the experimenter and was instructed to vary his judgments around a particular standard. In all, seven different pairs of people were tested, with the arbitrary standard (introduced by the confederate) ranging from 5 to 20 cm. For the first 50 judgment trials, the two participants in each pair made their judgments together (sometimes the naïve participant responded first, sometimes the confederate responded first). For the second set of 50 judgment trials, however, the naïve participant was tested alone. The results are shown in Figure 8.2. The blue line represents the naïve participant's responses during the first 50 trials, when the confederate was present and gave responses that remained consistently around a standard of between 5 to 20 cm; the purple line represents the naïve participant's responses during the second set of 50 trials, when the confederate was no longer present. The figure shows that the naïve participant's individual responses in the second set of trials remained very close to the standard established during the first 50 trials. Thus, the arbitrary standard introduced by the confederate clearly established a group norm, and that norm then carried over to influence the naïve participant's judgments when alone.

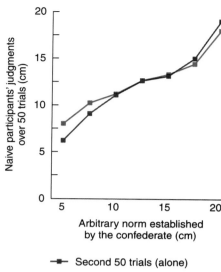

FIGURE 8.2 Naïve participants' judgments of movement on the first 50 trials and the second 50 trials

Adapted from Sherif, 1937, An experimental approach to the study of attitudes, *Sociometry*, 1, 90–98.

Multigenerational Norms. Taken together, Sherif's early experiments (1935, 1936, 1937) showed that group norms are spontaneously established and carry over into individual judgments. Of course, in everyday life, many norms have been around for a long time. We do not typically know how a particular norm got started, nor for how many generations the norm has been passed along. For example, the norm that servers in restaurants should be given tips has been common in our society for many years.

Mark MacNeil and Muzafer Sherif (1976) showed that the transmission of a norm from generation to generation is something that can be modelled in the laboratory. These researchers established an arbitrary group norm in groups of four male high school students; three members of the group were planted by the experimenter. The three experimental confederates established an arbitrary group norm of about 30 cm over a series of 30 judgment trials. After a brief rest, one of the three confederates left the group and was replaced by a new naïve participant. The new group then provided 30 more sets of judgments, with the same arbitrary group norm being continued by the two remaining confederates. This process was then repeated, until all of the confederates had finally been replaced with naïve participants by the fourth generation. In the fifth generation, the original naïve participant was replaced with a new one. The study continued for 11 generations, each one involving the replacement of the oldest group member with a new member. After 11 generations, responses were beginning to drift from the initial group norm of 30 cm, but not far—the original standard was still evident. Norms can persist long after their original instigators are gone.

Asch's Length Judgment Studies

If you imagined yourself as one of the "naïve" participants in Sherif's autokinetic experiments, you could probably see yourself going along with the others. After all, the judgment was an ambiguous one. But now imagine yourself participating in a very different experiment. In this study, social norms about the range of appropriate responses (as in Sherif's studies) are not really relevant, because the task is simple and clear-cut.

When you arrive at the laboratory, seven other students (just like you) are waiting to begin. The group is seated and told that this is an experiment involving the discrimination of lengths of lines. On each trial, you are shown one "standard" line, and three "comparison" lines. Your task is simply to indicate which of the three comparison lines matches the standard line in length. You can try the judgment out for yourself by using the set of lines shown in Figure 8.3. Unlike the Sherif experiments, this judgment is not ambiguous at all. One of the comparison lines is *exactly* the same length as the standard, and the two other comparison lines differ from the standard by at least 2 cm. The lines are printed in a dark black ink, and each is 1 cm wide. There is a single correct answer (in this case, comparison line #3). The task is so easy that students rarely make an error when they make the judgments alone.

As the experiment begins, you learn that each member of the group is to announce his or her judgment out loud so the entire group can hear. You happen to be seated in the second row of chairs, and six students announce their judgments before it is your turn. At first, everything proceeds smoothly. For the first two comparison trials, everyone else sees the lines the same way you do. But then something strange happens for the third set of lines. The six students who go before you all announce the wrong answer. Instead of selecting the line that matches exactly, they *all* select a line 2 cm longer than the standard line. You can't believe it. You rub your eyes. You wonder if you have missed something, or has the entire group gone crazy? What would you do in this circumstance? Would you give the correct answer even though it goes against what everyone else has said, or would you conform to the others' response? Whatever your decision, the same dilemma occurs on the fourth set of lines: everyone who goes before you selects the comparison line that is 2.5 cm shorter than the standard. Would you give the correct answer, or conform?

Solomon Asch (1951, 1952, 1956), who spent most of his career at Swarthmore College in Pennsylvania, did a series of experiments just like this. In his studies, seven members of each group were confederates of the experimenter, instructed to give the wrong answer on designated trials. Only one participant (to whom we will refer as the "critical participant") was naïve about the experimental situation. In total, the experiment included 12 trials on which the other students (the confederates) unanimously selected the wrong comparison line. In the face of this pressure, only 23% (28 out of 123) of the critical participants always gave the correct answer and went against the group on all 12 trials. These students remained completely independent.

FIGURE 8.3

Sample stimulus trial from Asch's length judgment studies

From Asch, S.E. (1951). "Effects of group pressure upon the modification and distortion of judgments," in H. Guetzkow, ed., *Groups, Leadership and Men* (pp. 177–190).

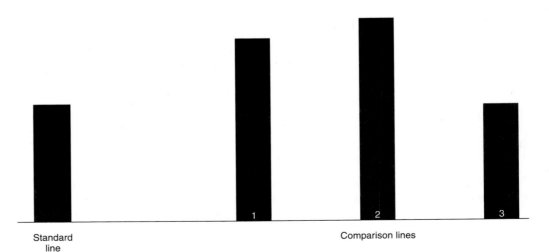

Standard line

Comparison lines

1 2 3

The remaining 77% of the critical participants went along with the group on at least one of the 12 trials. Across the 12 trials, 45% of the critical participants gave between 1 and 6 wrong answers, and 32% gave between 7 and 12 wrong answers. So, at one extreme, a substantial number of critical participants (23%) remained completely independent, but at the other extreme, an even larger number of critical participants (32%) yielded to group pressure many times by giving 7 or more wrong answers.

The Crutchfield Apparatus. Asch's procedure was very effective at generating conformity pressure. Being confronted by seven other people who disagree with your judgment in a face-to-face setting creates powerful social influence. But Asch's procedure also required many experimental confederates and involved elaborate stage-setting. The confederates needed to be carefully trained, and, like any theatre production, their acting potentially differed from session to session. Also, there was the possibility that the confederates would act differently depending on how the critical participant responded.

To improve efficiency, flexibility, and control, Richard Crutchfield (1955) at the University of California at Berkeley developed a clever procedure for studying conformity. Rather than using confederates, the **Crutchfield apparatus** simulates the responses of other people. When participants arrive for the experiment (usually in groups of five), they are seated in separate cubicles. Each cubicle contains an electrical panel with five rows of 11 lights and one row of 11 switches. The experimenter explains that each of the five participants controls one row of lights. Participants are told that they will answer questions projected on the wall facing the cubicles, so everyone can see the question at the same time. They are also told that, as each person indicates his or her response (by throwing one of the 11 switches), a corresponding light will be illuminated on the panel in all cubicles. Thus, each participant believes that he or she will learn about the responses of others and that his or her own responses will be publicly known.

In reality, the experimenter controls all of the lights and is able to simulate patterns involving a wrong but unanimous majority. The procedure is very efficient, because no confederates are needed and all five participants can be treated as "critical participants." The procedure also affords a high degree of experimental control. On any given judgment trial, each person can be instructed to respond in any of the possible serial positions (first, second, third, fourth, or fifth). Also, by controlling the lights, the experimenter can create any pattern of responses among the "other participants."

Crutchfield (1955) used his apparatus to reproduce the original Asch (1951) experiment involving judgments of line lengths with a unanimous majority of other respondents providing the wrong answer. Crutchfield's findings were very similar to those of Asch. In addition to line length judgments, Crutchfield employed a variety of other tasks, involving perceptual judgments, attitudes and opinions, personal preferences, and assessments of factual material. On virtually all of these tasks, participants showed some conformity to the judgments of others. The only exception was for judgments that involved selecting which of two drawings was preferred. In this case of expressing personal preferences, there was little or no effect of group pressure.

Nature of the Task. The *amount* of conformity found in Asch-type experiments, or using the Crutchfield apparatus, depends on features of the judgment task (Allen, 1965). One feature is the ambiguity of the task: conformity is more likely when tasks are ambiguous. For example, in a study by Crutchfield (1955), participants were required to solve a number series that, in fact, had no solution. The other

Crutchfield apparatus

a machine that consists of an electrical panel with several rows of lights; it allows the efficient study of conformity by simulating the responses of numerous hypothetical participants (simulated) participants unanimously provided the same incorrect answer, and 79% of the participants went along with it. This context is quite similar to Sherif's studies using the autokinetic effect.

Conformity is also influenced by the *difficulty* of the task. Can you guess the nature of this effect? Do you think that people are more likely to conform to others' responses when a task is difficult or when it is easy? Reasons can be generated for either prediction. On the one hand, difficult tasks might increase conformity because people are less certain of their own answer. On the other hand, difficult tasks might reduce conformity because it is okay to differ from others when a task is difficult. Imagine that you were asked a difficult trivia question: Would you be more strongly influenced by others' responses than on an easier question? If you think that you would be more influenced on difficult questions, your intuition matches the findings in social psychological experiments (e.g., Baron, Vandello, & Brunsman, 1996; Coleman, Blake, & Mouton, 1958). For example, in an experiment at New York University using Asch's procedures, Morton Deutsch and Harold Gerard (1955) had participants make line length judgments in two series. For one series, the lines were in plain view—a relatively easy task. But for the other series, a more difficult judgment was required. Here, the lines were removed before participants made their judgments, forcing people to rely on their memory of the lines. More conformity was found when judgments were based on memory than when the lines were in plain sight.

Why do ambiguous and difficult tasks produce more conformity than clear and easy tasks? To answer this question, let's return to the distinction between informational and normative influence. On ambiguous or difficult tasks (e.g., Sherif's studies), other people's responses exert both *informational* and *normative* influence, whereas on clear and easy tasks (e.g., Asch's studies), only *normative* influence occurs. Put another way, on ambiguous or difficult tasks, the individual not only feels some normative pressure to go along with others' judgments (which is also true on clear and easy tasks), but the individual also uses the others' judgments as a source of information about the correct answer (which is *not* true on clear and easy tasks). The additional impact of informational influence increases the overall rate of conformity on ambiguous and difficult tasks.

Individual Differences. Not everyone conforms. Remember that 23% of the critical participants in Asch's (1956) experiment *never* yielded to the group pressure. Is there something consistently different in the personality traits or other characteristics of people who stay independent compared to people who consistently yield? Researchers investigating individual differences in conformity on various tasks (not only line judgments) have found that people who remain independent are somewhat higher in their motivation to achieve (McClelland, Atkinson, Clark, & Lowell, 1953) and in their leadership ability (Crutchfield, 1955) than people who conform. Also, compared to conformers, people who remain independent tend to be less concerned about obtaining the approval of others (Strickland & Crowne, 1962), less authoritarian (Petersen & Dietz, 2000), and less conscientious (Roccas, Sagiv, Schwartz, & Knafo, 2002). Finally, there is evidence that individuals with high self-esteem are less likely to conform than individuals with low self-esteem (Santee & Maslach, 1982; Singh & Prasad, 1973; Stang, 1972), especially when high self-esteem is based on intrinsic qualities like honesty or generosity, as opposed to extrinsic things like achievements (see Arndt, Schimel, Greenberg, & Pyszczynski, 2002).

What profile emerges from these various characteristics? Perhaps most clearly, it seems that a strong sense of self is associated with remaining independent, as reflected in such qualities as high self-esteem, high motivation to achieve, high leadership ability, and minimal concern about others' approval. These individuals

8.1
ONLINE
LAB

seem to be more confident about their own judgments and, therefore, less influenced by others' judgments. We should bear in mind, however, that these qualities do not predict conformity perfectly; in fact, individual differences correlate relatively weakly with conformity and are only part of the puzzle of why and when people conform.

Age differences in conformity have also been explored. When attention is limited to children and teenagers, researchers have found that conformity to same-age peers increases during elementary school, peaks around grade 9, and then declines up to the university years (e.g., Berndt, 1979). Presumably, grade 9 is about the time when adolescents are most concerned about being popular and not being ridiculed (see Janes & Olson, 2000). When attention is limited to adults between the ages of 18 and 85, there is a general tendency for conformity to decrease as age increases (e.g., Pasupathi, 1999). As adults grow older, it seems that they gradually feel less pressure to agree with others, although some degree of conformity pressure remains throughout the life span.

© Mark Richards/PhotoEdit

Older adults tend to be less conforming than younger adults.

Effects of Group Size. Do larger unanimous majorities produce greater conformity in settings like those in Asch's experiments? That is, does conformity increase as the size of the unanimous group grows? This issue was one of the first things investigated by Asch (1951), who found that conformity did increase as the size of the group grew from one to three. Unanimous groups numbering more than three, however, did not produce further increases in conformity.

In a later experiment, Harold Gerard, Roland Wilhelmy, and Edward Conolley (1968) at the University of California found that conformity continued to increase when the size of the majority grew beyond three. These researchers' results, presented in Figure 8.4, show that conformity rose rapidly as the group size grew from one to five, but additional increases in size had no impact on conformity (indeed, there was a downward turn for groups of six). Taken together, the studies on group size indicate that increases in the group beyond four or five members have relatively little effect on conformity.

We should note, however, that these laboratory studies did not extend to very large groups, such as crowds of 25, 100, or even more. It seems likely that very large groups do, indeed, exert more conformity pressure than small groups. For example, members of the Solar Temple in Switzerland faced the weight of the entire group of more than 20 people when the mass suicides were committed. A group of more than 20 people, all pressing for obedience, must have generated enormous pressure to conform.

How to Make Conformity Disappear. If we want to understand what is going on in the conformity situation developed by Asch, one useful strategy is to find out what makes conformity *disappear.* Two rather different methods have been found to reduce very substantially the level of conformity exhibited in the original Asch studies. Learning about these two methods provides insight into why people often yield to a unanimous but obviously wrong majority.

In a variation on the original experiment, Asch (1956) made one change. Instead of having the "critical participants" announce their judgments out loud (public responses), he had them silently record their judgments in

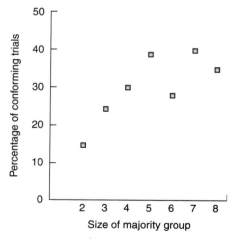

FIGURE 8.4 Percentage of conforming trials as the size of the group increases

From Gerard et al., "Conformity and group size," *Journal of Personality and Social Psychology,* 8(1), 79–82, 1968. Copyright © 1968 by the American Psychological Association.

writing (private responses). The other alleged participants (the confederates) still announced their answers out loud; this procedure was justified by leading the critical participant to believe that he or she had arrived late and, therefore, would have to provide answers in a different manner than the other participants. This shift to private, confidential judgments by the critical participant produced a dramatic reduction in conformity. Deutsch and Gerard (1955) also found a substantial reduction in conformity when judgments were anonymous rather than face-to-face with the opposing majority. In a similar vein, more recent research has shown that individuals are more likely to conform to other people's judgments when they must communicate their judgments to those people than when they do not have to communicate their judgments (Pennington & Schlenker, 1999; Quinn & Schlenker, 2002). Taken together, these results suggest that participants in the original conformity experiments did not privately accept the incorrect judgments of the majority, but instead conformed publicly because of normative pressure.

In another variation on the original experiment that greatly reduced conformity, Asch (1951) broke up the unanimity of the group facing the critical participant. In this variation, one of the experimental confederates deviated from the other confederates by announcing the correct answer. The presence of just one "partner"—someone else who called it the same way as the critical participant—virtually *eliminated* yielding to the majority. Thus, a little social support was all that participants needed to stand up against the majority in this context (Allen, 1975). Again, these results show that conforming participants in the original experiments were simply conforming in public and would have given the correct answer if there had been any crack in the wall of pressure against them.

Cultural Differences in Conformity

Most conformity experiments using the procedures of Sherif and Asch have been conducted in North America. But a number of conformity experiments have been done in other parts of the world, including Western and Northern Europe, Japan, South America, and Africa. Do these different cultures produce different rates of conformity?

Individualism Versus Collectivism. We have discussed the dimension of individualism versus collectivism in earlier chapters (Hofstede, 2001; Markus, Kitayama, & Heiman, 1996; Triandis, 1995). It seems plausible to predict that people from individualist cultures (e.g., North America and Western Europe) will conform less than people from collectivist cultures (e.g., Asia, South America). After all, individualism implies a strong personal identity based on one's unique features (an *independent* self), whereas collectivism implies commonality and interconnections with others (an *interdependent* self). Also, compared to people in individualist cultures, people in collectivist cultures are more concerned about their relationships with others, value tradition more highly, and define themselves more in terms of their social roles. All of these factors should increase conformity in collectivist cultures compared to individualist cultures. These comments also recall our discussion of individual differences in conformity, where we noted that a strong sense of self was associated with low rates of conformity.

By the mid-1990s, more than 100 conformity experiments had been conducted around the world using a line judgment task, either in the face-to-face procedure employed by Asch or in the Crutchfield apparatus. Rod Bond and Peter Smith (1996) at the University of Sussex in England reviewed 133 of these experiments. When they compared experiments done in different cultures, they confirmed that conformity was indeed higher in collectivist than in individualist countries. In fact, culture predicted participants' conformity even more strongly than did other influential factors, such as size of the group. These results show that people's socialization into either individualist or collectivist cultures has important effects on their tendency to go along with others when the answer is clearly wrong.

Individual Differences in Independent Versus Interdependent Self-Concepts. People from individualist cultures tend to have independent self-concepts, whereas those from collectivist cultures tend to have interdependent self-concepts. Nevertheless, people vary in their self-concepts even within the same culture. For example, some people in a collectivist culture have relatively independent self-concepts compared to others in their culture. Given the results of Bond and Smith (1996), it seems straightforward to predict that people whose self-concepts are independent will conform less than people whose self-concepts are interdependent.

Theodore Singelis (1994) at the University of Hawaii developed a scale to measure the extent to which individuals' self-concepts are independent or interdependent. Sample items from this scale are presented in Know Yourself 8.1: "Self-Construal Scale." You can answer these items to find out whether your own self-concept is primarily independent or interdependent. Although we are unaware of any direct tests of correlations between scores on this scale and conformity, this hypothesis would be interesting to pursue.

Gender Differences in Conformity

Do you think that women and men differ in their conformity to others' opinions and perceptions? If there is a gender difference, why does it occur?

Reviewers of the conformity literature have concluded that there is a small overall gender difference in conformity, such that women conform slightly more than do men (e.g., Bond & Smith, 1996; Eagly & Carli, 1981). Our choices of words, "small" and "slightly," are deliberate—the effect is not large, and many men conform more than many women (the distributions overlap). Various reasons have been offered for the gender difference. One suggestion is that most conformity researchers have been men, who may have been unconsciously biased toward finding greater independence among men than women (e.g., Eagly & Carli, 1981). Another suggestion is that the topics in conformity studies have typically been "masculine," with the result that women were less confident in their judgments than men and, therefore, more susceptible to social influence (e.g., Sistrunk & McDavid, 1971). A third suggestion is that women are more concerned about harmony in social relationships than are men, which makes them less willing to disagree with others (e.g., Eagly, 1978).

All of these possibilities are plausible, but another important qualification is that the gender difference in conformity appears only when participants' responses are public—that is, only when their responses will be communicated to other members of the group (e.g., Eagly & Chrvala, 1986; Eagly, Wood, & Fishbaugh, 1981). When responses are *private*, women do *not* conform more than men, but when responses are *public*, a gender difference often appears. This pattern of greater conformity in public suggests that women may be somewhat more susceptible to *normative influence* than men. Why would a gender difference in susceptibility to normative influence exist? Perhaps women's historically disadvantaged status has required them to be careful about deviating from others' judgments—they have to pick and choose when to disagree (see Wood & Eagly, 2002). On average, women are physically smaller than men and often fill less

Know Yourself 8.1
Self-Construal Scale

Please indicate the extent to which you agree or disagree with each of the following statements by circling the appropriate number on the answer scale.

1. It is important for me to maintain harmony within my group.

1	2	3	4	5	6	7
Strongly disagree	Disagree	Slightly disagree	Neutral	Slightly agree	Agree	Strongly agree

2. I am comfortable with being singled out for praise or rewards.

1	2	3	4	5	6	7
Strongly disagree	Disagree	Slightly disagree	Neutral	Slightly agree	Agree	Strongly agree

3. My happiness depends on the happiness of those around me.

1	2	3	4	5	6	7
Strongly disagree	Disagree	Slightly disagree	Neutral	Slightly agree	Agree	Strongly agree

4. I am the same person at home that I am at school.

1	2	3	4	5	6	7
Strongly disagree	Disagree	Slightly disagree	Neutral	Slightly agree	Agree	Strongly agree

5. I often have the feeling that my relationships with others are more important than my own accomplishments.

1	2	3	4	5	6	7
Strongly disagree	Disagree	Slightly disagree	Neutral	Slightly agree	Agree	Strongly agree

6. Being able to take care of myself is a primary concern for me.

1	2	3	4	5	6	7
Strongly disagree	Disagree	Slightly disagree	Neutral	Slightly agree	Agree	Strongly agree

7. I should take into consideration my parents' advice when making education/career plans.

1	2	3	4	5	6	7
Strongly disagree	Disagree	Slightly disagree	Neutral	Slightly agree	Agree	Strongly agree

8. I feel comfortable using someone's first name soon after I meet them, even when they are much older than I am.

1	2	3	4	5	6	7
Strongly disagree	Disagree	Slightly disagree	Neutral	Slightly agree	Agree	Strongly agree

9. It is important to me to respect decisions made by the group.

1	2	3	4	5	6	7
Strongly disagree	Disagree	Slightly disagree	Neutral	Slightly agree	Agree	Strongly agree

10. I enjoy being unique and different from others in many respects.

1	2	3	4	5	6	7
Strongly disagree	Disagree	Slightly disagree	Neutral	Slightly agree	Agree	Strongly agree

11. I will stay in a group if they need me, even when I'm not happy with the group.

1	2	3	4	5	6	7
Strongly disagree	Disagree	Slightly disagree	Neutral	Slightly agree	Agree	Strongly agree

12. My personal identity, independent of others, is very important to me.

1	2	3	4	5	6	7
Strongly disagree	Disagree	Slightly disagree	Neutral	Slightly agree	Agree	Strongly agree

SCORING: Add up the numbers you circled on all of the odd-numbered questions (1, 3, 5, 7, 9, and 11). This score represents the extent to which your self-concept is *interdependent*: scores can range from 6 to 42, and higher scores reflect a more interdependent self-construal. Also add up the numbers you circled on the even-numbered questions (2, 4, 6, 8, 10, and 12). This score represents the extent to which your self-concept is *independent*; scores can range from 6 to 42, and higher scores reflect a more independent self-construal. You can compare your scores for the interdependent and independent items to see whether you have predominantly one kind of self-construal.

Sample items from Singelis, T. M., "The measurement of independent and interdependent self-construals," *Personality and Social Psychology Bulletin, 20,* 580–591, Table 1, p. 585. Reprinted by permission of Sage Publications, Inc.

powerful social roles—both of which make deviating from a group relatively risky. These power differentials may explain, at least in part, the gender difference in conformity.

   ## Compliance: Doing as Others Want

Sometimes our behaviour is influenced by direct requests from other people, a type of conformity called *compliance*. Others may ask us to lend them our lecture notes, lend them some money, sign a petition calling for stronger action by the Canadian government to curb carbon dioxide emissions, or do some other favour for them. The requesters typically imply that we can refuse if we want to, though they would appreciate our compliance. Social psychologists have been interested in identifying factors that increase or decrease compliance with these sorts of requests and have documented an array of techniques that can be effective in getting people to act in the desired way (see Cialdini, 2001; Cialdini & Goldstein, 2004; Cialdini & Trost, 1998; Pratkanis & Aronson, 2001). We discuss six compliance techniques in this section. Some of the techniques rely on basic processes we have described in previous chapters (e.g., self-perception, dissonance, heuristics); others rely on social norms implying that compliance is the "proper" response. You may recognize some or all of these techniques, because they probably have been used by others to gain your compliance (and maybe even by you to gain others' compliance).

The Foot-in-the-Door Technique

We mentioned the **foot-in-the-door technique** in our discussion of how cults recruit new members in Chapter 7 (see page 278). This technique refers to the fact that if you can get someone to agree to a small request, then he or she is more likely to also agree to a much larger, related request. Jonathan Freedman, who is at the University of Toronto, conducted the first demonstration of this technique (Freedman & Fraser, 1966), and several other Canadian researchers also conducted important early investigations of the foot-in-the-door, including Patricia Pliner of the Erindale campus of the University of Toronto (Pliner, Hart, Kohl, & Saari, 1974) and Clive Seligman of the University of Western Ontario (Seligman, Bush, & Kirsch, 1976). In the initial study by Freedman and Fraser, researchers went door-to-door to homeowners and asked if the residents would be willing to have a large "Drive Carefully" sign installed in their front yards. The residents were shown a picture of another home with a poorly lettered sign obstructing much of the home's front. This was the large request—the one to which compliance was ultimately sought. When the large request was made without any prior contact, only 16% of homeowners agreed. But other residents were first contacted and asked a much smaller request, such as signing a petition or posting a small sign in their windows. When the larger request was then made two weeks later, more than 55% of the residents agreed to it. Thus, the initial contact and small request (the foot in the door) dramatically increased compliance. The foot-in-the-door effect has been replicated many times and in many contexts (see Burger, 1999), including the Internet (Guéguen & Jacob, 2001). It is probably one of the most common compliance techniques in everyday life.

Why does the foot-in-the-door technique work? What psychological mechanisms explain why agreement to a small request increases the likelihood of subsequent

foot-in-the-door technique
a strategy to increase compliance, based on the fact that agreement with a small request increases the likelihood of agreement with a subsequent larger request

Complying with a small request, such as signing a petition, increases the chances that someone will also comply with a larger request.

agreement to a larger request? Researchers have focused on two, related processes: self-perception and consistency.

Self-Perception Processes. We introduced *self-perception theory* in Chapter 4 (see page 128) and referred to it again briefly in Chapters 6 and 7. Daryl Bem (1972) hypothesized that people sometimes infer their internal states, such as attitudes and emotions, from their behaviour and the situation in which the behaviour occurred. How does self-perception relate to the foot-in-the-door technique? When people agree to an initial, small request, they may engage in a self-perception process whereby they label themselves as "helpful" because they willingly complied with the request. Therefore, when the second request is made, these individuals are more likely to agree because, after all, *they are helpful people*—a label that might not have existed, or not have been as prominent in their minds, if they had not agreed to the first request. Thus, the initial request stimulated a self-perception of helpfulness, which subsequently increased compliance with the second request (Beaman, Cole, Preston, Klentz, & Steblay, 1983; Burger, 1999; Dolinski, 2000; but see Gorassini & Olson, 1995).

Consistency Processes. A second process potentially involved in the foot-in-the-door technique is a desire for consistency. In the preceding chapter, we described *dissonance theory* (see page 240). Leon Festinger (1957) hypothesized that people want their attitudes and behaviours to be consistent with one another and are distressed by inconsistencies. We also mentioned impression management theory (see page 249), which postulates that people want to *appear* consistent to others and are embarrassed by public inconsistencies. Both of these motivations (to *be* consistent and to *appear* consistent) could contribute to the foot-in-the-door technique. After agreeing to an initial request, even a small one, people may feel that refusing a second, related request would be (or would appear) inconsistent (see Burger, 1999; Greenwald, Carnot, Beach, & Young, 1987).

Individual Differences in Preferences for Consistency (PFC). In Chapter 7, we presented the *preference for consistency scale*, developed by Robert Cialdini, Melanie Trost, and Jason Newsom (1995), in Know Yourself 7.1 (see page 254). People who score high on this scale agree with statements such as "I want to be described by others as a stable, predictable person" and "I make an effort to appear consistent to others." We also mentioned in Chapter 7 that people who score high in PFC exhibit stronger dissonance effects than do people who score low in PFC.

If the foot-in-the-door technique is caused, at least in part, by a desire for consistency, then people who score high in PFC may be more susceptible to the technique than people who score low in PFC. In fact, this is exactly what Cialdini and his colleagues (1995) found in an experiment using the foot-in-the-door technique (see also Guadagno, Asher, Demaine, & Cialdini, 2001).

The Door-in-the-Face Technique

Robert Cialdini and his colleagues at Arizona State University (Cialdini, Vincent, Lewis, Catalan, Wheeler, & Darby, 1975) wondered if the *opposite* of the foot-in-the-door technique might also, ironically, increase compliance with a second request. The **door-in-the-face technique** begins by making a very *large* request—one that is sure to be *turned down*. Once denied, the request is then followed by a *smaller* request—the one to which compliance is ultimately sought. The expectation is that these individuals, who have turned down one request, will be more likely to agree to a second request (we will explain why later!).

For example, in one study (Cialdini et al., 1975, Experiment 1), students were approached on a university campus and asked if they would be willing to accompany a group of juvenile delinquents on a two-hour trip to the zoo. For some students, this was the only request they received; as expected, most people declined (only 16% agreed). For other students, this request had been preceded by an even *larger* request: Would they be willing to serve as a counsellor to juvenile delinquents for at least two years? *Nobody* agreed to this initial large request. Yet when the large request was followed by the smaller request, fully 50% of the students agreed to accompany the group on a two-hour trip to the zoo. Thus, refusing a large request increased compliance with a smaller (but, in this case, still quite substantial) request.

How does the door-in-the-face technique work? It cannot be via self-perception or consistency processes (which contribute to the foot-in-the-door technique), because these processes would operate to make people who decline the first request *less* likely to agree to the second request as well (e.g., if they label themselves as unhelpful). What, then, causes greater compliance after a refusal? Cialdini and his colleagues (1975) proposed that a critical factor is the **norm of reciprocity.** Before we explain how this norm may account for the door-in-the-face technique, we need to define the norm itself: the norm of reciprocity is that we should reciprocate (give back in return) favours done for us. For example, if someone invites us to dinner, lends us money, or helps us in some other way, we should return the favour. You may have had the experience of receiving a birthday gift from someone and thinking, "Oops, I didn't give *him* (or her) a gift on his (or her) birthday." Did you feel guilty? If so, the norm of reciprocity may explain why: you know that if you received a gift, then you should have given a gift. The norm of reciprocity is very strong in Canada and appears to exist to some extent in most cultures around the world (Gouldner, 1960).

How does the norm of reciprocity explain the door-in-the-face technique? Cialdini and his colleagues (1975) suggested that when someone presents a second, smaller request following the refusal of a larger request, this second request may be seen as a *concession* on his or her part—a compromise in response to the initial refusal: "Well, then, would you at least be willing to . . . ?" Admittedly, this notion of a concession by the requester is rather illogical, because the target did not *ask* him or her to make the first request! Nevertheless, the target is susceptible to seeing the second request

door-in-the-face technique
a strategy to increase compliance, based on the fact that refusal of a large request increases the likelihood of agreement with a subsequent smaller request

"Excuse me, sir, would you be willing to volunteer four hours of your time at a homeless shelter next Saturday afternoon?"

norm of reciprocity
the principle that we should give back in return any favours that are done for us

as a compromise on the requester's part. Therefore, given that the requester has made a concession by lowering the demand, the target should make a concession in return (reciprocity); the most obvious concession would be to agree to the smaller request, which produces the door-in-the-face effect.

To get the door-in-the-face technique to work, the initial request must be large enough that most people will decline it, but it cannot be so outrageous that people consider it illegitimate (Schwarzwald, Raz, & Zvibel, 1979). If the initial request is illegitimate, then the requester will simply be ignored or dismissed. Also, the second request must be relatively close in time to the declined request, presumably because a long delay eliminates the perception that the two requests are connected—which is necessary if the second request is to be interpreted as a concession or compromise (Cann, Sherman, & Elkes, 1975).

The Free-Gift Technique

free-gift technique

a strategy to increase compliance, based on the fact that giving someone a small gift increases the likelihood of agreement with a subsequent request

It is possible to take advantage of the norm of reciprocity in a more straightforward way than the door-in-the-face technique. Specifically, *giving a small gift* to someone, or *doing a small favour* for someone, will make him or her feel indebted, which should increase willingness to comply with a subsequent request. A real-life example of this **free-gift technique** procedure comes from charities, which often mail small unsolicited gifts to potential donors, such as address labels, greeting cards, or calendars. The cover letter usually says that the gift is unconditional, but "a donation would certainly be appreciated." Recipients often feel enough pressure to reciprocate that they make a donation they would not have made if the gift had not been received. "Free gift," indeed.

Most of us can probably think of times when we have done a favour for someone we will need in the near future. Buying a drink for a friend before asking him or her to help you move might be an example. An experiment reported by Cornell University's Dennis Regan (1971) illustrated how the free-gift technique can be used to gain compliance. The real participants in this study were Cornell students paired with another student, who was actually an accomplice of the experimenter. In the "favour" condition of the experiment, the confederate went to get a soda and returned with an extra one for the unsuspecting student. In the "no-favour" condition, the confederate left the room for the same amount of time but returned with nothing. When the main part of the study was over, the confederate asked the naïve student to purchase some raffle tickets. Presumably feeling a need to return the earlier favour of a free soda, students in the favour condition responded by purchasing nearly twice as many raffle tickets as did students in the no-favour condition (for a related compliance technique, see Horvitz & Pratkanis, 2002).

Giving someone a small, free gift makes it more likely that he or she will then reciprocate by donating some money in return.

The Low-Ball Technique

Imagine yourself in the showroom of a car dealership. You have just made the deal of your life: a great car, all the features you want, and at a bargain price. As the paperwork is being prepared, you are imagining yourself driving home in that new car. Then the salesperson returns with some bad news. It seems the manager will not allow the deal to go through because the dealership would be losing just too much money. You were so close to having that car. But, for another $1000, the car can still be yours! You decide to go through with it—what's another thousand dollars? If you have fallen for this trick of the compliance trade, you have been the victim of the **low-ball technique.** The salesperson may never have intended to sell the car for the lower price and probably did not go to see the manager while you sat and waited.

The low-ball technique involves offering something at a given price and then raising the price after the individual agrees to the purchase. In an experimental demonstration of low-balling, university students were called on the telephone to be scheduled for participation in a psychology experiment (Cialdini, Cacioppo, Bassett, & Miller, 1978). Students in the control condition were told, right up front, that the experiment would need to be scheduled for 7:00 A.M. Even for that early time of day, 31% made the appointment and 24% actually showed up. In the low-ball condition, students were asked if they would agree to participate, but they were not told at what time. Only after they agreed were they told the time of day. Among these students, 56% made the appointment and 53% showed up at the designated time and place.

The *low-ball technique* involves offering something at a given price and then raising the price after the individual agrees to the purchase.

low-ball technique

a strategy to increase compliance, in which something is offered at a given price, but then, after agreement, the price is increased

Why does the low-ball technique work? One process may be a desire for consistency, such that people want to act consistently with their initial decision, or perhaps fear that they would look inconsistent if they did not carry through with the decision. Another, probably stronger component (at least in the car purchase example) may be *postdecisional dissonance* produced by the commitment. We explained in Chapter 7 that postdecisional dissonance leads to more favourable evaluations of the chosen alternative (see page 246). When people decide to buy a particular car and then go through the process of negotiating a price with the salesperson, they have made a private and public commitment to the car (see Burger & Cornelius, 2003). To justify this choice and commitment to themselves, people are likely to enhance their evaluation of the car. Thus, when the salesperson returns with the bad news, the purchaser now has an even more favourable attitude toward the car than he or she did before the negotiations. Hence, he or she is more likely to follow through on the purchase at the higher price.

The effectiveness of the low-ball technique is not limited to car sales and appointments for experiments. Among other applications, modified low-ball techniques have been shown to be successful in raising money for a museum (Brownstein & Katzev, 1985) and in getting people to abstain from smoking (Joule, 1987).

The Scarcity Technique

Scarcity is a quality that sells products. An artist's works become more valuable posthumously because no additional works will be forthcoming; parents climb all over one another trying to buy one of the few remaining samples of the latest rage for their children; and people rush to buy snow shovels or snow blowers when they think supplies might be getting short because the winter's first big storm is expected. It appears that if people think they may not be able to get something, then, masochistically, they really want that thing! Robert Cialdini (2001) summed up this effect of scarcity very clearly: "opportunities seem more valuable to us when they are less available" (p. 205).

The **scarcity technique** relies on these positive connotations of scarcity. This technique is one of the favourite methods used by retail stores to boost sales. How many times have you heard advertising appeals like these: *Hurry, a limited time offer! Only five left at this price! This sale will not be repeated!* The implications are clear: if you

scarcity technique

a strategy to increase the attractiveness of a product by making it appear rare or temporary

© Photodisc Green/Getty Images

Stores often try to utilize the *scarcity technique.*

liking technique

a strategy to increase compliance, based on the fact that people are more likely to assist others they find appealing than others they do not find appealing

don't act now, you will miss a fantastic opportunity. In fact, manufacturers sometimes deliberately produce products in limited numbers or offer them for a limited time to inflate the price and increase demand (e.g., some Disney videos). Making a product appear to be a scarce commodity increases its perceived value.

A simple demonstration of the scarcity technique was reported by Stephen Worchel, Jerry Lee, and Akanbi Adewole (1975). Students at the University of North Carolina were given a chocolate chip cookie and asked to taste it and then rate it on several scales. In one condition, the cookie was taken from a jar containing ten cookies. In another condition, the jar contained only two cookies, creating an experimental version of a scarce resource. Even though the cookies were all identical, they were rated as more desirable when they were taken from the two-cookie jar than from the ten-cookie jar.

The Liking Technique

We are more likely to comply with the requests of people we like than with the requests of people we dislike (Cialdini, 2001). This **liking technique** may not strike you as an earth-shattering revelation, but some of its implications may surprise you. Liking can be based on a variety of qualities and still exert an impact on compliance: we are more likely to be influenced by people who are physically attractive, people whom we know, people who are similar to us, and people who are trustworthy. In short, just about any source of likeability or attractiveness increases a requester's success.

Why does likeability increase compliance effectiveness? There are probably two main processes involved. First, we want to please and make happy people whom we like. It is rewarding for us to please them (and painful for us to displease them), so we are more likely to help them when requested to do so. Second, there is a *heuristic* that often contributes to this effect; we discussed heuristics in Chapter 3 (see page 84) and Chapter 7 (see page 259). Heuristics are simple, informal rules or shortcuts that we use to make judgments under some conditions, primarily when the decision is not terribly important. One heuristic that most of us follow is "I help people I like."

You have surely experienced the influence of this liking technique: when a friend asks a favour or when an outgoing and attractive salesperson makes a pitch, it is hard to resist. It is easier to say *no* to a stranger or to resist the suggestions of an unfriendly, dislikeable salesperson. The positive effect of liking lies at the heart of several compliance-producing techniques. For example, we are more likely to comply with the request of someone who has just flattered us than of someone who has not (Drachman, DeCarufel, & Insko, 1978), even if the flattery is as simple as the other person remembering our name (Howard, Gengler, & Jain, 1995).

Liking can even come from rather fleeting and arbitrary sources and still be influential. Dariusz Dolinski, Magdalena Nawrat, and Izabela Rudak (2001) at the University of Opole in Poland showed that very brief conversations between a confederate and a participant can increase compliance with a subsequent request. For example, in one experiment, a female university student approached other students individually in their dormitories and asked whether they would help out collecting money, books, and toys for children in an orphanage. Some participants were simply asked this request directly (after an opening "Hi!"); among this group, only 28% agreed. Other participants were exposed to a brief conversation prior to the request. Specifically, the woman asked them, "Hi! Is this session [examination period] going to be hard for you? How many exams are you taking? So, how are you feeling before the session?" Among participants exposed to this minimal conversation, 68% agreed to help out with the collections. The researchers suggested that this kind of conversation is characteristic of encounters with friends and acquaintances, so it serves as a heuristic to elicit responses like those directed to friends and acquaintances (see also Burger, Soroka, Gonzago, Murphy, & Somervell, 2001).

In another set of studies, Jerry Burger and his colleagues at Santa Clara University (Burger, Messian, Patel, del Prado, & Anderson, 2004) showed that university students were more likely to comply with another student's request (either for feedback on an essay or for money for a charity) when they shared a birthday, or a first name, or a "fingerprint type" with the student than when they did not have these coincidental similarities. In each study, the shared feature approximately doubled the rate of compliance or the size of donations. Taken together, these studies suggest that relatively minor manipulations of liking can have very substantial effects on compliance.

We have described six techniques that increase the likelihood that people will comply with another person's request. These techniques are used systematically by compliance professionals (salespersons, advertisers, real estate agents, etc.) and haphazardly by most of the rest of us. By studying the techniques—summarized in the accompanying Concept Review—we can arm ourselves against unwanted influence by watching for telltale signs of the techniques.

One unfortunate consequence of conformity and compliance pressure can be unhealthy behaviours, including alcohol, drug, and tobacco use. Exposure to these behaviours is an inevitable part of young people's lives, and the extent to which the exposure has a negative impact depends, at least in part, on the individuals' ability to resist compliance pressure. We discuss this issue in Social Psychology in Your Life: "Alcohol, Drug, and Tobacco Use."

CONCEPT REVIEW
Compliance Techniques

Technique	Description	Example
Foot-in-the-door technique	Agreeing to a small request increases the likelihood of agreeing to a second, larger request.	A struggling student asks a more talented classmate to explain something from the class, and then asks if the classmate would be willing to study together regularly.
Door-in-the-face technique	Refusing a large request increases the likelihood of agreeing to a second, smaller request.	Someone asks to borrow $100, and then reduces the request to $20 after the first request is refused.
Free-gift technique	Receiving a small gift increases the likelihood of agreeing to a subsequent request.	A charity sends free address labels to potential donors with a request for a contribution.
Low-ball technique	Agreeing to purchase something at a given price increases the likelihood of agreeing to purchase it at a higher price.	A car salesperson offers a car at a good price but is then "forced" by the "manager" to raise the price after the customer has agreed to the initial offer.
Scarcity technique	Making a product appear rare or temporary increases its attractiveness.	A store advertises a "limited time offer" for a product.
Liking technique	People are more likely to help others whom they like.	A salesperson flatters a customer to appear likeable.

Social Psychology in Your Life   *Alcohol, Drug, and Tobacco Use*

Do you smoke cigarettes? Do you drink alcohol? Have you ever tried marijuana? What about your friends? Do any of them have a substance abuse problem?

Chances are good that by late adolescence, most people have used alcohol, tobacco, or marijuana. For example, the Ontario Student Drug Use Survey in 2005 found that approximately two-thirds of the students in grades 7 to 12 in Ontario reported having consumed alcohol at some point in their lives, and approximately one-third reported having tried cigarettes and marijuana (Adlaf & Paglia-Boak, 2005). Think about the social conditions that foster these behaviours among young people. Very often, they involve social influence processes, such as conformity pressure and compliance techniques (Cohen & Fromme, 2002). People may go along with others to fit in, to be cool—because others are doing it. When the basic mechanisms of social influence are understood, it is not so surprising or puzzling that many young adults use or experiment with alcohol, drugs, or tobacco.

How, then, can we prevent people from getting involved with these substances? Historically, most prevention campaigns have used a combination of information and fear to curb substance abuse. As we discussed in the preceding chapter, fear appeals can be effective if they convince listeners that they are personally susceptible to a problem. But it is often difficult to convince young people that they may develop substance abuse problems. Also, information and fear

campaigns do not teach people any skills for resisting conformity and compliance pressure. Such skills might be important when young people encounter pressure in daily activities and at social events.

Some recent prevention programs have made specific attempts to address influence resistance skills. A good example is Project ALERT (Ellickson & Bell, 1990), a senior elementary school program that uses what we know about social norms and peer influence to prevent adolescent drug use. ALERT consists of 11 lessons in grade 7 and 3 lessons in grade 8. Teachers follow a curriculum to achieve several goals. One important goal is to change students' beliefs about drug and smoking norms. It turns out that most children overestimate the number of their peers who have used drugs and cigarettes, and overestimate the number who are favourable toward drug use and smoking. By providing accurate information, the program helps students realize that there is substantial social support for *not* using drugs and cigarettes. A second goal of the ALERT program is to provide specific skills to help young people resist conformity pressure. For example, students are helped to identify pro-drug pressures from peers, the media, and even parents (who might model cigarette or alcohol use). Students also discuss and rehearse ways to respond to these pressures. Small group activities are an important component of this program, as opposed to lectures.

A large-scale evaluation of Project ALERT was reported by Phyllis Ellickson,

Conformity pressure sometimes induces young adults to smoke.

Daniel McCaffrey, Bonnie Ghosh-Dastidar, and Douglas Longshore (2003). Forty-eight clusters of elementary schools in South Dakota were assigned randomly to the ALERT program or a control condition. More than 4000 students in grade 7 participated in the study. Before the program began, the experimental and control students were equivalent in alcohol, cigarette, and marijuana usage.

Eighteen months later, the students were surveyed again. The results were dramatic: students who had participated in the ALERT program reported substantially less substance use. Specifically, ALERT participants were significantly less likely to have used cigarettes, to have used marijuana, and to have *misused* alcohol (e.g., getting sick, binge drinking). The reductions in these outcome measures ranged from 19% to 39%, which represent major reductions. The focus on providing social skills for resisting influence appeared to work. Presumably, when students subsequently encountered conformity pressure, they were better able to withstand it.

  ## Obedience: Doing as Others Command

Obedience refers to conformity that results from another person's command or order (i.e., failing to obey was not presented as an option). We are taught from an early age to obey the commands of our parents. We learn quickly that disobedience can be

costly—the withdrawal of rewards, or even punishment. By the age of three or four, most children also know that police officers and doctors have special authority status, and it is best to obey their instructions. By the time we enter formal schooling environments (at the ripe old of age of five or six), most of us already know that the teacher is in command and obedience is expected.

The **norm of obedience to authority** refers to people's knowledge that legitimate authorities should be obeyed. This norm is powerful enough in our society that just the trappings of authority can be sufficient to produce obedience. For instance, when passers-by on a street were randomly approached and instructed to give a dime to a stranger, obedience was much greater when the individual was wearing the uniform of a security guard than when the same individual was wearing street clothes (Bickman, 1974).

It is easy to see how the trappings of authority can be used to extract obedience to small demands. It is also understandable that real authority typically elicits obedience. After all, people usually occupy positions of authority for a reason. Police officers are trained to keep the peace, doctors have special knowledge and skills to treat disease, and teachers are assigned the responsibility of guiding and training our children. An authority structure is especially important in the military, where soldiers are thoroughly trained to obey the orders of a superior officer.

So it is a good thing that we usually comply with the requests and obey the commands of legitimate authorities. Much of our social structure depends on respect and influence being given to authority figures. At the same time, however, our willingness to obey authorities may create a vulnerability to *destructive* social influence. What if a person of authority commands you to do something that conflicts with other important and valued goals? Suppose, for example, that an authority insists that you cause harm to another person. Would you obey? The norm of obedience to authority would press you to obey. But at the same time, you are not the kind of person who would deliberately cause harm to another, which would push you away from obedience. Which force would win in the end? When Stanley Milgram put this question to experimental test, the results were both surprising and disturbing.

norm of obedience to authority
the principle that we should obey legitimate authorities

Milgram's Obedience Studies

Stanley Milgram conducted one of the most famous sets of studies in the history of social psychology. During his career, Milgram was a professor at Harvard University, Yale University, and the City University of New York. His research was designed to explore the determinants of destructive obedience. To appreciate the significance of his work, we need to go over the procedure in some detail.

The Basic Procedure. Milgram (1963) devised a laboratory situation for studying obedience to authority. The goal of Milgram's obedience research was to create a setting that would be involving and realistic for the participants, but that would also permit a high degree of experimental control. Participants were recruited through advertisements in the local newspaper. When they arrived at the laboratory (at Yale University in New Haven, Connecticut), they were greeted by an experimenter and by one other person who also arrived as a participant. In fact, the other "participant" was really the experimenter's accomplice (confederate). The experimenter explained that this was an investigation of memory and learning. One of the two participants would be assigned the role of "learner" and the other the role of "teacher." The two then drew slips of paper from a hat to determine who would be the learner and who would be the teacher. The drawing was rigged so that the naïve participant was always the teacher and the confederate was always the learner.

FIGURE 8.5 The "shock machine" in Milgram's obedience studies

© 1965 by Stanley Milgram. From *Obedience* (film). Courtesy of Alexandra Milgram.

The experimenter went on to explain that this particular study was looking at the role of punishment in the learning process. The teacher would administer a memory test to the learner. Whenever the learner made a mistake, the teacher was to administer an electric shock. The learner was then strapped into a chair next to a wall, and electrodes were attached to his wrist.

The teacher was then taken to a different room and seated in front of a shock-generating machine. This machine was an instrument panel consisting of 30 switches in a horizontal row (see Figure 8.5). The switch at the far left was labelled "15 volts," and each successive switch was labelled in 15-volt increments, reaching "450 volts" at the far right. Verbal designations were also attached to sets of four switches—from left to right: Slight Shock, Moderate Shock, Strong Shock, Very Strong Shock, Intense Shock, Extreme Intensity Shock, and Danger: Severe Shock. The last two switches were simply labelled "XXX."

The teacher was given a "sample" shock from the 45-volt switch, which was enough to give a bit of a jolt. The teacher was instructed to administer an electric shock each time the learner made a mistake on the memory test. The key instruction was that the teacher was to move one level higher after each mistake. If the teacher expressed concern or wanted to stop at any point, the experimenter responded with a series of planned prods. The first prod was "Please continue" or "Please go on." The second prod was "The experiment requires that you continue." The third prod was "It is absolutely essential that you continue." The fourth prod was "You have no other choice, you *must* go on." These prods were always given in sequence, and only until the teacher obeyed. If the teacher still refused to go on after the fourth prod, the study was halted.

Several additional features of the laboratory setup should be mentioned. The experimenter was carefully trained to play the role of an authority. He was dressed in a grey coat, and maintained a stern (but not mean) appearance throughout the procedure. The learner was also specially trained for the role; he was a mild-mannered and likeable 47-year-old accountant. The study was clearly connected with Yale University—an institution generally held in very high regard. The "teachers" (the only naïve participants in the study) were recruited from the community. There were 40 of them, all male, between the ages of 20 and 50. They represented a variety of occupations and educational levels. They were paid $4 for their participation, but they were told that payment was solely for coming to the laboratory, and that the money was theirs to keep no matter what happened during the study.

The responses of the learner were all programmed. He gave wrong answers about 75% of the time. When the 300-volt shock level was reached, the teacher could hear a pounding on the wall, presumably from the learner banging on the wall next to his chair. The same thing happened after the 315-volt shock. After that point, the learner no longer responded to the test questions and no sounds were heard from him. The experimenter told the teacher that no answer was to be considered a wrong answer, and prodded him to continue. Although the teachers never knew it, keep in mind that the "learner" never received an electric shock. It was all an elaborate show.

What Would You Do? That is the basic procedure of Milgram's (1963) initial study. Imagine yourself as the teacher. How far would you go? Would you administer even a single shock? Would you go all the way to the end (30 switches)? When Milgram asked students and colleagues to predict what 100 hypothetical "teachers" would do, they agreed that only a very small percentage would go all the way to the end. They guessed that very few teachers would even go beyond the "Very Strong Shock" level (195–240 volts; switches 13–16). When Milgram (1974) asked 31 university students to predict their *own* behaviour in such a study, not a single one predicted obedience to the end (to the 450-volt level). In fact, the highest prediction was to switch 14 (210 volts). On average, these students predicted that they would stop after switch 9 or 10.

The First Study. When Milgram (1963) did his first study, just as it has been described here, he found that 26 of the 40 teachers, or 65%, were completely obedient—they continued to press the electric shock switches all the way to the end (switch 30; 450 volts). The first point at which *any* teacher refused to go on was at switch 20 (300 volts; the last of the "Intense Shock" switches). On average, these participants playing the role of teacher gave a maximum shock corresponding to switch 27.

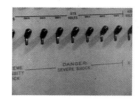

"[Scream of agony] Let me out of here! Let me out of here! My heart's bothering me! Let me out, I tell you! Let me out! Let me out! Let me out of here! Let me out! Let me out! Let me out!"

Variations on the Theme. The results of the first obedience study were surprising, to say the least. Nobody, including Milgram, expected to find obedience to that extent. The results prompted Milgram to conduct a number of variations on the original study (reported in Milgram, 1974). In the first variation (the second obedience study), more extensive vocal feedback was programmed from the learner. Remember that the original study involved pounding on the wall by the learner starting at the 300-volt shock level. In this variation, the teacher could hear protests from the learner starting at a much earlier stage. At first, the learner could be heard exclaiming in pain. The protests got louder, and at 150 volts (switch 10), the learner yelled that he wanted to stop and that his heart was bothering him. The protests grew in their intensity at each succeeding shock level. Of the 40 new "teachers" who participated in Study 2, 25 of them (62.5%) were completely obedient (going all the way to shock level 30). On average, they gave a maximum shock corresponding to switch 25.

In a third study, the learner was moved into closer proximity of the teacher. Instead of being seated in an adjacent room, the learner was seated in the same room. Forty more "teachers" participated; 16 of them (40%) were fully obedient. The average maximum shock in this study was switch 21. In a fourth study, the teacher was required to hold the learner's hand down on a plate to receive the electric shock. Forty more "teachers" were tested; 12 of them (30%) went all the way to shock level 30, with an average maximum shock of switch 18.

The results of the first four studies are graphed in Figure 8.6, which shows how the average maximum shock decreased across the studies. Even though obedience was still very high in the fourth study, it was clearly decreasing as the learner was brought into closer and closer proximity of the teacher (Milgram, 1974). Milgram continued to explore variations on the basic theme. He moved the laboratory away from Yale University, he changed the personnel who played the roles of learner and experimenter, and he had women participate as teachers. Still, the average maximum shock rarely went lower than switch number 20.

In another variation of the study (Milgram, 1974), the naïve participant acted as one of the "teachers," but was not responsible for actually pressing the shock-generating switch. Instead, another teacher (actually the experimenter's confederate) was assigned the job of pressing the switches. The naïve teachers were in a position to halt the procedure by refusing to go on at any point. Although they were not pressing the switches themselves, they would be passively permitting a peer to cause harm by simply continuing to participate as an assistant. And that's precisely what happened. Out of 40 teachers, 37 of them permitted the other teacher to continue all the way to switch number 30. When they were one

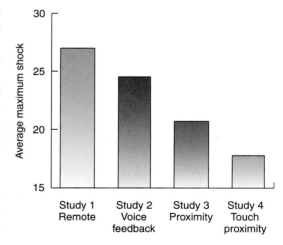

FIGURE 8.6 Average maximum shock delivered by "teachers" in Milgram's first four obedience studies

From S. Milgram, *Obedience to Authority: An Experimental View*, p. 36. Copyright © 1974 by Stanley Milgram. Reprinted by permission of HarperCollins Publishers.

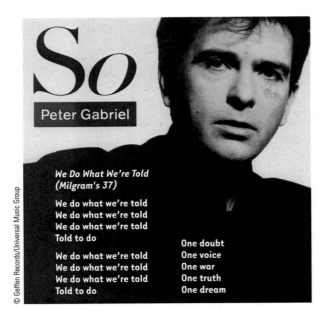

Lyrics from Peter Gabriel's song "We Do What We're Told (Milgram's 37)."

step removed from the act itself, almost all of the naïve teachers were willing to serve as accessories to the act. This result was so disturbing that it moved singer/songwriter Peter Gabriel to record "We Do What We're Told" (subtitled "Milgram's 37").

What Makes Obedience Go Away?   The results of the obedience studies were very troubling. It is hard to believe that people would obey authority to the extent of causing physical harm to another person for no good reason. Is it possible that people are naturally aggressive, and that the teachers were just taking the opportunity to unleash their aggressive urges? As it turns out, this is probably not a valid explanation for the results. When Milgram (1974) allowed the teachers to *select their own shock level* (rather than prodding them to continue up the scale), remarkably little "aggression" was observed. Only one teacher (out of 40) ever pushed switch number 30. Almost all of them stayed below switch number 10, and on average they gave a maximum shock corresponding to switch number 6. So, clearly, people would prefer *not* to administer intense shocks to another person.

What, then, can be done to liberate people from the destructive influence of the authority? In one variation on the basic procedure (Milgram, 1974), two experimenters were in charge. Both had all the trappings of authority, and both proceeded in complete agreement until the teacher got to switch number 10. At that point, one of the experimenters delivered the standard prod for the teacher to continue. But the other experimenter instructed the teacher to stop. Of the 20 teachers in this study, one had stopped just before the disagreement (at switch 9), 18 refused to continue precisely at the point of the experimenters' disagreement (switch 10), and the one remaining teacher refused to continue after switch 11. At last, a procedure was identified that effectively halted teachers along the escalating scale of switches. In an important sense, however, this was still a case of obedience to authority—only now, teachers were able to choose which of two equal authorities they would obey. Their choice was the authority who commanded them to stop.

The Legacy of the Obedience Studies

Milgram's studies have had a profound influence. Within the field of social psychology, they stirred an intense debate about research ethics, and led ultimately to the enactment of regulations regarding the treatment of human participants in research. Beyond the field of social psychology, the studies became widely known and widely cited—perhaps more than any other program of research in psychology (Miller, 1986). The research has been extended in many directions (Miller, 1986) and has been used to help understand crimes of obedience (e.g., Kelman & Hamilton, 1989).

Beyond the Original Obedience Studies.   Several studies have replicated or extended the basic obedience study (e.g., Blass, 1991; Miller, 1986). Studies have been conducted with participants in other countries, with children, and with other procedural variations. The same basic result is consistently obtained: many people readily accept the influence of an authority, even when that means causing potential harm to another person. One interesting application of this concept has been to the nurse–physician relationship. Several studies have shown that nurses will often carry out the orders of a physician even when there is good reason to believe that potential harm could come to the patient (Hofling, Brotzman, Dalrymple, Graves, & Pierce, 1966; Krackow & Blass, 1995).

Obedience in Society: How Far Can We Generalize? In Milgram's (1963) original paper, he motivated the study of obedience to authority by noting how obedience pressures could be implicated in the atrocities committed by German soldiers under the Nazi regime. In the very first paragraph of his paper, Milgram noted the following:

> Gas chambers were built, death camps were guarded, daily quotas of corpses were produced with the same efficiency as the manufacture of appliances. These inhumane policies may have originated in the mind of a single person, but they could only be carried out on a massive scale if a very large number of persons obeyed orders. (p. 371)

The experimental analysis of obedience has been used to understand other tragic events and crimes, including the My Lai massacre during the Vietnam War and the Watergate scandal (see Kelman & Hamilton, 1989). Are such extensions and applications valid? After all, the laboratory version of obedience developed by Milgram is a far cry from the settings and the social conditions that were operating at the time of such historical incidents. Indeed, critics of Milgram's approach (e.g., Baumrind, 1964) have argued that there is only a very weak parallel, at best. In reply, Milgram (1964) pointed out that the events of the Holocaust provided the *incentive* to begin a formal analysis of obedience to authority; the intent was not, nor could it be, to re-create those events in the laboratory.

Yet sometimes events in the news remind us of Milgram's findings. For example, in 1992, soldiers of the Canadian Airborne Regiment were deployed to the African country of Somalia at the request of the United Nations to help re-establish order in the country, which was in chaos after years of famine and civil war. Less than six months later, the Canadian public learned that at least two Canadian soldiers had tortured and murdered a 16-year-old Somalian prisoner, Shidane Arone. Subsequent discovery of photos showing one of the Canadian soldiers, Clayton Matchee, grinning beside a bloodied Arone shocked both military officials and the Canadian public—how could this young man have engaged in such behaviour? Abuse of prisoners is something done by other, immoral armies, not the Canadian military. But there was no possible denial—the photos were unambiguous. Why did this murder occur? The two soldiers claimed that they were just following orders from senior officers to be rough on Somalian looters (an allegation the military denied). In another bizarre turn in the case, Matchee attempted to hang himself and suffered severe brain damage, leaving him with the mental ability of a five-year-old; to the present day, he has been judged incompetent to stand trial. The second soldier was convicted of manslaughter and served five years in a military prison.

Milgram's research probably does inform us about destructive obedience in our society. His studies documented that people are more obedient to authority than most of us realize. At the same time, his research identified some of the factors that influence obedience, including the proximity of the victim, the actions of other people in the setting, and situational cues in the immediate environment (e.g., the labels on the shock generator). His participants were not blindly obedient—their actions were affected by relevant factors around them (although the overall level of obedience was higher than we might wish).

One perspective on Milgram's research that is not always recognized is that participants were placed in a situation that involved a slow escalation of aggression, which made it difficult for them to stop at any particular point. If a teacher had delivered a shock of 150 volts, why would a shock of 165 volts be immoral? And if the teacher had delivered a shock of 165 volts, why would a shock of 180 volts be immoral? And so on, up the scale on the shock generator, until teachers found themselves administering intense shocks. Thus, participants became slowly committed to their role in the study, once they began administering shocks after the learner's first error. This escalating commitment made a later decision to disobey very difficult. Perhaps Milgram's studies offer a warning that resistance to unethical commands must begin immediately, before people commit themselves in any way to their role in the setting.

The Question of Research Ethics. A serious criticism levelled against Milgram's obedience studies was that they involved the unethical treatment of human participants in psychological research (Baumrind, 1964; Kelman, 1967). The concern was that naïve participants were brought into a situation that could cause them serious emotional harm, without being informed at the outset of what they might experience. Milgram (1964) defended the research and pointed out that the vast majority of participants indicated afterwards that they were glad to have been in the study. A follow-up interview, conducted one year after the study, suggested that none of the participants had suffered any psychological harm.

Some researchers have used active role-playing as a way of reducing ethical concerns about research on obedience (e.g., Meeus & Raaijmakers, 1995). In role-playing studies, participants are placed in a full physical replication of the original obedience studies, but they know that shocks are not being administered and the setting is staged. They are instructed to act as they would if the situation were real. These role-playing studies have produced results that are quite similar to the original studies.

In the next, concluding section of the chapter, we turn from the specifics of conformity, compliance, and obedience to a broader perspective, identifying some of the underlying processes common to all of these behaviours. Researchers are interested in these general mechanisms in order to develop models of conformity that have the widest possible application.

General Mechanisms Underlying Conformity, Compliance, and Obedience

Research on social influence has produced a remarkable array of results. Social psychologists now know some of the factors that produce conformity to others' actions, can identify numerous techniques that are effective in getting people to comply with requests, and understand something about humans' vulnerability to authority. But are there general processes or motivations that apply to all of these domains? In the following pages, we describe three perspectives that have some applicability to conformity, compliance, and obedience.

Informational and Normative Influence: Accuracy and Social Motivation

The first perspective comes from the distinction we introduced at the beginning of the chapter between informational influence and normative influence. These two types of influence represent different underlying motivations.

Accuracy Motivation. People are motivated to have a correct understanding of events in the world, to make accurate decisions, and generally to be competent in dealing with their environments. One important way that people achieve these accuracy goals is by observing, copying, or interrogating others. For example, by engaging in social comparison, people can evaluate their beliefs and modify them, if necessary, to be more similar to others' beliefs. By watching and imitating experts, people can benefit from their experience and knowledge. When people encounter ambiguous tasks like the one in Sherif's studies, they can look to others for guidance about the appropriate response.

All of these examples refer to *informational influence* from other people. That is, people are an important source of information about the world, and it often makes sense to conform to their actions or attitudes.

Social Motivation. Part of being human is a desire to establish and maintain social relationships. Indeed, to survive and thrive, humans *need* other people; we are inherently social creatures. This need for affiliation and interpersonal relationships underlies, at least in part, conformity, compliance, and obedience. Even when the nature of a relationship with another person is minimal, such as the relationships between participants in a study (e.g., between the various group members in Asch's experiments), people try to be agreeable and to make others like them. You may recall from our discussion of *impression management* in Chapter 4 that one *self-presentation goal* that is almost always active in people's minds is to appear likeable, even to strangers (see page 143). Conforming to others' opinions and judgments is one way to get them to like us.

These examples refer to *normative influence* from others. That is, people want to be liked and respected by others, and conformity sometimes represents individuals' attempts to maintain positive relationships or avoid unpleasant interactions. In an interesting study that illustrated this kind of normative influence, University of Toronto social psychologist Romin Tafarodi and his colleagues (Tafarodi, Kang, & Milne, 2002) showed that members of visible minorities (e.g., Chinese Canadians) sometimes conform to the judgments of the majority group in order to be accepted by the majority group.

The connections between informational/normative influence and accuracy/social motivation are summarized in the accompanying Concept Review.

The importance of social attachments and positive interpersonal relationships is made very clear by the devastating psychological effects of *ostracism*—the exclusion of someone from a group (Gruter & Masters, 1986). Ostracism has been shown to produce a range of negative reactions, including depression, anxiety, and feelings of helplessness (e.g., Leary, 1990; Sommer, Williams, Ciarocco, & Baumeister, 2001). Ostracism, or the threat of ostracism, also increases individuals' conformity to the

CONCEPT REVIEW
Informational/Normative Influence and Accuracy/Social Motivation

Concept	Description	Interconnections
Informational influence	Influence from other people that derives from their serving as sources of information	Often caused by accuracy motivation
Normative influence	Influence from other people that derives from perceptions of what behaviour is considered proper and improper	Often caused by social motivation
Accuracy motivation	The desire to make accurate judgments and decisions	One important source of informational influence
Social motivation	The desire to establish and maintain social relationships	One important source of normative influence

Ostracism from a group is an extremely painful experience.

norms of the group: people try to show their loyalty to the group by conforming to the actions and attitudes of group members, hoping to avoid exclusion (e.g., Baumeister & Leary, 1995; Leary & Baumeister, 2000; Rudman & Fairchild, 2004; Williams, Cheung, & Choi, 2000).

More subtle evidence suggesting that it can be painful to disagree with others was reported by John Bassili (2003) of the University of Toronto. Bassili summarized the results of four attitude surveys that were conducted over the telephone. Canadian respondents were asked to state their position on a variety of social issues, such as "Do you think that large companies should have quotas to ensure a fixed percentage of women are hired, or should women get no special treatment?" and "Do you think that it should be against the law to write or speak in a way that promotes hatred toward a particular racial or religious group?" Participants' responses were recorded, as well as the *speed* of each response (reaction time). Bassili found that people who held the *more* common view answered significantly more quickly, on average, than did people who held the *less* common view on 20 of the 36 items, whereas the reverse was true (significantly faster responses by people who held the *less* common view) on only 2 of the 36 items (the other 14 items showed no significant differences in either direction). For instance, on the quota question, 39% of respondents thought that quotas were a good idea, whereas 58% supported no quotas (3% had no opinion). The average response times for these groups were 5.19 seconds for the quota position (the less common view) and 4.56 seconds for the no-quota position (the more common view). Similarly, response times for the hatred question differed for respondents holding different positions. In this case, 30% thought that it should *not* be against the law to promote hatred, whereas 69% thought that it should be against the law. Respondents who expressed the first position (less common view) took an average of 5.27 seconds, whereas respondents who expressed the second position (more common view) took an average of 3.27 seconds.

Why do people who hold less common views on an issue answer questions about that issue more slowly than people who hold the more common view? Bassili (2003) suggested that there is implicit pressure to conform to the more common positions in society, and people who hold less common positions feel hesitant about reporting their opinion. The possible negative responses of others inhibit those with less common views from expressing their attitudes (see also Christensen, Rothgerber, Wood, & Matz, 2004).

Terror Management Theory

terror management theory

a model hypothesizing that recognition of their own mortality raises anxiety in humans, which they can reduce by affirming and conforming to their cultural worldview

A second perspective on conformity comes from a theory with the intriguing name of **terror management theory,** which was developed primarily by Jeff Greenberg at the University of Arizona, Sheldon Solomon at Skidmore College, and Tom Pyszczynski at the University of Colorado (Greenberg, Solomon, & Pyszczynski, 1997; Solomon, Greenberg, & Pyszczynski, 1991). Building on work in cultural anthropology (e.g., Becker, 1962), these theorists suggested that humans face a unique problem among animal species: we know that we are mortal—that, one day, we will die. This awareness of our mortality is hypothesized to be deeply threatening; in fact, it is hypothesized to arouse potentially paralyzing terror. This hypothesis may strike you as implausible, because you do not feel terror about your own mortality. But terror management theorists would say that your lack of terror is the result of protective strategies that you have been taught during socialization or have developed on your own.

How do humans control the terror caused by knowing that we will die? Terror management theorists propose that humans embrace *cultural worldviews*—cultural conceptions of reality. For instance, people take comfort in cultural belief systems (norms, religious teachings, etc.) that impose stability on the world and give meaning to their existence. Importantly, cultural worldviews also provide a sense of immortality. Some people derive from their cultural worldview a belief in *literal* immortality—they will live on after death (e.g., religious beliefs in heaven, reincarnation, afterlife, etc.); such beliefs obviously help to reduce terror about one's own physical mortality. But even without believing in literal immortality, a cultural worldview can give people a feeling of *symbolic* immortality because they know that things like their children, their valued achievements, and important social institutions will live on after their own death. This symbolic immortality is hypothesized to reduce the threat of one's own physical demise.

Terror management theory has been applied to many different topics in social psychology, including research on self-esteem, aggression, attitudes, and prejudice. The fundamental point the theory makes in each of these domains is that belief in a cultural worldview can serve the function of managing death-related anxiety. For example, prejudice and aggression against members of outgroups may protect individuals from a fear of death by confirming their own group's values and ideology. If prejudice and aggression against outgroup members do serve this function, then prejudice and aggression may be more extreme when individuals have been *reminded* of their own mortality—and exactly this effect has been documented in research (e.g., Greenberg, Pyszczynski, Solomon, Rosenblatt, Veeder, Kirkland, et al., 1990; Harmon-Jones, Greenberg, Solomon, & Simon, 1996). In a similar vein, the University of Alberta's Jeff Schimel and his colleagues have shown that reminding people of their own mortality increases their use of stereotypes (Schimel, Simon, Greenberg, Pyszczynski, Solomon, Waxmonsky, & Arndt, 1999).

What relevance does terror management theory have to understanding conformity? This theory hypothesizes that conformity to social values and cultural worldviews can serve to protect people from death anxiety. By conforming to a group's

© AP Photo/Doug Kanter

Terror management theory hypothesizes that thinking about our mortality arouses anxiety.

norms and beliefs, people show others (and perhaps convince themselves) that this cultural worldview is valid. Validating one's cultural worldview allows people to be more confident that it will live on past their own death. Thus, conformity to a group's norms and beliefs can, indirectly, provide a sense of symbolic immortality. Presumably, conformity can be in the form of copying other group members' behaviours, complying with requests from group members, or obeying the commands of group leaders.

If conformity to one's cultural worldview protects against fear of mortality, then making people aware of their mortality should heighten their commitment to, and endorsement of, cultural values. This effect has been documented in several studies. For example, Jeff Greenberg and his colleagues (Greenberg, Pyszczynski, Solomon, Simon, & Breus, 1994) induced some participants at the University of Arizona to think about their own death by answering two questions: "Please briefly describe the emotions that the thought of your own death arouses in you" and "Jot down, as specifically as you can, what you think will happen to you physically as you die and once you are physically dead." After answering these questions, participants were given two essays about the United States allegedly written by different foreign students. One essay was pro-American, focusing on freedom, opportunities, and safety, whereas the other was anti-American, focusing on economic inequities, materialism, and lack of sympathy for people. Participants then rated the authors of the essays (e.g., intelligence) and indicated their agreement with the arguments in the essay. Participants who had been induced to think about their own death rated the pro-American author much more positively than the anti-American author and agreed much more with the content of the pro-American essay than the anti-American essay; in contrast, participants in a control condition who were not induced to think about their own death were only slightly more positive about the pro-American author and essay. Presumably, when their own mortality was salient,

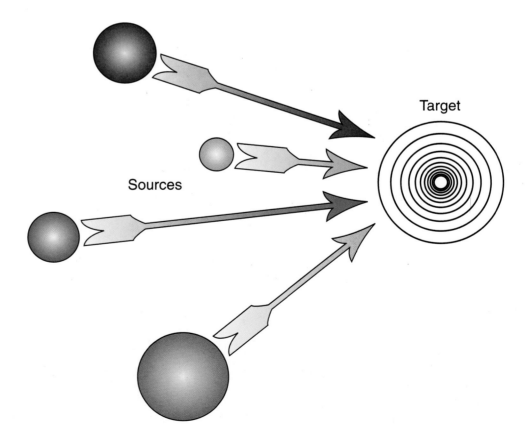

FIGURE 8.7 A pictorial representation of social impact theory, showing the influence of strength, immediacy, and number of sources on a target

Adapted from Latané, 1981, "The psychology of social impact," *American Psychologist*, 36, 343–356.

participants wanted to reaffirm the values of American society, because this cultural worldview gave their lives meaning and provided symbolic immortality (see also Landau, Solomon, Greenberg, Cohen, Pyszczynski, Arndt, et al., 2004).

Terror management theory provides a unique perspective on conformity. It views conformity as one means to achieve a goal that people may not recognize in themselves—namely, to control the anxiety created by awareness of their own mortality. The theory does not claim that fear of death is the only cause of conformity—people may conform for other reasons as well (e.g., relying on others to make an accurate decision). Nevertheless, this approach renders understandable some instances of conformity that would otherwise seem difficult to explain.

Social Impact Theory

Perhaps the broadest and most comprehensive attempt to explain social influence has been **social impact theory** (Latané, 1981; Tanford & Penrod, 1984). This theory conceives of social influence as being the result of *social forces* (pressures from other people) that operate on a target. The theory uses the metaphor of *physical* forces, such as light or sound, that can affect an object. The overall influence of a set of social forces depends on the forces' strength, immediacy, and number. *Strength* refers to the *intensity* of each social force, which reflects things like status, power, or credibility. Your boss can exert more influence on you than can a co-worker because your boss has more power over you. *Immediacy* refers to the *closeness* of each social force, which can reflect either physical or psychological proximity. Someone standing right next to you can exert more influence than someone communicating by e-mail, because face-to-face interaction is more immediate. *Number* refers simply to the *quantity* of social forces present. Five friends trying to get you to do something can produce more influence than one friend because there are more sources of pressure.

A schematic version of this view of social influence is shown in Figure 8.7. The amount of influence bearing on a target is a function of the strength of each source (depicted by the size of each source's circle), the immediacy of each source (depicted by the distance between each source and the target), and the total number of sources (Latané, 1981).

Mathematical models are quite rare in social psychology because the concepts and principles in the field are usually difficult to express in quantitative terms (see Fiske, 2004). Because social impact theory views social forces as akin to physical forces, it offers formulas that specify quite precisely the relationships between (1) the strength, immediacy, and number of social forces and (2) overall social influence. These formulas can capture important features of social influence.

For example, one principle of social impact theory deals specifically with the relation between the *number* of social forces and overall social influence. The principle is called the **psychosocial law** (Latané, 1981) and expresses the relation in terms of a mathematical equation. For our purposes, the important point about the equation is that it predicts that as the *number* of social forces increases, overall social influence also increases *but at a declining rate.* That is, each additional source of influence will have a diminishing impact on overall social influence. For example, increasing the number of sources from five to six will have less impact than increasing the number from two to three.

This reasoning may sound familiar to you, because it is exactly what Harold Gerard, Roland Wilhelmy, and Edward Conolley (1968) found when they investigated the effects of group size on conformity in the Asch line judgment task. We talked earlier about this experiment (see page 292), which showed that conformity increased as the size of the incorrect majority increased, but only up to a certain point. A graphical version of the findings is reproduced in Figure 8.8.

social impact theory
a model that conceives of influence from other people as being the result of social forces acting on individuals, much as physical forces can affect an object

psychosocial law
a principle in social impact theory that specifies the nature of the relation between the size of a group and its social influence. The principle predicts that as the number of social forces increases, overall social influence also increases, but at a declining rate.

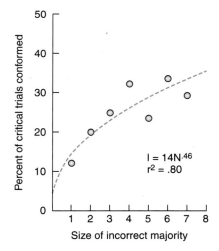

FIGURE 8.8 Fitting the psychosocial law equation from social impact theory to the data of Gerard, Wilhelmy, and Conolley (1968)

Adapted from Latané, 1981, "The psychology of social impact," *American Psychologist, 36,* 343–356.

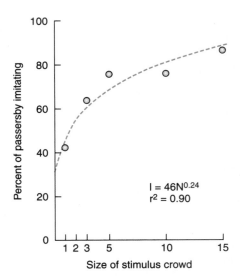

FIGURE 8.9 Fitting the psychosocial law equation from social impact theory to the data of Milgram, Bickman, and Berkowitz (1969)

Adapted from Latané, 1981, "The psychology of social impact," *American Psychologist*, 36, 343–356.

In the graph, the actual results of the 1968 experiment are depicted as open circles. The dashed curve is the predicted function generated by the equation from the psychosocial law; the curve does a good job of capturing the pattern of results (Latané, 1981).

Another simple study of social influence also illustrates the predictive accuracy of the psychosocial law. Stanley Milgram, Leonard Bickman, and Leonard Berkowitz (1969) conducted a field experiment in the streets of New York City. These researchers had between 1 and 15 assistants stop on a sidewalk and begin looking up at the sixth floor of a building. Unknown to naïve passers-by, their responses were being recorded—in particular, whether they looked up as well. When even 1 confederate was looking up, 42% of the passers-by also looked up. When the group of confederates was 15, 86% of the passers-by looked up. But once again, with each added group member, the size of the increase in conformity diminished. These results are shown in Figure 8.9, where again the original results are depicted as open circles and the dashed curve represents the predicted function generated by the psychosocial law equation, which does an excellent job of capturing the observed data (Latané, 1981).

Social impact theory has been used to describe many of the conformity and compliance effects discussed in this chapter. Equations from the theory predict results from a range of experiments quite well. The major shortcoming is that the theory and others like it (e.g., Tanford & Penrod, 1984) do not really *explain* what is happening inside the minds and bodies of the people who are being influenced. The equations provide a good *description* of social influence effects, but they do not tell us much about *why* social influence occurs.

It remains for future theorists to understand why the equations from social impact theory work so well and to translate them into psychological processes. Perhaps the other general mechanisms we have described—informational versus normative influence and terror management theory—will provide some of the conceptual basis for an integrative model.

The act of looking up is contagious.

© Stuart Hannagan/Getty Images

Chapter Summary

In this chapter, we reviewed social psychological research on three kinds of social influence. **Conformity** refers to *any* change in behaviour caused by another person or group. **Compliance** refers to a change in behaviour that is *requested* by another person or group. **Obedience** refers to a change in behaviour that is *ordered* by another person or group. Conformity is the most general of these concepts and, in fact, encompasses compliance and obedience.

Conforming behaviours happen for two principal reasons. **Informational influence** occurs when people are influenced by others because of a desire to be correct and to obtain valuable information. **Normative influence** occurs when people are influenced by others to gain rewards or avoid punishment. These kinds of influence can occur simultaneously.

People sometimes go along with the behaviour of others because of **social norms**—socially defined standards of proper and improper behaviour. In a series of studies, Muzafer Sherif used the **autokinetic effect** to study the emergence of norms. The autokinetic effect refers to the fact that in a darkened room, a stationary point of light will appear to move. When asked to estimate the amount of movement of the light—an ambiguous task—people are influenced by the responses of others, and norms that emerge in groups are maintained when members respond individually.

Solomon Asch studied conformity on a task in which the correct answer was obvious. Participants often conformed on a line judgment task when several experimental confederates had unanimously given the same, clearly incorrect answer. The **Crutchfield apparatus** was developed to study conformity more efficiently than using Asch's original procedure. The Crutchfield apparatus consists of an electrical panel with several rows of lights; it simulates the responses of numerous hypothetical participants.

Conformity researchers found that conformity was greater when tasks were ambiguous and difficult. Conformity also increased with larger groups, but only up to about four or five members. Studies in different cultures have yielded higher rates of conformity in collectivist cultures than in individualist cultures. Researchers have also uncovered a small gender difference, with women tending to conform somewhat more than men, but only when responses are public.

A variety of compliance techniques have been identified. The **foot-in-the-door technique** reflects that agreement to a small request results in higher rates of agreement to a subsequent, larger request. This technique may rely on self-perception processes and/or a desire for consistency. The **door-in-the-face technique** reflects that refusal of a very large request results in higher rates of agreement to a subsequent, smaller request. This technique probably relies on the **norm of reciprocity,** which is that we should reciprocate favours done for us. The **free-gift technique** also relies on the norm of reciprocity; it involves giving someone a small gift in order to increase the likelihood that he or she will comply with a subsequent request. The **low-ball technique** occurs when something is offered at a given price but then, after agreement, the price is increased. Even though the modified deal is less attractive, people have committed themselves to the course of action and may have engaged in postdecisional dissonance reduction. The **scarcity technique** involves making a product appear scarce or temporary to increase its attractiveness. The **liking technique** reflects the fact that we are more likely to comply with the requests of people we like than with the requests of people we dislike. This technique may rely on the fact that we want to please people we like and on the heuristic that we help people we like.

The **norm of obedience to authority** refers to people's knowledge that legitimate authorities should be obeyed. A series of studies by Stanley Milgram showed how powerful this norm is in our society. On the insistence of a person of authority (an experimenter in a lab coat), participants were willing to administer what they believed to be painful electric shocks to an innocent victim. The rate of obedience was influenced systematically by cues in the setting (e.g., the proximity of the victim), but the overall level of obedience was unexpectedly high. These studies raised considerable awareness about people's susceptibility to authoritative commands.

Several general mechanisms may apply across the domains of conformity, compliance, and obedience. Informational influence, which reflects a motive to make accurate judgments, and normative influence, which reflects a motive to maintain social relationships, can be applied to all of the topics in this chapter. **Terror management theory** hypothesizes that recognition of their own mortality raises anxiety in humans, which they can reduce by conforming to the values and standards of their group—that is, their cultural worldview. **Social impact theory** conceives of social influence as being the result of social forces acting on individuals, much as physical forces can affect an object. The theory provides mathematical models of conformity and compliance. For example, the **psychosocial law** specifies the nature of the relation between the size of a group and its social influence; the principle predicts that as the number of social forces increases, overall social influence also increases, but at a declining rate.

Key Terms

autokinetic effect (290)

compliance (287)

conformity (287)

Crutchfield apparatus (293)

door-in-the-face technique (301)

foot-in-the-door technique (299)

free-gift technique (302)

informational influence (288)

liking technique (304)

low-ball technique (303)

norm of obedience to authority (307)

norm of reciprocity (301)

normative influence (289)

obedience (287)

psychosocial law (317)

scarcity technique (303)

social impact theory (317)

social norm (289)

terror management theory (314)

Social Psychology Alive on the Web

SOCIAL PSYCHOLOGY ALIVE: ONLINE LABS

To perform the following experiment and see how you compare to other students, go to Social Psychology Lab, which can be accessed through ThomsonNOW™.

- 8.1 Judging Groups

SOCIAL PSYCHOLOGY ALIVE: QUIZZING AND PRACTICE TESTS

You can access our Web site directly by going to http://www.socialpsychologyalive.nelson.com for online quizzes, flash cards, and Internet links.

WEB SITES OF INTEREST

- A Web site featuring the work of Stanley Milgram is available at http://www.stanleymilgram.com.

- A Web site with information about Project ALERT is at http://www.projectalert.com.

INFOTRAC® COLLEGE EDITION

For additional readings, explore InfoTrac® College Edition, your online library of archived journal articles and periodicals dating back 22 years. If your instructor ordered InfoTrac® College Edition with this book, you can access it from your CD-ROM, or go directly to http://www.infotrac-college.com and use the passcode from the InfoTrac® College Edition card that came with your book. For this chapter, try these search terms: *conformity, compliance, obedience, informational influence, normative influence, social norms, foot-in-the-door, door-in-the-face, lowball, terror management, social impact theory.*

Social Psychology Alive: The Workbook

To apply what you've learned in this chapter to the real world, go to Chapter 8 of *Social Psychology Alive: The Workbook*:

- Can a Strategy Based on Social Norms Reduce College Drinking?
- Design Your Own Persuasion Campaign
- Studying Conformity with the Crutchfield Apparatus: A Computerized Demonstration

- Are You Inclined to Comply with Others? Test Your Need for Consistency!
- Social Norms and Suicide Bombings
- The Conformity and Obedience Experiments and Research Ethics
- Reacting to Requests and Demands

Social Psychology Alive: The Videos

To see video on the topics and experiments discussed in this chapter, you can go either to ThomsonNOW™ or to the CD-ROM, if your instructor assigned either one, to the following sections:

- Just Following Orders: Obedience to Authority
- Getting What You Want: Two Compliance Strategies in Action

To Learn More

This list contains citations to books or articles that can help you learn more. These readings are good places to start if you want to gain a deeper understanding of the topics in this chapter.

- Cialdini, R. B. (2001). *Influence: Science and practice* (4th ed.). Boston: Allyn & Bacon.
- Osherow, N. (1999). Making sense of the nonsensical: An analysis of Jonestown. In E. Aronson (Ed.), *Readings about the social animal* (8th ed., pp. 71–88). New York: Worth.
- Turner, J. C. (1991). *Social influence.* Pacific Grove, CA: Brooks/Cole.
- Milgram, S. (1974). *Obedience to authority.* New York: Harper & Row.

NEL

Stereotypes, Prejudice, and Discrimination

In 2001, Aaron Webster was a 41-year-old photographer living in Vancouver. His friends and family describe him as a gentle, friendly, and intelligent man. He was also openly gay. On November 17, 2001, Webster had the misfortune of crossing paths with a group of three or four young men aged 17 or 18, who were looking for someone, preferably homosexual, to beat up. Webster was walking in an area of Vancouver's Stanley Park where gay men were known to gather. The group of men swarmed him, viciously beating him with a baseball bat, a pool cue, and a golf club. Webster collapsed to the ground after a blow to the back of his neck, which tore his vertebral artery. The attackers ran away. Webster was found by his close friend Tim Chisholm, who called an ambulance and then comforted Aaron in his arms as he died.

How can we understand this sort of murderous behaviour? How can people hate enough to kill a person they do not even know? Three young men were eventually convicted of manslaughter in Webster's death, two of whom were juveniles (under 18 years of age) at the time of the crime and therefore could be sentenced only to a maximum of two years in a youth detention centre plus one year of house arrest; a third man, who was 18 at the time of the attack, was sentenced to six years in prison.

The sort of animosity exhibited in the killing of Aaron Webster, based simply on someone belonging to a group, is called **prejudice.** Prejudice can be formally defined as a negative attitude toward members of a group, which is often very strongly held. The term derives from the fact that the perceiver "prejudges" the targets (hence, prejudice), disliking them based only on their group membership. Although it is possible to be positively prejudiced toward a group (e.g., to prejudge members of an occupational group favourably), social psychologists have been interested in understanding negative prejudice. In this chapter, we will use the term prejudice to refer specifically to a negative attitude toward members of a group.

One possible consequence of prejudice is negative, harmful behaviour (e.g., aggression) toward people based on their group membership. **Discrimination** is the term used to refer to such actions. Whereas prejudice is an attitude, discrimination is a behaviour. Again, although positive discrimination can occur (sometimes called reverse discrimination), such as giving special or preferential treatment to members of an ethnic group, social psychologists have focused on harmful behaviour toward members of a group, and, in this chapter, we will use the term in this specific manner. Negative treatment can range from relatively mundane actions such as avoiding or not speaking to members of a group all the way to horrible actions such as attempting to systematically eliminate an ethnic group through banishment or murder (an action referred to as **genocide**). We opened the chapter with an example of extreme discrimination: the murder of a gay man. Social psychologists have devoted much time and energy to trying to understand why people treat others badly based simply on group membership.

prejudice

a negative attitude toward members of a group, which is often very strongly held

discrimination

negative, harmful behaviour toward people based on their group membership

genocide

an attempt to systematically eliminate an ethnic group through banishment or murder

CBC TV Archive Sales

Aaron Webster was murdered on November 17, 2001, in Vancouver.

An important concept in this chapter will be stereotypes, which we defined in Chapter 3 as individuals' beliefs that members of a group share particular attributes (see page 73). Unlike prejudice and discrimination—terms that social psychologists use to refer specifically to negative attitudes or actions—stereotypes can be either positive or negative. Stereotypes of some groups are largely positive (e.g., scientists), whereas stereotypes of other groups are largely negative (e.g., criminals). Negative stereotypes can provide the basis for prejudice and discrimination.

In this chapter, we discuss social psychological theory and research on stereotypes, prejudice, and discrimination (see also Brewer & Brown, 1998; Fiske, 1998; Jones, 1997; Nelson, 2002; Zanna & Olson, 1994). We address both the causes and consequences of these concepts. We begin by considering the magnitude of prejudice and discrimination today. We then turn to the sources of prejudice, focusing primarily on racial and ethnic prejudice. These sources of prejudice include stereotypes (a cognitive concept) and several emotional factors. We then discuss prejudice and discrimination directed against women, which is called sexism. Next, we take the perspective of people who are victims of prejudice and discrimination, describing two programs of research that have examined victimization from the inside. We then briefly discuss genocide. Our final section describes various strategies that have been proposed to reduce prejudice and discrimination.

Prejudice and Discrimination Today

Before we begin our analysis of the causes and consequences of prejudice and discrimination, let's consider how widespread these problems are today. On the one hand, it is quite easy for us to look around the world and find recent examples of ethnic conflict and religious hatred. The Middle East, Sudan, Iraq, Bosnia, Rwanda, Northern Ireland, the Philippines, Afghanistan, Somalia—the list goes on and on. Groups seem unable or unwilling to find peaceful solutions to longstanding disagreements. The high frequency of conflict and war around the globe is discouraging to say the least. On the other hand, racial and religious confrontations in Canada seem rarer today than 20 or 30 years ago. Indeed, most Canadians claim to have relatively favourable attitudes toward most minority groups. These considerations are encouraging, but should we believe what we are told? Do you think that prejudice and discrimination are declining in Canada?

It is probably true that blatant, overt discrimination is less common today than 20 or 30 years ago (see Schuman, Steeh, Bobo, & Krysan, 1997), although it certainly still exists (e.g., see Bushman & Bonacci, 2004; Mellor, 2003). Discrimination has been made illegal, and equal access has become mandatory policy for employers in the public and private sectors. Social norms now censure prejudice, and people are less likely to express negative feelings publicly. But some groups are still victims of hate crimes, as noted in the opening story. Also, some people have become more sophisticated at hiding their prejudice; they may feel negatively toward minority groups but try to avoid displaying discrimination.

Further, some people may even be fooling themselves into thinking they are unprejudiced when, in fact, they remain biased against members of disadvantaged groups. Can you think of a time when you heard someone say something that revealed an unrecognized prejudice toward a group? One of the authors of this book recalls an event related to Canadian actress Margot Kidder, best known for playing Lois Lane opposite Christopher Reeve's Superman in four movies between 1978 and

1987. Kidder suffers from bipolar disorder (a mental illness, usually treatable with medication, which is characterized by alternating periods of extreme highs and extreme lows). In 1996, Kidder was found wandering confused and lost in Los Angeles. Shortly after this event, Kidder came up in a conversation at a party, and several people laughed out loud at the mention of her name. They did not seem to recognize the demeaning stereotype of mental illness their laughter revealed. The concept of *implicit attitudes* was introduced in Chapter 6 (see page 194) and defined as individuals' automatic—and often unconscious—evaluations of a target. Some people possess unfavourable implicit attitudes toward disadvantaged groups but are not consciously aware of these negative automatic responses.

John Dovidio of the University of Massachusetts and Samuel Gaertner of the University of Delaware (1998, 2000; Gaertner & Dovidio, 1986) have argued that "old-fashioned," blatant racial discrimination has been replaced by more subtle and ambiguous discrimination (see also Katz & Hass, 1988; McConahay, 1986; Sears & Henry, 2003). Dovidio and Gaertner proposed that many majority group members (e.g., White Canadians) have *ambivalent,* or conflicted, feelings toward minorities (e.g., Aboriginal and Asian Canadians). Majority group members often support equal opportunities and regard themselves as unprejudiced and nondiscriminatory, but simultaneously harbour some negative beliefs and hostile feelings toward minority groups. Dovidio and Gaertner labelled this "new" or "modern" kind of prejudice **aversive racism,** because those who hold these views do not consider themselves to be prejudiced and would find any accusation of being prejudiced aversive (unpleasant or upsetting). Nevertheless, aversive racists are hypothesized to exhibit discrimination under some circumstances. Specifically, Dovidio and Gaertner predicted that many majority group members would exhibit discrimination toward minorities when the circumstances made negative treatment justifiable, thereby providing an excuse (perhaps even to themselves) for discrimination.

For example, Dovidio and Gaertner (2000) reported data from two different samples of White Americans, one obtained in 1989 and the other in 1999. The researchers predicted that the more recent sample would report less *blatant prejudice* toward Blacks than the earlier sample, but there would be little change over the ten-year period in *discriminatory behaviour* when the circumstances provided an excuse.

aversive racism

a "modern" kind of prejudice held by people who do not consider themselves prejudiced and who would find any accusation of being prejudiced aversive, but who nevertheless harbour some negative beliefs and hostile feelings toward members of minority groups

Aversive racists consider themselves unprejudiced but harbour some negative beliefs or feelings toward minority groups such as Blacks.

Participants reported their explicit attitudes toward Blacks by indicating the extent of their agreement with such statements as "I would mind it if a Black family with about the same income and education as my own would move next door to my home." In a second, separate session, participants were asked to evaluate a male candidate for a peer-counselling program at their university. The candidate was either White or Black and possessed either strong, ambiguous, or weak qualifications. Participants made a yes/no decision about whether the applicant should be recommended for the counselling position. The researchers predicted that when the applicant's qualifications were clear (either strong or weak), participants would assess White and Black applicants similarly, but when the qualifications were ambiguous, participants would assess the White applicant more positively than the Black applicant.

The items assessing explicit attitudes toward Blacks revealed less prejudice in 1999 than in 1989. Thus, as predicted, blatant prejudice declined over the ten-year period. What about participants' yes/no decisions for the job applicants? Figure 9.1 presents the percentages of participants who decided that the White or Black applicant *should* be recommended for the position. When the applicant's qualifications were strong, participants at both time periods recommended him whether he was White or Black. When the applicant's qualifications were weak, participants at both time periods did not recommend him whether he was White or Black. But now for the critical results: when the applicant's qualifications were ambiguous, participants recommended the White applicant more often than the Black applicant, and the effect in 1999 (77% vs. 40%) was just as strong as, or even a bit stronger than, the effect in 1989 (75% vs. 50%). Thus, although the more recent sample reported less blatant, overt prejudice, this sample evaluated the Black applicant with ambiguous qualifications just as negatively as the previous sample. Discrimination continued to occur when the circumstances masked it (see also Fiske, 2002).

These and other data suggest that some majority group members continue to harbour prejudice against minority groups, but either lie about it when reporting their attitudes or perhaps even deny it to themselves. Because many people may be unwilling to admit, or be unaware of, negative feelings toward racial or ethnic groups (see Crandall & Eshleman, 2003), direct questions such as "How favourable is your attitude toward Aboriginal Canadians?" may be an ineffective way to assess prejudice.

To address this problem, some researchers have used indirect measures of racial attitudes. For example, the *Implicit Association Test (IAT)*, which we described in Chapter 6 (see page 203), has been used to assess respondents' automatic, implicit atti-

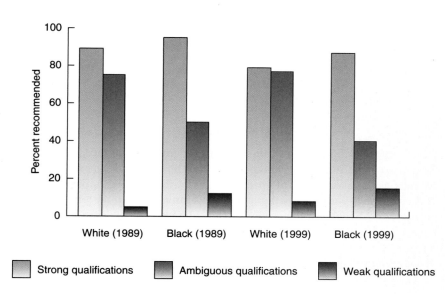

FIGURE 9.1 Percentage of White and Black applicants recommended for peer-counselling position in 1989 and 1999

From Dovidio & Gaertner, "Aversive racism and selection decisions: 1989 and 1999," *Psychological Science*, 11, 315–319, Table 1, p. 317, 2000. Reprinted by permission of Blackwell Publishing.

tudes toward minority groups (e.g., McConnell & Leibold, 2001). Facial EMG, which we also described in Chapter 6 (see page 203), has been used as a physiological measure of prejudice (Vanman, Saltz, Nathan, & Warren, 2004).

Stereotypes: Cognitive Sources of Prejudice and Discrimination

One major contribution of social psychology to understanding prejudice has been to identify common cognitive processes that can establish or maintain prejudice (e.g., see Fiske, 1998; Kunda, 1999). This cognitive perspective does not imply that prejudice is acceptable, but it does suggest that prejudice is the byproduct of "normal" human thinking processes. The key element in the cognitive view of prejudice is *stereotypes*.

As mentioned earlier, stereotypes are individuals' beliefs that members of a group share particular attributes. Someone might believe that doctors are intelligent and compassionate, hockey players are strong and aggressive, or Roman Catholics are religious and family-oriented. Robert Gardner (1994) of the University of Western Ontario has shown that most Canadians have well-developed stereotypes about the two principal linguistic groups in Canada: Anglophones and Francophones. Stereotypes qualify as one kind of *schema*—namely, schemas that represent human groups. We explained in Chapter 3 that schemas serve important functions for us: they allow us to sort objects into categories, to make assumptions about those objects, and thereby to impose meaning and predictability on our environment. We called this process *going beyond the information given*. When you categorize a plant as poison ivy, what do you "gain"? Most importantly, you gain information that the plant will cause an itchy rash if you touch it, based on the assumption that this particular poison ivy plant is similar to other poison ivy plants.

In much the same way, we make assumptions about people when we categorize them into groups based on stereotypes. When you categorize a woman as an RCMP officer, what do you gain? You can probably assume such things as she wants to uphold the law, she is armed, and she will help you if asked to do so. These assumptions can be made quickly and effortlessly and will provide a solid basis for behavioural decisions. Thus, stereotypes "efficiently" provide us with information about target persons that can guide behaviour; they allow us to make rapid inferences about target persons (Bodenhausen, 1988; Gilbert & Hixon, 1991; Pratto & Bargh, 1991).

Two Costs of Stereotypes: Oversimplification and Negativity

Unfortunately, although they simplify our judgments, stereotypes also have some big costs associated with using them: oversimplification and excessive negativity. First, we may assume *too much* uniformity or similarity within groups of people, especially with respect to large collections such as ethnic groups, nationalities, genders, and occupations. Recall our discussion of the *outgroup homogeneity effect* in Chapter 3 (see page 74); this term refers to the tendency for perceivers to overestimate the similarity within groups to which they do not belong. Think about your own perceptions of some nationalities—say, Iranians or North Koreans. Do you tend to think of people in these countries as all being quite similar to one another?

When a woman is categorized as an RCMP officer, several assumptions about her can be made quickly and effortlessly.

CP Photo/Don Denton

The reality is that, in contrast to categories of inanimate objects and plants, categories of humans tend not to be uniform or predictable. Poison ivy plants *always* cause an itchy rash when touched; apples *always* grow on trees; fire is *always* hot. In contrast, lawyers are *not* always wealthy; women are *not* always emotional; hockey players are *not* always aggressive. Stereotypes of large groups are oversimplified and, when applied to a particular individual, often inaccurate. Some stereotypes may have a kernel of truth, but none will apply to everyone in the group. Thus, when we rely on stereotypes to categorize and draw inferences about targets, we frequently make assumptions about them that are wrong.

A second cost of stereotypes is that they are often unfavourable in tone. Although some stereotypes consist mainly of positive characteristics (e.g., the common stereotypes of doctors, university students, and astronauts), other stereotypes contain negative traits (e.g., some people's stereotypes of ethnic minorities, car salesmen, or Americans). Why are stereotypes often unfavourable? One reason is that stereotypes may refer to groups that are believed to be competing with the perceiver's group for desired resources (we elaborate the role of competition in prejudice later). If perceptions of outgroups are tinged by perceived competition, they may become negative. There is also some evidence that being in a bad mood leads perceivers to interpret their stereotypes of some minority groups more negatively (e.g., Esses & Zanna, 1995). For example, believing that immigrants are close-knit might normally be seen as neutral or even positive (e.g., family-loving), but when a perceiver is in a bad mood, he or she might interpret "close-knit immigrants" as cliquish or secretive—negative characteristics. Negative emotions, then, can both elicit and intensify unfavourable stereotypes.

Another reason that stereotypes are often negative is that people may be unfamiliar with members of the targeted group and feel anxious or uncomfortable when interacting with them; people may label their anxiety as dislike for the group. Thus, unfamiliarity and anxiety may spill over into mistrust and hostility (see Plant, 2004; Plant & Devine, 2003; Stephan & Stephan, 1985). Anxiety about interacting with members of the outgroup will also lead people to avoid such interactions altogether.

Stereotypes Distort Information Processing

The fact that stereotypes are oversimplified and excessively negative might not be so problematic if we processed information in an unbiased way. For example, imagine that someone initially assumes, erroneously, that a young woman, Michelle, is conceited simply because she is from a wealthy family (whereas she is actually quite modest); this erroneous view will be corrected if the perceiver remains open to new information (so long as he or she continues to interact with Michelle, which might *not* be the case when stereotype-based expectations are negative). Unfortunately, as discussed in Chapter 3, humans are *not* open and unbiased processors of information related to stereotypes. Stereotypes (like other schemas) guide attention and interpretation in such a way as to increase the probability that perceivers' expectancies will be *confirmed*. The perceiver in our example is quite likely to decide that Michelle is, indeed, conceited.

Stereotypes Guide Attention. Stereotypes can distort information processing in several ways. One way is by affecting what perceivers *notice* about members of the stereotyped group. Generally, perceivers are sensitive to, and looking for, information that *confirms* the stereotype. In our example, the perceiver is likely to notice anything boastful Michelle says about herself, because the perceiver will be expecting such comments. (As we noted in our discussion of schemas in Chapter 3, very unexpected information can also grab our attention under certain conditions; see Olson, Roese, & Zanna, 1996; Plaks, Stroessner, Dweck, & Sherman, 2001.)

In an experiment by Bodenhausen (1988), a defendant in a criminal case was more likely to be judged guilty when his name was Carlos Ramirez than when his name was Robert Johnson.

© David Young-Wolff/PhotoEdit

Social psychologists have conducted experiments demonstrating that stereotypes can bias attention. For example, using a simulated courtroom setting, Northwestern University social psychologist Galen Bodenhausen (1988) gave participants information about a legal case involving a 24-year-old man accused of criminal assault. The information provided to participants was mixed: some supported a guilty verdict and some supported an innocent verdict. For example, the victim and the defendant were observed quarrelling in a bar earlier in the evening (evidence supporting a guilty verdict), but no eyewitnesses could positively identify the attacker (evidence supporting an innocent verdict). Before reading the case materials, some participants learned that the defendant was Robert Johnson of Dayton, Ohio, whereas other participants learned that the defendant was Carlos Ramirez of Albuquerque, New Mexico. A common, harmful stereotype of Hispanic American men is that they are aggressive (e.g., Marin, 1984); therefore, Bodenhausen thought that participants who believed the defendant was Hispanic might pay more attention to evidence suggesting aggression than participants who believed the defendant was White.

Consistent with Bodenhausen's predictions, participants who believed the defendant was Carlos Ramirez recalled a higher percentage of the evidence that supported a guilty verdict than did participants who believed the defendant was Robert Johnson. Also, participants in the Ramirez condition gave more extreme judgments of guilt than did participants in the Johnson condition. It appears that the stereotype of Hispanic men increased participants' attention to the evidence supporting a guilty verdict. This study has disturbing implications for the legal system, because a member of a minority group was judged more harshly than a member of the majority group, based on exactly the same information (only the name was changed).

Stereotypes Guide Interpretation. Stereotypes also distort information processing by affecting how perceivers *interpret* the behaviour of people in the group (e.g., Sekaquaptewa & Espinoza, 2004). Actions that are ambiguous will tend to be interpreted as consistent with expectations. Consequently, behaviours that do not necessarily support the stereotype will strengthen it. In our Michelle example, the perceiver may interpret neutral or ambiguous comments by Michelle as conceited.

An example of how stereotypes can affect the interpretation of ambiguous behaviour in a racial context was provided by Andrew Sagar of Elizabethtown College and Janet Schofield of the University of Pittsburgh (1980). These researchers showed grade 6 boys' drawings of Black and White models engaged in potentially aggressive behaviours (e.g., one child taking a pencil away from another child without asking permission). The authors hypothesized that exactly the same actions would be rated as more aggressive when performed by a Black model than by a White model because a common, damaging stereotype of Blacks is that they can be aggressive or hostile. As predicted, actions were rated as more threatening and less playful when they were performed by a Black model than when they were performed by a White model (see also Duncan, 1976). Sagar and Schofield included both Black and White participants in their study. Unexpectedly, the bias toward interpreting the behaviour as more aggressive when performed by a Black model than when performed by a White model was equally strong for Black and White participants. The researchers concluded from this finding that the differential interpretations reflected knowledge of a cultural stereotype rather than personal prejudice.

Joshua Correll, Bernadette Park, Charles Judd, and Bernd Wittenbrink (2002) conducted a fascinating, and disturbing, set of studies at the University of Colorado, which utilized a video game procedure. The game required White participants to decide as quickly as possible whether a male target person was armed or unarmed. Sometimes the target person's skin colour was black, and sometimes it was white. A photo of a target person was presented on a video screen, and participants were instructed to push one button (labelled *shoot*) if he was armed, but another button

9.1
ONLINE LAB

(labelled *don't shoot*) if he was unarmed. Participants earned points if they responded correctly and lost points if they responded incorrectly. They were told that the participants who scored highest in the game would receive monetary prizes. On a given trial, participants had to respond very quickly (in less than one second) to earn any points with a correct response; this rule was necessary to keep participants from responding slowly to avoid errors, and also to make the situation more comparable to real-life decisions faced by police officers, who must decide quickly whether a suspect is armed or unarmed.

Figure 9.2 presents samples of the photos used in the experiments. Each target appeared in each of the backgrounds for some participants. The armed targets held either a silver snub-nosed revolver or a black pistol; the unarmed targets held either an aluminum can, silver camera, black cell phone, or black wallet.

Across three experiments with White participants, the researchers found that participants were *faster* to judge correctly that Black targets were armed than to judge correctly that White targets were armed. The harmful stereotype of young Black men as aggressive or dangerous appeared to prime participants to identify a Black target as armed more quickly than a White target. In contrast, participants were *slower* to judge correctly that Black targets were unarmed than to judge correctly that White targets were unarmed. The stereotype of Black men interfered with participants' ability to identify a Black target as unarmed, compared to a White target.

There was another disturbing aspect of Correll and his colleagues' results: errors. Figure 9.3 presents the mean number of errors per 20 trials in responding to Black and White armed and unarmed targets from one of the experiments (the other studies yielded similar patterns of errors). When confronted with an unarmed target, participants were more likely to erroneously push the *shoot* button when the target was Black than when the target was White. In contrast, when confronted with an armed target, participants were more likely to erroneously push the *don't shoot* button when the target was White than when the target was Black. If these errors are applied to the context of real-life behaviour, they lead to the prediction that unarmed Black men are more likely to be shot in error by police officers than are unarmed White men (see also Greenwald, Oakes, & Hoffman, 2003; Payne, 2001; Payne, Lambert, & Jacoby, 2002).

FIGURE 9.2 Target and background example scenes from video game

Correll, Park, Judd, & Wittenbrink, 2002

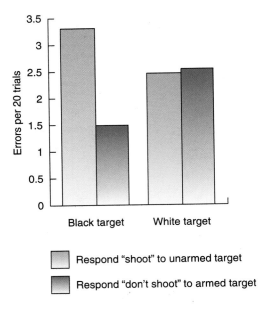

FIGURE 9.3 Mean numbers of errors in responses to unarmed and armed Black and White targets

From Correll et al., "The police officer's dilemma: Using ethnicity to disambiguate potentially threatening individuals," *Journal of Personality and Social Psychology*, 83, 1314–1329, Table 1, p. 1317, 2002. Copyright © 2002 by the American Psychological Association. Reprinted by permission.

One final result from these studies is important to mention. In a fourth experiment, Correll and his colleagues recruited *both* Black and White participants from the community (at bus stations, malls, and food courts in Denver). Exactly the same pattern of biased responding in the video game was obtained in this study, and the pattern was equally strong for Black and White participants. That is, even Black participants erroneously interpreted unarmed Black targets as armed more often than unarmed White targets (recall that Sagar & Schofield, 1980, also found identical effects with White and Black participants).

The occurrence of the bias within Black participants suggests that the impact of targets' skin colour on judgments of whether they were armed or unarmed reflected knowledge of a cultural stereotype rather than personal prejudice. In other words, the errors probably occurred because stereotypes distorted how the situation was interpreted, not because all participants disliked, or were prejudiced toward, Black targets (see also Judd, Blair, & Chapleau, 2004; Payne et al., 2002). These conclusions are reminiscent of some famous studies conducted many years earlier at the City University of New York, in which Kenneth Clark and Mamie Clark (1947) asked Black and White children to choose dolls to play with. Some dolls had black skin and some had white skin. Both Black and White children tended to choose white dolls as toys. Some commentators interpreted these findings as indicating "self-hatred" among Blacks, but another interpretation is that Black children were aware of the cultural stereotype that white skin is more valued than black skin and were conforming to this stereotype (a pattern of responding that declined when school integration and the black pride movement weakened the cultural stereotype; e.g., Hraba & Grant, 1970).

In Canada, Barry Corenblum of Brandon University in Manitoba has conducted several studies in which White and Aboriginal Canadian children were asked to express their preferences for light- versus dark-coloured objects, including White versus Aboriginal dolls, white versus brown stuffed rabbits, and white versus brown cups (e.g., Corenblum & Annis, 1987; Corenblum & Wilson, 1982). Results documented a consistent pro-light bias for all types of objects in both White and Aboriginal children. Corenblum concluded that these results do not appear to reflect an attempt by Aboriginal children to escape their minority group label by identifying with objects associated with the majority group. Instead, children of both racial groups have internalized the general societal preference for light-coloured objects.

Returning to the laboratory data collected by Correll and his colleagues (2002) examining the effects of race on misperceptions of weapons, these findings are worrisome, because real-life police officers must make similar decisions under conditions that can be stressful and threatening. For example, when police officers confront a suspect, they must make rapid decisions about whether the suspect is armed and whether his or her actions are threatening. Perhaps tragic errors occur more often when the suspect is Black rather than White. It is impossible to be certain, of course, that distorted interpretations caused any specific incident, but the findings in social psychological research are disturbing. One possible real-world example of these processes is described in the accompanying box, Social Psychology in Your Life: "The Shooting of Amadou Diallo."

The Potential Vicious Cycle of Stereotypes

Imagine that, as part of a group assignment in an abnormal psychology course, you must interview a hospitalized male paranoid schizophrenic patient at a psychiatric institution. Think about how you would feel just before meeting the patient. Think

Social Psychology in Your Life   *The Shooting of Amadou Diallo*

ATTENTION, POLICE! I AM ABOUT TO REACH INTO MY POCKET FOR A KLEENEX! I WILL MAKE NO SUDDEN MOVES! MY HANDS WILL BE VISIBLE AT ALL TIMES! PLEASE DO NOT, REPEAT, **NOT** OPEN FIRE....

© Steve Sack/Star Tribune, Minneapolis

In 1999, Amadou Diallo was a 22-year-old Black man living in New York City. He was born in the West African country of Liberia and lived at various times in Guinea, Thailand, and Singapore. His father, Saikou Diallo, was a businessman who travelled extensively. Amadou moved to New York in 1996, where he hoped eventually to go to school to obtain computer training. He first got a job as a deliveryman, and later worked as a street peddler selling gloves, socks, and videotapes in Manhattan. He worked 12 hours a day, 6 days a week, and was saving money for his return to school.

Amadou was a practising Muslim who often studied the Koran. He was a quiet, polite young man who shared a small apartment in the South Bronx with two other men. He loved to read and was also an avid sports fan. His favourite North American sport was basketball, and his favourite player was Michael Jordan.

On February 4, 1999, just after midnight, Amadou came home from work, but decided to go back out to get something to eat. After eating nearby, he returned to his apartment building. As he entered the vestibule of his building,

a group of four White plainclothes police officers called out to him from the street and ordered him not to move. Amadou turned toward them and reached into his pants pocket. All four police officers immediately opened fire, shooting a total of 41 bullets at Amadou.

Amadou was hit by 19 bullets and died instantly. It turned out that he was unarmed and was reaching into his pocket to get his wallet. He had no criminal record.

The four police officers were from the Street Crimes Unit of the NYPD and were looking for a serial rape suspect. They claimed that Amadou resembled the suspect they were seeking and said they believed he was reaching for a gun when he put his hand into his pocket.

The shooting of Amadou Diallo outraged many people and galvanized the Black community into action to protest how police officers treat members of minority groups. Three days after the shooting, hundreds of people attended a rally outside Amadou's apartment building, and several other protests followed, involving numerous celebrities, including former New York mayor David Dinkins and actress Susan Sarandon. Singer Bruce Springsteen wrote a song titled "American Skin:

41 Shots," which questioned why so many shots were fired and implied that Amadou's black skin was the reason he was killed.

Under intense pressure, authorities eventually brought charges of second-degree murder against the four police officers. In the highly publicized trial, all four officers were ultimately acquitted of all criminal charges. Their actions were judged to have been a tragic but justifiable mistake.

Why was Amadou Diallo shot that night? Did the fact that he was Black contribute to the police officers' decisions to open fire? Would they have given a White man the benefit of the doubt and waited until they saw what was in his hand? Did they view Amadou as suspicious because their stereotypes of Blacks were negative?

We cannot know with certainty why Amadou Diallo was shot. Research by social psychologists, however, such as the study we described by Correll and his colleagues (2002), shows that erroneous judgments about unarmed Black targets are more likely than parallel errors about White targets. Perhaps teaching police officers about this unconscious bias would motivate them to confirm that *any* suspect is armed before opening fire.

Amadou Diallo was shot 41 times by White police officers on February 4, 1999.

Reprinted with permission from the New York Post, Feb. 5, 1999, Copyright, NYP Holdings, Inc.

Finally ... see Monica speak · Hussein flies home to die

NEW YORK POST

IN COLD BLOOD

Police kill unarmed man in hail of 41 bullets

STILL THE GREATEST / Ali gets Wheaties box

about how close you would sit to him, whether you would smile a lot or remain serious, and how personal your questions would be.

For many of us, our stereotypes of paranoid schizophrenic patients would probably influence our behaviour in this meeting. We would feel nervous before meeting the patient; we would not sit close to him during the interview; and we would avoid personal questions. These effects are understandable. Our stereotypes provide a guide for how to behave toward other people, and our stereotype of paranoid schizophrenic patients includes such things as unpredictable, strange, hostile, and maybe even dangerous.

But let's consider a further issue: Do you think that the *patient's* behaviour might be influenced by *your* behaviour? That is, might he behave in certain ways because of how you behave toward him? If he notices that you are nervous and that you are staying a safe distance from him, he might infer that you do not like him and act differently than he would have acted if you had been more relaxed and friendly. The irony is that his behaviour might be affected in such a way as to *confirm* what you expected: he might act in a hostile fashion and thereby confirm your suspicion that he is unpredictable and dangerous. This process is depicted in Figure 9.4.

Self-Fulfilling Prophecies. This sequence of events, where (1) a perceiver's stereotype or expectancy about a target influences the perceiver's behaviour toward the target, and (2) the perceiver's behaviour toward the target then elicits the expected behaviour from the target (i.e., the target's behaviour confirms the perceiver's stereotype or expectancy), is called a **self-fulfilling prophecy.** In essence, the perceiver has acted in such a way as to make his or her own prophecy come true (Rosenthal, 2003).

Many fascinating studies in social psychology have demonstrated that stereotypes can influence the perceiver's behaviour (see Wheeler & Petty, 2001, for a review) and the perceiver's behaviour, in turn, can elicit the expected behaviour from the target: a self-fulfilling prophecy in the domain of stereotypes. For example, in a famous set of studies on this topic, Carl Word, Mark Zanna, and Joel Cooper (1974) recruited Princeton University students to serve as interviewers of applicants for a job. All participants (interviewers) were White. The researchers gave the interviewers a set of questions they could ask the applicants and told them to ask as few or as many of the questions as they wished. Unbeknownst to the interviewers, the job applicants were actually accomplices of the experimenter who had been trained to respond consistently to the interviewer's questions. Some of the job applicants were White and some were Black. The job interviews were videotaped, and the interviewers' behaviours were subsequently coded. It turned out that the White interviewers treated White and

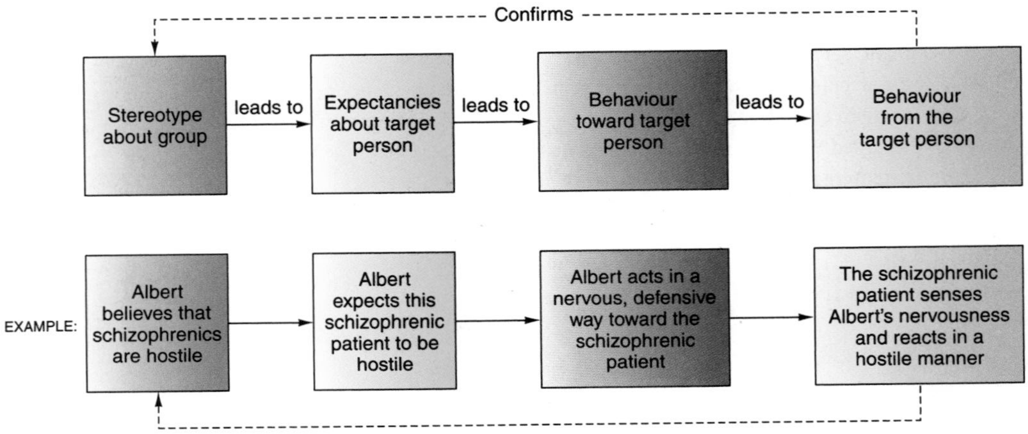

self-fulfilling prophecy

a process in which a perceiver's expectancy about a target person influences the perceiver's behaviour toward the target person in such a way as to elicit the expected actions from the target person

FIGURE 9.4 Self-fulfilling prophecy

Black applicants differently. For instance, the interviews with White applicants lasted longer than the interviews with Black applicants. Also, the interviewers exhibited more nonverbal behaviours that Mehrabian (1968) has labelled "immediacy" (e.g., eye contact, forward body lean) while interviewing the White applicants than while interviewing the Black applicants. Thus, the White applicants were exposed to more favourable and intimate nonverbal behaviours than were the Black applicants.

Given that White and Black job applicants were treated differently, an important question is whether such treatment would actually influence the performance of real applicants. Word and his colleagues (1974) tested this question in a second experiment. This time, the participants (all White) served as job applicants, and the interviewers were accomplices of the experimenter. The interviewers were White and were trained to treat job applicants either in the manner that White applicants had been treated in the first experiment (longer interview, more eye contact, and forward body lean) or in the manner that Black applicants had been treated in the first experiment (shorter interview, less eye contact, and backward body lean). The job applicants were videotaped, and their performance was subsequently evaluated by judges who did not know which condition each applicant was in. These judges rated the performances of applicants who received longer interviews and more intimate nonverbal behaviour as significantly better than the performances of applicants who received shorter interviews and less intimate nonverbal behaviour. Thus, the differential treatment of White and Black applicants in the first experiment was shown to be enough to create differences in the actual performance of the applicants in the second experiment.

These data suggest that stereotypes can produce expectancies about a target individual, which can then alter the perceiver's actions in ways that elicit the expected behaviour from the target (see also Chen & Bargh, 1997; Olson et al., 1996). Given that stereotypes of minority groups can be unfavourable, self-fulfilling prophecies may often be damaging and harmful. For instance, expecting members of a group to be unfriendly might actually produce unfriendly actions from them (caused by the perceiver's own behaviour toward the group members). Negative stereotypes can produce vicious cycles that perpetuate prejudice and discrimination against disadvantaged groups.

White interviewers might treat Black and White job applicants differently.

We should not exaggerate the inevitability of self-fulfilling prophecies. If targets are *aware* of someone's expectancy for them, they may work to *disprove* it, especially when it is negative (see Hilton & Darley, 1991; Miller & Turnbull, 1986; Neuberg, 1994; Stukas & Snyder, 2002). But in many cases, targets are unaware that perceivers have strong expectancies for them, which makes self-fulfilling prophecies more likely. Also, targets may sometimes behave consistently with a negative stereotype simply to maintain a smooth interaction (see Snyder & Haugen, 1995). Finally, as we will discuss in detail shortly (in the section on *stereotype threat*), even when individuals are aware that someone expects them to do poorly, their attempt to disconfirm that expectancy can sometimes actually hurt their performance—in colloquial terms, people sometimes "choke" when trying to disprove a negative stereotype about their group.

Do Stereotypes Influence Our Perceptions If We Disagree with Them?

All of us are aware of stereotypes that we don't personally endorse. We know that some people possess negative stereotypes about groups that we admire. Examples of groups targeted by negative stereotypes include Aboriginal Canadians, elderly persons, immigrants, Jews, Muslims, gays and lesbians, overweight persons, and recipients of welfare. What is your view of these groups? Whether your own views are positive or negative, you can probably identify some of the characteristics that are part of the negative stereotypes.

Let's use recipients of welfare as an example. Negative beliefs about welfare recipients can include that they are lazy, unintelligent, and dishonest (trying to cheat the system). The trait of laziness may be the most common belief: "If they really wanted a job, they could get off welfare." What do you think of this belief? Do you endorse it or reject it?

When people agree with a stereotype, it may not be surprising that it influences what they notice and how they interpret behaviour, as we have described in previous sections. But what happens when someone *knows* a stereotype but does *not* endorse it? If someone is aware that welfare recipients are often viewed as lazy, but does not agree with this generalization, can the simple knowledge of the stereotype somehow influence his or her perceptions? In other words, can stereotypes influence our perceptions even if we disagree with them?

subliminal priming procedure

a method of activating a schema or stereotype by flashing words or pictures very briefly on a computer screen in front of a participant

Some social psychological research has suggested an affirmative answer to this question. For example, Patricia Devine (1989) of the University of Wisconsin used a **subliminal priming procedure** to activate the stereotype of Blacks in some of her White participants. A subliminal priming procedure involves flashing a word or picture very briefly (sometimes as little as 1/100th of a second) on a computer screen in front of the participant. At these fast exposure speeds, participants can only see a flash of light and cannot even say whether the presentation was a word. Nevertheless, it turns out that participants do perceive such stimuli subconsciously, and concepts related to the words or pictures become activated in memory (see Bargh & Pietromonaco, 1982).

Half of Devine's participants were exposed to extremely brief presentations of words that were related to the stereotype of Black Americans, such as *Negroes*, *ghetto*, and *blues*. The remaining participants were exposed to extremely brief presentations of neutral words that were unrelated to the Black American stereotype. Devine assumed that a common stereotype of Black American men includes the trait of *hostility;* she also assumed that only some of her White participants would agree with this stereotype, but almost all of them would be aware of it.

All participants then completed a task in which they were given a written description of a young man (whose race was unspecified, so he was probably assumed to be

White) who engaged in several actions that were ambiguous with respect to hostility; his actions could be viewed as assertive (positive) or hostile (negative). Participants rated the hostility of the young man.

Participants for whom the stereotype of Black Americans had been activated rated the man as more hostile than did participants for whom the stereotype had not been activated. Thus, activating the stereotype increased the likelihood that ambiguous actions would be interpreted as hostile, presumably because hostility was part of the stereotype. It is important to note that none of the words used to prime the Black American stereotype (e.g., Negroes, ghetto) was directly related to hostility. Hostility was activated indirectly, via the stereotype.

Devine also measured participants' levels of reported prejudice against Black Americans, and it is here that she addressed the issue of whether stereotypes influence perceptions even in people who do not endorse them. Surprisingly, she found that exposure to words related to the stereotype of Black Americans increased the perceived hostility of ambiguous behaviour for both prejudiced and unprejudiced participants. Even people who did not consciously endorse the stereotype of Black Americans (unprejudiced participants) showed an effect of the priming manipulation. Given that, in real life, encountering a Black person will almost certainly activate the stereotype of Blacks, Devine's findings imply that there might be a general bias to interpret Blacks' actions as hostile, which will serve to reinforce the stereotype.

Implicit Intergroup Bias. This notion that stereotypes can automatically influence judgments without the perceiver's awareness has been termed **implicit intergroup bias** (see Blair, 2001). It is *implicit* because it is not deliberate and may be unrecognized by the perceiver. It is *intergroup bias* because it reflects distorted, usually unfavourable judgments about members of an outgroup. Researchers have documented implicit intergroup bias against several groups, including women, Blacks, and the elderly (e.g., Banaji & Greenwald, 1994; Cunningham, Nezlek, & Banaji, 2004; Greenwald, McGhee, & Schwartz, 1998; Levy, 1996; Wittenbrink, Judd, & Park, 2001). Implicit intergroup bias is similar to negative implicit attitudes toward a group, which are spontaneous negative feelings toward members of a group, of which the perceiver may be unaware. Devine's (1989) findings suggest that everyone may show some implicit intergroup bias, even those who disagree with a common stereotype.

Other researchers have reached different conclusions, however. For example, York University's Kerry Kawakami and her colleagues (Kawakami, Dion, & Dovidio, 1998) found that, in a group of Canadian university students, low-prejudiced White participants showed no evidence whatsoever of implicit intergroup bias against Black Canadians, whereas high prejudiced White participants did show such bias (see also Fazio, Jackson, Dunton, & Williams, 1995; Lepore & Brown, 1997; Wittenbrink, Judd, & Park, 1997). These findings are comforting for people who reject negative stereotypes of minority groups and do not want their own judgments to be unconsciously affected by the stereotypes. Some research also suggests that unprejudiced individuals actually seek out information to *disconfirm* common stereotypes (e.g., Wyer, 2004). Further, there is evidence that people who exhibit weak or no implicit intergroup bias also tend to behave in other positive ways toward the target group (e.g., Dovidio, Kawakami, & Gaertner, 2002; Hugenberg & Bodenhausen, 2003, 2004). Finally, there is evidence that implicit intergroup bias can be reduced by deliberate attempts to be open-minded (for a review, see Blair, 2002). For example, University of California at Los

implicit intergroup bias

distorted judgments about members of a group based on a stereotype, which can occur without the person's awareness

Implicit intergroup bias has been documented in perceivers' judgments about the elderly.

PhotoDisc Green/Getty Images

Angeles social psychologists Brian Lowery, Curtis Hardin, and Stacey Sinclair (2001) found that instructing participants to be "as unprejudiced as possible" significantly reduced implicit intergroup bias against Blacks on a subsequent task (see also Barden, Maddux, Petty, & Brewer, 2004; Blair, Ma, & Lenton, 2001; Dasgupta & Asgari, 2004; Dasgupta & Greenwald, 2001; Maddux, Barden, Brewer, & Petty, 2005).

Meta-Stereotypes

To this point in the chapter, we have focused on people's stereotypes of groups and how these stereotypes affect information processing and behaviour. For example, an individual's stereotype of Aboriginal Canadians might influence how he or she interprets the actions of an Aboriginal Canadian man encountered in downtown Edmonton.

But there is a second, mirror-image perspective on stereotypes. The University of Manitoba's Jacquie Vorauer coined the term **meta-stereotypes** to refer to a person's beliefs about the stereotype that outgroup members hold concerning his or her own group (Vorauer, Main, & O'Connell, 1998). For example, a White Canadian may believe that Aboriginal Canadians hold a negative stereotype of his or her group (i.e., of White Canadians). Meta-stereotypes vary according to which particular outgroup is considered. For example, the same White Canadian may believe that Asian Canadians hold a different stereotype of his or her group than do Aboriginal Canadians.

Vorauer and her colleagues (1998) surveyed White introductory psychology students at the University of Manitoba and found that there was substantial agreement among the participants on how White Canadians were viewed by Aboriginal Canadians. Some of the most common elements of this meta-stereotype were that Aboriginal Canadians consider White Canadians to be unfair, materialistic, egocentric, prejudiced, selfish, closed-minded, and arrogant. Note that these meta-stereotypes may or may not conform to how Aboriginal Canadians *actually* view White Canadians; they refer to White Canadians' *beliefs* about how they are viewed by Aboriginal Canadians.

Vorauer and her colleagues (Vorauer, Hunter, Main, & Roy, 2000; Vorauer et al., 1998) showed that meta-stereotypes influence people's expectations about their interactions with members of the outgroup. For example, people who believe that their group is viewed negatively by an outgroup tend to anticipate unpleasant interactions with members of that outgroup. As we mentioned in our discussion of self-fulfilling prophecies, anxiety about interacting with someone might lead to defensive behaviour that could, paradoxically, elicit reactions consistent with negative expectancies. Thus, believing that members of an outgroup evaluate one's ingroup negatively might cause hostile, aversive interactions. Clearly, it is important to understand the processes underlying meta-stereotypes. This relatively new topic seems likely to receive increased attention from social psychologists in the coming years.

meta-stereotype

a person's beliefs about the stereotype that outgroup members hold concerning his or her own group

Emotional Sources of Prejudice and Discrimination

We have focused so far in this chapter on stereotypes as a cause of prejudice, but negative attitudes toward specific groups sometimes spring from other, noncognitive sources. Theorists have identified several emotional or motivational processes that can contribute to prejudice and discrimination. For example, prejudice sometimes results from negative emotions such as frustration, anger, and hostility. Prejudice may also sometimes satisfy basic motives such as the need to evaluate the self positively. In this section, we discuss four theoretical models of prejudice that revolve around emotional or motivational factors.

Frustration and Prejudice: Scapegoat Theory

One of the oldest explanations of prejudice is that people become frustrated during difficult economic times and vent their frustration on weak, scapegoat targets (Allport, 1954; Berkowitz, 1962). From this perspective, prejudice involves the dominant group's "lashing out" at subordinate groups because of frustration and disappointment. Members of the disadvantaged group serve merely as scapegoats: they had little or no direct role in causing the frustration, but provide a convenient target of blame. Hence, this perspective on prejudice is known as **scapegoat theory.**

In Chapter 11, we discuss the role of frustration in aggression more generally, but at this point we limit our attention to how frustration can lead to prejudice and discrimination. In one of the most famous investigations of scapegoat theory, Carl Hovland and Robert Sears (1940) examined the correlation between the number of lynchings of Black Americans in the deep south of the United States between 1882 and 1930 and the price of cotton over the same period. The researchers hypothesized that Black men became the targets of angry, frustrated White Americans when cotton prices were low. Consistent with this reasoning, Hovland and Sears found a significant negative correlation between cotton prices and lynchings: as prices went down, lynchings went up.

Another example of a group that was targeted during times of economic difficulty was Jews in Nazi Germany in the late 1930s. Hitler roused anger against Jews in the Third Reich by claiming they had too much economic power and blaming them for the impact of the worldwide depression on Germany. Jews were an identifiable group who were already disliked by many Germans, and when Hitler initiated his campaign of misinformation, some Germans latched on to his message. The accusations from

scapegoat theory

a theory proposing that prejudice occurs because members of dominant groups use discrimination against members of weak target groups to vent their frustration and disappointment

© Time Life Pictures/Getty Images

In Nazi Germany, Jews were wrongly blamed for the country's economic problems. In this photo, Jewish citizens are being rounded up and taken to trains for transportation to concentration camps.

Hitler provided an excuse for some Germans to vent their frustrations by aggressing viciously against Jewish men, women, and children.

Perceived Competition and Prejudice: Realistic Group Conflict Theory

Another perspective on prejudice, which shares some elements with the frustration model, focuses on perceived competition between groups for scarce resources. When groups in society are believed to be competing with one another for such things as jobs, housing, political power, and health care, hostility can be aroused. This competitive hostility can lead, in turn, to prejudice. The effects of perceived competition have been articulated in a theory called **realistic group conflict theory** (Campbell, 1965; Pettigrew, 1978).

Many incidents in history illustrate this consequence of perceived competition, including wars over disputed claims for land (e.g., the conflict between India and Pakistan over Kashmir) and legal battles over natural resources (e.g., lawsuits initiated by First Nations peoples for the rights to land, mining, and fishing resources in Canada). But perhaps the clearest example is prejudice against immigrants (see Verkuyten, 2004; Zárate, Garcia, Garza, & Hitlan, 2004). In many countries, immigrants have been perceived to be competing directly with current residents for jobs and social benefits. Immigrants are accused of taking jobs away from native-born workers. There have been demonstrations in Great Britain, Germany, France, and many other countries where protesters (often composed of right-wing groups like skinheads and associated "hooligans," to use the British term) have denounced immigration and promoted hatred of immigrants. University of Western Ontario social psychologist Victoria Esses has studied attitudes toward immigrants for many years and has concluded that perceived competition from immigrants for jobs, health care, and other resources often leads people to oppose open, lenient immigration policies (e.g., see Esses, Dovidio, Jackson, & Armstrong, 2001).

A famous demonstration of the effects of competition was provided by Muzafer Sherif and his colleagues (Sherif, Harvey, White, Hood, & Sherif, 1961) in a study of 11-year-old boys at a summer camp (known as the *Robber's Cave experiment*). Two groups of boys at a camp learned that they would be competing in sporting events for several days, and the winning team would receive some very nice prizes. Almost immediately, the two groups expressed substantial hostility and prejudice toward one another and engaged in "discriminatory" behaviour such as stealing things from members of the other group. As predicted by realistic group conflict theory, introducing competition between the groups elicited strong dislike and derogation of the outgroup (see also Judd & Park, 1988).

Sometimes groups perceive not only competition for scarce resources from members of outgroups, but also threats to important values. People may believe that members of another group (e.g., Pakistani immigrants to Canada) bring with them a set of values and customs that threaten the status quo. This cultural threat can produce intergroup anxiety, resentment, and prejudice (Esses, Haddock, & Zanna, 1993; Stephan & Stephan, 1985; Zárate et al., 2004). The competition is not economic, but rather symbolic.

University of Manitoba social psychologists Charmaine Mohipp and Marian Morry (2004) found that perceived threats to symbolic beliefs were associated with negative attitudes toward gay men and lesbians among heterosexual university students. That is, the more gay men and lesbians were perceived to violate such matters as the traditional meaning of family and marriage, the more negative the attitudes toward these groups were (see also DeSteno, Dasgupta, Bartlett, & Cajdric, 2004).

realistic group conflict theory

a theory proposing that when groups in society are perceived to be competing with one another for resources, intergroup hostility can be aroused, which leads to prejudice

Self-Enhancement Motivation: Social Identity Theory

The frustration and competition perspectives articulated to this point focus on how negative affect (frustration, hostility, anger) can generate prejudice. A third affect-related factor in prejudice involves a potential *positive* emotional benefit of derogating outgroups: feeling good about the self, or self-enhancement.

We have noted many times in this book that people want to see themselves favourably (see, in particular, the sections on *self-serving judgments* in Chapters 3 and 4). One way to judge the self positively is in relative terms: "I am better than you." If another person is evaluated negatively, then the perceiver will probably conclude that he or she is better than the other. Feeling superior to another person can be gratifying, because it indirectly confirms one's own worth.

Self-enhancement happens not only at the individual level ("I am better than you") but also at the group level ("My group is better than your group"). We described *social identity theory* in Chapter 5 (see page 158). According to this theory (Tajfel, 1978; Tajfel & Turner, 1986), one important component of people's identity is their group memberships. Just as we strive for a positive personal identity, we also strive for a positive social (group) identity. Deciding that our ingroup is better than an outgroup is one way to enhance our self-esteem (see Aberson, Healy, & Romero, 2000; Fein & Spencer, 1997; Rubin & Hewstone, 1998). Recall our discussion of the *minimal group paradigm* in Chapter 5 (see page 159), which involves assigning individuals to groups on the basis of a trivial feature (e.g., whether they allegedly overestimate or underestimate the number of dots shown on a screen). Even when groups are formed in these meaningless, arbitrary ways, people show ingroup favouritism: they give members of their ingroup more resources than members of an outgroup.

These findings imply that a positive social identity makes us feel good. Consistent with this reasoning, researchers have found that when people's ingroup performs better than an outgroup, they report higher self-esteem and more positive judgments of their own abilities. A somewhat light-hearted demonstration of this effect was provided by Edward Hirt, Dolf Zillman, Grant Erickson, and Chris Kennedy (1992), who had students at Indiana University watch a live basketball game involving the Hoosiers (the university's team). After the game (in an allegedly unrelated study), participants reported their self-esteem and estimated their own future performance on a number of tasks (e.g., an anagrams task involving five-letter scrambled words, a motor skills task involving throwing velcro-covered balls onto a felt dart board, and a social skills task involving asking members of the opposite sex to go to a concert). When the Hoosiers won the game, participants reported higher self-esteem and made more optimistic predictions about their own future performance than when the Hoosiers lost the game. Thus, when their ingroup (university team) proved to be superior to an outgroup (another university team), people felt better about themselves.

Past studies indicate that derogating members of an outgroup can enhance self-esteem. Perhaps prejudice can be motivated, therefore, by a desire for self-enhancement. Some people who are highly prejudiced may be trying to make themselves feel good in comparison. A context that seems analogous to prejudice is peer ridicule among high school students. Groups of teenagers often engage in merciless ridicule of other teens. Why does this happen? Do they realize how painful it is to the target? Perhaps their motivation is to make themselves feel superior.

The film *The Eye of the Storm* (1971) showed how teacher Jane Elliott decided to give her grade 3, all-White class a firsthand experience of prejudice. She divided the class into two groups based on eye colour. She then declared that children with blue eyes were superior to children with brown eyes. For an entire day, she made blue-eyed children feel good about themselves and brown-eyed children feel disadvantaged. Then on the next day, she declared that she was wrong the day before, and it was actually brown-eyed children who were superior to blue-eyed children. After this second day of making one group feel superior to the other, things returned to normal

"I watched what had been marvelous, cooperative, wonderful, thoughtful children turn into nasty, vicious, discriminating little third graders in the space of fifteen minutes."

on the third day. One of the most interesting observations made by Ms. Elliott in the film was that, each day, the children in the "superior" group changed dramatically from their normal personalities, becoming arrogant, insulting, and condescending to children in the "inferior" group. She noted that it was as if the children really *wanted* to feel and act in this superior manner, and her eye-colour rules "released" this inherent tendency. Perhaps the children's behaviour reflected a basic human desire for a positive social identity.

A Unifying Model: Integrated Threat Theory

integrated threat theory

a theory proposing that prejudice results from four types of threats: realistic threats, symbolic threats, threats stemming from intergroup anxiety, and threats arising from negative stereotypes

A relatively recent addition to theories of prejudice was proposed by Walter Stephan and Cookie Stephan (2000) of New Mexico State University, a model they labelled **integrated threat theory.** These researchers suggested that negative attitudes toward an outgroup can result from four different kinds of threats: realistic threats, symbolic threats, threats stemming from intergroup anxiety, and threats arising from negative stereotypes. This model unifies several other perspectives on prejudice. Stephan and Stephan chose the term *threats* to refer to the fact that prejudiced people expect members of the disliked outgroup to behave in ways that are detrimental to ingroup members. These "detrimental" actions may include (but are not limited to) taking jobs away from ingroup members, challenging the ingroup's fundamental values, or simply making ingroup members feel uncomfortable during interactions.

How do Stephan and Stephan define each type of threat? (1) *Realistic threats* are those emphasized by realistic group conflict theory—that is, competition for jobs, political power, or other scarce resources. The outgroup is perceived to pose a significant threat to the material well-being of the ingroup. (2) *Symbolic threats* refer to perceived threats to the ingroup's important attitudes, beliefs, and values. In this case, the values of the outgroup are thought to be different from those of the ingroup; given that the ingroup believes in the moral correctness of its own views, the outgroup may be seen as threatening the moral fibre of the community. (3) Threats from *intergroup anxiety* arise when people feel uncertain and anxious about interacting with members of the outgroup. A lack of familiarity with the outgroup and its customs can create awkwardness and discomfort before and during interactions. (4) Finally, threats from *negative stereotypes* occur when people believe that members of the outgroup possess undesirable characteristics (e.g., aggressiveness, untrustworthiness) that may lead to detrimental actions toward the ingroup.

Think about your own attitudes toward outgroups. Are there any outgroups that make you feel uncomfortable? Immigrants, gays and lesbians, Aboriginal Canadians, Blacks—do you feel threatened by any of these groups? Perhaps you can recognize some of the elements of integrated threat theory in your own feelings, such as perceived competition for resources or discomfort during interactions.

Integrated threat theory hypothesizes that these four threats arouse aversive feelings toward the outgroup, such as anxiety, frustration, hostility, and anger, thus leading to negative intergroup attitudes (prejudice). One compelling aspect of the theory is that it can be applied equally well to understanding either the attitudes of the majority group toward minority groups or the attitudes of minority groups toward the majority group. In an interesting Canadian application of the theory, Brandon University's Barry Corenblum, together with Walter Stephan, recruited 110 White and 127 Aboriginal Canadians from Manitoba. Several First Nations were represented in the Aboriginal sample, including Ojibwa, Cree, and Métis. Participants completed measures of each type of perceived threat (realistic, symbolic, intergroup anxiety, and negative stereotypes), as well as attitudes toward the outgroup. Results for both groups supported the usefulness of three threats for predicting prejudice: symbolic threat, intergroup anxiety, and stereotype threat. These three variables predicted White respondents' degree of prejudice toward Aboriginal Canadians, as well as Aboriginal Canadians' degree of prejudice toward White Canadians. The fourth type of threat in the theory (realistic threats) predicted White respondents' attitudes toward Aboriginals but not Aboriginal respondents' attitudes toward Whites. It will be interesting to see how future tests of this theory turn out in the coming years (see also Stephan, Boniecki, Ybarra, Bettencourt, Ervin, Jackson, et al., 2002).

Another examination of the relation between threats and prejudice was conducted by Canadian social psychologist Stewart McCann (1999) at Cape Breton University in Sydney, Nova Scotia. McCann conducted an archival analysis of fluctuations in the memberships of fundamentalist, authoritarian churches in the United States over the period 1928 to 1986. McCann hypothesized that authoritarian churches might become more popular during times of high economic or political threat, because these churches tend to reject outgroups (e.g., nonbelievers) and to offer simple, clear answers for all problems (e.g., punishment from God). Using an index of social, economic, and political threat (SEPT; McCann & Stewin, 1990) for each year, McCann found that, indeed, increased threats were associated with larger memberships in fundamentalist churches (e.g., Southern Baptist) but not in more liberal churches (e.g., Presbyterian). To the extent that fundamentalist churches condone prejudice against outgroups more than liberal churches do, these data are consistent with the hypothesis that threats increase prejudice.

The various emotional sources of prejudice and discrimination are summarized in the accompanying Concept Review.

CONCEPT REVIEW
Emotional Sources of Prejudice and Discrimination

Emotional Source	*Relevant Theory*	*Description*	*Example*
Frustration	Scapegoat theory	People vent their frustrations from daily life by lashing out against members of a weak minority group	Gay bashing: Looking for gay men to beat up simply because it gets rid of feelings of frustration and stress
Perceived competition	Realistic group conflict theory	People dislike members of a group who are thought to be competing for scarce resources such as jobs or land	Disliking immigrants because they are believed to take jobs away from native-born workers
Self-enhancement	Social identity theory	People form negative impressions of members of an outgroup in order to make their own group seem superior	Laughing at the unusual customs or beliefs of a minority religious group in order to make the majority religious view seem superior
Threats	Integrated threat theory	People dislike members of a group who are competing for scarce resources, hold different attitudes and values, arouse anxiety, or are believed to possess undesirable characteristics	Avoiding contact with disabled people because interactions are awkward and anxiety-provoking

Sexism: Prejudice and Discrimination Against Women

To this point, we have focused on minority groups (e.g., Blacks, Aboriginal Canadians, gays and lesbians, immigrants) in our discussion of prejudice and discrimination. But there is another group in society that, historically, has been a target of discrimination. This group is different from the others we have discussed in that it is not a "minority" group at all—in fact, its members constitute approximately half of the humans on the planet. We refer, of course, to women.

In most societies around the world, men have occupied and continue to occupy the principal positions of power, wealth, and status. Although women have made gains over the past few decades, they remain underrepresented in positions of influence in most countries and badly disadvantaged in others. Women are subjected to prejudice, as well as both intentional and unintentional discrimination. Prejudice and discrimination directed against women because of their gender is called **sexism.**

Because women constitute approximately 50% of the population, virtually everyone has extensive experience with and exposure to women—a factor that makes this group distinct from other targets of discrimination. Also, almost all men (the dominant group in most societies) love and care about many women, including their mothers, wives, daughters, and female friends. So the problem is not so much that men dislike women, but rather that men do not always treat women as their equals. This unequal treatment has significant, detrimental effects on the lives of many women. In the current section, we discuss some of the causes and consequences of sexism.

sexism

prejudice and discrimination directed against women because of their gender

Sexism Today

In Canada today, most men consider themselves to be fair-minded and unbiased toward women. But are these self-perceptions accurate? Do you think most men's true beliefs about women are egalitarian, or are most men instead chauvinistic? Perhaps sexist attitudes and actions have simply become more subtle and elusive—paralleling our earlier discussion of racial prejudice.

Francine Tougas of the University of Ottawa and her colleagues (Tougas, Brown, Beaton, & Joly, 1995) have argued that, indeed, sexism has become more sophisticated than it used to be (see also Swim, Aikin, Hall, & Hunter, 1995). **Neosexism** refers to a modern and more subtle form of sexism, which includes beliefs that women are no longer disadvantaged, together with antagonism toward women's demands for special treatment. The accompanying Know Yourself 9.1: "Neosexism Scale" presents Tougas and her colleagues' (1995) scale. How would you answer these items?

Tougas and her colleagues administered the neosexism scale to two samples of Canadian men and found that, as predicted, men's scores on the neosexism scale correlated with their attitudes toward affirmative action programs that give preferential treatment to women, such that neosexists were more opposed to such programs. The researchers hypothesized that neosexist beliefs arise when men think that their own interests are best served by a hierarchical system in which men have more power than women (see also Beaton, Tougas, & Joly, 1996; Tougas, Crosby, Joly, & Pelchat, 1993).

Another perspective on modern sexism was provided by Peter Glick of Lawrence University and Susan Fiske of Princeton

neosexism

a subtle form of sexism, which includes beliefs that women are no longer disadvantaged and antagonism toward women's demands for better treatment

Sexism is prejudice or discrimination directed against women because of their gender.

Know Yourself 9.1
Neosexism Scale

Please indicate the extent to which you agree or disagree with each of the following statements by circling the appropriate number on the answer scale.

1. Discrimination against women in the labour force is no longer a problem in Canada.

1	2	3	4	5	6	7
Strongly Disagree			Undecided			Strongly Agree

2. I consider the present employment system to be unfair to women.

1	2	3	4	5	6	7
Strongly Disagree			Undecided			Strongly Agree

3. Women shouldn't push themselves where they are not wanted.

1	2	3	4	5	6	7
Strongly Disagree			Undecided			Strongly Agree

4. Women will make more progress by being patient and not pushing too hard for change.

1	2	3	4	5	6	7
Strongly Disagree			Undecided			Strongly Agree

5. It is difficult to work for a female boss.

1	2	3	4	5	6	7
Strongly Disagree			Undecided			Strongly Agree

6. Women's requests in terms of equality between the sexes are simply exaggerated.

1	2	3	4	5	6	7
Strongly Disagree			Undecided			Strongly Agree

7. Over the past few years, women have gotten more from government than they deserve.

1	2	3	4	5	6	7
Strongly Disagree			Undecided			Strongly Agree

8. Universities are wrong to admit women in costly programs such as medicine, when in fact, a large number will leave their jobs after a few years to raise their children.

1	2	3	4	5	6	7
Strongly Disagree			Undecided			Strongly Agree

9. In order not to appear sexist, many men are inclined to overcompensate women.

1	2	3	4	5	6	7
Strongly Disagree			Undecided			Strongly Agree

10. Due to social pressures, firms frequently have to hire unqualified women.

1	2	3	4	5	6	7
Strongly Disagree			Undecided			Strongly Agree

11. In a fair employment system, men and women would be considered equal.

1	2	3	4	5	6	7
Strongly Disagree			Undecided			Strongly Agree

SCORING: Score Items 1 and 3–10 using the answer scales as presented (1-2-3-4-5-6-7); Items 2 and 11 are reverse-scored (that is, 7-6-5-4-3-2-1). Add up the 11 items to get your overall neosexism score. Possible scores range from 11 to 77, and higher scores represent greater neosexism.

ambivalent sexism inventory

a measure of stereotyped attitudes toward women, which is composed of two dimensions, one positive and one negative: benevolent sexism and hostile sexism

benevolent sexism

positive but paternalistic attitudes toward women

hostile sexism

negative attitudes toward women who violate the traditional stereotype of women

University (1996), who suggested that men often hold *ambivalent* attitudes toward women. Recall from Chapter 6 that ambivalent attitudes contain both positive and negative elements (see page 234). Glick and Fiske argued that many men have mixed responses to women. On the one hand, these men have positive (if somewhat paternalistic) attitudes toward women in the sense that they like women and want to "protect" the women in their lives. On the other hand, these men have negative, hostile attitudes toward women who violate the traditional stereotype, such as feminists. Glick and Fiske developed a measure that they labelled the **ambivalent sexism inventory,** which included items to assess these two dimensions of sexism, which were labelled **benevolent sexism** and **hostile sexism.** Sample items for each dimension are presented in Know Yourself 9.2: "Ambivalent Sexism Inventory." See how you would answer these items.

Glick and a large number of collaborators (Glick, Fiske, Mladinic, Saiz, Abrams, Masser, et al., 2000) administered the ambivalent sexism inventory to large samples in 19 countries around the world, including the United States, Australia, Cuba, Nigeria, Chile, Turkey, Japan, and Botswana (but not Canada). The researchers were then able to calculate the average benevolent sexism and average hostile sexism scores in each country. They also obtained from the United Nations two measures of gender equality in each country, based on such things as women's participation in the economy and politics. Results showed that the levels of both benevolent sexism and hostile sexism in a country were negatively correlated with the measures of gender equality in that country. Countries where respondents exhibited more sexism (whether benevolent or hostile) tended to give women less access to economic and political arenas. Even measured at national levels, sexist attitudes were associated with gender discrimination and inequality.

Gender Stereotypes

In Chapter 5, we defined *gender stereotypes* as beliefs about the characteristics that are associated with men and women (see page 170). We noted that although there are some characteristics on which men and women actually differ significantly (e.g., aggressiveness, romantic attraction), many people *believe* that the sexes differ on a wide variety of characteristics.

The traditional view of men is that they are strong, aggressive, dominant, independent, and mathematical, whereas the traditional view of women is that they are warm, compassionate, indecisive, emotional, and verbally skilled (e.g., see Bergen & Williams, 1991). You might note that the characteristics believed to be associated with women are not necessarily negative; for example, it is presumably good to be warm and compassionate. In fact, women are often evaluated more positively than men, whose stereotype has been characterized as "bad but bold" (Glick, Lameiras, Fiske, Eckes, Masser, Volpato, et al., 2004). Characteristics that are associated with women, however, are not ones that would lead to positions of power and status, especially compared to the characteristics believed to be associated with men. Women are perceived as warmer than men, but also as less competent than men (Fiske, Cuddy, Glick, & Xu, 2002). Thus, gender stereotypes mirror the division of roles between men and women in society and can make it difficult for women to achieve positions of power and status (e.g., see Eagly & Karau, 2002).

Origins of Gender Stereotypes. Where do gender stereotypes come from? Why do people believe that men and women differ on various traits? Think about your own beliefs about the characteristics of men and women: Where did your beliefs come from?

Know Yourself 9.2
Ambivalent Sexism Inventory

Please indicate the extent to which you agree or disagree with each of the following statements by circling the appropriate number on the answer scale

BENEVOLENT SEXISM SCALE

1. Women should be cherished and protected by men.

0	1	2	3	4	5
Disagree Strongly	Disagree Somewhat	Disagree Slightly	Agree Slightly	Agree Somewhat	Agree Strongly

2. Men are complete without women.

0	1	2	3	4	5
Disagree Strongly	Disagree Somewhat	Disagree Slightly	Agree Slightly	Agree Somewhat	Agree Strongly

3. Women, compared to men, tend to have a superior moral sensibility.

0	1	2	3	4	5
Disagree Strongly	Disagree Somewhat	Disagree Slightly	Agree Slightly	Agree Somewhat	Agree Strongly

4. Men should be willing to sacrifice their own well-being in order to provide financially for the women in their lives.

0	1	2	3	4	5
Disagree Strongly	Disagree Somewhat	Disagree Slightly	Agree Slightly	Agree Somewhat	Agree Strongly

5. Many women have a quality of purity that few men possess.

0	1	2	3	4	5
Disagree Strongly	Disagree Somewhat	Disagree Slightly	Agree Slightly	Agree Somewhat	Agree Strongly

6. A good woman should be set on a pedestal by her man.

0	1	2	3	4	5
Disagree Strongly	Disagree Somewhat	Disagree Slightly	Agree Slightly	Agree Somewhat	Agree Strongly

HOSTILE SEXISM SCALE

1. Women exaggerate problems they have at work.

0	1	2	3	4	5
Disagree Strongly	Disagree Somewhat	Disagree Slightly	Agree Slightly	Agree Somewhat	Agree Strongly

2. Feminists are making entirely reasonable demands of men.

0	1	2	3	4	5
Disagree Strongly	Disagree Somewhat	Disagree Slightly	Agree Slightly	Agree Somewhat	Agree Strongly

3. Once a woman gets a man to commit to her, she usually tries to put him on a tight leash.

0	1	2	3	4	5
Disagree Strongly	Disagree Somewhat	Disagree Slightly	Agree Slightly	Agree Somewhat	Agree Strongly

4. Most women interpret innocent remarks or acts as being sexist.

0	1	2	3	4	5
Disagree Strongly	Disagree Somewhat	Disagree Slightly	Agree Slightly	Agree Somewhat	Agree Strongly

5. Many women are actually seeking special favours, such as hiring policies that favour them over men, under the guise of asking for "equality."

0	1	2	3	4	5
Disagree Strongly	Disagree Somewhat	Disagree Slightly	Agree Slightly	Agree Somewhat	Agree Strongly

6. Women seek to gain power by getting control over men.

0	1	2	3	4	5
Disagree Strongly	Disagree Somewhat	Disagree Slightly	Agree Slightly	Agree Somewhat	Agree Strongly

SCORING: For each scale (benevolent sexism and hostile sexism), score Items 1, 3, 4, 5, and 6 using the answer scales as presented (0-1-2-3-4-5); Item 2 in each scale is reverse-scored (that is, 5-4-3-2-1-0). Add up the six items in each scale to get your overall benevolent sexism or hostile sexism score. Possible scores on each scale range from 0 to 30, and higher scores represent greater sexism.

Sample items from Glick and Fiske, "The ambivalent sexism inventory: Differentiating hostile and benevolent sexism," *Journal of Personality and Social Psychology*, 70, 491–512, 1996. Copyright © 1995 by Peter Glick and Susan T. Fiske. Reprinted by permission.

One important factor is parental socialization: boys and girls are often raised differently. Boys are typically encouraged to be assertive, to engage in independent exploration, and to be physically active; girls are typically encouraged to be compassionate, to engage in quiet play, and to be polite. These parenting patterns teach boys to be self-confident and girls to be nurturant and also lead children to expect similar characteristics in other boys and girls.

Religious institutions also contribute to gender stereotypes. In many religions, men and women are treated differently and/or assigned different roles in the church. For instance, women are required to pray separately from men in some religions, such as Islam. Positions of power in most religions are dominated by men. For example, women cannot become priests in the Roman Catholic Church. These traditions teach young people that men and women differ in significant ways and are best suited to specific roles in society. There is some evidence that stronger religious beliefs are correlated with greater endorsement of stereotypical gender roles (Morgan, 1987).

Another source of gender stereotypes is the mass media. Men and women are portrayed in stereotypical ways in many television shows and movies. Some counterstereotypic portrayals occur, of course, but most characters fall into typical gender roles. For example, sitcoms usually portray women as very concerned about their physical appearance and as highly emotional. Music videos often portray women as sex objects. These characterizations may serve to influence young viewers' beliefs about gender traits and roles.

It is also likely that distorted interpretations and self-fulfilling prophecies serve to strengthen gender stereotypes. For instance, people may interpret a man's request for help as assertive, but a woman's request for help as submissive. In terms of self-fulfilling prophecies, people's actions may elicit stereotype-consistent behaviour. For instance, if parents expect their sons to be independent and decisive, they may act toward their sons in ways that evoke independent and decisive behaviour (e.g., insisting they make a speedy decision). In contrast, if parents expect their daughters to be nurturant and compassionate, they may act toward their daughters in ways that evoke such behaviours (e.g., sending them to visit a sick relative).

Accuracy of Gender Stereotypes.

The *accuracy* of gender stereotypes is a complex issue. We have mentioned several origins of stereotypes that may not have a basis in reality (e.g., media portrayals of men and women). But some researchers have argued that there is a "kernel of truth" in gender stereotypes (and in other domains of interpersonal perception as well; see Jussim, 1991). What should we conclude about the accuracy of gender stereotypes?

Sex differences that parallel the content of gender stereotypes, including aggressiveness and concern for others' feelings, have been documented in research actually comparing men and women. Also, Janet Swim (1994) asked men and women to estimate the sizes of the gender differences on numerous characteristics that had yielded reliable male–female differences in past research. She found that perceivers were generally quite good at judging the sizes of gender differences, which suggests that gender stereotypes have a factual basis.

But there is also evidence that gender stereotypes considerably exaggerate any current gender differences (e.g., Diekman, Eagly, & Kulesa, 2002). Carol Martin (1987) conducted an interesting study at the University of British Columbia in Vancouver. She asked men and women to indicate whether various characteristics were self-descriptive and also to estimate the percentage of men and women who possess the same characteristics. Martin used the self-ratings of men and women as a rough estimate of *actual* sex differences. These responses produced a few substantial differences between the sexes (e.g., on self-ratings of egotistical, cynical, and whiney) and a few smaller differences. She used the estimated percentages of each gender to assess *perceived* sex differences (i.e., stereotypes). These estimates of men and women as groups revealed many more significant differences than did the self-ratings. Indeed, participants judged that men and women as groups differed on virtually every trait that was measured. On 34 of 40 traits, perceived sex differences (based on ratings of the groups) were significantly larger than actual sex differences (based on self-ratings; see also Allen, 1995). Some traits were believed to differ substantially between the genders but were not actually endorsed differentially by men and women, including independent, helpful, and kind.

In a similar vein, Malcolm Grant, Cathryn Button, Abraham Ross, and Ted Hannah (1997) of Memorial University in St. John's, Newfoundland, asked men and women to report their own attitudes and also to estimate the average attitudes of men and women on such issues as immigration policies, pornography, rock videos, and nudist camps. Paralleling the results of Martin (1987), these researchers found that participants predicted significantly larger attitudinal sex differences than actually existed on most issues.

These findings show that, like other stereotypes, gender stereotypes are certainly oversimplifications—in this case, oversimplifications of men and women. Although the two genders may differ, on average, on a few characteristics, these differences are smaller than most of us believe. Also, differences *within* each sex (comparing different men or different women) are always larger than average differences *between* the two sexes. And most of us believe that men and women differ on some traits where there are no real differences at all. Thus, when gender stereotypes are used to form impressions of a particular target, they will often be inaccurate.

Of course, even if gender stereotypes ha_____ ernel of truth, this does not mean that gender differences are inevitab_____ n if men and women actually differ at the present time in how a_____ n average), it is possible that socialization that treated boys and g_____ reduce or eliminate this difference. We must distinguish betwee_____ ferences (which do exist on some characteristics) and *inevitable o_____ nces (which may be very few in number). In Chapter 5, we disc_____ rical and social sources of gender differences (e.g., see Buss & K_____ & Eagly, 2002) and suggested that both kinds of factors play s_____ rchers will have to disentangle the contributions of biology an_____

In conclusion, gender stereotypes exa_____ nces and include features that reflect, in whole or in part, the _____ assigned to men and women (see Abele, 2003; Diekman & Eagly_____ 1999). These observations imply that societies should not lim_____ opportunities on the basis of their gender.

Prejudice Against Overweight Wo____

Obesity is a devastating stigma in our culture. _____ ight are the targets of widespread prejudice and discriminatio_____ rd ridicule to denial of employment. A negative, damaging _____ verweight individuals is common in our society. Compared to nor_____ght persons, obese individuals are perceived as less attractive, less intelligent, less popular, less athletic, and less successful (e.g., Crandall, 1994; Harris, Harris, & Bochner, 1982; Hebl & Heatherton, 1997).

One reason that obese individuals are evaluated negatively is that they are often seen as personally responsible for being overweight—their weight is believed to reflect entirely their poor eating habits and lack of willpower. Tragically, obese individuals

Prejudice and discrimination directed against people who are overweight is common in our society.

often agree with these perceptions and, therefore, blame themselves for being ridiculed and rejected.

Although both overweight women and overweight men are subject to prejudice and negative treatment, the impact of being overweight is greater on women, because physical appearance is more highly valued for women than men in our culture (Crocker, Cornwell, & Major, 1993; Roehling, 1999). Consistent with this reasoning, researchers have found that although being overweight is associated with lower self-esteem in both women and men, the connection is stronger among women (Miller & Downey, 1999).

How bad is discrimination against overweight women? Michelle Hebl and Laura Mannix (2003) of Rice University found that if a man was simply sitting beside an overweight woman, even when the two were strangers, he was judged more negatively than if he was sitting beside a normal-weight woman. In perhaps the most disturbing demonstration of discrimination against overweight women, University of Kansas social psychologist Christian Crandall (1995) found that females who were heavier than average were less likely to receive financial support from their parents for university education than were normal-weight females; no such effect was found for males. Data also showed that there was no association between weight and family income or between weight and academic credentials (e.g., high school grades) among women, so it appears that the financial support statistics occurred because parents were discriminating against their own heavy-weight daughters.

Fear of Obesity Among Normal-Weight Women.

Given the profound negative consequences of obesity for women, it may not be surprising that even normal-weight women tend to be very concerned about their weight. Patricia Pliner, Shelly Chaiken, and Gordon Flett (1990) surveyed 639 visitors to a museum in Toronto. The sample included women and men of various ages from 10 to 79 years. The researchers found that women reported more anxiety about their eating habits, less satisfaction with their physical appearance, and more concern about their body weight than did men. Moreover, these sex differences occurred across the entire life span. Figure 9.5 presents the mean responses of men and women at each age group on a measure of **appearance self-esteem,** which assessed respondents' satisfaction with their looks. Higher bars represent greater satisfaction with one's physical appearance. The figure shows that women were less satisfied than men at every age in the sample.

appearance self-esteem

an individual's satisfaction with his or her physical looks

Why are so many women dissatisfied with their body shapes and sizes? One reason is that they are constantly exposed to unrealistic standards of thinness. In the mass media, female models, actors, and even reporters tend to be physically attractive and very thin. Magazine advertisements, for example, show so-called supermodels who are starvation-skinny. The term "heroin chic" has been used to describe models who are so thin and wasted that they appear to be heroin addicts, yet are presented as beautiful and sexy. Researchers have found that women's exposure to thin media images is associated with negative self-concepts and eating patterns. For example, Marian Morry of the University of Manitoba and Sandra Staska of the University of Winnipeg (2001) found that women who reported that they read beauty magazines internalized thin standards of beauty and were more likely to report eating problems. In another study, Toronto social psychologists Jennifer Mills, Janet Polivy, Peter Herman, and Marika Tiggemann (2002) found that women who reported that they were dieting rated their ideal body size

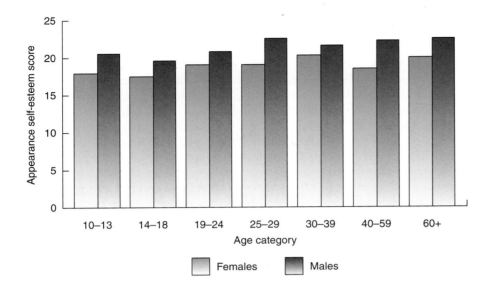

FIGURE 9.5 Mean appearance self-esteem for females and males at each age group

From Pliner et al., "Gender differences in concern with body weight and physical appearance over the lifespan," *Personality and Social Psychology Bulletin*, 16, 263–273, Table 1, p. 268, 1990. Reprinted by permission of Sage Publications.

as smaller following exposure to seven advertisements featuring very thin models (see also Stice & Shaw, 1994); exposure to the thin models did not influence perceived ideal sizes for women who were not dieting.

Fear of gaining weight can affect even athletic women. The University of Florida's Heather Hausenblas and the University of Western Ontario's Albert Carron (1999) reviewed 92 studies examining eating disorders among athletes and found that female athletes experienced more problems with *anorexia nervosa* (starvation brought on by an intense fear of gaining weight) and *bulimia* (binge eating followed by purging) than did female nonathletes. Eating disorders were especially common in what the authors called *aesthetic sports,* which involved subjective evaluations that might be based on appearance, such as gymnastics, figure skating, dance, and diving.

Women are frequently exposed to unrealistic standards of thinness in the media.

The Victim's Perspective: Prejudice and Discrimination from the Inside

To this point, we have focused on the causes of prejudice, discrimination, and sexism, trying to understand why people sometimes develop negative attitudes and behave in discriminatory ways toward members of other groups. But what about the people who are the *victims* of prejudice and discrimination? What are their lives like?

Think about your own experiences. Are you a member of any minority or disadvantaged groups? Some of you belong to ethnic or religious minority groups. Many of you are women, who can face significant discrimination, as noted in the preceding section. But even those of you who are not members of groups that are typically considered to be disadvantaged (e.g., Caucasian males) may be able to think of times when your group membership hurt you or was held against you. University students might be denied rental housing; men are sometimes viewed suspiciously as babysitters or child-care workers; varsity athletes might have to contend with a stereotype that they are not academically competent; and so on. Can you think of instances when you were judged in a biased way because you belonged to a certain group? How did this experience make you feel? What would it be like to be greeted with hostility or suspicion frequently throughout your life?

Social psychologists have directed less attention to the experiences of disadvantaged group members than to the causes of prejudice, largely because a long-term goal of research has been to *reduce* prejudice and discrimination. Thus, we have focused on the people who *are* prejudiced rather than the *targets* of prejudice. But it is also important to study the consequences of being a victim of prejudice. Some of the very first work in this area was conducted by Canadian social psychologists Ken Dion at the University of Toronto and Brian Earn at the University of Guelph (Dion & Earn, 1975; Dion, Earn, & Yee, 1978). In the last 10 or 20 years, many other researchers have also contributed to the investigation of the psychology of victimization (e.g., see the book edited by Swim & Stangor, 1998).

Before turning to this research, we should note that the most significant consequence of being a member of a severely disadvantaged group (e.g., an ethnic minority group) is probably not psychological but rather material: one's life is more difficult economically and occupationally than the lives of members of advantaged groups. Members of disadvantaged groups are more likely to live in poverty, to be the victims of violence, and to be denied opportunities than are members of majority or dominant groups in society. The term *disadvantaged* can be taken quite literally: the lives of these individuals are objectively more difficult than the lives of members of advantaged groups.

But prejudice and discrimination also have psychological consequences, because being the victim of discrimination is stressful. For example, Mindi Foster of Wilfrid Laurier University in Waterloo, Ontario, has shown that experiences of discrimination are associated with such symptoms as depression and anxiety, especially when victims' beliefs lead them to blame themselves for the discrimination (Foster, 2000; Foster & Tsarfati, 2005; see also Branscombe, Schmitt, & Harvey, 1999; Williams & Williams-Morris, 2000). Iowa State University social psychologists Frederick Gibbons, Meg Gerrard, and their colleagues (Gibbons, Gerrard, Cleveland, Wills, & Brody, 2004) found that experiences of discrimination were associated not only with emotional distress (e.g., feelings of worthlessness and anxiety), but also with greater use of alcohol and illegal drugs. The researchers argued that discrimination increased individuals' substance use because the alcohol and drugs were being used to reduce the emotional distress caused by discrimination.

Clearly, it is important to study how prejudice and discrimination affect their victims. In this section, we consider two lines of social psychological research that have focused specifically on members of minority or subordinate groups: research on the *personal–group discrimination discrepancy* and research on *stereotype threat*.

The Personal–Group Discrimination Discrepancy

Return again to your own experiences of discrimination, when membership in a group has hurt you. Thinking about whatever group this may be, how would you answer the following question: Have you experienced more, less, or about the same amount of discrimination as the average member of your group? For example, if you are a woman, have you experienced more, less, or about the same amount of gender discrimination as the average woman? If you are an Asian Canadian, have you experienced more, less, or about the same amount of racial discrimination as the average Asian Canadian? If your discrimination experiences have been based on being a university student, have you experienced more, less, or about the same amount of discrimination against students as the average university student?

Social psychologists studying members of disadvantaged groups have uncovered an interesting pattern in people's judgments of their own experiences of discrimination relative to the average member of their group: respondents consistently report that they have personally experienced *less* discrimination than the average member of their group. In other words, people who belong to groups that are targets of discrimination report that their own experiences have been less frequent or less serious than the experiences of the "typical" member of their group. This tendency for most people to report less personal discrimination than the typical member of their group cannot be accurate, because it is statistically impossible for *most people* to be less than *average*.

This phenomenon has been labelled the **personal–group discrimination discrepancy,** because personal discrimination is seen as discrepant from group discrimination: people report less personal discrimination than discrimination aimed at their group. Did your own answer follow this pattern? If so, your judgment is consistent with findings that have been obtained with *many* different disadvantaged groups. For example, Donald Taylor of McGill University, Stephen Wright of Simon Fraser University, and their colleagues have surveyed members of several disadvantaged groups and collected reports of personal discrimination (e.g., Poore, Gagne, Barlow, Lydon, Taylor, & Wright, 2002; Taylor, Wright, Moghaddam, & Lalonde, 1990; Taylor, Wright, & Porter, 1993). These surveys have yielded consistent evidence of the personal–group discrimination discrepancy. For instance, they found that Inuit adults living in remote Arctic communities reported having personally experienced less discrimination than the average Inuit adult; similarly, immigrant women in Montreal reported that their personal experiences of discrimination had been less frequent than those of the average immigrant woman. Faye Crosby (1984), who is at the University of California at Santa Cruz, found that working women in the United States reported having personally experienced less gender discrimination in their workplace than the average woman. Researchers have also found the personal–group discrimination discrepancy in surveys of single mothers receiving government assistance in London, Ontario (Olson, Roese, Meen, & Robertson, 1995), Chinese and Pakistani residents of Toronto (Dion & Kawakami, 1996), and other disadvantaged groups (for reviews, see Olson & Hafer, 1996; Taylor et al., 1993).

Why does this bias occur? Why do people consistently report less-than-average discrimination directed against themselves? Faye Crosby (1984) argued that motivational factors are important. She suggested that members of disadvantaged groups want to see themselves as experiencing relatively little discrimination because this allows them to feel that they have more control over their lives. Being a victim of discrimination means that your life is affected by others who dislike or have negative expectations for you, which might induce feelings of helplessness. In contrast, believing that discrimination does not occur much in one's own life maintains a perception of control. Similarly, Gordon Hodson of Brock University and Victoria Esses of the University of Western Ontario obtained evidence suggesting that the personal–group discrimination discrepancy reflects, at least in part, that people want to distance themselves from negative attributes associated with their group, such as being a target of discrimination (Hodson & Esses, 2002; see also Quinn & Olson, 2003).

Another motivational factor may be that denying personal discrimination gives members of minority groups an excuse for not doing anything about prejudice against their group. People who exhibit bigotry often belong to powerful or dominant groups in society, so taking action against bigots can be dangerous or costly. If members of minority groups see themselves as relatively untouched by discrimination, they can rationalize (to themselves and to other people) their own inaction.

People may also avoid saying that they have personally experienced discrimination because such claims are seen by others as whiney or complaining (see Kaiser & Miller, 2001). There are social costs associated with claiming discrimination, and these costs may cause members of minority groups to publicly minimize their own experiences of discrimination (Sechrist, Swim, & Stangor, 2004). Unfortunately, this avoidance may prevent people who really do experience discrimination from confronting the obstacles they face in their daily lives.

personal–group discrimination discrepancy
the tendency for people to report that they as individuals have experienced less negative treatment based on their group membership than the average member of their group

In addition to being motivated to *understate* discrimination directed against themselves *personally* for the reasons discussed above, members of disadvantaged groups might also be motivated to *exaggerate* discrimination at the *group* level (i.e., exaggerate how much discrimination the "typical" member of their group experiences). Such exaggeration could contribute to the personal–group discrimination discrepancy. Why might people exaggerate discrimination against their group? If one's group is the target of a lot of discrimination, then it deserves special programs such as affirmative action or social assistance. Thus, by exaggerating group-level discrimination, individuals may be hoping to provide a justification for these programs, which might benefit them personally.

Cognitive factors may also contribute to the personal–group discrimination discrepancy. For example, people may compare the discriminatory events in their own lives (a small sample) with all the discriminatory events they have heard about from other people and in the news. Their personal experiences with discrimination may seem quite minimal in comparison to the breadth of events involving others.

Stereotype Threat

stereotype threat

the pressure experienced by individuals who fear that if they perform poorly on a task, their performance will appear to confirm an unfavourable belief about their group

A second line of research on the effects of being a victim of prejudice has focused on the impact of negative social stereotypes on performance. In 1995, Claude Steele and Joshua Aronson published an important paper on **stereotype threat.** Stereotype threat occurs when individuals believe that if they perform poorly, their performance will appear to confirm an unfavourable stereotype about their group. Stereotype threat puts pressure on people to do as well as possible in order to discredit the negative stereotype. Unfortunately, this added pressure can itself cause poor performance—people can "choke" under the pressure.

For example, Black men and women know that some observers hold a negative, harmful stereotype that Blacks perform relatively poorly on academic tasks. Thus, whenever Blacks work on explicitly intellectual tasks, they may worry that if they perform poorly, they will confirm this stereotype in the eyes of some prejudiced people. They may feel that they "represent" their group and, therefore, must perform well to disconfirm the stereotype. This pressure—or stereotype threat—can impair performance. Whites may not face this kind of pressure when performing academic tasks.

Steele and Aronson (1995) documented this phenomenon with Black students at Stanford University—an elite institution where it might be expected that all students would be confident about their academic abilities. Steele and Aronson recruited Black and White students and administered a difficult test constructed from items from the verbal section of the Graduate Record Examination (GRE). Half of the participants (both Black and White) took the test under conditions that were expected to elicit stereotype threat among the Black students. These individuals were told that the study was investigating "various personal factors involved in performance on problems requiring reading and verbal reasoning abilities" and that they would receive feedback on their own abilities after the test. The remaining participants completed the test under more relaxed and nonevaluative conditions; they were not told that the test assessed verbal abilities and did not expect feedback on their own abilities after the test.

Figure 9.6 presents the performance data in each condition for Black and White students. As predicted, Black participants performed just as well as White students in the relaxed condition, but Black participants performed significantly worse than White students in the stereotype-threat condition. Note also that the performance of White participants was not affected by the threat manipulation, whereas the

Blacks can experience *stereotype threat* when they write an academic exam.

© Jose Luis Pelaez, Inc./CORBIS

performance of Black participants declined in the stereotype-threat condition compared to the relaxed condition.

These data show that stereotype threat can impair the performance of Black students. As if dealing with objective disadvantage were not enough, Blacks must also carry the weight of representing their group when they perform academic tasks. The added pressure of this responsibility may interfere with clear thinking; thus, their performance can deteriorate. Unfortunately, this pressure-induced decrement in performance might be interpreted by prejudiced observers as evidence that the negative stereotype is accurate.

Blacks are not the only target of negative stereotypes regarding performance on academic or other tasks. For example, another stereotype that some people hold is that women are less skilled at mathematics than are men. University of Waterloo social psychologist Steven Spencer and his colleagues Claude Steele and Diane Quinn (1999) tested whether women might, under certain conditions, experience stereotype threat on tests of mathematics, which would impair their performance. These researchers recruited university men and women, all of whom were skilled at math: all participants had taken at least one semester of calculus, had received at least a B in the course, and had previously scored in the top 15% of their age group on the math subsection of the Scholastic Aptitude Test. Further, all participants had completed a survey in which they indicated agreement with the following two statements: "I am good at math" and "It is important to me that I am good at math."

Participants completed a difficult test taken from the advanced GRE for mathematics. Half of the participants were administered the test under conditions that were expected to arouse stereotype threat among women: they were told that this test had shown significant gender differences in performance in the past. The remaining participants were administered the test under conditions that were expected to prevent stereotype threat: they were told that this test had never shown gender differences in the past.

Figure 9.7 presents the mean performance scores for women and men in the nonthreatening and threatening conditions. As predicted, women performed just as well as men in the nonthreatening condition. In contrast, women in the stereotype-threat condition performed significantly worse than did men in this condition (and also significantly worse than did women in the nonthreatening condition).

These data are striking in that the affected women were highly talented at mathematics; it may seem surprising that people who are good at something can be so negatively affected (see also Sekaquaptewa & Thompson, 2003). In fact, however, it turns out that people for whom a domain of ability is important (and who therefore care about how they perform in that domain) are *more* susceptible to stereotype threat than people who are less invested in the domain (Stone, 2002; Stone, Lynch, Sjomeling, & Darley, 1999). For instance, women who care about their mathematics ability are more susceptible to stereotype threat on math tests than are those who do not; similarly, Blacks who care about academic achievement are more susceptible to stereotype threat on academic tasks than are those who do not. Presumably, people who do not care about their performance in a particular domain will not experience additional pressure from stereotype threat—after all, they *don't care* about this domain. Of course, people who do care about the domain must also be aware of a negative stereotype of their group in order for stereotype threat to occur (Brown & Pinel, 2003). There is also evidence that people who identify strongly with their group will be more affected by stereotype threat than people who identify only weakly with their group (Schmader, 2002).

Joshua Aronson and his colleagues (Aronson, Lustina, Good, Keough, Steele, & Brown, 1999) showed that stereotype threat can even affect the performance of members of typically "advantaged" groups under the appropriate circumstances.

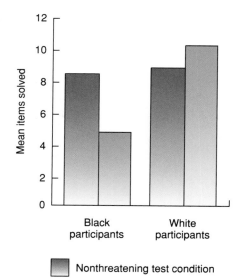

FIGURE 9.6 Performance by Black and White participants in nonthreatening and stereotype-threat test conditions

From Steele and Aronson, "Contending with stereotype: African-American intellectual test performance and stereotype threat," *Journal of Personality and Social Psychology*, 69, 797–811, Fig. 2, p. 802, 1995. Copyright © 1995 by the American Psychological Association. Reprinted by permission.

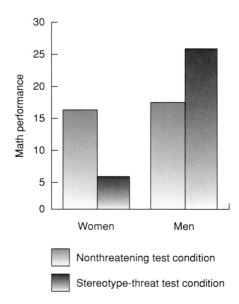

FIGURE 9.7 Performance by women and men in nonthreatening and stereotype-threat test conditions

From Spencer et al., "Stereotype threat and women's math performance," *Journal of Experimental Social Psychology,* 35, 4–28, Fig. 2, p. 13, 1999. Reprinted by permission of Elsevier.

These researchers administered a difficult mathematics test to White male Stanford University students who were selected to be strong in mathematics (similar to the selection criteria for participants in Spencer et al.'s 1999 experiment). Note that the common stereotype of White males is that they are *good* at math.

Half of the participants were told that the experiment was designed to investigate the phenomenal math achievement of Asian students and to try to understand the "growing gap in academic performance between Asian and White students." This alleged purpose was expected to induce stereotype threat in these White males, who would fear confirming the relatively inferior performance by Whites compared to Asians. The remaining participants did not hear anything about Asian students prior to taking the test.

Men in the stereotype-threat condition performed significantly worse (an average of 6.55 correct answers out of 18 questions) than did men in the non-threatening condition (an average of 9.58 correct answers). Thus, stereotype threat was documented for White men in mathematics when an allegedly even more talented group was highlighted as a possible comparison.

What mechanisms explain stereotype threat? How does the pressure of stereotype threat impair performance? One clearly important factor is emotional arousal: when people perform a test under conditions that create stereotype threat, they exhibit more numerous nonverbal signs of anxiety (Bosson, Haymovitz, & Pinel, 2004), as well as higher levels of sympathetic arousal (e.g., heart rate, blood pressure; O'Brien & Crandall, 2003). Other emotions may also occur: people report feeling disappointed and sad, perhaps because conditions producing stereotype threat accentuate a negative stereotype of their group (Keller & Dauenheimer, 2003). Stereotype threat also appears to reduce people's mental capacity—their ability to retain information in memory (Croizet, Després, Gauzins, Huguet, Leyens, & Méot, 2004; Schmader & Johns, 2003). This reduction in memory capacity probably occurs because feelings of anxiety and disappointment are distracting. Obviously, reduced memory capacity will hurt performance on difficult tests. The processes involved in stereotype threat are illustrated in Figure 9.8.

Are there ways to reduce the impact of stereotype threat on vulnerable populations? Thomas Ford of Western Michigan University and his colleagues (Ford, Ferguson, Brooks, & Hagadone, 2004) found that people who use humour to cope with stress are better able to deal with stereotype threat. Why does humour help? Ford and his colleagues found that using humour to deal with stress was associated with lower levels of anxiety, resulting in better performance. There is also evidence

FIGURE 9.8 Processes involved in stereotype threat

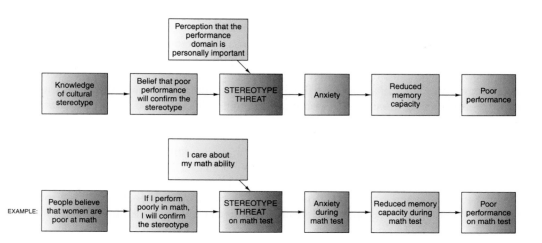

that exposure to a role model who violates the negative stereotype alleviates the negative effects of stereotype threat. For example, in one study, reading about four individual women who had succeeded in architecture, law, medicine, and invention significantly improved women's performance on a difficult math test under conditions of stereotype threat (McIntyre, Paulson, & Lord, 2003; see also Marx & Roman, 2002).

In another interesting study, the University of Alberta's Jeff Schimel and his colleagues (Schimel, Arndt, Banko, & Cook, 2004) found that women's performance on a math test under conditions of stereotype threat was *not* impaired if those women had recently confirmed their own self-worth by describing how one of their most important characteristics expressed their identity and values. These data suggest that, at least in part, stereotype threat hurts performance because people's self-concepts are threatened.

   # Genocide

We have discussed many negative consequences of prejudice, including distorted information processing, interpersonal aggression, job discrimination, and stereotype threat. But the worst consequence of prejudice is undoubtedly *genocide,* which we defined at the beginning of the chapter as an attempt to systematically eliminate an ethnic group through banishment or murder. Human history is unfortunately filled with instances of genocide, including many in the last century.

The most infamous case of genocide is probably the Holocaust, committed by the Nazis during the Second World War. The Holocaust involved the murder of about 6 million Jews in Germany and other Nazi-occupied countries. The slaughter was terrible. For instance, out of about 600 000 Jews in Hungary at the beginning of the war, approximately 450 000 (75%) were murdered.

" . . The SS people walked up and down, and [indicated] with thumb up to go right, and thumb down to go left. I was chosen to the right, some of my friends to the left. The right was chosen to work; the left was chosen to go to the gas chambers."

The Second World War may seem a distant event. We can find several instances of genocide in the past 15 years. In 1994, approximately 800 000 people were murdered in Rwanda in only 100 days (a killing rate five times higher than the Nazis' slaughter of Jews; see Prunier, 1995). The genocide was committed by extremist members of the majority ethnic group in Rwanda, the Hutus, who targeted members of the minority ethnic group, the Tutsis, as well as moderate Hutus. Roving gangs armed with machetes brutally massacred men, women, and children. One of the many troubling aspects of this tragedy was that it occurred despite the presence of United Nations peacekeeping troops.

Between 1992 and 1995, civil war in Bosnia and Herzegovina (one of several independent states that emerged from the former Yugoslavia in Europe) killed up to 250 000 people. Tens of thousands of these deaths were murders of civilians. For instance, Radislav Drstic, a Bosnian Serb general, was convicted in 1999 of murdering up to 8000 Bosnian Muslims in Srebrencia in 1995. This civil war in Bosnia and Herzegovina was not the end of ethnic conflict in the region. In 1998–1999, between 5000 and 10 000 ethnic Albanians were murdered in Kosovo (a province in Serbia, another state that emerged from Yugoslavia) by Serbian forces, and about 500 000 ethnic Albanians were displaced. Slobodan Milosevic, the president of Serbia at the time, was arrested in 2001 and charged with committing crimes against humanity during the Kosovo conflict.

In the most recent case of apparent genocide, up to 180 000 Black Sudanese civilians have been killed since 2003 in the Darfur region of Sudan by Arab Sudanese

Between 1975 and 1978, Pol Pot and the Khmer Rouge murdered approximately 1.7 million Cambodians, more than 20% of the country's population.

militias. There had been conflict for many years between the nomadic Arabs and the Black farmers. In addition to the killings, approximately 2.5 million Black Sudanese have been displaced and face starvation in refugee camps. International relief efforts have been hampered by interference from Sudanese authorities. An agreement that was reached with the Sudanese government in May 2006 to end the hostilities has not been entirely successful.

Some flagrant cases of mass murder were based on politics and education more than ethnicity, including brutal purges by Joseph Stalin in the U.S.S.R. in the 1930s and 1940s and by Mao Zedong in China in the 1950s, 1960s, and 1970s. For instance, it is estimated that during the so-called Cultural Revolution in China between 1966 and 1976, several million Chinese citizens were killed, including most of the country's intellectual elite. The Chinese Communists also supported Pol Pot and his Khmer Rouge in Cambodia, who conducted an equally bloody purge between 1975 and 1978. The Khmer Rouge murdered about 1.7 million Cambodians (more than 20% of the population), including virtually every influential thinker and known opponent to the Pol Pot regime.

Causes of Genocide

Genocide is such an extreme event that it almost defies explanation. How can anyone deliberately and systematically slaughter defenceless civilians? It is, of course, impossible to conduct experimental research on extreme harm-doing, for ethical reasons. But theorists can apply findings from research on less extreme aggression to try to understand genocide. Also, social scientists have sought to identify common elements in historical cases of genocide; these theorists have included social psychologists (e.g., Baumeister, 1997; Staub, 1989, 1999; Staub, Pearlman, & Miller, 2003; Waller, 2002) and political scientists (e.g., Adelman, 2000, 2004). We summarize a few insights from this literature in the following paragraphs.

Genocide is almost always preceded by what University of Massachusetts social psychologist Ervin Staub (1989, 1999) calls *difficult life conditions*. These conditions may consist of serious economic problems, major political changes or turmoil, and intense conflict between groups in a society. Difficult life conditions create both material and psychological deprivation; that is, people in the society are suffering in terms of basic physical needs (e.g., food, housing) and basic psychological needs (e.g., security, positive identity, sense of control). For instance, the political breakup of Yugoslavia after the 1980 death of its long-time Communist dictator, Marshall Tito, led to extreme instability. The new independent republics that emerged from Yugoslavia faced severe economic hardship, including high levels of unemployment. These conditions aggravated pre-existing tensions and conflict among the numerous ethnic groups in the region and undoubtedly contributed to the murders in Bosnia and Kosovo.

A second prerequisite for genocide appears to be the *dehumanization or devaluation of the outgroup* (Bar-Tal, 1990; Opotow, 2001; Staub, 1989; Waller, 2002). There is often a long history of hostility between the groups, but difficult life conditions intensify the antagonism and derogation. Members of the outgroup may be seen as subhuman and, therefore, not deserving of the usual rights and protections given to members of society. For example, in Rwanda, the majority Hutus had long disliked the Tutsis, who held many positions of influence. Mistrust and derogation of the Tutsis increased prior to the genocide because of rumours and propaganda spread by extremist factions within Hutu society. John Ellard, a social psychologist at the University of

Calgary, has written about some of the conditions that can lead to the *demonization* of an individual or group, which means that the target is perceived as truly evil (Ellard, Miller, Baumle, & Olson, 2002). For example, claiming that a group takes pleasure in others' suffering can lead observers to label the group as evil.

A third element in many cases of genocide is *excessive respect for authority* (Baumeister, 1997; Staub, 1989; Waller, 2002). If people in a dominant group are overly trusting of authorities' claims and interpretations of events, they may accept exaggerated accusations without supportive evidence. Obedient individuals may also carry out harmful acts when ordered to do so, even if they have personal doubts about the morality of their behaviour. Highly respectful cultures also look to their leaders for direction, which gives autocratic rulers like Adolf Hitler, Mao Zedong, and Pol Pot even more power. Respect for authority was very high in most of the countries mentioned earlier as cases of genocide, including Germany, China, Serbia, and Cambodia.

Genocide does not appear suddenly, without warning; there is always *a gradual escalation of aggression and violence.* This escalation means that people slowly become committed to harming the outgroup (Baumeister, 1997; Staub, 1999). Gangs of thugs might begin by threatening or beating up victims; when observers see aggression occurring without punitive consequences, they become more likely to copy such behaviour. What begins as isolated scare tactics and intimidation can transform into widespread violence and murder. Nazi Germany provided a clear example of this escalation. Anti-Semitic acts gradually increased after Hitler's rise to power in 1933. As it became clear that authorities would accept lawless behaviour toward Jews, groups of Nazi sympathizers became more aggressive. On the night of November 9, 1938, a coordinated set of attacks took place against Jewish homes, businesses, and synagogues—an event that became known as *Kristallnacht,* or the Night of Broken Glass. About 100 Jews were killed, and thousands of Jewish businesses were destroyed. This event signalled to all Germans that Jewish citizens were legitimate targets of violence.

Finally, genocide cannot occur without *passive bystanders.* Therefore, to understand incidents of mass murder, it is necessary to understand why people who could have intervened did not do so (Adelman, 2004; Baumeister, 1997; Staub, 1989, 1999). One important influence is, of course, fear of the aggressors. It can be dangerous to try to intervene in genocide, as many moderate Hutus learned in Rwanda—sometimes paying with their lives. Another factor is bureaucratic red tape and slow decision making. For example, a U.N. peacekeeping force in Rwanda when the violence began was directly prohibited by the United Nations from intervening because such action would violate the force's mandate, which was simply to observe; by the time the U.N. Security Council realized the foolishness of its policy, the slaughter was over. A third factor contributing to passivity is simple imitation: if other people do not intervene, then they must support the violence. As a result, bystanders who do not support the violence tolerate it because they assume everyone else supports it.

These five factors do not "explain" genocide. Nothing can provide compelling reasons for mass murder. Moreover, there have been countless cases of difficult life conditions that did not lead to genocide despite the presence of other factors such as dehumanization and excessive respect for authority. Nevertheless, the factors seem to have been present in many cases of genocide, which suggests they may be precipitating conditions. Other triggers are probably also necessary, and the specific causes of genocide undoubtedly differ from incident to incident. Although we are unlikely to develop a checklist that can predict genocide before it occurs, there is reason to hope that understanding the causes of this extreme form of harm-doing might suggest strategies for defusing potential hotspots. Along these lines, some of the social psychologists cited in this section (e.g., Ervin Staub, Daniel Bar-Tal) have worked with governments and humanitarian organizations to increase communication and decrease hostility in longstanding conflicts such as in the Middle East and in the former Yugoslavia.

Reducing Prejudice and Discrimination

If you were put in charge of a government agency whose goal was to reduce prejudice and discrimination, what would you do? Where do you think the limited money and resources could best be directed to improve relations between ethnic, racial, and religious groups? Should we focus on majority group members and try to change their attitudes? Should we emphasize educational programs for children in the school system? Should we introduce social programs designed to give minority groups more access to resources? What about the problems of negative stereotypes about women, the elderly, gays and lesbians, and other groups: How can we discredit these beliefs and promote greater understanding and tolerance?

Thinking about these issues brings home the fact that the problems of prejudice and discrimination are extremely complex and challenging. There is likely no single "best" way to attack the problems. Prejudice and discrimination have multiple causes; thus, multifaceted programs will be necessary to have a significant impact. But social psychologists have been at the forefront of designing and testing techniques to reduce prejudice and discrimination. Some of these techniques can be quite effective, and a broad-based approach utilizing numerous strategies might be highly successful. In the following paragraphs, we describe some of the research that has investigated how to reduce prejudice and discrimination and discuss the implications of these studies for real-life programs.

Dissonance and Prejudice Reduction

In Chapter 7, we discussed a variety of ways that attitudes can be changed. Some of these techniques can be applied to prejudice, which is a negative intergroup attitude.

One theory we described was Festinger's (1957) *dissonance theory* (see pages 239–255). Dissonance theory proposes that people want their attitudes, beliefs, and behaviours to be consistent with one another; if they become aware of inconsistencies, they feel bad and are motivated to restore consistency. Research derived from dissonance theory has documented that if people are induced to behave in a counterattitudinal fashion, they often change their attitudes to be more consistent with the behaviour. For instance, if university students write an essay arguing in favour of increasing tuition (a position that almost all students oppose), they subsequently become more favourable toward increasing tuition.

Michael Leippe and Donna Eisenstadt (1994) adapted the essay-writing technique to attack racial attitudes. White students at Adelphi University were asked to write an essay arguing in favour of doubling the percentage of the university's scholarship funds that would be specifically directed to Black students only. Half of the participants were simply told to write this essay (*low-choice* condition), and half were asked whether they would be willing to write the essay—instructions designed to make them feel that their essay writing was voluntary (*high-choice* condition). In addition, half of the participants signed their essay and recorded their phone number on a consent form (*public* condition), and half prepared the essay privately and never recorded their name or phone number on any of their materials (*private* condition). The researchers predicted that either high choice or high publicity would arouse dissonance, which participants would reduce by changing their racial attitudes to be more favourable toward Blacks. Racial attitudes were measured in an allegedly different study that followed the essay-writing task. Participants answered ten items measuring pro-Black attitudes (e.g., "Too many Blacks still lose out on jobs and promotions because of their skin colour").

Figure 9.9 presents the attitudes reported by participants in each condition who complied with the request to write a pro-Black essay; higher bars reflect more favourable attitudes toward Blacks. As predicted, the results showed

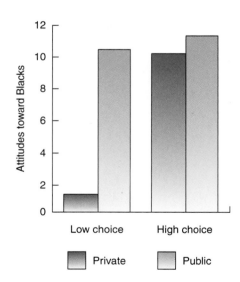

FIGURE 9.9 Attitudes toward Blacks following pro-Black essay in each condition

From Leippe and Eisenstadt, "Generalization of dissonance reduction: Decreasing prejudice through induced compliance," *Journal of Personality and Social Psychology*, 67, 395–413, Table 1, p. 401, 1995. Copyright © 1994 by the American Psychological Association. Reprinted by permission.

that participants who wrote an essay under *either* high-choice *or* high-publicity conditions (the low-choice/public condition, high-choice/private condition, and high-choice/public condition) reported more favourable attitudes than did participants in the low-choice/private condition. Thus, performing a behaviour that communicated a positive racial attitude significantly improved racial attitudes when the behaviour was either voluntary or public (or both).

The procedure in the public conditions of Leippe and Eisenstadt's study might remind you of the experiment by Leanne Son Hing of Guelph University and her colleagues that we described in Chapter 7 (Son Hing, Li, & Zanna, 2002; see page 253). Son Hing and her colleagues used the *hypocrisy paradigm* to arouse dissonance in students about their behaviour toward Asian Canadians. In the hypocrisy condition, participants were asked to make a public statement about the importance of fair treatment of Asian students and were then reminded of their own past failures to behave consistently with this position. Son Hing and her colleagues showed that participants exposed to this induction of hypocrisy exhibited more pro-Asian behaviour: they recommended smaller cuts to the budget of the Asian Students Association at their university than did participants who did not experience the hypocrisy manipulation.

The Contact Hypothesis and Prejudice Reduction

One straightforward idea for making people less prejudiced is to show them by direct exposure that members of the targeted group deserve decent treatment. This approach is based on the **contact hypothesis,** which predicts that contact between members of different groups will produce more positive intergroup attitudes (Allport, 1954; Pettigrew, 1986). You may recall the *mere exposure effect* discussed in Chapter 6 (see page 206), which refers to the tendency for attitudes toward an object to become more favourable as people are repeatedly exposed to it (Zajonc, 1968). The contact hypothesis is compatible with this positive effect of familiarity.

contact hypothesis
the idea that exposure to members of an outgroup will produce more favourable attitudes toward that group

Many researchers have reported correlational data showing that greater contact is associated with more favourable intergroup attitudes. For instance, Charmaine Mohipp and Marian Morry (2004) found that increased contact with gays and lesbians was associated with more favourable attitudes toward these groups among heterosexual students at the University of Manitoba (see also Whitely, 1990). Robert Altemeyer (1994), who is also at the University of Manitoba, found that prejudiced individuals reported having had relatively little contact in childhood with members of outgroups. Of course, correlational data are ambiguous in the sense that they cannot distinguish whether contact is producing positive attitudes or whether positive attitudes are encouraging more contact (see Islam & Hewstone, 1993). It is quite possible that both directions are operating.

Researchers have also found that more frequent contact between members of different language groups is associated with more positive feelings and lower levels of stress during intergroup interactions. For example, Richard Clément, who is at the University of Ottawa, and Kimberly Noels, who is at the University of Alberta, have found that greater previous contact between Francophone and Anglophone Canadians is associated with more positive attitudes toward future intergroup interactions, probably due in part to improved language skills that result from interactions with members of the linguistic outgroup (e.g., Clément & Noels, 1992; Clément, Noels, & Deneault, 2001; Noels & Clément, 1996).

A real-world test of the contact hypothesis was provided by the decision to desegregate classrooms in the United States in the 1950s and 1960s. This decision was based, in part, on the assumption that contact between racial groups would reduce prejudice. Early evaluations of the effects of desegregation were decidedly mixed, however, with evidence suggesting that the attitudes of some White children toward minority groups actually became more *negative* after desegregation (see Stephan, 1986). Why would contact with children of different racial groups fail to produce more favourable attitudes?

If contact is to have a positive effect, the interactions between the individuals should be positive, or at least neutral. Simply throwing racial or ethnic groups together in a school setting does not ensure that contact between the children will be positive—indeed, hostility, suspicion, and rejection can intensify negative attitudes within each group. How can contact be structured in order for exposure to have positive effects?

Researchers and educators have come to realize that several prerequisites must be met if contact is to have a positive effect on intergroup attitudes (Brewer & Miller, 1984; Pettigrew, 1998; Pettigrew & Tropp, 2000; Stephan, 1986). In other words, certain *kinds* of contact can be beneficial. What are these prerequisites? We will mention four.

First, the groups must be approximately *equal in status* before contact will be conducive to positive attitudes (Amir, 1969; Stephan, 1986). When one group is lower in status than the other, resentment can arise within both groups. In the United States, desegregation has often involved bussing inner-city Black children to suburban, predominantly White schools; the Black and White children are unlikely to have equal status in this situation.

Second, the groups must be involved in *cooperative behaviour* together (Bettencourt, Brewer, Croak, & Miller, 1992; Sherif et al., 1961). There must be shared activities between the groups, and the groups must have interdependent goals, such that each group relies on the other to some extent. Competition between groups, on the other hand, is harmful to intergroup attitudes (as we noted in the section on realistic group conflict theory). Schools often fail to meet this prerequisite, because students from different groups do not need to cooperate to fulfill assignments; indeed, students might feel that they are *competing* with students in other ethnic groups for attention of the teacher, grades, and so on.

A third requirement for intergroup contact to be beneficial is *support from legitimate authorities,* such as teachers, parents, and school board trustees (Allport, 1954; Stephan, 1986). If multicultural values are not supported by the teacher and by the students' parents at home, then intergroup contact is unlikely to have much benefit. Children often adopt their parents' attitudes on important issues, and if the parents oppose contact with outgroup members, children may be resistant and resentful themselves.

Finally, contact must be reasonably *intimate* or *personally important* if it is to improve intergroup attitudes (Amir, 1969; Pettigrew, 1998; van Dick et al., 2004). It is not enough for children to be in the same class or to see one another in the schoolyard. Children must talk to one another, play together, form intergroup friendships, and come to know one another reasonably well before attitudes are likely to change substantially. The contact should be significant enough to be personally meaningful to the individuals.

How or why does intergroup contact produce more favourable attitudes toward an outgroup (assuming that the contact is equal status, cooperative, supported by authorities, and intimate)? A key element appears to be anxiety reduction (see Paolini, Hewstone, Cairns, & Voci, 2004; Plant & Devine, 2003). When people have had little exposure to members of an outgroup, they may feel anxious about interacting with those individuals. Such anxiety will cause them to avoid possible interactions (Plant, 2004; Stephan & Stephan, 1989). In contrast, having some positive experiences with members of an outgroup reduces anxiety and encourages additional interactions. For instance, majority group children who are initially anxious about playing with Aboriginal Canadian children because they lack interracial exposure will become more comfortable after experiencing some positive intergroup interactions. The reduction in anxiety will be associated with more favourable attitudes toward, and more frequent interactions with, Aboriginal Canadian children. Along these lines, Victoria Esses of the University of Western Ontario has shown that emotional reactions to members of an outgroup are strong determinants of willingness to interact with that outgroup in the future (Esses & Dovidio, 2002), so it is essential that people overcome their anxiety about intergroup interactions. Positive intergroup contact may be the best avenue for achieving this goal.

Positive intergroup contact can also reduce other factors besides anxiety that lead to prejudice. For instance, when people work together cooperatively, negative stereotypes may be disconfirmed. People learn that members of the outgroup are not aggressive, arrogant, or whatever negative characteristics had previously been attributed to them. Positive contact also shows that the values and attitudes of the two groups are more similar than previously thought, which will reduce the perceived symbolic threat from the outgroup.

The University of Manitoba's Jacquie Vorauer (whose work on meta-stereotypes was mentioned earlier) has identified yet another reason why contact may improve intergroup attitudes. Vorauer showed that nonprejudiced people often believe that their actions communicate strong attraction to outgroup members and a desire to interact with them (e.g., by smiling, by making a positive comment, etc.), but those targets may not perceive such messages (Vorauer, 2005; Vorauer & Kumhyr, 2001). In other words, nonprejudiced people who want to interact with outgroup members may believe that they are exhibiting strong interest in such interactions, but in fact their actions may not be so clear and unambiguous. This miscommunication is probably due, in part, to inexperience with intergroup interactions. Thus, greater contact and behavioural experience with outgroup members should help to overcome this misunderstanding.

Social psychologist Elliot Aronson developed a teaching method he called the **jigsaw classroom** that can be used in classrooms to bring about positive interracial contact. This method is described in Social Psychology in Your Life: "The Jigsaw Classroom."

jigsaw classroom
a method of teaching designed to foster positive interracial contact, which involves forming small, culturally diverse groups of students who are each given one part of the material to be learned

Categorization Processes and Prejudice Reduction

Prejudiced perceivers categorize targets as members of a disliked outgroup. Such categorization is necessary before the bigot's negative stereotype can be applied to the target. Perhaps if we can alter the categorization process somehow, we can reduce prejudice. Several theorists have offered possible strategies.

One proposed approach is to discourage any categorization at all: we should judge other people as individual persons rather than as members of groups. For instance, an individual should be perceived as Takoda Daniel, rather than as an Aboriginal Canadian woman. This approach has been called *personalization* (versus *categorization*) or, in the context of racial prejudice, the **colour-blind approach** (Brewer & Brown, 1998; Brewer & Miller, 1984; Jones, 1997; Nelson, 2002). Although this idea has some merit, categorization is a process that is automatic, at least in part, and therefore virtually impossible to eliminate. Comparisons of the colour-blind approach with alternative strategies have not always supported its effectiveness (e.g., Richeson & Nussbaum, 2004).

A second strategy is to encourage "higher-level," or *superordinate,* categorizations that encompass both the perceiver and the target (Brewer & Brown, 1998; Dovidio, ten Vergert, Stewart, Gaertner, Johnson, Esses, et al., 2004; Gaertner, Dovidio, Anastasio, Bachman, & Rust, 1993). For example, rather than categorizing individuals as Francophone or Anglophone Canadians, members of both groups should be seen simply as Canadians. The rationale is that emphasizing shared memberships (or common identities) will reduce prejudice based on subcategories because outgroup members will be seen as part of the self. There is some evidence that this approach can reduce bias against outgroups (e.g., Gaertner et al., 1993; Galinsky & Moskowitz, 2000).

A third idea has produced the most encouraging results. This approach involves accepting group categorizations as inevitable but encouraging *mutual respect* for different groups. This perspective is known as **multiculturalism:** different cultural groups within a society will each maintain their own identity while simultaneously respecting other groups. Multiculturalism is the official policy of the federal government in Canada. Thus, Canadian policy encourages minorities to maintain their

colour-blind approach
the hypothesis that to reduce prejudice, people should be encouraged to categorize other people as individual persons rather than as members of groups

multiculturalism
the hypothesis that to reduce prejudice, different cultural groups within a society should each maintain their own identity while simultaneously respecting all other groups

Social Psychology in Your Life   *The Jigsaw Classroom*

In typical classrooms in elementary schools, students compete with one another for their teacher's attention, as well as for grades. This competitive atmosphere does not encourage positive relationships with other students, perhaps especially not with students who are perceived to belong to an outgroup, such as a different racial or ethnic group.

To address this problem, Elliot Aronson designed the jigsaw classroom (Aronson, 1990; Aronson, Stephan, Sikes, Blaney, & Snapp, 1978). The jigsaw classroom is structured in such a way as to induce children to cooperate. It is designed for use in elementary schools, with the goal of promoting positive intergroup attitudes among the children. It makes all students equal in status and dependent on one another for learning.

In the jigsaw method, children work in small groups (five or six students), each of which is composed of children from different ethnic groups. When the group works on an assignment, each child is given one part of the relevant information. For example, if the group is studying whales, one child will receive information from the teacher about what whales eat, another will receive information about where whales are found, another will receive information about the different species of whales, and so on. This feature explains why Aronson named his method the *jigsaw classroom:* each child is given one part of the total information, just as a jigsaw puzzle is composed of numerous parts that fit together to form the whole.

Each child will eventually present his or her information to the small group, and after all of the presentations, a test will be given to everyone in the group to assess their knowledge about the various topics. Importantly, students in the group will be able to obtain information about a topic *only* from the child in their group assigned to that topic, not from the teacher or children in other groups. Therefore, all children are dependent on all of the other children in their group for a full understanding of the topic.

After children receive their initial information, those who are assigned the same topic meet together to discuss the material and prepare their presentation. For instance, the children assigned to what whales eat (one from each group) meet together to go over the information and make sure they understand it. These meetings allow students who might have initial difficulty with the material to improve their comprehension. The students also prepare and rehearse their presentation.

When all of the children are ready to present their information, they return to their groups. Each child gives his or her presentation, and then the other children in the group ask questions, discuss the material, and identify the key details. Children become quite expert at interviewing other children and drawing out from each presenter the most important information.

The jigsaw classroom gives each member in the group an essential part to play in learning about a topic. It encourages listening, cooperative discussion, and engagement with the other children in the group. Given that each group includes members from different ethnic or racial groups, the jigsaw method facilitates cooperative intergroup contact.

Note that the jigsaw classroom creates all of the prerequisites for intergroup contact to be beneficial: (1) the children have equal status; (2) members of the groups must cooperate with one another and share a common goal; (3) the intergroup contact is supported and encouraged by the teacher, who is the primary legitimate authority in the setting; and (4) the interactions between children will be relatively intimate, in that they must talk together for extended periods of time.

Several investigators have tested the effectiveness of the jigsaw method versus traditional classroom procedures. Consistently, the jigsaw classroom has been shown to produce more positive intergroup attitudes than traditional classrooms (Aronson, 1990; Aronson et al., 1978; Desforges et al., 1991). Interestingly, the jigsaw classroom has also been shown to produce equal or better performance on tests of knowledge. These findings indicate that the jigsaw classroom deserves widespread implementation.

© Bob Daemmrich/PhotoEdit

In a jigsaw classroom, children work together in small groups to learn about a topic.

cultural identities within the diverse composition of the nation. This idea sounds wonderful, but is it possible to achieve? Some research suggests that it might be.

For instance, Christopher Wolsko and his colleagues at the University of Colorado (Wolsko, Park, Judd, & Wittenbrink, 2000) gave White participants either a message advocating a multicultural approach to improving intergroup relations (e.g., we need to appreciate our diversity and recognize and accept each group's positive and negative qualities), a message advocating a colour-blind approach to improving intergroup relations (e.g., we must recognize that all men and women are created equal, and we are, first and foremost, a nation of individuals), or no message. On subsequent measures, participants in both message conditions reported more favourable attitudes toward Blacks than did participants in the control condition. Interestingly, participants in the multicultural message condition were more willing to assign characteristics to Blacks as a group than were participants in either the colour-blind message or no message conditions, but these characteristics were both positive (e.g., humorous) and negative (e.g., superstitious) in valence. Thus, the multicultural perspective seemed to increase participants' willingness to stereotype, but on both favourable and unfavourable features, and the overall effect on attitudes was positive. The authors suggested that the multicultural perspective is ultimately more likely to succeed than the colour-blind approach because the maintenance of ethnic and cultural identity is important for psychological well-being and therefore should be encouraged within a cooperative, multifaceted society (see also Richeson & Nussbaum, 2004; Rudman, Ashmore, & Gary, 2001).

Multiculturalism means that ethnic groups within a society maintain their cultural traditions and respect other ethnic groups.

Anti-Discrimination Legislation

We have discussed several techniques that could be used to reduce prejudice. What about the undesirable behavioural consequences of prejudice, namely, *discrimination*? Can we influence people's behaviour directly? Is it a good idea to do so?

In fact, most societies do try to influence discrimination directly: they declare it illegal. In Canada and many other countries around the world, anti-discrimination legislation makes it illegal for employers, landlords, and other authorities to base decisions on individuals' race, religion, sex, age, physical mobility, sexual orientation, or other irrelevant features. These laws make no attempt to outlaw prejudice—it is impossible to prohibit feelings and attitudes. But it *is* possible to control the behavioural manifestations of prejudice by making discrimination illegal.

As a student of social psychology, do you think anti-discrimination legislation is a good idea? Will it have a positive or negative effect on public attitudes? Might the short-term and long-term effects differ?

Most social psychologists believe that anti-discrimination legislation will have largely positive effects, especially over the long term. Although the most important benefit of anti-discrimination legislation is to directly improve the lives of minority group members by reducing damaging behaviour toward them, there may be other positive effects as well. In particular, there are reasons to believe that anti-discrimination legislation will reduce prejudice over time (i.e., change intergroup attitudes in a favourable direction).

Both dissonance theory and self-perception theory predict that people may change their attitudes to be consistent with their behaviour (see Chapters 4 and 7). Dissonance theory states that people feel bad when their attitudes and behaviours are inconsistent; self-perception theory states that people infer their attitudes from their behaviours. Thus, if prejudiced people treat minority group members in a nondiscriminatory fashion, both theories would predict that those individuals might shift their attitudes toward being unprejudiced. The effects of dissonance and self-perception are limited, however, to conditions in which people perceive their behaviour to be voluntary. When anti-discrimination legislation is first passed, prejudiced people probably know that they are changing their behaviour because of the law, not voluntarily; attitude change is unlikely at this time. But over time, nondiscriminatory behaviour may become more of a habit, and people may forget that the law was the original reason for their current behaviour. When the salience of the law fades, people are likely to consider their behaviour to be voluntary, at which point both dissonance and self-perception processes will operate to make attitudes consistent with behaviour.

Same-Sex Marriage Laws. On June 28, 2005, the Canadian House of Commons voted 158 to 133 to adopt legislation legalizing same-sex marriage in Canada. In so doing, Canada became the third country in the world to declare gay and lesbian marriages lawful. Religious groups and institutions are not forced to sanctify same-sex marriages if they oppose them; the law applies to civil weddings. The legislation resulted from several prior legal verdicts that found the traditional definition of marriage violated the Charter of Rights and Freedoms, which guarantees equality for all Canadians.

Just eight months earlier, on November 2, 2004, 11 states in the United States voted on constitutional amendments to ban same-sex marriages. All 11 anti-same-sex-marriage amendments were supported, most by very large margins. These anti-same-sex-marriage votes represented, in part, a backlash against the Massachusetts Supreme Judicial Court, which in May 2004 granted gays and lesbians the right to marry in that state—the first such decision in the United States.

Same-sex marriage is a controversial issue in both countries. Many people feel passionately about one side or the other. Banning same-sex marriage is probably not seen as an act of "discrimination" by many who support this view. Nevertheless, disallowing same-sex marriage means that some people will be denied, on the basis of their sexual orientation, a fundamental right that is available to others—namely, to have their relationship with their partner recognized as a legal union.

Does making same-sex marriage *legal* influence attitudes toward gays and lesbians? It seems likely that recognizing same-sex marriages will, over time, reduce prejudice against gays and lesbians. For one thing, same-sex marriages should become more common, so mere exposure will presumably work to make attitudes toward these unions more favourable. Also, as explained earlier, dissonance and self-perception processes seem likely to improve attitudes over time. Finally, as elaborated in the next paragraph, the law establishes a social norm that same-sex relationships deserve equal respect and protections as heterosexual relationships.

Norms Against Discrimination. Laws have an educative function: they can be used to teach important values and principles. That is, laws help to establish *norms* in society, which are rules or guidelines about what behaviours are acceptable and unacceptable. Norms influence people in two ways: they can be internalized, such that people accept that the norms define "good" behaviour, and they also put external pressure on people to conform, because failure to follow norms might result in punishment or rejection. Because most of us consider discrimination to be a bad thing, it is important to show that discrimination will not be tolerated. Anti-discrimination legislation does that.

There is also evidence that social norms coming from *interpersonal* sources (rather than from laws) are influential in the area of stereotypes and prejudice. Researchers have shown that having someone verbally express an anti-racist view inhibits others from expressing prejudiced views, presumably because a social norm against showing prejudice is invoked by the first person's comments (e.g., Blanchard, Lilly, & Vaughn, 1991). This effect occurs in both prejudiced and unprejudiced individuals, because no one wants to be rejected. But people who are low in prejudice also experience *guilt* when they become aware that they have acted in a manner that might be seen as prejudiced. This guilt motivates unprejudiced persons to change their behaviour to be more nondiscriminatory (Monteith, 1993, 1996).

"We also see very large numbers of people giving ratings of zero to lesbians and gay men, meaning that they have very hostile feelings."

Outlook for the Future

So what is the outlook for the future, given these various perspectives on reducing prejudice and discrimination? Can effective programs be developed to ameliorate these important social problems? We think that the answer to this question is *yes*.

Encouraging contact between groups is probably the most important step, particularly among children in the school system. It is very difficult, though not impossible, to change the attitudes of highly prejudiced adults (Cook, 1969, 1990), so children should probably be our focus. As well as fostering equal-status contact (e.g., in a jigsaw classroom), schools should teach norms of multicultural tolerance. Engendering a positive attitude toward diversity is important.

At the societal level, legislation against discrimination minimizes the impact of prejudice, establishes a norm of tolerance, and probably influences attitudes in a desirable direction over time. Public education campaigns might also be beneficial. Procedures that elicit dissonance (e.g., by inducing feelings of hypocrisy) can be effective, although they may be difficult to apply to large numbers of individuals.

Prejudice underlies many of the problems we face in our world. Negative attitudes toward members of particular groups are a fundamental cause of human conflict and misery, ranging from interpersonal hostility to war and genocide. Social psychology has important things to contribute to the fight against prejudice, such as Elliot Aronson's idea of the jigsaw classroom. We need to convince politicians and lawmakers to give more of these ideas a try.

Chapter Summary

Prejudice is a negative attitude toward members of a group, which is often very strongly held. **Discrimination** is negative, harmful behaviour toward people based on their group membership. Perhaps the most extreme form of discrimination is **genocide,** which is an attempt to systematically eliminate an ethnic group through banishment or murder.

Blatant prejudice is probably less common today than it was 20 or 30 years ago, but discrimination based on racial, ethnic, or other group membership still occurs, especially when the circumstances provide an excuse for negative treatment. The term **aversive racism** has been used to refer to people who do not consider themselves prejudiced and who would find any accusation of being prejudiced aversive, but who nevertheless harbour some negative beliefs and hostile feelings toward members of minority groups.

Stereotypes are individuals' beliefs that members of a group share particular attributes. Stereotypes are almost always oversimplified and often excessively negative. Unfavourable stereotypes can lead to prejudice and discrimination. Stereotypes distort information processing about members of the target group. Stereotypes can also create vicious cycles by leading people to behave toward members of a group in ways that actually elicit the expected actions from those members; this process is called a **self-fulfilling prophecy.**

Stereotypes can influence perceivers' judgments without their awareness—effects that are called **implicit intergroup biases.** Researchers have documented implicit intergroup biases for numerous target groups; these studies have often used **subliminal priming procedures,** which involve flashing words or pictures very briefly on a computer screen in front of the participant.

A **meta-stereotype** is a person's beliefs about the stereotype that outgroup members hold concerning his or her own group. Meta-stereotypes influence individuals' expectations about their interactions with members of the outgroup, and these expectations can then alter the interaction itself.

Several emotional sources of prejudice and discrimination have been proposed. The **scapegoat theory** of prejudice proposes that members of the dominant group use discrimination against members of weak target groups to vent their frustration and disappointment. The disadvantaged targets may have had little or no role in causing the frustration, but provide a convenient target of blame. **Realistic group conflict theory** proposes that when groups in society are perceived to be competing with one another for resources, intergroup hostility can be aroused, which leads to prejudice. Social identity theory proposes that prejudice can make people feel good about themselves because they see their own group as better than the derogated outgroup. **Integrated threat theory** unifies several other theories by proposing that prejudice toward an outgroup results from four types of perceived threats: realistic threats, symbolic threats, threats stemming from intergroup anxiety, and threats arising from negative stereotypes.

Prejudice and discrimination directed against women because of their gender is called **sexism.** One measure of sexism is the neosexism scale; **neosexism** is a modern, subtle form of sexism, which includes beliefs that women are no longer disadvantaged and antagonism toward women's demands for better treatment. A second measure of sexism is the **ambivalent sexism inventory.** This scale includes items to assess two dimensions of sexism: **benevolent sexism,** which involves positive but paternalistic attitudes toward women (e.g., women are good but need protection), and **hostile sexism,** which involves negative attitudes toward women who violate the traditional stereotype (e.g., feminists).

Gender stereotypes are beliefs about the characteristics that are associated with men and women. Gender stereotypes may be accurate in some respects, but they also exaggerate current sex differences.

People who are overweight are the targets of prejudice and discrimination in our society. Obesity is a particularly devastating stigma for women because physical appearance is more highly valued for women than for men in our culture. Therefore, women tend to be very concerned about their weight. Measures of **appearance self-esteem,** which assess respondents' satisfaction with their physical looks, show that women are less satisfied with their appearance than men at all age levels.

The **personal–group discrimination discrepancy** refers to the tendency for people to report that they as individuals have experienced *less* negative treatment than the average member of their group. For instance, most women report that they have experienced less discrimination based on their gender than has the typical woman.

Stereotype threat occurs when individuals believe that if they perform poorly on a task, their performance will appear to confirm an unfavourable belief or stereotype about their group. Stereotype threat puts pressure on people to do as well as possible in order to discredit the negative stereotype, and this pressure can itself lead to poor performance. Stereotype threat impairs performance by arousing anxiety and reducing memory capacity.

One idea for reducing prejudice is through direct contact with members of the disliked group. This idea is based on the **contact hypothesis,** which predicts that exposure to members of an outgroup will produce more favourable attitudes toward that group. It turns out that intergroup contact must meet several prerequisites in order to produce positive attitudes, including equal status and cooperative behaviour. A teaching method that encourages positive interracial contact among elementary school children is the **jigsaw classroom.** In this method, small, culturally diverse groups of students are formed, and each student receives one part of the material to be learned.

Another idea for reducing prejudice is the **colour-blind approach,** which suggests that we should categorize other people as individual persons rather than as members of groups. A contrasting perspective is **multiculturalism,** which proposes that different cultural groups within a society should each maintain their own identity while simultaneously respecting all other groups.

Key Terms

ambivalent sexism
  inventory (346)

appearance self-esteem (350)

aversive racism (326)

benevolent sexism (346)

colour-blind approach (363)

contact hypothesis (361)

discrimination (324)

genocide (324)

hostile sexism (346)

implicit intergroup bias (337)

integrated threat theory (342)

jigsaw classroom (363)

meta-stereotypes (338)

multiculturalism (363)

neosexism (344)

personal–group discrimination
  discrepancy (353)

prejudice (324)

realistic group conflict
  theory (340)

scapegoat theory (339)

self-fulfilling prophecy (334)

sexism (344)

stereotype threat (354)

subliminal priming
  procedure (336)

Social Psychology Alive on the Web

SOCIAL PSYCHOLOGY ALIVE: ONLINE LABS

To perform the following experiment and see how you compare to other students, go to Social Psychology Lab, which can be accessed through ThomsonNOW™:

- 9.1 Don't Shoot

SOCIAL PSYCHOLOGY ALIVE: QUIZZING AND PRACTICE TESTS

You can access our Web site directly by going to http://www.socialpsychologyalive.nelson.com for online quizzes, flash cards, and Internet links.

INFOTRAC® COLLEGE EDITION

For additional readings, explore InfoTrac® College Edition, your online library of archived journal articles and periodicals dating back 22 years. If your instructor ordered InfoTrac® College Edition with this book, you can access it from your CD-ROM, or go directly to http://www.infotrac-college.com and use the passcode from the InfoTrac® College Edition card that came with your book. For this chapter, try these search terms: *prejudice, discrimination, stereotypes, aversive racism, self-fulfilling prophecy, realistic group conflict, sexism, gender stereotypes, stereotype threat, contact hypothesis, jigsaw classroom, multiculturalism.*

Social Psychology Alive: The Workbook
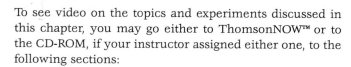

To apply what you've learned in this chapter to what happens in the real world, go to Chapter 9 of *Social Psychology Alive: The Workbook*:

- The Death Penalty and Aversive Racism
- Understanding How Stereotypes Can Be Self-Fulfilling: The Use of a Positive Test Strategy
- Don't Shoot!

- Sexism and Music
- Thin Is In
- Math Is (NOT) Just for Boys
- The Pernicious Effects of Prejudice
- Multiculturalism Versus Colour Blindness on the College Campus

Social Psychology Alive: The Videos

To see video on the topics and experiments discussed in this chapter, you may go either to ThomsonNOW™ or to the CD-ROM, if your instructor assigned either one, to the following sections:

- Prized Eyes: Stereotypes and Prejudice Then and Now
- Genocide: Mike Jacob's Story
- Sexual Stigma: Hating People for the People They Love

To Learn More

This list contains citations to books or articles that can help you learn more. These readings are good places to start if you want to gain a deeper understanding of the topics in this chapter.

- Whitely, B. E., Jr., & Kite, M. (2006). *Psychology of prejudice and discrimination.* Belmont, CA: Wadsworth.

- Oskamp, S. (Ed.). (2000). *Reducing prejudice and discrimination.* Mahwah, NJ: Erlbaum.
- Swim, J. K., & Stangor, C. (Eds.). (1998). *Prejudice: The target's perspective.* New York: Academic Press.

NEL

Group Dynamics and Intergroup Relations

The Liberal Party of Canada was the dominant political party in Canada during the 20th century. The party was in power for 72 of the 100 years, and every leader of the party during the century served at least once as prime minister of Canada. This success reflected many things, but one factor was the generally moderate positions taken by the Liberal Party on social and economic issues. A common stereotype of Canadians is that they are "middle-of-the-road," and there is probably some truth to this perception. The Liberal Party, which is near the centre of the political spectrum, often reflected moderation better than the other parties: more liberal than the Progressive Conservative Party on the right but more conservative than the New Democratic Party on the left.

The Liberal Party had many effective leaders during the century, including Wilfrid Laurier, William Lyon Mackenzie King, and Lester Pearson. Probably the most famous, arguably the best, and certainly the most charismatic of these leaders was Pierre Elliott Trudeau. Trudeau was elected leader of the Liberal Party in 1968 and two months later won the first of his three majority governments. Handsome, brilliant, and fluently bilingual (the son of a Quebecois father and a mother of Scottish descent), he was instantly popular across the country. The term "Trudeaumania" was coined to describe the reactions of Canadians to the new political celebrity. He dated movie stars, drove sports cars, and wore fashionable clothes.

But Trudeau was more than just appearance. He was instrumental in many important pieces of legislation. He liberalized laws regarding homosexuality and abortion. He created the Official Languages Act, which guaranteed bilingual services across the country. He was the principal author of a new Canadian Constitution, which included the Charter of Rights and Freedoms.

The Liberal Party of Canada has been a highly successful group, in the sense that it has governed the country more than any other party. Pierre Elliott Trudeau was a highly successful leader of this group, in the sense that he was elected several times and introduced many policies that shaped the Canadian landscape. In the remainder of this chapter, we will use the Liberal Party (or Canadian political parties more generally) and Pierre Trudeau to illustrate a number of issues in the study of how groups operate.

group dynamics

the social psychological study of groups and group processes

The topic of this chapter is the social psychological study of groups and group processes, an area of research often called **group dynamics.** Groups play a huge role in our lives: many of our daily activities occur in face-to-face groups (e.g., family, friends) and, more broadly, our ability to live a free and prosperous life depends on large groups such as nations. There are also new kinds of groups emerging today: the advent of the Internet has made it easy for people to communicate and form virtual groups. Indeed, the Internet can be considered an incubator of groups, some dangerous and some worthwhile. It is possible to find Web sites and chat groups that promote hatred and racism, but it is also possible to find ones that encourage helpfulness and positive thinking. This is an exciting (and scary) time to be studying groups.

Pierre Elliott Trudeau was a charismatic and influential prime minister of Canada between 1968 and 1984.

We begin our coverage of group dynamics by defining what social psychologists mean by a group. Then we turn our attention to individuals within groups: how does the presence of other people affect individuals' performances and actions? Moving to a group level of analysis, we discuss how groups make decisions; we describe conditions that can lead to poor decision making and how to avoid these conditions. Next, we turn to the issue of leadership and discuss both how leaders are chosen and which kinds of leaders are most effective in different groups. We close the chapter with our broadest level of analysis: how do groups interact with other groups? This discussion of intergroup relations addresses how cultural groups change when in contact with one another, as well as processes of intergroup conflict, including factors that heighten intergroup tensions and ways that such tensions can be reduced or managed.

A necessary place to begin our discussion of group dynamics is by defining what social psychologists mean by the term **group.** *The most common definition of a group in social psychology is two or more people who are interacting and/or influencing one another. This definition highlights two points. First, an obvious requirement for a group is that there must be at least two people (!), and of course most groups are larger than two. Second, the members of a group must be interacting with one another in some way, or at least influencing one another (Burn, 2004; Levine & Moreland, 1994). For example, if passengers on a plane have no interaction and pay no attention to one another, then they do not constitute a group in the sense that social psychologists use the term. On the other hand, if the passengers talk to one another, feel some bond with one another, or otherwise influence one another, then they might constitute a meaningful group. These observations suggest that, instead of drawing a hard line between "groups" and "nongroups," it may be sensible to think about collections of individuals as ranging along a continuum from little or no "group character" to a great deal of "group character." Passengers on a plane usually have little or no group character, but occasionally they have a lot of group character—such as the passengers on United Flight 93 who rose up against the terrorist hijackers on September 11, 2001, forcing the plane to crash in Pennsylvania before reaching its intended target.*

group
two or more persons who are interacting with one another and/or influencing one another

Social psychologists have directed most of their attention to groups of two different sizes. First, researchers interested in such topics as group productivity and group decision making have focused on small groups—usually between three and seven members, though potentially up to groups of 20 (Cartwright & Zander, 1968; Kerr, Aronoff, & Messe, 2000; Levine & Moreland, 1998). This size has made it possible for researchers to create small groups in the laboratory and to examine the processes underlying performance and judgment. Most of the groups within which our daily activities occur are small in size, such as our family, co-workers, and leisure groups, so this is a crucial size to understand. Second, researchers interested in such topics as intergroup conflict and international relations have focused on large

© Michael Newman/PhotoEdit

Most of the groups within which our daily activities occur are small in size.

collectives (more than 20 members), such as nations, religions, ethnic groups, and political parties (Brown, 1988; Taylor & Moghaddam, 1994). These researchers cannot create collectives in the laboratory, but instead have investigated how individuals perceive large collectives. For example, individual participants may be asked to report their impressions of large groups or their recommendations about how their ingroup should behave toward particular outgroups. It is important to understand collectives because they are the basis for many critical decisions, such as whether to make peace or war.

● ● ●   # Individual Performance and Behaviour in Group Settings

We begin our discussion of group dynamics at an individual level of analysis. That is, before getting into how groups operate as a unit, we need to consider how individuals change when they experience certain aspects of group settings, such as the presence of other people or the anonymity created by being in a group.

Social Facilitation: The Effects of an Audience

Imagine playing a familiar electronic game—one that you play very well—by yourself, with no one watching. Now imagine playing the same game in front of an audience of three or four friends. In which circumstance do you think you would perform better? Would you excel, or would you choke, in front of the audience?

Now imagine a different scenario. Imagine playing a *new* electronic game that you have never played before, which requires some unusual manipulations of the controller or keyboard, by yourself with no one watching. Now imagine playing the same novel game in front of three or four friends. Which performance do you think would be better in this case?

These hypothetical scenarios capture one of the oldest questions in social psychology: the effects of the presence of other people on an individual's performance. You may recall our description, in the section on the history of social psychology in Chapter 1 (see Social Psychology in Your Life: "The First Social Psychology Experiment," page 19), of the first publication of a social psychology experiment by Norman Triplett (1898). Triplett conducted a study in which children were asked to wind a fishing reel either alone or with another child doing the same task and found that the children performed better when another child was also present. Triplett concluded that people perform better in the presence of others—an effect that became known as **social facilitation.**

social facilitation

the effects of the presence of other people on individual performance, which will usually be improved performance on simple tasks and impaired performance on complex tasks

But it turned out that subsequent studies specifically testing the effects of an audience on individuals' performance yielded inconsistent findings. Participants in some studies did better when an audience was present than when one was not (e.g., Travis, 1925), whereas participants in other studies did better when alone than when an audience was present (e.g., Pessin, 1933). These contradictory findings slowly eroded interest in the issue, and researchers turned to other questions.

In 1965, however, Robert Zajonc of the University of Michigan rekindled interest in social facilitation (this is the same researcher who identified the *mere exposure effect* described in Chapter 6, see page 206). Zajonc observed that most studies that had shown an *improvement* in performance in front of an audience utilized relatively *simple* tasks, whereas most studies that had shown a *decrease* in performance in front of an audience utilized relatively *complex* tasks. Zajonc hypothesized that the presence of other people increases the probability of the **dominant responses** on a task. The dominant responses on a task are the ones that are most likely to occur when the person is alone. When a task is simple or is something that people have done many times (e.g., driving a car), the dominant responses will be correct ones or well-practised ones (e.g., stepping on the gas, steering the car). When a task is complex or novel, however (e.g., someone attempting to juggle three balls for the first time), the dominant responses are more likely to be incorrect ones (e.g., tossing the balls badly, failing to catch a ball). Zajonc predicted that these tendencies will be *heightened* by the presence of an audience.

dominant response

the action that is most likely to occur in a situation or on a task when the individual is alone

Consistent with Zajonc's hypothesis, research has shown that performance on simple, well-learned tasks typically improves in front of an audience, whereas performance on complex, novel tasks typically worsens in front of an audience (see Baron, Moore, & Sanders, 1978; Bond & Titus, 1983; Geen & Gange, 1977). Why do audiences increase the likelihood of dominant responses? Zajonc proposed that the presence of other people is physiologically arousing (e.g., causing faster heart rate), perhaps because the individual is anxious about performing well in front of others (Cottrell, Wack, Sekerak, & Rittle, 1968; Sanna, 1992). Zajonc knew that previous research by cognitive psychologists had shown that physiological arousal restricts individuals' range of attention: people can focus only on a few cues in the setting (e.g., Easterbrook, 1959). Zajonc suggested that when a task is simple, this narrowed focus of attention actually improves performance because it blocks out distractions, but when a task is complex, the narrowed focus of attention makes it difficult for the individual to attend to all of the cues necessary for good performance.

An interesting study of social facilitation was conducted at the University of California at Santa Barbara by Jim Blascovich, Wendy Mendes, Sarah Hunter, and Kristen Salomon (1999). Participants were presented with two-digit numbers on a computer screen (25, 97, 34, 81, etc.) and had to push one of two response keys. The participants had to figure out that they were supposed to push one key when the number was smaller than 68 and the other key when the number was larger than 68. They were not told about the number 68 in advance, so they had to discover this "rule" by trial and error (correct/incorrect feedback was given on each trial). Participants performed the task either alone or in front of two other students (one male and one female). When participants were allowed to *practise* this task for 25 trials before being tested (which made it an *easy* task because they had already figured out that 68 was the critical number), they performed better in front of an audience than alone. When participants were required to do this task without any practice, however (which made it a *difficult* task because they had not yet figured out the critical number), they performed significantly worse in front of an audience than alone. Thus, the presence of other people improved performance on a simple task but worsened performance on a difficult task.

Let's return to the question about whether you would perform better on a familiar electronic game alone or in front of an audience. Because this game is familiar to you, the dominant responses during the game should be the correct ones. Zajonc would predict, therefore, that an audience would *improve* your performance. But what about a new and challenging electronic game? In this case, the game is novel and relatively difficult, so the dominant responses are probably incorrect. Zajonc would predict, therefore, that an audience would *harm* your performance. Do these predictions match your own intuitions? The flowchart in Figure 10.1 depicts the processes involved in social facilitation.

It is interesting to think about the implications of research on social facilitation for where students should study. Will students learn material better if they study alone in their room or in the presence of other people in the library? If the material is very simple or already very familiar, then students may be better off studying in the library, because the presence of others should narrow their focus of attention and

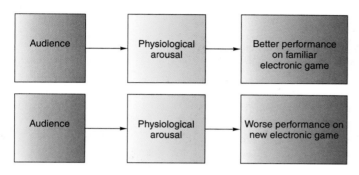

EXAMPLES:

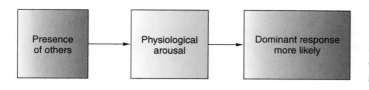

FIGURE 10.1 Social facilitation

possibly improve their retention. On the other hand, if the material is very complex or unfamiliar, then the narrowed focus of attention in the library might cause students to overlook aspects of the material, so they may be better off studying alone.

Social Loafing: Goofing Off When Others Can Do the Work

The social facilitation literature focuses on tasks that are performed individually, such as winding a fishing reel or figuring out which response key to push when a number is presented. What about tasks that involve *group* performance and where individual contributions are not identifiable? What happens when we are a small (and often invisible) part of a collective effort? From one perspective, it seems possible that being part of a group will increase our effort by motivating us—we'll give our all for the team! But from another perspective, it seems possible that we might slack off and let others do the work—why kill ourselves when no one will be able to identify our contribution anyway? If you have participated in group projects for courses, where all students in the group receive the same grade, you may have found that some group members did not really put in a full effort.

Bibb Latané, Kipling Williams, and Stephen Harkins (1979) coined the term **social loafing** to capture the idea that people may slack off in groups. In contrast to social facilitation, which is assumed to involve arousal (caused by the presence of others), social loafing is assumed to involve relaxation or reduced motivation (caused by believing that one's personal contribution is unidentifiable). To test whether social loafing occurs, Latané and his colleagues asked Ohio State University students to cheer as loudly as possible while blindfolded and wearing headphones to mask the sounds. The researchers led participants to believe on some trials that they were cheering alone, but on other trials that they were cheering together with one or five other participants. In actuality, participants always responded alone, and their individual cheers were recorded. Figure 10.2 presents the results of the study. Participants cheered the loudest when they thought they were performing alone (perceived group size of one), whereas they cheered only 82% as intensely when they believed one other person was also cheering (perceived group size of two) and only 74% as intensely when they believed five others were also cheering (perceived group size of six).

Many studies have investigated social loafing (for a review, see Karau & Williams, 1993), and the effect is a reliable one: the larger the group, the less effort individuals tend to exert on joint tasks. One necessary component for social loafing is individual anonymity; if people believe that their own performance within the group will be identifiable, social loafing disappears (e.g., Williams, Harkins, & Latané, 1981). In the next section of the chapter, we discuss another phenomenon that reflects, at least in part, being anonymous and unidentifiable in groups: *deindividuation*.

Do you think that social loafing is more likely in some groups than in others? It turns out that one factor influencing social loafing is the importance of the group to members. People are less likely to loaf when the group is important or meaningful to them than when the group is relatively

social loafing

the reduction of effort that people often exhibit when working in a group where individual contributions are unidentifiable

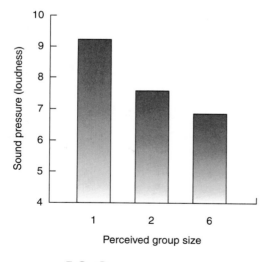

FIGURE 10.2 Loudness of cheering as a function of perceived group size

From Latané et al., "Many hands make light the work: The causes and consequences of social loafing," *Journal of Personality and Social Psychology*, 37, 822–832, Fig. 2, p. 827, 1979. Copyright © 1979 by the American Psychological Association. Reprinted by permission.

unimportant (e.g., Brickner, Harkins, & Ostrom, 1986). These findings suggest that in real-life groups whose members consider the group's goals to be worthwhile and believe the group is making a valuable contribution, social loafing is less likely. For instance, members of campaign teams for a political party (the Liberals or others) are probably unlikely to exhibit social loafing even when their individual actions are unidentifiable, because they believe that it is important to get their candidate elected.

Another factor that influences social loafing is the cohesiveness or attractiveness of the group itself. When the group is composed of friends or people who are attractive for other reasons, an individual's motivation is increased and social loafing declines (e.g., Hardy & Latané, 1988). Again, these data suggest that in real-life groups where people value their membership (such as in political parties), social loafing is less likely.

Social loafing occurs when people do not exert maximal effort because individual contributions are not identifiable.

Is social loafing *intentional*? That is, do people *deliberately* slack off in groups, or is the reduction in effort unconscious and unintentional? The answer is *both*. Sometimes, people *know* that they are not giving maximum effort, such as when a lazy student does as little work as possible in a group project. But sometimes people do not realize that their effort has been affected, such as in the study described earlier that used a cheering task (Latané et al., 1979). It seems unlikely that participants in this study deliberately cheered less loudly when they believed others were also cheering; instead, the belief that others were cheering probably unconsciously reduced participants' motivation to yell as loudly as possible.

Gender and Cultural Differences in Social Loafing. There are also some interesting data on *who* is most likely to exhibit social loafing. One relevant characteristic is gender: men are more likely to do it than women. In fact, studies using groups composed *only* of women have generally found no evidence of social loafing at all (see Karau & Williams, 1993). Although various possible explanations for this gender difference probably occur to our female readers, most theorists suspect that the difference occurs because women are more group-oriented and more concerned about collective outcomes than are men, who tend to be more individualistic in their orientation. Women's focus on group outcomes motivates them to exert maximum effort even when their individual contributions are not identifiable.

If this reasoning about the cause of gender differences in social loafing is correct, then more social loafing might also be expected in individualistic cultures such as Canada than in collectivistic cultures such as China. After all, people who have been socialized in a culture that emphasizes independence and individual achievements (individualistic cultures) may be less concerned about group outcomes than people who have been socialized in a culture that emphasizes interdependence and group achievements (collectivistic cultures). At least one study has produced this pattern of findings: Christopher Earley (1989) at the University of Minnesota found significant social loafing in a sample of participants from the United States, but no evidence of social loafing in a sample of participants from China. Thus, social loafing is at least partly a reflection of Western values and culture.

Deindividuation: Immersion in a Group

Feelings of anonymity contribute to social loafing, as we have noted. But anonymity can have other consequences as well. In particular, social psychologists have proposed that being a member of a group can sometimes produce a state of **deindividuation**

deindividuation

a psychological state in which people lose their sense of personal identity and feel immersed in a group

(Festinger, Pepitone, & Newcomb, 1952), which refers to a loss of personal identity and a sense of immersion in a group: people feel relatively anonymous and can be caught up in the actions of those around them. Wearing clothes that make identification difficult (e.g., the same uniform as other people in a setting, or a costume that conceals one's identity) can heighten deindividuation. Numerous studies have shown that when people are deindividuated, they are more likely to engage in socially undesirable behaviour (e.g., Prentice-Dunn & Rogers, 1989; Zimbardo, 1969).

Theorists have proposed different psychological processes through which deindividuation affects behaviour (see Mullen, Migdal, & Rozell, 2003). One perspective is that deindividuation weakens people's inhibitions against performing harmful or socially disapproved actions. A second perspective is that deindividuation heightens people's responsiveness to external cues, which may be either negative or positive. A third perspective is that deindividuation increases people's adherence to norms that emerge in a group. We discuss each of these perspectives in the following paragraphs.

Some theorists have argued that deindividuation weakens people's inhibitions against acting in ways that violate norms, such as selfish or aggressive behaviour. From this perspective, deindividuation is hypothesized to "release" people from their normal ethical constraints. For example, the concept of deindividuation has been used to explain negative, anti-normative actions such as theft, vandalism, and interpersonal violence (e.g., Mullen, 1986; Silke, 2003a). If deindividuation dissolves inhibitions, then an interesting legal issue is whether a state of deindividuation could be considered an extenuating circumstance (i.e., an excuse) for criminal actions committed while part of a large group of people (e.g., "He couldn't help himself—being immersed in the group swept away his inhibitions!"). Although it may sound implausible to posit deindividuation as an excuse, this strategy has already been used successfully by some lawyers (see Colman, 1991).

An illustrative study of deindividuation, investigating relatively mild anti-normative behaviour, was conducted by Ed Diener, Scott Fraser, Arthur Beaman, and Roger Kelem (1976). These researchers observed the actions of costumed children on Halloween in 27 different homes in the Seattle area. Inside the front door of each home was a table with a large bowl full of bite-sized candy bars and a smaller bowl full of coins (pennies and nickels). When children came to the door, a woman greeted them and invited them inside. Half of the children were randomly assigned to the *nonanonymous condition:* the woman asked them their names and where they lived. The remaining children were not asked their names or addresses (*anonymous condition*). It was also noted whether the children were alone or in a group of between two and six children. After the children entered the home, the woman said that she needed to return to her work in another room. She instructed the children to take *one* of the candy bars, and then exited the room. There was an unobtrusive observer positioned behind a backdrop who recorded the behaviour of the children.

Figure 10.3 presents the percentage of children who took more than one candy bar or who took money as well as candy from the table. These data show that children were more likely to break the rules when they were anonymous rather than nonanonymous and when they were in a group rather than alone. The authors concluded that anonymity produced deindividuation in the children, especially when they were in a group, which reduced their inhibitions and led them to behave more greedily or selfishly than they normally would have.

Prisons can induce deindividuation. Typically, both prisoners and guards wear uniforms, and names are often replaced with impersonal numbers. If guards feel unaccountable when interacting with prisoners, they may act maliciously. Philip Zimbardo (1972) conducted a study at Stanford University, where university men volunteered to take part in a simulated prison. The volunteers were randomly assigned to the roles of guards or prisoners and received uniforms appropriate to

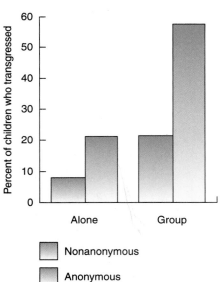

FIGURE 10.3 Percent of children who transgressed (took more than one candy bar or both candy and money)

From Diener et al., "Effects of deindividuation variables on stealing among Halloween trick-or-treaters," *Journal of Personality and Social Psychology*, 33, 178–183, Table 1, p. 181, 1976. Copyright © 1976 by the American Psychological Association. Reprinted by permission.

their roles; the guards also were given mirrored sunglasses to increase their sense of anonymity. All participants were given a list of rules to be followed by the prisoners, and the guards were told to enforce these rules. Zimbardo planned to continue the simulation for two weeks. Interactions between the guards and prisoners became so aggressive and insulting, however, that the simulation was terminated after just six days. Zimbardo reported that the guards had resorted to several control tactics that were degrading or cruel, which they justified by arguing that the prisoners would not otherwise obey the rules. This study suggests that deindividuation in a prison setting can produce unacceptable behaviour by guards. These findings may remind you of the actions of the Canadian soldiers who tortured and murdered a 16-year-old prisoner in Somalia, which we mentioned briefly in Chapter 8 in our discussion of obedience. Perhaps deindividuation contributed to this awful event.

Guard: "What is happening to Prisoner 189?"

Prisoners (in unison): "Prisoner 189 is being punished, Mr. Correctional Officer!"

Guard: "Say it five times—make sure you remember it!"

A different perspective on deindividuation was proposed by Kenneth Gergen and his colleagues at Swarthmore College (Gergen, Gergen, & Barton, 1973). These researchers suggested that deindividuation increases people's responsiveness to external cues, such as noticeable features of the setting, and these cues might sometimes be *prosocial* in nature. A study that supported this perspective was conducted by Robert Johnson and Leslie Downing (1979). Female participants at the University of Georgia wore either cloaks like those of the Ku Klux Klan (negative cue) or nursing uniforms (positive cue). In addition, some participants remained highly identifiable despite the clothing because they wore large nametags, whereas others did not have nametags and were expected to feel deindividuated because of the similarity of their cloaks or uniforms. All participants were asked to make recommendations about the intensity of electric shocks that should be administered to a "learner" in a verbal learning task. Compared to the identifiable condition, deindividuation (no nametags) led to *more* aggression in the KKK cloak condition but to *less* aggression in the nursing uniform condition. Thus, deindividuated participants responded either more negatively or more positively than identifiable participants, depending on the situational cues.

A third perspective on deindividuation was presented by Tom Postmes and Russell Spears (1998) at the University of Amsterdam. These researchers reviewed 60 studies that investigated deindividuation and agreed with past theorists that this state was reliably associated with increases in undesirable behaviour, especially for larger groups. They hypothesized, however, that the effects were not due to people being "released" from normal constraints when in large groups. Instead, they suggested that large groups (and the anonymity they provide) serve to *increase people's adherence to emerging norms in that group,* which are sometimes aggressive or self-serving. For example, a political protest rally might turn into a riot; this occurs not because people become "uninhibited" and therefore ignore social norms, but rather because a new norm of *aggression against authority* develops in the group. People feel part of the group and adopt its central norms, including the idea that it is okay to attack police or to damage property to make a political statement. Or consider the worst kind of mob violence—lynch mobs in the southern United States in the 1800s and early 1900s (Mullen, 1986). Groups of White men would search for a Black man accused of some act; if found, he might be hanged immediately without any opportunity to defend himself. Did this behaviour reflect disinhibition from

© AP/Wide World Photos/Mark Foley

Does *deindividuation* increase aggressive behaviour by prison guards?

social constraints or did it reflect the emergence of a norm within the mob that it was appropriate to punish the Black man? Perhaps both processes operated to some extent.

Postmes, Spears, and their colleagues have also speculated that a state of deindividuation can occur during Internet communication (e.g., Postmes, Spears, Sakhel, & de Groot, 2001; Spears, Lea, Corneliussen, Postmes, & ter Haar, 2002). They propose that the anonymity of computer-mediated communication elicits a sense of immersion into online groups, a diminishment of personal identity, and a willingness to follow unconventional norms within those virtual groups. For instance, think about Internet chat rooms. The anonymity provided by chat rooms can produce a willingness to be more candid than during face-to-face interactions. Contributors to a chat room may conform to group norms that they would not obey offline. For instance, expressing racist beliefs or describing sexual fantasies may be normative in an online group, and people who would not admit to such things in daily life may conform to the group norm.

It remains for future researchers to resolve questions about the psychological processes involved in deindividuation. Whether feelings of anonymity produced by being in a group release individuals from inhibitions, increase responsiveness to external cues, or increase adherence to emerging group norms must be disentangled in empirical research. Everyone agrees that deindividuation occurs, but there is disagreement about its mechanisms.

Decision Making in Groups

One of the most important functions fulfilled by groups is decision making. Most of the critical decisions made in all societies occur at the level of groups: political groups make decisions about international affairs, Supreme Court justices make decisions about legal principles, military groups make decisions about troop deployment and battlefield strategy, and so on. Many of the decisions that affect each of us in our daily lives are also made by groups: families decide where to go on vacation, work groups decide how to divide the responsibilities on a new project, friendship groups decide who will serve as the designated driver prior to going to a bar, and so on. Group decisions are a pervasive part of life, so it is important for social psychologists to understand how groups make decisions.

In this section, we discuss three issues related to group decision making. First, we describe how bad decisions can result from a desire to avoid disagreement in a group. Second, we discuss how majority ideas tend to intensify in a group. Third, we consider how one or a few people can sometimes make a big difference in a group.

Groupthink: Bad Decisions Because of Pressure to Agree

It seems reasonable to expect that groups have the potential to make better decisions than individuals. Groups have access to more information than a single person. Groups also provide multiple perspectives on an issue, which should help to identify problems with proposed solutions. The phrase "Two heads are better than one" seems to capture accurately the potential for groups to make good decisions.

But groups do *not* always make good choices. In fact, sometimes they make *terrible* decisions, such as when the directors of a drug company decide to introduce a new product despite safety concerns or when a group of generals makes a military decision that proves disastrous. What happened in these cases? Why didn't the decision-making group assess the options better and make a sounder judgment?

There are many reasons for bad decisions, of course. Sometimes, the correct course of action is highly uncertain and/or all of the options involve risks, as when a financial management company is trying to decide how to invest its clients' money. At other times, groups lack the necessary expertise to make informed judgments, as when a volunteer organization mismanages its budget because of a lack of relevant experience. These examples do not represent failures of the group to process information—the decision was either very difficult (for anyone), or the group lacked relevant knowledge (and had little chance from the start of making a well-informed choice).

Bad decisions can also be made, however, when the group has all the information it needs to make a good decision. In this case, the bad decision results from poor group functioning, as when the group engages in biased or faulty reasoning based on the information available to them. These cases are interesting because they were *unnecessary*—they could have been prevented if the group had operated more effectively. In this section, we describe one common source of error in group decision making.

Irving Janis (1972, 1982) of Yale University coined the term **groupthink** to refer to a way of thinking that can occur in decision-making groups, when pressure to agree leads to biased appraisal of options and poor decisions. The fundamental idea of groupthink is that when members of a group are highly motivated to agree with the leader and with one another, they do not express their reservations openly and do not criticize one another. Because many or all of the members are engaging in the same self-censorship, everybody believes that everyone else in the group strongly supports the decision. The result can be poor decisions that are not based on a thorough analysis of the options.

Janis hypothesized that groupthink is most likely to occur in certain kinds of groups. One important condition is that the group is highly cohesive. **Group cohesiveness** refers to the strength of the forces acting on group members to stay in the group (Festinger, 1950; Mullen & Cooper, 1994; Shaw, 1976). In highly cohesive groups, members are strongly motivated to remain: they like the other members, membership is prestigious, and/or they receive tangible benefits from being in the group. Thus, members of highly cohesive groups do not want to be ostracized or excluded from the group, which leads them to conform and to avoid criticizing other members' ideas. (We should note that group cohesiveness can have positive consequences as well. For example, members of highly cohesive groups are willing to work hard and make sacrifices for the group. Also, cohesiveness can help groups survive difficult events. Notwithstanding these potential benefits, group cohesiveness can have a stifling effect on discussion.)

A second important factor contributing to groupthink is a *directive leader*. Directive leaders openly express their own opinions—often before any discussion has occurred—and control subsequent conversation in the group. When a leader is highly directive, group members know exactly where he or she stands, which puts pressure on them to agree. Also, because directive leaders control the group's discussion, it can be difficult for members to raise questions or concerns.

A third factor that makes groups vulnerable to groupthink is high stress. Stress can arise for several reasons, including when a group faces external threat or when there is severe time pressure to make a decision. Whatever its cause, stress makes members feel even more pressure to follow the leader's opinion and to avoid rocking the boat. Stress intensifies the effects of group cohesiveness and directive leadership on the tendency for group members to keep their reservations to themselves.

Symptoms of Groupthink. If we see a group making bad decisions, how can we tell if groupthink is responsible? Janis identified eight *symptoms* of groupthink, which are described in Table 10.1. These symptoms are thought to occur in most cases of groupthink, although some will not apply to particular cases. All of the symptoms reflect group members' desires to agree and to maintain a positive group feeling. The symptoms cause faulty assumptions, inadequate assessment of possible

groupthink
a way of thinking that can occur in decision-making groups when pressure to agree leads to inadequate appraisal of options and poor decisions

group cohesiveness
the combined strength of all forces acting on members of a group to remain in the group

TABLE **10.1**
Symptoms of Groupthink

1. *An illusion of invulnerability:* If a group feels invincible, it tends to make decisions that are very risky; there is no need for caution because the group cannot lose. This symptom is interconnected with some of the other symptoms such as rationalization of warnings.

2. *Rationalization of warnings:* An essential element of good decision making is to assess carefully any possible problems with an option. If warning signals are discounted or rationalized as being harmless, then risky and low-quality decisions may occur. Rationalization of warnings is related to the illusion of invulnerability: rationalization can result in perceived invulnerability, and perceived invulnerability can encourage rationalization.

3. *An unquestioned belief in the inherent morality of the group:* Most of us believe that we are moral and ethical people. When a group assumes that it is inherently moral, it can fail to recognize that self-interest might be colouring its perspective. This failure may lead the group to ignore ethical aspects of its decisions, which can result in decisions that appear to others to be selfish or corrupt.

4. *Stereotyped views of enemy leaders:* Negative stereotypes about an outgroup are often believed to apply especially well to the leaders of that outgroup. When a group views enemy leaders as evil, it will be unwilling to negotiate with those leaders, increasing the chance of aggression. When a group views enemy leaders as weak and stupid, it may underestimate those leaders and make decisions that are risky or foolish. This symptom can contribute to an illusion of invulnerability—the first symptom above.

5. *Pressure on group members who challenge the consensus:* Highly cohesive groups usually want agreement and harmony. Therefore, it is upsetting when someone in the group criticizes assumptions or tentative decisions. Social pressure from other group members may be directed at these individuals, which will communicate that dissent is inconsistent with being a loyal member of the group. This social pressure can result in the exclusion of important information from discussion.

6. *Self-censorship of misgivings, questions, and counterarguments:* Because group members want agreement and know that dissent is inconsistent with being a loyal member of the group, they often engage in self-censorship by not expressing their doubts about ideas or assumptions. Like social pressure on people who raise questions, self-censorship can result in the exclusion of important information from the discussion.

7. *An illusion of unanimity:* Members of the group will often believe that everyone agrees with a tentative decision (partly because of social pressure on critics and self-censorship). This illusion that unanimity exists will further inhibit discussion. Perceived unanimity can lead to risky decisions and a failure to consider ethical aspects of the decision.

8. *Emergence of self-appointed mindguards:* Janis suggested that in highly cohesive groups, one or more members sometimes act as *mindguards*—people who protect the "mind" of the leader by shielding him or her from criticisms, doubts, and so on (a mental version of *bodyguards,* who protect the leader's physical well-being). These mindguards are self-appointed: they decide themselves that their actions are necessary for the peace of mind of the leader and the harmony of the group. Mindguards sometimes intercept people who might want to criticize a tentative decision and deny them access to the group.

Adapted from Janis, 1972, pp. 197—198

options, a willingness to take excessive risks, and, ultimately, poor decisions. The groupthink process is depicted in the flowchart in Figure 10.4.

Groupthink may help us to understand why some tragic events occurred. For instance, in May 2000, the drinking water system in the small Ontario town of Walkerton (population 4800) became contaminated with deadly bacteria, primarily *E. coli.* By the time the system was cleansed, more than 2300 people had become ill, and seven people eventually died. The community was traumatized, and the

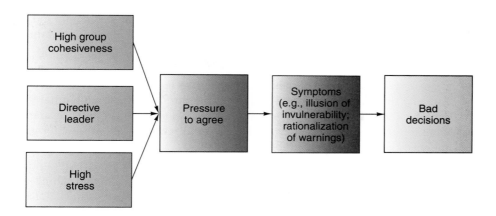

FIGURE 10.4
Groupthink process

outbreak inflicted enormous costs on families and businesses. Other cities throughout Ontario wondered about the safety of their own water systems.

Was the Walkerton tragedy an example of groupthink? Based on information that became public during a provincial inquiry that followed the events, it seems plausible to suggest that groupthink was at least partly responsible. For example, the individuals most directly responsible for monitoring the water system, Stan and Frank Koebel, were far too complacent about the water system. In particular, they had unrealistic beliefs about the potential for contamination. They were so resistant to the idea that the water could be unhealthy that they continued to drink it themselves even after test results indicated the presence of bacteria. Also, there should have been more careful monitoring of these two men by the Public Utilities Commission (PUC), but commission members simply accepted uncritically the men's assurances that the water was safe. In fact, the PUC had received a report in 1998 from the Ministry of the Environment indicating that trace amounts of *E. coli* bacteria had been found in some water samples and urging very careful monitoring of the water system, but nothing was done about this report. In general, a variety of improper operating practices had become routine in the Walkerton water system, and there was little or no monitoring by appropriate authorities. It was a disaster waiting to happen.

Which of the specific symptoms of groupthink listed in Table 10.1 were present in the Walkerton tragedy? The Koebel brothers and the members of the PUC appeared to view the water system as relatively invulnerable (#1). They engaged in numerous rationalizations of warnings, including the dismissal of the test results in 1998 indicating bacterial problems (#2). Neither the Koebel brothers nor the PUC seemed to understand or realize their ethical responsibilities to the public; they seemed to view themselves as inherently moral (#3). The standard procedure in the PUC seemed to be to accept the Koebel brothers' reports without rocking the boat (#5), which led the various PUC members to believe that everyone else on the commission thought everything was okay (#7). Taken together, these various symptoms suggest that groupthink was indeed operating in Walkerton.

Avoiding Groupthink. Janis (1972, 1982) identified several decision-making strategies that could be implemented in

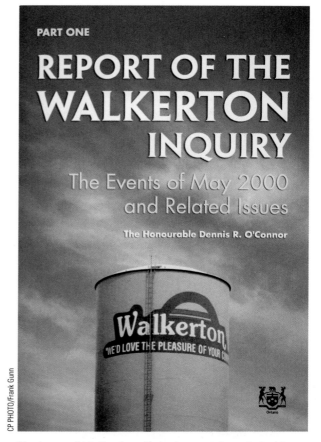

CP PHOTO/Frank Gunn

The town of Walkerton, Ontario, was devastated in May 2000 by the contamination of its water system with deadly bacteria.

cohesive groups to reduce the likelihood of groupthink. Three recommendations, which address different elements of groupthink, seem particularly important:

1. The leader should be nondirective and allow other group members to express their opinions before stating his or her view. One cause of groupthink is that members do not want to challenge or upset the leader. When leaders begin meetings by announcing their position or preference, pressure on other group members to agree is immediately introduced. To avoid groupthink, leaders should remain quiet and neutral early in the discussion, allowing other group members to express their opinions freely.

2. A norm of openness and candour should be established in the group (a norm that may have to originate from the leader). A major cause of groupthink is that members seek consensus and are loath to criticize or raise questions. But if the leader makes it clear that frank discussion is desirable and that all suggestions must be evaluated thoroughly, members will be more willing to raise questions about proposed ideas. Of course, instituting this norm will not have much impact if people who do criticize are then condemned by the leader or other members. But if members are rewarded for raising questions, the likelihood of groupthink can be greatly reduced. Janis suggested that it might even be possible to designate one member at each meeting (a different member each time) as the *devil's advocate,* whose specific role is to question everything.

3. People from outside the group should be included in the decision-making process. Highly cohesive groups often insulate themselves from outsiders. They want consensus, so the prospect of a different opinion is unattractive. But to make good decisions, it is important that groups seek out all possible views and involve as many relevant experts as possible in the decision-making process. Thus, outside experts should be invited to meetings of the group to share their ideas.

To avoid *groupthink,* decision-making groups should involve outside experts in their decisions.

Empirical Tests of Groupthink Predictions. Janis (1972, 1982) used the concept of groupthink to understand several historical examples of bad decisions (similar to our discussion of the Walkerton events). Case studies of this kind are interesting but do not test the model directly. Although there has not been a lot of empirical research on groupthink, some studies have been conducted (for reviews, see Esser, 1998; Mullen, Anthony, Salas, & Driskell, 1994; Park, 1990). Researchers have primarily investigated two predictions from Janis's model, relating to the effects of group cohesiveness and leadership styles. These issues have usually been explored by creating groups in the laboratory, manipulating cohesiveness and/or leadership style, and observing the decision-making process.

With regard to group cohesiveness, Janis predicted that highly cohesive groups are more likely to show evidence of groupthink than are less cohesive groups. Empirical support for this prediction, however, has been limited. Researchers have found that highly cohesive groups discourage dissent and produce more confident decisions, as predicted by Janis, but also that members of cohesive groups report *less* self-censorship, which is inconsistent with Janis's predictions (e.g., Moorhead & Montanari, 1986; Turner, Pratkanis, Probasco, & Leve, 1992).

Empirical tests of the effects of leadership style have been more consistently supportive of Janis's reasoning (Esser, 1998). For example, Matie Flowers (1977) of Syracuse University trained a confederate to lead a group in a highly directive or nondirective way and found that groups with directive leaders used less information and produced fewer possible solutions than did groups with nondirective leaders. Carrie Leana (1985) of the University of Florida identified directive or nondirective leaders based on group members' ratings of the leader's style in previous decisions; she found that groups with directive leaders produced fewer possible solutions and more frequent acquiescence to the leader's preferred position than did groups with nondirective leaders. In general, the evidence supports the hypothesis that an open leadership style is likely to produce a better and more broadly based decision than a directive leadership style (but see Peterson, 1997, for a different perspective).

It is interesting to apply this hypothesis that open leaders will be more effective than directive leaders to political parties and committees. The parliamentary system in Canada puts pressure on MPs to support their party's agenda even if they do not personally agree with it. Cabinet ministers, in particular, must toe the line with regard to the prime minister's statements and policies. This system gives the prime minister a great deal of power and probably predisposes him or her toward a directive leadership style. Perhaps decisions would be better if a more open process was adopted.

Other research relevant to groupthink has found that more information is considered by a group when there is a norm of critical thinking than when there is a norm of consensus seeking (Postmes, Spears, & Cihangir, 2001). Finally, research by Brock University's Gordon Hodson and the University of Western Ontario's Richard Sorrentino has shown that there are individual differences in how people respond to directive versus nondirective leaders (Hodson & Sorrentino, 1997); some people actually prefer and respond more positively to directive than nondirective leaders.

Group Polarization: Moving Toward the Majority View

One of the authors of this book recently participated in an interesting meeting of the psychology department's appointments committee, which is responsible for hiring new professors. The committee had to make a difficult decision, because it could approve job offers to only two of three highly qualified candidates who had all impressed the department during their interviews. The candidates came from different areas of psychology, so it was not obvious how to compare them. The meeting began with some preliminary comments from the department chairperson, and then each member expressed his or her own initial views on who should receive the two job offers. No candidate was selected by all of the members, but two candidates were named more often than the third. Next, the chair invited discussion of the candidates, and the committee members talked for almost an hour about the candidates. After this discussion, the chair called a vote on who should receive the two offers.

Can you predict the outcome of this process? Do you think that the candidate who received the fewest initial nominations was selected or not? On the one hand, it is plausible to speculate that people who *did* initially name this least-preferred candidate might feel threatened by their minority status in the committee and argue forcefully in favour of this individual, resulting in his or her ultimately being chosen to receive an offer. On the other hand, it is plausible that people who initially named the least-preferred candidate might feel foolish or intimidated and keep their mouths shut during the discussion, resulting in the candidate's not receiving an offer.

What actually happened? At the end of the discussion, the two candidates who had initially been named by the most committee members were selected *unanimously* to receive the job offers. Not a single committee member included the initially least-preferred candidate in his or her set of two choices.

group polarization

the tendency for group discussion to strengthen the initial leanings of the members in a group

This outcome is a classic example of group polarization. Perhaps someday, after reading and studying the following material, you might also recognize group polarization in your own experiences of group decision making.

Group polarization refers to the tendency for group discussion to strengthen the initial leanings of the members in a group. Whatever position or option is initially (pre-discussion) preferred by the majority of group members will tend to become even more widely preferred after group discussion (e.g., support for the two initially preferred candidates in the appointments committee meeting became unanimous after discussion).

Let's do an exercise to illustrate group polarization. Consider the following two situations and think about what you would recommend in each case:

1. The coach of a low-ranked basketball team in a tournament is scheduled to play one of the top-ranked teams. She thinks that her team might be able to surprise the other team by using an unusual defensive strategy, but she knows it is risky and might backfire. Would you encourage her to try the risky defence or would you recommend a more cautious approach?

2. The father of a young family is able to provide adequately for his family but does not have much money for luxuries. He hears from an acquaintance that a company is developing a new product that might greatly increase the value of its stock, although there is some risk that the product will fail. The young man is thinking about cashing in his life insurance policy to purchase stocks in the company. Would you encourage him to buy stocks or to be more cautious?

It turns out that most university students would encourage the coach to use the risky defence but discourage the father from buying the risky stocks (Myers & Lamm, 1976; Stoner, 1968; Wallach, Kogan, & Bem, 1962). How did your inclinations match these tendencies? But now the important question: What happens when university students discuss these situations in a group and *then* indicate what the individuals should do? Group polarization is what happens: after discussion, even more students recommend that the coach *should* try the risky defence, and even more students recommend that the father should *not* buy the risky stocks. The positions that most people initially preferred tend to become even more widely endorsed after group discussion.

The group polarization effect has been obtained in many studies examining a wide variety of discussion topics (e.g., Blascovitch, Ginsburg, & Veach, 1975; Brauer, Judd, & Gliner, 1995; Knox & Safford, 1976; Madsen, 1978; Whyte, 1993). The effect has been found when groups discuss political attitudes, sex education, racetrack betting, investment decisions, and many other topics. In each case, whatever inclination existed in the group prior to discussion was even more popular after discussion.

Research on group polarization in the past decade has taken the effect in new directions. For example, Markus Brauer, Charles Judd, and Vincent Jacquelin (2001) investigated whether groups would show polarization of *stereotypes*. If most members of a group believe that another target group is characterized by certain traits, will discussion make the stereotype more widely held and perhaps stronger? To test this question, Brauer and his colleagues created a stereotype in the laboratory. Students at the University of Colorado were given fictitious information about a group of adolescent boys, which emphasized negative qualities, including selfishness and violence. Some participants then engaged in discussion with other participants about their impressions of the group of boys before reporting their stereotypes, whereas other participants reported their stereotypes without engaging in any discussion. Figure 10.5 presents the mean ratings of selfishness and violence by participants who did and did not engage in group discussion. The results showed that participants who first discussed their impressions with other participants reported stronger

FIGURE 10.5 Ratings of target group on selfishness and violence

From Brauer et al., "The communication of social stereotypes: The effects of group discussion and information distribution on stereotypic appraisals," *Journal of Personality and Social Psychology*, 81, 463–475, Table 3, p. 470, 2001. Copyright © 2001 by the American Psychological Association. Reprinted by permission.

stereotypes—higher ratings of selfishness and violence—than did participants who rated the group without engaging in any discussion.

The implications of this study are somewhat worrisome. It suggests that if people share a common stereotype, then discussing it among themselves will tend to reinforce it. Perhaps this process contributes to the strong stereotypes that sometimes exist within groups (e.g., within families, peer groups, or cultural groups). Thus, group polarization may contribute to intergroup hostility (see also Myers & Bishop, 1970).

There are other settings where group polarization might also be problematic. For instance, in penitentiaries, antisocial attitudes may be intensified by interactions and conversations among prisoners. On the Internet, people expressing their opinions on racist or sexually exploitative Web sites might strengthen each other's attitudes and cause their dysfunctional views to become more common.

Causes of Group Polarization.

Why does the group polarization effect occur? Two principal explanations have been offered for the phenomenon (see Eagly & Chaiken, 1993; Isenberg, 1986). The first explanation focuses on the arguments that are presented during group discussion. People usually argue in favour of their own view on an issue. This means that the majority of arguments offered during a discussion are likely to support whatever view was predominant before the discussion began. Because most arguments offered during the discussion favour the predominant view, members of the group are most likely to be persuaded in that direction, which results in group polarization (Vinokur & Burnstein, 1974).

The second explanation, which is *not* incompatible with the first, focuses on people's desire to appear knowledgeable and intelligent. Group discussion lets everyone know each other's positions; members learn which view is endorsed by the majority. There is then social pressure to move in the direction of the preferred view, because members do not want to appear ill informed or unyielding (Sanders & Baron, 1977).

Notice that these two causes of group polarization parallel the concepts of *informational influence* and *normative influence* introduced in our discussion of conformity in Chapter 8 (see pages 288–289). Group discussion leads to polarized judgments because members of the group use other members' arguments as a source of information (informational influence) and because they feel social pressure to move toward the dominant view (normative influence).

Jury decision making is one of the most interesting applications of the concept of group polarization. This topic is described in Social Psychology in Your Life: "Group Polarization in the Courtroom."

We should mention that social psychologists interested in how juries make decisions have investigated other issues in addition to group polarization (e.g., see Schuller & Ogloff, 2001; Simon, 1975; Wrightsman, 1991). To take one example, Canadian social psychologist Regina Schuller of York University has conducted a wide-ranging program of research investigating the conditions under which juries are influenced by *expert testimony*—information relevant to a case that is presented by an outside, presumably unbiased, authority (Schuller, 1992; Schuller & Cripps, 1998; Schuller, McKimmie, & Janz, 2004; Schuller & Rzepa, 2002). Schuller has particularly focused on expert testimony about the concept of *battered woman syndrome* in trials of women who are accused of murdering their abusive husbands. This concept proposes that when women have been repeatedly physically abused, they develop an emotional state (or disorder) that can lead them to exhibit sudden and extreme aggression against their husband, sometimes without strong provocation. Schuller's research has found that when an expert presents information about the battered woman syndrome, explaining that such women are terrified for their own and their children's safety, juries are significantly more lenient in their judgments about the woman defendant. Schuller's findings indicate that jurors use expert testimony to interpret other information in the case.

Social Psychology in Your Life *Group Polarization in the Courtroom*

Juries are a crucial element of justice systems around the world. Juries make decisions about the guilt or innocence of defendants—a responsibility that is enormously important. How do juries go about reaching their decisions? Through discussion: the members discuss the details of the case. Social psychologists have observed that, like any other group discussions, jury deliberations are likely to produce group polarization (see Hans & Vidmar, 1986; Hastie, Penrod, & Pennington, 1983). That is, the predominant leaning toward a guilty or innocent verdict among jurors prior to discussion predicts the final outcome quite well, because discussion tends to favour the initially preferred decision.

Specifically, researchers have found that the results of an initial, pre-deliberation vote among the jurors predicts the final outcome: If most jurors are leaning toward conviction, then the unanimous decision is likely to be guilty, whereas if most jurors are leaning toward acquittal, then the unanimous decision is likely to be not guilty. This group

polarization effect has been found among simulated juries created in the laboratory (e.g., Davis, Kerr, Atkin, Holt, & Meek, 1975), as well as in real juries. Harry Kalven and Hans Zeisel (1966) surveyed people who had served on actual juries and found that the final verdict was almost always consistent with the majority view in an initial vote held before discussion began. Thus, jury deliberations typically led the group to a final decision that corresponded to the pre-discussion tendency.

One important qualification to the group polarization effect in juries is that it occurs more strongly for verdicts of *innocent* than for verdicts of *guilty* (Kalven & Zeisel, 1966; MacCoun & Kerr, 1988). That is, when most jurors initially lean toward acquittal, the final verdict is very likely to be acquittal, whereas when most jurors initially lean toward conviction, the final verdict is less predictable (though still more likely to be guilty than innocent).

Why would an initial leaning toward guilty be less influential on the final

verdict than an initial leaning toward innocent? Robert MacCoun and Norbert Kerr (1988) argued that jurors take to heart the principle of *beyond reasonable doubt:* they know that they should convict only if they are certain that the defendant is guilty beyond reasonable doubt. This principle leads jurors to require more evidence to convict than to acquit. Therefore, even when a guilty verdict is initially preferred by most jurors, acquittal might nevertheless prevail because all that must happen is that some doubt be introduced into the minds of the jurors who hold the majority view.

In juries, group polarization is greater for verdicts of innocent than for verdicts of guilty.

Minority Influence: The Power of the Few

Group polarization reflects the impact of the majority on group decisions. The initially preferred position (the *majority* position) tends to become more strongly supported after discussion. This effect constitutes the norm in social influence: more often than not, groups will exhibit polarization toward the dominant view during discussion and decision making. This effect probably reflects that most arguments will favour the majority view and that people feel social pressure to agree with the majority.

But the majority does not *always* carry the day—the minority view in a group can sometimes be profoundly influential. What conditions foster minority influence? We address this question first by discussing the qualities that characterize influential minority groups. We then turn to the question of whether exposure to a minority view stimulates creative thinking. We close with a discussion of how social impact theory conceptualizes minority influence.

Confidence and Persistence. Perhaps the best-known researcher on minority influence is French social psychologist Serge Moscovici, who wrote extensively on this issue (e.g., Moscovici, 1980; Moscovici & Doise, 1994). Moscovici argued that minorities can be successful in their influence only if they are firm and resolute in their position. That is, members of a minority subgroup must show that they are confident in their view and will not yield to majority pressure. Confidence within a minority raises questions in the minds of people who hold the majority view: "Why are these people so confident? Could their views be correct?" Members of a minority must persist in their position unwaveringly and also remain consistent among themselves. Evidence of either waffling on the issue or divisions within the minority subgroup greatly reduces its impact on the majority.

At the same time as remaining resolute, minorities should try to avoid appearing too rigid, extremist, or impervious to information (Papastamou & Mugny, 1990). Instead, they must seem reasonable and logical, *but also resolute in their opinion on this issue.* One way for a minority to achieve these appearances is by agreeing with the majority on other issues. Such agreement gives the members of the minority more credibility when they disagree, because they have shown that they do not always hold deviant views. When members of a minority disagree with the majority on virtually everything, their views are likely to be dismissed.

This reasoning can be applied to political parties in Canada. When a party is not in power and faces a majority government, the most effective way for it to have influence might be to avoid partisan opposition to every policy of the governing party. Instead, the weaker party should agree on some issues with the majority party, because disagreement on other issues will then be interpreted as reflecting legitimate substantive differences.

The fact that minority influence can occur does not mean that it is either easy or painless. People who take unpopular positions in any group usually face conformity pressure and may be rejected (Bassili, 2003; Evans, 2001; Levine, 1989; Schachter, 1951). Serving as a voice of dissent is usually thankless, and always difficult. Nevertheless, perhaps our discussion of minority influence will help you to remain resolute in the future when you are certain that you hold a correct, but unpopular, view on an important issue.

Unique Effects of Minority Influence? Moscovici and other researchers interested in minority influence (e.g., Nemeth, 1987) have argued that minorities have a special kind of influence on others in the group. These researchers have suggested that exposure to a minority view stimulates *divergent thinking*—novel, creative thoughts that consider alternative approaches to a problem. Because a minority voice underscores the fact that different views on the issue are possible, people in the majority are provoked to think carefully and to consider new perspectives (see Martin, Hewstone, & Martin, 2003). Even if the minority does not convince the majority to change its decision on a specific issue, it may elicit delayed effects on other judgments or tasks.

These effects of minorities are believed to differ from those of majorities, which are characterized as eliciting *convergent thinking*—standard or typical approaches to a problem. When exposed to a majority, people are pressured to conform to the majority view, as well as to suppress counterarguments.

Charlan Nemeth of the University of California at Berkeley has reported data showing that exposure to a minority view increases people's subsequent willingness to take an unpopular position themselves. In one study (Nemeth & Chiles, 1988), participants took part in a colour-judging task, in which they had to identify slides as blue or green. Some participants were exposed to confederates who gave unusual colour judgments (e.g., calling a blue slide green), whereas other participants were not exposed to these minority judgments. All participants then took part in a conformity study utilizing Solomon Asch's (1956) line-judging task (see pages 291–292). Asch's task required participants to identify which of several lines on a card matched the length of a line on a second card. The correct answer was always obvious, but before giving their responses, participants heard a set of confederates unanimously give erroneous line judgments on some trials. Asch found that participants often conformed with the confederates by giving the wrong answer. In the study by Nemeth and Chiles (1988), participants who had been exposed to a minority view in the colour-judging task were much less likely to conform on the line-judging task than were participants who had not been exposed to a minority view in the first task. Seeing someone express a minority judgment on a previous task increased participants' willingness to disagree with the majority on the line-judging task.

Social Impact Theory. Not all social psychologists agree that minority influence is qualitatively different from majority influence. In Chapter 8, we described *social impact theory* (see pages 317–318), which asserts that social influence is the result of psychological "forces" acting on an individual (Latané, 1981; Wolf, 1987). This theory interprets "social pressure" quite literally: people experience psychological forces pressing on them, just as they experience physical forces such as sound and weight.

Factors assumed to influence the social pressure felt by an individual include the number, strength, and closeness (immediacy) of sources of influence. When many people exert strong pressure in close proximity to the target, such as when several members of a family urge the father to stop smoking, successful social influence is more likely. Social impact theorists do not distinguish between majority and minority sources of influence; they hypothesize that both majorities and minorities exert their influence through similar processes. If minorities sometimes appear to have unusual impact, it may be because the strength or closeness of their influence is heightened in some way. For instance, the fact that minority views are often unexpected may increase their psychological strength. Similarly, minorities that are firm and resolute may be more influential than timid minorities because confidence translates into stronger social pressure.

Researchers will undoubtedly continue to debate the parallels between minority and majority influence. We suspect that the underlying processes of influence are similar, but minorities are likely to have some unique effects on subsequent tasks, such as increasing willingness to express dissent.

In the following section, we turn from research on groups as a whole to investigations of one specific member of the group: the leader. How leaders emerge in groups and why some leaders are more effective than others are important questions if we want to understand the functioning and performance of groups.

Leadership

The most important individual in a group is usually the leader. (Our earlier discussion of the role of the leader in creating groupthink illustrates this point.) The leader typically guides the group toward its goals, serves as a representative of the group, and tries to maintain morale. We will articulate some of the leader's functions shortly. Given the importance of this individual, it is not surprising that both social and industrial-organizational psychologists have been very interested in leadership. Two fundamental questions have received the most attention from researchers: "Who is *selected* (or emerges) as the leader of a group?" and "Who makes an *effective* (or successful) leader?"

The issues of emergence and effectiveness have been examined from three different perspectives on leadership: trait, situational, and interactionist approaches. Trait approaches focus on the characteristics of people who become leaders; situational approaches focus on external factors that influence the selection and effectiveness of leaders; and interactionist approaches investigate the combined effects of traits and situational factors. We discuss each of these approaches separately. But first, we need to define some relevant terms.

Definitions of Leader and Leadership Effectiveness

Think about groups to which you belong, such as your family, sports teams, friendship groups, work groups, religious groups, recreational clubs, or other groups. Can you identify a primary "leader" in all of these groups? If not, why not?

When you think carefully about various groups, it is surprising how complicated the issue of leadership becomes. Leaders can do *many* different things for their group, and leaders can become leaders in *many* different ways. Moreover, some groups have *several* leaders, whereas others have *no* clear leader. Sometimes, members in the same group even disagree about who should be considered the leader of their group.

Defining a Leader. So how can we define or identify a leader? There are numerous possibilities, but we will mention only three (see Burn, 2004; Chemers & Ayman, 1993; Hollander, 1985; Levine & Moreland, 1998; Shaw, 1976). (1) In some groups, the leader is the person who holds a formal position of authority, perhaps involving an election. These kinds of leaders are relatively easy to identify; examples include the prime minister or a provincial premier, the chairperson of a committee, and the judge in a courtroom. (2) If there is no formal leadership position, another way to define a leader is to say that he or she is the person who is so named by most members. Thus, we might ask members of a friendship group to identify the leader of their clique; there might be disagreement among members, but the leader would be defined as the person who received the most "votes." (3) A third way to define the leader is in terms of his or her *impact* on the group. For instance, the leader could be considered the person who exerts the most influence on members of the group, or who can best motivate members to work hard or to behave in a certain way. From this perspective, members of a group might not even realize who the true leader is; for example, there might be an "official" leader who fills a position of authority (e.g., the coach of a hockey team), but the "real" leader might be someone who inspires the other members to work hard (e.g., a star player). This third approach is exemplified by the concept of **transformational leaders.** Transformational leaders are leaders who *transform* the members of their group—these individuals stimulate fundamental changes in how members view themselves and the group (Bass & Avolio, 1993; House & Shamir, 1993; Ross & Offermann, 1997). Obviously, transformational leaders have a large impact on their group. For example, Mother Teresa radically changed how the nuns in her order saw themselves and their mission on earth. Traditionally, her order had emphasized prayer and contemplation, but Mother Teresa transformed the group into a problem-focused organization dedicated to helping the poor in the Calcutta slums. She inspired her followers by example and elicited great loyalty.

Pierre Trudeau qualified as a leader on all of these criteria at some point in his life. He served as leader of the Liberal Party and as prime minister of Canada, both

transformational leaders
individuals who produce fundamental changes in how members of a group view themselves and the group

Mother Teresa was a transformational leader.

important, formal positions of authority. Informally, he was viewed by many federalists as their symbolic leader during two referenda campaigns that were held in Quebec regarding separation. And he certainly had a large impact on the Liberal Party and Canada—he played a major role in the establishment of the Official Languages Act, the Charter of Rights and Freedoms, and other important pieces of legislation.

Functions Fulfilled by Leaders. Part of the difficulty in defining leadership comes from the fact that leaders can fulfill so many different functions for their groups. In specific groups, certain functions will be most important, but across groups there is an amazing diversity of things that leaders do (see Cartwright & Zander, 1968; Hollander, 1985; Vroom & Yetton, 1973). Table 10.2 describes ten possible functions of leaders, and this list does *not* constitute an exhaustive catalogue of the possibilities.

Some theorists have suggested that the various functions fulfilled by leaders fall into two major categories: task achievement and group maintenance (Bales & Slater, 1955; Hollander, 1985). The **task achievement function** involves all of the things necessary for group productivity, such as providing expert advice or training, planning how to achieve the goals of the group, distributing tasks to members, developing policies, monitoring and evaluating performance, and so on. The **group maintenance function** involves all of the things related to morale in the group, such as motivating members to remain committed, resolving disputes between members, and providing counselling to troubled members. In some groups, different individuals may emerge to fulfill these two functions; the two leaders are referred to as the **task leader** and the **socioemotional leader.**

Defining Leadership Effectiveness. The wide range of functions potentially fulfilled by leaders complicates any attempt to define and measure leadership

task achievement function
aspects of leadership that relate to group productivity

group maintenance function
aspects of leadership that relate to morale in the group

task leader
an individual who takes charge of issues related to productivity in a group

socioemotional leader
an individual who takes charge of issues related to morale in a group

---

TABLE **10.2**
Functions Potentially Fulfilled by Leaders

Leader Function	Definition	Example
Expert	Teaches skills to members	Dance instructor demonstrates movements to students
Planner	Plans how to achieve group goals	Military officer plans attack
Executive	Assigns tasks to members	Head chef assigns food preparation duties to kitchen staff in restaurant
Policymaker	Develops policies to guide group	Retail store manager implements new commission-based salary for salespersons
Performance appraiser	Evaluates members' performance	Supervisor provides formal evaluation of subordinate's job performance
External representative	Represents group to outside groups and individuals	Political leader visits foreign country
Motivator	Motivates members to perform and remain in group	Football coach gives emotional pre-game pep talk to players
Arbitrator	Resolves conflicts between members	Parent intervenes between fighting children and suggests solution
Exemplar	Sets example and inspires members	Religious leader lives exemplary life
Counsellor	Helps members deal with personal problems	University residence adviser counsels students on how to cope with first-year stressors

effectiveness. How can we assess the effectiveness of leaders when they fill such different roles in different groups? One leader might be an effective planner, whereas another might be an effective motivator. How can we compare these two individuals?

Just as there are different ways to define or identify a leader, there are different ways to define or measure leadership effectiveness (see Chemers & Ayman, 1993; Forsyth, 1999; Hollander, 1985). A common approach, especially in research in industrial-organizational psychology, has been to define an effective leader as one whose group is highly *productive.* When groups produce an output that can be quantified (e.g., counting the number of products assembled), this definition makes particular sense.

A second approach has been to define an effective leader as one whose group members are very *satisfied.* If the members of the group are happy, isn't that enough to consider the leader effective? This definition is particularly appropriate for groups whose primary purpose is socializing (e.g., friendship groups, social clubs).

A third approach to leadership effectiveness has been to define an effective leader as someone who has a large *impact* on the group. If a leader moves the group significantly toward its goals, then he or she is effective. But what if a leader has a large impact on a group but moves it in his or her own directions rather than toward the group's original goals? Adolf Hitler had a large impact on Germany, but he moved the country in a despicable direction that was abhorred by many Germans. Should we consider him to have been an effective or ineffective leader? Some theorists have argued that leader effectiveness should be defined in terms of achieving only the group's goals (which would assess Hitler as ineffective), whereas others have argued that any kind of impact, even the achievement of selfish goals, should be considered equally influential (which would assess Hitler as more effective).

What made Martin Luther King Jr., a great leader?

Finally, a straightforward way of defining leadership effectiveness—and the most common method in social psychological research—has been in terms of *group members' ratings of the leader's effectiveness.* This allows members to focus on whatever aspect of leadership they personally consider to be important (productivity, morale, etc.) when evaluating the leader.

Having clarified what we mean by leaders, functions of leaders, and leadership effectiveness, we can now turn to the three approaches mentioned earlier that have been taken by social psychologists interested in leadership. We begin with the trait approach.

Great Person Theory: Trait Approaches to Leadership

Much of the research on leadership has taken an individual difference perspective, trying to identify the personal characteristics that predict being chosen as a leader or being a successful leader. This **trait approach to leadership** has been called **Great Person theory:** great leaders are assumed to possess rare qualities that make them effective. When most of us think of famous leaders, such as Pierre Trudeau, Martin Luther King Jr., or Winston Churchill, we presume that they achieved their

trait approach to leadership
the perspective that people become leaders, or perform well as leaders, because of their individual characteristics, such as intelligence and charisma

Great Person theory
the hypothesis that exceptional leaders possess extraordinary qualities and skills—consistent with the trait approach to leadership

positions of influence because they were special in some way—charismatic, intelligent, decisive. This is the trait approach.

Most studies in this tradition have used correlational designs, in which people who achieve leadership positions (in naturally occurring or laboratory-created groups) are compared to people who do not. Researchers have measured a variety of personal characteristics that might predict leadership: physical features (e.g., height, gender), abilities (e.g., intelligence, task expertise), and personality traits (e.g., extraversion, need for achievement).

These studies have produced some interesting findings. For instance, people who emerge as leaders tend to be somewhat *taller* than nonleaders, at least among men (e.g., Stodgill, 1974). Does this surprise you? A more reassuring result is that leaders tend to be more capable or intelligent than nonleaders (e.g., Lord, DeVader, & Alliger, 1986).

There is also some evidence that these characteristics (height and intelligence) predict not only leader *emergence* but also leader *effectiveness*. Canadian social psychologist Stewart McCann (1992), who is at Cape Breton University in Sydney, Nova Scotia, conducted an archival analysis in which he calculated the correlations between several characteristics of past American presidents and their ratings of effectiveness by historians. Presidents who were tall and intelligent tended to receive higher ratings of effectiveness than did shorter and less intelligent presidents (see also Simonton, 1987). The result for intelligence makes sense, but what processes might explain the effect of height on presidential greatness? One possibility is that tall people are more physically intimidating and therefore more likely to influence others successfully. Another possibility is that a height stereotype exists, such that tall individuals are viewed as more talented or more forceful than short individuals, and this stereotype results in tall individuals having more influence.

Gender and Leadership. Leaders are also more likely to be male than female. Alice Eagly of Northwestern University and Steven Karau of Southern Illinois University (1991) examined a total of 110 comparisons of men and women in groups that were initially leaderless but that required members to rate the leadership abilities of each other or to elect a leader. Men received higher ratings or were elected as leader in 74 of the 110 comparisons (67%). A small number (15) of the comparisons involved ratings of *social* leadership skills, such as empathy or likeability; in these comparisons, women almost always received higher ratings than men (87%). Eagly and Karau suggested that men are more likely to emerge as the task leader of a group, whereas women are more likely to emerge as the socioemotional leader of a group.

Why do these gender differences occur? Why are men more likely to emerge as task leaders—which is probably the most common type of leader—than women? Eagly and Karau (1991, 2002) speculated that the findings reflected the operation of gender stereotypes, which characterize men as *agentic* (e.g., assertive, controlling) and women as *communal* (e.g., sympathetic, helpful). Perhaps men are more likely to *seek* positions as task leaders than are women because the positions are consistent with their gender role; or perhaps group members are more likely to *select* men than women as task leaders because they think that men will be more skilled or more comfortable in the role. Or perhaps both of these processes contribute.

Gender also influences the perceived effectiveness of leaders. Alice Eagly, Steven Karau, and Mona Makhijani (1995) reviewed prior studies that compared the effectiveness of male versus female leaders. Measures of *effectiveness* in these studies included group productivity, members' ratings of the leader's effectiveness, and frequency counts of "effective leader behaviours" by trained judges (usually scored from videotapes of the group). When the results of all studies were

When the leader's role in a group calls for such things as directing and controlling members, a female leader may be evaluated more negatively than a male leader.

combined, leaders performed better when the role demands of the leadership position matched their gender. That is, men tended to perform better (had more productive groups, were rated as a more effective leader, etc.) than women when the leader's role called for traditionally masculine strengths (e.g., it required the ability to direct and control people), whereas the reverse direction tended to occur when the leader's role called for traditionally feminine strengths (e.g., it required the ability to cooperate and get along with other people). This pattern is consistent with the finding mentioned previously that men are more likely to be chosen as task leaders, whereas women are more likely to be chosen as socioemotional leaders. Again, given that positions requiring task leadership are probably more common than positions requiring socioemotional leadership, these biases in evaluations favour men in most cases (see also Eagly & Karau, 2002; Ridgeway, 2001; Sczesny & Kuhnen, 2004).

We have noted that leaders are evaluated more favourably when their role demands match their gender; it may not be surprising, therefore, that men and women adopt different styles when they do become leaders (Carli, 2001; Rudman & Glick, 2001). Alice Eagly and Blair Johnson, who is at the University of Connecticut, concluded on the basis of a literature review that men are more likely than women to adopt a controlling, autocratic leadership style, whereas women are more likely than men to adopt an open, democratic leadership style (Eagly & Johnson, 1990). The autocratic style chosen by men fits the stereotype that men are dominant and controlling, and the democratic style chosen by women fits the stereotype that women are nurturant and cooperative (see Atwater, Carey, & Waldman, 2001; Eagly, Makhijani, & Klonsky, 1992; Foels, Driskell, Mullen, & Salas, 2000; Rudman & Kilianski, 2000).

Personality and Leadership. Researchers have also identified a number of personality dimensions that are associated with emerging as the leader of a group. The University of Florida's Timothy Judge and his colleagues (Judge, Bono, Ilies, & Gerhardt, 2002) reviewed more than 70 studies that had investigated personality predictors of leader *emergence*. Across this large set of studies, the researchers found that people who become leaders tend to be more *extraverted* (outgoing), more *conscientious* (reliable), and more *open to new experiences* (flexible) than those who do not become leaders. Judge and his colleagues also identified about 15 studies that specifically assessed leadership *effectiveness* and found that the same dimensions (extraversion, conscientiousness, and openness) predicted effectiveness significantly across the set of studies.

An illustrative study was conducted by the University of Western Ontario's Lorne Campbell and his colleagues (Campbell, Simpson, Stewart, & Manning, 2003). In this study, four-person all-male groups of students were asked to discuss how teaching at their university could be made more effective. These students had previously completed several personality measures. Some groups were observed by either an attractive female evaluator or an attractive male evaluator, whose task was ostensibly to observe and rate participants' performance at the discussion task; other groups had no evaluator present during the discussion. After the task was completed, all participants rated one another's leadership skills. Results showed that extraverts were rated as possessing more leadership skills than introverts, but this pattern occurred only when the groups were observed by a woman. The researchers speculated that extraverts are more motivated than introverts to make a favourable impression in situations where status hierarchies are salient—such as when an attractive woman is observing them in an all-male group.

In Know Yourself 10.1: "Extraversion, Conscientiousness, and Openness," we reproduce a very brief measure of these three dimensions (Gosling, Rentfrow, & Swann, 2003). Each of the dimensions has been shown to relate to leadership, but even as a package, they explain only a part of why people become leaders. See how you would answer the items.

In another interesting investigation of personality and leadership, Richard Sorrentino and Nigel Field (1986) of the University of Western Ontario tested whether the variables of achievement motivation and affiliation motivation were related to leadership. *Achievement motivation* reflects the extent to which people are attracted to, rather than frightened by, performance settings. People who are high in achievement motivation enjoy performance tasks and thrive on challenges, whereas people who are low in achievement motivation avoid performance settings and tend to choke in challenging situations. *Affiliation motivation* reflects the extent to which people approach or avoid *social* settings. People who are high in affiliation motivation are comfortable in social settings and seek them out, whereas people who are low in affiliation motivation are uncomfortable in social settings and try to avoid them.

How might these dimensions predict who will emerge as a leader? Sorrentino and Field hypothesized that high levels of achievement motivation and high levels of affiliation motivation would both be associated with becoming a leader because leaders should want to perform well and should enjoy interacting with others. To test these hypotheses, introductory psychology students completed measures of achievement and affiliation motivation early in a school term. Based on students' scores, the researchers constructed 12 groups of four members each: one member was high in both achievement and affiliation motivation, one member was low in both motivations, one member was high in achievement but low in affiliation motivation, and one member was high in affiliation but low in achievement motivation. Each group came into the lab on five separate occasions. At each session, the group worked for between one and two hours on an involving, complex problem-solving task. For instance, at one session, group members had to rank-order a list of materials in terms of their importance for survival in the Arctic. At another session, group members had to try to break a computer code. After the final problem-solving task in the fifth session, group members rated one another on a variety of leadership skills and nominated two members as leaders of the group.

Know Yourself 10.1
Extraversion, Conscientiousness, and Openness

Here are a number of personality traits that may or may not apply to you. Please circle a number on each scale to indicate the extent to which you see yourself in that way.

1. I see myself as extraverted.

1	2	3	4	5	6	7
Disagree strongly	Disagree moderately	Disagree a little	Neither agree nor disagree	Agree a little	Agree moderately	Agree strongly

2. I see myself as dependable.

1	2	3	4	5	6	7
Disagree strongly	Disagree moderately	Disagree a little	Neither agree nor disagree	Agree a little	Agree moderately	Agree strongly

3. I see myself as open to new experiences.

1	2	3	4	5	6	7
Disagree strongly	Disagree moderately	Disagree a little	Neither agree nor disagree	Agree a little	Agree moderately	Agree strongly

4. I see myself as reserved.

1	2	3	4	5	6	7
Disagree strongly	Disagree moderately	Disagree a little	Neither agree nor disagree	Agree a little	Agree moderately	Agree strongly

5. I see myself as disorganized.

1	2	3	4	5	6	7
Disagree strongly	Disagree moderately	Disagree a little	Neither agree nor disagree	Agree a little	Agree moderately	Agree strongly

6. I see myself as conventional.

1	2	3	4	5	6	7
Disagree strongly	Disagree moderately	Disagree a little	Neither agree nor disagree	Agree a little	Agree moderately	Agree strongly

7. I see myself as enthusiastic.

1	2	3	4	5	6	7
Disagree strongly	Disagree moderately	Disagree a little	Neither agree nor disagree	Agree a little	Agree moderately	Agree strongly

8. I see myself as self-disciplined.

1	2	3	4	5	6	7
Disagree strongly	Disagree moderately	Disagree a little	Neither agree nor disagree	Agree a little	Agree moderately	Agree strongly

9. I see myself as complex.

1	2	3	4	5	6	7
Disagree strongly	Disagree moderately	Disagree a little	Neither agree nor disagree	Agree a little	Agree moderately	Agree strongly

10. I see myself as quiet.

1	2	3	4	5	6	7
Disagree strongly	Disagree moderately	Disagree a little	Neither agree nor disagree	Agree a little	Agree moderately	Agree strongly

(*Continued on next page*)

11. I see myself as careless.

1	2	3	4	5	6	7
Disagree strongly	Disagree moderately	Disagree a little	Neither agree nor disagree	Agree a little	Agree moderately	Agree strongly

12. I see myself as uncreative.

1	2	3	4	5	6	7
Disagree strongly	Disagree moderately	Disagree a little	Neither agree nor disagree	Agree a little	Agree moderately	Agree strongly

SCORING:

1. *Extraversion:* Items 1 and 7 are scored using the answer scales as presented (1-2-3-4-5-6-7); Items 4 and 10 are reverse-scored (that is, 7-6-5-4-3-2-1). Add up your score on all four items for your total extraversion score. Possible scores range from 4 to 28, and higher scores reflect greater extraversion.

2. *Conscientiousness:* Items 2 and 8 are scored using the answer scales as presented; Items 5 and 11 are reverse-scored. Add up your score on all four items for your total conscientiousness score. Possible scores range from 4 to 28, and higher scores reflect greater conscientiousness.

3. *Openness to new experiences:* Items 3 and 9 are scored using the answer scales as presented; Items 6 and 12 are reverse-scored. Add up your score on all four items for your total openness score. Possible scores range from 4 to 28, and higher scores reflect greater openness to new experiences.

From Gosling et al., " A very brief measure of the Big-Five personality domains," *Journal of Research in Personality*, 37, 504–528, 2003. Reprinted by permission of Elsevier.

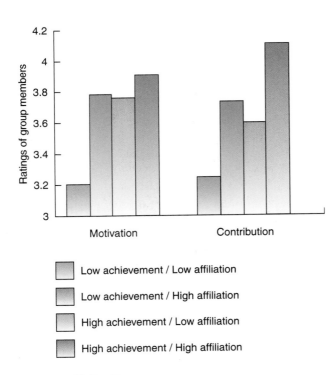

FIGURE 10.6 Ratings of motivation and contribution of group members

From Sorrentino and Field, "Emergent leadership over time: The functional value of positive motivation," *Journal of Personality and Social Psychology*, 50, 1091–1099, Table 1, p. 1094, 1986. Copyright © 1986 by the American Psychological Association. Reprinted by permission.

Figure 10.6 presents the mean ratings received by each personality type on two leadership dimensions: how motivated they were to help the group reach its goal, and how much they contributed to attaining the group's goal. The figure shows that participants who were high in both achievement and affiliation motivation tended to receive the highest ratings, and participants who were low in both achievement and affiliation motivation tended to receive the lowest ratings. Participants' nominations for leaders were also informative: the individual who was high in both achievement and affiliation motivation was nominated as one of the two leaders by 34 of the 36 other participants. Thus, the high-high person was almost always seen as a leader by the other members of the group.

Talent or Talk? What do you think are the implications of the findings we have described so far for the importance of *talent* in leadership emergence? Do people who emerge as leaders deserve to do so because of relevant skills and knowledge, or do leaders instead emerge on the basis of characteristics that shouldn't matter? Some of the findings seem to support a talent interpretation (e.g., intelligence, achievement motivation, affiliation motivation), whereas others suggest that irrelevant factors play a role (e.g., height, gender).

One specific aspect of this talent question has been investigated directly in some clever research by social psychologists. The issue involves the relative importance of the *quality* versus the *quantity* of contributions to a group. Does it matter for leadership emergence whether someone makes good rather than poor suggestions? You have probably been in a group in which one individual dominated the conversation but rarely said anything helpful. These sorts of people don't become leaders, do they? Surely the quality of contributions is more important than the quantity?

Maybe not. In a classic study conducted in London, Ontario, Richard Sorrentino and Robert Boutillier (1975) directly investigated the importance of quality and quantity of contributions to a group. Their research is noteworthy because it was an *experimental* test of a factor that might affect leader emergence. All of the studies we have described to this point have involved *measuring* existing traits—a correlational approach; Sorrentino and Boutillier *manipulated* the quality and quantity of individuals' contributions to a group.

Male students at the University of Western Ontario came to the laboratory in groups of three, together with a fourth male who was actually a confederate of the experimenter. Participants were taken to separate rooms and told that they would perform a problem-solving task as a group; the rooms had audio connections that allowed participants to speak to one another. The goal of the group was to maximize the number of points they earned on a task. Each trial of the task required the group to select one response from among several alternatives; based on information they had been given, as well as the payoffs on preceding trials, it was possible for the group to decode a pattern that could guide their choices.

The confederate followed a script that varied his contributions to fit one of four patterns. The *high-quality* scripts involved offering the correct answer on 11 of the 15 trials and the incorrect answer on 4 trials; the *low-quality* scripts involved offering 4 correct and 11 incorrect answers on the 15 trials. The *high-quantity* scripts involved many comments in addition to the offered answers; the *low-quantity* scripts involved very few comments in addition to the offered answers. The entire session lasted approximately one hour.

After completion of all 15 trials, participants rated one another's leadership abilities. Figure 10.7 presents the mean rating in each condition of the confederate's overall leadership skills (combining separate ratings of his task and socioemotional leadership skills). The figure shows that the *number* of the confederate's comments had a large impact on ratings of his leadership skills (the two right-hand bars are higher than the two left-hand bars), whereas the *correctness* of the confederate's comments had less impact. Statistical analyses revealed a significant effect of the quantity manipulation but no effect of the quality manipulation. In terms of perceived leadership ability, it appeared to matter *how much* the confederate talked, rather than the *quality* of what he said.

Were participants in this study illogical or deficient in their evaluations? The authors speculated that the findings may not be absurd at all. Perhaps people who participate a lot in group discussions are seen as being highly *motivated* to belong to the group. Even if their contributions are not always stellar, these individuals are seen as trying their best. Such motivation is believed to be necessary to lead a group. In contrast, individuals who speak infrequently, even if their comments are almost always good ones, are seen as low in motivation to belong to the group— they are not exerting a lot of effort on behalf of the group. Such individuals are not regarded as appropriate leaders (see also Anderson, John, Keltner, & Kring, 2001; Mullen, Salas, & Driskell, 1989). Thus, relying on quantity of participation as a basis for judgments of leadership potential may be at least somewhat rational.

So what should we conclude about the trait approach to leadership? For example, do these findings help us to understand Pierre Trudeau's effectiveness as a leader? Did he possess characteristics identified in social psychological research? The answer is that he probably did possess a rare combination of qualities. There is no doubt that he was highly intelligent. He was also friendly and extraverted, with strong social skills. Although we cannot know for sure, he was probably high in both achievement motivation and affiliation motivation. His personal charisma undoubtedly contributed to his effectiveness as a leader.

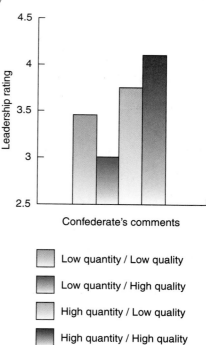

FIGURE 10.7 Ratings of leadership ability of confederate

From Sorrentino and Boutillier, "The effect of quantity and quality of verbal interaction on rating of leadership ability," *Journal of Experimental Social Psychology*, 11, 403–411, Table 1, p. 408, 1975. Reprinted by permission of Elsevier.

Being in the Right Place at the Right Time: Situational Approaches to Leadership

We have described evidence showing that certain characteristics increase the likelihood that an individual will emerge as the leader of a group. It is important, however, to avoid overstating this point with regard to everyday groups. In fact, most people are perfectly capable of serving as the leader of small groups—and most of us *are* the leader of one or more groups in our lives (family, friends, clubs, work groups, committees, etc.). Leaders of most groups do not need great oratorical skills or exceptional ambition; they simply need the commitment to do the necessary work and the goodwill of other members in the group. From this admittedly unromantic perspective, it becomes clear that leadership can be mundane or routine.

Indeed, it can sometimes be difficult to find *anyone* to serve as the leader of a group. For instance, university clubs often have subcommittees that are given specific responsibilities, such as organizing social events, maintaining membership lists, or advertising the club's events. Finding people who are willing to lead (chair) these subcommittees can be difficult; there tend to be a lot of lowered heads and averted gazes when the president of the club calls for volunteers on election night.

Emerging as leader, then, sometimes reflects being in the right place at the right time (or, depending on one's perspective, being in the wrong place at the wrong time). Traits and skills may be largely irrelevant—it was the leader's turn, or the leader was the only one willing to take on the position, or the leader happened to walk into the room exactly when the group was searching for a nominee! This perspective is known as the **situational approach to leadership:** external, situational factors can influence the selection of the leader.

What are some of these situational factors that affect leadership emergence? Believe it or not, one factor can be the seating arrangements at an initial group meeting. In a classic study (Howells & Becker, 1962), participants were required to work together in groups of five on several tasks at a rectangular table, with two individuals on one side and three individuals on the other side of the table. When later asked to identify the leader of the group, participants were significantly more likely to select someone on the two-person side than on the three-person side. Why? The authors suggested that communication tends to go back and forth across a table; thus, participants on the two-person side would be directing comments to more people (three rather than two), which would facilitate the perception that they were the leader.

Another situational factor that can affect leadership emergence is external threat. When a group perceives external threat, its members look for strong leadership to deal with the threat. The anxiety aroused by the threat motivates members to find an authority figure to guide them through the problem. For example, after the attacks of September 11, 2001, many Americans rallied around U.S. president George W. Bush and supported his decisions to initiate wars in Afghanistan and Iraq. Support for these military operations declined, however, as the casualties mounted, the weapons of mass destruction remained undiscovered, and the original terrorism faded in memory. As in this case, some members of a group may come to regret their enthusiastic endorsement of an extreme response to a threatening situation.

As a final example of the situational approach to leadership, consider the role of seniority in many organizations. People who have belonged to groups the longest are often seen as the ones who should serve as leaders, irrespective of their standing on relevant skills like intelligence or motivation. Seniority frequently seems to be the "default" basis for selecting leaders. Thus, when a group has a lot of turnover, the probability increases that a particular individual will eventually serve as leader. The University of North Carolina's Chet Insko and his colleagues (Insko et al., 1980) conducted an interesting study that explored the role of seniority. Participants in the study were assigned to four-person groups that worked on making simple products

situational approach to leadership

the perspective that external, situational factors, such as seating arrangements, can influence who will become leader of a group

External threats often prompt people to support their leaders.

(folding paper into particular shapes). Over the course of five hours, members were removed from groups and replaced with a new member. This renewal continued for a total of nine "generations." Almost without exception, groups developed a seniority rule for assuming the role of leader: the longest-serving group member became leader when the current leader was removed from the group. Why was seniority used to select leaders? The authors argued that this rule made sense for several reasons. First, more senior members were more experienced in making the product; second, newer members tended to be unfamiliar to other members and therefore seemed risky as choices for leader; and third, seniority was unambiguous and provided a simple rule for the orderly succession of leadership. These points may often apply to real-life groups as well, so perhaps it makes sense that groups rely, at least in part, on seniority in selecting leaders.

Person and Situation: Interactionist Approaches to Leadership

Social psychologists usually take an integrative approach to understanding social behaviour: dispositions and situational factors combine to influence actions (e.g., see the section entitled "Interactions Between Persons and Situations" in Chapter 5, pages 174–180). In the current context, the **interactionist approach to leadership** predicts that certain kinds of people are likely to emerge as leaders (or to be effective leaders) under one set of conditions, whereas other kinds of people are likely to emerge as leaders (or to be effective leaders) under a different set of conditions. Many individuals can become leaders (or can be effective leaders) if the appropriate situational factors are present.

The best-known interactionist approach to leadership is Fred Fiedler's (1967, 1978) **contingency model of leadership effectiveness.** Although the details of this theory have been only partially supported, it remains a useful way of viewing the topic of leadership. Fiedler selected the name *contingency model* because the theory assumes that the effectiveness of a particular style of leadership is *contingent* (depends) on situational factors.

Fiedler distinguished between two major categories of leadership styles: task-oriented leaders and relationship-oriented leaders (these styles correspond quite closely to our earlier distinction between *task leader* and *socioemotional leader*). Task-oriented leaders are primarily concerned with the performance and success of their group; they want group members to be productive. Relationship-oriented leaders, on the other hand, are primarily concerned with interpersonal relationships and morale in the group; they want group members to be happy.

The way that Fiedler proposed measuring this leadership style is interesting. His technique involves asking respondents to think of their *least-preferred co-worker*—that is, the person whom they *disliked* working with the most in all of their work experiences. Respondents are then asked to rate this incompetent or disagreeable co-worker on a number of personality dimensions. Of course, most people rate this person quite negatively, but some rate him or her *more* negatively than do others. Fiedler assumed that those individuals who give extremely negative ratings to their least-preferred co-worker are task-oriented because they cannot see anything positive in a person who was difficult to work with. In contrast, he assumed that those individuals who give less negative ratings to their least-preferred co-worker are relationship-oriented because they seem to find even this disagreeable person tolerable (they must like everybody!).

The key aspect of Fiedler's model is the prediction that task-oriented leaders will be more effective than relationship-oriented leaders in some situations, whereas the reverse will be true in other situations. When the group situation is *favourable* for the leader (e.g., the leader has a lot of power and group members

interactionist approach to leadership

the perspective that certain kinds of people are likely to emerge as leaders (or to be effective leaders) under one set of conditions, whereas other kinds of people are likely to emerge as leaders (or to be effective leaders) under a different set of conditions

contingency model of leadership effectiveness

a theory that predicts that task-oriented leaders will be more successful than relationship-oriented leaders in groups where the situation is either very favourable or very unfavourable for the leader, whereas relationship-oriented leaders will be more successful than task-oriented leaders in groups where the situation is mixed for the leader like the leader), Fielder predicted that task-oriented leaders will do better because they continue to push group members even when things are going well, whereas relationship-oriented leaders tend to relax in this situation. When the group situation is *mixed* for the leader (e.g., the leader has little power but group members like the leader), relationship-oriented leaders are hypothesized to do better because they are more skillful at maintaining the morale and motivation of group members in this mixed situation. Finally, when the group situation is *unfavourable* for the leader (e.g., the leader has little power and group members dislike the leader), task-oriented leaders are once again hypothesized to do better because they keep trying to push group members even under terrible circumstances, whereas relationship-oriented leaders tend to withdraw or give up when they are disliked and have no power.

Researchers have tested the contingency model of leadership effectiveness by creating groups in the laboratory that possess either favourable, mixed, or unfavourable conditions for the leader (for reviews of such studies, see Chemers, 2000; Northouse, 1997; Peters, Hartke, & Pohlmann, 1985; Strube & Garcia, 1981). For instance, some leaders are given substantial power to control the members' rewards and punishments, whereas other leaders have little power to influence members' outcomes. Groups are assigned either a task-oriented or a relationship-oriented leader (based on the leader's ratings of his or her least-preferred co-worker). These studies have provided some support for the predictions outlined above, but the results have been inconsistent. For example, a study may confirm one or two predictions from the theory but fail to support another. The amount of research on Fiedler's model has gradually declined in the face of these weakly supportive data.

If we focus on the interactionist approach to leadership more generally, rather than Fiedler's specific theory, the conclusion that different styles of leadership are more effective in different conditions seems justifiable (see Chemers, 2000; Peterson, 1997; Van Vugt, Jepson, Hart, & De Cremer, 2004). Unfortunately, broad models that can integrate all of the findings are not yet available. Nevertheless, the interactionist perspective is a good place for us to conclude our consideration of leadership, because it makes the point that, given the appropriate situation, most of us can be effective leaders. Although many of the great leaders in history probably possessed rare combinations of characteristics like exceptional intelligence, charisma, and ambition, the average individual can do just fine in many everyday groups. The three general approaches to leadership are summarized in the accompanying Concept Review.

CONCEPT REVIEW
Approaches to Leadership

Approach	Description	Examples of Variables
Trait approach	Goal is to identify the personal characteristics that predict being chosen a leader or being a successful leader	Height, intelligence, extraversion
Situational approach	Goal is to identify external, situational factors that influence being chosen a leader	Seating position, external threat, seniority
Interactionist approach	Goal is to understand how dispositional and situational factors combine to influence who is chosen a leader or who makes an effective leader	Contingency model, task-oriented vs. relationship-oriented leaders

Intergroup Relations

To this point, we have presented individual-level and *intra*group-level analyses—that is, we have discussed psychological processes that occur *within* a particular person or group (and affect performance, decision making, and leadership). It is also important, however, to understand how different groups relate to one another—*inter*group processes. The significance of intergroup relations is perhaps most obvious in the international sphere, where issues of war and peace apply. But everyday life also involves many intergroup perceptions and interactions; for instance, all of us have stereotypes of various ethnic, occupational, and gender groups, and all of us interact with people who belong to social and demographic groups different from our own. In the following paragraphs, we discuss some social psychological research that has explored intergroup relations (see also Brewer & Brown, 1998; Deutsch & Coleman, 2000; Taylor & Moghaddam, 1994; Worchel & Austin, 1986). We begin by discussing the intergroup process of *acculturation*, which refers to how two or more cultural groups adjust and change as a result of contact with one another. Because of the special significance of *negative* relations between groups, we then turn to intergroup *conflict*. We separately discuss factors that *escalate* conflict and factors that *reduce* conflict.

Acculturation

As we noted in our discussion of prejudice reduction in Chapter 9, Canada has pursued a *multiculturalism* policy with regards to ethnic diversity. That is, federal and provincial governments have tried to encourage ethnic and cultural groups within Canada to maintain their own identities while simultaneously respecting all other groups. This policy contrasts with the dominant perspective in the United States, where the *melting pot* analogy reflects the goal of assimilating all ethnic groups into one American identity. In both countries (and elsewhere around the globe), the process of acculturation occurs when different cultural groups interact.

Acculturation has been defined by Queen's University's John Berry (2005) as the "process of cultural and psychological change that takes place as a result of contact between two or more cultural groups and their individual members" (p. 698). Acculturation occurs at the group level, such as when ethnic groups change their traditions to better fit a new environment, and at the individual level, such as when individuals from a minority cultural group internalize values of the dominant cultural group into their personal identities.

Canadian social psychologists have been at the forefront of research on acculturation and have investigated the experiences of many different ethnic groups in Canada. For example, Richard Clément at the University of Ottawa and Kimberly Noels at the University of Alberta have studied the acculturation of Anglophones and Francophones living in predominantly French and predominantly English contexts, respectively (e.g., Clément, Michaud, & Noels, 1998; Clément, Noels, & Deneault, 2001; Noels, Pon, & Clément, 1996). The University of Guelph's Saba Safdar and York University's Clarry Lay have studied Iranian immigrants to southwestern Ontario (e.g., Safdar & Lay, 2003; Safdar, Lay, & Struthers, 2003).

Theoretical models of acculturation have distinguished between four different goals that can be pursued by cultural groups who are in contact with one another (e.g., Berry, 1997, 2005; Clément & Noels, 1992). *Integration* refers to the goal of identifying with one's own cultural group and also with the alternative culture(s). For example, Chinese immigrants to Toronto might remain connected to their Chinese heritage and also develop a new Canadian identity. *Separation* refers to the goal of identifying only with one's own cultural group and not at all with the alternative

acculturation

the process of cultural and psychological change that takes place as a result of contact between two or more cultural groups and their individual members culture(s). In this instance, those same Chinese immigrants might choose to retain their Chinese identity and resist adopting any new Canadian customs or values. *Assimilation* refers to the goal of identifying only with the alternative culture(s) and rejecting one's own cultural group. This would then mean that the Chinese immigrants might reject their Chinese identity and internalize a new, Canadian identity instead. Finally, *marginalization* is not really a goal, but refers to the situation where individuals lose their own identity but do not feel connected to the alternative culture(s). The Chinese immigrants might feel disconnected from their Chinese heritage but not identify with their new Canadian culture either.

A policy of multiculturalism (as in Canada) aims to create *integration* of immigrant groups, whereas a melting pot policy (as in the United States) aims to create *assimilation* among immigrant groups. Although both goals have positive features, John Berry (1997) has argued that immigrant groups are most likely to adapt effectively to a new environment when they strive for integration. Integration allows immigrants to retain familiar customs, language, and social networks while simultaneously establishing connections to the new cultural context.

An excellent example of Canadian research on the acculturation process was conducted recently by Safdar, Lay, and Struthers (2003). These researchers interviewed 166 Iranian immigrants to southwestern Ontario. The average age of the respondents was 34, and they had been in Canada for an average of seven years. The goal of the research was to investigate factors that were associated with three outcomes: maintaining their Iranian culture, having contact with the new Canadian culture, and health (both physical and psychological). The researchers measured many possible predictors of these outcomes, including respondents' self-esteem, perceived linguistic competence in English, social support, strength of Iranian identity, and frequency of stressful life events.

Results showed that respondents were more likely to maintain their Iranian culture when they identified strongly with their ethnic heritage and when they had close connections to their family. Respondents had greater contact with the new Canadian culture when they had good skills in English and when they had Canadian friends who supported them. Respondents reported better health when they had a low frequency of stressful life events and high levels of self-esteem and perceived control. This study demonstrates that the extent to which immigrants adapt effectively to their new country depends on both personal characteristics (e.g., self-esteem, ethnic identification) and external characteristics (e.g., stressful events, social support). Further research on acculturation is important if we want to help immigrant groups thrive within our multicultural society.

Development and Escalation of Intergroup Conflict

Several points that we made in earlier chapters suggest that relations between groups can often become strained, resulting in intergroup conflict. For example, we have noted previously that memberships in groups constitute an important part of people's identities (Ashmore, Deaux, & McLaughlin-Volpe, 2004). If you were asked to describe yourself, some of your answers would probably involve groups, such as "I am a Polish Canadian," "I am a student at the University of Saskatchewan," or "I am a psychology major." Recall from Chapters 5 and 9 our discussions of *social identity theory* (see pages 158 and 341). This theory (Tajfel, 1970, 1978) postulates that we want to maintain a positive identity, including a positive view of the groups to which we belong. To achieve this positive social identity, we sometimes belittle members of outgroups and/or give preferential treatment to members of our ingroups. For instance, we might express negative comments about students at other universities, or we might vote for another psychology major in an election for student government. These actions sometimes reflect an active attempt to make our own groups seem better than other groups. People who identify strongly with an ingroup are especially likely to want to heighten the status of that group relative to other groups (e.g., Stürmer & Simon, 2004; Van Vugt & Hart, 2004).

In a similar vein, the University of Western Ontario's Bertram Gawronski and his colleagues (Gawronski, Bodenhausen, & Banse, 2005) have argued that people naturally try to differentiate between their ingroup and various outgroups, which can lead them to assume that outgroups possess the opposite characteristics from those of the ingroup. Given that the ingroup is usually viewed positively, this differentiation process can lead to negative views of outgroups. Of course, negative views can engender mistrust, hostility, and discrimination between groups. In other words, they can elicit prejudice and intergroup conflict.

Another relevant concept was introduced in Chapter 3, "Social Cognition." In our discussion of stereotypes, we noted that people tend to see members of a group as similar to one another (to see them as a relatively uniform group). Individuals exhibit this tendency toward perceiving group uniformity even for groups to which they belong (ingroups), but the effect tends to be stronger in perceptions of outgroups ("They're all alike!"). The exaggeration of similarity within outgroups is called the *outgroup homogeneity effect,* as we noted in Chapter 3 (see page 74).

A final aspect of intergroup situations that increases the likelihood of conflict can be illustrated with a thought experiment. Imagine that you are playing a game of chess or checkers with another student. How competitive would you be? Now imagine that the student you are playing attends another university and is wearing a sweatshirt from the school. How competitive would you be in this case? If you think that you might be more competitive in the second situation, where group identities are emphasized, than in the first situation, where only individual identities are clear, your intuition matches the results of social psychological research.

Chester Insko, John Schopler, and their colleagues at the University of North Carolina (e.g., Insko, Thibaut, Moehle, Wilson, Diamond, Gilmore, et al., 1990; Schopler, Insko, Graetz, Drigotas, Smith, & Dahl, 1993) conducted numerous experiments in which participants played games against other participants. Sometimes the players were on their own, playing as an individual against another individual. Other participants played on behalf of a group, representing a three-person team that had been randomly formed at the beginning of the session. Participants played games in which they could employ either a strategy of cooperation or a strategy of competition. When participants represented a group, they were significantly more competitive and less cooperative than when they played as individuals. Thus, when a situation was perceived as involving intergroup behaviour, it elicited greater competitiveness than when it involved only interpersonal behaviour (for a review, see Wildschut, Pinter, Vevea, Insko, & Schopler, 2003). The researchers argued that intergroup situations elicit greater greed and greater fear of being exploited than do interpersonal situations (see also Winquist & Larson, 2004).

The factors we have discussed (social identity theory, differentiation, negative stereotypes about outgroups, the outgroup homogeneity effect, and the tendency for intergroup situations to elicit competition) suggest that intergroup contexts may be predisposed to degenerate into conflict. Conflict is not inevitable, of course, but it may often occur. Next, we consider three factors that can escalate a minor conflict into a major one: threats, self-presentation goals, and dehumanization.

Courtesy of James Olson

When intergroup identities are obvious, people tend to be more competitive.

Threats. Can you think of a recent occasion when you used a threat to try to influence another person? Perhaps you threatened a roommate by saying that you would move out of the apartment if she didn't start keeping the kitchen and bathroom clean. Or perhaps, as a babysitter, you threatened a child by saying that you would tell his parents that he had been bad if he did not go to bed immediately. Or perhaps you threatened an acquaintance that you'd "get" him somehow if he didn't stop spreading a rumour about you.

Almost all of us use threats occasionally. How effective are threats at inducing compliance? Do they have any "side effects"? Let's consider this issue by looking at the opposite side of the coin: Can you think of times when you were threatened by someone who wanted to influence you? Perhaps your parents threatened to ground you if you disobeyed them in some way. Perhaps a friend threatened to drive off without you if you did not arrive at her apartment on time. Perhaps a supervisor threatened to fire you if you did not perform better. How did these threats make you feel? Were they effective at influencing your behaviour?

When people think about being the *target* of a threat, they almost always recognize the problems with using threats to influence behaviour. Most of us feel very angry when others threaten us, even if we understand why they are doing so. We feel like they are taking away our freedom to make up our own mind, or they are acting as if they control us. In fact, threats often make us want to do exactly the *opposite* of what the other person is telling us to do, so he or she won't threaten us again in the future. But even if the threat is severe enough to make us change our behaviour, it leaves us feeling unhappy and upset. Threats can leave seeds of discontent and smouldering anger. None of us likes to be controlled by threats.

Despite the strong intuition that it is unproductive for other people to threaten us, we are much less likely to recognize that our own use of threats against others may be equally harmful (see Kemmelmeier & Winter, 2000). Think again about a time that you threatened another person. Didn't it seem obvious to you that the threat was necessary and justified, even fair? Anyone else would have done the same thing. The other person should have understood this point, right? In reality, however, most people respond to our threats in exactly the same way we respond to others' threats—badly.

There have been some fascinating studies in social psychology documenting the destructive effects of threats. Using threats can escalate a conflict between individuals or groups. In one of the earliest studies of threat, Morton Deutsch and Robert Krauss (1960) assigned participants to play the roles of managers of competing trucking companies. Their job was to move trucks back and forth from one location to another on a game map as quickly as possible; the more trips they made, the more profit they would reap. Both companies had a possible shortcut that would increase their profits, but there was a problem: the shortcut included a *one-lane* section. In this one-lane section, trucks could not pass one another, so if two trucks from the competing companies met, they would be stuck unless one backed up to allow the other to pass. If the companies cooperated, however, they could take turns using the shortcut and increase both companies' profits.

The crucial manipulation in the study was that Deutsch and Krauss gave some participants a "threat" that they could use. Specifically, some participants were given a gate they could place on the one-way section that would stop all trucks from using the road. Players could use this gate as a threat to try to force the other company to obey commands. Sometimes neither company had a gate, sometimes only one company had a gate (the *unilateral threat condition*), and sometimes both companies had a gate (the *bilateral threat condition*).

How did the presence of threats influence outcomes? Companies made significantly *less* money when one company had a gate (the unilateral threat condition) than when there were no gates. Further, companies made even *less* money when both companies had a gate (the bilateral threat condition) than when only one company had a gate. Thus, gates reduced companies' profits, and the more gates there were, the less profit was earned. The presence of threats somehow changed the dynamics of the game, such that cooperation was less likely, and profits were therefore reduced.

These findings are not surprising when we think again about how we feel when someone else threatens us. Threats make us angry, and anger rarely encourages cooperation. So when threats are used in a conflict, the two parties generally stop communicating and try to intimidate one another instead of finding a constructive solution.

What are the practical implications of these findings? In the context of international relations, they suggest that the use of threats by one country toward another (e.g., the threat of invasion, or the threat of nuclear weapons) may escalate hostility and conflict. Although threats may effectively influence behaviour (e.g., a country may conform to demands in the face of a nuclear threat), they may also heighten negative feelings and perceptions.

The use of threats heightens hostility and conflict

Thus, if it is possible to exert influence without threats, such a strategy seems preferable in most cases. Similarly, governing political parties, such as the Conservative or Liberal parties of Canada, should not threaten other parties in the House of Commons if cooperation will be needed on subsequent pieces of legislation. Threats may elicit partisan shouting matches rather than constructive dialogue.

Self-Presentation Goals. Intergroup relations are influenced by self-presentation goals, just like interpersonal relations. You may recall from Chapter 4, "Social Perception," our discussion of how people try to control others' impressions of them. We focused in that discussion on two goals of self-presentation that are virtually always present in interpersonal settings: to appear likeable and to appear competent.

Appearing competent is probably also a goal in most intergroup situations, but appearing likeable to other groups is not necessarily seen as important. For example, two ethnic groups that are in conflict may not care whether the other group likes them. Instead, another self-presentation goal of many groups is to appear *powerful* or *strong*. The impression of strength is important because other groups will be more likely to follow a powerful group's recommendations. Indeed, the importance of appearing strong is one reason why threats tend to arouse resistance and resentment. Groups that have been threatened by another group do not want to appear weak. If a group timidly bows to the pressure of a threat from another group, it may be seen as easy to push around, which will encourage the other group (and anyone else who witnesses the timid submission) to use threats again in the future. This reasoning helps us to understand why groups sometimes behave in ways that seem counterproductive during a conflict. Groups are concerned about their "image" or "reputation" (see Brown, 1968).

Dehumanizing the Enemy. Threats and the desire to appear strong can escalate intergroup conflict, as we have noted. But these factors seem insufficient to account for many of the extreme historical cases of intergroup violence, such as genocide, which we discussed in Chapter 9 (see pages 357–359). As we noted in our earlier discussion, one of the prerequisites for extreme harm-doing seems to be a perception that the target group is subhuman or inferior to the perpetrating group (e.g., see Bar-Tal, 1990; Staub, 1989; Waller, 2002). This process of **dehumanization** allows people to inflict pain and suffering on members of the target group without worrying about the morality of their behaviour. By viewing the target group as subhuman, the perpetrating group may see the normal rules of justice and fairness as irrelevant (Opotow, 1994, 2001; Opotow & Weiss, 2000). Treatment of members of the target group can then be similar to the treatment of animals, who are not normally

dehumanization

the process of perceiving members of a group as subhuman or inferior to members of one's own group; it allows people to inflict pain and suffering on the group without worrying about the morality of their behaviour

In the 18th and 19th centuries, slavery was rationalized by some Whites through a process of *dehumanization*.

seen as possessing the same rights as humans. For instance, this perception characterized many White American plantation owners' views of Black slaves in the 1700s and 1800s. Blacks stolen violently from Africa were seen as very different from White Americans—as not having the same feelings and needs as Whites. Apparently, it did not occur to egotistical slaveholders that they were destroying personal and family lives with their actions.

Another perception that leads to detrimental behaviour is seeing a target group as evil or malevolent. Evil people *deserve* to be treated badly (see Hafer & Olson, 2003). Many historical cases of genocide were preceded by propaganda campaigns depicting the target group as treacherous, immoral, and corrupt. For example, Adolf Hitler blamed an evil "Jewish conspiracy" for many of Germany's problems in the 1930s. His paranoid speeches fed a pre-existing anti-Semitism among the German population. Hitler characterized the Jewish minority as untrustworthy and dangerous. His message that the Jews were villainous eventually persuaded the majority of Germans either to support or to passively tolerate his murderous campaign (Bar-On, 2001).

Cultural Differences in Conflict Escalation. There is some evidence that members of collectivistic cultures, such as China and Japan, approach situations of interpersonal and intergroup conflict with a more cooperative, open-minded attitude than do members of individualistic cultures, such as North America and Western Europe, which may reduce the likelihood of a conflict's escalating in collectivistic cultures. For example, Kimberly Wade-Benzoni and her colleagues (Wade-Benzoni, Okumura, Brett, Moore, Tenbrunsel, & Bazerman, 2002) found that Japanese participants were more likely to deal with a conflict by cooperating with other people in the dispute and by dividing resources equally among all claimants than were American participants. In a similar vein, Michele Gelfand and her colleagues (Gelfand, Higgins, Nishii, Raver, Dominguez, Murakami, et al., 2002) found that Japanese participants did not see their own behaviour in a dispute as fairer than the behaviour of other disputants, whereas American participants showed a strong tendency to consider their own behaviour in the conflict to be fairer than their opponents' actions. Perceiving one's own behaviour as fairer than one's opponents' actions is likely to escalate a situation of minor conflict into one of high conflict and mistrust. Thus, the individualistic perspective that is predominant in North America and Western Europe may increase the likelihood of severe intergroup conflict compared to the collectivistic perspective (see also Carnevale & Leung, 2001; Mayer, 2000).

terrorism

actual or threatened violence against civilians for alleged political purposes

Terrorism. Terrorism represents perhaps the ultimate escalation tactic in a conflict. **Terrorism** can be defined as actual or threatened violence against civilians for alleged political purposes (McCauley & Segal, 1987). It can take the form of a suicide car bomb in a marketplace, a random shooting spree at a train station, an airplane crashed into a skyscraper, or a variety of other murderous actions targeting innocent people.

One important observation about terrorism is that its psychological impact far exceeds its material or physical impact (see Silke, 2003b). Terrorist actions that kill only a handful of people and damage limited property can nevertheless receive worldwide media coverage, cause widespread fear, and stimulate hugely expensive government self-protection programs. The number of people killed by terrorism each year is dwarfed by the number of victims of road accidents, mishaps in the workplace, and various diseases. Yet terrorism probably causes more anxiety than any of these other threats.

Another point about terrorism is that it often reflects a desire to create fear and confusion, rather than to resolve an issue or conflict. Terrorists typically do not want to negotiate; their goal is often to bring anarchy to a society—the breakdown of social control. Further, terrorist organizations are highly secretive, so it is hard for authorities to communicate with them unless they have a political wing. These features of terrorism make it extremely difficult to control or eliminate.

So what can governments do to reduce the terrorist threat facing them? One response that is often taken is military action against the terrorists or supporters of the terrorists. For example, the war in Afghanistan can be seen as a response to the events of September 11, 2001. The long-term effectiveness of military responses to terrorism has been questioned, however, by some social scientists (e.g., see Plous & Zimbardo, 2004). Perhaps the major problem with military action is that civilians will almost inevitably be killed in addition to terrorists, and these deaths of noncombatants may reinforce impressions that the country battling terrorism is selfish and aggressive, making it easier for terrorists to recruit new members.

Improving vigilance and security within one's own country can offer some protection but does not address the underlying problem. International actions are also required. Scott Plous and Philip Zimbardo (2004) suggested that increasing foreign aid to countries that are working actively to fight terrorism might be effective. This approach makes terrorism more difficult to practise. A related strategy is to work for broad international consensus on issues of human rights, so alliances can be built that will cooperate in the long-term battle against terrorism.

Fathali Moghaddam (2005) argued that, in the long run, the only way to combat terrorism effectively is to address the social problems that motivate terrorist actions. People join terrorist organizations, in part, because they feel frustrated by their inability to produce change through legitimate channels. Moghaddam argued that we must reduce this sense of hopelessness by nourishing democracy around the world. For example, we should support governments that work to improve the educational, professional, and political opportunities available to their citizens. These kinds of reforms may forestall the emergence of the next generation of terrorists.

Reduction of Intergroup Conflict

It is not inevitable that conflict will spiral out of control. Sometimes, groups find solutions to disagreements and evolve strategies for cooperative behaviour. Several factors increase the likelihood that intergroup conflict will be reduced.

Communication. Perhaps the most important factor in the reduction of conflict is communication. If the opposing groups do not exchange information and suggestions, it is very unlikely that a resolution satisfactory to both sides will be found. In contrast, open and continued communication between antagonistic groups greatly increases the chances of reducing the intensity of the conflict.

The importance of communication was documented in a couple of studies by Morton Deutsch and Robert Krauss, which used the trucking game they previously developed. In one study (Deutsch & Krauss, 1962), participants were forced to communicate on every trial. This procedure reduced the negative impact of threats, but only when just one company had a gate. If both companies had gates (threats), not even forced communication was enough to avoid conflict and poor outcomes.

The researchers suggested that communication did not have stronger positive effects because participants were not necessarily exchanging positive, constructive information. Indeed, they reported that many participants in the study used the mandatory communication as an opportunity to deliver a verbal threat! In a subsequent study using the trucking game (Krauss & Deutsch, 1966), the researchers explicitly tutored some participants in how to communicate fair proposals. These participants were instructed to take the other player's perspective and to work for a strategy that was fair to both sides. The remaining participants did not receive this tutoring about constructive communication. Results showed that the tutored participants obtained significantly better outcomes than did the nontutored participants, even when both players had gates (threats). Thus, when communication was moulded to be constructive in nature, it helped to reduce conflict and encourage cooperation.

How, exactly, does communication serve to reduce conflict? Dean Pruitt (1998) suggested that communication can have a variety of positive effects (see also Kerr & Kaufman-Gilliland, 1994; Orbell, van de Kragt, & Dawes, 1988; Tyler & Blader, 2000). For one thing, communication usually leads the opposing sides to generate ideas and strategies for how to cooperate. Without communication, each side is likely to focus instead on strategies for exploiting its opponent. Second, while discussing ideas for cooperation, group members may make public statements that commit them to cooperate. This commitment increases the chances that people will actually follow through with cooperative behaviour. Third, communication can increase people's confidence that the *other* side will cooperate. In other words, communication tends to increase trust between the opponents. Finally, communication often makes connections or similarities between the opponents more apparent. For instance, the groups might recognize that they share a common identity (e.g., as humans), or they might realize that they both want the same goal (e.g., an equitable solution).

For all of these reasons, communication is a key element in conflict reduction. We will return to the importance of communication in Chapter 12, "Helpful Social Behaviour," when we talk about cooperation. Communication also plays an important role in effective governance by political parties. For example, members of legislative committees typically come from different parties, but they discuss the relevant issues jointly. This communication facilitates balanced, constructive approaches to issues.

Trust. We just mentioned trust as one of the possible, positive consequences of communication. Trust means that individuals or groups think that another person or group has good intentions and will not take advantage of them. Trust turns out to be a critical factor influencing cooperation (see Webb & Worchel, 1986). For example, organizational researchers have found that cooperative behaviours are more common in companies in which employees trust one another and management (e.g., Kramer, 1999; Zaheer, McEvily, & Perrone, 1998). When individuals or groups do not trust one another, they are unwilling to act in ways that leave themselves vulnerable. Cooperation usually requires putting oneself in a position where exploitation is possible (e.g., allowing the other person or group to use shared resources), so a lack of trust reduces the chances of cooperation.

Recall also that intergroup settings tend to elicit more competitiveness than interpersonal settings (Insko et al., 1990; Schopler et al., 1993), and one cause of this effect is that groups fear being exploited by other groups more than individuals fear being exploited by other individuals. This reasoning suggests that groups will generally be trusted less than individuals, which has indeed been found (Insko & Schopler, 1998). Thus, intergroup settings elicit not only competitiveness, but also distrust.

There is an unfortunate asymmetry in the ease of creating versus destroying trust. It can take a long time for secure trust to develop between two groups. In contrast, trust can be dissolved very quickly—often a single action is sufficient to eliminate trust. For instance, friendly neighbours can quickly become enemies if one family calls the police to complain about noise at a party hosted by the other family. This asymmetry (with trust being harder to create than to destroy) means that intergroup relations are often characterized by a lack of trust, especially when groups have a long history of interaction.

Can conflict ever be reduced if groups do not trust one another? Daniel Bar-Tal (2000) argued that longstanding intergroup disputes, such as the Arab–Israeli conflict in the Middle East, create a **conflictive ethos,** which is an atmosphere of distrust and hatred. To reduce conflict significantly, an **ethos of peace** must develop, which is an atmosphere of acceptance and cooperation. But how can this atmosphere be created between opponents in an intractable conflict? A few procedures make groups more willing to cooperate in the absence of trust (Deutsch, 1973; Pruitt, 1998). One strategy is to make a decision reversible (rather than final and unchangeable), which allows each side to withdraw if the other fails to cooperate. For example, a decision to share important resources might be made contingent on certain conditions, with the understanding that the decision will be reversed if the conditions are not met. A second strategy is to divide a significant cooperative move into many smaller and less risky moves, which allows each side to minimize its losses if the other side fails to cooperate. For instance, a loan of $10 million might be broken down into ten loans of $1 million made over a period of time. A third procedure is to find an external group or authority who will supervise the planned cooperation, preferably a well-respected and powerful neutral party. For example, the United Nations might be recruited to supervise the return of territory from one side to the other. If these strategies can be used to elicit initial cooperation, then a broader process of reconciliation can begin.

Unilateral Conciliatory Initiatives.

Imagine that you are the representative of a group that has a substantial history of suspicion and conflict with another group. For instance, imagine that you work for a large company and represent a group of employees who have had bitter negotiations with management in the past. Your group does not trust management's motives, and management appears to believe that your group is a bunch of lazy and greedy workers. Over the last few years, management has taken several actions and instituted some rules that have annoyed your group, such as installing cameras to monitor workers, refusing to allow workers to take personal phone calls at work, and threatening layoffs if profits don't increase. Your group has also engaged in some confrontational behaviour, such as a work slowdown for several weeks, letter campaigns complaining about the company to local politicians, and even threats of an illegal walkout. Simply put, things can't get much worse in terms of intergroup relations.

Can you think of anything that might quickly and significantly change the nature of the relationship between your group and management? Is there something that could happen that would be a very positive influence? Sale of the company might work, but it could also result in layoffs or cutbacks. Increased demand for the product or new contracts with other businesses would undoubtedly make the company more secure, but would it necessarily improve labour–management relations?

What if management suddenly announced that it was discontinuing one of its actions or rules that have annoyed members of your group? For instance, without any explicit request from your group, management quietly removed all cameras from the building. This action was not accompanied by any new demands on your group; it was a unilateral move by management.

Social psychologists studying intergroup relations have proposed that unilateral actions of this sort can be very effective in reducing intergroup conflict and tension. The term used to refer to these actions is **unilateral conciliatory initiatives** (Osgood, 1962; Pruitt, 1998). One side undertakes the action (hence, *initiative*) without any explicit demands for similar concessions from the other side (hence, *unilateral*), and the action represents a significant concession, thereby implying a sincere motive for reconciliation (hence, *conciliatory*). Because the action is spontaneous and no demands are attached, the opposing group is likely to believe that it represents a real attempt to ease tensions. You may recall our discussion of the *norm of reciprocity* in Chapter 8 (see page 301)—favours should be returned in

conflictive ethos

an atmosphere of distrust and hatred that can develop in longstanding disputes

ethos of peace

an atmosphere of acceptance and cooperation, which can facilitate the resolution of disputes

unilateral conciliatory initiatives

actions to reduce conflict that one group takes without any request from the opponent and without any explicit demands for concessions from the opponent kind—which is a strong norm in most cultures around the world. Given the norm of reciprocity, the opposing group is likely to feel that it should respond to a unilateral conciliatory initiative with a concession of its own. As a result, one or two concessions by one side can trigger a dramatic de-escalation of tension and suspicion—the opposite of a vicious cycle.

There are some famous examples of the effectiveness of unilateral conciliatory initiatives in international relations. For instance, in the 1980s, the United States and the former Soviet Union greatly reduced international tensions near the end of the so-called Cold War when each side made unilateral reductions in nuclear armaments. Soviet president Mikhail Gorbachev and U.S. president Ronald Reagan independently announced significant reductions in their nuclear arsenals. These announcements consistently led the other side to make a reciprocal concession. A collective determination to reduce the threat of war produced enormous changes in the relationship between these superpowers.

It takes courage and determination to perform a unilateral conciliatory initiative. The side that takes the action puts itself at risk of exploitation; indeed, it is this vulnerability that makes the action effective at reducing tension. These actions may be most effective when the initiator is equal or greater in power than the opponent. If the side that initiates the action is more powerful, then the action is very likely to be seen as genuine, whereas a concession by a weak opponent may be seen as an act of desperation that does not call for a reciprocal concession (Lindskold & Aronoff, 1980).

Our international examples throughout this section of the chapter underscore the importance of knowledge about intergroup conflict—how it develops and how it can be reduced. There is more than just group productivity or employee satisfaction involved; the very survival of our species may hang in the balance. Concepts like unilateral conciliatory initiatives might literally save our lives if we can effectively communicate our knowledge to relevant leaders. If you wonder sometimes about the importance of social psychology, think back to this topic of intergroup conflict and reflect on the nuclear capabilities of many countries.

In the 1980s, Ronald Reagan and Mikhail Gorbachev each performed *unilateral conciliatory initiatives*, which helped to end the Cold War.

© Bettmann/CORBIS

Chapter Summary

Group dynamics is the social psychological study of groups and group processes. By **group,** social psychologists mean two or more persons who are interacting with one another and/or influencing one another. Social psychologists have focused on groups of two different sizes: small groups range from 2 to 20 members, and large collectives consist of groups larger than 20.

Social facilitation refers to the effects of the presence of other people on individual performance. When a task is simple or well learned, the presence of other people tends to produce better performance. When a task is difficult or novel, the presence of other people tends to produce worse performance. These two findings reflect that the presence of other people is arousing, which increases the probability of the **dominant responses** (the responses that are most likely to occur when the person is alone).

Social loafing refers to the reduction in effort that people often exhibit when working in a group where individual contributions are unidentifiable. Social loafing tends to increase with larger groups and with increased anonymity.

Deindividuation refers to a psychological state in which people lose their sense of personal identity and feel immersed in a group. Large groups and clothing that reduces identifiability can produce deindividuation. Deindividuation tends to increase socially undesirable behaviour, but it is unclear whether this finding reflects that being in a group releases people from inhibitions, increases their responsiveness to external cues, or increases adherence to emerging group norms.

Groups often must make decisions. **Groupthink** refers to a way of thinking that can occur in decision-making groups when pressure to agree leads to biased appraisal of options and poor decisions. Groupthink is hypothesized to occur mainly in groups that are high in **group cohesiveness,** which refers to the combined intensity of all forces acting on group members to stay in a group. Groupthink produces a number of symptoms that involve illusions, rationalizations, and excessive risk taking.

Another phenomenon that occurs in group decision making is **group polarization.** Group polarization refers to the tendency for group discussion to strengthen the initial leanings of the members in a group. Group polarization has been shown to occur in juries, but the effect is stronger for initial leanings toward acquittal than for initial leanings toward conviction.

Although majorities usually prevail in group discussion, minorities sometimes exert considerable influence. Minorities are more likely to be influential if they are firm and resolute in their position. Some theorists have argued that the nature of minority influence is qualitatively different from the nature of majority influence. For example, minorities may stimulate divergent thinking, which consists of novel and creative thoughts, whereas majorities may stimulate convergent thinking, which consists of typical or standard approaches to a problem.

Research on leadership has focused on two issues: "Who becomes a leader?" (leadership emergence) and "Who makes a good leader?" (leadership effectiveness). There are many different kinds of leaders, including **transformational leaders**, who stimulate fundamental changes in the way group members view themselves and the group. Leaders can fulfill many functions in a group, which fall into two major categories. The **task achievement function** involves all of the things necessary for group productivity. The **group maintenance function** involves all of the things related to morale in the group. In some groups, different individuals may fulfill these two categories of functions; the two leaders are labelled the **task leader** and the **socioemotional leader.**

The **trait approach to leadership,** also called **Great Person theory,** tries to identify the personal characteristics that are associated with being chosen as a leader or with being a successful leader, such as intelligence and charisma. The **situational approach to leadership** tries to identify external, situational factors that can influence leadership emergence, such as physical seating arrangements. The **interactionist approach to leadership** predicts that certain kinds of people are likely to emerge as leaders (or to be effective leaders) under one set of conditions, whereas other kinds of people are likely to emerge as leaders (or to be effective leaders) under a different set of conditions. For example, the **contingency model of leadership effectiveness** predicts that task-oriented leaders will be more effective than relationship-oriented leaders in groups where the situation is either very favourable or very unfavourable for the leader, whereas relationship-oriented leaders will be more effective than task-oriented leaders when the situation is mixed for the leader.

Acculturation is the process of cultural and psychological change that takes place as a result of contact between two or more cultural groups and their individual members. Different goals regarding acculturation can be pursued by cultural groups. Integration refers to the goal of identifying with one's own cultural group and also with the alternative culture. Separation refers to the goal of identifying only with one's own cultural group. Assimilation refers to the goal of identifying only with the alternative culture. Marginalization occurs when individuals lose their own cultural identity and do not feel connected to the alternative culture either.

Intergroup relations are often negative. The use of threats tends to escalate conflict between groups. Extreme forms of intergroup violence, such as genocide, may be facilitated by perceptions that the target group is subhuman or inferior. This **dehumanization** of members of the target group allows people to inflict pain and suffering without worrying about the morality of their behaviour. **Terrorism** refers to actual or threatened violence against civilians for alleged political purposes. Terrorism often has more psychological impact than material or physical impact. Unfortunately, it is very difficult to control or eliminate terrorism.

To reduce intergroup conflict, communication and trust are very important. Longstanding disputes create a **conflictive ethos,** which is an atmosphere of distrust and hatred. Reducing conflict requires developing an **ethos of peace,** which is an atmosphere of acceptance and cooperation. **Unilateral conciliatory initiatives** occur when one group takes a step to reduce conflict without any explicit demands for concessions by the other side; such actions can significantly ease intergroup conflict.

Key Terms

acculturation (403)

conflictive ethos (411)

contingency model of leadership effectiveness (401)

dehumanization (407)

deindividuation (377)

dominant response (375)

ethos of peace (411)

Great Person theory (393)

group (373)

group cohesiveness (381)

group dynamics (372)

group maintenance function (392)

group polarization (386)

groupthink (381)

interactionist approach to leadership (401)

situational approach to leadership (400)

social facilitation (374)

social loafing (376)

socioemotional leader (392)

task achievement function (392)

task leader (392)

terrorism (408)

trait approach to leadership (393)

transformational leaders (391)

unilateral conciliatory initiatives (411)

Social Psychology Alive on the Web

SOCIAL PSYCHOLOGY ALIVE: ONLINE LABS

To perform the following experiment and see how you compare to other students, go to Social Psychology Lab, which can be accessed through ThomsonNOW™.

• 10.1 Judging Leadership

SOCIAL PSYCHOLOGY ALIVE: QUIZZING AND PRACTICE TESTS

You can access our Web site directly by going to http://www.socialpsychologyalive.nelson.com for online quizzes, flash cards, and Internet links.

INFOTRAC® COLLEGE EDITION

For additional readings, explore InfoTrac® College Edition, your online library of archived journal articles and periodicals dating back 22 years. If your instructor ordered InfoTrac® College Edition with this book, you can access it from your CD-ROM, or go directly to http://www .infotrac-college.com and use the passcode from the InfoTrac® College Edition card that came with your book. For this chapter, try these search terms: *groups, social facilitation, social loafing, deindividuation, group productivity, groupthink, group cohesiveness, group polarization, minority influence, leader, leadership, conflict, dehumanization, terrorism.*

Social Psychology Alive: The Workbook

To apply what you've learned in this chapter to what happens in the real world, go to Chapter 10 of *Social Psychology Alive: The Workbook:*

- How Do You Define a Group and Its Leader?
- Can You Demonstrate These Trademarks of Group Behaviour?
- Experiment A: Social Facilitation: Will They Excel or Choke?
- Experiment B: Groupthink: Let's All Follow the Leader

- Masks and the Mob
- Decisions About the War in Iraq and Groupthink
- Is Your Group Susceptible to Groupthink?
- Preparing Yourself to Be a Jury Foreperson
- What Do You Prefer in a Leader?
- Judging Leadership
- So You Want to Be a Diplomat: Preparing for Your Job with the Department of Foreign Affairs
- Taking Steps to Promote Tolerance

Social Psychology Alive: The Videos

To see video on the topics and experiments discussed in this chapter, you can go either to ThomsonNOW™ or to the CD-ROM, if your instructor assigned either one, to the following section:

- Imprisoned in a Role: The Stanford Prison Study

To Learn More

This list contains citations to books or articles that can help you learn more. These readings are good places to start if you want to gain a deeper understanding of the topics in this chapter.

- Burn, S. M. (2004). *Groups: Theory and practice.* Belmont, CA: Thomson/Wadsworth.

- Forsyth, D. R. (2006). *Group dynamics* (4th ed.). Belmont, CA: Thomson Learning/Wadsworth.
- Chemers, M. M., & Ayman, R. (Eds.). (1993). *Leadership theory and research: Perspectives and directions.* San Diego, CA: Academic Press.

NEL

Aggression and Violence

*T*aber is a small town of about 7000 people in southern Alberta. On April 28, 1999, shortly after 1:00 P.M., a 14-year-old boy (who cannot be identified because of his age) entered W. R. Myers High School in Taber with a semi-automatic rifle. He encountered two 17-year-old boys in the hallway and shot them both. One of the victims, Jason Lang, later died of his wounds. The shooter continued down the hall and threatened several other students but did not fire his weapon. He was convinced by another student, a friend, to put down his gun and was then arrested by an unarmed policeman who was in the school as a resource officer.

Speculation immediately focused on the coincidence that the shootings in Taber followed only eight days after the highly publicized shootings at Columbine High School in Colorado in which Eric Harris and Dylan Klebold killed 13 people. Was the Taber shooting a case of copycat killing—was the boy modelling his actions on those of Harris and Klebold, who had been featured continuously on television and in the print media for the previous week?

Students who knew the shooter described him as an unpopular kid who had been the target of teasing from other students. The boy's mother claimed that he was the victim of incessant bullying and had shown signs of depression. Perhaps the boy was provoked by name-calling; nobody likes to be ridiculed, and perhaps his anger got so intense that an act of retaliation was inevitable. He certainly overreacted, but many of us have responded to teasing with some form of aggression.

Whatever the specific cause(s) of the boy's actions, he showed that people are capable of extreme forms of aggression. Understanding the nature of human aggression, especially knowing the factors that increase or decrease it, is one of social psychology's most important challenges.

In this chapter, we describe social psychological research on aggression and violence. We begin by defining aggression and distinguishing among different varieties of aggressive behaviour. With this necessary background about the concept of aggression, we turn to theories of aggression—models that attempt to explain why aggression occurs. There are numerous theories that present quite different approaches to aggression (as implied by our brief analysis of the Taber shootings), as well as a recent theory that combines several prior models to provide a relatively comprehensive analysis. We then turn to the effects on aggression of several factors, including personality traits, alcohol, and heat. Next, we discuss the social context of aggression by focusing on the role of cultural factors, as well as aggression on the playground, in close relationships, and in groups. We then discuss effects of the media, including violence on television, violent video games, and pornography. We close the chapter by discussing how aggression in society might be controlled and reduced.

Definition and Varieties of Aggression

The first thing we need to do is define what we mean by the term *aggression*. In everyday conversation, the term has many meanings. For example, people may talk about someone having an *aggressive attitude* or a musician *playing a piece aggressively*. Although these are legitimate uses of the term, they differ from the meaning intended by social psychologists. First, when social psychologists talk about aggression, they refer specifically to observable behaviour. Although thoughts and attitudes can lead to aggression, they are not themselves a form of aggression. Second, harm or potential harm is involved in all cases of aggression—but not all harm-doing should be labelled aggression. Consider the physician or dentist whose intent is to help, but whose behaviour can cause pain. Or consider a salesperson who knowingly sells us something at a higher price than we would have paid elsewhere (and therefore causes financial harm). Do we want to label these behaviours as true aggression?

In wrestling with these kinds of ambiguities, Leonard Berkowitz (1993) summed up the social psychological definition of **aggression** as "any form of behavior that is intended to injure someone physically or psychologically" (p. 3). Notice that the inclusion of *intent* to harm would make the physician's behaviour something other than aggression and the emphasis on *injury* (physical or psychological) would make the salesperson's behaviour something other than aggression.

When aggression is intended to cause *extreme* injury—such as death—we call it **violence.** Notice that violence is always a form of aggression, but not all aggression is violence because it is not always aimed at causing extreme injury (Anderson & Bushman, 2002a). For instance, shooting or stabbing someone is aggressive and violent; insulting or pushing someone is aggressive but not violent.

Several types or varieties of aggression need to be identified before we turn to theoretical models of the causes of aggression.

Hostile and Instrumental Aggression

When we think about some of the most common kinds of aggression (e.g., insults, pushes), they often involve negative emotional states such as anger, frustration, or hatred. Aggression that results from these sorts of negative emotions has been called **hostile aggression** (Buss, 1961). Hostile aggression is often impulsive rather than planned, and the primary goal is to hurt the target.

But people also commit aggressive acts in order to achieve more distant goals than simply hurting the target. For example, when a parent spanks a child, the motivation may be to teach the child to control some undesired behaviour. When a robber knocks someone to the ground, the robber's ultimate goal is to grab a purse or wallet. Admittedly, in both of these cases, there is the intent to inflict some pain or arouse some fear, but the principal underlying motive is a more distant goal—to teach a lesson or to steal something of value. Aggression that is motivated by goals other than harming the target has been called **instrumental aggression** (Buss, 1961). Instrumental aggression is often premeditated or planned rather than impulsive.

You may be tempted to think of hostile aggression and instrumental aggression as an *either/or* dichotomy—that aggressive behaviour is either hostile or instrumental. Such an assumption would be a mistake, however, because aggression is more complicated than that. People's motives for aggression are often multifaceted. Brad Bushman and Craig Anderson (2001a) gave a compelling example to make this point. Eric Harris and Dylan Klebold, who perpetrated the Columbine High School shootings, carefully planned their actions—they did research, they mapped out their

aggression
behaviour that is intended to injure someone physically or psychologically

violence
aggression that is intended to cause extreme injury

hostile aggression
harm-doing that arises out of negative emotions such as anger, frustration, or hatred

instrumental aggression
harm-doing that is motivated by goals other than hurting the target, such as obtaining something of value

steps, they even rehearsed the scenario. These facts would seem to make their actions consistent with instrumental aggression. In the aftermath of Columbine, however, it became clear that Harris and Klebold were also very angry young men. They nurtured a great deal of hostility, often aimed at the athletes at their school who had been known to anger and provoke them. These facts make their actions consistent with hostile aggression. This episode illustrates that aggressive behaviour can be caused by several factors simultaneously (see also Aronson, 2000). In fact, most acts of aggression reflect some mixture of anger and a desire to achieve more distant goals.

Therefore, the distinction between hostile and instrumental aggression is only occasionally useful for precisely classifying a particular aggressive act (Bushman & Anderson, 2001a). Nevertheless, the distinction is often helpful in thinking about why aggression occurs.

Earlier, we gave as an example of instrumental aggression a parent's decision to spank a child. Presumably, spanking is intended to teach the child a lesson and to modify the child's behaviour in some way. Does spanking actually work? Is it effective in achieving the parent's distant goals? The accompanying box, Social Psychology in Your Life: "Is Corporal Punishment Effective?" discusses this issue.

Relational Aggression

Aggression starts early in social life. By the time children reach school age, they have developed a fairly diverse repertoire of aggressive behaviours, including non-physical aggression. For example, even at preschool age, especially among girls, we can observe some forms of psychological harm-doing (Crick, Casas, & Mosher, 1997; Underwood, 2003). Whereas boys tend to exhibit physical aggression, girls are more likely to rely on **relational aggression** (Crick & Grotpeter, 1995). Relational aggression is behaviour that is intended to damage another person's peer relationships. Have you seen people use social exclusion or rumour spreading as a means of inflicting harm on others? This is relational aggression: it may leave no physical damage, but it can inflict very significant psychological damage. The accompanying Concept Review summarizes the types of aggression we have described.

relational aggression

behaviour that is intended to damage another person's peer relationships

Nicki Crick and her colleagues at the University of Minnesota have investigated relational aggression. In one study (Crick et al., 1997), measures of the physical and relational aggression of preschoolers were obtained from teachers and from the children themselves. For example, the teachers were asked to rate the relational aggressiveness of students on items such as these:

- Tries to get others to dislike a peer
- Verbally threatens to keep a peer out of the play group if the peer doesn't do what the child asks

In addition to the teachers' ratings, the children were asked to indicate which of their peers engaged in relational aggression. This was done by showing each child pictures of his or her peers, and asking him or her to point to the pictures that corresponded to:

- Kids who say they won't invite someone to their birthday party if they can't have their own way
- Kids who tell other kids that they can't play with the group unless they do what the group wants them to do

Social Psychology in Your Life
Is Corporal Punishment Effective?

An important practical question that has been put to psychological science is whether or not the spanking of children is effective as a method of discipline (Gershoff, 2002; Kazdin & Benjet, 2003). First, it is important to be clear about what we mean by *spanking* and *corporal punishment*. Spanking typically refers to the hitting of a child with an open hand, usually on the extremities such as the buttocks. The intent of spanking is to punish by producing some pain, but without causing physical injury such as bruising. Corporal punishment is the more general term used in reference to "the use of physical force with the intention of causing a child to experience pain but not injury for the purpose of correction or control of the child's behavior" (Straus, 1994, p. 4). Corporal punishment encompasses both spanking and the use of objects (paddles, belts, etc). Both of these concepts differ from *physical abuse,* which is the intentional infliction of injury.

Elizabeth Thompson Gershoff (2002) reviewed the literature on corporal punishment. She found that spanking a child is an effective way of achieving immediate compliance. But this was really the only "positive" effect of corporal punishment. The evidence indicates that such punishment does not produce long-term compliance, which would reflect the child's acceptance of the moral lesson presumably being taught by corporal punishment. Indeed, the use of corporal punishment is associated with a variety of negative effects in children: greater aggression, higher degrees of delinquent and antisocial behaviour, lower quality of the parent–child relationship, lower mental health, and an increased chance of physical abuse.

A word of caution: these findings are almost entirely correlational. So we don't know whether the relationship between corporal punishment and children's aggression means that the punishment causes increased aggression, or a child's aggressive behaviour elicits corporal punishment, or both; it is also possible that some third variable is influencing both the use of corporal punishment and aggressive behaviour in children. Still, the array of associations found between the use of corporal punishment and negative outcomes (some of which extend into adulthood) is a chilling cause for concern.

The American Academy of Pediatrics and the American Psychological Association caution parents not to hit their children. In addition to the evidence just cited, there are other good theoretical reasons why corporal punishment should be avoided. For example, we will soon be describing research on the modelling of aggression: children imitate adults, including their aggressive behaviour. What are children being taught when their parents hit them? They may imitate this behaviour by hitting other people to teach them a lesson. The best parenting advice provided by the research suggests that nonphysical methods—timeouts, suspension of privileges, grounding—are more effective forms of punishment in producing long-term changes in behaviour (Kazdin & Benjet, 2003).

Spanking tends to produce short-term, but not long-term, compliance.

To complement these measures, other assessments were designed to reflect overt, physical aggression. For example, the teachers were asked to rate students on such items as:

- Hurts other children by pinching them
- Pushes or shoves other children

Similarly, the children picked out their peers to identify:

- Kids who push or shove other kids
- Kids who throw things at other kids when they don't get their way

CONCEPT REVIEW
Types of Aggression

Type	Description	Examples
Aggression (all)	Behaviour that is intended to injure someone physically or psychologically	Punch, insult
Hostile aggression	Aggression that results from negative emotional states such as anger, frustration, or hatred	Road rage, jealousy-induced assault
Instrumental aggression	Aggression that is motivated by goals other than harming the target	Armed robbery, parental spanking
Relational aggression	Behaviour that is intended to damage another person's peer relationships	False gossip, ridicule

In the teachers' assessments, boys were judged as engaging in more overt (physical) aggression than girls. In contrast, girls were judged as engaging in more relational aggression than boys. When the children were grouped based on the teacher ratings, 12% of the boys but only 3% of the girls were categorized as physically aggressive, whereas 26% of the girls but none of the boys were categorized as relationally aggressive. Thus, even at four to five years of age, children showed important gender differences in their forms of aggressive actions.

It is interesting to note that this pattern of results was not observed in the preschoolers' ratings. At this young age, children had not yet developed a reliable sense of assigning aggressive inclinations to their peers. Other studies have shown, however, that it does not take long for children to sort these things out. By the time they reach grade school, teachers and children show a high degree of consensus on which children rely more on physical versus relational aggression (Crick, 1996; Crick & Grotpeter, 1995; Grotpeter & Crick, 1996). And the evidence bears out that girls more than boys generally rely on social forms of aggression (Galen & Underwood, 1997).

One result of using social exclusion or spreading rumours about others is the possibility that others will come to dislike you. Even among preschoolers, Crick and her colleagues (1997) found signs of social maladjustment among girls who used relational aggression. Some evidence suggests that this relationship continues into young adulthood: Nicole Werner and Nicki Crick (1999) found that relational aggression among university students was associated with peer rejection and antisocial personality.

But we should not be too quick to draw a final conclusion. It appears that aggressive behaviour can sometimes be associated with *popularity*. Amanda Rose, Lance Swenson, and Erika Waller (2004) at the University of Missouri recently found that among older (grade 7 and 9) youths, both overt and relational aggression were positively related to popularity. It seems that aggression can sometimes be "cool" and lead to increased rather than decreased peer acceptance. This is reminiscent of our observation in Chapter 6 that people who use *ridicule* to control others may be seen as clever. More research is needed to untangle the complex relationship between aggression and popularity.

Boys engage in more physical aggression than do girls.

© Peter Marlow/Magnum Photos

Theories of Aggression

Having defined and clarified relevant terms, we can now turn to the question of when and why people engage in aggressive (and sometimes violent) behaviour. We begin with a general framework that integrates several previous models, each of which is then reviewed separately. We conclude by returning to the general framework and elaborating its key features.

General Aggression Model (GAM)

A broad framework for answering the question of why people behave aggressively was developed by social psychologist Craig Anderson, who is at Iowa State University, and his colleagues (Anderson, 1997; Anderson & Bushman, 2002a; Anderson, Deuser, & DeNeve, 1995; Bartholow, Anderson, Carnagey, & Benjamin, 2005; Lindsay & Anderson, 2000). Anderson brought together decades of social psychological thinking about aggression in what he called the **general aggression model (GAM).** A simplified version of the GAM is shown in Figure 11.1.

The fundamental idea is that aggressive behaviour is the result of a chain of psychological processes. People respond to situational events (e.g., someone insults them or frustrates them) by generating some or all of the following: aggressive thoughts, aggressive feelings, and physiological arousal. Some people are more likely than others to respond to situational events with aggressive thoughts and feelings; this idea is reflected in the category of *individual differences* in the model. The aggressive thoughts, feelings, and arousal within the person increase the probability of aggressive behaviour, but the individual must first interpret the situation as one in which aggression is appropriate (e.g., he has been insulted, feels angry, and must defend his honour). How do people decide whether aggression is appropriate? The GAM uses the

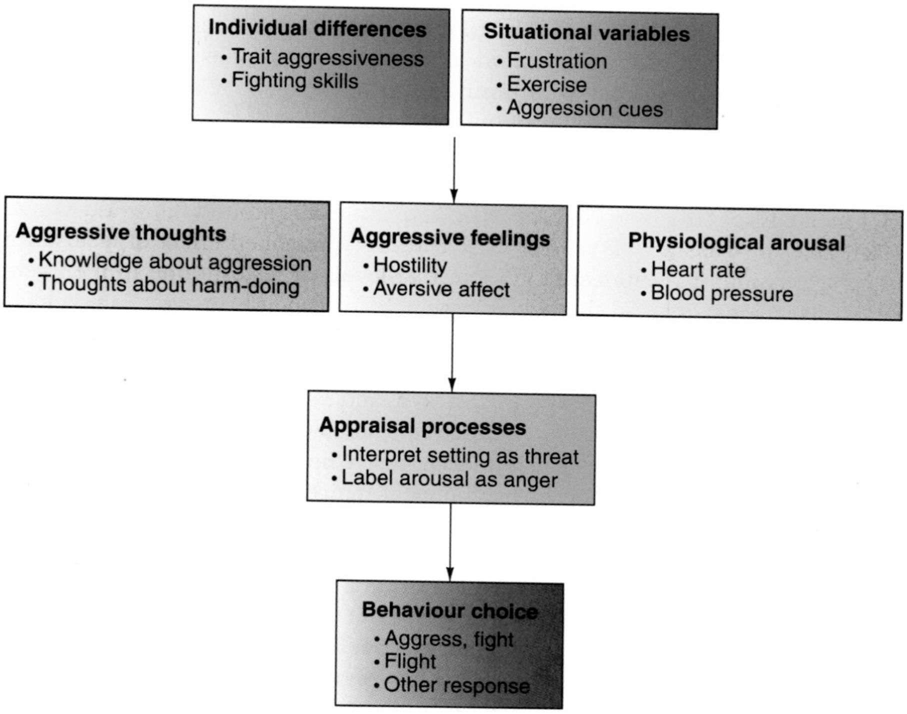

general aggression model (GAM)

a broad theory that conceptualizes aggression as the result of a chain of psychological processes, including situational events, aggressive thoughts and feelings, and interpretations of the situation

FIGURE 11.1 Simplified version of the general aggression model

From Anderson, "Effects of violent movies and trait hostility on hostile feelings and aggressive thought," *Aggressive Behavior*, 23, 161–178, 1997. Reprinted by permission of Wiley-Liss, Inc., a subsidiary of John Wiley & Sons, Inc.

term *appraisal processes* to represent this decision. For instance, if the individual appraises (or interprets) the setting as one involving danger or threat, the interpretation may lead directly to aggressive behaviour.

We will elaborate each of these steps in a later section. One of the nice features of the GAM is that it pulls together five rich theoretical traditions in the study of aggression, which we review in the following sections:

- Biological influences on aggression
- Frustration and aggression
- Excitation transfer
- Social learning theory
- Cognitive neoassociation model

Biological Influences on Aggression

Human aggression is undoubtedly influenced by biological processes. For example, the emotion of anger, which often precedes aggression, is associated with physiological arousal. Anger-induced physiological arousal is spontaneous and innate—people do not have to "learn" to feel this state. Evidence of biological influences on aggression comes from numerous sources; we discuss two in the following paragraphs: hormonal activity and evolutionary processes. Later in the chapter we will discuss the effects of alcohol on aggression; these findings also represent a biological effect.

Hormonal Activity and Aggression. Researchers have long assumed that hormones play an important role in aggressive behaviour in nonhuman animals (e.g., Archer, 1988; Lorenz, 1966). The role of hormones in human aggression, however, is more controversial and almost certainly smaller. The clearest evidence with humans relates to the possible role of the male sex hormone testosterone. James Dabbs and his colleagues at Georgia State University (e.g., Dabbs, Carr, Frady, & Riad, 1995; Dabbs, Frady, Carr, & Besch, 1987) investigated the relation between testosterone levels and violent aggression among prison inmates. Prisoners who were convicted of violent crimes were found to have higher levels of testosterone than prisoners who were convicted of nonviolent crimes.

It is possible that the higher levels of testosterone in men than women explain, at least in part, gender differences in violent aggression (e.g., the fact noted in Chapter 5 that men commit between 70% and 90% of the murders around the world; see Archer, 1994; Daly & Wilson, 1988). Consistent with this presumed effect of testosterone on male aggression, it is interesting to note that levels of testosterone in men generally peak in their mid-20s and then decline, which corresponds to age-related changes in violent crime (peaking among men in their mid-20s and then declining).

In a review and analysis of 45 studies on the testosterone–aggression relation, social psychologists Angela Book, Katherine Starzyk, and Vernon Quinsey (2001), who are at Queen's University in Kingston, Ontario, concluded that there is a small but reliable relation between testosterone levels and aggressive behaviour. Of course, because these data are correlational, they do not definitively indicate causation. For example, some researchers have suggested that aggressive behaviour might increase levels of testosterone (e.g., Mazur & Lamb, 1980). Nevertheless, it seems clear that testosterone and aggression are related to one another, perhaps in a reciprocal fashion (see Geen, 1998).

Evolutionary Processes. Some theorists have proposed that the human tendency toward aggression is innate and has evolved because it served a survival function in our evolutionary past. For example, a *fight-or-flight* response to threat presumably increased our ancestors' chances of surviving attacks from predators or competitors by preparing our ancestors to engage in self-defensive aggression (or escape). Similarly, more complex forms of aggression may also reflect, in part, evolutionary pressures.

Margo Daly and Martin Wilson at McMaster University in Hamilton, Ontario, identified male sexual jealousy as a common precipitator of aggression and argued that evolutionary pressures selected for this emotional state (Daly & Wilson, 1988; Wilson & Daly, 1985). These researchers argued that men have evolved to aggress against other men who threaten the paternity of offspring borne by their female mates. Thus, a man may respond with jealousy and aggression when other men try to initiate sexual liaisons with a woman with whom he has had sexual relations (e.g., his partner). Daly and Wilson suggested that the high rates of homicide among men in their 20s (who are in their prime reproductive years), which often involve some type of sexual jealousy, are consistent with this perspective.

Of course, even if aggression in humans has evolved because it has survival value, this does not mean that humans cannot inhibit their aggressive behaviour. That is, an aggressive impulse can be consciously suppressed when aggressive behaviour would be counterproductive. Indeed, as the following sections reveal, cognitive processes play a critical role in determining whether a situation that could elicit aggression actually does so.

Frustration and Aggression

One of the earliest efforts to develop a general theory of human aggression took place at Yale University by John Dollard, Neal Miller, Leonard Doob, O. H. Mowrer, and Robert Sears (1939). At the heart of their theory was a rather simple conjecture: "aggression is always a consequence of frustration" (p. 1). Although it may sound implausible to propose that all aggression comes from just one cause, these theorists defined frustration broadly enough to encompass many settings. *Frustration* occurs whenever an individual's efforts to obtain a desired goal are interfered with or otherwise blocked. For example, if traffic is slow, you may feel frustrated because your goal is to get to a particular location. If you receive a failing mark on a test, you may feel frustrated because your goal is to pass the course. If you experience pain when someone hits you, you may feel frustrated because your goal is to avoid pain. Based on this broad definition of frustration, Dollard and his co-workers proposed the **frustration–aggression hypothesis,** which actually contained two components. One component was that frustration always leads to some form of aggression, and the other was that frustration is the only cause of aggression. Thus, according to this view, frustration and aggression are inextricably tied to one another.

An experiment conducted by Russell Geen (1968) illustrates how the frustration–aggression relation can be studied in the laboratory. This study employed a procedure that is frequently used in research on aggression. Male students at the University of Wisconsin arrived in pairs for an experiment allegedly concerned with the effects of punishment on learning. They were told that the experiment would involve the administration of electric shocks, and that one of the two students at each session would act as the teacher and one as the learner. This setup probably reminds you of the Milgram obedience experiments described in Chapter 8, but participants were not *ordered* to administer shocks in this study. One of the students was a confederate, and it was this student who was always given the role of learner.

Prior to this alleged learning task, the real participant was assigned to one of four experimental conditions. In one condition, frustration was induced by having the participant work on a jigsaw puzzle that was described as being a test of intelligence. Unknown to the participant, the puzzle had no solution! Certainly a frustrating experience. Participants in a second condition worked on a jigsaw puzzle that was

frustration–aggression hypothesis
the twin propositions that frustration always leads to some form of aggression and frustration is the only cause of aggression

Being unable to complete a jigsaw puzzle is frustrating.

solvable. As they worked on the puzzle, however, the confederate interfered and prevented them from finishing. In a third condition, the confederate allowed the participant to finish his puzzle but insulted his intelligence by suggesting that his puzzle was not very difficult. Rather than inducing frustration, this condition was expected to induce *anger*. A fourth, control condition was included in which participants simply completed a solvable puzzle while seated alone.

Following the puzzle procedure, participants were given an opportunity to engage in aggression against the confederate. The participant played the role of teacher in a series of learning trials. Every time the learner (actually the confederate) made a mistake on the learning task, the teacher could "punish" him by delivering an electric shock. Thus, the participant was provided with an opportunity to inflict harm. Using this procedure, the extent of aggression could be indexed in different ways, such as by counting the number of electric shocks given or by gauging the intensity of the shocks selected. In reality, this was all a setup—no electric shocks were actually delivered. But the participant didn't know that. As far as he was concerned, depressing the shock button was causing another person some degree of harm.

What happened? Figure 11.2 presents the number of shocks delivered in each condition. Participants in the two frustration conditions delivered many more shocks than did participants in the control condition. As a result of being frustrated, these "teachers" took the opportunity to harm the "learner." Notice that *both* frustration conditions produced equally high levels of aggression. Whether the frustration was caused by task difficulty or by interference from a person, the frustration caused an increase in aggression. One other result was important: participants in the insult condition showed even higher levels of aggression—they delivered the most electric shocks of all. These participants, who were presumably angered rather than frustrated, seized the opportunity to be aggressive toward the person who had provoked them.

Geen's (1968) experiment highlights a problem with the original frustration–aggression hypothesis. Specifically, the results showed that factors other than frustration—in this case, anger—can also cause aggression. Indeed, ever since its introduction, the hypothesis that frustration is the *only* cause of aggression has been the target of criticism. In response to data like those collected by Geen, researchers investigating the frustration–aggression link (e.g., Berkowitz, 1989) have modified their claims by proposing that frustration *sometimes* causes aggression and aggression is *sometimes* caused by frustration. As the qualifications "sometimes" imply, factors other than frustration are recognized as possible causes of aggression. This more defensible position is sometimes called the *revised frustration–aggression hypothesis*.

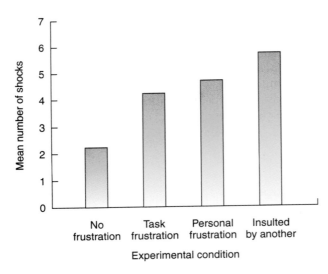

FIGURE 11.2 Number of shocks delivered in each condition

From Geen, "Effects of frustration, attack, and prior training in aggressiveness upon aggressive behavior," *Journal of Personality and Social Psychology*, 9, 316–321, 1968. Copyright © 1968 by the American Psychological Association. Reprinted by permission.

Displaced Aggression. Two final aspects of the frustration–aggression hypothesis deserve brief mention. Dollard and his colleagues initially assumed that frustration-induced aggression would always be directed at the person who caused the frustration. It was soon recognized, however, that even when frustration does lead to aggression, people may not direct their aggression toward the actual source. For one thing, it may be unwise or dangerous to do so. If the person who blocks you from obtaining a desired goal is stronger or more powerful than you, then you might be smart to inhibit your aggression. Or if that person has left the scene, it may not even be possible to retaliate against him or her. Under these circumstances, people may direct their aggression elsewhere. This phenomenon is known as

displaced aggression. For example, if you experience frustration at work because your boss gives you a poor performance evaluation or treats you badly in some other way, you may exhibit aggression against a subordinate or even against members of your own family later after you return home. The idea of displaced aggression has been supported in many studies (for a review, see Marcus-Newhall, Pedersen, Carlson, & Miller, 2000).

Although displaced aggression can occur without the unfortunate target having done anything to provoke it (e.g., someone comes home from a frustrating day at work and kicks a sleeping dog), it often occurs in response to a minor triggering frustration. For example, someone who experiences frustration at work but cannot retaliate against the boss may later hit a family member who is slightly annoying at the dinner table. This kind of aggression, called *triggered displaced aggression,* may often be far more intense than would be expected from the relatively minor trigger. These reactions illustrate the proverbial phrase "the straw that broke the camel's back": a small triggering event (one more piece of straw; a minor frustration) elicits a large response (a broken back; extreme aggression). Norman Miller at the University of Southern California and his colleagues have developed a model of triggered displaced aggression that specifies the conditions under which it is most likely to occur (see Miller, Pedersen, Earleywine, & Pollock, 2003; Pedersen, Gonzales, & Miller, 2000; Vasquez, Denson, Pedersen, Stenstrom, & Miller, 2005).

Catharsis. A second interesting aspect of Dollard and his colleagues' thinking has not been so well supported. Specifically, aggression was assumed to relieve frustration and, therefore, to reduce any further aggression. This effect was called **catharsis.** Perhaps the best way to think about catharsis is by drawing an analogy to hydraulics: frustration causes pressure to build up inside you. As the pressure builds, there is an increasing need to release it. We often speak of people whose anger "boils over." One outlet for all this pressure may be aggressive behaviour. And once you do it, the pressure is reduced. Your impulse to be aggressive is relieved or even eliminated. In short, catharsis implies that aggressive behaviour reduces the likelihood of additional aggression.

This is a provocative idea, and some early experiments seemed to confirm the idea of catharsis (e.g., Doob & Wood, 1972). Most experiments, however, have *not* found the effect to be reliable (see Baron & Richardson, 1994). In fact, the *opposite* effect has more often been obtained. That is, when people are provided an opportunity for aggression (or observe aggression) against a source of frustration, it usually serves to heighten, rather than lessen, subsequent aggression (e.g., Bushman, 2002; Bushman, Baumeister, & Stack, 1999). Why might a heightening effect occur? One possibility is that any aggression in a situation makes subsequent aggression seem more appropriate: a norm is established that aggression is permissible. Another possibility is that the initial act of aggression leads people to see themselves as aggressive, and this self-perception increases the likelihood of subsequent aggressive responses. Whatever the cause of a heightening effect, catharsis does *not* appear to occur: engaging in aggressive behaviour does not reliably reduce the probability of subsequent aggression.

Excitation Transfer

A theoretical perspective known as *excitation transfer* begins with an assumption that aversive arousal leads to aggression. This assumption was actually borrowed from research on the frustration–aggression hypothesis, which assumed that aggressive behaviour is preceded by frustration—a form of emotional arousal. For example, in a paper discussing the revised frustration–aggression hypothesis, Leonard Berkowitz (1989) described frustration as producing a state of aversive and uncomfortable

displaced aggression
harm-doing that is directed at someone or something that was not the actual source of frustration

catharsis
the idea that aggressive behaviour releases people's pent-up frustration and reduces the likelihood of subsequent aggression

Can arousal from exercise increase aggression?

arousal, which presumably explains why frustration can lead to aggression. A variety of early experiments had confirmed that physiological arousal (e.g., blood pressure, heart rate) increases when people are frustrated or angered (e.g., Gambaro & Rabin, 1969; Hokanson & Shetler, 1961; Kahn, 1966). If aversive arousal causes or heightens aggression, then the passage of time (cooling off), listening to soothing music, or otherwise distracting oneself with pleasant things may reduce aggression by reducing aversive arousal. Consistent with this reasoning, Vladimir Konečni (1975a, 1975b), who obtained his doctorate at the University of Toronto, showed that aggressive behaviour was reduced by having insulted or angered participants engage in activities known to reduce aversive arousal, such as those just mentioned. These data support the idea that aversive arousal increases aggressive behaviour.

If aversive arousal leads to aggression, then an interesting question is whether arousal from sources *other than* frustration or anger can also produce (or increase) aggression. Many situations that do not involve frustration or anger can cause a person to become aroused, including exercise, viewing sporting events, and exposure to sexually themed material. Can these sources of arousal cause an increase in aggressive behaviour, even though the arousal itself did not come from being angered or provoked? The answer to this question appears to be *yes*.

In a classic experiment conducted at the University of Indiana, Dolf Zillmann, Aaron Katcher, and Barry Milavsky (1972) led participants to believe that they were interacting with another person in a study of the effects of punishment on learning. In one condition, the "partner" delivered a series of moderately painful electric shocks to the participant, based on the participant's responses to attitude questions. These shocks were expected to anger the participant and to motivate an aggressive retaliation. In the other condition, the "partner" was much less provocative and delivered only a few mild electric shocks in response to the participant's attitude expressions.

Following one of these two conditions, participants completed a second, allegedly unrelated experiment having to do with motor behaviour. Some participants sat quietly at a table performing a nonstrenuous task (threading small discs with off-centre holes). Other participants spent the same amount of time pedalling a stationary bicycle. Measures of physiological arousal (heart rate, blood pressure, and skin temperature) confirmed that participants in the bicycle-pedalling condition experienced much greater arousal than did those in the disc-threading condition.

All participants then had an opportunity to retaliate against the "partner" by delivering electric shocks in a teacher–learner procedure (similar to the one used by Geen, 1968). That is, the participant played the role of teacher and the "partner" played the role of learner. Alleged responses of the learner were pre-programmed so that errors were deliberately made, and the teacher's job was to select an intensity of electric shock as punishment.

To summarize, participants were exposed initially to a procedure that either elicited anger or did not, which was followed by either vigorous or quiet motor activity. Of the resulting four conditions, only one produced a high level of aggression: when participants *both* were angered *and* spent the intervening time on the exercise bicycle. Presumably, the arousal produced by riding the bicycle was labelled as anger or became attached to participant's anger, resulting in more aggressive behaviour. Figure 11.3 summarizes the results in each of the four conditions. Zillmann and his colleagues referred to the effect in the *anger + arousal* condition as **excitation transfer**: unrelated physiological arousal can be linked to anger-related thoughts and cognitions, and ultimately increase anger-related aggression. In the condition where participants were angered but then spent some time quietly performing a nonstrenuous task, anger-induced arousal presumably dissipated over time.

excitation transfer

the idea that physiological arousal from sources other than frustration or anger can be linked to anger-related thoughts and cognitions, thereby increasing aggression

One of the interesting things about excitation transfer is that it can increase aggressive behaviour even when people are no longer consciously aware of a state of arousal. Dolf Zillmann and Jennings Bryant (1974) found that the transfer of excitation increased aggression after participants had left the arousing setting and their physiological arousal had partly dissipated. These findings imply that an arousing event (e.g., a raucous sports game or a boisterous concert) may cause people to respond to insults or other provocation with greater intensity of aggression even after they have left the arousing setting.

	Arousal	No arousal
Anger	Aggression	No aggression
No anger	No aggression	No aggression

FIGURE 11.3 Diagram of conditions in Zillmann, Katcher, and Milavsky experiment, 1972

Social Learning Theory

The perspectives on aggression we have described (frustration–aggression and excitation transfer) assume that physiological arousal is a key cause of aggression. But how do people *learn* to be aggressive in the first place? Where do they acquire knowledge about how to hit, push, or insult others? **Social learning theory** (Bandura, 1973; Bandura & Walters, 1963) proposes that humans learn many kinds of responses, including aggressive ones, by observing other people (who may *not* be *intentionally* demonstrating the responses). For example, children may watch other children and adults during their daily activities. Watching other people both shows us how to perform a behaviour and teaches us whether that behaviour will be rewarded or punished (based on whether the people we watch are rewarded or punished). A social learning perspective on aggression posits that people often learn aggressive behaviours by observing others being rewarded (or, at least, not being punished) for aggressive actions, and then imitate or model those responses. Individuals' personal experiences of rewards or punishments following their own aggression then further shape their behaviour. This perspective raises obvious concerns about depictions of violence in the mass media, because children (and adults) can presumably learn aggressive behaviour from the media.

social learning theory
an approach proposing that humans learn many kinds of responses, including aggressive ones, by observing others; observation shows people both how to perform a behaviour and whether that behaviour will be rewarded or punished

Let us describe one of the classic experimental demonstrations of social learning. This study used Bobo dolls, which are inflatable dolls with a weighted, rounded bottom, so they always bounce back if you try to knock them over. They are typically painted with a smiling clown's face. Albert Bandura, a Canadian who is a professor at Stanford University, and his colleagues Dorothea Ross and Sheila Ross (1963) gave nursery school children the opportunity to play with a Bobo doll. The children, who ranged in age from three to five years, were first divided into three experimental groups and one control group. One experimental group observed an adult model acting very aggressively toward a Bobo doll. The model punched the doll, sat on it and punched it in the nose, hit it on the head with a mallet, tossed it in the air, and kicked it around the room, all the while saying things like "Sock him in the nose," "Hit him down," "Throw him in the air," "Kick him," and "Pow." This kind of behaviour is far more aggressive than what children would ordinarily or spontaneously do, but provided a number of very specific things for the children to learn. A second experimental group saw the same adult model perform the same actions, but in a film rather than live. The third experimental group watched a cartoon version of aggressive behaviour, in which a cartoon cat was shown being aggressive with the Bobo doll. The control group of children did not see any aggressive models.

After witnessing these aggressive acts (in the experimental conditions), the child was led to another room. The room was filled with highly attractive toys—a young child's dream! The child definitely wanted to play with some of those toys. But it was not to be. The experimenter explained that these were her very best toys, and that

After watching an adult aggress against a Bobo doll, children were likely to engage in imitative aggression against a similar doll.

cognitive neoassociation model of aggression

a theory of harm-doing proposing that aversive events activate the schemas for fight and flight, which elicit the emotions of anger and fear; whether people respond with aggression or escape depends on the pattern of cues in the situation

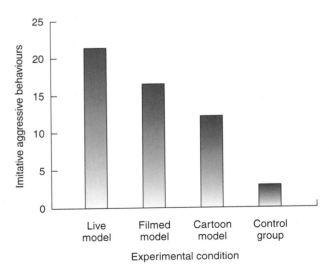

FIGURE 11.4 Number of acts of imitative aggression in each condition

From Bandura et al., "Imitation of film-mediated aggressive models," *Journal of Abnormal and Social Psychology,* 66, 3–11, 1963. Copyright © 1963 by the American Psychological Association. Reprinted by permission.

she did not let just anyone play with them. No, these toys were being reserved for some *other* children. Talk about frustrating. Indeed, this was the point. To provide some instigation for aggression, the children were deliberately frustrated by being denied access to these wonderful toys.

The child was then led to yet another room containing a variety of less dazzling, everyday toys. These toys included nonaggressive toys, such as a tea set, crayons, dolls, cars, and trucks. But also available in the room was a small Bobo doll, a mallet, and other aggressive toys such as dart guns and a suspended tetherball with a face painted on it. The child was given 20 minutes of free play time, during which observations were made of aggressive behaviour. Figure 11.4 presents the average levels of imitative aggression exhibited by children in each group. Children in the control group engaged in very few of the aggressive actions that had been specifically modelled by the adult, confirming that children of this age are unlikely to spontaneously engage in aggressive actions against a Bobo doll. This is not to say that aggression was absent in the control group; in fact, children in the control group were just as likely as children in the experimental groups to engage in aggression that had not been modelled by the adult, such as gun play. However, children in the experimental groups were far more likely to also exhibit imitative aggression: striking the Bobo doll, kicking it, tossing it in the air, and so on. Thus, these children had learned a specific way to act aggressively when frustrated.

Social learning theory identifies the learning processes involved in aggressive behaviour. It does not dispute the role of frustration or aversive arousal in the *instigation* of aggression; instead, it focuses on how people learn specific patterns of aggressive responding, which will be exhibited when they are angry or frustrated. For example, young hockey players learn to fight by watching their heroes in the National Hockey League; they will imitate the aggressive behaviour when they have been angered or frustrated in a game. Note that other sports are just as arousing and frustrating as hockey, such as football and basketball, but are much less disrupted by fighting than hockey. Why? One explanation is that the norms of hockey treat fighting as acceptable, so players use it to release frustration and to intimidate other players. In most other sports, fighting is not valued or approved, so players do not engage in it. The key difference is that fighting is often rewarded in hockey but usually punished in other sports.

One of the important lessons of the social learning approach is that people acquire knowledge about aggressive behaviour. The next perspective builds on this point.

Cognitive Neoassociation Model

Over time, people pick up knowledge about aggression and aggressive behaviour, which gets stored and organized in memory. For example, by watching others and by acquiring information in the environment, people learn that certain situations and feelings are associated with aggressive responding. You will recall from Chapter 3, "Social Cognition," that human memory is organized around *schemas* and *associative networks* that connect those schemas. Once a schema becomes *activated* in memory, it tends to bring to mind other schemas through a process of *spreading activation.*

These basic features of social cognition were used by Leonard Berkowitz (1990; Berkowitz & Heimer, 1989) at the University of Wisconsin to develop a **cognitive neoassociation model of aggression.** The idea is that aggression results from a process of spreading activation. Initially, an unpleasant event arouses negative affect (negative emotion). This negative affect then simultaneously activates two distinct schemas, or response tendencies. One is the tendency to *fight*—the type of responses we associate with aggression or harm-doing. The other is the tendency toward *flight*—the type of responses we associate with escape or avoidance. Through a process of spreading activation, these two schemas further activate *anger* (the emotion associated with fight) and *fear* (the emotion associated with flight).

If an unpleasant event causes you to simultaneously experience anger and fear, how do you decide to act on one versus the other? How does frustration or provocation or any other unpleasant event ultimately lead to the choice between aggression versus running away? The answer is that it depends on the pattern of cues in the situation. If other events or cues in the situation produce relatively greater activation of schemas related to anger, then aggression is more likely to be the result. If other cues are more likely to activate schemas related to fear, then flight is the more probable response.

Many different objects and symbols can serve as aggression-related cues.

What sorts of cues will activate anger and aggression? Unfortunately, aggression-related cues are very common. Guns, knives, aggressive song lyrics, violent movies, insulting phrases, and hostile symbols are readily associated in North American culture with anger and aggression. According to the cognitive neoassociation model of aggression, the presence of such cues in the environment will lead to more aggressive behaviour in response to aversive arousal. Most of the research on this hypothesis has supported it.

A classic experiment was conducted by Leonard Berkowitz and Anthony LePage (1967). Student participants at the University of Wisconsin received either one or seven electric shocks from a partner (actually a confederate of the experimenter). The students were then given an opportunity to return electric shocks back to their partner, presumably as a method for evaluating his performance; the duration of these shocks (how long the shock lever was held down) was recorded. In some conditions, the table at which the participant was seated was empty except for the shock button. In other conditions, however, a 12-gauge shotgun and a .38-calibre revolver were lying on the table near the shock button—they were described as belonging to the participant's partner (this cover story might not work today). As shown in Figure 11.5, the participants clearly retaliated with shocks of greater duration when they had earlier received seven rather than one shock themselves. In addition, however, the extent of retaliation to seven shocks was significantly greater when weapons were present than when they were absent.

Some researchers (e.g., Page & Scheidt, 1971) suggested that this "weapons effect" was the result of *demand characteristics,* which we defined in Chapter 2 as cues in a study that suggest to participants how they are supposed to respond (see page 50). The idea is that participants guessed that the guns were supposed to make them more aggressive, so they responded to confirm this hypothesis. Subsequent studies have produced evidence arguing against the role of demand characteristics, however. The basic effect has been found numerous times in different settings with different aggression cues (e.g., Bartholow et al., 2005; Leyens & Parke, 1975; Turner, Layton, & Simons, 1975) and has been confirmed in comprehensive reviews of the literature (e.g., Bettencourt & Kernahan, 1997). Thus, the conclusion that aggressive cues, such as weapons, can increase aggressiveness seems valid.

GAM Again

This brings us back to the *general aggression model (GAM)* with which we began our discussion of theories of aggression (see Figure 11.1, page 423). How do the specific theories fit into this general model? The category of *situational variables* in the GAM encompasses elements of several specific theories, including frustration (from the frustration–aggression hypothesis), exercise (from excitation transfer), and aggression

11.1
ONLINE
LAB

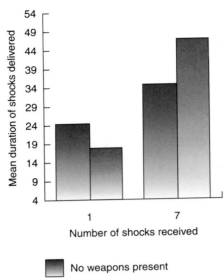

FIGURE 11.5 Duration of shocks delivered in each condition

From Berkowitz and LePage, "Weapons as aggression-eliciting stimuli," *Journal of Personality and Social Psychology*, 7, 202–207, 1967. Copyright © 1967 by the American Psychological Association. Reprinted by permission.

cues (from the cognitive neoassociation model). These sources of arousal and cognition initiate a process that can lead to aggression. The category of *individual differences* in the GAM is relatively distinct from the specific theories we have covered, but the next section, "Influences on Aggression," will discuss some of these variables.

The three categories of *aggressive thoughts*, *aggressive feelings*, and *physiological arousal* in the GAM capture elements of each of the specific theories. For example, hormone levels may be associated with differences in physiological arousal in response to provocation, and the excitation transfer perspective assumes that arousal from any source can heighten aggressive responding. The frustration–aggression hypothesis postulates that aggressive feelings (e.g., hostility) result from frustrating circumstances. Social learning theory and the cognitive neoassociation model emphasize the importance of knowledge and thoughts about aggression.

The category of *appraisal processes* in the GAM is probably most closely connected to the cognitive neoassociation model of aggression, which posits that when anger schemas are activated, the response tendency to *fight* will guide behaviour. The excitation transfer perspective is also related to the category of *appraisal processes*, because it assumes that arousal from any source can be (mis)interpreted as anger.

Finally, the category of *behavioural choice* in the GAM encompasses elements of social learning theory and the cognitive neoassociation model. Social learning theory addresses how people learn aggressive responses, and the cognitive neoassociation model posits that either *fight* or *flight* responses can occur depending on the strength of the activation of anger versus fear schemas.

The GAM provides a useful framework for future research on aggression. Each step in the model identifies important aspects of the transition from negative events to aggressive behaviour. In the following sections, we describe additional research on factors that influence aggression. Although these studies were not specifically guided by the GAM, they can be seen as relevant to one or more of the categories in the model. The various theories of aggression are summarized in the accompanying Concept Review.

CONCEPT REVIEW
Theories of Aggression

Theory	Description/Key Features	Limitations/Outlook
General aggression model (GAM)	Aggressive behaviour is the result of a chain of processes; this model integrates the other theories	A recent model that provides a useful framework for future research
Biological influences on aggression	Aggression is affected by hormones and other physiological factors	Humans can inhibit or suppress innate aggressive impulses
Frustration–aggression hypothesis	Interference with obtaining desired goals causes aggression	Factors other than frustration cause aggression; catharsis does not occur
Excitation transfer model	Arousal from any source can produce or increase aggression	Does not address the most common causes of aggression
Social learning theory	Individuals learn aggressive responses by observing other people	Focuses on how aggression is learned rather than when aggression will occur
Cognitive neoassociation model	Unpleasant events arouse negative emotions, which cause aggression if aggression cues in the situation activate *fight* and *anger* schemas	Applies recent work in social cognition to aggression

● ● ●   Influences on Aggression

Most of the current research on aggression is aimed at understanding its determinants—factors that cause an increase or decrease in aggressive behaviour. In this
section, we discuss several of these influences.

Individual Differences

Have you ever noticed that some people are more aggressive than others? They may
be defensive and argumentative, especially when criticized. Or they may just seem
more likely than most people to respond to unpleasant events with aggression rather
than walking away or some other less confrontational response. The GAM includes
a category of influences on aggression labelled *individual differences* (see Figure 11.1,
page 423). Why are some people more aggressive? We mention three relevant dimensions here.

Narcissism. In Chapter 5, "The Person in the Situation," we discussed the dimension of *narcissism,* which refers to an excessive love for the self (see page 167). People
who are high in narcissism have inflated views of their self-worth, which are not connected to reality. We noted in Chapter 5 that narcissistic individuals tend to be defensive about criticism that threatens their high ego. Therefore, when criticized,
narcissistic individuals often respond with hostility and aggression—a response
labelled *threatened egotism* (see Baumeister, Smart, & Boden, 1996; Baumeister,
Bushman, & Campbell, 2000; Bushman & Baumeister, 1998; Twenge & Campbell,
2003). Thus, one cause of individual differences in aggression is narcissism.

Trait Aggressiveness. Arnold Buss and Mark Perry (1992) observed that
some people are more likely to respond to *any* provocation with aggression than are
other individuals. They labelled this dimension **trait aggressiveness** and developed
the **Aggression Questionnaire (AQ)** to measure it. The AQ consists of four related
dimensions: physical aggression, verbal aggression, anger, and hostility. Selected
items from the scale are reproduced in Know Yourself 11.1: "Trait Aggressiveness."
People who score high on this scale are hypothesized to be more aggressive. Do you
consider yourself to be an aggressive person? Answer the items in the Know
Yourself feature to see whether the descriptions tend to be characteristic or uncharacteristic of you. Buss and Perry (1992) presented evidence showing that scores on
the AQ correlated with ratings of participants' aggressiveness obtained from
acquaintances (that is, high scorers were rated as more aggressive by acquaintances
than were low scorers).

   Brad Bushman (1996) wondered whether people who score high on the AQ also possess more elaborate schemas related to aggression. This idea was based on the cognitive neoassociation model of aggression described earlier. To test the hypothesis,
Bushman selected 160 students to participate in his study: 80 had scored very high on
the AQ and 80 had scored very low. Bushman asked these students to examine pairs of
words and to evaluate how "similar, associated, or related" each word pair was. The
words were drawn from two sets: a set of 10 aggressive words (blood, butcher, choke,
fight, gun, hatchet, hurt, kill, knife, wound) and a set of ten ambiguous words (alley,
animal, bottle, drugs, movie, night, police, red, rock, stick). The ambiguous words were
selected so they could be interpreted as reflecting aggressiveness but would not necessarily be so interpreted. When the words were paired in all possible combinations, they
fell into three word-pair categories: aggressive–aggressive, aggressive–ambiguous, and
ambiguous–ambiguous.

trait aggressiveness
*a disposition that represents how
likely people are to respond to
provocations with aggression*

Aggression Questionnaire (AQ)
*a scale that measures individual
differences in trait aggressiveness*

Know Yourself 11.1
Trait Aggressiveness

Please indicate for each of the following items how *characteristic* or *uncharacteristic* it is of *you* by circling the appropriate number on the answer scale.

1. Once in a while, I cannot control my urge to strike another person.

         1   2   3   4   5
   Extremely uncharacteristic   Extremely characteristic

2. When people annoy me, I may tell them what I think of them.

         1   2   3   4   5
   Extremely uncharacteristic   Extremely characteristic

3. I have trouble controlling my temper.

         1   2   3   4   5
   Extremely uncharacteristic   Extremely characteristic

4. I wonder why sometimes I feel so bitter about things.

         1   2   3   4   5
   Extremely uncharacteristic   Extremely characteristic

5. If somebody hits me, I hit back.

         1   2   3   4   5
   Extremely uncharacteristic   Extremely characteristic

6. I can't help getting into arguments when people disagree with me.

         1   2   3   4   5
   Extremely uncharacteristic   Extremely characteristic

7. Sometimes I fly off the handle for no good reason.

         1   2   3   4   5
   Extremely uncharacteristic   Extremely characteristic

8. When people are especially nice, I wonder what they want.

         1   2   3   4   5
   Extremely uncharacteristic   Extremely characteristic

SCORING: Add up all of the circled numbers for your overall trait aggressiveness score. Possible scores range from 8 to 40, and higher scores represent more trait aggressiveness.

Sample items from Buss and Perry, "The aggressional questionnaire," *Journal of Personality and Social Psychology*, 63, 452–459, 1992. Copyright © 1992 by the American Psychological Association. Reprinted by permission.

Most of the students judged the aggressive-aggressive word pairs (e.g., fight–gun) to be very similar and related to each other. Even for these word pairs, however, the students who scored high on the AQ tended to rate them as *more* similar than did the students who scored low on the AQ. A more interesting difference occurred for the aggressive-ambiguous word pairs, such as blood–animal, hurt–rock, or knife–stick. If people who score high on the AQ tend to have well-developed schemas related to aggression, then they should more readily perceive aggressive connections between these pairs. As predicted, students who had high scores on the AQ, compared to those with low scores, rated the aggressive-ambiguous word pairs as significantly more similar to one another. Thus, people who scored high on a measure of trait aggressiveness seemed to possess relatively elaborate schemas of aggression. The two groups of participants did not differ in their ratings of the similarity of ambiguous–ambiguous word pairs.

Executive Functioning. Effective social behaviour requires continual planning and monitoring. For example, in order to work toward a goal, people must decide a strategy to achieve the goal, assess their progress, and, if necessary, make changes to their initial plan. These sorts of higher-order cognitive processes are called **executive functioning**, because they represent attempts to organize and coordinate several simpler tasks simultaneously (Luria, 1980). Neurological research has indicated that executive functioning is controlled by the frontal lobes of the brain (e.g., Petrides, 1985).

Several studies have found that poor performance on measures of executive functioning is associated with more aggression in response to provocation (e.g., Giancola, 1995; Lau & Pihl, 1994). The usual explanation for this finding is that people with poor executive functioning have difficulty processing multiple pieces of information simultaneously; thus, they fail to notice cues in the setting that typically inhibit aggression (e.g., cues indicating that aggression will be punished).

For example, Darcy Santor and his colleagues at Dalhousie University in Halifax (Santor, Ingram, & Kusumakar, 2003) led 15- and 16-year-old participants to believe that they were competing in a reaction time task with another participant; in reality, there was no second person, and the experimenter provided pre-programmed responses to the actual participant. All participants had previously completed measures of executive functioning. The alleged competitors exchanged verbal messages with one another at the end of each trial by selecting a message from a set of options. These messages ranged from relatively positive ones (e.g., "Keep trying, you can do better"; "Come on, you should be better than that") to extremely negative ones (e.g., "You're a loser"; "I'm kicking your sorry ass"). Results showed that when the alleged partner's behaviour was provocative, participants with poor executive functioning were more aggressive than participants with good executive functioning. Specifically, when the messages participants received from their partner became increasingly negative over trials, poor executive functioning was associated with more aggression (choosing more negative messages to send to the hypothetical competitor). When the partner's messages became increasingly positive over trials, on the other hand, there was no difference in aggression by participants with poor versus good executive functioning. Thus, deficits in executive functioning were associated with stronger aggression under circumstances that were provocative. Presumably, participants with poor executive functioning were less influenced by cues suggesting the inappropriateness of aggression (e.g., the experimental setting, the presence of the experimenter, etc.).

executive functioning
higher-order cognitive processing that organizes and coordinates lower-level elements of behaviour such as planning and monitoring progress toward goals

Alcohol

We often hear of aggressive behaviour in the context of drunken brawls, barroom fights, and other settings in which people have consumed alcohol. One Canadian study found that more than half of the people who committed a violent crime had been drinking alcohol before the event (Murdoch, Pihl, & Ross, 1990). Experimental evidence also confirms that alcohol does indeed increase aggression (Bushman & Cooper, 1990). The typical experiment in this area uses a procedure originally developed by Stuart Taylor (1967). Participants are asked to consume a beverage that may or may not contain alcohol. In the alcohol conditions, participants drink a mixture containing about 2/5 vodka and 3/5 ginger ale, and they end up consuming about 43 grams of vodka for every 18 kilograms of body weight (Gantner & Taylor, 1992). In the control or placebo conditions, the cocktail consists entirely of ginger ale.

© Paul Edmonston/CORBIS

Alcohol intoxication tends to increase aggressive behaviour.

However, even in the placebo conditions, the researcher might place a small amount of vodka around the rim of the glass so that participants cannot easily guess that they have been assigned to the placebo condition.

From that point forward, the typical experiment looks like those we described earlier. The participants are angered or provoked, and then provided an opportunity to retaliate (e.g., by administering electric shocks). Across dozens of experiments like this, it is clear that the consumption of alcohol causes an increase in aggressive behaviour.

Research by Peter Hoaken at the University of Western Ontario and Robert Pihl at McGill University has shown that both men and women become more aggressive when they are intoxicated, but the effect is stronger for men (Hoaken, Campbell, Stewart, & Pihl, 2003; Hoaken & Pihl, 2000). A survey of Ontario adults aged 18 to 60 provided results consistent with this notion that alcohol is more likely to be involved in male than female aggression. Kathryn Graham and Samantha Wells (2001) of the University of Western Ontario found that the majority of men who reported having been involved in an incident of aggression in the last year also reported that they had been drinking alcohol prior to the event, whereas the majority of women who reported having been involved in an incident of aggression in the last year reported that alcohol had not been consumed prior to the event. Thus, male violence seems to be more closely associated with alcohol consumption than female violence, although intoxication increases aggression for both sexes (see also Wells, Graham, Speechley, & Koval, 2005; Wells, Graham, & West, 2000).

Why does alcohol intoxication increase aggression? Several processes contribute to the effects of alcohol (see Hoaken et al., 2003; Pihl & Peterson, 1995; Pihl, Peterson, & Lau, 1993). First, alcohol is a depressant, which affects the brain in such a way that normal inhibitions against aggression are often reduced (Graham, 1980). Second, alcohol has indirect effects on aggression by causing changes in thought, perception, and interpretation. You may recall from Chapter 6, "Attitudes and Social Behaviour," our discussion of the concept of *alcohol myopia* (Steele & Josephs, 1990; see page 211). Alcohol intoxication reduces cognitive capacity and produces a narrowing of attention. Fewer environmental cues than normal can be monitored when an individual is intoxicated. As a result, the most obvious external cues have more impact on behaviour than usual; if these cues are consistent with aggressive behaviour, then aggression is more likely by an intoxicated than by a sober person. Think about the places where people drink: these settings are often loud, crowded, or competitive. By causing a person to focus in on these particular aspects of the environment, alcohol can have the effect of increasing the tendency to respond aggressively.

Recent research by Peter Hoaken has identified a third way that alcohol may increase aggression: it reduces individuals' physiological stress-responses to threats (Hoaken et al., 2003). That is, when faced with a provoking situation (e.g., an insult or a shove in a bar), intoxicated individuals do not experience their typical (sober) level of fear about being punished for an aggressive response (e.g., fear of being beaten up or fear of being charged with assault). Consequently, intoxicated individuals are more likely to respond aggressively to a provocation.

Heat

Another factor known to affect aggression is temperature. Both anecdotal stories and empirical research tell us that aggressive behaviour is more likely to occur when it is hot. For example, crime statistics show that deadly assault is more frequent in hot years than in relatively cooler years (Anderson, Bushman, & Groom, 1997). Generally, field studies show that heat increases aggression, and many laboratory experiments show the same (see Anderson, 1989). Some experiments in this area show that people become increasingly aggressive as the temperature of the room goes up—but only to a certain point (Baron, 1979). Once the heat becomes excessive, aggression actually goes down. Perhaps people simply want to escape the extreme heat, or perhaps their energy is sapped by the highest temperatures.

Why do increases in heat, at least to a certain point, cause increases in aggression? One possibility is that heat makes people uncomfortable and angry, thereby causing aversive arousal that contributes to aggressive behaviour, consistent with an excitation transfer effect. Another possibility is that heat activates cognitive schemas of aggression or violence (perhaps because of physical discomfort), which might increase aggressive responding. An experiment by Craig Anderson and his colleagues (Anderson et al., 1995) provided some support for both of these possible explanations. Participants who had been randomly assigned to sit in a hot room showed significant increases in both aversive arousal and aggressive thoughts compared to participants who had been randomly assigned to sit in a room with a comfortable temperature.

The Social Context of Aggression

The causes and characteristics of aggression change across different social settings. In this section, we consider a few contextual aspects of aggression. We begin by discussing the influence of *culture* on aggression: some cultures condone or permit aggression as an acceptable way to handle conflict more than do other cultures. We then discuss some of the particular social contexts in which aggression appears: on the playground, in close relationships, and in groups.

Culture and Aggression

Social learning theory teaches us that people *learn* how to be aggressive. Our aggressive behaviours are shaped by the environment, especially what we observe in others. If people are immersed from an early age in a culture that encourages and supports aggressive behaviour, then we should not be surprised to find that the people of that culture display a propensity for violence.

If social and cultural environments play a role in shaping aggressive behaviour, then we should find considerable variability in the violence of different cultures and countries. Consistent with this reasoning, Dane Archer and Rosemary Gartner examined a variety of violence-related crimes in 110 countries over the period from 1900 to 1970. Archer and Gartner (1984) looked at the statistics on such crimes as homicide, rape, and assault. When they compared countries, they found that some exhibited a greater propensity for violence than others. For example, of all the industrial nations around the world, the United States had the highest rate of homicides during this period. Why? The researchers suggested that it was because of the ease with which firearms can be obtained in the United States.

Of course, the United States is itself a quilt of varying norms, customs, traditions, and subcultures. And regional differences in violence do exist within the United States. Perhaps the most important of these regional differences is that the homicide rate is greater in southern parts of the country than in northern parts. This finding is one of those results for which a multitude of explanations could be developed. Try to explain this effect yourself. Perhaps it is due to differences in climate. We know that the American South is warmer than the North, and we have already reviewed evidence showing a relationship between heat and aggression. Or perhaps it has something to do with the deeper poverty of the South: poor economic conditions create a breeding ground for frustration and violence. And it may have occurred to you that the southern history of slavery and racial conflict might still be exerting a residual effect.

These are all reasonable explanations, and each probably contributes at least in part to the observed regional differences in homicide rates. But social psychologists Richard Nisbett and Dov Cohen (1996) suggested that another factor was important. These researchers proposed that the people of the southern United States belong to a **culture of honour**—a culture in which White non-Hispanic men, in particular, are taught from an early age to defend their honour and their reputation for strength and toughness. According to this view, when a southern man is insulted, thus threatening his reputation, the proper response is one of dominance, violence, or aggression.

culture of honour

a social network in which men are taught from an early age to defend their reputation for strength by responding to insults or threats with aggression

Nisbett and Cohen marshalled considerable evidence for this interpretation. They linked the culture of honour with a regional history of people deriving their livelihood from the herding of animals. Unlike the North, much of the southern United States was settled chiefly by immigrant herders from Ireland, Scotland, and Wales. Nevertheless, not all parts of the southern United States have roots in a herding economy; in support of Nisbett and Cohen's analysis, homicide rates within the southern United States are substantially higher in the *herding* regions (the hills and dry plains) than in the *farming* regions.

The relationship between insults and aggression in the southern culture of honour has also been studied in the laboratory. Cohen and Nisbett and their colleagues Brian Bowdle and Norbert Schwarz (1996) observed White male students at the University of Michigan who had been raised in the South or the North of the United States. The procedure was designed to deliver an insult to the experimental participant and then measure an aggression-related outcome. Participants were first asked to complete a short questionnaire and then take it to a table at the end of a long and narrow hallway. Cohen and his colleagues (1996) described what happened next:

> As the participant walked down the hall, a confederate of the experimenter walked out of a door marked "Photo Lab" and began working at a file cabinet in the hall. The confederate had to push the file drawer in to allow the participant to pass by him and drop his paper off at the table. As the participant returned seconds later and walked back down the hall toward the experimental room, the confederate (who had re-opened the file drawer) slammed it shut on seeing the participant approach and bumped into the participant with his shoulder, calling the participant an "asshole." (p. 948)

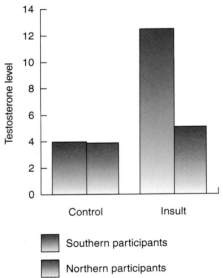

FIGURE 11.6 Changes in testosterone levels for southern and northern participants in each condition

From Cohen et al., "Insult, aggression, and southern culture of honor: An 'experimental ethnography,'" *Journal of Personality and Social Psychology*, 70, 945–960, 1996. Copyright © 1996 by the American Psychological Association. Reprinted by permission.

In one of the experiments, the aggression-related outcome focused on changes in participants' hormone levels. The researchers measured cortisol levels, which is a hormone associated with stress and arousal. They also measured testosterone levels, which, as we mentioned earlier, is a hormone associated with aggressive and dominant behaviour. Both hormones can be assessed from a small sample of saliva, and saliva samples were taken prior to the insult and again right afterwards. Figure 11.6 compares the testosterone results for southern and northern participants who had either been insulted or assigned to a no-insult control condition (the results for cortisol were similar). It is clear that the southern and northern participants responded to the insult in different ways. The southern participants showed elevated testosterone levels, indicating a readiness to respond with aggression.

Lest you think that a "macho" concern with reputation is exclusive to men from the southern United States, a survey of Ontario residents by Kathryn Graham and Samantha Wells (2001) at the University of Western Ontario indicates otherwise. These researchers found that male aggression often results from real or perceived insults in public settings, frequently bars. Men appear to be sensitive to threats to their honour and ready to defend their image physically. The researchers speculated that this kind of aggression "could be reduced by redefining the acceptability of male-to-male aggression" (p. 618).

These findings indicate that cultural factors affect how people respond to provocations. Norms about appropriate responses to insults and threats can influence the aggressiveness of people's actions. In the accompanying box, Social Psychology in Your Life: "Aggression on the Highway," we discuss another form of aggression that is common in our culture: road rage.

Social Psychology in Your Life   *Aggression on the Highway*

A new form of aggressive behaviour has been recognized in the past two decades: road rage. Although anger on the highways has probably been with us for a long time, its aggressive consequences are receiving more attention today. Canadian psychologists Reginald Smart and Robert Mann (2002) were able to find 59 cases of road rage described in Canadian newspapers between 1998 and 2000, involving 4 deaths and 43 injuries. The American Automobile Association (1997) estimated that more than 10 000 incidents of aggression on the highways occurred in the United States between 1990 and 1996. These incidents resulted in more than 200 deaths and more than 12 000 injuries.

It is easy to understand how the highway can be a breeding ground for aggression. Traffic jams produce frustration, and the discomfort of sitting for long periods in a car (especially in hot weather) can produce aversive arousal. Combine these factors with even a small provocation by another driver, and aggression will be elicited from some people.

One strategy for reducing road rage is to focus on characteristics of high-anger drivers, with the goal of developing interventions that might curtail their aggressive driving. Jerry Deffenbacher and his colleagues at Colorado State University have shown that when high-anger drivers recognize their problem and indicate a desire to control it, interventions can be effective in reducing their risky behaviours (e.g., Deffenbacher, Filetti, Richards, Lynch, & Oetting, 2003; Deffenbacher, Huff, Lynch, Oetting, & Salvatore, 2000). These interventions teach high-anger drivers to recognize potentially frustrating and confrontational situations and to reinterpret them as noncompetitive. One specific strategy is to teach *empathy*: the angry driver is told to put himself or herself in the other driver's place. This new perspective often reduces hostility. A key to successful treatment, however, is the admission of a problem. Some angry drivers refuse to acknowledge their problem, and psychological interventions are ineffective for them.

What can you do for yourself? Try to avoid being an angry driver. Don't let another driver's provocation be interpreted as a cause for retaliation. The American Automobile Association (1999) recommends that you avoid offending others in your driving habits and do not get engaged in an escalation of hostility. Try putting yourself in the other driver's place, and try deliberate relaxation techniques such as deep breathing and counting to ten. Everyone loses when aggression appears on the highway.

© Anthony Redpath/CORBIS

Road rage has been associated with many deaths and injuries.

School bullies tend to be rejected by most of their peers.

Aggression on the Playground

One of the most active areas of research on aggression focuses on children and the development of aggressive behaviour (Coie & Dodge, 1998). In this section, we briefly summarize some of this interesting and important developmental work.

Anger emerges as a distinct emotional response within the first six months of life (Stenberg & Campos, 1990). Between the ages of one and two years, children begin to target aggressive behaviour at others. Presumably because of socialization pressures, physical aggression tends to decline and be replaced by verbal aggression as children approach their schooling years. Still, some children continue to engage in physical aggression to control their peers.

Earlier in the chapter, we noted that relational aggression is sometimes associated with peer rejection and sometimes with peer acceptance. When John Coie and Janis Kupersmidt (1983) assembled small groups of previously unacquainted fourth-grade boys, those boys who most often started fights and engaged in both physical and verbal aggression tended to be rejected by the others. Similarly, Kenneth Dodge (1983) found that second-grade boys rejected peers who engaged in verbal aggression and hitting during the initial periods of becoming acquainted.

Two additional observations, however, complicate the issue (Coie & Dodge, 1998). The first is that aggressive behaviour is sometimes viewed as appropriate and justified. For example, children view aggression positively when their peers use it to stand up for themselves (Lancelotta & Vaughn, 1989).

The second observation is that there are subgroups among aggressive children, some of whom are not rejected by their peers. Karen Bierman and her colleagues at Pennsylvania State University (Bierman, Smoot, & Aumiller, 1993) classified elementary school boys into four distinct groups that represented the crossing of two dimensions: boys were classified as either aggressive or not aggressive on the one hand, and as rejected or not rejected by their peers on the other hand. This resulted in the four combinations shown in Figure 11.7. The two subgroups of aggressive boys were equally aggressive, whether they were rejected by their peers or not. The primary thing that distinguished the *rejected* aggressive boys was that they engaged in additional antisocial actions: they were also more argumentative and disruptive than their nonrejected counterparts.

As children get older, they typically learn to use behaviours other than aggression as means for resolving conflict and achieving goals. Yet some children and adolescents continue to engage in physical and verbal aggression, often targeting specific individuals. In the research literature, an everyday term is used to describe such children and adolescents: *school bullies* (Perry, Williard, & Perry, 1990). School bullies tend to fall into the category of rejected and aggressive. Because they are rejected by many of their peers, their main source of affiliation is among themselves (Coie & Dodge, 1998). This fact is a serious problem, because bullies find themselves in a social environment that reinforces and encourages their antisocial behaviour: their friends all do it, and their victims tend to avoid rather than confront their aggression. School bullies are at high risk of school failure, which in turn makes the rest of their life more difficult.

	Rejected	Not rejected
Aggressive	Aggressive–rejected	Aggressive–not rejected
Not aggressive	Rejected–not aggressive	Neither rejected nor aggressive

FIGURE 11.7 Combinations of rejected or not rejected aggressive or not aggressive boys

From Bierman et al., "Characteristics of aggressive-rejected, aggressive (nonrejected), and rejected (nonaggressive) boys," *Child Development*, 64, 139–151, 1993. Reprinted by permission of Blackwell Publishing.

Understanding the development of aggression in children is essential if we hope to intervene to teach adaptive social skills. Such interventions will be an important topic in future research.

Aggression in Close Relationships

When we think about our close relationships—the ones with parents, children, siblings, and lovers—we prefer to focus on the positive and fulfilling aspects of those relationships. Yet even in the closest of relationships, violent aggression sometimes enters the scene. It has been estimated that 25% or more of intimate couples have experienced at least one episode of physical aggression within the relationship (Straus & Gelles, 1990). In fact, women are more likely to be physically abused by current or former male partners than by strangers (Koss, Goodman, Browne, Fitzgerald, Keita, & Russo, 1994). Murder is one of the leading causes of death among children and youth, and most homicides of infants are committed by their parents or caretakers (Finkelhor, 1997). These are sobering statistics and emphasize a need to focus on and understand violence in the context of close relationships.

Most of the research on aggression in close relationships has focused on heterosexual married couples. In this context, it is important to distinguish between psychological aggression and physical aggression. Examples of psychological aggression against a partner include public humiliation, threats of harm, or destruction of a partner's possessions. Physical aggression includes pushing, hitting, burning, kicking, using a weapon, or otherwise causing direct physical harm to a partner. Daniel O'Leary and his colleagues at the State University of New York at Stony Brook have investigated violence in married couples. One longitudinal study of early marriages found that psychological aggression is a good predictor of later physical aggression (Murphy & O'Leary, 1989). Another large-scale study, involving more than 10 000 couples, found that women were more likely to be the victims of physical aggression when their husbands suffered from an alcohol or drug problem, depression, low income, or the stress of marital discord (Pan, Neidig, & O'Leary, 1994). Not surprisingly, incidents of aggression early in a marriage are very predictive of a marriage breaking apart (Rogge & Bradbury, 1999).

Batterers. We have noted that husbands sometimes engage in psychological and physical aggression against their wives. What kind of men direct aggressive behaviour toward female partners? Work in clinical psychology suggests that subgroups of batterers share certain characteristics. In particular, research by Amy Holtzworth-Munroe and her colleagues at Indiana University has shown that violent husbands generally fall into one of three subgroups (Holtzworth-Munroe, 2000; Holtzworth-Munroe & Stuart, 1994; Holtzworth-Munroe, Stuart, & Hutchinson, 1997; see also Waltz, Babcock, Jacobson, & Gottman, 2000):

- *Family-only:* These are the least violent men, and they rarely exhibit aggressive behaviour outside the home. Their aggression can typically be traced to stress, poor relationship skills, and perhaps exposure to marital violence when they were children. Family-only aggressors tend to regret their actions, and interventions can produce a positive change in behaviour.

Women are more likely to be physically abused by current or former male partners than by strangers.

- *Dysphoric/borderline:* These are relatively more violent men, who sometimes engage in severe physical abuse. Although focused mainly on their wives, these men occasionally exhibit aggressive behaviour outside the home. But more important, these men exhibit signs of psychological distress: depression, anxiety, fear of rejection, extreme mood swings, and poor relationships skills. Dysphoric/borderline aggressors often have a history of being abused by their own parents, and it is much more difficult to bring about a positive change in behaviour.

- *Generally violent/antisocial:* These are violent men who do not discriminate in their aggression—it just happens that their wives are more often available as targets. Substance abuse, criminal behaviour, and other signs of antisocial personality characteristics are common among these men. They harbour hostile attitudes toward women and generally consider violence to be an acceptable way of interacting with others. They are extremely resistant to interventions designed to reduce their violence against their wives.

These distinctions among batterers are important because husbands who engage in family-only aggression are most amenable to interventions that can curb their violence and allow them to develop a healthier marital relationship (Holtzworth-Munroe, 2000). Thus, the limited resources available for interventions should probably be directed primarily at these husbands. Law enforcement may be the only way to deal with the more violent batterers. The distinctions also illustrate the idea from the *general aggression model* that there are individual differences in people's tendencies to have aggressive thoughts and feelings.

Effects on Children. Domestic violence is often witnessed by children. As we noted above, one characteristic of many men who abuse their wives is that they once witnessed their own parents' violence. Many (but not all) children who are exposed to violence between their parents show adverse consequences in their own psychological adjustment, interactions with peers, and progress in school (Kitzmann, Gaylord, Holt, & Kenny, 2003). Consistent with social learning accounts of aggressive behaviour, surveys and longitudinal studies have found that children who are exposed to domestic violence between their parents are at increased risk, as adults, of either perpetrating or being the victim of violence in their own close relationships (e.g., Ehrensaft, Cohen, Brown, Smailes, Chen, & Johnson, 2003).

For example, Marilyn Kwong, Kim Bartholomew, Antonia Henderson, and Shanna Trinke (2003) of Simon Fraser University conducted a telephone survey of 1249 adults in the Vancouver area. Respondents answered a set of questions about physical aggression between their parents (father to mother or mother to father) and from each parent to themselves (father to self or mother to self). Respondents also answered questions about both physical and psychological aggression within their own intimate relationships as adults, either by them directed against their partner or by their partner directed against them (self to partner or partner to self). Virtually all of the measures of violence in respondents' family histories correlated with virtually all of the measures of violence in respondents' adult intimate relationships. In other words, those individuals who witnessed or experienced violence during their childhoods were more likely to be involved in violent relationships as adults. Violence begat violence. It is not a cliché to say that interventions are needed to break the cycle of violence that is passed on from one generation to the next.

Aggression in Groups

To this point, the type of aggression we have focused on has been that of individuals aggressing against other individuals. Sometimes, however, people behave aggressively in the context of a social group. Riots, lynchings, and the behaviour of unruly crowds at sporting events are often cited as examples of *mob violence.* A **mob** is "a crowd acting under strong emotional conditions that often lead to violence or illegal acts" (Staub & Rosenthal, 1994, p. 281). Mob violence can reflect organized leadership, such as the planned actions of the Ku Klux Klan, but more often it is relatively unorganized and even spontaneous, such as violence that occurs at sporting events or during political protests.

We have discussed in previous chapters two social psychological processes that might contribute to mob violence. One is *deindividuation,* which we defined in Chapter 10 as a loss of personal identity and a sense of immersion in a group (see page 377). Deindividuation tends to occur in large groups and may reduce individuals' sense of responsibility for their actions, which can then decrease their inhibitions against committing violence. A second process is *conformity pressure,* which can lead individuals to copy the behaviour of others even when the action runs contrary to what those individuals would ordinarily do when alone (see Chapter 8, "Conformity, Compliance, and Obedience").

Several laboratory studies have provided experimental evidence that deindividuation can increase aggressive behaviour. For instance, Steven Prentice-Dunn and Ronald Rogers (1980; Rogers & Prentice-Dunn, 1981) at the University of Alabama developed a laboratory procedure that either induced deindividuation or emphasized participants' personal identities. Participants arrived for the experiment in small groups of four or five. Unknown to the participants, one member of the group was always an accomplice who worked for the experimenter. As is frequently done in laboratory experiments on aggression, the situation was set up so that the naïve participants believed that they could administer electric shocks to a victim.

Some participants were randomly assigned to a condition that fostered a sense of deindividuation: these participants were never addressed by name, were told that their individual levels of electric shocks would not be known to the experimenter, believed that they would never meet the recipient (victim) of the shocks, and heard

mob

a crowd acting under strong emotional conditions that often lead to violence or illegal acts

Mob violence is often unplanned and unorganized.

the experimenter accept full responsibility for the victim's well-being. Participants in the identity-enhancing condition, in contrast, wore nametags, were addressed by their first names, were led to believe that their individual choices of electric shocks would be known to the experimenter, anticipated meeting the victim afterwards, and were given personal responsibility for any harm done to the victim.

All participants then completed a procedure that allowed them to administer electric shocks to the experimental accomplice. Participants exhibited significantly more aggression (administered more electric shock) when they were in a state of deindividuation than when their personal identity was emphasized. Presumably, deindividuation weakened participants' restraints against aggression.

Although mob violence occurs, it is important to remember that people often gather in large groups or crowds without engaging in aggressive or violent acts. Just as people seldom act aggressively when alone, groups seldom engage in violence without some kind of instigating event (Staub & Rosenthal, 1994). What kind of events can precipitate mob violence? Typically, they are events that make people *angry*. Most of the riots that have occurred in North American cities can be traced to specific events that instilled anger among the participants (Downes, 1968). For example, an occurrence (or perceived occurrence) of police brutality can spark a riot (Stark, 1972), such as occurred in April 2001 in Quebec City when city police responded to a few rock-throwing demonstrators at the Summit of the Americas with a barrage of tear gas that affected many innocent bystanders and incited wider acts of violence by the crowd. A combination of anger and deindividuation produced by a large group can be a recipe for aggressive behaviour. These kinds of events illustrate that people may respond to situational variables with aggressive thoughts and feelings, as predicted by the *general aggression model.*

Media Effects on Aggression

To this point, we have focused on *person-to-person* ways of transmitting aggression, such as interpersonal frustration, modelling effects, and cultural learning. The *mass media,* including television, movies, and the Internet, have the potential to magnify these person-to-person processes many times over. For example, millions of viewers watch particular episodes of a television show, and most of us surf the Internet at least occasionally. This enormous exposure explains why social psychologists have been very interested in studying the possible effects of the mass media on aggression. The media fit into the category of *situational variables* in the GAM: television programs or video games can elicit aggressive thoughts, feelings, and arousal within individuals, which may eventually lead to aggressive behaviour.

The primary reason social psychologists are concerned about possible effects of the media is that violence is so common in television, movies, and video games. Think about your own exposure to media violence: viewing television programs with frequent episodes of aggression, listening to popular music with violent lyrics, watching aggressive sports, and playing video games with violent content. It is very difficult to avoid exposure to media violence in Canada. Have you ever noticed yourself acting differently because of violence you saw on television? Some defenders of the television and movie industries have suggested that violent programs actually provide safe and harmless outlets for aggressive impulses.

The question of whether the media cause or encourage aggressive behaviour is at the centre of a great societal debate. Some of the person-to-person processes we have covered in the chapter raise serious concerns about possible negative effects of media violence. But these studies were not designed to investigate the media directly. In the following paragraphs, we turn to research that has specifically investigated the effects of the mass media on aggressive behaviour.

Television Violence

One of the best examples of social psychological research on the effects of exposure to violent television programming was reported recently by a research team at the University of Michigan led by L. Rowell Huesmann (Huesmann, Moise-Titus, Podolski, & Eron, 2003). This study actually started in the late 1970s, with a sample of more than 500 eight- and nine-year-old children in the Chicago area who were followed over a period of three years (Huesmann & Eron, 1986). The children were observed and tested to determine the amount of their exposure to TV violence, the degree to which they identified with aggressive television characters, and the extent of their aggressive behaviour with peers. Results from this initial wave of observation showed that the more aggressive children were also the ones who watched more television, indicated a preference for violent shows, and more strongly identified with the aggressive characters in those shows. It was the combination of heavy exposure to television violence and identification with aggressive characters that particularly predicted aggressive behaviour.

You may be thinking that childhood aggression is just a normal part of growing up. We have already noted that many children hit and push each other on the playground, but this is hardly the kind of aggression we worry about among adult members of society. Hold that thought. Fast-forward 15 years, when the original sample of children studied by Huesmann and Eron are in their early 20s. It is the 1990s, and the children are now young adults: they have jobs and spouses, and some have already been convicted of violent crimes.

Huesmann and his colleagues were able to locate and re-interview nearly 400 of the participants from the earlier study. The measures of aggression used in the follow-up study reflected the kinds of aggression we *do* worry about among adult members of society: indirect aggression such as stealing things; verbal aggression such as calling a person names or mocking another's abilities; physical aggression such as hitting, kicking, or shoving people; spousal abuse; and criminal violence. Now 15 years later, the earlier results were confirmed. The most aggressive adults were the ones who, as children, had watched more violence on television and had identified more strongly with the aggressive characters. This was true for both the men and the women, and was independent of socioeconomic status, intellectual ability, and other demographic variables (Huesmann et al., 2003).

What are the processes through which exposure to violent television programming might increase aggressive behaviour? Several of the factors discussed previously in the chapter could be involved. Perhaps most directly, violence on television presents models of aggressive behaviour, who teach viewers how to aggress and typically show that aggression has positive consequences. Violent programming can also prime hostile and aggressive thoughts, as well as elicit aggressive feelings (e.g., anger at the "bad guys" and satisfaction when they are shot). Frequent violence on television might also desensitize viewers to aggression, making violent behaviour seem more normal and acceptable.

The findings of Huesmann and his colleagues (2003) are sobering. Long-term exposure to television violence is correlated with aggressive behaviour within viewers who identify strongly with violent characters. Of course, these data are correlational, so we cannot be certain about cause and effect (e.g., aggressive people may be attracted to aggressive television), a point emphasized by some critics, including University of Toronto social psychologist Jonathan Freedman (1984, 1992). But numerous experimental studies have also been conducted, and they have

Children who watch a lot of violent television programming tend to be more aggressive than children who watch less violent television programming.

generally shown a significant effect of exposure to violent television programs on aggression (for summaries, see Geen, 1998; Paik & Comstock, 1994; Wood, Wong, & Chachere, 1991). Many of these experimental studies were admittedly artificial (and therefore lacked mundane realism—see page 56), but when combined with the field studies make for a convincing indictment of violent television programming (Anderson et al., 2003; Anderson & Bushman, 2002b; Bushman & Anderson, 2001b; Johnson, Cohen, Smailes, Kasen, & Brook, 2002).

It is interesting to consider the "size" of the effect of viewing television violence on aggressive behaviour. Just how "big" or "significant" is television's impact on aggression?

Brad Bushman and Craig Anderson (2001b) compared the size of television's effect on aggression to other effects that help us to interpret the importance of the findings. Figure 11.8 presents the relative sizes of several effects. The first column represents the effect of smoking on lung cancer; the second column represents the effect of viewing violent television programs on aggression; the third column represents the effect of playing violent video games on aggression (which we discuss in the next section); and the fourth column represents the effect of calcium intake on bone mass. You can see from the figure that the effect of violent television on aggressive behaviour is not as strong as the effect of smoking on lung cancer, but it is larger than the effect of calcium intake on bone mass—a finding that is considered well proven by medical researchers.

In summary, it seems that a specific mixture of variables involving violent television is predictive of adult aggressive behaviour. Not everyone is negatively affected by television violence. But elevated adult aggression is found among men and women who, as children, (1) *watched a lot of violent television,* and (2) *identified strongly with aggressive characters featured on television.* These results make good social psychological sense. Watching a lot of violent television programs provides repeated opportunities to learn aggressive

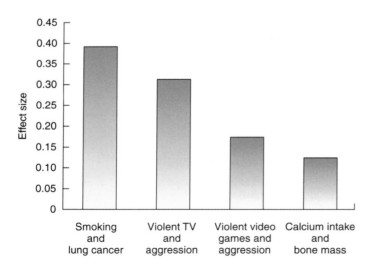

FIGURE 11.8 Comparisons of the effect of television violence on aggression with other effects

From Bushman and Anderson, "Media violence and the American public: Scientific facts versus media misinformation," *American Psychologist*, 56, 477–489, 2001. Copyright © 2001 by the American Psychological Association. Reprinted by permission.

behaviours. Identifying strongly with aggressive television characters motivates viewers to copy the characters' behaviour. After all, violence seemed to work on television, so it might be effective in dealing with one's own problems as well. This hypothesized process through which violent television can influence behaviour is depicted in the flowchart in Figure 11.9.

Violent Video Games

The advent of violent video games in the past 15 years has added a new wrinkle to media aggression. Unlike television, video games are highly *interactive*: players make rapid-fire decisions to behave aggressively in the games. The immediate satisfaction of seeing an enemy destroyed might be a strong reinforcement for aggression. Also, playing violent video games seems likely to elicit aggressive thoughts and emotions, which might influence subsequent behaviour. On the other hand, the violence in video games is less realistic than the violence on television (e.g., the characters are animated), which might reduce its impact.

"[People who play a lot of violent video games] will start making more aggressive decisions about how they'll respond to ambiguous or threat situations, conflict situations, than they would have if they had not spent so many hours basically practicing how to be an aggressive person."

The first video games came out in the late 1970s, but violent games became common only in the 1990s with titles like *Mortal Kombat* and *Street Fighter*. More recent games have become increasingly graphic in their portrayal of violence (e.g., *Grand Theft Auto*, *Halo 2*). Statistics indicate that the majority of regular video game players identify *violent* games as their favourites. Many parents and educators have expressed concern about aggressive video games, particularly after events of schoolyard violence such as the Columbine shootings in 1999—Eric Harris and Dylan Klebold enjoyed playing *Doom*, a highly graphic shooting game. In 2000, the mayor of Indianapolis introduced a law banning children under 18 from playing violent arcade video games unless accompanied by an adult (Halladay & Wolf, 2000).

Despite the fact that violent video games have been around only 10 or 15 years, numerous studies have examined the connections between playing these games and aggression. Most studies have been correlational (that is, they simply measured violent video game use and aggression), but some have been experimental (that is, participants were randomly assigned to play violent or nonviolent video games and then given an opportunity to engage in aggression). The measures of aggression have ranged from aggression against inanimate objects (e.g., a Bobo doll) to aggression against another person (e.g., delivering electric shock to someone).

Researchers who have reviewed this literature, however, have made different judgments about the evidence. Mark Griffiths (1999) concluded that all of the published studies on violent video games to that date had enough methodological problems to prevent any clear conclusion. Lillian Bensley and Juliet Van Eenwyk (2001) similarly argued that "current research evidence is not supportive of a major concern that

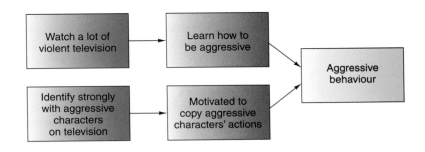

FIGURE 11.9
Hypothesized effects of television violence on behaviour

Playing violent video games may increase subsequent aggression.

violent video games lead to real-life violence" (p. 256). But Craig Anderson and Brad Bushman (2001) came to another conclusion based on a statistical analysis of 33 investigations of the effects of playing violent video games on aggressive behaviour by children and young adults. Across the set of studies, there was a small but statistically significant effect, such that playing violent video games increased aggression. The size of this effect is depicted in Figure 11.8 (page 446) relative to some other findings, including the effect of violent television on aggressive behaviour. The figure shows that the impact of video games is smaller than the impact of violent television (see also Sherry, 2001), but nevertheless larger than such widely accepted findings as the impact of calcium intake on bone mass.

The most consistent evidence that playing violent video games can increase aggressive behaviour has been obtained in studies that used young children (ages ten and under) and that measured aggression by observing the children at play (Bensley & Van Eenwyk, 2001; Griffiths, 1999). For example, University of Mississippi social psychologists A. Roland Irwin and Alan Gross (1995) randomly assigned seven- or eight-year-old boys to play either an aggressive martial arts video game or a nonaggressive but equally arousing motorcycle race video game. After playing the game, the boys interacted with another child in a setting where a variety of toys were available. During this free play period, the boys who had played the martial arts game exhibited more physical aggression toward toys (e.g., punching or kicking a toy) and more verbal aggression toward the other child (e.g., threats or insults) than did the boys who had played the racing game.

If we accept the evidence that violent video games can have undesirable effects, what should we do about it? For instance, should violent video games be banned or legally restricted? Should we instead leave the issue to parents, who should monitor their children's leisure activities (but who do *not* always do so)? These are difficult questions that relate more to social policy than social psychological research. Anderson and Bushman (2001) made an interesting suggestion at the end of their review of research on violent video games; they speculated that video games could potentially be developed that would teach and reinforce *nonviolent* solutions to social conflicts. Although some video games already exist that allow "prosocial" actions (e.g., *The Sims*), few games specifically reward positive, nonviolent responses by the characters. Given that video games appear capable of teaching antisocial responses, perhaps they could be designed to teach prosocial responses instead.

Pornography

A final question about the effects of the media on aggression relates to sexually explicit materials. The term *pornography* is often used in a general way to refer to sexual materials, such as sexually explicit videotapes, men's magazines, and Web sites with sexual content. Critics sometimes claim that pornography increases aggressive behaviour, especially sexual aggression such as rape. A close look at the literature indicates that the picture is rather complicated.

The first thing we need to do is differentiate among types of pornography. James Check, a social psychologist at York University, and William Fisher, a social psychologist at the University of Western Ontario, have suggested that three types of sexually explicit materials should be distinguished, although the boundaries between the categories are not precise (Check & Guloien, 1989; Fisher & Barak, 2001). **Erotica** is sexually explicit material that depicts nonviolent, consensual sexual activity (e.g., a couple engaging in consensual sexual intercourse). **Degrading pornography** is sexually explicit material that debases or dehumanizes people, usually women (e.g., a woman having serial sexual intercourse with several men). **Violent pornography** is sexually explicit material that depicts aggressive, hostile sexual

erotica

sexually explicit material that depicts nonviolent, consensual sexual activity

degrading pornography

sexually explicit material that debases or dehumanizes people, usually women

violent pornography

sexually explicit material that depicts aggressive, hostile sexual activity

activity (e.g., sexual assault). The effects of these three kinds of materials on viewers' attitudes and actions probably differ.

It appears that *erotica* has few, if any, negative effects. For example, Charlene Senn of the University of Windsor and Serge Desmarais of the University of Guelph (2004) recruited women to watch either erotica or degrading pornography with a same-sex friend or with their male partner. Whereas women who watched degrading pornography reported negative moods, those who watched erotica reported relatively positive moods; it did not matter whether they watched the videos with a friend or partner. Other research has shown that when sought out and viewed by couples, erotica results in a short-term increase in their typical sexual activity (see Fisher, 1986). Experiments in which participants have been given an opportunity for aggression after viewing erotica (e.g., after viewing photographs of nudes) have generally found that erotica *reduced* aggression (see Allen, D'Alessio, & Brezgel, 1995). Thus, the portrayal of nonviolent, consensual sexual activity seems to have positive, not negative, effects on aggressiveness.

The effects of degrading or violent pornography are less clear. Depending on whom you talk to, you might be convinced that degrading pornography causes unfavourable attitudes toward women and violent pornography causes aggression against women, or you might be convinced that it is unclear from current research how these stimuli affect attitudes and behaviour in natural settings. Before we elaborate on this controversy, we want to describe a couple of illustrative studies.

In one of the best-known experiments on the effects of pornography, Ed Donnerstein (1980) randomly assigned male participants at the University of Wisconsin to view one of three films. One group of men watched a mild and neutral control film—it had nothing to do with either sex or violence. A second group watched an explicit depiction of heterosexual sex—it was highly erotic, but did not contain any suggestion of aggression, force, or violence between the depicted couple. A third group of men watched a film that was both sexually explicit and aggressive—it portrayed a violent sexual assault.

After viewing one of the films, participants were provided an opportunity to deliver electric shocks to another person. Half of the time, this other person was a woman, and half of the time, it was a man. Results showed an increase in aggression (as measured by the number and intensity of electric shocks) when participants had viewed the violent sexual assault and then had an opportunity to be aggressive toward a woman. The nonviolent, erotic film did not produce any more (nor less) aggression than did the neutral film, and the violent sexual assault film caused an increase in aggression only when the target of that aggression was female and not male.

Not surprisingly, Donnerstein's results received a lot of attention and raised concerns about the negative impact of violent pornography—which is widely available in adult video stores (and now on the Internet). But some researchers expressed doubts about the conclusion that violent pornography causes aggression. For example, William Fisher and Guy Grenier (1994) asked male participants at the University of Western Ontario to write a short essay, which was then evaluated very unfavourably by a female co-participant (actually an accomplice of the experimenter). After receiving this negative evaluation, the male participants were asked whether they would be willing to rate some pretest materials for a study on pornography. All participants agreed, at which point they watched a videotape that depicted a violent sexual assault. After viewing this violent pornography, participants served as the "teacher" in a memory task over an intercom, on which the female co-participant (who had evaluated their essay negatively) was the "learner" in a different room. She made numerous errors on the memory task; participants indicated verbally to her on each trial whether her response was correct or incorrect. After the memory task was completed, participants were told that, if they wished, they could provide an overall evaluation to the woman in one of two ways: they could speak with her over the intercom to give their overall evaluation of her performance, or they could deliver between one and ten electric shocks to the woman to indicate their evaluation (with one or few shocks meaning a good performance, and many shocks meaning a poor performance). (A plausible cover story was given for this shock option.) But participants were also given a third option: because the woman already knew how many mistakes she had made, the participant could simply leave the laboratory immediately if he wished. Only 14% of the men chose to deliver any electric shocks to the woman. The remaining 86% did not engage in any aggression, deciding instead either to leave the experiment (64%) or to provide a verbal evaluation (21%). The authors concluded that exposure to pornography does not motivate men to be aggressive against women—at least, it doesn't motivate them enough to want to remain in an experiment to shock someone who frustrated them.

So what are we to conclude about the effects of violent pornography? Some researchers (e.g., Fisher & Barak, 2001; Fisher & Grenier, 1994) argue that existing data are insufficient to conclude that pornography increases aggression or sexual assault. In this regard, these authors point to police data showing that the incidence of forcible sexual assault in the United States decreased between the years of 1995 and 1999—a period when pornographic materials of all sorts were becoming much more widely available over the Internet. Other researchers (e.g., Malamuth & Check, 1985; Seto, Maric, & Barbaree, 2001) argue that violent pornography is harmful for some men who view it. Specifically, these researchers believe that men who are already predisposed to engage in sexual aggression may be negatively influenced by watching violent pornography, such that they are even more likely to behave violently. These researchers agree that violent pornography has little or no behavioural effect on most people (though it may affect attitudes toward sexuality and women), but they link it to aggression by a few high-risk individuals. Neil Malamuth, who began his academic career at the University of Manitoba, and his colleagues (Malamuth, Addison, & Koss, 2000) suggested that men with a predisposition toward sexual aggression interpret the same pornography differently from nonaggressive men. For example, men with a controlling, hostile approach to sexuality may be more likely than nonaggressive men to pick out images in violent pornography that reinforce links between power, sex, and aggression.

The issue of the effects of violent pornography on aggression will undoubtedly receive more attention from researchers over the next decade. Canadians Charlene Senn and Serge Desmarais (2001, 2004) have argued cogently that sex researchers need to create naturalistic viewing conditions for their studies and to recruit both women and men as participants. The impact of pornography is an important social question that needs to be answered. Even if it can be indisputably established that certain kinds of pornography have negative effects on some individuals, however, the solution will remain uncertain. Introducing legislation to make depictions of certain sexual acts among adults illegal would be both difficult to define precisely and difficult to enforce. Education about the negative effects of violent pornography is an appealing approach, but would such efforts reach the relatively few individuals who are most at risk?

Controlling Aggression and Violence

Social psychologists have learned a great deal about the causes and consequences of human aggressive behaviour. What ideas does this knowledge provide about how aggression and violence might be controlled?

The distinction between hostile and instrumental aggression may be relevant to the issue of controlling aggression. To reduce aggression that results primarily from negative emotional arousal (hostile aggression), one approach might be to teach people how to *control* their negative emotions, such as anger, so aggressive behaviour does not necessarily follow from arousal. To reduce aggression that is designed to obtain a desired goal (instrumental aggression), the most direct approach is probably to teach people alternative, nonaggressive strategies. Finally, another, more general approach to reducing aggression would be to reduce aversive environments that cause pain and frustration. We consider each of these ideas in the following paragraphs, but begin with a very simple idea: reduce the availability of guns.

Gun Control

One straightforward strategy for reducing the negative consequences of aggression is to reduce the availability of guns. Guns may not cause aggression, but they can increase the likelihood that aggressive impulses will have serious consequences like death or physical injury.

Evidence for a connection between guns and injuries comes from comparisons of crime statistics in the United States and Canada. For example, the 2001 murder rate in the United States, where guns are relatively easily obtained and are present in many households, was almost three times as high as the murder rate in Canada, where gun controls are stricter and fewer households own a gun (5.5 murders per 100 000 population in the United States versus 1.8 murders per 100 000 population in Canada). The rates for homicide committed with a firearm differed even more dramatically, with the U.S. rate almost five times as high as the Canadian rate. In contrast, the two countries were very similar in the rates of most nonviolent crimes in 2001, such as break and enter, motor vehicle theft, and other theft.

Comparisons are even more dramatic when particular cities in the United States are identified. For example, the total number of murders in 2001 in Canada, with a population of approximately 30 million, was 554. The city of Chicago, with a population of less than 3 million, had a total of 666 murders in 2001. Detroit, with a population of less than 1 million, had a total of 395 murders in 2001—a rate of 41.3 murders per 100 000 population, compared to Canada's rate of 1.8 murders per 100 000 population.

Of course, these are correlational data, and the United States and Canada (or Detroit and Canada) differ in many ways that might influence homicide rates besides the availability of guns. To take just two examples, there is greater poverty in the United States, and the weather is hotter. But if American and Canadian cities that are matched with one another on some of these dimensions are compared, similar conclusions are reached. For example, a group of researchers from the University of Washington in Seattle (Sloan, Kellerman, Reay, Ferris, Koepsell, Rivara, et al., 1988) compared various statistics from Seattle and Vancouver between 1980 and 1986. Seattle and Vancouver have similar populations, average incomes, and climates. During the period studied, the murder rate was 1.63 times higher in Seattle than Vancouver, a difference that was almost entirely due to murders by handguns, which were 4.8 times higher in Seattle than Vancouver. In contrast, burglary rates were similar in the two cities. The researchers speculated that the greater availability of guns in Seattle was responsible for the differences in murder rates.

Many people own one or more guns for self-protection. But guns in the home are much more likely to be used for purposes other than self-defence. For example, the presence of a gun in the home makes it five times more likely that a family member will commit suicide. A gun triples the probability of a homicide in the home (e.g., the murder of a spouse). A gun in the home is 22 times more likely to kill a family member or friend (accidentally, during a fight, or by suicide) than to kill in self-defence.

Gun control legislation is controversial. Some gun owners strongly defend their right to bear arms, particularly in the United States. The gun registry that was established in Canada by the Liberal government in 1995 has been a financial disaster, proving much more expensive than originally expected (approximately $1.5 billion as of 2005 instead of the anticipated $100 million), and the Conservative government that was elected in 2006 pledged to change or abolish the registry. On the other hand, it does seem plausible that stricter gun controls would, over time, lower the number of handgun deaths in the United States.

Controlling Anger

One approach to reducing aggressive behaviour that is compatible with the *general aggression model* focuses on controlling anger. The GAM emphasizes the role of aggression-related feelings, thoughts, and arousal. According to the model, anger, frustration, or similar emotions *combine* with aggression- or violence-related thoughts to create a tendency to act aggressively. If the aggression-related thoughts can be short-circuited, then aggressive behaviour should be less likely.

For example, people can be taught how to control their anger by changing their thoughts (Novaco, 1975). Jerry Deffenbacher and his colleagues at Colorado State University, whose work with angry drivers is described in Social Psychology in Your Life: "Aggression on the Highway" (page 439), developed an intervention for general anger reduction along these lines (Deffenbacher, Thwaites, Wallace, & Oetting, 1994). University students who identified themselves as having problems with anger and who desired some help with anger management were recruited into the study. The intervention consisted of **cognitive-relaxation coping skills training,** or **CRCS** for short. In this training, people are first taught a series of relaxation skills—how to keep themselves calm and tension-free. Next, they are introduced to the idea of **cognitive restructuring,** learning to reduce their anger by recognizing and modifying their thoughts and attributions. For example, they are taught to think about the fact that another person who has provoked them probably did not *intend* to do so. The final step is to imagine or visualize situations that arouse anger, and then to use the relaxation and cognitive restructuring skills to reduce that anger.

The CRCS intervention has been shown to be effective in producing a reduction in anger, both in the short term and over the long term (Deffenbacher, Oetting, Huff, & Thwaites, 1995). It has also been shown to work well with adolescents (Deffenbacher, Lynch, Oetting, & Kemper, 1996). Thus, this intervention has considerable promise and may eventually be used more widely in the educational system.

cognitive-relaxation coping skills training (CRCS)

an intervention program designed to reduce anger, which involves teaching people a set of relaxation techniques and ways to modify their anger-related thoughts

cognitive restructuring

recognizing and modifying anger-related thoughts and attributions; it forms part of CRCS training

Teaching Alternatives to Aggression

Reducing aggression that results primarily from trying to obtain a desired goal (instrumental aggression) is challenging, because this kind of aggression is seen as *necessary* for achieving the goal. For example, when a parent punishes a child for disobedience, or when a schoolyard bully takes a desired toy away from another child, the aggression is seen as the means to an end.

The best approach to reducing instrumental aggression is probably to convince people that nonaggressive strategies are more successful in the long run. For example, parents can be informed that corporal punishment is ineffective (see Social Psychology in Your Life: "Is Corporal Punishment Effective?" on page 421) and can be taught how to use timeouts and grounding (these techniques also model nonviolence in parents' own actions). Aggressive schoolchildren can be taught that bullying makes them unpopular and can be shown how to reduce conflict in other ways.

Programs that teach children effective, nonaggressive approaches to problem solving have been developed for use in elementary schools (e.g., Eargle, Guerra, & Tolan, 1994). One important skill these programs try to teach is *communication*—children are taught to *talk* about problems and conflicts with peers instead of reacting aggressively. Another important goal of these school programs is to teach *empathy*—putting oneself in the shoes of another and imagining how that person feels. As we noted in our discussion of road rage, empathy often reduces aggressive behaviour (e.g., Richardson, Hammock, Smith, & Gardner, 1994). More generally, improving children's social skills and problem-solving strategies can reduce their reliance on aggressive tactics to achieve goals.

Reducing Aversive Environments

Many aggressive acts occur because people find themselves in aversive environments. Hot, crowded settings elicit discomfort; a slap from another person elicits pain; poverty is associated with hunger. These states of discomfort, pain, and hunger can lead to aggression, as predicted by the *frustration–aggression hypothesis*, the *excitation transfer effect*, and the integrative *GAM*. If it were possible to

Aversive environments increase aggressive behaviour.

reduce the number of aversive environments in society, the amount of aggression would be reduced as well.

How could aversive environments be reduced? Some strategies are difficult to implement but would have substantial impact. For example, poverty is strongly linked with aggression and violence, so ensuring that more people have enough to eat, a decent place to live, and reasonable prospects for employment would certainly help. Of course, these actions are political, not psychological, but it is important to recognize that social policies can significantly affect the amount of societal violence.

Physical discomfort and pain also cause aggression, so actions that reduce pain and suffering would reduce aggression as well. Even small actions to reduce others' discomfort can have great effect when done many times over by large numbers of people. For example, such actions could include municipalities' providing air-conditioned shelters during the summer for those who need them, police officers' minimizing the use of aggressive tactics with suspects or protesters, and even personal decisions by individuals to refrain from criticizing others. Trying to minimize others' discomfort is actually a big part of living and working successfully in families and social groups. Actions that make the world a less hostile place for others have the added benefit of reducing the amount of aggression that might affect us personally.

Chapter Summary

Aggression is behaviour that is intended to injure someone physically or psychologically. When aggression is intended to cause *extreme* injury, we call it **violence.** Aggression can take many forms. **Hostile aggression** is harm-doing that arises out of negative emotions like anger, frustration, or hatred. In contrast, **instrumental aggression** refers to harm-doing that is motivated by a more distant goal, such as teaching someone a lesson or obtaining something of value. One example of instrumental aggression is corporal punishment, which refers to the use of physical force (including spanking) with the intention of causing a child to experience pain but not injury for the purpose of correction or control of the child's behaviour. **Relational aggression** is behaviour that is intended to damage another person's peer relationships.

Social psychologists have conducted a great deal of research investigating the causes of aggression and violence. A general framework for research on aggression is provided by the **general aggression model** (or **GAM**), which conceptualizes aggression as the result of a chain of psychological processes. People respond to situational events by generating aggressive thoughts, aggressive feelings, and/or physiological arousal; in turn, these states initiate appraisal (interpretation) processes that can lead to aggressive behaviour.

Biological processes undoubtedly influence aggression. For example, a relation exists between the male sex hormone testosterone and aggressive behaviour. The **frustration–aggression hypothesis** proposes that frustration always leads to some form of aggression and that frustration is the only cause of aggression. Although studies have shown that frustration can indeed cause aggression, other factors such as anger also play a role. **Displaced aggression** occurs when people cannot be aggressive toward the actual source of their frustration, so they direct aggression elsewhere. The **catharsis** effect proposes that aggressive behaviour releases people's pent-up frustration and reduces the likelihood of subsequent aggression. Researchers have found, however, that catharsis does not typically occur; in fact, the opposite is typically true.

Aggressive behaviour is often preceded by some form of emotional and physiological arousal. This arousal can even come from sources unrelated to aggression, such as exercise. Researchers have shown that arousal from any source can be linked to anger-related thoughts and can ultimately cause an increase in aggressive behaviour—an effect that has been called **excitation transfer.**

Social learning theory proposes that humans learn many kinds of responses, including aggressive ones, by observing other people. Watching other people shows us both how to perform a behaviour and whether that behaviour will be rewarded or punished. The **cognitive neoassociation model of aggression** is based on the idea that aversive or unpleasant events activate the schemas for *fight* and *flight,* which themselves elicit the emotions of anger and fear. Whether people respond with aggression or escape depends on the pattern of cues in the situation. This hypothesis has been supported in studies showing the "weapons effect": participants are more likely to behave aggressively when aggressive cues (e.g., weapons) are present in the environment.

Not everyone is equally aggressive. Individuals who are high in narcissism have inflated views of their self-worth and often respond to criticism with hostility and aggression—a response that has been labelled threatened egotism. Also, some people are more likely to respond to any provocation with aggression than are other people—an individual difference that has been termed **trait aggressiveness.** The **Aggression Questionnaire (AQ)** measures trait aggressiveness. People who score high on the AQ have elaborate schemas related to aggression. Finally, people who have poor **executive functioning** also tend to be more aggressive in response to provocation; executive functioning refers to higher-order cognitive processing that organizes and coordinates lower-level elements of behaviour such as planning and monitoring progress toward goals.

Alcohol typically causes an increase in aggressive behaviour. This conclusion comes from studies that compared conditions in which alcohol was consumed with placebo conditions in which participants believed they were given alcohol but actually received nonalcoholic fluids. Heat also tends to increase aggressive behaviour. Heat may create aversive arousal that increases aggressive behaviour and may activate aggression-related cognitions.

Cultural factors also influence aggression. It has been proposed that many people in the southern United States were raised in a **culture of honour**—a culture in which men are taught from an early age to defend their honour and their reputation for strength and toughness. Within this culture, when a man is insulted or his reputation

threatened, the proper response is one of dominance, violence, or aggression.

Children often engage in aggression. Once at school, physical aggression tends to be replaced by verbal aggression, but some children remain physically aggressive. Some, but not all, of these aggressive children are rejected by their peers. One group of aggressive and rejected individuals consists of *school bullies,* who often target their aggressive behaviour toward specific individuals.

Violence also occurs in close relationships. Some men are physically abusive to their female partners. These batterers fall into three subgroups: those who are aggressive primarily at home (family-only), those who exhibit signs of psychological distress (dysphoric/borderline), and those who are generally violent (generally violent/antisocial). Children who witness domestic violence are very often adversely affected.

A **mob** is a crowd acting under strong emotional conditions that often lead to violence or illegal acts. Mob violence may be caused by deindividuation, which is a loss of personal identity and a sense of immersion in a group, or by conformity pressure, which can lead individuals to copy the behaviour of others even when the action runs contrary to how they would normally behave.

Longitudinal research on the relation between television viewing and aggressive behaviour has found that children who (1) watched a lot of violent television and (2) identified strongly with aggressive characters featured on television were more likely to exhibit aggressive behaviour as adults than were children who did not meet these criteria. These correlational findings are supported by experiments that have demonstrated a significant effect of viewing television violence on aggressive behaviour. There is also evidence that playing violent video games is associated with a significant increase in aggression, especially among young children.

Erotica is sexually explicit material that depicts nonviolent, consensual sexual activity. This kind of material generally reduces aggressive responding. **Degrading pornography** is sexually explicit material that debases or dehumanizes people, usually women. **Violent pornography** is sexually explicit material that depicts aggressive, hostile sexual activity. Some, but not all, researchers have argued that violent pornography makes men who were already predisposed to engage in sexual aggression more likely to behave violently.

Ideas for controlling aggression include controlling anger, teaching alternatives to aggression, and reducing aversive environments. With regard to anger control, **cognitive-relaxation coping skills training (CRCS)** involves teaching people a series of relaxation skills and introducing them to the idea of **cognitive restructuring,** which involves modifying their thoughts to reduce anger.

Key Terms

aggression (419)

Aggression Questionnaire
  (AQ) (433)

catharsis (427)

cognitive neoassociation model
  of aggression (430)

cognitive restructuring
  (452)

cognitive-relaxation coping skills
  training (CRCS) (452)

culture of honour (438)

degrading pornography (448)

displaced aggression (427)

erotica (448)

excitation transfer (428)

executive functioning (435)

frustration–aggression
  hypothesis (425)

general aggression model
  (GAM) (423)

hostile aggression (419)

instrumental aggression (419)

mob (443)

relational aggression (420)

social learning theory (429)

trait aggressiveness (433)

violence (419)

violent pornography (448)

Social Psychology Alive on the Web

SOCIAL PSYCHOLOGY ALIVE: ONLINE LABS

To perform the following experiment and see how you compare to other students, go to Social Psychology Lab, which can be accessed through ThomsonNOW™.

- 11.1 Sentencing

SOCIAL PSYCHOLOGY ALIVE: QUIZZING AND PRACTICE TESTS

You can access our Web site directly by going to http://www.socialpsychologyalive.nelson.com for online quizzes, flash cards, and Internet links.

INFOTRAC® COLLEGE EDITION

For additional readings, explore InfoTrac® College Edition, your online library of archived journal articles and periodicals dating back 22 years. If your instructor ordered InfoTrac® College Edition with this book, you can access it from your CD-ROM, or go directly to http://www.infotrac-college.com and use the passcode from the InfoTrac® College Edition card that came with your book. For this chapter, try these search terms: *aggression, violence, relational aggression, frustration, excitation transfer, social learning, domestic violence, mob, erotica, pornography.*

Social Psychology Alive: The Workbook

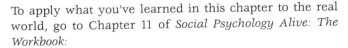

To apply what you've learned in this chapter to the real world, go to Chapter 11 of *Social Psychology Alive: The Workbook:*

- Venting Your Rage
- Girls and Aggression

- Violence and the Media
- Violent Video Games and Aggressive Behaviour
- Sentencing
- School Violence

Social Psychology Alive: The Videos

To see video on the topics and experiments discussed in this chapter, you can go either to ThomsonNOW™ or to the CD-ROM, if your instructor assigned either one, to the following section:

- Teach Me a Lesson: Learning to Be Violent

To Learn More

This list contains citations to books or articles that can help you learn more. These readings are good places to start if you want to gain a deeper understanding of the topics in this chapter.

- Baron, R. A., & Richardson, D. (1994). *Human aggression*. New York: Plenum Press.

- Berkowitz, L. (1993). *Aggression: Its causes, consequences, and control*. New York: McGraw-Hill.

- Underwood, M. K. (2003). *Social aggression among girls*. New York: Guilford Press.

Helpful Social Behaviour

*W*hen the massive waves, or tsunami, hit the beaches of Indonesia and other countries along the Indian Ocean on December 26, 2004, they were up to 9 metres tall and travelling between 50 and 100 kilometres per hour—much too fast to outrun. The source of the waves was a violent earthquake, measuring 9.0 on the Richter scale (the most powerful earthquake in the world in 40 years), which occurred off the west coast of Sumatra, one of the islands comprising Indonesia in the Indian Ocean. The displacement of the ocean floor triggered immense ripples in the water that moved along the entire depth of the ocean, releasing unimaginable amounts of energy. In the open seas, the surface waves travelled up to 1000 kilometres per hour, faster than most jet planes. Although there is a warning system for tsunamis in the Pacific Ocean, one does not exist for tsunamis in the Indian Ocean. Therefore, areas that were not breached for several hours nevertheless received no warning of the impending devastation. Most of the damage from the tsunami was caused not by the initial wave front, but instead by the huge mass of water that came in behind. The depth of the water along the flooded areas rose very suddenly, and the sheer weight of the water pulverized objects in its path, reducing buildings to their foundations and crushing vehicles, homes, and people. Many people who were not killed instantly were swept out to sea when the surge of water receded.

The extent of the devastation did not become clear immediately. Initial estimates of a few thousand casualties rose dramatically over the following weeks, reaching almost 250 000 deaths by the end of April 2005, four months after the event. In Indonesia alone, 165 000 lives were lost. Other countries badly hurt by the tsunami included Sri Lanka with 31 000 deaths, India with 16 000 deaths, and Thailand with 5400 deaths. The

© AP/Wide World Photos/Achmad Ibrahim

The tsunami on December 26, 2004, caused enormous damage along the coastlines of the Indian Ocean, including this town of Banda Aceh, Indonesia.

number of people left homeless and destitute by the tsunami was also in the hundreds of thousands, and these numbers included untold children left orphaned by the deaths of both parents.

Perhaps just as extraordinary as the tsunami was the helping response from the rest of the world, including Canada, to victims of the event. In the weeks following December 26, 2004, the Canadian government pledged millions of dollars to the relief effort. The Canadian DART (Disaster Assistance Response Team), which consists of almost 200 members, was sent to Sri Lanka, where it spent many weeks helping victims. The team included medical personnel, water-purification equipment, engineers to rebuild infrastructure like roads and bridges, and communications facilities to coordinate relief efforts.

Even more amazing was the response of individuals and small groups across the country. Individual Canadians made special contributions to agencies despite recent holiday spending; schoolchildren from across Canada collected money in tin cans for victims; Canadian churches, synagogues, and mosques held auctions to raise funds; and sports teams played fundraising games to raise money. The government said it would match all private donations that were made to tsunami relief efforts before January 11, 2005; in this two-week time period, Canadians donated almost $150 million. The tragedy of December 26 was terrible, but the helping response from Canadians and the rest of the world was inspiring.

The purpose of this chapter is to describe social psychological research on helpful behaviour. We will return to people's responses to the tsunami at several points in the chapter to illustrate theoretical concepts. We begin by defining relevant terms, including helping *and* prosocial behaviour. *Armed with this background information, we consider a debate in social psychology about the motivation that underlies helping behaviour: Are helpers sometimes motivated purely by a concern for others' welfare, or do helpers always provide assistance in order to make themselves feel good? This debate about* altruism versus egoism *is difficult to resolve, and many researchers have therefore turned to the more straightforward task of identifying factors that influence helping, such as norms, guilt, and modelling. We describe some of these factors. Next, we discuss* volunteerism— *a type of helping behaviour that is usually not a response to a specific event or request but rather a commitment to provide assistance to a worthwhile organization. We then consider a specific form of helping behaviour that has received a lot of attention in the popular press: bystander intervention in emergencies. We identify the psychological processes that are involved in the decision to provide emergency helping. After a brief discussion of cultural differences in helping behaviour, we shift gears and consider the* recipients *of help: Are they typically thankful to receive assistance, or do they sometimes experience negative emotions? Then we discuss another form of prosocial behaviour besides helping:* cooperation in settings known as social dilemmas, *in which actions that seem beneficial in the short term can be disastrous in the long run. Finally, we close the chapter with a discussion of* social support, *which is a form of helping behaviour that is typically substantial in nature and directed at family members or close friends. It turns out that this form of support has considerable impact on recipients' physical and mental well-being.*

Helping Behaviour

Helpful social behaviour, or **helping,** can be defined as behaviour intended to assist another person; the recipient may or may not have requested assistance, but the helper perceives that aid is needed. You are being helpful when you provide directions to a lost driver, hold the door open for a stranger, pick up packages that have been dropped, or let someone in a hurry cut before you in the coffee line at Tim Hortons. These forms of helping are not very costly, and most of us give and receive

helping
behaviour that is intended to assist another person

such benefits every day. Helping in these ways is so common that we often take them for granted as just a basic element of social life. But other forms of helping can be more costly. People may go out of their way to return a lost wallet, offer assistance after an accident, or help to free a stranger's car stuck in the snow. Not everyone does these things, but they occur frequently. Some forms of helping are less tangible than holding open a door or pushing a car out of the snow. Often we are needed—or we need others—to provide moral support, some encouraging words, or a shoulder to cry on. This kind of emotional helping and social support is common among families and friends, and it contributes in important ways to a happy and healthy life.

A broader category of behaviour is **prosocial behaviour,** which can be defined as any action that provides benefit to other people (Batson, 1998). Prosocial behaviour encompasses helping, but it also includes actions that are not necessarily intended to assist others, such as following the rules in a game, being honest, and cooperating with others in social situations.

prosocial behaviour
any action that provides benefit to others

Types of Helping

As our examples in the preceding paragraphs illustrate, there are many different ways in which a person can help others. Because of this diversity, it is useful to identify some basic categories of helping behaviours. Anne McGuire (1994) asked students at Vassar College to describe instances of helping that they had personally experienced, either as the helper or as the recipient, and involving either friends or strangers. The students described nearly 1500 examples of such help. These helping behaviours varied in terms of their relative frequencies, costs, benefits, causes, and consequences. McGuire proposed that the behaviours fell into four major categories. As shown in Table 12.1,

TABLE 12.1
Four Basic Categories of Helping Behaviours

Category	Examples
Casual helping	Giving someone a snack
	Answering a short question
	Lending a pen
Emergency helping	Offering assistance or calling for help after an accident or injury
	Returning a wallet or money
	Taking someone to the hospital in an emergency
Substantial personal helping	Giving a ride longer than 30 kilometres
	Doing laundry for someone
	Sending homemade food
Emotional helping	Giving moral support; being supportive
	"Being there" for someone; providing security and loyalty
	Comforting someone

Adapted from McGuire, 1994, "Helping behaviors in the natural environment: Dimensions and correlates of helping." *Personality and Social Psychology Bulletin, 20*; 45—56.

these categories consisted of casual helping, emergency helping, substantial personal helping, and emotional helping. Casual helping and emergency helping typically involve strangers, whereas substantial personal helping and emotional helping typically involve family or friends. Casual helping and emotional helping can be relatively simple to perform, whereas substantial personal helping and emergency helping are potentially more difficult. Each of these categories of helping has different causes and consequences, and we will refer back to them at various points in the chapter.

In a similar effort to understand the basic dimensions of helping, Australian social psychologists Philip Pearce and Paul Amato (1980) looked at the similarities and differences among 62 helping situations. This analysis identified three major dimensions along which helping behaviours vary. The first dimension is the degree to which helping is planned or formal versus spontaneous or informal. As an example, chaperoning juvenile delinquents on a trip to the zoo is usually planned well in advance, whereas giving the correct directions to a stranger on the street is usually done spontaneously. The second dimension of helping situations involves the seriousness of the problem. Giving someone change to make a phone call is not a particularly serious situation, whereas giving help to a heart attack victim is very serious. The third dimension found by Pearce and Amato involves a distinction between "giving what you have" and "doing what you can." When you donate money to a charity or share food with friends, you are providing help by *giving what you have.* When you break up a fight or pick up a dropped package for someone, you are providing help by *doing what you can.*

When you help a neighbour shovel her driveway, you are providing help by *doing what you can.*

Courtesy of James Olson

Can you envision how these dimensions might relate to the categories of helping identified by McGuire (1994)? Casual helping is typically unplanned and not serious; it can involve either giving what you have (e.g., giving money to a street musician) or doing what you can (e.g., opening a door for another person). Like casual helping, emergency helping is also usually unplanned, but it is serious and always involves doing what you can (e.g., contacting the police after an accident). Substantial personal helping is typically planned; it is often serious and can involve either giving what you have (e.g., donating a significant sum of money) or doing what you can (e.g., providing long-term social support to a sick relative). Finally, emotional helping is usually planned and involves doing what you can; it can be either serious (e.g., comforting a friend who has lost a family member) or not serious (e.g., expressing encouragement to someone who will soon write an exam). Thinking about the intersection of these two categorization schemes underscores just how diverse helping behaviours can be.

Altruism Versus Egoism

Social psychologists have been very interested in the question of *why* individuals help others (e.g., Batson, 1991; Schroeder, Penner, Dovidio, & Piliavin, 1995). What motivates individuals to offer assistance to people whom they often don't even know? After all, most types of helping impose some cost on the helper, such as time, money, or even physical danger. Yet despite these costs, helping behaviours happen frequently. Two basic explanations have been proposed to account for helping behaviours.

Help Others and Help Yourself.   Think back to some instances in which you have helped another person. Perhaps you provided local directions, gave some change to a homeless person, held the door open for someone in a wheelchair, or donated money to a charity. You certainly provided a benefit to another person. But didn't you also feel pretty good about yourself? And those pats on the back or looks of approval from others didn't hurt either. Maybe the reward was just an internal one—wouldn't Mom be proud of me? These points illustrate that one consequence of helping others is that it makes *you* feel good too. And what about those times when you chose *not* to help another in need? You passed by a motorist in distress, avoided eye contact with a panhandler, or didn't offer directions to a stranger who was clearly lost. Did you feel a twinge of guilt? Perhaps you tried to rationalize it, but those looks of disapproval from others hurt. It does not take long for us to learn that helping is associated with rewards and other positive outcomes, and that not helping is associated with punishments and other negative outcomes. In the end, perhaps our prosocial actions are really driven by a self-centred desire to obtain rewards and avoid punishments. This is an **egoistic motivation** for helping. The outcome of helping may indeed provide some benefit to another, but the helper's true motivation—the end goal—is to gain some benefit for the self.

Helping Others for Others' Sake.
Yet surely there are times when the intent of the helper is to benefit another without regard for personal rewards or punishments. An **altruistic motivation** for helping occurs when the helper's end goal is simply to provide some benefit to another. The helper may gain some benefit along the way, but that is not the reason for helping. Try to think of instances of pure altruism—helping that is motivated only out of a concern for another's welfare. Suppose a man discovers that his five-year-old daughter is trapped inside a burning building. Without concern for his own life, the man rushes in to save his daughter. Does this count as altruism? Certainly the man is concerned more about the welfare of another person than about himself. And it is doubtful that he is motivated by a desire for public recognition or social approval. Or consider a woman who offers to donate one of her kidneys to a sister who will surely die without the transplant. The operation is painful and dangerous. It is hard to imagine anything other than an altruistic motivation.

The distinction between egoistic and altruistic motivations for helping, however, is not clear-cut. The problem is that we cannot directly observe the reason for people's helping; we must somehow infer the underlying motivation or internal state of the helper. This has proven to be extremely difficult. Consider, for example, an anonymous donor who gave a large sum of money to help victims of the tsunami, but who refused to be identified or otherwise given credit. Is this altruism or egoism? Perhaps the donor was acting on the pure desire to help others, with no concern about gaining social approval or self-satisfaction, which would be an altruistic motivation. But it is also possible that the donor was acting on the need to feel useful, or to compensate for the guilt of having refused an earlier request for assistance, which would be egoistic reasons for helping. We could ask the donor directly, but he or she may be reluctant or unable to reveal the true reason. And it is quite possible that both motivations contribute simultaneously—a mixture of altruism and egoism.

The Evolution of Altruism?
Perhaps a more basic question relevant to the issue of altruism versus egoism is: Why would people *ever* be altruistic? It hardly seems to be in one's self-interest to make a large sacrifice in favour of another person. There is plenty to be lost when an individual risks his or her own life to save another person, and we can list many reasons for not helping. What, then, would motivate a person to be altruistic? One explanation is an evolutionary one, based on the principle of **inclusive fitness** (Hamilton, 1964). This principle refers to the idea that some social behaviours have been selected during the course of evolution because they increase the survival of our *genes*—not necessarily within us, but within other relatives (Kenrick, Li, & Butner, 2003). For example, a father who rescues his daughter is improving the odds that some of his own genes will survive—whether or

egoistic motivation

a motive for helping in order to obtain rewards or avoid punishments

altruistic motivation

a motive for helping purely for the sake of providing benefit to another person

inclusive fitness

the principle that some social behaviours have been selected during the course of evolution because they increase the survival of our genes not he survives. In early human history, people lived in small hunter–gatherer bands, in which members were highly interdependent and often related. Therefore, altruism toward any member of the band could potentially benefit one's own genes as well.

Inclusive fitness may explain why people are willing to sacrifice their own personal resources (including their lives) in favour of offspring and other close genetic relatives (Dawkins, 1976; Kenrick et al., 2003). When Eugene Burnstein, Christian Crandall, and Shinobu Kitayama (1994) asked university students in the United States and Japan whom they would most likely help in a number of everyday and life-and-death situations, the students said they would rather help a brother (close kin) than a nephew or a cousin (more distant kin). Other research has shown that people provide more social support to close relatives than to distant relatives and say they would distribute more money from a lottery win to close relatives than to distant relatives (Neyer & Lang, 2003; Webster, 2003).

Dennis Krebs, who is at Simon Fraser University in Burnaby, British Columbia, and Kathy Denton, who is at Douglas College in New Westminster, British Columbia, argued that humans evolved to behave in ways that uphold *systems of cooperation* among members of a band or larger group (Krebs, 2005; Krebs & Denton, 1999, 2005). That is, helping (and other moral behaviour) occurs because systems of cooperation benefit everybody in a group—individuals may give help at one time but receive help at another time.

If altruism toward members of one's ingroup can have survival benefits for people's genes, then some sort of motivational or emotional state presumably evolved in humans to induce them to behave altruistically toward similar others. The state of *empathy* might be the motivational mechanism for altruistic behaviour (Hoffman, 1981).

Imagine that you have just observed a friend accidentally touch the red-hot element of a stove. "Ouch! That hurts!" you exclaim. You can almost feel the pain yourself. This ability to comprehend how another person experiences a situation is known as **empathy** (Davis, 1996). You may recall from Chapter 11, "Aggression and Violence," that empathy reduces the likelihood of aggressive behaviour (e.g., it can reduce road rage; see page 439). Empathy for someone in need increases the likelihood that an individual will be helpful to that person (e.g., Levy, Freitas, & Salovey, 2002; Schlenker & Britt, 2001).

We are more likely to feel empathy with others who are similar to us because their similarity makes it easier to imagine what they are feeling. Empathy is also easier with familiar others because our knowledge of them makes it easier to put ourselves in their shoes. These factors will work to make us especially empathic with ingroup members and with kin, who tend to be similar and well known to us. Thus, by evolving the capacity for empathy, humans evolved a motivation that induced helpful behaviour selectively directed toward ingroup members and genetic relatives.

Empathy–Altruism Hypothesis.

Some social psychologists have suggested that the helping triggered by empathy is often altruistic—it is not motivated out of a concern for one's own well-being. According to this **empathy–altruism hypothesis,** feelings of empathy for a person can lead to behaviour that is truly aimed at helping that person, such as an adult's altruism toward a child in need (Batson, 1991, 1998).

On the other hand, the empathy–helping relationship can be interpreted as yet another version of egoistic motivation. The *real* reason you help is to escape your own distress. Suppose you see that another person is in need of help—he or she has just dropped a bag of groceries, and canned goods are rolling in every direction. How would that make you feel? If you empathize, it should cause you to experience some distress yourself—almost as if it were you who had dropped the bag. This is not a pleasant feeling, and most people would want to make themselves feel better.

The principle of *inclusive fitness* provides one explanation for why people behave altruistically toward close genetic relatives.

empathy

the ability to comprehend how another person is experiencing a situation

empathy–altruism hypothesis

the idea that feelings of empathy for a person can lead to behaviour that is motivated solely by wanting to help that person

How? By helping to pick up the cans. The victim will be grateful, and others will see you as a kind and generous person. And in the process, you will have shed your own distress. These two competing interpretations of the effects of empathy are depicted in the flowchart in Figure 12.1.

How can the empathy–altruism hypothesis be tested against an egoistic interpretation of empathy? This has proven to be difficult, and it has led to heated debate in the research literature. Let's look at a couple of examples of how this debate has developed. If you are interested in learning more, social psychologist Mark Davis (1996), who is at Eckerd College in St. Petersburg, Florida, provides a very nice summary of this research controversy.

Suppose you find that a person is in need of help. You empathize—you feel his or her pain. You could help, but doing so will cause some distress or discomfort for yourself. Daniel Batson and his colleagues (Batson, Duncan, Ackerman, Buckley, & Birch, 1981) created a laboratory version of this situation. Female students at the University of Kansas arrived at the laboratory for what they thought was a study of task performance under stressful conditions. The students were told that they would be paired with another female student, and that one of them would be randomly selected to perform a task under aversive conditions while the other would observe. The aversive conditions involved performing a memory task while receiving electric shocks at random intervals. In fact, there was no second student. Under the guise of showing up late, the participants were told that the "other student" had been led to another room, but that she could be observed through a closed-circuit television monitor. What the real participants actually saw on the monitor was a prerecorded video.

A drawing was then held, which was rigged so that the real participant always drew the role of observer and the other student—her name was Elaine—always drew the role of worker. It became clear during the course of observation that Elaine (actually a videotaped actor) was quite distressed upon receiving the first few shocks. When the experimenter (appearing as part of the videotaped act) expressed concern, Elaine explained that a childhood experience—being thrown by a horse onto an electric fence—had made her especially sensitive to electric shock. The experimenter offered to end the study, but Elaine said that she wanted to go on. Then the experimenter proposed that the observer might be willing to change places with her. That was fine with Elaine, so the experimenter went to ask the real participant if she would be willing to trade places and receive the electric shocks in Elaine's place.

Unknown to the participants in the experiment, they had been randomly assigned to one of four conditions. Two conditions were designed to create high empathy for

ALTRUISTIC INTERPRETATION:

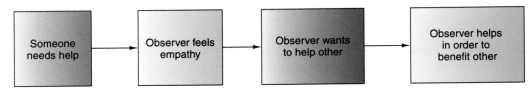

EGOISTIC INTERPRETATION:

FIGURE 12.1
Altruistic and egoistic interpretations of how empathy leads to helping

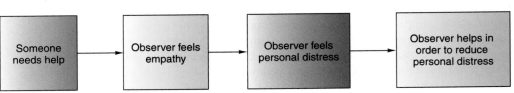

Elaine, whereas two created low empathy. In the high-empathy conditions, the student learned that she and Elaine were very similar in their attitudes and values (on the basis of a survey completed earlier in the semester). In the low-empathy conditions, the student learned that she and Elaine were very different in their attitudes and values. The empathy–altruism hypothesis predicts that the high-empathy conditions should arouse altruistic motivation, whereas the low-empathy conditions should arouse egoistic motivation.

A second manipulation was designed to make it either easy or difficult for the participants to avoid watching Elaine continue to receive the shocks. In the easy escape conditions, the participant was told that if she did not trade places, she would *not* continue to observe Elaine receive the remaining shocks—these instructions provided an easy escape from the distress of watching Elaine suffer. In the difficult escape conditions, however, the participant was told that if she did not trade places, she would continue to observe Elaine receiving the shocks.

Participants then had to decide whether or not to help by trading places. When it was difficult to escape, the choice was expected to be to help whether participants were egoistically or altruistically motivated. After all, if they were egoistically motivated, then helping was the best way to reduce their own distress, since they would otherwise be forced to watch Elaine receive more shocks. And if they were altruistically motivated, then helping was the only way to reduce Elaine's distress. Either way, helping was likely to occur. The more interesting circumstance was when escape was easy. If participants were egoistically motivated, then choosing not to help (escaping) was the best way to minimize their own distress—they wouldn't have to observe Elaine anymore and they wouldn't have to receive the shocks themselves. But if they were altruistically motivated, then helping was still the only way to reduce Elaine's distress.

The results of the study are presented in Figure 12.2. The only condition in which low helping rates occurred was when low empathy had been induced and escape from watching Elaine's suffering was easy. In both of the high-empathy conditions, in which altruistic motivation was presumably aroused, more than 80% of the participants offered to trade places with Elaine, irrespective of how easy it was for them to escape. In the low-empathy conditions, helping depended on ease of escape. When escape was difficult, more than 60% of the participants offered to trade places, but presumably for egoistic reasons. When escape was easy, on the other hand, only 18% offered to help.

The results from this experiment are consistent with the empathy–altruism hypothesis, and similar patterns of results have been obtained in other experiments reported by Batson and his colleagues (e.g., Batson, O'Quin, Fultz, Vanderplas, & Isen, 1983; for reviews, see Batson, 1991, 1998; Davis, 1996). These studies call our attention especially to the combination of high empathy and easy escape. It is this combination of factors that is hypothesized to reflect altruistic motivation when people help.

But Robert Cialdini of Arizona State University and Mark Schaller of the University of British Columbia (Cialdini, Schaller, Houlihan, Arps, Fultz, & Beaman, 1987; Schaller & Cialdini, 1990, 1998) have challenged this interpretation. In particular, they suggest that the combination of high empathy and a suffering victim causes observers to feel sadness, even when escape is easy. People don't like to feel sad and will often help a victim in distress in an effort to make themselves feel better (Baumann, Cialdini, & Kenrick, 1981)—an egoistic rather than altruistic motivation for helping. Cialdini and Schaller and their colleagues conducted their own version of the experiment done by Batson and his colleagues, but with some additional conditions and measures. Cialdini and his colleagues found two results that point to egoistic helping under conditions of high empathy and easy escape. First, the amount of helping was directly related to the extent of the observer's reported sadness: the more sadness

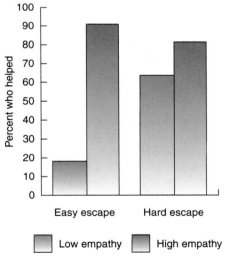

FIGURE 12.2 Percent who helped in each condition

From Batson et al., "Is empathic emotion a source of altruistic motivation?" *Journal of Personality and Social Psychology,* 40, 290–302, Table 2, p. 296, 1981. Copyright © 1981 by the American Psychological Association. Reprinted by permission.

reported by the observer, the more likely it was that help was offered. Second, when the observers were led to believe that helping would not relieve their sadness, they no longer offered to help. Thus, even under conditions designed to bring out altruistic helping, it is difficult to rule out egoistic concerns entirely.

An Unresolved Debate. Researchers continue to address this matter of egoistic versus altruistic motivations for helping. On one side of the debate are those who believe that helping is almost always the result of egoistic motivations (e.g., Maner, Luce, Neuberg, Cialdini, Brown, & Sagarin, 2002). On the other side are those who believe that empathy elicits pure altruism in some circumstances (e.g., Batson, Chang, Orr, & Rowland, 2002; Batson, et al., 2003). The jury is still out on this one. Perhaps it doesn't matter whether people help because they want to make themselves feel better or because they care only about the other person, so long as they help. After all, no matter why it occurs, helping is a good thing. It may be more important simply to identify the factors that influence whether people help or not. Many social psychologists have taken this perspective, not worrying about the underlying motivation behind helping but simply focusing on situational and personal variables that predict helping. In the next section, we review some of these factors.

Factors Influencing Helping

In the following paragraphs, we discuss six factors that influence helping behaviour. The research we describe has focused on low-cost helping to strangers, mainly because this kind of helping can be studied in a controlled fashion relatively easily (e.g., by staging an event that may elicit helping). This kind of helping falls into the category of *casual helping* identified by McGuire (1994). In terms of Pearce and Amato's (1980) dimensions underlying helping, most of these studies focused on helping that is spontaneous and not very serious. We should note, however, that the principles we discuss in this section probably apply to any kind of helping, including actions that fall into McGuire's categories of substantial personal helping and emotional helping.

norm of social responsibility

the rule or guideline that we should help those who need help, if possible

Social Norms. One explanation for helping behaviour, perhaps especially low-cost helping, is that it is prescribed by *social norms,* which are culturally defined rules or guidelines about what behaviours are proper and improper (see Chapter 8, page 289). For example, the **norm of social responsibility** dictates that we should help those who need help (Berkowitz, 1972). It is easy to demonstrate this norm. Try it for yourself: simply approach a stranger in a public place and ask if he or she would tell you the time of day. In all likelihood, you will receive the help you request. Bibb Latané and John Darley (1970) had their students at Columbia University walk the streets of New York City making simple requests of passers-by. More than 80% agreed to tell a student what time it was or how to get to Times Square. Even the more intrusive request of change for a quarter was granted by 73% of the strangers. Although these figures may not surprise you, such high rates of compliance show that people generally accept the norm that they should be helpful when it is simple to do so. Fewer people were willing to reveal their names (39%) or to give the student a dime (34%). But when Latané and Darley's students tacked on an explanation for wanting a dime—"I need to make a telephone call" or "My wallet has been stolen"—they doubled their chances of getting the money. Help is given to those who appear to have a need.

It seems likely that media coverage following the tsunami on December 26, 2004, as well as the helpful responses of governments and organizations, made some people think about the norm of social responsibility. Awareness of the norm may then have motivated some people to make a contribution.

Another social norm is the *norm of reciprocity*, which we defined in Chapter 8 as the principle that we should give back in return any favours that are done for us (see page 301; Gouldner, 1960). This norm instructs us to help those who have helped us in the past and can be utilized to increase our chances of receiving help. When Latané and Darley's (1970) students volunteered their names before asking for a dime, they improved their success from 34% to 50%. A one-for-one trade of the same "commodity" works even better—when the students gave their own name, they were able to get 59% of the strangers to reciprocate by revealing their names.

Shalom Schwartz (1977) of the Hebrew University of Jerusalem pointed out that social norms will guide helping only to the extent that those norms have been internalized and incorporated as part of individuals' own values. Schwartz referred to these as **personal norms**—expectations for oneself in particular situations. If you have internalized the norm of social responsibility, and you see it as appropriate or fitting in a particular helping situation, then you are likely to help. On the other hand, if you have not adopted this norm as an important personal value, or you don't see it as applying in the situation, then you are less likely to help. Schwartz's model explains why broad social norms fail to predict helping for some people (see Batson, 1998).

personal norms
guidelines that have been internalized to become expectations for oneself in particular situations

Modelling Helpful Behaviour. Observing the actions of a helpful model increases individuals' helpfulness (e.g., Sarason, Sarason, Pierce, Shearin, & Sayers, 1991). A classic demonstration of this effect was reported by James Bryan and Mary Ann Test (1967). On two consecutive Saturday afternoons, a broken-down car was planted on a busy road in Los Angeles. It was a Ford Mustang, with a flat left-rear tire and an inflated spare leaning against it. Any passer-by could easily see the flat tire and a woman standing by the car waiting for some help. An experimenter watched from nearby, counting the number of cars that passed and the number of motorists who stopped to offer assistance. In the model condition, an Oldsmobile had been planted about 400 metres before the Mustang. Motorists could see that the Oldsmobile was raised by a jack under the left-rear bumper while a woman was watching a man changing the flat tire. In the control condition, there was no Oldsmobile. In each condition, the experimenters waited for 2000 would-be helpers to pass by. How often did the woman receive help with her Mustang? In the control condition, 35 motorists stopped to offer assistance. In the model condition, 58 stopped—a significant increase.

The effect of models can be seen in the influence of parents on their children's helpfulness. Studies have shown that children whose parents modelled helping were more helpful than children whose parents did not model helping (e.g., Mussen & Eisenberg-Berg, 1977). Presumably, modelling helpful behaviour teaches children how to be helpful and shows them that helping brings positive consequences for the helper and the recipient (Batson, 1998; Grusec, 1991).

Modelling probably also played a role in responses to the 2004 tsunami. People saw that others were responding generously, including others who were similar to them. These models then led observers to act similarly.

Blaming the Victim. How would you respond if someone came up to you in a bar and asked you for some money to make a phone call, explaining that his wallet had

The *norm of social responsibility* tells us to help those who need help.

The children of parents who model helpful behaviour tend to become more helpful themselves.

just world theory

a model proposing that humans need to believe that the world is a fair place where people generally get what they deserve

been stolen a few minutes ago? What if he asked you for money to make a phone call and explained that he had spent his last money on a beer a few minutes ago?

This example illustrates the point that people are more receptive to the requests of victims who did not get themselves into trouble in the first place. If victims brought about their own problems, then observers tend to blame them and are less likely to offer help. For example, Greg Schmidt and Bernard Weiner (1988) asked students at the University of California at Los Angeles to indicate their willingness to lend their notes from a previous class to another student who needed the notes either because of eye problems that had made it difficult for him to see or because he had gone to the beach instead of class. Participants also reported the extent to which they felt sympathy and anger about the request. Results showed that participants reported more willingness to lend the notes for medical reasons than for a deliberate decision to skip class, and this greater likelihood of helping was associated with reports of more sympathy and less anger. Thus, when the victim was blameworthy, participants were less willing to help.

This mention of blaming the victim may remind you of our brief discussion of Melvin Lerner's **just world theory** in Chapter 2 (see page 34), where we used the model to illustrate some characteristics of theories and hypotheses. Lerner (1980), who taught at the University of Waterloo, hypothesized that humans *need* to believe that the world is a fair and just place, where individuals receive approximately what they deserve: good people tend to get rewarded, and bad people tend to suffer. When observers see individuals who are suffering innocently—through no fault of their own—their belief in a just world is threatened. One straightforward way to deal with this threat is to help the victim(s) directly, which can restore justice to the situation (see Haynes & Olson, 2006). Responses from around the world to victims of the tsunami in December 2004 probably reflected, in part, people's recognition that the situation was terribly unjust. The victims were blameless, and helping them restored at least some justice to the situation. Thus, the belief in a just world can motivate helping.

But the belief in a just world can sometimes interfere with helping. When victims cannot easily be helped, especially when their suffering is also expected to continue, the situation is very threatening to the belief in a just world. Carolyn Hafer of Brock University in St. Catharines, Ontario (see Hafer, 2000; Hafer & Bègue, 2005), has shown that when people read about a suffering victim, thoughts related to justice and injustice occur spontaneously. If helping is not an option, then people may protect their belief by convincing themselves either that the victims did something to cause their own suffering or that the victims are "bad people" who, in some sense, *deserve* to suffer. By blaming the victims for their plight or devaluing their worthiness, people can maintain their belief in a just world and rationalize their own inaction. Indeed, people sometimes *look* for reasons to blame victims so they do not have to offer help.

Canadian social psychologist Aaron Kay and his colleagues (Kay, Jost, & Young, 2005) suggested that people want to believe that the society in which they live is fair; the authors labelled attempts to confirm this belief *system justification*. They showed that a desire to justify the social system can lead people both to derogate victims and to enhance (perceive as better) people who are successful. After all, if the system is fair, then people who do poorly must be unskilled or unmotivated, whereas people who succeed must be skilled and motivated. Unfortunately, these system justifications might lead people to avoid helping victims.

Good Mood. Have you ever noticed that when you feel good, you are a little more helpful or kindly to others? It's as if the warm glow of positive feelings causes you to be more helpful. Alice Isen and Paula Levin (1972) conducted two simple but well-known experiments to confirm this intuition. In one experiment, cookies were distributed to students who were studying in the library. A control group of other students who were studying in the same library did not receive the cookies. A few minutes later, the experimenter approached each student and asked if he or she would be willing to help out by serving as a confederate in an experiment. The students who had received a cookie were more likely to volunteer and to offer more of their time than the students who had not received a cookie. In a second experiment, good mood was induced by having shoppers in a mall find an unexpected dime in the coin return slot of a public telephone. A control group of shoppers had used the same phone but did not find the unexpected money. After a shopper left the phone, the experimenter followed alongside and then dropped a manila folder full of papers. Almost 90% of the shoppers who had found the unexpected dime stopped to help the experimenter pick up the papers. In contrast, only 1 out of 25 shoppers in the control group offered such help. The effects of a good mood on helping have been replicated many times (e.g., Carlson, Charlin, & Miller, 1988; Cunningham, Shaffer, Barbee, Wolff, & Kelly, 1990), and seem to last for about ten minutes after the positive mood has been induced (Isen, Clark, & Schwartz, 1976).

Guilt. To this point, we have considered only instances in which another's misfortune was not a result of the *helper's* actions—the helper did not *cause* the other person to need help. But sometimes we are the cause of another person's need for help—you bump into somebody and cause the person to drop a package, you spill coffee on a stranger, or you accidentally let a door slam in someone's face. It's embarrassing and it can make you feel guilty. But will it increase your chances of offering to help? The answer is yes (e.g., Carlsmith & Gross, 1969; Cunningham, Steinberg, & Grev, 1980). Moreover, people will not only try to rectify the victim's misfortune, but they will also be more helpful to others whom they did not affect.

In a classic study of guilt and helping, Vladimir Konečni (1972) utilized pedestrians on the streets of Toronto. To get a sense of the baseline rate of helping, an experimenter walked toward pedestrians and, at a distance of about 4 metres, dropped some computer key-punched cards. As he knelt down to pick them up, he said to the passerby, "Please don't step on them." Even though they were not directly asked to help, 16% nevertheless offered to assist. In a guilt-inducing condition, the experimenter approached from behind and, at the moment he caught up, brushed the pedestrian's arm and then dropped the computer cards. As before, the experimenter knelt down to pick up the cards. Under these conditions, in which the pedestrian was made to feel partly responsible for the mishap, 39% offered to assist. A third condition showed that the guilt generalized to helping others. In this condition, the experimenter was carrying some books when he absentmindedly bumped into the pedestrian, causing the books to fall. The experimenter quickly picked them up, muttering, "They are not mine, and you have to do this." About 60 metres down the walkway, another experimenter staged the same card-dropping accident used in the baseline condition. Now 42% of the pedestrians who had been made to feel guilty a minute or two earlier offered to help.

Individual Differences in Helping: The Altruistic Personality.

Some people just seem to have a helpful personality. You know the type: always willing to lend a helping hand, frequently expressing concern about the welfare of others, and constantly being kind to strangers. Other people prefer to mind their own business and do not typically show much empathy or concern about others' needs. These observations suggest that people differ in their basic predispositions to be helpful. This view was explored by Samuel and Pearl Oliner (1988) at Humboldt State University, who tried to understand why, in Nazi Europe, some ordinary men and women were willing to risk their own lives to rescue Jews. Trying to distinguish between *rescuers* and *nonrescuers* during the Holocaust, the Oliners suggested that rescuers' actions were determined by "their own personal qualities . . . it was the values learned from their parents which prompted and sustained their involvement" (p. 142). (Recall our earlier discussion of parental modelling.) Through the course of extensive interviews, the Oliners concluded that rescuers differed from nonrescuers in their relationships with their parents. Rescuers consistently reported a warm and stable relationship with their parents—a kind of relationship that has been labelled a *secure attachment* (see Chapter 13's discussion of close relationships). Nonrescuers, on the other hand, tended to report less positive relationships with their parents.

Experimental research on personality and helping has focused primarily on individual differences in *empathy,* the ability to imagine what another person is experiencing. The **Interpersonal Reactivity Index (IRI),** developed by Mark Davis (1983, 1996), was designed to measure such differences. The IRI has four parts or subscales:

- *Perspective Taking* measures the extent to which a person routinely takes the point of view of others.
- *Empathic Concern* measures the tendency of a person to experience sympathy or compassion for others.
- *Personal Distress* reflects the degree to which a person experiences distress or discomfort in response to another's extreme distress.
- *Fantasy* reflects a tendency to imagine oneself in hypothetical situations.

Selected items from the scale are reproduced in Know Yourself 12.1: "Interpersonal Reactivity Index." People who score high on this scale are hypothesized to be more empathic. Answer the items in the Know Yourself feature to see whether they tend to describe you well or not.

Research has examined whether high scores on these scales are related to helping. For example, Gustavo Carlo, Nancy Eisenberg, and their colleagues (Carlo, Eisenberg, Troyer, Switzer, & Speer, 1991) gave students at Arizona State University the option of changing places with another student (a confederate of the experimenter) who was very upset performing an unpleasant task. Some participants were told that they would have to watch the other student complete additional trials on the task if they did not switch places (difficult escape), whereas other participants were told that they would not have to watch additional trials (easy escape). Recall from our previous discussion of the empathy–altruism hypothesis that empathy would be expected to predict helping best when escape is easy (because most people will help when escape is difficult, irrespective of their empathy). As predicted, Carlo, Eisenberg, and their colleagues found that individual differences in altruistic personality traits (including the IRI scales of Perspective Taking, Empathic Concern, and Personal Distress) predicted helping significantly when the escape from watching the distressed victim was easy. Empathic individuals were helpful even when they did not "have" to be (i.e., even when escape was easy).

The same group of researchers (Eisenberg et al., 2002) reported the results of a longitudinal study of 32 individuals who were first interviewed when they were four or five years old and then interviewed again 11 times over the next 20 years. At the very first session, the children were observed in free play interactions with other children, and their behaviour was coded for the frequency of several helpful acts toward other children, such as sharing toys and offering comfort. At later sessions, a variety of self-report measures of empathy and altruism were obtained. We can mention only a few of the findings here. In general, the researchers found that participants' scores on measures of altruistic personality traits were relatively stable

Interpersonal Reactivity Index (IRI)

a measure reflecting the extent to which people feel empathy in response to others' experiences

Know Yourself 12.1
Interpersonal Reactivity Index

For each of the following items, please indicate how well it describes you by circling the appropriate number on the answer scale.

1. I try to look at everybody's side of a disagreement before I make a decision.

   1   2   3   4   5

   Does not describe me well   Describes me very well

2. I often have tender, concerned feelings for people less fortunate than me.

   1   2   3   4   5

   Does not describe me well   Describes me very well

3. In emergency situations, I feel apprehensive and ill at ease.

   1   2   3   4   5

   Does not describe me well   Describes me very well

4. I daydream and fantasize, with some regularity, about things that might happen to me.

   1   2   3   4   5

   Does not describe me well   Describes me very well

5. I sometimes try to understand my friends better by imagining how things look from their perspective.

   1   2   3   4   5

   Does not describe me well   Describes me very well

6. When I see someone being taken advantage of, I feel kind of protective toward them.

   1   2   3   4   5

   Does not describe me well   Describes me very well

7. I sometimes feel helpless when I am in the middle of a very emotional situation.

   1   2   3   4   5

   Does not describe me well   Describes me very well

8. I really get involved with the feelings of the characters in a novel.

   1   2   3   4   5

   Does not describe me well   Describes me very well

9. Before criticizing somebody, I try to imagine how I would feel if I were in their place.

   1   2   3   4   5

   Does not describe me well   Describes me very well

10. I would describe myself as a pretty soft-hearted person.

    1   2   3   4   5

    Does not describe me well   Describes me very well

11. Being in a tense emotional situation scares me.

    1   2   3   4   5

    Does not describe me well   Describes me very well

12. When I watch a good movie, I can very easily put myself in the place of a leading character.

    1   2   3   4   5

    Does not describe me well   Describes me very well

SCORING:

1. *Perspective Taking:* Add up the circled numbers for Items 1, 5, and 9 for your overall perspective-taking score. Possible scores range from 3 to 15, and higher scores reflect a stronger tendency to take other people's perspectives.

2. *Empathic Concern:* Add up the circled numbers for Items 2, 6, and 10 for your overall empathic concern score. Possible scores range from 3 to 15, and higher scores reflect more empathic concern.

3. *Personal Distress:* Add up the circled numbers for Items 3, 7, and 11 for your overall personal distress score. Possible scores range from 3 to 15, and higher scores reflect a stronger tendency to feel distressed in emotional settings.

4. *Fantasy:* Add up the circled numbers for Items 4, 8, and 12 for your overall fantasy score. Possible scores range from 3 to 15, and higher scores reflect a greater tendency to imagine oneself in hypothetical situations.

5. *Total Interpersonal Reactivity:* Add up the scores for all four subscales for your overall interpersonal reactivity score. Possible scores range from 12 to 60, and higher scores reflect a stronger reactivity to the experiences of others.

Sample items from Davis, "Measuring individual differences in empathy: Evidence for a multidimensional approach," *Journal of Personality and Social Psychology*, 44, 113–126, 1983.

over time: individuals who scored high in empathy and altruism in early sessions also tended to score high in later sessions. Perhaps the most remarkable finding was that individual differences in altruistic personality traits measured at ages 24 or 25 (including the IRI scales of Perspective Taking and Empathic Concern) were significantly correlated with the frequency with which those individuals had shared toys with other children during free play 20 years earlier. Sharing behaviour at an early age was predictive of altruistic traits in young adulthood.

It would be interesting to investigate whether people who responded to the 2004 tsunami by making a donation or organizing a money-raising event would score highly on the IRI. Perhaps being able to empathize with (imagine themselves in the situation of) victims of the tragedy motivated them to help. The accompanying Concept Review summarizes the factors that influence helping.

Volunteerism

volunteerism

unpaid helping behaviour that is given willingly to a worthwhile cause or organization

The studies reviewed in the preceding section focused largely on helpful actions toward individuals who need assistance at a particular time. But there is another category of helping behaviour that is not in response to a specific need or request for help. This kind of helping usually involves deliberation and forethought, extends over time, can be substantial in size, and often benefits strangers. We refer here to **volunteerism**—unpaid helping behaviour given willingly to a worthwhile cause or service organization. Volunteerism falls into the category of *substantial personal helping* in McGuire's categorization scheme. In 2000, 27% of Canadians over the age of 14 engaged in some form of volunteerism, contributing, on average, 162 hours (National Survey of Giving, Volunteering, and Participating, 2000). The accompanying box, Social Psychology In Your Life: "Who Volunteers in Canada?" provides some additional data about volunteers.

Do you volunteer your time to a worthwhile cause? If so, what is your motivation? Do you volunteer because you enjoy it, or are you motivated by wanting to help others? Social psychologists have directed less attention to volunteerism than to other forms of helping behaviour, but researchers have begun to investigate what motivates individuals to be volunteers and what kinds of experiences as volunteers keep them involved.

CONCEPT REVIEW
Factors Influencing Helping

Factor	Description	Example
Social norms	Culturally defined guidelines about proper and improper behaviour	Norm of social responsibility: we should help those who need help
Models	Helpful actions by other people	Observe someone helping to change a flat tire
Blame	Victim's responsibility for getting into the situation	Help victims only when they did not get themselves into trouble in the first place
Good mood	Positive emotions from any cause	Find an unexpected quarter in the coin return slot of a public telephone
Guilt	Feeling partly responsible for the victim's situation	Bump into someone, who drops what he or she is carrying
Individual differences	Ability to experience empathy and visualize oneself in the victim's place	Scores on the Interpersonal Reactivity Index (IRI)

Social Psychology in Your Life

Who Volunteers in Canada?

The National Survey of Giving, Volunteering, and Participating is conducted every few years by Statistics Canada. The most recent survey for which detailed analyses are available was conducted in 2000. This survey was completed by almost 15 000 Canadians, who comprised a representative sample of the Canadian population over the age of 14.

The survey revealed interesting patterns of volunteering across different groups.

Table 12.2 presents the rates of volunteering and, among volunteers, the average numbers of hours contributed, within a variety of demographic groups. The volunteer rate across age groups was quite consistent, except for lower levels among people aged 25 to 34 and those

over 65. Presumably, the latter statistic reflects health problems and other practical difficulties faced by the elderly. Notice that those aged 65 and older who did volunteer contributed the highest average number of hours of any age group. The precise reason for the lower rate of helping among adults aged 25 to 34 is unclear; perhaps these persons are

TABLE 12.2
Volunteering in Canada in 2000 by Age, Sex, Education, Income, and Religiosity

	Volunteer Rate	Average Hours
Age		
15—24	29%	130
25—34	24%	131
35—44	30%	153
45—54	30%	158
55—64	28%	181
65+	18%	269
Sex		
Male	25%	170
Female	28%	155
Education Level		
Less than high school	19%	154
High school diploma	23%	150
Some postsecondary	33%	173
Postsecondary diploma	28%	165
University degree	39%	166
Household Income		
< $20 000	17%	207
$20 000–$39 999	21%	179
$40 000–$59 999	26%	162
$60 000–$99 999	32%	145
$100 000 or more	39%	150
Religiosity		
Very religious	41%	200
Not very religious	26%	156

Adapted from the Statistics Canada publication 2000 National Survey of Giving, Volunteering and Participating. Catalogue 89M0017XCB, August 17, 2001.

(Continued on next page)

busy getting established in careers and starting families, with the result that they have little time or energy for volunteering.

Women were somewhat more likely to volunteer than men, though male volunteers contributed somewhat more hours than female volunteers. In general, volunteer rates went up as education increased. Similarly, volunteering was greater as household incomes increased, perhaps because any costs of volunteering (e.g., transportation) are less significant for more wealthy individuals. Finally, religiosity was associated with more volunteering (although some of these hours were undoubtedly dedicated to the religious institutions that people attended).

The survey also asked respondents whether they had had a variety of early life experiences that might be expected to predict volunteering later in life. Table 12.3 presents some of these findings. Participants were more likely to volunteer if their parents had volunteered, suggesting a modelling effect. Participants were also more likely to volunteer if they had been involved in various groups, including religious groups, youth groups, student government, and team sports. These data are correlational and, therefore, might reflect the influence of other factors, such as financial wealth, which makes membership in groups and participation

TABLE 12.3
Volunteering in Canada in 2000 by Early Life Experiences

	Volunteer Rate
Parents Volunteered	
Yes	42%
No	24%
Active in Religious Group	
Yes	38%
No	23%
Belonged to Youth Group	
Yes	35%
No	20%
Active in Student Government	
Yes	38%
No	23%
Participated in Team Sports	
Yes	31%
No	21%
Received Help from Others	
Yes	35%
No	20%

Adapted from the Statistics Canada publication 2000 National Survey of Giving, Volunteering and Participating, Catalogue 89M0017XCB, August 17, 2001.

in sports more affordable. Nevertheless, it is interesting that those who were generally active in groups as children were more likely to become volunteers later in life. Finally, participants were more likely to volunteer if they had received help in the past from volunteers. Understanding why people do or do not volunteer might allow charitable groups to recruit volunteers more effectively. Studies of the motives that might underlie volunteerism are discussed in the text.

Allen Omoto and Mark Snyder (1995) surveyed volunteers at AIDS organizations across the United States. The researchers proposed five distinct reasons (motives) why people might volunteer their time and developed a scale to measure these motives. They conceptualized two of the motives (values and community concern) as primarily other-oriented, or "humanitarian," motives and three (understanding, personal development, and esteem enhancement) as primarily self-oriented, or "egoistic," motives. Each hypothesized motive is listed below with two sample items from the scale:

- *Values.* Because I enjoy helping other people. Because of my personal values, convictions, and beliefs.
- *Community concern.* Because of my concern and worry about the gay community. To help members of the gay community.
- *Understanding.* To understand AIDS and what it does to people. To learn more about how to prevent AIDS.

- *Personal development.* To challenge myself and test my skills. To meet new people and make new friends.
- *Esteem enhancement.* To feel better about myself. To feel needed.

Omoto and Snyder (1995) used their measures of these motives, as well as participants' reports of personal experiences as a volunteer, to predict how long the participants had served as AIDS volunteers. The results were interesting. First, satisfaction with one's experiences as a volunteer predicted tenure: participants who had served the longest reported being very satisfied with their experiences as a volunteer (e.g., their experiences had been interesting, and they looked forward to their volunteer work). Second, Omoto and Snyder found that the relatively self-oriented, egoistic motives for being a volunteer were associated with longer tenure. That is,

What motivates people to become volunteers?

participants who joined the organization to gain understanding about AIDS, to develop themselves personally, or to enhance their esteem tended to be long-serving volunteers. In contrast, joining because of one's values or because of concern about the gay community did not predict length of service as a volunteer.

Louis Penner and Marcia Finkelstein (1998), however, reported a somewhat different pattern of findings in another sample of volunteers at AIDS organizations in the United States. Penner and Finkelstein replicated the finding that satisfaction with one's experiences as a volunteer was important. But in terms of the motives identified by Omoto and Snyder (1995), Penner and Finkelstein found that the only significant predictor of participants' length of service was the other-oriented motive of values: people who joined because they enjoy helping other people tended to be long-serving volunteers. Penner and Finkelstein also included a measure of individual differences in empathy, which included items from the Perspective Taking, Empathic Concern, and Personal Distress subscales of the Interpersonal Reactivity Index described on page 473. High scores on this measure of empathy were associated with longer service as a volunteer. Thus, Penner and Finkelstein's findings suggest that humanitarian motives and an empathic personality describe long-serving volunteers (see also Simon, Stürmer, & Steffens, 2000).

Mark Davis, Jennifer Hall, and Marnee Meyer (2003) at Eckerd College in St. Petersburg, Florida, surveyed volunteers in nine different organizations, only one of which was AIDS related. These researchers obtained additional evidence that satisfaction with one's experiences as a volunteer predicts helping: the extent to which participants were satisfied with their volunteer experiences strongly predicted the amount of time they donated per week. Also, the researchers found that the extent to which participants felt that their motives for joining the group had been fulfilled—whether those motives were other-oriented or self-oriented—predicted their satisfaction with their experiences. Thus, it appears that either humanitarian or egoistic motives can increase volunteerism, so long as individuals feel that their motives are being met by the volunteer experience.

In an interesting extension of work on the motives underlying volunteering, Marc Kiviniemi, Mark Snyder, and Allen Omoto (2002) of the University of Minnesota found that respondents who had only one principal motive for becoming a volunteer (e.g., personal development) reported less stress and more satisfaction with their volunteer activities than did respondents who had two or more important motives for becoming a volunteer (e.g., personal development and community concern). Why might this effect of multiple motives occur? Perhaps conflict between the different motives, with each being satisfied by different experiences, causes stress and dissatisfaction (see also Grube & Piliavin, 2000). So it may be advantageous to have just one overriding reason for volunteering, because roles and activities in the charitable organization can then be chosen to satisfy the single central motive.

Emergency Helping

On February 12, 1993, two ten-year-old boys, Robert Thompson and Jon Venables, kidnapped and murdered two-year-old James Bulger in Liverpool, England. The case was shocking and tragic in many respects, including the ages of those involved. But in terms of a social psychological analysis of helping in emergency settings, one important part of this incident was that several adults saw the three boys together and wondered whether something was wrong but did not pursue their suspicions. Thompson and Venables, who were troubled boys with a history of theft and truancy, saw Bulger at a shopping mall and decided to kidnap him "just for the hell of it." They took him by the hand and led him out of the mall (security cameras at the mall videotaped them leaving, which led to their arrests after Bulger's body was found). It seems that their initial intentions were to beat up Bulger and leave him lost. They first took the boy to an isolated area beside a canal, where they picked him up and dropped him on his head, which caused a big bruise and cut on his forehead. They then walked around aimlessly for about two hours with the little boy, trying to decide what to do and where to leave him. It was during this period that they were seen by several adults. Most of these adults assumed that the boys were brothers and the older boys were trying to deal with an uncooperative younger brother. One elderly woman noticed that Bulger was crying and injured; she approached the boys and asked them what the problem was. The boys said they had just found Bulger lost at the bottom of the hill. The woman suggested the boys take Bulger to the police station down the road, but then did nothing as the boys went off in the opposite direction. Later, another woman who was walking a dog saw the bruise on Bulger's head and said she would accompany the boys to the police station, but when another adult who was present refused to watch her dog, she didn't argue when the boys said they knew the way

Why didn't the adults who saw two-year-old James Bulger in the company of Robert Thompson (left) and Jon Venables (right) investigate the situation more thoroughly?

© MER/CORBIS SYGMA

© MER/CORBIS SYGMA

and walked off. Eventually, the boys took Bulger to another isolated location next to railroad tracks, where they beat him severely and left him dying. His body was found two days later.

Why didn't the adults investigate more carefully when they were suspicious about the boys? There was no physical intimidation involved—the ten-year-olds were children themselves. Primarily, it seems that the witnesses were uncertain about the seriousness of the situation. Some assumed that the boys were related; others probably didn't want to get involved and convinced themselves that nothing was wrong. The two women who directly confronted the boys had no particular reason to doubt their story about having found the two-year-old, although the subsequent actions of the boys (heading off in the wrong direction) should perhaps have triggered deeper suspicion and additional actions. The end result is that we are left with a terrible tragedy that took one boy's life and brought enormous pain to several families.

Social psychologists have been interested in the processes involved in deciding to intervene in a potential emergency. Anne McGuire (1994) included *emergency helping* as one of her four major categories of helping behaviour, which we summarized at the beginning of this chapter. You may have read about cases of bystander apathy, where someone was assaulted on a subway or sidewalk, or someone collapsed in a public place, and people did nothing to intervene or help the victim. What goes through the minds of bystanders in these kinds of situations?

The Decision Tree. Bibb Latané of Florida Atlantic University and John Darley of Princeton University conducted one of the most famous series of studies in social psychology to investigate the dynamics of bystander intervention in emergencies. Their research was guided by a theoretical analysis that specified a series of decisions that must be made before a person will intervene in an emergency. This **decision tree** is presented in Figure 12.3. Latané and Darley (1970) proposed that in order for intervention to occur, five separate things must happen: the individual must (1) notice the event, (2) interpret the event as an emergency, (3) accept personal responsibility for helping, (4) decide on an appropriate form of assistance, and (5) implement the action. If *any* of these steps does not occur, then the individual will not intervene. For example, someone might notice an event and interpret it as an emergency, but if he or she does not assume responsibility for helping, intervention will not happen.

In the following paragraphs, we discuss each step in the decision tree. We also describe some fascinating experiments that have illuminated the psychological processes that underlie the first three steps. We conclude by identifying some techniques that people can use to improve the odds that they will receive help in an emergency.

Notice the Event. Before intervention in an emergency can occur, one requirement is that people must notice the event. This point may seem obvious, but the real world is full of distractions and complications that can interfere with attention to emergencies. John Darley and Daniel Batson (1973) used a simple manipulation to interfere with participants' awareness of events around them: time pressure.

Participants in this experiment were students attending the Princeton Theological Seminary. The students were told that they would be delivering a talk on one of two topics in another building.

decision tree

a set of five steps that must be completed before an individual will intervene in an emergency situation

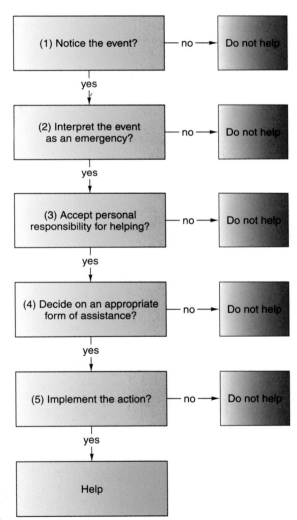

FIGURE 12.3 The decision tree leading to bystander intervention in emergencies

Data from Latané and Darley, *The unresponsive bystander: Why doesn't he help?* Copyright © 1970. Adapted by permission of Pearson Education, Inc.

*"And who is my neighbour?"
Jesus replied, "A man was going
down from Jerusalem to Jericho,
and he fell among robbers, who
stripped him and beat him, and
departed, leaving him half dead.
Now by chance a priest was going
down the road; and when he saw
him he passed by on the other
side. So likewise a Levite, when
he came to the place and saw
him, passed by on the other side.
But a Samaritan, as he jour-
neyed, came to where he was;
and when he saw him, he had
compassion, and went to him
and bound his wounds, pouring
on oil and wine; then he set him
on his own beast and brought
him to an inn, and took care of
him. And the next day he took
out two dennarii and gave them
to the innkeeper, saying 'Take
care of him; and whatever more
you spend, I will repay you when
I come back.' Which of these
three, do you think, proved
neighbour to him who fell among
the robbers?" He said, "The one
who showed mercy on him." And
Jesus said to him, "Go and do
likewise." [Luke 10:29–37 RSV]*

For half of the students, the assigned topic was the parable of the Good Samaritan (see sidebar). For the other half of the students, the assigned topic was unrelated to the theme of helping. The students were given directions to the other building and then were exposed to the manipulation of time pressure: some of the students were told that they really had to hurry because they were already late (high-hurry condition); other students were told that they should not delay because they had just enough time to make it (intermediate-hurry condition); a third group was told that there was no rush because they had lots of time to get there (low-hurry condition).

On their way to the other building, the students passed by a "victim" who was sitting slumped in a doorway, in probable need of assistance (he was actually an actor playing the part). The manipulation of time pressure exerted a strong effect on whether participants stopped to help the victim: the percentage of students who helped was 63% in the low-hurry condition, 45% in the intermediate-hurry condition, and only 10% in the high-hurry condition. Participants in the high-hurry condition typically claimed that they did not see the victim in the doorway. Thus, even the first step of noticing the event can sometimes derail helping.

Interestingly, the topic of the participants' talk (Good Samaritan or unrelated to helping) had no effect on helping. It may seem ironic that *seminary* students on their way to give a talk about the *Good Samaritan parable* helped only 10% of the time when they were in a rush, but these findings underscore the importance of situational factors such as time pressure.

Interpret the Event as an Emergency. Before people will intervene in an event, they must interpret it as an emergency—as a situation that calls for action of some kind. We mentioned earlier that it seems likely this step played a role in the James Bulger case. Many real-life events are ambiguous. Is this man sick or drunk? Did that person call "help" or simply cough? Are those boys fighting or just fooling around? The response that will be made in each of these cases depends on observers' interpretations.

Latané and Darley (1968) illustrated the importance of how events are interpreted in a clever study. Students attending Columbia University were invited to a discussion of problems in the lives of students at an urban university. When they arrived for the discussion, they were directed to a waiting room to complete a preliminary questionnaire. Some of the students were seated alone, whereas others were seated with two other students. Soon after they were seated, a clearly visible stream of white smoke began entering the room through a vent. The smoke continued to come into the room throughout the session, eventually becoming thick enough to partially obscure participants' vision.

When the students were waiting alone, about 75% of them got up to report the problem within two minutes—they interpreted the situation as one that might be dangerous. But when the students were working in groups of three, only 38% of the groups reported the smoke. In a third condition, two of the three students were actually confederates of the experimenter and only one person in each group was a real participant. The confederates were instructed to remain passive and indifferent. Only 10% of the real participants in these groups reported the smoke.

What was going through participants' minds? Those who did not report the smoke typically said that they assumed the smoke was not dangerous or was part of the experiment. But why was this conclusion more frequent in the second and third conditions, where multiple bystanders were present? Latané and Darley suggested that participants in these conditions were looking at the other participants to decide whether or not the situation was serious. When they saw other people doing nothing (e.g., the two passive confederates in the third

George P. Chomas/Shutterstock

Is this man sick or drunk? Before offering someone help, people must interpret the event as an emergency.

condition), they concluded that the situation must not be an emergency. Or, at least, they were uncertain enough about the situation that they did not want to possibly make a fool of themselves by getting up and investigating the smoke. In the single-participant condition, people did not have these other individuals affecting how they interpreted the situation, so they were more likely to decide that they should do something.

It is noteworthy that this experiment investigated a situation in which participants *themselves* may have been in danger, yet bystander apathy still occurred. Inaction was more "dangerous" than action because failing to respond to a real fire has far worse consequences than responding when there is no real fire. In real-life emergencies, it is often dangerous for people to intervene, and their inaction may sometimes be "rational" in the sense that they could be hurt. But in this smoke study, inaction was potentially dangerous, yet participants often failed to act when other people were present.

Accept Personal Responsibility for Helping. The third step in the decision tree is that the person must accept personal responsibility for intervening. For example, if someone witnesses a fight at a sports event where many police are present, he or she is unlikely to feel responsible for breaking up the fight.

Darley and Latané (1968) demonstrated the importance of perceived responsibility in another study. Male students at New York University believed they were having a discussion with either one, two, or five other students. In fact, the "discussion" was all prerecorded, and only one naïve student participated at a time. When the naïve student arrived for the study, he was seated in a small room off a corridor containing a number of other small rooms. Once seated, the student was fitted with headphones and listened to the remaining instructions. He was told that he would be participating in a discussion with one, two, or five other students, and that all the students would take turns talking for two minutes about themselves and their personal problems. It was explained that the headphones and the separate cubicles would help protect everyone's anonymity. The experimenter would *not* be listening, and only the *speaker's* microphone would be turned on at any given time. During one of the other students' second turn speaking (actually a prerecording), he could be heard having a seizure. He said that he was having a problem, and that he could really use some help. The experimenter waited in the corridor to observe how long it took the naïve student to come out of the room to look for help (recall that only the speaker's microphone was allegedly turned on).

When the group size was believed to be two—just the student and the seizure victim—every single student got up to help within three minutes. When the group size appeared to be three—the student, the victim, and one other—85% of the students responded within three minutes. But when the group size appeared to be six—the student, the victim, and four others—only 62% of the students ever responded to the victim's plea for help. Thus, the greater the number of perceived bystanders, the less likely a participant was to come to the victim's aid.

What explains the reduced helping in the (apparently) larger groups? Personal responsibility is probably the critical factor. Participants who believed that other people were present felt less personal responsibility for helping the victim, because others could help just as well. Their *interpretation* of the event seems unlikely to have been affected by the other alleged bystanders because they were always by themselves in a room. Rather, their beliefs about how many other people were present influenced whether they felt responsible for helping the victim.

Abraham Ross, a social psychologist at Memorial University in St. John's, Newfoundland, conducted several well-known studies of bystander intervention (e.g., Ross, 1971; Ross & Braband, 1973). One experiment showed that the presence of another person does not always reduce helping. Specifically, Ross and Braband (1973) found that when an emergency occurred while a male participant was sitting with a *blind* person, the participant was just as likely to respond as when participants were alone. Presumably, participants knew that the blind person could not respond, so they continued to feel personally responsible for helping.

In another experiment, by Bibb Latané and Judith Rodin (1969), the presence of a bystander probably influenced both participants' interpretation of the situation and their sense of responsibility for helping. Imagine that you have just arrived for a consumer marketing research study, and you are seated alone in a small room to complete a questionnaire. The marketing representative tells you that she will be working in the office next door. The two rooms are separated by a collapsible divider. As you are working, you can hear the woman climbing on a chair, probably trying to reach something on a bookcase. Then you suddenly hear a loud crash and a scream. "Oh, my god, my foot . . . I . . . I . . . can't move it!" The woman moans in obvious pain. "Oh, my ankle! I can't get this thing off me!" What would you do? Would you get up to check on her?

When Latané and Rodin conducted this experiment with students at Columbia University, 70% offered to help, usually by getting up from their seat and opening the room divider. But that was when the students were alone. Other students were brought together in pairs—two strangers seated at the same table working on their questionnaires. In only 40% of the two-participant groups did either member of the pair come to her assistance. It was even worse when the experimenter planted a confederate to sit in the room with an unknowing student. The confederate was instructed to be passive: during the emergency he looked up, shrugged his shoulders, and then went back to work on his questionnaire. In these cases, fewer than 10% of the naïve participants went to check on the woman.

In this experiment, bystanders presumably had dual effects. When the other person did not immediately assist the woman, participants were more likely to think, "she's probably fine" (benign interpretation of the event) and "it's not my responsibility anyway" (denial of personal responsibility). Each of these inferences would reduce the likelihood that individuals would intervene.

This inhibitory effect of bystanders on the likelihood of an individual's helping is called the **bystander effect.** The bystander effect can be defined as follows: the likelihood that an individual will intervene in an emergency goes down as the number of bystanders increases. For example (*these figures are hypothetical*), individual bystanders may intervene 75% of the time in a particular emergency situation when alone, whereas these same individuals may intervene only 50% of the time when two other people are also present and only 30% of the time when five other people are also present. The bystander effect does *not* necessarily mean that victims are less likely to receive help when many bystanders are present than when only one is present. Instead, the effect refers to the probability that a *specific person* will intervene; the probability goes down as the number of bystanders increases. The bystander effect can be caused by the impact of bystanders on how events are interpreted, on feelings of responsibility to help, or both.

It is possible that even *thinking about being in a group* may have a diffusing effect on perceived responsibility for helping. Stephen Garcia, Kim Weaver, Gordon Moskowitz, and John Darley (2002) at Princeton University used a priming procedure to get participants to visualize being with a group: participants were asked to imagine that they had won a dinner for themselves and some of their friends at their favourite restaurant. Some participants were asked to imagine that they had won dinner for themselves and 30 of their friends; others were asked to imagine that they had won dinner for themselves and ten friends; and others were asked to imagine that they had won dinner for themselves and one friend. All participants then answered a question about this imaginary dinner that was intended simply to justify the imagination task. Next, the critical question (allegedly unconnected to the imagination task) was posed: participants were asked to estimate how much of their salary they expected to give to charities after they were well established in a career. Participants who had imagined a dinner with 30 friends estimated giving a smaller

bystander effect

the likelihood that an individual will intervene in an emergency goes down as the number of bystanders increases

Fifty women were harassed and groped in broad daylight in the midst of crowds in Central Park. Not only were the women's cries for help ignored, bystanders videotaped the assaults.

percentage of their salary to charity than did participants who had imagined a dinner with ten friends, who in turn estimated giving a smaller percentage of their salary to charity than did participants who had imagined a dinner with one friend. A follow-up study showed that the same imagination task influenced participants' willingness to volunteer extra time for research. The researchers labelled these findings the *implicit bystander effect,* because simply thinking about being in a group produced an effect parallel to the original bystander effect.

Decide on an Appropriate Form of Assistance. Even when people have noticed and interpreted an event as an emergency and accepted personal responsibility for helping, they must still decide how to intervene. Sometimes this step will stymie potential helpers: How can they effectively assist? For example, individuals may sometimes lack the ability to help, such as when they do not know how to administer CPR to an apparent heart-attack victim. Or people may be unsure why someone has lost consciousness: Did the person choke, or have a heart attack, or what? People may also lack the necessary tools to help, such as when they see a boat in difficulty on the water; if they lack a means of offering help (e.g., their own boat), they may remain indecisive. It is true that in virtually every circumstance, people could, at the very least, seek help by dialling 911 or looking for other helpers, but if an individual is trying to think of more immediate assistance, he or she may remain inactive.

People are more likely to intervene in an emergency when they possess relevant skills, such as knowing how to administer CPR to a heart-attack victim.

Implement the Decision to Help. Finally, even when people have noticed and interpreted an event as an emergency, accepted personal responsibility for helping, and decided how to help, they may not implement that decision for a number of reasons. Perhaps the most common cause of hesitation in real-life emergencies is perceived danger—the costs of helping are potentially too high. For example, people are hesitant to intervene in cases of assault or robbery because they may be injured. Indeed, police recommend against intervening in dangerous situations. People may also fear "becoming involved" because, in the future, the perpetrator may seek them out or they may have to go to court to testify. Another reason people may not implement a decision to help is potential embarrassment. We have been socialized to respect others' privacy and do not want to offer help that will be rejected by the victim or criticized by observers. Thus, even when we think a person needs help and we know how to help, we may waver for fear of a negative response from the victim or others in the situation.

Improving the Odds. Armed with this knowledge about intervention in emergencies, there are things you can do to improve the chances that you will get help when you need it. Ambiguity or uncertainty should probably be your chief concern: people are less likely to help when they are uncertain that an emergency is happening. Lack of perceived personal responsibility is also an important culprit: diffusion of responsibility in a crowded situation means that individuals are less likely to step forward with assistance than if they were alone. Sometimes, others' initial reactions to an emergency are to experience fear or guilt, which will focus their attention inward on themselves or motivate them to leave the situation. Getting people to focus attention on you and *your* distress is likely to increase their empathy and helping.

Knowing these facts, Robert Cialdini (2001) suggested a very simple and straight-forward way to help yourself in an emergency: "You, sir, in the blue jacket, I need your help. Call an ambulance" (p. 118). These two sentences (or something similar) are short, simple, and to the point. They clarify the situation ("I need your help"), assign personal responsibility to an individual, and identify a specific action that will assist you. You should say similar things to several bystanders if possible.

Fortunately, people often do complete the five steps necessary to intervene in an emergency. Bystander apathy may be more common than we would like, but we should not downplay the heroics of some bystanders. Sometimes emergency settings elicit remarkable acts of courage and selflessness.

Cultural Differences in Helping

Given the previously described evidence that factors such as social norms and mod-elling influence helping behaviour, it seems very likely that the culture into which people are socialized will affect their helping response in different settings. Yet, sur-prisingly little research has examined cross-cultural differences in helping behaviour (Moghaddam, Taylor, & Wright, 1993).

In one investigation designed to understand how culture might influence the *development* of helping behaviour, Harvard University psychologists Beatrice and John Whiting (Whiting, Whiting, & Longabaugh, 1975) studied the social and family settings of children living in six locations, all small farming communities but in dif-ferent cultures:

- Nyansongo, Kenya
- Juxtlahuaca, Mexico
- Tarong, Philippines
- Taira, Japan
- Khalapur, India
- Orchard Town, United States

In each locale, the researchers observed the structure of household chores, the divi-sion of family and work responsibilities, and the helping behaviour of children. Examples of helpful behaviour included direct help when needed (e.g., giving food to another, scratching another's insect bite), providing social support (e.g., consoling a crying baby, praising another's help), and maintaining positive relationships (e.g., greeting others in a friendly way, holding another's hand).

One important difference between these cultures was the extent to which children were socialized to be nurturant and responsible. Most notably in Kenya, Mexico, and the Philippines, children were expected to help with the house-hold chores, the farming work of the family, and caring for younger siblings. In short, children in these cultures were socialized to take responsibility for family life. It was in these same cultures that the children scored highest in helpful behaviours. In contrast, children in the United States were socialized to be competitive in school and were typically assigned very few family responsibilities. The Orchard Town children scored the lowest in helpful behav-iours. Although considerable variability was found within each culture, it was clear that children's orientation toward others versus themselves was affected by their socialization.

When children are socialized to take some responsibility for family life, they may become more helpful in other ways as well.

We have discussed in previous chapters the dimension of individualism–collectivism (see Sorrentino, Cohen, Olson, & Zanna, 2005; Triandis, 1995). Could this difference between cultures influence people's willingness to help others? Joan Miller, David Bersoff, and Robin Harwood (1990) of Yale University compared the views of children and adults living in the United States with those living in India concerning perceived responsibilities for helping others. Participants were asked whether there was a moral obligation to help people in various situations, or whether helping was instead a matter of choice. In both the United States and India, people were seen as having a moral responsibility to help their children and generally to help others in life-threatening situations. However, when it came to less serious situations and giving help to friends or strangers, the Americans regarded helping as a matter of personal choice, not moral obligation. The Indians saw things differently. Hindu culture places greater emphasis on interdependence, social duty, and mutual aid. The Indians viewed helping as a moral responsibility even when the need was less serious or when strangers were involved.

There is also evidence that, when they do give help, people from individualist cultures think it is fine to discuss one's helpfulness publicly, whereas people from collectivist cultures consider it inappropriate to tell others (Fu, Lee, Cameron, & Xu, 2001). This difference probably reflects, in part, the stronger expectations for helpfulness that exist in collectivist cultures, where helping is not really something to brag about—it is simply expected. The findings may also reflect a greater emphasis on modesty in collectivist cultures compared to individualist cultures.

The Recipient's Reaction to Help

To this point in the chapter, we have focused on the *helper*—the motives that underlie helping, the factors that encourage people to help, and so on. But there is another side to helping: the person being helped. When someone suffers a heart attack, receiving help can mean the difference between life and death. But sometimes people do not like to be on the receiving end of help. In this section, we look at the recipient's view of helping: what it feels like to need help, and what it might say about our ability. Help can be a positive and supportive thing. But needing help, especially from strangers, can sometimes threaten our self-esteem.

Have you ever refused an offer of help? Perhaps you were carrying a load of heavy packages, and a stranger asked if you needed some help. You feel the strain building in your muscles and wonder if you really can make it out the door by yourself. "No, thanks, I can handle it," you reply. Or have you ever been lost in an unfamiliar part of town? You had no idea where you were, yet you continued to drive past gas stations where help was readily available.

Why do we sometimes resist seeking help, or even refuse an offer of help? And why does receiving help sometimes make us feel worse rather than better? Social psychological research has identified several possible reasons (Fisher, Nadler, & Whitcher-Alagna, 1982; Nadler & Fisher, 1986).

Norm of Reciprocity. One view is that the acceptance of aid puts you in another's debt. We have previously discussed the norm of reciprocity, which states that when someone helps you, you should help him or her in return. When the help is minor and casual, it is possible that a simple "Thank you" will suffice. But the debt is greater when someone goes out of his or her way to help. People do not generally like to be in such social debt and may be reluctant to request or accept help if they have doubts about their ability to reciprocate.

Martin Greenberg and Solomon Shapiro (1971) provided a nice illustration of this principle in a well-known early study. Students at the University of Pittsburgh participated in what they thought was a study of physical disability and work performance. Upon arrival, the student was joined by another student who was actually a confederate working for the experimenter. It was explained to the students that they would each be playing the role of a disabled worker who is trying to meet a production quota. One student—always the naïve participant—was assigned the role of a worker with a *motor* disability. This was simulated by placing the student's preferred arm in a sling. The other student—always the confederate—was assigned the role of a worker with a *visual* disability, which was simulated by wearing an eye patch and a pair of sunglasses. The students were told that they would be working on two tasks. The first task would be to construct paper boxes from sheets of paper—a task deliberately chosen because of its difficulty for the naïve student with a simulated motor disability. The second task would be to check sheets of paper for typographical errors and to circle each error with a red pen, which was chosen because of its potential difficulty for the confederate-student with a simulated visual disability. The students were told that a quota would be set for each task, and that money could be earned by meeting and exceeding the quota. The students were also told that if one finished early, the other could ask for help:

> If either of you needs help from the other in order to meet your quota, feel free to request such assistance. Of course, neither of you is obliged to help the other. If you would like to help the other person you must first wait until he asks for assistance. Keep in mind the fact that you are not in competition with each other and that both of you can earn 50 cents and more. (p. 294)

Before they went to work on their quotas, the students were given a practice period on each of the two tasks. As expected, the naïve student—who had a simulated motor disability—had a difficult time with the box-making task and was not able to finish during the allotted practice period. The other student—the confederate—was able to finish the box-making task well before the practice time was up. Practice on the typographical error task was next. The naïve student was always able to finish well within the allotted practice time. Here is where the experimental manipulation was introduced. In the reciprocation condition, the confederate was not able to complete the second task before the end of the practice time. In the no-reciprocation condition, however, the confederate finished the second task at just about the same time as the naïve participant. What were Greenberg and Shapiro trying to do? The naïve student always knew he or she would have difficulty with the box-making task, and that the other student—who could do it easily—would be a good source of help. In the reciprocation condition, an opportunity for reciprocation had been created: the naïve student was almost certain to be in a position to offer help on the typographical error task, because the confederate-student had struggled during the practice period. In the no-reciprocation condition, however, the opportunity for reciprocation was very unlikely, because the other student (the confederate) appeared to be good at both tasks. How often would students in the two conditions ask the other student for help?

The results were very clear. When the students perceived that they would later have an opportunity to reciprocate, 71% asked for assistance in meeting their box-making quota on the first task. But when the students expected no such opportunity for reciprocation, only 37% requested help. Knowing that they would be able to repay the favour on the second task, students in the reciprocation condition were more favourable toward receiving help.

Threat to Self-Esteem. We all need help from time to time, and often we are glad to accept help when it is offered. But what does it say about you when you need help? It may signify nothing more than one of those everyday situations in which all of us, at one time or another, could use a little help. Sometimes we get lost and could use some directions. The need for such help does not mean that you are unintelligent or less capable than anyone else. But in other settings, finding yourself in need of help could suggest that you are not a very capable person—especially when you discover that nobody else seems to need help. Have you ever found yourself trying to learn a new subject, and you just couldn't get it? At first, you make the attribution that it is a very difficult subject, or the teacher is lousy. But then you discover that all of your friends—people who are very similar to you in other respects—are having an easier time with the subject. Now needing help seems to expose a weakness. It makes you look less intelligent and less capable than you thought. It can be a threat to your self-esteem.

Arie Nadler, Jeffrey Fisher, and Siegfried Streufert (1976) demonstrated one case in which receiving help actually hurts. Purdue University students played a game in which they could win money if they performed well. Although they played the game in an isolated cubicle, the students were told that they had been matched with a "pair-mate" with whom they would interact later. The pair-mate was actually fictitious and simply provided a way to create threat to the real participant's self-esteem. The experiment was arranged so that, at one point, the student learned that he and his pair-mate were either very similar in their attitudes, values, and interests or very dissimilar.

Sometimes receiving help can threaten the recipient's self-esteem.

When the game began, the students discovered that it was extremely challenging and would be difficult to win. As the student proceeded through the game, his earnings dwindled and he was very close to being eliminated. His pair-mate was doing much better and was in a position to share some of his earnings to help keep the real participant in the game. In one condition of the experiment, the pair-mate did come through with some assistance by delivering a donation to the real student. In another condition, no such donation was made. So here we have four conditions in which a student either received help or not from another student who was portrayed as either very similar or very dissimilar. Nadler and his colleagues (1976) reasoned that receiving help from someone who was very similar and who appeared to be performing much better on the same task would pose a threat to one's self-esteem: it would make a person feel less worthy and less intelligent. And that is exactly what they found. Students in this combination of conditions described themselves as feeling sadder, less confident, less intelligent, and less able, even though their actual performance was exactly the same as that of participants who did not receive help or who received help from a dissimilar other. This deflating effect was especially true among the students who had rated themselves earlier in the semester as having high self-esteem. The more positively participants thought of themselves, the more they were threatened by another person who was similar to them, outperformed them, and then helped them. It actually hurt these participants' self-esteem to receive assistance from such a person.

The Helper's Reason for Helping. We have identified two conditions under which people may not respond positively to help from others: when they cannot reciprocate the help and when the help threatens their self-esteem. Daniel Ames, Francis Flynn, and Elke Weber (2004) at Columbia University proposed that a third determinant of people's reactions to help is their perceptions of why the helper decided to help—his or her *reason for helping*. Think about occasions when someone has helped you. Did you wonder why they did so?

Ames and his colleagues suggested that when people receive help, they try to figure out why the help was offered, because this information tells them how the helper feels about them: Does he or she care about me? If people decide that the helper cares about them, then they feel positively about the help, want to interact with the helper again in the future, and want to reciprocate the helping. But if people decide that the helper was guided by considerations other than caring, then they feel less positively and are less motivated to interact again in the future and to reciprocate the help.

The researchers suggested that when recipients of help think about why they received help, they typically contemplate three main reasons: because of liking/caring, because of a cost–benefit calculation, or because of role demands (see also Morris, Podolny, & Ariel, 2000). The *liking/caring* explanation indicates that the helper is helping "from the heart" and is not necessarily expecting anything in return. Paradoxically, this absence of reciprocation pressure makes recipients more likely to want to reciprocate! The *cost–benefit* explanation indicates that the helper deliberately weighed potential rewards for himself or herself against potential costs of helping. This "cold, calculating" decision to help implies that the helper does not necessarily like the recipient and is probably expecting something in return. The *role demands* explanation indicates that the helper felt it was his or her obligation, or duty, to help, such as when a police officer gives help or when a co-worker's job responsibilities include assisting on a particular task. This reason for helping implies that the helper does not necessarily like the recipient and may even feel superior in the sense that he or she "is responsible" for the welfare of the recipient.

Ames and his colleagues (2004) conducted several studies in which participants either read descriptions of hypothetical situations in which they might receive help, or described actual experiences of receiving help, and then reported how they would or did feel in the situation. Results supported the prediction that helping motivated by caring produces the most positive responses from the recipient. The researchers suggested that recipients' perceptions of the reasons for the helping influence their judgments about the nature of their relationship with the helper: the caring explanation implies a close, affectionate relationship, whereas the cost–benefit and role demands explanations imply a more formal, businesslike relationship.

Individual Differences in Gratitude.

dispositional gratitude

an individual differences variable reflecting the extent to which people feel thankful for receiving help from others

Michael McCullough of Southern Methodist University, Robert Emmons of the University of California at Davis, and their colleagues have taken a very different approach to understanding recipients' reactions to helping: these researchers have conceptualized **dispositional gratitude** as an individual difference variable, with some people being more inclined toward feeling thankful for receiving help than other people (McCullough, Emmons, & Tsang, 2002; McCullough, Kilpatrick, Emmons, & Larson, 2001). At one end of this dimension are people who always seem grateful for any help they receive. These individuals are likely to thank others explicitly and to recognize help they received. At the other end of the dimension are people who might informally be labelled "ingrates." These individuals never thank anyone for help and do not seem even to know that their success is partly due to others' efforts.

McCullough and his colleagues (2002) developed a six-item scale to measure dispositional gratitude, which is reproduced in Know Yourself 12.2: "Dispositional Gratitude." Answer the items to see how you score on this dimension.

McCullough and his colleagues (2002) found that scores on the measure of dispositional gratitude were correlated with measures of happiness, life satisfaction, and optimism, such that grateful people tended to be happier, more satisfied with life, and more optimistic than ungrateful people. In contrast, ungrateful people reported more anxiety and depression than did grateful individuals. Of course, these are correlational data, so we cannot know whether being grateful makes people happier, whether being happy makes people feel grateful, or whether some third factor influences both happiness and gratitude. Nevertheless, it seems clear that feeling grateful is associated with other positive states.

Scores on the gratitude scale also correlated with the Perspective Taking and Empathic Concern subscales of the Interpersonal Reactivity Index: grateful individuals tended to take other people's perspectives more (to be more empathic) than ungrateful individuals. Finally, McCullough and his colleagues (2002) obtained from participants the names of people who knew them well; these individuals

© Guerorgui Pinkhassov/Magnum Photos

Some people are more *dispositionally grateful* for receiving help than are other people.

Know Yourself 12.2
Dispositional Gratitude

Please indicate how much you agree or disagree with each of the following items by circling the appropriate number on the answer scale.

1. I have so much in life to be thankful for.

1	2	3	4	5	6	7
Strongly disagree	Disagree	Slightly disagree	Neutral	Slightly agree	Agree	Strongly agree

2. If I had to list everything that I felt grateful for, it would be a very long list.

1	2	3	4	5	6	7
Strongly disagree	Disagree	Slightly disagree	Neutral	Slightly agree	Agree	Strongly agree

3. When I look at the world, I don't see much to be grateful for.

1	2	3	4	5	6	7
Strongly disagree	Disagree	Slightly disagree	Neutral	Slightly agree	Agree	Strongly agree

4. I am grateful to a wide variety of people.

1	2	3	4	5	6	7
Strongly disagree	Disagree	Slightly disagree	Neutral	Slightly agree	Agree	Strongly agree

5. As I get older, I find myself more able to appreciate the people, events, and situations that have been part of my life history.

1	2	3	4	5	6	7
Strongly disagree	Disagree	Slightly disagree	Neutral	Slightly agree	Agree	Strongly agree

6. Long amounts of time can go by before I feel grateful to something or someone.

1	2	3	4	5	6	7
Strongly disagree	Disagree	Slightly disagree	Neutral	Slightly agree	Agree	Strongly agree

SCORING: Items 1, 2, 4, and 5 are scored in the way they appear (1-2-3-4-5-6-7), but Items 3 and 6 are scored in the reverse direction (7-6-5-4-3-2-1). Add up your scores across all of the items for your total dispositional gratitude score. Possible scores range from 6 to 42, and higher scores reflect more dispositional gratitude.

Sample items from McCullough et al., "The grateful disposition: A conceptual and empirical topography," *Journal of Personality and Social Psychology*, 82, 112–127, 2002. Copyright © 2002 by the American Psychological Association. Reprinted by permission.

were subsequently contacted and asked to rate the participant on a variety of measures, including helpful behaviour (e.g., how often the target person goes out of his or her way to do favours for others; how often the target person volunteers time to help others). Higher scores on the measure of dispositional gratitude were associated with higher scores on the peer ratings of helpful behaviours. Thus, people who were grateful for help they received also tended to be more helpful to others. This finding might serve as a lesson for all of us: perhaps we should make more effort to feel thankful for the help we receive from others—we might even become more helpful ourselves. The various factors influencing how the recipients of help react to the assistance are summarized in the accompanying Concept Review.

Social Dilemmas: Cooperating for the Common Good

Self-interest, or egoistic motivation, is a powerful force. In some facets of life, being concerned primarily for one's own well-being seems natural and even makes sense: it is a competitive, dog-eat-dog world, so looking out for number one may be the key to survival.

But there are also situations in which a narrow focus on one's own short-term rewards can be counterproductive. In these situations, individual, competitive motives conflict with group, cooperative motives. These settings also tend to contrast short-term against long-term considerations. The term used to refer to these situations is *social dilemmas*. Some of the greatest threats to human survival will require cooperation and sacrifice of immediate personal gain if we are to defeat them. Nowhere is this more evident than in the erosion of natural resources and the environment; we must all conserve, thereby giving up some individual gain, in order for the world to remain healthy.

cooperation

collaborative behaviour with other people that takes into account both one's own outcomes and the outcomes of the others

The behaviour we discuss in this section is **cooperation:** collaborative behaviour with other people that takes into account both one's own interests and the interests of the others. Cooperation is one form of *prosocial behaviour*—behaviour that provides benefit to others. Cooperation is not necessarily *helping behaviour* (behaviour intended to assist another person); for example, it does not fit into any of McGuire's (1994) four categories of helping behaviour (see Table 12.1, page 462). Rather, it is joint behaviour that balances self- and other interests and often takes a long-term perspective.

Definition of Social Dilemmas

social dilemma

a situation in which selfish choices produce better immediate outcomes for the individual than do cooperative choices, but long-term outcomes for everyone will suffer if everyone behaves selfishly

A **social dilemma** is a situation in which individual interests conflict with interests of the group. All social dilemmas are characterized by two features: (1) selfish choices produce better immediate outcomes for the individual than do cooperative choices, but (2) long-term outcomes for everyone will suffer if everyone behaves selfishly (Schroeder, 1995). These characteristics make choices between selfishness and cooperation very difficult. For example, when a stock of resources is fixed, taking as much as possible may often appear to be the best way to come out ahead. But at what cost? Your own immediate personal outcomes may be maximized, but if everybody makes the same selfish decisions, the pool of resources will soon be depleted. Cooperation may entail giving up some of your own potential benefit so that, in the long run, everyone comes out ahead. The nature of this dilemma was nicely illustrated in a story about farmers, cattle, and an open pasture recounted by Garrett Hardin (1968).

The *tragedy of the commons* can be illustrated with cases of shared pastures being overgrazed.

Tragedy of the Commons. Hardin (1968) described how shared but fixed resources can quickly become depleted if everyone seeks to maximize their own outcomes—a **tragedy of the commons**. Imagine a common pasture—open and free to all—that is capable of sustaining 100 cows. Ten farmers each have ten cows grazing in that pasture. Because the number of cows equals exactly the capacity of the pasture, the collective benefit is maximized. But individual farmers are also seeking to maximize their own personal benefits. "What harm would it do," thinks a farmer, "if I add one more cow?" That farmer's benefit will increase by almost 10%. The cost of one more cow would be very small—the pasture will be stressed a small amount, and so the productivity of each cow will be slightly diminished. But the cost would be spread over 100 other cows and nine other farmers, and so the cost to any single cow or farmer will be very small. Adding one more cow may therefore seem to be the rational and sensible thing to do. Of course, the other farmers might get the same idea—all being rational, sensible, and seeking to maximize their own gains. Soon, the pasture contains 110 cows. Again, at this point, farmers may decide that one more cow added by them wouldn't hurt much, and soon 120 cows are in the pasture. If all of the farmers continue to pursue their selfish interests, the pasture's resources will be fully depleted and no longer capable of sustaining even a single cow. In the end, every farmer loses—a tragedy born out of each individual's seeking to maximize his or her own outcomes.

Hardin (1968) cited several examples of the tragedy of the commons. Overgrazing of common pastures is a real problem. The world's oceans are also treated as a commons, and the result has been overharvesting of fish and whales to the point of driving many species toward extinction. For example, northern cod were at one time abundant in the waters off Newfoundland, but overfishing between 1950 and 1990 decimated their numbers; a ban on cod fishing was imposed by the Canadian government in 1992 and recently renewed in 2003. Environmental pollution is another example of the tragedy of the commons: the garbage, sewage, and carbon dioxide contributed by one person is hardly enough to cause noticeable harm to the environment, but the sum of many small individual contributions can add up to irreparable harm to all. Indeed, global warming, which has almost certainly been worsened by industrial and automotive pollution, now represents a true threat to all humans. In every case, the short-term pursuit of self-interest and maximization of self-benefits creates a long-term cumulative and collective loss.

The Prisoner's Dilemma. A variation of the commons problem that social psychologists have utilized in the laboratory is the **prisoner's dilemma game**. One of the first social psychologists to use this game was Anatol Rapoport (1960), who was a professor at the University of Toronto. This game also forces a choice between selfishness and cooperation. Imagine that two partners in crime are being held in separate cells at police headquarters. They stand accused of a series of robberies, but a confession is needed to make the most serious charges stick. Without the confession, enough evidence is available to convict them only of minor crimes, and each would receive a one-year sentence. The prosecutor promises to recommend less than the maximum ten-year sentence if a confession is made. If both confess, they both receive eight-year

tragedy of the commons
the depletion of a communal resource, such as a shared cow pasture for a group of farmers, because each individual pursues selfish interests

prisoner's dilemma game
a simulated social dilemma that requires participants to make choices between acting selfishly and cooperatively when selfishness looks better initially but can damage long-term joint outcomes of the players

payoff matrix

a table representing the outcomes for each player in a prisoner's dilemma game based on the players' combined choices

12.1
ONLINE
LAB

sentences. If only one confesses, that one gets just three months, and the other gets ten years. The main catch is that each prisoner must make a decision independently and without communicating with the other. All of the possible outcomes are summarized in the **payoff matrix** shown in Table 12.4 (Luce & Raiffa, 1957). The "cooperative" choice for each suspect is to *not confess*—it will produce the best collective outcomes. But there is a strong temptation to act selfishly, or *confess*. In fact, confessing is the rational thing to do. If you think that your partner will make the cooperative choice (not confess), then you come out ahead by confessing (three months vs. one year). If you think that your partner will confess, then you still come out ahead by confessing (eight years vs. ten years). But notice that if both make this same "rational" choice to confess, then both end up worse off (eight years) than if the two had cooperated by not confessing (one year).

The hypothetical dilemma of the two prisoners lacks one important quality of real-life social dilemmas: repeated "trials" over time. If a prisoner needs to make a one-time decision to confess or not confess, it is indeed rational to be selfish by confessing. But in almost all social dilemmas, there will be a continuing relationship between the people involved, and early decisions will exert strong effects on later decisions. For example, to return to the tragedy of the commons, if farmers learn that one of the other farmers has added a cow, then they may be more likely to add a cow themselves. So a situation that could have remained cooperative is rendered selfish and competitive by the actions of one person.

In fact, when researchers use the prisoner's dilemma game to study behaviour in social dilemmas, they require participants to play many trials of the game. Hence, participants never actually hear the hypothetical story of the two prisoners, nor is the game labelled "the prisoner's dilemma game." Instead, the game is described simply as a multi-trial game in which participants select one of two possible responses on each trial, and their payoffs on each trial are determined by the combined choices. Participants are also typically given a copy of a payoff matrix (like the one in Table 12.4, but with the labels Person 1, Person 2, Response A, and Response B, and with the payoffs expressed in points rather than prison sentences).

Decision Making in Social Dilemmas

How do people in social dilemmas decide whether to act selfishly or cooperatively? University of Toronto social psychologist J. Mark Weber and his colleagues (Weber, Kopelman, & Messick, 2004) proposed that people are guided primarily by their perceptions of what behaviour is *appropriate* in the situation: "What does a person

---

TABLE 12.4
A Payoff Matrix for the Prisoner's Dilemma Game

	Prisoner 2's Decision:	
	Not Confess **(Cooperative response)**	**Confess** **(Selfish response)**
Prisoner 1's Decision:		
Not Confess **(Cooperative response)**	Both prisoners get a 1-year sentence	Prisoner 1 gets a 10-year sentence; Prisoner 2 gets a 3-month sentence
Confess **(Selfish response)**	Prisoner 1 gets a 3-month sentence; Prisoner 2 gets a 10-year sentence	Both prisoners get an 8-year sentence

After Luce & Raiffa, 1957, Games and decisions: Introduction and critical survey, New York: Wiley.

like me do in a situation like this?" Based on features of the situation itself, social norms, personal experiences in similar situations, and dispositional traits related to cooperativeness, people might judge a particular social dilemma to be a setting in which either selfish or cooperative responses are appropriate. This perception of appropriate behaviour will guide the individuals' actual responses.

What does the word *appropriate* mean in this model? Responses that are judged "appropriate" in a setting might be those that are considered morally right, or those that are expected to produce the best outcomes, or those that are believed to be typical for this setting. The specific meaning of appropriate varies across individuals and even across situations for the same person. This model of decision making is appealing because it integrates research on many factors that have been shown to affect cooperative behaviour in social dilemmas. In the following paragraphs, we review some of the literature on social dilemmas, using the appropriateness model as an integrative framework.

Situational Labels. There is a lot of evidence that the way individuals *label* a social dilemma influences their behaviour. In a simple but compelling demonstration of this idea, Israeli social psychologist Varda Liberman, together with Steven Samuels and Lee Ross (a Canadian professor at Stanford University), had either university students or Israeli pilots play a seven-trial version of the prisoners' dilemma game (Liberman, Samuels, & Ross, 2004). For some participants, the game was given a label that implied cooperation (e.g., the Community Game), whereas for others it was given a label that implied selfishness or competition (e.g., the Wall Street Game). This simple manipulation of the game's name exerted a huge impact on cooperation, such that the cooperatively labelled game elicited approximately twice as many cooperative responses as the competitively labelled game. Why did the labels exert such a strong effect? Presumably, the label of the game influenced participants' perceptions of what responses were appropriate, including how other players were likely to respond and whether selfish responses were ethical or unethical.

Priming. It is possible to affect participants' responses in social dilemmas more subtly than with overt situational labels. Specifically, *priming* the schema of cooperation or competition can influence reactions. For example, University of Waterloo social psychologist Aaron Kay, together with Lee Ross (2003), required participants to rearrange five-word sequences into proper sentences using four of the five words. A total of 24 sequences were provided, and 16 of the sequences created four-word sentences related either to cooperation (e.g., "helped friend computer she her" could be rearranged into "she helped her friend") or competition (e.g., "today is tournament often the" could be rearranged into "the tournament is today"). Participants then read about a multi-trial prisoner's dilemma game and were asked how they would respond in such a game. Those participants who had their schema of *cooperation* primed reported that they would behave more cooperatively than did those participants who had their schema of *competition* primed. Presumably, the priming manipulation influenced how participants thought about the game, which affected whether cooperative or selfish responses were considered appropriate.

In another study of priming effects, Arjaan Wit at the University of Leiden in the Netherlands and Norbert Kerr at Michigan State University gave participants the opportunity to divide some money among several "bank accounts," including a private account for themselves and a group account that would be divided among all six participants who were taking part at the session (Wit & Kerr, 2002). Before making this division, participants were exposed to a manipulation designed to make either an individual or a collective perspective salient (prominent). Specifically, some participants were told that each of the six participants would individually throw dice to determine the percentage of money in the bank accounts they would receive (individual perspective), whereas other participants were told that the experimenter would throw dice one time to determine the percentage of money in each account all six participants would receive (collective perspective). This simple procedure had a significant impact on how much participants assigned to their own private account: the individual perspective led participants to put more money into their private account than did the collective perspective. Presumably, making a collective perspective salient increased the perceived appropriateness of sharing responses (see also De Cremer & van Dijk, 2002; Kramer & Brewer, 1984).

Social Norms. Earlier in the chapter, the concept of social norms was used to explain why people might engage in helpful behaviour. For example, the norm of social responsibility dictates that we should help others who are in need. Similarly, there is evidence that cooperation in social dilemmas is influenced by norms. In one experiment, Harvey Hornstein and his colleagues at Columbia University (Hornstein, LaKind, Frankel, & Manne, 1975) made a cooperative norm especially salient by having students listen to a (fictitious) news story about a man who donated his kidney to a total stranger. Other groups of students listened to a news story featuring antisocial behaviour, and still others heard no news story at all; the norm of social responsibility was not expected to be activated in these conditions. The students then played a prisoner's dilemma game in which they had to choose between a cooperative and a selfish strategy. The students were more likely to choose the cooperative strategy, and to assume that their partner would also do so, after hearing the story that involved helpful behaviour than in the other two conditions.

Making people aware of social norms for cooperation may be a good way to increase cooperative strategies relating to the environment. Joseph Hopper and Joyce McCarl Nielsen (1991) found that Denver, Colorado, residents were more likely to participate in a community recycling program when they perceived that their own neighbourhood had a norm for recycling. Why do norms affect cooperative behaviour? Norms represent shared views of what is appropriate behaviour in the situation, including what is fair or unfair for those involved (see Schroeder, Steel, Woodell, & Bembenek, 2003).

Actions of Similar Models. People's behaviour in social dilemmas is also influenced by the actions of other people, especially those who are similar in important ways. This point was demonstrated in a study by Craig Parks, Larry Sanna, and Susan Berel (2001). Washington State University students played a multi-trial prisoner's dilemma game, but before actually starting were given information about how three (fictitious) previous participants had behaved. Additional background information about these alleged previous participants made them seem either very similar or very dissimilar to a typical university student. Participants' own responses on the subsequent social dilemma task were significantly affected by the alleged actions of similar others: participants cooperated more when similar models were believed to have cooperated than when similar models were believed to have responded selfishly. The alleged responses of very dissimilar models had no impact on participants' responses on the task. These findings suggest that the actions of similar others influenced perceptions of appropriate behaviour in the social dilemma.

Communication. Communication in social dilemmas tends to increase cooperative responses. In the original scenario of two criminal suspects facing the dilemma of whether or not to confess, part of their difficulty is that they are not allowed to talk to one another. Communication

When people believe that their neighbourhood has a norm for recycling, they are more likely to recycle themselves.

might allow the prisoners to express their intentions to cooperate. This idea was put to experimental test by Robyn Dawes, Jeanne McTavish, and Harriet Shaklee (1977) at the University of Oregon. A variation of the prisoner's dilemma was created so that participants in small groups had to make a choice between a cooperative and a competitive response. The game was set up so that the payoff for a particular participant would be very high if he or she chose a selfish response and most of the others chose a cooperative strategy. The greater the number of selfish responses, however, the lower the payoff—and if numerous participants chose the selfish option, the payoff actually turned negative! In this case, the cooperative strategy clearly maximized the collective payoff.

In one condition of the experiment, the participants were not permitted to talk with one another before making their individual decisions; 70% of these participants responded selfishly. In another condition, the participants were given ten minutes to discuss their dilemma before making their decisions; the selfish response rate was cut to 28% here. A little bit of communication went a long way to enhancing cooperation and maximizing the collective outcome, presumably because people discussed the benefits of cooperation and were convinced that it was the appropriate response (see also Kerr & Kaufman-Gilliland, 1994; Tazelaar, Van Lange, & Ouwer-kerk, 2004). This effect of communication may remind you of our discussion of intergroup conflict in Chapter 10, where we suggested that communication between groups may be the most important factor in the reduction of conflict.

Individual Differences in Cooperativeness: Social Value Orientation.

Earlier in the chapter, we talked about the altruistic personality—people who are especially helpful toward others. Researchers interested specifically in social dilemmas have identified an individual difference variable that predicts people's responses in such settings. The variable is known as **social value orientation,** and three major orientations are normally distinguished. *Individualists* are primarily concerned with maximizing their own outcomes. *Competitors* are primarily concerned with maximizing their own outcomes relative to others' outcomes. *Prosocials* are primarily concerned with maximizing the total outcomes of everyone in the setting.

Social value orientation is typically assessed by asking people to select which of three hypothetical distributions of money or points they would prefer (Van Lange & Kuhlman, 1994). For example, they might be asked to choose among the following three options: Option A pays 600 points to the self and 300 points to an unknown other, Option B pays 500 points to the self and 100 points to the other, and Option C pays 500 points to the self and 500 points to the other. Option A is the individualistic choice because it maximizes personal points. Option B is the competitive choice because it maximizes the difference between the points assigned to the self and the other. Option C is the prosocial choice because it maximizes the total points for self and other combined (see Steinel & De Dreu, 2004). In similar fashion, participants are asked to choose one of three alternatives on nine different items. If they make a particular type of choice (e.g., competitive) on at least six of the nine items, then they are considered to have a specific social value orientation (e.g., competitor). If they do not choose one type of option on at least six items, then they are assumed to have mixed motives and are not included in tests of social value orientation.

Researchers have found that people with a prosocial value orientation cooperate more often in social dilemmas than do individualists or competitors (e.g., Kramer, McClintock, & Messick, 1986; Roch & Samuelson, 1997; Smeesters, Warlop, Van Avermaet, Corneille, & Yzerbyt, 2003; Utz, 2004). Prosocials also expect other people to cooperate, respond positively to others' cooperation, and remain optimistic about future cooperation (e.g., Liebrand, Jansen, Rijken, & Suhre, 1986; Parks & Rumble, 2001; Parks, Sanna, & Posey, 2003). In research on the related topic of negotiation, researchers have found that prosocial negotiators are less contentious and engage in

social value orientation

a disposition that reflects individual differences in cooperativeness in social dilemmas; three orientations are typically distinguished: individualists, competitors, and prosocials

CONCEPT REVIEW
Factors Influencing Cooperation in Social Dilemmas

Factor	Description	*Example of Relevant Manipulation or Measure*
Labels	Cooperative versus competitive labels increase or decrease cooperation	Use Community Game versus Wall Street Game as label for the prisoner's dilemma game
Priming	Activating the schema of cooperation or competition increases or decreases cooperation	Have participants rearrange sentences relating to cooperation or competition
Social norms	Cooperative norms will increase cooperation when they are salient	Have participants read an article about an organ donor
Models	Actions of similar others can increase or decrease cooperation	Tell participants about the responses of previous participants who were similar to typical students
Communication	Allowing people to communicate can increase cooperation	Give participants 10 minutes to converse before choosing responses
Individual differences	Social value orientation influences cooperation	Measure whether participants are individualists, competitors, or prosocials

more problem solving than individualistic or competitive negotiators (see De Dreu, Weingart, & Kwon, 2000).

How does social value orientation influence people's behaviour? Prosocials consider cooperation in social dilemmas to be the appropriate behaviour, whereas competitors and individualists consider self-interested actions to be appropriate (Weber et al., 2004). Specifically, prosocials consider cooperation to be morally correct and also the most rational choice in terms of maximizing personal outcomes in the long run. Competitors and individualists often consider cooperative responses to be "weak" and expect selfish responses to maximize personal outcomes in the long run (Liebrand et al., 1986).

The factors we have discussed that influence cooperation in social dilemmas are summarized in the accompanying Concept Review.

 ## Social Support

I get by with a little help from my friends.
—*John Lennon and Paul McCartney (1967)*

Social Support Networks

Two of the four categories of helping behaviours we described at the beginning of this chapter (McGuire, 1994; see Table 12.1) have received relatively little discussion so far (except for the section on volunteerism): substantial personal helping and emotional helping. One difference between these two categories and casual or emergency helping is who does them—strangers versus acquaintances. Whereas casual and emergency helping are typically done by strangers, substantial personal helping and emotional helping are typically done by friends and family members. Thus, the availability and quality of this kind of helping depend considerably on a **social support network:** people who can be called upon for help and who will provide it when needed, such as family members, friends, neighbours, and other acquaintances.

Social support has received less attention as a research topic from social psychologists than have casual and emergency helping, although clinical psychologists have studied this topic for several decades. Recently, however, social psychologists have become more actively involved in research on social support and have generated interesting findings from a variety of theoretical perspectives (e.g., Abend & Williamson, 2002; Feeney & Collins, 2001; Neff & Karney, 2005; Neyer & Lang, 2003; Simpson, Rholes, Oriña, & Grich, 2002; Taylor, Sherman, Kim, Jarcho, Takegi, & Dunagan, 2004). In this section, we review some of this work, as well as some important findings by clinical psychologists.

social support network

people who can be called upon for help and who will provide help when needed, such as family, friends, and neighbours

Perceived Availability of Social Support Versus Actual Receipt of Social Support.

Social support networks serve at least two functions (Stroebe & Stroebe, 1996). Specifically, it is important to distinguish between the *perceived availability* of social support and the *actual receipt* of social support. On the one hand, people may believe that family and friends are available should they ever be needed; this *perceived availability* of social support presumably gives people confidence that they can deal with stress and a feeling that others care for them. On the other hand, people must truly receive social support when they need it; this *actual receipt* of social support encompasses helping with physical tasks, expressing emotional support, and providing information that helps individuals cope with their situation.

It turns out that the benefits of a social support network have been easier to document for one kind of social support than for the other. Which kind would you expect to be associated more strongly with positive outcomes, the perceived availability of social support or the actual receipt of social support? Perhaps surprisingly, data suggest that *perceiving* help is nearby is more consistently connected to well-being than is actually *receiving* help when needed (Wethington & Kessler, 1986). We will discuss this interesting result shortly.

Measuring the Perceived Availability of Social Support.

To measure people's perceptions that others are available if needed, Irwin Sarason and his colleagues at the University of Washington (Sarason, Levine, Basham, & Sarason, 1983) developed a Social Support Questionnaire (SSQ). This scale consists of 27 items that ask respondents to list all of the people on whom they can rely in a variety of circumstances, and to rate how satisfied they are with these social supports. Respondents who nominate many people providing support and who report high satisfaction receive higher scores on the SSQ. Here are some sample items:

- Whom can you really count on to listen to you when you need to talk?

- Whom could you really count on to help you out in a crisis situation, even though they would have to go out of their way to do so?

Jupiter Images

A *social support network* consists of people who can be called on for help when it is needed, such as family members and friends.

- Whom can you really count on to be dependable when you need help?
- With whom can you totally be yourself?
- Who do you feel really appreciates you as a person?

Measuring the Actual Receipt of Social Support. To measure how much social support people have actually received, Manuel Barrera, Irwin Sandler, and Thomas Ramsay (1981) at Arizona State University developed the Inventory of Socially Supportive Behaviours (ISSB). This scale consists of 40 instances of helping that people might have received. Each item is rated for its frequency of occurrence during the past month, on a scale from 1 (not at all) to 5 (about every day). Respondents who report more frequent occurrence of the social support behaviours receive higher scores on the ISSB. Here are some sample items:

- Expressed interest and concern in your well-being
- Joked and kidded to try to cheer you up
- Told you that you are OK just the way you are
- Gave you some information on how to do something
- Was right there with you (physically) in a stressful situation

Social Support and the Reciprocity Norm. One interesting aspect of social support networks is that they provide help without the pressure of immediate reciprocation (although social support in close relationships may be most beneficial when each partner supports the other; see Gleason, Iida, Bolger, & Shrout, 2003). The terminally ill and the very old depend heavily on their social support networks even though they are the least able members of the network to ever reciprocate for the physical, financial, and emotional support they receive. Of course, these individuals often have a history of providing support to others in the past.

Toni Antonucci and James Jackson (1990) at the University of Michigan proposed the metaphor of a social support network being like a *bank*. You make deposits when you are able, and you take withdrawals when you need them. There is no expectation of one-to-one reciprocation between members of a social support network. Rather, it is a collective bank to which its members contribute and from which its members are entitled to draw. It is not coincidental that a person's social support network primarily comprises others with whom close interpersonal relationships are enjoyed—relatives, spouses, children, parents, and close friends. In Chapter 13, we will learn that close relationships often move beyond a one-for-one exchange of benefits to something more like a communal sharing of benefits (Clark & Mills, 1979). In communal relationships, the receipt of a benefit creates no specific obligation to return that benefit: from each according to their ability, and to each according to their need.

Social Support and Health

Research on the effects of social support has focused on its potential health benefits, both physical and mental. Why or how might social support be beneficial to well-being? There are at least four ways that social support might improve recipients' mental or physical health (Schaefer, Coyne, & Lazarus, 1981; Wills, 1991):

- *Informational support* provides advice, instructions, directions, and generally useful information about health-related topics. Examples include giving advice about helpful exercise routines and finding out where to obtain needed medication.
- *Instrumental support* is the provision of physical assistance or material resources that provide aid. These resources could include providing physical care during

an illness, lending money, or providing other services and resources that may be needed by someone in distress.

- *Companionship support* provides company to the person in need, creating a sense of belonging. Sitting with or reading to a sick friend, going shopping, or having lunch together are examples of companionship support.

- *Emotional support* is the giving of acceptance and reassurance, providing a source of intimacy and confidence. Expressing love, comforting when sad, and discussing fears are examples of emotional support.

Health Consequences of the Perceived Availability of Social Support.

The evidence is quite clear and consistent that perceiving a wide social support network has positive effects on health and well-being. For example, perceiving that a wide social support network is available if necessary has been shown to improve recovery from physical illness, to reduce the negative impact of stressful events, and to protect against depression (e.g., Cortina, 2004; Cross & Vick, 2001; House, Landis, & Umberson, 1988; Katz, Monnier, Libet, Shaw, & Beach, 2000; Lindorff, 2000; McCaskill & Lakey, 2000). Believing that they can call on a social support network increases individuals' feelings of control: if necessary, they can face problems together with friends and family (Cohen, 2004).

Demonstration

The purpose of the study is to make the guests sick. A cold virus is placed into the nose, and the volunteers are sequestered at a local motel for six days, where they're tested daily to see just how sick they get.

In one well-known early study, Lisa Berkman and S. Leonard Syme (1979) surveyed almost 5000 adults living in Alameda County, California, in 1965. The adults ranged in age from 30 to 69. For the following nine years (through 1974), the sample was followed and deaths were recorded. Throughout the period of study, the residents who had reported relatively poor social networks in 1965 were twice as likely to die as those who had reported relatively good social networks (the quality of social networks was defined in terms of the number and extent of social relationships, including marriage, family and friends, church membership, and other group affiliations).

Heart disease is one aspect of physical health that seems clearly influenced by the perceived availability of social support. Between 1974 and 1989, more than 1300 patients at Duke Medical Center were enrolled in a study of coronary artery disease and social support (Williams et al., 1992). The patients all had significant coronary artery disease, and records were kept of those who died as a result of their heart problems. A simple measure of social support availability was obtained: the patients were asked whether or not they were married or had a close confidant on whom they could rely. During one five-year period, the unmarried patients who did not have a close confidant were more than three times as likely to die as were the married patients or those who did have a confidant. Even when a variety of other socioeconomic factors were taken into account (e.g., income, number of dependents, education), the most important predictor of mortality was the presence versus absence of a spouse or confidant (see also King, Reis, Porter, & Norsen, 1993).

Health Consequences of the Actual Receipt of Social Support.

In contrast to clear evidence showing that the perceived availability of social support is beneficial to people's health, it has proven more difficult to connect the *actual receipt* of social support with positive outcomes. Indeed, several studies have found that people receiving more social support reported *worse* symptoms and problems (e.g., Barrera, 1981; Bolger, Zuckerman, & Kessler, 2000; Neuling & Winefield, 1988). How is this possible when the receipt of social support should presumably make people feel better, not worse? One reason may be that the data have often been correlational. People may have received a lot of social support *because their health was bad,* rather than the social support actually being harmful (Stroebe & Stroebe,

1996). But this criticism does not apply to all of the studies that have failed to show positive effects of actual receipt of social support.

For example, New York University social psychologist Niall Bolger and his colleagues (Bolger, Foster, Vinokur, & Ng, 1996) interviewed 102 breast cancer patients at two different times: the women were visited in their homes at four months and ten months after diagnosis. At each session, the women were asked about physical impairments and emotional distress (anxiety, depression). In addition, at each session, the spouse or "significant other" (often the patient's daughter) reported the amount of social support he or she was currently providing to the patient. This was done by rating how much he or she was doing such things as:

- Providing encouragement and reassurance when she needs it
- Providing her with direct help (doing things for her, giving her things she needs)
- Listening to her when she needs to talk about things that are important to her
- Saying things that raise her self-confidence
- Giving her useful information or advice when she needs it

Because well-being and social support were each measured twice, the researchers could examine how the two concepts changed and influenced one another over time. The results showed that physical limitations caused by the breast cancer led to increased social support, as would be expected. However, social support did not appear to improve physical recovery or to reduce distress over time: support had no effect. Even more troubling was the finding that patients who experienced a lot of emotional distress subsequently received *less* social support from their support person; in other words, social support appeared to be *eroded* by the patient's distress. The researchers suggested that support givers may have seen emotional distress as something the patient should be able to control, so they reduced support because they felt unappreciated or because it was simply unpleasant being around the patient.

How should we interpret the apparent lack of benefit of actually received social support? In 1986, Darrin Lehman of the University of British Columbia, John Ellard of the University of Calgary, and Camille Wortman of the State University of New York at Stony Brook reported a survey of individuals who had lost either a spouse or a child in a motor vehicle accident. Respondents were asked to describe social support attempts that they had received from other people, either helpful or unhelpful. Respondents were able to identify numerous support attempts of each kind. Some of the most frequently mentioned helpful supports were the opportunity to express feelings and simply being together with someone who cared for them. Some of the most frequently mentioned unhelpful support attempts were giving advice and encouraging them to recover. Thus, some forms of social support may not be helpful at all. For example, telling people that it is time for them to get over their loss may be more likely to create anger than to facilitate recovery. Of course, these findings may reflect, in part, misperceptions by the recipients of the support; perhaps the individuals offering support intended their actions to be interpreted differently (see Lakey, Adams, Neely, Rhodes, Lutz, & Sielky, 2002; Lutz & Lakey, 2001).

Niall Bolger and his colleagues (2000) made an interesting observation about this issue. These researchers proposed that when people recognize that they have received social support, this recognition can have an emotional cost. Recall our discussion earlier in the chapter that receiving help may sometimes threaten self-esteem (Nadler et al., 1976). Such a reduction in self-esteem might counteract any benefit from the social support. To test this idea, Bolger and his colleagues studied 68 heterosexual couples in which one person was preparing to write the New York State Bar Examination to become a lawyer—a stressful event. Participants completed a brief questionnaire each day for five weeks, indicating their emotional feelings and social support (the person preparing for the bar exam reported any social support he or she had received, and the other member of the dyad reported any social support he or she had provided).

Results showed that when the person preparing for the exam reported receiving social support, he or she tended to report *more distress* on the following day. Thus, knowing that they had received social support appeared to make people feel worse, perhaps because the support threatened their self-esteem. Also, many acts of social support reported by the support giver were *not* reported by the recipient, suggesting that people do not always recognize everything that is done for them. The researchers labelled these unrecognized acts of support "invisible" social support. The most interesting finding of all was that "invisible" acts of support were associated with the recipient reporting *less distress* on the following day! In other words, acts of social support that were reported by the giver but *not* recognized as such by the recipient tended to have a positive impact. The researchers suggested that when it is "invisible," social support does not threaten self-esteem.

In closing, perhaps the actual receipt of social support does have beneficial effects on health in some circumstances (e.g., when the support is unrecognized) or for some people (see Feeney & Collins, 2003; Frazier, Tix, & Barnett, 2003). It may seem strange that receiving social support can ever have *negative* effects on well-being, but the data suggest that this can sometimes be the case. It will be interesting to see whether future research identifies more clearly the conditions under which received support is either beneficial or harmful.

Chapter Summary

Helping is behaviour that is intended to assist another person. It is one type of **prosocial behaviour,** which is any action that provides benefit to other people. Helping behaviour falls into a number of distinct categories, including casual helping, emergency helping, substantial personal helping, and emotional helping.

People often help because of an **egoistic motivation**—a desire to obtain rewards or to avoid punishments. It is also possible that people sometimes help out of an **altruistic motivation**—purely for the sake of providing benefit to another, without regard for self-gain. One explanation why humans have evolved to be altruistic is based on the principle of **inclusive fitness,** which is the idea that some social behaviours have been selected during the course of evolution because they increase the survival of our genes. **Empathy** is the ability to comprehend how another person is experiencing a situation. The **empathy–altruism hypothesis** proposes that feelings of empathy for a person can lead to behaviour that is motivated solely by wanting to help that person.

Social norms are culturally defined rules or guidelines about what behaviours are proper and improper. Several norms are relevant to helping behaviour. For example, the **norm of social responsibility** dictates that we should help those who need help, if possible. The norm

of reciprocity states that we should return favours to others who have helped us. These norms will guide behaviour only when they have become **personal norms** for the individual—when they have been internalized to become expectations for oneself in particular situations.

Seeing another person model helpful behaviour increases helping. On the other hand, perceiving the victim as responsible for his or her own problems reduces helping. Such victim blaming may help to protect people's belief in a just world even when they see others suffering; this belief is hypothesized to be important in **just world theory.** Good mood and feelings of guilt are two other factors that have been shown to increase helping.

Some people are more helpful than others. One variable that predicts helpful behaviour is individual differences in empathy, which can be measured by the **Interpersonal Reactivity Index (IRI).** The IRI has four parts, which assess different aspects of empathy: perspective taking, empathic concern, personal distress, and fantasy.

Volunteerism is unpaid helping behaviour that is given willingly to a worthwhile cause or service organization. Several motives for engaging in volunteer behaviour have been identified. One important predictor of continuing volunteerism is satisfaction with one's volunteer experiences.

Social psychologists interested in emergency helping have suggested that a series of decisions must be made before a bystander will intervene in an emergency. This **decision tree** consists of the following steps: the bystander must (1) notice the event, (2) interpret the event as an emergency, (3) accept personal responsibility for intervening, (4) decide on an appropriate form of assistance, and (5) implement the action. If any of the steps does not occur, the bystander will not intervene. The inhibitory effects of the presence of other people on these steps produce the **bystander effect:** the likelihood that an individual will intervene in an emergency goes down as the number of bystanders increases.

People who receive help sometimes respond negatively. One reason may be that they do not want to feel obligated to reciprocate the help. Another possibility is that receiving help threatens their self-esteem. Finally, the helper's reason for helping can affect the recipient's reaction: when helping is done because of liking/caring, recipients typically respond positively, whereas when helping is done because of a cost–benefit analysis or because of role demands, recipients may respond negatively.

Dispositional gratitude refers to the extent to which people feel thankful for receiving help from others. People who are high on this dimension are more likely than people low on the dimension to recognize help they received, to feel grateful for help, and to be helpful themselves.

Cooperation is collaborative behaviour with other people that takes into account both one's own outcomes and the outcomes of the others. Cooperative behaviour is essential in settings known as **social dilemmas,** which are situations in which selfish choices produce better immediate outcomes for the individual than do cooperative choices, but long-term outcomes for everyone will suffer if everyone behaves selfishly. One example of a social dilemma is the tragedy of the commons—the depletion of a communal resource, such as a shared cow pasture for a group of farmers, because each individual pursues selfish interests. A simulated social dilemma is created in the **prisoner's dilemma game,** in which participants make choices between acting selfishly and acting cooperatively when selfishness looks better initially but can damage long-term joint outcomes of the players. Each prisoner's dilemma game has a **payoff matrix** associated with it, which specifies the outcomes for each player based on their combined choices.

People's actions in social dilemmas depend on their perceptions of what behaviour is appropriate in the situation. These perceptions of appropriate behaviour can be influenced by labels, priming, social norms, actions of other people, and communication with other individuals. There are also stable individual differences in people's cooperativeness in social dilemmas, which have been labelled **social value orientation.** Three social value orientations are typically distinguished: *individualists* are primarily concerned with maximizing their own outcomes, *competitors* are primarily concerned with maximizing their outcomes relative to others' outcomes, and *prosocials* are primarily concerned with maximizing the total outcomes of everyone in the setting.

Social support networks are people who can be called upon for help and who will provide help when needed, such as family, friends, and neighbours. Some kinds of helping behaviour, such as substantial personal helping and emotional helping, are provided mainly by individuals' social support networks. It is important to distinguish between the *perceived availability* of social support and the *actual receipt* of social support. Many studies have found that perceiving a wide network of support that can be called upon if necessary is associated with positive health outcomes, including longevity and recovery from coronary artery disease. It has been more difficult to show positive health benefits of actually receiving social support, perhaps because receiving support threatens recipients' self-esteem. It has been suggested that unrecognized social support, called *invisible* social support, may have beneficial health effects.

Key Terms

altruistic motivation (464)

bystander effect (482)

cooperation (490)

decision tree (479)

dispositional gratitude (488)

egoistic motivation (464)

empathy (465)

empathy–altruism hypothesis (465)

helping (461)

inclusive fitness (464)

Interpersonal Reactivity Index (IRI) (472)

just world theory (470)

norm of social responsibility (468)

payoff matrix (492)

personal norms (469)

prisoner's dilemma game (491)

prosocial behaviour (462)

social dilemma (490)

social support network (497)

social value orientation (495)

tragedy of the commons (491)

volunteerism (474)

Social Psychology Alive on the Web

SOCIAL PSYCHOLOGY ALIVE: ONLINE LABS

To perform the following experiment and see how you compare to other students, go to Social Psychology Lab, which can be accessed through ThomsonNOW™.

- 12.1 Prisoner's Dilemma

SOCIAL PSYCHOLOGY ALIVE: QUIZZING AND PRACTICE TESTS

You can access our Web site directly by going to http://www.socialpsychologyalive.nelson.com for online quizzes, flash cards, and Internet links.

INFOTRAC® COLLEGE EDITION

For additional readings, explore InfoTrac® College Edition, your online library of archived journal articles and periodicals dating back 22 years. If your instructor ordered InfoTrac® College Edition with this book, you can access it from your CD-ROM, or go directly to http://www.infotrac-college.com and use the passcode from the InfoTrac® College Edition card that came with your book. For this chapter, try these search terms: *helping, prosocial behavior, altruism, empathy, bystander intervention, cooperation, social dilemma, prisoner's dilemma, social value orientation, social support.*

Social Psychology Alive: The Workbook

To apply what you've learned in this chapter to what happens in the real world, go to Chapter 12 of *Social Psychology Alive: The Workbook:*

- Can You Demonstrate the Social Norms of Casual Helping?
- Why Do People Donate Blood?
- Relief Cowboy: What Motivates Professional Relief Workers?
- Holocaust Rescuers and Bystanders
- Good Samaritan Laws

- Vacationing as a Volunteer
- Cooperation Versus Competition: Will You Choose to Compete?
- The Story of Kitty Genovese
- The Carnegie Hero Fund Commission: Heroes Do Exist!
- Thoughts on Helping by Authors, Philosophers, and Leaders
- How Can I Help?

Social Psychology Alive: The Videos

To see video on the topics and experiments discussed in this chapter, you can go either to ThomsonNOW™ or to the CD-ROM, if your instructor assigned either one, to the following section:

- Thanks for Nothing: Bystander Apathy
- Sick of Solitude: The Link Between Sociability and Health

To Learn More

This list contains citations to books or articles that can help you learn more. These readings are good places to start if you want to gain a deeper understanding of the topics in this chapter.

- Schroeder, D. A., Penner, L. A., Dovidio, J. F., & Piliavin, J. A. (1995). *The psychology of helping and altruism: Problems and puzzles.* New York: McGraw-Hill.

- Schroeder, D. A. (1995). *Social dilemmas: Perspectives on individuals and groups.* Westport, CT: Praeger.
- Stroebe, W., & Stroebe, M. (1996). The social psychology of social support. In E. T. Higgins & A. W. Kruglanski (Eds.), *Social psychology: Handbook of basic principles* (pp. 597–621). New York: Guilford.

NEL

Liking, Loving, and Close Relationships

*F*rank and Betty met during their first year in university. For Frank, it was love at first sight. "She was so beautiful," recalls Frank, "her smile just lit up the room. From the first time I met her, I knew that Betty and I were meant for each other." It took Betty a little longer to warm up to Frank. "He was nice enough, and very handsome. But it wasn't until our fourth or fifth date that I realized how much we had in common." Frank and Betty married soon after graduation. After 50 years of marriage, they are still very much in love. When Frank battled prostate cancer a few years ago, Betty never left his side. Frank credits his quick recovery and current good health to the love and support provided by Betty. "Of course I was there," replies Betty. "He has always been there for me."

Billy has followed a different path when it comes to romance. At age 38, none of his many relationships has lasted more than six months. "I guess I'm afraid of commitment," quips Billy. "I'm more the 'love 'em and leave 'em' kind of guy." Billy likes to "play the field," and bounces from one relationship to another.

More than any other topic in social psychology, research on close and intimate relationships highlights that we are, indeed, social beings. From our earliest moments as infants, and continuing through the oldest ages of adulthood, the close relationships and attachments we form with other people provide the basic foundations of social life. It is in the context of our intimate social relationships that we experience some of our most intense emotions—happiness, joy, love, desire, sorrow, despair, dejection, and heartache.

Most close relationships begin with an initial attraction and sense of liking for another person, just as Frank and Betty described in their relationship. Why is it that we are attracted to some people but not to others? On what basis do we develop a liking for one person but not another? And is beauty in the eye of the beholder, or is it possible that some people are just more attractive than others? These questions are among those answered by research on liking and attraction. Some people are more attractive than others, with some interesting social consequences. But the affection that grows into a close relationship depends on many factors beyond those that simply meet the eye.

dyadic relationships

relationships that develop between two people

As we explore the nature and development of close interpersonal relationships, our focus will be on **dyadic relationships**: relationships that develop between two people. The very first close dyadic relationship is the one formed between an infant and a primary caregiver (usually the mother). The social world of the infant revolves around this relationship, and it can have a profound influence on social development later in life. Social life grows rapidly in childhood, and it is not long before children begin establishing close relationships with others—siblings, peers, and other adults. These relationships help to shape a child's social identity, and establish basic patterns of social interaction that carry into adulthood.

Starting in adolescence and early adulthood, people begin to establish intimate relationships. Romance and sex become an important part of social life. The rewards can be great—a sense of satisfaction, happiness, and even good health. But the costs can be great too. When a relationship ends or goes bad, the result can be loneliness, sadness, depression, and even poor health. Despite the downside, it seems that we are compelled to form close and intimate social relationships throughout the span of our lives. The ability to establish close relationships—to experience love and intimacy with other people—is a fundamental part of being human.

Attraction

Do you like everyone you meet? Probably not. Most of us take a liking to some people but not to others. Why is this? What causes you to like one person, to be indifferent to another, and to dislike yet others? Your grandmother might tell you that opposites attract—that you like other people whose interests and backgrounds complement your own, and that you seek out the company of those who have different and unique perspectives. On the other hand, common folk wisdom has it that birds of a feather flock together: similarity rather than difference breeds liking and attraction for another. So which is it? Do opposites attract, or do we prefer those who are just like us?

Suppose that your friend is playing matchmaker and sets you up for a blind date. What's your first thought? You can admit it—you are probably wondering if this mystery date is good-looking. "Well," replies your friend, "beauty is more than skin deep. Looks aren't everything. Besides, he has a great personality." As you desperately look for a way out of this date, you begin to wonder why good looks and physical attraction are so important when it comes to potential romantic partners. "It really shouldn't matter," you tell yourself. But it does. Research on **interpersonal attraction** has shown that not only do birds of a feather flock together, but we also prefer the good-looking birds.

> **interpersonal attraction**
> *the study of attraction or liking between two or more people*

Propinquity

Before two people can become lovers, or friends, or even mere acquaintances, they must first meet. The meeting can be face to face, it can be through the mail, or it can happen through the Internet. Regardless of the medium, a relationship cannot develop between two people until they meet. When Sam Cooke wrote a song about being alone on a Saturday night, he correctly identified the problem:

> If I could meet 'em I could get 'em
> but as yet I haven't met 'em
> that's how I'm in the state I'm in

This is why you go to parties and hang out in the common areas of the residence—to meet people. When lonely hearts ask for advice, the columnists always suggest getting involved in activities with other people—at church, in a volunteer organization, wherever you can meet other people who share your interests. You may take this wisdom for granted, but the circumstances and causes of initial attraction often start with the boy or girl next door, simply because you are very likely to meet. The term **propinquity** captures this idea well: nearness or proximity in physical space, which creates the opportunity to meet another person. Despite the ready access to others provided by information technology (e-mail, instant messaging, and so on), physical proximity seems to play an important role in interpersonal communication and attraction (Burgoon, Bonito, Ramirez, Dunbar, Kam, & Fischer, 2002).

> **propinquity**
> *nearness or proximity in physical space, which creates the opportunity to meet another person*

The Likelihood of Meeting. Whether you live in a residence, an apartment, or a house, you probably live in the vicinity of other people. The typical apartment complex is a good example—hundreds of people living in close proximity. Out of all your neighbours, you are likely to run into some more than others. How often the paths of two neighbours cross will depend in large part on **spatial ecology**: the physical layout of the buildings and the distance separating apartments. Leon Festinger, Stanley Schachter, and Kurt Back (1950) took advantage of apartment life to study the effects of spatial ecology on the formation and development of friendships.

> **spatial ecology**
> *the physical layout of buildings and the distance separating different buildings, rooms, and other spaces*

This classic study took place at two new housing projects—Westgate and Westgate West—which were built for married veteran students at the Massachusetts Institute of Technology in the mid-1940s. Because they were new developments, the students were assigned to houses or apartments based only on their order on a waiting list. This created an ideal opportunity to study the formation and development of friendships. The residents did not initially know one another, and they had no control over which particular house or apartment they were assigned. They were initially strangers, some of whom were destined to cross paths more often than others merely because of the physical arrangement of houses and apartments.

Consider the Westgate West apartments. These were former Navy barracks. Each had ten apartments, with five to a floor. A schematic diagram of a Westgate West building is shown in Figure 13.1. The arrangement of the apartment units meant that the residents were likely to see some of their neighbours more than others. The residents of apartments 2 and 3 were next-door neighbours, whereas those in apartments 6 and 10 were separated by three other apartments. This difference in physical distance made it much more likely that the people in apartments 2 and 3 would bump into one another than would the people in apartments 6 and 10. But another kind of distance—**functional distance**—also played an important role at Westgate West. Notice that two apartments—1 and 5—were located right in front of the stairs. This meant that the residents of those two first-floor apartments were more likely to see their upstairs neighbours than were the other first-floor residents. Physically, their apartments were quite far apart, but functionally they were close together.

At one point in the study, the residents of Westgate and Westgate West were asked to name the three people they most often saw socially. The results showed a very clear effect of propinquity. The friends who were named most often were those who lived within closer physical *and* functional proximity. The lucky residents of the end apartments on the first floor (1 and 5) enjoyed a large number of friendships with the second-floor residents. The location at the foot of the stairs created a short functional distance to their second-floor neighbours. Indeed, this functional proximity was more important in determining mutual friendships than was physical proximity.

Meeting Does Not Guarantee Liking. Neighbours don't always get along. In fact, some neighbours hate one another. This suggests that living within close proximity of another is not a guarantee that you will become best friends. In fact, you could become bitter enemies. One reason is that your neighbours could do things that bother you—they may play the stereo too loud, fail to cut the grass, or constantly park their car in front of your house. In short, your neighbour can spoil the environment. Ebbe Ebbesen, Glenn Kjos, and Vladimir Konečni (1976) suggested that propinquity could just as easily produce disliking for your neighbour as it could a good friendship. To test this idea, they conducted a study very similar to the Westgate study, only this time it was done in an Irvine, California, housing development. The residents were asked to indicate three neighbours whom they liked *and* three neighbours whom they disliked. Just as Festinger, Schachter, and Back (1950)

functional distance

compared to physical distance, the closeness between two places in terms of the opportunities for interaction

FIGURE **13.1**

Spatial arrangement of the apartments at Westgate West

From Festinger, Schachter, and Back, *Social Pressures in Informal Groups: A Study of Human Factors in Housing,* 1950. Reprinted by permission of HarperCollins Publishers, Inc.

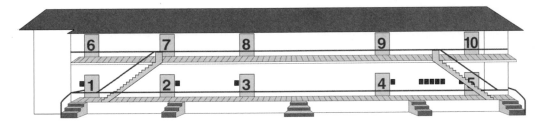

had found decades earlier, the liked neighbours were the ones who lived in closer proximity. And just as Ebbesen, Kjos, and Konečni suspected, the disliked neighbours were also the ones who lived within closer proximity. When an interviewer asked these residents why they disliked some of their close neighbours, it was most often because the neighbour did things to spoil their living environment. It seems that propinquity does not always lead to liking.

The simple fact that people live next door does not necessarily mean that they like each other.

Similarity

One reason that propinquity matters is that it provides the opportunity and setting for the exchange of personal information (Brockner & Swap, 1976; Segal, 1974). Exchanging information—discovering whether you are similar or dissimilar—is one of the principal ways in which people decide whether or not they like each other.

Compatible Attitudes. When you strike up a conversation with your neighbour, what do you talk about? Perhaps you comment on the recent snowfall or the latest hike in banking fees at the Bank of Nova Scotia, but that does not lay the foundation for a close and meaningful relationship. If you really want to establish some basis for a friendship, it is much more important to find out what the other person thinks and feels about current events, social and political issues, religion, morality, music, and literature. People find others more attractive and likeable the more similar they are in their attitudes, beliefs, and preferences (Byrne, 1971; Klohnen & Luo, 2003). This is known as the **attitude-similarity effect**. For example, Donn Byrne and Gerald Clore (1966) had students at the University of Texas learn about a stranger's attitudes by either reading the stranger's responses to an attitude scale, listening to a tape recording of the stranger indicating his or her attitudes, or viewing a colour movie of the stranger expressing his or her attitudes. Regardless of how it was presented, students found the stranger more attractive the more his or her attitudes were similar to their own (see also Klohnen & Luo, 2003; Luo & Klohnen, 2005). Our attraction toward similar others need not be based on deep similarities, such as attitudes and values. John Jones, Brett Pelham, and their colleagues (Jones, Pelham, Carvallo, & Mirenberg, 2004) found that people are more likely to marry someone whose first or last name is similar to their own!

Marian Morry at the University of Manitoba has pointed out that, just as similarity leads to liking, the reverse is also true: liking leads to perceived similarity (Morry, 2005a). For example, when participants wrote about a positive event that had occurred in an ongoing friendship, they subsequently reported being more similar to their friend than when they wrote about a negative event that had occurred in a friendship. Presumably, thinking about the positive event produced more liking for the friend (or more satisfaction with the friendship), which then led to greater perceived similarity.

The relationship between similarity and attraction can be viewed from another perspective, however. Milton Rosenbaum (1986) at the University of Iowa suggested that it is not so much that we are attracted to similar others, but rather that we are repulsed by dissimilar others. In the absence of any information about another person, we often tend to assume that we are similar in our attitudes and values. Adding information that tells us we are indeed similar should not cause a major change from our default assumption. However, learning that another

attitude-similarity effect
the idea that people find others more attractive and likeable the more similar they are in their attitudes, beliefs, and preferences

13.1
ONLINE
LAB

repulsion hypothesis

the idea that people find others less attractive and less likeable if they differ substantially in their attitudes, beliefs, and preferences

self-disclosure

the process of people revealing to one another increasingly personal and intimate details about themselves

person is actually quite different from ourselves should cause an adjustment—downward!—in our liking for that person. Rosenbaum calls this the **repulsion hypothesis,** and several studies have found support for the idea (Chen & Kenrick, 2002; Rosenbaum, 1986).

Self-Disclosure. The development of a close dyadic relationship depends on both people revealing to one another increasingly personal and intimate details about themselves—a process known as **self-disclosure** (Derlega, Metts, Petronio, & Margulis, 1993; Reis, 2000). People who are willing to disclose intimate details about themselves are generally better liked than those who are less inclined to self-disclose. We also tend to reveal personal things about ourselves to others whom we initially like, and we tend to like others as a result of having disclosed personal information to them (Collins & Miller, 1994). For example, Canadian social psychologist Marian Morry (2005b) asked participants to complete several questionnaires about a nonromantic opposite-sex friendship. She found that satisfaction with the friendship was positively correlated both with how much respondents self-disclosed to the friend and how much the friend self-disclosed to respondents.

People do vary in their willingness or ability to engage in self-disclosure. Are you the type of person who is willing to completely and fully discuss with others your personal habits, deepest feelings, and worst fears? If so, then you are a high discloser. If you are the kind of person who is reluctant to discuss these things with others, then you are a low discloser. Not only do people differ in how much they self-disclose *to* others, but they also differ in how much they elicit disclosure *from* others (Miller, Berg, & Archer, 1983). Are you the type of person who can easily get people to open up, who enjoys listening to people, and who can keep other people talking about themselves? If so, then you are an opener—a person who is good at getting others to disclose intimate details about themselves.

Lynn Carol Miller, John Berg, and Richard Archer (1983) designed the Opener Scale to measure individual differences in people's ability to get other people to "open up" and to engage in intimate self-disclosure. Students at the University of Texas at Austin were classified as high or low disclosers, and as high or low openers. The students were then paired in all four combinations of discloser and opener status. One member in each pair was instructed to ask the other a series of questions in an effort to get acquainted. Some of the questions were fairly innocuous, such as "What do you dislike about your classes?" Other questions were more intimate, such as "What things in your past do you feel guilty about?" or "What attracts you to members of the opposite sex?" The high disclosers were willing to reveal intimate personal information to just about anyone, but the low disclosers were more comfortable revealing intimate personal details to partners who had good rather than poor opener abilities.

Facial Beauty

Even before you strike up a conversation with a stranger, you have already taken in a great deal of information. One of the first things you notice when you meet another person face to face is his or her face. In the process of getting acquainted and deciding whether you like another person, do looks matter to you? If you are like most people, looks do matter (Hatfield & Sprecher, 1986). Most of us respond more favourably to, and show more interest in, attractive than unattractive people. It seems to start early in infancy: babies show a preference for attractive over unattractive faces, they show more positive responses to attractive than unattractive strangers, and they prefer attractive to unattractive dolls (Langlois, Roggman, & Rieser-Danner, 1990).

As children grow older, physical attraction continues to play an important role in interpersonal relationships.

Perhaps infants don't know better, and we do often hear that children can be cruel. But as adults, have we not learned that beauty is in the eye of the beholder, that we should never judge a book by its cover, and that beauty is only skin deep? The answer to all three questions seems to be no. A review of the research on facial attractiveness shows that beauty is *not* in the eye of the beholder, that people *do* judge "books" by their "covers," and that beauty is *sometimes* more than skin deep (Langlois, Kalakanis, Rubenstein, Larson, Hallam, & Smoot, 2000).

Shared Perceptions of Beauty. A common assumption is that standards of beauty are culture-specific, and that children within a particular culture gradually learn what is and is not considered attractive. The research evidence, however, does not support this assumption. Even very young infants show a preference for faces that adults have judged as attractive (Langlois, Ritter, Roggman, & Vaughn, 1991; Ramsey, Langlois, Hoss, Rubenstein, & Griffin, 2004). When people are asked to rate the attractiveness of strangers' faces, they show remarkable agreement (Berscheid & Walster, 1974). The consistency even cuts across cultural boundaries (Bernstein, Lin, & McClellan, 1982; Cunningham, 1986). Asian, Hispanic, Black, and White students show very strong agreement in their judgments of the physical attractiveness of Asian, Hispanic, Black, and White photographed faces (Cunningham, Roberts, Barbee, Druen, & Wu, 1995). People of all ages and cultural backgrounds seem to share a common view of what is, and what is not, an attractive face. But what is it, exactly, that makes a face attractive?

The Components of Facial Features. One way to answer this question is to measure specific features of the face. Does facial attractiveness depend on the length of your nose, the shape of your eyes, the height of your cheekbones, the fullness of your lips, the slant of your forehead, or the thickness of your eyebrows? Facialmetrics is one approach to studying facial beauty. As Figure 13.2 shows, facialmetrics involves the measurement of a large number of facial features, such as the size of a nose or the width of a smile. Researchers using this approach have found that women rate male faces as more attractive when those faces feature prominent cheekbones, a large chin, and a wide smile (Cunningham, Barbee, & Pike, 1990). Women also show a preference for male faces in which the height of the eyes does not deviate too far from average. Men, on the other hand, indicate preferences for female targets with large eyes, a small nose and chin, prominent cheekbones, high eyebrows, large pupils, and a large smile (Cunningham, 1986). Research at the University of Western Ontario by Sampo Paunonen and his colleagues (Paunonen, Ewan, Earthy, Lefave, & Goldberg, 1999) has shown that judges also use facial features to infer personality traits. The size of targets' eyes seems particularly important. For both male and female targets, smaller eyes lead perceivers to attribute more masculinity, less nurturance, and less empathy than larger eyes.

Average Faces Are Attractive Faces. The facialmetric approach has shown that some facial features are related to attractiveness, but others are not. And in some cases, such as height of the eyes, it is deviance from the average that makes a face less attractive. Yet this still does not answer the question of what particular combination of features makes one face more attractive than another. Nor does it explain the remarkable consistency across ages and cultures in what people consider attractive in a face. Rather than dissecting the face into hundreds of possible features, Judith Langlois and Lori Roggman (1990) at the University of Texas approached the problem from a different angle. They noted two things. First, evolutionary pressures and natural selection generally favour average rather than extreme population features. Second, starting early in infancy, people routinely form prototypes or

People of all ages and cultural backgrounds seem to share a common view of what is, and what is not, considered an attractive face.

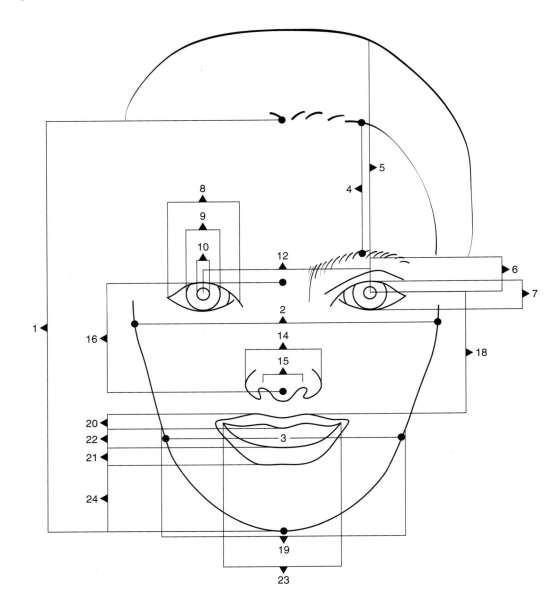

FIGURE 13.2
Facialmetrics involves the measurement of different facial features, such as width of pupil (10), length of nose (16), and width of smile (23).

From Cunningham, "Measuring the physical in physical attractiveness: Quasi-experiments on the sociobiology of female facial beauty," *Journal of Personality and Social Psychology,* 50(5), 925–935. Copyright © 1986 by the American Psychological Association. Reprinted by permission.

cognitive schemas that capture the central or average features of the many instances and exemplars of a particular category (see Chapter 3, "Social Cognition," and Chapter 4, "Social Perception"). Putting these two observations together, Langlois and Roggman made a fascinating prediction: Faces will be judged as more attractive the closer they are to the average of the population of faces.

To test this prediction, pictures of faces were digitized into a standard 512 × 512 matrix. Composite faces were then created by calculating the arithmetic average across 2, 4, 8, 16, or 32 faces. Figure 13.3 illustrates the averaging process, and Figure 13.4 shows examples of what happens when you average across multiple digitized faces. Male and female university students were asked to rate the attractiveness of both the individual and the various composite faces. The students showed a clear preference for the 16- and 32-face composites, rating them as more attractive than the individual faces that were used to create them. It seems that averaged faces are more appealing than individual instances. Does this imply that the best-looking faces are just average and undistinguished (Alley & Cunningham, 1991)? Not according to Langlois, Roggman, and Lisa Musselman (1994),

(A)

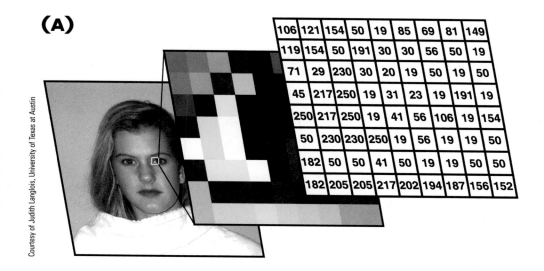

(B)

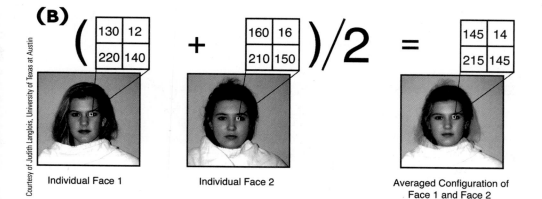

Individual Face 1   Individual Face 2   Averaged Configuration of
                                                        Face 1 and Face 2

Courtesy of Judith Langlois, University of Texas at Austin

FIGURE 13.3 Faces can be digitized (A) and then multiple faces can be averaged to create a composite (B).

From Langlois, Roggman, and Musselman, "What is average and what is not average about attractive faces?" *Psychological Science,* 5(4), 214–220, 1994. Reprinted by permission of Blackwell Publishing.

who point out that averaged faces are anything but common. They simply represent the best example or prototype of what a face looks like. Perhaps because of their apparent familiarity, people find such prototypical faces very attractive (Berscheid & Reis, 1998).

Bodily Features

Most of the research on physical attraction focuses on facial features (Berscheid & Reis, 1998). But the human body offers more than just the face as a basis for judging attractiveness. People differ in their height, weight, body shape, hair colour, skin colour, and odour. For these dimensions, a number of important consistencies have been found, but also some interesting cultural differences.

Body Types. People come in all different shapes and sizes. Some people are lean and muscular; others are softer and rounder. One aspect of body type that has shown consistent relationship to rated attractiveness is the waist-to-hip ratio—the ratio of waist circumference to hip circumference. For most adult women, the waist is narrower than the hips and so the waist-to-hip ratio is less than 1.0. Of course women vary quite a bit, with some whose waist is much narrower than their hips, and others whose waist and hips are about the same. For most adult men, the waist

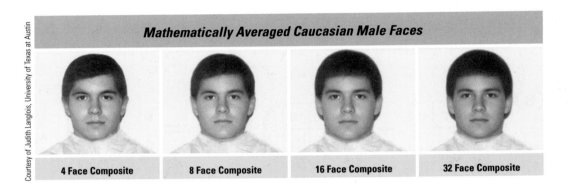

FIGURE 13.4
The effects of averaging across 4, 8, 16, or 32 faces. Faces are judged as more attractive the greater the number of faces contributing to the composite.

From Web site for Langlois, Roggman, and Musselman, "What is average and what is not average about attractive faces?" *Psychological Science,* 5(4), 214–220, 1994. Reprinted by permission of Blackwell Publishing.

Courtesy of Judith Langlois, University of Texas at Austin

and hips are nearly the same in circumference, and so the waist-to-hip ratio is much closer to 1.0. But men vary too, with some whose hips extend further around than their waists. Figures 13.5 and 13.6 show examples of male and female bodies that vary in their waist-to-hip ratios.

Devendra Singh (1993) of the University of Texas asked male university students to rate the attractiveness of female figures that varied in their waist-to-hip ratios. The men rated line drawings just like the ones in Figure 13.5. Results showed that the female figures were judged as more attractive when they exhibited a low rather than a high waist-to-hip ratio. In another study, Singh (1995) asked female university students to make similar ratings of male figures varying in waist-to-hip ratios. The women rated line drawings just like the ones in Figure 13.6. In contrast to the earlier study involving the ratings made by men of female figures, the women judged the male figures in this study as more attractive when they exhibited a waist-to-hip ratio closer to 1.0. It seems that men prefer women whose waist is

FIGURE 13.5 Line drawings illustrate female waist-to-hip ratios of 0.7, 0.8, 0.9, and 1.0 (from left to right). Males judge females with lower waist-to-hip ratios as more attractive

From Singh, "Adaptive significance of female physical attractiveness: Role of waist-to-hip ratio," *Journal of Personality and Social Psychology,* 65(2), 293–307. Copyright © 1993 by the American Psychological Association. Reprinted by permission.

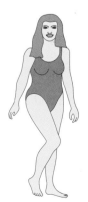

FIGURE 13.6
Line drawings illustrate male waist-to-hip ratios of 0.7, 0.8, 0.9, and 1.0 (from left to right). Females judge males with higher waist-to-hip ratios as more attractive.

From Singh, "Female judgment of male attractiveness and desirability for relationships: Role of waist-to-hip ratio and financial status," *Journal of Personality and Social Psychology*, 69(6), 1089–1101, 1995, Figure 1, p. 1091. Copyright © 1995 by the American Psychological Association. Reprinted by permission.

narrower than their hips (see also Streeter and McBurney, 2003), whereas women prefer men who have a relatively tapered look with hips and waist approximately the same in circumference.

Going beyond their impact on perceived attractiveness, the University of Western Ontario's Lorne Campbell and his colleagues (Campbell, Simpson, Stewart, & Manning, 2002) investigated whether waist-to-hip ratios in men had any predictive value for the men's overt behaviours. Campbell and his colleagues found that men with waist-to-hip ratios close to 1.0 (the ratio preferred by women) behaved more dominantly and were rated as more leader-like in all-male group discussions than men with smaller waist-to-hip ratios. Interestingly, this effect occurred only when a female observer was watching and evaluating the group members; the researchers hypothesized that this condition elicited some intrasexual competition among the men. Why did waist-to-hip ratios predict dominance behaviours? One possibility is that higher waist-to-hip ratios in men are associated with higher levels of testosterone, a hormone that produces secondary sex characteristics and is associated with aggression (Anderson, 1994).

Weight. In some cultures, thinness is considered most attractive, but elsewhere the cultural ideal is a plump body (Symons, 1979). In North America, thin is in and there is a pervasive stigma attached to being overweight (Crandall, 1994; Crocker, Cornwell, & Major, 1993). But why should preferences for body weight differ across cultures? One explanation is that attitudes about weight are communicated through a culture's customs and media. If the culture equates thinness with beauty, then members of the culture will learn to prefer thin bodies. If the cultural tradition is to value plumpness, then members of the culture will learn to prefer heavier bodies.

Height. What's your height preference in a date? Do you prefer someone who is taller than you, shorter than you, or about the same height? The apparent rule for heterosexual dating is that males should be taller (Berscheid & Walster, 1974). But perhaps not too tall. When William Graziano, Thomas Brothen, and Ellen Berscheid (1978) at the University of Minnesota asked women to rate the attractiveness of potential male dates, they indicated a preference for males of medium height (approximately 1.8 m). The short males (approximately 1.7 m) and the tall males (approximately 1.9 m) were judged as less attractive.

© Randy Faris/CORBIS

Judgments of body shape show that men prefer women whose waist is narrower than their hips, but women prefer men whose waist and hips are nearly the same in circumference.

Body Odour. Most of us spend a good deal of time and money making ourselves smell good. We use underarm deodorant, brush our teeth with scented toothpaste, and dab ourselves with perfume or cologne. We assume that some of our natural body odours might be unattractive to others, perhaps even offensive. People who have a pleasant body odour *are* judged as more attractive than those who smell bad (Levine & McBurney, 1986). We are especially hard on people who know they smell bad and who could do something about it. John Levine and Donald McBurney (1977) of the University of Pittsburgh created some descriptions of hypothetical people described as having a severe body odour problem. In one description, the target person was described as being aware and able to control the problem. In other descriptions, the target person was either unaware of the problem, unable to control it, or both. When university students were asked to evaluate each malodorous target person, they were much less favourable when the target was both aware and able to control the problem.

The factors that influence interpersonal attraction are summarized in the accompanying Concept Review.

CONCEPT REVIEW
Interpersonal Attraction

Source of Information	Description	Effect	Example
Propinquity	Nearness or proximity in physical space, which creates the opportunity to meet another person.	Next-door neighbours are more likely to know one another. This can lead to either increased or decreased liking.	Residents of neighbouring apartments are more likely to socialize and become friends.
Similarity	Sharing similar attitudes, values, and beliefs with another person.	The greater the similarity between two people, the greater the liking.	Learning that you and a stranger feel the same way about the major political parties will lead to increased liking.
Repulsion	People exhibit extremely dissimilar attitudes, values, and beliefs.	The greater the dissimilarity between two people, the less the liking.	You dislike another person when you discover major differences in your religious beliefs.
Self-disclosure	Disclosing intimate details about yourself to another person.	People who disclose intimate details about themselves are liked better.	Talking to another person about things that frighten you leads to increased attraction
Facial features	Aspects of a person's face, such as size of a nose, width of a smile, slant of forehead, or thickness of eyebrows.	People are judged as more beautiful when their facial features are closest to the average.	A person with eyes very close together is judged as less attractive than others with more average spacing between their eyes.
Bodily features	Aspects of a person's body, such as body type, weight, height, or body odour.	For men, a waist-to-hip ratio close to 1.0 is judged as most attractive. For women, a waist-to-hip ratio less than 1.0 is judged as most attractive.	A pear-shaped man is judged as less attractive than a man with a tapered body type.

The Evolutionary Significance of Good Looks

Many of the results we just reviewed may make sense in terms of your own experience. But why should these factors matter, and why the differences between genders on some preferences? Why are people with a pleasant body odour judged as more attractive? Why does a person's weight matter when it comes to perceptions of attractiveness? Social psychologists often draw on evolutionary theory to explain these effects (Barrett, Dunbar, & Lycett, 2002).

For example, Devendra Singh (1993, 1995) draws on evolutionary theory to explain the effects of waist-to-hip ratios (see also Campbell et al., 2002). Until boys and girls reach puberty, they have very similar waist-to-hip-ratios (both usually very close to 1.0). It all changes when females reach the age of menarche and become biologically capable of reproducing. This is when the hips of most young women become relatively larger than their waist. It is an outwardly visible signal to males that a female is capable of reproduction. As males mature, they tend to take on a more tapered look, but their hip-to-waist ratio stays roughly the same. This too is a signal of a male's reproductive ability: a waist-to-hip ratio closer to 1.0 is an outwardly visible signal to females that a male is in good health and capable of contributing his part to reproduction.

Accounting for the effects of body weight on attraction, an evolutionary view would emphasize that body weight serves as an outwardly visible signal of reproductive potential. Indeed, cultures that exhibit a preference for plump bodies are also ones where food resources are scarce. In that particular environmental context, greater body fat is a signal of greater reproductive potential (Symons, 1979). In North America, where food resources are not scarce, thinness may be a signal of relatively better reproductive health.

Other research shows that facial attractiveness is strongly related to the perceived health of the model's skin (B. C. Jones, Little, Burt, & Perrett, 2004; B. C. Jones, Little, Feinberg, Penton-Voak, Tiddeman, & Perrett, 2004), and we seem to prefer faces that display symmetry—relative similarity of the left and right sides (e.g., Hume & Montgomerie, 2001). The preference for symmetric faces appears to exist across cultures, and even young infants show the preference (Noor & Evans, 2003; Rhodes, Geddes, Jeffery, Dziurawiec, & Clark, 2002; Rhodes, Yoshikawa, Clark, Lee, McKay, & Akamatsu, 2001). Again drawing from an evolutionary explanation, it may be the case that nice skin and symmetrical faces communicate information about a person's overall state of health. In fact, Canadian researchers Deborah Hume and Robert Montgomerie (2001) at Queen's University found that women with attractive faces had experienced fewer health problems than had women with unattractive faces, and men with attractive faces came from wealthier backgrounds than did men with unattractive faces. To the extent that health and privileged rearing environments are associated with reproductive fitness, our species may be specially tuned to find features that signal these qualities more attractive.

The Social Benefits of Good Looks

The evidence is that some people are, indeed, better looking than others. But physical attractiveness is just a surface feature. What do good looks have to do with the more important internal qualities of a person, such as intelligence, character, personality, skills, or competence?

What Is Beautiful Is Good. We are frequently admonished to never judge a book by its cover, but when it comes to making judgments about other people, that's exactly what we do. University of Toronto social psychologist Karen Dion and her

what is beautiful is good

the inference that attractive people possess other desirable traits and abilities in addition to their good looks

colleagues (Dion, Berscheid, & Walster, 1972) famously suggested that people regularly make the inference that **what is beautiful is good:** attractive people possess other desirable traits and abilities in addition to their good looks. For example, subsequent researchers found that, based on nothing more than photographs, attractive babies were judged by adults as smarter, as easier to care for, and as causing parents fewer problems than unattractive babies (Stephan & Langlois, 1984). The same thing happened when kindergartners and fourth-graders were asked to consider photographs of second-graders. The attractive second-graders were judged as smarter, friendlier, and less mean than unattractive second-graders (Langlois & Stephan, 1977). In study after study, attractive people have been judged as more socially competent and socially skilled than unattractive people (Eagly, Ashmore, Makhijani, & Longo, 1991; Feingold, 1992b).

The accompanying feature, Social Psychology in Your Life: "Preparing for Your Day in Court," discusses how physical attractiveness may influence court decisions.

The *what is beautiful is good* stereotype does not apply to every personal quality. For example, attractive and unattractive people are judged as no different in their

Social Psychology in Your Life   *Preparing for Your Day in Court*

The benefits of being attractive extend well beyond the domain of liking and friendships. In fact, physical attractiveness can be on your side when you find yourself in a court of law, whether you are there as a witness, as a plaintiff, as a defendant, or as a lawyer. If you find yourself in one of these situations, you should attend to how you look.

During the 1950s, an ambitious program of research known as the Chicago Jury Project compared the decisions reached by actual juries with the decisions that would have been reached by judges. In about 3500 cases in which they knew what the juries had decided, Harry Kalven and Hans Zeisel (1966) asked judges to render their own hypothetical verdicts. In about 14% of the cases, the judges said they would have convicted the defendant even though the jury had actually voted to acquit. Why did the jury let the defendant go in those cases? Often, the defendant was attractive or the victim was unattractive (or both). In another 14% of the cases, the judges said they would have acquitted even though the

jury had actually voted to convict the defendant. Why did the jury convict in those cases? This time, the defendant was often unattractive or the victim was attractive (or both). In other research, Victoria Esses of the University of Western Ontario and Christopher Webster of the Clarke Institute of Psychiatry in Toronto (1988) showed that physically unattractive defendants were more likely to be classified as "dangerous offenders" under the Canadian Criminal Code. Physically unattractive offenders are also more likely to receive severe sentences (Stewart, 1980).

This attractiveness bias has also been demonstrated in laboratory studies, in which mock or pretend jurors generally rate physically attractive defendants as less guilty and as deserving less punishment than unattractive defendants (Berg & Vidmar, 1975; Bray & Noble, 1987; Efran, 1974; Mitchell & Byrne, 1973; Reynolds & Sanders, 1975; Rumsey, 1976; Rumsey, Allgeier, & Castore, 1978; Vidmar & Crinklaw, 1974). But don't depend on

your good looks to always get you off the hook. Laboratory studies have shown that being physically attractive can backfire on defendants who *used* their attractiveness to perpetrate a crime. Harold Sigall and Nancy Ostrove (1975) of the University of Maryland found that attractive defendants who had been accused of burglary received shorter sentences than did unattractive defendants—just as the previous studies would have predicted. However, attractive defendants who were accused of swindling received *longer* sentences than did unattractive defendants. It seems that people take offence when criminals deliberately use their good looks to take advantage of others.

Does this evidence mean that attractiveness of trial participants controls the outcome in the majority of cases? Not at all. A defendant's (or plaintiff's) personal attributes, including attractiveness, are especially important when other information is lacking or extremely ambiguous. But usually, what determines the outcome of a case is the strength of the evidence.

integrity or concern for others (Eagly et al., 1991). But keep in mind that most of the research has been conducted in North America, with North Americans judging other North Americans. Within this individualist cultural context, social competence and social skills are more highly valued than concern for others (Triandis, 1995). Now consider the very different context found in many Asian cultures, where concern for others and group allegiance are among the most highly prized personal qualities (Triandis, 1995). When students in Korea (a more collectivist culture) were asked to rate the photographs of other Korean students, the more attractive people were judged as higher in integrity and concern for others (Wheeler & Kim, 1997). Taking the cultural context into account, it would seem that what is beautiful is *culturally* good.

The Real Benefits of Beauty. Now we know that some people are better looking than others and that it is common to make a variety of positive inferences about good-looking people. But do good-looking people actually possess the desirable qualities and abilities that we assume they do? The answer is *sometimes yes* and *sometimes no* (Feingold, 1992b). Averaging over dozens of studies, it is true that physically attractive people are more popular, more socially skilled, and more sexually experienced than unattractive people. Presumably, these differences occur because attractive people are sought after by others, so they become confident in social situations, develop good social skills, and have more opportunities for relationships that might lead to sexual behaviour. But attractive people are far from perfect, especially when you look beyond their social skills. For example, attractive and unattractive people do not differ in their intelligence or mental health.

Friendships

To this point in the chapter, we have discussed why people come to like one another, and the physical features that people find most and least attractive. But that's only the beginning when it comes to the close relationships we form with others. How does that initial sense of liking or attraction eventually grow into a deeper and closer relationship? Early in your life, you almost certainly developed very close relationships with the adults who cared for you—your mother, your father, and others. As you grew, friends became an increasingly important part of your life. Most adults can still name their best childhood friends, and you may count some of those people among your close friends today. Of course, you don't develop close friendships with everyone you meet, or even with everyone whom you like and find attractive. In this section, we will explore theories and research that help us to understand how and why we develop friendships with some people but not with others.

You will notice that much of this section focuses on friendships among children. When it comes to adults, the research attention has been on romantic relationships rather than on friendships. Nevertheless, it is instructive to examine how children become friends. Much of what guides the formation of friendships in childhood also applies to the close relationships we form as adults.

Friendships Among Children

In most settings, children spend much of their time in the company of other children—around the neighbourhood, in school, and on sports teams (Ellis, Rogoff, & Cromer, 1981). As we discussed earlier, it is propinquity that provides the opportunity for children to develop close relationships with their peers.

Of the many possible dyads that can be formed, only a relatively few will result in close friendships. Children are more likely to become friends when they are alike in age, sex, ethnicity, race, and interests.

friendships

dyadic relationships involving mutual liking

sociometric rating procedure

within a group of acquaintances, each person is asked to name everyone whom he or she considers a friend. Two peers within that social network are then considered to be friends if each nominates the other as a friend

popular children

children who are named frequently by others in a sociometric rating procedure

rejected-aggressive children

children who are unpopular because they commonly engage in disruptive aggressive behaviours

rejected-withdrawn children

children who are spurned by their peers because of their social awkwardness and immaturity

Of the many possible dyads that can be formed, only a relatively few will result in close **friendships.** What distinguishes a friend from a mere acquaintance? The method most often used to establish that two people are friends is a **sociometric rating procedure.** Within a group of acquaintances, each person is asked to name everyone whom he or she considers a friend. Two peers within that social network are then considered to be friends if each one nominates the other as a friend.

Under what conditions does a mere acquaintanceship develop into a closer friendship? The strongest determinant is similarity: children are more likely to become friends when they are alike in age, sex, ethnicity, race, and interests (Hartup, 1989). Children quickly discover the dimensions along which they are similar. Kenneth Rubin, who began his career at the University of Waterloo, and his colleagues (Rubin, Lynch, Coplan, Rose-Krasnor, & Booth, 1994) assembled four unfamiliar seven-year-olds together in a room and observed their social interactions and approaches to playing. When each child was asked to indicate which of the other children was preferred as a playmate, they tended to select the one whose behavioural style was most similar to their own. In adolescence (as in adulthood), it is similarity in attitudes, life goals, and intelligence that helps to establish a friendship (Smollar & Youniss, 1982).

Some kinds of similarity are easy to recognize—the outwardly visible signs of age, sex, and race. But how do children learn about their similarities and differences when it comes to interests, preferences, attitudes, or goals in life? Just like adults, children rely on a process of self-disclosure: revealing to one another increasingly personal and intimate details. Children who are successful in communicating with another, and sharing information about themselves, are more likely to develop a close friendship (Gottman, 1983). A friendship will continue to grow as long as the children cooperate and reciprocate in their exchanges, and learn how to resolve their conflicts in a peaceful way (Hartup, 1989; Newcomb & Bagwell, 1995).

Popularity. Some children enjoy many friendships, while others seem to have few. What is it that distinguishes popular children from the unpopular ones? **Popular children** are the ones who are named frequently by others in a sociometric rating procedure. They are good at maintaining positive relationships with their peers, and tend to avoid drawing attention to themselves. They join in play with others without disrupting what the others are doing, they play constructively, they communicate clearly about their feelings and interests, and they are generally cooperative and sensitive to others' interests (Newcomb, Bukowski, & Pattee, 1993). Popular children can be aggressive in the sense of being assertive, but their aggression rarely disrupts the activities of others. In addition to their social skills and competence, popular children also tend to be more physically attractive (Langlois, 1986).

Unpopularity. Some children are unpopular because they frequently engage in disruptive aggressive behaviours. These children are called **rejected-aggressive children.** They exhibit the opposite of the qualities that make children popular: they tend to brag about and call attention to themselves, are uncooperative in peer groups, and are relatively insensitive to others' interests and needs. They tend to be rejected by their peers because of their aggressiveness. Other children are spurned by their peers for a very different reason—because of their social awkwardness and immaturity. These are known as **rejected-withdrawn children.** They just never seem to "fit in," and over time they develop low self-esteem, avoid playing with others, and frequently become the victims of bullying attacks (Hodges, Malone, & Perry, 1997).

Most studies of popularity involve observation of peers who are already acquainted. To watch the emergence of popularity, Kenneth Dodge (1983) observed the interactions in a group of initially unacquainted second-grade boys. Each group had eight boys, who were observed during a series of one-hour play sessions. The play sessions took place in a large room full of toys and furniture. The boys were free to play with the toys, climb on the furniture, engage in rough-and-tumble play, or to sit off by themselves if they wanted. After two weeks of these play sessions, some of the boys had emerged as popular within the group, while others were clearly suffering from peer rejection. What did these two groups of children do differently? For one thing, the rejected children were frequently aggressive; the popular children were not. The popular and rejected children engaged in about the same amount of social conversation with their

Some children are rejected by their peers because of aggressive behaviour. Others are rejected because of their social awkwardness and immaturity.

peers during the first play session; but by the eighth play session, the popular children were engaging in social conversation twice as often as the rejected children. Similar to the findings of many other studies, among these second-grade boys, the popular children were more physically attractive than their rejected peers. In a similar study, John Coie and Janis Kupersmidt (1983) determined the popularity status within groups of fourth-grade boys who already knew each other. When the boys were then placed into new groups of unacquainted peers, they quickly reestablished their old social status: boys who were previously popular emerged as popular in the new group, and boys who were previously rejected found themselves rejected once again.

How Peers Exert Their Influence. It is a common observation that children and adolescents are influenced by their peers (Harris, 1995). Thomas Berndt (1979) asked groups of 3rd, 6th, 9th, and 11th–12th graders whether or not they would go along with the antisocial behaviour of their peers. The antisocial behaviours included such things as cheating, stealing, and minor destruction of property. As an example, here is one of the scenarios that the children considered:

> You are with a couple of your best friends on Halloween. They're going to soap windows, but you're not sure whether you should or not. Your friends all say you should, because there's no way you could get caught. What would you *really* do? (Berndt, 1979, p. 610)

The children were asked to indicate whether or not they would engage in the described behaviour, and how certain they were about their choice. As you can see in Figure 13.7, peer conformity increased from the 3rd through the 9th grade, but then showed a reduction among 11th–12th graders. At least until early adolescence, then, children show increasing peer conformity. The reduction among 11th–12th graders, whose average age was 18, reflects a developmental trend toward greater autonomy in late adolescence and young adulthood.

Peer conformity is a classic example of normative social influence (Chapter 8). Remember that normative influence occurs because of social pressures, rewards, and norms. Fitting in with your peers, and fearing their rejection, brings heavy social pressure to conform. As children grow and develop during the grade school

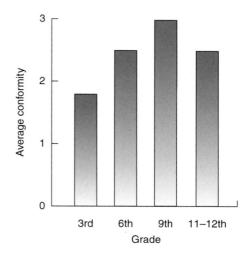

FIGURE 13.7 Conformity with peers' antisocial behaviour increases from 3rd to 9th grade, but then declines somewhat in 11th—12th grade.

Data from Berndt, 1979, "Developmental changes in conformity to peers and parents," Study 1. *Developmental Psychology*, 15(6), 608–616.

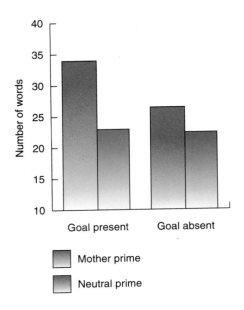

FIGURE 13.8 Number of words generated in five minutes

Adapted from Fitzsimons & Bargh, "Thinking of you: Nonconscious pursuit of interpersonal goals associated with relationship partners" *Journal of Personality and Social Psychology, 84,* 148–164, Figure 3, p. 158, 2003. Copyright © 2003 by the American Psychological Association. Reprinted by permission.

years, they become more sensitive to social norms, and their motivation to be accepted and liked by their peers increases.

But people also exert influence in more subtle ways than peer pressure. In fact, simply thinking about significant others can automatically activate goals and elicit actions related to those individuals. Canadian social psychologist Gráinne Fitzsimons, who is at the University of Waterloo, and John Bargh, who is at Yale University, demonstrated this idea of automatic activation of goals in a clever experiment (Fitzsimons & Bargh, 2003). University students were asked at the beginning of a semester to identify goals they currently pursued with regard to their mother. Approximately half of the participants said that they tried to please their mother by performing well academically; the remaining participants did not mention this particular goal. Several months later, all participants came to a laboratory for an experiment. Their first task was described as a memory test, but it was actually a priming task. Half of the participants answered a variety of questions about their mother (e.g., describe your mother's appearance), and half answered neutral, non-interpersonal questions (e.g., describe your bedroom). All participants then completed a challenging word-generation task in which they had to create as many words as possible from a set of seven letters in five minutes.

Figure 13.8 presents the results on this intellectual task. As the figure shows, among participants who identified pleasing their mother academically as one of their current goals at the beginning of the semester (*goal present*), those who were primed with their mother generated more words from the set of letters than did participants who were primed with neutral questions. By thinking about their mother, the former individuals appeared to be motivated to perform better—that is, thoughts of their mother seemed to activate the goal of performing well on an intellectual task. On the other hand, if participants did not identify pleasing their mother academically as a goal at the beginning of the semester (*goal absent*), then their performance was not influenced by the priming manipulation (mother vs. neutral). Thus, simply thinking about a significant person in one's life can automatically activate goals related to that person. People may not even realize that their actions are being influenced by thoughts about others (see also Fitzsimons, Shah, Chartrand, & Bargh, 2005).

Friendships Among Adults

As we mentioned earlier, friendship formation among adults has received relatively little research attention (Derlega & Winstead, 1986). We know a fair amount about what adults find attractive in one another, the important role of attitude similarity as a determinant of liking, and the value that adults place in self-disclosure. Yet we do not know much about how adults move from initial attraction and sense of liking to a deeper, closer friendship. Nor do we know much about how adult friendships develop over time. Some initial insight, however, was provided in a study conducted by Robert Hays (1985) at the University of Texas.

At the very beginning of their first year in university, students were recruited for a 12-week longitudinal study of friendship development. At the outset, each student was asked to name two people of their same sex whom they did not know before school began but with whom they thought they might become friends. Then every three weeks, the students completed a variety of questionnaires asking about their dyadic interactions with their budding friends.

Whatever led the students to initially nominate someone as a potential friend did not always result in a close friendship—about 63% of the potential friendships actually developed into close friendships by the end of the school term. One thing that predicted the success of a friendship was propinquity—a good friendship was more likely to develop between roommates or dorm-mates than between two students who lived in different buildings or in different parts of town. As the relationships developed over time, the students reported increasing levels of intimacy in their personal exchanges. At the outset, the would-be friends might discuss local, regional, or world events (a low level of intimacy). But as time went by, the friends were more likely to discuss things such as their current sexual activities (clearly a more intimate revelation). Indeed, self-disclosure of increasingly intimate details became a very important part of the growing friendships.

Beverley Fehr (2004) of the University of Winnipeg found that both women and men agree that intimacy in same-sex friendships is more likely when the friends engage in such behaviours as self-disclosure and providing emotional support. Men, however, are less likely to choose to engage in those behaviours than women. Perhaps men simply desire less intimacy in their same-sex friendships than women, or perhaps men fear that self-disclosure and emotional expressiveness will be negatively perceived by male friends (see also Bank & Hansford, 2000).

Rejection

Nobody likes to feel rejected, yet social exclusion can start early in social life. In Chapter 8 on conformity, we discussed evidence that social ostracism is agonizing (e.g., Bassili, 2003; Sommer et al., 2001). Indeed, social relationships are so integral and important in our lives that when others exclude or reject us, it creates a feeling that can best be described as *painful*. Recent research suggests that the pain we feel may be deeply rooted in our brains. Naomi Eisenberger, Matthew Lieberman, and Kipling Williams (2003) engaged people in a simulated game of three-way catch. It became evident at some point that the participant was being excluded by the other two players. Here's the interesting feature of the study: the participants' brains were being scanned all the time using a method called functional magnetic resonance imaging (fMRI). The brain scans showed that social rejection in the three-way game of catch caused a response in the participants' brains that is very similar to the experience of physical pain.

Geoff MacDonald, a Canadian professor at the University of Queensland in Australia, and Mark Leary of Wake Forest University (2005) recently provided a fascinating review of research suggesting that social and physical pain operate through the same pain system. That is, the two forms of pain share common physiological mechanisms. The authors argued that overlap between social and physical pain was an evolutionary development that aided humans to respond to threats of exclusion. Thus, it may be true that rejection hurts—quite literally!

 ## Attachment

It may seem logical at this point to jump right into the topic of close and intimate relationships in adulthood. We will get to that topic soon. But first it is useful to step back and consider an integrative theoretical approach to understanding relationships: the theory of attachment. Rather than drawing a distinction between the relationships we form as children and the relationships we form as adults, attachment theory suggests that the same basic processes govern our close relationships throughout the span of our lives.

Attachment Theory

Have you ever watched a litter of very young puppies? They spend most of their time playing, exploring the world, eating, and sleeping. They certainly seem to enjoy one another, and usually enjoy playing with people too. But what happens when a puppy is suddenly frightened, or finds that it has strayed too far from its familiar surroundings? Will the puppy take comfort if you hold it, pet it, and speak softly? Probably not. Most puppies will still show signs of distress—they whine, wiggle, and shake, frantically searching for their *mother*. Only the puppy's mother will do. Very early in life, those puppies become very *attached* to their mother. Indeed, we are always cautioned never to separate a puppy from its mother too early; we are told that it can cause harm. People are not much different. Infants like to play and to explore, but they also become upset when they get separated from their mother or whomever else they are especially attached to. When babies become distressed, not just anyone is able to provide comfort and relief—only that special person will do, the one to whom the infant is closely attached.

British developmental psychologist John Bowlby (1969) used the concept of attachment to explain how and why people develop close relationships. Bowlby's **attachment theory** focused primarily on the infant and his or her caregiver, but the theory of attachment has also been used to account for the relationships that develop between close friends and lovers throughout the life span (Colin, 1996). Bowlby emphasized an *ethological* approach, which focuses on innate behaviours that have been shaped during the course of evolution. Babies are cute—their faces, smiles, and body proportions seem to invite a positive response from adults. Positive attention from adults leads to a positive response from the infant, and before you know it, a close relationship is developing. In Bowlby's view, both the infant and the adult come biologically prepared to develop attachments. The process is not instantaneous, however; it unfolds over time, and depends on each member of the dyad learning how to respond appropriately to the other.

attachment theory
Bowlby's theory concerning the development and the effects of the emotional bond between an infant and its caregiver; also used to account for the relationships that develop between close friends and lovers throughout the life span

Social smiles between an infant and mother mark the beginning of a close emotional attachment.

Infant Attachment

Most of attachment theory, and the research conducted to support the theory, has been developed in the context of infant–caregiver relationships. In this section, we will discuss some of that research. As you are reading about *strange situations* and *forms of attachment*, think about how these ideas might apply to the attachments and relationships we form as adults.

The Strange Situation. How do we take Bowlby's (1969) theory and test it in the laboratory? Canadian psychologist Mary Ainsworth created a situation involving several brief episodes during which the experimenters could observe the baby's responses to strangers, separation from mother, and reunions with mother (Ainsworth, Blehar, Waters, & Wall, 1978). The procedure is known as the **strange situation.** The mother and baby are introduced to the experimental room, which contains a variety of toys and play objects. The mother and baby are left alone for a few minutes, and their behaviour is observed and recorded through a one-way mirror. Then a stranger (the experimenter) enters the room, and soon begins conversing with the mother. The stranger then approaches the baby as the mother unobtrusively leaves the room. For the next few minutes, the stranger sits quietly in the room allowing the baby to explore and to play with toys. The mother then returns for a reunion with her baby. Another few minutes pass, then the mother says "bye bye" and leaves the baby alone in the room. Remember that the experimenters are observing and recording the baby's responses the whole time. After the baby has been left alone for a few minutes (less if severe signs of distress are observed), the stranger re-enters the room, and offers comfort if the baby is clearly upset. The mother then returns for a final reunion.

What do babies actually do in the strange situation? Observation of one-year-old infants indicates a range of emotional responses: protest, despair, and detachment. But infants vary in their specific patterns of response. Not all infants display signs of distress, and not all show detachment. Generally, infants fall into one of three categories (Colin, 1996):

- *Secure.* By far the most common pattern, **secure attachment** is seen when the baby actively explores the room when left alone with the mother, gets upset when the mother leaves the room, is clearly happy when the mother returns, and may even seek close physical proximity with her in an effort to relieve distress. This pattern is called *secure* attachment because the baby is clearly using its mother as a safe haven and a secure base from which it feels safe to explore a novel situation. Across many studies, about 62% of North American infants show the secure attachment pattern (Campos, Barrett, Lamb, Goldsmith, & Stenberg, 1983).

- *Resistant.* One pattern of **insecure attachment** is seen among babies who prefer to stay close to the mother rather than actively exploring the room, who become very upset when the mother leaves the room, and who appear to be upset or angry when the mother returns. During the reunion episodes, these babies try to remain near their mothers, yet they usually resist any physical contact initiated by her. It seems that these infants want to cling to their mothers, but they clearly have become angry with her. This pattern is usually

strange situation
developed by Mary Ainsworth, a procedure involving several brief episodes during which experimenters observe a baby's responses to strangers, separation from mother, and reunions with mother

secure attachment
the most common pattern seen in the strange situation procedure, in which the baby actively explores the room when left alone with mother, gets upset when mother leaves the room, is clearly happy when mother returns, and may seek close physical proximity with her in an effort to relieve distress; the baby uses its mother as a safe haven and a secure base from which it feels safe to explore a novel situation

insecure attachment
a pattern seen in the strange situation, in which the baby does not use its mother as a safe haven and secure base from which to explore a novel situation

Different forms of attachment are expressed in distinct emotional expressions: (left) enjoying comfort and safety; (middle) being angry; and (right) being aloof and ignoring.

resistant insecure attachment

a pattern seen in the strange situation, in which the baby prefers to stay close to mother rather than actively explore the room, becomes very upset when mother leaves the room, and appears to be upset or angry when mother returns, trying to remain near the mother but usually resisting any physical contact initiated by her; sometimes called ambivalent or anxious-ambivalent insecure attachment

avoidant insecure attachment

a pattern seen in the strange situation, in which the baby basically ignores the mother, usually shows no strong signs of disturbance when she leaves the room, and avoids the mother during reunion episodes or greets her return rather casually

called **resistant insecure attachment.** Because of the vacillation between approach and avoidance, the pattern is sometimes called *ambivalent* or *anxious-ambivalent insecure attachment* (Cassidy & Berlin, 1994). About 15% of North American infants show this attachment pattern (Campos et al., 1983).

- *Avoidant.* A second pattern of insecure attachment is seen among babies who basically ignore their mothers, and usually show no strong signs of disturbance when she leaves the room. These babies are often observed to avoid their mothers during reunion episodes, or at least to greet her return rather casually. This is why the pattern is usually called **avoidant insecure attachment.** About 23% of North American infants show this pattern (Campos et al., 1983).

Is It Universal?   Attachment theory emphasizes the biological roots of emotional attachment and draws upon evolutionary theory for support. It is therefore often assumed that attachment behaviours are universal: that North American infants behave the same way as do infants in Japan, Africa, or Europe. Indeed, infants from all around the world have been tested in the strange situation procedure—from Israeli kibbutzim to Japan, from Uganda to The Netherlands. In some cultures, the strange situation is very strange indeed. For example, Japanese infants rarely experience separation from their mothers. As a result, they often show signs of extreme distress in the strange situation (Takahashi, 1990). Kibbutz-raised infants usually have multiple caregivers, but rarely do they come into contact with strangers (Sagi, 1990). When comparisons are made between two cultures (e.g., Canada versus Japan), large differences are often found in how much distress infants experience in the strange situation. Despite these differences, the secure pattern of attachment is clearly the most frequently observed pattern around the world. The insecure patterns, however, are more culture-specific: the avoidant pattern occurs with greater frequency in North American and Western European countries, perhaps because of cultural preferences for children to become independent quickly, whereas the resistant pattern is more common in Israel, Japan, and other Asian countries, perhaps because of cultural

The development of close attachments is a universal experience.

© Robert Holmes/CORBIS

emphasis on emotional dependence among family members (Harwood & Miller, 1991; van IJzendoorn & Kroonenberg, 1988).

Learning About Relationships. Those first early attachments provide the infant with knowledge about and experience with close relationships. Over time, the infant begins to develop a mental representation, schema, or **working model of a close relationship**: the feelings, thoughts, beliefs, and expectations learned during the course of those first close relationships (Colin, 1996). For the securely attached infant, the working model or relationship schema indicates that other people can be trusted and relied upon to provide a safe haven, to be nurturing and supportive, and to provide a partnership in life. The securely attached infant also learns that he or she is a person who is worthy of trust, love, and support. But for insecurely attached infants, the world of close relationships seems very different. These infants develop a working model that close relationships sometimes involve acceptance, but at other times rejection; that sometimes the other person is accessible, but at other times inaccessible; that the other person can be responsive and caring on some occasions, but unresponsive and uncaring on others. The insecurely attached infant learns that he or she may *not* be a person who is worthy of trust, love, and support. How does an infant or young child respond to such frustration and emotional pain? Avoidant infants respond by inhibiting or blocking thoughts and actions that make them aware of the other; resistant infants respond by expressing anger or ambivalence toward the other.

Attachment Beyond Infancy. The kind of attachment observed during infancy is usually stable over time and still evident in the early grade-school years. Mary Main and Jude Cassidy (1988) of the University of California at Berkeley found that the attachment pattern observed when infants were 12 months old was usually still evident when the children were six years old. The attachment pattern is most stable over time when there has been little disruption or change in the child's life. Major disruptions—such as parents' divorce or a dramatic change in socioeconomic circumstances—can produce more variability in attachment. This probably happens because of the effects a major disruption can have on a caregiver's ability to maintain a positive and supportive relationship (Ackerman, Izard, Schoff, Youngstrom, & Kogos, 1999; Conger et al., 1992). Suddenly finding yourself unemployed or a single parent can have a chilling effect—at least temporarily—on the relationship with your child. The other side to this issue is that a secure attachment can provide some protection or buffer against the harmful effects of an impoverished or disrupted social environment. Even in unfavourable environments, many children do manage to adapt effectively, developing competence in social and academic domains. Children who demonstrate this kind of resilience in the face of adversity usually have had the benefits of a close and positive relationship with their parents, good connections with members of an extended family, and relationships with supportive role models outside of the family (Masten & Coatsworth, 1998).

Adult Attachment

When John Bowlby (1969) wrote about emotional attachments, he was focusing primarily on the emotional, behavioural, and cognitive responses of infants and young children: the positive and secure emotional bonds that typically develop between infant and primary caregiver, the distress and anxiety when they become separated, and the relief and comfort-seeking that usually occurs upon reunion. Until the 1980s, research on emotional attachment focused almost exclusively on the relationship between child

working model of a close relationship
the feelings, thoughts, beliefs, and expectations learned during the course of an infant's first close relationships

and primary caregiver. Yet, Bowlby thought of attachment as a lifelong quality of human relationships—as a process that begins during infancy, but one that continues to influence and guide all of the close relationships we form in adolescence and adulthood. Bowlby assumed that the mental representation—the working model—of close relationships formed during childhood persisted throughout adulthood.

A Theory of Adult Attachment. In 1987, Cindy Hazan of Cornell University and Phillip Shaver of the University of California at Davis proposed that the concept of attachment could be used to describe and understand close relationships in adulthood. To develop a theory of **adult attachment,** they translated each of the three major patterns of attachment found among infants—secure, resistant (anxious/ambivalent), and avoidant—into their adult forms. The trick for doing this was to think about attachment in terms of an adult's close relationships with other adults rather than a child's relationship with his or her caregiver. Hazan and Shaver developed three brief descriptions to represent the different attachment patterns:

> *Secure.* I find it relatively easy to get close to others and am comfortable depending on them. I don't often worry about being abandoned or about someone getting too close to me.
>
> *Anxious/Ambivalent.* I find that others are reluctant to get as close as I would like. I often worry that my partner doesn't really love me or won't want to stay with me. I want to get very close to my partner, and this sometimes scares people away.
>
> *Avoidant.* I am somewhat uncomfortable being close to others; I find it difficult to trust them completely, difficult to allow myself to depend on them. I am nervous when anyone gets too close, and often, love partners want me to be more intimate than I feel comfortable being. (Shaver & Hazan, 1993, p. 35)

Adults Are Not Children. Shaver and Hazan (1993) acknowledged some important differences between attachment in early childhood compared to adulthood. For one thing, adult attachment relationships are far more reciprocal: adults are able to exchange roughly equivalent benefits, whereas children and their caregivers bring very different needs and contributions to the relationship. Attachment between children and adults typically involves a parent–child relationship, in which the ultimate goal is to raise healthy offspring. Attachment among adults typically involves a romantic relationship between peers in which the prominent elements are companionship, intimacy, and sex.

Despite these differences, the major functions of early attachment can also be found in adult attachment. Adults seek to maintain close proximity in an attachment relationship. Even as an adult, separation from your romantic partner can make you feel sad or lonely, and reunions can make you feel happy and warm. As an adult, you face threats and challenges in life, and a romantic partner can provide support, understanding, and a safe haven to help you through it. Adults do not pursue the same kinds of play and exploration as children, but they do rely on romantic attachments to provide a secure base for work and adult forms of play.

One centrepiece of attachment theory is the concept of a *working model*: a person's mental representation of relationships. Kim Bartholomew of Simon Fraser University and Dale Griffin of the University of British Columbia (Bartholomew, 1990; Bartholomew & Horowitz, 1991; Griffin & Bartholomew, 1994) have made a distinction between two aspects of an adult's working model of attachment. One is the working model of other people: your thoughts, beliefs, and judgments about whether or not other people can be trusted and relied upon to provide support and protection. The other is the working model of the self: perceptions of yourself as a person who is (or is not) worthy of support and protection and to whom others are likely (or unlikely) to respond in a positive and helpful way. A secure pattern of adult attachment occurs

adult attachment

the concept of attachment used to describe and understand close relationships in adulthood by translating each of the three major patterns of attachment found among infants— secure, anxious/ambivalent, and avoidant—into their adult forms when both working models (of other and of self) are positive; an insecure pattern of attachment occurs when one or both working models are negative. McGill University's Mark Baldwin has shown that individuals who have an anxious attachment style are more sensitive to possible rejection by others. That is, the concept of interpersonal rejection is more accessible in these individuals' minds, which might predispose them to suspect that their partner does not care for them (Baldwin & Dandeneau, 2005; Baldwin & Meunier, 1999). Similarly, Susan Boon of the University of Calgary, together with Dale Griffin (1996), found that individuals who have an anxious attachment style tend to compare their relationship to an ideal standard, which makes them feel dissatisfied, whereas individuals who have a secure attachment style take a more positive perspective on their relationship by focusing on what they gain from it compared to having no relationship.

How Do We Measure Adult Attachment? To do research on early attachment, it was necessary to create a method for measuring attachment. That's why Mary Ainsworth invented the strange situation procedure. That method clearly won't do for adults. Instead, researchers rely on an adult's own description or rating of his or her attachment relationships. One approach was developed by Nancy Collins and Stephen Read (1990) at the University of Southern California. These researchers designed the Adult Attachment Scale (AAS), which consists of 18 questions intended to classify adults into one of the three attachment patterns. It focuses only on attachment relationships experienced as an adult with other adults. The complete set of scale items is shown in Know Yourself 13.1: "The Adult Attachment Scale." Try the scale for yourself.

Play and Work. For infants and young children, differences in attachment style are related to differences in exploration and play (Ainsworth et al., 1978). Secure infants will readily explore new settings, try new toys, and generally go about mastering their environments. Resistant children are too worried about maintaining close proximity with their primary caregiver to engage in the sort of exploration that leads to mastery, but they may engage in exploratory activity in an effort to gain their caregiver's attention and approval. Avoidant children use exploration and play as a way of keeping busy, of distracting themselves from thoughts or awareness of their primary caregiver. How do these differences in play and exploration translate into adult attachment? Cindy Hazan and Phillip Shaver (1990) suggested that work represents the adult version of exploration and mastery. After classifying adults according to the three styles of attachment, they asked a variety of questions about work and relationships. Securely attached adults reported that they enjoy and value work, are not very concerned about failure, and do not let work interfere with their important personal relationships. Anxious/ambivalent adults seem to use work as a way to gain respect and approval from others, but sometimes loaf after receiving praise. Avoidant adults appear to use work as a way to avoid social interactions, and they are generally less satisfied with their jobs.

Attachment and Daily Social Interactions. You may have noticed a major difference between studies of infant–child attachment and studies of adult attachment. In the case of children, their behaviours, emotional responses, and social interactions are usually observed and recorded as they happen, by an outside observer. In contrast, adults are simply relied upon to provide their own reports of past events. To remedy this, and to get a better idea of how adult attachment style might influence everyday interactions, Marie-Cecile Tidwell, Harry Reis, and Phillip Shaver (1996) used a method called **event sampling.** Students at the State University of New York at Buffalo were asked to keep a social interaction diary for one week. This involved filling out a standard diary form for every social interaction lasting more

event sampling
a method used to study adult attachment that involves the recording of information about a person's social interactions over a period of time

Know Yourself 13.1
The Adult Attachment Scale

Rate the extent to which each statement below describes your feelings on a scale ranging from not at all characteristic (1) to very characteristic (5):

1. I find it difficult to allow myself to depend on others.

   1   2   3   4   5

   Not at all characteristic   Very characteristic

2. People are never there when you need them.

   1   2   3   4   5

   Not at all characteristic   Very characteristic

3. I am comfortable depending on others.

   1   2   3   4   5

   Not at all characteristic   Very characteristic

4. I know that others will be there when I need them.

   1   2   3   4   5

   Not at all characteristic   Very characteristic

5. I find it difficult to trust others completely.

   1   2   3   4   5

   Not at all characteristic   Very characteristic

6. I am not sure that I can always depend on others to be there when I need them.

   1   2   3   4   5

   Not at all characteristic   Very characteristic

7. I do not often worry about being abandoned.

   1   2   3   4   5

   Not at all characteristic   Very characteristic

8. I often worry that my partner does not really love me.

   1   2   3   4   5

   Not at all characteristic   Very characteristic

9. I find others are reluctant to get as close as I would like.

   1   2   3   4   5

   Not at all characteristic   Very characteristic

10. I often worry my partner will not want to stay with me.

    1   2   3   4   5

    Not at all characteristic   Very characteristic

11. I want to merge completely with another person.

    1   2   3   4   5

    Not at all characteristic   Very characteristic

12. My desire to merge sometimes scares people away.

    1   2   3   4   5

    Not at all characteristic   Very characteristic

13. I find it relatively easy to get close to others.

    1   2   3   4   5

    Not at all characteristic   Very characteristic

14. I do not often worry about someone getting too close to me.

1	2	3	4	5
Not at all characteristic				Very characteristic

15. I am somewhat uncomfortable being close to others.

1	2	3	4	5
Not at all characteristic				Very characteristic

16. I am nervous when anyone gets too close.

1	2	3	4	5
Not at all characteristic				Very characteristic

17. I am comfortable having others depend on me.

1	2	3	4	5
Not at all characteristic				Very characteristic

18. Often, love partners want me to be more intimate than I feel comfortable being.

1	2	3	4	5
Not at all characteristic				Very characteristic

SCORING: Items 3–4, 8–14, and 17 are scored as shown (1-2-3-4-5); items 1–2, 5–7, 15–16, and 18 are reverse-scored (5-4-3-2-1).

These items are grouped into three sets:

- Items 1–6 represent trust in others.
- Items 7–12 reflect anxiety in relationships.
- Items 13–18 relate to closeness and intimacy.

Each set has possible scores from 6 to 30, with higher scores reflecting more of the dimension.

than ten minutes. The standard diary form, shown in Figure 13.9, was to be completed as soon as possible after each interaction. In this way, the major social interaction events in each student's day were sampled and recorded. In addition to keeping their diaries for one week, the students were classified in terms of attachment style.

One thing was clear in this study: students who were classified as avoidant experienced a variety of negative emotions in their daily social interactions with others. Compared to the other students, the interactions recorded in their diaries revealed more sadness, frustration, worry, tension, and embarrassment. Compared to the secure students, the avoidant students also spent less time and were less comfortable in their opposite-sex interactions.

Lorne Campbell of the University of Western Ontario and his colleagues (Campbell, Simpson, Boldry, & Kashy, 2005) also used a diary procedure to examine how attachment styles relate to daily experiences. Dating partners completed diaries each day for 14 days, in which they described any interactions with their partner and their current perceptions of the relationship. Results showed that participants who were more anxiously attached reported more conflicts with their dating partners, and these perceived conflicts were associated with lower satisfaction ratings and more pessimistic estimates of the stability of the relationship. Anxiously attached individuals seemed more sensitive to problems in their relationship and more negatively affected by perceived conflicts than securely attached individuals.

The Adult Version of a Safe Haven. Children and adults sometimes find themselves experiencing distress and anxiety. We know this happens for children in the strange situation procedure. In that setting, securely attached children will seek

ATTACHMENT AND SOCIAL INTERACTIONS

Social Security No. ____________________

Date: ________ Time: ________ a.m. or p.m.? Length: _____ hrs. _____ min.

Who initiated the interaction? _____ I did. _____ Other did. _____ It was mutual.

Was this a phone call? _____ Yes _____ No

Initials of other(s): _____ _____ _____
Sex of other(s): _____ _____ _____

If more than three others, number of males _____ females _____

Intimacy	superficial	1	2	3	4	5	6	7	meaningful
I disclosed	very little	1	2	3	4	5	6	7	a great deal
Other disclosed	very little	1	2	3	4	5	6	7	a great deal
Quality (How pleasant was it?)	unpleasant	1	2	3	4	5	6	7	very pleasant
I helped/supported other	very little	1	2	3	4	5	6	7	a great deal
Other helped/supported me	very little	1	2	3	4	5	6	7	a great deal
Degree of disagreement/conflict	very little	1	2	3	4	5	6	7	a great deal
Degree of closeness/camaraderie	very little	1	2	3	4	5	6	7	a great deal
Who mainly influenced or controlled the interaction?	I did	1	2	3	4	5	6	7	other did
My level of satisfaction	dissatisfied	1	2	3	4	5	6	7	very satisfied
I got from the interaction	less than expected/ hoped for	1	2	3	4	5	6	7	more than expected/ hoped for

Nature of interaction: Job Task Conversation Leisure activity Other: ________

Approximate content of the interaction (what you were doing and talking about):________

During the interaction (or immediately after it), how much did you feel . . .

happy/encouraged	not at all	1	2	3	4	5	6	7	a great deal
sad/disappointed	not at all	1	2	3	4	5	6	7	a great deal
frustrated/irritated	not at all	1	2	3	4	5	6	7	a great deal
rejected/left out	not at all	1	2	3	4	5	6	7	a great deal
comfortable/relaxed	not at all	1	2	3	4	5	6	7	a great deal
needed/appreciated	not at all	1	2	3	4	5	6	7	a great deal
bored/distant	not at all	1	2	3	4	5	6	7	a great deal
caring/warm	not at all	1	2	3	4	5	6	7	a great deal
hurt/treated badly	not at all	1	2	3	4	5	6	7	a great deal
worried/anxious	not at all	1	2	3	4	5	6	7	a great deal
stimulated/invigorated	not at all	1	2	3	4	5	6	7	a great deal
tense/ill at ease	not at all	1	2	3	4	5	6	7	a great deal
successful/productive	not at all	1	2	3	4	5	6	7	a great deal
sexually interested/aroused	not at all	1	2	3	4	5	6	7	a great deal
envious/jealous	not at all	1	2	3	4	5	6	7	a great deal
accepted/like you belonged	not at all	1	2	3	4	5	6	7	a great deal
embarrassed/self-conscious	not at all	1	2	3	4	5	6	7	a great deal
disgusted/disapproving	not at all	1	2	3	4	5	6	7	a great deal
ashamed/guilty	not at all	1	2	3	4	5	6	7	a great deal
imposed upon/intruded upon	not at all	1	2	3	4	5	6	7	a great deal
tired/low in energy	not at all	1	2	3	4	5	6	7	a great deal

FIGURE 13.9 The social interaction diary. Research participants completed this form for every social interaction lasting more than 10 minutes.

From Reis and Wheeler, "Studying social interaction with the Rochester Interaction Record," in *Advances in Experimental Social Psychology*, ed. M. P. Zanna (vol. 24, pp. 269–318, 2004). Reprinted by permission of Elsevier.

out their caregiver for comfort and relief—a safe haven. And the securely attached caregiver will provide it. This is clearly one of the benefits of a secure attachment relationship. The same benefit seems to apply for adults. Jeffry Simpson, William Rholes, and Julia Nelligan (1992) studied 83 dating couples at Texas A & M University. When each couple arrived at the laboratory, they were seated together and completed a series of questionnaires that included assessments of their attachment styles. The female partner was then escorted alone to another room, where she was told, "In the next few minutes, you are going to be exposed to a situation and set of experimental procedures that arouse considerable anxiety and distress in most people" (Simpson et al., 1992, p. 437). She was then shown a dark room containing some ominous psychophysiological recording equipment. The experimenter explained that the room was not quite ready yet, and led the woman back to the room where her male partner was waiting. It was during this waiting period that the experimenter was most interested in observing the interactions of the partners.

The procedure was designed to make the woman feel distressed and anxious. Nothing was said to her partner as the experimenter left the couple alone in the waiting room. What the unsuspecting couple didn't know was that their interactions for the next five minutes were recorded by a video camera hidden in the room. What would the women do? Would they seek comfort and relief from their partners? And what would the men do? Would they offer support and reassurance? Well, the securely attached women who had reported feeling very anxious were observed to seek out their partners during this waiting period for both emotional support and physical comfort. And the securely attached male partners responded by providing emotional support and by making reassuring comments. In contrast, when the avoidant women were feeling anxious, they were *less* likely to seek out support from their partner during the waiting period. The avoidant males were not very supportive either: the more his partner experienced anxiety, the less emotional support or concern the avoidant male was likely to express for her well-being (see also Campbell, Simpson, Kashy, & Rholes, 2001).

Finding Satisfaction in Romance. As you read about the results from past studies, did it occur to you that securely attached adults might enjoy more fulfilling and satisfying romantic relationships compared to their insecurely attached friends? This appears to be true, but gender differences make the picture somewhat more complicated. Lee Kirkpatrick and Keith Davis (1994) followed 354 university-student couples who were involved "in steady or serious dating relationships" for a three-year longitudinal study of attachment style and stability in romantic relationships. Although many of the couples stayed together over the three-year period, many others broke up. Overall, most of the students—about 75%—showed the secure attachment pattern. As a result, the majority of dating couples involved a secure–secure pair. About 14% of the men and women showed the avoidant pattern, but they seemed to avoid one another: none of the dating couples involved an avoidant–avoidant pair! At the beginning of the study, the avoidant men reported the least satisfaction in their relationships; the secure and anxious men were happier. Yet, after three years, it was the anxious men who were more likely to have broken up. The pattern for women differed. It was the anxious women who were least satisfied at the outset, with the secure and avoidant women happier, yet the avoidant women were more likely to break up during the ensuing three years.

Close Relationships in Adulthood

The concept of attachment has been very useful in helping to understand the origin and nature of close relationships. Yet, attachment theory is only one of many related perspectives on the formation and development of close relationships in adulthood. Adults relate to one another in a variety of ways; the closest relationships involve intimacy, love, and long-time partnerships. Some of our close relationships endure, maturing and growing deeper over time. Other close relationships weaken over time, occasionally ending in bitterness and hostility. Theory and research sheds light on when, how, and why our close relationships work this way.

Dimensions of Adult Relationships

In 1959, John Thibaut and Harold Kelley wrote an influential book on the social psychology of groups—how two or more people interact and come to depend on one another. The simplest group is two people: a dyad. A key aspect of close

interdependence

a sharing of contributions and outcomes by two people

dyadic relationships (e.g., romantic partners) is that they involve some degree of **interdependence:** a sharing of contributions and outcomes. Thibaut and Kelley observed that people in a close relationship see themselves as a unit, sharing in both the costs and the rewards of one another's outcomes. When your partner receives good news or a reward, it is just as though the good news or reward were for you—you enjoy the outcome as though it were your own. And when times are tough—when your partner is disappointed or hurt—you share the pain. One of the interesting consequences of interdependence is that people will often behave in ways that benefit their partner even if it is costly to themselves. In the long run, they will share in the benefit they provided to their partner. Using the concept of interdependence to understand close relationships was first suggested by Thibaut and Kelley (1959), later expanded by Kelley (1979), and most recently elaborated by Canadian social psychologist John Holmes (2002; Holmes & Cameron, 2005), who is at the University of Waterloo. The interdependence perspective has become an influential approach in the study of close dyadic relationships.

Closeness. Some close relationships involve a very high degree of interdependence. Harold Kelley (1983) described high interdependence as follows:

> A high degree of interdependence between two people is revealed in four properties of their interconnected activities: (1) the individuals have *frequent* impact on each other, (2) the degree of impact per each occurrence is *strong,* (3) the impact involves *diverse* kinds of activities for each person, and (4) all of these properties characterize the interconnected activity series for a relatively long *duration* of time. (p. 13)

Ellen Berscheid, Mark Snyder, and Allen Omoto (1989) of the University of Minnesota followed up on this idea by developing a scale—the Relationship Closeness Inventory (RCI)—to assess the frequency, diversity, and strength of the interdependence between two people. Students were asked to complete the RCI twice: once in reference to their closest, deepest, and most intimate relationship, and once in reference to a relationship that was considered to be not very close or intimate. As expected, the close relationships involved sharing in a greater number (diversity) of activities and spending more time (frequency) with the close other in those activities. The strength of interdependence was assessed by asking the students to indicate the amount of influence the other person had on their thoughts, feelings, and behaviour. As expected, the close other was rated as having more influence than the nonclose other.

Providing Benefits for the Other. One aspect of interdependence is that the partners in a dyad provide benefits for one another. Margaret Clark of Carnegie-Mellon University and Judson Mills of the University of Maryland (1979, 1993) distinguished between two different ways in which benefits are provided in relationships. In some cases, the partners engage in an equal exchange of benefits: you scratch my back, and I'll scratch yours. When you are invited to a friend's house for dinner, you return the favour in kind; on holidays or birthdays, you exchange gifts of roughly equal value with your friends. These are examples of an **exchange relationship:** the partners tend to keep track of what they have given and what they have received, and they strive to keep the books balanced. In exchange relationships, the norm of reciprocity (see page 301 in Chapter 8) is expected to apply.

You can probably imagine a number of your relationships that are based on the rules of exchange. Yet, other relationships—perhaps those you have with a romantic partner or a family member—typically involve a different set of rules. In these relationships, you may find yourself providing or receiving benefits primarily when they are needed.

exchange relationship

a relationship in which the partners tend to keep track of what they have given and what they have received, and strive to keep the books balanced

In these cases, the rule is not to provide a benefit for a benefit, but rather to provide a benefit for a need. Clark and Mills referred to this as a **communal relationship:** the receipt of a benefit creates no specific obligation to return that benefit. Responding to the needs of your partner is the benefit in a communal relationship. These features of communal relationships may remind you of the concept of *social support networks* (see page 497 in Chapter 12), where support is provided without expectation of reciprocation.

Equity and Fairness. Whether your relationship is exchange or communal, your satisfaction may depend on how *fair* you perceive it to be (Adams, 1965). For example, the rules that govern an exchange relationship create pressure to return one benefit with another of comparable value. Failing to return a benefit, or reciprocating with one of either lesser or greater value, creates an inequity in the relationship and will be seen as unfair. Likewise, the rules that govern a communal relationship create pressure to provide benefits when needed, and to accept them when needed. Over time, it is the give-and-take in response to needs that keeps the communal relationship balanced and fair. **Equity theory** was developed to help formalize the idea of perceived fairness or balance in interpersonal relationships (Walster, Walster, & Berscheid, 1978), including close dyadic relationships (Hatfield, Traupmann, Sprecher, Utne, & Hay, 1985). An *equitable* relationship is one in which both partners perceive that they are receiving relatively fair outcomes. When one partner contributes more to a relationship, that partner might expect relatively more in return. Equity is an interesting problem in communal relationships, because the benefits contributed by one partner may be very different from the benefits contributed by the other.

How much do equity and social exchange really matter in close relationships? This is one of those cases in which it matters for most people some of the time, and for some people most of the time (Sprecher & Schwartz, 1994). For example, concerns about equity seem to make a difference during the initial stages of a developing romantic relationship. Elaine Walster, G. William Walster, and Jane Traupmann (1978) contacted students at the University of Wisconsin who were in casual or steady dating relationships. The students were first asked a number of questions about how equitable or inequitable they perceived their dating relationships to be: how their own contributions and benefits to the relationship stacked up against their partner's. These questions were used to classify the students as being underbenefited (outcomes were less than they deserved), equitably treated (outcomes were fair compared to contributions), or overbenefited (outcomes were more than they deserved).

The students also completed a survey about the intimacy of their sexual relationship. For example, they were asked how "far" they had gone with their partner (from kissing to intercourse and oral sex), how long they knew each other before they had sexual intercourse, and their reasons for having sex (they wanted it, their partner wanted it, or they both wanted it). Results showed that the students who described their relationships as relatively equitable were also more sexually intimate—not because one or the other partner wanted it, but because they both wanted it. Similar studies have found that dating men and women are more content, satisfied, and happy when they perceive themselves to be treated equitably in their relationship (Traupmann, Hatfield, & Wexler, 1983).

Diane Holmberg and Samantha MacKenzie (2002) of Acadia University in Wolfville, Nova Scotia, found that people involved in a dating relationship were more satisfied with the relationship if it was developing in the way they thought relationships typically *should* develop (their *schema* for relationships). For example, people often have beliefs about how quickly behaviours like kissing, hugging, saying "I love you," and having sexual intercourse should occur in a relationship. When respondents' personal relationships were developing in line with their schemas for

communal relationship
a relationship in which the receipt of a benefit creates no specific obligation to return that benefit; responding to the needs of your partner is the benefit

equity theory
the idea of perceived fairness or balance in interpersonal relationships, such that both partners perceive that they are receiving relatively equal outcomes

relationships, they were happier. Given that *equitable* treatment is part of most people's beliefs about how relationships should develop, these findings are consistent with research on equity theory.

Extreme Interdependence. Very close relationships involve a high degree of interdependence and the sharing of benefits on a communal rather than an exchange basis. These relationships seem to involve the merging of two selves. Your partner becomes, in some sense, a part of you—and you become a part of your partner. The distinction between *you* and *me* becomes blurred, and you begin to think of yourselves as *we*.

Arthur and Elaine Aron, who are at the University of New York at Stony Brook, expanded on this idea (Aron, Aron, Tudor, & Nelson, 1991) and even developed a method for measuring the extent to which a person perceives overlap between his or her own self and the other. Earlier, George Levinger (1988) suggested that a relationship between two people can be drawn as two overlapping circles: the more the overlap, the greater the intimacy. The Arons used this idea to create the Inclusion of Other in the Self (IOS) scale (Aron, Aron, & Smollan, 1992). The scale, which is shown in Figure 13.10, is quite straightforward: you simply select the pair of circles that best describes your close relationship; the greater the overlap, the higher is your score on the IOS scale. Try it for yourself. Think about your closest romantic relationship, and choose the pair that best describes it. University students who score higher on the IOS scale also report greater intimacy and positive emotions about the other. Among people who are married, higher IOS scores go with perceptions of deeper commitment and greater marital satisfaction. Generally, people interpret the overlapping circles of the IOS as reflecting the degree of interconnectedness with a close other.

An Investment Model of Relationships. Close relationships are like investments. You put a lot into them, and you expect something in return. As we learned in our discussion of interdependence and equity theory, people are happiest when their close relationship returns are in proportion to their investments. People are unhappy when they feel that they are underbenefiting—when their returns are perceived as low relative to their investments. Does this mean that close relationships end when one or both partners feel underbenefited? Not necessarily. Even when you sense the return on your investment is less than desired, you may be reluctant to abandon it. After all, you may already have put substantial personal resources into the relationship, and to walk away would be giving up what you have already put in. You may decide to ride out the storm, just like a bad run in the stock market, in the hope that things will get better. Or you may decide to stick with the relationship because all of the alternatives look worse.

Please circle the picture below that best describes your relationship:

FIGURE 13.10

Inclusion of Other in the Self scale

From Aron, Aron, and Smollen, "Inclusion of Other in the Self scale and the structure of interpersonal closeness," *Journal of Personality and Social Psychology*, 63(4), 596–612. Copyright © 1992 by the American Psychological Association. Reprinted by permission.

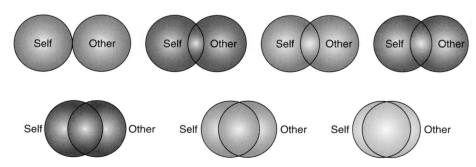

This analogy has been developed by Caryl Rusbult, who is at the University of North Carolina. Rusbult (1983) proposed an **investment model of close relationships.** According to this model, satisfaction and stability in a relationship depend on the balance or trade-off between the positive and negative aspects of the relationship (see also Kelley, 1983). For example, an individual will be satisfied and motivated to remain in a relationship if he or she perceives (a) the benefits of staying as relatively high and (b) the value of the alternatives as relatively low. But an individual will be motivated to leave a relationship if he or she perceives (a) low benefits in remaining and (b) high value in alternatives. In one test of this model, Rusbult (1983) followed dating couples for seven months and found that couples were more likely to remain together when satisfaction increased and quality of alternatives decreased over time, whereas couples were more likely to break up when satisfaction decreased and quality of alternatives increased over time (see also Drigotas & Rusbult, 1992).

An important part of the investment model is the idea that people compare the value of their current relationship with the value of available alternatives. In some cases, people may choose to stay in a bad relationship because the alternatives are no better, and may even be worse. This helps to explain why a person would stay in an abusive relationship. Along these lines, Rusbult and John Martz (1995) interviewed women who had sought refuge at a shelter for battered women. Even though the women had good reason to leave their partners, many of them expressed a strong desire to remain in the relationship. This pattern was greater among those women who had no better alternatives—those with less education, poor financial resources, and no means of transportation.

Commitment. Individuals vary in how *committed* they are to their relationship. John Lydon of McGill University has conducted some well-known research on the role of commitment in close relationships. Lydon, Kimberly Burton, and Danielle Menzies-Toman (2005) defined **commitment** as "the motivation to maintain and sustain a relationship even in the face of adversity" (p. 126). Lydon and his colleagues argued that people become committed to a relationship when it provides meaning to their lives and when they are highly interdependent with their partner. When commitment is high, people are not tempted by alternative opportunities and can weather bumpy events in the relationship. As a result, couples who express greater commitment to a relationship are more likely to stay together than are couples who express less commitment.

Lydon and his colleagues have conducted several studies documenting the role of commitment in close relationships (e.g., Lydon, Fitzsimons, & Naidoo, 2003; Lydon, Meana, Sepinwall, Richards, & Mayman, 1999). One interesting finding is that individuals who are highly committed to a romantic relationship usually evaluate an attractive alternative partner less positively than individuals who are low in commitment. That is, when an attractive alternative partner is encountered, people who are committed to a relationship often devalue this individual (rate him or her as less attractive than do control participants), presumably as a way of protecting their current, high-commitment relationship.

It sometimes happens that one partner feels more committed to the relationship than the other. What happens when one partner is relatively content, but the other is less content or even wants out? In these cases, the stability of the relationship is determined mostly by the weak-link partner. Mark Attridge, Ellen Berscheid, and Jeffry Simpson (1995) interviewed dating couples at Texas A & M University. The couples were then contacted six months later and asked if they were still dating. As previous studies had found, the couples who had expressed greater commitment to the relationship were more likely to still be together. But whether or not the couple was still dating was determined mostly by the partner who felt less satisfied and less dependent on the relationship. The less commitment expressed by *that* partner, the more likely it was that the couple would separate.

investment model of close relationships

according to this model, satisfaction and stability in a relationship depend on the balance or trade-off between the positive and negative aspects of the relationship, with the idea that people compare the value of their current relationship with the value of available alternatives

commitment

the motivation to maintain and sustain a relationship even in the face of adversity

Positive or Accurate Appraisals from One's Partner? An interesting issue in adult close relationships concerns whether people prefer their partner to have (1) a positive, perhaps even *overly* positive impression of them, or (2) a realistic, even if somewhat negative, impression of them. For example, imagine that someone considers himself to be a worrier, who sometimes gets too anxious about upcoming events that are not really very threatening. Will this person be happier if his close relationship partner has an impression of him that he is brave and fearless or will he be happier if his partner accurately believes that he is rather anxious? On the one hand, perceptions of being brave indicate how much his partner thinks of him, but on the other hand, accurate perceptions show that his partner recognizes his weaknesses but wants to stay with him anyway. These two kinds of appraisals from one's partner are often called *enhancing* (positive) versus *verifying* (accurate).

Some researchers have argued that people usually prefer enhancing, positive appraisals from their partner (e.g., Murray, Holmes, & Griffin, 1996a), whereas other researchers have argued that people usually prefer verifying, accurate appraisals from their partner (e.g., Swann, De La Ronde, & Hixon, 1994). Lorne Campbell and his colleagues at the University of Western Ontario (Campbell, 2005; Campbell, Lackenbauer, & Muise, in press) have attempted to identify the conditions under which people prefer each kind of appraisal. For example, the length of the relationship may be important. Campbell and his colleagues (2006) recruited 103 students who were involved in a romantic relationship for at least three months. The average length of time participants had been together was two and a half years. Participants were led to believe that their partner saw them either accurately or overly positively on a dimension that they previously stated was important to them. If participants' self-views on this dimension were negative (which makes verifying versus enhancing appraisals different), then those who were in long-term relationships responded more positively to accurate, verifying appraisals than to positive, enhancing appraisals. Specifically, a verifying appraisal on a negative trait led participants to believe that their partner saw the best in them and ignored their faults, compared to an enhancing appraisal on the same trait. Thus, although globally positive feedback might make people in a short-term relationship feel good, it may be more important in a long-term relationship to know that your partner recognizes both your strengths and your weaknesses. After all, accurate appraisals provide a solid, realistic base on which to build intimacy and trust.

Love

Our discussion of close relationships, interdependence, and commitment has danced around the idea of love. Poets and philosophers, musicians and writers, parents and advice columnists—all have their own definitions of love. The view emerging from social psychology is that love can be many different things, depending in large part on the nature of the relationship. The love you feel for your parents is different from the love you feel for your romantic partner. People profess love of Canada, love for animals, and brotherly love. Indeed, Beverley Fehr of the University of Winnipeg and James Russell of the University of British Columbia (1991) listed 84 different types of love that were mentioned by participants in a survey. These researchers proposed that the concept of love encompasses a wide variety of feelings and relationships, though all types share some basic elements such as caring and unselfishness. Closer scrutiny of the concept of love will help us to understand more about this very important and universal aspect of human experience.

Passionate Love. Sometimes we think of love as involving strong and intense feelings, infatuation, arousal, and a deep sense of passion. This is the kind of love that Elaine Hatfield and G. William Walster (1978) called **passionate love.** Here is their definition:

> A state of intense longing for union with another. Reciprocated love (union with the other) is associated with fulfillment and ecstasy. Unrequited love (separation) with emptiness, anxiety, or despair. A state of profound physiological arousal. (p. 9)

Hatfield (1988) described passionate love as a form of excitement involving a mixture of intense positive and negative emotions. It is euphoria, happiness, tranquillity, anxiety, panic, and despair all wrapped up in the relationship we have—or might have—with another. Sometimes our passion for another is reciprocated, as when two people are *falling in love.* At other times, our passion is not reciprocated. We can still have fantasies about another, and this can be the source of great pleasure. But unrequited love is also associated with strong negative emotions—just think about those times in your life when you developed a deep crush on someone who hardly knew you existed.

Companionate Love. Passionate love is intense and exciting, and seems to be a very important part of being in love. But it is not the kind of love that sustains a long-term relationship or close attachment. Indeed, we can experience passionate love even in the absence of intimacy. In contrast, the kind of love that develops in a close and intimate relationship is **companionate love,** which Hatfield and Walster (1978) defined as "the affection we feel for those with whom our lives are deeply entwined" (p. 9). Certainly, passionate love is a part of those kinds of relationships, but intimacy and closeness only develop with companionate love.

Styles of Love. Some of us fall head over heels in love with every potential romantic partner we meet. Others are attracted only to a particular type. And some of us take a long time to warm up, preferring to ease slowly into romantic relationships. Canadian sociologist John Alan Lee (1988) of the University of Toronto elaborated on the idea that people might differ in their styles of love. Lee identified three primary **love styles,** but also recognized that people may change their preferred style over their lifetimes. Some people may even prefer more than one style at a time, blending two or three styles, or perhaps using different styles with different partners. Recent studies show that the same primary love styles can be found among those who live in very different cultures (Kanemasa, Taniguchi, Daibo, & Ishimori, 2004).

Clyde and Susan Hendrick (1986), who are at Texas Tech University, developed the Love Attitudes Scale as a way to measure the various styles of love. As we describe some of Lee's love styles, we will use items from the Love Attitudes Scale to illustrate them.

The three primary love styles are *eros, storge,* and *ludus.*

Some people know exactly what physical type turns them on, and become intensely excited when they meet a person who comes close to the ideal. *Eros*—named for the Greek god of love—is an erotic style of loving, which begins with a powerful physical attraction. Whether it is the colour of another's hair, height, body type, or facial features, erotic lovers know what they want, and they experience love when they see

passionate love
The kind of love that involves strong and intense feelings, infatuation, arousal, and a deep sense of passion

companionate love
the kind of love that develops in a close and intimate relationship; the affection we feel for those with whom our lives are deeply entwined

love styles
the idea that people differ in their styles of love; the three primary styles are eros, storge, and ludus

"When I date someone, it doesn't take me long to figure out whether it's going to work or not. I get a sense right away if there's good chemistry between us. I think chemistry is the most important thing—it's how I know that I've found my 'one and only.'"

it. In one study, Australian social psychologists Julie Fricker and Susan Moore (2002) found that people experience greater satisfaction in their romantic relationships the more they can be described by the eros love style. The intensity of eros may lessen over time, and ultimately develop into a more relaxed style. On the Love Attitudes Scale (Hendrick & Hendrick, 1986), eros is indicated by agreement with statements such as these:

My lover and I have the right physical "chemistry" between us.

Our lovemaking is very intense and satisfying.

I feel that my lover and I were meant for each other.

In ancient Greek conceptions, *storge* (pronounced *store-gay*) referred to the kind of affection or love that develops between siblings or playmates. It is not the intense excitement or passion of eros. Rather, it is the kind of love that develops when people enjoy similar activities, start up a friendship, and then slowly build an affection and sense of commitment. Storgic lovers do not have a particular type in mind, and generally do not go looking for love. It is a much more sedate style of loving, one that is not typically accompanied by the kinds of things that erotic lovers do, such as staring into their lover's eyes and professing their love out loud. On the Love Attitudes Scale, storge is indicated by agreement with statements such as these:

The best kind of love grows out of a long friendship.

Love is really a deep friendship, not a mysterious, mystical emotion.

Genuine love first requires caring for a while.

For some people, love is just a game. They bounce from lover to lover, preferring not to settle down in any single long-term close relationship. They are rovers. If they can't be with the one they love, then they love the one they are with. The term *ludus*—the Latin word for game or play—is a fitting description for this style of love. People who prefer this style appear to derive satisfaction from a life filled with numerous but shorter-lived love experiences. Yet those who clearly fall into the ludus category of love style seem to experience less satisfaction in their romantic relationships than do others, such as those who are better described by eros (Fricker & Moore, 2002). On the Love Attitudes Scale, ludus is indicated by agreement with statements such as these:

I enjoy playing the "game of love" with a number of different partners.

I try to keep my lover a little uncertain about my commitment to him/her.

I have sometimes had to keep two of my lovers from finding out about each other.

Just as primary colours can be mixed to produce a large palette of hues, so can the primary love styles be blended to create many secondary styles of love. Among these, Lee (1988) identified three especially interesting ones, termed *mania*, *pragma*, and *agape*.

Some people are preoccupied with their lover. These lovers are very possessive and can become intensely jealous. At the same time, they are insecure and need repeated assurances that they are loved. What they fear most is unrequited love. It is almost as though a manic lover is in love with the idea of being in love, rather than being in love with a particular person. Lee (1988) described the manic lover as having the ludus style, but without the confidence. On the Love Attitudes Scale, *mania* is indicated by agreement with statements such as these:

> When my lover doesn't pay attention to me, I feel sick all over.
>
> When I am in love, I have trouble concentrating on anything else.
>
> Sometimes I get so excited about being in love that I can't sleep.

The combination of ludus and storge produces *pragma*—from the Greek root for *pragmatic*. Some people keep an informal list of qualities they desire in a lover—the closer the match, the greater the love. Compatibility is the goal. On the Love Attitudes Scale, pragma is indicated by agreement with statements such as these:

> One consideration in choosing a partner is how he/she will reflect on my career.
>
> Before getting very involved with anyone, I try to figure out how compatible his/her hereditary background is with mine in case we ever have children.
>
> I try to plan my life carefully before choosing a lover.

The kind of love style that is so often preached and so rarely practised is *agape*—selfless, giving, altruistic love. The agapic lover considers it a duty to love another who is in need of love, even in the absence of any sense of emotional attachment or eros. On the Love Attitudes Scale, agape is indicated by agreement with statements such as these:

> I cannot be happy unless I place my lover's happiness before my own.
>
> I would endure all things for the sake of my lover.
>
> I would rather suffer myself than let my lover suffer.

Three Components of Love. In trying to make sense of all the different distinctions and styles of love, Yale University's Robert Sternberg (1986) proposed that love can best be understood in terms of three basic components: intimacy, passion, and commitment. Intimacy is that sense of closeness or connectedness you experience when you feel understood and cared for by another. Passion is the intense physical and sexual attraction you may feel for another. Commitment in the short term is a decision to love someone, and in the long term a dedication to maintain that love. By placing each component at the three corners of a triangle, Sternberg suggests that a large variety of love experiences can be understood as combinations of the three components (see Figure 13.11). Indeed, almost all of the forms of liking and loving that we have discussed can be found in Sternberg's **triangular theory of love.**

triangular theory of love
the idea that a wide variety of love experiences can be understood as combinations of three basic components: intimacy, passion, and commitment

Intimacy in the absence of passion and commitment is a deep friendship. Passion without intimacy and commitment is infatuated love. And commitment without intimacy and passion is empty love. By combining the three basic components, we get the many and varied forms of love. Companionate love is the combination of intimacy and commitment. With all three components present, we have complete or consummate love; in the absence of all three components, we are left with nonlove.

Cultural Dimensions of Love. They say that love makes the world go around. But is love experienced everywhere in the world in the ways we have discussed here? People in a wide variety of cultures do indeed show all the signs of

FIGURE 13.11

A triangular theory
of love

From Sternberg, "A triangular theory of
love," *Psychological Review*, 93(2),
119–135. Copyright © 1986 by the
American Psychological Association.
Reprinted by permission.

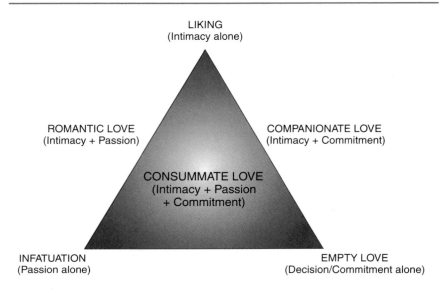

	Component of love		
Kind of love	*Intimacy*	*Passion*	*Decision/ commitment*
Nonlove	–	–	–
Liking	+	–	–
Infatuated love	–	+	–
Empty love	–	–	+
Romantic love	+	+	–
Companionate love	+	–	+
Fatuous love	–	+	+
Consummate love	+	+	+

LIKING
(Intimacy alone)

ROMANTIC LOVE
(Intimacy + Passion)

COMPANIONATE LOVE
(Intimacy + Commitment)

CONSUMMATE LOVE
(Intimacy + Passion
+ Commitment)

INFATUATION
(Passion alone)

EMPTY LOVE
(Decision/Commitment alone)

FATUOUS LOVE
(Passion + Commitment)

experiencing one or more of the love styles reviewed above (Hatfield & Rapson,
1996). The companionate form of love, which is really an emotional attachment,
seems especially prevalent. But some historians and anthropologists have suggested that passionate love is not such a universal experience. For them, romantic
passion is a refinement of Western European culture and rarely found elsewhere in
the world (Jankowiak, 1995). Yet, when William Jankowiak and Edward Fischer
(1992) looked at the evidence, it was clear that romance and passion was enjoyed
from sub-Saharan Africa to East Asia, from the Pacific Islands to South America.
Out of 166 different cultures, passionate love was documented in 147 of them.
So, while it is true that romantic passion is not found *everywhere,* it is found in
most places.

Gender Differences in Conceptions of Love. Canadian psychologists
Beverley Fehr and Ross Broughton (2001) at the University of Winnipeg found that
women and men differ somewhat in their conceptions of love. Although the two sexes
agree on many aspects of love (e.g., the importance of affection and commitment),
women are more likely than men to conceptualize love in terms of its companionate
features, such as friendship and nurturance, whereas men are more likely than
women to conceptualize love in terms of its passionate features, such as romance and

sexual attraction. These differences might sometimes be problematic if individuals in a heterosexual relationship expect the other person to demonstrate his or her love in exactly the same way that they do.

Conflict in Close Relationships

All relationships involve conflict, at least occasionally. Two people in a close, intimate relationship cannot agree on everything; disagreements are inevitable. Consequently, an important determinant of the long-term success of relationships is the effectiveness of the couple's strategies for resolving conflict. Conflict can either mushroom into a major confrontation that threatens the whole relationship or be addressed constructively and perhaps even revitalize the relationship.

John Holmes, who is at the University of Waterloo, and Sandra Murray, who obtained her Ph.D. at Waterloo under the supervision of Holmes and now teaches at the State University of New York at Buffalo, provided a comprehensive analysis of conflict in close relationships (Holmes & Murray, 1996). These researchers noted that a critical element in relationship conflict is the individuals' *construals*, or interpretations, of the issues underlying the conflict. Often, disagreements occur over issues that are not really fundamental to the relationship, such as a partner's moodiness, a minor but irritating habit, or an isolated act of selfishness. Even though an initial conflict may involve a trivial issue, individuals can escalate the significance of the disagreement, such as interpreting a thoughtless comment as a sign that one's partner no longer cares about the relationship. This sort of overgeneralization of the conflict is made more likely by anger and defensiveness—emotions that often occur during conflict.

Perceived Regard. One of the most important predictors of whether people escalate minor conflicts into major ones seems to be their perceptions of their partner's *regard*, or caring, for them. Some individuals feel confident in their relationship and in their partner's caring for them, whereas others are less certain that their partner has positive regard for them. This difference in perceived regard is important because it can influence how people react to minor conflicts.

Sandra Murray, John Holmes, and their colleagues have conducted numerous studies investigating how *perceived regard* is related to the impact of minor conflicts in relationships. One variable that correlates with perceived regard is self-esteem. That is, self-esteem can be used as an indicator of people's confidence in their relationship: individuals with high self-esteem generally believe that their partner values them, whereas individuals with low self-esteem generally underestimate their partner's evaluation of them (e.g., Murray, Holmes, & Griffin, 2000). In one series of studies, participants who were in dating relationships were led to believe that their partner perceived problems in the relationship (Murray, Rose, Bellavia, Holmes, & Kusche, 2002). Low–self-esteem individuals reacted badly to this information, concluding that their partner's commitment to the relationship might be weakening. In return, low–self-esteem individuals provided less favourable evaluations of their partner. High–self-esteem individuals, on the other hand, did not react badly to the news that their partner perceived problems in the relationship, continuing to report that their partner cared for them and continuing to evaluate their partner favourably. Thus, people who lacked confidence in the relationship (low–self-esteem participants) read too much into possible problems and reacted in defensive, counterproductive ways, such as derogating their partner.

In another study (Murray, Bellavia, Rose, & Griffin, 2003), married or cohabiting couples were recruited through advertisements to keep a diary for 21 days, in which they recorded their experiences and emotions at work and at home. Rather than using self-esteem to assess confidence in the relationship, participants were asked at the beginning of the study to report their perceptions of how their partner evaluated them on 20 interpersonal qualities (e.g., kind, controlling, patient, moody). Some participants believed that their partner evaluated them very positively (i.e., *high regard*), and some believed that their partners had less favourable perceptions of them (i.e., *low regard*). Results showed that participants who believed their partners had low regard for them overreacted to negative interactions, such as a moody partner, by feeling very hurt. Further, these individuals then behaved more negatively toward their partner in subsequent interactions. Thus, people who lacked confidence in their relationship were more likely to behave in ways that actually hurt the relationship than were those who had more confidence about their partner's regard for them.

Trust is another concept that correlates with perceived regard (i.e., with confidence in a partner's caring). Highly trusting individuals feel secure in their partner's love and optimistic about the future of the relationship, whereas individuals who are low in trust for their partner are more doubtful about their partner's love and more pessimistic about the future of the relationship. John Rempel, who is at St. Jerome's University in Waterloo, Ontario, together with Michael Ross and John Holmes of the University of Waterloo (2001), recruited 35 married couples and asked them to complete a scale that measured trust and then to discuss a problem in their relationship for 15 minutes. Participants' statements during the discussion were coded for valence (favourable versus unfavourable) and target (relationship, self, partner, external factors). Highly trusting participants tended to make favourable statements while discussing the problem, and their statements often referred to the relationship. Low-trust participants, on the other hand, made more negative statements while discussing the problem, and these statements more often focused on external factors. The authors concluded that individuals' trust "acts as a 'filter' through which events in a relationship are perceived and interpreted" (p. 57). In general, high trust is associated with relationship-enhancing interpretations and actions, whereas low trust is associated with relationship-diminishing interpretations and actions (see also Rempel, Holmes, & Zanna, 1985).

There is also evidence that the way people publicly describe a conflict in their relationship can change their subsequent perceptions of it. For example, Ian McGregor of York University and John Holmes (1999) found that instructing participants to describe a relationship conflict from a particular perspective (e.g., from their partner's perspective) influenced their evaluations of that conflict eight weeks later, such that they evaluated the event more consistently with whatever perspective they had been asked to take. Similarly, University of Waterloo researchers Jessica Cameron, Michael Ross, and John Holmes (2002) found that if people were asked to describe something they had done that hurt their intimate partner, they tended to describe the transgression in ways that minimized its implications for the relationship. More interestingly, they also subsequently expressed greater optimism about the future of the relationship. These findings show that how individuals publicly talk about their relationship can actually change their perceptions of the relationship.

Beyond Heterosexual Relationships

When it comes to research on close relationships in adulthood, it is almost always assumed that we are talking about heterosexual dyads—a man and a woman. Yet women fall in love with women, and men fall in love with men. Lesbians and gay men become closely attached, and they enjoy intimate and romantic relationships. What do we know about close relationships when the partners are of the same biological sex? For a long time, this question was simply ignored. It was not until the 1980s and 1990s that researchers started to pay serious attention to lesbian, gay, and bisexual close relationships (D'Augelli & Patterson, 1995).

Gay and lesbian couples do not differ from married heterosexual couples in the quality of their relationships. Lawrence Kurdek and J. Patrick Schmitt (1986) surveyed four groups of couples who were living together and considered their relationships to be monogamous. The four groups included 44 married heterosexual couples, 35 cohabiting heterosexual couples, 50 gay couples, and 56 lesbian couples. The married, gay, and lesbian couples did not differ in the quality of their relationships: all three groups reported the same degree of love and liking for their partners, and satisfaction with the relationship. The cohabiting heterosexual couples experienced lower relationship quality: they reported less liking for their partner and lower relationship satisfaction. Within the context of their dyadic relationships, the gay and lesbian couples were just as happy as were the married heterosexual couples. However, the gay and lesbian couples perceived less social support from their families than did either of the heterosexual groups, emphasizing the stigma that is often associated with homosexuality.

The things that make heterosexual couples happy and satisfied in their relationships are basically the same things that make lesbian and gay couples happy in theirs (Kurdek, 1995). Satisfaction is greater when both partners feel that they share in decision making (Kurdek & Schmitt, 1986), when the perceived rewards of the relationship are greater than the perceived costs (Kurdek, 1991), and when the couple engages in productive and positive methods for resolving their conflicts and problems (Kurdek, 1991). Shared decision making is one aspect of equality in a relationship, and the lesbian couples in Kurdek and Schmitt's (1986) survey reported more sharing in their decision making than did any of the other groups. This is consistent with earlier studies in which lesbian couples emphasized the importance of equality in their relationships (Blumstein & Schwartz, 1983).

One issue that gay and lesbian couples face, which heterosexual couples do not, is *coming out* to family and acquaintances. Homosexual couples face possible rejection

Gay and lesbian couples do not differ from married heterosexual couples in the quality of their relationships.

if their sexual orientation is devalued by their family. Susan Boon and Jeff Miller (1999) at the University of Calgary examined this issue. These researchers found that gay and bisexual men were more likely to reveal their sexual identities to their mothers when they had high trust in their relationship with their mother. High trust presumably gave men confidence that disclosure would not irreparably harm their family relationships.

Few researchers have investigated *attachment* processes in homosexual couples, but some relevant research was conducted recently by Kim Bartholomew and her colleagues at Simon Fraser University (Landolt, Bartholomew, Saffrey, Oram, & Perlman, 2004; Stanley, Bartholomew, & Oram, 2004). In one study (Landolt et al., 2004), a sample of 191 gay and bisexual men completed questionnaires about their childhood relationships and their adult attachment styles. Results showed that parental rejection during childhood, especially rejection by fathers, was associated with greater attachment anxiety in respondents' gay relationships as adults. These findings are interesting because stereotypes of gay men often imply close childhood relationships with their mothers, which might be expected to make maternal rejection more predictive of insecure adult attachment. In fact, though, paternal rejection was more strongly associated with anxious attachment styles. We can expect more research on attachment in homosexual relationships over the next few years.

Chapter Summary

In this chapter, we reviewed the social psychology of close relationships: attraction, attachment, and close relationships from childhood through adulthood. Our focus was on **dyadic relationships**, which are relationships that develop between two people, such as a parent and a child or two romantic partners.

The study of **interpersonal attraction** starts with a consideration of **spatial ecology,** which calls our attention to close **functional distance** and **propinquity** that create the opportunity for exchanging personal information. We discover information about others, and reveal information about ourselves, through a process called **self-disclosure.** This can lead to liking, or it can lead to disliking. We like others whose attitudes and values are similar to our own (the **attitude-similarity effect**) and dislike others whose attitudes and values are dissimilar to our own (the **repulsion hypothesis**).

We also like others who are physically attractive. Faces are perceived as especially attractive when they are most like the average or prototypical face. Bodies are perceived as most attractive when they signal reproductive fitness. For example, women show a preference for male bodies in which the waist-to-hip ratio is close

to 1.0. Men show a preference for female bodies in which the waist-to-hip ratio is substantially less than 1.0. Attractive people enjoy a number of social benefits—they are judged by others as more competent, and may be less likely to be convicted of a crime. At the root of these effects is the assumption that **what is beautiful is good.** Although attractive people do not enjoy all of the benefits attributed to them, it is sometimes the case that attractive people are more socially skilled than unattractive people.

Once two people decide they like one another, they may develop a deeper **friendship.** A **sociometric rating procedure** is commonly used to identify friendships within a group of acquaintances; two people are considered friends when each one nominates the other as a friend. Most research on friendships has been conducted with children, who establish their friendships on the basis of similarity, physical attraction, and self-disclosure. Some children enjoy many friendships, and tend to emerge as **popular children** even in new social groupings. Other children have very few friendships: **rejected-aggressive children** and **rejected-withdrawn children** tend to emerge as unpopular in new social groupings. Friendships among adults follow a developmental trajectory involving increasing levels of intimate self-disclosure.

John Bowlby's **attachment theory** provides a general framework for understanding the origin and maintenance of close relationships throughout the life span. Infants and their caregivers form emotional attachments, which provide the infant with a secure base and a safe haven for exploring the world. One hallmark of an emotional attachment is the occurrence of emotional distress upon separation. The **strange situation** procedure was designed to observe the response of infants when they become separated from their caregiver. Most infants show a **secure pattern of attachment,** but some show an **avoidant** or a **resistant** pattern of **insecure attachment.** Early attachment experiences form the basis for a person's **working model of a close relationship.** Attachment theory has been extended to the study of **adult attachment,** where forms of both the secure and insecure attachment patterns are found among adults in their close and romantic relationships. Because the strange situation procedure cannot be used to assess attachment in adults, questionnaire measures of adult attachment have been developed, including the Adult Attachment Scale (AAS). In testing the relation between attachment styles and relationship experiences, researchers often use **event sampling** methods to have adults report on their close relationships. In general, adults who have secure patterns of attachment with their partner enjoy more fulfilling romantic relationships than those who have insecure patterns of attachment.

Adult close relationships take many forms. A close relationship involves some degree of **interdependence. Exchange relationships** are based on the equal exchange of benefits, whereas **communal relationships** are based on provision of benefits when they are needed. **Equity theory** is used to explain how people keep track of, and are affected by, the equality of exchanges in close relationships.

An analogy can be drawn between close relationships and investments, which is the central idea underlying the **investment model of close relationships.** According to this model, satisfaction and stability in a relationship depend on the balance between the positive and negative aspects of the relationship. Relationship stability also depends on the individuals' **commitment** to the relationship, which refers to their motivation to maintain and sustain the relationship even in the face of adversity.

Love is the emotional experience of a close relationship. **Passionate love** is an intense state of longing for union with another. **Companionate love** is more like an emotional attachment. People differ in their **love styles,** from the erotic passionate style of eros, to the practical and goal-oriented style of pragma. The **triangular theory of love** identifies intimacy, passion, and commitment as its three basic elements. Research in cultures around the world indicates that passionate love is a nearly universal experience.

All relationships experience conflict. An important determinant of the long-term success of a relationship is the couple's ability to defuse conflicts and deal with disagreements constructively. When people believe that their partner values them and has positive regard for them, they tend to weather relationship storms better. In contrast, people who lack confidence in the relationship (who are uncertain whether their partner cares for them) tend to read too much into minor conflicts and react in defensive, counterproductive ways, such as derogating their partner.

Although there has not been a lot of research on gay and lesbian relationships, the work that has been done indicates that the same things that make heterosexual couples happy and satisfied in their relationships also make gay and lesbian couples happy in theirs. There is also some evidence that early childhood experiences are predictive of gay men's attachment styles as adults, similar to evidence for heterosexual individuals.

Key Terms

Social Psychology Alive on the Web

SOCIAL PSYCHOLOGY ALIVE: ONLINE LABS

To perform the following experiment and see how you compare to other students, go to Social Psychology Lab, which can be accessed through ThomsonNOW™.

- 13.1 Attitudes

SOCIAL PSYCHOLOGY ALIVE: QUIZZING AND PRACTICE TESTS

You can access our Web site directly by going to http://www.socialpsychologyalive.nelson.com for online quizzes, flash cards, and Internet links.

INFOTRAC® COLLEGE EDITION

For additional readings, explore InfoTrac® College Edition, your online library of archived journal articles and periodicals dating back 22 years. If your instructor ordered InfoTrac® College Edition with this book, you can access it from your CD-ROM, or go directly to http://www.infotrac-college.com and use the passcode from the InfoTrac® College Edition card that came with your book. For this chapter, try these search terms: *propinquity, self-disclosure, interpersonal attraction, friendship, attachment, love.*

Social Psychology Alive: The Workbook

To apply what you've learned in this chapter to the real world, go to Chapter 13 of *Social Psychology Alive: The Workbook.*

- Do the Westgate Findings Hold for Your Dorm or Apartment Building?
- Exploring Attitude Similarity and Liking
- What Determines Physical Attractiveness?
- Are You Headed for Court? What You Need to Know

- Does Your Attachment Style Affect Your Interactions with Other People?
- Can You Find True Love in Cyberspace?
- Do You Need an Excuse to Watch a Movie?
- Match That Tune!
- Dress for Success!

Social Psychology Alive: The Videos

To see video on the topics and experiments discussed in this chapter, you can go either to ThomsonNOW™ or to the CD-ROM, if your instructor assigned either one, to the following section:

- How Do I Love Thee? Expressions of Love Styles

To Learn More

This list contains citations to books or articles that can help you learn more. These readings are good places to start if you want to gain a deeper understanding of the topics in this chapter.

- Brehm, S. S., Miller, R. S., Perlman, D., & Campbell, S. M. (2002). *Intimate relationships* (3rd ed.). New York: McGraw-Hill.

- Sternberg, R. J., & Barnes, M. L. (1988). *The psychology of love.* New Haven, CT: Yale University Press.

- Reis, H. T., & Patrick, B. C. (1996). Attachment and intimacy: Component processes. In E. T. Higgins and A. W. Kruglanski (Eds.), *Social psychology: Handbook of basic principles.* New York: Guilford Press, pp. 523–563.

Social Psychology in Your Life

Steve majored in psychology as an undergraduate and then spent four more years studying social psychology in graduate school. After another year working as a postdoctoral fellow in social psychology, Steve was hired as an assistant professor at a major university. His job was to teach and do research in his specialized field—social psychology. With a new job and exciting research to do, Steve was ready to finally join the ranks of professional social psychologists. The only thing he lacked was a car—he had no way to get to work.

On his first day in town, Steve headed to a local car dealership. He knew all the tricks of the trade. He was determined to get a good deal on a new car and not fall victim to the social influence tactics of a car salesperson. Steve figured that being a social psychologist made him immune to the tricks and techniques of the car dealer. "Low-balling won't work on me!" he thought confidently. Being forewarned is being forearmed, or so he thought.

It turns out that Steve got snookered. He paid way too much for a car he didn't really want to buy in the first place. The car he took for a test drive was a model with more options than Steve wanted. "Don't worry about it," remarked the salesman. "It'll only cost you a few dollars more each month. And just imagine yourself driving around town in this car." Back in the showroom, the salesman offered a good price for the car. "Just give me $5 and your driver's licence, so I can go show the manager that you are serious," he explained. Returning with a sad look, he said that the dealer would be losing money at that price. For another $1000, though, he could make a deal. Again, the salesperson urged Steve to "imagine yourself behind the wheel of that nice-looking car."

Steve could really see himself driving around in that car. He took the deal. And then came all the "necessary" extras—undercoating, extended warranty, floor mats, and on and on. By the time he finished, Steve had spent thousands of dollars more than he intended. As he drove off the lot, he realized that he had been taken. "How can I be so gullible?" he screamed to himself. Yet by the time he arrived at home, Steve was quite happy with the outcome. In the span of about an hour, he had convinced himself that he deserved the nicer car, and that the price he paid was fair. Besides, the poor car salesman had his own family to support and really needed the commission.

The true story of Steve's experience when buying a car highlights two important aspects of using social psychology in your own life. On the one hand, it reinforces the value of social psychological principles. Whether he knew it or not, the car salesman was relying on techniques of social influence, all of which we reviewed in Chapter 8.

On the other hand, Steve's story reminds us of the extraordinary difficulty in using the principles of social psychology to change our own behaviour. In thinking about the applications of social psychology, it is tempting to seek practical advice on how to use social psychology to improve your own life. A number of books suggest a variety of such personal uses of social psychology (a good example is Lovaglia, 2000), dealing with problems such as depression, motivation,

Purchasing a car highlights many aspects of social psychology.

personal prejudices, and resisting influence. However, the truth is that knowing social psychology does not make you immune to social influence, stereotypes, prejudice, dissonance, obedience, groupthink, social loafing, or anything else you have learned about in this book. Social psychology may help you to better understand the real influences in your life, but translating that knowledge into practical action, especially applied to yourself, may be the most difficult challenge of all.

One way to appreciate the practical use of social psychology is by looking at how people use the principles and methods of social psychology in their jobs. As it turns out, social psychology has been put to good use in a variety of occupational settings. In this chapter, we provide a small sampling of careers in which knowledge of social psychology can be very useful. We also talk about career options for those who choose to make a career out of social psychology.

The future is quite bright for the maturing field of social psychology. New knowledge is accumulating rapidly, and thousands of social psychologists continue to work on refining and extending the theories and principles reviewed in this book. Later in this chapter, we will offer some modest speculation about exciting new directions for social psychology.

Social Psychology and Your Career

Some people choose to make a career out of social psychology. All three authors of this book proudly identify themselves as social psychologists. Most of the authors who are cited throughout the book are social psychologists. They are busy conducting research, as well as teaching in the classroom. A career in research and teaching in social psychology can be rewarding and fulfilling.

You do not need to make a career of social psychology, however, to benefit from its insight. You will find that social psychology can be used to increase your success in almost any occupation. Perhaps you plan to go into business. Surely, this will involve the need to work in the context of an organization; it may lead to a career in marketing or advertising. If this sounds like you, your knowledge of social psychology will come in handy. Perhaps you want to enter the world of health care—to become a doctor, a physician's assistant, an emergency medical technician, a nutritionist, or a physical therapist. If this is your goal, social psychology will support you. Perhaps you aspire to be a teacher—an elementary or high school educator or a college or university professor. Your knowledge of social psychology will make you a better teacher.

In this section, we provide a few examples of how knowledge of social psychology can be put to use in your career. In some cases, we describe people who earned advanced degrees in social psychology. In other cases, we discuss how general knowledge of social psychology can be useful without the need for obtaining an advanced degree. Keep in mind that we have barely scratched the surface of social psychology in this book. For every chapter, advanced university courses drill down much deeper. If you think that social psychology will be relevant to your career aspirations, we urge you to learn more and enroll in specialized courses. You can also learn more about the usefulness of social psychological knowledge by reading books on the topic of *applied social psychology*, such as the recent Canadian volume edited by Frank Schneider, Jamie Gurman, and Larry Coutts (2005).

Business and Organizations

Throughout this book, we have described social psychological research that relates to businesses and organizations. It should therefore come as no surprise that those who come armed with an understanding of social psychology can be of great value in these settings. People who work in direct sales can draw from a variety of social psychological principles, as illustrated in the opening to this chapter. In larger organizations, social psychology is used by those who work in human resources departments to help with hiring decisions, performance assessments, interpersonal conflicts, and other social dynamics in the workplace. Companies that develop and market products rely on social psychological insight from the initial design stages of a product, through product testing, to the marketing and advertising of the product.

If you are heading for business school, rest assured that more social psychology is in your future. You may want to hold on to your social psychology textbooks—you will need them! You will probably complete a course on consumer behaviour, which includes a heavy dose of theory and research on attitudes (Chapter 6), persuasion (Chapter 7), and social influence (Chapter 8). In all likelihood, you will take a course on organizations, which will focus in part on such topics as group dynamics and leadership (Chapter 10). And most business schools require a course on research methods, which will be strongly oriented toward the research methods of social psychology (Chapter 2).

Many large companies in Canada and elsewhere operate their own research departments, where they employ a staff of scientists. The process of developing and testing new products, and ultimately marketing them, relies on a team of people with expertise in such fields as engineering, chemistry, biology, economics, finance, and social psychology. The research methods used in such settings are fundamentally the same as those used in the studies described in this book. Yet, the corporate research setting also differs substantially from the university research setting. There are at least three important differences between doing research in a corporate setting and doing it in an academic setting (Garfein, 1997). First, an academic researcher publishes articles in scientific journals with the goal of sharing that research with all who are interested. In the world of business research, most of the results stay within the company. When such research is shared, it is done much less formally than in scientific journals. Second, the audience for academic researchers is primarily other academic researchers within one's own area of specialization (e.g., other social psychologists). In the corporate world, the audience for one's research includes managers, colleagues who are not themselves social psychologists, and possibly business customers. These people require clear, audience-friendly, and action-oriented presentations. Finally, academic research is usually an individual process, whereas corporate research environments tend to be organized around teams of researchers, which requires the social psychologist to work hand in hand with researchers from different fields. It is almost always a multidisciplinary research environment.

The accompanying box, An Interesting Career: "Social Psychology Meets the Insurance Business," highlights the career of Rod Hancock, a social psychologist who pursued a career in the insurance industry. As Hancock's experiences show, social psychological training produces a highly flexible set of skills.

Government

The Canadian federal and provincial governments include a variety of departments and agencies that rely on people with expertise in social psychology. Some government organizations are in the business of actually doing research, others provide funding for research in universities, and still others enact, monitor, and

An Interesting Career

Social Psychology Meets the Insurance Business

When Rod Hancock finished work on his Ph.D. in the 1970s, he knew that a career in university research was not for him. He enjoyed research and was good at it, but did not feel that he was passionate enough about it to make it his career.

A fortunate circumstance was that Hancock's wife had connections to an insurance brokerage company in London, Ontario, called McFarlan Rowlands Insurance. The president of the company interviewed Rod and immediately offered him a job. Rod accepted and became involved in various aspects of the company, including sales, identifying new insurance directions for the company, and making sure that employee and customer satisfaction remained high. His familiarity with social psychology helped in all of these tasks. For instance, Hancock's understanding of principles of influence improved his sales techniques. His ability to think about issues from different perspectives

helped him to identify new directions for the company. His knowledge of human motivation enhanced his ability to assess and increase employee and customer satisfaction.

Hancock's performance at the company was outstanding, and he rose quickly through the ranks. In 1984, he took over as president of the company! His guidance has made McFarlan Rowlands one of the premiere insurance brokerages in the country. An interesting consequence of Hancock's training was that he actively pursued the business of insuring Canadian psychologists (e.g., providing liability insurance to clinical, social, and organizational psychologists involved in private practice), a part of the insurance industry about which he had insider knowledge. This aspect of the business has done extremely well. McFarlan Rowlands is now the officially sanctioned provider of professional liability programs to psychologists and mental

health providers throughout Canada, and Hancock regularly attends the annual convention of the Canadian Psychological Association, where he continues to follow new research in social psychology.

Courtesy of Rodney Hancock

Rod Hancock pursued a career in the insurance business.

enforce government regulations. Table 14.1 provides a sampling of such departments and agencies within Canadian governments.

Research. The research staffs of agencies such as the Department of National Defence or Correctional Services Canada conduct their own studies and often contribute to the scientific literature, just as university-based academic researchers do. One major difference is that the research conducted in these organizations tends to be driven by the priorities of the government, rather than the priorities of the individual researchers (Cooper, 1997). This is very similar to the situation we described earlier in businesses and corporations, where the research agenda is set by the company's priorities. The research conducted in government agencies often relates to federal policies, addressing questions about the functioning of government institutions (such as the Canadian military) or the consequences of federal regulations (in places such as prisons). Because the research in government agencies is closely connected with national policies, it can have a broad impact.

Funding. Funding agencies of the federal and provincial governments provide the money for doing research. Much of the Canadian social psychology research that we have discussed in this book was made possible through grants from the

TABLE 14.1
Examples of Canadian Federal Departments and Councils to Which Social Psychology Makes a Contribution

Research	Funding	Regulation
Department of National Defence	Social Sciences and Humanities Research Council of Canada	Health Canada
Correctional Services Canada	Natural Sciences and Engineering Research Council of Canada	Transportation Safety Board of Canada
Sport Canada	Canadian Institutes of Health Research	Canadian Environmental Assessment Agency

Social Sciences and Humanities Research Council of Canada or the Canadian Institutes of Health Research. When researchers need money to conduct their research, they can apply for grants from these and other public and private sources. The funding agencies have developed very elaborate systems for reviewing grant proposals. Not only do they evaluate the scientific merit of the proposed research, they also take into account the relevance to society and the likelihood that the research will contribute to the solution of an important problem (e.g., curing a disease). Scientific experts work in the funding agencies to help manage the review and funding process.

One of this book's authors (Steven Breckler) worked for nearly ten years as a program officer at the National Science Foundation in the United States, where he had responsibility for the distribution of funding for social psychological research. Far from being government bureaucrats, program officers help agencies to set funding priorities, develop new funding opportunities for researchers in their fields, manage the review of proposals, and serve as the primary point of contact for researchers. This work can be extremely rewarding.

Regulation. The regulatory agencies of the federal and provincial governments are responsible for ensuring compliance with laws and regulations. Social psychologists have advised government agencies on a wide array of issues related to safety and health, including airline cockpit and cabin safety, driving and traffic safety (recall our discussion of road rage in Chapter 11), and strategies for increasing recycling behaviours. The areas of responsibility for these regulatory agencies bear directly on social behaviour, dealing with issues of compliance, obedience, and social judgment.

Law

We have already mentioned how social psychologists work in government agencies that are related to laws and regulations. People who know social psychology are also in high demand in other ways that interact with the law and legal systems. For example, a large number of consulting companies employ social psychologists to help advise lawyers and their clients when it comes to jury selection and trial strategies. Social psychologists also provide guidance to police departments and law enforcement agencies to help improve their handling of criminal investigations.

The multidisciplinary field of criminal justice draws from many facets of social psychology, including psychological theories of criminal behaviour, policing strategies, courtroom process, racial profiling, gangs, drug crimes, and terrorism (Schmalleger, 2004; Wrobleski & Hess, 2006). Although lawyers do not typically obtain advanced training in social psychology, their work can often be improved by a fundamental understanding of social psychological principles.

Over the past 25 years, a number of large consulting companies have been established in Canada and the United States to help lawyers and their clients prepare for their days in court (Kressel & Kressel, 2004). These companies conduct small experiments for their clients, often modelled very closely on social psychology experiments. A mock courtroom might be built, and actors hired to portray the roles of judge, lawyers, clients, and witnesses. Participants are then recruited from the community to play the role of jurors. In different experimental conditions, different lines of argument can be tried out or different approaches to structuring the trial can be tested. The pretend jurors are then sent to deliberate, and their discussions are carefully observed and noted. The results may provide good guidance for lawyers and their clients. These consulting companies are constantly hiring people who have varying degrees of knowledge about the theories and methods of social psychology. The accompanying box, An Interesting Career: "Social Psychologist as Trial Consultant," describes the career of trial consultant Joy Stapp.

The courtroom is a rich social environment

An Interesting Career

Social Psychologist as Trial Consultant

Joy Stapp went to graduate school in social psychology. After spending several years working at the American Psychological Association, she took a job with a large trial consulting firm in Houston, Texas, marking the beginning of an interesting and successful career as a trial consultant. Stapp ultimately left the large firm to start her own company with partner Nancy Singleton. The firm of Stapp Singleton develops recommendations for trial strategy that are based on empirical research. "My background is in social psychology, and my partner, Nancy Singleton, has a doctorate in social anthropology. Our perspectives are quite different, but we share a belief in the experimental method and are sensitive to the biases that can skew our results. We are concerned with issues of reliability and validity—concepts that are not

always familiar to our attorney clients and their corporate clients" (Stapp, 1996, p. 12).

Stapp explains that some trial consultants focus most of their attention on jury selection. Others devote their energy to preparing witnesses and effective exhibits. Stapp Singleton works mainly on developing an effective trial strategy, one that "shapes juror perceptions during voir dire [jury selection] and opening statements, is supported by the presentations of the evidence through witnesses and exhibits, is reinforced in closing arguments, and leads to a favourable verdict

Joy Stapp pursued an interesting career as a trial consultant.

for our clients" (Stapp, 1996, p. 12). This approach clearly embraces more of the social psychological richness of a trial, and emphasizes the importance of skills in research methodology. Like most who work as trial consultants, Joy Stapp was not trained specifically for this kind of work. Her background in social psychology coupled with the opportunity to apply her research skills in a different area created the right mix to launch an interesting career.

Research by Gary Wells has helped to provide guidelines for the collection of eyewitness information.

Social psychology has also been put to very productive use in advising police departments in their use of criminal lineups. Social psychologist Gary Wells, who began his career at the University of Alberta before moving to Iowa State University, helped to develop a guide for law enforcement agencies and their collection of eyewitness evidence. Some of the research that formed the basis for this guide was discussed in Chapter 3. The U.S. Department of Justice picked up on this work, and commissioned a special report (Technical Working Group for Eyewitness Evidence, 1999) for distribution to law enforcement agencies—a good example of social psychologists' reaching out to cops on the beat to help them better do their jobs. Time will tell whether local police departments utilize this work to improve the way they handle eyewitness evidence. If you happen to pursue a career in law enforcement, one of your contributions can be to recognize such applications and to draw upon them.

A career as a lawyer is one that you may not immediately associate with expertise in social psychology. But consider the many different instances in which a lawyer could make good use of social psychology. As we just mentioned, the courtroom setting is one that is rich in social psychological phenomena: persuasion, social influence, and group (jury) decision making. Even outside the courtroom, lawyers get involved with interpersonal conflict, negotiation, and sometimes very emotional clients. In many respects, a career in law is a career in applied social psychology. Earlier, we advised students heading off to business school to hold on to their social psychology textbooks. The advice also applies if you plan to attend law school!

Health and Medicine

Increasingly, social psychologists and those with some knowledge of social psychology are pursuing careers in health-care settings. Health psychology itself is a multidisciplinary field, drawing from medicine, biology, psychology, and other social and behavioural sciences. Health psychologists work in a wide array of settings. Some conduct basic research in universities, especially in medical schools and schools of public health. Others work in public foundations and organizations dedicated to conducting research on particular health problems. The accompanying box, An Interesting Career: "A Social Psychologist Working to Improve Health," describes the health-related career of Louis Gliksman. Still others work in primary care, joining teams of health-care professionals in hospitals, clinics, and rehabilitation centres.

The guiding model in health psychology is known as the **biopsychosocial model,** which emphasizes that good health and illness are determined by a combination of biological, social, and psychological factors. Acceptance of the biopsychosocial model is growing within the medical community, which is facilitating more effective and comprehensive health care. Indeed, throughout this book, we introduced connections between social psychology and health. We hope you remember the following selected examples (see Friedman & Silver, 2005, or Taylor, 2002, for more detailed treatments):

biopsychosocial model

model that emphasizes that good health and illness are determined by a combination of biological, social, and psychological factors

Social interaction is an important part of health care.

- Chapter 4 ("Social Perception: Perceiving the Self and Others"): In Canadian social psychologist Tory Higgins's *self-discrepancy theory,* perceived discrepancies between the actual self and either the ideal self or the ought self are hypothesized to be associated with specific kinds of emotions and behaviours. Higgins proposed that failure to reach our ideals can lead to depression, whereas failure to live up to our obligations can lead to anxiety. As it happens, the most common psychological complaints reported to clinical psychologists and psychiatrists are depression and anxiety. Higgins's work on self-discrepancy theory links a particular pattern of self-perceptions to each of these two states.
- Chapter 6 ("Attitudes and Social Behaviour"): Following from the reasoned-action model of attitude-behaviour relationships, we discussed the *IMB model*

An Interesting Career

A Social Psychologist Working to Improve Health

Louis Gliksman always had an interest in health-related behaviours. After completing his Ph.D. in social psychology at the University of Western Ontario in 1981, he was recruited by the Addiction Research Foundation (ARF)—a Canadian research-oriented organization focusing on the determinants and consequences of addictions, including tobacco, alcohol, and drugs. In 1999, the ARF merged with the Clarke Institute of Psychiatry, the Queen Street Mental Health Centre, and the Donwood Institute to assume a broader mandate and scope under the new moniker the Centre for Addiction and Mental Health (CAMH). Its goals are "to develop and disseminate resources and services that will improve the lives of people with mental health and addiction problems" (Centre for Addiction and Mental Health, 2003, p. 52).

Over the years, Gliksman has conducted research on a variety of fascinating topics. His samples have included university students, Aboriginal Canadians, and representative community samples. For example, he has conducted research on the prevalence of binge drinking on university campuses in Canada, as well as the

incidence of alcohol problems more generally among young people. He has developed and investigated programs in Canada, the United States, and South Africa to reduce the harm of consuming alcohol, such as teaching servers in bars to recognize when they should stop serving a patron. Gliksman has also studied aggression and violence in bar settings, including problems that result from provocative actions by bouncers. He has investigated the relation between illicit opiates (e.g., heroin) and crime in Canada, as well as the cost-effectiveness of Drug Treatment Courts in Toronto. He has also been involved in numerous international projects, including an investigation of the barriers to treatment for drug-addicted HIV-positive women in Rio de Janeiro, an investigation of alcohol interventions in Latin America, and a Global Alcohol Database project housed in Geneva, Switzerland.

Social psychological knowledge and training have greatly assisted Gliksman's health-oriented research for the CAMH. He is currently the director of the Social, Prevention and Health Policy Research Department at CAMH. This department

Louis Gliksman works in the field of health research and promotion.

includes staff with diverse backgrounds, including criminology, history, nursing, psychology, and sociology. The research conducted by this group is truly interdisciplinary, utilizing theories and approaches that are both exciting and creative.

In addition to his many research projects and administrative responsibilities at CAMH, he sits on a number of national and international advisory and planning bodies. Gliksman has also maintained involvement with academic psychology: for many years, he was an associate professor of psychology at Brescia University College, where he taught psychology to undergraduates, and he is still an affiliate professor with the University of Western Ontario's Psychology Department.

of AIDS-preventive behaviour, which was developed by Jeffrey Fisher of the University of Connecticut and his brother William Fisher of the University of Western Ontario (Fisher & Fisher, 1992). The IMB (Information, Motivation, and Behavioural skills) model helps to identify the most important determinants of "safer sex behaviours," such as using a condom during intercourse and refusing to have unsafe sex. When a person makes decisions about engaging in risky sexual behaviours, it is important to know that those decisions are influenced by information the person possesses, the person's motivation to perform risky or safer behaviours, and the person's skill at performing preventive behaviours correctly.

- Chapter 7 ("Attitude Change"): We focused on the effectiveness of persuasive communications that arouse fear. Fear appeals are very common in health-related advertising campaigns. Good examples can be found in efforts to stop people from smoking or abusing drugs, or to encourage people to engage in safe sex (by emphasizing the negative consequences of not doing so). Although there is a limit on the effectiveness of fear appeals, the research shows that the arousal of fear *increases* the impact of messages on attitudes and behavioural intentions. The usual explanation of this finding is that fear is an aversive state, which people want to reduce; people accept the recommendations of the message because doing so reduces their fear.

- Chapter 12 ("Helpful Social Behaviour"): The evidence is quite clear and consistent that perceiving a wide social support network has positive effects on health and well-being. For example, perceiving that a wide social support network is available if necessary has been shown to improve recovery from physical illness, to reduce the negative impact of stressful events, and to protect against depression. It is less clear whether the actual receipt of social support helps or hurts, suggesting that more research is needed to better understand the relationship between social support and health.

Education

Effective teachers possess a good understanding of social behaviour and interpersonal relationships. They recognize how social processes bear on learning and education outcomes. If you plan to be a teacher—no matter what subject or grade level—the principles of social psychology will help you do a better job. Traditionally, most teachers in training complete a course in developmental psychology. This makes sense, because effective teaching depends on an understanding of how children grow and develop. Increasingly, teacher education programs are adding social psychological principles to the list of fundamental prerequisites for a career in education. This recognizes that the social context of learning is clearly important for teachers to understand.

A background in social psychology can be helpful in a variety of careers relating to education and learning. In addition to its value for teachers, social psychology is an important part of research in educational psychology. As in other fields we have touched upon, educational psychology is itself a blend of many distinct areas of psychology. It draws together the theory and research traditions of cognitive psychology, developmental psychology, social psychology, psychometrics, neuroscience, and other areas. Although cognitive and developmental psychologists have traditionally been the principal contributors to research on education and learning, social psychologists have increasingly been conducting influential research on academic achievement. Good examples are found in a recent book edited by Joshua Aronson (2002b), who is a social psychologist doing research and teaching in the School of Education at New York University. In this book, a variety of social psychological perspectives are brought to bear on improving academic achievement (see also American Psychological Association, 1997). Just a few examples will give you a good sense of how social psychology can offer important insight:

- In the typical classroom, children are prodded and motivated by external rewards: gold stars, the honour roll, the teachers' praise. The carrot is always dangling just within reach. However, social psychology tells us that this may not be the best way to nurture long-term motivation and achievement. Instead, people tend to do better and to achieve more when they are motivated by internal goals—when they learn and achieve because they enjoy it, because it is fun, because it will help them achieve other worthwhile goals. This is the difference between extrinsic motivation (concrete rewards) and intrinsic motivation (being driven from within). Academic achievement is greater when learners are driven by intrinsic motivation, as research by Robert Vallerand of the University of Quebec at Montreal has shown (e.g., Vallerand, 1997; Vallerand, Fortier, & Guay, 1997; Vallerand & Ratelle, 2002). Indeed, the most successful teachers are those who manage to engage students' intrinsic motivations (Deci & Ryan, 2002; Lepper & Woolverton, 2002).

- One of the problems that poor-performing students face is the debilitating effects of failure. They blame themselves, and others go along by attributing their failure to stable, internal factors. As we often see with depression, academic failure can lead to a vicious self-fulfilling spiral of continued failure. A fascinating set of interventions, inspired by attribution theory, can help. In an early study (Miller, Brickman, & Bolen, 1975), one classroom of students was subjected to the classic scenario: the teacher tried to explain (quite rationally) to the students why they needed to do well in math. In another classroom, the teacher used a little social psychology. The students in this class were simply told that they were good at math—that they were the high math performers. Whether it was true or not, the attribution of high math ability was attached to the students in this class. These students did better on a standard math test when compared to those who got the classic persuasion treatment. More recent research shows that a variety of attribution-inspired interventions succeed in motivating students to do well (Wilson, Damiani, & Shelton, 2002).

- Recall from Chapter 9, where we introduced the idea of *stereotype threat*, how awareness of one's membership in a stigmatized group can have negative consequences for important performance tests (J. Aronson, 2002a). In a recent study at the University of Arizona, Michael Johns, Toni Schmader, and Andy Martens (2005) showed that teaching women about stereotype threat is an effective way of reducing its detrimental effects on their math test performance. More generally, it is important for teachers to understand that a student's identity as a member of a socially stigmatized group can have an important bearing on academic success.

© Bruce Ayres/Stone/Getty Images

Social psychology provides important insight into the social environment of the classroom.

Basic Research

To this point, we have deliberately focused on career opportunities and areas of application that take social psychology and social psychologists far from the university-based research laboratory. We hope to have convinced you that social psychology is relevant in a variety of settings, and that an understanding of social psychology will be useful no matter where your career interests lie. For some, those career ambitions are to stay at a university and continue doing basic research in social psychology.

So what's it like to be a research social psychologist, and how do you get to be one? Most of us started right where you are today: completion of an introductory course and a burning desire to learn more. We took advanced courses in social psychology, and rounded out our education by taking courses in other subdisciplines of psychology. Many social psychologists got hooked by getting involved in research—first as a participant (a research subject), and then as a research assistant.

If you want to pursue a career in research following undergraduate studies, then graduate school is most likely the next step. Many outstanding graduate training programs in Canada offer a Ph.D. in social psychology. Graduate training averages about five years, so prepare yourself for the continuing life of a student. Most programs involve another two or three years of coursework and the beginning of a research apprenticeship. You will learn how to plan and conduct a program of research, how to present your research to colleagues, and how to publish your research in scientific journals. You will focus your attention on a well-specified problem in social psychology, and you will master all there is to know about that problem. All of this hard work will culminate in a doctoral dissertation—your own contribution to science and a demonstration that you are finally ready to join the ranks of full-fledged social psychologists.

For those who pursue a university-based research career, one of the major obstacles is finding a job. Faculty positions in a specific area (such as social psychology) are not available every year at every school. You need to be prepared to hunt far and wide, and in all likelihood to move far away from where you live. It is an exciting time when you finally get to set up your own research laboratory, plan your own program of research, and help to train the next generation of social psychologists. Life as a university professor is great. The hours are flexible (but long!), the campus setting is familiar and comfortable, and you get to interact with students and other faculty. Even with all these benefits, it is not an easy job. Junior faculty are under constant pressure to publish their research, to obtain funding, and to otherwise contribute to the academic community.

College and University Teaching

Many social psychologists find teaching at colleges or small universities to be the most rewarding career choice. They like to spend their time with students, acquainting future generations with the principles of social psychology. This is also hard work. In addition to teaching their courses, faculty at teaching-oriented schools are expected to supervise students' research projects and to keep abreast of the ever-growing literature in their field.

Graduate schools typically offer their students the opportunity to spend time in the classroom. Indeed, this is where many instructors initially learned the great joy and satisfaction of teaching. If you think this might be where your interest lies, we can offer a little advice: most Ph.D. programs devote little time to the explicit training of future teachers. The emphasis tends to be on the training of future researchers. This means that you will need to devote special attention to acquiring and refining your own teaching skills. Don't be dissuaded—most universities offer resources for learning how to be an effective teacher. But you will probably need to look beyond your immediate training program.

● ● ● The Future of Social Psychology

One of the greatest joys of studying social psychology is that the science keeps evolving. The chapters of this book have been organized to reflect the major areas on which social psychology has focused and will continue to focus. Every so often, new approaches and new problems gain the attention of social psychologists. Although we can't predict the future with great precision, we can see on the horizon at least two areas that promise to grab significant attention from social psychologists over the next decade. One is based on our growing ability to understand how the human brain supports cognition and emotion. The other relates to the emergence of new technologies that promise to transform science and society.

Social Behaviour and the Brain

Advances in cognitive science and neuroscience make it possible to look inside the brain as people engage in everyday perception and thought. To a large extent, technology has facilitated this progress. One method, functional magnetic resonance imaging (fMRI), helps us to identify areas of the brain that are involved in emotion and cognition. Much of the research in this area focuses on very fundamental cognitive processes, such as visual perception or the manipulation of numerical information. Recently, however, social psychologists have drawn on these methods to learn more about the connection between the brain and social behaviour (Ochsner & Lieberman, 2001), and the specialty field of **social neuroscience** is beginning to take shape (Cacioppo, 2002; Cacioppo et al., 2002; Cacioppo, Berntson, Sheridan, & McClintock, 2000). Research in this area is focusing on such classic social psychology problems as social cognition (Mitchell, Heatherton, & Macrae, 2002), decision making (Camerer, 2003; Sanfey, Rilling, Aronson, Nystrom, & Cohen, 2003), and aggression (Davidson, Putnam, & Larson, 2000; Harmon-Jones & Sigelman, 2001).

One very promising area of social neuroscience research focuses on people's perceptions, cognitions, and emotions concerning ethnic groups. In earlier chapters (especially Chapter 9), we focused a lot of attention on stereotypes, prejudice, and discrimination. In the past few years, teams of social psychologists, cognitive psychologists, and neuroscientists have used the methods of neuroimaging to gain deeper insight into these phenomena (Eberhardt, 2005).

For example, research shows that overt, explicit expressions of racial prejudice have declined over the past few decades. Yet, as we discussed in Chapter 9, measures of racial prejudice that are disguised in their true intent continue to reveal that people harbour racial prejudice and negative stereotypes. The picture emerging from this research suggests that people can sometimes control their expressions of prejudice, but other times not. The first, automatic response that people show often indicates some degree of bias, but if you give these same people the opportunity to control their responses, then their overt expressions of prejudice tend to go away.

It must take a fair degree of cognitive effort and control to suppress an initial, automatic bias. This is where brain imaging becomes a very useful and powerful tool. Research in neuroscience has helped to identify a specific region of the brain that is heavily involved in cognitive control, attention, judgment, and critical thinking.

social neuroscience

an emerging area of research combining the perspectives of social psychology and neuroscience to understand the relationship between the brain and social behaviour

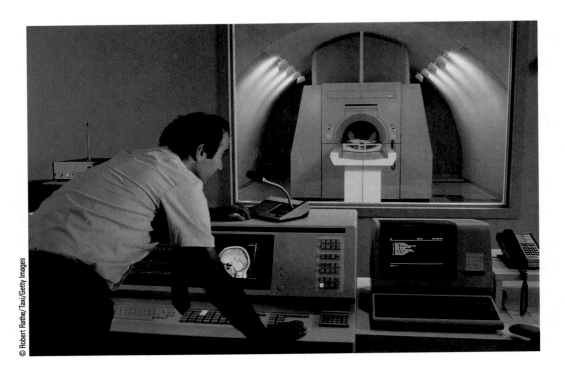

Magnetic resonance imaging (MRI) technology is used in social neuroscience research.

executive function

the set of advanced cognitive processes involved in cognitive control, attention, judgment, and critical thinking

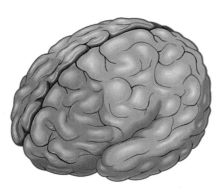

FIGURE 14.1 The blue shaded region shows the location of the prefrontal cortex.

Adapted from *The Prefrontal Cortex* by J. M. Fuster, 1989.

Collectively, these advanced cognitive processes are called **executive function.** The region of the brain associated with executive function is the prefrontal cortex, which is highlighted in Figure 14.1.

Recent experiments have blended social psychology with neuroscience by looking at activity in the brain as participants are exposed to racial information. In a typical experiment, White participants might be shown pictures of both White and Black faces. In social psychology experiments, racial bias is often revealed by implicit measures over which participants have little control, but such bias is not usually evident on explicit measures over which participants can exercise their control. Until recently, of course, it was presumed or theorized that participants engaged in some form of cognitive control—executive function—when responding to explicit measures. With neuroimaging methods, we can now look more directly into the brains of participants to see if, indeed, they do engage in extra cognitive control in response to faces from a race different than their own.

The accumulating evidence confirms that exposure to different-race faces produces a significant activation in portions of the prefrontal cortex (Cunningham, Johnson, Raye, Gatenby, Gore, & Banaji, 2004; Richeson, Baird, Gordon, Heatherton, Wyland, Trawalter, et al., 2003). When racially biased White participants are exposed to Black faces, regions of the prefrontal cortex show a lot more activity than when they are exposed to White faces. It would seem that racially biased participants engage in a lot of cognitive effort to control their responses. The results of two such studies are shown in Figures 14.2 and 14.3.

Even without relying on high-tech brain-imaging devices, cognitive neuroscientists have developed other strategies for understanding how brain processes might be involved in perception and cognition. One common approach is to study research participants who show brain-related cognitive disorders. If the main focus is on memory, then researchers might examine memory-related processes among people who suffer from amnesia or Alzheimer's disease. If the main focus is on motor behaviour, then researchers might focus on people who suffer from Parkinson's disease. In both cases, the logic is that we can learn about the role of brain processes by including in our studies people who suffer from brain disorders that are known to produce specific deficits.

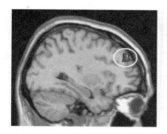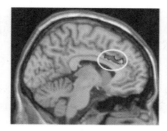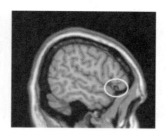

FIGURE 14.2 Imaging results from Cunningham et al. (2004) show increased prefrontal cortex (PFC) activity in White participants' responses to Black versus White faces.

From Cunnigham, Johnson, Raye, Gatenby, Gore, Banaji, "Separable Neural components in the processing of Black and White faces," *Psychological Science*, Vol. 15, Number 12. Copyright 2004, American Psychological Society.

How might this help in our effort to learn more about social behaviour? Let's take a look at an experiment reported by Matthew Lieberman, Kevin Ochsner, Daniel Gilbert, and Daniel Schacter (2001) at Harvard University. These researchers were interested in the cognitive underpinnings of attitude change produced by *cognitive dissonance*. In Chapter 7 we explained how the unpleasant feelings produced by dissonant cognitions motivate people to do something to change their state. One common way for people to reduce their dissonance is by changing their attitudes to make them more consonant with their behaviour. What Lieberman and his colleagues wanted to know is whether people need to be explicitly aware of the discrepancy between their attitudes and behaviour—whether people need to remember that they recently engaged in counterattitudinal behaviour—in order for them to engage in dissonance-reducing attitude change.

To answer this question, the researchers compared unimpaired adults with patients who were suffering from anterograde amnesia—a form of memory loss in which people are unable to form new memories that can be recognized and retrieved. Using a standard *free-choice paradigm* (described in Chapter 7), Lieberman and his colleagues (2001) found that amnesiacs showed just as much attitude change as did the control participants. These results were used to support the view that people need not remember that they have engaged in attitude-discrepant behaviours to nevertheless engage in dissonance-reducing attitude change.

Emerging Technologies

The emergence of new technologies, especially information technologies, is starting to show an impact in social psychology. In Chapter 2, we talked about the Internet as providing an important new context for collecting data (Birnbaum, 2000, 2001). We also described how immersive virtual environments can be used to create social

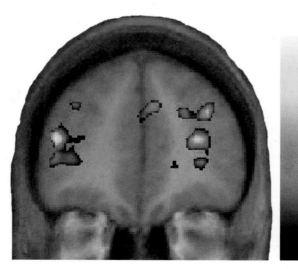

FIGURE 14.3 Imaging results from Richeson et al. (2003) show increased prefrontal cortex (PFC) activity in White participants' responses to Black versus White faces.

From Cunnigham, Johnson, Raye, Gatenby, Gore, Banaji, "Separable Neural components in the processing of Black and White faces," *Psychological Science*, Vol. 15, Number 12. Copyright 2004, American Psychological Society.

Social communication is often mediated by computers.

environments for research (Bailenson, Blascovich, Beall, & Loomis, 2003; Blascovich, Loomis, Beall, Swinth, Hoyt, & Bailenson, 2001).

Immersive Environments. Consider how immersive virtual environments might play an important role in the future of social psychology. Throughout this book, we have described examples of research involving the use of an experimenter's confederate—a person working for the experimenter who is trained to behave or respond in very specific ways. Research confederates were an important part of Asch's conformity experiments, Milgram's obedience experiments, Sherif's normative influence experiments, and Latané and Darley's emergency bystander experiments (to cite just a few examples).

The use of a live "plant" in social psychology experiments is often critical for setting the necessary social stage. Yet we also know that it introduces additional sources of variability into the experimental setting. Suppose the confederate behaves differently on different days, or at different times of the same day. What if the confederate's behaviour interacts with characteristics of the real participants? Perhaps a confederate will respond differently to tall respondents than to short ones. All of these possibilities create important threats to the validity of an experiment. Social psychologists would place a high value on gaining additional control over these variables.

The technology of immersive virtual environments may offer the methodological solution. Although the technology is still in its infancy, it is easy to see how it affords a high degree of control. Everything about the "situation" presented to participants is constructed and controlled by a computer. A nice illustration is offered in a recent experiment by Jeremy Bailenson and Nick Yee (2005) at Stanford University. These researchers were interested in a phenomenon that Tanya Chartrand and John Bargh had earlier called the *chameleon effect* (Chartrand & Bargh, 1999). Chartrand and Bargh found that participants automatically mimic the motor behaviours of a stranger, and that people generally like others who engage in such mimicry. Following the tradition of social psychological research, these experiments featured the use of a live confederate.

Bailenson and Yee wanted to know if the same effect would be observed under the more controlled conditions of an immersive virtual environment. To find out, they created a digital chameleon: a computer-controlled agent in immersive virtual reality. Figure 14.4 shows a participant in the experimental apparatus. Within this virtual environment, participants "interacted" with the virtual agent. The digital chameleon was programmed either to mimic the participant's head movements (with a four-second delay) or to respond with the prerecorded movements of another participant. As the virtual agent was moving its head, it verbally presented a persuasive argument. Results showed that the agent was more persuasive and better liked when it mimicked the participant's own head movements.

Another fascinating use of immersive virtual environments relates to the burgeoning fields of cognitive and social neuroscience. Research in these areas depends heavily on neuroimaging technology. The current state of that technology requires that research participants lie still in a very confined space. This creates a special challenge in presenting stimulus materials. It is relatively easy to show still photographs or computer-generated images as people's brains are being scanned. It is much harder to create engaging social situations for people when they are lying flat on their backs inside the tunnel of a magnetic resonance imaging device. The recent advances in immersive virtual environment technology may offer a solution (Tarr & Warren, 2002). A realistic virtual environment can be created for participants, even when they are in the confines of the imaging device.

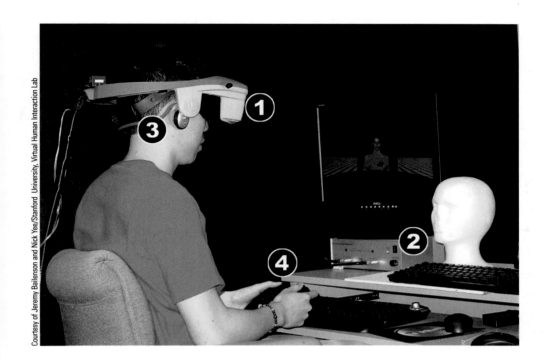

FIGURE 14.4 A participant engaged in Bailenson and Yee's (in press) immersive virtual environment system. The components are: (1) orientation tracking sensor, (2) image generator, (3) head-mounted display, and (4) game pad input device.

Courtesy of Jeremy Bailenson and Nick Yee/Stanford University, Human Interaction Lab.

The Internet. Whenever new technology is introduced, people worry about its impact on society. This is especially true of communications technology, whose history includes the introduction of telephones and television. In both cases, the technology was greeted with a sort of ambivalence—excitement about its benefits, but apprehension about its consequences. Internet technology is today's centre of attention. Internet technology goes well beyond its use as simply another method in the social psychologist's toolbox (Chapter 2). The Internet, instant messaging, and chat rooms have pervaded social life. The Internet has become one of the main ways in which people communicate, and it provides an important new medium for the delivery of persuasive messages. This makes Internet-mediated communication a social phenomenon in its own right (Kiesler, 1997).

Researchers are beginning to examine social behaviour within this technological context (e.g., Brym & Lenton, 2001; Calvert, 2002; Katz & Rice, 2002; Kiesler & Kraut, 1999; Kraut, Patterson, Lundmark, Kiesler, Mukophadhyay, & Scherlis, 1998), and we expect that this will become a booming area of research in the next decade. In some ways, the Internet is a sort of moving target for doing research, especially on social behaviour, because it is changing and evolving itself. For example, in one major longitudinal study conducted in the late 1990s, Robert Kraut and his colleagues at Carnegie Mellon University (Kraut et al., 1998) followed people over a period of one to two years, just after Internet accessibility became available in their homes. Participants in this study made heavy use of the Internet, especially for communication with others. At that time, Internet use appeared to cause a decline of communication among family members within the households: they experienced declines in the sizes of their social circles and increases in depression and loneliness. In a more recent follow-up study of the same households (Kraut, Kiesler, Boneva, Cummings, Helgeson, & Crawford, 2002), however, those negative consequences had evaporated. Indeed, during the intervening years, it appears that Internet use in this sample was associated with relatively positive outcomes.

Increasingly, the Internet is being used as a means of meeting new people for possible romantic relationships. Robert Brym of the University of Toronto and

People are sometimes reluctant to accept the products of new technology.

Nanotechnology may someday be a big frontier for social and behavioural science.

Rhonda Lenton of McMaster University conducted a large survey of online dating in Canada in 2000–2001. They reported that more than 1 million Canadians had visited an online dating site. Those who used online dating services were not unsociable offline. For example, about half of the users of online dating services belonged to an organization or club offline, and most had friends they saw socially. About two-thirds of the users of online dating services had met someone face-to-face whom they first met on the Internet, and about one-quarter of the users had met at least one person they regarded as a "partner." Surprisingly, the researchers concluded that online dating seemed to be safer than conventional dating: only 10% of people who went out on a date with someone they met online reported being frightened. Brym and Lenton concluded that online services are a viable avenue for meeting potential partners.

The technology that allows electronic interpersonal communication also has a potential application in the field of social neuroscience. As we just discussed, one challenge of doing research with magnetic resonance imaging technology is that it constrains the social situation. Recently, researchers have been using Internet technology to allow for social interaction while two people are separately ensconced in the imaging equipment (Montague et al., 2002).

New Technologies. It is fun to imagine what other new technologies might intersect the world of social psychology. One likely intersection is that social psychologists will probably be involved in assessing the societal impact of new technologies. Often, people are skeptical or even fearful of new technologies. A good example is in public resistance to the use of genetically modified foods. This may not be high on the list of Canadian concerns (Hallman, Hebden, Aquino, Cuite, & Lang, 2003), but across Europe, people are reluctant to consume genetically modified foods and often protest the development of such foods. The subject has become an important part of European thought, attitudes, and values (Cook, Kerr, & Moore, 2002; Koivisto Hursti & Magnusson, 2003; Laros & Steenkamp, 2004; Miles & Frewer, 2003). Efforts to understand how people respond to the introduction of new technologies, however, has not yet drawn much research attention from social psychologists.

Another interesting example is in the area of nanotechnology: technology that allows us to manipulate matter at the level of individual atoms or molecules. As with genetically modified foods, social psychologists may begin investigating the social consequences of this new technology, especially if people are reluctant to adopt nanotechnology because they fear negative and aversive results (Roco & Bainbridge, 2001). In the area of research methods, it may be that this technology will produce new tools that permit unprecedented opportunities for observing and recording affective, cognitive, and behavioural processes (Roco & Bainbridge, 2002). Whatever new technologies the future holds, it is likely that social psychologists will play a role in understanding them—both their social consequences and the advances in research methods that they might allow.

Chapter Summary

This is the end—the last summary of the last chapter. In this chapter, we highlighted the many interesting career possibilities that are enabled by a background in social psychology, including in business, government, law, health, education, research, and teaching. We also engaged in a little forecasting, suggesting that emerging frontiers in social psychology can be found at the intersections with neuroscience and with new technologies.

Key Terms

biopsychosocial model (558)   **executive function** (564)   **social neuroscience** (563)

Social Psychology Alive on the Web

SOCIAL PSYCHOLOGY ALIVE: QUIZZING AND PRACTICE TESTS

You can access our Web site directly by going to http://www.socialpsychologyalive.nelson.com for online quizzes, flash cards, and Internet links.

INFOTRAC® COLLEGE EDITION

For additional readings, explore InfoTrac® College Edition, your online library of archived journal articles and periodicals dating back 22 years. If your instructor ordered InfoTrac® College Edition with this book, you can access it from your CD-ROM, or go directly to http://www.infotrac-college.com and use the passcode from the InfoTrac® College Edition card that came with your book. For this chapter, try these search terms in combination with *social psychology: careers, consumer behavior, marketing, biopsychosocial model, education, teaching, social neuroscience, immersive virtual environments, Internet.*

Social Psychology Alive: The Workbook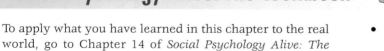

To apply what you have learned in this chapter to the real world, go to Chapter 14 of *Social Psychology Alive: The Workbook.*

- Name That Job

- Proverbs, Adages, and Platitudes: A Look Back at Chapter 1
- The Practical Relevance of Social Psychology

Developing a Measure of a Social Psychological Construct

In the following paragraphs, we outline the basic steps involved in developing a measure of a social psychological construct. The construct might be a disposition (trait), attitude, set of beliefs, or other stable concept (see Chapter 6 for additional information specifically on developing measures of attitudes). We assume that the construct is not so simple or straightforward that it can be assessed with a single item (e.g., "Do you support or oppose bringing back the death penalty?").

The steps we describe are those needed to produce a *self-report* measure, which means that respondents provide their answers directly and describe their own traits and behaviours. Self-report measures assume that respondents are able and willing to answer honestly. In Chapter 6, we discuss some of the limitations of self-report measures (see pages 201–202), so you might want to review these points before proceeding. In particular, self-report measures can be influenced by socially desirable responding, such that participants' answers are influenced by a desire to make themselves look good. Thus, if the construct is one on which there is a socially "good" or "correct" position (or, conversely, a negative or unpopular position), self-report measures can be problematic. We will assume that the construct to be measured lends itself to a self-report approach.

Step 1: Get a Clear Idea of What the Construct Means

Before researchers can develop a measure of a construct, they must have a clear idea of what it means. They formulate an appropriate definition of the construct, as well as provide a detailed analysis of what it represents. What are the key elements in the construct? What behaviours reflect the construct? Does the construct have different facets/components, or is it a simple, one-dimensional concept? Are there synonyms for the construct (words that mean the same thing) that help to clarify its meaning?

For example, imagine that we want to measure the construct of *shyness*. The first step in designing a measure would be to define shyness and think about its key elements and behaviours. We might define shyness as *a tendency to feel discomfort and self-consciousness in the presence of other people.* This definition would mean that we should obtain self-reports of discomfort and self-consciousness in social settings rather than ratings of how people feel in private settings. Are there different components of shyness? We might say yes, shyness can involve physical symptoms like blushing, psychological symptoms like anxiety in public, and behavioural symptoms like avoiding social situations. We would therefore want to assess each of these components of shyness. We might also recognize that shyness can be evidenced in many different settings, including interactions with strangers, interactions with opposite-sex others, giving talks in front of a group, and other social situations. We would therefore try to ask about shyness behaviours and reactions in each of these possible settings; perhaps some people are shy with specific target groups but not others, whereas some people are shy in just about all social settings.

Step 2: Develop Items for the Self-Report Measure

The second step in developing a self-report measure of a construct is to design or collect a reasonably large set of statements or questions that the researcher thinks reflect the construct. This step can be more challenging than expected: it is often easy to think of one or two items that clearly measure a construct but very difficult to think of many more. There is no "correct" number of questionnaire items to generate, but broad concepts like personality traits are best assessed by many items—10, 20, or even more. If the concept is relatively simple and unidimensional (e.g., attitudes toward a social issue, such as the importance of a strong military), then fewer items are needed—as few as three or four items may be enough.

The statements or questions developed for the scale should possess a number of characteristics, which are summarized below.

- *Aim for clear wording.* Each questionnaire item should be clear and unambiguous in its meaning. Words should be common ones that all respondents will understand. Sentences should be relatively short and simple in both grammar and meaning. Furthermore, unless the questionnaire is designed to be sex-specific, the items should apply to both men and women.

- *Aim for nonredundancy.* Questionnaire items should be distinct and different from one another in some way. Avoid the simple rephrasing of existing items. It is fine to have some similarly worded items (e.g., "Tests make me anxious" and "I get nervous before exams"), but if the construct is so simple that there are *only* two or three ways it can be described, then keep the measure short.

- *Aim for comprehensiveness.* Include questionnaire items that assess each facet or component of the construct. By including items that reflect the various elements, you help ensure that the measure is comprehensive and captures the construct's full range. At the same time, avoid items that reflect related but distinct constructs. For example, a measure of aggression should not have large numbers of items related to anger; otherwise your scale might be measuring some mix of the two constructs.

- *Aim for a balanced scale.* Include some items in which a response of "agree" reflects *more* of the construct and other items in which a response of "agree" reflects *less* of the construct. If all of the questionnaire items are phrased in the same direction (an unbalanced scale), then a general tendency to agree with statements will bias respondents' total scores on the scale. In other words, include different items on which the same response (e.g., "strongly agree") means contrasting things. For example, a measure of tidiness or neatness should *not* include only items like "I am a neat person," "I usually clean up after myself," and "Materials on my desk are always well organized," because these are all worded in the same direction: agreement reflects greater tidiness. It should also include some items on which *disagreement* reflects greater tidiness, such as "I often leave dirty dishes in the sink" and "People sometimes tell me I am a slob."

- *Avoid double negatives:* Do not include statements or items that are double negatives (e.g., "I never state that I do not support reinstating capital punishment"), because they are confusing and difficult to understand.

- *Avoid two-component items.* Do not use questionnaire items that include two separate points, because participants may agree with one part but not the other. For example, asking participants to rate agreement with the statement "Prisoners are treated too well and we should bring back capital punishment" is problematic, because respondents may feel differently about the two components (treating prisoners less well versus bringing back capital punishment).

- *Avoid items that have a strong positive or negative connotation.* For instance, even the most authoritarian person may be unwilling to publicly endorse the statement "I believe the torture of war prisoners is warranted." Similarly, even the least helpful person might feel compelled to agree with an altruism item such as "It is only proper to help the sick and needy."

Each item in the measure must have a "response scale" on which participants circle a number, a word, or a phrase to indicate their answer. The most common response scales are agreement (e.g., "strongly disagree" to "strongly agree"), self-descriptiveness (e.g., "very untrue of me" to "very true of me"), and degree or strength (e.g., "not at all" to "extremely"). The answer scale for an item always includes several possible responses; the most common number of options is probably 7, but anywhere from 5-point to 11-point scales are common. Responses are generally scored from 1 to 7 (or 1 to 5, or 1 to 11, etc.) such that higher scores reflect *more* of the construct being measured. Thus, if the measure is intended to assess tidiness, high scores should reflect greater tidiness; if the measure is intended to assess support for capital punishment, high scores should reflect stronger support for capital punishment.

Let's continue our example of developing a measure of shyness. What are some questionnaire items that conform to these guidelines and that could be used to measure shyness? Ten sample items are listed below, with a one-sentence instruction explaining how responses should be made:

Please indicate the extent to which you disagree or agree with each of the following statements by circling one of the numbers on the answer scale.

1. I feel self-conscious when other people watch me entering a room.

1	2	3	4	5	6	7
Strongly disagree			Neutral			Strongly agree

2. My friends would describe me as outgoing.

1	2	3	4	5	6	7
Strongly disagree			Neutral			Strongly agree

3. I feel awkward interacting with members of the opposite sex.

1	2	3	4	5	6	7
Strongly disagree			Neutral			Strongly agree

4. Large parties are very enjoyable for me.

1	2	3	4	5	6	7
Strongly disagree			Neutral			Strongly agree

5. I feel comfortable introducing myself to other students in my classes.

1	2	3	4	5	6	7
Strongly disagree			Neutral			Strongly agree

6. Blushing is *not* a problem for me.

| 1 | 2 | 3 | 4 | 5 | 6 | 7 |
Strongly disagree   Neutral   Strongly agree

7. I dislike speaking in front of a group.

| 1 | 2 | 3 | 4 | 5 | 6 | 7 |
Strongly disagree   Neutral   Strongly agree

8. I am a shy person.

| 1 | 2 | 3 | 4 | 5 | 6 | 7 |
Strongly disagree   Neutral   Strongly agree

9. I enjoy meeting new people.

| 1 | 2 | 3 | 4 | 5 | 6 | 7 |
Strongly disagree   Neutral   Strongly agree

10. I often avoid social settings.

| 1 | 2 | 3 | 4 | 5 | 6 | 7 |
Strongly disagree   Neutral   Strongly agree

A total score on this scale would be calculated by adding up participants' responses across all items, with higher scores representing more shyness. Thus, all items that reflect more shyness when respondents *agree* with them (Items 1, 3, 7, 8, and 10) would be scored using the response scale exactly as it appears below the items—from 1 (strongly disagree) to 7 (strongly agree). However, all items that reflect more shyness when respondents *disagree* with them (Items 2, 4, 5, 6, and 9) would be scored by *reversing* the scale as it appears below the items: responses would be scored from 7 (strongly disagree) to 1 (strongly agree). For example, if respondents circled "2" on the answer scale, they would be assigned a score of 6, or if they circled "5" on the answer scale, they would be assigned a score of 3. Possible total scores on the 10 items would range from 10 (if a respondent answered every item by circling the least shy response and received a score of 1 on each of the 10 items) to 70 (if a respondent answered every item by circling the most shy response and received a score of 7 on each of the 10 items).

But these total scores would assume that all 10 items in the questionnaire are "good" or "effective" items. This assumption must actually be tested before the researcher's job is done. We describe how to assess the quality of the items in the next section.

Step 3: Assess the Quality of the Items

After a researcher has come up with questionnaire items that seem to be worded clearly, are balanced, and reflect the breadth of the construct, the next step is to evaluate the quality of these items. Are they, in fact, all accurate reflections of the same underlying construct? Do they "hold together" as a scale? Are they unambiguous?

There are two very common ways to assess the quality of the items in a scale: examining the item–total correlations and conducting a factor analysis. We will explain the first procedure in some detail, but factor analysis is complex enough that we will only outline its purposes or goals. If you want to do a factor analysis (after understanding what it is intended to do), you can ask for assistance from someone who is relatively expert in statistics and computer analysis.

Item–Total Correlations. In any initial pool of statements designed by a researcher, there will probably be some items that are ambiguous, poorly phrased, or even unrelated to the construct being measured. These questionnaire items will not contribute meaningfully to respondents' scores and should be identified and removed from the questionnaire. For example, suppose that a researcher wanting to measure shyness included the following statement in the original set: "I occasionally wonder what people think of me." The researcher might have expected this item to reflect shyness, with shy people agreeing with the statement more than nonshy people. But perhaps *everyone* wonders occasionally what other people think of them, so this item might elicit high agreement from both shy and nonshy respondents. If this is the case, then the item does not reflect shyness and should be eliminated.

Item–total correlations help to identify such ineffective statements. To compute item–total correlations, we must first calculate respondents' total scores across all items. Although these total scores include the bad items as well as the good items, they provide an initial estimate of the construct for each person. Next, taking one item at a time, participants' responses on that item are correlated with their total scores. If scores on the item correlate significantly with the total scores (that is, people who score high on that one item also tend to score high on the total scores), then it is assumed to be an effective item. But if the item does *not* correlate significantly with the total scores, then it is assumed to be an ineffective item, because participants' answers do not appear to reflect the intended construct. That is, someone who agrees with that item is just as likely to be high on the construct as low. After all items have been tested in this manner, the ineffective items are dropped from the scale. The remaining items can then be included in a revised measure for future studies (or as a basis for recalculating the current participants' scores if the researcher wants to do so).

Factor Analysis. Factor analysis is a statistical procedure that shows which items in a scale tend to "go together" to form a *factor*. A factor can be thought of in this context as an underlying theme to the items. Factor analysis identifies how many factors or themes exist in the set of items and which items form each factor. The researcher can interpret what a factor means by looking at the specific items that form the factor. In many cases, the researcher expects or hopes that *all* of the items in a scale will form just one factor, because the construct is conceptualized as unidimensional (e.g., degree of liking for chocolate) and so the items should represent that one theme. But sometimes the construct may be expected to have two or even more factors, because it has different components or elements. Earlier, we explained the importance of getting a clear idea of what the construct means—Step 1 in the process of developing a measure. This understanding of the construct will presumably include the number of components that are expected. For example, it has been proposed that the construct of risk taking is made up of four distinct but related facets: physical risk taking, monetary risk taking, social risk taking, and ethical risk taking. A factor analysis would test whether this four-factor structure is, in fact, exhibited in a set of items on risk taking.

Step 4: Assess the Validity of the Scale

Item–total correlations and factor analysis indicate whether your questionnaire's items are all measuring the same construct, but those methods do not tell you whether it is the construct you intended to measure. To be confident that scores on the new measure actually reflect what they are supposed to reflect (the *validity* of the measure; see page 39 in Chapter 2), the researcher should also collect data showing that the measure correlates with other, established measures of the construct (if they exist) or with appropriate, related constructs. That is, the researcher should document the validity of the scale by showing that it predicts other things that are conceptually related. These "other things" can include measures of behaviour, personality traits, beliefs, or anything else that *should* correlate with the new measure.

For example, to establish the validity of a measure of shyness, a researcher might try to show that scores on the scale correlate significantly with other known measures of shyness. (You may be wondering why a researcher would develop a new measure of a construct if other measures already exist. The existing measures may not be appropriate for the researcher's goals for a variety of reasons. For example, existing measures may have been developed for use with a different population or may not capture all components of the construct.) Alternatively, the researcher can think about other constructs that are relevant to shyness. One such measure could be peer judgments of shyness—ratings of participants' shyness by their friends. If the new measure is valid, then people who score high in shyness on the new measure should be rated as more shy by their friends than people who score low in shyness. Other measures could consist of participants' self-reports of *behaviours* that presumably reflect shyness, such as the number of parties they have attended in the last month, or the number of new friends they have made while at university. Presumably, people who score high in shyness on the new measure will report having attended fewer parties and having made fewer new friends than people who score low in shyness.

Another way to demonstrate the validity of a measure of shyness could involve constructing controlled settings where participants' shyness could be observed and rated. For example, participants could be brought into the laboratory to interact for ten minutes with one or two assistants of the experimenter. Scores on the new shyness measure should predict how much conversation participants initiate during the interaction, with shy participants initiating less conversation than nonshy participants. Participants could also be asked following the interaction to rate their feelings of discomfort; scores on the measure of shyness should predict ratings of discomfort during the interaction, with shy participants reporting more discomfort than nonshy participants.

Conclusion

We have outlined four steps in the development of a self-report measure of a social psychological construct: (1) get a clear idea of what the construct means, (2) develop items for the measure, (3) assess the quality of the items, and (4) assess the validity of the scale. These steps are necessary no matter what construct is being measured— a personality trait or a more limited concept such as an attitude or a belief. This process of developing a measure represents the challenge of *operational definitions* discussed in Chapter 2 (see page 35). Theoretical ideas must be translated into testable questions, and psychological constructs must be translated into measurable responses before good empirical research can be conducted. By developing sound measures of social psychological constructs, researchers can collect the data necessary to evaluate important theories in psychology.

Glossary

accessibility the ease with which a schema comes to awareness

acculturation the process of cultural and psychological change that takes place as a result of contact between two or more cultural groups and their individual members

actor–observer difference a pattern of differences in attributions in which actors tend to make external attributions for their own behaviour, whereas observers tend to make internal attributions for the same actions

actual self a conception of the self describing our perception of how we really are

adult attachment the concept of attachment used to describe and understand close relationships in adulthood by translating each of the three major patterns of attachment found among infants—secure, anxious/ambivalent, and avoidant—into their adult forms

aggression behaviour that is intended to injure someone physically or psychologically

Aggression Questionnaire (AQ) a scale that measures individual differences in trait aggressiveness

alcohol myopia the tendency for intoxication to reduce cognitive capacity, which results in a narrowing of attention

altruistic motivation a motive for helping purely for the sake of providing benefit to another person

ambivalent attitudes evaluations of targets that include both positive and negative elements

ambivalent sexism inventory a measure of stereotyped attitudes toward women, which is composed of two dimensions, one positive and one negative: benevolent sexism and hostile sexism

appearance self-esteem an individual's satisfaction with his or her physical looks

archival research correlational investigations that are based on pre-existing information obtained by researchers, such as historical records, newspaper articles, or other forms of public data

attachment theory Bowlby's theory concerning the development and the effects of the emotional bond between an infant and its caregiver; also used to account for the relationships that develop between close friends and lovers throughout the life span

attitude an individual's evaluation of a target along a good–bad dimension

attitude-similarity effect the idea that people find others more attractive and likeable the more similar they are in their attitudes, beliefs, and preferences

attributions causal judgments about why an event or behaviour occurred

augmentation principle a rule of attribution that states that the perceived role of a cause will be augmented (increased) if other factors are present that would work against the behaviour

autobiographical memory stored information about the self, such as goals, personality traits, past experiences, and other qualities

autokinetic effect in a darkened room, a stationary point of light will appear to move periodically

automatic process a judgment or thought that we cannot control, which occurs without intention, very efficiently, and sometimes beneath our awareness

availability heuristic the tendency to base a judgment on how easily relevant examples can be generated

aversive racism a "modern" kind of prejudice held by people who do not consider themselves prejudiced and who would find any accusation of being prejudiced aversive, but who nevertheless harbour some negative beliefs and hostile feelings toward members of minority groups

avoidant insecure attachment a pattern seen in the strange situation, in which the baby basically ignores the mother, usually shows no strong signs of disturbance when she leaves the room, and avoids the mother during reunion episodes or greets her return rather casually

behavioural intention an individual's plan to perform or not perform an action

behaviourism an approach in psychology that assumes that behaviour can be explained purely in terms of stimulus–response connections established through experience and reinforcement

benevolent sexism positive but paternalistic attitudes toward women

bias blind spot the tendency to think that biases and errors in judgments are more common in others than in ourselves

biopsychosocial model model that emphasizes that good health and illness are determined by a combination of biological, social, and psychological factors

blank lineup a group of individuals that does not include the suspect; everyone in the lineup is known to be innocent

bystander effect the likelihood that an individual will intervene in an emergency goes down as the number of bystanders increases

categorization the process of recognizing and identifying something

catharsis the idea that aggressive behaviour releases people's pent-up frustration and reduces the likelihood of subsequent aggression

central route to persuasion persuasion that occurs when attitude change results from a careful analysis of the information in a persuasive communication

chronic accessibility the degree to which schemas are easily activated for an individual across time and situations

cognitive dissonance theory a model proposed by Leon Festinger, which states that awareness of consonant cognitions makes us feel good, whereas awareness of dissonant cognitions makes us feel bad. Further, the unpleasant feelings produced by dissonant cognitions motivate us to do something to change our state.

cognitive miser model a view of information processing that assumes people usually rely on heuristics to make judgments and only engage in careful, thoughtful processing when necessary

cognitive neoassociation model of aggression a theory of harm-doing proposing that aversive events activate the schemas for *fight* and *flight,* which elicit the emotions of anger and fear; whether people respond with aggression or escape depends on the pattern of cues in the situation

cognitive response theory a model of persuasion that assumes that the impact of a message on attitudes depends on the thoughts evoked by the message

cognitive restructuring recognizing and modifying anger-related thoughts and attributions; it forms part of CRCS training

cognitive-relaxation coping skills training (CRCS) an intervention program designed to reduce anger, which involves teaching people a set of relaxation techniques and ways to modify their anger-related thoughts

collectivist cultures cultures in which people are seen as interdependent beings who should contribute to harmonious group functioning

colour-blind approach the hypothesis that to reduce prejudice, people should be encouraged to categorize other people as individual persons rather than as members of groups

commitment the motivation to maintain and sustain a relationship even in the face of adversity

communal relationship a relationship in which the receipt of a benefit creates no specific obligation to return that benefit; responding to the needs of your partner is the benefit

companionate love the kind of love that develops in a close and intimate relationship; the affection we feel for those with whom our lives are deeply entwined

compatibility principle a theory stating that a measure of attitudes will correlate highly with a measure of behaviour only when the two measures are matched in terms of being general/broad or specific/narrow

compliance a change in behaviour that is requested by another person or group

conflictive ethos an atmosphere of distrust and hatred that can develop in longstanding disputes

conformity any change in behaviour caused by another person or group

consonant cognitions beliefs that are consistent or compatible with one another

contact hypothesis the idea that exposure to members of an outgroup will produce more favourable attitudes toward that group

contingency model of leadership effectiveness a theory that predicts that task-oriented leaders will be more successful than relationship-oriented leaders in groups where the situation is either very favourable or very unfavourable for the leader, whereas relationship-oriented leaders will be more successful than task-oriented leaders in groups where the situation is mixed for the leader

controlled process a judgment or thought that we command, which is intentional, requires significant cognitive resources, and occurs within our awareness

cooperation collaborative behaviour with other people that takes into account both one's own outcomes and the outcomes of the others

correlational research studies in which investigators measure two or more concepts and see whether the concepts are associated with one another

correspondence bias the tendency to assume that people's actions and words reflect their personality, their attitudes, or some other internal factor, rather than external or situational factors

counterfactual thoughts reflections on how past events might have turned out differently

covariation model of attribution an attribution theory proposing that we make causal judgments by determining whether a particular behaviour correlated with a person, a situation, or some combination of persons and situations

Crutchfield apparatus a machine that consists of an electrical panel with several rows of lights; it allows the efficient study of conformity by simulating the responses of numerous hypothetical participants

culture the set of values, beliefs, and behaviours shared by a group of people and communicated from one generation to the next

culture of honour a social network in which men are taught from an early age to defend their reputation for strength by responding to insults or threats with aggression

debriefing a postexperimental procedure in which participants are given a full and complete description of the study's design, purpose, and expected results; if there has been any deception during the study, it must be identified and explained in the debriefing

decision tree a set of five steps that must be completed before an individual will intervene in an emergency situation

defensive high self-esteem a positive self-view that is fragile and vulnerable to threat

degrading pornography sexually explicit material that debases or dehumanizes people, usually women

dehumanization the process of perceiving members of a group as subhuman or inferior to members of one's own group; it allows people to inflict pain and suffering on the group without worrying about the morality of their behaviour

deindividuation a psychological state in which people lose their sense of personal identity and feel immersed in a group

demand characteristics cues in a study that suggest to participants how they are supposed to respond

dependent variable a concept that is measured by the researcher after the manipulation(s) in an experiment; it is typically expected to be affected by the manipulation(s)

destructive cult a rigidly structured group, led by a charismatic leader, that recruits and retains members using manipulative, deceptive techniques

discounting principle a rule of attribution which states that the perceived role of a cause will be discounted (reduced) if other plausible causes are also present

discrimination negative, harmful behaviour toward people based on their group membership

displaced aggression harm-doing that is directed at someone or something that was not the actual source of frustration

display rules norms in a culture for how and when emotions should be expressed

dispositional gratitude an individual differences variable reflecting the extent to which people feel thankful for receiving help from others

dispositional optimism a disposition that represents the extent to which people have positive, confident expectations about their own future outcomes

dispositions individuals' consistencies across time and settings in a specific type of feeling, thought, and/or action, which make individuals different from other people

dissonant cognitions beliefs that are inconsistent or logically discrepant with one another

dominant response the action that is most likely to occur in a situation or on a task when the individual is alone

door-in-the-face technique a strategy to increase compliance, based on the fact that refusal of a large request increases the likelihood of agreement with a subsequent smaller request

downward counterfactual thoughts reflections on how past events might have turned out worse

downward social comparison social comparison with people who are worse off or less skilled than we are

dyadic relationships relationships that develop between two people

effort justification paradigm a research methodology used to test dissonance theory that arouses dissonance by getting people to invest time or energy to achieve a goal that may not be worthwhile

egoistic motivation a motive for helping in order to obtain rewards or avoid punishments

elaboration likelihood model a theory of attitude change that specifies the conditions under which people will think carefully about the content of a persuasive message. It distinguishes between two types of processing: the central route to persuasion and the peripheral route to persuasion.

empathy the ability to comprehend how another person is experiencing a situation

empathy–altruism hypothesis the idea that feelings of empathy for a person can lead to behaviour that is motivated solely by wanting to help that person

equity theory the idea of perceived fairness or balance in interpersonal relationships, such that both partners perceive that they are receiving relatively equal outcomes

erotica sexually explicit material that depicts nonviolent, consensual sexual activity

ethos of peace an atmosphere of acceptance and cooperation, which can facilitate the resolution of disputes

evaluative conditioning a process by which objects come to evoke positive or negative affect simply by their association with affect-inducing events

event sampling a method used to study adult attachment that involves the recording of information about a person's social interactions over a period of time

exchange relationship a relationship in which the partners tend to keep track of what they have given and what they have received, and strive to keep the books balanced

excitation transfer the idea that physiological arousal from sources other than frustration or anger can be linked to anger-related thoughts and cognitions, thereby increasing aggression

executive function the set of advanced cognitive processes involved in cognitive control, attention, judgment, and critical thinking

executive functioning higher-order cognitive processing that organizes and coordinates lower-level elements of behaviour such as planning and monitoring progress toward goals

experimental realism the extent to which the study's setting feels realistic and involving to participants and elicits spontaneous behaviour

experimental research investigations in which the researcher manipulates one concept (or more than one) and assesses the impact of the manipulation(s) on one or more other concepts

explicit attitudes evaluations that people can report consciously

external validity the extent to which research results can be generalized beyond the current sample, setting, and other characteristics of the study

extraneous variables potential sources of error in the experiment that should be controlled; they encompass everything in the experiment except the independent and dependent variables

facial electromyography (facial EMG) a procedure for measuring muscle contractions in the face that may be sensitive to positive versus negative responses to a stimulus

factorial design experiment an experimental study that involves two or more independent variables

false consensus effect the tendency to assume that other people share our own attitudes and behaviours to a greater extent than is actually the case

false hope syndrome the tendency to try repeatedly but unsuccessfully to achieve a goal because of unrealistic expectations about the likelihood of success

field experiment an experimental study that is conducted in a setting outside the laboratory; it tends to produce high mundane realism and external validity

foot-in-the-door technique a strategy to increase compliance, based on the fact that agreement with a small request increases the likelihood of agreement with a subsequent larger request

free choice paradigm a research methodology used to test dissonance theory that arouses dissonance by getting people to choose between two or more alternatives

free-gift technique a strategy to increase compliance, based on the fact that giving someone a small gift increases the likelihood of agreement with a subsequent request

friendships dyadic relationships involving mutual liking

frustration–aggression hypothesis the twin propositions that frustration always leads to some form of aggression and frustration is the only cause of aggression

functional distance compared to physical distance, the closeness between two places in terms of the opportunities for interaction

general aggression model (GAM) a broad theory that conceptualizes aggression as the result of a chain of psychological processes, including situational events, aggressive thoughts and feelings, and interpretations of the situation

genocide an attempt to systematically eliminate an ethnic group through banishment or murder

Gestalt theory an approach in psychology that assumes that people's overall, subjective interpretations of objects are more important than the objects' physical features, and that objects are perceived in their totality, as a unit, rather than in terms of their individual features

Great Person theory the hypothesis that exceptional leaders possess extraordinary qualities and skills—consistent with the trait approach to leadership

group two or more persons who are interacting with one another and/or influencing one another

group cohesiveness the combined strength of all forces acting on members of a group to remain in the group

group dynamics the social psychological study of groups and group processes

group maintenance function aspects of leadership that relate to morale in the group

group polarization the tendency for group discussion to strengthen the initial leanings of the members in a group

groupthink a way of thinking that can occur in decision-making groups when pressure to agree leads to inadequate appraisal of options and poor decisions

hard sell an advertising strategy that relies on presenting information about the positive features of a product

helping behaviour that is intended to assist another person

heuristic an informal rule or shortcut that is used to make everyday judgments

heuristic persuasion attitude change resulting from cues that indicate that the position advocated in a message is valid

heuristic processing superficial analysis of a message that focuses on cues indicating the validity or invalidity of the advocated position

hindsight bias the tendency for people to overestimate the predictability of known outcomes

hostile aggression harm-doing that arises out of negative emotions such as anger, frustration, or hatred

hostile media phenomenon the tendency for people who feel strongly about an issue to believe that the media coverage of the issue is biased against their side

hostile sexism negative attitudes toward women who violate the traditional stereotype of women

hypocrisy paradigm a research methodology used to test dissonance theory that arouses dissonance by having people publicly promote a socially desirable behaviour and then be made aware that they have not always exhibited the behaviour themselves in the past

hypothesis a specific prediction about what should occur if a theory is valid; it provides the means by which a theory can be tested

ideal self a conception of the self describing our perception of how we would ideally like to be

identity the characteristics that individuals think define them and make up their most important qualities

illusion of control the tendency to overestimate our control of situations and events

illusory correlation the belief that two variables are related to one another when, in fact, they are not

IMB model of AIDS-preventive behaviour a theory postulating that information, motivation, and behavioural skills guide individuals' protective actions in the sexual domain

immersive virtual environments technology computer programs that construct an imaginary setting in which participants behave; the computer controls the visual and auditory information and allows participants to respond as if the scene was real

Implicit Association Test (IAT) a reaction time procedure that provides a measure of implicit attitudes; participants sort targets into a "good" category or a "bad" category, and the speed at which the sorting is completed is taken as a measurement of implicit attitude toward the object

implicit attitudes automatic evaluative responses to a target, which may occur without awareness

implicit intergroup bias distorted judgments about members of a group based on a stereotype, which can occur without the person's awareness

impression management the deliberate control of one's public behaviour to create a certain impression

impression management theory an alternative to dissonance theory that argues that participants in dissonance experiments want to appear consistent to the experimenter and therefore lie about their attitudes

inclusive fitness the principle that some social behaviours have been selected during the course of evolution because they increase the survival of our genes

independent variable a concept or factor that is manipulated by the researcher in an experiment; its causal impact on one or more other variables is assessed in the experiment

individualist cultures cultures in which people are seen as independent beings who possess stable abilities, traits, and attitudes

induced compliance paradigm a research methodology used to test dissonance theory that arouses dissonance by getting people to engage in counterattitudinal behaviour. In this paradigm, participants are induced to comply with an experimenter's request that they behave in a way that is inconsistent with their attitudes.

informational influence influence from other people that is motivated by a desire to be correct and to obtain accurate information

informed consent a procedure by which participants are told beforehand what to expect in the study and are reminded that they can withdraw at any time

ingratiation behaviour designed to make someone like us

insecure attachment a pattern seen in the strange situation, in which the baby does not use its mother as a safe haven and secure base from which to explore a novel situation

instrumental aggression harm-doing that is motivated by goals other than hurting the target, such as obtaining something of value

integrated threat theory a theory proposing that prejudice results from four types of threats: realistic threats, symbolic threats, threats stemming from intergroup anxiety, and threats arising from negative stereotypes

interaction result showing that the effect of one experimental manipulation depends on the level of another experimental manipulation; it can only be observed in a factorial design experiment

interactionist approach to leadership the perspective that certain kinds of people are likely to emerge as leaders (or to be effective leaders) under one set of conditions, whereas other kinds of people are likely to emerge as leaders (or to be effective leaders) under a different set of conditions

interdependence a sharing of contributions and outcomes by two people

internal validity the extent to which research yields clear causal information; it tends to be low in correlational research and high in experimental research

interpersonal attraction the study of attraction or liking between two or more people

Interpersonal Reactivity Index (IRI) a measure reflecting the extent to which people feel empathy in response to others' experiences

intuitive scientists untrained scientists who try to make causal judgments in a rational, scientific manner

investment model of close relationships according to this model, satisfaction and stability in a relationship depend on the balance or trade-off between the positive and negative aspects of the relationship, with the idea that people compare the value of their current relationship with the value of available alternatives

jeer pressure the conformity pressure that is produced by seeing someone ridiculed by another person

jigsaw classroom a method of teaching designed to foster positive interracial contact, which involves forming small, culturally diverse groups of students who are each given one part of the material to be learned

just world theory a model proposing that humans need to believe that the world is a fair place where people generally get what they deserve

learned helplessness a state of apathy in which we simply give up trying to achieve our goals

Life Orientation Test (LOT) a measure of dispositional optimism

Likert-type scale an attitude measurement technique that requires respondents to indicate the extent of their agreement or disagreement with several statements on an issue

liking technique a strategy to increase compliance, based on the fact that people are more likely to assist others they find appealing than others they do not find appealing

looking glass self the tendency to internalize other people's judgments about us into our self-concept

love styles the idea that people differ in their styles of love; the three primary styles are *eros*, *storge*, and *ludus*

low-ball technique a strategy to increase compliance, in which something is offered at a given price, but then, after agreement, the price is increased

main effect the effect of one experimental manipulation on the dependent variable, averaged across all levels of other experimental manipulations

mere exposure effect the tendency for repeated contact with an object, even without reinforcement, to increase liking for the object

meta-stereotype a person's beliefs about the stereotype that outgroup members hold concerning his or her own group

minimal group paradigm a procedure in which participants are divided into groups based on trivial features or information

mob a crowd acting under strong emotional conditions that often lead to violence or illegal acts

mood-congruent recall the idea that positive feelings will activate positive memories and negative feelings will activate negative memories

multiculturalism the hypothesis that to reduce prejudice, different cultural groups within a society should each maintain their own identity while simultaneously respecting all other groups

mundane realism the extent to which the study's setting looks and feels like the outside world; it increases the external validity of research results

narcissism a disposition that represents the extent to which people have excessive love for themselves

neosexism a subtle form of sexism, which includes beliefs that women are no longer disadvantaged and antagonism toward women's demands for better treatment

nonverbal behaviour actions and cues that communicate meaning in ways other than by words

norm of obedience to authority the principle that we should obey legitimate authorities

norm of reciprocity the principle that we should give back in return any favours that are done for us

norm of social responsibility the rule or guideline that we should help those who need help, if possible

normative influence influence from other people that is motivated by a desire to gain rewards or avoid punishment

obedience a change in behaviour that is ordered by another person or group

object-appraisal function a function of attitudes in which attitudes provide rapid evaluative judgments of targets, facilitating approach or avoidance

observational studies correlational investigations in which researchers watch participants and code measures from the observed behaviour, either "live" or from videotapes

operational definition a specific, observable response that is used to measure a concept

optimal distinctiveness theory a model hypothesizing that people want to maintain a balance between similarity to other people and individuality from other people

ought self a conception of the self describing our perception of how we think we should or ought to be

outgroup homogeneity effect the tendency for people to overestimate the similarity within groups to which they do not belong

overjustification effect an inference that we performed a potentially enjoyable activity for external reasons (e.g., for a reward) rather than because we enjoyed it

parental investment hypothesis the idea that having children is more costly for women than for men, which has led to the evolution of some differences between the sexes in the characteristics they seek in mates

participant-observation research a special type of observational study in which a researcher actually joins an ongoing group to observe the members' behaviour

passionate love the kind of love that involves strong and intense feelings, infatuation, arousal, and a deep sense of passion

payoff matrix a table representing the outcomes for each player in a prisoner's dilemma game based on the players' combined choices

perfectionism a disposition that represents the extent to which individuals strive for error-free performance

peripheral cues simple features or heuristics that are assumed to indicate that a message is valid

peripheral route to persuasion persuasion that occurs when attitude change results from noncognitive factors; it encompasses evaluative conditioning and mere exposure

personal norms guidelines that have been internalized to become expectations for oneself in particular situations

personal–group discrimination discrepancy the tendency for people to report that they as individuals have experienced less negative treatment based on their group membership than the average member of their group

planning fallacy the tendency for people to underestimate how long it will take to complete a task

popular children children who are named frequently by others in a sociometric rating procedure

power distance the extent to which a culture accepts an unequal distribution of influence within the society

preference for consistency (PFC) a disposition that represents the extent to which people desire predictability and consistency within their own responses and within others' responses

prejudice a negative attitude toward members of a group, which is often very strongly held

priming the process by which the activation of a schema increases the likelihood that the schema will be activated again in the future

prisoner's dilemma game a simulated social dilemma that requires participants to make choices between acting selfishly and cooperatively when selfishness looks better initially but can damage long-term joint outcomes of the players

propaganda a persuasive attempt that is motivated by an ideology, or set of values, and that is deliberately biased in its presentation of information

propinquity nearness or proximity in physical space, which creates the opportunity to meet another person

prosocial behaviour any action that provides benefit to others

protection motivation theory a model that articulates how threatening messages can influence attitudes and behaviour

psychometrics a subdiscipline within psychology that is devoted to understanding and refining methods for psychological measurement

psychosocial law a principle in social impact theory that specifies the nature of the relation between the size of a group and its social influence; the principle predicts that as the number of social forces increases, overall social influence also increases, but at a declining rate

random assignment a procedure by which each participant in an experiment is equally likely to take part in any of the experimental conditions; it controls extraneous variable problems arising from characteristics of the participants

random sampling a recruitment process in which every person in a particular population has exactly the same probability of being in the study; it produces a representative sample

realistic group conflict theory a theory proposing that when groups in society are perceived to be competing with one another for resources, intergroup hostility can be aroused, which leads to prejudice

reconstructive memory the process of trying to rebuild the past based on cues and estimates

reference group a collection of people that serves as a standard of comparison for an individual, whether in terms of attitudes, values, or behaviour

rejected-aggressive children children who are unpopular because they commonly engage in disruptive aggressive behaviours

rejected-withdrawn children children who are spurned by their peers because of their social awkwardness and immaturity

relational aggression behaviour that is intended to damage another person's peer relationships

relative deprivation a feeling of anger or resentment about our outcomes based on comparisons with better-off others

reliability the extent to which a measure is free of "random" fluctuations, both over time and across judges

representative sample a group of respondents that accurately reflects a larger population from which it was drawn and to which the researcher wants to generalize the results

representativeness heuristic the tendency to judge the likelihood that a target belongs to a category based on how similar the target is to the typical features of the category

repulsion hypothesis the idea that people find others less attractive and less likeable if they differ substantially in their attitudes, beliefs, and preferences

Research Ethics Board (REB) a committee that must approve all studies before they can be started; it ensures that the procedures will not cause unacceptable harm to participants

resistant insecure attachment a pattern seen in the strange situation, in which the baby prefers to stay close to mother rather than actively explore the room, becomes very upset when mother leaves the room, and appears to be upset or angry when mother returns, trying to remain near the mother but usually resisting any physical contact initiated by her; sometimes called ambivalent or anxious-ambivalent insecure attachment

scapegoat theory a theory proposing that prejudice occurs because members of dominant groups use discrimination against members of weak target groups to vent their frustration and disappointment

scarcity technique a strategy to increase the attractiveness of a product by making it appear rare or temporary

schemas mental representations of objects or categories, which contain the central features of the object or category as well as assumptions about how the object or category works

secure attachment the most common pattern seen in the strange situation procedure, in which the baby actively explores the room when left alone with mother, gets upset when mother leaves the room, is clearly happy when mother returns, and may seek close physical proximity with her in an effort to relieve distress; the baby uses its mother as a safe haven and a secure base from which it feels safe to explore a novel situation

secure high self-esteem a positive self-view that is confidently held

self-affirmation theory an alternative to dissonance theory that argues that people are threatened by behaviour that challenges their self-worth and can deal with this threat by reaffirming an important value

self-concept all information about the self in memory

self-disclosure the process of people revealing to one another increasingly personal and intimate details about themselves

self-discrepancy theory a theory proposing that perceived differences between the actual self and the ideal self produce depression, and perceived differences between the actual self and the ought self produce anxiety

self-efficacy the belief that we are capable of performing a particular behaviour that is required for a certain goal

self-esteem a disposition that represents people's judgments of their own worthiness

self-fulfilling prophecy a process in which a perceiver's expectancy about a target person influences the perceiver's behaviour toward the target person in such a way as to elicit the expected actions from the target person

self-handicapping the tendency to seek, create, or claim inhibitory factors that interfere with performance and thus provide an explanation for potential failure

self-handicapping scale a scale that measures how often people engage in self-handicapping behaviour

self-monitoring a disposition that represents the extent to which people rely on external or internal cues to guide their behaviour

self-oriented perfectionism a disposition that represents the extent to which individuals set extremely high standards for themselves and are satisfied only when their performance is flawless

self-perception theory a theory proposing that we often judge our own internal states by reviewing our past behaviour and inferring internal states consistent with our behaviour unless there were clear external causes of our behaviour

self-presentation impression management

self-promotion behaviour designed to make someone respect us

self-serving judgments perceptions or comparisons that enhance the perceived worth of the self

semantic differential scale an attitude measurement technique that requires respondents to rate a target on several evaluative dimensions (such as good–bad and favourable–unfavourable)

sequential lineup the procedure of showing an eyewitness each individual in the group separately rather than together in a simultaneous lineup

sexism prejudice and discrimination directed against women because of their gender

single-factor experiment an experimental study that involves only one independent variable

situational approach to leadership the perspective that external, situational factors, such as seating arrangements, can influence who will become leader of a group

social cognition the study of how information about people is processed and stored

social comparison the process of comparing ourselves to others in order to judge the self

social construals how individuals personally interpret or perceive a social situation

social contract the idea that human societies have developed basic rules of social and moral conduct, which members of the societies implicitly agree to follow

social dilemma a situation in which selfish choices produce better immediate outcomes for the individual than do cooperative choices, but long-term outcomes for everyone will suffer if everyone behaves selfishly

social facilitation the effects of the presence of other people on individual performance, which will usually be improved performance on simple tasks and impaired performance on complex tasks

social identity theory a model hypothesizing that people want to have positive appraisals of groups to which they belong

social impact theory a model that conceives of influence from other people as being the result of social forces acting on individuals, much as physical forces can affect an object

social learning theory an approach proposing that humans learn many kinds of responses, including aggressive ones, by observing others; observation shows people both how to perform a behaviour and whether that behaviour will be rewarded or punished

social loafing the reduction of effort that people often exhibit when working in a group where individual contributions are unidentifiable

social neuroscience an emerging area of research combining the perspectives of social psychology and neuroscience to understand the relationship between the brain and social behaviour

social norm a rule or guideline in a group or culture about what behaviours are proper and improper

social psychology the scientific study of how individuals' thoughts, feelings, and behaviours are influenced by other people

social support network people who can be called upon for help and who will provide help when needed, such as family, friends, and neighbours

social value orientation a disposition that reflects individual differences in cooperativeness in social dilemmas; three orientations are typically distinguished: individualists, competitors, and prosocials

socialization the process by which infants are moulded into acceptable members of their society

socially desirable responding a form of responding that involves giving answers that portray the respondent in a positive light

socially prescribed perfectionism a disposition that represents the extent to which individuals believe that other people expect exceptional performance from them and will judge them negatively if such standards are not achieved

socioemotional leader an individual who takes charge of issues related to morale in a group

sociometric rating procedure within a group of acquaintances, each person is asked to name everyone whom he or she considers a friend. Two peers within that social network are then considered to be friends if each nominates the other as a friend

soft sell an advertising strategy that relies on the use of images, emotions, symbols, or values to promote a product

spatial ecology the physical layout of buildings and the distance separating different buildings, rooms, and other spaces

spontaneous self-concept the aspects of identity that are in conscious awareness at a given point in time

stereotype a set of characteristics that a perceiver associates with members of a group

stereotype threat the pressure experienced by individuals who fear that if they perform poorly on a task, their performance will appear to confirm an unfavourable belief about their group

strange situation developed by Mary Ainsworth, a procedure involving several brief episodes during which experimenters observe a baby's responses to strangers, separation from mother, and reunions with mother

subjective norm an individual's feelings of social pressure to perform or not perform an action

subliminal priming procedure a method of activating a schema or stereotype by flashing words or pictures very briefly on a computer screen in front of a participant

survey a correlational study in which the researcher asks questions to respondents, either in a printed questionnaire, on a computer, over the telephone, or during an interview

systematic processing careful, deliberative analysis of the arguments in a message

systematic-heuristic model a theory of attitude change that distinguishes between two types of processing that can occur in response to a persuasive message: systematic processing and heuristic processing

task achievement function aspects of leadership that relate to group productivity

task leader an individual who takes charge of issues related to productivity in a group

terror management theory a model hypothesizing that recognition of their own mortality raises anxiety in humans, which they can reduce by affirming and conforming to their cultural worldview

terrorism actual or threatened violence against civilians for alleged political purposes

theory an explanation of why an event or outcome occurs; it identifies the underlying causes of an event or phenomenon

theory of reasoned action a model of behaviour that views humans as rational decision makers who behave on the basis of logical beliefs

threatened egotism a hostile, aggressive response to criticism from others, which has been linked to narcissism

tragedy of the commons the depletion of a communal resource, such as a shared cow pasture for a group of farmers, because each individual pursues selfish interests

trait aggressiveness a disposition that represents how likely people are to respond to provocations with aggression

trait approach to leadership the perspective that people become leaders, or perform well as leaders, because of their individual characteristics, such as intelligence and charisma

transformational leaders individuals who produce fundamental changes in how members of a group view themselves and the group

triangular theory of love the idea that a wide variety of love experiences can be understood as combinations of three basic components: intimacy, passion, and commitment

"Type A" coronary-prone behaviour pattern a constellation of characteristics, including impatience, anger, and hostility, that has been linked to heart disease

uncertainty orientation a disposition that represents the extent to which people want to learn new things about themselves and their environment

unilateral conciliatory initiatives actions to reduce conflict that one group takes without any request from the opponent and without any explicit demands for concessions from the opponent

unobtrusive measures assessments that are taken without the realization of participants, thereby minimizing socially desirable responding

upward counterfactual thoughts reflections on how past events might have turned out better

upward social comparison social comparison with people who are better off or more skilled than we are

validity the extent to which a measure really assesses what it is supposed to assess—whether scores on the measure actually reflect the assumed underlying concept

value-expressive function a function of attitudes in which attitudes communicate individuals' identity and values

values broad, abstract standards or goals that people consider to be important guiding principles in their life

violence aggression that is intended to cause extreme injury

violent pornography sexually explicit material that depicts aggressive, hostile sexual activity

volunteerism unpaid helping behaviour that is given willingly to a worthwhile cause or organization

what is beautiful is good the inference that attractive people possess other desirable traits and abilities in addition to their good looks

working model of a close relationship the feelings, thoughts, beliefs, and expectations learned during the course of an infant's first close relationships

References

Aaker, J. L., Benet-Martínez, V., & Garolera, J. (2001). Consumption symbols as carriers of culture: A study of Japanese and Spanish brand personality constructs. *Journal of Personality and Social Psychology, 81,* 492–508.

Abbey, A. (1987). Misperceptions of friendly behaviour as sexual interest: A survey of naturally occurring incidents. *Psychology of Women Quarterly, 11,* 173–194.

Abele, A. E. (2003). The dynamics of masculine-agentic and feminine-communal traits: Findings from a prospective study. *Journal of Personality and Social Psychology, 85,* 768–776.

Abend, T. A., & Williamson, G. M. (2002). Feeling attractive in the wake of breast cancer: Optimism matters, and so do interpersonal relationships. *Personality and Social Psychology Bulletin, 28,* 427–436.

Aberson, C. L., Healy, M., & Romero, V. (2000). Ingroup bias and self-esteem: A meta-analysis. *Personality and Social Psychology Review, 4,* 157–173.

Aboud, F. E., & Doyle, A. B. (1996). Parental and peer influences on children's racial attitudes. *International Journal of Intercultural Relations, 20,* 371–383.

Abrahamson, A. C., Baker, L. A., & Caspi, A. (2002). Rebellious teens? Genetic and environmental influences on the social attitudes of adolescents. *Journal of Personality and Social Psychology, 83,* 1392–1408.

Abrams, D., Ando, K., & Hinkle, S. (1998). Psychological attachment to the group: Cross-cultural differences in organizational identification and subjective norms as predictors of workers' turnover intentions. *Personality and Social Psychology Bulletin, 24,* 1027–1039.

Abramson, L. Y., Metalsky, G. I., & Alloy, L. B. (1989). Hopelessness depression: A theory-based subtype of depression. *Psychological Review, 96,* 358–372.

Ackerman, B. P., Izard, C. E., Schoff, K., Youngstrom, E. A., & Kogos, J. (1999). Contextual risk, caregiver emotionality, and the problem behaviors of six- and seven-year-old children from economically disadvantaged families. *Child Development, 70,* 1415–1427.

Adams, J. S. (1965). Inequity in social exchange. In L. Berkowitz (Ed.), *Advances in experimental social psychology* (Vol. 2, pp. 267–299). New York: Academic Press.

Adams, M., & Adams, J. (1991). Life events, depression, and perceived problem solving alternatives in adolescents. *Journal of Child Psychology and Psychiatry, 32,* 811–820.

Adelman, H. (2000). Rwanda revisited: In search for lessons. *Journal of Genocide Research, 2,* 431–44.

Adelman, H. (2004). The theory and history of genocide. *International History Review, 26,* 89–96.

Adlaf, E. M., & Paglia-Boak, A. (2005). *Drug use among Ontario students 1977–2005. CAMH Research Document Series, No. 17.* Toronto: Centre for Addiction and Mental Health.

Adorno, T. W., Frenkel-Brunswik, E., Levinson, D. J., & Sanford, R. N. (1950). *The authoritarian personality.* New York: Harper.

Ainsworth, M. D. S., Blehar, M. C., Waters, E., & Wall, S. (1978). *Patterns of attachment : A psychological study of the strange situation.* Hillsdale, NJ: Erlbaum.

Ajzen, I. (1985). From actions to intentions: A theory of planned behavior. In J. Kuhl & J. Beckman (Eds.), *Action control: From cognition to behavior* (pp. 11–39). New York: Springer-Verlag.

Ajzen, I. (1991). Theory of planned behavior. *Organizational Behavior and Human Decision Processes, 50,* 179–211.

Ajzen, I., & Fishbein, M. (1977). Attitude-behavior relations: A theoretical analysis and review of empirical research. *Psychological Bulletin, 84,* 888–918.

Ajzen, I., & Fishbein, M. (1980). *Understanding attitudes and predicting social behavior.* Englewood Cliffs, NJ: Prentice-Hall.

Albarracín, D., Johnson, B. T., & Zanna, M. P. (Eds.). (2005) *Handbook of attitudes and attitude change.* Mahwah, NJ: Erlbaum.

Albarracín, D., & Wyer, R. S., Jr. (2000). The cognitive impact of past behavior: Influences on beliefs, attitudes, and future behavioral decisions. *Journal of Personality and Social Psychology, 79,* 5–22.

Alicke, M. D. (1985). Global self-evaluation as determined by the desirability and controllability of trait adjectives. *Journal of Personality and Social Psychology, 3,* 1621–1630.

Alicke, M. D. (2000). Evaluating social comparison targets. In J. Suls & L. Wheeler (Eds.), *Handbook of social comparison: Theory and research* (pp. 271–293). New York: Kluwer Academic/Plenum.

Allen, B. P. (1995). Gender stereotypes are not accurate: A replication of Martin (1987) using diagnostic vs. self-report and behavioral criteria. *Sex Roles, 32,* 583–600.

Allen, M., D'Alessio, D., & Brezgel, K. (1995). A meta-analysis summarizing the effects of pornography: II. Aggression after exposure. *Human Communication Research, 22,* 258–283.

Allen, V. L. (1965). Situational factors in conformity. In L. Berkowitz (Ed.), *Advances in experimental social psychology* (Vol. 2, pp. 133–175). New York: Academic Press.

Allen, V. L. (1975). Social support for nonconformity. In L. Berkowitz (Ed.), *Advances in experimental social psychology* (Vol. 8, pp. 1–43). New York: Academic Press.

Alley, T. R., & Cunningham, M. R. (1991). Averaged faces are attractive, but very attractive faces are not average. *Psychological Science, 2,* 123–125.

Allison, S. T., Messick, D. M., & Goethals, G. R. (1989). On being better but not smarter than others: The Muhammad Ali effect. *Social Cognition, 7,* 275–296.

Allport, G. W. (1935). Attitudes. In C. Murchison (Ed.), *The handbook of social psychology* (pp. 798–844). Worcester, MA: Clark University Press.

Allport, G. W. (1954). *The nature of prejudice.* Reading, MA: Addison-Wesley.

Allport, G. W. (1985). The historical background of social psychology. In G. Lindzey & E. Aronson (Eds.), *The handbook of social psychology* (3rd ed., Vol. 1, pp. 1–46). New York: Random House.

Allport, G. W., & Kramer, B. M. (1946). Some roots of prejudice. *Journal of Psychology, 22,* 9–39.

Altemeyer, B. (1994). Reducing prejudice in right-wing authoritarians. In M. P. Zanna & J. M. Olson (Eds.), *The psychology of prejudice: The Ontario symposium* (Vol. 7, pp. 131–148). Mahwah, NJ: Erlbaum.

Alwin, D. F., Cohen, R. L., & Newcomb, T. M. (1991). *Political attitudes over the life span: The Bennington women after fifty years.* Madison: University of Wisconsin Press.

American Automobile Association. (1997). *Aggressive driving: Three studies.* Washington, DC: American Automobile Association Foundation for Traffic Safety.

American Automobile Association. (1999). *Controlling road rage: A literature review and pilot study.* Washington, DC: American Automobile Association Foundation for Traffic Safety.

American Psychological Association (1997). Learner-centered psychological principles: A framework for school redesign and reform. Available from http://www.apa.org/ed/lcp.html.

American Psychological Association. (2001). *Publication manual of the American Psychological Association* (5th ed.). Washington, DC: American Psychological Association.

Ames, D. R., Flynn, F. J., & Weber, E. U. (2004). It's the thought that counts: On perceiving how helpers decide to lend a hand. *Personality and Social Psychology Bulletin, 30,* 461–474.

Amir, Y. (1969). Contact hypothesis in ethnic relations. *Psychological Bulletin, 71,* 319–341.

Amodio, D. M., Harmon-Jones, E., & Devine, P. G. (2003). Individual differences in the activation and control of affective race bias as assessed by startle eyeblink response and self-report. *Journal of Personality and Social Psychology, 84,* 738–753.

Anderson, C. A. (1989). Temperature and aggression: Ubiquitous effects of heat on occurrence of human violence. *Psychological Bulletin, 106,* 74–96.

Anderson, C. A. (1997). Effects of violent movies and trait hostility on hostile feelings and aggressive thoughts. *Aggressive Behavior, 23,* 161–178

Anderson, C. A., Berkowitz, L., Donnerstein, E., Huesmann, L., Johnson, J. D., Linz, D., et al. (2003). The influence of media violence on youth. *Psychological Science in the Public Interest, 4,* 81–110.

Anderson, C. A., & Bushman, B. J. (2001). Effects of violent video games on aggressive behavior, aggressive cognition, aggressive affect, physiological arousal, and prosocial behavior: A meta-analytic review of the scientific literature. *Psychological Science, 12,* 353–359.

Anderson, C. A., & Bushman, B. J. (2002a). Human aggression. *Annual Review of Psychology, 53,* 27–51.

Anderson, C. A., & Bushman, B. J. (2002b). Media violence and the American public revisited. *American Psychologist, 57,* 448–450.

Anderson, C. A., Bushman, B. J., & Groom, R. W. (1997). Hot years and serious and deadly assault: Empirical tests of the heat hypothesis. *Journal of Personality and Social Psychology, 73,* 1213–1223.

Anderson, C. A., Deuser, W. E., & DeNeve, K. M. (1995). Hot temperatures, hostile affect, hostile cognition, and arousal: Tests of a general model of affective aggression. *Personality and Social Psychology Bulletin, 21,* 434–448.

Anderson, C., John, O. O., Keltner, D., & Kring, A. M. (2001). Who attains social status? Effects of personality and physical attractiveness in social groups. *Journal of Personality and Social Psychology, 81,* 116–132.

Anderson, M. (1994). *Sexual selection.* Princeton, NJ: Princeton University Press.

Antonucci, T. C., & Jackson, J. S. (1990). The role of reciprocity in social support. In I. G. Sarason, B. R. Sarason & G. R. Pierce (Eds.), *Social support: An interactional view* (pp. 173–198). New York: Wiley.

Archer, D. (1997). Unspoken diversity: Cultural differences in gestures. *Qualitative Sociology, 20,* 79–105.

Archer, D. & Akert, R. M. (1977). Words and everything else: Verbal and nonverbal cues in social interpretation. *Journal of Personality and Social Psychology, 35,* 443–449.

Archer, D., & Gartner, R. (1984). *Violence and crime in cross-national perspective.* New Haven, CT: Yale University Press.

Archer, J. (1988). *The behavioural biology of aggression.* Cambridge: Cambridge University Press.

Archer, J. (Ed.). (1994). *Male violence.* New York: Routledge.

Argyle, M., Alkema, F., & Gilmour, R. (1971). The communication of friendly and hostile attitudes by verbal and nonverbal signals. *European Journal of Social Psychology, 1,* 385–402.

Arkes, H. R., Wortmann, R. L., Saville, P. D., & Harkness, A. R. (1981). Hindsight bias among physicians weighing the likelihood of diagnoses. *Journal of Applied Psychology, 66,* 252–254.

Arkin, R. M., & Baumgardner, A. H. (1985). Self-handicapping. In J. H. Harvey & G. Weary (Eds.), *Attribution: Basic issues and applications* (pp. 169–202). New York: Academic Press.

Armitage, C. J., & Conner, M. (2000). Attitude ambivalence: A test of three key hypotheses. *Personality and Social Psychology Bulletin, 26,* 1421–1432.

Arndt, J., Schimel, J., Greenberg, J., & Pyszczynski, T. (2002). The intrinsic self and defensiveness: Evidence that activating the intrinsic self reduces self-handicapping and conformity. *Personality and Social Psychology Bulletin, 28,* 671–683.

Aron, A., Aron, E. N., & Smollan, D. (1992). Inclusion of other in the self scale and the structure of interpersonal closeness. *Journal of Personality and Social Psychology, 63,* 596–612.

Aron, A., Aron, E. N., Tudor, M., & Nelson, G. (1991). Close relationships as including other in the self. *Journal of Personality and Social Psychology, 60,* 241–253.

Aronson, E. (1968). Dissonance theory: Progress and problems. In E. Aronson, R. Abelson, W. McGuire, T. Newcomb, M. Rosenberg, & P. Tannenbaum (Eds.), *Theories of cognitive consistency: A sourcebook* (pp. 5–27). Chicago, IL: Rand McNally.

Aronson, E. (1990). Applying social psychology to desegregation and energy conservation. *Personality and Social Psychology Bulletin, 16,* 118–132.

Aronson, E. (2000). *Nobody left to hate: Teaching compassion after Columbine.* New York: Freeman.

Aronson, E., & Carlsmith, J. M. (1968). Experimentation in social psychology. In G. Lindzey & E. Aronson (Eds.), *The handbook of social psychology* (2nd ed., Vol. 2, pp. 1–79). Reading, MA: Addison-Wesley.

Aronson, E., Ellsworth, P. C., Carlsmith, J. M., & Gonzales, M. H. (1990). *Methods of research in social psychology* (2nd ed.) New York: McGraw-Hill.

Aronson, E., Fried, C. B., & Stone, J. (1991). Overcoming denial and increasing the use of condoms through the induction of hypocrisy. *American Journal of Public Health, 81,* 1636–1638.

Aronson, E., & Mills, J. (1959). The effect of severity of initiation on liking for a group. *Journal of Abnormal and Social Psychology, 59,* 177–181.

Aronson, E., Stephan, C., Sikes, J., Blaney, N., & Snapp, M. (1978). *The jigsaw classroom.* Beverly Hills, CA: Sage.

Aronson, J. (2002a). Stereotype threat: Contending and coping with unnerving expectations. In J. Aronson (Ed.), *Improving academic achievement: Impact of psychological factors on education* (pp. 279–301). New York: Academic Press.

Aronson, J. (Ed.) (2002b). *Improving academic achievement: Impact of psychological factors on education.* New York: Academic Press.

Aronson, J., Lustina, M. J., Good, C., Keough, K., Steele, C. M., & Brown, J. (1999). When White men can't do math: Necessary and sufficient factors in stereotype threat. *Journal of Experimental Social Psychology, 35,* 29–46.

Arrowood, A. J., & Amoroso, D. M. (1965). Social comparison and ordinal position. *Journal of Personality and Social Psychology, 2,* 101–104.

Asch, S. E. (1951). Effects of group pressure upon the modification and distortion of judgments. In H. Guetzkow (Ed.), *Groups, leadership and men* (pp. 177–190). Pittsburgh, PA: Carnegie Press.

Asch, S. E. (1952). *Social psychology.* New York: Prentice-Hall.

Asch, S. E. (1956). Studies of independence and conformity: I. A minority of one against a unanimous majority. *Psychological Monographs: General and Applied, 70*(9), 1–70.

Ashmore, R. D., Deaux, K., & McLaughlin-Volpe, T. (2004). An organizing framework for collective identity: Articulation and significance of multidimensionality. *Psychological Bulletin, 130,* 80–114.

Aspinwall, L. G., Kemeny, M. E., Taylor, S. E., Schneider, S. G., & Dudley, J. P. (1991). Psychosocial predictors of gay men's AIDS risk-reduction behavior. *Health Psychology, 10,* 432–444.

Atkin, C., & Block, M. (1983). Effectiveness of celebrity endorsers. *Journal of Advertising Research, 23*, 57–61.

Attridge, M., Berscheid, E., & Simpson, J. A. (1995). Predicting relationship stability from both partners versus one. *Journal of Personality and Social Psychology, 69*, 254–268.

Atwater, L. E., Carey, J. A., & Waldman, D. A. (2001). Gender and discipline in the workplace: Wait until your father gets home. *Journal of Management, 27*, 537–566.

Ausubel, D. P. (1955). Relationships between shame and guilt in the socializing process. *Psychological Review, 62*, 378–390.

Axsom, D., & Cooper, J. (1985). Cognitive dissonance and psychotherapy: The role of effort justification in inducing weight loss. *Journal of Experimental Social Psychology, 21*, 149–160.

Axtell, R. (1991). *Gestures: The do's and taboos of body language around the world.* New York: Wiley.

Baccus, J. R., Baldwin, M. W., & Packer, D. J. (2004). Increasing implicit self-esteem through classical conditioning. *Psychological Science, 15*, 498–502.

Backer, T. E., Rogers, E. M., & Sopory, P. (1992). *Designing health communication campaigns: What works?* Newbury Park, CA: Sage.

Bailenson, J. N., Blascovich, J., Beall, A. C., & Loomis, J. M. (2003). Interpersonal distance in immersive virtual environments. *Personality and Social Psychology Bulletin, 29*, 819–833.

Bailenson, J. N., & Yee, N. (2005). Digital chameleons: Automatic assimilation of nonverbal gestures in immersive virtual environments. *Psychological Science, 16*, 814–819.

Baldwin, M. W. (1992). Relational schemas and the processing of social information. *Psychological Bulletin, 112*, 461–484.

Baldwin, M. W. (Ed.). (2005). *Interpersonal cognition.* New York: Guilford.

Baldwin, M. W., & Dandeneau, S. D. (2005). Understanding and modifying the relational schemas underlying insecurity. In M. W. Baldwin (Ed.), *Interpersonal cognition* (pp. 33–61). New York: Guilford.

Baldwin, M. W., Fehr, B., Keedian, E., Seidel, M., & Thomson, D. W. (1993). An exploration of the relational schema underlying attachment styles: Self-report and the lexical decision approaches. *Personality and Social Psychology Bulletin, 19*, 746–754.

Baldwin, M. W., & Meunier, J. (1999). The cued activation of attachment relational schemas. *Social Cognition, 17*, 209–227.

Baldwin, M. W., & Sinclair, L. (1996). Self-esteem and "if . . . then" contingencies of interpersonal acceptance. *Journal of Personality and Social Psychology, 71*, 1130–1141.

Bales, R. F., & Slater, P. (1955). Role differentiation in small decision-making groups. In T. Parsons & R. F. Bales (Eds.), *The family, socialization, and interaction processes* (pp. 259–306). Glencoe, IL: Free Press.

Banaji, M. R., & Greenwald, A. G. (1994). Implicit stereotypes and prejudice. In M. P. Zanna & J. M. Olson (Eds.), *The psychology of prejudice: The Ontario symposium* (pp. 55–76). Hillsdale, NJ: Erlbaum.

Bandura, A. (1973). *Aggression: A social learning analysis.* Englewood Cliffs, NJ: Prentice-Hall.

Bandura, A. (1977). Self-efficacy: Toward a unifying theory of behavior change. *Psychological Review, 84*, 191–215.

Bandura, A. (1986). *Social foundations of thought and action.* Englewood Cliffs, NJ: Prentice-Hall.

Bandura, A. (1991). Human agency in social cognitive theory. *American Psychologist, 44*, 1175–1184.

Bandura, A., Ross, D., & Ross, S. (1963). Imitation of film-mediated aggressive models. *Journal of Abnormal and Social Psychology, 66*, 3–11.

Bandura, A., & Walters, R. H. (1963). *Social learning and personality development.* New York: Holt, Rinehart, and Winston.

Bank, B. J., & Hansford, S. L. (2000). Gender and friendship: Why are men's best same-sex friendships less intimate and supportive? *Personal Relationships, 7*, 1–23.

Barden, J., Maddux, W. W., Petty, R. E., & Brewer, M. B. (2004). Contextual moderation of racial bias: The impact of social roles on controlled and automatically activated attitudes. *Journal of Personality and Social Psychology, 87*, 5–22.

Barefoot, J. C. (1992). Developments in the measurement of hostility. In H. S. Friedman (Ed.), *Hostility, coping and health* (pp. 13–31). Washington, DC: American Psychological Association.

Bargh, J. A. (1994). The four horsemen of automaticity: Awareness, intention, efficiency, and control in social cognition. In R. S. Wyer, Jr., & T. K. Srull (Eds.), *Handbook of social cognition: Vol 1. Basic processes* (2nd ed., pp. 1–40). Hillsdale, NJ: Erlbaum.

Bargh, J. A., Bond, R. N., Lombardi, W. L., & Tota, M. E. (1986). The additive nature of chronic and temporary sources of construct accessibility. *Journal of Personality and Social Psychology, 50*, 869–879.

Bargh, J. A., & Pietromonaco, P. (1982). Automatic information processing and social perception: The influence of trait information presented outside of conscious awareness on impression formation. *Journal of Personality and Social Psychology, 43*, 437–449.

Bar-On, D. (2001). The bystander in relation to the victim and the perpetrator: Today and during the Holocaust. *Social Justice Research, 14*, 125–148.

Baron, R. A. (1979). Aggression and heat: The "long hot summer" revisited. In A. Baum, J. E. Singer, & S. Valins (Eds.), *Advances in environmental psychology* (pp. 57–84). Hillsdale, NJ: Erlbaum.

Baron, R. A., & Richardson, D. (1994). *Human aggression.* New York: Plenum Press.

Baron, R. S. (2000). Arousal, capacity, and intense indoctrination. *Personality and Social Psychology Review, 4*, 238–254.

Baron, R. S., Logan, H., Lilly, J., Inman, M., & Brennan, M. (1994). Negative emotion and message processing. *Journal of Experimental Social Psychology, 30*, 181–201.

Baron, R. S., Moore, D., & Sanders, G. S. (1978). Distraction as a source of drive in social facilitation research. *Journal of Personality and Social Psychology, 36*, 816–824.

Baron, R. S., Vandello, J. A., & Brunsman, B. (1996). The forgotten variable in conformity research: Impact of task importance on social influence. *Journal of Personality and Social Psychology, 71*, 915–927.

Barrera, M., Jr. (1981). Social support in the adjustment of pregnant adolescents: Assessment issues. In B. H. Gottlieb (Ed.), *Social networks and social support* (pp. 69–96). Beverly Hills, CA: Sage.

Barrera, M., Jr., Sandler, I. N., & Ramsay, T. B. (1981). Preliminary development of a scale of social support: Studies on college students. *American Journal of Community Psychology, 9*, 435–447.

Barrett, L., Dunbar, R., & Lycett, J. (2002). *Human evolutionary psychology.* Princeton, NJ: Princeton University Press.

Bar-Tal, D. (1990). Causes and consequences of delegitimization: Models of conflict and ethnocentrism. *Journal of Social Issues, 46*(1), 65–81.

Bar-Tal, D. (2000). From intractable conflict through conflict resolution to reconciliation: Psychological analysis. *Political Psychology, 21*, 351–365.

Bartholomew, K. (1990). Avoidance of intimacy: An attachment perspective. *Journal of Social and Personal Relationships, 7*, 147–178.

Bartholomew, K., & Horowitz, L. M. (1991). Attachment styles among young adults: A test of a four-category model. *Journal of Personality and Social Psychology, 61*, 226–244.

Bartholow, B. D., Anderson, C. A., Carnagey, N. L., & Benjamin, A. J., Jr. (2005). Interactive effects of life experience and situational cues on aggression: The weapons priming effect in hunters and nonhunters. *Journal of Experimental Social Psychology, 41,* 48–60.

Bass, B. M., & Avolio, B. J. (1993). Transformational leadership: A response to critiques. In M. M. Chemers & R. Ayman (Eds.), *Leadership theory and research: Perspectives and directions* (pp. 49–80). San Diego, CA: Academic Press.

Bassili, J. N. (1996). Meta-judgmental versus operative indexes of psychological attributes: The case of measures of attitude strength. *Journal of Personality and Social Psychology, 71,* 637–653.

Bassili, J. N. (2003). The minority slowness effect: Subtle inhibitions in the expression of views not shared by others. *Journal of Personality and Social Psychology, 84,* 261–276.

Bassili, J. N., & Brown, R. D. (2005). Implicit and explicit attitudes: Research, challenges, and theory. In D. Albarracin, B. T. Johnson, & M. P. Zanna (Eds.), *The handbook of attitudes* (pp. 543–574). Mahwah, NJ: Erlbaum.

Bassili, J. N., & Smith, M. C. (1986). On the spontaneity of trait attribution: Converging evidence for the role of cognitive strategy. *Journal of Personality and Social Psychology, 50,* 239–245.

Batson, C. D. (1991). *The altruism question: Toward a social-psychological answer.* Hillsdale, NJ: Erlbaum.

Batson, C. D. (1998). Altruism and prosocial behavior. In D. T. Gilbert, S. T. Fiske, & G. Lindzey (Eds.), *The handbook of social psychology* (Vol. 2, 4th ed., pp. 317–356). Boston, MA: McGraw-Hill.

Batson, C. D., Chang, J., Orr, R., & Rowland, J. (2002). Empathy, attitudes, and action: Can feeling for a member of a stigmatized group motivate one to help the group? *Personality and Social Psychology Bulletin, 28,* 1656–1666.

Batson, C. D., Duncan, B. D., Ackerman, P., Buckley, T., & Birch, K. (1981). Is empathic emotion a source of altruistic motivation? *Journal of Personality and Social Psychology, 40,* 290–302.

Batson, C. D., Lishner, D. A., Carpenter, A., Dulin, L., Harjusola-Webb, S., Stocks, E. L., Gale, S., Hassan, O., & Sampat, B. (2003). "... As you would have them do unto you": Does imagining yourself in the other's place stimulate moral action? *Personality and Social Psychology Bulletin, 29,* 1190–1201.

Batson, C. D., O'Quin, K., Fultz, J., Vanderplas, M., & Isen, A. M. (1983). Influence of self-reported distress and empathy on egoistic versus altruistic motivation to help. *Journal of Personality and Social Psychology, 45,* 706–718.

Baumann, D. J., Cialdini, R. B., & Kenrick, D. T. (1981). Altruism as hedonism: Helping and self-gratification as equivalent responses. *Journal of Personality and Social Psychology, 40,* 1039–1046.

Baumeister, R. F. (1982). A self-presentational view of social phenomena. *Psychological Bulletin, 91,* 3–26.

Baumeister, R. F. (1997). *Evil: Inside human violence and cruelty.* New York: Freeman.

Baumeister, R. F. (1998). The self. In D. T. Gilbert, S. T. Fiske, & G. Lindzey (Eds.), *Handbook of social psychology* (4th ed., Vol. 1, pp. 680–740). New York: McGraw-Hill.

Baumeister, R. F., Bushman, B. J., & Campbell, W. K. (2000). Self-esteem, narcissism, and aggression: Does violence result from low self-esteem or from threatened egotism? *Current Directions in Psychological Science, 9,* 26–29.

Baumeister, R. F., & Leary, M. R. (1995). The need to belong: Desire for interpersonal attachments as a fundamental human motivation. *Psychological Bulletin, 117,* 497–529.

Baumeister, R. F., Smart, L., & Boden, J. M. (1996). Relation of threatened egotism to violence and aggression: The dark side of high self-esteem. *Psychological Review, 103,* 5–33.

Baumeister, R. F., & Twenge, J. M. (2003). The social self. In T. Millon & M. J. Lerner (Eds.), *Handbook of psychology: Personality and social psychology* (Vol. 5, pp. 327–352). Hoboken, NJ: Wiley.

Baumgardner, A. H. (1990). To know oneself is to like oneself: Self-certainty and self-affect. *Journal of Personality and Social Psychology, 58,* 1062–1072.

Baumrind, D. (1964). Some thoughts on the ethics of research: After reading Milgram's "Behavioral study of obedience." *American Psychologist, 19,* 421–423.

Beach, S. R. H., & Tesser, A. (2000). Self-evaluation maintenance and evolution. In J. M. Suls & L. Wheeler (Eds.) *Handbook of social comparison: Theory and research* (pp. 123–140). New York: Kluwer Academic/Plenum.

Beaman, A. L., Cole, C. M., Preston, M., Klentz, B., & Steblay, N. M. (1983). Fifteen years of foot-in-the-door research: A meta-analysis. *Personality and Social Psychology Bulletin, 9,* 181–196.

Beaton, A. M., Tougas, F., & Joly, S. (1996). Neosexism among male managers: Is it a matter of numbers? *Journal of Applied Social Psychology, 26,* 2189–2203.

Becker, E. (1962). *The birth and death of meaning.* New York: Free Press.

Bem, D. J. (1967). Self-perception: An alternative interpretation of cognitive dissonance phenomena. *Psychological Review, 74,* 183–200.

Bem, D. J. (1972). Self-perception theory. In L. Berkowitz (Ed.), *Advances in experimental social psychology* (Vol. 6, pp. 1–62). New York: Academic Press.

Bem, S. L. (1981). *Bem Sex Role Inventory professional manual.* Stanford, CA: Consulting Psychologists Press.

Bem, S. L. (1984). Androgyny and gender schema theory: A conceptual and empirical integration. In T. B. Sonderegger (Ed.), *Nebraska symposium on motivation: Psychology and gender* (Vol. 32, pp. 179–226). Lincoln: University of Nebraska Press.

Benjamin, L. T., Cavell, T. A., & Shallenberger, W. R. (1984). Staying with initial answers on objective tests: Is it a myth? *Teaching of Psychology, 11,* 133–141.

Benoit, W. L., & Strathman, A. (2004). Source credibility and the elaboration likelihood model. In J. S. Seiter & R. H. Gass (Eds.), *Perspectives on persuasion, social influence, and compliance gaining* (pp. 95–111). Boston, MA: Pearson Education.

Bensley, L., & Van Eenwyk, J. (2001). Video games and real-life violence: Review of the literature. *Journal of Adolescent Health, 29,* 244–257.

Berg, K. S., & Vidmar, N. (1975). Authoritarianism and recall of evidence about criminal behavior. *Journal of Research in Personality, 9,* 147–157.

Bergen, D. J., & Williams, J. E. (1991). Sex stereotypes in the United States revisited: 1972–1988. *Sex Roles, 24,* 413–423.

Berglas, S., & Jones, E. E. (1978). Drug choice as a self-handicapping strategy in response to non-contingent success. *Journal of Personality and Social Psychology, 36,* 405–417.

Berkman, L. F., & Syme, S. L. (1979). Social networks, host resistance, and mortality: A nine-year follow-up study of Alameda County residents. *American Journal of Epidemiology, 109,* 186–204.

Berkowitz, L. (1962). *Aggression: A social psychological analysis.* New York: McGraw-Hill.

Berkowitz, L. (1972). Social norms, feelings, and other factors affecting helping and altruism. In L. Berkowitz (Ed.), *Advances in experimental social psychology* (Vol. 6, pp. 63–108). New York: Academic Press.

Berkowitz, L. (1989). Frustration-aggression hypothesis: Examination and reformulation. *Psychological Bulletin, 106,* 59–73.

Berkowitz, L. (1990). On the formation and regulation of anger and aggression: A cognitive-neoassociationistic analysis. *American Psychologist, 45,* 494–503.

Berkowitz, L. (1993). *Aggression: Its causes, consequences, and control.* New York: McGraw-Hill.

Berkowitz, L., & Heimer, K. (1989). On the construction of the anger experience: Aversive events and negative priming in the formation of feelings. In L. Berkowitz (Ed.), *Advances in experimental psychology* (Vol. 22, pp. 1–37). San Diego, CA: Academic Press.

Berkowitz, L., & LePage, A. (1967). Weapons as Aggression-Eliciting Stimuli. *Journal of Personality and Social Psychology, 7*, 202–207.

Berndt, T. J. (1979). Developmental changes in conformity to peers and parents. *Developmental Psychology, 15*, 608–616.

Bernstein, D. M., Atance, C., Loftus, G. R., & Meltzoff, A. (2004). We saw it all along: Visual hindsight bias in children and adults. *Psychological Science, 15*, 264–267.

Bernstein, I. H., Lin, T., & McClellan, P. (1982). Cross- vs. within-racial judgments of attractiveness. *Perception and Psychophysics, 32*, 495–503.

Berry, J. W. (1997). Immigration, acculturation and adaptation. *Applied Psychology: An International Review, 46*, 5–34.

Berry, J. W. (2005). Acculturation: Living successfully in two cultures. *International Journal of Intercultural Relations, 29*, 697–712.

Berscheid, E., Graziano, W., Monson, T., & Dermer, M. (1976). Outcome dependency: Attention, attribution, and attraction. *Journal of Personality and Social Psychology, 34*, 978–989.

Berscheid, E., & Reis, H. T. (1998). Attraction and close relationships. In D. T. Gilbert, S. T. Fiske, & G. Lindzey (Eds.), *Handbook of social psychology* (4th ed., Vol. 2, pp. 193–281). New York: McGraw-Hill.

Berscheid, E., Snyder, M., & Omoto, A. (1989). The relationship closeness inventory: Assessing the closeness of interpersonal relationships. *Journal of Personality and Social Psychology, 57*, 792–807.

Berscheid, E., & Walster, E. (1974). Physical attractiveness. In L. Berkowitz (Ed.), *Advances in experimental social psychology* (Vol. 7, pp. 157–215). New York: Academic Press.

Bettencourt, B. A., Brewer, M. B., Croak, M. R., & Miller, N. (1992). Cooperation and the reduction of intergroup bias: The role of reward structure and social orientation. *Journal of Experimental Social Psychology, 28*, 301–319.

Bettencourt, B., & Kernahan, C. (1997). A meta-analysis of aggression in the presence of violent cues: Effects of gender differences and aversive provocation. *Aggressive Behavior, 23*, 447–456.

Bickman, L. (1974). The social power of a uniform. *Journal of Applied Social Psychology, 4*, 47–61.

Bierman, K. L., Smoot, D. L., & Aumiller, K. (1993). Characteristics of aggressive-rejected, aggressive (nonrejected), and rejected (nonaggressive) boys. *Child Development, 64*, 139–151.

Birnbaum, M. H. (Ed.). (2000). *Psychological experiments on the Internet*. San Diego, CA: Academic Press.

Birnbaum, M. H. (2001). *Introduction to behavioral research on the Internet*. Upper Saddle River, NJ: Prentice Hall.

Bizer, G. Y., & Krosnick, J. A. (2001). Exploring the structure of strength-related features: The relation between attitude importance and attitude accessibility. *Journal of Personality and Social Psychology, 81*, 566–586.

Bjorkvist, K., Osterman, K., & Lagerspetz, K. M. J. (1994). Sex differences in covert aggression among adults. *Aggressive Behavior, 20*, 27–33.

Blaine, B., & Crocker, J. (1993). Self-esteem and self-serving biases in reactions to positive and negative events: An integrative review. In R. F. Baumeister (Ed.), *Self-esteem: The puzzle of low self-regard* (pp. 55–85). New York: Plenum.

Blair, I. V. (2001). Implicit stereotypes and prejudice. In G. B. Moskowitz (Ed.), *Cognitive social psychology: The Princeton Symposium on the legacy and future of social cognition* (pp. 359–374). Mahwah, NJ: Erlbaum.

Blair, I. V. (2002). The malleability of automatic stereotypes and prejudice. *Personality and Social Psychology Review, 6*, 242–261.

Blair, I. V., Ma, J. E., & Lenton, A. P. (2001). Imagining stereotypes away: The moderation of implicit stereotypes through mental imagery. *Journal of Personality and Social Psychology, 81*, 828–841.

Blair, M. E., & Shimp, T. A. (1992). Consequences of an unpleasant experience with music: A second-order negative conditioning perspective. *Journal of Advertising, 21*, 35–44.

Blanchard, F. A., Lilly, T., & Vaughn, L. A. (1991). Reducing the expression of racial prejudice. *Psychological Science, 2*, 101–105.

Blanton, H., Cooper, J., Skurnik, I., & Aronson, J. (1997). When bad things happen to good feedback: Exacerbating the need for self-justification with self-affirmations. *Personality and Social Psychology Bulletin, 23*, 684–692.

Blascovich, J., Ginsburg, G. P., & Veach, T. L. (1975). A pluralistic explanation of choice shifts on the risk dimension. *Journal of Personality and Social Psychology, 31*, 422–429.

Blascovich, J., Loomis, J., Beall, A. C., Swinth, K. R., Hoyt, C. L., & Bailenson, J. N. (2001). Immersive virtual environment technology as a methodological tool for social psychology. *Psychological Inquiry, 13*, 103–124.

Blascovich, J., Mendes, W. B., Hunter, S. B., & Salomon, K. (1999). Social "facilitation" as challenge and threat. *Journal of Personality and Social Psychology, 77*, 68–77.

Blass, T. (1991). Understanding behavior in the Milgram obedience experiment: The role of personality, situations, and their interactions. *Journal of Personality and Social Psychology, 60*, 398–413.

Bless, H. (2001). Mood and the use of general knowledge structures. In L. L. Martin & G. L. Clore (Eds.), *Theories of mood and cognition: A user's guidebook* (pp. 9–26). Mahwah, NJ: Erlbaum.

Blumstein, P., & Schwartz, P. (1983). *American couples*. New York: William Morrow.

Bochner, S., & Insko, C. A. (1966). Communicator discrepancy, source credibility, and attitude change. *Journal of Personality and Social Psychology, 4*, 614–621.

Bodenhausen, G. V. (1988). Stereotypic biases in social decision making and memory: Testing process models of stereotype use. *Journal of Personality and Social Psychology, 55*, 726–737.

Bodenhausen, G. V., Kramer, G. P., & Susser, K. (1994). Happiness and stereotypic thinking in social judgment. *Journal of Personality and Social Psychology, 66*, 621–632.

Bolger, N., Foster, M., Vinokur, A. D., & Ng, R. (1996). Close relationships and adjustments to a life crisis: The case of breast cancer. *Journal of Personality and Social Psychology, 70*, 283–294.

Bolger, N., Zuckerman, A., & Kessler, R. C. (2000). Invisible support and adjustment to stress. *Journal of Personality and Social Psychology, 79*, 953–961.

Bonanno, G. A., Field, N. P., Kovacevic, A., & Kaltman, S. (2002). Self-enhancement as a buffer against extreme adversity: Civil war in Bosnia and traumatic loss in the United States. *Personality and Social Psychology Bulletin, 28*, 184–196.

Bond, C. F., & Titus, L. J. (1983). Social facilitation: A meta-analysis of 241 studies. *Psychological Bulletin, 94*, 265–292.

Bond, R., & Smith, P. B. (1996). Culture and conformity: A meta-analysis of studies using Asch's (1952b, 1956) line judgment task. *Psychological Bulletin, 119*, 111–137.

Book, A. S., Starzyk, K. B., & Quinsey, V. L. (2001). The relationship between testosterone and aggression: A meta-analysis. *Aggression and Violent Behaviour, 6*, 579–599.

Boon, S. D., & Griffin, D. W. (1996). The construction of risk in relationships: The role of framing in decisions about intimate relationships. *Personal Relationships, 3*, 293–306.

Boon, S. D., & Lomore, C. D. (2001). Admirer-celebrity relationships among young adults: Explaining perceptions of celebrity influence on identity. *Human Communication Research, 27*, 432–465.

Boon, S. D., & Miller, J. R. (1999). Exploring the links between interpersonal trust and the reasons underlying gay and bisexual males' disclosure of their sexual orientation to their mothers. *Journal of Homosexuality, 37*(3), 45–68.

Booth-Kewley, S., & Friedman, H. S. (1987). Psychological predictors of heart disease: A quantitative review. *Psychological Bulletin, 101,* 343–362.

Bornstein, R. F. (1989). Exposure and affect: Overview and meta-analysis of research, 1968–1987. *Psychological Bulletin, 106,* 265–289.

Bornstein, R. F., & D'Agostino, P. R. (1992). Stimulus recognition and the mere exposure effect. *Journal of Personality and Social Psychology, 63,* 545–552.

Bosson, J. K., Haymovitz, E. L., & Pinel, E. C. (2004). When saying and doing converge: The effects of stereotype threat on self-reported versus nonverbal anxiety. *Journal of Experimental Social Psychology, 40,* 247–255.

Bourhis, R. Y. (1994). Power, gender, and intergroup discrimination: Some minimal group experiments. In M. P. Zanna & J. M. Olson (Eds.), *The psychology of prejudice: The Ontario symposium* (Vol. 7, pp. 171–208). Hillsdale, NJ: Erlbaum.

Bower, G. H. (1981). Mood and memory. *American Psychologist, 36,* 129–148.

Bowers, K. S., & Farvolden, P. (1996). Revisiting a century-old Freudian slip: From suggestion disavowed to the truth repressed. *Psychological Bulletin, 119,* 355–380.

Bowlby, J. (1969). *Attachment and loss.* New York: Basic Books.

Brandon, R., & Davies, C. (1973). *Wrongful imprisonment.* London: Allen & Unwin.

Branscombe, N. R., Schmitt, M. T., & Harvey, R. D. (1999). Perceiving pervasive discrimination among African Americans: Implications for group identification and well-being. *Journal of Personality and Social Psychology, 77,* 135–149.

Brauer, M., Judd, C. M., & Gliner, M. D. (1995). The effects of repeated attitude expressions on attitude polarization during group discussions. *Journal of Personality and Social Psychology, 68,* 1014–1029.

Brauer, M., Judd, C. M., & Jacquelin, V. (2001). The communication of social stereotypes: The effects of group discussion and information distribution on stereotypic appraisals. *Journal of Personality and Social Psychology, 81,* 463–475.

Bray, R. M., & Noble, A. M. (1987). Authoritarianism and decisions of mock juries: Evidence of jury bias and group polarization. In L. S. Wrightsman, S. M. Kassin, & C. E. Willis (Eds.), *In the jury box: Controversies in the courtroom* (pp. 83–94). Thousand Oaks, CA: Sage.

Breckler, S. J. (1984). Empirical validation of affect, behavior, and cognition as distinct components of attitude. *Journal of Personality and Social Psychology, 47,* 1191–1205.

Breckler, S. J., & Wiggins, E. C. (1989). Affect versus evaluation in the structure of attitudes. *Journal of Experimental Social Psychology, 25,* 253–271.

Brehm, J. W. (1956). Post-decision changes in desirability of alternatives. *Journal of Abnormal and Social Psychology, 52,* 384–389.

Brendl, C. M., Markman, A. B., & Messner, C. (2001). How do indirect measures of evaluation work? Evaluating the inference of prejudice in the Implicit Association Test. *Journal of Personality and Social Psychology, 81,* 760–773.

Brescoll, V., & LaFrance, M. (2004). The correlates and consequences of newspaper reports of research on sex differences. *Psychological Science, 15,* 515–520.

Brewer, M. B. (1991). The social self: On being the same and different at the same time. *Personality and Social Psychology Bulletin, 17,* 475–482.

Brewer, M. B. (1993). Social identity, distinctiveness, and in-group homogeneity. *Social Cognition, 11,* 150–164.

Brewer, M. B., & Brown, R. J. (1998). Intergroup relations. In D. T. Gilbert, S. T. Fiske, & G. Lindzey (Eds.), *Handbook of social psychology* (4th ed., Vol. 2, pp. 554–594). Boston, MA: McGraw-Hill.

Brewer, M. B., & Miller, N. (1984). Beyond the contact hypothesis: Theoretical perspectives on desegregation. In N. Miller & M. B. Brewer (Eds.), *Groups in contact: The psychology of desegregation* (pp. 281–302). New York: Academic Press.

Brickner, M. A., Harkins, S. G., & Ostrom, T. M. (1986). Effects of personal involvement: Thought-provoking implications for social loafing. *Journal of Personality and Social Psychology, 51,* 763–769.

Brigham, J. C. (1990). Target person distinctiveness and attractiveness as moderator variables in the confidence-accuracy relationship in eyewitness identifications. *Basic and Applied Social Psychology, 11,* 101–115.

Brindberg, D., & Durand, J. (1983). Eating at fast-food restaurants: An analysis using two behavioral intention models. *Journal of Applied Social Psychology, 13,* 459–472.

Brinthaupt, T. M., Moreland, R. L., & Levine, J. M. (1991). Sources of optimism among prospective group members. *Personality and Social Psychology Bulletin, 17,* 36–43.

Brockner, J., & Swap, W. C. (1976). Effects of repeated exposure and attitudinal similarity on self-disclosure and interpersonal attraction. *Journal of Personality and Social Psychology, 33,* 531–540.

Brosius, H., & Engel, D. (1996). The causes of third-person effects: Unrealistic optimism, impersonal contact, or generalized negative attitudes toward media influence? *International Journal of Public Opinion Research, 8,* 142–162.

Brown, B. R. (1968). The effects of need to maintain face on interpersonal bargaining. *Journal of Experimental Social Psychology, 4,* 107–122.

Brown, J. D. (1986). Evaluations of self and others: Self-enhancement biases in social judgments. *Social Cognition, 4,* 353–376.

Brown, L. S. (1997). The private practice of subversion: Psychology as tikkun olam. *American Psychologist, 52,* 449–462.

Brown, R. J. (1988). *Group processes: Dynamics within and between groups.* Oxford, UK: Blackwell.

Brown, R. P., & Pinel, E. C. (2003). Stigma on my mind: Individual differences in the experience of stereotype threat. *Journal of Experimental Social Psychology, 39,* 626–633.

Brownstein, R. J., & Katzev, R. D. (1985). The relative effectiveness of three compliance techniques in eliciting donations to a cultural organization. *Journal of Applied Social Psychology, 15,* 564–574.

Bruner, J. S. (1957). Going beyond the information given. In H. Gruber, G. Terrell, & M. Wertheimer (Eds.), *Contemporary approaches to cognition* (pp. 41–69). Cambridge, MA: Harvard University Press.

Bryan, J. H., & Test, M. A. (1967). Models and helping: Naturalistic studies in aiding behavior. *Journal of Personality and Social Psychology, 6,* 400–407.

Brym, R. J., & Lenton, R. L. (2001). *Love online: A report on digital dating in Canada.* Toronto, ON: MSN.CA.

Buckhout, R. (1974). Eyewitness testimony. *Scientific American, 231,* 23–31.

Buehler, R., & Griffin, D. (2003). Planning, personality, and prediction: The role of future focus in optimistic time predictions. *Organizational Behavior and Human Decision Processes, 92,* 80–90.

Buehler, R., Griffin, D., & MacDonald, H. (1997). The role of motivated reasoning in optimistic time predictions. *Personality and Social Psychology Bulletin, 23,* 238–247.

Buehler, R., Griffin, D., & Ross, M. (1994). Exploring the "planning fallacy": Why people underestimate their task completion times. *Journal of Personality and Social Psychology, 67,* 366–381.

Buehler, R., Griffin, D., & Ross, M. (2002). Inside the planning fallacy: The causes and consequences of optimistic time predictions. In T. Gilovich, D. Griffin, & D. Kahneman (Eds.),

Heuristics and biases: The psychology of intuitive judgment (pp. 250–270). Cambridge, UK: Cambridge University Press.

Burger, J. M. (1999). The foot-in-the-door compliance procedure: A multiple-process analysis and review. *Personality and Social Psychology Review, 3,* 303–325.

Burger, J. M., & Cornelius, T. (2003). Raising the price of agreement: Public commitment and the lowball compliance procedure. *Journal of Applied Social Psychology, 33,* 923–934.

Burger, J. M., Messian, N., Patel, S., del Prado, A., & Anderson, C. (2004). What a coincidence! The effects of incidental similarity on compliance. *Personality and Social Psychology Bulletin, 30,* 35–43.

Burger, J. M., Soroka. S., Gonzago, K., Murphy, E., & Somervell, E. (2001). The effect of fleeting attraction on compliance to requests. *Personality and Social Psychology Bulletin, 27,* 1578–1586.

Burgoon, J. K., Bonito, J. A., Ramirez, A., Dunbar, N. E., Kam, K., & Fischer, J. (2002). Testing the interactivity principle: Effects of mediation, propinquity, and verbal and nonverbal modalities in interpersonal interaction. *Journal of Communication, 52,* 657–677.

Burn, S. M. (2004). *Groups: Theory and practice.* Belmont, CA: Thomson/Wadsworth.

Burnstein, E., Crandall, C., & Kitayama, S. (1994). Some neo-Darwinian decision rules for altruism: Weighing cues for inclusive fitness as a function of the biological importance of the decision. *Journal of Personality and Social Psychology, 67,* 773–789.

Bushman, B. J. (1996). Individual differences in the extent and development of aggressive cognitive-associative networks. *Personality and Social Psychology Bulletin, 22,* 811–819.

Bushman, B. J. (2002). Does venting anger feed or extinguish the flame? Catharsis, rumination, distraction, anger and aggressive responding. *Personality and Social Psychology Bulletin, 28,* 724–731.

Bushman, B. J., & Anderson, C. A. (2001a). Is it time to pull the plug on the hostile versus instrumental aggression dichotomy? *Psychological Review, 108,* 273–279.

Bushman, B. J., & Anderson, C. A. (2001b). Media violence and the American public: Scientific facts versus media misinformation. *American Psychologist, 56,* 477–489.

Bushman, B. J., & Baumeister, R. F. (1998). Threatened egotism, narcissism, self-esteem, and direct and displaced aggression: Does self-love or self-hate lead to violence? *Journal of Personality and Social Psychology, 75,* 219–229.

Bushman, B. J., Baumeister, R. F., & Stack, A. D. (1999). Catharsis, aggression, and persuasive influence: Self-fulfilling or self-defeating prophecies? *Journal of Personality and Social Psychology, 76,* 367–376.

Bushman, B. J., & Bonacci, A. M. (2004). You've got mail: Using e-mail to examine the effect of prejudiced attitudes on discrimination against Arabs. *Journal of Experimental Social Psychology, 40,* 753–759.

Bushman, B. J., & Cooper, H. M. (1990). Effects of alcohol on human aggression: An integrative research review. *Psychological Bulletin, 107,* 341–354.

Buss, A. H. (1961). *The psychology of aggression.* New York: Wiley.

Buss, A. H., & Perry, M. (1992). The aggression questionnaire. *Journal of Personality and Social Psychology, 63,* 452–459.

Buss, D. M. (1989). Sex differences in human mate preferences: Evolutionary hypotheses tested in 37 cultures. *Behavioral and Brain Sciences, 12,* 1–49.

Buss, D. M. (1996). The evolutionary psychology of human social strategies. In E. T. Higgins & A. W. Kruglanski (Eds.), *Social psychology: Handbook of basic principles* (pp. 3–38). New York: Guilford.

Buss, D. M. (1999). *Evolutionary psychology: The new science of the mind.* Boston, MA: Allyn & Bacon.

Buss, D. M., & Kenrick, D. T. (1998). Evolutionary social psychology. In D. T. Gilbert, S. T. Fiske, & G. Lindzey (Eds.), *The handbook of social psychology* (4th ed., Vol. 2, pp. 982–1026). Boston: McGraw-Hill.

Button, C. M., Grant, M. J., Hannah, T. E., & Ross, A. S. (1993). The dimensions underlying perceived attitudes: Liberalism and concern for traditional values. *Canadian Journal of Behavioural Science, 25,* 230–252.

Buunk, B. P. (1995). Comparison direction and comparison dimension among disabled individuals: Toward a refined conceptualization of social comparison under stress. *Personality and Social Psychology Bulletin, 21,* 316–330.

Buunk, B. P., Oldersma, F. L., & de Dreu, C. K. W. (2001). Enhancing satisfaction through downward comparison: The role of relational discontent and individual differences in social comparison orientation. *Journal of Experimental Social Psychology, 37,* 452–467.

Byrne, D. E. (1971). *The attraction paradigm.* New York: Academic Press.

Byrne, D. E., & Clore, G. L. (1966). Predicting interpersonal attraction toward strangers presented in three different stimulus modes. *Psychonomic Science, 4*(6), 239–240.

Cacioppo, J. T. (2002). Social neuroscience: Understanding the pieces fosters understanding the whole and vice versa. *American Psychologist, 57,* 819–831.

Cacioppo, J. T. (2004). Common sense, intuition, and theory in personality and social psychology. *Personality and Social Psychology Review, 8,* 114–122.

Cacioppo, J. T., Berntson, G. G., Adolphs, R., Carter, C. S., Davidson, R. J., McClintock, M., et al. (Eds.). (2002). *Foundations in social neuroscience.* Cambridge, MA: MIT Press.

Cacioppo, J. T., Berntson, G. G., Sheridan, J. F., & McClintock, M. (2000). Multilevel integrative analyses of human behavior: Social neuroscience and the complementing nature of social and biological approaches. *Psychological Bulletin, 126,* 829–843.

Cacioppo, J. T., Bush, L. K., & Tassinary, L. G. (1992). Microexpressive facial actions as a function of affective stimuli: Replication and extension. *Personality and Social Psychology Bulletin, 18,* 515–526.

Cacioppo, J. T., Marshall-Goodell, B. S., Tassinary, L. G., & Petty, R. E. (1992). Rudimentary determinants of attitudes: Classical conditioning is more effective when prior knowledge about the attitude stimulus is low rather than high. *Journal of Experimental Social Psychology, 28,* 207–233.

Cacioppo, J. T., Martzke, J. S., Petty, R. E., & Tassinary, L. G. (1988). Specific forms of facial EMG response index emotions during an interview: From Darwin to the continuous flow hypothesis of affect-laden information processing. *Journal of Personality and Social Psychology, 54,* 592–604.

Cacioppo, J. T., & Petty, R. E. (1985). Central and peripheral routes to persuasion: The role of message repetition. In L. F. Alwitt & A. A. Mitchell (Eds.), *Psychological processes and advertising effects* (pp. 91–111). Hillsdale, NJ: Erlbaum.

Cacioppo, J. T., Petty, R. E., Losch, M. E., & Kim, H. S. (1986). Electromyographic activity over facial muscle regions can differentiate the valence and intensity of affective reactions. *Journal of Personality and Social Psychology, 50,* 260–268.

Calvert, S. L. (2002). The social impact of virtual environment technology. In K. M. Stanney (Ed.), *Handbook of virtual environments: Design, implementation, and applications.* (pp. 663–680). Mahwah, NJ: Erlbaum.

Camerer, C. F. (2003). Strategizing in the brain. *Science, 300,* 1673–1675.

Cameron, J. J., Ross, M., & Holmes, J. G. (2002). Loving the one you hurt: Positive effects of recounting a transgression against an intimate partner. *Journal of Experimental Social Psychology, 38,* 307–314.

Campbell, D. T. (1957). Factors relevant to validity of experiments in social settings. *Psychological Bulletin, 54,* 297–312.

Campbell, D. T. (1965). Ethnocentric and other altruistic motives. In D. Levine (Ed.), *Nebraska Symposium on Motivation* (Vol. 13, pp. 238–311). Lincoln: University of Nebraska Press.

Campbell, J. D. (1990). Self-esteem and clarity of self-concept. *Journal of Personality and Social Psychology, 59,* 538–549.

Campbell, L. (2005). Responses to verifying and enhancing appraisals from romantic partners: The role of trait importance and trait visibility. *European Journal of Social Psychology, 35,* 663–675.

Campbell, L., Lackenbauer, S., & Muise, A. (2006). When is being known or adored by romantic partners most beneficial? Self-perceptions, relationship length, and responses to partner's verifying and enhancing appraisals. *Personality and Social Psychology Bulletin, 32,* 1283–1294.

Campbell, L., Simpson, J. A., Boldry, J., & Kashy, D. A. (2005). Perceptions of conflict and support in romantic relationships: The role of attachment anxiety. *Journal of Personality and Social Psychology, 88,* 510–531.

Campbell, L., Simpson, J. A., Kashy, D. A., & Rholes, W. S. (2001). Attachment orientations, dependence, and behavior in a stressful situation: An application of the actor-partner interdependence model. *Journal of Social and Personal Relationships, 18,* 821–843.

Campbell, L., Simpson, J. A., Stewart, M., & Manning, J. (2003). Putting personality in social context: Extraversion, emergent leadership, and the availability of rewards. *Personality and Social Psychology Bulletin, 29,* 1547–1559.

Campbell, L., Simpson, J. A., Stewart, M., & Manning, J. G. (2002). The formation of status hierarchies in leaderless groups: The role of male waist-to-hip ratio. *Human Nature, 13,* 345–362.

Campos, J. J., Barrett, K., Lamb, M. E., Goldsmith, H., & Stenberg, C. R. (1983). Socioemotional development. In M. M. Haith & J. J. Campos (Eds.), *Handbook of child psychology* (Vol. 2, pp. 783–915). New York: Wiley.

Cann, A., Sherman, S. J., & Elkes, R. (1975). Effects of initial request size and timing of a second request on compliance: The foot in the door and the door in the face. *Journal of Personality and Social Psychology, 32,* 774–782.

Cannon, W. B. (1932). *The wisdom of the body.* New York: Norton.

Caporael, L. R., & Brewer, M. B. (1995). Hierarchical evolutionary theory: There is an alternative and it's not creationism. *Psychological Inquiry, 6,* 31–80.

Cardeña, E., Butler, L. D., & Spiegel, D. (2003). Stress disorders. In I. B. Weiner (Series Ed.) & G. Stricker & T. A. Widiger (Vol. Eds.), *Handbook of psychology: Vol. 8. Clinical psychology* (pp. 229–249). Hoboken, NJ: Wiley.

Carli, L. L. (2001). Gender and social influence. *Journal of Social Issues, 57,* 725–742.

Carlo, G., Eisenberg, N., Troyer, D., Switzer, G., & Speer, A. L. (1991). The altruistic personality: In what contexts is it apparent? *Journal of Personality and Social Psychology, 61,* 450–458.

Carlsmith, J. M., & Gross, A. E. (1969). Some effects of guilt on compliance. *Journal of Personality and Social Psychology, 11,* 232–239.

Carlson, M., Charlin, V., & Miller, N. (1988). Positive mood and helping behavior: A test of six hypotheses. *Journal of Personality and Social Psychology, 55,* 211–229.

Carlston, D. E., & Skowronski, J. J. (1994). Savings in the relearning of trait information as evidence for spontaneous trait generation. *Journal of Personality and Social Psychology, 66,* 840–856.

Carnevale, P. J., & Leung, K. (2001). Cultural dimensions of negotiation. In M. A. Hogg & S. Tindale (Eds.), *Blackwell handbook of social psychology: Group processes* (pp. 482–496). Oxford, UK: Blackwell.

Cartwright, D. S., & Zander, A. (Eds.). (1968). *Group dynamics: Research and theory* (3rd ed.). New York: Harper & Row.

Carver, C. S., Coleman, A. E., & Glass, D. C. (1976). The coronary-prone behavior pattern and the suppression of fatigue on a treadmill test. *Journal of Personality and Social Psychology, 33,* 460–466.

Carver, C. S., Ganellen, R. J., Froming W. J., & Chambers, W. (1983). Modeling: An analysis in terms of category accessibility. *Journal of Experimental Social Psychology, 19,* 403–421.

Carver, C. S., Pozo, C., Harris, S. D., Noriega, V., Scheier, M. F., Robinson, D. S., Ketcham, A. S., Moffat, F. L., Jr., & Clark, K. C. (1993). How coping mediates the effects of optimism on stress: A study of women with early stage breast cancer. *Journal of Personality and Social Psychology, 65,* 375–391.

Cassidy, J., & Berlin, L. J. (1994). The insecure/ambivalent pattern of attachment: Theory and research. *Child Development, 65,* 971–991.

Centre for Addiction and Mental Health (2003). *Research Annual Report 2003.* Toronto, ON: CAMH.

Chaiken, S. (1980). Heuristic versus systematic processing and the use of source versus message cues in persuasion. *Journal of Personality and Social Psychology, 39,* 752–766.

Chaiken, S. (1987). The heuristic model of persuasion. In M. P. Zanna, J. M. Olson, & C. P. Herman (Eds.), *Social inference: The Ontario symposium* (Vol. 5, pp. 3–39). Hillsdale, NJ: Erlbaum.

Chaiken, S., & Baldwin, M. W. (1981). Affective-cognitive consistency and the effect of salient behavioral information on the self-perception of attitudes. *Journal of Personality and Social Psychology, 41,* 1–12.

Chaiken, S., & Maheswaran, D. (1994). Heuristic processing can bias systematic processing: Effects of source credibility, argument ambiguity, and task importance on attitude judgment. *Journal of Personality and Social Psychology, 66,* 460–473.

Chan, D. K.-S., Cheung, S. F., Gray, A., Ip, A., & Lee, B. (2004). Identifying the psychosocial correlates of condom use by female sex workers in Hong Kong. *AIDS Care, 16,* 530–539.

Chang, E. C., & Asakawa, K. (2003). Cultural variations on optimistic and pessimistic bias for self versus a sibling: Is there evidence for self-enhancement in the West and for self-criticism in the East when the reference group is specified? *Journal of Personality and Social Psychology, 84,* 569–581.

Chang, E. C., Asakawa, K., & Sanna, L. J. (2001). Cultural variations in optimistic and pessimistic bias: Do Easterners really expect the worst and Westerners really expect the best when predicting future life events? *Journal of Personality and Social Psychology, 81,* 476–491.

Chang, E. C., & Sanna, L. J. (2001). Negative attributional style as a moderator of the link between perfectionism and depressive symptoms: Preliminary evidence for an integrative model. *Journal of Counseling Psychology, 48,* 490–495.

Chapman, L. J. (1967). Illusory correlation in observational report. *Journal of Verbal Learning and Verbal Behavior, 6,* 151–155.

Chapman, L. J., & Chapman, J. P. (1967). Genesis of popular but erroneous diagnostic observations. *Journal of Abnormal Psychology, 72,*193–204.

Chapman, L. J., & Chapman J. P. (1969). Illusory correlation as an obstacle to the use of valid psycho-diagnostic signs. *Journal of Abnormal Psychology, 74,* 272–280.

Chartrand, T. L., & Bargh, J. A. (1999). The chameleon effect: The perception-behavior link and social interaction. *Journal of Personality and Social Psychology, 76,* 893–910.

Chassin, L., Presson, C. C., & Sherman, S. J. (1984). Cigarette smoking and adolescent psychosocial development. *Basic and Applied Social Psychology, 5,* 295–315.

Check, J. V., & Guloien, T. H. (1989). Reported proclivity for coercive sex following repeated exposure to sexually violent pornography, nonviolent dehumanizing pornography, and erotica. In D. Zillman & J. Bryant (Eds.), *Pornography: Research advances and policy considerations* (pp. 159–184). Hillsdale, NJ: Erlbaum.

Chemers, M. M. (2000). Leadership research and theory: A functional integration. *Group Dynamics: Theory, Research, and Practice, 4,* 27–43.

Chemers, M. M., & Ayman, R. (Eds.). (1993). *Leadership theory and research: Perspectives and directions.* San Diego, CA: Academic Press.

Chen, F. F., & Kenrick, D. T. (2002). Repulsion or attraction? Group membership and assumed attitude similarity. *Journal of Personality and Social Psychology, 83,* 111–125.

Chen, M., & Bargh, J. A. (1997). Nonconscious behavioral confirmation processes: The self-fulfilling consequences of automatic stereotype activation. *Journal of Experimental Social Psychology, 33,* 541–560.

Cheng, P. W., & Novick, L. R. (1992). Covariation in natural causal induction. *Psychological Review, 99,* 365–382.

Chesney, M. A., & Rosenman, R. H. (Eds.). (1985). *Anger and hostility in cardiovascular and behavioral disorders.* Washington, DC: Hemisphere.

Cho, H., & Witte, K. (2004). A review of fear-appeal effects. In J. S. Seiter & R. H. Gass (Eds.), *Perspectives on persuasion, social influence, and compliance gaining* (pp. 223–238). Boston, MA: Pearson Education.

Choi, I., & Nisbett, R. E. (1998). Situational salience and cultural differences in the correspondence bias and the actor-observer bias. *Personality and Social Psychology Bulletin, 24,* 949–960.

Choi, N., & Fuqua, D. R. (2003). The structure of the Bem Sex-Role Inventory: A summary report of 23 validation studies. *Educational and Psychological Measurement, 63,* 872–887.

Christensen, P. N., Rothgerber, H., Wood, W., & Matz, D. C. (2004). Social norms and identity relevance: A motivational approach to normative behavior. *Personality and Social Psychology Bulletin, 30,* 1295–1309.

Cialdini, R. B. (2001). *Influence: Science and practice* (4th ed.). Boston, MA: Allyn & Bacon.

Cialdini, R. B., Borden, R., Thorne, A., Walker, M., Freeman, S., & Sloane, L. T. (1976). Basking in reflected glory: Three (football) field studies. *Journal of Personality and Social Psychology, 34,* 366–375.

Cialdini, R. B., Cacioppo, J. T., Bassett, R., & Miller, J. A. (1978). Low-ball procedure for producing compliance: Commitment then cost. *Journal of Personality and Social Psychology, 36,* 463–476.

Cialdini, R. B., & Goldstein, N. J. (2004). Social influence: Compliance and conformity. *Annual Review of Psychology, 55,* 591–621.

Cialdini, R. B., Schaller, M., Houlihan, D., Arps, K., Fultz, J., & Beaman, A. L. (1987). Empathy-based helping: Is it selflessly or selfishly motivated? *Journal of Personality and Social Psychology, 52,* 749–758.

Cialdini, R. B., & Trost, M. R. (1998). Social influence: Social norms, conformity, and compliance. In D. T. Gilbert, S. T. Fiske, & G. Lindzey (Eds.), *The handbook of social psychology* (3rd ed., Vol. 2, pp. 151–192). Boston, MA: McGraw-Hill.

Cialdini, R. B., Trost, M. R., & Newsom, J. T. (1995). Preference for consistency: The development of a valid measure and the discovery of surprising behavioral implications. *Journal of Personality and Social Psychology, 69,* 318–328.

Cialdini, R. B., Vincent, J. E., Lewis, S. K., Catalan, J., Wheeler, D., & Darby, B. L. (1975). Reciprocal concessions procedure for inducing compliance: The door-in-the-face technique. *Journal of Personality and Social Psychology, 31,* 206–215.

Clark, K. B., & Clark, M. P. (1947). Racial identification and preference in Negro children. In T. M. Newcomb & E. L. Hartley (Eds.), *Readings in social psychology* (pp. 169–178). New York: Holt, Rinehart, & Winston.

Clark, M. S., & Mills, J. (1979). Interpersonal attraction in exchange and communal relationships. *Journal of Personality and Social Psychology, 37,* 12–24.

Clark, M. S., & Mills, J. (1993). The difference between communal and exchange relationships: What it is and is not. *Personality and Social Psychology Bulletin, 19,* 684–691.

Clay, C. (1987). *No freedom for the mind: A study of the cult phenomenon from a Canadian perspective.* Burlington, ON: Trinity Press.

Clément, R., Baker, S. C., & MacIntyre, P. D. (2003). Willingness to communicate in a second language: The effects of context norms and vitality. *Journal of Language and Social Psychology, 22,* 190–209.

Clément, R., Michaud, C., & Noels, K. A. (1998). Acculturative effects of social support during intergroup contact situations. *Revue Québécoise de Psychologie, 19,* 189–210.

Clément, R., & Noels, K. A. (1992). Towards a situated approach to ethnolinguistic identity: The effects of status on individuals and groups. *Journal of Language and Social Psychology, 11,* 203–232.

Clément, R., Noels, K. A., & Deneault, B. (2001). Interethnic contact, identity, and psychological adjustment: The mediating and moderating roles of communication. *Journal of Social Issues, 57,* 559–577.

Clore, G. L., & Gormly, J. B. (1974). Knowing, feeling, and liking: A psychophysiological view. *Journal of Research in Personality, 8,* 218–230.

Clore, G. L., Schwarz, N., & Conway, M. (1994). Affective causes and consequences of social information processing. In R. S. Wyer, Jr., & T. K. Srull (Eds.), *Handbook of social cognition: Vol. 1. Basic processes* (2nd ed., pp. 323–417). Hillsdale, NJ: Erlbaum.

Cohen, A. R. (1962). An experiment on small rewards for discrepant compliance and attitude change. In J. W. Brehm & A. R. Cohen (Eds.), *Explorations in cognitive dissonance* (pp. 73–79). New York: Wiley.

Cohen, C. E. (1981). Person categories and social perception: Testing some boundaries of the processing effects of prior knowledge. *Journal of Personality and Social Psychology, 40,* 441–452.

Cohen, D., & Hoshino-Browne, E. (2005). Insider and outsider perspectives on the self and social world. In R. M. Sorrentino, D. Cohen, J. M. Olson, & M. P. Zanna (Eds.), *Culture and social behavior: The Ontario symposium* (Vol. 10, pp. 49–76). Mahwah, NJ: Erlbaum.

Cohen, D., & Nisbett, R. E. (1997). Field experiments examining the culture of honor: The role of institutions in perpetuating norms about violence. *Personality and Social Psychology Bulletin, 23,* 1188–1199.

Cohen, D., Nisbett, R. E., Bowdle, B. F., & Schwarz, N. (1996). Insult, aggression, and the southern culture of honor: An "experimental ethnography." *Journal of Personality and Social Psychology, 70,* 945–960.

Cohen, E. S., & Fromme, K. (2002). Differential determinants of young adult substance use and high-risk sexual behavior. *Journal of Applied Social Psychology, 32,* 1124–1150.

Cohen, G. L., Aronson, J., & Steele, C. M. (2000). When beliefs yield to evidence: Reducing biased evaluation by affirming the self. *Personality and Social Psychology Bulletin, 26,* 1151–1164.

Cohen, S. (2004). Social relationships and health. *American Psychologist, 59,* 676–684.

Coie, J. D., & Dodge, K. A. (1998). Aggression and antisocial behavior. In N. Eisenberg (Ed.), *Social, emotional, and personality development* (5th ed., Vol. 4, pp. 779–862). New York: Wiley.

Coie, J. D., & Kupersmidt, J. B. (1983). A behavioral analysis of emerging social status in boys' groups. *Child Development, 54,* 1400–1416.

Colby, K. M. (1968). A programmable theory of cognition and affect in individual personal belief systems. In R. P. Abelson,

E. Aronson, W. J. McGuire, T. M. Newcomb, M. J. Rosenberg, & P. H. Tannenbaum (Eds.) *Theories of cognitive consistency: A source book* (pp. 520–525). Chicago: Rand McNally.

Coleman, J. F., Blake, R. R., & Mouton, J. S. (1958). Task difficulty and conformity pressures. *Journal of Abnormal and Social Psychology, 57,* 120–122.

Colin, V. L. (1996). *Human attachment.* Philadelphia: Temple University Press.

Collins, N. L., & Miller, L. C. (1994). Self-disclosure and liking: A meta-analytic review. *Psychological Bulletin, 116,* 457–475.

Collins, N. L., & Read, S. J. (1990). Adult attachment, working models, and relationship quality in dating couples. *Journal of Personality and Social Psychology, 58,* 644–663.

Collins, R. L. (1996). For better or worse: The impact of upward social comparisons on self-evaluations. *Psychological Bulletin, 34,* 366–375.

Collins, R. L. (2000). Among the better ones: Upward assimilation in social comparison. In J. M. Suls & L. Wheeler (Eds.), *Handbook of social comparison: Theory and research* (pp. 159–171). New York: Kluwer Academic/Plenum.

Colman, A. M. (1991). Crowd psychology in South African murder trials. *American Psychologist, 46,* 1071–1079.

Colvin, C. R., & Block, J. (1994). Do positive illusions foster mental health? An examination of the Taylor and Brown formulation. *Psychological Bulletin, 116,* 3–20.

Colvin, C. R., Block, J., & Funder, D. C. (1995). Overly positive evaluations and personality: Negative implications for mental health. *Journal of Personality and Social Psychology, 68,* 1152–1162.

Conger, R. D., Conger, K. J., Elder, G. H., Lorenz, F. O., Simmons, R. L., & Whitebeck, L. B. (1992). A family process model of economic hardship and adjustment of early adolescent boys. *Child Development, 63,* 526–541.

Conway, M., & Ross, M. (1984). Getting what you want by revising what you had. *Journal of Personality and Social Psychology, 47,* 738–748.

Cook, A. J., Kerr, G. N., & Moore, K. (2002). Attitudes and intentions towards purchasing GM food. *Journal of Economic Psychology, 23,* 557–572.

Cook, S. W. (1969). Motives in a conceptual analysis of attitude-related behavior. In W. J. Arnold & D. Levine (Eds.), *Nebraska Symposium on Motivation* (Vol. 17, pp. 179–231). Lincoln: University of Nebraska Press.

Cook, S. W. (1990). Toward a psychology of improving justice: Research on extending the equality principle to victims of social injustice. *Journal of Social Issues, 46*(1), 147–161.

Cooley, C. H. (1902). *Human nature and the social order.* New York: Charles Scribner's Sons.

Cooper, C. (1997, March/April). An interesting career in psychology: Social science analyst in the public sector. *Psychological Science Agenda, 10*(2), 8.

Cooper, J. (1980). Reducing fears and increasing assertiveness: The role of dissonance reduction. *Journal of Experimental Social Psychology, 16,* 199–213.

Cooper, J. (1998). Unlearning cognitive dissonance: Toward an understanding of the development of dissonance. *Journal of Experimental Social Psychology, 34,* 562–575.

Cooper, J., Bennett, E. A., & Sukel, H. L. (1996). Complex scientific testimony: How do jurors make decisions? *Law and Human Behavior, 20,* 379–394.

Cooper, J., & Fazio, R. H. (1984). A new look at dissonance theory. In L. Berkowitz (Ed.), *Advances in experimental social psychology* (Vol. 17, pp. 229–264). New York: Academic Press.

Cooper, J., Zanna, M. P., & Taves, P. A. (1978). Arousal as a necessary condition for attitude change following induced compliance. *Journal of Personality and Social Psychology, 36,* 1101–1106.

Corenblum, B. (2003). What children remember about ingroup and outgroup peers: Effects of stereotypes on children's processing of information about group members. *Journal of Experimental Child Psychology, 86,* 32–66.

Corenblum, B., & Annis, R. C. (1987). Racial identity and preference in Native and White Canadian children. *Canadian Journal of Behavioural Science, 19,* 254–265.

Corenblum, B., Annis, R., & Young, S. (1996). Effects of own group success or failure on judgements of task performance by children of different ethnicities. *European Journal of Social Psychology, 26,* 777–798.

Corenblum, B., & Stephan, W. G. (2001). White fears and Native apprehensions: An integrated threat theory approach to intergroup attitudes. *Canadian Journal of Behavioural Science, 33,* 251–268.

Corenblum, B., & Wilson, A. E. (1982). Ethnic preference and identification among Canadian Indian and White children: Replication and extension. *Canadian Journal of Behavioural Science, 14,* 50–59.

Correll, J., Park, B., Judd, C. M., & Wittenbrink, B. (2002). The police officer's dilemma: Using ethnicity to disambiguate potentially threatening individuals. *Journal of Personality and Social Psychology, 83,* 1314–1329.

Cortina, L. M. (2004). Hispanic perspectives on sexual harassment and social support. *Personality and Social Psychology Bulletin, 30,* 570–584.

Cottrell, N. B., Wack, D. L., Sekerak, G. J., & Rittle, R. H. (1968). Social facilitation of dominant responses by the presence of an audience and the mere presence of others. *Journal of Personality and Social Psychology, 9,* 245–250.

Cousins, N. (1979). *Anatomy of an illness.* New York: Norton.

Cozzarelli, C. (1993). Personality and self-efficacy as predictors of coping with abortion. *Journal of Personality and Social Psychology, 65,* 1224–1236.

Crandall, C. S. (1994). Prejudice against fat people: Ideology and self-interest. *Journal of Personality and Social Psychology, 66,* 882–894.

Crandall, C. S. (1995). Do parents discriminate against their heavyweight daughters? *Personality and Social Psychology Bulletin, 21,* 724–735.

Crandall, C. S., & Eshleman, A. (2003). A justification-suppression model of the expression and experience of prejudice. *Psychological Bulletin, 129,* 414–446.

Crano, W. D., & Brewer, M. B. (2002). *Principles and methods of social research* (2nd ed.). Mahwah, NJ: Erlbaum.

Crawford, M. T., & McCrea, S. M. (2004). When mutations meet motivations: Attitude biases in counterfactual thought. *Journal of Experimental Social Psychology, 40,* 65–74.

Crelia, R. A., & Tesser, A. (1996). Attitude heritability and attitude reinforcement: A replication. *Personality and Individual Differences, 21,* 803–808.

Crick, N. R. (1996). The role of overt aggression, relational aggression, and prosocial behavior in the prediction of children's future social adjustment. *Child Development, 67,* 2317–2327.

Crick, N. R., Casas, J. F., & Mosher, M. (1997). Relational and overt aggression in preschool. *Developmental Psychology, 33,* 579–588.

Crick, N. R., & Grotpeter, J. K. (1995). Relational aggression, gender, and social-psychological adjustment. *Child Development, 66,* 710–722.

Crites, S. L., Jr., Fabrigar, L. R., & Petty, R. E. (1994). Measuring the affective and cognitive properties of attitudes: Conceptual and methodological issues. *Personality and Social Psychology Bulletin, 20,* 619–634.

Crocker, J. (1981). Judgment of covariation by social perceivers. *Psychological Bulletin, 90,* 272–292.

Crocker, J., Cornwell, B., & Major, B. (1993). The stigma of overweight: Affective consequences of attributional ambiguity. *Journal of Personality and Social Psychology, 64,* 60–70.

Crocker, J., & Park, L. E. (2004). The costly pursuit of self-esteem. *Psychological Bulletin, 130,* 392–414.

Crocker, J., Sommers, S. R., & Luhtanen, R. K. (2002). Hopes dashed and dreams fulfilled: Contingencies of self-worth and graduate school admissions. *Personality and Social Psychology Bulletin, 28,* 1275–1286.

Croizet, J.-C., Després, G., Gauzins, M.-E., Huguet, P., Leyens, J.-P., & Méot, A. (2004). Stereotype threat undermines intellectual performance by triggering a disruptive mental load. *Personality and Social Psychology Bulletin, 30,* 721–731.

Crosby, F. (1976). A model of egoistical relative deprivation. *Psychological Review, 83,* 85–113.

Crosby, F. (1984). The denial of personal discrimination. *American Behavioral Scientist, 27,* 371–386.

Cross, S. E., & Vick, N. V. (2001). The interdependent self-construal and social support: The case of persistence in engineering. *Personality and Social Psychology Bulletin, 27,* 820–832.

Croyle, R. T., & Cooper, J. (1982). Dissonance arousal: Physiological evidence. *Journal of Personality and Social Psychology, 45,* 782–791.

Crutchfield, R. S. (1955). Conformity and character. *American Psychologist, 10,* 191–198.

Cunningham, M. (2001). The influence of parental attitudes and behaviors on children's attitudes toward gender and household labor in early adulthood. *Journal of Marriage and the Family, 63,* 111–122.

Cunningham, M. R. (1986). Measuring the physical in physical attractiveness: Quasi-experiments on the sociobiology of female facial beauty. *Journal of Personality and Social Psychology, 50,* 925–935.

Cunningham, M. R., Barbee, A. P., & Pike, C. L. (1990). What do women want? Facialmetric assessment of multiple motives in the perception of male facial physical attractiveness. *Journal of Personality and Social Psychology, 59,* 61–72.

Cunningham, M. R., Roberts, A. R., Barbee, A. P., Druen, P. B., & Wu, C. (1995). "Their ideas of beauty are, on the whole, the same as ours": Consistency and variability in the cross-cultural perception of female physical attractiveness. *Journal of Personality and Social Psychology, 68,* 261–279.

Cunningham, M. R., Shaffer, D. R., Barbee, A. P., Wolff, P. L., & Kelly, D. J. (1990). Separate processes in the relation of elation and depression to helping: Social versus personal concerns. *Journal of Experimental Social Psychology, 26,* 13–33.

Cunningham, M. R., Steinberg, J., & Grev, R. (1980). Wanting to and having to help: Separate motivations for positive mood and guilt-induced helping. *Journal of Personality and Social Psychology, 38,* 181–192.

Cunningham, W. A., Johnson, M. K., Raye, C. L., Gatenby, J. C., Gore, J. C., & Banaji, M. R. (2004). Separable neural components in the processing of black and white faces. *Psychological Science, 15,* 806–813.

Cunningham, W. A., Nezlek, J. B., & Banaji, M. R. (2004). Implicit and explicit ethnocentrism: Revisiting the ideologies of prejudice. *Personality and Social Psychology Bulletin, 30,* 1332–1346.

Cunningham, W. A., Preacher, K. J., & Banaji, M. R. (2001). Implicit attitude measures: Consistency, stability, and convergent validity. *Psychological Science, 12,* 163–170.

Cutler, B. L., & Penrod, S. D. (1995). *Mistaken identification: The eyewitness, psychology and the law.* New York: Cambridge University Press.

Cutrona, C. E., & Troutman, B. R. (1986). Social support, infant temperament, and parenting self-efficacy: A mediational model of post-partum depression. *Child Development, 57,* 1507–1518.

D'Augelli, A. R., & Patterson, C. J. (Eds.). (1995). *Lesbian, gay, and bisexual identities over the lifespan.* New York: Oxford University Press.

Dabbs, J. M., Carr, T. S., Frady, R. L., & Riad, J. K. (1995). Testosterone, crime, and misbehaviour among 692 male prison inmates. *Personality and Individual Differences, 18,* 627–633.

Dabbs, J. M., Frady, R. L., Carr, T. S., & Besch, N. F. (1987). Saliva testosterone and criminal violence in young adult prison inmates. *Psychosomatic Medicine, 49,* 174–182.

Daly, M., & Wilson, M. (1988). *Homicide.* New York: Aldine deGruyter.

Darley, J. M., & Batson, C. D. (1973). "From Jerusalem to Jericho": A study of situational and dispositional variables in helping behavior. *Journal of Personality and Social Psychology, 27,* 100–108.

Darley, J. M., & Gross, P. H. (1983). A hypothesis-confirming bias in labelling effects. *Journal of Personality and Social Psychology, 24,* 20–33.

Darley, J. M., & Latané, B. (1968). Bystander intervention in emergencies: Diffusion of responsibility. *Journal of Personality and Social Psychology, 8,* 377–383.

Darwin, C. (1872). *The expression of the emotions in man and animals.* London: Murray.

Das, E. H. H. J., de Wit, J. B. F., & Stroebe, W. (2003). Fear appeals motivate acceptance of action recommendations: Evidence for a positive bias in the processing of persuasive messages. *Personality and Social Psychology Bulletin, 29,* 650–664.

Dasgupta, N., & Asgari, S. (2004). Seeing is believing: Exposure to counterstereotypic women leaders and its effect on the malleability of automatic gender stereotyping. *Journal of Experimental Social Psychology, 40,* 642–658.

Dasgupta, N., & Greenwald, A. G. (2001). On the malleability of automatic attitudes: Combating automatic prejudice with images of admired and disliked individuals. *Journal of Personality and Social Psychology, 81,* 800–814.

Davidson, R. J., Putnam, K. M., & Larson, C. L. (2000). Dysfunction in the neural circuitry of emotion regulation: A possible prelude to violence. *Science, 289,* 591–594.

Davis, C. G., Lehman, D. R., Wortman, C. B., Silver, R. C., & Thompson, S. C. (1995). The undoing of traumatic life events. *Personality and Social Psychology Bulletin, 21,* 109–124.

Davis, J. H., Kerr, N. L., Atkin, R. S., Holt, R., & Meek, D. (1975). The decision processes of 6- and 12-person mock juries assigned unanimous and two-thirds majority rules. *Journal of Personality and Social Psychology, 32,* 1–14.

Davis, M. H. (1983). Measuring individual differences in empathy: Evidence for a multidimensional approach. *Journal of Personality and Social Psychology, 44,* 113–126.

Davis, M. H. (1996). *Empathy: A social psychological approach.* Boulder, CO: Westview.

Davis, M. H., Hall, J. A., & Meyer, M. (2003). The first year: Influences on the satisfaction, involvement, and persistence of new community volunteers. *Personality and Social Psychology Bulletin, 29,* 248–260.

Dawes, R. (1989). Statistical criteria for establishing a truly false consensus effect. *Journal of Experimental Social Psychology, 25,* 1–17.

Dawes, R. M., McTavish, J., & Shaklee, H. (1977). Behavior, communication, and assumptions about other people's behavior in a commons dilemma situation. *Journal of Personality and Social Psychology, 35,* 1–11.

Dawkins, R. (1976). *The selfish gene.* New York: Oxford University Press.

Day, D. M. (2005). Applying social psychology to the criminal justice system. In F. W. Schneider, J. A. Gruman, & L. M. Coutts (Eds.), *Applied social psychology: Understanding and addressing social and practical problems* (pp. 257–282). Thousand Oaks, CA: Sage.

De Cremer, D., & van Dijk, E. (2002). Reactions to group success and failure as a function of identification level: A test of the goal-transformation hypothesis in social dilemmas. *Journal of Experimental Social Psychology, 38,* 435–442.

De Dreu, C. K. W., Weingart, L. R., & Kwon, S. (2000). Influence of social motives on integrative orientation: A meta-analytic review and test of two theories. *Journal of Personality and Social Psychology, 78,* 889–905.

De Houwer, J., Thomas, S., & Baeyens, F. (2001). Associative learning of likes and dislikes: A review of 25 years of research on human evaluative conditioning. *Psychological Bulletin, 127,* 853–869.

de Rivera, J. (1997). Estimating the number of false memory syndrome cases. *American Psychologist, 52,* 996–997.

Deary, I. J., Whiteman, M. C., Starr, J. M., Whalley, L. J., & Fox, H. C. (2004). The impact of childhood intelligence on later life: Following up the Scottish mental surveys of 1932 and 1947. *Journal of Personality and Social Psychology, 86,* 130–147.

Deaux, K., & LaFrance, M. (1998). Gender. In D. T. Gilbert, S. T. Fiske, & G. Lindzey (Eds.), *The handbook of social psychology* (4th ed., Vol. 1, pp. 788–827). New York: McGraw-Hill.

DeBono, K. G., & Packer, M. (1991). The effects of advertising strategy on perceptions of product quality. *Personality and Social Psychology Bulletin, 17,* 194–200.

Deci, E. L., & Flaste, R. (1995). *Why we do what we do: The dynamics of personal autonomy.* New York: Putnam.

Deci, E. L., & Ryan, R. M. (1985). *Intrinsic motivation and self-determination in human behavior.* New York: Plenum.

Deci, E. L., & Ryan, R. M. (2002). The paradox of achievement: The harder you push, the worse it gets. In J. Aronson (Ed.), *Improving academic achievement: Impact of psychological factors on education* (pp. 61–87). New York: Academic Press.

Deffenbacher, J. L., Filetti, L. B., Richards, T. L., Lynch, R. S., & Oetting, E. R. (2003). Characteristics of two groups of angry drivers. *Journal of Counseling Psychology, 50,* 123–132.

Deffenbacher, J. L., Huff, M. E., Lynch, R. S., Oetting, E. R., & Salvatore, N. F. (2000). Characteristics and treatment of high-anger drivers. *Journal of Counseling Psychology, 47,* 5–17.

Deffenbacher, J. L., Lynch, R. S., Oetting, E. R., & Kemper, C. C. (1996). Anger reduction in early adolescents. *Journal of Counseling Psychology, 43,* 149–157.

Deffenbacher, J. L., Oetting, E. R., Huff, M. E., & Thwaites, G. A. (1995). Fifteen-month follow-up of social skills and cognitive-relaxation approaches to general anger reduction. *Journal of Counseling Psychology, 42,* 400–405.

Deffenbacher, J. L., Thwaites, G. A., Wallace, T. L., & Oetting, E. R. (1994). Social skills and cognitive-relaxation approaches to general anger reduction. *Journal of Counseling Psychology, 41,* 386–396.

Demers, A., Kairouz, S., Adlaf, E. M., Gliksman, L., Newton-Taylor, B., & Marchand, A. (2002). Multilevel analysis of situational drinking among Canadian undergraduates. *Social Science and Medicine, 55,* 415–424.

Denton, K., & Krebs, D. (1990). From the scene to the crime: The effect of alcohol and social context on moral judgment. *Journal of Personality and Social Psychology, 59,* 242–248.

DePaulo, B. M., & Friedman, H. S. (1998). Nonverbal communication. In D. Gilbert, S. T. Fiske, & G. Lindzey (Eds.), *The handbook of social psychology* (4th ed., Vol. 2 pp. 3–40). New York: McGraw-Hill.

Derlega, V. J., Metts, S., Petronio, S., & Margulis, S. T. (1993). *Self-disclosure.* Newbury Park, CA: Sage.

Derlega, V. J., & Winstead, B. A. (1986). *Friendship and social interaction.* New York: Springer-Verlag.

Desforges, D. M., Lord, C. G., Ramsey, S. L., Mason, J. A., Van Leeuwen, M. D., West, S. C., & Lepper, M. R. (1991). Effects of structured cooperative contact on changing negative attitudes toward stigmatized social groups. *Journal of Personality and Social Psychology, 60,* 531–544.

DeSteno, D., Dasgupta, N., Bartlett, M. Y., & Cajdric, A. (2004). Prejudice from thin air: The effect of emotion on automatic intergroup attitudes. *Psychological Science, 15,* 319–324.

DeSteno, D., Petty, R. E., Rucker, D.D., Wegener, D. T., & Braverman, J. (2004). Discrete emotions and persuasion: The

role of emotion-induced expectancies. *Journal of Personality and Social Psychology, 86,* 43–56.

Deutsch, M. (1973). *The resolution of conflict.* New Haven, CT: Yale University Press.

Deutsch, M., & Coleman, P. T. (Eds.). (2000). *The handbook of conflict resolution.* San Francisco: Jossey-Bass.

Deutsch, M., & Gerard, H. B. (1955). A study of normative and informational social influences upon individual judgment. *Journal of Abnormal and Social Psychology, 51,* 629–636.

Deutsch, M., & Krauss, R. M. (1960). The effect of threat upon interpersonal bargaining. *Journal of Abnormal and Social Psychology, 61,* 181–189.

Deutsch, M., & Krauss, R. M. (1962). Studies of interpersonal bargaining. *Journal of Conflict Resolution, 6,* 52–76.

Devine, P. G., (1989). Stereotypes and prejudice: Their automatic and controlled components. *Journal of Personality and Social Psychology, 56,* 5–18.

Dickerson, C., Thibodeau, R., Aronson, E., & Miller, D. (1992). Using cognitive dissonance to encourage water conservation. *Journal of Applied Social Psychology, 22,* 841–854.

Diekman, A. B., & Eagly, A. H. (2000). Stereotypes as dynamic constructs: Women and men of the past, present, and future. *Personality and Social Psychology Bulletin, 26,* 1171–1188.

Diekman, A. B., Eagly, A. H., & Kulesa, P. (2002). Accuracy and bias in stereotypes about the social and political attitudes of women and men. *Journal of Experimental Social Psychology, 38,* 268–282.

Diener, E., Fraser, S. C., Beaman, A. L., & Kelem, R. T. (1976). Effects of deindividuation variables on stealing among Halloween trick-or-treaters. *Journal of Personality and Social Psychology, 33,* 178–183.

Dion, K. K., Berscheid, E., & Walster, E. (1972). What is beautiful is good. *Journal of Personality and Social Psychology, 24,* 285–290.

Dion, K. L., & Earn, B. M. (1975). The phenomenology of being a target of prejudice. *Journal of Personality and Social Psychology, 32,* 944–950.

Dion, K. L., Earn, B. M., & Yee, P. H. (1978). The experience of being a victim of prejudice: An experimental approach. *International Journal of Psychology, 13,* 197–214.

Dion, K. L., & Kawakami, K. (1996). Ethnicity and perceived discrimination in Toronto: Another perspective on the personal/ group discrimination discrepancy. *Canadian Journal of Behavioural Science, 28,* 203–213.

Dodge, K. A. (1983). Behavioral antecedents of peer social status. *Child Development, 54,* 1386–1399.

Dolinski, D. (2000). On inferring one's beliefs from one's attempt and consequences for subsequent compliance. *Journal of Personality and Social Psychology, 78,* 260–272.

Dolinski, D., Nawrat, M., & Rudak, I. (2001). Dialogue involvement as a social influence technique. *Personality and Social Psychology Bulletin, 27,* 1395–1406.

Doll, J., & Ajzen, I. (1992). Accessibility and stability of predictors in the theory of planned behavior. *Journal of Personality and Social Psychology, 63,* 754–765.

Doll, J., & Orth, B. (1993). The Fishbein and Ajzen theory of reasoned action applied to contraceptive behavior: Model variants and meaningfulness. *Journal of Applied Social Psychology, 23,* 395–415.

Dollard, J., Miller, N. E., Doob, L. W., Mowrer, O. H., & Sears, R. R. (1939). *Frustration and aggression.* New Haven, CT: Yale University Press.

Donnerstein, E. (1980). Aggressive erotica and violence against women. *Journal of Personality and Social Psychology, 39,* 269–277.

Doob, A. N., & Wood, L. E. (1972). Catharsis and aggression: Effects of annoyance and retaliation on aggressive behavior. *Journal of Personality and Social Psychology, 22,* 156–162.

Dooley, D. (2001). *Social research methods* (4th ed.). Upper Saddle River, NJ: Prentice-Hall.

Dovidio, J. F., & Gaertner, S. L. (1998). On the nature of contemporary prejudice: The causes, consequences, and challenges of aversive racism. In J. Eberhardt & S. T. Fiske (Eds.), *Confronting racism: The problem and the response* (pp. 3–32). Newbury Park, CA: Sage.

Dovidio, J. F., & Gaertner, S. L. (2000). Aversive racism and selection decisions: 1989 and 1999. *Psychological Science, 11,* 315–319.

Dovidio, J. F., Kawakami, K., & Gaertner, S. L. (2002). Implicit and explicit prejudice and interracial interaction. *Journal of Personality and Social Psychology, 82,* 62–68.

Dovidio, J. F., Kawakami, K., Johnson, C., Johnson, B., & Howard, A. (1997). On the nature of prejudice: Automatic and controlled processes. *Journal of Experimental Social Psychology, 33,* 510–540.

Dovidio, J. F., ten Vergert, M., Stewart, T. L., Gaertner, S. L., Johnson, J. D., Esses, V. M., Riek, B. M., & Pearson, A. R. (2004). Perspective and prejudice: Antecedents and mediating mechanisms. *Personality and Social Psychology Bulletin, 30,* 1537–1549.

Downes, B. T. (1968). Social and political characteristics of riot cities: A comparative study. *Social Science Quarterly, 49,* 504–520.

Downey, G., Freitas, A. L., Michaelis, B., & Khouri, H. (1998). The self-fulfilling prophecy in close relationships: Rejection sensitivity and rejection by romantic partners. *Journal of Personality and Social Psychology, 75,* 545–560.

Drachman, D., DeCarufel, A., & Insko, C. A. (1978). The extra credit effect in interpersonal attraction. *Journal of Experimental Social Psychology, 14,* 458–465.

Drigotas, S. M., & Rusbult, C. E. (1992). Should I stay or should I go? A dependence model of breakups. *Journal of Personality and Social Psychology, 62,* 62–87.

Duck, J. M., Hogg, M. A., & Terry, D. J. (1998). Perceived self-other differences in persuasibility: The effects of interpersonal and group-based similarity. *European Journal of Social Psychology, 28,* 1–21.

Duff, S. J., & Hampson, E. (2000). A beneficial effect of estrogen on working memory in post-menopausal women taking hormone replacement therapy. *Hormones and Behavior, 38,* 262–276.

Duff, S. J., & Hampson, E. (2001). A sex difference on a novel spatial working memory task in humans. *Brain and Cognition, 47,* 470–493.

Duncan, B. L. (1976). Differential social perception and attribution of intergroup violence: Testing the lower limits of stereotyping of Blacks. *Journal of Personality and Social Psychology, 34,* 590–598.

Duncan, C. P., & Nelson, J. E. (1985). Effects of humor in a radio advertising experiment. *Journal of Advertising, 14*(2), 33–40.

Dunkley, D. M., Blankstein, K. R., Halsall, J., Williams, M., & Winkworth, G. (2000). The relation between perfectionism and distress: Hassles, coping, and perceived social support as mediators and moderators. *Journal of Counseling Psychology, 47,* 437–453.

Dunning, D. (1993). Words to live by: The self and definitions of social concepts and categories. In J. M. Suls (Ed.), *Psychological perspectives on the self* (Vol. 4, pp. 99–126). Hillsdale, NJ: Erlbaum.

Dunning, D., Meyerowitz, J. A., & Holzberg, A. (1989). Ambiguity and self-evaluation: The role of idiosyncratic trait definitions in self-serving assessments of ability. *Journal of Personality and Social Psychology, 57,* 1082–1090.

Dunning, D., & Perretta, S. (2002). Automaticity and eyewitness accuracy: A 10- to 12-second rule for distinguishing accurate from inaccurate positive identifications. *Journal of Applied Psychology, 87,* 951–962.

Dweck, C. S. (1986). Motivational processes affecting learning. *American Psychologist, 41,* 1040–1048.

Dweck, C. S., Goetz, T. E., & Strauss, N. L. (1980). Sex differences in learned helplessness: IV. An experimental and naturalistic study of failure. *Journal of Personality and Social Psychology, 38,* 441–452.

Dweck, C. S. & Leggett, E. L. (1988). A social-cognitive approach to motivation and personality. *Psychological Review, 95,* 256–273.

Eagly, A. H. (1978). Sex differences in influenceability. *Psychological Bulletin, 85,* 86–116.

Eagly, A. H. (1987). *Sex differences in social behavior: A social-role interpretation.* Hillsdale, NJ: Erlbaum.

Eagly, A. H. (1995). The science and politics of comparing women and men. *American Psychologist, 50,* 145–158.

Eagly, A. H., Ashmore, R. D., Makhijani, M. G., & Longo, L. C. (1991). What is beautiful is good, but . . . : A meta-analytic review of research on the physical attractiveness stereotype. *Psychological Bulletin, 110,* 109–128.

Eagly, A. H., & Carli, L. L. (1981). Sex of researchers and sex-typed communications as determinants of sex differences in influenceability: A meta-analysis of social influence studies. *Psychological Bulletin, 90,* 1–20.

Eagly, A. H., & Chaiken, S. (1984). Cognitive theories of persuasion. In L. Berkowitz (Ed.), *Advances in experimental social psychology* (Vol. 17, pp. 267–359). New York: Academic Press.

Eagly, A. H., & Chaiken, S. (1993). *The psychology of attitudes.* Fort Worth, TX: Harcourt Brace Jovanovich.

Eagly, A. H., & Chaiken, S. (1998). Attitude structure and function. In D. Gilbert, S. Fiske, & G. Lindzey (Eds.), *The handbook of social psychology* (4th ed., Vol. 1, pp. 269–322). New York: McGraw-Hill.

Eagly, A. H., Chen, S., Chaiken, S., & Shaw-Barnes, K. (1999). The impact of attitudes on memory: An affair to remember. *Psychological Bulletin, 125,* 64–89.

Eagly, A. H., & Chrvala, C. (1986). Sex differences in conformity: Status and gender role interpretations. *Psychology of Women Quarterly, 10,* 203–220.

Eagly, A. H., & Johnson, B. T. (1990). Gender and leadership style: A meta-analysis. *Psychological Bulletin, 108,* 233–256.

Eagly, A. H., & Karau, S. J. (1991). Gender and the emergence of leaders: A meta-analysis. *Journal of Personality and Social Psychology, 60,* 685–710.

Eagly, A. H., & Karau, S. J. (2002). Role congruity theory of prejudice toward female leaders. *Psychological Review, 109,* 573–598.

Eagly, A. H., Karau, S. J., & Makhijani, M. G. (1995). Gender and the effectiveness of leaders: A meta-analysis. *Psychological Bulletin, 117,* 125–145.

Eagly, A. H., Makhijani, M. G., & Klonsky, B. G. (1992). Gender and the evaluation of leaders: A meta-analysis. *Psychological Bulletin, 111,* 3–22.

Eagly, A. H., & Wood W. (1999). The origins of sex differences in human behavior. *American Psychologist, 54,* 408–423.

Eagly, A. H., Wood, W., & Fishbaugh, L. (1981). Sex differences in conformity: Surveillance by the group as a determinant of male nonconformity. *Journal of Personality and Social Psychology, 40,* 384–394.

Eargle, A., Guerra, N., & Tolan, P. (1994). Preventing aggression in inner-city children: Small group training to change cognitions, social skills, and behavior. *Journal of Child and Adolescent Group Therapy, 4,* 229–242.

Earley, P. C. (1989). Social loafing and collectivism: A comparison of the United States and the People's Republic of China. *Administrative Science Quarterly, 34,* 565–581.

Easterbrook, J. A. (1959). The effects of emotion on cue utilization and the organization of behavior. *Psychological Review, 66,* 183–201.

Eaves, L. J., Eysenck, H. J., & Martin, N. G. (1989). *Genes, culture, and personality: An empirical approach.* London, UK: Academic Press.

Ebbesen, E. B., Kjos, G. L., & Konecni, V. J. (1976). Spatial ecology: Its effects on the choice of friends and enemies. *Journal of Experimental Social Psychology, 12,* 505–518.

Eberhardt, J. L. (2005). Imaging race. *American Psychologist, 60,* 181–190.

Edwards, K., & Smith, E. E. (1996). A disconfirmation bias in the evaluation of arguments. *Journal of Personality and Social Psychology, 71,* 5–24.

Efran, M. G. (1974). The effect of physical appearance on the judgment of guilt, interpersonal attraction, and severity of recommended punishment in a simulated jury task. *Journal of Research in Personality, 8,* 45–54.

Ehrensaft, M. K., Cohen, P., Brown, J., Smailes, E., Chen, H., & Johnson, J. G. (2003). Intergenerational transmission of partner violence: A 20-year prospective study. *Journal of Consulting and Clinical Psychology, 71,* 741–753.

Eisenberg, N., Guthrie, I. K., Cumberland, A., Murphy, B. C., Shepard, S. A., Zhou, Q., & Carlo, G. (2002). Prosocial development in early adulthood: A longitudinal study. *Journal of Personality and Social Psychology, 82,* 993–1006.

Eisenberger, N. I., Lieberman, M. D., & Williams, K. D. (2003). Does rejection hurt? An fMRI study of social exclusion. *Science, 302,* 290–292.

Ekman, P., & Friesen, W. V. (1969a). Nonverbal leakage clues to deception. *Psychiatry, 32,* 88–106.

Ekman, P., & Friesen, W. V. (1969b). The repertoire of nonverbal behavior: Categories, origins, usage, and coding. *Semiotica, 1,* 49–98.

Ekman, P., Friesen, W. V., O'Sullivan, M., Chan, A., Diacoyanni-Tarlatzis, I., Heider, K., Krause, R., LeCompte, W. A., Pitcairn, T., Ricci-Bitti, P. E., Scherer, K., Tomita, M., & Tzavaras, A. (1987). Universals and cultural differences in the judgments of facial expressions of emotion. *Journal of Personality and Social Psychology, 53,* 712–717.

Elfenbein, H. A., & Ambady, N. (2002). On the universality and cultural specificity of emotion recognition: A meta-analysis. *Psychological Bulletin, 128,* 203–235.

Elfenbein, H. A., & Ambady, N. (2003). Universals and cultural differences in recognizing emotions. *Current Directions in Psychological Science, 12,* 159–164.

Ellard, J. H., Miller, C. D., Baumle, T.-L., & Olson, J. M. (2002). Just world processes in demonizing. In M. Ross & D. T. Miller (Eds.), *The justice motive in everyday life* (pp. 350–362). Cambridge, UK: Cambridge University Press.

Ellickson, P. L., & Bell, R. M. (1990). Drug prevention in junior high: A multisite longitudinal test. *Science, 247,* 1299–1305.

Ellickson, P. L., McCaffrey, D. F., Ghosh-Dastidar, B., & Longshore, D. L. (2003). New inroads in preventing adolescent drug use: Results from a large-scale trial of project ALERT in middle schools. *American Journal of Public Health, 93,* 1830–1836.

Ellis, S., Rogoff, B., & Cromer, C. C. (1981). Age segregation in children's social interactions. *Developmental Psychology, 17,* 399–407.

Epley, N., & Dunning, D. (2000). Feeling "holier than thou": Are self-serving assessments produced by errors in self- or social prediction? *Journal of Personality and Social Psychology, 79,* 861–875.

Esser, J. K. (1998). Alive and well after 25 years: A review of groupthink research. *Organizational Behavior and Human Decision Processes, 73,* 116–141.

Esses, V. M., & Dovidio, J. F. (2002). The role of emotions in determining willingness to engage in intergroup contact. *Personality and Social Psychology Bulletin, 28,* 1202–1214.

Esses, V. M., Dovidio, J. F., Jackson, L. M., & Armstrong, T. L. (2001). The immigration dilemma: The role of perceived group competition, ethnic prejudice, and national identity. *Journal of Social Issues, 57,* 389–412.

Esses, V. M., Haddock, G., & Zanna, M. P. (1993). Values, stereotypes, and emotion as determinants of intergroup attitudes. In D. M. Mackie & D. L. Hamilton (Eds.), *Affect, cognition, and stereotyping: Interactive processes in group perception* (pp. 137–166). New York: Academic Press.

Esses, V. M., Haddock, G., & Zanna, M. P. (1994). The role of mood in the expression of intergroup stereotypes. In M. P. Zanna & J. M. Olson (Eds.) *The psychology of prejudice: The Ontario symposium* (pp. 77–101). Hillsdale, NJ: Erlbaum.

Esses, V. M., & Maio, G. R. (2002). Expanding the assessment of attitude components and structure: The benefits of open-ended measures. In W. Stroebe & M. Hewstone (Eds.), *European review of social psychology* (Vol. 12, pp. 71–102). Chichester, UK: Wiley.

Esses, V. M., & Webster, C. D. (1988). Physical attractiveness, dangerousness, and the Canadian Criminal Code. *Journal of Applied Social Psychology, 18,* 1017–1031.

Esses, V. M., & Zanna, M. P. (1995). Mood and the expression of ethnic stereotypes. *Journal of Personality and Social Psychology, 69,* 1052–1068.

Evans, R. (2001). Examining the informal sanctioning of deviance in a chat room culture. *Deviant Behavior, 22,* 195–210.

Fabrigar, L. R., MacDonald, T. K., & Wegener, D. T. (2005). The structure of attitudes. In D. Albarracín, B. T. Johnson, & M. P. Zanna (Eds.), *The handbook of attitudes* (pp. 79–124). Mahwah, NJ: Erlbaum.

Fabrigar, L. R., Priester, J. R., Petty, R. E., & Wegener, D. T. (1998). The impact of attitude accessibility on elaboration of persuasive messages. *Personality and Social Psychology Bulletin, 24,* 339–352.

Fazio, R. H. (1990). Multiple processes by which attitudes guide behavior: The MODE model as an integrative framework. In M. P. Zanna (Ed.), *Advances in experimental social psychology* (Vol. 23, pp. 75–109). San Diego, CA: Academic Press.

Fazio, R. H. (2000). Accessible attitudes as tools for object appraisal: The costs and benefits. In G. R. Maio & J. M. Olson (Eds.), *Why we evaluate: Functions of attitudes* (pp. 1–36). Mahwah, NJ: Erlbaum.

Fazio, R. H., Jackson, J. R., Dunton, B. C., & Williams, C. J. (1995). Variability in automatic activation as an unobtrusive measure of racial attitudes: A bona fide pipeline? *Journal of Personality and Social Psychology, 69,* 1013–1027.

Fazio, R. H., & Williams. C. J. (1986). Attitude accessibility as a moderator of the attitude-perception and attitude-behavior relations: An investigation of the 1984 presidential election. *Journal of Personality and Social Psychology, 51,* 505–514.

Fazio, R. H., & Zanna, M. P. (1981). Direct experience and attitude-behavior consistency. In L. Berkowitz (Ed.), *Advances in experimental social psychology* (Vol. 14, pp. 161–202). San Diego, CA: Academic Press.

Fazio, R. H., Zanna, M. P., & Cooper, J. (1977). Dissonance and self-perception: An integrative view of each theory's proper domain of application. *Journal of Experimental Social Psychology, 13,* 464–479.

Feeney, B. C., & Collins, N. L. (2001). Predictors of caregiving in adult intimate relationships: An attachment theoretical perspective. *Journal of Personality and Social Psychology, 80,* 972–994.

Feeney, B. C., & Collins, N. L. (2003). Motivations for caregiving in adult intimate relationships: Influences on caregiving behavior and relationship functioning. *Personality and Social Psychology Bulletin, 29,* 950–968.

Fehr, B. (2004). Intimacy expectations in same-sex friendships: A prototype interaction-pattern model. *Journal of Personality and Social Psychology, 86,* 265–284.

Fehr, B., & Broughton, R. (2001). Gender and personality differences in conceptions of love: An interpersonal theory analysis. *Personal Relationships, 8,* 115–136.

Fehr, B., & Russell, J. A. (1991). The concept of love viewed from a prototype perspective. *Journal of Personality and Social Psychology, 60,* 425–438.

Fein, S., & Spencer, S. J. (1997). Prejudice as self-image maintenance: Affirming the self through derogating others. *Journal of Personality and Social Psychology, 73,* 31–44.

Feingold, A. (1992a). Gender differences in mate selection preferences: A test of the parental investment model. *Psychological Bulletin, 112,* 125–139.

Feingold, A. (1992b). Good-looking people are not what we think. *Psychological Bulletin, 111,* 304–341.

Feldman Barrett, L., & Barrett, D. J. (2001). An introduction to computerized experience sampling in psychology. *Social Science Computer Review, 19,* 175–185.

Festinger, L. (1950). Informal social communication. *Psychological Review, 57,* 271–282.

Festinger, L. (1954). A theory of social comparison processes. *Human Relations, 7,* 117–140.

Festinger, L. (1957). *A theory of cognitive dissonance.* Stanford, CA: Stanford University Press.

Festinger, L., & Carlsmith, J. M. (1959). Cognitive consequences of forced compliance. *Journal of Abnormal and Social Psychology, 58,* 203–210.

Festinger, L., Pepitone, A., & Newcomb, T. (1952). Some consequences of de-individuation in a group. *Journal of Abnormal and Social Psychology, 47,* 382–389.

Festinger, L., Riecken, H. W., & Schachter, S. (1956). *When prophecy fails.* Minneapolis: University of Minnesota Press.

Festinger, L., Schachter, S., & Back, K. (1950). *Social pressures in informal groups: A study of human factors in housing.* New York: Harper & Row.

Fiedler, F. E. (1967). *A theory of leadership effectiveness.* New York: McGraw-Hill.

Fiedler, F. E. (1978). The contingency model and the dynamics of the leadership process. In L. Berkowitz (Ed.), *Advances in experimental social psychology* (Vol. 11, pp. 59–112). New York: Academic Press.

Fiedler, K., Nickel, S., Muehlfriedel, T., & Unkelbach, C. (2001). Is mood congruency an effect of genuine memory or response bias? *Journal of Experimental Social Psychology, 37,* 201–214.

Fincham, F. D., & Bradbury, T. N. (1993). Marital satisfaction, depression, and attributions: A longitudinal analysis. *Journal of Personality and Social Psychology, 64,* 442–452.

Finkelhor, D. (1997). The homicides of children and youth: A developmental perspective. In G. K. Kantor & J. L. Jasinski (Eds.), *Out of the darkness: Contemporary perspectives on family violence* (pp. 17–34). Thousand Oaks, CA: Sage.

Fischhoff, B. (1975). Hindsight ≠ Foresight: The effects of outcome knowledge on judgment under uncertainty. *Journal of Experimental Psychology: Human Perception and Performance, 3,* 288–299.

Fishbein, M., & Ajzen, I. (1975). *Belief, attitude, intention and behavior: An introduction to theory and research.* Reading, MA: Addison-Wesley.

Fisher, J. D., & Fisher, W. A. (1992). Changing AIDS risk behavior. *Psychological Bulletin, 111,* 455–474.

Fisher, J. D., Fisher, W. A., Misovich, S. J., Kimble, D. L., & Malloy, T. E. (1996). Changing AIDS risk behavior: Effects of an intervention emphasizing AIDS risk reduction information, motivation, and behavioral skills in a college student population. *Health Psychology, 15,* 238–250.

Fisher, J. D., Nadler, A., & Whitcher-Alagna, S. (1982). Recipient reactions to aid. *Psychological Bulletin, 91,* 27–54.

Fisher, W. A. (1986). A psychological approach to human sexuality: The Sexual Behavior Sequence. In D. Byrne & K. Kelley (Eds.), *Alternative approaches to the study of sexual behavior* (pp. 113–172). Hillsdale, NJ: Erlbaum.

Fisher, W. A., & Barak, A. (2001). Internet pornography: A social psychological perspective on Internet sexuality. *Journal of Sex Research, 38,* 312–323.

Fisher, W. A., Fisher, J. D., & Rye, B. J. (1995). Understanding and promoting AIDS-preventive behavior: Insights from the theory of reasoned action. *Health Psychology, 14,* 255–264.

Fisher, W. A., & Grenier, G. (1994). Violent pornography, antiwoman thoughts, and antiwoman acts: In search of reliable effects. *Journal of Sex Research, 31,* 23–38.

Fiske, A. P., Haslam, N., & Fiske, S. T. (1991). Confusing one person with another: What errors reveal about the elementary forms of social relations. *Journal of Personality and Social Psychology, 60,* 656–674.

Fiske, A. P., Kitayama, S., Markus, H. R., & Nisbett, R. E. (1998). The cultural matrix of social psychology. In D. T. Gilbert, S. T. Fiske, & G. Lindzey (Eds.), *The handbook of social psychology* (4th ed., Vol. 2, pp. 915–981). Boston, MA: McGraw-Hill.

Fiske, S. T. (1998). Stereotyping, prejudice, and discrimination. In D. T. Gilbert, S. T. Fiske, & G. Lindzey (Eds.), *The handbook of social psychology* (4th ed., Vol. 2, pp. 357–411). Boston, MA: McGraw-Hill.

Fiske, S. T. (2002). What we know now about bias and intergroup conflict, the problem of the century. *Current Directions in Psychological Science, 11,* 123–128.

Fiske, S. T. (2004). Mind the gap: In praise of informal sources of formal theory. *Personality and Social Psychology Review, 8,* 132–137.

Fiske, S. T., Cuddy, A. J. C., Glick, P., & Xu, J. (2002). A model of (often mixed) stereotype content: Competence and warmth respectively follow from perceived status and competition. *Journal of Personality and Social Psychology, 82,* 878–902.

Fiske, S. T., & Taylor, S. E. (1991). *Social cognition* (2nd ed.). New York: McGraw-Hill.

Fitzsimons, G. M., & Bargh, J. A. (2003). Thinking of you: Nonconscious pursuit of interpersonal goals associated with relationship partners. *Journal of Personality and Social Psychology, 84,* 148–164.

Fitzsimons, G. M., Shah, J., Chartrand, T. L., & Bargh, J. A. (2005). Goals and labors, friends and neighbors: Self-regulation and interpersonal relationships. In M. W. Baldwin (Ed.), *Interpersonal cognition* (pp. 103–125). New York: Guilford.

Flowers, M. L. (1977). A laboratory test of some implications of Janis' groupthink hypothesis. *Journal of Personality and Social Psychology, 35,* 888–896.

Foels, R., Driskell, J. E., Mullen, B., & Salas, E. (2000). The effects of democratic leadership on group member satisfaction: An integration. *Small Groups Research, 31,* 676–701.

Ford, T. E., Ferguson, M. A., Brooks, J. L., & Hagadone, K. M. (2004). Coping sense of humor reduces effects of stereotype threat on women's math performance. *Personality and Social Psychology Bulletin, 30,* 643–653.

Forgas, J. P. (1992). Affect and social perception: Research evidence and an integrative theory. In W. Stroebe & M. Hewstone (Eds.), *European review of social psychology* (Vol. 3, pp. 183–223). Chichester, England: Wiley.

Forgas, J. P., & Bond, M. H. (1985). Cultural influences on the perception of interaction episodes. *Personality and Social Psychology Bulletin, 11,* 75–88.

Forgas, J. P., Levinger, G., & Moylan, S. J. (1994). Feeling good and feeling close: Affective influences on the perception of intimate relationships. *Personal Relationships, 1,* 165–184.

Försterling, F. (2001). *Attribution: An introduction to theories, research, and applications.* Philadelphia, PA: Taylor and Francis Group.

Forsyth, D. R. (1999). *Group dynamics* (3rd ed.). Pacific Grove, CA: Brooks/Cole.

Foster, M. D. (2000). Positive and negative responses to personal discrimination: Does coping make a difference? *Journal of Social Psychology, 140,* 93–106.

Foster, M. D., & Tsarfati, E. M. (2005). The effects of meritocracy beliefs on women's well-being after first-time gender discrimination. *Personality and Social Psychology Bulletin, 31,* 1730–1738.

Frazier, P. A., Tix, A. P., & Barnett, C. L. (2003). The relational context of social support: Relationship satisfaction moderates the relations between enacted support and distress. *Personality and Social Psychology Bulletin, 29,* 1133–1146.

Freedman, J. L. (1984). Effects of television violence on aggressiveness. *Psychological Bulletin, 96,* 227–246.

Freedman, J. L. (1992). Television violence and aggression: What psychologists should tell the public. In P. Suedfeld & P. E. Tetlock (Eds.), *Psychology and social policy* (pp. 179–189). Washington, DC: Hemisphere.

Freedman, J. L., & Fraser, S. C. (1966). Compliance without pressure: The foot-in-the-door technique. *Journal of Personality and Social Psychology, 4,* 195–202.

Frey, D. (1986). Recent research on selective exposure to information. In L. Berkowitz (Ed.), *Advances in experimental social psychology* (Vol. 19, pp. 41–80). San Diego, CA: Academic Press.

Fricker, J., & Moore, S. (2002). Relationship satisfaction: The role of love styles and attachment styles. *Current Research in Social Psychology, 7*(11), 182–204.

Friedman, H. S. (Ed.). (1992). *Hostility, coping and health.* Washington, DC: American Psychological Association.

Friedman, H. S., & Schustack, M. W. (2003). *Personality: Classic theories and modern research.* Boston, MA: Allyn & Bacon.

Friedman, H. S., & Silver, R. C. (Eds.). (2005). *The Oxford handbook of health psychology.* New York: Oxford University Press.

Friedman, M., & Rosenman, R. H. (1974). *Type A behavior and your heart.* New York: Knopf.

Fu, G., Lee, K., Cameron, C. A., & Xu, F. (2001). Chinese and Canadian adults' categorization and evaluation of lie- and truth-telling about prosocial and antisocial behaviors. *Journal of Cross-Cultural Psychology, 32,* 720–727.

Gaertner, S. L., & Dovidio, J. F. (1986). The aversive form of racism. In J. F. Dovidio & S. L. Gaertner (Eds.), *Prejudice, discrimination, and racism* (pp. 61–89). Orlando, FL: Academic Press.

Gaertner, S. L., Dovidio, J. F., Anastasio, P. A., Bachman, B. A., & Rust, M. C. (1993). The common ingroup identity model: Recategorization and the reduction of intergroup bias. In W. Stroebe & M. Hewstone (Eds.), *European review of social psychology* (Vol. 4, pp. 1–26). New York: Wiley.

Galanter, H. (1989). *Cults: Faith, healing, and coercion.* New York: Oxford University Press.

Galen, B. R., & Underwood, M. K. (1997). A developmental investigation of social aggression among children. *Developmental Psychology, 33,* 589–600.

Galinsky, A. D., & Moskowitz, G. B. (2000). Perspective-taking: Decreasing stereotype expression, stereotype accessibility, and in-group favoritism. *Journal of Personality and Social Psychology, 78,* 708–724.

Gambaro, S., & Rabin, A. I. (1969). Diastolic blood pressure responses following direct and displaced aggression after anger arousal in high- and low-guilt subjects. *Journal of Personality and Social Psychology, 12,* 87–94.

Gangestad, S. W., & Simpson, J. A. (2000). The evolution of human mating: Trade-offs and strategic pluralism. *Behavioral and Brain Sciences, 23,* 573–587.

Gantner, A. B., & Taylor, S. P. (1992). Human physical aggression as a function of alcohol and threat of harm. *Aggressive Behavior, 18,* 29–36.

Garcia, S. M., Weaver, K., Moskowitz, G. B., & Darley, J. M. (2002). Crowded minds: The implicit bystander effect. *Journal of Personality and Social Psychology, 83,* 843–853.

Gardner, R. C. (1985). *Social psychology and second language learning.* London, UK: Arnold.

Gardner, R. C. (1994). Stereotypes as consensual beliefs. In M. P. Zanna & J. M. Olson (Eds.), *The psychology of prejudice: The Ontario symposium* (pp. 1–31). Hillsdale, NJ: Erlbaum.

Gardner, R. C., & Clément, R. (1990). Social psychological perspectives on second language acquisition. In H. Giles & W. P. Robinson (Eds.), *Handbook of social psychology* (pp. 495–517). Chichester, UK: Wiley.

Gardner, R. C., & Lambert, W. E. (1959). Motivational variables in second language acquisition. *Canadian Journal of Psychology, 13,* 266–272.

Gardner, W. L., Gabriel, S., & Hochschild, L. (2002). When you and I are "we," you are not threatening: The role of self-expansion in social comparison. *Journal of Personality and Social Psychology, 82,* 239–251.

Gardner, W. L., Gabriel, S., & Yee, A. Y. (1999). "I" value freedom, but "we" value relationships: Self-construal priming mirrors cultural differences in judgment. *Psychological Science, 10,* 321–326.

Garfein, R. (1997, May/June). An interesting career in psychology: International market research consultant. *Psychological Science Agenda, 10*(3), 7.

Gawronski, B., & Bodenhausen, G. V. (2005). Accessibility effects on implicit social cognition: The role of knowledge activation and retrieval experiences. *Journal of Personality and Social Psychology, 89,* 672–685.

Gawronski, B., Bodenhausen, G. V., & Banse, R. (2005). We are, therefore they aren't: Ingroup construal as a standard of comparison for outgroup judgments. *Journal of Experimental Social Psychology, 41,* 515–526.

Gawronski, B., Deutsch, R., & Seidel, O. (2005). Contextual influences on implicit evaluation: A test of additive versus contrastive effects of evaluative context stimuli in affective priming. *Personality and Social Psychology Bulletin, 31,* 1226–1236.

Gawronski, B., & Strack, F. (2004). On the propositional nature of cognitive consistency: Dissonance changes explicit, but not implicit attitudes. *Journal of Experimental Social Psychology, 40,* 535–542.

Gawronski, B., Strack, F., & Bodenhausen, G. V. (in press). Attitudes and cognitive consistency: The role of associative and propositional processes. In R. E. Petty, R. H. Fazio, & P. Briñol (Eds.), *Attitudes: Insights from the new wave of implicit measures.* Mahwah, NJ: Erlbaum.

Gawronski, B., Walther, E., & Blank, H. (2005). Cognitive consistency and the formation of interpersonal attitudes: Cognitive balance affects the encoding of social information. *Journal of Experimental Social Psychology, 41,* 618–626.

Geary, D. C. (1999). *Male, female: The evolution of human sex differences.* Washington, DC: American Psychological Association.

Geen, R. G. (1968). Effects of frustration, attack, and prior training in aggressiveness upon aggressive behavior. *Journal of Personality and Social Psychology, 9,* 316–321.

Geen, R. G. (1998). Aggression and antisocial behavior. In D. T. Gilbert, S. T. Fiske, & G. Lindzey (Eds.), *The handbook of social psychology* (4th ed., Vol. 2, pp. 317–356). Boston, MA: McGraw-Hill.

Geen, R. G., & Gange, J. J. (1977). Drive theory of social facilitation: Twelve years of theory and research. *Psychological Bulletin, 84,* 1267–1288.

Gelfand, M. J., Higgins, M., Nishii, L. H., Raver, J. L., Dominguez, A., Murakami, F., Yamaguchi, S., & Toyama, M. (2002). Culture and egocentric perceptions of fairness in conflict and negotiation. *Journal of Applied Psychology, 87,* 833–845.

Gerard, H. B., Wilhelmy, R. A., & Conolley, E. S. (1968). Conformity and group size. *Journal of Personality and Social Psychology, 8,* 79–82.

Gergen, K. J., Gergen, M. M., & Barton, W. H. (1973). Deviance in the dark. *Psychology Today, 7,* 129–130.

Gershoff, E. T. (2002). Corporal punishment by parents and associated child behaviors and experiences: A meta-analytic and theoretical review. *Psychological Bulletin, 128,* 539–579.

Giancola, P. R. (1995). Evidence for sorsolateral and orbital prefrontal cortical involvement in the expression of aggressive behaviour. *Aggressive Behaviour, 21*, 431–450.

Gibbons, F. X., Gerrard, M., Cleveland, M. J., Wills, T. A., & Brody, G. (2004). Perceived discrimination and substance use in African American parents and their children: A panel study. *Journal of Personality and Social Psychology, 86*, 517–529.

Gilbert, D. T. (1989). Thinking lightly about others: Automatic components of the social inference process. In J. A. Bargh & J. S. Uleman (Eds.), *Unintended thought* (pp. 189–211). New York: Guilford.

Gilbert, D. T., & Hixon, J. G. (1991). The trouble of thinking: Activation and application of stereotypic beliefs. *Journal of Personality and Social Psychology, 60*, 509–517.

Gilbert, D. T., & Malone, P. S. (1995). The correspondence bias. *Psychological Bulletin, 117*, 21–38.

Gilbert, D. T., Pelham, B. W., & Krull, D. S. (1988). On cognitive busyness: When person perceivers meet persons perceived. *Journal of Personality and Social Psychology, 54*, 733–740.

Giles, M., Liddell, C., & Bydawell, M. (2005). Condom use in African adolescents: The role of individual and group factors. *AIDS Care, 17*, 729–739.

Gilovich, T. (1991). *How we know what isn't so: The fallibility of human reason in everyday life.* New York: Macmillan.

Gilovich, T., Griffin, D, & Kahneman, D. (Eds.). (2002). *Heuristics and biases: The psychology of intuitive judgment.* New York: Cambridge University Press.

Gilovich, T., Vallone, R., & Tversky, A. (1985). The hot hand in basketball: On the misperception of random sequences. *Cognitive Psychology, 17*, 295–314.

Giner-Sorolla, R., & Chaiken, S. (1994). The causes of hostile media judgments. *Journal of Experimental Social Psychology, 30*, 165–180.

Glass, D. C. (1977). *Behavioral patterns, stress, and coronary disease.* Hillsdale, NJ: Erlbaum.

Gleason, M. E. J., Iida, M., Bolger, N., & Shrout, P. E. (2003). Daily supportive equity in close relationships. *Personality and Social Psychology Bulletin, 29*, 1036–1045.

Gleicher, F., & Petty, R. E. (1992). Expectations of reassurance influence the nature of fear-stimulated attitude change. *Journal of Experimental Social Psychology, 28*, 86–100.

Glick, P., DeMorest, J. A., & Hotze, C. A. (1988). Self-monitoring and beliefs about partner compatibility in romantic relationships. *Personality and Social Psychology Bulletin, 14*, 485–494.

Glick, P., & Fiske, S. T. (1996). The ambivalent sexism inventory: Differentiating hostile and benevolent sexism. *Journal of Personality and Social Psychology, 70*, 491–512.

Glick, P., Fiske, S. T., Mladinic, A., Saiz, J. L., Abrams, D., Masser, B., et al. (2000). Beyond prejudice as simple antipathy: Hostile and benevolent sexism across cultures. *Journal of Personality and Social Psychology, 79*, 763–775.

Glick, P., Lameiras, M., Fiske, S. T., Eckes, T., Masser, B., Volpato, C., et al. (2004). Bad but bold: Ambivalent attitudes toward men predict gender inequality in 16 nations. *Journal of Personality and Social Psychology, 86*, 713–728.

Goethals, G. R. (1986a). Fabricating and ignoring social reality: Self-serving estimates of consensus. In J. M. Olson, C. P. Herman, & M. P. Zanna (Eds.), *Relative deprivation and social comparison: The Ontario symposium* (Vol. 4, pp. 135–157). Hillsdale, NJ: Lawrence-Erlbaum.

Goethals, G. R. (1986b). Social comparison theory: Psychology from the lost and found. *Personality and Social Psychology Bulletin, 12*, 261–278.

Goethals, G. R., & Darley, J. M. (1977). Social comparison theory: An attributional approach. In J. M. Suls & R. L. Miller (Eds.), *Social comparison processes: Theoretical and empirical perspectives* (pp. 259–278). Washington, DC: Hemisphere.

Goethals, G. R., & Klein, W. M. P. (2000). Interpreting and inventing social reality: Attributional and constructive elements in social comparison. In J. M. Suls & L. Wheeler (Eds.), *Handbook of social comparison: Theory and research* (pp. 23–44). New York: Kluwer Academic/Plenum.

Goethals, G. R., Messick, D. M., & Allison, S. T. (1991). The uniqueness bias: Studies of constructive social comparison. In J. M. Suls & T. A. Wills (Eds.), *Social comparison research: Contemporary theory and research* (pp. 149–176). Hillsdale, NJ: Erlbaum.

Goffman, E. (1959). *The presentation of self in everyday life.* Oxford, England: Doubleday.

Goffman, E. (1967). *Interaction ritual.* Oxford, England: Aldine.

Goldstein, D. G., & Gigerenzer, G. (2002). Models of ecological rationality: The recognition heuristic. *Psychological Review, 109*, 75–90.

Gollwitzer, P. M. (1999). Implementation intentions: Strong effects of simple plans. *American Psychologist, 54*, 493–503.

Gorassini, D. R., & Olson, J. M. (1995). Does self-perception change explain the foot-in-the-door effect? *Journal of Personality and Social Psychology, 69*, 91–105.

Gosling, S. D., Rentfrow, P. J., & Swann, W. B., Jr. (2003). A very brief measure of the Big-Five personality domains. *Journal of Research in Personality, 37*, 504–528.

Gottfredson, L. S., & Deary, I. J. (2004). Intelligence predicts health and longevity, but why? *Current Directions in Psychological Science, 13*, 1–4.

Gottman, J. M. (1983). How children become friends. With commentary by William G. Graziano. *Monographs of the Society for Research in Child Development, 38*(2, Serial No. 201).

Gouldner, A. W. (1960). The norm of reciprocity: A preliminary statement. *American Sociological Review, 25*, 161–178.

Govan, C. L., & Williams, K. D. (2004). Changing the affective valence of the stimulus items influences the IAT by re-defining the category labels. *Journal of Experimental Social Psychology, 40*, 357–365.

Graham, K. (1980). Theories of intoxicated aggression. *Canadian Journal of Behavioral Sciences, 12*, 141–158.

Graham, K., & Wells, S. (2001). The two worlds of aggression for men and women. *Sex Roles, 45*, 595–622.

Grant, M. J., Button, C. M., Hannah, T. E., & Ross, A. S. (2003). The role of ideological consistency in attitude inferences. *Current Research in Social Psychology, 9*(3).

Grant, M. J., Button, C. M., Ross, A. S., & Hannah, T. E. (1997). Accuracy of attitude stereotypes: The case of inferences based on gender. *Canadian Journal of Behavioural Science, 29*, 83–91.

Grant, M. J., Hannah, T. E., Ross, A. S., & Button, C. M. (1995). Structure and processing of the perceived attitudes of others: Beyond "liberal" and "conservative." *Social Behavior and Personality, 23*, 1–22.

Graziano, W. G., Brothen, T., & Berscheid, E. (1978). Height and attraction: Do men and women see eye-to-eye? *Journal of Personality, 46*, 128–145.

Greaven, S. H., Santor, D. A., Thompson, R., & Zuroff, D. C. (2000). Adolescent self-handicapping, depressive affect, and maternal parenting styles. *Journal of Youth and Adolescence, 29*, 631–646.

Greenberg, J., Pyszczynski, T., Solomon, S., Rosenblatt, A., Veeder, M., Kirkland, S., & Lyon, D. (1990). Evidence for terror management theory II: The effects of mortality salience on reactions to those who threaten or bolster the cultural worldview. *Journal of Personality and Social Psychology, 58*, 308–318.

Greenberg, J., Pyszczynski, T., Solomon, S., Simon, L., & Breus, M. (1994). Role of consciousness and accessibility of death-related thoughts in mortality salience effects. *Journal of Personality and Social Psychology, 67*, 627–637.

Greenberg, J., Solomon, S., & Pyszczynski, T. (1997). Terror management theory of self-esteem and cultural worldviews: Empirical assessments and conceptual refinements. In M. P. Zanna (Ed.), *Advances in experimental social psychology* (Vol. 29, pp. 61–139). San Diego, CA: Academic Press.

Greenberg, M. S., & Shapiro, S. P. (1971). Indebtedness: An adverse aspect of asking for and receiving help. *Sociometry, 34,* 290–301.

Greenwald, A. G. (1968). Cognitive learning, cognitive response to persuasion, and attitude change. In A. G. Greenwald, T. C. Brock, & T. M. Ostrom (Eds.), *Psychological foundations of attitudes* (pp. 147–170). New York: Academic Press.

Greenwald, A. G., & Banaji, M. R. (1995). Implicit social cognition: Attitudes, self-esteem, and stereotypes. *Psychological Review, 102,* 4–27.

Greenwald, A. G., Banaji, M. R., Rudman, L. A., Farnham, S. D., Nosek, B. A., & Mellott, D. S. (2002). A unified theory of implicit attitudes, stereotypes, self-esteem, and self-concept. *Psychological Review, 109,* 3–25.

Greenwald, A. G., Carnot, C. G., Beach, R., & Young, B. (1987). Increasing voting behavior by asking people if they expect to vote. *Journal of Applied Psychology, 72,* 315–318.

Greenwald, A. G., McGhee, D. E., & Schwartz, J. L. K. (1998). Measuring individual differences in implicit cognition: The implicit association test. *Journal of Personality and Social Psychology, 74,* 1464–1480.

Greenwald, A. G., Oakes, M. A., & Hoffman, H. G. (2003). Targets of discrimination: Effects of race on responses to weapon holders. *Journal of Experimental Social Psychology, 39,* 399–405.

Griffin, D., & Bartholomew, K. (1994). Models of the self and other: Fundamental dimensions underlying measures of adult attachment. *Journal of Personality and Social Psychology, 67,* 430–445.

Griffiths, M. (1999). Violent video games and aggression: A review of the literature. *Aggression and Violent Behavior, 4,* 203–212.

Grotpeter, J. K., & Crick, N. R. (1996). Relational aggression, overt aggression, and friendship. *Child Development, 67,* 2328–2338.

Grube, J. A., & Piliavin, J. A. (2000). Role identity, organizational experiences, and volunteer performance. *Personality and Social Psychology Bulletin, 26,* 1108–1119.

Grusec, J. (1991). The socialization of altruism. In M. S. Clark (Ed.), *Prosocial behavior* (pp. 9–33). Newbury Park, CA: Sage.

Gruter, M., & Masters, R. D. (1986). Ostracism as a social and biological phenomenon: An introduction. *Ethology and Sociobiology, 7,* 149–158.

Guadagno, R. E., Asher, T., Demaine, L. J., & Cialdini, R. B. (2001). When saying yes leads to saying no: Preference for consistency and the reverse foot-in-the-door effect. *Personality and Social Psychology Bulletin, 27,* 859–867.

Guéguen, N., & Jacob, C. (2001). Fund-raising on the web: The effect of an electronic foot-in-the-door on donation. *CyberPsychology & Behavior, 4,* 705–709.

Guglielmi, R. S. (1999). Psychophysiological assessment of prejudice: Past research, current status, and future directions. *Personality and Social Psychology Review, 3,* 123–157.

Guimond, S., & Dubé-Simard, L. (1983). Relative deprivation theory and the Quebec nationalist movement: The cognition-emotion distinction and the personal-group deprivation issue. *Journal of Personality and Social Psychology, 44,* 526–535.

Haddock, G., & Zanna, M. P. (1998). On the use of open-ended measures to assess attitudinal components. *British Journal of Social Psychology, 37,* 129–149.

Haddock, G., Rothman, A. J., Reber, R., & Schwarz, N. (1999). Forming judgments of attitude certainty, intensity, and importance: The role of subjective experiences. *Personality and Social Psychology Bulletin, 25,* 771–782.

Hafer, C. L. (2000). Do innocent victims threaten the belief in a just world? *Journal of Personality and Social Psychology, 79,* 165–173.

Hafer, C. L., & Bègue, L. (2005). Experimental research on just-world theory: Problems, developments, and future challenges. *Psychological Bulletin, 131,* 128–167.

Hafer, C. L., & Olson, J. M. (2003). An analysis of empirical research on the scope of justice. *Personality and Social Psychology Review, 7,* 311–323.

Hafer, C. L., Reynolds, K. L., & Obertynski, M. A. (1996). Message comprehensibility and persuasion: Effects of complex language in counterattitudinal appeals to laypeople. *Social Cognition, 14,* 317–337.

Hall, J. A. (1984). *Nonverbal sex differences: Communication accuracy and expressive style.* Baltimore: Johns Hopkins University Press.

Halladay, J., & Wolf, R. (2000, July 18). Indianapolis OKs restrictions on violent video game usage. *USA Today,* p. A5.

Hallman, W. K., Hebden, W. C., Aquino, H. L., Cuite, C. L., & Lang, J. T. (2003). *Public perceptions of genetically modified foods: A national study of American knowledge and opinion.* New Brunswick, NJ: Food Policy Institute, Cook College, The State University of New Jersey.

Halpern, D. F. (1992). *Sex differences in cognitive abilities* (2nd ed.). Hillsdale, NJ: Erlbaum.

Halpern, D. F. (2004). A cognitive-process taxonomy for sex differences in cognitive abilities. *Current Directions in Psychological Science, 13,* 135–139.

Hamilton, D. L., & Gifford, R. K. (1976). Illusory correlation in interpersonal perception: A cognitive basis of stereotypic judgments. *Journal of Experimental Social Psychology, 12,* 392–407.

Hamilton, D. L., & Sherman, J. W. (1994). Stereotypes. In R. S. Wyer, Jr., & T. K. Srull (Eds.), *Handbook of social cognition. Volume 2: Applications* (2nd ed., pp. 1–68). Hillsdale, NJ: Erlbaum.

Hamilton, W. D. (1964). The genetical evolution of social behavior. I and II. *Journal of Theoretical Biology, 7,* 1–52.

Hampson, E. (2002). Sex differences in human brain and cognition: The influence of sex steroids in early and adult life. In J. B. Becker, S. M. Breedlove, D. Crews, & M. McCarthy (Eds.), *Behavioral endocrinology* (2nd ed., pp. 579–628). Cambridge, MA: MIT Press.

Han, S., & Shavitt, S. (1994). Persuasion and culture: Advertising appeals in individualistic and collectivistic societies. *Journal of Experimental Social Psychology, 30,* 326–350.

Hans, V. P., & Vidmar, N. (1986). *Judging the jury.* New York: Plenum.

Hansen, R. D., & Hall, C. A. (1985). Discounting and augmenting facilitative and inhibitory forces: The winner takes almost all. *Journal of Personality and Social Psychology, 49,* 1482–1493.

Hansen, R. D., & Hansen, C. H. (1988). Repression of emotionally tagged memories: The architecture of less complex emotions. *Journal of Personality and Social Psychology, 55,* 147–169.

Harackiewicz, J. M., & Elliot, A. J. (1998). The joint effects of target and purpose goals on intrinsic motivation: A mediational analysis. *Personality and Social Psychology Bulletin, 24,* 675–689.

Hardin, G. (1968). The tragedy of the commons. *Science, 162,* 1243–1248.

Hardy, C., & Latané, B. (1988). Social loafing in cheerleaders: Effects of team membership and competition. *Journal of Sport and Exercise Psychology, 10,* 109–114.

Harmon-Jones, E., Brehm, J. W., Greenberg, J., Simon, L., & Nelson, D. E. (1996). Evidence that the production of aversive consequences is not necessary to create cognitive dissonance. *Journal of Personality and Social Psychology, 70,* 5–16.

Harmon-Jones, E., Greenberg, J., Solomon, S., & Simon, L. (1996). The effects of mortality salience on intergroup bias between minimal groups. *European Journal of Social Psychology, 26,* 677–681.

Harmon-Jones, E., & Harmon-Jones, C. (2002). Testing the action-based model of cognitive dissonance: The effect of action orientation on postdecisional attitudes. *Personality and Social Psychology Bulletin, 28,* 711–723.

Harmon-Jones, E., & Mills, J. (Eds.). (1999). *Cognitive dissonance: Progress on a pivotal theory in social psychology.* Washington, DC: American Psychological Association.

Harmon-Jones, E., & Sigelman, J. (2001). State anger and prefrontal brain activity: Evidence that insult-related relative left-prefrontal activation is associated with experienced anger and aggression. *Journal of Personality and Social Psychology, 80,* 797–803.

Harris, J. R. (1995). Where is the child's environment? A group socialization theory of development. *Psychological Review, 102,* 458–489.

Harris, J. R. (1998). *The nurture assumption: Why children turn out the way they do.* New York: Free Press.

Harris, M. B., Harris, R. J., & Bochner, S. (1982). Fat, four-eyed, and female: Stereotypes of obesity, glasses, and gender. *Journal of Applied Social Psychology, 12,* 503–516.

Harris, P. (1996). Sufficient grounds for optimism? The relationship between perceived controllability and optimistic bias. *Journal of Social and Clinical Psychology, 15,* 9–52.

Hartup, W. W. (1989). Social relationships and their developmental significance. *American Psychologist, 44,* 120–126.

Harwood, R. L., & Miller, J. G. (1991). Perceptions of attachment behavior: A comparison of Anglo and Puerto Rican mothers. *Merrill-Palmer Quarterly, 37,* 583–599.

Hassan, S. (1988). *Combating cult mind control.* Rochester, VT: Park Street Press.

Hastie, R. (1981). Schematic principles in human memory. In E. T. Higgins, C. P. Herman, & M. P. Zanna (Eds.), *Social cognition: The Ontario symposium* (Vol. 1, pp. 39–88). Hillsdale, NJ: Erlbaum.

Hastie, R., Penrod, S. D., & Pennington, N. (1983). *Inside the jury.* Cambridge, MA: Harvard University Press.

Hatfield, E. (1988). Passionate and companionate love. In R. J. Sternberg & M. L. Barnes (Eds.), *The psychology of love* (pp. 191–217). New Haven, CT: Yale University Press.

Hatfield, E., & Rapson, R. L. (1996). *Love and sex: Cross-cultural perspectives.* Boston, MA: Allyn & Bacon.

Hatfield, E., & Sprecher, S. (1986). *Mirror, mirror: The importance of looks in everyday life.* Albany, NY: State University of New York Press.

Hatfield, E., Traupmann, J., Sprecher, S., Utne, M., & Hay, J. (1985). Equity in intimate relations: Recent research. In W. Ickes (Ed.), *Compatible and incompatible relationships* (pp. 91–117). New York: Springer.

Hatfield, E., & Walster, G. W. (1978). *A new look at love.* Reading, MA: Addison-Wesley.

Hausenblas, H. A., & Carron, A. V. (1999). Eating disorder indices and athletes: An integration. *Journal of Sport and Exercise Psychology, 21,* 230–256.

Hawkins, S. A., & Hastie, R. (1990). Hindsight: Biased judgments of past events after the outcomes are known. *Psychological Bulletin, 107,* 311–327.

Haynes, G. A., & Olson, J. M. (2006). Coping with threats to just-world beliefs: Derogate, blame, or help? *Journal of Applied Social Psychology, 36,* 664–682.

Hays, R. B. (1985). A longitudinal study of friendship development. *Journal of Personality and Social Psychology, 48,* 909–924.

Hazan, C., & Shaver, P. R. (1987). Romantic love conceptualized as an attachment process. *Journal of Personality and Social Psychology, 52,* 511–524.

Hazan, C., & Shaver, P. R. (1990). Love and work: An attachment-theoretical perspective. *Journal of Personality and Social Psychology, 59,* 270–280.

Hazlewood, J. D., & Olson, J. M. (1986). Covariation information, causal questioning, and interpersonal behavior. *Journal of Experimental Social Psychology, 22,* 276–291.

Hebl, M. R., & Heatherton, T. F. (1997). The stigma of obesity: The differences are black and white. *Personality and Social Psychology Bulletin, 24,* 417–426.

Hebl, M. R., & Mannix, L. M. (2003). The weight of obesity in evaluating others: A mere proximity effect. *Personality and Social Psychology Bulletin, 29,* 28–38.

Heider, F. (1958). *The psychology of interpersonal relations.* New York: Wiley.

Heilman, M. E., Block, C. J., & Martell, R. F. (1995). Sex stereotypes: Do they influence perceptions of managers? *Journal of Social Behavior and Personality, 10,* 237–252.

Heine, S. J., & Lehman, D. R. (1995). Cultural variation in unrealistic optimism: Does the West feel more invulnerable than the East? *Journal of Personality and Social Psychology, 68,* 595–607.

Heine, S. J., & Lehman, D. R. (1997a). Culture, dissonance, and self-affirmation. *Personality and Social Psychology Bulletin, 23,* 389–400.

Heine, S. J., & Lehman, D. R. (1997b). The cultural construction of self-enhancement: An examination of group-serving biases. *Journal of Personality and Social Psychology, 72,* 1268–1283.

Helgeson, V. S., & Mickelson, K. (1995). Motives for social comparison. *Personality and Social Psychology Bulletin, 21,* 1200–1209.

Helgeson, V. S., & Taylor, S. E. (1993). Social comparisons and adjustment among cardiac patients. *Journal of Applied Social Psychology, 23,* 1171–1195.

Henderlong, J., & Lepper, M. R. (2002). The effects of praise on children's intrinsic motivation: A review and synthesis. *Psychological Bulletin, 128,* 774–795.

Hendrick, C., & Hendrick, S. (1986). A theory and method of love. *Journal of Personality and Social Psychology, 50,* 392–402.

Hendrick, S. S., Hendrick, C., & Adler, N. L. (1988). Romantic relationships: Love, satisfaction, and staying together. *Journal of Personality and Social Psychology, 54,* 980–988.

Herek, G. M. (1986). The instrumentality of attitudes: Toward a neofunctional theory. *Journal of Social Issues, 42*(2), 99–114.

Herek, G. M., & Capitanio, J. P. (1998). Symbolic prejudice or fear of infection? A functional analysis of AIDS-related stigma among heterosexual adults. *Basic and Applied Social Psychology, 20,* 230–241.

Hewitt, P. L., & Flett, G. L. (1991). Perfectionism in the self and social contexts: Conceptualization, assessment, and association with psychopathology. *Journal of Personality and Social Psychology, 60,* 456–470.

Hewstone, M., & Jaspars, J. (1983). A re-examination of the role of consensus, consistency and distinctiveness: Kelley's cube revisited. *British Journal of Social Psychology, 22,* 41–50.

Higgins, E. T. (1987). Self-discrepancy: A theory relating self and affect. *Psychological Review, 94,* 319–340.

Higgins, E. T. (1989). Knowledge accessibility and activation: Subjectivity and suffering from unconscious sources. In J. S. Uleman & J. A. Bargh (Eds.), *Unintended thought* (pp. 75–123). New York: Guilford Press.

Higgins, E. T. (1996). Knowledge activation: Accessibility, applicability, and salience. In E. T. Higgins & A. W. Kruglanski (Eds.), *Social psychology: Handbook of basic principles* (pp. 133–168). New York: Guilford Press.

Higgins, E. T. (2004). Making a theory useful: Lessons handed down. *Personality and Social Psychology Review, 8,* 138–145.

Higgins, E. T., Bond, R. N., Klein, R., & Strauman, T. (1986). Self-discrepancies and emotional vulnerability: How magnitude, accessibility, and type of discrepancy influence affect. *Journal of Personality and Social Psychology, 51,* 5–15.

Higgins, E. T., King, G. A., & Mavin, G. H. (1982). Individual construct accessibility and subjective impressions and recall. *Journal of Personality and Social Psychology, 43,* 35–47.

Higgins, E. T., Klein, R., & Strauman, T. (1985). Self-concept discrepancy theory: A psychological model for distinguishing among different aspects of depression and anxiety. *Social Cognition, 3,* 51–76.

Higgins, R. L., Snyder, C. R., & Berglas, S. (Eds.). (1990). *Self-handicapping: The paradox that isn't.* New York: Plenum.

Hilton, D. J., & Slugoski, B. R. (1986). Knowledge based causal attribution: The abnormal conditions focus model. *Psychological Review, 93*, 75–88.

Hilton, J. L., & Darley, J. M. (1991). The effects of interaction goals on person perception. In M. P. Zanna (Ed.), *Advances in experimental social psychology* (Vol. 24, pp. 235–267). San Diego, CA: Academic Press.

Hirt, E. R., Deppe, R. K., & Gordon, L. J. (1991). Self-reported versus behavioral self-handicapping: Empirical evidence for a theoretical distinction. *Journal of Personality and Social Psychology, 61*, 981–991.

Hirt, E. R., McCrea, S. M., & Kimble, C. E. (2000). Public self-focus and sex differences in behavioral self-handicapping: Does increasing self-threat still make it "just a man's game"? *Personality and Social Psychology Bulletin, 26*, 1131–1141.

Hirt, E. R., Zillman, D., Erickson, G. A., & Kennedy, C. (1992). Costs and benefits of allegiance: Changes in fans' self-ascribed competencies after team victory versus defeat. *Journal of Personality and Social Psychology, 63*, 724–738.

Hoaken, P. N. S., & Pihl, R. O. (2000). The effects of alcohol intoxication on aggressive responses in men and women. *Alcohol and Alcoholism, 33*, 47–54.

Hoaken, P. N. S., Campbell, T., Stewart, S. H., & Pihl, R. O. (2003). Effects of alcohol on cardiovascular reactivity and the mediation of aggressive behaviour in adult men and women. *Alcohol and Alcoholism, 38*, 84–92.

Hodges, E. V., Malone, M. J., & Perry, D. G. (1997). Individual risk and social risk as interacting determinants of victimization in the peer group. *Developmental Psychology, 33*, 1032–1039.

Hodson, G., & Esses, V. M. (2002). Distancing oneself from negative attributes and the personal/group discrimination discrepancy. *Journal of Experimental Social Psychology, 38*, 500–507.

Hodson, G., & Olson, J. M. (2005). Testing the generality of the name letter effect: Name initials and everyday attitudes. *Personality and Social Psychology Bulletin, 31*, 1099–1111.

Hodson, G., & Sorrentino, R. M. (1997). Groupthink and uncertainty orientation: Personality differences in reactivity to the group situation. *Group Dynamics: Theory, Research, and Practice, 1*, 144–155.

Hoffman, M. L. (1981). Is altruism part of human nature? *Journal of Personality and Social Psychology, 40*, 121–137.

Hofling, C. K., Brotzman, E., Dalrymple, S., Graves, N., & Pierce, C. (1966). An experimental study in nurse-physician relationships. *Journal of Nervous and Mental Disease, 143*, 171–180.

Hofstede, G. H. (1980). *Culture's consequences: International differences in work-related values.* Beverly Hills, CA: Sage.

Hofstede, G. H. (1991). *Cultures and organizations: Software of the mind.* London, UK: McGraw-Hill.

Hofstede, G. H. (2001). *Culture's consequences: Comparing values, behaviors, institutions, and organizations across nations* (2nd ed.). Thousand Oaks, CA: Sage.

Hokanson, J. E., & Shetler, S. (1961). The effect of overt aggression on physiological arousal level. *Journal of Abnormal and Social Psychology, 63*, 446–448.

Holland, R. W., Verplanken, B., & van Knippenberg, A. (2002). On the nature of attitude-behavior relations: The strong guide, the weak follow. *European Journal of Social Psychology, 32*, 869–876.

Hollander, E. P. (1985). Leadership and power. In G. Lindzey & E. Aronson (Eds.), *The handbook of social psychology* (3rd ed., Vol. 2, pp. 485–537). New York: Random House.

Holmberg, D., & MacKenzie, S. (2002). So far so good: Scripts for romantic relationship development as predictors of relational well-being. *Journal of Social and Personal Relationships, 19*, 777–796.

Holmes, J. G. (2002). Interpersonal expectations as the building blocks of social cognition: An interdependence theory perspective. *Personal Relationships, 9*, 1–26.

Holmes, J. G., & Cameron, J. (2005). An integrative review of theories of interpersonal cognition: An interdependence theory perspective. In M. W. Baldwin (Ed.), *Interpersonal cognition* (pp. 415–447). New York: Guilford.

Holmes, J. G., & Murray, S. L. (1996). Conflict in close relationships. In E. T. Higgins & A. W. Kruglanski (Eds.), *Social psychology: Handbook of basic principles* (pp. 622–654). New York: Guilford.

Holtzworth-Munroe, A. (2000). A typology of men who are violent toward their female partners: Making sense of the heterogeneity in husband violence. *Current Directions in Psychological Science, 9*, 140–143.

Holtzworth-Munroe, A., & Stuart, G. L. (1994). Typologies of male batterers: Three subtypes and the differences among them. *Psychological Bulletin, 116*, 476–497.

Holtzworth-Munroe, A., Stuart, G. L., & Hutchinson, G. (1997). Violent versus nonviolent husbands: Differences in attachment patterns, dependency, and jealousy. *Journal of Family Psychology, 11*, 314–331.

Hoorens, V., & Nuttin, J. M. (1993). Overvaluation of own attributes: Mere ownership or subjective frequency? *Social Cognition, 11*, 177–200.

Hoorens, V., & Ruiter, S. (1996). The optimal impact phenomenon: Beyond the third person effect. *European Journal of Social Psychology, 26*, 599–610.

Hopper, J. R., & Nielsen, J. M. (1991). Recycling as altruistic behavior: Normative and behavioral strategies to expand participation in a community recycling program. *Environment and Behavior, 23*, 195–220.

Hornsey, M. J., & Jetten, J. (2004). The individual within the group: Balancing the need to belong with the need to be different. *Personality and Social Psychology Review, 8*, 248–264.

Hornstein, H. A., LaKind, E., Frankel, G., & Manne, S. (1975). Effects of knowledge about remote social events on prosocial behavior, social conception, and mood. *Journal of Personality and Social Psychology, 32*, 1038–1046.

Horvitz, T., & Pratkanis, A. R. (2002). A laboratory demonstration of the fraudulent telemarketers' 1-in-5 prize tactic. *Journal of Applied Social Psychology, 32*, 310–317.

Hoshino-Browne, E., Zanna, A. S., Spencer, S. J., & Zanna, M. P. (2004). Investigating attitudes cross-culturally: A case of cognitive dissonance among East Asians and North Americans. In G. Haddock & G. R. Maio (Eds.), *Contemporary perspectives on the psychology of attitudes* (pp. 375–397). London, UK: Psychology Press.

Hoshino-Browne, E., Zanna, A. S., Spencer, S. J., Zanna, M. P., Kitayama, S., & Lackenbauer, S. (2005). On the cultural guises of cognitive dissonance: The case of Easterners and Westerners. *Journal of Personality and Social Psychology, 89*, 294–310.

House, J. S., Landis, K. R., & Umberson, D. (1988). Social relationships and health. *Science, 241*, 540–545.

House, R. J., & Shamir, B. (1993). Toward the integration of transformational, charismatic, and visionary theories. In M. M. Chemers & R. Ayman (Eds.), *Leadership theory and research: Perspectives and directions* (pp. 81–107). San Diego, CA: Academic Press.

Houston, D. A., & Fazio, R. H. (1989). Biased processing as a function of attitude accessibility: Making objective judgments subjectively. *Social Cognition, 7*, 51–66.

Hovland, C. I, & Sears, R. (1940). Minor studies in aggression: VI. Correlation of lynchings with economic indices. *Journal of Psychology, 9*, 301–310.

Hovland, C. I., & Weiss, W. (1951). The influence of source credibility on communication effectiveness. *Public Opinion Quarterly, 15*, 635–650.

Hovland, C. I., Janis, I. L., & Kelley, H. H. (1953). *Communication and persuasion*. New Haven, CT: Yale University Press.

Howard, D. J., Gengler, C., & Jain, A. (1995). What's in a name? A complimentary means of persuasion. *Journal of Consumer Research, 22*, 200–211.

Howells, L. T., & Becker, S. W. (1962). Seating arrangement and leadership emergence. *Journal of Abnormal and Social Psychology, 64*, 148–150.

Hraba, J., & Grant, G. (1970). Black is beautiful: A reexamination of racial preference and identification. *Journal of Personality and Social Psychology, 16*, 398–402.

Huesmann, L. R., & Eron, L. D. (Eds.). (1986). *Television and the aggressive child: A cross-national comparison*. Hillsdale, NJ: Erlbaum.

Huesmann, L. R., Moise-Titus, J., Podolski, C.-L., & Eron, L. D. (2003). Longitudinal relations between children's exposure to TV violence and their aggressive and violent behavior in young adulthood: 1977–1992. *Developmental Psychology, 39*, 201–221.

Huff, R., Rattner, A., & Sagarin, E. (1986). Guilty until proven innocent. *Crime and Delinquency, 32*, 518–544.

Hugenberg, K., & Bodenhausen, G. V. (2003). Facing prejudice: Implicit prejudice and the perception of facial threat. *Psychological Science, 14*, 640–643.

Hugenberg, K., & Bodenhausen, G. V. (2004). Ambiguity in social categorization: The role of prejudice and facial affect in race categorization. *Psychological Science, 15*, 342–345.

Hui, C. H. (1988). Measurement of individualism-collectivism. *Journal of Research in Personality, 22*, 17–36.

Hull, J. G., & West, S. G. (1982). The discounting principle in attribution. *Personality and Social Psychology Bulletin, 8*, 208–213.

Hume, D. K., & Montgomerie, R. (2001). Facial attractiveness signals different aspects of "quality" in women and men. *Evolution and Human Behavior, 22*, 93–112.

Hyde, C. R. (1999). *Pay it forward*. New York: Simon & Schuster.

Hyman, I. E., Jr., Husband, T. H., & Billings, F. J. (1995). False memories of childhood experiences. *Applied Cognitive Psychology, 9*, 181–197.

Insko, C. A., & Schopler, J. (1998). Differential distrust of groups and individuals. In C. Sedikides, J. Schopler, & C. A. Insko (Eds.), *Intergroup cognition and intergroup behavior* (pp. 75–107). Mahwah, NJ: Erlbaum.

Insko, C. A., Schopler, J., Hoyle, R. H., Dardis, G. J., & Graetz, K. A. (1990). Individual-group discontinuity as a function of fear and greed. *Journal of Personality and Social Psychology, 58*, 68–79.

Insko, C. A., Thibaut, J. W., Moehle, D., Wilson, M., Diamond, W. D., Gilmore, R., Solomon, M. R., & Lipsitz, A. (1980). Social evolution and the emergence of leadership. *Journal of Personality and Social Psychology, 39*, 431–448.

Irwin, A. R., & Gross, A. M. (1995). Cognitive tempo, violent video games, and aggressive behavior in young boys. *Journal of Family Violence, 10*, 337–350.

Isbell, L. M. (2004). Not all happy people are lazy or stupid: Evidence of systematic processing in happy moods. *Journal of Experimental Social Psychology, 40*, 341–349.

Isen, A. M., Clark, M., & Schwartz, M. F. (1976). Duration of the effect of good mood on helping: "Footprints on the sands of time." *Journal of Personality and Social Psychology, 34*, 385–393.

Isen, A. M., & Levin, P. F. (1972). The effect of feeling good on helping: Cookies and kindness. *Journal of Personality and Social Psychology, 21*, 384–388.

Isen, A. M., Means, B., Patrick, R., & Nowicky, G. (1982). Some factors influencing decision making strategy and risk-taking. In M. S. Clark & S. T. Fiske (Eds.), *Affect and cognition: The 17th annual Carnegie Mellon symposium on cognition* (pp. 243–261). Hillsdale, NJ: Erlbaum.

Isen, A. M., Shalker, T. E., Clark, M., & Karp, L. (1978). Affect accessibility of material in memory, and behavior: A cognitive loop. *Journal of Personality and Social Psychology, 36*, 1–12.

Isenberg, D. J. (1986). Group polarization: A critical review and meta-analysis. *Journal of Personality and Social Psychology, 50*, 1141–1151.

Islam, M. R., & Hewstone, M. (1993). Dimensions of contact as predictors of intergroup anxiety, perceived out-group variability, and out-group attitude: An integrative model. *Personality and Social Psychology Bulletin, 19*, 700–710.

James, W. (1890/1948). *Psychology*. Cleveland, OH: World Publishing.

Jamieson, D. W., Lydon, J. E., & Zanna, M. P. (1987). Attitude and activity preference similarity: Differential bases of interpersonal attraction for low and high self-monitors. *Journal of Personality and Social Psychology, 53*, 1052–1060.

Janes, L. M. (2003). *The effects of goals on self-assessment versus self-protection*. Doctoral dissertation, University of Western Ontario, London, Ontario.

Janes, L. M., & Olson, J. M. (2000). Jeer pressure: The behavioral effects of observing ridicule of others. *Personality and Social Psychology Bulletin, 26*, 474–485.

Janis, I. L. (1972). *Victims of groupthink*. Boston, MA: Houghton Mifflin.

Janis, I. L. (1982). *Groupthink* (2nd ed.). Boston, MA: Houghton Mifflin.

Janis, I. L., & Feshbach, S. (1953). Effects of fear-arousing communications. *Journal of Abnormal and Social Psychology, 48*, 78–92.

Jankowiak, W. R. (1995). *Romantic passion: The universal experience?* New York: Columbia University Press.

Jankowiak, W. R., & Fischer, E. F. (1992). A cross-cultural perspective on romantic love. *Ethnology, 31*, 149–155.

Jemmott, J. B., Jemmott, L. S., & Fong, G. T. (1992). Reductions in HIV risk-associated sexual behaviors among Black male adolescents: Effects of an AIDS prevention intervention. *American Journal of Public Health, 82*, 372–377.

Jessop, D. J. (1982). Topic variation in levels of agreement between parents and adolescents. *Public Opinion Quarterly, 46*, 538–559.

Johns, M., Schmader, T., & Martens, A. (2005). Knowing is half the battle: Teaching stereotype threat as a means of improving women's math performance. *Psychological Science, 16*, 175–179.

Johnson, D. J., & Rusbult, C. E. (1989). Resisting temptation: Devaluation of alternative partners as a means of maintaining commitment in close relationships. *Journal of Personality and Social Psychology, 57*, 967–980.

Johnson, J. G., Cohen, P., Smailes, E. M., Kasen, S., & Brook, J. S. (2002). Television viewing and aggressive behavior during adolescence and adulthood. *Science, 295*, 2468–2471.

Johnson, J. T., Boyd, K. R., & Magnani, P. S. (1994). Causal reasoning in the attribution of rare and common events. *Journal of Personality and Social Psychology, 66*, 229–242.

Johnson, R. D., & Downing, L. L. (1979). Deindividuation and valence of cues: Effects on prosocial and antisocial behavior. *Journal of Personality and Social Psychology, 37*, 1532–1538.

Jones, B. C., Little, A. C., Burt, D. M., & Perrett, D. I. (2004). When facial attractiveness is only skin deep. *Perception, 33*, 569–576.

Jones, B. C., Little, A. C., Feinberg, D. R., Penton-Voak, I. S., Tiddeman, B. P., & Perrett, D. I. (2004). The relationship between shape symmetry and perceived skin condition in male facial attractiveness. *Evolution and Human Behavior, 25*, 24–30.

Jones, E. E. (1979). The rocky road from acts to dispositions. *American Psychologist, 34*, 107–117.

Jones, E. E. (1990). *Interpersonal perception*. New York: Macmillan.

Jones, E. E., & Berglas, S. C. (1978). Control of attributions about the self through self-handicapping strategies: The appeal of alcohol and the role of underachievement. *Personality and Social Psychology Bulletin, 4*, 200–206.

Jones, E. E., & Harris, V. A. (1967). The attribution of attitudes. *Journal of Experimental Social Psychology, 3*, 1–24.

Jones, E. E., & Nisbett, R. E. (1972). The actor and the observer: Divergent perceptions of the causes of behavior. In E. E. Jones, D. E. Kanouse, H. H. Kelley, R. E. Nisbett, S. Valins, & B. Weiner (Eds.), *Attribution: Perceiving the causes of behavior* (pp. 79–94). Morristown, NJ: General Learning Press.

Jones, E. E., & Pittman, T. S. (1982). Toward a general theory of strategic self-presentation. In J. M. Suls (Ed.), *Psychological perspectives on the self* (Vol. 1, pp. 231–262). Hillsdale, NJ: Erlbaum.

Jones, E. E., & Rhodewalt, F. (1982). *Self-handicapping scale.* Unpublished scale, Department of Psychology, Princeton University, and Department of Psychology, University of Utah.

Jones, E. E., & Wortman, C. (1973). *Ingratiation: An attributional approach.* Morristown, NJ: General Learning Press.

Jones, J. M. (1997). *Prejudice and racism* (2nd ed.). New York: McGraw-Hill.

Jones, J. T., Pelham, B. W., Carvallo, M., & Mirenberg, M. C. (2004). How do I love thee? Let me count the Js: Implicit egotism and interpersonal attraction. *Journal of Personality and Social Psychology, 87,* 665–683.

Jones, J. T., Pelham, B. W., & Mirenberg, M. C. (2002). Name letter preferences are not merely mere exposure: Implicit egotism as self-regulation. *Journal of Experimental Social Psychology, 38,* 170–177.

Jordan, C. H., Spencer, S. J., & Zanna, M. P. (2003). "I love me . . . I love me not": Implicit self-esteem, explicit self-esteem, and defensiveness. In S. J. Spencer, S. Fein, M. P. Zanna, & J. M. Olson (Eds.), *Motivated social perception: The Ontario symposium* (Vol. 9, pp. 117–145). Mahwah, NJ: Erlbaum.

Jordan, C. H., Spencer, S. J., Zanna, M. P., Hoshino-Browne, E., & Correll, J. (2003). Secure and defensive high self-esteem. *Journal of Personality and Social Psychology, 85,* 969–978.

Joule, R. V. (1987). Tobacco deprivation: The foot-in-the-door technique versus the low-ball technique. *European Journal of Social Psychology, 17,* 361–365.

Judd, C. M., Blair, I. V., & Chapleau, K. M. (2004). Automatic stereotypes vs. automatic prejudice: Sorting out the possibilities in the Payne (2001) weapon paradigm. *Journal of Experimental Social Psychology, 40,* 75–81.

Judd, C. M., & Park, B. (1988). Out-group homogeneity: Judgments of variability at the individual and group levels. *Journal of Personality and Social Psychology, 54,* 778–788.

Judge, T. A., Bono, J. E., Ilies, R., & Gerhardt, M. W. (2002). Personality and leadership: A qualitative and quantitative review. *Journal of Applied Psychology, 87,* 765–780.

Judge, T. A., Erez, A., Bono, J. E., & Thorsen, C. J. (2002). Are measures of self-esteem, neuroticism, locus of control, and generalized self-efficacy indicators of a common core construct? *Journal of Personality and Social Psychology, 83,* 693–710.

Jussim, L. (1991). Social perception and social reality: A reflection-construction model. *Psychological Review, 98,* 54–73.

Jussim, L., Soffin, S., Brown, R., Ley, J., & Kohlhepp, K. (1992). Understanding reactions to feedback by integrating ideas from symbolic interactionism and cognitive evaluation theory. *Journal of Personality and Social Psychology, 62,* 402–421.

Kacmar, K. M., Delery, J. E., & Ferris, G. R. (1992). Differential effectiveness of applicant impression management tactics on employment interview decisions. *Journal of Applied Social Psychology, 16,* 1250–1272.

Kahn, M. (1966). The physiology of catharsis. *Journal of Personality and Social Psychology, 3,* 278–286.

Kahneman, D. (2003). A perspective on judgment and choice. *American Psychologist, 58,* 697–720.

Kahneman, D., & Frederick, S. (2002). Representativeness revisited: Attribute substitution in intuitive judgment. In T. Gilovich, D. Griffin, & D. Kahneman (Eds.), *Heuristics and biases: The psychology of intuitive judgment* (pp. 49–81). New York: Cambridge University Press.

Kahneman, D., & Miller, D. T. (1986). Norm theory: Comparing reality to its alternatives. *Psychological Review, 93,* 136–153.

Kahneman, D., & Tversky, A. (1973). On the psychology of prediction. *Psychological Review, 80,* 237–251.

Kaiser, C. R., Major, B., & McCoy, S. K. (2004). Expectations about the future and the emotional consequences of perceiving prejudice. *Personality and Social Psychology Bulletin, 30,* 173–184.

Kaiser, C. R., & Miller, C. T. (2001). Stop complaining! The social costs of making attributions to discrimination. *Personality and Social Psychology Bulletin, 27,* 254–263.

Kalven, H., & Zeisel, H. (1966). *The American jury.* Boston, MA: Little, Brown.

Kanemasa, Y., Taniguchi, J., Daibo, I., & Ishimori, M. (2004). Love styles and romantic love experiences in Japan. *Social Behavior and Personality, 32,* 265–282.

Kaplan, K. J. (1972). On the ambivalence-indifference problem in attitude theory and measurement: A suggested modification of the semantic differential technique. *Psychological Bulletin, 77,* 361–372.

Karau, S. J., & Williams, K. (1993). Social loafing: A meta-analytic review and theoretical integration. *Journal of Personality and Social Psychology, 65,* 681–706.

Kardes, F. R., Sanbonmatsu, D. M., Voss, R. T., & Fazio, R. H. (1986). Self-monitoring and attitude accessibility. *Personality and Social Psychology Bulletin, 72,* 468–474.

Kashima, Y., Kokubo, T., Kashima, E. S., Boxall, D., Yamaguchi, S., & Macrae, K. (2004). Culture and self: Are there within-culture differences in self between metropolitan areas and regional cities? *Personality and Social Psychology Bulletin, 30,* 816–823.

Kashima, Y., Yamaguchi, S., Kim, U., Choi, S.-C., Gelfand, M. J., & Yuki, M. (1995). Culture, gender, and self: A perspective from individualism-collectivism research. *Journal of Personality and Social Psychology, 69,* 925–937.

Kasser, T., Koestner, R., & Lekes, N. (2002). Early family experiences and adult values: A 26-year, prospective longitudinal study. *Personality and Social Psychology Bulletin, 28,* 826–835.

Kasser, T., Ryan, R. M., Zax, M., & Sameroff, A. J. (1995). The relations of maternal and social environments to late adolescents' materialistic and prosocial values. *Developmental Psychology, 31,* 907–914.

Katz, D. (1960). The functional approach to the study of attitudes. *Public Opinion Quarterly, 24,* 163–204.

Katz, I., & Hass, R. G. (1988). Racial ambivalence and American value conflict: Correlational and priming studies of dual cognitive structures. *Journal of Personality and Social Psychology, 55,* 893–905.

Katz, J. E., & Rice, R. E. (2002). *Social consequences of Internet use: Access, involvement, and interaction.* Cambridge, MA: MIT Press.

Katz, J., Monnier, J., Libet, J., Shaw, D., & Beach, S. R. H. (2000). Individual and crossover effects of stress on adjustment in medical student marriages. *Journal of Marital and Family Therapy, 26,* 341–351.

Kawakami, K., Dion, K. L., & Dovidio, J. F. (1998). Racial prejudice and stereotype activation. *Personality and Social Psychology Bulletin, 24,* 407–416.

Kawakami, K., & Dovidio, J. (2001). The reliability of implicit stereotyping. *Personality and Social Psychology Bulletin, 27,* 212–225.

Kawakami, K., Dovidio, J. F., & Dijksterhuis, A. (2003). Effect of social category priming on personal attitudes. *Psychological Science, 14,* 315–319.

Kay, A. C., Jost, J. T., & Young, S. (2005). Victim derogation and victim enhancement as alternate routes to system justification. *Psychological Science, 16,* 240–246.

Kay, A. C., & Ross, L. (2003). The perceptual push: The interplay of implicit cues and explicit situational construals on behavioral intentions in the prisoner's dilemma. *Journal of Experimental Social Psychology, 39,* 634–643.

Kazdin, A. E., & Benjet, C. (2003). Spanking children: Evidence and issues. *Current Directions in Psychological Science, 12,* 99–103.

Keller, J., & Dauenheimer, D. (2003). Stereotype threat in the classroom: Dejection mediates the disrupting threat effect on women's math performance. *Personality and Social Psychology Bulletin, 29,* 371–381.

Kelley, H. H. (1967). Attribution theory in social psychology. In D. Levine (Ed.), *Nebraska Symposium on Motivation* (Vol. 15, pp. 192–238). Lincoln: University of Nebraska Press.

Kelley, H. H. (1973). The process of causal attribution. *American Psychologist, 28,* 107–128.

Kelley, H. H. (1979). *Personal relationships: Their structures and processes.* Hillsdale, NJ: Erlbaum.

Kelley, H. H. (1983). *Close relationships.* New York: W. H. Freeman.

Kelly, C., & Breinlinger, S. (1995). Attitudes, intentions, and behavior: A study of women's participation in collective action. *Journal of Applied Social Psychology, 25,* 1430–1445.

Kelman, H. C. (1967). Human use of human subjects: The problem of deception in social psychological experiments. *Psychological Bulletin, 67,* 1–11.

Kelman, H. C., & Hamilton, V. L. (1989). *Crimes of obedience: Toward a social psychology of authority and responsibility.* New Haven, CT: Yale University Press.

Kemmelmeier, M., & Winter, D. G. (2000). Putting threat into perspective: Experimental studies on perceptual distortion in international conflict. *Personality and Social Psychology Bulletin, 26,* 796–809.

Kennamer, J. D. (1990). Self-serving biases in perceiving the opinions of others. *Communication Research, 17,* 393–404.

Kenrick, D. T., Ackerman, J., & Ledlow, S. (2003). Evolutionary social psychology: Adaptive predispositions and human culture. In J. Delamater (Ed.), *Handbook of social psychology* (pp. 103–122). New York: Kluwer/Plenum.

Kenrick, D. T., Li, N. P., & Butner, J. (2003). Dynamical evolutional evolutionary psychology: Individual decision rules and emergent social norms. Psychological Review, 110, 3–28.

Kernis, M. H. (1984). Need for uniqueness, self-schemas, and thought as moderators of the false-consensus effect. *Journal of Personality and Social Psychology, 35,* 381–391.

Kernis, M. H., & Paradise, A. W. (2002). Distinguishing between secure and fragile forms of high self-esteem. In E. L. Deci & R. M. Ryan (Eds.), *Handbook of self-determination research* (pp. 339–360). Rochester, NY: University of Rochester Press.

Kernis, M. H., & Waschull, S. B. (1995). The interactive roles of stability and level of self-esteem: Research and theory. In M. P. Zanna (Ed.), *Advances in experimental social psychology* (Vol. 27, pp. 93–141). San Diego, CA: Academic Press.

Kerr, N. L., Aronoff, J., & Messe, L. A. (2000). Methods of small group research. In H. T. Reis & C. M. Judd (Eds.), *Handbook of research methods in social psychology* (pp. 160–189). Cambridge, UK: Cambridge University Press.

Kerr, N. L., & Kaufman-Gilliland, C. M. (1994). Communication, commitment, and cooperation in social dilemmas. *Journal of Personality and Social Psychology, 66,* 513–529.

Kiesler, S. (1997). *Culture of the Internet.* Mahwah, NJ: Erlbaum.

Kiesler, S., & Kraut, R. (1999). Internet use and ties that bind. *American Psychologist, 54,* 783–784.

Kihlstrom, J. F. (1994). Hypnosis, delayed recall, and the principles of memory. *International Journal of Clinical and Experimental Hypnosis, 42,* 337–345.

Kim, M., & Hunter, J. E. (1993). Attitude-behavior relations: A meta-analysis of attitudinal relevance and topic. *Journal of Communication, 43,* 101–142.

Kinder, D. R. (1998). Opinion and action in the realm of politics. In D. T. Gilbert, S. T. Fiske, & G. Lindzey (Eds.), *The handbook of social psychology* (4th ed., Vol. 2, pp. 778–867). New York: McGraw-Hill.

King, K. B., Reis, H. T., Porter, L. A., & Norsen, L. H. (1993). Social support and long-term recovery from coronary artery surgery: Effects on patients and spouses. *Health Psychology, 12,* 56–63.

Kirk, R. E. (2003). Experimental design. In J. A. Schinka & W. F. Velicer (Eds.), *Handbook of psychology: Volume 2. Research methods in psychology* (pp. 3–32). Hoboken, NJ: Wiley.

Kirkpatrick, L. A., & Davis, K. E. (1994). Attachment style, gender, and relationship stability: A longitudinal analysis. *Journal of Personality and Social Psychology, 66,* 502–512.

Kitayama, S., & Markus, H. R. (Eds.). (1994). *Emotion and culture: Empirical studies of mutual influence.* Washington, DC: American Psychological Association.

Kitayama, S., Snibbe, A. C., Markus, H. R., & Suzuki, T. (2004). Is there any "free" choice? Self and dissonance in two cultures. *Psychological Science, 15,* 527–533.

Kitayama, S., & Uchida, Y. (2003). Explicit self-criticism and implicit self-regard: Evaluating self and friend in two cultures. *Journal of Experimental Social Psychology, 39,* 476–482.

Kitzmann, K. M., Gaylord, N. K., Holt, A. R., & Kenny, E. D. (2003). Child witnesses to domestic violence: A meta-analytic review. *Journal of Consulting and Clinical Psychology, 71,* 339–352.

Kiviniemi, M. T., Snyder, M., & Omoto, A. M. (2002). Too many of a good thing? The effects of multiple motivations on stress, cost, fulfillment, and satisfaction. *Personality and Social Psychology Bulletin, 28,* 732–743.

Kling, K. C., Ryff, C. D., Love, G., & Essex, M. (2003). Exploring the influence of personality on depressive symptoms and self-esteem across a significant life transition. *Journal of Personality and Social Psychology, 85,* 922–932.

Klohnen, E. C., & Luo, S. (2003). Interpersonal attraction and personality: What is attractive—self similarity, ideal similarity, complementarity or attachment security? *Journal of Personality and Social Psychology, 85,* 709–722.

Knight, G. P., Fabes, R. A., & Higgins, D. A. (1996). Concerns about drawing causal inferences from meta-analyses: An example in the study of gender differences in aggression. *Psychological Bulletin, 119,* 410–421.

Knox, R. E., & Safford, R. K. (1976). Group caution at the racetrack. *Journal of Experimental Social Psychology, 12,* 317–324.

Koestner, R., Lekes, N., Powers, T. A., & Chicoine, E. (2002). Attaining personal goals: Self-concordance plus implementation intentions equals success. *Journal of Personality and Social Psychology, 83,* 231–244.

Koivisto Hursti, U.-K., & Magnusson, M. K. (2003). Consumer perceptions of genetically modified and organic foods. What kind of knowledge matters? *Appetite, 41,* 207–209.

Konečni, V. J. (1972). Some effects of guilt on compliance: A field replication. *Journal of Personality and Social Psychology, 23,* 30–32.

Konečni, V. J. (1975a). Annoyance, type and duration of postannoyance activity, and aggression: The "cathartic effect." *Journal of Experimental Psychology: General, 104,* 76–102.

Konečni, V. J. (1975b). The mediation of aggressive behavior: Arousal level versus anger and cognitive labeling. *Journal of Personality and Social Psychology, 32,* 706–712.

Korotkov, D., & Hannah, T. E. (2004). The five-factor model of personality: Strengths and limitations in predicting health status, sick role and illness behaviour. *Personality and Individual Differences, 36,* 187–199.

Koss, M. P., Goodman, L. A., Browne, A., Fitzgerald, L. F., Keita, G. P., & Russo, N. F. (1994). *No safe haven: Male violence against women at home, at work, and in the community.* Washington, DC: American Psychological Association.

Krackow, A., & Blass, T. (1995). When nurses obey or defy inappropriate physician orders: Attributional differences. *Journal of Social Behavior and Personality, 10,* 585–594.

Kramer, R. (1999). Trust and distrust in organizations: Emerging perspectives, enduring questions. *Annual Review of Psychology, 50,* 569–598.

Kramer, R. M., & Brewer, M. B. (1984). Effects of group identity on resource use in a simulated commons dilemma. *Journal of Personality and Social Psychology, 46,* 1044–1057.

Kramer, R. M., McClintock, C. G., & Messick, D. M. (1986). Social values and cooperative response to a simulated resource conservation crisis. *Journal of Personality, 54,* 576–592.

Krantz, D. S., Glass, D. C., & Snyder, M. L. (1974). Helplessness, stress level, and the coronary-prone behavior pattern. *Journal of Experimental Social Psychology, 10,* 284–300.

Kraus, S. J. (1995). Attitudes and the prediction of behavior: A meta-analysis of the empirical literature. *Personality and Social Psychology Bulletin, 21,* 58–75.

Krauss, R. M., & Deutsch, M. (1966). Communication in interpersonal bargaining. *Journal of Personality and Social Psychology, 4,* 572–577.

Kraut, R., Kiesler, S., Boneva, B., Cummings, J. N., Helgeson, V., & Crawford, A. M. (2002). Internet paradox revisited. *Journal of Social Issues, 58*(1), 49–74.

Kraut, R., Patterson, M., Lundmark, V., Kiesler, S., Mukophadhyay, T., & Scherlis, W. (1998). Internet paradox: A social technology that reduces social involvement and psychological well-being? *American Psychologist, 53,* 1017–1031.

Krebs, D. L. (2005). An evolutionary reconceptualization of Kohlberg's model of moral development. In R. Burgess & K. MacDonald (Eds.), *Evolutionary perspectives on human development* (pp. 243–274). Thousand Oaks, CA: Sage.

Krebs, D. L., & Denton, K. (1999). On the relations between moral judgment and moral behavior. In D. Garz, F. Oser, & W. Althof (Eds.), *The context of morality* (pp. 240–263). Frankfurt: Suhrlcamp.

Krebs, D. L., & Denton, K. (2005). Toward a more pragmatic approach to morality: A critical examination of Kohlberg's model. *Psychological Review, 112,* 629–649.

Kressel, N. J., & Kressel, D. F. (2004). *Stack and sway: The new science of jury consulting.* Boulder, CO: Westview Press.

Kreuger, J. (1988). On the perception of social consensus. In M. P. Zanna (Ed.), *Advances in experimental social psychology* (Vol. 30, pp. 164–240). New York: Academic Press.

Kreuger, J. (1998). Enhancement bias in descriptions of self and others. *Personality and Social Psychology Bulletin, 24,* 505–516.

Kruger, J., & Burrus, J. (2004). Egocentrism and focalism in unrealistic optimism (and pessimism). *Journal of Experimental Social Psychology, 40,* 332–340.

Kruger, J., Wirtz, D., & Miller, D. T. (2005). Counterfactual thinking and the first instinct fallacy. *Journal of Personality and Social Psychology, 88,* 725–735.

Kruglanski, A. W. (1996). Motivated social cognition: Principles of the interface. In E. T. Higgins & A. W. Kruglanski (Eds.), *Social psychology: Handbook of basic principles* (pp. 493–520). New York: Guilford Press.

Kruglanski, A. W., & Higgins, E. T. (Eds.). (2004). Special Issue: Theory construction in social personality psychology: Personal experiences and lessons learned. *Personality and Social Psychology Review, 8*(2).

Krull, D. S., Loy, M. H., Lin, J., Wang, C., Chen, S., & Zhao, X. (1999). The fundamental fundamental attribution error: Correspondence bias in individualist and collectivist cultures. *Personality and Social Psychology Bulletin, 25,* 1208–1219.

Kuhn, M. H., & McPartland, T. S. (1954). An empirical investigation of self-attitudes. *American Sociological Review, 19,* 68–76.

Kumkale, G. T., & Albarracín, D. (2004). The sleeper effect in persuasion: A meta-analytic review. *Psychological Bulletin, 130,* 143–172.

Kunda, Z. (1990). The case for motivated reasoning. *Psychological Bulletin, 108,* 480–498.

Kunda, Z. (1999). *Social cognition: Making sense of people.* Cambridge, MA: MIT Press.

Kunda, Z., & Nisbett, R. E. (1986). The psychometrics of everyday life. *Cognitive Psychology, 18,* 195–224.

Kunda, Z., & Thagard, P. (1996). Forming impressions from stereotypes, traits and behaviors: Parallel constraint satisfaction theory. *Psychological Review, 103,* 284–308.

Kurdek, L. A. (1991). Correlates of relationship satisfaction in cohabiting gay and lesbian couples: Integration of contextual, investment, and problem-solving models. *Journal of Personality and Social Psychology, 61,* 910–922.

Kurdek, L. A. (1995). Lesbian and gay couples. In A. R. D'Augelli & C. J. Patterson (Eds.), *Lesbian, gay, and bisexual identities over the lifespan* (pp. 243–261). New York: Oxford University Press.

Kurdek, L. A., & Schmitt, J. P. (1986). Relationship quality of partners in heterosexual married, heterosexual cohabiting, and gay lesbian relationships. *Journal of Personality and Social Psychology, 51,* 711–720.

Kurman, J. (2001). Self-enhancement: Is it restricted to individualistic cultures? *Personality and Social Psychology Bulletin, 27,* 1705–1716.

Kwong, M. J., Bartholomew, K., Henderson, A. J. Z., & Trinke, S. J. (2003). The intergenerational transmission of relationship violence. *Journal of Family Psychology, 17,* 288–301.

LaFrance, M., Hecht, M. A., & Paluck, E. L. (2003). The contingent smile: A meta-analysis of sex differences in smiling. *Psychological Bulletin, 129,* 305–334.

Lakey, B., Adams, K., Neely, L., Rhodes, G., Lutz, C. J., & Sielky, K. (2002). Perceived support and low emotional distress: The role of enacted support, dyad similarity and provider personality. *Personality and Social Psychology Bulletin, 28,* 1546–1555.

Lancelotta, G. X., & Vaughn, S. (1989). Relation between types of aggression and sociometric status: Peer and teaching perceptions. *Journal of Educational Psychology, 81,* 86–90.

Landau, M. J., Solomon, S., Greenberg, J., Cohen, F., Pyszczynski, T., Arndt, J., Miller, C. H., Ogilvie, D. M., & Cook, A. (2004). Deliver us from evil: The effects of mortality salience and reminders of 9/11 on support for President George W. Bush. *Personality and Social Psychology Bulletin, 30,* 1136–1150.

Landolt, M. A., Bartholomew, K., Saffrey, C., Oram, D., & Perlman, D. (2004). Gender nonconformity, childhood rejection, and adult attachment: A study of gay men. *Archives of Sexual Behavior, 33,* 117–128.

Langer, E. J. (1975). The illusion of control. *Journal of Personality and Social Psychology, 32,* 311–328.

Langer, E. J. (1977). The psychology of chance. *Journal for the Theory of Social Behaviour, 7,* 185–207.

Langlois, J. H. (1986). From the eye of the beholder to behavioral reality: Development of social behaviors and social relations as a function of physical attractiveness. In C. P. Herman, M. P. Zanna, & E. T. Higgins (Eds.), *Physical appearance, stigma, and social behavior: The Ontario symposium* (Vol. 3, pp. 23–51). Hillsdale, NJ: Erlbaum.

Langlois, J. H., Kalakanis, L., Rubenstein, A. J., Larson, A., Hallam, M., & Smoot, M. (2000). Maxims or myths of beauty? A meta-analytic and theoretical review. *Psychological Bulletin, 126,* 390–423.

Langlois, J. H., Ritter, J. M., Roggman, L. A., & Vaughn, L. S. (1991). Facial diversity and infant preferences for attractive faces. *Developmental Psychology, 27,* 79–84.

Langlois, J. H., & Roggman, L. A. (1990). Attractive faces are only average. *Psychological Science, 1,* 115–121.

Langlois, J. H., Roggman, L. A., & Musselman, L. (1994). What is average and what is not average about attractive faces? *Psychological Science, 5,* 214–220.

Langlois, J. H., Roggman, L. A., & Rieser-Danner, L. A. (1990). Infants' differential social responses to attractive and unattractive faces. *Developmental Psychology, 26,* 153–159.

Langlois, J. H., & Stephan, C. W. (1977). The effects of physical attractiveness and ethnicity on children's behavioral attributions and peer preferences. *Child Development, 48,* 1694–1698.

LaPiere, R. T. (1934). Attitudes vs. actions. *Social Forces, 13,* 230–237.

Laros, F. J. M., & Steenkamp, J.-B. E. M. (2004). Importance of fear in the case of genetically modified food. *Psychology and Marketing, 21,* 889–908.

Larsen, J. T., McGraw, A. P., Mellers, B. A., & Cacioppo, J. T. (2004). The agony of victory and the thrill of defeat: Mixed emotional reactions to disappointing wins and relieving losses. *Psychological Science, 15,* 325–330.

Lassiter, G. D., Geers, A. L., Munhall, P. J., Ploutz-Snyder, R. J., & Breitenbecher, D. L. (2002). Illusory causation: Why it occurs. *Psychological Science, 13,* 299–305.

Latané, B. (1981). The psychology of social impact. *American Psychologist, 36,* 343–356.

Latané, B., & Darley, J. M. (1968). Group inhibition of bystander intervention in emergencies. *Journal of Personality and Social Psychology, 10,* 215–221.

Latané, B., & Darley, J. M. (1970). *The unresponsive bystander: Why doesn't he help?* New York: Appleton-Century-Crofts.

Latané, B., & Rodin, J. (1969). A lady in distress: Inhibiting effects of friends and strangers on bystander intervention. *Journal of Experimental Social Psychology, 5,* 189–202.

Latané, B., Williams, K. P., & Harkins, S. G. (1979). Many hands make light the work: The causes and consequences of social loafing. *Journal of Personality and Social Psychology, 37,* 822–832.

Lau, M. A., & Pihl, R. O. (1994). Alcohol and the Taylor aggression paradigm: A repeated measures study. *Journal of Studies on Alcohol, 55,* 701–706.

Lavine, H., Thomsen, C. J., Zanna, M. P., & Borgida, E. (1998). On the primacy of affect in the determination of attitudes and behavior: The moderating role of affective-cognitive ambivalence. *Journal of Experimental Social Psychology, 34,* 398–421.

Leana, C. R. (1985). A partial test of Janis' groupthink model: Effects of group cohesiveness and leader behavior on defective decision making. *Journal of Management, 11,* 5–17.

Leary, M. R. (1990). Responses to social exclusion: Social anxiety, jealousy, loneliness, depression, and low self-esteem. *Journal of Social and Clinical Psychology, 9,* 221–229.

Leary, M. R. (1995). *Self-presentation: Impression management and interpersonal behavior.* Madison, WI: Brown & Benchmark.

Leary, M. R., & Baumeister, R. F. (2000). The nature and function of self-esteem: Sociometer theory. In M. P. Zanna (Ed.), *Advances in experimental social psychology* (Vol. 32, pp. 1–62). San Diego, CA: Academic Press.

Leary, M. R., & Kowalski, R. (1995). *Social anxiety.* New York: Guilford.

Leary, M. R., & Shepperd, J. A. (1986). Behavioral self-handicaps versus self-reported self-handicaps: A conceptual note. *Journal of Personality and Social Psychology, 51,* 1265–1268.

Leathers, D. G. (1997). *Successful nonverbal communication: Principles and applications.* Boston: Allyn & Bacon.

Lee, F., Hallahan, M., & Herzog, T. (1996). Explaining real life events: How culture and domain shape attributions. *Personality and Social Psychology Bulletin, 22,* 732–741.

Lee, J. A. (1988). Love-styles. In R. J. Sternberg & M. L. Barnes (Eds.), *The psychology of love* (pp. 38–67). New Haven, CT: Yale University Press.

Lehman, D. R., Ellard, J. H., & Wortman, C. B. (1986). Social support for the bereaved: Recipients' and providers' perspectives on what is helpful. *Journal of Consulting and Clinical Psychology, 54,* 438–446.

Leippe, M. R., & Eisenstadt, D. (1994). Generalization of dissonance reduction: Decreasing prejudice through induced compliance. *Journal of Personality and Social Psychology, 67,* 395–413.

Lepore, L., & Brown, R. (1997). Category and stereotype activation: Is prejudice inevitable? *Journal of Personality and Social Psychology, 72,* 275–287.

Lepper, M. R., & Greene, D. (Eds.). (1978). *The hidden costs of reward.* Hillsdale, NJ: Erlbaum.

Lepper, M. R., Greene, D., & Nisbett, R. E. (1973). Undermining children's interest with extrinsic rewards: A test of the "overjustification effect." *Journal of Personality and Social Psychology, 28,* 129–137.

Lepper, M. R., & Woolverton, M. (2002). The wisdom of practice: Lessons learned from the study of highly effective tutors. In J. Aronson (Ed.), *Improving academic achievement: Impact of psychological factors on education* (pp. 135–158). New York: Academic Press.

Lerner, M. J. (1977). The justice motive in social behavior: Some hypotheses as to its origins and forms. *Journal of Personality, 45,* 1–52.

Lerner, M. J. (1980). *The belief in a just world: A fundamental delusion.* New York: Plenum Press.

Lerner, M. J., & Simmons, C. H. (1966). The observer's reaction to the "innocent victim": Compassion or rejection? *Journal of Personality and Social Psychology, 4,* 203–210.

Leventhal, H., & Cameron, L. (1994). Persuasion and health attitudes. In S. Shavitt & T. C. Brock (Eds.), *Persuasion: Psychological insights and perspectives* (pp. 219–249). Boston, MA: Allyn & Bacon.

Levine, J. M. (1989). Reaction to opinion deviance in small groups. In P. Paulus (Ed.), *Psychology of group influence* (2nd ed., pp. 187–231). Hillsdale, NJ: Erlbaum.

Levine, J. M., & McBurney, D. H. (1977). Causes and consequences of effluvia: Body odor awareness and controllability as determinants of interpersonal evaluation. *Personality and Social Psychology Bulletin, 3,* 442–445.

Levine, J. M., & McBurney, D. H. (1986). The role of olfaction in social perception and behavior. In C. P. Herman, M. P. Zanna, & E. T. Higgins (Eds.), *Physical appearance, stigma, and social behavior: The Ontario symposium* (Vol. 3, pp. 179–217). Hillsdale, NJ: Erlbaum.

Levine, J. M., & Moreland, R. L. (1994). Group socialization: Theory and research. In W. Stroebe & M. Hewstone (Eds.), *European review of social psychology* (Vol. 5, pp. 305–336). Chichester, UK: Wiley.

Levine, J. M., & Moreland, R. L. (1998). Small groups. In D. T. Gilbert, S. T. Fiske, & G. Lindzey (Eds.), *Handbook of social psychology* (4th ed., Vol. 2, pp. 415–469). Boston, MA: McGraw-Hill.

Levine, J. M., & Moreland, R. L. (2004). Collaboration: The social context of theory development. *Personality and Social Psychology Review, 8,* 164–172.

Levine, R. (2003). *The power of persuasion: How we are bought and sold.* Hoboken, NJ: Wiley.

Levinger, G. (1988). Can we picture "love"? In R. J. Sternberg & M. L. Barnes (Eds.), *The psychology of love* (pp. 139–158). New Haven, CT: Yale University Press.

Levy, B. (1996). Improving memory in old age through implicit self-stereotyping. *Journal of Personality and Social Psychology, 71,* 1092–1107.

Levy, S. R., Freitas, A. L., & Salovey, P. (2002). Construing action abstractly and blurring social distinctions: Implications for perceiving homogeneity among, but also empathizing with and helping, others. *Journal of Personality and Social Psychology, 83,* 1224–1238.

Lewin, K. (1951). *Field theory in social science* (D. Cartwright, Ed.). New York: Harper.

Leyens, J.-P., & Parke, R. D. (1975). Aggressive slides can induce a weapons effect. *European Journal of Social Psychology, 5,* 229–236.

Liberman, V., Samuels, S. M., & Ross, L. (2004). The name of the game: Predictive power of reputations versus situational labels in determining prisoner's dilemma game moves. *Personality and Social Psychology Bulletin, 30,* 1175–1185.

Lieberman, M. D., Ochsner, K. N., Gilbert, D. T., & Schacter, D. L. (2001). Do amnesics exhibit cognitive dissonance reduction? The role of explicit memory and attention in attitude change. *Psychological Science, 12,* 135–140.

Liebrand, W. B., Jansen, R. W., Rijken, V. M., & Suhre, C. J. (1986). Might over morality: Social values and the perception of other players in experimental games. *Journal of Experimental Social Psychology, 22,* 203–215.

Lifton, R. J. (1961). *Thought reform and the psychology of totalism: A study of "brainwashing" in China.* New York: Norton.

Likert, R. (1932). A technique for the measurement of attitudes. *Archives of Psychology, 140,* 5–53.

Linder, D. E., Cooper, J., & Jones, E. E. (1967). Decision freedom as a determinant of the role of incentive magnitude in attitude change. *Journal of Personality and Social Psychology, 6,* 245–254.

Lindorff, M. (2000). Is it better to perceive than receive? Social support, stress and strain for managers. *Psychology, Health, and Medicine, 5,* 271–286.

Lindsay, D. S., Hagen, L., Read, J. D., Wade, K. A., & Garry, M. (2004). True photographs and false memories. *Psychological Science, 15,* 149–154.

Lindsay, J. J., & Anderson, C. A. (2000). From antecedent conditions to violent actions: A general affective aggression model. *Personality and Social Psychology Bulletin, 26,* 533–547.

Lindsay, R. C. L., Brigham, J. C., Brimacombe, C. A. E., & Wells, G. L. (2002). Eyewitness research. In J. Ogloff (Ed.), *Taking psychology and law into the twenty-first century: Perspectives in law and psychology* (Vol. 14, pp. 199–223. New York: Kluwer Academic/Plenum Publishers).

Lindsay, R. C. L., Nosworthy, G. J., Martin, R., & Martynuck, C. (1994). Using mug shots to find suspects. *Journal of Applied Psychology, 79,* 121–130.

Lindsay, R. C. L., Pozzulo, J. D., Craig, W., & Corber, S. (1997). Simultaneous lineups, sequential lineups, and showups: Eyewitness identification decisions of adults and children. *Law and Human Behavior, 21,* 391–404.

Lindskold, S., & Aronoff, J. (1980). Conciliatory strategies and relative power. *Journal of Experimental Social Psychology, 16,* 187–196.

Litt, M. D., Tennen, H., Affleck, G., & Klock, S. (1992). Coping and cognitive factors in adaptation to in vitro fertilization failure. *Journal of Behavioral Medicine, 15,* 351–369.

Lockwood, P., & Kunda, Z. (1997). Superstars and me: Predicting the impact of role models on the self. *Journal of Personality and Social Psychology, 73,* 91–103.

Lockwood, P., Marshall, T. C., & Sadler, P. (2005). Promoting success or preventing failure: Cultural differences in motivation by positive and negative role models. *Personality and Social Psychology Bulletin, 31,* 379–392.

Loftus, E. F. (1979). *Eyewitness testimony.* Cambridge, MA: Harvard University Press.

Loftus, E. F. (2004). Memories of things unseen. *Current Directions in Psychological Science, 13,* 145–147.

Loftus, E. F., & Ketcham, K. (1994). *The myth of repressed memory: False memories and allegations of sexual abuse.* New York: St. Martin's Press.

Loftus, E. F., Miller, D. G., & Burns, H. J. (1978). Semantic integration of verbal information into a visual memory. *Journal of Experimental Psychology: Human Learning and Memory, 4,* 19–31.

Loftus, E. F., & Palmer, J. C. (1974). Reconstruction of automobile destruction: An example of the interaction between language and memory. *Journal of Verbal Learning and Verbal Behavior, 13,* 585–589.

Loomis, J. M., Blascovich, J., & Beall, A. C. (1999). Immersive virtual environment technology as a basic research tool in psychology. *Behavior Research Methods, Instruments, & Computers, 31,* 557–564.

Lord, C. G., Ross, L., & Lepper, M. R. (1979). Biased assimilation and attitude polarization: The effects of prior theories on subsequently considered evidence. *Journal of Personality and Social Psychology, 37,* 2098–2109.

Lord, R. G., DeVader, & Alliger, G. M. (1986). A meta-analysis of the relation between personality traits and leadership perceptions: An application of validity generalization procedures. *Journal of Applied Psychology, 71,* 402–410.

Lorenz, K. (1966). *On aggression.* New York: Harcourt, Brace and World.

Losier, G. F., & Koestner, R. (1999). Intrinsic versus identified regulation in distinct political campaigns: The consequences of following politics for pleasure versus personal meaningfulness. *Personality and Social Psychology Bulletin, 25,* 287–298.

Lovaglia, M. J. (2000). *Knowing people: The personal use of social psychology.* Boston, MA: McGraw-Hill.

Lowery, B. S., Hardin, C. D., & Sinclair, S. (2001). Social influence effects on automatic racial prejudice. *Journal of Personality and Social Psychology, 81,* 842–855.

Luce, R. D., & Raiffa, H. (1957). *Games and decisions: Introduction and critical survey.* New York: Wiley.

Luginbuhl, J., & Palmer, R. (1991). Impression management aspects of self-handicapping: Positive and negative effects. *Personality and Social Psychology Bulletin, 17,* 655–662.

Luo, S., & Klohnen, E. C. (2005). Assortative mating and marital quality in newlyweds: A couple-centered approach. *Journal of Personality and Social Psychology, 88,* 304–326.

Luria, A. (1980). *Higher cortical functions in man.* New York: Basic Books.

Lutz, C. J., & Lakey, B. (2001). How people make support judgments: Individual differences in the traits used to infer supportiveness in others. *Personality and Social Psychology Bulletin, 81,* 1070–1079.

Lydon, J. E., Burton, K., & Menzies-Toman, D. (2005). Commitment calibration with the relationship cognition toolbox. In M. W. Baldwin (Ed.), *Interpersonal cognition* (pp. 126–152). New York: Guilford.

Lydon, J. E., Fitzsimons, G. M., & Naidoo, L. (2003). Devaluation versus enhancement of attractive alternatives: A critical test using the calibration paradigm. *Personality and Social Psychology Bulletin, 29,* 349–359.

Lydon, J. E., Meana, M., Sepinwall, D., Richards, N., & Mayman, S. (1999). The commitment calibration hypothesis: When do people devalue attractive alternatives? *Personality and Social Psychology Bulletin, 25,* 152–161.

MacCoun, R. J., & Kerr, N. L. (1988). Asymmetric influence in mock jury deliberation: Jurors' bias for leniency. *Journal of Personality and Social Psychology, 54,* 21–33.

MacDonald, G., & Leary, M. R. (2005). Why does social exclusion hurt? The relationship between social and physical pain. *Psychological Bulletin, 131,* 202–223.

MacDonald, T. K., & Ross, M. (1999). Assessing the accuracy of predictions about dating relationships: How and why do lovers' predictions differ from those made by observers? *Personality and Social Psychology Bulletin, 25,* 1417–1429.

MacDonald, T. K., Zanna, M. P., & Fong, G. T. (1995). Decision making in altered states: Effects of alcohol on attitudes toward drinking and driving. *Journal of Personality and Social Psychology, 68,* 973–985.

MacDonald, T. K., Zanna, M. P., & Fong, G. T. (1996). Why common sense goes out the window: Effects of alcohol on intentions to use condoms. *Personality and Social Psychology Bulletin, 22,* 763–775.

MacHovec, F. J. (1989). *Cults and personality.* Springfield, IL: Charles C. Thomas.

MacIntyre, P. D., Baker, S. C., Clément, R., & Conrod, S. (2001). Willingness to communicate, social support and language learning orientations of immersion students. *Studies in Second Language Acquisition, 23,* 369–388.

MacIntyre, P. D., Clément, R., Dörnyei, Z., & Noels, K. A. (1998). Conceptualizing willingness to communicate in a second language: A situational model of second language confidence and affiliation. *Modern Language Journal, 82,* 545–562.

MacLeod, C., & Campbell, L. (1992). Memory accessibility and probability judgments: An experimental evaluation of the availability heuristic. *Journal of Personality and Social Psychology, 63,* 890–902.

MacLin, O. H., MacLin, M. K., & Malpass, R. S. (2001). Race, arousal, attention, exposure, and delay: An examination of factors moderating face recognition. *Psychology, Public Policy, and Law, 7,* 134–152.

MacMartin, C., & Yarmey, A. D. (1999). Rhetoric and the recovered memory debate. *Canadian Psychology, 40,* 343–358

MacNeil, M. K., & Sherif, M. (1976). Norm change over subject generations as a function of arbitrariness of prescribed norms. *Journal of Personality and Social Psychology, 34,* 762–773.

Maddux, J. E., & Rogers, R. W. (1983). Protection motivation and self-efficacy: A revised theory of fear appeals and attitude change. *Journal of Experimental Social Psychology, 19,* 469–479.

Maddux, W. W., Barden, J., Brewer, M. B., & Petty, R. E. (2004). Saying no to negativity: The effects of context and motivation to control prejudice on automatic evaluative responses. *Journal of Experimental Social Psychology, 41,* 19–35.

Madsen, D. B. (1978). Issue importance and choice shifts: A persuasive arguments approach. *Journal of Personality and Social Psychology, 36,* 1118–1127.

Main, M., & Cassidy, J. (1988). Categories of response to reunion with the parent at age 6: Predictable from infant attachment classifications and stable over a 1–month period. *Developmental Psychology, 24,* 415–426.

Maio, G. R., Esses, V. M., & Bell, D. W. (2000). Examining conflict between components of attitudes: Ambivalence and inconsistency are distinct constructs. *Canadian Journal of Behavioural Science, 32,* 58–70.

Maio, G. R., & Olson, J. M. (1998). Values as truisms: Evidence and implications. *Journal of Personality and Social Psychology, 74,* 294–311.

Maio, G. R., & Olson, J. M. (Eds.). (2000a). *Why we evaluate: Functions of attitudes.* Mahwah, NJ: Erlbaum.

Maio, G. R., & Olson, J. M. (2000b). What *is* a value-expressive attitude? In G. R. Maio & J. M. Olson (Eds.), *Why we evaluate: Functions of attitudes* (pp. 249–269). Mahwah, NJ: Erlbaum.

Major, B., Cozzarelli, C., Sciacchitano, A. M., Cooper, M. L., Testa, M., & Mueller, P. M. (1990). Perceived social support, self-efficacy, and adjustment to abortion. *Journal of Personality and Social Psychology, 59,* 452–463.

Malamuth, N. M., & Check, J. V. (1985). The effects of aggressive pornography on beliefs in rape myths: Individual differences. *Journal of Research on Personality, 19,* 299–320.

Malamuth, N. M., Addison, T., & Koss, M. (2000). Pornography and sexual aggression: Are there reliable effects and can we understand them? *Annual Review of Sex Research, 11,* 26–91.

Maner, J. K., Luce, C. L., Neuberg, S. L., Cialdini, R. B., Brown, S., & Sagarin, B. J. (2002). The effects of perspective taking on motivations for helping: Still no evidence for altruism. *Personality and Social Psychology Bulletin, 28,* 1601–1610.

Marcus-Newhall, A., Pedersen, W. C., Carlson, M., & Miller, N. (2000). Displaced aggression is alive and well: A meta-analytic review. *Journal of Personality and Social Psychology, 78,* 670–689.

Marin, G. (1984). Stereotyping Hispanics: The differential effect of research method, label, and degree of contact. *International Journal of Intercultural Relations, 8,* 17–27.

Markman, K. D., Gavanski, I., Sherman, S. J., & McMullen, M. N. (1993). The mental simulation of better and worse possible worlds. *Journal of Experimental Social Psychology, 29,* 87–109.

Marks, G., & Miller N. (1987). Ten years of research on the false-consensus effect: An empirical and theoretical review. *Psychological Bulletin, 102,* 72–90.

Markus, H. R., & Kitayama, S. (1991). Culture and the self: Implications for cognition, emotion, and motivation. *Psychological Review, 98,* 224–253.

Markus, H. R., Kitayama, S., & Heiman, R. J. (1996). Culture and "basic" psychological principles. In E. T. Higgins & A. W. Kruglanski (Eds.), *Social psychology: Handbook of basic principles* (pp. 857–913). New York: Guilford Press.

Markus, H. R., & Kunda, Z. (1986). Stability and malleability of the self-concept. *Journal of Personality and Social Psychology, 51,* 858–866.

Martin, C. L. (1987). A ratio measure of sex stereotyping. *Journal of Personality and Social Psychology, 52,* 489–499.

Martin, C. L., Ruble, D. N., & Szkrybalo, J. (2002). Cognitive theories of early gender development. *Psychological Bulletin, 128,* 903–933.

Martin, L. L., Seta, J. J., & Crelia, R. A. (1990). Assimilation and contrast as a function of people's willingness and ability to expend effort in forming an impression. *Journal of Personality and Social Psychology, 59,* 38–49.

Martin, R. A. (2001). Humor, laughter, and physical health: Methodological issues and research findings. *Psychological Bulletin, 127,* 504–519.

Martin, R., Hewstone, M., & Martin, P. Y. (2003). Resistance to persuasive messages as a function of majority and minority status. *Journal of Experimental Social Psychology, 39,* 585–593.

Marx, D. M., & Roman, J. S. (2002). Female role models: Protecting women's math test performance. *Personality and Social Psychology Bulletin, 28,* 1183–1193.

Masten, A. S., & Coatsworth, J. D. (1998). The development of competence in favorable and unfavorable environments. *American Psychologist, 53,* 205–220.

Masuda, T., & Kitayama, S. (2004). Perceiver-induced constraint and attitude attribution in Japan and the US: A case for the cultural dependence of the correspondence bias. *Journal of Experimental Social Psychology, 40,* 409–416.

Matheson, K., & Dursun, S. (2001). Social identity precursors to the hostile media phenomenon: Partisan perceptions of coverage of the Bosnian conflict. *Group Processes and Intergroup Relations, 4,* 116–125.

Matsumoto, D. (1996). *Culture and psychology.* Pacific Grove, CA: Brooks/Cole.

Matthews, K. A. (1982). Psychological perspectives on the Type A behavior pattern. *Psychological Bulletin, 91,* 293–323.

Matthews, K. A. (1988). Coronary heart disease and Type A behaviors: Update on and alternative to the Booth-Kewley and Friedman (1987) quantitative review. *Psychological Bulletin, 104,* 373–380.

Mayer, B. (2000). *The dynamics of conflict resolution: A practitioner's guide.* San Francisco: Jossey-Bass.

Mayo, C., & Henley, N. M. (Eds.). (1981). *Gender and nonverbal behavior.* New York: Springer-Verlag.

Mazur, A., & Lamb, T. A. (1980). Testosterone, status, and mood in human males. *Hormones and Behaviour, 14,* 236–246.

McArthur, L. Z. (1972). The how and what of why: Some determinants and consequences of causal attribution. *Journal of Personality and Social Psychology, 18,* 195–224.

McCann, C. D., & Endler, N. S. (Eds.). (1990). *Depression: New directions in theory, research, and practice.* Toronto: Wall & Emerson.

McCann, S. J. H. (1992). Alternative formulas to predict the greatness of U.S. presidents: Personological, situational, and zeitgeist factors. *Journal of Personality and Social Psychology, 62,* 469–479.

McCann, S. J. H. (1999). Threatening times and fluctuations in American church memberships. *Personality and Social Psychology Bulletin, 25,* 325–336.

McCann, S. J. H., & Stewin, L. L. (1990). Good and bad years: An index of American social , economic, and political threat. *Journal of Psychology, 124,* 601–617.

McCaskill, J. W., & Lakey, B. (2000). Perceived support, social undermining, and emotion: Idiosyncratic and shared perspectives of adolescents and their families. *Personality and Social Psychology Bulletin, 26*, 820–832.

McCaul, K. D., O'Neill, H. K., & Glasgow, R. E. (1988). Predicting the performance of dental hygiene behaviors: An examination of the Fishbein and Ajzen model and self-efficacy expectations. *Journal of Applied Social Psychology, 18*, 114–128.

McCauley, C. R., & Segal, M. E. (1987). Social psychology of terrorist groups. In C. Hendrick (Ed.), *Group processes and intergroup relations: Review of personality and social psychology* (Vol. 9, pp. 231–256). Thousand Oaks, CA: Sage.

McClelland, D. C., Atkinson, J. W., Clark, R. A., & Lowell, E. L. (1953). *The achievement motive.* New York: Appleton-Century-Crofts.

McConahay, J. B. (1986). Modern racism, ambivalence, and the modern racism scale. In J. F. Dovidio & S. L. Gaertner (Eds.), *Prejudice, discrimination, and racism* (pp. 91–125). Orlando, FL: Academic Press.

McConnell, A. R., & Leibold, J. M. (2001). Relations among the Implicit Association Test, discriminatory behavior, and explicit measures of racist attitudes. *Journal of Experimental Social Psychology, 37*, 435–442.

McCullough, M. E., Emmons, R. A., & Tsang, J.-A. (2002). The grateful disposition: A conceptual and empirical topography. *Journal of Personality and Social Psychology, 82*, 112–127.

McCullough, M. E., Kilpatrick, S. D., Emmons, R. A., & Larson, D. B. (2001). Is gratitude a moral affect? *Psychological Bulletin, 127*, 249–266.

McDougall, W. (1908). *An introduction to social psychology.* London, UK: Methuen.

McFarland, C., & Buehler, R. (1998). The impact of negative affect on autobiographical memory: The role of self-focused attention to moods. *Journal of Personality and Social Psychology, 75*, 1424–1440.

McFarland, C., Buehler, R., & MacKay, L. (2001). Affective responses to social comparisons with extremely close others. *Social Cognition, 19*, 547–586.

McFarland, C., & Miller, D. T. (1994). The framing of relative performance feedback: Seeing the glass as half empty or half full. *Journal of Personality and Social Psychology, 66*, 1061–1073.

McFarland, C., & Ross, M. (1987). The relationship between current impressions and memories of self and dating partners. *Personality and Social Psychology Bulletin, 13*, 228–238.

McGregor, I. (2003). Defensive zeal: Compensatory conviction about attitudes, values, goals, groups, and self-definitions in the face of personal uncertainty. In S. J. Spencer, S. Fein, M. P. Zanna, & J. M. Olson (Eds.), *Motivated social perception: The Ontario symposium* (Vol. 9, pp. 73–92). Mahwah, NJ: Erlbaum.

McGregor, I., & Holmes, J. G. (1999). How storytelling shapes memory and impressions of relationship events over time. *Journal of Personality and Social Psychology, 76*, 403–419.

McGregor, I., & Marigold, D. C. (2003). Defensive zeal and the uncertain self: What makes you so sure? *Journal of Personality and Social Psychology, 85*, 838–852.

McGregor, I., Zanna, M. P., Holmes, J. G., & Spencer, S. J. (2001). Compensatory conviction in the face of personal uncertainty: Going to extremes and being oneself. *Journal of Personality and Social Psychology, 80*, 472–488.

McGuire, A. M. (1994). Helping behaviors in the natural environment: Dimensions and correlates of helping. *Personality and Social Psychology Bulletin, 20*, 45–56.

McGuire, W. J. (1969). The nature of attitudes and attitude change. In G. Lindzey & E. Aronson (Eds.), *Handbook of social psychology* (2nd ed., Vol. 3, pp. 136–314). Reading, MA: Addison-Wesley.

McGuire, W. J., McGuire, C. V., & Winton W. (1979). Effect of household sex composition on the salience of one's gender in the spontaneous self-concept. *Journal of Experimental Social Psychology, 15*, 77–90.

McGuire, W. J., & Padawer-Singer, A. (1976). Trait salience in the spontaneous self-concept. *Journal of Personality and Social Psychology, 33*, 743–754.

McIntyre, R. B., Paulson, R. M., & Lord, C. G. (2003). Alleviating women's mathematics stereotype threat through salience of group achievements. *Journal of Experimental Social Psychology, 39*, 83–90.

Medin, D. L. (1989). Concepts and conceptual structure. *American Psychologist, 44*, 1469–1481.

Medvec, V., H., Madey, S. F., & Gilovich, T. (1995). When less is more: Counterfactual thinking and satisfaction among Olympic medalists. *Journal of Personality and Social Psychology, 69*, 603–610.

Meeus, W. H. J., & Raaijmakers, Q. A. W. (1995). Obedience in modern society: The Utrecht studies. *Journal of Social Issues, 51*, 155–176.

Mehrabian, A. (1968). Relationship of attitudes to seated posture, orientation, and distance. *Journal of Personality and Social Psychology, 10*, 26–30.

Mehrabian, A. (1972) *Nonverbal communication.* Chicago: Aldine-Atherton.

Meissner, C. A., & Brigham, J. C. (2001). Thirty years of investigating the own-race bias in memory for faces: A meta-analytic review. *Psychology, Public Policy, and Law, 7*, 3–35.

Mellor, D. (2003). Contemporary racism in Australia: The experiences of Aborigines. *Personality and Social Psychology Bulletin, 29*, 474–486.

Mendelsohn, H. (1973). Some reasons why information campaigns can succeed. *Public Opinion Quarterly, 37*, 50–61.

Meyer, J. R., Nash, J. D., McAlister, A. L., Maccoby, N., & Farquhar, J. W. (1980). Skills training in a cardiovascular health education campaign. *Journal of Consulting and Clinical Psychology, 48*, 129–142.

Mezulis, A. H., Abramson, L. Y., Hyde, J. S., & Hankin, B. L. (2004). Is there a universal positivity bias in attributions? A meta-analytic review of individual, developmental, and cultural differences in the self-serving attributional bias. *Psychological Bulletin, 130*, 711–747.

Michener, H. A., DeLamater, J. D., & Myers, D. G. (2003). *Social psychology* (5th ed.). Belmont, CA: Wadsworth.

Midgley, C., & Urdan, T. (1995). Predictors of middle school students' use of self-handicapping strategies. *Journal of Early Adolescence, 15*, 398–411.

Miles, S., & Frewer, L. J. (2003). Public perception of scientific uncertainty in relation to food hazards. *Journal of Risk Research, 6*, 267–283.

Milgram, S. (1963). Behavioral study of obedience. *Journal of Abnormal and Social Psychology, 67*, 371–378.

Milgram, S. (1964). Issues in the study of obedience: A reply to Baumrind. *American Psychologist, 19*, 848–852.

Milgram, S. (1974). *Obedience to authority: An experimental view.* New York: Harper & Row.

Milgram, S., Bickman, L., & Berkowitz, L. (1969). Note on the drawing power of crowds of different size. *Journal of Personality and Social Psychology, 13*, 79–82.

Miller, A. G. (1986). *The obedience experiments: A case study of controversy in social science.* New York: Praeger.

Miller, C. T., & Downey, K. T. (1999). A meta-analysis of heavyweight and self-esteem. *Personality and Social Psychology Review, 3*, 68–84.

Miller, D. T., & Turnbull, W. (1986). Expectancies and interpersonal processes. *Annual Review of Psychology, 37*, 233–256.

Miller, D. T., Turnbull, W., & McFarland, C. (1990). Counterfactual thinking and social perception: Thinking about what might have been. In M. P. Zanna (Ed.), *Advances in experimental social psychology* (Vol. 23, pp. 305–331). New York: Academic Press.

Miller, J. G. (1984). Culture and the development of everyday social explanation. *Journal of Personality and Social Psychology, 46*, 961–978.

Miller, J. G., Bersoff, D. M., & Harwood, R. L. (1990). Perceptions of social responsibilities in India and in the United States: Moral imperatives or personal decisions? *Journal of Personality and Social Psychology, 58*, 33–47.

Miller, L. C., Berg, J. H., & Archer, R. L. (1983). Openers: Individuals who elicit intimate self-disclosure. *Journal of Personality and Social Psychology, 44*, 1234–1244.

Miller, L. C., Cooke, L. L., Tsang, J., & Morgan, F. (1992). Should I brag? Nature and impact of positive and boastful disclosures for women and men. *Human Communication Research, 18*, 364–399.

Miller, N., Pedersen, W. C., Earleywine, M., & Pollock, V. E. (2003). A theoretical model of triggered displaced aggression. *Personality and Social Psychology Review, 7*, 75–97.

Miller, R. L., Brickman, P., & Bolen, D. (1975). Attribution versus persuasion as a means for modifying behavior. *Journal of Personality and Social Psychology, 31*, 430–441.

Mills, J. S., Polivy, J., Herman, C. P., & Tiggemann, M. (2002). Effects of exposure to thin media images: Evidence of self-enhancement among restrained eaters. *Personality and Social Psychology Bulletin, 28*, 1687–1699.

Mills, J., & Blankstein, K. R. (2000). Perfectionism, intrinsic vs. extrinsic motivation, and motivated strategies for learning: A multidimensional analysis of university students. *Personality and Individual Differences, 29*, 1191–1204.

Mills, J., & Jellison, J. M. (1967). Effect on opinion change of how desirable the communication is to the audience the communicator addressed. *Journal of Personality and Social Psychology, 56*, 82–92.

Miquelon, P., Vallerand, R. J., Grouzet, F. M. E., & Cardinal, G. (2005). Perfectionism, academic motivation, and psychological adjustment: An integrative model. *Personality and Social Psychology Bulletin, 31*, 913–924.

Mischel, W., Cantor, N., & Feldman, S. (1996). Principles of self-regulation: The nature of willpower and self-control. In E. T. Higgins & A. W. Kruglanski (Eds.), *Social psychology: Handbook of basic principles* (pp. 329–360). New York: Guilford Press.

Mitchell, H. E., & Byrne, D. (1973). The defendant's dilemma: Effects of jurors' attitudes and authoritarianism on judicial decisions. *Journal of Personality and Social Psychology, 25*, 123–129.

Mitchell, J. P., Heatherton, T. F., & Macrae, C. N. (2002). Distinct neural systems subserve person and object knowledge. *Proceedings of the National Academy of Sciences, 99*, 15238–15243.

Miyamoto, Y., & Kitayama, S. (2002). Cultural variation in correspondence bias: The critical role of attitude diagnosticity of socially constrained behavior. *Journal of Personality and Social Psychology, 83*, 1239–1248.

Moghaddam, F. M. (2005). The staircase to terrorism: A psychological exploration. *American Psychologist, 60*, 161–169.

Moghaddam, F. M., Taylor, D. M., & Wright, S. C. (1993). *Social psychology in cross-cultural perspective.* New York: Freeman.

Mohipp, C., & Morry, M. M. (2004). The relationship of symbolic beliefs and prior contact to heterosexuals' attitudes toward gay men and lesbian women. *Canadian Journal of Behavioural Science, 36*, 36–44.

Montada, L., & Lerner, M. J. (Eds.). (1998). *Responses to victimizations and belief in a just world.* New York: Plenum Press.

Montague, P. R., Berns, G. S., Cohen, J. D., McClure, S. M., Pagnoni, G., Dhamala, M., et al. (2002). Hyperscanning: Simultaneous fMRI during linked social interactions. *Neuroimage, 16*, 1159–1164.

Monteith, M. J. (1993). Self-regulation of prejudiced responses: Implications for progress in prejudice reduction efforts. *Journal of Personality and Social Psychology, 65*, 469–485.

Monteith, M. J. (1996). Affective reactions to prejudice-related discrepant responses: The impact of standard salience. *Personality and Social Psychology Bulletin, 22*, 48–59.

Moorhead, G., & Montanari, J. R. (1986). An empirical investigation of the groupthink phenomenon. *Human Relations, 39*, 399–410.

Moreland, R. L., & Beach, S. R. (1992). Exposure effects in the classroom: The development of affinity among students. *Journal of Experimental Social Psychology, 28*, 255–276.

Moretti, M. M., Segal, Z. V., McCann, C. D., Shaw, B. F., Miller, D. T., & Vella, D. (1996). Self-referent versus other-referent information processing in dysphoric, clinically depressed, and remitted depressed subjects. *Personality and Social Psychology Bulletin, 22*, 68–80.

Morf, C. C., & Rhodewalt, F. (1993). Narcissism and self-evaluation maintenance: Explorations in object relations. *Personality and Social Psychology Bulletin, 19*, 668–676.

Morgan, M. Y. (1987). The impact of religion on gender-role attitudes. *Psychology of Women Quarterly, 11*, 301–310.

Morris, M. W., & Larrick, R. P. (1995). When one cause casts doubt on another: A normative analysis of discounting in causal attribution. *Psychological Review, 102*, 331–355.

Morris, M. W., & Peng, K. (1994). Culture and cause: American and Chinese attributions for social and physical events. *Journal of Personality and Social Psychology, 67*, 949–971.

Morris, M. W., Podolny, J. M., & Ariel, S. (2000). Missing relations: Incorporating relational constructs into models of culture. In P. C. Earley & H. Singh (Eds.), *Innovations in international and cross-cultural management* (pp. 52–90). Thousand Oaks, CA: Sage.

Morry, M. M. (2005a). Relationship satisfaction as a predictor of similarity ratings: A test of the attraction-similarity hypothesis. *Journal of Social and Personal Relationships, 22*, 561–584.

Morry, M. M. (2005b). Allocentrism and friendship satisfaction: The mediating roles of disclosure and closeness. *Canadian Journal of Behavioural Science, 37*, 211–222.

Morry, M., & Staska, S. L. (2001). Magazine exposure: Internalization, self-objectification, eating attitudes, and body satisfaction in male and female university students. *Canadian Journal of Behavioural Science, 33*, 269–279.

Morton, J. B., & Trehub, S. E. (2001). Children's understanding of emotion in speech. *Child Development, 72*, 834–843.

Moscovici, S. (1980). Toward a theory of conversion behavior. In L. Berkowitz (Ed.), *Advances in experimental social psychology* (Vol. 13, pp. 209–239). New York: Academic Press.

Moscovici, S., & Doise, W. (1994). *Conflict and consensus.* London, UK: Sage.

Mullen, B. (1986). Atrocity as a function of lynch mob composition: A self-attention perspective. *Personality and Social Psychology Bulletin, 12*, 187–197.

Mullen, B., Anthony, T., Salas, E., & Driskell, J. E. (1994). Group cohesiveness and quality of decision making: An integration of tests of the groupthink hypothesis. *Small Group Research, 25*, 189–204.

Mullen, B., & Cooper, C. (1994). The relation between group cohesiveness and performance: An integration. *Psychological Bulletin, 115*, 210–227.

Mullen, B., Migdal, M. J., & Rozell, D. (2003). Self-awareness, deindividuation, and social identity: Unraveling theoretical paradoxes by filling empirical lacunae. *Personality and Social Psychology Bulletin, 29*, 1071–1081.

Mullen, B., Salas, E., & Driskell, J. E. (1989). Salience, motivation, and artifact as contributions to the relation between participation rate and leadership. *Journal of Experimental Social Psychology, 25*, 545–559.

Murdoch, D., Pihl, R. O., & Ross, D. (1990). Alcohol and crimes of violence: Present issues. *International Journal of the Addictions, 25,* 1065–1081.

Murphy, C. M., & O'Leary, K. D. (1989). Psychological aggression predicts physical aggression in early marriage. *Journal of Consulting and Clinical Psychology, 57,* 579–582.

Murphy, S. T., Monahan, J. L., & Zajonc, R. B. (1995). Additivity of nonconscious affect: Combined effects of priming and exposure. *Journal of Personality and Social Psychology, 69,* 589–602.

Murray, S. L., Bellavia, G. M., Rose, P., & Griffin, D. W. (2003). Once hurt, twice hurtful: How perceived regard regulates daily marital interaction. *Journal of Personality and Social Psychology, 84,* 126–147.

Murray, S. L., Haddock, G., & Zanna, M. P. (1996). On creating value-expressive attitudes: An experimental approach. In C. Seligman, J. M. Olson, & M. P. Zanna (Eds.), *The psychology of values: The Ontario symposium* (Vol. 8, pp. 107–133). Mahwah, NJ: Erlbaum.

Murray, S. L., & Holmes, J. G. (1997). A leap of faith? Positive illusions in romantic relationships. *Personality and Social Psychology Bulletin, 23,* 586–604.

Murray, S. L., Holmes, J. G., & Griffin, D. W. (1996a). The benefits of positive illusions: Idealization and the construction of satisfaction in close relationships. *Journal of Personality and Social Psychology, 70,* 79–98.

Murray, S. L., Holmes, J. G., & Griffin, D. W. (1996b). The self-fulfilling nature of positive illusions in romantic relationships: Love is not blind, but prescient. *Journal of Personality and Social Psychology, 71,* 1155–1180.

Murray, S. L., Holmes, J. G., & Griffin, D. W. (2000). Self-esteem and the quest for felt security: How perceived regard regulates attachment processes. *Journal of Personality and Social Psychology, 78,* 478–498.

Murray, S. L., Holmes, J. G., MacDonald, G., & Ellsworth, P. C. (1998). Through the looking glass darkly? When self-doubts turn into relationship insecurities. *Journal of Personality and Social Psychology, 75,* 1459–1480.

Murray, S. L., Rose, P., Bellavia, G. M., Holmes, J. G., & Kusche, A. G. (2002). When rejection stings: How self-esteem constrains relationship-enhancement processes. *Journal of Personality and Social Psychology, 83,* 556–573.

Mussen, P., & Eisenberg-Berg, N. (1977). *Roots of caring, sharing, and helping.* San Francisco: W. H. Freeman.

Mussweiler, T. (2003). Comparison processes in social judgment: Mechanisms and consequences. *Psychological Review, 110,* 472–489.

Mussweiler, T., Rüter, K., & Epstude, K. (2004). The man who wasn't there: Subliminal social comparison standards influence self-evaluation. *Journal of Experimental Social Psychology, 40,* 689–696.

Mussweiler, T., & Strack, F. (2000). Consequences of social comparison: Selective accessibility, assimilation, and contrast. In J. M. Suls & L. Wheeler (Eds.), *Handbook of social comparison: Theory and research* (pp. 253–270). New York: Kluwer Academic/Plenum.

Myers, D. G., & Bishop, G. D. (1970). Discussion effects on racial attitudes. *Science, 169,* 778–789.

Myers, D. G., & Lamm, H. (1976). The group polarization phenomenon. *Psychological Bulletin, 83,* 602–627.

Nadler, A., & Fisher, J. D. (1986). The role of threat to self-esteem and perceived control in recipient reaction to help: Theory development and empirical validation. In L. Berkowitz (Ed.), *Advances in experimental social psychology* (Vol. 19, pp. 81–122). New York: Academic Press.

Nadler, A., Fisher, J. D., & Streufert, S. (1976). When helping hurts: The effects of donor-recipient similarity and recipient self-esteem on reactions to aid. *Journal of Personality, 44,* 392–409.

Nail, P. R., MacDonald, G., & Levy, D. A. (2000). Proposal of a four-dimensional model of social response. *Psychological Bulletin, 126,* 454–470.

Nasco, S. A., & Marsh, K. L. (1999). Gaining control through counterfactual thinking. *Personality and Social Psychology Bulletin, 25,* 556–568.

National Survey of Giving, Volunteering, and Participating (2000). *Caring Canadians, involved Canadians.* Toronto, ON: Canadian Centre for Philanthropy.

Neff, L. A., & Karney, B. R. (2005). Gender differences in social support: A question of skill or responsiveness? *Journal of Personality and Social Psychology, 88,* 79–90.

Nelson, T. D. (2002). *The psychology of prejudice.* Boston, MA: Allyn & Bacon.

Nemeth, C. J. (1987). Influence processes, problem solving and creativity. In M. P. Zanna, J. M. Olson, & C. P. Herman (Eds.), *Social influence: The Ontario symposium* (Vol. 5, pp. 237–246). Hillsdale, NJ: Erlbaum.

Nemeth, C. J., & Chiles, C. (1988). Modelling courage: The role of dissent in fostering independence. *European Journal of Social Psychology, 18,* 275–280.

Neuberg, S. L. (1994). Expectancy-conformation processes in stereotype-tinged social encounters: The moderating role of social goals. In M. P. Zanna & J. M. Olson (Eds.), *The psychology of prejudice: The Ontario symposium* (Vol. 7, pp. 103–130). Hillsdale, NJ: Erlbaum.

Neuling, S. J., & Winefield, H. R. (1988). Social support and recovery after surgery for breast cancer: Frequency and correlates of supportive behaviors by family, friends and surgeon. *Social Science and Medicine, 27,* 385–392.

Neumann, R., Hülsenbeck, K., & Seibt, B. (2004). Attitudes toward people with AIDS and avoidance behavior: Automatic and reflective bases of behavior. *Journal of Experimental Social Psychology, 40,* 543–550.

Newby-Clark, I. R., Buehler, R., Koehler, D. J., & Griffin, D. (2000). People focus on optimistic scenarios and disregard pessimistic scenarios while predicting task completion times. *Journal of Experimental Psychology: Applied, 6,* 171–182.

Newby-Clark, I. R., McGregor, I., & Zanna, M. P. (2002). Thinking and caring about cognitive inconsistency: When and for whom does attitudinal ambivalence feel uncomfortable? *Journal of Personality and Social Psychology, 82,* 157–166.

Newcomb, A. F., & Bagwell, C. L. (1995). Children's friendship relations: A meta-analytic review. *Psychological Bulletin, 117,* 306–347.

Newcomb, A. F., Bukowski, W. M., & Pattee, L. (1993). Children's peer relations: A meta-analytic review of popular, rejected, neglected, controversial, and average sociometric status. *Psychological Bulletin, 113,* 99–128.

Newcomb, T. M. (1943). *Personality and social change.* New York: Dryden.

Newcomb, T. M. (1963). Persistence and regression of changed attitudes: Long-range studies. *Journal of Social Issues, 19,* 3–14.

Newcomb, T. M., Koeing, K. E., Flacks, R., & Warwick, D. P. (1967). *Persistence and change: Bennington College and its students after 25 years.* New York: Wiley.

Newman, L. S. (1991). Why are traits inferred spontaneously? A developmental approach. *Social Cognition, 9,* 221–253.

Neyer, F. J., & Lang, F. R. (2003). Blood is thicker than water: Kinship orientation across adulthood. *Journal of Personality and Social Psychology, 84,* 310–321.

Nickerson, R. S. (2001). The projective way of knowing: A useful heuristic that sometimes misleads. *Current Directions in Psychological Science, 10,* 168–172.

Nisbett, R. E., & Cohen, D. (1996). *Culture of honor: The psychology of violence in the south.* Boulder, CO: Westview Press.

Nisbett, R. E., & Wilson, T. D. (1977). Telling more than we can know: Verbal reports on mental processes. *Psychological Review, 84,* 231–259.

Noels, K. A. (2003). Learning Spanish as a second language: Learners' orientations and perceptions of their teachers' communication style. *Language Learning, 53* (Suppl. 1), 97–136.

Noels, K. A., & Clément, R. (1996). Communicating across cultures: Social determinants and acculturative consequences. *Canadian Journal of Behavioural Science, 28,* 214–228.

Noels, K. A., Pelletier, L. G., Clément, R., & Vallerand, R. J. (2000). Why are you learning a second language? Motivational orientations and self-determination theory. *Language Learning, 50,* 57–85.

Noels, K. A., Pons, G., & Clément, R. (1996). Language, identity, and adjustment: The role of linguistic self-confidence in the acculturation process. *Journal of Language and Social Psychology, 15,* 246–264.

Noor, F., & Evans, D. C. (2003). The effect of facial symmetry on perceptions of personality and attractiveness. *Journal of Research in Personality, 37,* 339–347.

Norenzayan, A., Choi, I., & Nisbett, R. E. (2002). Cultural similarities and differences in social inference: Evidence from behavioral predictions and lay theories of behavior. *Personality and Social Psychology Bulletin, 28,* 109–120.

Northouse, P. G. (1997). *Leadership: Theory and practice.* Thousand Oaks, CA: Sage.

Novaco, R. W. (1975). *Anger control.* Lexington, MA: Lexington Books.

Nuttin, J. M. (1987). Affective consequences of mere ownership: The name-letter effect in twelve European languages. *European Journal of Social Psychology, 17,* 381–402.

O'Brien, L. T., & Crandall, C. S. (2003). Stereotype threat and arousal: Effects on women's math performance. *Personality and Social Psychology Bulletin, 29,* 782–789.

Ochsner, K. N., & Lieberman, M. D. (2001). The emergence of social cognitive neuroscience. *American Psychologist, 56,* 717–734.

O'Connor, D. R. (2002). *Report of the Walkerton inquiry: The events of May 2000 and related issues.* Toronto: Ontario Ministry of the Attorney General.

Oettingen, G., & Mayer, D. (2002). The motivating function of thinking about the future: Expectations versus fantasies. *Journal of Personality and Social Psychology, 83,* 1198–1212.

O'Keefe, G. J. (1985). "Taking a bite out of crime": The impact of a public information campaign. *Communication Research, 12,* 147–178.

Oliner, S. P., & Oliner, P. M. (1988). *The altruistic personality.* New York: Free Press.

Olson, J. M. (1992). Self-perception of humor: Evidence for discounting and augmentation effects. *Journal of Personality and Social Psychology, 62,* 369–377.

Olson, J. M., Buhrmann, O., & Roese, N. J. (2000). Comparing comparisons: An integrative perspective on social comparison and counterfactual thinking. In J. M. Suls & L. Wheeler (Eds.), *Handbook of social comparison: Theory and research* (pp. 379–398). New York: Kluwer Academic/ Plenum.

Olson, J. M., & Hafer, C. L. (1996). Affect, motivation, and cognition in relative deprivation research. In R. M. Sorrentino & E. T. Higgins (Eds.), *Handbook of motivation and cognition* (Vol. 3, pp. 85–117). New York: Guilford.

Olson, J. M., Hafer, C. L., Couzens, A., & Kramins, I. (2000). You're OK, I'm OK: The self-presentation of affective reactions to deprivation. *Social Justice Research, 13,* 359–371.

Olson, J. M., Roese, N. J., & Zanna, M. P. (1996). Expectancies. In E. T. Higgins & A. W. Kruglanski (Eds.), *Social psychology: Handbook of basic principles* (pp. 211–238). New York: Guilford Press.

Olson, J. M., Roese, N. J., Meen, J., & Robertson, D. J. (1995). The preconditions and consequences of relative deprivation: Two field studies. *Journal of Applied Social Psychology, 25,* 944–964.

Olson, J. M., & Stone, J. (2005). The influence of behavior on attitudes. In D. Albarracín, B. T. Johnson, & M. P. Zanna (Eds.), *The handbook of attitudes* (pp. 223–271). Mahwah, NJ: Erlbaum.

Olson, J. M., & Zanna, M. P. (1987). Understanding and promoting exercise: A social psychological perspective. *Canadian Journal of Public Health, 78,* S1–S7.

Olson, J. M., Vernon, P. A., Harris, J. A., & Jang, K. L. (2001). The heritability of attitudes: A study of twins. *Journal of Personality and Social Psychology, 80,* 845–860.

Olson, M. A., & Fazio, R. H. (2004). Reducing the influence of extrapersonal associations on the Implicit Association Task: Personalizing the IAT. *Journal of Personality and Social Psychology, 86,* 653–667.

Omoto, A. M., & Snyder, M. (1995). Sustained helping without obligation: Motivation, longevity of service, and perceived attitude change among AIDS workers. *Journal of Personality and Social Psychology, 68,* 671–686.

Opotow, S. (1994). Predicting protection: Scope of justice and the natural world. *Journal of Social Issues, 50* (3), 49–63.

Opotow, S. (2001). Reconciliation in times of impunity: Challenges for social justice. *Social Justice Research, 14,* 149–170.

Opotow, S., & Weiss, L. (2000). Denial and the process of moral exclusion in environmental conflict. *Journal of Social Issues, 56,* 475–490.

Orbell, J. M., van de Kragt, A. J. C., & Dawes, R. M. (1988). Explaining discussion-induced cooperation. *Journal of Personality and Social Psychology, 54,* 811–819.

Orne, M. T. (1962). On the social psychology of the psychological experiment: With particular reference to demand characteristics and their implications. *American Psychologist, 17,* 776–783.

Osgood, C. E. (1962). *An alternative to war or surrender.* Urbana: University of Illinois Press.

Osgood, C. E., Suci, G. J., & Tannenbaum, P. H. (1957). *The measurement of meaning.* Urbana: University of Illinois Press.

Osherow, N. (1999). Making sense of the nonsensical: An analysis of Jonestown. In E. Aronson (Ed.), *Readings about the social animal* (8th ed., pp. 71–88). New York: Worth.

Oskamp, S., & Schultz, P. W. (2005). *Attitudes and opinions* (3rd ed.). Mahwah, NJ: Erlbaum.

Ottati, V. C., Tindale, R. S., Edwards, J., Bryant, F. B., Heath, L., O'Connell, D. C., et al. (Eds.). (2002). *The social psychology of politics.* New York: Plenum.

Owens, T. J. (2003). Self and identity. In J. Delamater (Ed.), *Handbook of social psychology* (pp. 205–232). New York: Kluwer Academic/Plenum.

Oyserman, D., Coon, H. M., & Kemmelmeier, M. (2002). Rethinking individualism and collectivism: Evaluation of theoretical assumptions and meta-analyses. *Psychological Bulletin, 128,* 3–72.

Page, M. M., & Scheidt, R. J. (1971). The elusive weapons effect: Demand awareness, evaluation apprehension, and slightly sophisticated subjects. *Journal of Personality and Social Psychology, 20,* 304–318.

Paik, H., & Comstock, G. (1994). The effects of television violence on antisocial behavior: A meta-analysis. *Communication Research, 21,* 516–546.

Pan, H. S., Neidig, P. H., & O'Leary, K. D. (1994). Predicting mild and severe husband-to-wife physical aggression. *Journal of Consulting and Clinical Psychology, 62,* 975–981.

Paolini, S., Hewstone, M., Cairns, E., & Voci, A. (2004). Effects of direct and indirect cross-group friendships on judgments of Catholics and Protestants in Northern Ireland: The mediating role of an anxiety-reduction mechanism. *Personality and Social Psychology Bulletin, 30,* 770–786.

Papastamou, S., & Mugny, G. (1990). Synchronic consistency and psychologization in minority influence. *European Journal of Social Psychology, 20,* 85–98.

Park, B. (1986). A method for studying the development of impressions of real people. *Journal of Personality and Social Psychology, 51,* 907–917.

Park, W. (1990). A review of research on groupthink. *Journal of Behavioral Decision Making, 3,* 229–245.

Parks, C. D., & Rumble, A. C. (2001). Elements of reciprocity and social value orientation. *Personality and Social Psychology Bulletin, 27,* 1301–1309.

Parks, C. D., Sanna, L. J., & Berel, S. R. (2001). Actions of similar others as inducements to cooperate in social dilemmas. *Personality and Social Psychology Bulletin, 27,* 345–354.

Parks, C. D., Sanna, L. J., & Posey, D. C. (2003). Retrospection in social dilemmas: Thinking about the past affects future cooperation. *Journal of Personality and Social Psychology, 84,* 988–996.

Pasupathi, M. (1999). Age differences in response to conformity pressure for emotional and nonemotional material. *Psychology and Aging, 14,* 170–174.

Paulhus, D. L. (1984). Two-component models of socially desirable responding. *Journal of Personality and Social Psychology, 46,* 598–609.

Paulhus, D. L. (1998). Interpersonal and intrapsychic adaptiveness of trait self-enhancement: A mixed blessing? *Journal of Personality and Social Psychology, 74,* 1197–1208.

Paunonen, S. V., Ewan, K., Earthy, J., Lafave, S., & Goldberg, H. (1999). Facial features as personality cues. *Journal of Personality, 67,* 555–583.

Pavlov, I. P. (1927). *Conditional reflexes.* London, UK: Oxford University Press.

Payne, B. K. (2001). Prejudice and perception: The role of automatic and controlled processes in misperceiving a weapon. *Journal of Personality and Social Psychology, 81,* 181–192.

Payne, B. K., Lambert, A. J., & Jacoby, L. L. (2002). Best laid plans: Effects of goals on accessibility bias and cognitive control in race-based misperceptions of weapons. *Journal of Experimental Social Psychology, 38,* 384–396.

Pearce, P. L., & Amato, P. R. (1980). A taxonomy of helping: A multidimensional scaling analysis. *Social Psychology Quarterly, 43,* 363–371.

Pedersen, W. C., Gonzales, C., & Miller, N. (2000). The moderating effect of trivial triggering provocation on displaced aggression. *Journal of Personality and Social Psychology, 78,* 913–927.

Pelham, B. W. (1999). *Conducting experiments in psychology: Measuring the weight of smoke.* Pacific Grove, CA: Brooks/Cole.

Pelham, B. W., Koole, S. L., Hardin, C. D., Hetts, J. J., Seah, E., & DeHart, T. (2005). Gender moderates the relation between implicit and explicit self-esteem. *Journal of Experimental Social Psychology, 41,* 84–89.

Pelham, B. W., Mirenberg, M. C., & Jones, J. T. (2002). Why Susie sells seashells by the seashore: Implicit egotism and major life decisions. *Journal of Personality and Social Psychology, 82,* 469–487.

Pelletier, L. G., Séguin-Lévesque, C., & Legault, L. (2002). Pressure from above and pressure from below as determinants of teachers' motivation and teaching behaviors. *Journal of Educational Psychology, 94,* 186–196.

Peng, K., & Knowles, E. D. (2003). Culture, education, and the attribution of physical causality. *Personality and Social Psychology Bulletin, 29,* 1272–1284.

Penner, L. A., & Finkelstein, M. A. (1998). Dispositional and structural determinants of volunteerism. *Journal of Personality and Social Psychology, 74,* 525–537.

Pennington, J., & Schlenker, B. R. (1999). Accountability for consequential decisions: Justifying ethical judgments to audiences. *Personality and Social Psychology Bulletin, 25,* 1067–1081.

Perloff, L. S. (1983). Perceptions of vulnerability to victimization. *Journal of Social Issues, 39,* 41–61.

Perloff, R. M. (1989). Ego-involvement and the third person effect of televised news coverage. *Communication Research, 16,* 236–262.

Perloff, R. M. (2003). *The dynamics of persuasion: Communication and attitudes in the 21st century* (2nd ed.). Mahwah, NJ: Erlbaum.

Perry, D. G., Williard, J. C., & Perry, L. C. (1990). Peers' perceptions of the consequences that victimized children provide aggressors. *Child Development, 61,* 1310–1325.

Pessin, J. (1933). The comparative effects of social and mechanical stimulation on memorizing. *American Journal of Psychology, 45,* 263–270.

Peters, L. H., Hartke, D. D., & Pohlmann, J. T. (1985). Fiedler's contingency theory of leadership: An application of the meta-analysis procedures of Schmidt and Hunter. *Psychological Bulletin, 97,* 274–285.

Petersen, L.-E., & Dietz, J. (2000). Social discrimination in a personnel selection context: The effects of an authority's instruction to discriminate and followers' authoritarianism. *Journal of Applied Social Psychology, 31,* 206–220.

Peterson, R. S. (1997). A directive leadership style in group decision making can be both virtue and vice: Evidence from elite and experimental groups. *Journal of Personality and Social Psychology, 72,* 1107–1121.

Petrides, M. (1985). Deficits on conditional associative-learning tasks after frontal- and temporal-lobe lesions in man. *Neuropsychologia, 23,* 610–614.

Pettigrew, T. F. (1978). Three issues in ethnicity: Boundaries, deprivations, and perceptions. In J. M. Yinger & S. J. Cutler (Eds.), *Major social issues: A multidisciplinary view* (pp. 25–49). New York: Free Press.

Pettigrew, T. F. (1986). The intergroup contact hypothesis reconsidered. In M. Hewstone & R. Brown (Eds.), *Contact and conflict in intergroup encounters* (pp. 169–195). New York: Basil Blackwell.

Pettigrew, T. F. (1998). Intergroup contact theory. *Annual Review of Psychology, 49,* 65–85.

Pettigrew, T. F., & Tropp, L. R. (2000). Does intergroup contact reduce prejudice? Recent meta-analytic findings. In S. Oskamp (Ed.), *Reducing prejudice and discrimination* (pp. 93–114). Mahwah, NJ: Erlbaum.

Petty, R. E., & Cacioppo, J. T. (1981). *Attitudes and persuasion: Classic and contemporary approaches.* Dubuque, IA: Brown.

Petty, R. E., & Cacioppo, J. T. (1983). Source factors and the elaboration likelihood model of persuasion. *Advances in Consumer Research, 11,* 668–682.

Petty, R. E., & Cacioppo, J. T. (1986). The elaboration likelihood model of persuasion. In L. Berkowitz (Ed.), *Advances in experimental social psychology* (Vol. 19, pp. 123–205). New York: Academic Press.

Petty, R. E., Cacioppo, J. T., & Goldman, R. (1981). Personal involvement as a determinant of argument-based persuasion. *Journal of Personality and Social Psychology, 41,* 847–855.

Petty, R. E., Cacioppo, J. T., & Schumann, D. (1983). Central and peripheral routes to advertising effectiveness: The moderating role of involvement. *Journal of Consumer Research, 10,* 134–148.

Petty, R. E., & Krosnick, J. A. (1995). *Attitude strength: Antecedents and consequences.* Mahwah, NJ: Erlbaum.

Petty, R. E., Rucker, D. D., Bizer, G. Y., & Cacioppo, J. T. (2004). The elaboration likelihood model of persuasion. In J. S. Seiter & R. H. Gass (Eds.), *Perspectives on persuasion, social influence, and compliance gaining* (pp. 65–89). Boston, MA: Pearson Education.

Petty, R. E., Wells, G. L., & Brock, T. C. (1976). Distraction can enhance or reduce yielding to propaganda: Thought disruption versus effort justification. *Journal of Personality and Social Psychology, 34,* 874–888.

Phillips, D. P. (1977). Motor vehicle fatalities increase just after publicized suicide stories. *Science, 196,* 1464–1465.

Pickett, C. L., Gardner, W. L., & Knowles, M. (2004). Getting a cue: The need to belong and enhanced sensitivity to social cues. *Personality and Social Psychology Bulletin, 30,* 1095–1107.

Pihl, R. O., & Peterson, J. B. (1995). Drugs and aggression: Correlations, crime and human manipulative studies and some proposed mechanisms. *Journal of Psychiatric Neurosciences, 20,* 141–149.

Pihl, R. O., Peterson, J. B., & Lau, M. A. (1993). A biosocial model of the alcohol-aggression relationship. *Journal of Studies on Alcohol, 11,* 128–139.

Plaks, J. E., Stroessner, S. J., Dweck, C. S., & Sherman, J. W. (2001). Person theories and attention allocation: Preferences for stereotypic versus counterstereotypic information. *Journal of Personality and Social Psychology, 80,* 876–893.

Plant, E. A. (2004). Responses to interracial interactions over time. *Personality and Social Psychology Bulletin, 30,* 1458–1471.

Plant, E. A., & Devine, P. G. (2003). The antecedents and implications of interracial anxiety. *Personality and Social Psychology Bulletin, 29,* 790–801.

Pliner, P., Chaiken, S., & Flett, G. (1990). Gender differences in concern with body weight and physical appearance over the lifespan. *Personality and Social Psychology Bulletin, 16,* 263–273.

Pliner, P., Hart, H., Kohl, J., & Saari, D. (1974). Compliance without pressure: Some further data on the foot-in-the-door technique. *Journal of Experimental Social Psychology, 10,* 17–22.

Plous, S. L., & Zimbardo, P. G. (2004). How social science can reduce terrorism. *The Chronicle of Higher Education,* September 10, 2004, B9–B10.

Polivy, J., & Herman, C. P. (2002). If at first you don't succeed: False hopes of self-change. *American Psychologist, 57,* 677–689.

Poore, A. G., Gagne, F., Barlow, K. M., Lydon, J. E., Taylor, D. M., & Wright, S. C. (2002). Contact and the personal/group discrimination discrepancy in an Inuit community. *Journal of Psychology, 136,* 371–382.

Pope, K. S. (1996). Memory, abuse, and science: Questioning claims about the false memory syndrome epidemic. *American Psychologist, 51,* 957–974.

Postmes, T., & Spears, R. (1998). Deindividuation and antinormative behavior: A meta-analysis. *Psychological Bulletin, 123,* 238–259.

Postmes, T., Spears, R., & Cihangir, S. (2001). Quality of decision making and group norms. *Journal of Personality and Social Psychology, 80,* 918–930.

Postmes, T., Spears, R., Sakhel, K., & de Groot, D. (2001). Social influence in computer-mediated communication: The effects of anonymity on group behavior. *Personality and Social Psychology Bulletin, 27,* 1243–1254.

Powers, T. A., Koestner, R., & Topciu, R. A. (2005). Implementation intentions, perfectionism, and goal progress: Perhaps the road to hell *is* paved with good intentions. *Personality and Social Psychology Bulletin, 31,* 902–912.

Powers, T. A., Zuroff, D. C., & Topciu, R. A. (2004). Covert and overt expressions of self-criticism and perfectionism and their relation to depression. *European Journal of Personality, 18,* 61–72.

Pratkanis, A., & Aronson, E. (2001). *Age of propaganda: The everyday use and abuse of persuasion* (Rev. ed.). New York: Freeman.

Pratto, F., & Bargh, J. A. (1991). Stereotyping based on apparently individuating information: Trait and global components of sex stereotypes under attention overload. *Journal of Experimental Social Psychology, 27,* 26–47.

Prentice-Dunn, S., & Rogers, R. W. (1980). Effects of deindividuating situational cues and aggressive models on subjective deindividuation and aggression. *Journal of Personality and Social Psychology, 39,* 104–113.

Prentice-Dunn, S., & Rogers, R. W. (1989). Deindividuation and the self-regulation of behavior. In P. B. Paulus (Ed.), *The psychology of group influence* (2nd ed., pp. 86–109). Hillsdale, NJ: Erlbaum.

Price, P. C., Pentecost, H. C., & Voth, R. D. (2002). Perceived event frequency and the optimistic bias: Evidence for a two-process model of personal risk judgments. *Journal of Experimental Social Psychology, 38,* 242–252.

Priester, J. R., & Petty, R. E. (1996). The gradual threshold model of ambivalence: Relating the positive and negative bases of attitudes to subjective ambivalence. *Journal of Personality and Social Psychology, 71,* 431–449.

Prochaska, J. O., DiClemente, C. C., & Norcross, J. C. (1992). In search of how people change: Applications to addictive behaviors. *American Psychologist, 47,* 1102–1114.

Pronin, E., Lin, D. Y., & Ross, L. (2002). The bias blind spot: Perceptions of bias in self versus others. *Personality and Social Psychology Bulletin, 28,* 369–381.

Pruitt, D. G. (1998). Social conflict. In D. T. Gilbert, S. T. Fiske, & G. Lindzey (Eds.), *Handbook of social psychology* (4th ed., Vol. 2, pp. 470–503). Boston, MA: McGraw-Hill.

Prunier, G. (1995). *The Rwanda crisis: History of a genocide.* New York: Columbia University Press.

Quinn, A., & Schlenker, B. R. (2002). Can accountability produce independence? Goals as determinants of the impact of accountability on conformity. *Personality and Social Psychology Bulletin, 28,* 772–783.

Quinn, K. A., & Olson, J. M. (2003). Framing social judgment: Self-ingroup comparison and perceived discrimination. *Personality and Social Psychology Bulletin, 29,* 228–236.

Radcliffe, N. M., & Klein, W. M. P. (2002). Dispositional, unrealistic, and comparative optimism: Differential relations with the knowledge and processing of risk information and beliefs about personal risk. *Personality and Social Psychology Bulletin, 28,* 836–846.

Ramirez, J. M. (1993). Acceptability of aggression in four Spanish regions and a comparison with other European countries. *Aggressive Behavior, 19,* 185–197.

Ramsey, J. L., Langlois, J. H., Hoss, R. A., Rubenstein, A. J., & Griffin, A. M. (2004). Origins of a stereotype: Categorization of facial attractiveness by 6-month-old infants. *Developmental Science, 7,* 201–211.

Rankin, R. F., & Campbell, D. T. (1955). Galvanic skin response to Negro and White experimenters. *Journal of Abnormal and Social Psychology, 51,* 30–33.

Rapoport, A. (1960). *Fights, games, and debates.* Ann Arbor: University of Michigan Press.

Raskin, R., & Hall, C. S. (1979). A narcissistic personality inventory. *Psychological Reports, 45,* 590.

Raskin, R., & Terry, H. (1988). A principal-components analysis of the Narcissistic Personality Inventory and further evidence of its construct validation. *Journal of Personality and Social Psychology, 54,* 890–902.

Regan, D. T. (1971). Effects of a favor and liking on compliance. *Journal of Experimental Social Psychology, 7,* 627–639.

Regan, P. C., Snyder, M., & Kassin, S. M. (1995). Unrealistic optimism: Self-enhancement or person positivity? *Personality and Social Psychology Bulletin, 21,* 1073–1082.

Reis, H. T. (2000). Self-disclosure. In A. E. Kazdin (Ed.), *Encyclopedia of psychology* (Vol. 17, pp. 210–212). Washington, DC: American Psychological Association.

Rempel, J. K., Holmes, J. G., & Zanna, M. P. (1985). Trust in close relationships. *Journal of Personality and Social Psychology, 49,* 95–112.

Rempel, J. K., Ross, M., & Holmes, J. G. (2001). Trust and communicated attributions in close relationships. *Journal of Personality and Social Psychology, 81,* 57–64.

Reynolds, D. E., & Sanders, M. S. (1975). Effect of defendant attractiveness, age, and injury on severity of sentence given by simulated jurors. *Journal of Social Psychology, 96,* 149–150.

Rhodes, G., Geddes, K., Jeffery, L., Dziurawiec, S., & Clark, A. (2002). Are average and symmetric faces attractive to infants? Discrimination and looking preferences. *Perception, 31*, 315–321.

Rhodes, G., Yoshikawa, S., Clark, A., Lee, K., McKay, R., & Akamatsu, S. (2001). Attractiveness of facial averageness and symmetry in non-Western cultures: In search of biologically based standards of beauty. *Perception, 30*, 611–625.

Rhodewalt, F. (1990). Self-handicappers: Individual differences in the preference for anticipatory, self-protective acts. In R. L. Higgins, C. R. Snyder, & S. Berglas (Eds.), *Self-handicapping: The paradox that isn't* (pp. 69–106). New York: Plenum.

Rhodewalt, F., & Fairfield, M. (1991). Claimed self-handicaps and self-handicappers: The relation of reductions in intended effort to performance. *Basic and Applied Social Psychology, 16*, 397–416.

Rhodewalt, F., Sanbonmatsu, D. M., Tschanz, B., Feick, D. L., & Waller, A. (1995). Self-handicapping and interpersonal trade-offs: The effects of claimed self-handicaps on observers' performance evaluations and feedback. *Personality and Social Psychology Bulletin, 21*, 1042–1050.

Richardson, D., Hammock, G., Smith, S., & Gardner, W. (1994). Empathy as a cognitive inhibitor of interpersonal aggression. *Aggressive Behavior, 20*, 275–289.

Richeson, J. A., Baird, A. A., Gordon, H. L., Heatherton, T. F., Wyland, C. L., Trawalter, S., et al. (2003). An fMRI investigation of the impact of interracial contact on executive function. *Nature Neuroscience, 6*, 1323–1328.

Richeson, J. A., & Nussbaum, R. J. (2004). The impact of multiculturalism versus color-blindness on racial bias. *Journal of Experimental Social Psychology, 40*, 417–423.

Ridgeway, C. L. (2001). Gender, status, and leadership. *Journal of Social Issues, 57*, 637–656.

Robins, R. W., Hendin, H. M., & Trzesniewski, K. H. (2001). Measuring global self-esteem: Construct validation of a single-item measure and the Rosenberg Self-Esteem Scale. *Personality and Social Psychology Bulletin, 27*, 151–161.

Roccas, S., Sagiv, L., Schwartz, S. H., & Knafo, A. (2002). The big five personality factors and personal values. *Personality and Social Psychology Bulletin, 28*, 789–801.

Roch, S. G., & Samuelson, C. D. (1997). Effects of environmental uncertainty and social value orientation in resource dilemmas. *Organizational Behavior and Human Decision Processes, 70*, 221–235.

Roco, M. C., & Bainbridge, W. S. (2001). *Societal implications of nanoscience and nanotechnology.* Arlington, VA: National Science Foundation.

Roco, M. C., & Bainbridge, W. S. (2002). *Converging technologies for improving human performance: Nanotechnology, biotechnology, information technology and cognitive science.* Arlington, VA: National Science Foundation.

Roehling, M. (1999). Weight-based discrimination in employment: Psychological and legal aspects. *Personnel Psychology, 52*, 969–1016.

Roese, N. J. (1994). The functional basis of counterfactual thinking. *Journal of Personality and Social Psychology, 66*, 805–818.

Roese, N. J. (1997). Counterfactual thinking. *Psychological Bulletin, 121*, 133–148.

Roese, N. J. (2005). *If only: How to turn regret into opportunity.* New York: Broadway Books.

Roese, N. J., & Olson, J. M. (1995). Counterfactual thinking: A critical overview. In N. J. Roese & J. M. Olson (Eds.), *What might have been: The social psychology of counterfactual thinking* (pp. 1–55). Mahwah, NJ: Erlbaum.

Roese, N. J., & Olson, J. M. (1997). Counterfactual thinking: The intersection of affect and function. In M. P. Zanna (Ed.), *Advances in experimental social psychology* (Vol. 29, pp. 1–59). San Diego, CA: Academic Press.

Rogers, C. R. (1961). *On becoming a person.* Boston: Houghton Mifflin.

Rogers, R. W. (1983). Cognitive and physiological processes in fear appeals and attitude change: A revised theory of protection motivation. In J. T. Cacioppo & R. E. Petty (Eds.), *Social psychophysiology: A sourcebook* (pp. 153–176). New York: Guilford.

Rogers, R. W., & Mewborn, C. R. (1976). Fear appeals and attitude change: Effects of a threat's noxiousness, probability of occurrence, and the efficacy of coping responses. *Journal of Personality and Social Psychology, 34*, 54–61.

Rogers, R. W., & Prentice-Dunn, S. (1981). Deindividuation and anger-mediated interracial aggression: Unmasking regressive racism. *Journal of Personality and Social Psychology, 41*, 63–73.

Rogge, R. D., & Bradbury, T. N. (1999). Till violence does us part: The differing roles of communication and aggression in predicting adverse marital outcomes. *Journal of Consulting and Clinical Psychology, 67*, 340–351.

Rohan, M. J., & Zanna, M. P. (1996). Value transmission in families. In C. Seligman, J. M. Olson, & M. P. Zanna (Eds.), *The psychology of values: The Ontario symposium* (Vol. 8, pp. 233–276). Mahwah, NJ: Erlbaum.

Rokeach, M. (1973). *The nature of human values.* New York: Free Press.

Rose, A. J., Swenson, L. P., & Waller, E. M. (2004). Overt and relational aggression and perceived popularity: Developmental differences in concurrent and prospective relations. *Developmental Psychology, 40*, 378–387.

Rosenbaum, M. E. (1986). The repulsion hypothesis: On the nondevelopment of relationships. *Journal of Personality and Social Psychology, 51*, 1156–1166.

Rosenberg, M. (1979). *Conceiving the self.* New York: Basic Books.

Rosenberg, M. J., & Hovland, C. I. (1960). Cognitive, affective, and behavioral components of attitudes. In C. I. Hovland & M. J. Rosenberg (Eds.), *Attitude organization and change* (pp. 1–14). New Haven, CT: Yale University Press.

Rosenthal, R. (2003). Covert communication in laboratories, classrooms, and the truly real world. *Current Directions in Psychological Science, 12*, 151–154.

Ross, A. S. (1971). Effect of increased responsibility on bystander intervention: The presence of children. *Journal of Personality and Social Psychology, 19*, 306–310

Ross, A. S., & Braband, J. (1973). Effect of increased responsibility on bystander intervention: II. The cue value of a blind person. *Journal of Personality and Social Psychology, 25*, 254–258.

Ross, E. A. (1908). *Social psychology.* New York: Macmillan.

Ross, L. (1977). The intuitive psychologist and his shortcomings. In L. Berkowitz (Ed.), *Advances in experimental social psychology* (Vol. 10, pp. 173–220). San Diego, CA: Academic Press.

Ross, L., Amabile, T. M., & Steinmetz, J. L. (1977). Social roles, social control, and biases in social-perception processes. *Journal of Personality and Social Psychology, 35*, 485–494.

Ross, L., Greene, D., & House, P. (1977). The "false consensus effect": An egocentric bias in social perception and attribution processes. *Journal of Experimental Social Psychology, 13*, 279–301.

Ross, L., & Nisbett, R. E. (1991). *The person and the situation: Perspectives of social psychology.* New York: McGraw-Hill.

Ross, M. (1989). Relation of implicit theories to the construction of personal histories. *Psychological Review, 96*, 341–357.

Ross, M., & Wilson, A. E. (2002). It feels like yesterday: Self-esteem, valence of personal past experiences, and judgments of subjective distance. *Journal of Personality and Social Psychology, 82*, 792–803.

Ross, M., Xun, W. Q. E., & Wilson, A. E. (2002). Language and the bicultural self. *Personality and Social Psychology Bulletin, 28*, 1040–1050.

Ross, S. M., & Offermann, L. R. (1997). Transformational leaders: Measurement of personality attributes and work group performance. *Personality and Social Psychology Bulletin, 23,* 1078–1086.

Rothbart, M., Evans, M., & Fulero, S. (1979). Recall for confirming events: Memory processes and the maintenance of social stereotypes. *Journal of Experimental Social Psychology, 15,* 343–355.

Roy, M. M., Christenfeld, N. J. S., & McKenzie, C. R. M. (2005). Underestimating the duration of future events: Memory incorrectly used or memory bias? *Psychological Bulletin, 131,* 738–756.

Rozin, P., Lowery, L., Imada, S., & Haidt, J. (1999). The CAD triad hypothesis: A mapping between three moral emotions (contempt, anger, disgust) and three moral codes (community, autonomy, divinity). *Journal of Personality and Social Psychology, 76,* 674–686.

Ruback, R. B., & Juieng, D. (1997). Territorial defense in parking lots: Retaliation against waiting drivers. *Journal of Applied Social Psychology, 27,* 821–834.

Rubin, K. H., Lynch, D., Coplan, R., Rose-Krasnor, L., & Booth, C. L. (1994). "Birds of a feather . . . ": Behavioral concordances and preferential personal attraction in children. *Child Development, 65,* 1778–1785.

Rubin, M., & Hewstone, M. (1998). Social identity theory's self-esteem hypothesis: A review and some suggestions for clarification. *Personality and Social Psychology Review, 2,* 40–62.

Ruble, D. N., & Goodnow, J. J. (1998). Social development in childhood and adulthood. In D. T. Gilbert, S. T. Fiske, & G. Lindzey (Eds.), *The handbook of social psychology* (4th ed., Vol. 1, pp. 741–787). New York: McGraw-Hill.

Rudman, L. A. (1998). Self-promotion as a risk factor for women: The costs and benefits of counterstereotypical impression management. *Journal of Personality and Social Psychology, 74,* 629–645.

Rudman, L. A., Ashmore, R. D., & Gary, M. L. (2001). "Unlearning" automatic biases: The malleability of implicit prejudice and stereotypes. *Journal of Personality and Social Psychology, 81,* 856–868.

Rudman, L. A., & Fairchild, K. (2004). Reactions to counterstereotypic behavior: The role of backlash in cultural stereotype maintenance. *Journal of Personality and Social Psychology, 87,* 157–176.

Rudman, L. A., & Glick, P. (2001). Prescriptive gender stereotypes and backlash toward agentic women. *Journal of Social Issues, 57,* 743–762.

Rudman, L. A., & Kilianski, S. E. (2000). Implicit and explicit attitudes toward female authority. *Personality and Social Psychology Bulletin, 26,* 1315–1328.

Rumsey, M. G. (1976). Effects of defendant background and remorse on sentencing judgments. *Journal of Applied Social Psychology, 6,* 64–68.

Rumsey, M. G., Allgeier, E. R., & Castore, C. H. (1978). Group discussion, sentencing judgments, and the leniency shift. *Journal of Social Psychology, 105,* 249–257.

Rusbult, C. E. (1983). A longitudinal test of the investment model: The development (and deterioration) of satisfaction and commitment in heterosexual involvements. *Journal of Personality and Social Psychology, 45,* 101–117.

Rusbult, C. E., & Martz, J. M. (1995). Remaining in an abusive relationship: An investment model analysis of nonvoluntary dependence. *Personality and Social Psychology Bulletin, 21,* 558–571.

Russell, J. A. (1994). Is there universal recognition of emotion from facial expression? A review of the cross-cultural studies. *Psychological Review, 115,* 102–141.

Russell, J. A., & Fehr, B. (1987). Relativity in the perception of emotion in facial expressions. *Journal of Experimental Psychology: General, 116,* 223–237.

Russell, J. A., Suzuki, N., & Ishida, N. (1993). Canadian, Greek, and Japanese freely produced emotion labels for facial expressions. *Motivation and Emotion, 17,* 337–351.

Safdar, S., & Lay, C. H. (2003). The relations of immigrant-specific and immigrant-nonspecific daily hassles to distress controlling for psychological adjustment and cultural competence. *Journal of Applied Social Psychology, 33,* 299–320.

Safdar, S., Lay, C. H., & Struthers, W. (2003). The process of acculturation and basic goals: Testing a multidimensional individual difference acculturation model with Iranian immigrants in Canada. *Applied Psychology: An International Review, 52,* 555–579.

Sagar, H. A., & Schofield, J. W. (1980). Racial and behavioral cues in Black and White children's perceptions of ambiguously aggressive acts. *Journal of Personality and Social Psychology, 39,* 590–598.

Sagarin, B. J., Cialdini, R. B., Rice, W. E., & Serna, S. B. (2002). Dispelling the illusion of invulnerability: The motivations and mechanisms of resistance to persuasion. *Journal of Personality and Social Psychology, 83,* 526–541.

Sagi, A. (1990). Attachment theory and research from a cross-cultural perspective. *Human Development, 33,* 10–22.

Salovey, P., Rothman, A. J., & Rodin, J. (1998). Health behavior. In D. T. Gilbert, S. T. Fiske, & G. Lindzey (Eds.), *The handbook of social psychology* (4th ed., Vol. 2, pp. 633–683). New York: McGraw-Hill.

Salovey, P., & Wegener, D. T. (2002). Communicating about health: Message framing, persuasion, and health behavior. In J. Suls & K. Wallston (Eds.), *Social psychological foundations of health and illness.* Oxford: Blackwell.

Sande, G. N., Goethals, G. R., & Radloff, C. E. (1988). Perceiving one's own traits and others': The multifaceted self. *Journal of Personality and Social Psychology, 54,* 13–20.

Sanders, G. S., & Baron, R. S. (1977). Is social comparison irrelevant for producing choice shifts? *Journal of Experimental Social Psychology, 13,* 303–314.

Sanfey, A. G., Rilling, J. K., Aronson, J. A., Nystrom, L. E., & Cohen, J. D. (2003). The neural basis of economic decision-making in the ultimatum game. *Science, 300,* 1755–1758.

Sanna, L. J. (1992). Self-efficacy theory: Implications for social facilitation and social loafing. *Journal of Personality and Social Psychology, 62,* 774–786.

Sanna, L. J., & Turley, K. J. (1996). Antecedents to spontaneous counterfactual thinking: Effects of expectancy violation and outcome valence. *Personality and Social Psychology Bulletin, 22,* 906–919.

Santee, R. T., & Maslach, C. (1982). To agree or not to agree: Personal dissent amid social pressure to conform. *Journal of Personality and Social Psychology, 42,* 690–700.

Santor, D. A., Ingram, A., & Kusumakar, V. (2003). Influence of executive functioning difficulties on verbal aggression in adolescents: Moderating effects of winning and losing and increasing and decreasing levels of provocation. *Aggressive Behaviour, 29,* 475–488.

Santor, D. A., Messervey, D., & Kusumakar, V. (2000). Measuring peer pressure, popularity, and conformity in adolescent boys and girls: Predicting school performance, sexual attitudes, and substance abuse. *Journal of Youth and Adolescence, 29,* 163–182.

Sarason, I. G., Levine, H. M., Basham, R. B., & Sarason, B. R. (1983). Assessing social support: The social support questionnaire. *Journal of Personality and Social Psychology, 44,* 127–139.

Sarason, I. G., Sarason, B. R., Pierce, G. R., Shearin, E. N., & Sayers, M. H. (1991). A social learning approach to increasing blood donations. *Journal of Applied Social Psychology, 21,* 896–918.

Satow, K. (1975). Social approval and helping. *Journal of Experimental Social Psychology, 11,* 501–509.

Schachter, S. (1951). Deviation, rejection, and communication. *Journal of Abnormal and Social Psychology, 46,* 190–207.

Schacter, D. L. (1996). *Searching for memory: The brain, the mind, and the past.* New York: Basic Books.

Schaefer, C., Coyne, J. C., & Lazarus, R. S. (1981). The health-related functions of social support. *Journal of Behavioral Medicine, 4,* 381–406.

Schafer, R. (1967). Ideals, the ego ideal, and the ideal self. In R. R. Holt (Ed.), *Motives and thought: Psychoanalytic essays in honor of David Rapaport* [Special Issue], *Psychological Issues, 5,* 131–174.

Schaller, M., & Cialdini, R. B. (1990). Happiness, sadness, and helping: A motivational integration. In E. T. Higgins & R. M. Sorrentino (Eds.), *Handbook of motivation and cognition: Foundations of social behavior* (Vol. 2, pp. 265–296). New York: Guilford.

Schaller, M., & Cialdini, R. B. (1998). The economics of empathic helping: Support for a mood management motive. *Journal of Experimental Social Psychology, 24,* 163–181.

Scheier, M. F., & Carver, C. S. (1985). Optimism, coping and health: Assessment and implications of generalized outcome expectancies, *Health Psychology, 4,* 219–247.

Scheier, M. F., Matthews, K. A., Owens, J., Magovern, G. J., Sr., Lefebvre, R. C., Abbott, R. A., & Carver, C. S. (1989). Dispositional optimism and recovery from coronary artery bypass surgery: The beneficial effects on physical and psychological well-being. *Journal of Personality and Social Psychology, 57,* 1024–1040.

Schiaffino, K. M., & Revenson, T. A. (1992). The role of perceived self-efficacy, perceived control, and causal attributions in adaptation to rheumatoid arthritis: Distinguishing mediator from moderator effects. *Personality and Social Psychology Bulletin, 18,* 709–718.

Schimel, J., Arndt, J., Banko, K. M., & Cook, A. (2004). Not all self-affirmations were created equal: The cognitive and social benefits of affirming the intrinsic (vs. extrinsic) self. *Social Cognition, 22,* 75–99.

Schimel, J., Arndt, J., Pyszczynski, T., & Greenberg, J. (2001). Being accepted for who we are: Evidence that social validation of the intrinsic self reduces general defensiveness. *Journal of Personality and Social Psychology, 80,* 35–52.

Schimel, J., Simon, L., Greenberg, J., Pyszczynski, T., Solomon, S., Waxmonsky, J., & Arndt, J. (1999). Stereotypes and terror management: Evidence that mortality salience enhances stereotypic thinking and preferences. *Journal of Personality and Social Psychology, 77,* 905–926.

Schimmack, U., Oishi, S., Furr, R. M., & Funder, D. C. (2004). Personality and life satisfaction: A facet-level analysis. *Personality and Social Psychology Bulletin, 30,* 1062–1075.

Schlenker, B. R. (1980). *Impression management: The self-concept, social identity, and interpersonal relations.* Monteray, CA: Brooks/ Cole.

Schlenker, B. R., & Britt, T. W. (2001). Strategically controlling information to help friends: Effects of empathy and friendship strength on beneficial impression management. *Journal of Experimental Social Psychology, 37,* 357–372.

Schmader, T. (2002). Gender identification moderates stereotype threat effects on women's math performanace. *Journal of Experimental Social Psychology, 38,* 194–201.

Schmader, T., & Johns, M. (2003). Converging evidence that stereotype threat reduces working memory capacity. *Journal of Personality and Social Psychology, 83,* 440–452.

Schmalleger, F. (2004). *Criminal justice today: An introductory text for the 21st century* (8th ed.). Upper Saddle River, NJ: Prentice Hall.

Schmidt, F. L., & Hunter, J. E. (2003). Meta-analysis. In J. A. Schinka & W. F. Velicer (Eds.), *Handbook of psychology: Vol. 2. Research methods in psychology* (pp. 533–554). Hoboken, NJ: Wiley.

Schmidt, G., & Weiner, B. (1988). An attribution-affect-action theory of behavior: Replications of judgments of help-giving. *Personality and Social Psychology Bulletin, 14,* 610–621.

Schneider, F. W., Gruman, J. A., & Coutts, L. M. (Eds.). (2005). *Applied social psychology: Understanding and addressing social and practical problems.* Thousand Oaks, CA: Sage.

Schopler, J., Insko, C. A., Graetz, K. A., Drigotas, S., Smith, V. A., & Dahl, K. (1993). Individual-group discontinuity: Further evidence for mediation by fear and greed. *Personality and Social Psychology Bulletin, 19,* 419–431.

Schroeder, D. A. (Ed.). (1995). *Social dilemmas: Perspectives on individuals and groups.* Westport, CT: Praeger.

Schroeder, D. A., Penner, L. A., Dovidio, J. F., & Piliavin, J. A. (1995). *The psychology of helping and altruism: Problems and puzzles.* New York: McGraw-Hill.

Schroeder, D. A., Steel, J. E., Woodell, A. J., & Bembenek, A. F. (2003). Justice within social dilemmas. *Personality and Social Psychology Review, 7,* 374–387.

Schuette, R. A., & Fazio, R. H. (1995). Attitude accessibility and motivation as determinants of biased processing: A test of the MODE model. *Personality and Social Psychology Bulletin, 21,* 704–710.

Schuller, R. A. (1992). The impact of battered woman syndrome evidence on jury decision processes. *Law and Human Behavior, 16,* 597–620.

Schuller, R. A., & Cripps, J. (1998). Expert evidence pertaining to battered women: The impact of gender of expert and timing of testimony. *Law and Human Behavior, 22,* 17–31.

Schuller, R. A., McKimmie, B. M., & Janz, T. (2004). The impact of expert testimony in trials of battered women who kill. *Psychiatry, Psychology and Law, 11,* 1–12.

Schuller, R. A., & Ogloff, J. R. P. (Eds.). (2001). *Introduction to psychology and law: Canadian perspectives.* Toronto, ON: University of Toronto Press.

Schuller, R. A., & Rzepa, S. (2002). Expert testimony pertaining to battered woman syndrome: Its impact on jurors' decisions. *Law and Human Behavior, 26,* 655–673.

Schuman, H., Steeh, C., Bobo, L., & Krysan, M. (1997). *Racial attitudes in America* (2nd ed.). Cambridge, MA: Harvard University Press.

Schwartz, S. H. (1977). Normative influences on altruism. In L. Berkowitz (Ed.), *Advances in experimental social psychology* (Vol. 10, pp. 221–279). New York: Academic Press.

Schwartz, S. H. (1992). Universals in the content and structure of values: Theoretical advances and empirical tests in 20 countries. In M. P. Zanna (Ed.), *Advances in experimental social psychology* (Vol. 25, pp. 1–65). San Diego, CA: Academic Press.

Schwartz, S. H. (1996). Value priorities and behavior: Applying the theory of integrated value systems. In C. Seligman, J. M. Olson, & M. P. Zanna (Eds.), *Values: The Ontario symposium* (Vol. 8, pp. 1–24). Mahwah, NJ: Erlbaum.

Schwartz, S. H., & Bardi, A. (1997). Influences of adaptation to communist rule on value priorities in Eastern Europe. *Political Psychology, 18,* 385–410.

Schwartz, S. H., & Sagiv, L. (1995). Identifying culture-specifics in the content and structure of values. *Journal of Cross-Cultural Psychology, 26,* 92–116.

Schwarz, N. (1990). Feelings as information: Informational and motivational functions of affective states. In E. T. Higgins & R. M. Sorrentino (Eds.), *Handbook of motivation and cognition: Foundations of social behavior* (Vol. 2, pp. 527–561). New York: Guilford Press.

Schwarz, N., Bless, H., Strack, F., Klumpp, G., Rittenauer-Schatka, H., & Simons, A. (1991). Ease of retrieval of information: Another look at the availability heuristic. *Journal of Personality and Social Psychology, 61,* 195–202.

Schwarz, N., & Clore, G. L. (1996). Feelings and phenomenal experience. In E. T. Higgins and A. W. Kruglanski (Eds.), *Social psychology: Handbook of basic principles* (pp. 433–465). New York: Guilford Press.

Schwarz, N., & Vaughn, L. A. (2002). The availability heuristic revisited: Ease of recall and content of recall as distinct sources of information. In T. Gilovich, D. Griffin, & D. Kahneman (Eds.), *Heuristics and biases: The psychology of intuitive judgment* (pp. 103–119). New York: Cambridge University Press.

Schwarzwald, J., Raz, M., & Zvibel, M. (1979). The application of the door-in-the-face technique when established behavioral customs exist. *Journal of Applied Social Psychology, 9,* 576–586.

Sczesny, S., & Kuhnen, U. (2004). Meta-cognition about biological sex and gender-stereotypic physical appearance: Consequences for the assessment of leadership competence. *Personality and Social Psychology Bulletin, 30,* 13–21.

Sears, D. O., & Henry, P. J. (2003). The origins of symbolic racism. *Journal of Personality and Social Psychology, 85,* 259–275.

Sechrist, G. B., Swim, J. K., & Stangor, C. (2004). When do the stigmatized make attributions to discrimination occurring to the self and others? The roles of self-presentation and need for control. *Journal of Personality and Social Psychology, 87,* 111–122.

Sedikides, C. (1990). Effects of fortuitously activated constructs versus activated communication goals on person impressions. *Journal of Personality and Social Psychology, 58,* 397–408.

Sedikides, C., Gaertner, L., & Toguchi, Y. (2003). Pancultural self-enhancement. *Journal of Personality and Social Psychology, 84,* 60–79.

Sedikides, C., Rudich, E. A., Gregg, A. P., Kumashiro, M., & Rusbult, C. (2004). Are normal narcissists psychologically healthy? Self-esteem matters. *Journal of Personality and Social Psychology, 87,* 400–416.

Sedikides, C., & Strube, M. (1997). Self-evaluation: To thine own self be good, to thine own self be sure, to thine own self be true, and to thine own self be better. In M. P. Zanna (Ed.), *Advances in experimental social psychology* (Vol. 29, pp. 209–269). San Diego, CA: Academic Press.

Segal, M. W. (1974). Alphabet and attraction: An unobtrusive measure of the effect of propinquity in a field setting. *Journal of Personality and Social Psychology, 30,* 654–657.

Seiter, J. S., & Gass, R. H. (2004). *Perspectives on persuasion, social influence, and compliance gaining.* Boston, MA: Pearson Education.

Sekaquaptewa, D., & Espinoza, P. (2004). Biased processing of stereotype-incongruency is greater for low than high status groups. *Journal of Experimental Social Psychology, 40,* 128–135.

Sekaquaptewa, D., & Thompson, M. (2003). Solo status, stereotype threat, and performance expectancies: Their effects on women's performance. *Journal of Experimental Social Psychology, 39,* 68–74.

Seligman, C., Bush, M., & Kirsch, K. (1976). Relationship between compliance in the foot-in-the-door paradigm and size of first request. *Journal of Personality and Social Psychology, 33,* 517–520.

Seligman, C., Fazio, R. H., & Zanna, M. P. (1980). Effects of salience of extrinsic rewards on liking and loving. *Journal of Personality and Social Psychology, 38,* 453–460.

Seligman, C., & Katz, A. N. (1996). The dynamics of value systems. In C. Seligman, J. M. Olson, & M. P. Zanna (Eds.), *The psychology of values: The Ontario symposium* (Vol. 8, pp. 53–75). Mahwah, NJ: Erlbaum.

Seligman, M. E. P. (1975). *Helplessness: On depression, development, and death.* San Francisco: Freeman.

Senn, C. Y., & Desmarais, S. (2001). Are our recruitment practices for sex studies working across gender? The effect of topic and gender of recruiter on participation rates of university men and women. *Journal of Sex Research, 38,* 111–117.

Senn, C. Y., & Desmarais, S. (2004). Impact of interaction with a partner or friend on the exposure effects of pornography and erotica. *Violence and Victims, 19,* 645–658.

Seto, M. C., Maric, A., & Barbaree, H. E. (2001). The role of pornography in the etiology of sexual aggression. *Aggression and Violent Behavior, 6,* 35–53.

Shapiro, J. P., Baumeister, R. F., & Kessler, J. W. (1991). A three-component model of children's teasing: Aggression, humor, and ambiguity. *Journal of Social and Clinical Psychology, 10,* 459–472.

Sharkey, W. F. (1992). Use of and responses to intentional embarrassment. *Communication Studies, 43,* 257–275.

Sharp, M. J., & Getz, J. G. (1996). Substance use as impression management. *Personality and Social Psychology Bulletin, 22,* 60–67.

Shaver, P., & Hazan, C. (1993). Adult romantic attachment: Theory and evidence. In D. Perlman & W. H. Jones (Eds.), *Advances in personal relationships* (Vol. 4, pp. 29–70). Philadelphia, PA: Jessica Kingsley.

Shavitt, S. (1990). The role of attitude objects in attitude functions. *Journal of Experimental Social Psychology, 26,* 124–148.

Shavitt, S., Swan, S., Lowery, T. M., & Wanke, M. (1994). The interaction of endorser attractiveness and involvement in persuasion depends on the goal that guides message processing. *Journal of Consumer Research, 3,* 137–162.

Shaw, M. E. (1976). *Group dynamics: The psychology of small group behavior* (2nd ed.). New York: McGraw-Hill.

Sheldon, K. M., Elliot, A. J., Kim, Y., & Kasser, T. (2001). What's satisfying about satisfying events? Testing 10 candidate psychological needs. *Journal of Personality and Social Psychology, 80,* 325–339.

Sheppard, B. H., Hartwick. J., & Warshaw, P. R. (1988). The theory of reasoned action: A meta-analysis of past research with recommendations for modifications and future research. *Journal of Consumer Research, 15,* 325–343.

Shepperd, J. A., Maroto, J. J., & Pbert, L. A. (1996). Dispositional optimism as a predictor or health changes among cardiac patients. *Journal of Research in Personality, 30,* 517–534.

Shepperd, J. A., & McNulty, J. K. (2002). The affective consequences of expected and unexpected outcomes. *Psychological Science, 13,* 85–88.

Sherif, M. (1935). A study of some social factors in perception. *Archives of Psychology, 27*(187), 1–60.

Sherif, M. (1936). *The psychology of social norms.* Oxford, UK: Harper.

Sherif, M. (1937). An experimental approach to the study of attitudes. *Sociometry, 1,* 90–98.

Sherif, M., Harvey, O., White, B., Hood, W., & Sherif, C. (1961). *Intergroup conflict and cooperation: The Robber's Cave experiment.* Norman: University of Oklahoma, Institute of Group Relations.

Sherman, D. K., & Cohen, G. L. (2002). Accepting threatening information: Self-affirmation and the reduction of defensive biases. *Current Directions in Psychological Science, 11,* 119–123.

Sherman, D. K., Nelson, L. D., & Steele, C. M. (2000). Do messages about health risks threaten the self? Increasing the acceptance of threatening health messages via self-affirmation. *Personality and Social Psychology Bulletin, 26,* 1046–1058.

Sherman, S. J., Presson, C. C., & Chassin, L. (1984). Mechanisms underlying the false consensus effect: The special role of threat to the self. *Personality and Social Psychology Bulletin, 10,* 127–138.

Sherry, J. L. (2001). The effects of violent video games on aggression: A meta-analysis. *Human Communication Research, 27,* 409–431.

Shultz, T. R., & Lepper, M. R. (1996). Cognitive dissonance reduction as constraint satisfaction. *Psychological Review, 103,* 219–240.

Shultz, T. R., Leveille, E., & Lepper, M. R. (1999). Free choice and cognitive dissonance revisited: Choosing "lesser evils" versus "greater goods." *Personality and Social Psychology Bulletin, 25,* 40–48.

Sigall, H., & Ostrove, N. (1975). Beautiful but dangerous: Effects of offender attractiveness and nature of the crime on juridic judgment. *Journal of Personality and Social Psychology, 31*, 410–414.

Silke, A. (2003a). Deindividuation, anonymity, and violence: Findings from Northern Ireland. *Journal of Social Psychology, 143*, 493–499.

Silke, A. (Ed.). (2003b). *Terrorists, victims, and society: Psychological perspectives on terrorism and its consequences.* Chichester, UK: Wiley.

Silverman, I., Choi, J., Mackewn, A., Fisher, M., Moro, J., & Olshansky, E. (2000). Evolved mechanisms underlying wayfinding: Further studies on the hunter-gatherer theory of spatial sex differences. *Evolution and Human Behavior, 21*, 201–213.

Simon, B., Stürmer, S., & Steffens, K. (2000). Helping individuals or group members? The role of individual and collective identification in AIDS volunteerism. *Personality and Social Psychology Bulletin, 26*, 497–506.

Simon, R. J. (1975). *The jury system in America: A critical overview.* Newbury Park, CA: Sage.

Simonton, D. K. (1987). *Why presidents succeed: A political psychology of leadership.* New Haven, CT: Yale University Press.

Simpson, J. A., Rholes, W. S., & Nelligan, J. S. (1992). Support seeking and support giving within couples in an anxiety-provoking situation: The role of attachment styles. *Journal of Personality and Social Psychology, 62*, 434–446.

Simpson, J. A., Rholes, W. S., Oriña, M. M., & Grich, J. (2002). Working models of attachment, support giving, and support seeking in a stressful situation. *Personality and Social Psychology Bulletin, 28*, 598–608.

Sinclair, L., & Kunda, Z. (1999). Reactions to a Black professional: Motivated inhibition and activation of conflicting stereotypes. *Journal of Personality and Social Psychology, 77*, 885–904.

Sinclair, L., & Kunda, Z. (2000). Motivated stereotyping of women: She's fine if she praised me but incompetent if she criticized me. *Personality and Social Psychology Bulletin, 26*, 1329–1342.

Sinclair, R. C. (1988). Mood, categorization breadth, and performance appraisal: The effects of order of information acquisition and affective state on halo, accuracy, information retrieval, and evaluations. *Organizational Behavior and Human Decision Processes, 42*, 22–46.

Singelis, T. M. (1994). The measurement of independent and interdependent self-construals. *Personality and Social Psychology Bulletin, 20*, 580–591.

Singh, D. (1993). Adaptive significance of female physical attractiveness: Role of waist-to-hip ratio. *Journal of Personality and Social Psychology, 65*, 293–307.

Singh, D. (1995). Female judgment of male attractiveness and desirability for relationships: Role of waist-to-hip ratio and financial status. *Journal of Personality and Social Psychology, 69*, 1089–1101.

Singh, U. P., & Prasad, T. (1973). Self-esteem, social-esteem, and conformity behaviour. *Psychologia: An International Journal of Psychology in the Orient, 16*, 61–68.

Sistrunk, F., & McDavid, J. W. (1971). Sex variable in conformity behavior. *Journal of Personality and Social Psychology, 17*, 200–207.

Skowronski, J. J., Carlston, D. E., & Isham, J. T. (1993). Implicit versus explicit impression formation: The differing effects of overt labeling and covert priming on memory and impressions. *Journal of Experimental Social Psychology, 29*, 17–41.

Sloan, J. H., Kellerman, A. L., Reay, D. T., Ferris, J. A., Koepsell, T., Rivara, F. P., et al. (1988). Handgun regulations, crime, assaults, and homicide: A tale of two cities. *New England Journal of Medicine, 319*, 1256–1261.

Smart, R. G., & Mann, R. E. (2002). Deaths and injuries from road rage: Cases in Canadian newspapers. *Canadian Medical Association Journal, 167*, 761–762.

Smeesters, D., Warlop, L., Van Avermaet, E., Corneille, O., & Yzerbyt, V. (2003). Do not prime hawks with doves: The interplay of construct activation and consistency of social value orientation on cooperative behavior. *Journal of Personality and Social Psychology, 84*, 972–987.

Smith, C. P. (Ed.). (1992). *Motivation and personality: Handbook of thematic content analysis.* New York: Cambridge University Press.

Smith, E. R. (1994). Social cognition contributions to attribution theory. In P. G. Devine, D. L. Hamilton, & T. M. Ostrom (Eds.), *Social cognition: Impact on social psychology* (pp. 77–108). San Diego, CA: Academic Press.

Smith, E. R. (1998). Mental representations and memory. In D. Gilbert, S. T. Fisk & G. Lindzey (Eds.), *Handbook of social psychology* (4th ed., Vol. 1, pp. 391–445). Boston, MA: McGraw-Hill.

Smith, E. R., & DeCoster, J. (2000). Dual process models in social and cognitive psychology: Conceptual integration and links to underlying memory systems. *Personality and Social Psychology Review, 4*, 108–131.

Smith, M. B., Bruner, J. S., & White, R. W. (1956). *Opinions and personality.* New York: Wiley.

Smith, P. B., & Bond, M. H. (1994). Social psychology across cultures: Analysis and perspectives. Boston: Allyn & Bacon.

Smith, R. H. (2000). *Assimilative and contrastive emotional reactions to upward and downward social comparisons.* In J. M. Suls & L. Wheeler (Eds.), *Handbook of social comparison: Theory and research* (pp. 173–200). New York: Kluwer Academic/Plenum.

Smith, S. M., Lindsay, R. C. L., & Pryke, S. (2000). Postdictors of eyewitness errors: Can false identifications be diagnosed? *Journal of Applied Psychology, 85*, 542–550.

Smith, S. M., Lindsay, R. C. L., Pryke, S., & Dysart, J. E. (2001). Postdictors of eyewitness errors: Can false identifications be diagnosed in the cross-race situation? *Psychology, Public Policy, and Law, 7*, 153–169.

Smith, T. W., Snyder, C. R., & Perkins, S. (1983). On the self-serving function of hypochondriacal complaints: Physical symptoms as self-handicapping strategies. *Journal of Personality and Social Psychology, 44*, 787–797.

Smith, W. P., & Arnkelsson, G. R. (2000). Stability of related attributes and the inference of ability through social comparison. In J. M. Suls & L. Wheeler (Eds.), *Handbook of social comparison: Theory and research* (pp. 45–66). New York: Kluwer Academic/ Plenum.

Smollar, J., & Youniss, J. (1982). Social development through friendship. In K. H. Rubin & H. S. Ross (Eds.), *Peer relationships and social skills in childhood* (pp. 279–298). New York: Springer-Verlag.

Snyder, C. R., & Fromkin, H. L. (1980). *Uniqueness: The human pursuit of difference.* New York: Plenum.

Snyder, M. (1974). Self-monitoring of expressive behavior. *Journal of Personality and Social Psychology, 30*, 526–537.

Snyder, M. (1987). *Public appearances, private realities: The psychology of self-monitoring.* New York: Freeman.

Snyder, M., Berscheid, E., & Glick, P. (1985). Focusing on the exterior and the interior: Two investigations of the initiation of personal relationships. *Journal of Personality and Social Psychology, 48*, 1427–1439.

Snyder, M., & Cantor, N. (1998). Understanding personality and social behavior: A functionalist strategy. In D. T. Gilbert, S. T. Fiske, & G. Lindzey (Eds.), *The handbook of social psychology* (4th ed., Vol. 1., pp. 635–679). Boston, MA: McGraw-Hill.

Snyder, M., & Gangestad, S. (1986). On the nature of self-monitoring: Matters of assessment, matters of validity. *Journal of Personality and Social Psychology, 51*, 125–139.

Snyder, M., & Haugen, J. A. (1995). Why does behavioral confirmation occur? A functional perspective on the role of the target. *Personality and Social Psychology Bulletin, 21*, 963–974.

Snyder, M., & Swann, W. B., Jr. (1976). When actions reflect attitudes: The politics of impression management. *Journal of Personality and Social Psychology, 34*, 1034–1042.

Snyder, M. L., & Jones, E. E. (1974). Attitude attribution when behavior is constrained. *Journal of Experimental Social Psychology, 10*, 585–600.

Solomon, S., Greenberg, J., & Pyszczynski, T. (1991). A terror management theory of social behavior: The psychological functions of self-esteem and cultural worldviews. In M. P. Zanna (Ed.), *Advances in experimental social psychology* (Vol. 24, pp. 91–159). San Diego, CA: Academic Press.

Solso, R. L., & MacLin, M. K. (2002). *Experimental psychology: A case approach* (7th ed.). Boston, MA: Allyn & Bacon.

Sommer, K. L., Williams, K. D., Ciarocco, N. J., & Baumeister, R. F. (2001). When silence speaks louder than words: Explorations into the intrapsychic and interpersonal consequences of social ostracism. *Basic and Applied Social Psychology, 23*, 225–243.

Son Hing, L. S., Li, W., & Zanna, M. P. (2002). Inducing hypocrisy to reduce prejudicial responses among aversive racists. *Journal of Experimental Social Psychology, 38*, 71–78.

Sorrentino, R. M., & Boutillier, R. G. (1975). The effect of quantity and quality of verbal interaction on ratings of leadership ability. *Journal of Experimental Social Psychology, 11*, 403–411.

Sorrentino, R. M., Cohen, D., Olson, J. M., & Zanna, M. P. (Eds.). (2005). *Culture and social behavior: The Ontario symposium* (Vol. 10). Mahwah, NJ: Erlbaum.

Sorrentino, R. M., & Field, N. (1986). Emergent leadership over time: The functional value of positive motivation. *Journal of Personality and Social Psychology, 50*, 1091–1099.

Sorrentino, R. M., & Hewitt, E. (1984). Uncertainty-related properties of achievement tasks revisited. *Journal of Personality and Social Psychology, 4*, 884–899.

Sorrentino, R. M., & Higgins, E. T. (1986). Motivation and cognition: Warming up to synergism. In R. M. Sorrentino & E. T. Higgins (Eds.), *Handbook of motivation and cognition* (pp. 3–19). New York: Guilford Press.

Sorrentino, R. M., & Roney, C. J. R. (2000). *The uncertain mind: Individual differences in facing the unknown.* Philadelphia, PA: Psychology Press.

Sorrentino, R. M., Short, J. C., & Raynor, J. O. (1984). Uncertainty orientation: Implications for affective and cognitive views of achievement behavior. *Journal of Personality and Social Psychology, 46*, 189–206.

Spears, R., Lea, M., Corneliussen, R. A., Postmes, T., & ter Haar, W. (2002). Computer-mediated communication as a channel for social resistance: The strategic side of SIDE. *Small Group Research, 33*, 555–574.

Spence, J. T. (1993). Gender-related traits and gender ideology: Evidence for a multifactorial theory. *Journal of Personality and Social Psychology, 64*, 624–635.

Spencer, S. J., Steele, C. M., & Quinn, D. M. (1999). Stereotype threat and women's math performance. *Journal of Experimental Social Psychology, 35*, 4–28.

Sporer, S. L. (1993). Eyewitness identification accuracy, confidence, and decision times in simultaneous and sequential lineups. *Journal of Applied Psychology, 78*, 22–33.

Sporer, S. L. (2001). The cross-race effect: Beyond recognition of faces in the laboratory. *Psychology, Public Policy, and Law, 7*, 170–200.

Sporer, S. L., Penrod, S. D., Read, J. D., & Cutler, B. L. (1995). Choosing, confidence, and accuracy: A meta-analysis of the confidence-accuracy relation in eyewitness identification studies. *Psychological Bulletin, 118*, 315–327.

Sprecher, S., & Schwartz, P. (1994). Equity and balance in the exchange of contributions in close relationships. In M. J. Lerner & G. Mikula (Eds.), *Entitlement and the affectional bond* (pp. 11–41). New York: Plenum.

Srull, T. K., & Wyer, R. S., Jr. (1980). Category accessibility and social perception: Some implications for the study of person memory and interpersonal judgments. *Journal of Personality and Social Psychology, 38*, 841–856.

Stang, D. J. (1972). Conformity, ability, and self-esteem. *Representative Research in Social Psychology, 3*, 97–103.

Stangor, C., Lynch, L., Duan, C., & Glass, B. (1992). Categorization of individuals on the basis of multiple social features. *Journal of Personality and Social Psychology, 62*, 207–218.

Stangor, C., & McMillan, D. (1992). Memory for expectancy-congruent and expectancy-incongruent information: A review of the social and social developmental literatures. *Psychological Bulletin, 111*, 42–61.

Stanley, J. L., Bartholomew, K., & Oram, D. (2004). Gay and bisexual men's age-discrepant childhood sexual experiences. *Journal of Sex Research, 41*, 381–389.

Stapp, J. (1996, January/February). An interesting career in psychology: Trial consultant. *Psychological Science Agenda, 9*, 12.

Stark, R. (1972). *Police riots, collective violence and law enforcement.* Belmont, CA: Wadsworth.

Staub, E. (1989). *The roots of evil: The origins of genocide and other group violence.* New York: Cambridge University Press.

Staub, E. (1999). The origins and prevention of genocide, mass killing and other collective violence. *Peace and Conflict: Journal of Peace Psychology, 5*, 303–337.

Staub, E., Pearlman, L. A., & Miller, V. (2003). Healing the roots of genocide in Rwanda. *Peace Review, 15*, 287–294.

Staub, E., & Rosenthal, L. H. (1994). Mob violence: Cultural-societal sources, instigators, group processes, and participants. In L. D. Eron, J. H. Gentry, & P. Schlegel (Eds.), *Reason to hope: A psychosocial perspective on youth and violence* (pp. 281–313). Washington, DC: American Psychological Association.

Steele, C. M. (1988). The psychology of self-affirmation: Sustaining the integrity of the self. In L. Berkowitz (Ed.), *Advances in experimental social psychology* (Vol. 21, pp. 261–302). New York: Academic Press.

Steele, C. M., & Aronson, J. (1995). Contending with a stereotype: African-American intellectual test performance and stereotype threat. *Journal of Personality and Social Psychology, 69*, 797–811.

Steele, C. M., & Josephs, R. A. (1990). Alcohol myopia: Its prized and dangerous effects. *American Psychologist, 45*, 921–933.

Steele, C. M., & Liu, T. J. (1981). Making the dissonance act unreflective of self: Dissonance avoidance and the expectancy of a value-affirming response. *Personality and Social Psychology Bulletin, 7*, 393–397.

Steele, C. M., & Liu, T. J. (1983). Dissonance processes as self-affirmation. *Journal of Personality and Social Psychology, 45*, 5–19.

Steele, C. M., Southwick, L. L., & Critchlow, B. (1981). Dissonance and alcohol: Drinking your troubles away. *Journal of Personality and Social Psychology, 41*, 831–846.

Steele, C. M., Spencer, S. J., & Lynch, M. (1993). Dissonance and affirmational responses: Resilience against self-image threats. *Journal of Personality and Social Psychology, 64*, 885–896.

Steinel, W., & De Dreu, C. K. W. (2004). Social motives and strategic misrepresentation in social decision making. *Journal of Personality and Social Psychology, 86*, 419–434.

Stenberg, C., & Campos, J. (1990). The development of anger expressions in infancy. In N. Stein, T. Trabasso, & B. Leventhal (Eds.), *Concepts in emotion.* Hillsdale, NJ: Erlbaum.

Stephan, C. W., & Langlois, J. H. (1984). Baby beautiful: Adult attributions of infant competence as a function of infant attractiveness. *Child Development, 55*, 576–585.

Stephan, W. G. (1986). Effects of school desegregation: An evaluation 30 years after *Brown.* In L. Saxe & M. Saks (Eds.), *Advances in applied social psychology* (Vol. 4, pp. 181–286). New York: Academic Press.

Stephan, W. G., Boniecki, K. A., Ybarra, O., Bettencourt, A., Ervin, K. S., Jackson, L. A., McNatt, P. S., & Renfro, C. L. (2002). The role of threats in the racial attitudes of Blacks and Whites. *Personality and Social Psychology Bulletin, 28*, 1242–1254.

Stephan, W. G., & Stephan, C. W. (1985). Intergroup anxiety. *Journal of Social Issues, 41*(3), 157–175.

Stephan, W. G., & Stephan, C. W. (1989). Antecedents of intergroup anxiety in Asian-Americans and Hispanic-Americans. *International Journal of Intercultural Relations, 13*, 203–219.

Stephan, W. G., & Stephan, C. W. (2000). An integrated threat theory of prejudice. In S. Oskamp (Ed.), *Reducing prejudice and discrimination* (pp. 23–46). Mahwah, NJ: Erlbaum.

Sternberg, R. J. (1986). A triangular theory of love. *Psychological Review, 93*, 119–135.

Sternberg, R. J., & Kolligan, J. (Eds.). (1990). *Competence considered*. New Haven, CT: Yale University Press.

Stevens, C. K., & Kristof, A. L. (1995). Making the right impression: A field study of applicant impression management during job interviews. *Journal of Applied Psychology, 80*, 587–606.

Stewart, J. E. (1980). Defendant's attractiveness as a factor in the outcome of criminal trials: An observational study. *Journal of Applied Social Psychology, 10*, 348–361.

Stice, E., & Shaw, H. E. (1994). Adverse effects of the media portrayed thin-ideal on women and linkages to bulimic symptomatology. *Journal of Social and Clinical Psychology, 13*, 288–308.

Stodgill, R. M. (1974). *Handbook of leadership*. New York: Free Press.

Stone, J. (1999). What exactly have I done? The role of self-attribute accessibility in dissonance. In E. Harmon-Jones & J. Mills (Eds.), *Cognitive dissonance: Progress on a pivotal theory in social psychology* (pp. 175–200). Washington, DC: American Psychological Association.

Stone, J. (2001). Behavioral discrepancies and the role of construal processes in cognitive dissonance. In G. B. Moskowitz (Ed.), *Cognitive social psychology: The Princeton symposium on the legacy and future of social cognition* (pp. 41–58). Mahwah, NJ: Erlbaum.

Stone, J. (2002). Battling doubt by avoiding practice: The effects of stereotype threat on self-handicapping in White athletes. *Personality and Social Psychology Bulletin, 28*, 1667–1678.

Stone, J. (2003). Self-consistency for low self-esteem in dissonance processes: The role of self-standards. *Personality and Social Psychology Bulletin, 29*, 846–858.

Stone, J., Aronson, E., Crain, A. L., Winslow, M. P., & Fried, C. B. (1994). Inducing hypocrisy as a means of encouraging young adults to use condoms. *Personality and Social Psychology Bulletin, 20*, 116–128.

Stone, J., & Cooper, J. (2001). A self-standards model of cognitive dissonance. *Journal of Experimental Social Psychology, 37*, 228–243.

Stone, J., & Cooper, J. (2003). The effect of self-attribute relevance on how self-esteem moderates dissonance processes. *Journal of Experimental Social Psychology, 39*, 508–515.

Stone, J., Lynch, C. I., Sjomeling, M., & Darley, J. M. (1999). Stereotype threat effects on Black and White athletic performance. *Journal of Personality and Social Psychology, 77*, 1213–1227.

Stone, J., Wiegand, A. W., Cooper, J., & Aronson, E. (1997). When exemplification fails: Hypocrisy and the motive for self-integrity. *Journal of Personality and Social Psychology, 72*, 54–65.

Stoner, J. A. F. (1968). Risky and cautious shifts in group decisions: The influence of widely held values. *Journal of Experimental Social Psychology, 4*, 442–459.

Strack, F., & Deutsch, R. F. (2004). Reflective and impulsive determinants of social behavior. *Personality and Social Psychology Bulletin, 8*, 220–247.

Strack, F., Schwarz, N., Bless, H., Kubler, A., & Wanke, M. (1993). Awareness of the influence as a determinant of assimilation versus contrast. *European Journal of Social Psychology, 23*, 53–62.

Straus, M. A. (1994). *Beating the devil out of them: Corporal punishment in American families*. New York: Lexington Books.

Straus, M. A., & Gelles, R. J. (1990). *Physical violence in American families: Risk factors and adaptation to violence in 8,145 families*. New Brunswick, NJ: Transaction.

Streeter, S. A., & McBurney, D. H. (2003). Waist-hip ratio and attractiveness: New evidence and a critique of a "critical test." *Evolution and Human Behavior, 24*(2), 88–98.

Strickland, B. R., & Crowne, D. P. (1962). Conformity under conditions of simulated group pressure as a function of the need for social approval. *Journal of Social Psychology, 58*, 171–181.

Stroebe, W., & Stroebe, M. (1996). The social psychology of social support. In E. T. Higgins & A. W. Kruglanski (Eds.), *Social psychology: Handbook of basic principles* (pp. 597–621). New York: Guilford Press.

Stroessner, S. J. & Plaks, J. E. (2001). Illusory correlation and stereotype formation: Tracing the arc of research over a quarter century. In G. Moskovitz (Ed.), *Cognitive social psychology: The Princeton symposium on the legacy and future of social cognition*. Mahwah, NJ: Erlbaum.

Strube, M., & Garcia, J. (1981). A meta-analysis investigation of Fiedler's contingency model of leadership effectiveness. *Psychological Bulletin, 90*, 307–321.

Stukas, A. A., Jr., & Snyder, M. (2002). Targets' awareness of expectations and behavioral confirmation in ongoing interactions. *Journal of Experimental Social Psychology, 38*, 31–40.

Sturges, J. W., & Rogers, R. W. (1996). Preventive health psychology from a developmental perspective: An extension of protection motivation theory. *Health Psychology, 15*, 158–166.

Stürmer, S., & Simon, B. (2004). The role of collective identification in social movement participation: A panel study in the context of the German gay movement. *Personality and Social Psychology Bulletin, 30*, 263–277.

Suls, J. M., Martin, R., & Wheeler, L. (2002). Social comparison: Why, with whom, and with what effect? *Current Directions in Psychological Science, 11*, 159–163.

Swann, W. B., Jr., De La Ronde, C., & Hixon, J. G. (1994). Authenticity and positivity strivings in marriage and courtship. *Journal of Personality and Social Psychology, 66*, 857–869.

Swenson, O. (1987). *The perilous path of cultism*. Caronport, SK: Briercrest Books.

Swim, J. K. (1994). Perceived versus meta-analytic effect sizes: An assessment of the accuracy of gender stereotypes. *Journal of Personality and Social Psychology, 66*, 21–36.

Swim, J. K., Aikin, K. J., Hall, W. S., & Hunter, B. A. (1995). Sexism and racism: Old-fashioned and modern prejudices. *Journal of Personality and Social Psychology, 68*, 199–214.

Swim, J. K., & Stangor, C. S. (Eds.). (1998). *Prejudice: The target's perspective*. New York: Academic Press.

Symons, D. (1979). *The evolution of human sexuality*. New York: Oxford University Press.

Tafarodi, R. W. (1998). Paradoxical self-esteem and selectivity in the processing of social information. *Journal of Personality and Social Psychology, 74*, 1181–1196.

Tafarodi, R. W., Kang, S.-J., & Milne, A. B. (2002). When different becomes similar: Compensatory conformity in bicultural visible minorities. *Personality and Social Psychology Bulletin, 28*, 1131–1142.

Tajfel, H. (1970). Experiments in intergroup discrimination. *Scientific American, 223*(2), 96–102.

Tajfel, H. (Ed.). (1978). *Differentiation between social groups: Studies in the social psychology of intergroup relations*. London, UK: Academic Press.

Tajfel, H., & Turner, J. C. (1986). The social identity theory of intergroup behavior. In S. Worchel & W. G. Austin (Eds.), *The psychology of intergroup relations* (2nd ed., pp. 7–24). Chicago: Nelson-Hall.

Takahashi, K. (1990). Are the key assumptions of the "strange situation" procedure universal? A view from Japanese research. *Human Development, 33,* 23–30.

Tanford, S., & Penrod, S. (1984). Social influence model: A formal integration of research on majority and minority influence processes. *Psychological Bulletin, 95,* 189–225.

Tang, S, & Hall, V. C. (1995). The overjustification effect: A meta-analysis. *Applied Cognitive Psychology, 9,* 365–404.

Tarr, M. J., & Warren, W. H. (2002). Virtual reality in behavioral neuoscience and beyond. *Nature Neuroscience, 5* (Supplement), 1089–1092.

Taylor, D. M., & Moghaddam, F. M. (1994). *Theories of intergroup relations: International social psychological perspectives* (2nd ed.). Westport, CT: Praeger.

Taylor, D. M., Wright, S. C., Moghaddam, F. M., & Lalonde, R. N. (1990). The personal/group discrimination discrepancy: Perceiving my group, but not myself, to be a target for discrimination. *Personality and Social Psychology Bulletin, 16,* 254–262.

Taylor, D. M., Wright, S. C., & Porter, L. E. (1993). Dimensions of perceived discrimination: The personal/group discrimination discrepancy. In M. P. Zanna & J. M. Olson (Eds.), *The psychology of prejudice: The Ontario symposium* (Vol. 7, pp. 233–255). Hillsdale, NJ: Erlbaum.

Taylor, S. E. (2002). *Health psychology* (5th ed.). New York: McGraw-Hill.

Taylor, S. E., & Brown, J. D. (1988). Illusion and well-being: A social psychological perspective on mental health. *Psychological Bulletin, 103,* 193–210.

Taylor, S. E., & Brown, J. D. (1994). Positive illusions and well-being revisited: Separating fact from fiction. *Psychological Bulletin, 116,* 21–27.

Taylor, S. E., Kemeny, M. E., Reed, G. M., Bower, J. E., & Gruenewald, T. L. (2000). Psychological resources, positive illusions, and health. *American Psychologist, 55,* 99–109.

Taylor, S. E., Klein, L. C., Lewis, B. P., Gruenewald, T. L., Gurung, R. A. R., & Updegraff, J. A. (2000). Biobehavioral responses to stress in females: Tend-and-befriend, not fight-or-flight. *Psychological Review, 107,* 411–429.

Taylor, S. E., Lerner, J. S., Sherman, D. K., Sage, R. M., & McDowell, N. K. (2003a). Portrait of the self-enhancer: Well adjusted and well liked or maladjusted and friendless? *Journal of Personality and Social Psychology, 84,* 165–176.

Taylor, S. E., Lerner, J. S., Sherman, D. K., Sage, R. M., & McDowell, N. K. (2003b). Are self-enhancing cognitions associated with healthy or unhealthy biological profiles? *Journal of Personality and Social Psychology, 85,* 605–615.

Taylor, S. E., & Lobel, M. (1989). Social comparison activity under threat: Downward evaluation and upward contacts. *Psychological Bulletin, 96,* 569–575.

Taylor, S. E., Sherman, D. K., Kim, H. S., Jarcho, J., Takagi, K., & Dunagan, M. S. (2004). Culture and social support: Who seeks it and why? *Journal of Personality and Social Psychology, 87,* 354–362.

Taylor, S. E., Wayment, H. A., & Carillo, M. (1996). Social comparison, self-regulation, and motivation. In R. M. Sorrentino & E. T. Higgins (Eds.), *Handbook of motivation and cognition: The interpersonal context* (Vol. 3, pp. 3–27). New York: Guilford.

Taylor, S. P. (1967). Aggressive behavior and physiological arousal as a function of provocation and the tendency to inhibit aggression. *Journal of Personality, 35,* 297–310.

Tazelaar, M. J. A., Van Lange, P. A. M., & Ouwerkerk, J. W. (2004). How to cope with "noise" in social dilemmas: The benefits of communication. *Journal of Personality and Social Psychology, 87,* 845–859.

Technical Working Group for Eyewitness Evidence. (1999). *Eyewitness evidence: A guide for law enforcement.* Washington, DC: U.S. Department of Justice.

Tedeschi, J. T., Schlenker, B. R., & Bonoma, T. V. (1971). Cognitive dissonance: Private ratiocination or public spectacle? *American Psychologist, 26,* 685–695.

Tennen, H., & Affleck, G. (1987). The costs and benefits of optimistic explanations and dispositional optimism. *Journal of Personality, 55,* 377–393.

Tennen, H., & Affleck, G. (1993). The puzzles of self-esteem: A clinical perspective. In R. F. Baumeister (Ed.), *Self-esteem: The puzzle of low self-regard* (pp. 241–262). New York: Plenum.

Tesser, A. (1988). Toward a self-evaluation maintenance model of social behavior. In L. Berkowitz (Ed.), *Advances in experimental social psychology* (Vol. 21, pp. 181–227). New York: Academic Press.

Tesser, A. (1993). The importance of heritability in psychological research: The case of attitudes. *Psychological Review, 100,* 129–142.

Tesser, A. (2000). On the confluence of self-esteem maintenance mechanisms. *Personality and Social Psychology Review, 4,* 290–299.

Tesser, A., Millar, M., & Moore, J. (1988). Some affective consequences of social comparison and reflection processes: The pain and pleasure of being close. *Journal of Personality and Social Psychology, 54,* 49–61.

Thibaut, J. W., & Kelley, H. H. (1959). *The social psychology of groups.* New York: Wiley.

Thompson, M. M., Zanna, M. P., & Griffin, D. W. (1995). Let's not be indifferent about (attitudinal) ambivalence. In R. E. Petty & J. A. Krosnick (Eds.), *Attitude strength: Antecedents and consequences* (pp. 361–386). Mahwah, NJ: Erlbaum.

Thornton, B., & Moore, S. (1993). Physical attractiveness contrast effect: Implications for self-esteem and evaluations of the social self. *Personality and Social Psychology Bulletin, 19,* 474–480.

Tice, D. M., & Baumeister, R. F. (1990). Self-esteem, self-handicapping, and self-presentation: The strategy of inadequate practice. *Journal of Personality, 58,* 443–464.

Tidwell, M.-C. O., Reis, H. T., & Shaver, P. R. (1996). Attachment, attractiveness, and social interaction: A diary study. *Journal of Personality and Social Psychology, 71,* 729–745.

Todman, J., & Day, K. (2006). Computer anxiety: The role of psychological gender. *Computers in Human Behaviour, 22,* 856–869.

Tougas, F., Brown, R., Beaton, A. M., & Joly, S. (1995). Neosexism: Plus ça change, plus c'est pareil. *Personality and Social Psychology Bulletin, 21,* 842–849.

Tougas, F., Crosby, F., Joly, S., & Pelchat, D. (1993). Men's attitudes toward affirmative action: Justice and intergroup relations at the cross-roads. *Social Justice Research, 8,* 57–71.

Towles-Schwen, T., & Fazio. R. H. (2001). On the origins of racial attitudes: Correlates of childhood experiences. *Personality and Social Psychology Bulletin, 27,* 162–175.

Townsend, J. M., & Wasserman, T. (1998). Sexual attractiveness: Sex differences in assessment and criteria. *Evolution and Human Behavior, 14,* 171–191.

Towson, S. M. J. (2005). Social psychological theory. In F. W. Schneider, J. A. Gruman, & L. M. Coutts (Eds.), *Applied social psychology: Understanding and addressing social and practical problems* (pp. 19–34). Thousand Oaks, CA: Sage.

Trafimow, D., & Sheeran, P. (1998). Some tests of the distinction between cognitive and affective beliefs. *Journal of Experimental Social Psychology, 34,* 378–397.

Traupmann, J., Hatfield, E., & Wexler, P. (1983). Equity and sexual satisfaction in dating couples. *British Journal of Social Psychology, 22,* 33–40.

Travis, L. E. (1925). The effect of a small audience upon eye-hand coordination. *Journal of Abnormal and Social Psychology, 20,* 142–146.

Triandis, H. C. (1989). The self and social behavior in differing cultural contexts. *Psychological Review, 96,* 506–520.

Triandis, H. C. (1994). *Culture and social behavior.* New York: McGraw-Hill.

Triandis, H. C. (1995). *Individualism and collectivism*. Boulder, CO: Westview Press.

Triandis, H. C., McCusker, C., & Hui, C. H. (1990). Multimethod probes of individualism and collectivism. *Journal of Personality and Social Psychology, 59,* 1006–1020.

Triplett, N. (1898). The dynamogenic factors in pacemaking and competition. *American Journal of Psychology, 9,* 507–533.

Trivers, R. L. (1972). Parental investment and sexual selection. In B. Campbell (Ed.), *Sexual selection and the descent of man* (pp. 136–179). Chicago: Aldine.

Trope, Y. (1986). Identification and inferential processes in dispositional attribution. *Psychological Review, 93,* 239–257.

Trope, Y., Cohen, O., & Maoz, Y. (1988). The perceptual and inferential effects of situational inducements on dispositional attribution. *Journal of Personality and Social Psychology, 55,* 165–177.

Tschanz, B. T., & Rhodewalt, F. (2001). Autobiography, reputation, and the self: On the role of evaluative valence and self-consistency of the self-relevant information. *Journal of Experimental Social Psychology, 37,* 32–48.

Turner, C. W., Layton, J. F., & Simons, L. S. (1975). Naturalistic studies of aggressive behavior: Aggressive stimuli, victim visibility, and horn honking. *Journal of Personality and Social Psychology, 31,* 1098–1107.

Turner, M. E., Pratkanis, A. R., Probasco, P., & Leve, C. (1992). Threat, cohesion, and group effectiveness: Testing a social identity maintenance perspective on groupthink. *Journal of Personality and Social Psychology, 63,* 781–796.

Tversky, A., & Kahneman, D. (1973). Availability: A heuristic for judging frequency and probability. *Cognitive Psychology, 5,* 207–232.

Twenge, J. M., & Campbell, W. K. (2003). "Isn't it fun to get the respect that we're going to deserve?" Narcissism, social rejection, and aggression. *Personality and Social Psychology Bulletin, 29,* 261–272.

Tyler, T. R., & Blader, S. L. (2000). *Cooperation in groups: Procedural justice, social identity, and behavioral engagement.* Philadelphia: Psychology Press.

Uleman, J. S., Newman, L. S., & Moskowitz, G. B. (1996). People as flexible interpreters: Evidence and issues from spontaneous trait inference. In M. P. Zanna (Ed.), *Advances in experimental social psychology* (Vol. 28, pp. 211–279). San Diego, CA: Academic Press.

Underwood, M. K. (2003). *Social aggression among girls.* New York: Guilford Press.

Utz, S. (2004). Self-activation is a two-edged sword: The effects of I primes on cooperation. *Journal of Experimental Social Psychology, 40,* 769–776.

Vallerand, R. J. (1997). Toward a hierarchical model of intrinsic and extrinsic motivation. In M. P. Zanna (Ed.), *Advances in experimental social psychology* (Vol. 29, pp. 271–360). San Diego, CA: Academic Press.

Vallerand, R. J., Fortier, M. S., & Guay, F. (1997). Self-determination and persistence in a real-life setting: Toward a motivational model of high school dropout. *Journal of Personality and Social Psychology, 72,* 1161–1176.

Vallerand, R. J., & Ratelle, C. F. (2002). Intrinsic and extrinsic motivation: A hierarchical model. In E. L. Deci & R. M. Ryan (Eds.), *Handbook of self-determination research* (pp. 37–63). Rochester, NY: University of Rochester Press.

Vallone, R. P., Ross, L., & Lepper, M. R. (1985). The hostile media phenomenon: Biased perception and perceptions of media bias in coverage of the Beirut massacre. *Journal of Personality and Social Psychology, 49,* 577–585.

van der Velde, F. W., & van der Pligt, J. (1991). AIDS-related health behavior: Coping, protection motivation, and previous behavior. *Journal of Behavioral Medicine, 14,* 429–451.

van Dick, R., Wagner, U., Pettigrew, T. F., Christ, O., Wolf, C., Petzel, T., Castro, V. S., & Jackson, J. S. (2004). Role of perceived importance in intergroup contact. *Journal of Personality and Social Psychology, 87,* 211–227.

van IJzendoorn, M. H., & Kroonenberg, P. M. (1988). Cross-cultural patterns of attachment: A meta-analysis of the strange situation. *Child Development, 59,* 147–156.

Van Lange, P. A. M., & Kuhlman, D. M. (1994). Social value orientations and impressions of partner's honesty and intelligence: A test of the might versus morality effect. *Journal of Personality and Social Psychology, 67,* 126–141.

Van Lange, P. A. M., & Sedikides, C. (1998). Being more honest but not necessarily more intelligent than others: Generality and explanations for the Muhammad Ali Effect. *European Journal of Social Psychology, 28,* 675–680.

Van Overwalle, F., & Jordens, K. (2002). An adaptive connectionist model of cognitive dissonance. *Personality and Social Psychology Review, 6,* 204–231.

Van Reekum, C. M., Van den Berg, H., & Frijda, N. H. (1999). Cross-modal preference acquisition: Evaluative conditioning of pictures by affective olfactory and auditory cues. *Cognition and Emotion, 13,* 831–836.

Van Vugt, M., & Hart, C. M. (2004). Social identity as social glue: The origins of group loyalty. *Journal of Personality and Social Psychology, 86,* 585–598.

Van Vugt, M., Jepson, S. F., Hart, C. M., & De Cremer, D. (2004). Autocratic leadership in social dilemmas: A threat to group stability. *Journal of Experimental Social Psychology, 40,* 1–13.

Vanman, E. J., Saltz, J. L., Nathan, L. R., & Warren, J. A. (2004). Racial discrimination by low-prejudiced Whites: Facial movements as implicit measures of attitudes related to behavior. *Psychological Science, 15,* 711–714.

Vargas, P. T., von Hippel, W., & Petty, R. E. (2004). Using partially structured attitude measures to enhance the attitude-behavior relationship. *Personality and Social Psychology Bulletin, 30,* 197–211.

Vasquez, E. A., Denson, T. F., Pedersen, W. C., Stenstrom, D. M., & Miller, N. (2005). The moderating effect of trigger intensity on triggered displaced aggression. *Journal of Experimental Social Psychology, 41,* 61–67.

Verkuyten, M. (2004). Emotional reactions to and support for immigrant policies: Attributed responsibilities to categories of asylum seekers. *Social Justice Research, 17,* 293–314.

Vidmar, N., & Crinklaw, L. D. (1974). Attributing responsibility for an accident: A methodological and conceptual critique. *Canadian Journal of Behavioural Science, 6,* 112–130.

Vignoles, V. L., Chryssochoou, X., & Breakwell, G. M. (2000). The distinctiveness principle: Identity, meaning, and the boundary of cultural relativity. *Personality and Social Psychology Review, 4,* 337–354.

Vinokur, A., & Burnstein, E. (1974). Effects of partially-shared persuasive arguments on group-induced shifts: A group-problem-solving approach. *Journal of Personality and Social Psychology, 29,* 305–315.

Vispoel, W. P. (1998). Reviewing and changing answers on computer-adaptive and self-adaptive vocabulary tests. *Journal of Educational Measurement, 35,* 328–345.

Visser, P. S., & Mirabile, R. R. (2004). Attitudes in the social context: The impact of social network composition on individual-level attitude strength. *Journal of Personality and Social Psychology, 87,* 779–795.

Vonk, R. (2002). Self-serving interpretations of flattery: Why ingratiation works. *Journal of Personality and Social Psychology, 82,* 515–526.

Vorauer, J. D. (2005). Miscommunications surrounding efforts to reach out across group boundaries. *Personality and Social Psychology Bulletin, 31,* 1653–1664.

Vorauer, J. D., Hunter, A. J., Main, K. J., & Roy, S. A. (2000). Meta-stereotype activation: Evidence from indirect measures for specific evaluative concerns experienced by members of dominant groups in intergroup interaction. *Journal of Personality and Social Psychology, 78*, 690–707.

Vorauer, J. D., & Kumhyr, S. (2001). Is this about you or me? Self- versus other-directed thoughts and feelings in response to intergroup interactions. *Personality and Social Psychology Bulletin, 27*, 706–719.

Vorauer, J. D., Main, K. J., & O'Connell, G. B. (1998). How do individuals expect to be viewed by members of lower status groups? Content and implications of meta-stereotypes. *Journal of Personality and Social Psychology, 75*, 917–937.

Vroom, V. H., & Yetton, P. W. (1973). *Leadership and decision-making*. Pittsburgh, PA: University of Pittsburgh Press.

Wade-Benzoni, K. A., Okumura, T., Brett, J. M., Moore, D. A., Tenbrunsel, A. E., & Bazerman, M. H. (2002). Cognitions and behavior in asymmetric social dilemmas: A comparison of two cultures. *Journal of Applied Psychology, 87*, 87–95.

Walker, I., & Smith, H. J. (Eds.). (2002). *Relative deprivation: Specification, development, and integration*. Cambridge, UK: Cambridge University Press.

Wallach, M., Kogan, N., & Bem, D. J. (1962). Group influence on individual risk taking. *Journal of Abnormal and Social Psychology, 65*, 75–86.

Waller, J. (2002). *Becoming evil: How ordinary people commit genocide and mass murder*. New York: Oxford University Press.

Waller, N. G., Kojetin, B. A., Bouchard, T. J., Jr., Lykken, D. T., & Tellegen, A. (1990). Genetic and environmental influences on religious interests, attitudes, and values: A study of twins reared apart and together. *Psychological Science, 1*, 138–142.

Walster, E., Walster, G. W., & Berscheid, E. (1978). *Equity: Theory and research*. Boston, MA: Allyn & Bacon.

Walster, E., Walster, G. W., & Traupmann, J. (1978). Equity and premarital sex. *Journal of Personality and Social Psychology, 36*, 82–92.

Walther, E. (2002). Guilty by mere association: Evaluative conditioning and the spreading attitude effect. *Journal of Personality and Social Psychology, 82*, 919–934.

Waltz, J., Babcock, J. C., Jacobson, N. S., & Gottman, J. M. (2000). Testing a typology of batterers. *Journal of Consulting and Clinical Psychology, 68*, 658–669.

Webb, W., & Worchel, S. (1986). Trust and distrust. In S. Worchel & W. G. Austin (Eds.), *The psychology of intergroup relations* (2nd ed.). Chicago: Nelson-Hall.

Weber, J. M., Kopelman, S., & Messick, D. M. (2004). A conceptual review of decision making in social dilemmas: Applying a logic of appropriateness. *Personality and Social Psychology Review, 8*, 281–307.

Webster, G. D. (2003). Prosocial behavior in families: Moderators of resource sharing. *Journal of Experimental Social Psychology, 39*, 644–652.

Wegener, D. T., & Petty, R. E. (1997). The flexible correction model: The role of naive theories in bias correction. In M. P. Zanna (Ed.), *Advances in experimental social psychology* (Vol. 29, pp. 141–208). San Diego, CA: Academic Press.

Weigel, R. H., & Newman, L. S. (1976). Increasing attitude-behavior consistency by broadening the scope of the behavioral measure. *Journal of Personality and Social Psychology, 33*, 793–802.

Weinstein, N. D. (1980). Unrealistic optimism about future life events. *Journal of Personality and Social Psychology, 39*, 806–820.

Weinstein, N. D. (1984). Why it won't happen to me: Perceptions of risk factors and susceptibility. *Health Psychology, 3*, 431–457.

Weinstein, N. D., & Klein, W. M. (1996). Unrealistic optimism: Present and future. *Journal of Social and Clinical Psychology, 15*, 1–8.

Weiss, E. M., Kemmier, G., Deisenhammer, E. A., Fleischhacker, W. W., & Delazer, M. (2003). Sex differences in cognitive function. *Personality and Individual Differences, 35*, 863–875.

Welch, D. (1983). *Nazi propaganda*. Beckenham, UK: Croom Helm.

Wells, G. L. (1993). What do we know about eyewitness identification? *American Psychologist, 48*, 553–571.

Wells, G. L., & Olson, E. A. (2001). The other-race effect in eyewitness identification: What do we do about it? *Psychology, Public Policy, and Law, 7*, 230–246.

Wells, G. L., Olson, E. A., & Charman, S. D. (2002). The confidence of eyewitnesses in their identifications from lineups. *Current Directions in Psychological Science, 11*, 151–154.

Wells, S., Graham, K., Speechley, M., & Koval, J. J. (2005). Drinking patterns, drinking contexts and alcohol-related aggression among late adolescent and young adult drinkers. *Addiction, 100*, 933–944.

Wells, S., Graham, K., & West, P. (2000). Alcohol-related aggression in the general population. *Journal of Studies on Alcohol, 61*, 626–632.

Werner, N. E., & Crick, N. R. (1999). Relational aggression and social-psychological adjustment in a college sample. *Journal of Abnormal Psychology, 108*, 615–623.

Werth, L., Strack, F., & Forster, J. (2002). Certainty and uncertainty: The two faces of the hindsight bias. *Organizational Behavior and Human Decision Processes, 87*, 323–341.

Wethington, E., & Kessler, R. C. (1986). Perceived support, received support, and adjustment to stressful life events. *Journal of Health and Social Behavior, 27*(March), 78–89.

Whalley, L. J., & Deary, I. J. (2001). Longitudinal cohort study of childhood IQ and survival up to age 76. *British Medical Journal, 322*, 1–5.

Wheeler, L., & Kim, Y. (1997). What is beautiful is culturally good: The physical attractiveness stereotype has different content in collectivistic cultures. *Personality and Social Psychology Bulletin, 23*, 795–800.

Wheeler, L., Martin, R., & Suls, J. M. (1997). The proxy model of social comparison for self-assessment of ability. *Personality and Social Psychology Review, 1*, 54–61.

Wheeler, S. C., & Petty, R. E. (2001). The effects of stereotype activation on behavior: A review of possible mechanisms. *Psychological Bulletin, 127*, 797–826.

White, J. R. (2003). Sex differences in personality in the United States and the Philippines: An investigation of cross-cultural universality. *Dissertation Abstracts International: Section B. The Sciences and Engineering, 63*, 3507.

White, K., & Lehman, D. R. (2005). Culture and social comparison seeking: The role of self-motives. *Personality and Social Psychology Bulletin, 31*, 232–242.

Whitely, B. E., Jr. (1990). The relationship of heterosexuals' attributions for the causes of homosexuality to attitudes toward lesbians and gay men. *Personality and Social Psychology Bulletin, 16*, 369–377.

Whiting, B. B., Whiting, J. W. M., & Longabaugh, R. (1975). *Children of six cultures: A psycho-cultural analysis*. Cambridge, MA: Harvard University Press.

Whyte, G. (1993). Escalating commitment in individual and group decision making: A prospect theory approach. *Organizational Behavior and Human Decision Processes, 54*, 430–455.

Wicker, A. W. (1969). Attitude versus actions: The relationship of verbal and overt behavioral responses to attitude objects. *Journal of Social Issues, 25*(4), 41–78.

Wiggins, E. C. (2000). Federal regulation. In A. E. Kazdin (Ed.), *Encyclopedia of psychology* (Vol. 4, pp. 1–2). Washington, DC: American Psychological Association.

Wilcox, G. B., Murphy, J. H., & Sheldon, P. S. (1985). Effects of attractiveness of the endorser on the performance of testimonial ads. *Journalism Quarterly, 62*, 548–552.

Wildschut, T., Pinter, B., Vevea, J. L., Insko, C. A., & Schopler, J. (2003). Beyond the group mind: A quantitative review of the interindividual-intergroup discontinuity effect. *Psychological Bulletin, 129*, 698–722.

Williams, D. R., & Williams-Morris, R. (2000). Racism and mental health: The African American experience. *Ethnicity and Health, 5,* 243–268.

Williams, G. C., Cox, E. M., Hedberg, V. A., & Deci, E. L. (2000). Extrinsic life goals and health-risk behaviors in adolescents. *Journal of Applied Social Psychology, 30,* 1756–1771.

Williams, K. D., Cheung, C. K. T., & Choi, W. (2000). Cyberostracism: Effects of being ignored over the internet. *Journal of Personality and Social Psychology, 79,* 748–762.

Williams, K. D., Harkins, S. G., & Latane, B. (1981). Identifiability as a deterrent to social loafing: Two cheering experiments. *Journal of Personality and Social Psychology, 40,* 303–311.

Williams, R. B., Barefoot, J. C., Califf, R. M., Haney, T. L., Saunders, W. B., Pryor, D. B., et al. (1992). Prognostic importance of social and economic resources among medically treated patients with angiographically documented coronary artery disease. *Journal of the American Medical Association, 267,* 520–524.

Wills, T. A. (1981). Downward comparison principles in social psychology. *Psychological Bulletin, 90,* 245–291.

Wills, T. A. (1991). Social support and interpersonal relationships. In M. Clark (Ed.), *Prosocial behavior* (pp. 265–289). Newbury Park, CA: Sage.

Wilson, A. E., & Ross, M. (2000). The frequency of temporal-self and social comparisons in people's personal appraisals. *Journal of Personality and Social Psychology, 5,* 928–942.

Wilson, A. E., & Ross, M. (2001). From chump to champ: People's appraisals of their earlier and present selves. *Journal of Personality and Social Psychology, 80,* 572–584.

Wilson, M., & Daly, M. (1985). Competitiveness, risk taking, and violence: The young male syndrome. *Ethology and Sociobiology, 6,* 59–73.

Wilson, T. D., Damiani, M., & Shelton, J. N. (2002). Improving the academic performance of college students with brief attributional interventions. In J. Aronson (Ed.), *Improving academic achievement: Impact of psychological factors on education* (pp. 89–108). New York: Academic Press.

Wilson, T. D., Lindsey, S., & Schooler, T. Y. (2000). A model of dual attitudes. *Psychological Review, 107,* 101–126.

Wilson, T. D., Wheatley, T. P., Kurtz, J. L., Dunn, E. W., & Gilbert, D. T. (2004). When to fire: Anticipatory versus postevent reconstrual of uncontrollable events. *Personality and Social Psychology Bulletin, 30,* 340–351.

Winquist, J. R., & Larson, J. R., Jr. (2004). Sources of the discontinuity effect: Playing against a group versus being in a group. *Journal of Experimental Social Psychology, 40,* 675–682.

Winter, L., & Uleman, J. S. (1984). When are social judgments made? Evidence for the spontaneousness of trait inferences. *Journal of Personality and Social Psychology, 47,* 237–252.

Wit, A. P., & Kerr, N. L. (2002). "Me versus just us versus us all" categorization and cooperation in nested social dilemmas. *Journal of Personality and Social Psychology, 83,* 616–637.

Witte, K., & Allen, M. (2000). A meta-analysis of fear appeals: Implications for effective public health campaigns. *Health Education and Behavior, 27,* 591–615.

Witte, K., Meyer, G., & Martell, D. (2001). *Effective health risk messages: A step-by-step guide.* Thousand Oaks, CA: Sage.

Wittenbrink, B., Judd, C. M., & Park, B. (1997). Evidence for racial prejudice at the implicit level and its relationship with questionnaire measures. *Journal of Personality and Social Psychology, 72,* 262–274.

Wittenbrink, B., Judd, C. M., & Park, B. (2001). Spontaneous prejudice in context: Variability in automatically activated attitudes. *Journal of Personality and Social Psychology, 81,* 815–827.

Wolf, S. (1987). Majority and minority influence: A social impact analysis. In M. P. Zanna, J. M. Olson, & C. P. Herman (Eds.), *Social influence: The Ontario symposium* (Vol. 5, pp. 207–235). Hillsdale, NJ: Erlbaum.

Wolfe, D. A. (1999). *Child abuse: Implications for child development and psychopathology.* Thousand Oaks, CA: Sage.

Wolsko, C., Park, B., Judd, C. M., & Wittenbrink, B. (2000). Framing interethnic ideology: Effects of multicultural and color-blind perspectives on judgments of groups and individuals. *Journal of Personality and Social Psychology, 78,* 635–654.

Wood, J. V. (1989). Theory and research concerning social comparisons of personal attributes. *Psychological Bulletin, 106,* 231–248.

Wood, J. V., & Van der Zee, K. (1997). Social comparisons among cancer patients: Under what conditions are comparisons upward and downward? In B. P. Buunk & F. X. Gibbons (Eds.), *Health, coping, and well-being* (pp. 299–328). Mahwah, NJ: Erlbaum.

Wood, J. V., Michela, J. L., & Giordano, C. (2000). Downward comparison in everyday life: Reconciling self-enhancement models with the mood-cognition priming model. *Journal of Personality and Social Psychology, 79,* 565–579.

Wood, W. (2000). Attitude change: Persuasion and social influence. *Annual Review of Psychology, 50,* 539–570.

Wood, W., & Eagly, A. H. (2002). A cross-cultural analysis of the behavior of women and men: Implications for the origins of sex differences. *Psychological Bulletin, 128,* 699–727.

Wood, W., & Kallgren, C. A. (1988). Communicator attributes and persuasion: Recipients' access to attitude-relevant information in memory. *Personality and Social Psychology Bulletin, 14,* 172–182.

Wood, W., Wong, F. Y., & Chachere, G. (1991). Effects of media violence on viewers' aggression in unconstrained social interaction. *Psychological Bulletin, 109,* 371–383.

Worchel, S., & Austin, W. G. (Eds.). (1986). *The social psychology of intergroup relations* (2nd ed.). Chicago: Nelson-Hall.

Worchel, S., Lee, J., & Adewole, A. (1975). Effects of supply and demand on ratings of object value. *Journal of Personality and Social Psychology, 32,* 906–914.

Word, C. H., Zanna, M. P., & Cooper, J. (1974). The nonverbal mediation of self-fulfilling prophecies in interracial interaction. *Journal of Experimental Social Psychology, 10,* 109–120.

Wrightsman, L. S. (1991). *Psychology and the legal system* (2nd ed.). Pacific Groves, CA: Brooks/Cole.

Wrobleski, H. M., & Hess, K. M. (2006). *Introduction to law enforcement and criminal justice* (8th ed.). Belmont, CA: Wadsworth.

Wyer, N. A. (2004). Not all stereotypic biases are created equal: Evidence for a stereotype-disconfirming bias. *Personality and Social Psychology Bulletin, 30,* 706–720.

Yarmey, A. D. (2001). Expert testimony: Does eyewitness memory research have probative value for the courts? *Canadian Psychology, 42,* 92–100.

Yarmey, A. D. (2003). Eyewitness identification: Guidelines and recommendations for identification procedures in the United States and Canada. *Canadian Psychology, 44,* 181–189.

Yarmey, A. D. (2004). Eyewitness recall and photo identification: A field experiment. *Psychology, Crime and Law, 10,* 53–68.

Yarmey, A. D., Jacob, J., & Porter, A. (2002). Person recall in field settings. *Journal of Applied Social Psychology, 32,* 2354–2367.

Zaheer, A., McEvily, B., & Perrone, V. (1998). Does trust matter? Exploring the effects of interorganizational and interpersonal trust on performance. *Organizational Science, 9,* 141–159.

Zajonc, R. B. (1965). Social facilitation. *Science, 149,* 269–274.

Zajonc, R. B. (1968). Attitudinal effects of mere exposure. *Journal of Personality and Social Psychology, 9* (Monograph suppl., No. 2, Pt. 2), 1–27.

Zanna, M. P. (2004). The naive epistemology of a working social psychologist (or the working epistemology of a naive social psychologist): The value of taking "temporary givens" seriously. *Personality and Social Psychology Review, 8,* 210–218.

Zanna, M. P., & Cooper, J. (1974). Dissonance and the pill: An attribution approach to studying the arousal properties of dissonance. *Journal of Personality and Social Psychology, 29,* 703–709.

Zanna, M. P., Detweiler, R. A., & Olson, J. M. (1984). Physiological mediation of attitude maintenance, formation, and change. In W. M. Waid (Ed.), *Sociophysiology* (pp. 163–195). New York: Springer-Verlag.

Zanna, M. P., Kiesler, C. A., & Pilkonis, P. A. (1970). Positive and negative attitudinal affect established by classical conditioning. *Journal of Personality and Social Psychology, 38,* 432–440.

Zanna, M. P., & Olson, J. M. (Eds.). (1994). *The psychology of prejudice: The Ontario symposium* (Vol. 7). Mahwah, NJ: Erlbaum.

Zanna, M. P., & Rempel, J. K. (1988). Attitudes: A new look at an old concept. In D. Bar-Tal & A. W. Kruglanski (Eds.), *The social psychology of knowledge* (pp. 315–334). Cambridge, UK: Cambridge University Press.

Zanna, M. P., & Sande, G. N. (1987). The effect of collective actions on the attitudes of individual group members: A dissonance analysis. In M. P. Zanna, J. M. Olson, & C. P. Herman (Eds.), *Social influence: The Ontario symposium* (Vol. 5, pp. 151–163). Hillsdale, NJ: Erlbaum.

Zárate, M. A., Garcia, B., Garza, A. A., & Hitlan, R. T. (2004). Cultural threat and perceived realisitic group conflict as dual predictors of prejudice. *Journal of Experimental Social Psychology, 40,* 99–105.

Zawadzki, B. (1948). Limitations on the scapegoat theory of prejudice. *Journal of Abnormal and Social Psychology, 43,* 127–141.

Zillmann, D., & Bryant, J. (1974). Effect of residual excitation on the emotional response to provocation and delayed aggressive behavior. *Journal of Personality and Social Psychology, 30,* 782–791.

Zillmann, D., Katcher, A. H., & Milavsky, B. (1972). Excitation transfer from physical exercise to subsequent aggressive behavior. *Journal of Experimental Social Psychology, 8,* 247–259.

Zimbardo, P. G. (1969). The human choice: Individuation, reason, and order vs. deindividuation, impulse, and chaos. In W. J. Arnold & D. Levine (Eds.), *Nebraska Symposium on Motivation* (Vol. 17, pp. 237–307). Lincoln: University of Nebraska Press.

Zimbardo, P. G. (1972). *The Stanford prison experiment.* Slide show produced by Philip G. Zimbardo, Inc.

Zimbardo, P. G., Weisenberg, M., & Firestone, I. (1965). Communication effectiveness in producing public conformity and private attitude change. *Journal of Personality, 33,* 233–255.

Zuckerman, M. (1995). Good and bad humors: Biochemical bases of personality and its disorders. *Psychological Science, 6,* 325–332.

Author Index

Subject Index